Bedouin Folktales from the North of Israel

Bedouin Folktales from the North of Israel

YOEL SHALOM PEREZ
AND
JUDITH ROSENHOUSE

Indiana University Press

This book is a publication of

Indiana University Press
Office of Scholarly Publishing
Herman B Wells Library 350
1320 East 10th Street
Bloomington, Indiana 47405 USA

iupress.org

Frontispiece by Vika Gorstain.

Manufactured in the United States of America

First printing 2022

Library of Congress Cataloging-in-Publication Data

Names: Rosenhouse, J., editor. | Perets, Yo'el Shalom, editor.
Title: Bedouin folktales from the north of Israel / edited by Judith Rosenhouse and Yoel Shalom Perez.
Identifiers: LCCN 2022027112 (print) | LCCN 2022027113 (ebook) | ISBN 9780253063823 (hardback) | ISBN 9780253063830 (paperback) | ISBN 9780253063847 (ebook)
Subjects: LCSH: Bedouins—Israel—Galilee—Folklore. | Women, Bedouin—Israel—Galilee—Folklore. | Tales—Israel—Galilee.
Classification: LCC GR286.2.B44 B44 2022 (print) | LCC GR286.2.B44 (ebook) | DDC 398.20933/45—dc23/eng/20220709
LC record available at https://lccn.loc.gov/2022027112
LC ebook record available at https://lccn.loc.gov/2022027113

CONTENTS

Foreword vii
Transcription and Abbreviations xiii

PART I · Stories of Love, Loyalty, and Devotion

1. Between the Sun and the Moon *3*
2. The Princess on the Island *21*
3. The Girl Who Fell into a Well *30*
4. The Ḥāǧǧ's Daughter and the Orator *38*
5. A Woman's Loyalty *47*
6. The King's Wife and the Poor Man *55*
7. Ǧuḥā and the Queen *63*
8. The Doe *68*
9. The Woman from the Sea *76*
10. The Raindrop Bubbles Will Testify *80*
    A. The Man and His Neighbor *80*
    B. Ḏā'eq 'Anṣāf (Tasting Justice) *82*
11. The Coffee Server *89*
12. The Old Man and the Girl, the Old Woman and the Young Man *101*
13. The Girl and Her Brother Who Became a Deer *106*
14. Do Good and Throw It into the Sea *119*
15. The Transposed Heads *125*
16. The Son Who Obeyed His Mother *132*
17. The Silent Princess and Smart Mḥammad *137*
18. The Two Notes (Smart Ḥasan) *145*
19. The Kidnapped Bride *152*
20. The Prince and His Two Wives *159*
21. In the Family *169*
    A. Between a Brother and His Sister *169*
    B. Between a Bride and Her Mother-in-Law *171*
22. The Replaced Bride *176*
23. The Dangerous Night-Watch *183*
    A. Šāṭer Ḥasan and His Nine Brothers *183*
    B. Seven Brides for Seven Brothers *200*
24. My Mother Slew Me; My Father Ate Me *211*
    A. The Green Bird *211*
    B. The Yellow Cow *213*
25. The Boy, the Uncle, and the Lover *220*
26. The Inheritance Case *227*

PART II · Stories about Ġūls and Demons

27. The Giant *245*
28. Frēṭ Rummān (Snow White) *255*
29. The Man Who Delivered a Daughter *268*
30. The Girl and Her Seven Brothers *272*
31. The Sickle Hand *284*
32. Bells Sound *305*
    A. Ǧbēna and the Jujube Tree *305*
    B. The Ǧinn and the Girl in Dog Clothes *311*
33. The Golden Palm Tree *322*
34. The Children and the Ogre *333*
    A. The Girls and the Ġūla *333*
    B. Grēʿa, Ḥmēda, and Ḥdaydūn *341*
    C. Nuṣṣ-ᵉNṣēṣ *350*
35. The Emīr's Daughter Who Flew to Switzerland *361*
36. The Golden Children *372*
    A. The Three Siblings and the Talking Birds *372*
    B. The Wicked Old Woman *377*
    C. The Emīr and the Slave *382*
37. The Ġūla, the Mallow Gatherer, and His Daughter *395*
38. The Two Brothers and the Ġūla *403*
39. Personal Narratives about Meetings with Ġūls *413*
    A. The Young Man and the Ġūla *413*
    B. The Ġūla Who Posed as a Tribe Member *416*
    C. The Groom and the Ġūla *417*
    D. The Ġūla in the Waterhole *418*
    E. Abu Xiḏᵉr and the Ġūla *418*
40. The Old Woman and the Ḥūt *425*

PART III · Animal Stories

41. The Man and the Wounded Snake *433*
    A. The Snake Story *433*
    B. The Shepherd and the Snake *435*
42. The Goat, the Kid, and the Ġūla *441*
43. The Lion Who Wanted to Know Man's Nature *446*
44. The Two Hunters *452*

Epilogue *463*

Bedouin Dialects in the North of Israel / Judith Rosenhouse 465
Bedouin Tribes in the Galilee: Historical and Settlement Background / Arnon Medzini 487
Maps 513
Bibliography 517
Index of Tale Types 527
Index of Motifs 531
Narrators List 537
Subject and Name Index 541

FOREWORD

IN 1970, THE FAMOUS French ethnographer Geneviève Calame-Griaule wrote in her article "For Ethnolinguistic Study of African Literatures on the Study of African Oral Literature" the following:[1]

> Rarely, the texts are given to us in their authentic form, that is to say in their original language, and accompanied by a faithful translation. If the documents published by the linguists fulfill these conditions, they generally lack the comments allowing locating them in the culture that produced them. Conversely, the texts, collected and extensively commented on by ethnologists, are unfaithful to the form of these texts.
>
> The exceptions to this rule make us aware of what we have lost and of the effort required for completing them. In order to attempt the total analysis of these literatures, it is absolutely necessary to be able to refer to the contextual and cultural context, which has molded a content of a wider, even universal heritage, into a new and unique form.
>
> The linguistic context alone makes it possible to specify the exact value of the terms used and the stylistic intentions of the narrator. The reference to the cultural context, on the other hand, will make us understand the choice of elements, their symbolic importance, the structural rules that determine their combination, the sociological interest of the narrative, etc. (Translated from French by Y. S. Perez)

This book reflects an interdisciplinary collaboration between two researchers—the one is a linguist and the other, a folklorist—aiming to realize to some extent Calame-Griaule's above quoted expectations. The book is intended for folklorists, anthropologists, and linguists as much as the wide public that cherishes learning about other cultures and wishes to be acquainted with the Arabic narrative tradition of the Middle East.

Yoel Shalom Perez is a folklorist who, in the 1980s, conducted extensive fieldwork focusing on the narrative tradition of Bedouin tribes in the north of Israel. He collected and recorded in Arabic, the original language, more than a hundred folktales, narrated mostly by Bedouin women from various tribes in the Galilee area.

Judith Rosenhouse is a linguist who, in those years, conducted the first linguistic research on the spoken language of the Bedouin tribes in the Galilee, as part of her linguistic specialization in colloquial Arabic dialects.

Our collaboration already had begun in the 1980s, when we helped each other in finding a few Bedouin folktales and translating them into Hebrew. After many years of separate research, this connection was resumed when Yoel was working on publishing his Hebrew book on the Bedouin tribes' folktales from the north of Israel.[2]

The Hebrew edition included almost all the stories that Yoel had collected. The texts were written in colloquial sedentary Arabic as used in Israel (not in the original Bedouin dialects). They were written in Hebrew alphabetic transcription and accompanied with translation into Hebrew. Almost each folktale was followed by Perez's folkloristic commentary, regarding cultural and social aspects. The book also contained an original comprehensive chapter, written by Rosenhouse for that book, about the Bedouin dialects in the north of Israel, and Medzini's original chapter on the historical and demographical background of the Bedouin tribes in the Galilee.

The current book combines work by the two authors, Perez and Rosenhouse. Rosenhouse transcribed and translated the stories into English directly from the Arabic recordings and added the linguistic, cultural, and sociolinguistic notes for each story she translated. She also revised the chapter on Bedouin dialects that appeared in the Hebrew volume by adding phonological, morphological, and syntactic descriptions, tables, and details that were not mentioned in the Hebrew version. Perez collected most of the stories in Arabic, arranged them by groups, following the folkloristic method, and translated several stories that he had recorded in Hebrew into English. He also wrote the commentary for each story or group of stories.

Twenty-seven informants from thirteen tribes were recorded. Twenty of the twenty-seven narrators were women, and seven, men. Most of the narrators were in their fifties when they told us their narratives. The list of the narrators and their tribes appears in an appendix at the end of the book.

In the current book, we present to English readers fifty-seven folktales from the one hundred tales that appear in the Hebrew book. These fifty-seven tales represent forty-two narrative types and reflect a wide range of narrative genres. In some cases, we present a few versions of the same story, demonstrating narrative variance and plot variance in the different versions. In other cases, we only mention such versions while noting their unique aspects, in comparison with the folktale presented in the book.

The first part of the book contains folktales of the novella type—realistic stories in which human characteristics, such as cleverness, erotica, love, loyalty, and cunning, are those that propagate the story plot. The second part of the book is dedicated to imaginary tales in which the protagonists contend with ghouls, demons, and other imaginary figures. Many of such stories were told by mothers to their children and fulfilled pedagogical roles in their upbringing, by emphasizing protagonists' character features worthy of imitation. The narrative types to which these folktales belong are frequent in all the Indo-European space, but they are unique in both the way the protagonists are portrayed and the atmosphere, which reflect the traditional Bedouin lifestyle. The belief in the existence of devils and demons of many forms and types was (and is still) common in Bedouin society.[3] The narrators still sometimes express this belief by metatextual utterances when they mention meetings with such creatures. A typical expression is *bʿīd ʿannak*, "[may it be] far from you" (also used for anything bad/evil that might occur). One chapter in the book deals with memorates, or personal stories in which the narrators tell about personal meetings they had with such demons, or about people they personally knew who experienced the same. The last part of the book deals with tales about meetings between the protagonists and various animals—snakes, lions, wolf, hyenas. While these stories have an imaginary nature, they are based on the narrator's acquaintance with the animal world in their vicinity.

Most of the stories are presented here in their original Bedouin Arabic dialect in phonemic/phonetic transcription and in accurate English translation.[4] Since Galilee dialects and other dialects in the north of Israel are so diverse, while the study of dialectal differences is not the main target of this volume, we do not often mention specific sedentary dialects. Moreover, for the translation of the folktales, Perez also contacted sedentary speakers of Arabic, without checking their specific origins or dialects. In addition, note the narrators' casual speech manner and the mixture of different dialectal features (Koiné and contact features) in their speech. All these factors lend the Arabic speech samples in this book the typical and realistic picture of modern Bedouin Arabic dialects and should be considered as such.

A comprehensive ethnographic, folkloristic, and linguistic commentary accompanies the folktales. In addition, the volume includes the revised and extended chapter on the Galilee Bedouin dialects and the chapter about the historical and demographical background of the Galilee Bedouin tribes.

In contrast with texts of Negev Bedouin tribes from the south of Israel, relatively few Galilee Bedouin stories and folktales have been collected and written down, and their dialects have rarely been studied (but cf. Rosenhouse, *Bedouin Arabic Dialects*). This aspect grants our volume a significant importance.

The book does not intend to be a methodological textbook of Galilee Bedouin dialects. Yet the chapter on the Bedouin dialects, and Galilee Bedouin dialects in particular, presents linguistic issues systematically. To facilitate reading, the abbreviations key and transcription tables (preceding the folktales) are presented directly after this foreword. The linguistic comments, partly discussing issues that have not been published so far, will contribute a basic and important understanding of many subjects. To enhance readers' attention, important linguistic points recur in the notes, in addition to their reference to adequate sections in the chapter on Bedouin dialects. A relatively long time has passed since the publication of Rosenhouse's (1984) book on the Galilee Bedouin's language. In this new collection as in that book, we demonstrate and highlight genuine features of Galilee Bedouin dialects and the impact of modernity and other regional dialects on their speech.

The Bedouin Arabic vocabulary in these tales reveals various lexical items that are not used in the sedentary dialects. We therefore often searched some dictionaries to find the origins and spread of such lexical items. For that purpose, we used mainly Al-Barghuthi's *Dictionary of Colloquial Palestinian Arabic Dialects* (2001) for the Palestinian dialects of the central hilly area of the country, Wehr's *Dictionary of Modern Written Arabic* (1971) for Modern Standard Arabic, and rarely Freytag's Arabic-Latin dictionary of Classical Arabic (1830–33). Barthélemy's *Dictionnaire arabe-français* (1939–1945/1966), a dictionary of Levant Sedentary dialects from the first half of the twentieth century that sometimes includes comments on Bedouin features, was also consulted quite often. Occasionally, we used Elihay's *Olive Tree Dictionary* (2005), though he hardly referred to Bedouin vocabulary, as well as the glossary in Shawarbah's *Grammar of Negev Arabic* (2012) and Henkin's *Negev Arabic* (2010) on Negev Bedouin Arabic. We mention these dictionaries only sporadically, for we did not aim at a systematic comparative study.

On the folkloristic level, the book portrays a broad picture of the local Bedouin narrative culture and illuminates its place in the wider circles of Islamic and Arabic narrative culture, and in the even wider circle of the Indo-European and African narrative world. For each story, the commentary part of the book brings parallels from Israel and the neighboring countries in both the Islamic and the Jewish cultural spaces and in other cultural spaces.

It can be assumed that the Bedouin narrative tradition has a deep link to the Jewish narrative tradition. Already in the *Jāhiliyya* period (the so-called "ignorance" period, which preceded Islam), there were strong links between Arab and Jewish tribes who lived in the Arabian Peninsula (today, Saudi Arabia). The prophet Muḥammad, who initiated Islam in the seventh century CE, knew well the Jewish narrative tradition, and the Qur'ān contains many stories from the Hebrew (Jewish) Bible. After the Muslims had conquered most of the Middle East, including the Land of Israel,[5] a continuous dialogue existed between Muslims and Jews all over the Middle Eastern Muslim Empire.

Therefore, it is not surprising that stories that were considered until recently as purely Jewish stories, such as "Solomon's Daughter in the Tower" and "Story of a Rat and a Pit," have Bedouin parallels in this volume. Over four centuries (1517–1917), the area of Egypt (until 1882), the Arabian Peninsula, the Land of Israel, Syria, and Iraq, up to Turkey, Greece, Bulgaria, and the Balkan, was united under the Ottoman Empire rule. This fact enabled movement of different peoples throughout the region. From the narrative perspective, we may speak about an Ottoman cultural space, which was common to Jews, Muslims, Christians, and people of other religions. Bedouin tribes from countries all over the empire—Kurdistan, Iraq, Syria, Transjordan, the Arabian Peninsula, and Egypt—reached the Galilee in the eighteenth and nineteenth centuries (see Medzini's chapter). They carried with them narrative traditions from their original countries. Since Jews were also living everywhere in the Ottoman Empire, no wonder we find Jewish folktales parallel to the Bedouin narratives.

We wish to express our deep thanks to all the men and women narrators whose folktales we present here and all the people who hosted us in their homes with kindness and good will, in the best Bedouin tradition. In particular, we would like to mention the two wonderful narrators from the ʿArab El-Ḥuğērāt tribe, Ṯalğe Mūsa and Ṣabḥa ʿAbūd. Between them, they made a crucial contribution to our book with sixteen folktales (about 30 percent of the stories). Both are now in their nineties. During the work on the book, we met with them again and even re-recorded them with their full cooperation.

Special thanks are extended to all those who helped us in the past and present regarding writing down the texts of the stories and their translation into Hebrew and their publication in the Hebrew version. **Bruria Horowitz** invested numerous hours in transcribing and writing down the recorded texts and translating them into Hebrew, without which the Hebrew book would not have been published. **ʿAli Sḥādeh** from the Arab village Kaukab Abu al-Hiǧa wrote down the recordings in Arabic. **Yehuda Katz** also recorded a story, which was translated into Hebrew and published back in 1980 (in Rosenhouse and Katz, *Texts in the Dialects of Bedouins in Israel*) and appears again in this volume, in Arabic transcription and English translation. **Assaf Golani and his team** made great efforts in the publishing of these stories in the Hebrew volume. Cordial thanks are due also to **Michael Greenberg** for the time devoted to editing the English text. **Dr. Roseland Daeem**, from Haifa, is gratefully thanked for her help in translating the story "The Coffee Server" into Hebrew and providing Arabic proverbs, which are now part of the book. Thanks to **Dr. Arnon Medzini** for his chapter about the history and demography of the Galilee Bedouin tribes, which appears in the Hebrew version of the book and in this English volume. We cordially thank **Professor Dan Ben-Amos** and **Professor El-Shamy** for their support and effective advice along the years.

We are grateful to the two anonymous reviewers of the manuscript, whose comments have contributed to its final form and much improved our work. Last, but not least, we would like to thank the team members of Indiana University Press: Jennika Baines, Sophia Herbert, Nancy Lila Lightfoot, Rachel Erin Rosolina, and Pete Feely. They were involved in the various stages of the production of this volume, and patiently and kindly helped us overcome all the difficulties on the way to the happy end.

We hope that the publication of this book will not only advance the linguistic, anthropological, and folkloristic research of Bedouin folktales in Israel but also contribute to the understanding between Arabs and Jews in Israel and elsewhere and promote peace in our region.

Yoel Perez and Judith Rosenhouse

Notes

1. Geneviève Calame-Griaule, "For Ethnolinguistic Study."

2. Perez, *Between the Sun and the Moon.*

3. This belief is based on the general view that everything that comes from Allah is for man's good. Anything that is not from him relates to devils and demons, who live in various places under the ground or in hiding above ground and may cause harm to people who harm them (cf. Piamenta, *Muslim Conception of God*; Lebling, *Legends of the Fire Spirits*).

4. Since the Galilee Bedouin speech in these folktales reveals much fluctuation in the pronunciation of certain vowels and consonants (cf. transcription and abbreviations below) the transcription is not only phonemic but also mostly phonetic, and same words may often differ in their pronunciations, even by one and the same speaker.

5. The Land of Israel (Hebrew: אֶרֶץ יִשְׂרָאֵל Modern: Eretz Yisrael) is the traditional Jewish name for an area of indefinite geographical extension in the southern Levant. Related biblical, religious, and historical English terms for this area include the Land of Canaan, the Promised Land, the Holy Land, and Palestine.

TRANSCRIPTION AND ABBREVIATIONS

THE TEXTS USE THE Semitists' accepted transcription method. This method serves also for Arabic words in the English translations of the stories, the commentaries and the tables of Arabic letter names, Bedouin tribes' and narrators' names, place names, etc. The Semitists' symbols are given in table 1 for the consonants and in table 2 for the vowels. On speech features, see the chapter on Bedouin Arabic dialects at the end of this book.

TABLE 1. Arabic Consonants in Semitists' Phonemic Method

Arabic letter name	Semitists' symbol	Arabic letter name	Semitists' symbol	Arabic letter name	Semitists' symbol
'Alif	'	Zaa'	z	Faa'	f
Baa'	b	Siin	s	Qaaf	q
Taa'	t	Šiin	š	Kaaf	k
Ṯaa'	ṯ	Ṣaad	ṣ	Laam	l
Jiim	ğ	Ḍaad	ḍ	Miim	m
Ḥaa'	ḥ	Ṭaa'	ṭ	Nuun	n
Xa'	x	Ḏ̣aa'	ḏ̣	Haa'	h
Daal	d	'Ain	ʿ	Waaw	w
Ḏaal	ḏ	Ġain	ġ	Yaa'	y
Raa'	r				

TABLE 2. Arabic Short and Long Vowels

Front vowel	Mid Vowel	Back Vowel
High i, ī		u, ū
Mid e, ē	ə	o, ō
Low	ā	

Table Comments

1. For pharyngealized or velarized consonants, a dot is placed under the consonant: *ṭ*, *ṣ*, *ḷ*, etc., except for *ḥ* (which is pharyngeal).

2. Some consonants have allophones in the Bedouin dialects: *q~g~x~ġ~'*; *ğ*—*ž*; k—č.

3. The dialects studied here also use consonants borrowed from Hebrew, English, and other languages using the symbols *c*, *p*, *v*.

4. Geminated consonants are marked by geminated symbols, such as *kabbar*, "enlarge"; *ğamma*, "they came"; *widdo*, "he wants"; etc. When a geminated consonant is followed by another consonant, we do not delete one of the geminated consonants, although the gemination is usually reduced and pronounced as a single consonant.

5. A main accent on a stressed syllable is marked by an accent on the accented vowel, as in *gháwa*, "coffee"; *ál-bugar*, "the cattle." However, accent is not always marked.

6. Hebrew words in the texts are marked by a small H at word beginning and end. In the English translation they are repeated in brackets, followed by the translation.

7. Long vowels are marked by a line above the vowel, as in, *gāḷ*, "he said"; *yōm*, "a day"; *dīn*, "religion."

8. The mid vowel ə is mainly used in unstressed epenthetic syllables. It has various phonetic timbres, affected by the consonantal and vowel environment. When an epenthetic vowel appears in the text, it is written as a small superscript symbol. However, this vowel is hardly used in this book.

9. Since vowels in these dialects do not always reflect different phonemes, different vowels can appear in the same word, even in the speech of the same narrator (cf. note 4, in the notes following the foreword, above).

Abbreviations and Symbols

C	Consonant
C1	1st root consonant
C2	2nd root consonant
C3	3rd root consonant
ColA	Colloquial Arabic
CS	Code switching
f.	Feminine
LA	Literary Arabic (Classical Arabic)
LA/MSA	Both Literary Arabic and Modern Standard Arabic are referred to
m.	Masculine
MSA	Modern Standard Arabic (equivalent to LA but in modern written texts)
pl.	Plural
sg.	Singular
Stress	Accent above the letter, e.g., *á*, *í*, *é*, *ú*
V	Vowel
1, 2, 3	Personal pronouns
1pl.	1st person plural
2f.sg.	2nd person feminine singular
3m.sg.	3rd person masculine singular

‘ ’	marks for translated terms into English
“ ”	quotation marks denoting spoken utterance (e.g., in a dialogue)
( )	Round brackets in the texts are usually used to explain unclear forms or words
( )	Round brackets in the translations often complement the text for coherent English
[ ]	Square brackets in the texts and the translations reflect utterances that are not part of the narrative, but a side utterance directed at or by members of the audience.

Slashes or square brackets for phonemic/phonetic symbols are not used in this book. Instead, *italic* fonts emphasize Arabic phonemes or words in the linguistic and sociolinguistic notes and in the chapter on Bedouin dialects.

PART I · Stories of Love, Loyalty, and Devotion

1. Between the Sun and the Moon

NARRATOR: Ibrāhīm Qwēder Ṣbēḥāt

TRIBE: *'Arab Rummāneh-Ṣbēḥāt*

IFA[1] 17414 September 2, 1982

1 ’amīr ʿarab xaḷḷaf min al-ġulām wāḥad, ’alla wāḥad.[2] min-čud-ma huwwa muʿtazz bīh, u-huwwa ’amīr ʿarab, ğāb lo mʿallem madrase xuṣūṣi, ’ay naʿam.	1 A Bedouin emīr had only one son (of boys). Because of his pride in him, and he was a Bedouin emīr, he brought for him a private schoolteacher, yes indeed.
6 ṣār yeʿallem fīh. yōm min el-’ayyām li-mʿallem qāl-lo,[3] “yā mḥimmad, ’aḷḷahumma ṣalli ʿala n-nebi muḥammad, ’in šuft ru’ya wa-nsarrēt fīha bi-n-nhār txarrifhā-š la-ḥada, wala l-’immak wa-la la-’abūk wa-la ’ili.”	6 He started teaching him. One day, the teacher said to him, “Oh Mḥimmad, Allah pray on the Prophet Muḥammad, if you see a dream and you are glad with it, do not tell it to anyone, not to your mother nor your father, or me.”
12 qāl-lo, “lēš, yā sīdi?” qāl-lo, “lamma tšūfha bi-l-manām bitšūfha b-tarīx ḥayātak, šāyif, ’in mā xarraftha. u-’in xarraftha—rāḥat, baṭṭal ^{i}tšūfha.”	12 He said to him, “Why, oh sir?” He said to him, “When you see it in your sleep, you will see it in your life (see?), if you do not tell it. And if you tell it, it will disappear, you will not see it [it will not come true].”
baqa lēle min-el-layāli šāf ru’ya—nāyem bēn eš-šam^{e}s u-bēn el-qamar. ’ansarr biha kṯīr hāy.	One night, he saw a dream—that he was sleeping between the sun and the moon. He was very glad with it, this one [the boy].
19 lamma aqʿadato ’ummo ziʿel min ’immo l(a)’anno r-ru’ya rāḥat lamma qaʿad u-fattaḥ.	19 When his mother woke him up, he was angry with his mother, because the dream disappeared when he got up and became awake.
lamma qām eṣ-ṣabi zaʿlān, ḥāwalat ta-yġassel—mā riḏī-š yġassel. ḥāwalat ta-yišrab šāy, yišrab qahwe—	When the boy got up angry, she tried to make him wash—he did not agree to wash himself. She tried to make him drink tea, drink coffee—

25 mā riḏ̣ī-š. ḥamal kitābo ʿala l-madrase, zaʿlān.

25 he did not agree [to do so]. He took his book and went to school angry.

27 rāḥat qālt l-abūh b-ad-dīwān. ʾabūh waddā-lo. rāḥ ǧābo. ḥačā-lo, “mā-lak zaʿlān? lēš mā ġasalteš? lēš mā šribteš šāy, lēš mā šribteš qahwa?” mā raddeš.

27 She went and told his father [who was] in the living room [guests’ room]. His father sent for him. And he [a servant] went and brought him. He said to him, “Why are you angry? Why haven’t you washed yourself? Why didn’t you drink tea and why didn’t you drink coffee?” He did not answer.

31 ḥalafo l-yamīn, “ʾin mā qu(l)t li šu mā lak, la-ʾabīʿak li-baʿīd!” [miṯel bīʿat il-ʿabīd—qabel kānu ybīʿu l-ʿabīd, bēʿa-muštara. fāhim?] eṣ-ṣabi ḏ̣aḷḷ muṣirr, mā riḏ̣īš yqūl-lo. ḥalaf ʿalē l-yamīn u-bāʿo. ʾanṭāh, sallem ʿala-l-ʿabd tabaʿo, qāl-lo: “rak(k)bo warāk ʿa-l-ǧawād u-rūḥ, xuḏo ʿa-ǧenīn ṯamma tqūl u-bīʿo.

31 He swore, “If you don’t tell me what is the matter with you, I will surely sell you to a far place.” (Like selling the slaves. In the past they used to sell slaves, buying and selling [them]. Do you understand?) The boy persisted—he did not agree to tell him. He [his father] swore and sold him. He gave him to his servant and told him, “Put him behind you on the horse and go to Ǧenin, there you will say [announce] and sell him.

39 ʾamma hā, bīʿu u-rudd raǧʿo hā, miš tgūl la-ʾabu-xalīl u-yḏ̣aḷḷ mabyūʿ fi bēto min šān yemīni, ʿala-nni ḥalaft yamīn bi-ṭ-ṭalāq min ʾummo. bīʿo la-ʾabu xalīl fa-iḏa mā rudd-eš, rudd raǧʿo, xuḏo minno, yaʿni min šān el-yamīn.”

39 “But this, sell him and get him back again, this [one]. Do not tell Abu Xalil, so that he will remain sold in his house because of my oath, because I swore to divorce his mother. Sell him to Abu Xalil and if he does not want [him], get [him] back again, take him back from him, that is, because of the oath.”

45 il-ʿabed rāḥ bāʿo, mā radd-eš ʿala l-ḥaki-hā. ʾabu xalīl xaḏo u-rawwaḥ ʿala blādo. ʾabu xalīl ǧāy sāyiḥ ʿala l-blād.

45 The slave went and sold him, the slave did not answer this talk. Abu Xalil took him and went home to his country. Abu Xalil had come as tourist to the country.

48 [taʿrif inte? ʾaywa.] ʾabu xalīl mabṣūṭ min hā-l-walad. walad—tiffāḥa, u-ʾadīb. ʾay naʿam.

48 (Do you know? Yes.) Abu Xalil [was] satisfied with the boy. The boy [was like] a [sweet] apple and polite. Yes, indeed.

51 ʾaǧat ʿēlto la-ʾabu xalīl qālat-lo, “yā-bnayy, ʾinte mā-lak-š lā ʾimm wa-lā ʾabb?” qāl-lha, “ʾili ʾimm wa-ʾabu. minnēn xliqᵉt ʾana?” qālat-lo, “čīf bāʿūk?” qāl-lha, “šufᵉt ruʾᵉya u-mā rḏ̣īt-eš ʾaqūl-lom ʿanna, u-lamma mā rḏ̣īt-eš ʾaqūl lhin ʿanna—maʿnātu, bāʿūni. ḥalaf ʾabūy ʿalayy bi-ṭ-ṭalāq min ʾimmi, u-ʾana mā rḏ̣īt-eš ʾaqūl-lo, ṭabʿan bāʿni.”

51 Abu Xalil’s wife came to the boy and said to him, “O my son, you, haven’t you got no mother or father?” He said to her, “I have a mother and a father. How [from where] was I born?” She said to him, “How did they sell you?” He said to her, “I saw a dream and did not want to tell them about it, and when I refused to tell them about it, it means, they sold me. My father swore to divorce my mother and I didn’t want to tell him, naturally he sold me.”

60 ṣārat tdalli ʿalēh ta-nno yqūl-lha. qāl-lha, "'int(i) 'aḥsan min 'immi u-'abūy? 'inno 'immi u-'abūy mā qult-illom, ta-'aqūl-leš 'inti?" ziʿlat minno u-t'ellamat minno. lamma ğa ğōzha qālat-lo . . . "eṣ-ṣabi, yā tiḥwā yā tbīʿa!" "lēš yā flāne?" qālat-lo, "yā ṛabb, fōqo-taḥto,"	60 She began to entice him to tell her. He said to her, "Are you better than my mother and father? I have not told my mother and father, so I will tell you?" She got angry with him and was hurt by him. When her husband came, she said to him, "The boy—either you drive him off or sell him." He said, "Why, oh so-and-so?" She said to him "Oh, Allah, his up is down" [things are mixed up with him].
68 la-'āxir ḥabsat b-ʿaqlo.[4] 'en-natīğe, fīh 'ilo qabīl, 'abu xalīl, 'amīr ʿarab, miṯl-ma tqūl, ra'īs dawli. fīh 'ilo qabīl, ṭabʿan m-maḥallāt ṯāni(ye).	68 In the end, she put it into his head. In short, Abu Xalil had a parallel colleague [one like him]; Abu Xalil [was] a Bedouin emīr, as you say, head of the state. He had a parallel, naturally, from other places.
72 en-natī(ğe), lamma ṭayyar ʿa-s-sūq, ye'ul-lehō, b-dūn mulāḥaẓa, 'ibno, 'iben qabīlo ğāy šammet hawa ʿala blādo, [fāhm yā sīdi?] al-madīne. šara ṣ-ṣabi,	72 When he went to the market [to sell the boy], by chance, there was his parallel's son coming to make a journey to his country, his town. He bought the boy.
76 lamma šarāh u-rawwaḥu, inḅaṣaṭ fīh. natīžt.e. maṯīl, miṯel-mā ṣār fī hōn, ṣār fī hnāk.	76 When he bought him and they went home, he was satisfied with him. In short . . . as happened to him here, happened to him there.
78 il-mara ḥāwalat ta-yqūl-la, mā rḏī-š yqūl-la. 'ay naʿam. qālat la-ğōzha, "aṣ-ṣabi hāḏa bīʿo, bidnā-š iyyāh, hāḏa siyāsto miš mlīḥa!"	78 The woman tried to make him tell her; he did not agree to tell her. Yes indeed. She said to her husband, "this boy—sell him, we do not want him. His behavior is not good."
82 n-natīğe, 'ağa huwwa, riʿāyitna-l-ʿazīz, u-qāl-lo yfawwato ʿala s-siğn, ḥaṭṭū fi ġurfe min ġuraf as-siğn . . . yōm, eṯnēn, ʿašara, ʿašrīn, yaʿalam 'aḷḷa, nisyū. 'ay naʿam.	82 In short, he came, he (our dear protegee), and said to him [to the jailer] to put him in jail, he put him in a room from the prison rooms. One day, two days, ten, twenty, Allah knows [how many]. They forgot about him. Yes indeed.
87 yōm, eṣ-ṣabi, yā sīdna el-ʿazīz, min ṭūl-mā ṣār-lo ġēr min el-ğūʿ u-l-ʿaṭaš, ṣār (y)ʿayyiṭ u-yibki u-yiddaʿi la-'aḷḷa subḥāno wa-taʿāla, yifriğ ʿanno.	87 One day, the boy, (o our dear sir), because of the long time of his hunger and thirst, he started crying and weeping and praying to Allah, may he be exalted and praised, to let him go free.
91 qāl: "atšaṭṭa"—tišaṭṭaḥ fī madīnt ar-rāwi, ṭilʿ(a) minha. w-illa hī dār ṭawīla ʿarīḍa, w-illa hī bīha qaṣer. wi-l-qaṣer, mā hī bint el-malik alli bī, yaʿani, bint ra'īs ed-dawla.	91 He said, "I will walk." He walked in the narrator's town. He went out of there. Lo, and it was a long and wide house and in it was a palace. And the palace—it was the king's daughter who was in it, that is, the daughter of the head of the state.

96 ṣār yfurr, ʾağa ʿala l-maṭbax, l-ʾakl bihabbel, mā-šā-ḷḷa, ʾin-natīže, ʾakal u-šireb, ʾay naʿam, u-riğeʿ maḥallo.

96 He started running and came to the kitchen. The food was steaming, thank Allah [as Allah willed]. In short, he ate and drank, yes, and returned to his place.

99 ʾay naʿam. natīžt-al-ʾamer, bint el-ʾamīr, ṭabʿan, ʾaw il-malik, ʾažat ṭallaʿat ʿala l-ʾakel. il-ʾakel maxtūš, maʾkūl minno. ḥakat maʿ immha ba-t-telefōn. qālat-ilha, "il-ʿabde bi-l-ğūʿ, zīdi l-ʾakel, ʾay naʿam. u-dīri bālek ʿa-l-ʿabde."

99 Yes indeed. In short, the emīr's daughter, naturally, or the king, came and looked at the food. The food had been eaten, someone had eaten from it. She talked with her mother on the phone. She said to her, "The slave girl is hungry, add to the food and watch the slave girl."

106 natīžt-al-ʾamer, ṣārat kull yōm tufqod el-ʾakel maʾkūl minno. ṣārat titraqqab. mīn illi byākol min al-ʾakl—hiyye l-ʿabde ʾaw ġērha. ṣadfat el-walad hāḏa, hu baʿd ma ʾakal u-widdo yrūḥ ʿala l-maḥall illi hū fīh.

106 In short, she started watching the food every day, [if it was] eaten. she started watching, who is that who eats from the food—is it the slave girl or someone else? By chance, she met the boy, after he had eaten and was going to return to the place in which he was [staying].

112 ʾin-natīğe, yōm min ha-l-ʾiyyām zaqṭato. qālat lo, "šu ʾinte, ʾins willa ğinn?" qāl-la, "lā, ʾins, ʾana ʾins." qālat-lo,"šū mṣībtak?" qāl-la, xarrafha ʿād, xarrafha qiṣṣto. xaḷḷato ʿindha. ʾaywa. ḥāwalat ʾinno yqūl-lha. qāl-lha, "baqul-(l)kīš." "ṭayyeb, mā-ʿalēš." qālat-lo, "ʿala kull ḥāl ʾaxallīk ʿindi hōn. fiš ḥada ʿendi ġēr la-ʾaḷḷa. xallīk ʿandi."

112 In short, on one of these days she caught him. She said to him, "What are you—a human or a ğinnie?" He said to her, "No, a human, I'm a human." She said to him, "What is your disaster?" He said to her, told her then, told her his story. She let him stay with her. She tried to make him tell her. He said to her, "I won't tell you." "Fine, never mind." She said to him, "In any case I'll let you be with me here. No one is with me except Allah. Stay at my place."

121 ḍaḷḷ ʿindha. ṭabʿan il-ʾakel illi ṣārat twaddīh ʾimmha ṣār yčaffi l-ğahitēn. yčaffi l-ğahitēn.

121 He remained with her. Naturally, the food that her mother began to send began to suffice for the two parties. To suffice for the two parties.

124 Yōm, ʾabu xalīl, yā sīdna l-ʿazīz, wadda la-ʾabu l-bint ğōz xēl. wāḥad kdīš u-wāḥad ʾaṣīl. ʾamma l-eṯnēn ğins wāḥad u-lōn wāḥad u-ṭūl wāḥad—ma-fiš wāḥad yizīd ʿan eṯ-ṯāni lā biṭ-ṭūl wa-lā bi-l-ḥağem.

124 One day, (o our dear sir,) Abu Xalil—sent to the girl's father two horses—a mule and a pedigree horse. But the two [were] one kind and one color and one length—one of them is not more than the other—neither in length nor in size.

130 qāḷ-lo, "(wi)ddak teʿrif-li l-ʾaṣīl min l-ᵉkdīš. ʾin ʿerifthin tiksab eṯ-ṯnēn [fāhim, yā-ba], u-banṭīk ğizi l-māl u-kaḏa. mā ʿerifthinn-eš bitirğiʿhen u-bitḥuṭṭ ğaza kaḏa." maʿalēš.

130 He said to him, "You must distinguish the pedigree [horse] from the mule. If you know them, you'll gain both of them (do you understand, o father/old man?) and I'll give you [as] a reward such money and so on as. If you do not know [distinguish] them, you'll return them [to me] and will pay such and such penalty." Fine.

135 baqa fi n-natīǧe, yā sīdna l-ʿazīz, ʿand el-ʾamīr illi ʿendo el . . . eṣ-ṣabi el-maḫčūm hāḏa. rakkibhen l-fawāres, rāḥu l-mīdān, ar-rās, ʿa-r-rās. il-kdīš mā inʿarafeš min el-ʾaṣīl. siyāq wāḥad, u-lōn wāḥad u-l-ḥaǧem wāḥad.	135 He came (in short, o our dear sir) to the emīr, who had this jailed boy. This one [the emīr] made cavalrymen ride them, they went to the hippodrome, [they ran] head to head [they made the same distance at the same time], the mule was not distinguished from the pedigree horse. One pace, one color, and one size.
141 ziʿil, en-natiīǧi, u-rā(ḥ) ʿend binto, ʿa-l-qaṣer. qālat-lo, "mā-lak yā-ba, šāyiftak miš mabṣūṭ." qāl-lha, "ʾusukti, yā-ba. il-malik el-flāni mwaddī-li	141 He was angry and went to his daughter in the palace. She said to him, "What's the matter, oh, Father, you look unhappy." He said to her, "Shut up, Daughter. The certain king has sent me
145 ǧōz xēl, el-lōn wāḥad, u-ṭūl wāḥad, u-kaḏa u-kaḏa, ḥatta neʿaref mīn el-ʾaṣīl umīn el-kdīš, u-mā ḥna-š ʿārfīn.	145 a pair of horses, of one color, and one length, etc., etc., to distinguish the pedigree horse from the mule, and we do not know.
148 lā el-xubara ʿārfīn, wa-lā l-xayyāla ʿārfīn. ba-ṭ-ṭrād qiyās wāḥad, miš nāfḏi ʿan baʿiḍha!"	148 Neither the experts know, nor the cavalrymen. In the race, they have one measure, the one does not overtake the other."
151 ʾaywa. ʿala kull ḥāl, rāḥat la-ṣ-ṣabi, qālat lo, "il-masʾale hēč hēč." qāl-lha, "ʾana baḥillha." rāḥat la-ʾabūha qālat-lo, "ġīb ʿanni ʾarbaʿa u-ʿišrīn sāʿa. baʿṭīk ǧawāb." ġāb ʿanha, yā sīdna l-ʿazīz.	151 Yes. In any case, she went to the boy and said to him, "The problem is so-and-so." He said to her, "I'll solve it." She went to her father and said to him, "Stay away from me for twenty-four hours. I'll give you an answer." He stayed away from her (o our dear sir).
156 qālt-lo, "šī?" qāl-lha: "bayyit kull ᵃḥṣān b-maḥall, u-xaḷḷīhen biǧ-ǧūʿ. l-ⁱkdīš—ḥaša s-sāmʿīn—min el-ǧūʿ biṣīr yōkol ṣōlo. il-ʾaṣīl biḏaḷḷ wāqef, lā bōkol, wa-lā . . . bišimm-ūš ṣōlo, mā bišimmō-š [fāhem, yā-bā], ʿala ʾiǧr wāḥad yiḏaḷḷ wāqef, il-ʾaṣīl. haḏāk yṣīr yeǧūl u-yōkol. b-il-kīlo."	156 She said to him [the boy], "What [anything]?" He said to her, "Let each horse stay in a separate place, and let them be hungry. The mule—asking the listeners' pardon—because of its hunger begins to eat its excrement, the pedigree horse will remain standing, will not eat nor smell its excrement, will not smell it (do you understand, o son). On one foot, he remains standing, the pedigree horse. That one [the mule] begins to walk and eat. Kilograms."
164 fiʿlan, lamma ǧarrbu . . . kānat . . . rabaṭūhin . . . fiʿlan ṣaḥīḥ. mʿanbiṭ čaʾinnu bōkel wi-l-ʾaṣīl wāqef ʿala ʾiǧr waḥade u-ḏāmer.ʾay naʿam. ʿirfom. waddar. kisibhen. ʾay naʿam.	164 In fact, when they tried (it), tied them, it was truly [the mule] digging as if he was eating and the pedigree horse was standing on one leg and was inert [getting thin]. They identified them. He lost [to him] and [the other] won them. Oh, yes.

168 haḏāk, yā sīdna l-ʿazīz, waddā-lo kamān ǧōz ǧawāher. ʾay naʿam. qāḷ-ḷo, "ʾiḏa l-māl. māl ed-dawli tabaʿak, biwāzen hāi el-ǧawhara, [fāhem, yā ʾaxi,] baʿṭīk binti, šames. [binto ʾisma šams. u-bint ʾaxi illi ʿindo ṣ-ṣabi ʾisimha l-qamar.]

168 That one [the other emīr], (o our dear sir) also sent to him a pair of pearls. Yes. He said to him, "If the money, all your state money, weighs against these pearls, (do you see, my brother?) I'll give you my daughter, Shams." (His daughter's name was Shams [Sun] and the daughter with whom the boy was, her name was Qamar [Moon].)

175 banṭīk binti u-badfaʿ ǧize, ǧaze māl . . . kull ḥayāti, yaʿani bakūn taḥt er-raʿiyye tabaʿak. w-in ma fakkētha tinṭīni el-qamar [fāhem, yā sīdi], ubitkūn ʿindi taḥt raʿīti kull ez-zamān, yaʿni, raʿiyye, tḥuṭṭ-e-ǧōze, yaʿani, ǧōze maʿāy." qāl-lo, "mnīḥ. lakān."

175 "I will give you my daughter and will pay a fine, money fine . . . all my life, that is, I'll be under your patronage. If you do not solve it, you will give me Qamar (do you understand, oh my sir?) and you will be under my patronage all the time, that is, patronage, you will pay me a fine, that is, a fine to me." He said to him, "Good. Let it be."

182 n-natīǧe, yā sīdi l-ʿazīz, qāl: "šū yixrib bēto [li-bʿīd]—mā ʾatyaso. ʾil-ǧawhara hāy—kull māli, māl el-ḥukūme biddhā-š, mā tkābi inno twāzinha? hātū-lna kabšet ḏahab." ḥaṭṭha b-il-mizān, ha-ḏ-ḏahabāt, hiyye baqat mlazqa bi-l-mīzān u-ḏ-ḏahab irtafaʿ. ʾe!

182 In short (my dear sir), he said, "May his house be ruined—far [from the listeners]—what a fool he is! This pearl—will not all my money and the government's money suffice to equal it? Give us a piece of gold." He put it in the scales, it stayed stuck to the scales and the [hand with] the gold rose [was lighter than the jewel]. Aye!

188 ṣār kull mā fīh ʿindo māl u-kull mā fīh ʿind ʿarabo māl, ǧābūh, ḏahab ṣāfi, yaʿni, muš ʿimle, bas ḏahab. ʾin-natīǧe, lamma iḥtār dalīlo, mā ḏall-ⁱš ʿind ʿarabo lā ḏahab la-n-niswān wa-lā ḏahab—

188 He began—all the money he had, and all the money his Bedouins had, they brought it, pure gold, that is, not coins, only gold. In short, when he got confused [literally: his proof was confused] there remained by his Bedouins neither gold for the women nor [hidden] gold—

193 maxzūn—illa ḥaṭṭ muqābel hāy el-ǧawhara, biš fāide. min el-ʿama, baʿīd il-ʿama, rāḥ qāl la-binto. ʾay naʿam. qālat-lo, "ǧīb ʿanna ʾarbaʿa u-ʿišrīn sāʿa."

193 stored—whatever he put against the jewel [had] no benefit [no use]. Because of his blind rage (let blindness be far [from your life]), he went and said [it] to his daughter. Yes, indeed. She said to him: "Stay away from me twenty-four hours."

197 ʾinna hī žtāmʿat maʿa-ṣ-ṣabi. ʾiṣ-ṣabi ʿindha, mxabba b-il-ⁱxzāne. lamma bīǧi ʾabūha bitxabbī.

197 She decidedly joined the boy. Now, the boy was at her place, hidden in the wardrobe. When her father came, she would hide him.

200 natīǧt il-ʾamer [yā sīdna l-ʿazīz], qālat-lo, "taʿāl, ʾel-masʾale hēč hēč." qāl-lha: "ʾana baḥillha, ʾimma b-šarṭ." qālt-lo, "šu š-šarṭ?" qāl-lha: "iš-šarṭ biddi š-šams u-l-qamar."

200 In short (our dear sir) she said to him, "Come, the problem is so-and-so." He said to her, "I'll solve it, but on condition." She said to him, "What is the condition?" He said to her, "The condition is that I want Shams and Qamar."

205 qālat lo, "šū bižmaʿna bī—b-ha-l-ḥači hāḏ?" qāl-lha: "qūli la-'abūč 'inno fīh ʿandak sağīn 'inti mitqalldo wa-ḥabso min tarīx keḏa. 'iftaḥ ʿalēh wa-fiqdo, 'in kānno ṭayyeb, šī 'ilak maškile balāṭ, biḥilla.	205 She said to him, "What will bring us together to this talk?" He said to her, "Tell your father that you have a prisoner whom you have tied up and jailed since this certain date. Open it [the cell] for him and check: if he's still well [alive]. The thing which you have and is difficult like a rock, he will solve it.
211 w-in čānno miyyet, maʿnāto (wi)ddak tkūn raʿāya, kull zamānak taḥt riʿāyet—'idārt-el-malek el-fulāniy. 'ana, lamman-ažtmaʿ fīh batʿāhad 'ana wiyyāh	211 "If he is dead, it means that all the time you will remain under the patronage of the certain king. I, when I meet him, I shall agree with him
215 —yihebiṭ-lek, yaʿṭīni š-šams u-l-qamar, 'ana baḥill-ha. mā ḥallētha, yiqṭaʿ rāsi."	215 —if he 'falls in' [agrees] with you, i.e., he will give me Shams and Qamar, I shall solve it. If I do not solve it—he will cut my head off."
218 qālat-lo, "maʿqūle." 'imma qāl-la, "ḥaḍrī-li, ḥaḍrī-li midd ᵉšʿīr mi(n)-šān tiġlī wa-'atġassal fīh mi(n)-šān badani sa-yuṣfurr." maʿnā yṣīr mrīḍ. [natīžt el-'amer, mā liyā, mā liyā.] 'aywā.	218 She said to him, "[This is] reasonable." He told her, "Prepare for me a *midd* [a weight unit] of barley and boil it and I'll wash myself in it in order that my body will become yellow"; that is, he will be ill. (The end of the thing is good, good [no harm on him].) Yes.
223 lamma ğa ('a)būha, qālat lo, "šuft ru'ya inno fīh ʿindak walad bi-s-siğen, hū lli biḥillha, iḏa baʿad fīh ḥayā" haḏāka nāsī: . . . min ṭūl al-waqet. nada, nada ʿala l-saǧǧīn, illi qāl-lo yisiğno, hāḏa hū.	223 When her father came to her, she said to him, "I saw a dream that you have a boy in your prison and he is the one who will solve it, if he's still alive." That one [the king] has forgotten him . . . He called, called for the jailer to whom he had said to jail him, that's it.
228 qāl-lo, "il-walad illi sağanto wa't fīh?" qāl-lo, "ḥaṭṭēto bi-l-maḥall el-fulāni." qāl-lo, "btiṭʿamo u-btisqīh, bitḥuṭṭ?" qāl-lo, "waḷḷa, 'ana nāsī. 'ēš widdak?"—min ṭūl es-sīre. rāḥu lāqūh [yā sīdna l-ʿazīz], lāqūh b-ḥālt-en-nizāʿ. mitġassel bmayyet el-šʿīr ʿend binto, ʿāmel ḥālo miyyet.	228 He said to him, "The boy whom you imprisoned, [some] time [ago] is there?" He said to him, "I've put him in a certain place." He said to him, "Do you feed him and let him drink and put (things for him)?" He said, "By Allah, I have forgotten him. What do you want?" because of the long time [story]. They went and found him (oh, our dear sir) in the state of dying—he had washed in the barley water at his daughter's [place]. He pretended to be dead.
236 ğābū, [natīğt el-'amr,] ğābū-lo dakātra u-ṣāru yġaḏḏu fīh u-'iši min ha- n-nōʿ. 'ačam min yōm, ṣiḥi, lamma ṭabʿan, hū fiyyū-š 'iši. natīžt el-'amer, atʿāhad hū w-iyyāh.	236 They brought him, in short, they brought doctors for him, and started feeding him and things of this kind [of treatment]. [After] a few days, he got better, when naturally he did not have anything [wrong]. In short, he (the emīr) met him (the boy).

241 qāl-lo, "nṭīni kitāb xaṭṭi wa-'imḏi ʿalēh tanni 'afikkha." qāl-lo, "šū biddak? šū biddak mistaʿidd 'aqaddim-lak." qāl-lo, "biddi š-šams wi-l-qamar. 'akṯar min hēk mā biddī-š minnak, wa-'ana (')ibn ʿflān min el-maḥall el-fulān" (šāyif, yā sīdu?) 'amḏa u-aʿṭāh. 'aywā.	241 He (the boy) said to him (the emīr), "Give me a handwritten letter and sign it in order that I will solve it." He said to him, "What do you want? Whatever you want, I'm willing to give you." He said to him, "I want Shams and Qamar and I want nothing else from you, and I am the son of a certain person from the certain place." ([Do you] see, sir?) He signed and gave it to him. Yes.
248 "hātu-li l-ǧawhara u-hātu-li l-mizān u-'ačam ḏahaba." qālu: "āh, šū hāḏa?" al-wazāra, "šū hāḏa, hāḏa lli biḥillha?" lamma ǧāb el-mizān, ḥaṭṭu, mulānu ḏ-ḏahab, u-ḥaṭṭu el-ǧawhara minna, u-ḥaṭṭu aḏ-ḏahabe minna, u-ǧāb nitfet ramḏa, ṭrāb, u-ḥaṭṭha ʿala ǧ-ǧawhara. tsāwu.	248 "Give me the pearl and give me the scales, and give me some gold pieces." They said, "Ah, what is this?" The ministers, "What is this? This one wants to solve it?" When he brought the scales and the gold, the pearl from one side, and they put some pieces of gold. He put some dried sand, earth, and put it on the pearl, the sides [of the scale, the pearls and the gold] got even.
255 qāl-lo, "šū hāy?" qāl-lo, "hāy ʿēn bani 'ādam; hāy maḥṣūra b-ʿēn bani 'ādam—ʿēn bani 'ādam tisbaʿ-š illa min at-trāb." qāl, "hāḏa ṣaḥīḥ."	255 He said to him [the boy], "What is this?" He said to him, "This is the eye of human beings, this is limited to humans—the human eye is not satisfied except from the ground." He said, "That is true."
260 ʿa-kull ḥāl, ittaṣal be-l-qamar u-š-šames u-tǧawwazhen u-riǧaʿ ʿal-(')abū.[5]	260 In any case, he united with Qamar and Shams, and married them and went back to his father.

Commentary

In the popular thinking of many cultures, dreams are considered to be message bearers from the future and symbols for the fulfillment of hidden wishes. The story "Between the Sun and the Moon" belongs to type ATU 725 ("A Dream about Future Greatness"). It is an adolescence story that reflects maturation processes and generational power struggles.

I recorded the story from Ibrahim Qwēder Ṣbēḥāt, a Bedouin janitor from the tribe Rummāneh-Ṣbēḥāt, who worked in the regional council Basmat-Tabʿūn (a Bedouin settlement near Kiryat Tivʿon). This is the only story I recorded from him. This narrative type is known all over Europe, Asia, and Africa. In the Israel Folktale Archives (IFA),[6] there are ten versions.[7]

Worthy of note is the version that Galit Hasan-Rokem recorded from the Moroccan storyteller Abraham Lugasi (IFA 9481). Lugasi's version is very long and very detailed. It was written down exactly as he told it, and it is very close to the Bedouin version above, containing most of the motifs that exist in the Bedouin story. It is interesting to compare the two, so I discuss it here broadly.

In Lugasi's version, the son refuses to tell his dream to his father, and his father punishes him—the son is thrown into the sea. The son swims to an island where a king has imprisoned his daughter to prevent her from meeting men (see in this context story 2, "The Princess on the Island"). The king's daughter falls in love with the son and marries him. Another king orders her father, the king, to prepare a special silver cup that will be exactly the same as the cup in his hand. No one can fulfill the mission, and the king arrives on the island to part with his daughter before the other king kills him, as he has killed many kings who failed to meet his demand. The king's daughter convinces her father that she will be able to make a similar cup. She secretly addresses her husband, and he does manage to make an identical copy. Her father, the king, hands the two cups over to the other king and wins his respect. The king's daughter reveals the secret to her father, and her father meets her husband and acknowledges him as his son-in-law. The son returns to his father and reconciles with him. An interesting Iraqi parallel is found in Inea Bushnaq's book *Arab Folktales*.[8]

The present Bedouin story takes place over a long period. It describes the hero's life from birth to adulthood. At the beginning of the story, the storyteller places foreshadowing in the mouth of the hero's teacher: "When you see it in your sleep, you will see it in your life." And indeed, the central axis of the story is a dream the hero has in his youth and fulfills as an adult.

In the beginning of the story, we hear about the good relationship between the father and his son: "Because of his pride in him, and he was a Bedouin emīr, he brought for him a private schoolteacher." The father cares about his son's education and brings him a private teacher. However, the same teacher indirectly causes a change in the father's attitude toward his son. The teacher warns his pupil that his dream will come true only if he keeps it to himself and does not tell it to anyone: "If you see a dream and you are glad with it, do not tell it to anyone, neither to your mother nor your father, or me." However, this advice causes a conflict between the boy and his parents, who do not accept the boy's attempt to resist, hold his own opinion, and rebel against their authority. The conflict begins between him and his mother, but she perpetuates the conflict rather than ignoring it. She rushes to tell the father about the son's behavior.

The father behaves recklessly. He vows that if the boy does not obey his request to reveal his secret, he will divorce his wife. The father, like the mother, does not try to solve the conflict peacefully. He escalates it, and in trying to suppress the boy's rebellion, he puts himself in the position of having to choose between the boy and his mother—between selling the boy and divorcing his wife. When the boy remains recalcitrant, the father must keep his word and choose his wife over his son.

It seems that the crisis reflects an oedipal struggle between the father and his son. The father perceives his son as a threat, as competition for the mother's love, and tries to keep him out of the house. However, once it actually happens, the father regrets his rashness and tries to rectify the situation by ordering a slave to sell the boy and then redeem him immediately.

The slave does not carry out the father's directives; as the narrator says it, "The slave did not answer this talk." He sells the boy and does not redeem him. Does he fulfill the father's innermost desire to get rid of his son, or is he perhaps jealous of the preferred status of his master's son and seeking revenge? The narrator does not give us a definite answer. From an artistic point of view, this fuzziness stimulates curiosity, leaves the situation unclear, and provides listeners some leeway. This part of the story thus creates the crisis between the two generations and the basis for further development of the plot.

However, this is not the only generational crisis in the story. The future bride of the hero manages a complex relationship with her parents, one that in a way is in opposition to the events in the hero's life. When the princess's mother thinks that the food she served her daughter was eaten by the slave, she does not exaggerate the crisis like the protagonist's mother but tries to solve the problem herself peacefully. On the other side the princess's mother harasses the hero, defames him in her talk with the *emīr*, and in fact causes the *emīr* to throw him into jail.

The narrator tells us that the hero's experiences with the wife of Abu Xalil, the first person to buy him as a slave, occurred again with a second buyer's wife, this time the emīr's wife. He tells us that the first woman "began to entice him to tell her," meaning she tries to seduce him sexually, and when he refuses the seduction, she turns to her husband and blames the hero for misconduct. It seems to be an accusation of sexual assault. The impression of the sexual assault complaint is strengthened by the description of the hero's beauty in an earlier paragraph: "The boy (was like) a (sweet) apple and polite." Later the same thing happens with the other woman. Therefore, we find here a hint, in parallel to the oedipal complex vis-à-vis the boy, of an Electra complex, as the girl and her mother compete for the affections of the same man.

The first woman, by the way, wonders about the circumstances that led to the hero's expulsion from his parents' house and being sold into slavery. The woman tries to understand how such a pretty and nice boy— "polite," as the narrator describes him—could be sold into slavery by his parents. The boy's answer is also interesting: "My father swore to divorce my mother and I did not want to tell him. *Naturally* he sold me." The boy takes for granted his father's decision and does not blame him. I will refer to his acceptance of this verdict when I discuss the connection between our story and the Islamic Qur'ān version of the biblical Joseph story.

However, let us return to the princess's relationship with her parents. Here we find a reverse symmetry. The girl encounters a problem: someone is eating her food. She turns to her mother for help. The experienced mother suspects her maidservant and advises her daughter to increase food rations and to keep an eye on the maidservant's actions. (The puzzling actions of the suspected handmaiden in a way parallel the puzzling behavior of the slave at the beginning of the story.) The mother does not tell the father what happened. She prefers to end the matter peacefully.

The daughter soon discovers the hero of the story in her room. Like her mother, she is impressed by his beauty and his nice manners. She falls in love with him and hides him. This is a rebellion against the customary rules of morality. Like the boy, she has an independent position of her own. The princess also has a secret that she must not reveal to her parents—neither to her mother nor to her father. Later she must resolve this conflict and find a way to inform her parents of the boy's presence without being condemned for inappropriate behavior.

Unlike the boy, the girl finds a middle ground; she *invents* a dream that allows her to reveal her secret to her parents and still achieve her goal of marrying the hero. The symmetry, then, is completed through a fictional dream that corresponds to the boy's real dream, one that would also come true and enable the girl to solve her critical crisis.

Another symmetrical plot point is the recklessness of the two fathers: the recklessness of the emīr, who falls into his opponent's trap and is tempted to take on solving the riddles, is equivalent to the recklessness of the father at the beginning of the story, which led to him selling his son into slavery.

Thus, the circle is completed, and both heroes— Muḥammad and the princess—overcome the youthful crises and accomplish their goals. In this respect, we can say that the story has a comedic character in the classic sense: The story begins with an initial problematic social crisis between the authority of "tribal elders" (the parents) and the younger generation, their children, who rebel against authority and demand change and renewal. The crisis is diminished, as it is in comedy, and the parental figures are not condemned but rather neutralized as they lose their power.

The struggle between the generations is a central axis of the whole story. The two young people fight for their right to keep their own place and to get the previous generation to legitimate their adulthood. It should be noted that the struggle goes beyond the family boundary. The boy must resist the seduction of the older women who covet him for his beauty and character, and later he must overcome the mistrust and contempt shown by the viziers when he comes to solve the riddle: "They said: 'Ah, what's this?' The ministers said: 'What is this? This one wants to solve it?'"

Up to this point, I have looked mainly at the content of the story and its literary structure. I have shown how both dreams—the "real" one and the fictional one—from a literary perspective, have a major role in the story: the whole story revolves around the dreams. Now we can ask, What is the role of the dreams in the *heroes' lives*?

It seems that the dream in this case is a form of communication. The hero's communication with himself and the basic spiritual experience within him form a sort of nucleus around which he develops his emerging personality. Freud argues that at the foundation of each dream there is a hidden wish. The dream of the hero is a dream of future greatness, an expression of his desire to find himself elevated to the heavenly bodies. However, the fulfillment of the dream does not happen by itself. The hero carries out his dream actively, by turning it into a measure and touchstone of his life. The important thing is not the specific content of the dream but rather the importance he attaches to it. The hero directs his life according to the principle he received from his teacher: keeping the secret. Each of the secondary heroes—the mother, the father, the two women, and the princess—is examined and judged by his or her attitude toward this secret. Only the princess, who is ready to accept the hero as he is, without trying to learn his secret—that is to say his crystallized independence—passes the test and therefore becomes the realization of his dream.

We know nothing about the other girl he marries, Abu Xalil's daughter. The names Sun and Moon (*Shams* and *Qamar* in Arabic) are not conventional. They appear in other contexts as literary heroines in Bedouin stories. Shams, Abu-Xalil's daughter, is not examined and judged by her attitude toward his secret, but one can assume that the hero knew her when he stayed in Abu-Xalil's house, and maybe he had some expectation of marrying her.

What is the role of the fictional dream in the princess's life? If we keep the idea of inverse symmetry that was proposed earlier, we could say that in her case there is a reverse movement. She has to *reconcile two opposites*. She is torn between loyalty to her parents and accepted tradition, on the one hand, and the need to follow her heart's desire, on the other. If the hero has fulfilled a dream, then it can be said that she was *fulfilling reality* through a fictional dream.

A closer look shows that the symmetry is not inverse but equivalent: each of the characters uses the dream to overcome obstacles and achieve a goal. Each of them tries to control his or her life and fate. He does it by clinging to the principle, while she does it by sophisticated manipulation of her father through a dream that never happened.

Her dream seems manipulative, and it is perceived—being false—as inferior in relation to the "real" dream of the hero. However, we must look at it in a broader perspective: The princess is facing a crisis, and it is not only her personal crisis. The fates of her father and the entire kingdom are at stake. Imagine the script of the story if the riddle had not been solved: the princess's father would have become a slave to Abu Xalil, she herself would have married him against her will, and the hero would have died of starvation.

The idea of a fictional dream was the initiative of the princess. The hero only offers her the outline. He wants to sign an agreement with the emīr that will ensure his release and his marriage to his beloved, Moon, and to the other girl, Sun. So he suggests that she tell the emīr about the forgotten prisoner, who can solve the riddle and is willing to guarantee it at the risk of losing his head. He also says that he will use the trick of barley water to pretend to be dying.

However, beyond this, he does not tell her how to put the plan into action. The princess is the one who has to execute the plan, explaining that she knows of the prisoner's existence and his fate—forgotten and starving—without raising the suspicion that she really knows him, and persuading her father that this forgotten prisoner has the knowledge necessary to solve the riddle.

The girl finds the perfect solution: she takes advantage of the Bedouin belief in dreams and their significance. She thus intelligently adapts her actions to the social customs of the tribe without giving up her ambitions. Her society has absolutely no tolerance for a girl who is having sex with a stranger (or even a friendly relationship, since the narrator does not tell us what happens while the hero stays in her room, leaving it to our imagination). Since Arab society attributes supernatural power to dreams, she describes a dream that removes any suspicion, and ensures that her father is convinced about the young boy's ability to solve the riddle that the experienced viziers have failed to solve. The narrator, whom I consider an unusual storytelling master, tells us later that the viziers disdained the boy's ability to solve the riddle, so indeed there was a real necessity to establish the status of the boy through a dream. Moreover, when the girl describes her dream to her father, she omits the boy's suggestion that he guarantee the solution with his life: "If I do not solve it—he will cut my head off." Instead, she says to her father, "I saw a dream that you have a boy in your prison and he is the one who will solve it, if he's still alive."

This is the point where our wonderful storyteller, with his natural eye for drama, feels that the most suspenseful moment in the story has arrived, and between the description of the boy's plan and the description of its actual implementation by the girl, he inserts the soothing words, "The end of the thing is good, good."

Thus, one can say that the young girl's fictional dream is not just a manipulation but a wonderful way to describe her proactive initiative in adapting herself to tribal tradition, fulfilling the desire of her heart, and saving her father and the entire kingdom. Moreover, it seems that the way the heroine chooses to face her problems is much more resourceful and imaginative than that of the hero, who persistently keeps his secret at all costs.

I have given the princess the status of a central hero, equivalent to the status of the hero, with good reason. Our narrator sings an ode to youth, and to the ways by which young people confront the world around them. He presents both the masculine way and the feminine way, and perhaps he prefers the feminine way.

In addition to discussing the dreams, it is also worthwhile to discuss the content of the riddles. The first riddle relates to the question of how to distinguish between a noble horse and a workhorse that look identical in their external appearances and skills. This riddle is rooted deeply in the Bedouin world, where breeding noble horses has always had great importance. However, beyond that is the hidden symbolism connected to the plot of the whole story: distinguishing between the horses is a metaphor for distinguishing between people. A person's true face is revealed in a state of crisis, when one is stressed and pressured. The noble horse that is not "tempted" and does not debase itself by eating its droppings is a symbol of the hero who keeps his dignity and values even at times of crisis. The hero manages to solve the riddle by relying on his life experience.

Noble origin is also an important issue in Bedouin society, which treats slaves and orphans contemptuously. With her questions, the first woman tries to find out whether the boy is an orphan, and he replies firmly, "I have a mother and a father. How (from where) am I born?" Toward the end of the story, the hero tells the emīr, "And I am the son of a certain person from a certain place"—that is to say, he emphasizes that he comes from a high-level family and is therefore worthy of marrying emīrs' daughters.

The second riddle is also a clearly symbolic one. It concerns the human greed that knows no bounds, and here we can say also that the hero solves it by relying on his experience with greedy women.

Dreams and the solving of riddles often evoke associations with the biblical story of Joseph. Indeed, if we compare our story to the Joseph story, we will find that the similarity is not coincidental.

The similarity is reflected in motifs as well as in the overall format of the story. The story of Joseph in the Bible is built as a long novella that describes the life of the hero from his birth until his death. Joseph was the eldest son of his previously barren mother, Rachel, and he became the pampered and favorite son of his father, Jacob. In his dream, he sees the heavenly bodies—the sun, the moon, and the stars—which symbolize his adolescent struggles and his future greatness. Thereafter, his father's attitude toward him changes, and he scolds his son for his dreams of greatness. Our story also covers an entire life story, from the birth of the hero to his adulthood and the moment when his dream comes true.

Since our story was told in an Islamic society, we must compare it not to the biblical tale of Joseph but to its later version in the Qur'ān, to which many elements were added from Midrashim and Islamic legends. An entire chapter in the Qur'ān (sūrah 12) is dedicated to Joseph's story. In later Islamic writings, there are expansions of the story. For example, in the Qur'ān, Jacob reacts to the dream about the sun, moon, and stars (the biblical dream of the grain sheaves is not mentioned in the Qur'ān) by saying, "O my son, do not relate your vision to your brothers, lest they plot and scheme against you. Satan is man's sworn enemy. And thus, your Lord will choose you, and will teach you the interpretation of events" (sūrah 12, 5–6). To a certain extent, Jacob plays the role of the teacher in our story, who instructs the hero to tell his dream to no one.

Joseph's brothers are jealous of his superior status and eventually sell him into slavery. In our story, the hero has no jealous brothers; the jealous figure is the slave who does not fulfill his master's instructions.

The act of selling the hero also finds its analogy in the Joseph story. Reuben does not intend to abandon his brother, but events evolve in such a way that, after Joseph is thrown into the pit, he is sold into slavery and taken from his homeland. In our story, as well, the hero's father intends to sell him for only a limited time, but the slave thwarts the father's intentions.

In the Bible, Joseph's voice is not heard at the time of the sale. He is completely passive. But later, when his brothers go to Egypt, we hear in their conversation an echo of what happened many years earlier: "And they said one to another: 'We are verily guilty concerning our brother, in that we saw the distress of his soul, when he besought us, and we would not hear; therefore is this distress come upon us'" (Genesis 42:21). In the Islamic narrative tradition, however, it was said of Joseph, "He bore his suffering in silence, and there was one saying in his mouth: everything is from Allah, and man should not doubt His deeds." There is also an echo of this acceptance in the words of the hero of our story: "I did not want to tell him. *Naturally* he sold me."

One of the most prominent elements in the Qur'ānic tradition is the description of Joseph's beauty, which is probably based on later Jewish traditions. According to the Qur'ān, the wife of the governor presents Joseph before her friends while they hold sharp knives; impressed by his beauty, they cut their fingers: "Some ladies in the city said, 'The governor's wife is trying to seduce her servant. She is deeply in love with him. We see she has gone astray.' And when she heard of their gossip, she invited them, and prepared for them a banquet, and she gave each one of them a knife. She said, 'Come out before them.' And when they saw him, they marveled at him, and cut their hands. They said, 'Good Allah, this is not a human, this must be a precious angel'" (sūrah 12, 30–31). In later Muslim sources, it is said that the governor's wife gave them apples and, peeling the apples, they cut their hands. This description appears also in a Jewish Midrash, where instead of apples she gives them citrons (Midrash Tanhuma 39:5).

This story has become a central theme in Islam, and the scene is depicted on many art objects—carpets, pictures, and miniatures—throughout the Muslim world.[9] In the Bedouin story, we find an echo in the narrator's remarks: "Abu Xalil was satisfied with the boy. The boy (was like) a (sweet) apple and polite."

Later, the temptation motif appears once again, and the hero is thrown into jail after an accusation of sexual harassment. Like Joseph, our hero is also forgotten and left to rot in jail, and his rescue, like Joseph's, is due to his ability to decipher obscure meanings. Joseph solves the ministers' and Pharaoh's dreams. The Bedouin hero solves the riddles that were presented to the emīr.

There is a strong connection between riddles and dreams. Joseph is a dream interpreter, but he also solves problems, using a guessing cup: "And Joseph said, What is this thing which you have done? Had you no thought that such a man as I would have power to see what is secret?" (Genesis 44:15).

Joseph marries Asenath, the daughter of Poti-phera, the priest of On—that is to say, a woman of high status. Our hero marries two emīrs' daughters. Midrash Bereshit (Genesis) Rabbah identifies Poti-phera with Potiphar and suggests that Joseph married the daughter of the woman who tried to seduce him (Midrash Bereshit Rabbah 86:3). Our story, as we have seen, follows the same script.

Another interesting analogy to the biblical Joseph stories is the use of the number two instead of three, the usual typological number in folktales. In Joseph stories, all the dreams appear in pairs: Joseph's two dreams, the ministers' two dreams, and Pharaoh's two dreams. In our story, we find the number two repeatedly: The hero finds himself in a dream between two celestial bodies—the sun and the moon. The hero twice refuses to reveal his secret, to his mother and to his father. The hero was sold twice. Two women try to force him to tell his secret. There are two riddles, and in each of them, two objects (two horses and two gems), and the hero marries two wives.

The two gems symbolize two eyes. The motif of a man's eyes being insatiable until they are covered with earth also appears in the Babylonian Talmud, in the story of Alexander's visit to heaven (Babylonian Talmud, Tamid 32b):

> As Alexander was journeying, he sat by a spring and began to eat bread. He had with him some salted fish, and as they were being washed, they gave off a sweet odour. He said, "This shows that this spring comes from the Garden of Eden." Some say that he took some of the water and washed his face with it; others say that he went alongside of it until he came to the door of the Garden of Eden. He cried out, "Open the door for me." They replied, "This is the gate of the Lord, the righteous shall enter into it." [Ps. 118:20] He replied, "I too am a king; I am also of some account, give me something." They gave him a cranium (with empty eyeballs). He went and weighed all his silver and gold against it, and it was not equal to it. He said to the Rabbis, "How is this?" They replied, "It is the eyeball of a human being, which is never satisfied." He said to them, "How can you prove that this is so?" They told him, "Take a little dust and cover this eye." And immediately it was weighed down; and so, it is written, "Hell and Destruction are never full and the eyes of man are never satiated." (Prov. 27:20)

This idea is expressed in an Arab proverb: "Nothing will fill the eye of the greedy except the dust" (*mā yemalli 'en al-ḥasūd 'ġēr al-trāb*).

In the Bedouin story, the hero is thrown into prison, and the emīr's daughter provides him with food. A similar episode appears in Midrash "Vayosha."[10] In this Midrash, Moses describes how he came to Midian and was thrown into prison by Jethro. Zipporah, Jethro's daughter, provides him with food from her father's table for seven years, and thus he manages to stay alive throughout his imprisonment. The description overlaps in many details with the Bedouin hero's description of being thrown into prison and his rescue:

> And every day Zipporah supported me from all the delicacies of her father, Jethro, until I completed seven years in the pit. Seven years later, Zipporah said to her father, "I remember, my father, that once you took one man who brought you the stick and you threw him into the pit and you made a great iniquity. If you want, open the pit and look: If he is dead, take him out and throw his carcass out so that his body will not be left stinky in your house, and if he is alive, you will know that he is a complete tsaddik [righteous]." He said to her, "My daughter, you speak well, do you remember his name?" She said to him, "I remember his name was Moses son of Amram." Immediately Jethro went and opened the pit and called, "Moses, Moses!" I replied, "Here I am!" And he took me out of there, kissed me on the head, and said, "Blessed is Allah who has kept you in the pit for seven years. I testify that He slays and revives. And I testify that you are a complete righteous man, and by your saying Egypt is destined to be destroyed, and by your saying the Egyptians will drown in the sea—Pharaoh and his army." And he gave me money, and gave me his daughter Zipporah as a wife, and made a stipulation with me that all the children that will be born in my house shall be half Jews, and half Ishmael. (Midrash Vayosha, 7–8)

One can assume another possible influence in the story of Sendebar (*The Seven Sages of Rome*—a cycle of stories of Sanskrit, Persian, and Hebrew origins), or Syntipass, in the Bedouin tale. In the frame story of Sendebar, the hero, the king's son, is also ordered by his teacher to keep a secret (actually not to talk for a certain time even to his father). The king's concubine tries to entice the hero to kill his father and marry her, and when he does not agree, she accuses him publicly of attempting to rape her. Here also the king is described as a reckless man who is ready to kill his son without inquiry.[11]

As mentioned, the story revolves around the dream motif. The analysis of the story clearly exposes a variety of beliefs related to the perception of dreams in the folktale. The dream serves as a precursor of a wish fulfillment, as a driving force in the hero's life, as an axis and guiding principle of his life, as a source of authority, and as an instrument by which the weak can overcome the strong. The dream is perceived, both from the perspective of the dreamers and from the perspective of the listeners, as a sign from heaven, a real message from Allah. In the popular thinking, there is a strong connection between dreams and riddles: the dreamer, like Joseph, is revealed as a solver of riddles.

Folktales pass from one generation to another, from father to son and from mother to daughter; thus, it is not surprising to find that the subject of relations between generations plays a central role in such stories. The story reflects the struggle between the two generations: the young people attempt to get their parents to treat them like adults who have the right to act on their desires. The story also emphasizes the extent to which parents' actions affect the fates of their children: the hero is sold into slavery because of the recklessness of his father, and the emīr's daughter might have shared the same fate because of her father's recklessness.

Finally, it can be said that folktales in general convey something of the spirit of a dream. As human beings, we live in a world with ambiguity and uncertainty, where things are more hidden than known. The folktale, like the dream, expresses a hidden wish in the heart of all of us: the desire to control our destiny instead of being a pawn in the hands of unknown forces. In the story, as in a dream, we have the possibility of weaving another reality that will strengthen our confidence in the world order, the triumph of justice over evil, and the fulfillment of our desires.

However, the good storyteller, as I show here and throughout this analysis, nevertheless succeeds in maintaining a certain ambiguity. Just as in a dream, there are unmistakably fundamental, enigmatic elements, and the heroes must interpret their dreams; thus, in a good story, things are not so cut and dried. The plot of the story has a convoluted course, and we, the listeners, do not know everything. We must fill in the gaps using our imagination.

This is true in stories as in real life—where we also must decode signs and interpret them throughout the course of our lives. This is a source of pain and sadness but also a source of beauty and excitement in dreams, in stories, and in reality.

Notes

1. IFA—The Israel Folktale Archives. See note 6 in this chapter.

2. A traditional older Bedouin folktale begins with a *traditional introduction* and ends with a *traditional ending.* These tale parts are sometimes set formulas (e.g., kān yā mā kān, "[it] was or was not") and in other cases short, accepted discourse elements (e.g., *hāḏa*, "this [m.sg.]," *hēna*, "here," etc.). However, the rush and bustle of modern life also has penetrated this realm of stories, and often these traditional folkloristic parts are missing, although the content of a story is somehow retained. Narrators may know the introduction and ending formulas but often fail to use them. This story, for example, begins without any such opening and ends without any formal ending. (In the end, we hear only that "the hero went back to his father.")

The nature of every Bedouin story differs from stories of sedentary (urban or rural) Arabic speakers. One of the most frequent and characteristic features is the narrator's *concise reference to the participants* in the story, the heroes, the heroines, and their accomplices. Since the story narrates events, the dialogue among the participants raises much of the interest. The narrator, whether a man or a woman, usually does not mention the speaker's name and just uses the verb *to say* in the third person ("*she/he/they said to him/her,*" etc.). The context should enable the listener/reader to understand who is speaking to whom and how the speakers are related. Many such examples are found throughout the folktales in this book, including this first story.

3. Another feature of Bedouin stories is the *conciseness of description.* As analyzed in the folkloristic commentary, many elements of the story are left hidden, unmentioned, and up to the listeners' imagination. This issue has been compared to other old stories as in the Bible, where brevity is the main model (cf. Goitein, *Narrative Art in the Bible*; Fishbane, *Biblical Text and Texture*; Bar-Efrat, *Narrative Art in the Bible*). Thus, the connection between this Bedouin story and biblical elements such as Joseph's story is visible not only on the level of contents but also on the level of style and linguistic discourse structures.

In the following parts of these notes, we continue to mention linguistic features that are typical of the Galilee Bedouin stories and Bedouin stories in general.

4. The Galilee Bedouins settled in the area more than a century ago. Therefore, their contacts with the local sedentary population have been affecting them in many ways, as we note in various stories in this book.

5. Frequent repetition of sentences is another feature of these Bedouin narratives, used for emphasis or effect, as rhetorical sentences. These issues are also noted throughout the book.

6. The Israel Folktale Archives (IFA), named in honor of its founder, Professor Dov Noy, was established in 1955. It contains about twenty-five thousand oral folk narratives passed down over the generations by newly arriving immigrants and veteran Israelis alike, including Jews, Arabs, Druze, Circassians, and others. The archives are presently housed at the University of Haifa. IFA has the largest collection of Jewish folktales in Israel and the world over. IFA plays an important role in advancing the cultural heritage of Israel's many ethnic communities and in encouraging open dialogue among cultures and ethnicities.

7. Morocco (6106, 9190, 9481), Egypt (7007), Turkey (1025), Yemen (6399), Iraq (1590), Kurdistan (6762), Iran (11571), and Samaritan version (1481).

8. Bushnaq, *Arab Folktales*, 326–31.

9. Brosh, *Biblical Stories in Islamic Painting*, 29–31, 48–73.

10. Midrash Vayosha is a short Midrash that interprets the two verses before Shirat Ha-Yam (Song of the Sea) (Exodus 14:30–31) and the verses of Shirat Ha-Yam itself (Exodus 15:1–18), according to their order. The Midrash was apparently held at the end of the eleventh or early twelfth centuries.

11. Epstein, *Tales of Sendebar*, 86.

2. The Princess on the Island

NARRATOR: Ṯalǧe Mūsa

TRIBE: *ʿArab el-Ḥuǧērāt*
IFA 17402 February 5, 1982

1 bī hā-l-emīr. ʿindo hā-l-binet.[1] hāḏ-al-binet hī ǧamīle, zēne, yaʿani. yōm min ḏāt al-ʾayyām, u-hal-ʿarab—ṣār ʾalli ʿindo walad yigūl, "biddi bint al-ʾamīr flān," yaʿani, miṯel ma tgūl bint el-ʾamīr mḥimmad, bidna bint al-ʾamīr.	1 There was this emīr, [and] he had a daughter. This daughter/girl was beautiful, pretty, that is. One day, these Bedouins, those who had a boy (male child), started to say, "I want [to marry] the certain emīr's daughter. That is, Emīr Mhammad's daughter, we want [to marry] the emīr's daughter."
7 šū gāl el-ʾamīr?[2] gāl, "tiǧi ʾaǧawwizha. hāḏi mitʿallme!" wēn ḥaṭṭha? ḥaṭṭa b-qaṣr ʿāli, lā tšūf lā ḏakar wa-lā ʾunṯa.	7 What did the emīr say? He said, "It will come; I will marry her off; she's a learned girl." Where did he put her? He put her in a high castle, she would see neither a male nor a female.
11 ṣārat an-nās titsammaʿ biha, miṯel wāḥad ygūl "ʾana biddi binto, ʾana biddi binto." qāl: "waḷḷāhi, illa ʾaḥammilha wa-aḥuṭha ib-hā-l-ǧazīre!"	11 The people started hearing about her and said, that is, "I want his daughter, I want his daughter." . . . He said, "By Allah, I'll carry her [off] and put her in this island,
15 ǧazīre bi-l-baḥar, miṯel ma tgūl, ǧazīre b-hā-l-baḥar, ʿāli, u-mā fī wāḥad yiʾdar yfūt-elha. yōm min ḏāt hā-l-ayyām ḥaṭṭ hā-l-bint hināk, hā-l-ǧazīre. šū biddo ysāwe? ʿalēha ḥaras, ḥaṭṭ hā-l-ḥaras ʿalēha.	15 an island in the sea, as you say, island in the sea, high [island], and no one will be able to come to her." One day, he put this girl there, on that island. What did he want to do? Guards. He put guards on her.
21 yōm hā-r-rāʿi. rāʿi miʿza, qāʿed hāḏa r-rāʿi ^{i}b-hā-š-šita. u-ṣārat bidha ad-dunya	21 One day, this shepherd, herdsman, was sitting, this shepherd, in the rain.

23 tišti, ʿala-ğanb al-baḥar. winn hā l-faras. fāṭse. gaṣṣ yaʿani ḏaherha, fāt eb-gaḷb al-faras, yaʿni fāṭse, fāṭse. widdo yiḏri. widdo yiḏru min kuṯr-el-mayy wi-min kuṯr-il-laḥm el-baḥar yrūḥ u-yīği.	23 It started raining, on the edge of the sea. Lo, there was a mare, a corpse. He cut her back and entered into the mare, that is, the corpse, corpse. He wanted to avoid, wanted to avoid—from the water abundance, and the sea [that] was coming and going.
28 ʾağa čalb. yōm-enn ač-čalb saḥab, biddo yōkl-el-faras. sew-ḥab al-faras, biya, u-l-zalame bīha, l-walad, r-rāʿi. saḥabo bīha, wēn axaḏo? la-ʿind el-bint . . . ač-čalb ba-l-baḥar, yefūt hāḏa ʿinda, huwwa, ʾaxaḏ al-faras u-hū yitxabbi, al-walad, ib-gaḷbha.	28 There came a dog. When the dog carried, wanted to eat the mare. It carried the mare, in it, with the man in it, the boy, the shepherd. It carried him in it. Where did it take him? To the girl. The dog in the sea, entered her [place]; it took the mare and he was hiding inside it, the boy, within it.
35 el-walad ma-hu šāʿer, inno b-gaḷb al-baḥar, ʿala wağh el-mayy māši, w-ač-čalb yimši. miši, ʾa - ḥaṭṭ, fāt ʿala ha-ğ-ğazīre. yōmin fāt ʿala hā-ğ-ğazīri, ʾağa ʿalēha. qaʿad ʿala hā-ğ-ğazīre. u-ṭṭallaʿ, iṭṭallaʿ—fiš ḥada. qaʿad ^{i}b-ğanb ha-l-qaṣar. hāḏa[3] biddo yōkol, biddo yišrab—fiš ʾiši. ṣār yiṭṭalleʿ, yiṭṭalleʿ	35 The shepherd, he did not feel, that he was in the sea, on the face of the water, walking, and the dog was going, going. Ah—It put down—entered this island. When it entered the island, he [the boy] went onto it. He sat on this island and looked and looked [around]—no one [was there]. He was sitting near the castle. This [man] wanted to eat, to drink—there was nothing. He started looking, looking [around].
43 šāfato. hiyye ^{i}ṭṭallaʿat min fōq willa hā-l-bane ʾādam. qālat-lo, "mnēn ğīt?" qāl-lha, "u-mnēn inte ğīti^{y}?" qālat-lo, "m(i)n an-naṣīb." qālat lo, "iṭlaʿ ğāy."	43 She saw him. She was looking from above and lo [there was] a human. She said to him, "Where did you come from?" He said to her, "And where did you come from?" She said to him, "By fate." She said to him, "Come up to me."
47 iṭlaʿ ğāt. ğā. ta-lli gāl-(l)ha mnēn. "ʾana kunt ʿa-šaṭṭ al-baḥar u-saḥabni, u-mā ʿrift tann šū ʾawṣalni, laʾēt." gāl-lha, "w-inti?"	47 He came up to her, and he said to her where he had come from. "I was on the sea beach, and suddenly it dragged me and I did not know what made me come here, I met. . . ." He said to her, "And you?"
50 gālat-lo, "ʾana, ʾabūya ḥiča fi wlād il-amīr u-mā biddo yğawwizni. yalla, taʿāl, biddna nitğawwaz."[4] hadōl eğ-ğimāʿa ittafagu maʿa baʿaḏhin. widdhin yitğawwazu. itğawwaza.	50 She said to him, "I, my father spoke with boys of the emīr and did not want to marry me off. Come on, come, we need to get married." These guys [the two of them] agreed with each other, they wanted to marry, and they got married.
55 yōm ʾabūha, min baʿed sabʿa—ṯamāni snīn, sitt—sabʿe snīn, ʾaḷḷāhu ʾaʿlam, la-wēnta, gāl "biddi ʾarūḥ ʾašūf binti—šu ṣār bīha. hī mātat? hī ṭābat? hī—šū?" rāḥ eb-hā-s-safīne la-ʿindha, laqa z-zalame ʿindha, gāl-lha; "šū hāḏ, yā-āba?"	55 One day, her father, after seven or eight years, six or seven years, Allah knows [how many] till when, [he] said, "I will go and see my daughter, what has become of her. Is she dead? Is she better? She—what?" He went in a boat to her, and found that man with her. He said to her, "What's this, o my daughter?"

61 qālat lo, "yā-ba, yā man ha-z-zimān šakk-lo gaḏa, mā lak ma binsawāh. ʼinta hazamtni min šān lā ašūf ar-riğāl. u-ʼaḻḻa baʿaṯ-li hā-r-rağul min el-baḥar u-ğāb li iyyāh, ğābo. ač-čalb ğarr li iyyā u-ğāb li iyyāh la-ʿindi." šāyif?	61 She said to him, "O father, the one for whom time has formed his fate, there is nothing that can be done [against it]. You left me so that I will not see men, and Allah sent me the man from the sea and brought him to me. It brought him, the dog carried him and brought him to me." See?
67 saḥab ḥālo, aṭlaʿha u-aṭlaʿo u-banā-lhin bēt šaʿar u-gaʿad aǧ-ǧimāʿa ʿend ʼabūha. ṣārat al-ʿarab tgūl, "ṭayyeb mnēn, tanno hāḏa ğawwaz binto?	67 He went away, took her out and took him out and built a tent for them and they stayed [lived] near her father's [place]. The Bedouins started to say, "Well, where has this one got his daughter married?
71 mā wadda binto tannha mā titğawwaz, wa-ʼağat mitğawze we-ğābat wāḥad ^{i}mʿāha?" ṣārat al-ʿarab titxarraf u-tgūl, "waḻḻāhi, bidna nšūf."	71 "Didn't he send his daughter so she does not marry and she comes married and brings someone with her?" The Bedouins started talking and saying, "By Allah, we want to see."
75 gāl-lhen, "taʿālu ta-axarrifko quṣṣ^{u}t binti. ʼana waddēt binti ʿa-ğ-ğazīre, ğazīrt el-baḥar, tanna ma tšūf hā-r-rğāl, u-ʼaḻḻa baʿaṯ-ilha wāḥad ʿala-hā-ğ-ğazīre u-ğawwazato.	75 He said to them, "Come, and I'll tell you my daughter's story. I took my daughter to the island, the island of the sea, so that she will not see men, and Allah sent one to her to the island and they got married.
80 ʼa, lehā hī, lawenn čān yeğības ta ʼala hū, aṭ-ṭēr. ywaddi-lha. aṭ-ṭēr ywaddi-lha ʼakel ʼabūha, ʼabūha ywaddi maʿ-eṭ-ṭēr—bī ṭēr miṯl-en-nisr, ywaddi-la tōkel. kull yōm ywaddī-la tōkel. yīği la-ʿinda, bil-ʼawwal yiğīb, bil-ʼawwal ilha, laḥāla. ṣār yiğīb essa la-ṯnēn—ʼilha u-la-ğōzhe. u-hāy hī l-xurrafiyye. hāy hī l-xurrafiyye, miš ʼiši.	80 "Yes, for her, her, if it would bring—only it, the bird. [It] would bring for her, [the bird] would bring her father's food. Her father would send it to her with the bird—there was a bird, like an eagle, it would take [food] for her to eat. Every day it would bring her [and she] would eat. It would come to her, in the beginning it brought—in the beginning it brought for her alone. It started bringing now for the two—for her and her husband." And this is the story. This is the story, it's nothing.

Commentary

This story was told by Ṯalğe Mūsa, from the ʿArab el-Ḥuğērāt tribe. She had married an Arab from the village of Kaukab Abu-l-Hiğa, and she lives there to this day. Another version was told by Ṣabḥa ʿAbūd, from the same tribe, who lives in the Bedouin village of Dahariya near Yodfat (Western Galilee). I have written down many of Ṯalğe's stories, some of which she had heard in childhood from wandering storytellers. Ṯalğe and Ṣabḥa worked with me in the flower fields of Yodfat and were the first informants I recorded.

"The Princess on the Island" is one of the Jewish oikotypes (local types) of the international type ATU 930A, "The Predestined Wife."[5]

Yoav Elstein has extensively reviewed the Hebrew versions and sources of the story, as has Aliza Shenhar.[6] The most known Hebrew version was published by Shlomo Buber, in the introduction to *Midrash Tanhuma* in 1885, and was based on a manuscript from the Bodleian Library in Oxford. Another version, published by A. M. Habermann, was based on a fragment of the Cairo Genizah in Cambridge.[7]

Here is the story from *Tanhuma*—Buber's manuscript:[8]

> It is told that King Solomon had a most beautiful daughter whose like could not be found in the whole land of Israel. He watched the stars to see who was her appointed spouse and who would wed her, and saw that this would be a certain poor man, and none would be poorer than he in Israel. What did he do then? He built a lofty tower in the sea and had walls around it on every side. Then he took his daughter and set her in that lofty tower and placed seventy eunuchs of the elders of Israel with her. In that tower he made no entrance in order that no man should be able to enter, but in it he placed ample provender and said, "Now let me see the acts and workings of His Name!"
>
> In due course, that poor man who was the maiden's destined spouse set out on a journey by night. Now he was ragged and barefoot, starving and thirsting, and had nothing on which to lie. He saw the carcass of an ox flung away in the field and crept in between the ribs to keep himself warm. There he fell asleep, and a huge bird came and took that carcass and bore it away to the roof of the tower above the maiden's room. There the bird consumed the flesh of the carrion, and there it stayed on the roof.
>
> At daybreak, the maiden left her room to go and walk on the roof as was her daily fashion, and there she saw that youth. "Who are you," she asked him, "and who brought you hither?" And he answered: "I am a Jew of the city of Acre, but a bird brought me hither." What did she do then? She took him to her room and clothed him and washed him and anointed him, and then he was shown to be so handsome that his like could not be found in all the regions of Israel.
>
> Now the maiden fell in love with him with all her heart and soul, and her soul was linked to his, and the young man was keen and shrewd and witty and a scribe. One day she said to him, "Are you prepared to hallow me as your wife?" "Would that I might!" said he to her. And what did he do? He let some blood and wrote her a marriage contract with a bride price stated therein, all with his blood, and he hallowed her to him and said: "Witness is the Lord this day and witnesses are Michael and Gabriel the angels!" And he joined with her after the fashion of all men, and she conceived from him.
>
> When the elders saw that she was pregnant, they said to her: "It seems that you are bearing a child within you." "True," she told them. "And from whom have you conceived?" they asked her. "What business is it of yours to know?" she answered. At that the faces of the elders fell, because they dreaded King Solomon and feared that he might bring charges against them. So, they sent for him to come and speak to them. Solomon took ship and came to them. And they told him: "Your majesty, this is how things are, and do not put any blame upon your servants!" When he heard this, he summoned his daughter and asked her what had happened. And she answered him: "The Holy and Blessed One brought me a good and handsome youth, a scholar and a scribe, and he has hallowed me to him for wife." She summoned the youth, and he came to the king and showed him the marriage contract he had made for the princess. Then the king asked him details of his father and his mother and his family and the city from which he came; and from his answers he understood that this was the one whom he had seen in the stars. Then he

rejoiced very much indeed and said: "Blessed is the Ever Present who gives a man his own!" And that is the point of the verse: "God sets the lonely in families" (Ps. 68:7).

I will not discuss the Hebrew versions of the story extensively but will make a few comments. This novella is centered on a marriage, which takes place without witnesses. In the *Tanhuma* version, the wedding ceremony happens prior to any sexual relationship. During the marriage ceremony, the young man says to the young woman, "Witness is the Lord this day and witnesses are Michael and Gabriel the angels!" In the Genizah version, the *kiddushin* (sanctification) is performed first by the act of sexual intercourse, and only after the girl is pregnant does the young man say, "We have no witnesses, before whom shall I sanctify you?" And the young woman answers: "We will put our heads out the window and say: God will be a witness, and when this is known to my father and he will ask us about the matter of *kiddushin* and who were the witnesses, we will tell him: The Lord was witness between us." It is interesting to note that in the *Tanhuma* version, it is the young man who initiates the choosing of God and his messengers as witnesses, while in the Genizah version the initiative comes from the girl.[9]

On the other hand, in both Bedouin versions, it seems that the problem of witnesses does not bother the narrators, and in both stories, the initiative to marry is that of the king's daughter.

At the beginning of the story, the girl surrenders passively to her father's whims, and, as the story progresses, she becomes increasingly active and proactive. In Ṣabḥa ʿAbūd's version, she descends from a tree, introduces herself to the boy, interrogates him, and eventually asks him to marry her. In Ṯalǧe's version, the young woman looks down at him from the palace roof, interrogates him, invites him to come up to her, and finally initiates the marriage (the division of roles is clear since she is a princess and he is a shepherd).[10] It is noteworthy that in the two Bedouin versions the young woman looks at the young man from above at the beginning of the encounter.

The king is the active figure at the beginning of the story. He tries to change fate. However, by the end of the story he accepts what has happened. The passive-active role of the daughter, as opposed to the active-passive role of the father, is closely linked to the struggle between the parents' and children's generations.

The king represents the older generation in the plot, while the princess and her beloved represent the younger. In addition to the king's attempt to challenge fate, there is an intergenerational struggle that ends with the victory of the young couple.

Regarding the spatial components of the story, it appears that the plot begins in the king's palace and continues into the middle of the sea, with no exact site defined. The king's daughter moves from the land, which is stable, to a less stable site, to the heart of the sea, and the young man, who begins his journey on land, eventually reaches the sea. The ever-changing sea symbolizes and marks the change, the transition to the unknown.

Sea and tower are also erotic symbols. Water sources, such as sea, pool, and well, are all distinctly female symbols, whereas a palace and tower are clearly masculine symbols. The combination of these two elements in the story hints at an erotic connection between the heroes. In an overwhelming majority of the stories about journeys taking place in the sea, as Dov Noy points out, "The sea passage brings the hero to sexual adventure,"[11] and our story certainly fits this pattern.

The young man starts at the social bottom as a simple man (a shepherd), hungry, thirsty, seeking cover from the rain, but by the end of the plot, he is the king's son-in-law. The spatial landmarks symbolize the upheaval: he begins his journey at a low site—the seashore—and ends it in a high place, a tower.

The contrast between the daughter and her father is also reflected in the protagonists' different relationships to Allah. In Ṣabḥa ʿAbūd's version, Allah is completely absent. On the other hand, in Ṯalǧe Mūsa's version, the name of Allah appears eight times in different forms. The final words of the story are "*kullu min Allah*"— "all [is] from Allah." It is likely that the variations stem from the different circumstances of the narrators' lives. Ṯalǧe Mūsa, who married a rural Arab, is a religious woman who strictly observes prayer and the fast of Ramadan and who was even crowned as a *Ḥāǧǧa* after her pilgrimage to Mecca. On the other hand, the first narrator is less religious.

In Ṯalǧe's version, at the beginning of the story, the father mentions Allah: "By Allah, I'll carry her [off] and put her in this island." The words "By Allah" (*waḷḷāhi*) are the usual form of oath, but here it seems as if the father tries Allah and challenges him. At the end of the story, he accepts the law: "And Allah sent one to her to the island and they got married."

On the other hand, to the daughter, Allah appears to be helping her personally and canceling her father's intention: "O father, the one for whom time has formed his fate, there is nothing that can be done [against it]. You left me so that I will not see men, and Allah sent me the man from the sea and brought him to me."

The same model for God's place in the story also characterizes the Hebrew version, cited above, where God appears four times: (1) in Solomon's words at the beginning of the story, "Now let me see the acts and workings of His Name!"; (2) in the boy's words during the wedding, "Witness is the Lord this day"; (3) in the young woman's words, "The Holy and Blessed One brought me a good and handsome youth"; (4) and in Solomon's words at the end of the story, "Blessed is the Ever Present who gives a man his own!" Solomon's words have a symmetrical structure. This is an intellectual process of experimentation and error, which ends with a principled conclusion: "who gives a man his own [wife]." In the words of the young man and woman, there is another symmetry. For them, divine intervention is not a question but an existing fact: The Lord witnesses everything; He is present in every moment. He takes care of me personally, says the girl: "The Holy and Blessed One brought *me* a good and handsome youth."

In the Hebrew version, the king imprisons the girl on the island in an attempt to change the fate recorded in the stars. At the end of the story, the king admits his failure and concludes, "Blessed is the Ever Present who gives a man his own [wife]." In Ṣabḥa ʿAbūd's version, the king decides arbitrarily: "My daughter—I do not want to marry her, and I do not want the boys to see her." However, at the end of the story, the king says to the young man, "This is your part and your destiny, child, and you are my son-in-law." This suggests that it was not an arbitrary whim of the king but an attempt to change his daughter's fate. In Ṯalǧe's version, the king incarcerates his daughter because he wants to keep her from unsuitable suitors: "It will come; I will marry her off; she's a learned girl." At the end, the daughter is the one who defies her father: "O father, that one for whom time has formed his fate, there is nothing that can be done [against it]. You left me so that I will not see men, and Allah sent me the man from the sea and brought him to me." Later, when the king tells his friends about what happened, he concludes: "I took my daughter to the island, the island of the sea, so that she will not see men, and Allah sent one to her to the island and they got married." The basic motif of the challenge to fate and the admission of the power of Allah at the end is thus clearly evident in both the Hebrew and Bedouin versions.

One last point of note is the function of the bird in the story. In the *Tanhuma* version, a large bird carries the bull's carcass to the tower and thus ends its part in the plot. In Ṣabḥa ʿAbūd's version, the bird is replaced by a wild animal that comes from the sea. In Ṯalǧe's version, a type of dog, whose nature has not been explained, appears. The large eagle-shaped bird in Ṣabḥa ʿAbūd's version fulfills another role: it provides food and drink for the young woman. Initially, the bird is described as acting on its own initiative out of pity, but later in the story, it is revealed that the bird also is familiar with the princess's story. After she marries the young man, it rushes to inform the king, and at his request, it brings the two spouses by air from the island to the king's palace. In Ṯalǧe's version, the bird is completely absent from the story, and the king arrives on the island in a ship, as occurs in the Hebrew version. In Ṯalǧe's version, unlike in Ṣabḥa ʿAbūd's version, the daughter is not abandoned to her fate on the island but is watched over by guards and lives in a palace established by the king on the island. The guards are only mentioned once. The bird, which brings food to the young woman and later also to her husband and which informs the king of events, is not mentioned in this version. The king visits the island because he wants to know what has happened to his daughter.

When Ṯalǧe finished telling her story, I asked if there was also a bird in the tale, and she remembered details she had forgotten to mention. She noted that it was a bird that brought the princess food on the king's errand, and, when it discovered that the girl had married, the bird cooperated with the couple and doubled the ration.

In the version brought by Habermann from the Cairo Genizah, a hoopoe brought the boy to the tower. Later, another bird, the *ḥantura*, whose nature is unclear, appears. This bird informs Solomon that the heavens agree to his daughter's marriage with the young man brought by the hoopoe. The *ḥantura* learned this when it visited heaven and saw Elijah bringing water to Abraham in honor of Solomon's daughter's marriage. Its knowledge of the celestial approval is reinforced when it visited the angels' mansion, where the event was celebrated simultaneously with the wedding on earth (the fact that the prophet Elijah was not yet born in Solomon's time does not bother the narrator particularly). It should also be noted that in this version the young man is brought to the princess in a horse skin, in a manner similar to that in the two Bedouin narratives.

The Bedouin versions correspond in many ways to the Genizah version, yet they more closely resemble the Hebrew version of the *Tanhuma*. The fact that the king converses with the bird may indicate that he is King Solomon, who according to both the Jewish and Muslim traditions knew the language of animals and birds. It is probable that the story entered the Muslim traditions from Jewish sources, but there is no firm evidence of this.

Elstein, who also discusses the Arab versions of the story, presents a version that was written by the theologian and historian Muḥammad al-Tabari (839–923) in the ninth century. In this version, the name of the bird is *Symruch*. The *symruch* initiates the incarceration of the young woman, "The Princess from the West," in its nest to prove to King Solomon that it can break fate's decree. Here the bird seems to fulfill two roles: it abducts the young woman and provides her with food. Later, the young man (who is "The Prince of the East" and not just a simple man) tricks the bird and reaches the nest in the skin of an animal, which the bird carries, without its knowledge. Again, the young woman shows initiative by tricking the bird and keeping the prince hidden. At the end of the story, the bird brings the princess to Solomon to show him that it has indeed succeeded in changing her predicted future. However, when the princess emerges from the skin, the prince and the son who was born to the couple step out, as well. The *symruch* flies away because of the shame of its failure and, afterward, is seen no more.

In a Moorish version of the story, "Solomon and the Gryphon," which was recorded in Algeria, the place of the bird who initiates imprisoning the girl in an isolated place is taken by a creature half-eagle and half-lion and not by King Solomon.[12]

In a Judeo-Spanish version by Rivka Arieli (IFA 12745), King Solomon assembles all the animals and declares that each person has a mate destined by heaven. To test the correctness of the declaration, one eagle abducts a girl and raises her in a mountain cave. A young man arrives there by chance and marries the young woman, and the couple has three children. When King Solomon assembles the animals again, the eagle, who wishes to refute the king's words, tells of the kidnapping of the young woman. At the king's request, it delivers her in a large chest. When the chest is opened, not only does the girl step out but so do her spouse and their three children, and the eagle admits the truth of the king's declaration.

Notes

1. One of the differences between speech and reading is that **speech is richer in prosodic means than normal written texts**. The human voice transmits many more meanings in a spoken message than punctuation does. Prosody includes **intonation (melodies), pauses, speech rate (quick or slow), amplitude (vocal force),** etc. Thus, grammatically defined sentences (i.e., utterances that have a subject and a predicate, for example) may be part of a larger intonation unit. However, an intonation unit may begin after a pause and end with a pause without comprising both subject and predicate sentence parts, thus not making a "grammatical sentence." This story, as many of the other stories in this book, begins with short grammatical sentences, split by short breaks (pauses). For example, "There was this emīr, (and) he had a daughter. This daughter/girl was beautiful, pretty, that is. One day, these Bedouins, those who had children, started to say, I want (to marry) the certain emīr's daughter." These first lines provide the setting of the story: two main characters—the emīr and his daughter—and the issue of her marriage options. We note this because no particle (at times named a "discourse marker") links these sentences in Arabic. (The English translation adds them in brackets to create a coherent English style.) The pauses may be short or long, which is audible in the recordings but not shown in the written texts. Compared with English discourse markers (or written punctuation marks), Arabic and its dialects use fewer particles than English does, and they appear in different places in the text. See these language-specific features in many points in this book.

2. A very frequent and characteristic style element of Bedouin narration is that the narrator asks a **rhetorical question and answers it immediately, by repeating it** (fully or partially). This structure precedes a direct speech utterance or any other sentence that the narrator uses. See **šū gāḷ el-'amīr? gāḷ,** "What did the emīr say? He said," (line 3). If the "answer" is not repeated, it may be a brief telegraphic (rhetorical) answer, as in line 8: **šū biddo ysāwe? ʿalēha ḥaras, ḥaṭṭ hā-l-ḥaras ʿalēha.** "What did he want to do? Guards on her. He placed these guards (to watch) on her."

3. Note 3, Story 1, Notes, mentions the concise style, which very often does not name participants or the overt verb subject. **Demonstrative particles** ("this," "that", "those") may occur instead of the noun mentioning the object or person referred to. In developmental discourse studies, the use of demonstratives instead of explicit nouns (or noun phrases) may indicate a speaker's limited style, vocabulary, or speech habits. However, the Bedouin narrators' use of this feature very often indicates conciseness as a linguistic feature.

4. Note that the girl marries the young man who arrived at her place without asking her father's permission. This was dictated by circumstances, but also by her own will. This may suggest that at least Galilee Bedouins can take into consideration the girl's opinion about the identity of her future husband, as we see in some other stories. In addition, the girl does not enable him to stay with her without the social, traditional, legal,-moral pledge regarding a woman's chastity.

5. Perez, "From the Source of Israel and Ishmael," 20.

6. Elstein, *Encyclopedia of the Jewish Story*, "Theme 'The King's Daughter Locked-Up in a Tower,'" 79–104; Shenhar, "The Folkloristic Sources od Bialik's Agadat Shelosha ve-Arba'ah," *Yeda-'Am*, 17, 28–32.

7. Habermann, "Ancient Version of the Origin," 88–91.

8. Buber, *Mavo Lemidrash Tanhuma (Introduction to Midrash Tanhuma)*, 21.

9. Despite the ambiguity regarding the dating of the *Tanhuma* manuscript by Buber, it seems to be earlier than the version published by Habermann. The version published by Habermann seems to have been written somewhere in the eleventh century and reflects, in terms of realism, the medieval period and knighthood in Europe.

10. Among the Bedouin tribes living in Saudi Arabia as opposed to the Bedouin tribes in the Galilee, it was not customary to marry women without first obtaining their consent to marriage. It is possible that the activism of the women in both stories suggests that these are ancient stories that reflect an ancient reality.

11. Noy, "Family Conflict in Folktales of Jewish Communities," 222.

12. Basset, "Salomon and the Griffin." *Moorish Literature*, 207.

3. The Girl Who Fell into a Well

NARRATOR: Nūra Ḥalīfa

TRIBE: *'Arab el-'Arāmša*
RECORDER: *Naomi Raies*
IFA: 14074 ca. 1981

Text

One day there is a girl [a young woman] and she—her parents moved from the village and she did not know where they went. [They were] Bedouins—moving from place to place. When she reached a place where there was a water pit, she tore her handkerchief and she put a piece [of it] inside. She would lower it down and take out the piece and suck it, from her thirst. And when she looked down into the pit, she fell.

A man came on a horse and he heard there was something going on in a water hole—noise. He looked—like that—from the door of . . . Yes, from above, he saw something walking, slipping there, passing through the water. Then she asked him to save her for she cannot go out. He said to her, "I'll save you, if you give yourself [have intercourse]—we're getting married!"

The girl, she had a hard time. She told him: "Forgive me, you will . . . it's a difficult thing for me, the parents and all that . . ." He says to her, "Then you will die in the pit!"

The more she asked him to save her, he said to her, "If you give and if you swear!"

She swears, "Yes, if you marry me all the time and ask me from my parents!"

He said to her, "OK."

He took her out and raped the girl with force. He told her, "I'm going to your parents and tomorrow and the day after tomorrow you'll be in my house."

He went and [behaved as if] he did not know the girl's house [address], and she gave him everything: where she was going, and who her parents were, and where they live. He did not recognize her anymore, he did not think of her. He found a woman from his family and married her.

This girl, she remained until thirty-three, thirty-five years. She did not get married. She could not marry anymore. If it is revealed to her parents or someone [that she is not a virgin], they would murder her.

Therefore, every time this girl, the new girl he married—every time they had a child, the child would die in the pit—in a water hole. The first boy went to play after a cat. He ran after it. The cat jumped over a water hole—the boy jumped into the hole and he died.

The second child he is going with his dad to get water [from] the pit and he looks down at his shadow inside—the boy enters the hole and dies.

The third child he went to play there. Going where they go—he went to play and died [in the pit].

[The] mother dreamed at night that an old sheikh came and told her, "Ask your husband what he did!"

And she believed this dream was true. In the morning, she said to her husband, "I don't let you go until you tell me . . . until you tell me what happened and what you did while you were single. We separate [we divorce] if you do not tell me!"

He said to her, "If I told you, you would have died—we would have separated [divorced] too!"

"No matter, but I do not want my children dying all the time in a water hole. There's something, I dreamed, a man came, a sheikh, at night, and told me, 'Ask your husband what he did!'"

And after she stood on his head [bothered or annoyed him] and did not want to leave him until he would tell her, he said to her, "I found a girl, and so and so I did to her!"

She said to him, "Go and look for the girl. My heart tells me: She's still waiting for you!"

He went looking for her and found her in a terrible bad state, and he saved her from this life, and he married her, and the girl who was his children's mother left and agreed to divorce. And the girl—he married the girl whom he took out of the water hole.

Commentary

The narrator, Nora Ḥalīfa, a member of ʿArab el-ʿArāmša tribe, located near the Lebanese border, told the story in Arabic, and her daughter translated it into broken Hebrew while listening. Unfortunately, the recorded Arabic source was not preserved.

The story of "The Girl Who Fell into the Well," or "The Weasel and the Well," as it is known in the Hebrew sources, is considered a Jewish oikotype of the international narrative type ATU 930A. The international type is classified among the fate stories. A king hears a prophecy that his son is going to marry a simple peasant girl; he tries to challenge fate and kill her, but his efforts fail, and the prophesized fate occurs. The international type has two well-known Jewish oikotypes: "The Weasel and the Well" (ATU 930A f) and "Solomon's Daughter in the Tower" (ATU 930A k). These two oikotypes also appear in the Bedouin culture space in northern Israel.

The story is mentioned in the Babylonian Talmud in tractate Taʿanit 8a, by its name only: "R. Ammi said, Rain falls only for the sake of Men of Faith, as it is said, 'Truth shall spring out of the earth; and righteousness shall look down from heaven' [Psalms 85, 11]. R. Ammi further said: 'Come and see how great the Men of Faith are as is evidenced from the episode of the Weasel and the Pit. If this is the case with one who trusts in the Weasel and the Pit how much more so if one trusts in the Holy One blessed be He!'"

Rashi (Rabbi Shlomo Yitzchaki [1040–1105]), in his commentary on this passage, explains that this is a familiar story. He summarizes its contents succinctly:

> *Hulda* and *Bor* [Weasel and the Well]—who killed two people. It is found in the legend: one man who gave his faith [promise] to one maid that he would marry her. She said, "Who attests?" And there was one pit and a weasel. The young man said: "The water pit and the weasel are witnesses." Later he passed his faith [broke off his promise] and married another and gave birth to two sons. One fell into the pit and died, and one was bitten by a weasel and died. His wife said to him, "What is it [what brought about] that our sons die a strange death?" And he said to her: "Thus and thus was the deed."[1]

A longer and fuller version appears in the *Millon Ha'Aruch* (Talmudic lexicon), a book by Rabbi Nathan Ben Jehiel of Rome (1035–c. 1110). Rabbi Nathan's version is built as a novella with a definite beginning and end. A similar version is found in *The Responsa of the Geonim*, and a later version appears in the writings of the Tosafists (medieval rabbis from France and Germany). Here is the version by Rabbi Nathan:

> Rabbi Hanina said: "Consider how great are witnesses who are sureties!" And whence do we know? From the weasel and the pit. And if this could befall with one who takes weasel and pit as witness and surety, how much more so with one who takes the Holy and Blessed One as witness.
>
> Once upon a time, a certain girl was going home. She was bedecked with gold and silver. But she lost her way and walked in uninhabited places. The noon hour came, she was thirsty and had no companions. Then she saw a well with a rope and bucket hanging from it. She took the rope of the bucket and climbed down and drank. But when she wished to climb up, she could not do so; and she wept and wailed and shouted aloud.
>
> A man passed by and heard her voice. He stood over the well, gazed down but could not distinguish anything. "Who are you?" he asked. "Of humankind or of the imps?" "I am of humankind." "Maybe you are an evil spirit and are deceiving me," said he. "No," she answered. "Swear to me," said he then, "that you are a human being." So, she took an oath. "What has happened?" he asked; and she told him the whole story. "If I bring you up," said he, "will you mate with me?" "Yes," said she; and he brought her up.
>
> Once he brought her up, he wished to mate with her. But she said to him, "Of which people are you?" "I am of Israel," said he, "I come from such and such a place and I am a *cohen* [priest]." Then she said to him: "I also belong to this and that family, well-known and distinguished people." And she went on: "A person like you, who belongs to the holy stock which the Holy and Blessed One selected and hallowed out of all Israel—do you wish to act like a brute beast without a marriage document and proper allowing? Come for me to my father and mother, and I shall plight my troth with you." So, they made a covenant with one another. And she asked, "Who will be witness between you and me?" Now a weasel was just passing in front of them. Said he, "By heaven! Let the weasel and the well be witnesses that we shall not play one another false." Then he went his way and she went hers.
>
> Now the girl remained true to her promise. If anybody came to seek her hand, she would reject him. When her family began to put pressure on her, she began to behave as though she were demented and began tearing her own garments and the garments of anybody who touched her. At last, people left her alone, and she remained true to that man.

As for him, once he had gone away from her his instinct possessed him, he forgot her, went to his city, engaged in his craft, and wedded a wife. She became pregnant and bore him a son. But when he was three months old, a weasel choked him. She became pregnant again and bore a son who fell into a pit. Then the man's wife said to him: "If your children had died in the ordinary way, I would have accepted the judgment and held it just. But now that they have perished in these strange fashions, I feel there must be a reason. Tell me all you have done!" Then he told her the whole story, and she said: "Go to the portion that was given you by the Holy and Blessed One."

He went away and sought her in her town. "She is demented," they said to him, "and anybody who wishes to wed her is treated in this and this way." Then he went to her father and told him the whole tale. And he went on: "I accept her with any blemishes there may be in her." The father called witnesses. Then he went to her, and she began to act after her fashion, but he merely said: "Weasel and pit." Then she answered him: "I, too, have kept my word."[2]

As far as I know, there is no written source of the story before the eleventh century. Since then, one meets the story in many different versions. It seems that this story was prevalent during the Talmudic period in the days of Rabbi Ami. Rabbi Ami, from the third generation of the *Amoraim* of the Land of Israel, was active in the late fourth century CE. He was a member of a family of priests, who immigrated to the Land of Israel from Babylon, settled in Caesarea, and later moved to Tiberias. Rabbi Ami was a disciple of Rabbi Yochanan and a colleague of Rabbi Abahu. It seems that the story was so familiar that the editor of the Talmud made do with mentioning its name and did not think he had to include the whole text. The story continued to be told orally among the people, and seven hundred years later, in the eleventh century, we find written versions of it.

My data does not allow me to determine whether the Bedouin version is a reincarnation of a Jewish version or a part of an independent development line that originated from earlier versions.[3]

'Eli Yassif doubts whether the two medieval sages who relate the story, Rashi in northern France and Rabbi Nathan Ben Jehiel in Italy, wrote down an ancient tradition that originated in the time of the sages.[4] He gives examples from other stories that support his hypothesis that these are medieval stories, based on realia details characteristic of medieval Europe and not of the Land of Israel of the Talmudic period.

In my opinion, the details of the story actually reinforce the assumption that this is a Talmudic story. The narrative motif of falling into a pit is known to us from many places in rabbinic literature.

Take, for example, the stories presented in the Mishna (Yevamot 16:4), and then the Talmudic story about the daughter of Nechonia the pit digger, who fell into a pit, as well as the Talmudic discussion about a child who fell into a pit (Babylonian Talmud, Yevamot 121b; Bava Kama 50a). In the Bedouin stories, recorded from informants in the north of Israel, this motif is repeated again and again.

In the Jerusalem Talmud, tractate Gittin, there is an extensive discussion of whether a man's voice heard from a pit is sufficient to indicate that he is a real person or whether eyewitness testimony of a man's reflection is also needed. In this context,

Rabbi Abin notes, "The demons were found in the pits as they are found in the fields" (Jerusalem Talmud, Gittin, chap. 6, p. 48, col. 2). In many of the stories I recorded, such as the story of Nuṣṣ-Nṣēṣ ("Half-Tiny Half," the Bedouin Tom Thumb), when the protagonist who has fallen into a well calls for help, the first question presented by rescuers is "Are you a human or a demon?" This question is repeated again and again in other Bedouin tales.

The fact that this question appears in Hebrew in the text of Rabbi Nathan's story ("Who are you, of humankind or of the imps?") reinforces the assumption that the story of the weasel and the well comes from the Land of Israel and not from Europe. In Pesikta Rabbati, a Midrash from the middle of the ninth century, this question is mentioned in an allegorical story about the prophet Jeremiah, who meets a disheveled woman dressed in black. The first thing he says is, "If you are a woman speak to me, and if you are a ghost go away from me" (Pesikta Rabbati, 26). In Midrash Ruth Zuta, a late Midrash written in the ninth century or so, Boaz asks Ruth a similar question when he discovers her sleeping at his feet in the threshing floor: "And the man trembled and swore to her, if you are a ghost go away from me, and if you are a human being, tell me. She said to him, I am a human being and I came to ask God to give me a part in your family" (Midrash Zuta-Ruth [Buber] 3:8).

The question "Who are you, of humankind or of the imps?" appear in many Bedouin folktales but is not found in Nūra Ḥalīfa's story. It is possible that the question existed in the Arabic record of the story but was dropped during the translation into Hebrew by the narrator's daughter.

Whether the Bedouin story was taken from Jewish sources or is an independent formation, there is no doubt that in terms of its structure, its content, and the manner in which it was told, it reflects a cultural worldview that is different from the Jewish worldview. The Bedouin version must be considered in relation to the Bedouin social and cultural context in which it occurs. The Jewish texts emphasize the loyalty motif. The young man who lifts the young woman from the pit does not rape her but promises to marry her. And yet, although the woman agrees to marry him against her will, she does not break her promise but makes every effort to maintain it, to the extent that she pretends to have a mental illness or epilepsy.

In contrast, in the Bedouin story, rape is actually carried out. The raped woman, as it emerges from the story, does not feel obliged to the rapist, and she extracts from him a promise by oath to marry her to save her honor and her life. The main motive is fear: the raped girl's fear of the fate that awaits her if her secret is exposed. Her chances of marrying someone else in this situation are nil, and in keeping with family honor, there is a good chance that her family will try not only to harm the rapist but also to kill her if the secret is revealed. The motive of fear is clearly evident from the woman's words: "The girl, she had a hard time. She told him: 'Forgive me, you will . . . it's a difficult thing for me, the parents and all that . . .'" So too in the narrator's comment, "She could not marry anymore. If it is revealed to her parents or someone [that she is not a virgin], they would murder her."

In two different cultural spaces, the same story reflects two different customs: the Bedouin listener receives a completely different message than the Jewish reader.

The Bedouin version is the only version in which it is explicitly stated that the man had raped the girl after she was lifted out of the pit, while in the Jewish sources it is only hinted: "Once he brought her up, he wished to mate with her."

In the Bedouin version, the man bluntly presses the young woman, forcing her to swear that she will be his wife even before he brings her out of the pit:

> He said to her, "I'll save you, if you give yourself [have intercourse]—we're getting married!"
>
> The girl, she had a hard time. She told him: "Forgive me, you will . . . it's a difficult thing for me, the parents and all that . . ." He says to her, "Then you will die in the pit!"
>
> The more she asked him to save her, he said to her, "If you give and if you swear!"
>
> She swears, "Yes, if you marry me all the time and ask me from my parents!"
>
> He said to her, "OK."

The two witnesses, the pit and the weasel (or in this case the cat), do not appear in this part of the story, but later we learn that both were silent witnesses to the oath, and, after the violation by the young man, they are the ones who punish him by causing the death of his children. In the Bedouin version, the man initiates the oath, but it seems that he does so to make sure that the young woman will surrender to him as soon as he takes her out of the pit and not because he intends to marry her.

In both the Hebrew and Bedouin versions, the main hero is the young woman, not the man. At the beginning of the story, it is quite clear that she is passive, and the young man is the one who advances and urges on, but already in the rescue stage, the female voice is clearly heard. The young woman is doing her best to cope with a situation that was imposed on her and not to accept it passively. Later on, the man is the one who becomes passive and defensive, whereas his children's mother and the woman who was abandoned take the lead in the plot.

In the Bedouin story, it would seem that the central figure is the second woman, whose children die in the pit. This version adds a component that does not appear in the Hebrew versions—a dream. The motif of a dream that is interpreted or revealed is very common in the folk narrative. In her dream, the second woman sees the figure of a sheikh, an authority figure who tells her, "Ask your husband what he did!" The woman intuits that the deaths of her three children in the pit are not accidental and that her husband is hiding a secret from her. In the Bedouin society in which she lives, her status vis-à-vis the man is inferior. She cannot force him to expose his secret, and she needs the support of an outside authority to face her husband and demand it. This hidden wish is expressed in a dream: the sheikh, who represents authority above the husband, appears and encourages her to deal with her husband.

Following the dream, the woman turns to her husband with a vigorous demand and threatens to leave the house: "And she believed this dream was true. In the morning, she said to her husband, 'I don't let you go until you tell me . . . until you tell me what happened, and what you did while you were single. We separate [we divorce] if you do not tell me!'"

The husband is not willing to reveal his secret despite the vigor of the demand, and then the woman uses the dream: "There's something, I dreamed, a man came, a sheikh, at night, and told me, 'Ask your husband what he did!'" The Bedouin society's respect for the dream is what ultimately compels the husband to reveal the truth. And here the narrator puts in the woman's mouth the sentence that in my opinion is the key in the whole story: "Go and look for the girl, my heart tells me: She's still waiting for you!"

The woman has discovered her husband's secret, which is the key to her suffering. Imagine the intensity of the shock she is experiencing. Her husband, the authoritative power in her life, is revealed to her, first as a rapist and secondly as a man without honor who broke the pledge he gave to the woman he raped and thereby caused the death of their children. What should she do? How should she behave? The woman is a victim of circumstances she has no control over. Now she knows the truth, and she has two choices. She can stop the circle of death, simply by separating from him and leaving him to his fate. Alternatively, she may require him to marry the other woman as a second wife (since Islamic law permits him to marry more than one woman) and hope that this act will be perceived by Divine Providence as an act of atonement and will allow her to bring children into the world and raise them.

She chooses the first option, which means for her another sacrifice: she will become an old divorcee whose chances of remarrying are nil. However, regard the way in which she informs her husband about her decision: "Go look for the girl, *my heart tells me*: She's still waiting for you!"

How much emotion and how much strength are hidden in this short sentence! Not only is she about to make another sacrifice, and this time by choice, but she also gathers all her mental strength and advises her husband to marry the girl. Even at the heart of her tragedy, she finds room to think about the well-being and happiness of her husband and of a woman she does not know personally. She accepts her fate and consciously abandons the possibility of living in a romantic triangle with the raped woman, with all that it would entail. She shows nobility and altruism in wanting to benefit the second victim in the affair, the woman whose honor was violated by her husband and who was abandoned to the fate of a spinster.

This characterization indicates the effect of the dream on the woman it did not just grant her the power to confront her husband. She experienced the dream as a sign from heaven and as proof that the death of her children was not accidental but a punishment from heaven for her husband's behavior. She felt that some gesture of correction was required from her, a sacrifice that would atone for her husband's actions.

What a great human drama! In the Jewish versions, the main point is the contrast between the breach of the commitment by the man and the fulfillment of the commitment by the woman. In the Bedouin story, this contrast no longer exists. For the raped woman, this is not a matter of allegiance but of avoiding the exposure of her dishonor. However, in both cases, the emphasis falls on the virtues of the woman and the shortcomings of the man.

Recall that the story was told by a *mother*, mediated by *her daughter*. The story is therefore told in a feminine society and from identification with the female characters in the story. Note that at the point where the dream is mentioned the narrator explicitly uses the term *mother*. Instead of saying, "The woman dreamed," she says, "[The] *mother* dreamed at night that an old sheikh came and told her, 'Ask your husband what he did!'"

It seems that when the Bedouin narrator describes the injured woman's behavior, she expresses a general feeling of sisterhood and revolt against the men who control their lives. At the same time, the authoritative figure "recruited" in the dream, to face the husband from the position of power, is a masculine figure. This figure is not only a source of authority in relation to her husband but also the one that determines to a large extent the woman's actions in the future.

Notes

1. Rashi, commentary on the Babylonian Talmud, Ta'anit 8a.
2. Bin Gorion, *Mimekor Israel*, 170–71.
3. A discussion of other aspects of the story's components and its place in folk literature is found in Yassif, *Hebrew Folktale*.
4. Yassif, *Hebrew Folktale*.

4. The Ḥāǧǧ's Daughter and the Orator

NARRATOR: Ṣabḥa ʿAbūd

TRIBE: *ʿArab el-Ḥuǧērāt*

IFA 12718 December 12, 1979

1 bū[1] ǧirān ṯnēn. wāḥad ʿendo walad u-bent. hā-z-zlima widdo[2] yrū(ḥ) ʿa-l- ḥaǧǧ. (ǧāro). widdo yrūḥ hū u-marto u-ʾibno. ʿa-l-ḥaǧǧ. hīn ʿando wāḥad ǧār, hā-ǧ-ǧār xaṭīb, yaʿani, lāff laffe, u-ʿindo dār, ktīr, hāḏa-l-ḥāǧǧ. gaḷ-ḷo, "b-aḷḷa, yā ǧāri, dīr bālak ʿa-l-bint, yaʿani, ʾana widd-arūḥ ʿala l-ḥaǧǧ." huwa nihaǧ, ʿa-l-ḥaǧǧ, huwa, z-zlima nihaǧ, hū u-marto u-ibno ʿa-l-ḥāǧǧ.	1 There were two neighbors. One had a son and a daughter. This man wanted to go to make a pilgrimage (his neighbor). He wanted to go, he and his wife and son. To the pilgrimage. Now, he had a neighbor, this neighbor was an orator [at the mosque], that is, wearing a *laffe* [rolled headkerchief] and had a big house. This Ḥāǧǧ [the pilgrim], he went off to the pilgrimage, he, the man, and his wife and son, he said to him, "By Allah, my neighbor, take care of my daughter, that is, I want to go to the pilgrimage." He went off to the pilgrimage, he, the man, and his wife and son, to the ḥāǧǧ.
11 ṣār kull yōm ydugg-ilha ʿal-bāb, hāḏa l-xaṭīb. tgul-lo, "mīn?" ygūl-la, "ʾani, l-xaṭīb." tgul-lo, "š-widdak?" ygul-lēha, "widdi tiftaḥi." tgul-lo, "laʾ." kull yōm, kull yōm, kull yōm. yōm—ṣār—gaʿad šahar ʾabūha ba-l-ḥaǧǧ, huwa u-marto u-ibno,	11 He began every day knocking at her door, this orator. She says to him, "Who [is it]?" He would say to her, "I, the orator." She says to him, "What do you want?" He says to her: "I want you to open." She says: "No." Every day, every day, every day. One day—he began—her father stayed in the pilgrimage a month, he and his wife and son.
18 ṣār yuktob makatīb ʾabel-ma yiǧūn, yuktob-lom makatīb ʾinno	18 He started writing letters before they come [back] writing to them that
20 bintkam qadd mā tīǧi ʿandīha nās u-ṣḥāb	20 "your daughter, many people and friends come to her,

22 u-widdha iyyāha, tīği la-ʿinda, u-ʾani māni ğādir amnaḥḥa (= amnaʿha).” u-hū čiḏb. bas huwwa widdo yifta(ḥ) ʿanda, u-hiyya mā rāḏia tiftaḥḥa ʿalē.	22 and they want her [or: she wants it/them], and I cannot prevent this.” It was a lie, but he wanted to go to her and she did not agree to it.
26 gāl, huwwa, aywa, ʾibno, hāḏa l-ḥāğğ, gāḷ, ʾā, la-ʾibno, “rūḥ, hāḏi barūde, u-rūḥ ṭuxxa wa-ʿabbi min dammha ginniyye u-hāt li iyyāha ta-ʾašrabo,” ʾabūha.	26 He said, he, yes, his son, this Ḥāğğ [the father], said, yes, to his son, “Go. This is a rifle, and go shoot her and fill up a bottle from her blood and give it to me to drink,” her father.
31 waḷḷa, miše, rāḥ el-walad. gaḏab—gaʿad yōmēn . . . ʿala ğanb ad-dār, b-ğamb dārha . . . ta-yšūf wāḥad yīği, ta-yšūf. [$_{H}$histakel. ʾaf aḥad lo ba$_{H}$]. gāḷ “hāḏa ḥarām ʾanni ʾaṭuxxa.”	31 By Allah, he went—the boy went. He took—he stayed two days near the house, at the side of the house, to see anyone that comes, to see ($_{H}$histakel. ʾaf ʾeḥad lo ba$_{H}$). He looked. No one came. He said, “It's a crime [it is not allowed] if I shoot her.”
36 gaḏab—siter ʿalē hā d-dār xamst-iyyām [Hhu histakel ʾalH] dār—gāḷ, “aftaḥi!” gāḷat lo, “mīn?” gāḷ-ḷha, “ʾaxūč.” gāḷat-lo, “ṭayyib.” fitḥat lo, u—ḥabbato, ḥabḥabato. ʾaxūha.	36 He took . . . he hid near her house five days. (HHu histakelH He looked at) the house—he said, “Open!” She said to him: “Who is it?” He said to her: “Your brother.” She said, “OK,” she opened and kissed and welcomed him—[it was] her brother.
41 huwwe mā šāf ʿalēha ʾiši, aywa, gāḷ-ḷha: “yā-xti, iḥna widna rrūḥ ʿa-maṭraḥ beʿīd.” mišam. mišam, yaʿani, maṭraḥ beʿid u-mā ṣiḥi yiḏbaḥḥa liʾanno mā šāf ʿalēha ʾiši.	41 He did not see on her anything [he did not find on her any blame]. Yes. He said to her, “O my sister, we shall go to a very far place.” They went, went, that is, to a distant place, and he did not feel [did not have the heart] to kill her because he did not find on her anything [wrong].
46 ḥarām inno yiḏbaḥḥa, miṯel ḥaḏāk yitrāṣad.	46 [It would be] a crime to kill her, like that [who] lies in ambush.
48 u-mā šāf ʿalēha iši. gāḷ ḥarām yiḏbaḥa. ʾaywa.	48 And he did not see anything on her. He said, “It's a crime to kill her.” Yes.
50 ğē la-ʿand maṭraḥ beʿīd, nifa-elha, lā hī ṭēra u-faras (HgadolH) hiya mā timši bal-ʾarḍ. hīna ʿand hā-l-ʿēn, u-ʿala ḏīf el-ʿēn ugaʿad taḥt aš-šağara. u-gāḷ-ḷa, “yā-xayta, xaḷḷīna nitrayyaḥ.”	50 He came to a distant place, he banished her, [where] no bird or mare, a (HgadolH) big [animal], would go on the ground. Here, near a spring, and on the edge of the spring, and he sat under the tree. He said to her, “O little sister, let's rest.”
55 tarayyaḥam. (gāḷat-lo) gāḷ-ḷa, “yā-xti, hīč hīč ʾani ṣār mʿāya, u-hāḏa l-xaṭīb gāḷ l-abūya inno gad-ma tīği ʿandeč nās. katab-ilna maktūb u-waddā-lna iyyāh. gāḷ-ḷi ta-ʸaḏbaḥeč ʾabūya, w-ani mā ṣḥīt ʾaḏbaḥeč, liʾanni mā šuft ʿalēč ʾiši, wa-ʾani widdi ʾadaššreč hīči.”	55 The rested (there). He said to her, “O my sister, so-and-so, I—it happened to me, and this orator told my father that how many people come to you, he wrote to us a letter and sent it to us. He told me to kill you, my father. I did not want to kill you because I did not see in you anything (wrong). I'll thus leave you.”

62 daššarha taḥt ha-š-šeğarāt b-ḥāḏ-ha-l-ʿēn. ḏaḷḷat u-hū daššarha u-rāḥ. u-hū māši madd ʿa-ṭēr u-ṭaxxo u-ḏibḥo ʿa-zaṭṭ dammo bi-l-ganniyye u-xaḏā la-ʾabō. gāḷ-ḷo, "ṭaxxētha?" gāḷ-ḷo, "ṭaxxētha." gāḷ-ḷo, "ḏ̣ibaḥtha?" gāḷ-ḷo, "ḏ̣ibaḥtha, naʿam." aywa.	62 He left her under the trees at that spring. She remained, and he left her and went [away]. When he was going, he caught a bird and shot it and killed it, and poured its blood in the goblet and took it to his father. He said to him, "Did you shoot her?" He said, "I shot her." He said to him, "Did you kill her?" He said to him, "I killed her, yes." Yes.
69 humma—hiyye ğāḷat, ṭilʿat ʿala ha:-š-šağara ʿala-nhā ʿa-ṣ-ṣōm. ṭalʿat ʿa-š-šağara. w-in hā-n-nās, zlām, xayyāle, min ʿarab ṯāni.	69 They—she went around [and then] climbed up the tree though she was fasting. She climbed up the tree. And lo, there [came] people, men, horsemen [riders] from another Bedouin tribe.
73 ğumma. daḥḥagam. ʾazgam xēlham ʿa-l-ʿēn u-mišam. ʾağa wāḥad minhom, daḥḥag winn zawālha b-al-ʿēn, b-al-mayy. maša, zawālha ba-l-ʿēn, miša, ṣār yaʿani, b-aṭ-ṭarīg, gāḷ-ḷhum: "ʾani nisēt ʾiši ʿa-l-ʿēn, widdi ʾarğaʿ." gāḷ-ḷo, "ṭayyeb."	73 They came, looked, and let their horses drink at the spring, and went. One of them came and saw her image in the spring, in the water. He went, her image was in the spring. He was, that is, on the way, he said to them, "I forgot something at the spring. I want to go back." He said to him, "All right."
80 riğeʿ, gāḷ-ḷha: "ʾinzili, ʾinzeli, ʿalēk ʾaḷḷah w-(ʾ)amān ʾaḷḷah w-il-xāyen yixūno ʾaḷḷah.[3] ʾanzili!" rakkabha warā u-xaḏāha ʿa-bēto. waḷḷa, gaʿadat eb-bēto šahar, [$_{H}$ḥodeš, ḥodeš, ḥodeš$_{H}$], ʾaḷḷa yaʿlam.	80 He returned and said to her, "Get down, get down, the security of Allah is on you, and the traitor—Allah will betray him. Come down!" He seated her on the horse behind him and took her to his house. By Allah, she stayed in his house a month ($_{H}$ḥodeš, ḥodeš, ḥodeš$_{H}$) month, month, month, Allah knows [how long].
86 ʿando mara, huwwa, u-ʿando wlād. (gāḷ-ḷo—gāḷ-ilha), ʿando ʾummo, gāḷ-ilha, "gūli-lha, hāḏi, mā tiğawwaz?" gāḷat-ilha ʾummo, gāḷat-ilha, "mā tizawwağīn? tāxḏīn ʾibn-al-malak?"	86 He had a wife and had children (he said to her, said to him) and his mother [at his place]. He said to her [to his mother], "Tell her, to this one, doesn't she want to marry?" She said to her, his mother [said to the girl], "Aren't you getting married? Will you take [only] the prince?"
91 gāḷat: "laʾ, ʾani widdi ʾāxoḏ hāḏa illi ğābni, hā-z-zalame illi ğābni, flān," ʾismo mḥammad. gāḷat ilha: "ʿindo mara wa-ʿindo wlād." gāḷat ilha, "lēš la? wa-ʾani ṯ-ṯāni(ya)." gāḷat-ilha, "ṭayyeb." gāḷ,"ṭayyeb."	91 She said to her, "No, I want to take this man who brought me, so-and-so." His name was Muhammad. She said to her, "He has a wife and he has children." She said, "Why not? And I'm the second [wife]." She said to her, "OK." He said, "Good."

97 ʿagad ʿagdo ʿalēha tağawwazha. limma tiğawwazha, yōm, rāḥat ʾiyyām u-ʾağat ʾayyām,[4] ṣar ʿindha wlād ^{a}ṯnēn. mišat. yōm, ʾağat ʿala miṯl-al-ʿakka. fātat—daḥḥagat ʿalē li-ghawa. willa ʾabūha u-hā-l-xaṭīb ba-l-^{i}ghawa bišrabu [$_{H}$yištu qafe$_{H}$].	97 He married her [legally]. When he married her, one day, days went and came [days in and days out], she had two children. She went. One day she went, she came to [a place] like Acre. She entered, looked at a coffeehouse and lo [there was] her father and the orator in the coffeehouse, drinking ($_{H}$yištu qafe$_{H}$) drinking coffee.
104 gālat-ilhum . . . rāḥat. ġābat. gaʿadat ğimʿa. bāgat ^{a}hdūm ğōzha u-libsat libs ^{e}zlām[5] u-rāḥat ʿa-le-ghawa u-gaʿadat ʿalēhom, [$_{H}$tište kafe. yištu qafe. nehene$_{H}$]. gāḷat-ilhum "kull wāḥad yxarref ʿala zimān šnu faʿal hā" aywa, šnū. haḏāk yxarref u-haḏāk yxarref. gāḷat-lo, "ʾani widdi ʾaxarrifkam šnu ṣār ^{i}mʿāya ^{i}b-ḥayāti."	104 She said to them. . . . She went, hid [herself], stayed [away] a week. She stole her husband's clothes, and put on men's clothes, and went to the coffeehouse and sat down near them. ($_{H}$tište kafe. yištu qafe. nehene$_{H}$) To drink coffee. They will drink coffee. Enjoying. She said to them, "Everyone will tell about a [past] time, what he's done. this [he]," yes. What. . . . This one tells and that one tells. She said to him, "I want to tell you what happened with me in my life."
113 gāḷ-ḷha "šnō?" gāḷat-ilhom, "ʾabuya rā-ʿa-hal-ḥağğ. ʿandin ʾabūya mā rāḥ ʿa-l-ḥağğ ʾabūya waṣṣa al-xaṭīb ʿaleyya." "šnu ʿād itxarrif?" yigul-lo l-xaṭīb "lā, xurrafītak muš ^{i}mlīḥe." ʾabūha ygūl "la, la, xarref." yiguḷ-ḷa, "aywa."	113 He said to her, "What?" She said to them, "My father went to the pilgrimage. When he went off to the pilgrimage, my father made the orator my guardian." "What are you telling?" the orator says to him. "No, your story is not good." Her father says, "No, no, tell [it]." He says to her, "Yes."
119 waḷḷa, gāḷat, "ʾabūya rāʿ-a-l-ḥağğ u-waṣṣa l-xaṭīb ʿaleyya. hāḏa l-xaṭīb kull yōm yīği, iṭugg-lī ʿa-l-bāb, yiguīl-li, "iftaḥi," ʾani mā widdi aftaḥ.	119 By Allah, she said, "My father went to this pilgrimage and made the orator my guardian. Every day, this orator he comes, knocks on my door, says to me, 'Open it.' I do not want to open.
123 ʿandin yōm māni fataḥt-lo, ʾabūya, liʾanno ğārna, yiguḷ-ḷo "dīr bālak ʿala binti. ʾinte miṯel ʾabūha," huwwa ṣār kull yōm yṭugg li ʿa-l-bāb u-ʾani mā widdi aftaḥ-lo. huwwa rāḥ. ʿandinma ğā ʾabūya biddo yīği, ṣār yuktob makatīb la-ʾabūya ʾinha miš ^{e}mlīḥa, u-btīği nās ʿendīha."	123 "When I did not open for him—my father—because [he was] our neighbor, he [had] said to him, 'Look after my daughter, you are like her father.' He began to knock at my door every day and I did not want to open it for him. He went, when my father was about to come [back], he began to write letters to my father, that she is not good, [that] people come to her."
131 ṣār ygul-lha l-xaṭīb "la, la txarref." ygūl-lha ʾabūha, "xarref." ʿandinmā xallaṣat gāḷat-ḷo, "ʾinte, hāḏ ʾabūya u-hāḏa l-xaṭīb," u-gāḷat, ṭallat hā-l-fard min ğenbha u-gawwaṣat al-xaṭīb.	131 The orator began to say to her, "No, no, do not tell." Her father said to her, "Tell." When she finished, she said, "You—this is my father and this is the orator." And she said, took out a pistol from her side and shot the orator.

Commentary

The story "The Ḥāğğ's Daughter and the Orator" belongs to the narrative type ATU 883A, "The Innocent and Slandered Maiden."

The narrative type is described as follows: In the absence of her father (parents), a relative (a friend, a clergyman, guardian) attempts to seduce a young woman. When she rejects him, he writes a slanderous letter (out of revenge) to her father accusing her of loose conduct. The father commands his son to kill his sister. Out of pity (believing in her innocence), the brother spares her and gives the liver (heart, blood) of an animal to the king as proof of the murder. The girl is abandoned.

A king (prince) finds her and marries her. When the king has to go to war (when the woman with her children want to pay a visit to her father), he tells a servant (officer, soldier, dignitary) or a relative (brother, uncle) to take care of (accompany) his wife.

A second attempt at seduction is made, and the woman's children are often killed. She escapes in men's clothes (disguised as soldier, officer, or shepherd) and works unrecognized as a servant in her father's house (in an inn, as a shepherd). Despite the slanderer's statement that the queen is dead (abducted, escaped, has murdered her children), the king searches for his wife (father searches for his daughter). Finally, all persons concerned meet together, and the woman in man's clothes tells them what happened (in the form of a tale). The family is reunited, and the evildoers are punished.[6]

In Europe, there are many literary adaptations of the story. The narrative type is common throughout Europe and Asia. In the Middle East, it is known in Iran, Iraq, Kuwait, Qatar, Syria, Israel, Jordan, Saudi Arabia, and Yemen. In Africa, it is known in Egypt, Sudan, Algeria, and Morocco.

As one can see, in the Bedouin version, only the first episode of seduction appears. The young woman, abandoned by her brother, is found by a hunter, who marries her with his mother's blessing. Dressing up in men's clothing is a one-time act, which takes place when the woman recognizes her father and the *khatib* (orator), who come to a café. She disguises herself so she can tell her story. At the end of the story, the daughter is the one who takes revenge on the *khatib* and kills him.[7] The husband plays no part, and it is not clear from the story whether he is even present in the café when his wife reveals her secret.

Sexual harassment, rape, and incest are not often dealt with as subjects or given public expression in traditional societies. Society expresses its opinion about these violent phenomena through "socially discrete" means—such as implicit criticism through poems and stories. Our story is an excellent example of this.

The preacher takes advantage of the situation of the young woman whom he promised to care for and tries to seduce her. When she does not respond, he takes revenge on her by sending a slanderous letter to her father. In view of the defamatory status, the girl cannot prove her innocence. She does not tell her brother about the *khatib*'s attempts to seduce her. This is typical behavior for victims of sexual assault, who often feel guilty about being attacked and prefer to hide what has happened. Even the brother, although he believes in his sister's blamelessness and therefore leaves her alive, does not dare to disagree with his father's words or admit that he did not carry out the cruel command. He cunningly hides from the father the fact that his daughter is alive. In more complex versions of the story, which appear in other cultural spaces, the attempt to seduce the protagonist, who in the continuation of the story is already a mature woman and a mother, repeats itself, and again this is done by exploiting the woman's weakness and isolation.

In the patriarchal Bedouin society, a woman always needs male protection, either at her father's house or at her husband's. The Bedouin proverb says, "Marriage (a husband) is protection (*Al ǧōz sitra*)"—that is, the transition to married life gives her the masculine protection that she had in her parents' home. Situations where a woman is left alone, without the presence of her father or husband, expose her to the dangers of sexual abuse.

Even when the protagonist has the opportunity to reveal the true face of someone who has abused her, she needs to masquerade in men's clothing and indirectly expose what happened, through a story. In other versions of the story, as illustrated by the narrative type, masquerading in men's clothing allows the heroine to maintain a normal life for long periods without fearing for her vulnerability as a defenseless woman.

In this story, the father's status in the patriarchal family as the ultimate authority, whom all family members must obey, is also clear. The son does not dare disobey his father's demand, and he uses a trick to avoid confrontation with his father. In a Jewish version of the story written by Varda Shilo, a daughter of a Kurdish Jewish family from Zakho, the narrator says of the brother, "He did what his father said, because the father's words should be honored, even if he is not just."[8]

The motif of drinking the blood of the murdered, P253.1, "Brother about to drink blood of seemingly guilty sister," appears in many folktales. In Judaism, the prohibition of eating blood is one of the seven most important prohibitions (Noah's commandments, which are also binding on Gentiles) in the Bible: "It shall be a perpetual statute for your generations throughout all your dwellings that ye eat neither fat nor blood" (Leviticus 3:17). Islam also forbids eating blood, but not as severely. For example, it is not necessary to salt the meat to absorb the blood before eating. In the Kurdish-Jewish story mentioned above, it is explicitly stated, "He went to his father and gave him the blood. [The father] drank it."[9] However, in this Jewish story, the characters are not Jewish but Muslim. This is, as I said, "socially discrete"—an attempt to transfer the plot of the story to another cultural space.

The blood motif conjures up the story of Joseph, whose bloodstained striped shirt was presented to Jacob as false proof of his death. The mention of the shirt also appears in the Qur'ān: "They [the brothers] brought his shirt with false [literally: lying, a lie] blood on it" (sūrah 12, 18).

The young woman's hiding in the tree and her revelation brought about by her reflection in the water are also recurring motifs in many Bedouin stories. From a literary-metaphorical point of view, it is possible that the reflection of the real woman in the water corresponds to the story she tells at the end of the plot, a story that reflects the real events she underwent.

The use of the narrative technique of a story within a story is common in folktales. It allows the narrator to give listeners an inner view of the oral storytelling art.

The image of the orator (*khatib*) is illuminated here in a negative light. This is a familiar theme in Bedouin folktales, as well as in other cultural spaces. The preacher in the mosque has authority and influence over believers. The story criticizes the exploitation that is occasionally employed by religious people who abuse their religious authority (motif K2284, "Treacherous priest.")

There is an Arabic version that was recorded in Bīr Zēt, not far from Rāmallah; however, its contents indicate its Bedouin origin.[10] This story, called "The Emīr's Daughter," is very different from the Bedouin story I recorded in the north of Israel. It is much more complex, closer to the international narrative type of the story. It contains three episodes in which Ḥamda, the heroine, is forced to face the accusation of wanton behavior: once from her father, once from her first husband, and once from her second husband. At the beginning of the story, her father suspects that she went astray and sends his servant to kill her. In the second episode, her brother-in-law tries to seduce her in her husband's absence, and when he is unable to do so, he falsely accuses her of misconduct. The husband believes his brother's words and abandons his wife in a deserted place. As in this tale, the woman hides among the branches of a tree reflected in the pool below. A prince who passes by discovers her, brings her to his house, and marries her through his mother's mediation. As in the Bedouin story, the prince requests that his mother ask the young woman whether she wants to marry him. In the prince's absence, his brother tries to seduce her (the narrator hints here: "The brother asks her for what is inappropriate"), and when she does not agree after his threat to murder her two sons, he kills them. Managing to escape, the heroine hides in a pit. Later she wears men's clothing and finds shelter with another emīr, who employs her to work in his fields. The brother who murdered her children libels her in front of her husband and claims that she is a *ġūla* who devoured her children. At the end of the story, the father and the two husbands meet at the emīr's house. The heroine tells the story of her life and reveals herself as a woman. The truth comes out, and the father and the two brothers who have falsely accused her are punished.

In the story from Bīr Zēt, two items stand out. First, the innocent heroine finds herself in situations where men try to seduce her, and second, neither her father nor any of her husbands endeavor to find out the truth and hear her version. Only at the end of the story can she tell her story and only when she is disguised as a man. The stories therefore reflect her inferior status as a woman who has neither power of expression nor the ability to deal with her detractors. On the other hand, both stories emphasize the fact that she is not forced to marry but rather asked to agree. The story from Bīr Zēt also emphasizes that each of the husbands, when putting her on his horse before marriage, is careful to preserve her honor: in the narrator's words, "He placed his sword between himself and her during the ride"—that is, he maintained her innocence as long as they were not married.

Another Palestinian version is found in Bushnaq's book.[11] A Syrian version is almost identical to the first part of the story from Bīr Zēt.[12] In the IFA archives, there are twelve Jewish versions of the story: six from Morocco, three from Kurdistan, two from Yemen, and one from Poland (a version that the narrator heard when he was in exile in Siberia, from a Russian prisoner).[13]

This story, with its many versions, thus presents, under a narrative cover, issues considered taboo in traditional society, allowing them to enter into the public consciousness in a way that condemns immoral acts and criticizes their implementers.

In some of the versions, the protagonist is portrayed not as a submissive and helpless female figure who is sexually harassed but as a resourceful woman who is capable of fighting for her honor and hurting or tricking those who harass her. Even in versions where she remains passive in the face of repeated attempts to hurt her and her children, she eventually finds a way to bring her justice to light and to punish those who harm her. In this respect, it is possible to view Ṣabḥa ʿAbūd's version as one of feminine encouragement and intensification—especially since it is told and transmitted by a woman.

Notes

1. An important particle is the word *bī/bū* ("there is"), which in sedentary dialects (in Israel) is *fī, fīh*. These prepositions have undergone grammaticalization from their original prepositional meanings, "in (it)" (*bī, fī*) and "with it" (*bi-*). These meanings exist next to the existential meaning ("there is"). Without a definite noun following the preposition, the meaning is existential only; for example, *bī zlima*, "there is a man." The difference between *bī* and *bū* follows from historically different derivations: *bi* + **hi* > *bī*, whereas *bi* + **hu* > *bū*.

2. This word, *widdo*, here translated as "he will," literally means "his will, his wish" (< widd+o)—that is to say, it is not a verb but an inflected noun, with a suffixed bound pronoun. In sedentary dialects (of Israel) this is pronounced as *biddo/baddo*, which has a prefixed /*bi-*, *ba-*/, "in, with" (*w* is deleted), to create the structure "in his wish," or "he wishes." Since this is a tenseless nominal structure, to refer to past or future actions Bedouins add a conjugated form of the verb "be," *kān, yekūn*, as in *kān widdo*, "he wanted," and *yekūn widdo*, "he will want." Note that widdo means not only "want" but also an obligation or a future action—"he/it has to (do)" or "he will (do)." The semantic ambiguity of *biddo/baddo* also exists in various sedentary dialects.

3. Like many folktales in other language societies, Arabic folktales, including these Bedouin tales, use narrative formulas of swearing, promises, and threats to emphasize the relevance or seriousness of some issue. The formulas in these Bedouin stories often involve rhymes and metric structures, such as *'alēk(i) 'aḷḷa w-'amān 'aḷḷa, w-al-xāyin yexūno 'aḷḷa* ("Allah and Allah's security is on you, and the traitor—Allah will betray him"). Note such formulas in other tales in this book.

4. The vowel system of Galilee Bedouin dialects has five short and five long vowels (*i, e, a, o, u; ī, ē, ā, ō, ū*). However, their use is not strictly limited to morphological patterns or rules (cf. Blanc, "Arabic Dialects of the Negev Bedouins," about Negev Bedouins). Certain vowels may occur instead of others in different cases, without any (phonetic) conditioning. Thus, *i/e*, *o/u*, *a/i*, and *a/u*, among others, may interchange. In this story we find, for example, the verb *come* pronounced as *iğa*, *ağa*, and even *ğa*. Many such examples occur in other words in the following stories. Our transcription generally follows the phonetic manner of pronunciation of each word as the narrator uttered it, so that various forms can reflect the same word in these texts. This process exists to some extent also in sedentary dialects, but in these narratives, it is frequent.

5. The subject of females' rights and status is very serious in the Arab (including Bedouin) world because women are considered a weak and vulnerable element of society. Men are therefore obliged to protect their female relatives (wives, mothers, sisters, daughters) at all costs. Because of the notion of "family honor," women cannot do all that they like and have to rely on their male relatives for security and respect. This story shows the girl's difficulties after a man's slander. Even when she wants to reveal the truth and take revenge on the

perpetrator, she has to steal her husband's clothes and disguise herself as a man to be able to sit with the men, speak, and be heard.

6. Uther, *The Types of International Folktales*, 1:506-507.

7. In another version I heard from her, it is the heroine's father who kills the *khatib* with a *shibriyeh* (dagger).

8. Shilo, *Lishana Deni*, 117.

9. Shilo, 119.

10. Schmidt and Kahle, *Volkserzählungen aus Palästina* 1:114–27; Patai, *Arab Folktales from Palestine and Israel*, 79–84.

11. Bushnaq, *Arab Folktales*, 361–66.

12. Bushnaq, 46–50.

13. Morocco: 1091, 4730, 5650, 6411, 11785, 13964; Kurdistan: 6962, 10263, 14784; Yemen: 55, 1350, 8496; Poland: 9999.

5. A Woman's Loyalty

NARRATOR: Ṣabḥa ʿAbūd

TRIBE: *ʿArab el-Ḥuǧērāt*
IFA 12723 December 12, 1979

Text

There was one couple, a man and a woman, who loved each other very much.

They said, "If one of us dies, the other will enter the grave too."

Some time passed, and the woman died.

The husband said, "Put me also in the grave."

They said, "All right."

They buried her and put him in the grave and covered [them].

After about two or three days, people pass by the cemetery, they hear voices of conversation from one of the graves. They went to open the grave and found both alive, both husband and wife—Allah let them live, arranged for her to get several years of his life. They took them and brought them home.

Some time passed, and people began to tell the story. The emīr heard about it.

He said to his friends, "He put himself in the grave for her, but I can bring her away from him [i.e., he was faithful to her to death, but she could be seduced]!"

He went to town and bought clothes and candies and presents to trade with. He took the goods and went near her house and began to declare his merchandise there.

The husband was not at home, and the woman—she went downstairs and began to ask him, "What is this?"

He said to her, "Come with me to our place, where we have a lot of beautiful goods."

The woman heard him and said, "Yes, I'm ready to go."

She went with him to his place.

He went to the people who sat with them and said to them, "Here, I brought her from him!"

The husband came home and did not find his wife. He looked for her a day, two days, three days, and could not find her. Finally, he found Bedouins and asked them.

They told him, "Let's go to the sheikh."

He went to the emīr and sat with him.

He asked him, "What are you looking for?"

He said, "I have a wife and she is gone."

He said to him, "Listen, your wife is here."

He gave him his wife. The husband took the woman and left.

The king said to his sons, "Wait for him to cross the sea and kill him and his wife!"

The sons followed him, and as they crossed the sea, they heard him say to her, "I have done so much for you, and you are going and betraying me?" He took a sword and cut off her head.

The sons came and told the king. The emīr sent to call him.

He said to him, "Now that you killed your wife, let me give you my daughter as wife."

And this man, he has two sons and a daughter from his first wife.

He said to the emīr, "I'm going to bring my children and come back to you."

He took them. On the way back, they came to a place with water, and the camels did not want to pass.

The daughter said to him, "This female camel will cross the water."

He asked her, "Why?"

She said to him, "Because her mother would also cross the water and not be afraid."

The man took a sword and cut off the daughter's head.

Commentary

The informant told me the story in Arabic, and I wrote down her words in Hebrew while trying to preserve her style as much as possible. The narrator used the words *king*, *prince*, and *sheikh* indiscriminately.

The story belongs to the narrative type ATU 1350, "The Soon-Consoled Widow" (previously AT 1350, "The Loving Wife"): a man feigns death in order to test his wife's faithfulness. The wife is eager to take the man who brings her the news for her new husband (lover).[1] The narrative type is well known both in Europe and in the Middle East.

The story is based on the popular belief that women are less faithful than men are. Already in Ecclesiastes, which is traditionally attributed to King Solomon, it is said, "Which yet my soul seeketh, but I find not: one man among a thousand have I found; but a woman among all those have I not found" (Ecclesiastes 7:28). In the Middle Ages, a popular story based on this verse was written about King Solomon, who wanted to clarify to the people and the *Sanhedrin* (the highest court of the ancient Jews during the Second Temple period) the meaning of the statement attributed to him. Solomon finds a couple who live in harmony and then turns secretly to the husband and offers him a senior position in the palace and his daughter's hand in marriage, provided that at night he cut off his wife's head with his sword. The husband hesitates, and, when night falls and he intends to cut off his wife's head, he sees her lying by his two young children and retracts his intention. The next day, he informs King Solomon that he cannot commit the crime. A month later, the king calls the wife. He suggests he will marry her if she cuts off her husband's head. The woman agrees, and

Solomon gives her a sword made of tin. After her husband falls asleep, she attempts to cut off his head. The husband awakens and understands what has happened. The next day, the two of them are invited to meet King Solomon and the *Sanhedrin*, and at the king's request, the husband tells the story: "So-and-so happened. I woke up and found my wife, who was about to kill me, if it were not made of tin, I would be dead. I pitied her, but she did not pity me."[2] Another story that largely corresponds to the Bedouin story is the story of the Matrona (Widow) from Ephesus (Matrona in Latin is both a lady and a widow), found in a novel called *Satyricon*, written in Latin in the first century CE and attributed to Petronius. Fragments that survived from the work were copied during the Middle Ages and printed in 1664, and the book was widely distributed in the Western world. It contains a mixture of poetry and prose. Its plot combines adventure and eroticism with philosophy and gastronomy. One of the stories tells of a woman from Ephesus who lost her husband and wept on his grave for five days without bringing anything to her mouth. At the same time, the governor of the town ordered the crucifixion of several bandits. The gallows were not far from the grave where the woman lamented the death of her beloved husband. One of the soldiers was assigned to guard the bodies to prevent them from being taken down and buried. At night, the soldier saw a light between the graves not far away and heard the widow crying. He was curious to know the cause. He left his post, went to the grave, and saw a cute woman weeping. He gave her his dinner to calm her hunger and begged her to stop crying. The woman responded to his pleas and ate. They began to talk, and in the end, the two fell in love, and the widow agreed to have sexual intercourse with him at her husband's grave. The next few nights, the soldier returned and brought her food and wine, and the two continued to make love at the grave. One night, when the soldier left his post to meet the widow, one of the robbers' relatives removed his body from the cross and brought it for burial. When the soldier discovered what had happened in his absence, he told the widow and informed her that he intended to kill himself before he could be brought to trial. He asked her to bury his body in the grave beside her husband's body.

The woman did not agree. "Heaven forbid that I should look at the same moment on the dead bodies of two men whom I love" (*Satyricon* 112).

She instructed the soldier to remove her husband's body from the coffin and hang it on the cross instead of the missing bandit. The soldier helped her to carry out her plan. The next day everyone wondered how the dead body found its way to the cross.

This ancient story has undergone many changes. In the Talmud (Kiddushin 2b), it is said (in Aramaic): "In that story about a woman who acted like this and took him out." The Talmud does not explain what this is about, but the Tosafists give the complete story in the name of Rabbeinu Chananel.[3]

> There was the case of one woman who was weeping and mourning at her husband's tomb and there was a person there guarding [the body of] one hanged at the King's command. And he came to this woman and seduced her and, and she succumbed to him. And when he came back to the [body of the] hanged man he did not find him, and he was worried for fear of the King. The woman said to him: Do not be afraid. Take my husband from his grave and hang him instead. And she took her husband

out and he hanged him. This proves that even in her sorrow her [evil] inclination overcomes her.

The story is also repeated extensively in the book *Sefer Sha'ashuim* (Book of delight)—a book written by Joseph Ibn Zabara in the twelfth century in Barcelona and based on many popular sources. In Joseph Ibn Zabara's version, the hanged man was bald; therefore, the woman tore off her husband's hair so no one would notice the cheating.

Another version of the story is found in the *Mishle Shualim* (Fox fables) of R. Berechiah Ben Natronai Ha-Nakdan (thirteenth century). The story is also known from *The Fables of Marie de France*, attributed to Mary de France (end of the twelfth century), and from another medieval book, *The Seven Sages of Rome*.[4]

In addition to the Bedouin story, there are in the IFA archive five parallels from Iraq, Iran, Yemen, and Morocco, as well as one parallel from Poland.[5] These Hebrew parallels are closer to the description of the international type. The Bedouin story, on the other hand, is quite different. It begins with the husband's declaration of allegiance, saying that he should be buried alive if his wife dies before him. This indeed happens, and the husband, faithful to his statement, wants to be buried next to his wife. Allah brings the woman back to life. The emīr hears about the case and tempts the woman in order to show the husband that his wife is not loyal to him. The woman is tempted and comes to the emīr's house. The husband, who is looking for her, goes to the emīr and hears about his wife's betrayal. He kills her and marries the emīr's daughter. Later he kills his daughter from his first wife after he concludes that the daughter will follow her mother's ways.

The belief in the strong connection between mother and daughter that causes a daughter to imitate her mother's actions is also very ancient. The prophet Ezekiel, on addressing his prophecy to Jerusalem, likens her to the daughter of Canaan and says: "Behold, every one that useth proverbs shall use this proverb against thee, saying, As is the mother, so is her daughter" (Ezekiel 16:44). The commentators agree that the prophet was using a familiar proverb that was common in his environment (Babylon of the sixth century BCE): the daughter follows her mother's path.

In the Jerusalem Talmud, in the course of conversation between Rabbi Yossi Ma'ony and Rabbi Yehuda Nesiah (the president of the *Sanhedrin* in Tiberias and the grandson of Rabbi Yehuda HaNasi, the editor of the Mishna), Rabbi Yehudah asks Rabbi Yossi about the meaning of the verse "For their mother hath played the harlot" (Hosea 2:7). According to Rabbi Yehuda Nesiah, the verse refers to Sarah, Abraham's wife and the mother of the people of Israel. Rabbi Yehuda wonders, "Can it be that our mother Sarah was a prostitute?" To this, Rabbi Yossi replies, "As is the mother, so is her daughter, as is this generation [age] so is the president [of the *Sanhedrin*], as is the president so is this generation." In other words, he uses the biblical quote cited earlier, and afterward, he brings biblical verses that prove the truth of his words.

In the Babylonian Talmud, Rabbi Akiba's daughter, who married Ben Azzai, allows him, like her mother, Rachel, to leave the house to study Torah far away. Once again, one encounters this statement: "The daughter of Rabbi Akiba acted in a similar way toward Ben Azzai. And this it is that people say 'Ewe follows ewe; a daughter's acts are like those of her mother'" (Babylon Talmud, Ketubot 63a).

Like the Bedouin story, the Talmud also depicts an animal in the household—in this case, a sheep—that imitates the actions of its predecessor. The image also relates to the name of Rabbi Akiba's wife, who, according to other Midrashic sources, had the name Rachel (in biblical Hebrew, *rachel* [pronounced raḥel] is a female sheep).

In the Arab culture space, there is also the perception that the daughter follows in her mother's footsteps. The expression "*ṭāl'a la-immha*" (takes after her mother) in spoken Arabic is used, usually with a negative and sarcastic connotation, for a daughter who imitates her mother's actions. The word *ṭāl'a* means "going out" or "rising." It is possible that the source of the expression is the proverb *ṭobb al-ğarra 'a-temmha betaṭla' al-bint li-ammha* (put the jar on its mouth—the girl takes after her mother).[6] This saying is used, both positively and negatively, to mean that the daughter takes after her mother. The proverb comes from a custom prevalent in Arab villages: mothers used to hang laundry or to deal with house affairs on the roof, which the girls were not allowed to enter unless they were called. When a mother needed something from her daughter, she would hit an upside-down jar lightly on the roof. The echoing noise signaled to the daughter that her mother was calling for her. Another Arabic proverb expresses the same idea: *farx il-baṭṭ 'awwām* (the duck's chick is a good swimmer). This one is said in a positive tone—when people succeed, it is said that they resemble their fathers or mothers.

Two other less common proverbs also describe a female chick imitating the act of the adult bird. The first is *bint il-wazzah 'awwāmah* (the goose's daughter is a good swimmer), and the second is *bint il-xawwāḍa xawwāḍa* (the swimmer's [or the sailor's] daughter swims, or the feminine sailor's daughter is also a feminine sailor). These two proverbs are said in condemnation of a daughter who, like her mother, goes astray.

The Bedouin story is built as a novella and has a realistic nature, with the exception of one supernatural event: Allah restores both spouses to life and gives the woman several years of life that he "borrows" from the husband. This motif of transferring years of life from one person to another (or from animals to humans) is known in many cultural spaces. The Zohar relates that Adam was expected to live a thousand years, but he agrees to give seventy years of his life to King David, who was supposed to die on the day he was born (Zohar, vol. b [Exodus: Pikudey], 235a).

A literary Arabic equivalent of the story is found in James Edward Hanauer's book *Folk-lore of the Holy Land: Moslem, Christian and Jewish*. The text he gives is adapted and presented in a framework story in which the hoopoe, unlike all the other birds, refuses King Solomon's demand to come and shade his wife with its wings on his wedding day. The king sends the other birds to bring it by force, and the hoopoe tells them several stories condemning women to explain its refusal to come to the king's aid. One of the stories it tells is a parallel to the Bedouin story. Here is Hanauer's version:

> A certain man had for wife a most beautiful woman of whom he was consumedly fond; and she was even fonder of him, for he was very rich.
>
> "Were I to die," she would sometimes sigh in his ear, "you would soon dry your eyes and take a better wife; whereas, if you died first, I should end my days in grief." "Nay, by Allah," replied the man fiercely. "Were you to die, I would renounce my business and weep on your grave seven years."

"Would you?" she cried, enraptured. "Oh, I would do more than that for your sweet memory!"

The woman, as it was decreed, died first, and the man, true to his vow, gave up his business, and mourned at her graveside night and day for seven long years, subsisting upon scraps of broken meat thrown to him by the charitable. His clothes turned to rags; his hair and beard hung about him like the fronds of maiden hair; his nails grew as long as eagle's talons, and his body became as emaciated as that of the leaf insect. (*Mantis religiosa*, called by the natives of the Jerusalem district "St George's mare," or "The Jew's mare.")

At the end of the seven years El-Khaḍr, being sent that way, saw the strange mourner, and inquired his story. The saint asked him whether he really believed that his wife, had she outlived him, would have done as much. "Of course," was the reply. "Do you think that, if she were now alive, she would still love you?" "Of course I do." "Well," said El-Khaḍr, "we shall see." He struck the grave with Moses' rod and bade it open, when the woman arose in her shroud, young and lovely as ever. El-Khaḍr, having hidden behind a monument, the woman saw only her husband. Horrified by his appearance, she cried, "Who are you, dreadful creature, more like a beast than a man? Why am I here in the graveyard? If you are a ghûl, I pray you not to eat me."

She shuddered still more when she learnt that the frightful creature was her faithful husband, and deferred going home with him till nightfall, saying that people would talk if she went through the streets in her grave-clothes. He sat down beside her, laid his head in her lap, and in the relief of again possessing her, fell sound asleep.

A sultan, journeying by that way, saw the couple near the open grave, and, struck by the woman's beauty in her shroud, he invited her to be his love. She laid her husband's head on the ground and stepped into a litter that was in readiness.

When the cavalcade was gone. El-Khaḍr came and woke the husband, telling him how his wife had been carried off, and suggesting that they should follow her. They started in pursuit and reached the palace soon after the Sultan's arrival there. El-Khaḍr demanded an audience, which, on account of his commanding presence, was instantly granted. The sultan was incredulous and very angry when El-Khaḍr proclaimed the identity of his companion, while the woman vehemently declared that the old fright had never been her husband. The saint offered to settle the question and commanded that the woman should resume her shroud and be taken back to the graveyard. The sultan, in awe of El-Khaḍr, was bound to submit, and the woman was brought to the brink of her former grave. She suddenly fell into it, a lifeless corpse; some say in consequence of a withering look from El-Khaḍr, and others, as the result of a blow from the beak of a great eagle, which suddenly swooped down out of heaven.

El-Khaḍr then closed the grave with a stroke of his rod; and by the command of Allah, her husband regained the seven years which he had lost. He was thus enabled to marry again and live long and happily with another wife, whom, having lost his illusions, he was wise enough to keep in her place.[7]

As in the Bedouin story, here also the wife returns to life because of a miraculous occurrence: the appearance of El-Khaḍr (as Muslims call Elijah). The husband does not "lend" years to his wife, but he miraculously recovers the seven years he wasted in futile mourning for his dead wife. In this story too, the king (sultan) acts as the seductive figure.

In his book *Why Did the Earth Laugh? Bedouins Narrate*, Mordechai Yonai relates an edited version of the Bedouin story called "The Emīr Who Did Not Trust Women."[8] No details about the origin of the story are given. In this version, the story begins with two brothers, one of whom had a son and the other, a daughter. They decide to marry their children to each other when they are of age. One of the brothers, the groom's father, is killed in battle; the second brother dies of grief over his brother's death. The elders of the tribe appoint the son as an emīr and seek to fulfill his father's will by marrying him to his cousin. His cousin conditions her marriage: "I will be your wife only if death does not separate us. If you die before me, I will be buried with you, and if I die before you, you will be buried with me." The groom accepts the condition. A short while later, the emīr sets out for a raid (*ghazu*), and his wife accompanies him. On the way, the woman dies, and the emīr, faithful to his oath, commands that he be buried alive beside her. Three days later, passersby hear voices coming from the grave. They open the grave and discover the couple alive. The rumor of the miracle reaches another emīr's ears. He decides to teach the groom a lesson. When the husband is absent from his home, he seduces the wife by bringing her delicacies, and she responds to his courtship, mounts his horse, and goes to his encampment. Looking for his wife, the betrayed emīr arrives at the tent of the emīr who kidnapped his wife, and his host tells him what has happened. At this point in the story, the betrayed husband asks the emīr if this is the nature of all women, and his host answers in the affirmative, saying, "All of them, even my mother." After this statement, the husband responds to the emīr's offer to examine this matter in practice and try to seduce his host's mother. The mother responds to his temptation, and the husband lets the emīr in on his secret. They decide to put the mother on trial. The husband informs her that he will come to take her at midnight, but first she must kill her son with the knife he gives her so that the son will not disturb him. The mother approaches her son's bed and stabs the body on it without realizing that it is a doll. The next morning, the emīr sends the husband along with the two women—the traitorous wife and his mother. At the same time, the emīr sends two young men to follow the husband. "Ride on your mares and quickly follow them," he tells them. "If they cross the water and they are on their way to their tribe, kill all three with the sword, but if they do not all cross the water, bring the emīr alive."

The two follow him. When they reach the stream, the emīr's camel refuses to cross it. The betrayed emīr pulls out his sword and cuts off the camel's legs. Then he accuses his wife and the emīr's mother of treachery and cuts off their heads, and then he slaughters the camel above them as a sign of their disgrace. He returns with the two followers to the emīr's tent. The latter praises him and offers his young sister in marriage.

This version explains a vague phrase in the Bedouin story: "The king said to his sons: Wait for him to cross the sea and kill him and his wife!" In the Bedouin story, the king had no reason to kill the betrayed husband, while here the emīr's mother was also involved. The emīr puts the husband on trial. He expects him to kill the two women. It seems that the stream marks the boundary between the area of the emīr's control and that of the husband. If the husband does not harm the women, even the emīr's mother will not be punished and will find refuge in the neighboring tribe, which will shame the emīr. In this version, no explanation is given for the camel's refusal to cross the water.

The motif "The crosser's daughter—crosses" is found in another Bedouin story in Yonai's book, "As the Daughter so Is the Mother."[9] The story was told to the author by Abu ʿAli El-Hēb, of the ʿArab El-Hēb tribe in the north of Israel. In this story, the protagonist is a ğ*ammāla*, one who belongs to a tribe of camel breeders who roam in the desert. Returning to his tent unexpectedly at midnight, he discovers that his wife is betraying him with a strange man. The man escapes from the tent, and the hero kills his wife, folds up his tent, and goes on a wandering journey, taking his young daughter with him. When they reach the river, the camels refuse to cross it. The young daughter turns to her father and says to him, "Do you remember, Father, that camel that always crossed the water and the herd followed her? Let us bring her daughter and she will cause the whole herd to cross." One night, following this statement, the father murders his daughter in her sleep.

The story I heard from Ṣabḥa ʿAbūd is thus a typical story of a patriarchal Bedouin society that maintains some beliefs about the traitorous nature of women. Bedouin society, as well as Arab society as a whole, is very serious about adultery on the part of the woman (although the male adulterer is also punished). It seems that the purpose of the story is to strengthen the man's control of his wife, and the story is a warning sign for women not to breach their loyalty and graze in foreign fields.[10]

As we have seen, the Bedouin story corresponds to a long series of similar stories from the Arab culture as well as from the Jewish cultural space, especially to medieval stories, and it matches the reality of Bedouin life as it was in Israel and neighboring countries until the beginning of the twentieth century.

Notes

1. Uther, *The Types of International Folktales*, 2:285.

2. Jelinek, *Bet ha_Midrash* vol. 4, 146–48 *Fables of King Solomon*, story 3.

3. Rabbeinu Chananel (Chananel Ben Chushiel) was one of the greatest Tosafists; his family moved from Rome in the second half of the tenth century and settled in the city of Kairouan in North Africa.

4. See Martin, *Fables of Marie de France*, 88–89, fable no. 25; Runte, Wikeley, and Farrell, *Seven Sages of Rome*, 197–203. For a comprehensive interpretation of the narrative type AT 1510, "The Matron of Ephesus," see Ben-Amos, *Folktales of the Jews*, 3:481–91.

5. Iraq: 141; Persian Kurdistan: 10218; Yemen: 8711; Morocco: 8146, 11647; Poland: 15130.

6. Dr. Roseland Daeem, a Christian Arab folklore researcher from Haifa, told us about these sayings. We do not know whether Galilee Bedouins know and use them.

7. Hanauer, *Folk-lore of the Holy Land*, 254–56.

8. Yonai, *Why Did the Earth Laugh?*, 99–105.

9. Yonai, 97–98.

10. In a Jewish-Libyan parallel found in the IFA (6445), this is highlighted at the end of the story: "The king learned that the Police Minister misused his position because of a widow who had forgotten her husband on the third day after his death. What did he do? He sent three policemen to bring the woman before him and ordered her to be tied to the tail of an untamed pony. The woman was dragged by the horse until her bones were crushed. This punishment has since been used as a sign and an example for women to remain faithful to their husbands and to remember them at least a week after their death."

6. The King's Wife and the Poor Man

NARRATOR: Zehiyya Ġrifāt

TRIBE: *ʿArab el-Ġrifāt*
IFA 17411 September 11, 1982

1 min hōn la-hōn,[1] ʾalla al-ʾamīr. u-hū wa-l-mara gāʿadīn ʿala-ha-l-baranda. lamman gaʿadu, kull mā yiği wāḥad fagīr yguḷ-ḷo [=tgūḷ-ḷo]: "hāḏa min marato, al-ġani—min marato." yōm, hāḏa gāḷ, "šū yaʿani al-ġani min marato w-al-fagīr min marato?" da ʿayyin ʿala wāḥad fagīr b-al-balad u-ğawwazha la-l-fagīr. rāḥ waddāha la-l-fagīr; gāḷ la-l-xadam "rūḥam xuḏūha ʿand-al-fagīr hāḏ."	1 From here thereto, there is this emīr. As he and the woman [his wife] are sitting on the terrace, when they were sitting, each time a poor man came by, she would say to him, "This is from his wife"; "the rich man is from his wife." One day this [emīr] said, "What does it mean 'the poor man is from his wife' and 'the rich man is from his wife'?" He looked for one in the town and married her to the poor man. He went and took her to the poor man and said to the servants, "Take her to this poor man."
11 lamman xaḏūha, ʿal-xā, wāḥad—mā ygūm, lā yaḥki, nāyem ʿa-l-farša ʿan-ha-š-šikel. giʿedat hāy ʿind^{a} ʾummo, al-fagīr. ʿando ʾummo. widdo yšuxx ygūl-la "qaʿʿīni." widdo yišrab—"ʾezgīni." "widdi ʾākul—ṭaʿmīni." u-huw nāyem ʿa-l-farša. gāḷat, "ʾā, malīḥ hāḏa ʿan ha-š-šikel?" l-al-xityāra "šū ykūn leč hāḏa?" gāḷat ilha, "ʾebni."	11 When they took her, [it was] to one who does not get up, does not talk, [and is] lying on the bed this way [all the time]. She stayed at his mother's, the poor man's [mother]. He had his mother [at home]. He wanted to piss he would say to her "make me," when he wanted to drink—"let me drink," "I want to eat—feed me." And he was lying on the bed. She said to her: "O, is it good this way?" To the old woman. "What is this (one) to you?" She said to her: "My son."
20 "kam sana ṣār-lek bi-l-mašġala-hāḏa?" gāḷat-ilha, "ṣār-li sabaʿtaʿšar sana."	20 "How many years have you been with this problem [issue, works]?" She said to her, "I've been [so] seventeen years."

23 gāḷat-la, “u-šū ysāwi?” rāḥat l-al-xadam, ğābat sabeʿ guḏbān rummān, sabeʿ guḏbān ḥadīd, sabeʿ guḏbān būlāḏ. (ʿaṣāy, teʿarifha.)

23 She said to her, “And what does he do?” She went to the servant, brought seven pomegranate sticks, seven iron sticks, and seven steel sticks. (Sticks, you know it.)

27 min ’awwal huwa gāḷ-ḷa, “qaʿʿī” ḏarbatu l-gaḏīb, kasratu ʿalēh. ʿād rāḥ ʿa-($_{H}$bēt šimuš$_{H}$) . . . gāl, “widdi ’ašrab,” ṯāni gaḏīb. rāḥ širib min el-barrād u-’ağa. gāḷ-ḷa, “widdi ’ākol” ḏirbato. fa-kasrat ʿalē el-guḏbān kullha. ṣār yerūḥ u-yišrab u-yīği laḥālo. u-sabaʿtaʿšar sina hu mġalleb ’ummo, teṭaʿmū u-tazgī—zalama kbīr.

27 On the first time he said “empty me,” she hit him with the stick, broke the stick on him. So he went to ($_{H}$bēt šimuš$_{H}$) W.C. He said, “I want to drink,” the second stick. He went and drank from the refrigerator and came (back). He said to her, “I want to eat,” she hit him. And she broke all the sticks on him. He began to go and drink and come back on his own. And seventeen years he was bothering his mother, feeding him and making him drink. [And he was] a big man.

35 lamman geḏbat . . . ṣār yerūḥ u-yīği. ṣār yerūḥ ʿala-aš-šuġul. yištġil. tḥuṭṭ-lo z-zuwwāda, w-irūḥ yištġal. u-mā ʿindo ’iši, fagīr. ʿindo xušše miṯl aṭ-ṭābūn. [btiʿraf šū ṭ-ṭābūn? bēto ṭābūn, fiš ʿendo.] ’ā.

35 When she took . . . he began to work. He worked. She would give him provisions [a lunch box], and he would go and work. He did not have anything—[he was] poor. He had a hut, like a baking oven. (Do you know what a taboon is? He has nothing. His house was [like] an oven, he had anything.) Yes.

40 lamman ṣār yištġel, yōm ’ağat gāflet ⁱğmāl. [man gabuḷ kānat en-nās twaddi ʿala ʿakka l-gamḥ, ’iši,]

40 When he began working, [there] came one day a camel caravan. In the past people were bringing wheat, anything, to Acre [ʿAkko].

43 mafīš bī zmān sayyarāt, bī ğmāl. gāḷu-ḷa: “txaḷḷi ṣāleḥ yrūḥ maʿāna u-

43 There were at that time no cars, there] were camels. They told her [the woman], “Will you let Ṣāleḥ go with us and

45 yāxoḏ el-’ağār bi-’ağarēn?” gāḷat-lo, “’ā, lēš lā?” ʿemlat-lo zuwwāda, u-ḥaṭṭat-lo zuwwāda u-rāḥ ᵉmʿā ž-žmāʿa.

45 take his fees doubled?” She said to him: “Yes, why not.” She made for him a provisions box and put for him the provisions and he went with the group.

48 miṯel ma-tgūḷ, ṣār ʿend bīr eṣ-ṣafa, ʿend bīr tabaʿ el-ē . . . magadīr eṣ-ṣafa, elli b-eš-šaʿab. hināka ḥaṭṭatu ta-yišrabu mayya, yitrayyaḥu. lamman ḥaṭṭatu hunāk widdhom yišrabu, mafiš ḥabel maʿāham. gālu, “mīn yinzal ʿa-l-bīr u-yāxoḏ ’ağāru bi-’ağarēn? tinzel, ya ṣāleḥ, u-nanṭīk el-’ağār bi-’ağarēn?” gāḷ-ḷo, “’ā, lēš lā.”

48 As you say, he was by Bīr Eṣ-Ṣafa, near a well . . . near the “purity quantities” [well][2] in Šaʿab. There they camped [for a while], they wanted to drink water, to rest. When they camped there and wanted to drink, they [saw that they] did not have a rope with them [to draw the water from the well]. They said, “Who would like to go down the well and will take his fee twice? Will you go down, Ṣāleḥ, and we’ll give you your fee double?” He said, “Yes, why not.”

57 nizel. al-ma—'azga eğ-ğmāl u-'azga š-šīx, ṭallaʿ, ʿaggad walla fa-l-bīr ğawwa. winn šāf el-basatīn, šāf hā-l-^{e}krūm, ar-rummān, at-tuffāḥ, al-ʿineb, wann zalama ḥūt, ġūl, gāʿed, u-waḥda nāime ʿala rekibto hōn, waḥda nāime ʿala rkibto hōn, ʿa-l-ġūḷ. [fhimt ʿalayya šlōn?] lamman nāmat alla-nadā, gāḷ-ḷo "as-salāma ʿalekom."	57 He went down [to] the water, gave water to the camels, and gave water to the old man [sheikh]. He looked and went on, and lo inside the well—and he saw orchards, what vineyards, pomegranates, apples, grapes, and lo a man, a ḥūt, a ġūl, sitting, and one [girl] sleeping on his knee from here and one girl sleeping on his knee from here, on the ġūl. (Did you understand me how?) When she was asleep, he called him, [and] said to him: "Peace on you" [Hello, good day].
66 gāḷ el-ġūḷ, "lōla huwwe salāmak ḏaḷḷ ib-kalāmak, l-axaḷḷi wuḥūš al-barr tismaʿ tagrīṭ ʿaḏmak!"[3] gāḷ-ḷo, "opp!" gāḷ-ḷo,	66 The ġūl said to him, "If your greeting had not remained in your words, I would have let the wild animals hear the chewing/gnawing of your bones." He said to him, "Woe." He said to him,
69 "tgūl, mīn 'aḥsan min aṯ-ṯintēn? min 'aḥibb 'akṯar min aṯ-ṯintēn, hal-as-sōda walla l-bēḍa?"[4] gāḷ-ḷo, "la, 'ana 'aḥibb" . . . gāḷ-ḷo, "ḥibb ḥabībak law kān ʿabd aswad." gāḷ-ḷo, "ʿifa aḷḷāh^{a} ʿannak."[5]	69 "Say, who is more beautiful between the two? Whom do I love more between the two, the black one or the white one?" He said to him, "No, I like" . . . He said to him, "Love your beloved even if she were a black slave." He said to him, "May Allah give you health."
75 lammin gāḷ-ḷo ʿan-ha-š-šikel, gāḷ-ḷo, "ağ-ğmāl, xaḷḷaṣ? xaḷḷaṣam? da, ragātam ʿanna"	75 When he [the ġūl] said to him this way, he [the man, Ṣāleḥ] said to him [the camel driver], "[The camels] finished? [The camels] finished [drinking]? This, their term (deadline) is (lifted) from us."
78 gāḷ-ḷo, "stanna, stanna šwayye," ṭāga hī, min ğawwīta hāl-bīr, ṭāga hēk, bīha l-krūm u-bīha kull(a) 'iši. rā(ḥ) ʿa-hā-r-rummāna, ğāb ṯalaṯ-^{i}kwāz rummān, anṭāha iyyāhen. gāḷ-ḷo, "xuḏ haḏōla, 'amāna la-ʿindak."	78 He [the ġūl] said to him, "Wait a little while, wait a little." There was a niche, inside the well, there was such a niche, where there were those orchards and everything. He [the ġūl] went to the pomegranate tree, brought three pomegranates, and gave them to him. He said to him, "Take these as a trust for those whom you have [your family]."
84 lamman xaḏa[6] aṯ-ṯlāṯ-^{i}kwāz er-rummān, u-ḥaṭṭhen, laffhen b-ʿobbo, mā widdo yewaddī bi-maṭraḥ, hinne ḏahab, miš rummān. huwwe biḥsabhen rummān, fagīr, ʿala nī(y)to.	84 When he took the three pomegranates and put them, folded them in his lap, he did not want to give them in a [hiding] place. They were of gold, not pomegrana tes. He thought they were pomegranates. He was poor, a simple [honest] man [who did not know them].

89 lamma xaḏ̣āhan, bī wāḥad min al-gāfla, bi-(yi)ʿāwad ʿala-ʾāsia, ʿala balado. lamman gāḷ-ḷo, "tāxaḏ-ha-l-ʾamāna maʿāk, la-ʾommi u-la-ʿēlti, honāk?"	89 When he took them, there was one from the caravan, who wanted to go back to Asia, to his town. When he said to him, "Will you take this trust with you to my mother and family there?"
93 gāḷ-ḷo, "ʾā." ḥaṭṭ ar-rummānāt b-gaḷb eṭ-ṭḥīnāt. ma xaḷḷa haḏāk yšūfo.	93 He said to him, "Yes." He put the pomegranates in the flour. He did not let that one see it [the pomegranates].
95 hināka nāda ʿa-rabʿa ṣallaḥō wa-aṭlaʿūh min al-bīr u-ḥaṭṭ al-ʾamāna u-ḥaṭṭ az-zuwwāda u-waddāhom la-marato, la-ʾommo. miš marato hiyya, hiyya-lli ḥaṭṭa l-ʾamīr ʿando, yaʿani.	95 Then he called his group and they helped him and took him out of the well. He put the trust and pomegranates put the provisions and gave them to his wife, his mother. Not his wife, that is, she was the one whom the emīr placed at his place.
100 lammin ḥaṭṭa ʿando, raddaha la-hināk, "hē, yā-(e)mm ṣāleḥ, ṣāleḥ baʿaṯ-ilku ʾamāna hōn, taʿāli xuḏi ha-l-ʾamāna." ǧatt il-mara illi ʿando, ʾaxḏat el-ʾamāna u-fawwatatha.	100 When he put it with him [with the man], he returned it there, "Oh, Mother of Ṣaleḥ, Ṣaleḥ has sent you a trust here. Come and take this trust." The woman who was at his place came out, took the trust, and brought it in.
105 haḏāka rāḥu ʿala ʿakka, maṯalan, ybīʿu l-gamḥ illi maʿāham, ba-l-ʾaǧār. hāḏi lamman. ʾummo mā šāfat al-hadiyye tabaʿha, ʾebenha lli baʿaṯha. al-mara-lli ʿindo illi šāfatha . . . mā ziʿlat hēk, winna kūz er-rummān, kullo ḏahab, aṯ-ṯāni kaḏālika miṯel, aṯ-ṯāleṯ miṯel kaḏālika. kulla ḏahab.	105 They went to Acre, for example, to sell what they had, at a price. This [woman] when . . . His mother did not see her present, which her son had sent. The woman who was at his place saw it. She was angry like that, [but] lo all the pomegranate was gold, the second one was also like that, the third was also like that. All was gold.
113 hāḏ-al-mara rāḥat ǧābat nās ᵉtʿammer, banat gaṣer, miṯel gaṣer ǧōzha b-at-tekmīl.	113 This woman went and brought people to build—they built a palace, exactly like her husband's palace.
116 gāmat[7] el-xušša, gāmat al-bēt, miṯel gaṣer al-ʾamīr tabaḥa ǧōzha, ʿamilt	116 She removed the hut, removed the house, and did a palace like the emīr's, her husband's. She made
118 el-gaṣar. šū ʿende gaṣer ǧōzha l-ʾamīr, ḥaṭṭat b-al-gaṣer.	118 the palace. Whatever he had in her husband's palace, the emīr, she put in this [new] palace.
120 ʾaǧa hāḏa l-fagīr, rawwaḥ, ydawwer ʿa-ha-l-xušša. xušša gabel[8], fiš bēt mlīḥ, fiš bēt ʿendo.	120 This poor man came, went back home, and was looking for the hut, [it was] a hut previously, not a nice house—he did not have a house.
123 ṭabb ʿalē – fī ḥaras ṯnēn, ḥaras ṯnēn ʿala bāb hā-l-gaṣer tabaʿo alli banato al-mara. gāḷ-ḷo, "ʿala ēš anti dāyer hōn?" al-ḥaras. gāḷ-ḷo, "ʾāni yamm ʿala l-ʿilm, ʿendi walāya ṯintēn. u-kānu bi-nitfet xušše hōn. ʾaḏkor ʾanna xuššti kānat hōn."	123 He entered—two guards came to him, two guards at the door of his palace, which the woman had built. He said to him, "What are you looking for here?" the guard [said]. He said to him, "I clearly know [am of the knowledge] that I have two ladies and they were in a small hut here. I remember that my hut was here."

130 rāḥ gāḷ l-al-malaka tabaʿtom. gāḷ-ḷa "hāḏa wāḥad hēk hēk, esmo ṣāleḥ, dāir ygūḷ kān fī xuššta hōn." gāḷat lo, "ā, hāḏa elna, tabaʿna, fawwtū."

130 He went and said to their queen, he said to her, "This one is so-and-so, his name is Ṣāleḥ and he says he has a hut here." She said to him, "Yes, he is of us, ours, let him in."

134 fawwatūh ʿal-ḥammām, ḥammamūh u-labbasū badlet ʾamīr, u-fawwatō. lamman fawwatō, waddat la-ǧōzha l-ʾawwalāni, l-al-ʾamīr ǧōzha, gāḷat-lo, "taʿāl, rūḥ ʾagul-lo tfaḍḍal ʿašāk el-lēla ǧbāl, ḏāt el-flāniyya, ʿala marto al-flāniyya." ʾaǧa l-ʾamīr, gāḷ-ḷo, "yā flān, (el-ġūl wazīr),

134 They brought him to the bathroom, bathed him and dressed him an emīr's suit, and brought him in. When they brought him in, she sent for her first husband, her husband the emīr, and said to him, "Come, go tell him please your dinner tonight is on the hill, at that same someone, on [the responsibility of] his wife." The emīr came and said to him, "O man (the ġūl is the wazīr),

142 "ʾani maʿazūm ʿala ʿaša. widdi mā yiṣīr, anni arū-ʿala hāḏa l-ʿaša hunāk, ʿazamna flān."

142 I am invited for dinner. I want. It's impossible [that] I will not go to this dinner there. That person invited us."

145 šū, naṭṭ el-wazīr gāḷ-ḷo, "walak, yā zalama, yinḍāf ʿindo hāḏ? hāḏa fagīr, ʿindo nitfet xušša." gāḷ-ḷo, "yaʿni, hū diʿāna, u-ʾana—widna ṛṛūḥ."

145 What, the wazīr jumped and said to him: "Woe, o man, would anyone be hosted by this [person]? He is poor, he has a small hut." He said to him, "That is it, he invited me and I—we will go."

149 lamma rāḥam hā-l-waggāfa, waggāfa waddathen, šū gaṣro. ēš hū b-bēto, bī. bas el-mara mā warrato ḥālha šēli, b-al-marra. ʿend el-ʿaša liga ha-l-ʾakel ʿala ṭ-ṭawlāt, liga l-mašrūbāt, liga kull ʾiši timām. itʿašša. lamma tʿaššam baʿd-es-sahriyya, yaʿani ʿand el-malak ʿāde ʾinha l-mara tidīr el-ʾakel ṯāni. ʿugb es-sahriyya dārat el-mara ʾakel ṯāni u-ʾaʿraḍat ʿalē.

149 When they went, the servant, servant led them. What a palace [his palace was]. All that he had in his house was there. But the woman did not reveal herself to him at all, at all. At the dinner he found the food on the tables, found drinks, found everything perfect. He had dinner. When they had had dinner, after the entertainment, the king had a habit that the woman would bring food again. After the entertainment, the woman brought the food again and revealed herself to him.

159 lamma ʾaʿraḍat ʿalē gāḷ-ḷa, "hu-anti alli hōn?" gālat lo, "hāḏa ʾana alli hōn." gāḷ-ḷa, "baʿdek ʿa-l-ʿahad walla baṭṭalti?" walla, yaʿni, xunti l-ʿahed? gāḷat, "la, baʿadni ʿa-l-ʿahad."[9] yaʿani ma ǧawwazato, l-az-zalama illi fātat ʿala l-bēt tabaʿo. gāḷat miṯel beʿada ʿala ǧōzha l-ʾamīr, hiyya iyyā.

159 When she revealed herself, he said to her, "Is it you who is here?" She said to him, "It's I who am here." He said to her, "Are you still keeping the oath or have you annulled it?" He said to her, that is, "Have you cheated on [broken] the oath?" She said, "No, I am still under the oath." That is, she had not married the man into whose house she entered. She said, as though she was still with her husband the emīr, she was with him.

167 gāḷ-ha: "ʿārfīn šū ṣār bēni u-bān hāy el-mara?" la-l-wazīr, gāḷ-ḷo, "laʾ,"

167 He said to them, "Do you know what went on between me and this woman?" to the wazīr. He said to him, "No."

169 u-li-hāḏa lli usmo ṣāleḥ. gāḷ-ḷo, "lā'." gāḷ, "hāḏ-al-mara, kull mā yimrog wāḥad min ʿendi alli hdūma mlīḥa, tegūl "hāḏa min marato." w-alli hdūmo mā mlīḥa, tgūl, "min marato."	169 And to that one whose name was Ṣāleḥ, he said to him, "No." He said, "This woman, each time someone would pass by [from] my place whose clothes were nice she would say, "This is from his wife." And that one whose clothes were not fine, she would say, "From his wife."
174 al-ġani tgūl "min marato," w-al-fagīr tgūl "min marato." ǧīt 'ani ḥaṭṭēta b-al-bēt—dawwart la-l-xadam, guḷt-ilam, "'ayya bēt fagīr tḥuṭṭu bīha ʿašan nšūf šū widha tiʿmal-lo hāḏi." tanni t'akkadet inn al-fagīr min marato wa-l-ġani min marato."	174 The rich man—she would say "from his wife" and the poor man—she would say "from his wife." I went and put her, looked for the servants and told them, "Any poor house you will put her in it so that we'll see what she will do to him, this one." Until I became sure, that the poor man is from his wife and the rich man is from his wife.
181 az-zalama, lamman gāḷ hēk, gāḷ-ḷha, "yalla ta-nrawwaḥ ʿa-l-bēt tabaʿna, yā man kānnek baʿadek ʿala l-ʿahed." ʿawāyed el-ʿarab, yaʿani ʿawāyidna. gāḷat-ḷo, "wēn 'arawwaḥ? mā 'arawwaḥ 'alla mā ǧibt binti, bintak, yā l-'amīr, la-ṣāleḥ.	181 The man, when he said this, he said to her, "Come on; let's go home to our house, if you are still on the oath." Bedouin habits. That is, our habits. She said to him, "Where shall I go home? I will not go home unless you give my daughter, your daughter, oh, emīr, to Ṣāleḥ [as wife]."
188 'ani ma teʿibt b-al-bēt hāḏa u-mā ltagēt hāḏa, tanni 'adaššro, muš ʿāmra la-ġēri, alla mā aǧīb binti, w-aḥuṭṭha b-il-bēt hāḏa, u-yāxoḏha z-zalama lue hāḏ." hāḏ-al-xurrāfa xallṣat hassaʿ, ġair awaṣṣlak ṯānia. mniḥa willa miṯluha?	188 "I haven't toiled with this house and haven't met this [man] so that I will [not] build for someone else, unless I bring my daughter and put her in this house and this man will take her [in marriage]." This story is finished now. I will give you another one [like it], good or similar?

Commentary

I wrote down two versions of the story from two different tribes. The first one, which is transcribed here, was told by Zehiyya Ġrifāt, a gifted narrator who married a member of another tribe, the Bedouin tribe of ʿArab el-Ḥuǧērāt and lived in an isolated house near Yodfat. The second story was narrated by Ṣabḥa ʿAbūd, from ʿArab el-Ḥuǧērāt.

The narrative type ATU 923B, "The Princess Who Was Responsible for Her Own Fortune," is common throughout the Mediterranean region and North Africa, as well as Europe and Asia. It appears in several forms. Following is a description of the main lines of this type, some of which are found in the Bedouin versions.

When a king asks his (three) daughters who is responsible for their good fortune (who has the blessing of the kingdom, wealth, and honor), the elder daughters answer that he is the one, but the youngest says that she herself (only Allah) is responsible (she states that a woman is responsible for her husband's fortune).

Her father becomes angry at her statement and forces her to marry a beggar (disabled man) with whom she must live in humble circumstances (she is driven forth).

Through his wife's wit (skill), the beggar becomes rich, becomes a king, or is cured of his disease.

The father visits the new king (rich man), recognizes his daughter, and is forced to admit that she is responsible for her own fortune.

In both Bedouin versions, it is the king's wife, and not one of his daughters, who declares that the husband's fortune depends on his wife. The king marries her to a poor man, and the queen manages to make him rich. At the end of the story, the king brings his wife back to the palace. In Zehiyya's version, the woman does not actually marry the poor man but only stays at home with his mother. In exchange for her returning to the palace, she demands that her husband, the king, marry her daughter to the poor man who has become rich: "She said to him, 'Where shall I go home? I will not go home unless you give my daughter, your daughter, oh, emīr, to Ṣāleḥ [as wife]. I haven't toiled with this house and haven't met this [man] so that I will [not] build for someone else, unless I bring my daughter and put her in this house and this man will take her [in marriage].'"

In Ṣabḥa ʿAbūd's story, the king divorces his wife after she makes her announcement, but he admits her innocence at the end; however, the narrative does not reveal whether she returns to the palace.

An Arabic version of the story was written down at the beginning of the twentieth century in Bīr Zēt, near Rāmallah.[10] The heroine in this version is the daughter of the sultan. Here, too, the husband finds himself in the well of a demon (*raṣad*—a demonic figure who hoards hidden treasures) and receives pomegranates full of pearls. As in Ṣabḥa ʿAbūd's story, in which the emīr identifies his wife by the taste of the food she cooks, so too does the sultan recognize the food that is served to him as food cooked by his daughter. According to the custom in Arab and Bedouin society, when a meal is served, the woman does not take part in it. At most, she comes to greet the guests at the end of the meal.

In Zehiyya's story, this issue is highlighted: "But the woman did not reveal herself to him at all, at all. At the dinner he found the food on the tables, found drinks, found everything perfect. He had dinner. When they had had dinner, after the entertainment, the king had a habit that the woman would bring food again. After the entertainment, the woman brought the food again and revealed herself to him." And so it is in Ṣabḥa ʿAbūd's story: "She went round, blessing them after the meal."

The *ġūl*'s question, which of his wives should he love, the white one or the black, and the hero's answer, "Love your beloved even if she were a black slave," appear in other Bedouin stories. The answer emphasizes the fact that virtues are not examined according to the color of a person's skin, and love is a matter of personal taste. In the Jewish version, recorded by Flora Cohen, who was born in Egypt (IFA 2875), the *ġūl* is replaced by an African Negro, and to his question of which girl is more beautiful, the white or the black, the hero answers, "Your beloved is whom you love, even if she is a black slave."

The story has several Jewish versions, which were written down in the IFA archive from immigrants from Arab countries.[11]

Notes

1. The phrase *min hōn la-hōn* is an opening expression (cf. chap. 1, note 2). It need not be understood literally, as a place description. It also means "the sway of time," denoting the vagueness of the time and place of the narrated story. Note the sedentary form *hōn* instead of the Galilee Bedouin form *hēn* ~ *hīn*. This is an example of the Bedouins' mixed dialects, due to contacts with the surrounding sedentary population.

2. There is a famous old well in the Galilee village Šaʿab, which is located to the southeast of Acre.

3. *lōla huwwe salāmak daḷḷ ʾb-kalāmak, l-axaḷḷi wuḥuūš al-barr tasmaʿ tagrīṭ ʿaḏāmak!*: "If your greeting had not remained in your speech, I would have let the wild animals hear the chewing/ gnawing of your bones." This narrative formula occurs in other stories with few variations. The sentence is conditional, with the particle *lōla*, "if not," in the opening part and *la-* at the final part of the sentence. (Cf. chap. 4, note 3).

4. *ʾas-sōda willa l-bēḏa*: "the black one [f.sg.] or the white one [f.sg.]." Color names in Arabic include names of Semitic origin, as well as other expressions. The meanings of color terms vary—some of them indicate colors as in European languages while others are entirely different. An example is the term *ʾabyaḏ*, "white [f.sg.]," which normally means white and also refers to human skin color (as a metaphor).

5. The expression *ʿafā ʾaḷḷahu ʿannak*, "may Allah forgive you," is used as a wish or blessing. As usual in such expressions, Allah is mentioned and alluded to for aid and support. Many blessings, greetings, and curses exist in any Arabic dialect. Cf. Piamenta, *Muslim Conception of God*; Rosenbaum, "Curses, Insults and Taboo Words."

6. A typical Bedouin verb form has the pattern *xáḏa* (cf. sedentary *ʾáxaḏ*/*ʾáxad* in Israel), "take." Cf. the verb "eat": *kála* vs. sedentary *ʾakal*. The process could have been *ʾakál* > *kál* > *kála*, if it were assimilated to the pattern of verbs such as *liga*, "to meet." This development could be related to the fact that the glottal stop is generally weak and tends to disappear in Arabic dialects. However, forms such as *xáḏa* tend to disappear from Galilee Bedouin dialects because of the leveling effects of sedentary dialects or MSA.

7. The verb *qām*/*gām* in MSA means "get up" and is used as an intransitive verb. In this text it is also a transitive verb, probably by omission of the first syllable (prefix) *ʾa* of the fourth verb measure. This phenomenon exists in other verbs, too.

8. The word *gabel*, "before," has various grammatical functions: it is used mainly as a time particle, functioning as a preposition and a noun. Its meanings are mainly "before (temporal point)," "past times" (noun), and the locative "in front of." Phonetically, its pronunciation in these Bedouin dialects includes forms such as *gabl* + suffix, *gabel, gabul*, and *gabol*, as well as a rare *qabl* (with MSA or rural *q* instead of *g*) and *ʾabel*, *ʾabel-mā* (with the urban glottal stop). When *-mā* or *-lā* is attached to it, it serves as a syntactic (subordinating) conjunction. These forms occur several times in this collection.

9. This story is presented very dryly and succinctly, with conciseness of descriptions (cf. chap. 1, note 3). The protagonists express no emotions by word or behavior, although this is a love story (of the emīr and his wife) full of difficulties and dangers for the protagonists to overcome.

10. Schmidt and Kahle, *Volkserzählungen aus Palästina*, 1:134–39, Story 40.

11. Egypt: 2875; Morocco: 8229, 11908, 12883, 13889, 15314; Kurdish Kurdistan: 6188.

7. Ǧuḥā and the Queen

NARRATOR: Ṣabḥa ʿAbūd

TRIBE: *ʿArab el-Ḫuǧērāt*
IFA 13259 ca. 1980

Text

Ǧuḥā was sitting at the king's [court]. One day he heard the king say to his wife, "Shall we go to the seacoast? Will we go for air [to take a walk]?"

He was with them. He, Ǧuḥā, heard. He went alone [to the place].

She said to him, "Where shall we go for air?"

He said to her, "To the sea of Tiberias."

They were on the beach with eucalyptus trees. Ǧuḥā went, climbed the tree. When he got on it, he stayed there to wait. Here sits the emīr's wife, she and her husband, playing *mingaleh*.

As they played, she said to him, "I want to bet: if I win, you will have to go before me naked in the sea, if you win, I will have to go naked before you!"

He said to her, "Good [OK]."

She won him. When she won him, he started walking in front of her and he was naked.

They sat down again. They played again and here he won. When he won, she began to come and go naked in front of him. When she goes to him, she brings her hair forward, and when she goes back, she puts her hair on her back.

When the emīr and his wife finished, Ǧuḥā came down from the tree, came to them and said, "Did you see my donkey?" Ǧuḥā said to them, "Did not you see my donkey?"

She looked at him and said, "Since when have you been here on the tree?"

He said to her, "From the beginning of the story I have been on the tree."

She said to him, "Oh Allah!"

They went to their house. She said to her husband, "I do not want Ǧuḥā to stay in our house anymore!"

He said to her, "Good [OK]." Her husband [said], "Send Ǧuḥā away."

She said to him, "You—tomorrow morning, take your articles and go away!"

He said to her, "OK."

He [Ǧuḥā] has millstones and he has a donkey. All day—and she looks down at him from the window—he takes the millstones and he does not put them, one from here and one from here [meaning he puts them both in one sack on one side of the donkey, and the donkey falls].

She laughed at him [and finally] said to him: "Ǧuḥā, put one from here and one from here!"

He said to her, "For heaven's sake [*daxīl rabbak*; literally: I am asking for the help of your Lord (Allah)]—you, why did you not talk [all this time]?"

She started to laugh [and Ǧuḥā remained at their home].

One day her husband fell ill.

When he fell ill, he said to him, "Ǧuḥā, amuse me."

Ǧuḥā began to amuse him. All night, and he amuses him. He amused him, and a nap fell on the emīr.

He said to him [to the emīr], "For heaven's sake [*daxīl rabbak*], when do you intend to die?"

The king laughed. From his laugh, the abscess in his throat exploded and he was healed.

He said, "People, by Allah, this Ǧuḥā—no one is like him: he caused me to laugh, and my pain was exploded [and I was healed]. And I—I did not leave a doctor in the world who did not try to heal me, and nothing helped."

Ǧuḥā stayed with him. He did not leave, and he would not go away. We're done.

Commentary

Ṣabḥa ʿAbūd narrated this folktale (and the others in this volume) without any details about its origin. She only said that she had heard stories from a traveling *ḥakawāti* ("storyteller"), and this may have been one of those stories. The commentary below refers to Nawi's *Arab Stories* (1972), and is probably based on Iraqi traditions, *Arabian Nights* (Burton, 1885–88), and similar sources.

This story is unusual among Ṣabḥa ʿAbūd's stories. This is an erotic story, the type that is commonly told in a male society.

Ǧuḥā (جُحا) is a well-known cultural hero throughout the Mediterranean region, in Israel and neighboring countries, Syria, Lebanon, Jordan, and Iraq. In North Africa, he is known as Shcha, and in Italy, Giufà. He is also well known in Jewish-Sephardic folklore. In Turkey and in Muslim countries throughout Asia, the same figure is replaced by Nasiruddin Hodja, and it is quite possible that this is the same figure. In Ṣabḥa ʿAbūd's story, Ǧuḥā plays the role of the emīr's companion. This role suggests a possible connection between our story and stories told in Iraq about Abū Nuwās, the court poet of Caliph Harun al-Rashid.

Abu Nuwās (756–814) was one of the greatest classical Arab poets. He was born in Persia to an Arab father and Persian mother. At a certain stage in his life, Abu Nuwās was forced into exile in Egypt after he was disowned by Harun al-Rashid because of a poem he wrote, in which he praised a family from the Persian elite that had opposed the caliph's rule and been slaughtered by him. After the death of Haroun al-Rashid in 809, Abu Nuwās returned to Baghdad and served as a poet in the court of Muḥammad al-Amin, Harun al-Rashid's son. It seems that Ṣabḥa ʿAbūd's story is based on this episode.

Abu Nuwās has become a popular hero in the Arab culture and is mentioned several times in the *Arabian Nights*. Many anecdotes portray him as a womanizer and a renegade. Abu Nuwās is also the name of a cult hero and a villain in Swahili culture in Africa as well as in Indonesia. In Ṣabḥa ʿAbūd's story, several elements link the image of Ǧuḥā to the image of Abu Nuwās: (1) the role he plays in the king's house, as both joker and healer, and (2) his exile from the royal court.

In his book *Arab Stories*, Eliahu Nawi includes the story "The Other Side of the Coin."[1] Nawy's story clarifies the relationship between the first part of Ṣabḥa ʿAbūd's story, in which Ǧuḥā appears as a voyeur in an intimate meeting between the royal couple, and the final part, in which he amuses the queen as he tries to load his two millstones on the same side of the donkey.

According to Nawi's story, the king seeks Abu Nuwās's advice regarding his intimate relationship with his wife, the queen, who repeatedly refuses his requests for intercourse, with the excuse that she has her period. Abu Nuwās asks the king, "And what about the other side?" The king understands the hint and goes to the queen uncharacteristically. After the queen finds out that Abu Nuwās is the one who advised the king to act as he did, she forces the king to exile him. Abu Nuwās masquerades as a poor farmer, stands under the queen's window, and, as in our story, tries to load the two millstones in a sack on one side of the donkey, causing them to fall again and again. Zubaydah, the queen, looks at his efforts until her patience snaps and she calls to him, "What a fool you are, put one on the other side." "Allah forbid, madam," Abu Nuwās responds. "I once advised the king to do so—and I was sentenced to exile!"

In the *Arabian Nights*, there is another story related to Ṣabḥa ʿAbūd's story—"The Caliph Harun al-Rashid and Queen Zubaydah in the Bath."[2] In this story, the queen stands naked in a pool hidden in the garden and sprinkles herself with water from a jar. Harun al-Rashid sneaks into the garden and looks at the naked queen. When she notices him, she hastens to cover her chest with both hands. The elated caliph goes away. A poem verse comes to his mind, but he cannot finish the rhyme. He tells his friend, Abu Nuwās, what happened and asks him to complete the poem. Abu Nuwās fulfills his wish and writes a continuation of the poem, in which he describes in detail the queen's beauty. In this story, the voyeur is the king himself, sharing the experience with his court poet. The description of the queen covering her chest with her hands but failing to completely hide her full breasts corresponds to Ṣabḥa ʿAbūd's story, where the queen tries to hide her nakedness with her hair.

In a comment, Richard Burton, the famous translator of the *Arabian Nights*, describes how the king and the queen play a game whose nature has not been clarified and in which the victor imposes a certain condition on the loser. At one point, the queen succeeds in defeating the king, and she forces him to lie with the ugliest, most foolish, and most disgusting maid in the palace kitchen, as revenge for the death of her son caused by the caliph.[3]

In his book *From the Arabic Folklore*, Abraham Ben-Shahar provides an Arabic version of the story he heard in Israel.[4] Here, too, the hero is Abu Nuwās. He looks for his donkey and climbs a tree near the king's palace to search from above. At the same time, Harun al-Rashid sits in the garden with his young wife. They play the game of *shatranǧ* (chess) and stipulate between them that the winner will see the nakedness of the loser. The queen loses, and she exposes her body to her husband's eyes and asks him, "Well, what did you see?" Harun al-Rashid replies, "I saw the world and what is in it" (*shuft a(l)-dunia u-mā fiha*). At that moment, Abu Nuwās calls from the top of the tree: "Perhaps you saw my donkey, too?"

Our narrator transfers the plot to the Sea of Galilee. This is a common phenomenon with storytellers, who describe the events as having occurred in their familiar environment. The king and the queen are playing the mingaleh game. Mingaleh (or mingal, mankal, mankala, مَنْقَل ,مِنْجَل) مَنْقَلَة is a shepherd's game that has been common among Bedouin peasants for centuries.[5] The game is mentioned in *Arabian Nights*: "Then I set before him somewhat of food and we ate; and I got ready perfumes for fumigating the hall, wherewith he was pleased. Moreover, I made him a Mankalah-cloth; and we played and ate sweetmeats and we played again and took our pleasure till nightfall."[6]

At the end of the story, Ǧuḥā is described as having succeeded in healing the king by joking with him and causing an abscess in the king's throat to explode (motif N640, "Accidental healing"; motif N641.0.1§, "Patient laughs so hard at comic actions (scenes) about him, thus abscess breaks (object in throat dislodged) and he is healed." This part of the tale appears as an independent story in different cultural spaces. In the IFA archives, there is an Arabic story narrated by Ibrahim Samaan of Rāmi in the Galilee (IFA 6819). A simple worker pretends to be a doctor and uses an enema. Calif Harun al-Rashid has an abscess in his throat. The imaginary doctor offers to give him an enema. The caliph bursts into laughter; the abscess ruptures, and his throat heals. Dan Ben-Amos refers extensively to Jewish folktales with a similar motif.[7]

Since no one has documented the rules of the game used by the Bedouins in the north of Israel, I present here a detailed account of the game, as I heard it from a young Bedouin from the ʿArab el-Ḥuǧērāt tribe. The game board consists of two rows of holes, one for each player. Each row has four holes called houses. In many cases, the holes were hewn in the bedrock, and one can find these in many places in Israel, especially near ancient winepresses and wineries. At the Nimrod Fortress (*qal'at namrūd*), for example, one can see a game board carved into one of the rocks. The pieces are sixty-four stones divided at the beginning of the game evenly among all the holes—eight stones in each hole. In the course of the game, each player tries to remove as many stones as possible from the board, and the game ends when there are no more stones on the board. The winner is the one who has managed to remove more stones. The winner of one game gets to choose one of the opponent's houses to keep, and when the next match begins, the winner has five holes and the loser three (unless the first game ended in a draw). The game series ends as soon as one of the players manages to obtain all eight houses.

The player sitting on the south side—the side facing Mecca—opens the game. The opening player takes eight stones from one of the houses in his or her possession and, moving counterclockwise, divides them among the houses, with each house receiving one stone in turn. It is clear that when the stones are redistributed, the empty house might acquire a new stone. The opponent, similarly, takes a group of stones on his or her side and divides it among the houses, while also moving counterclockwise. A player who creates a pair or a house with four stones—that is, places a stone in a house with either one or three stones—has the right to remove stones. There are additional rules:

A player who forms a group of four stones or a pair and also similarly forms the contents of the house before dropping the last stone into a pair or a group of four removes the contents of the two houses from the board. If, in the same move, the second house from the end also forms a couple or four stones, the player removes them as well, and so on, provided the houses with two or four stones appear in sequence without being interrupted by a house with an odd number of stones.

To complicate play, the anonymous inventor of the game added a limiting rule: a player who has not yet removed stones from the board is not allowed to divide a group containing one or three stones among the houses, even if such a group is found in the player's own house.

If during the course of the game all the houses of a certain player are empty (or the player's houses contain only groups of one or three stones and the player has not yet removed stones), the turn passes to the second player. This player continues to play until a new situation is created in which the second player can play as well.

The winner gains one of the opponent's houses. In the next game, the new owner of the house may play with stones in the same house, while the opponent may not.

Notes

1. Nawi, *Arab Stories*, 54–55.
2. Burton, *Arabian Nights*, vol. 5, Nights 385–86.
3. Burton, 10:127–28.
4. Ben-Shahar, *From the Arabic Folklore*, 89–90.
5. Teper, "Game Boards in the Rock," 21–23.
6. Burton, *Arabian Nights*, vol 1, night 15.
7. Ben-Amos, *Folktales of the Jews*, 1:536–41.

8. The Doe

NARRATOR: Šḥāde Rxayyim

TRIBE: *'Arab el-Sa'adiyya*

IFA 17415 September 2, 1982

1 kān bī ’amīr ʿarab. w-’amīr hā-l-ʿarab maʿā niswān ṯintēn . . . ʿendo niswān ṯintēn. bī waḥde xaḷḷafat ʿyāl ^{i}ṯnēn, u-bī waḥda xaḷḷafat walad wāḥad. walad wāḥad sammatu š-šāṭer mḥimmad.	1 There was a Bedouin emīr. And this Bedouin emīr had two wives. He had two wives. There is one who had two children, and one who had one child. One child, she named him Clever Mḥimmad.
6 kibrum al-uwlād, ṣārum ^{i}kbār. yiği abūhum, štarā-lhum, kull wāḥad, faras u-barūde.[1] taʿrif (al-ba-) waḥade sākna hināk. wa-hadīk sākna hināk. kull waḥda sākna la-ḥālha. ṭilʿum yōm ʿa-ṣ-ṣēd wa-ʿa-l-ganaṣ.[2] widdhom yiṣayyadom ḥağal, ’arāneb, ġuzlān, ’aḷḷa yaʿalam.	6 The children grew up, became big. Their father came, bought for them, each one, a mare and a rifle, you know, one wife [was] living there, and one was living there [elsewhere], each one was living alone [on her own]. They went one day to the hunting and trap hunting. They wanted to hunt partridges, rabbits, deer, Allah knows [what].
13 aṯ-ṯalāṯa (a)ṭlaʿam. aš-šāṭer ^{i}mḥimmad šāf ġazāla. lamma šāf ġazāla ṭradha. ḏaḷḷ warāha. hadlākum[3] ḏ̣ayyaʿū, mā ʿerfū wēn rāḥ. sāʿa ṣayyadum ḥağal, w-’iši, u-rikbum ʿa-l-xēl u-ḏ̣aḷḷum mʿawwdīn.	13 The three [of them] went out. Clever Mḥimmad saw a gazelle. When he saw a gazelle, he chased it. He kept [following] after it. Those [two brothers] lost him, did not know where he had gone. When they hunted partridge, and something like that, they rode the horses and went on, returning.
18 “wēn ’axūkum?” gāḷu-lhum, “waḷḷa šufnā ṭarad ġazāla u-mā nʿaref wēn rāḥ, ḏ̣ayyaʿnā.” hāḏ̣a ṣārat ’ummo ġēr al-^{i}bka wa-n-nōḥ.	18 “Where is your brother?” They said to them, “By Allah, we saw he was chasing a gazelle and we do not know where he went, we lost him.” Now, his mother had only weeping and mourning.

22 huwwa ḏ̣aḷḷ warāha, min aǧ-ǧibal hāḏ̣ l-aǧ-ǧibal hāḏ̣, u-hi tinhazim, al-ġazāla, muš ʿārf yṭuxx, ta-ġābat ʿalē š-šams. ġābat ʿalē š-šams, tiʿeref, ḥaṭṭ barūdto hēn ʿa-ḏrāʿo, u-rubaṭ faraso u-nām. ba-l-lēl ʿād yešūfa? mā ʿād yešūfa. ḏ̣aḷḷ nāyem ta-ṭelʿat aš-šam^{e}s.	22 He remained, after it [following the gazelle], from this mountain to that mountain, and it was running away, the gazelle, he could not shoot [it], until the sun set on him. The sun set on him—you know, he put his rifle here on his arm and tied his mare and slept. In the night can he see it? He cannot see it. He remained asleep until the sun rose.
29 lamma ṭelʿat aš-šams u-gām, daḥḥag alla l-ġazāle wāgfe ʿala gbāḷo hināk. ʾe—šu hā-š-šaġle hāḏi? madd ʿalēha ta-yeṭuxxa—inhezmat. ḏ̣aḷḷ warāha, (šāyef), ḏ̣aḷḷ warāha, yōmēn u-hī teʿāmlo l-muʿāmala hāḏi, min ǧibal la-ǧibal.	29 When the sun rose and he got up, he saw—lo, the gazelle standing in front of him there. E! What is this thing? He stretched to shoot it—it fled. He remained after it, (you see), he remained [chasing] after it, two days and it was treating him this treatment, from mountain to mountain.
35 la-ṯāleṯ yōm hilek, lā mayye, lā šurob, šu ha-š-šaġle hāḏi? walla, ġābat ʿalē š-šams, nām, gaʿad aṣ-ṣubaḥ, alla hī wāgfa hināk. gām madd ta-yeṭuxxa, mā ḏ̣aḷḷ minha maḏ̣būṭ, ^{i}nfadat. bī bēt šaʿar ba-l-baṭīn u-gāmat hā-l-ġazāla tḏ̣aḷḷ hanāk waḷḷa trū(ḥ)-ʿala ha-l-bēt.	35 On the third day he was dying—no water, no drink—what is this thing? By Allah, the sun set on him, he slept. He got up in the morning, lo—it was standing there. He got up, stretched to shoot it—nothing of it remained clear—it ran away. There was a tent in the valley and this gazelle went and remained there, she went into the tent.
42 ʾeh! lamma šāf hāḏa taʿaǧǧab, gāl-lak "šū ha-š-šagla hāḏi? ġazāla tfūt b-al-bēt?" gām ričeb al-faras u-ḥaṭṭ ha-l-barūda ǧiddāmo u-ḏ̣aḷḷ lāfi hū-l-bēt.	42 E! When he saw this, he was surprised. He said to you [to himself], "What is this thing? A gazelle entering a tent?" He rode his mare and put his rifle in front of him and continued turning to[ward] this tent.
46 hī, šū lābse? lābsa ǧild ġazāl u-miṯl al-ġazāl, miṯel mā yešūf al-ġōrill al-yōm w-iši. lamman ǧat ʿa-l-bēt ^{i}b-sāʿ šliḥatu, waddaratu u-libsat ha-l-(a)wāʿi . . . bdawiyye. ṣārat ^{e}bdawiyye.	46 She, what was she wearing? She was wearing the skin of a gazelle, and [was] like a gazelle, as you see a gorilla today and such. When she came to the tent, quickly she took it off, hid it and put on these clothes . . . Bedouin. She became a Bedouin [female].
51 ǧa ʿala ha-l-bēt "ʾahalan wa-sahalan". hū walad ^{e}ḥlewi čān. "ʾahlan wa-sahalan, tfaḏ̣ḏ̣al". gāḷ-ḷa, "yā-xti." gāḷat-ḷo, "xēr." gāḷ, "šuft ġazāla ǧat ʿala ha-l-bēt, mā šuft li iyyāha wēn rāḥat?" gāḷat-lo, "lā, walla, yā xūya, mā šuftha. hawwid, tfaḏ̣ḏ̣al."	51 He came to the tent. "Welcome, welcome." He was a handsome boy. "Welcome, welcome, please [enter]." He said to her, "Oh sister." She said to him, "What is the matter [is it good]?" He said, "I saw a gazelle coming to the tent; haven't you seen it, where it has gone?" She said to him, "No, by Allah, oh my brother, I haven't seen it. Please get off [the mare], please [come in]."

57 šnū az-zlima mayyet min ağ-ğūʿ^{a}, widdo yhawwid, widdo yišrab mayya. ḥawwal az-zlima, rabaṭat hā-l-faras. gāḷat, "widdak tākol, ğaʿān?" gāḷ-ḷa, "walla, yā-xti, ğaʿān, ṯāni yōm hināki ma li šarb." ğā(ʼa)bat lo ʼačel, kala u-širb u-fi-(a)mān eḷḷā. u-rāḥte, u-mā rayyaḥato šuft al-ġazāle. gāḷat-lo, "mā šuftha wala šēle šēle."	57 What, the man was dying of hunger, he wants to get off, to drink water. The man got off [the mare], she tied the mare and said, "Do you want to eat, are you hungry?" He said to her, "By Allah, my sister, hungry. The second day there [that] I haven't had a drink." She brought him food, he ate and drank and was happy [satisfied due to Allah's protection]. And bothered him the sight of the gazelle. She said to him, "I did not see it at all, not at all."
66 walla, šwayye, šwayye, ^{i}lla xwānha—ilha sabʿ exwān. hemma kāynīn b-aṣ-ṣēd u-marōḥīn,[4] šāfum al-faras ʿand al-bēt, bēt la-hālo, mā fī ʿindo ḥada šēle šēle.	66 By Allah, slowly, slowly, lo her brothers, she had seven brothers. They had been in the hunting and [as] they were going home, they saw the mare at the tent, a house on its own, nobody near it at all.
70 qālum," šu as-sīre? šū as-sīre? ʿandīna xayyāl." ğamma ʿa-l-bēt, gāḷū-lha, "yā binet," gāḷat-ilhum, "yā xēr." gāḷū-lha, "mīn hā-z-zlima alli hēn, ʼins walla ğinn?"	70 They said, "What is the matter? What is the matter? We have [at our place] a horseman." They came to the tent, and said to her, "O girl." She said to them, "Is there anything wrong?" They said to her, "Who is the man who is here—a human or a demon?"
75 gāḷat-ilhum, "mā-aguḷ-ḷukum alla mā tāxḏūn al-ʼīmān, mā tʿaṭūn al-ʼīmān ʿalē." gāḷū-la, "yā-xti, ʿalē l-ʼīmān, mā-ḥada yisaʼalū šēle šēle."	75 She said to them, "I'll tell you only if you give the security on him, if you give him the security." They said to her, "O my sister, he's got the security. No one will ask him anything at all, nothing at all."
79 lēš, hī waddaratu gabel la yiğum ixwānha, lamma šāfat ixwānha ğāyīn. xāfat yuḥkum maʿā u-yiḏarbū w-iši^{y} miš ^{i}mnīḥ. gāḷ-ḷa, "xalaṣ, hātī."	79 Why, she had hidden him before her brothers had come, when she saw that they were coming. She was afraid that they may talk with him and beat him or something not good. He [one brother] said to her, "That is it, bring him."
83 lamma ğābū, daḥḥagu ʿala l-walad, subḥān all^{a}-xlag. "ʼahalan wa-sahalan, tfaḏḏaḷ, šnū sīrtak?" gāḷ-ḷēhem, "walla, yā ʿammi, ṣār maʿāy kaḏa kaḏa. ʼani mā bī la-ʼummi ġēr ʼani. u-ṭilaʿet ʼani wa-xwāni ʿa-ṣ-ṣēd w-al-ganaṣ, u-šufet ha-l-ġazāle.	83 When she brought him, they looked at the boy, praise he who created [him]. "Welcome, welcome, please [partake the refreshments], what is your story?" He said, "By Allah, o my uncle, this and this happened to me. I—my mother has no one except me. And I went, I with my half brothers hunting and capturing [animals], and I saw this gazelle.
90 kull mā: widd(i)-aṭuxxa – tinhazem, ^{a}trūḥ hināk u-ḏaḷḷa, ʿa-l yōmēn, ta-šuft el-ġazāle ğat ʿala ha-l-bēt u-mā aʿrif wēn rāḥat."	90 "Whenever I want to shoot it, it flees, it goes there and stays, for two days, until I saw the gazelle come to this tent and I do not know where she has gone."

94 gāḷu-ḷo, “hī hāḏ al-ġazāle bnafsa.” (hāḏ al-ġazāle ʿal-’uxthom. hī, isemha ġazāle.) “fa-mā dām hīk ṣār maʿāk, iḥna widdna naʿṭīku, naʿagud-lak ^{a}ʿgādak u-nğawwzak. we-’inta ’axu ilne.”	94 They said to him, “She is this gazelle, herself.” (This gazelle, about their sister. She, her name was Gazelle.) “And as long as this happened to you, we wish to give you, tie with you the marriage ties and will marry you, and you are a brother to us.”
99 ğamm al-ğimāʿa ğawwazū ʿa-l-binet u-ʿamlu lo hā-l-ʿeres, u-fi-’amān aḷḷa.	99 The group came and married the girl [off] to him and made a wedding for him and everything was all right [they were living in Allah’s security].
101 ġāb ʿala-mmo, mudda ṣār ġāyeb. ğa siḥab ḥālo, gāḷ-ḷahum, ağ-ğimāʿa, gāḷ, “walla, widd(i)-arawwe(ḥ) ʿala hali. widd-arūḥ, widd-ašūf ’ummi, ’ašūf ’abūya, ’ašūf . . .”	101 The boy was lost [disappeared] for his mother, for a [long] while he was missing. He got up and came and said to them, the group, he said, “By Allah I want to go back home to my family. I want to see my mother, to see my father, to see . . .”
106 gāḷu-ḷo, “’ā, ’aḷḷa maʿāk.” ričeb wu-rakkabha warā ʿala hā-l-faras, u-yalla mrawwaḥ hū wiyyāha. yimčin yōmēn ṯalāṯa ta-waṣlum ahalum, miṯel hā-s-sāʿa, d-dinya tāle-n-nahār.	106 They said to him, “Yes, Allah be with you” [he was allowed to leave]. He rode and put her behind him on the mare and off they went home, he with her. He may have been on the way two or three days until they reached his family, at about this time of the day, in the afternoon.
111 ma-šāfum ahalum, šāfum šāṭer ^{e}mḥimmad mrawwaḥ u-hā-l-ʿarūs maʿā, u-hā-l-hay’a. šū lāgathu hā-l-ʿarab! qālum al-ʿarab “rāḥ, māt hāḏ̣.”	111 They did see, their family, they saw Clever Mḥimmad coming back home and this bride with him, and this delegation, what—how these Bedouins met him, they [the Bedouins] had said [to themselves], “He is gone, he died.”
115 lāgū bi-hā-z-zaġarīṭ u-hā-l-ġanāni u-ha-l-faraḥ alli widdak iyyā. u-hāy-hī xurrāfti rāḥat ʿalēk.	115 They met him with the joy cries [ululations] and these songs and all the joy which you [may] want. And this is my story, [which] has passed [gone] to you.

Commentary

“The Doe” was told by Šḥāde Rxayyim, a member of the ʿArab el-Saʿadiyya tribe, who lives in the Bedouin settlement of Basmat Ṭabʿūn, near Kiryat Tiv’on.

It is a poetic love story, to which I found no other Arab equivalent in the region near Israel. A prince named Clever Mḥammad sets out with his stepbrothers to hunt. He pursues a doe, and his brothers lose sight of him. After a three-day-long chase, the hero sees the deer enter a Bedouin tent. He follows it into the tent and discovers that the deer has disappeared, and in its place, a beautiful maiden welcomes him. She hosts him, feeds him, and gives him water. When the girl’s brothers return, the girl hides the hero, but after her brothers promise that they do not intend to harm him, she introduces him to them. The brothers inform the hero that their sister is the one he was pursuing and that they will marry her to him. Afterward, the married couple returns to the hero's house.

Stith Thompson, in his book *The Folktale*, discusses the narrative type AT 401, "The Princess Transformed into Deer," which to a certain extent resembles the plot of the Bedouin story.[5] A prince and his companions go hunting. In pursuit of a deer, they arrive at an abandoned castle. The hero manages to bring the enchanted deer back to its human form after spending three frightening days in the castle and grappling with terrible difficulties. Later, after marrying the girl, the prince loses her, goes on a quest for her, and eventually finds her. Thompson argues that the story has a limited circulation, and it appears in Europe and the Mediterranean but is not known south of Turkey. Uther includes this narrative type in the subtypes of ATU 400, "The Man on a Quest for His Lost Wife."[6] El-Shamy mentions two parallels from Iraq.[7] The main motif of the story is motif N773, "Adventure from following animal to cave (lower world)."

The image of a woman as a deer is ancient and appears in different cultural spaces. In the Song of Songs, the lover faces his beloved and tells her: "Thy two breasts are like two young roes that are twins" (Song of Songs 7:3). In the book of Proverbs, the author congratulates his readers: "Let thy fountain be blessed: and rejoice with the wife of thy youth. Let her be as the loving hind and pleasant roe; let her breasts satisfy thee at all times; and be thou ravished always with her love" (Proverbs 5:18–19). In the Middle Ages, Jewish poets like Rabbi Yehuda Halevi often used the image of deer in their poems.

But, to the best of my knowledge, the story of the transformation of a girl to a deer first appears in a monumental epic of about nine thousand verses composed by the greatest Jewish poet of Persia in the fourteenth century, Mevlana Shahin Shirazi (Our Lord Shahin of Shiraz), the epic *Ardashir Nameh*, written in 1332 CE. The following is a summary of the passage related to the image of a deer.

> One day Ardashir goes hunting with his friends. His two sons, Shiro, the eldest son whom Vashti bore, and Cyrus, the son of Queen Esther, accompany him on his way.
>
> Cyrus hunts thirty deer. His stepbrother, Shiro, chases a lovely deer that draws him into the heart of the forest. After losing his horse and his way, he decides to stay in the forest. At night, two lions attack him, but he manages to kill them. In the morning, he continues looking for a way through the forest. Ten days pass. On the tenth day, he is surrounded by a pack of wolves. Shiro fights for his life. A fire-breathing dragon comes to his aid, attacks the wolves, and kills them.
>
> Finally, he manages to find his lost horse. He continues on his way and encounters the deer he was pursuing. He chases her and comes to a wonderful garden with a pure-water pool adorned with wonderful flowers. The pursued deer plunges into the waters of the pond and disappears, and Shiro, weary from his journey, lies by the pool and falls asleep.
>
> When he awakes, he realizes that the garden and the pool have disappeared, and he stands in the middle of a magnificent landscape, which is as beautiful as the Garden of Eden. Soon seven slaves and ten handmaids appear before him and invite him by their mistress's command to come with them. Riding behind them, Shiro reaches a magnificent palace built of pure silver. A knight welcomes him and leads him into the palace. The palace courtyard has a pool surrounded by gold hoops, and silver fish swim in its waters.

When he enters the palace, a handsome princess greets him warmly. She informs him that on seeing his face during the hunt she fell in love with him, and therefore, she disguised herself as a deer and drew him to her palace, and as he approached, she challenged him and set wild animals on him.

The princess is Mahazad, daughter of Barkh, the king of China. Her father passed away two years previously and left her his kingdom. The kings of India and Babylon have courted her, but she gives her love to Shiro.

Shiro falls in love with the beautiful princess. He embraces her, and she returns his favor. The next day both of them go to the wonderful garden and sip together from the pool's water. Among the rosebushes that surround the garden, the prince sees the tombstone of Havrang the Wise, who founded the palace. On the dome of his tombstone stands a bird, constantly waving its wings. Mahazad utters a magic word, and the flapping stops. Through a hidden gate, two lions emerge and they follow them into a cave. In the cave, they find an inscription, which Havrang the Wise ordered to be engraved on his tombstone: "I am Havrang, who was the first and foremost of all the kings of Perry. Nothing remains forever. Pay attention to the world changes and do not trust someone who is not worthy of it." Havrang's words touch Shiro's heart profoundly. As he leaves the cave with his beloved, tears stream down his face. The mouth of the enchanted cave closes, and a season of love and joy begins for Shiro and Mahazad.

A year later, Mahazad gives birth to a son, Ardashir's grandson, whom they name Mahyar. Two nursemaids take care of him for two years. After three years, Shiro longs for his father. Mahazad performs magic, and in one night, with a large entourage, they pass a nine-months' journey up to the foot of Mount Alvond, not far from the location of Ardashir and his men.

It is likely that Shahin drew the story from earlier Persian sources; however, this is not the place to elaborate on the subject.

Another story resembling the plot of the Bedouin story is found in the Celtic culture space of Ireland in the Fenian Cycle. The Fianna were a group of mythical hunter-fighters from the Celtic period in Ireland, preceding the adoption of Christianity on the island (third century CE). They were led by Fionn Mac Cumhaill.

For centuries, stories about this group circulated among the people. In the eighth, ninth, and tenth centuries, there are many references in Irish literature to Fionn and his men in the context of fighting, hunting, and courting women. Stories about Fionn are an important part of Irish folktales and Scottish ballads to this day. One of the Fianna stories, corresponding to Thompson's description of the narrative type AT 401, describes the birth of Oisín, Fionn's son. A brief summary follows. In the course of hunting, Fionn and his men see a beautiful fawn. They chase it. The fawn stops and kneels. Fionn's dogs catch it, but instead of attacking it, they lick its face. Fionn orders them not to hurt the fawn. The fawn enters Fionn's house and disappears. That evening, a beautiful-looking woman enters Fionn's room and informs him that her name is Sadhbh and that she is the fawn he met on his way. She explains to him that the druid Fear Doirche of the Tuatha Dé Danann cast a spell on her after she rejected his love, and for three years, she has been condemned to wander in the forests in the form of a fawn. However, the spell will end in one place, Fionn's castle. Fionn falls in love with Sadhbh and gives up hunting and fighting to settle down with her, and soon she is pregnant.

Later, after Sadhbh is pregnant, Fionn leaves his fortress to fight Nordic invaders. In his absence, Fear Doirche, having put on Fionn's face, appears. Sadhbh exits the fort to meet him. The druid casts a spell on her, turns her back into a deer, and carries her off with him. Fionn returns from his travels and learns the bitter news.

For seven years, he searches for his wife, but he cannot find her. Then he finds a little naked boy in the middle of the forest. Fionn identifies him as the son of Sadhbh, his beloved; adopts him as a son; and calls him Oisín, which means "little deer."

A possible connection between the ancient Irish epic and a contemporary Bedouin story seems rather far-fetched, but as another story, the story of the woman who emerged from the sea, which I will discuss later, shows, it is very possible that certain Celtic motifs also penetrated Islamic culture. It should be remembered that between the fourth and the first centuries BCE, Celtic tribes arrived in Spain, Italy, Macedonia, and Turkey. At that time, Celtic merchants came to Egypt and intervened in local politics. There must have been cultural contacts between Celtic culture and Hellenistic culture, mutually influencing each other. The passage of stories and narrative motifs from place to place throughout the Indo-European cultural space is a familiar folkloric phenomenon. It is also possible that both the Celtic story and the Persian story derive from the same ancient source. Among the stories of the *Arabian Nights*, there are many about the transformation of women into animals as a result of spells and the evil eye.

The Bedouin story is captivating precisely because of its simplicity. It does not contain magic or sorcery. The girl is the one who wears the skin of a doe and pulls the hero to her tent. For three days, during which the hero does not eat or drink, he follows her resolutely. The folktale is short on emotional descriptions, but the chase seems to reflect a picture of a young man in love: an unrestrained and uncontrollable desire for the unattainable beloved, to the point of forgetting his physical needs. The meeting with the girl is also very charged. The surprised hero does not connect the beautiful girl in front of him with the deer he has pursued. Twice he asks her what happened to the deer that entered the tent, once when he arrives and once after he has eaten and drunk, and twice she denies the existence of the deer. The repetition emphasizes how much the deer occupies the hero's thoughts. We hear nothing about the feelings aroused in him by the sight of the girl's beauty. Nevertheless, it seems that the passion of hunting is slowly converted into his desire for the girl who generously hosts him, while, it seems, she is also examining him and his behavior. The next sentence in the story may hint at what happened: "By Allah, slowly, slowly, lo her brothers, she had seven brothers." The words "slowly, slowly," which seem to be out of place, suggest that during the brothers' absence, a slow process of falling in love occurred between the two.

The entire story is replete with characteristics from Bedouin life: a polygamous family; relationship between stepbrothers, sons of a common father; the father's gift of a horse and a rifle to his sons as a symbol of their coming of age; animal hunting; hospitality. Finally, the problem of entering the foreign tent of a woman while the men are absent, which is taboo in Bedouin society, is expressed, inter alia, by the girl's fear of her brothers' actions when they meet the stranger and by their exclamation when they see him, "Who is the man who is here—a human or a demon?" (as men do not do this).

All these details give the story a local Bedouin character. Yet the story exemplifies a universal emotion: the awakening of love. The girl appears in the story as an active figure who does not conform to the Arab perception, which still exists in many places, according to which a girl's marriage is initiated by her brothers and father. Perhaps this is an expression of a common custom in the Bedouin tribes in Arabia, who did not force a girl to marry against her will. It is also possible that the story, although told by a man, reflects the secret desire of Bedouin women to free themselves from patriarchal control and determine their fate on their own.

Notes

1. *yiǧi abūhum, štarā-lhum, kull wāḥad, faras u-bārūde*: "Their father came, bought for them, each one, a mare and a rifle." *ṭil'um yōm 'a-ṣ-ṣēd wa-'a-l-ganaṣ,* ***widdhom*** *yiṣayyadom ḥaǧal*; "They went one day to the hunting and shooting. They want to hunt partridges." Note verb tense changes between the past and the present: *yiǧi . . . štarā-lhum*; *ṭil'um . . . widdhom*. Such jumps from past to present and back appear very frequently in spontaneous oral speech including the stories. To express the present (time), Arabic uses an imperfect verb form or a nominal (verbless) form to express aspects of tangible, real-life events. Past tense verbs usually refer to the time of the narrated occurrence. But "historical present," indicated by imperfect verbs (or nominal sentences), exists in other languages (e.g., English). Brinton, "Historical Discourse Analysis." For Bedouin Arabic dialects, Henkin examined this discourse element in Negev narratives. Henkin, *Negev Arabic*, 142–45. Her material is similar to that of the Galilee Bedouin dialects: in men's narratives, the present tense is unmarked, whereas the past tense is marked; indeed, a man narrated the story in this chapter. Henkin also links tense use with background and plotline structures. However, in this respect Galilee Bedouin narratives are not as strictly structured as the Negev ones. (Cf. Piamenta, *Use of Tenses*, for verb use and meanings in sedentary Jerusalem Arabic, including "tense jumps.")

2. *aṣ-ṣēd w-il-ganaṣ*, "hunting and trap hunting," are two near-synonyms for an activity that was a major skill of the nomadic Bedouin men who did not raise farm animals. Sowayan, *Arabian Oral Historical Narrative*; Meron, Shehadi, and Masarwi, *Seed of Pomegranate*, 300.

3. *haḏlākum* is a lengthened form of the demonstrative pronoun for the plural, with two suffixes, *-āk* and *-um*. Usually, the base form of the plural is *haḏōl*, "these." *-ak* denotes the distal demonstrative, and *-um*, the plural. Demonstrative pronoun forms vary in the Arabic dialects (cf. Fischer, *Die demonstrative Bildungen der neuarabischen Dialekte*), including those of this collection (cf. Bedouin Dialects in the North of Israel at the back of this book).

4. The sentence *hemma kāynīn b-aṣ-ṣēd u-marōḥīn, šāfum al-faras 'and al-bēt* ("They had been in the hunting and as they were going home, they saw the mare at the tent") contains two clauses: the circumstantial clause (with present participle forms in the beginning) and the following main clause (with the verb in the past tense). The participles here indicate a prolonged activity, which took place in the past (cf. note 1, above). The verb form *marōḥīn* reveals this process: *murawwiḥīn* (present participle, m.pl.) > *murawwḥīn* > *murawḥīn* > *mrawḥīn* > *mrōḥīn* >*marōḥīn*.

5. Thompson, *The Folktale*, 94.

6. Uther, *Types of International Folktales.*

7. El-Shamy, *Types of the Folktale in the Arab World.*

9. The Woman from the Sea

NARRATOR: Unknown

TRIBE: *'Arab el-'Arāmša*
IFA 17426 September 1982

Text

I would like to tell you a story I heard from a woman in Lebanon who is married [to someone] in our place. A true story.

The woman, during the days [the time] of her grandfather, heard a story that one [man] was near the beach of Beirut and he had a watermelon field, and that watermelon field was at its season [the watermelons were full-grown]. Every day the watermelon owner comes and sees the watermelons hollow and eaten from the inside. Who did it? Nobody [was in sight].

One day he said, "I'll go and sleep there, I want to know who's eating the watermelons."

One night, he took a rifle and went to sleep at the watermelon field, at twelve o'clock at night. Suddenly he felt steps, and twenty men came out of the watermelon patch.

He jumped up and ran after this one, and ran after that one, what did he want? To shoot, to shoot them. He grabbed one and held it. It seems that it is a *ġūl* or a man, or a wild animal. He held it until morning. There was a hustle and bustle, "Doomsday" (*wa-qāmat al-qiyāmah*).[1] He did not release it until morning. He took it and brought it to the house.

In the morning, he showed it to all the people. He looked at it—[it had the] image of a human woman, a perfect human woman. He showed her to all the people. He asks her [talks to her], and she does not answer, [she is] shouting. Her voice is like a puppy's voice.

She stayed with him for a year. After all the people, the villagers and the neighbors, saw her, and outsiders came to see the wonderful story. She stayed with him a year at home. He married her, he saw [treated] her as a human woman, a young woman like all young women. She has perfect beauty.

Nine months after he married her, Allah gave them a child, and in the second year, he gave them a child again, and in the third year, he gave them a child. All the time he keeps his wife at home, ties her up, and locks her, he goes out—locks her, he enters—locks her. All the time the key in his pocket, [he is] afraid that she will run away.

One day he asked her, "Do you want to go to the sea?"

She said to him, yes—she shook her head, meaning yes.

He said to her, "I want to slaughter the child."

He went to an old man. The old man—he told him that he had done the deed, told him what had happened.

He [the old man] said to him: "She has a swelling in her throat, let it go out, grab it and cut it and throw it away, and she will become an ordinary human woman, she will speak like we do."

One day she shouted.

He said, "I do not know how I will capture [catch] her."

He asked her, "Do you want to go to the sea?"

She said to him, "I want to go to the sea"—she shook her head.

He grabbed the boy and told her, "I want to slaughter him in order that you go to the sea! The three children—I want to slaughter them."

He came, he wanted to drag the knife over her throat. When he dragged the knife across her throat, all the swelling in her throat came out. He grabbed it, cut it with scissors. There was some blood. He took her to one who healed her with Arabic medicine and she was healed.

When she was healed, after two or three days, she said to him, "If you let me go, I want to go to the sea, I do not want to take my children and go to the sea. I want to show you the people who live in the sea. There are people in the water as there are here on earth, more or less. They all live in the water."

This family is called *El-Baḥri* [the marine] family and they live to this day in Beirut.

Commentary

The ʿArab el-ʿArāmša tribe lives close to Adamit, near the northern border of Israel, not far from the Mediterranean Sea. Some members of the tribe live in Lebanon on the other side of the border. One family of its clan originated in Kurdistan.[2]

Connection between a human being and a woman who dwells in the sea appears in two other Bedouin stories that I collected in the Galilee: In the story "Seven Brides for Seven Brothers," a mermaid helps the hero to leap with his horse over the sea in his search for his kidnapped wife. In the story "The Three Siblings and the Talking Birds," a mermaid by the name of Fāṭma helps the hero rescue his beloved from a *ġūl*, who kidnapped her. (See chap. 36, "The Golden Children.")

The plot of our story takes place on the shores of Beirut (the capital of Lebanon.) The narrator does not tell us whether the visit actually materializes. He only notes that the family continues to live in Beirut.

Stories that explain the origins of customs, traditions, names of places and people, and natural or social phenomena are called etiological stories. Thus, for example, the book of Genesis explains that the serpent's lack of limbs is punishment for the seduction of Adam and Eve (Genesis 3). In addition, see the appearance of the rainbow as a sign of God's covenant with Noah (Genesis 9) and the prohibition on eating the *gid hanashe* (sinew of the thigh vein) by the children of Israel as a reminder of Jacob's fight with the angel near the ford of the Jabbok River (Genesis 32).

The story of the woman who emerged from the sea is ostensibly an etiological legend that explains the origin of the name of the Al-Baḥri family, that is, "the family of the sea." The narrator presents the story as a true event that happened and notes that she heard it from a Lebanese woman who married a member of the tribe.

The motif of a woman who comes from the sea is in wide circulation, known in different cultures. Stories about mermaids are common in Celtic culture. Thompson points out several motifs related to mermaids: B81.2, "Mermaid marries man"; B81.2.1, "Mermaid has son by human father."[3] These motifs appear mainly in northern European countries located along the coast. Motif B81, "Mermaid. Woman with tail of fish. Lives in sea," exists in many cultural spaces, including Greek mythology stories. The best-known story is that of Odysseus's encounter with the sirens, described in *The Odyssey.*

In the Babylonian Talmud, there is a discussion of dolphins: "Dolphins are fruitful and multiply by coupling with human beings. What are dolphins?—Said Rab Judah: Humans of the sea" (Babylonian Talmud, Bechorot 8:1). In the *Tosefta* it is said about them: "[They] give birth and raise [suck] from human beings"; that is, they can have fruitful relations with human beings. Rashi interprets: "*Dolphins are fruitful and multiply by coupling with human beings*—that if a man has intercourse with them, they can become pregnant from him. *Humans of the sea*—there are fish in the sea, which has half human shape and half a shape of fish, and in French they are called *shiriena* (from ancient French *sereine*—siren, mermaid)."

In *Arabian Nights*, there is a story about the mermaid Julnár.[4] A Persian slave is brought to the Persian king. The king falls in love with her and marries her. One day, after the king makes love to her, he declares that he would have been happy if she had brought a son to inherit his kingdom after his death and begs her to speak. She breaks her silence and informs him that she carries his son and heir. She tells him that she belongs to a family of human sea creatures who live in the sea, and only because of his great love for her, she did not jump out the window and flee to the sea. Later on, the story describes the prince's birth and his visit to his relatives under the water.

This story corresponds to a large extent to the Bedouin story. Here, too, there is a silent mermaid who marries a human being. It is also possible that the story of the swelling, which prevents the girl from speaking, is a somatic expression of a mental phenomenon. In medicine, there is a phenomenon of a protrusion in the throat area, due to a state of contradictory emotions, called *globus hystericus*—"neither swallowing nor vomiting." It seems that in both stories, the heroine's heart struggles between her longing for the sea and for her family and her loyalty to her husband and children, and this is expressed in the form of temporary silence.

The motif of muteness also appears in a Sephardic Jewish story called "The Boy and the Sea-Woman," written down by the folklorist and historian Meir (Max) Gruenwald in the 1930s in eastern Europe and published after his death.[5] In this story, the hero comes to an empty town. During the night, he watches a group of men and women rising from the sea and entering the town. He manages to catch a girl from the sea, and he marries her. The mermaid is mute. Afterward, the mermaid dies. According to the custom in the city where they live, the local people bury the living husband with his dead wife (a familiar motif from the Sindbad stories in *Arabian Nights*). After the husband manages to dig himself out of the grave, he discovers that he is on an island. At the end of the story, he meets three young men from the sea, who help him escape the island and return safely to land. Before they separate, the boys tell him that they are his sons who were born to him from the mermaid.

Notes

1. The idiom appears in the Qur'ān. The literal meaning is Doomsday—that is to say, big hustle and bustle.
2. Ben-David and Barkai, *Bedouins in the North of the Country*, 33.
3. Thompson, *Motif-Index of Folk Literature*.
4. Burton, *Arabian Nights*, 268–69, nights 738–39.
5. Gruenwald, *Tales, Songs & Folkways of Sephardic Jews*, 60–62.

10. The Raindrop Bubbles Will Testify

A. The Man and His Neighbor

NARRATOR: Ṣabḥa ʿAbūd

TRIBE: *ʿArab el-Ḥuğērāt*

IFA 17406 ca.1981

1 wāḥad bī ʿando mara. u-ʿando ğār. ʿendo ğār, u-rāyiḥ u-ğāro xāṭrīn ʿala . . . ʿakka,[1] aywa, miṯel ma tgūḷ,[2] xaṭram, rāḥam iṯnēnhum la-ḥālhom.	1 A man had a wife, and had a neighbor. He had a neighbor, and he went—he and his neighbor—tracking to . . . Acre, yes. As you would say, they tracked, went the two of them alone.
5 ʿendinma xaṭar,[3] u-hu māši b-hā-l-waʿar, ba-l-waʿar, yaʿani miṯel marğ, miṯel baṭṭōf, miṯl-al-baṭṭōf. waḷḷa, ğe gēʿad hu w-iyyā, ʾad-dinya tišti. gaʿad hu wiyyā ʿala ha-kōm ḥğār [$_{H}$yavanim$_{H}$].[4] teḥadda, daḥḥag ʿalē. gāḷ, "hassa ʾani lū ḏibaḥtak, mīn ddi-yigūl ʿannak?" gāḷ-ḷo, "bigabīš al-may tešhad ʿalēk." yaʿani al-mayy alli ma-tišti ad-dinya teṣīr tešhad ʿalē.	5 When he tracked and he—there was nothing in the open field, in the area, that is, like a valley, like Baṭṭōf. By Allah, he came, sat with him, it started raining. He sat with him on a heap of stones, ($_{H}$avanim$_{H}$) stones. He challenged, looked at him and said to him, "Now, if I kill you, who would tell about you?" He said to him, "The raindrop bubbles will testify [to it]." That is, the water which it rains will witness against him.
15 gāḷ-ḷo, "waḷḷāhi, ġēr aḏbaḥak w-aḥuṭṭak b-hā-r-riğim w-ašūf bagabīš al-mayy tašhad ʿalēk walla lā." gāḷ-ḷo, "ṭayyib." gaḏbo, gaḏbo u-ḏabaḥo, u-fataḥ ar-riğim u-dabbo b-ar-riğim, bal-ḥğār, b-al-[$_{H}$avanim$_{H}$].[5]	15 He said to him, "By Allah, I must kill you and will put you in this heap and I'll see if the raindrop bubbles will testify on you or not." He said to him, "OK." He seized him, seized him and killed him and opened up the stone heap, and threw him in the stone heap, in the stones, in the ($_{H}$avanim$_{H}$) stones.
21 rāḥ, rawwaḥ. hū ğāro. ʾabū, ğīrān.	21 He went, returned home. He was his neighbor. His father, [they were] neighbors.

22 yaʿani, aywa, gām ğe ğāro, gāḷ-ḷo, “mā-šuft-li ibni, flān?” gāḷ-ḷo, “lā waḷḷa, mā šufto.” hū ḏibḥo(!), essa ḥaṭṭo ba-hā-r-riğim. rāḥ ^{a}yṣayyid ʾabū, ydawwer ʿalē hīn, hīn, hīn—māš.	22 That is, yes, he went to his neighbor and said to him, “Haven’t you seen my son, so-and-so?” He said to him, “No, by Allah, I haven’t seen him.” He had killed him, he just put him in that stone heap. He went looking for him, his father, [he was] looking for him here, here, here—nothing.
27 yōm baʿad sintēn ṯalāṯe, giḍab—ṣārt ad-dinya tišti. ṣār yiḏ̣ḥak hāḏa. gāḷat-ḷo marto, gāḷat-ḷo, “baḷḷāhi, lēš inta ḏ̣ḥač^{e}t?” gāḷ-ḷha, “hēč ana ḏ̣ḥičt.”[6] gāḷat-ḷo, “lēš anta ḏ̣ḥačt?” gāḷ-ḷa, “hēč ana ḏ̣ḥičt.” gāḷat-ḷo, “widdak tguḷ-li lēš ^{e}ḏ̣ḥičt.” gāḷ-ḷha, “mā wid(di)-ʾagūḷ”	27 One day, after two or three years, he took—it started raining. He started laughing, that one [person]. She said to him, his wife, she said to him, “By Allah, why did you laugh?” He said to her, “Like that, I laughed.” She said to him, “Why did you laugh?” He said to her, “Just so, I laughed.” She said to him, “You must tell me why you laughed.” He said to her, “I do not want to tell.”
34 gāḷat-ḷo, “widdi agūḷ” gāḷat-ḷo min hīn, min hīn, min hīn, marto—gāḷ-ilha, gāḷ-ḷha “hu mā ʿād agūḷo.” kull wāḥad ʿindo ʿag^{u}ḷ mū lāzim yigūḷ la-marto.	34 She said to him, “I want [you] to say.” She spoke to him from here, from here, from here—he told her. He said to her, “It is something I don’t want to tell [it].” Anyone who has a brain is not obliged to tell his wife.
38 gāḷ-iḷha, “waḷḷa, ʾani, gabuḷ sitt ^{e}snīn hāḏa iḏa ruḥt ʾani w-al-walad, xaṭarna, w-ani ʿād ğīt ani wiyyāh, ʿand hā—mšīna, ruḥna ʿa-l-maṭraḥ, al-marğ al-eflāni.	38 He told her, “By Allah, I—six years ago, this [was] when I went, I with the boy, we went tracking, and I came with him, to that—we went, walked to the place, the certain valley.”
43 w-aḥna ğāʿadīn u-gut-lo, “hassa ʾani, lū ḏabaḥtak, mīn widdo ygūl ʿannak?”	43 As we were sitting, I said to him, “Now I, if I kill you, who will tell about you?”
45 winno ygūl “bigabīš al-mayy tešhad, tgūḷ ʿanni,” yaʿani, al-mayye—ad-dinya w-hī tišti, hāḏa al-mayy ygūl ʿanni.”	45 Lo—he says, “The raindrop bubbles will testify tell about me.” That is, “the water—raining, that water will tell about me.”
48 gut-lo, “walla ma-ṭāl bagabīš al-mayy tešhad ʿalēk, inni gār aḏbaḥak.”	48 I said to him, “By Allah, as long as raindrops will bear witness on you, I must [I have no choice but] kill you.”
50 ḏibaḥto, xanaqto, ḥaṭṭēto b-ha-r-riğim.” gāḷat-ḷo, “inta?” gāl, “ā.” gāḷat-lo, “bayyē”	50 “I killed him, strangled him, put him in that stone heap.” She said to him, “You?” He said, “Yes.” She said, “O, my! [father!]”
53 yōm tekāwan hū wiyyāha, yaʿani tekāwanam. waḷḷa, gāḷat, “bayyē, widdo yiḏbaḥni miṯel ma ḏbaḥ ^{a}flān.” ğābo—sameʿ abū, samaʿ axwāno, samaʿ . . . ṣār ḥarb bēnhum. aywa. ay, w-inta lōn (<šlōn) mā gut el-martak, hī martak. hāḏa hū.	53 One day he quarreled with her, that is, they quarreled. By Allah, she said, “O, my, he wants to kill me as he killed so-and-so.” He seized him—his father heard, his brothers heard, he heard . . . and a war broke out between them. Yes. Yes, whatever you tell your wife, she is your wife. That is it.

B. Ḏā'eq 'Anṣāf (Tasting Justice)

NARRATOR: Ibrahim ʿAli Ḥreb Ḥuğērāt
TRIBE: *'Arab el-Ḥuğērāt*
IFA 13247 June 1980

1 hēn-hīn bu bī ṯnēn. kānam ğāʿadīn taḥt ^{e}šğara. gām ğe wāḥad, wāḥad nāim w-wāḥad ğāʿad. gām wāḥad ṭalaʿ min xašmo nxale. gāḷ-ḷo, "ugʿod, ugʿod. bū hīna nxala ṭalʿat min xašmak."	1 Here, there is a man. . . . There are two. They were sitting under a tree. One—one was sleeping, one was awake. One [of them]—a bee came out of his nose. He said to him [to the other one], "Wake up, wake up, there is a bee that came out of your nose."
6 gāḷ-ḷo, "uskut, 'ana[7] ʿāref . . . 'eskut, 'eskut, 'ani ʿāref." gām gāḷ-ḷo, "'ana ʿārf hassa w-ana" u-hāḏa—(y)guḷ-ḷo, "'ana ʿārf ha-n-nxala wēn hiyye." gām rāḥam biḥsam[8] b-hāl-bīr. u-gāmam ligam bīr ḏahab.	6 He said to him, "Shut up, I know; shut up, shut up, I know." He said to him, "I know now" and this—he said to him, "I know this bee—where it is." They got up and looked for this well. And they found a well with gold.
12 gāḷam. gāḷ-ḷa, "ḥawwal inti." gāḷ-ḷo, "lā', m-ini mḥawwal."[9] gāḷ-ḷo, "la', ḥawwal." gām ḥawwal haḏāka, liga . . . liga ḏahab. ğe gāḷ-ḷo "šayyal-la, ʿabbī-li, wa-rafaʿa liya." hīn arfaʿa, gāḷ-ḷo, ygūḷ-ḷa "yaḷḷa aṭleʿani." gāḷ-ḷo, "yaḷḷa m-ini 'aṭlaʿak. xaḷḷīk." gām ğe sakkar. mā gidd yesakkar gāḷ-ḷo hāḏa,	12 They said—he said to him, "Get you down [to the well]." He said to him, "No, I'm not going down." He said to him, "No, go down." He descended, that one, found . . . found gold. He said to him, "Carry it, fill it for me and lift it for me." So, he lifted it. He said to him, he says to him, "Come on, get me out." He said to him, "Come on, I'm not getting you out. Remain [there]." He went and closed [the well]. Just before he was closing it, that one said to him,
20 "'iḏa ğābat marti ʿaği itsammi l-walad ḏā'eq 'anṣāf." gāḷ-ḷo, "ṭayyeb." fa-gām sakkar ʿalē nihā'iyyan.	20 "If my wife gives birth, let her name the boy "Tasting Justice." He said to him, "Good," and closed it on him finally.
23 rā-ʿala marto. gāḷat-ḷo, "wēn e . . . hāḏa?, wēn ṣāḥbak?" gāḷ-ḷa, "ana ğīt min darb, u-hū ğāy min darb." gāḷat-ḷo, "ṭayyeb." (la-mīn hāḏ, haḏāka?)	23 He went [back] to his wife. She said to him, "Where is er . . . that one? Where is your friend?" He said to her, "I've come from one way, and he is coming from [another] way." She said to him, "Good." (Whose is that?)
27 ṣār seḥbat šahar šharēn. gām gāḷat-ḷo, "mā ğe." walla inna yegūḷ-ḷa, gāmat ğābat ʿağe. sammato Ḏā'eq 'Anṣāf.	27 She carried [her pregnancy] a month or two months. She said to him, "He has not come [back]." And lo he says to her [the name]—she delivered a boy. She named him Tasting Justice.
30 willa hā-l-ʿağe rāḥ yilʿab maʿa w^{a}lād ṣaffo.	30 Lo, this boy went to play with children of his class.

gām ğa ʿalēhom malik. gāḷ-ḷo, "šnū 'ismak inti?" gāḷ-ḷo, "'ana-smi Ḏā'eq al-'Anṣāf." gāḷ-ḷo, "mīn sammāk?" gāḷ-ḷo, "'ommʷi." gāḷ-ḷo, "'iḏan, taʿāl maʿāy (la) 'ammak." rāḥ xaḏā (l)'ammo.	There came to them a king. He said to him, "You, what is your name?" He said to him, "My name is Tasting Justice." He said to him, "Who named you?" He said to him, "My mother." He said to him, "Then come with me to your mother." He went and took him to his mother.
gāḷat-ḷo, "ta-nifsi tabāʿ al-'anṣāf." gāḷ-ḷo hāḏa. gāḷ-ḷa, "hāḏa, ṣāḥbi hīyā . . . usammā sāḥbi. gal-li sammiyo Ḏā'eq al-'Anṣāf." gāḷat lo. gāḷ-ḷa, "yalla, taʿāli, gūlī-li wēn ṣāḥbo."	She said to him, "The same as Tasting Justice." He said to her [she said to him] this [man], "his friend [was] here." His wife said, and his friend named him, he [her dead husband] told me [the friend] to name him "Tasting Justice," she said to him. He said to her, "Come on, come tell me where his friend is."
gāḷum "ğe." yegūḷ-ḷo, "liffe, hāḏa, wēn huwwa?" walla, nno yegul-lo, "māt." walla yegūl-lo, "kaḏḏāb, 'eḥki ṣ-ṣaḥīḥ." gāḷ-ḷom, "gūḷ mawwatto, saqaṭ (h)ayya l-bīr u-daššarto."	They [others] said, "He has come." He said to him, "Turn, this [man], where is he?" Lo, he said to him, "He died." Lo, he says to him, "Liar, tell the truth." He said to them, "Say [that] I killed him. He fell into some well and I deserted him."
gāḷ-ḷo, "ʿand ayy bīr lli-daššarta." gām ğa hāḏa, sakkar ʿala l-bīr. gāḷ, "gāl-li, hawwid ha-s-sāʿa ʿaḏāmo ʿala l-bīr." hawwad. xaḏa ʿeḏa. ṭāḥ ʿaḏāmo. gāḷ-ḷo, "yalla, xaḷḷīk inta barḏo."	He said to him, "At which well did you leave him?" This one came and closed the well. He said, "Tell me, bring down now his bones to the well." He descended. He went and threw his bones. He said to him, "Come on, you stay [there], too."

Commentary

These two stories collected from the same tribe, of the ʿArab el-Ḥuğērāt, belong to the narrative type ATU 960, "The Sun Will Bring Everything to Light."

The belief that one's actions are viewed from above and that secrets will be revealed is ancient. Already in Ecclesiastes it is said: "Curse not the king, no not in thy thought; and curse not the rich in thy bedchamber: for a bird of the air shall carry the voice, and that which hath wings shall tell the matter" (Ecclesiastes 10:20). A similar idea appears in the parables of Jesus in the New Testament: "For there is nothing hid, which shall not be manifested; neither was any thing kept secret, but that it should come abroad" (Mark 4:22). It appears again in the Gospel according to Luke: "For nothing is secret, that shall not be made manifest; neither any thing hid, that shall not be known and come abroad" (Luke 8:17), and in another place: "For there is nothing covered, that shall not be revealed; neither hid, that shall not be known. Therefore whatsoever ye have spoken in darkness shall be heard in the light; and that which ye have spoken in the ear in closets shall be proclaimed upon the housetops" (Luke 12:2–3).

In Arabic, there are proverbs expressing a similar idea: "Tomorrow the snow will melt and the valley will be seen" (*bukra biḏūb aṯ-ṯalğ u-bibān al-marğ*), as well as "there is not even a spit under the stone to hide" (*mā fī bazqa taḥt ḥağar b-tixtfi*).

In folk narrative, this belief is expressed in many stories. One of the most famous is the legend of the Greek poet Ibycus, who lived in the second half of the sixth century BCE. According to the legend, Ibycus was attacked by bandits, who wounded him mortally. When it happened, a flock of cranes passed over him, and before he died, he cried, "The cranes will take my revenge!" The bandits left him there without attributing importance to his last words. A few weeks later, while one of the murderers was sitting in the open theater in Corinth, he saw cranes hovering in the sky and shouted: "These are the avengers sent by Ibycus!" An investigation was immediately launched. The murderer pleaded guilty and gave the authorities the names of the rest of the gang.

In the wake of the legend, the words "the cranes of Ibycus" became an epigram, expressing the idea that the gods punished the criminals in ways that could not be foreseen.

The Brothers Grimm's story "The Bright Sun Will Bring It to Light" tells about a tailor who attacked a Jew on the way to rob him and beat him to death.[10] Before he died, the Jew said, "The bright sun will bring it to light." As in the first Bedouin story, when the murderer sat with his wife, the sun shone on it and the reflection gleamed on the wall, and the tailor said, "Yes, it would like very much to bring it to light, and cannot!" His wife urged him to explain what he was saying, and after much entreaty, he told her what had happened. The woman told the story to her good friend, the story soon became widespread, and the murderer was punished.

In the legend of Ibycus, as in the Brothers Grimm's story and the Bedouin stories, the last words of the murdered are those that ultimately lead to the discovery of the crime (motif D1715, "Magic power of dying man's words"; motif N271.1, "The sun brings all to light. The murderer repeats as he sees the rays of the sun, the last words of the dying man, thus betraying the crime").

In their book, Meron, Shehadi, and Masarwi present a version of this story narrated by Rawḍeh Asʿad Ghanāim, from Bāqa al-Gharbiyya.[11] In that story, as in the first Bedouin story presented here, rainwater bubbles lead to the exposure of the murderer.

Another popular motif appears in the second Bedouin story: N271.2, "Murder revealed by unusual names of boys. The dying man leaves a message to name his sons 'O Allah' and 'O king' (or the like). This arouses the king's curiosity and brings the murder to light."

The reason for the murder in the first story is not a robbery but an argument. The adult murderer is depicted in the story as someone who does not believe in the power of Providence, unlike the boy who accompanies him, and he murders the boy to prove his claim. In the second story, as in many other versions of the story, the motivation for the murder is money.

In the first story, the narrator's metatext comment on the murderer is interesting: "He has no brains. Everyone who has brains does not have to tell his wife." The chauvinistic approach, which holds that women are not as good at keeping secrets as men, suggests that men should not share their secrets with their wives. A similar concept is expressed in the biblical story of Samson and his wives (Judges 14, 16). It is interesting that here a woman expressed this view.

In the second story, which the narrator heard from his grandmother in his childhood, appears to be another popular perception of the nature of women versus men: The mother opposes the appointment of her son as a judge. It seems that, to prevent further bloodshed, she does not want to raise the issue of the father's death. The son, in contrast, is determined to discover the meaning of his strange name, and he forces his mother to reveal the secret and thus to expose his father's killer.

The judge functions here as an investigative and judicial authority as well as an executive authority. He investigates an affair in which he himself is involved and carries out the verdict. In Deuteronomy it says: "If there be a controversy between men, and they come unto judgment, that the judges may judge them; then they shall justify the righteous, and condemn the wicked. And it shall be, if the wicked man be worthy to be beaten, that the judge shall cause him to lie down, and to be beaten before his face, according to his fault, by a certain number" (Deuteronomy 25:1–2). Although it is customary to interpret the biblical text to mean that the judge only orders the beating of the defendant as a punishment, a plain reading of the text affirms that the judge is also the one who executes the judgment. According to the biblical account, the beating is only a punishment, but in the Islamic tradition, extracting a confession from a defendant by beating, as described in the Bedouin story, is a common matter. In his book *Travels in Arabia Deserta*,[12] Charles M. Doughty describes an event in which a thief is caught in a convoy heading to Mecca, and the convoy members beat him with hard rods to force him to reveal where he buried the money.

Ibrahim ʿAli Ḥreb Ḥuğērāt told me two versions of the story. We brought here only one of them. In the second version he enlarged the story and added many details. What is special about the enlarged version of Ḏā'eq 'Anṣāf's story is the dream that begins the plot. The sleeping man sees in his dream a large tree and near the tree a pile of stones and under the pile there is a well full of gold. At the same time his friend sees a bee that emerges of the stone pile and enters into the dreamer nostril. The event can be viewed from three points of view: from the perspective of the dreamer, from the point of view of the friend, and from the point of view of the reader.

Four elements in the story link the dream to reality: a heap of stones, a bee, a well, and gold. Let us examine the interaction between the participants and the elements.

The story begins with the friend's point of view. Through his eyes, we see the image of the bee that emerges from the pile of stones near the tree and enters the nose of the sleeping man. At this stage, the viewer knows nothing about the gold or the well.

The dreamer, on the other hand, sees in his dream the tree and the heap of stones next to it, the well hidden beneath the heap, and the gold inside it. At this stage, the heap of stones and the tree are shared by both dream and reality.

When the dreamer awakes, he tells the viewer the contents of the dream (gold in the well), and the viewer updates him about what happened while he was asleep (a bee in the nose). Now both of them interpret the dream together, forming the necessary associative connection:

Golden bee → gold
Nose (nostril) → well

They come to a common conclusion: the gold lies in the well below the stone heap, or in the laconic phrase of the narrator, "They said: This may be the heap of stones."

In folk literature, many stories about dreams are followed by finding a treasure. They are associated with the narrative type ATU 1645, "The Treasure at Home." One of the best known is the story "The Treasure under the Bridge," which appears in Hasidic Jewish sources.[13] The story appears in the thirteenth century in *Maṭnawīye Ma'nawī*, the broad poetic work of Jalal Al-din al-Rumi, written between 1258 and 1273 CE. It is also included in *Arabian Nights* under the name "The Ruined Man Who Became Rich Again through a Dream."[14]

A prominent element in the story of Ḏā'eq 'Anṣāf is the bee, which enters the dreamer's nose. It is part of the narrative type ATU 1645A, "Dream of Treasure Bought": A king falls asleep under a tree. A servant sees an animal creep out of his mouth, run to a stream, and try to cross it. The servant lays his sword across the stream, and the animal runs over it, crosses the stream, and enters the opening in a mountain. Later the animal goes back into the mouth of the sleeping king. The king awakes and relates that he dreamed that he went over a stream on an iron bridge and entered a mountain where he found a great treasure. The servant tells the king what he has observed. The king looks into the mountain and discovers the great treasure, which he donates to the church.

The story is well known from literary sources written in the Middle Ages. In many versions, someone else buys the dream and finds the treasure: motif N531.3, "Dream of treasure bought. Treasure has been seen by man's soul absent in sleep in form of a fly. The purchaser of the dream finds the treasure." Thus, for example, a Japanese version of the story, told by a gifted narrator named Tsune Watanbe in 1967 in the village of Nomura, Japan, tells of two friends who set out to cut trees in the forest.[15] As they rest, one of them falls asleep, and after a while, just as he wakes up, his friend sees a bee stepping out of his nostril and flying away. The awakened man tells his friend that he has dreamed of a hidden gold treasure in the garden of a rich man from Osaka. The friend buys the dream for a fee. Later he travels to Osaka, arrives at the rich man's home, and asks for permission to dig in his garden to find the treasure, promising to share it. The rich man tries to deceive the man, and in the middle of the night, he digs with his servants in the garden but discovers that the jar that was supposed to hold the treasure is empty. He goes back to bury the jar in its hiding place, and the next day, he invites the guest to dig in the garden. He, too, discovers that the jar is empty, and he has to return home empty-handed. But when he returns home, he discovers that a rain of gold coins and other treasures entered his house at night and covered all the floors of the house.

What is interesting about the Japanese story is the motif of the bee, which comes out of the nostrils of the sleeping man. Probably here, too, the golden bee symbolizes the golden treasure. A folktale that was collected in Surinam from a Maronite informant, "Jauw's Dream," tells of two friends, one of whom sleeps and dreams while his friend remains awake.[16] The friend sees a little mouse come out of his sleeping friend's nostrils. He follows the mouse, which leads him to a thick tree in the forest. The mouse climbs the tree and disappears into the thicket. After a while, the mouse reappears, comes down from the tree, makes its way to the house of the two friends, and goes back into the sleeping friend's nostril. At that moment, the sleeping man wakes up and tells his friend that he has dreamed that he left the house, journeyed to the forest to a certain tree that grew there, climbed it, and found a crate full of gold. The friend takes him to the tree the mouse visited. The two climb up and find the treasure. The story ends with the two men wasting the treasure they have found, and so the gold coins spread throughout the world. Until then there were no known gold coins in the world.

It seems that in this story, as in other versions, the animal coming out of the nostrils of the sleeping man symbolizes his soul. Motif E721, "Soul wanders from body in sleep. Dreams explained as experiences of the soul on these wanderings," and motif E730, "Soul in animal form," appear in many folktales.

Notes

1. The narrator makes the story realistic by mentioning a nearby town, the city of Akko (Acre). Later on in the story, she mentions the valley Baṭṭōf, which is not far from where she lives, for the same purpose. Place names are not necessarily the real locations of occurrence of this (and other) tales.

2. *miṯel mā tgūḷ*, "as you'd say," is a frequent hedging phrase used by Bedouins as a discourse marker to express "as if, like, such as."

3. *'indinma xaṭar*, "when he traveled," is another particle (time adverb) constructed by adding *mā* to the preposition *'ind* and the relative particle base *inn*, "that." In LA/MSA, the preposition is *'indamā*, but the narrator apparently mixes it with the use of the particle *in ~ en* (cf. *inno*, in LA/MSA and Owens, "Historical Linguistics").

4. *yavaním/yabaním*, "stones," is apparently the Modern Hebrew word *'avaním*. The narrator apparently does not know the correct Hebrew form of the word.

5. *yōm, ba'ad sintēn ṯalāṯe, giva ṣār ad-dinya tišti*: "one day, after two, three years, after, rain began falling." *giva* may be derived from the verb *qefa*, "to follow, come after something," though it is pronounced here with a voiced *f*, or *v*.

Note that the following verb *ṣār* is in the m., though usually the word *dinya* is f. This may be because the verb precedes the noun subject, allowed in LA/MSA and the colloquial dialects and not a case of flawed planning of a spontaneous utterance.

6. *gāḷat-lo, "baḷḷāhi, lēš inta ḍ̣haček?" gāḷ-ḷha, "hēč ana ḍ̣hičt"*: "She said to him, his wife, she said to him, 'by Allah, why did you laugh?' He said to her, 'Like that, I laughed.'" The verb *laugh*—"you laughed" versus "I laughed"—has two forms here. Note the different vowel in the first syllable in each of these verbs. (Cf. chap. 4, note 4; chap. 15, note 5, which refer to vowel form volatility in Galilee Bedouin dialects.) In addition, note the added auxiliary vowel in *ḍ̣hačet* and its lack in *ḍ̣hičt*. These two forms seem to reflect two verb patterns of measure I: Ci/e/aCaC and CiCiC (e.g., *ketab*, "he wrote," and *raḥal*, "he roamed away," versus *nizil*, "he descended"), which the narrator mixed in this speech. An auxiliary (anaptyctic or epenthetic) vowel (e.g., *e* in *ḍ̣hačet*) is added, depending on the phonetic-articulatory environment, which makes it difficult to produce a consonant cluster without the auxiliary vowel. This causes part of the numerous variegated forms of the words in this collection of spontaneous speech.

7. Other cases where the narrator mixes Bedouin and sedentary morpho-phonetic features are when she says sedentary *'ana* and Bedouin *'ani*, "I," sedentary *inti* and Bedouin *'inta*, "you [m.sg.]" in sequence, as well as sedentary *gāḷat-lo*, "she said to him," versus Bedouin *gāḷ-ḷa*, "he said to him"—in other words, the vowel of the bound pronoun of the m. sg. third person is sometimes *a* and sometimes *o* in her speech. Note that for this bound person, the vowel *o* is the usual form in sedentary and certain Bedouin dialects, whereas *a* is used in a few Bedouin Galilee dialects for this suffixed pronoun.

8. Some of the narrator's words reflect a sedentary dialect and then are repeated in the Bedouin dialect. One such feature relates to the verb pattern (cf. the section on morphology

and tables 9 and 10 in the chapter on Galilee Bedouin dialects at the end of this book). The Bedouin verb patterns include CaCaC and CiCaC in verb measure I. The pattern with *a* in the first syllable appears if the first or second root consonant is a laryngeal or pharyngeal phoneme, while *i* occurs when those consonants are not laryngeal or pharyngeal (cf. *ḥaraṯ*, "plow," versus *kital*, "kill"). However, this narrator uses *ṭala'*, a form that would be characteristic of sedentary dialects. (In fact, sedentary speakers have *ṭile'* for this verb.) Where Bedouin dialects would be *ṭíla'*, *bᵉḥásam*. So the narrator partly keeps the Bedouin phonetic rule but not in the correct phonetic environment. See also *biḥsam* with sedentary *s* for the verb that in Galilee Bedouin dialects would be *bᵉḥáṯam*, with *a* and *ṯ*.

9. The narrator is a native Bedouin speaker despite the above phonetic mixtures, as attested in other morphological and lexical features. See, for example, Bedouin *šharēn* (sedentary *šahrēn*) "two months," in Story 10A; *ğe*, "he came" (sedentary: ağa); and *m-ini mḥawwal*, "I am not coming down" (sedentary: *'ana miš nāzil ~ biddīš 'anzel*).

10. Grimm, *The Original Folk and Fairy Tales of the Brothers Grimm*, story 115.

11. Meron, Shehadi, and Masarwi, *Seed of Pomegranate*, 255–58.

12. Doughty, *Travels in Arabia Deserta*, 1:14.

13. Berger, *Simchat Yisrael*, 49, "The Dream of Rabbi Isaac of Cracow." The story appears in other Hasidic sources and is also included in the stories of Rabbi Nachman of Breslov.

14. Burton, *Arabian Nights*, 289, night 351.

15. Dorson, *Folktales Told around the World*, 245–51.

16. Penard and Penard, "Surinam Folk-Tales," 239–50. Suriname is a tiny country that lies on the coast and borders Brazil in the south. In the past, it was a Dutch colony. Its diverse population includes the descendants of immigrants from North India, Creole people (descendants of black people and Europeans), descendants of Java immigrants from Indonesia and Maroons—descendants of black slaves who fled to Suriname.

11. The Coffee Server

NARRATOR: Ṯalǧe Mūsa

TRIBE: *ʿArab el-Ḥuǧērāt*

June 1, 2015

1 hāḏa ’amīr, ’amīr min zamān, ’amīr, ’amīr. ʿindu hā-l-bint, mā ʿindū-š wulād, ʿindu hā-l-binet. ʿindu ǧirāno hēn, eš—šābb, yaʿani, biḥibbha, widdu iyyāha, widdu iyyāha, yaʿani, bint ḥalāl, miš ġaṣbin ʿanha. hī bitḥibbu, bas abūha bidduš.[1]	1 This emīr, emīr from long ago, emīr, emīr. He has a daughter, he doesn't have sons—he has this daughter. He has these neighbors here. The boy courted the girl, that is, he loved her, he wanted her, that is, [she was] a decent girl, [he was] not forcing her. She loves him, but her father does not want.
8 ’abūha—bēt šaʿar, hadd u-raḥal. ʿa-maḥall ebʿīd, ebʿīd, ebʿīd, ebʿīd. hāḏa qām min-nōm eṣ-ṣubeḥ—lā fī byūt, wa-lā fī ʿarab.[2] wēn rāḥ hāḏ? gaʿad hā-š-šābb yifakkar. šū yifakker a š-šābb "biddi yilḥaq, biddi-iyyāha." qālu-la "ġēr elḥaq w-ašūf."	8 Her father—[has, lives in] a tent; he took it apart and went off. To a very, very, very, very distant place. This [boy] got up from sleep in the morning—there were no tents, no Bedouins. Where did this one go? The boy sat down to think. What does the boy think: "I want to follow, I want her." They [he] said to him[self], "I'll just follow and I will see."
15 ṣār yimši, bi-l-lel yimši u-b-in-nhār yinām. bi-lel yimši u-b-in-nhār yinām. ’aǧa ʿala hā-r-reʿyān ʿala hā-l-ʿēn. ʿēn mayye. ʿala hā-l-ʿēn, qālū-lo—gāl, "’as’alhen"	15 He began walking. He walked at night and slept during daytime. At night he walked and during daytime slept. He came to some shepherds at a spring, water spring. To the spring. They said to him—he said [to himself], "I'll ask them."
20 gāl "’as’alhen" gāl-(l(hin, "al-’amīr eflān?" qālu, "lā, miš mawǧūd ʿen(c)na."	20 He said, "I'll ask them." He said to them, "[Do you know where is] the certain emīr?" They said to him, "No, he is not with us."

22 el-ʿarab eṯ-ṯāniyīn, qabīle ṯāniye, “miši ʿalīna.” “’as’al qabīle ṯāniye, as’al,”	22 The other Bedouins, another tribe, “He went off from us.” “I’ll ask another tribe, I’ll ask,”
25 qāl, “wēn el-’amīr ^{e}flān?” qālu-lo: “hiyyā, huwwa hōn ʿin(d)na, b-il-ʿarab.”	25 he said. “Where is the certain emīr?” They said to him, “He is here, he is here with us, in the Bedouin [place].”
27 saḥab ḥālo ’ağa ʿalēhen, s-sāʿa sabʿa, eš-šābb ʿala hā-l-bēt, šū hā-l . . . ʿalem ’aḷḷa, kam sine u-huwwa dāyir ydawwer tanno leqīhen. qāl-la, “di n’ēt,”[3] qāl-la “hū lli-biddha nī’a.”	27 He went and came to them, seven o’clock, the boy [came] to the tent. What this . . . Allah knows how many years he was going around, searching, until he found them. He said to her [to himself], “Well, I’ve gone far.” He said [to himself], “This distance is what this [search] requires.”
32 qāl-lha, “biddi širbet mayy, ismaḥi, širbet mayy.” ṭallat ʿalē hēk, ti-tgūl la-’emmha, ti-tgūl-la, “yā yumma, hāḏa ʿabd min ʿabīd el-mawāli.” yaʿani ʿabed. ǧāwab hāḏa gāl-la,[4]	32 He said, to her, “I want a gulp of water, if you please, a gulp of water.” She looked at him like that, and says to her mother, says to her, “O mother, this is a slave from the Mawāli slaves”; that is, a slave. He answered her, said to her,
37 “’ana ʿabd min ʿabīd el-mawāli?	37 “Am I a slave of the Mawāli slaves?
38 ana min ğōrko(m) yā bīḏ̣ hāḏi iḥwāli,	38 I, because of your abuse, o white ones, this is my condition.
39 min ğōrčen, yā bīḏ̣, hāḏi ^{i}ḥwāli.	39 Because of your abuse, o white ones, this is my condition.
40 ṭallat ʿalayya, brātemha ʿadīd zawāwid (kāin biḥaṭṭū hōna).	40 She looked at me, her lips [have] many tattooed paints, (they used to put them here).
42 ṣār mit ʿalayya brātimha bū zawāwid.	42 I died for her lips which have tattoos.
43 mufarragan gozla, suwat al-^{e}hlāli.	43 Her hair is spread on her forehead, [she is] equal to the moon [in beauty].
44 ’ani ʿabd-aḷḷa, mā-ni ʿabd al-maxālīğ.	44 I am Allah’s slave, not a slave of living creatures.
45 ’alla min ğōrčen, yā bīḏ̣, hāḏi iḥwāli.”	45 But because of your abuse, o white ones, this is my condition.”
46 qālu-lo, “šū btištġel?” qāl-ilhen, “’ana qahawği. ’aštġil qahawği la-l-dalla alli b-aḏubb ḥaṭab u-b-aḏubb ğalle u-b-asawwi qahwa murra.” qaʿad[5] ʿindhin hā-(z)-zʿēne.[6]	46 They said to him, “What do you work?” He said to them, “I am a coffee man, I work as a coffee man, with the coffee pot, and I gather chopped wood and dung, and make bitter coffee.” This vagabond stayed with them.

50 yōm, ʿa-dōr qabel, kānat an-nās tiġzi ġaz^{a}w. yiġzu. ġazat el-ʿarab, ġazzāye, ġazat aṭ-ṭarš wa-ʾaxḏathum, rāḥat lu l-ben(t). gāḷat-ḷo, "yā ğallāl, rāḥ al-bōš[7] ^{e}mʿa r-reʿyān." gāḷ-ḷha, "yā ʿaḏbe, mā biyya alḥag el-xayyāl, ʾağriyya mā talḥag al-xayyāl."	50 One day, in the past, people would attack others. [They would] attack. They attacked the Bedouin, the raiders; they raided the sheep and goats and took them. The girl went to him and said to him, "O gatherer [dung gatherer], the sheep has gone [is lost] with the shepherds." He said to her, "O, sweet one, I cannot follow the horseman, my legs will not catch up with the horseman."
57 gāḷat-ḷo, "ʿendi ḏaxīra—sēf ʾabūya wa-l-iḥsān." gāḷ, lākin ʿa-hāl-ğawād, ṣār yirkab la-wara, yidīr wuğho ʿala ṭīz al-^{i}ḥṣān. gāḷat-ḷo, "mū hīč, mū hīč, yā ğobbān, mū hīč." mā hu mišān tiḥki maʿo. qālat-lo, "ʾirkab hēk."	57 She said to him, "I have ammunition: my father's sword and the horse." But this horse—he started riding it backward, turning his face toward the horse's bottom. She said to him, "Not like this, not like this, o coward, not like this." But he [did it] in order that she would talk with him. She said to him, "Ride like that."
63 hāḏa tanno baʿʿad ʿan al-ʿarab la-ġād,	63 This [one], until he got far from the Bedouin place to that direction,
64 nizel ʿan-il-^{i}ḥṣān, šaddad al-iḥzām tabaʿo u-ḍabbaṭo, u-ḥiml es-sēf u-rikeb u-miši^{y}. wēn miši^{y}? leḥigha, leḥig el-gōm elli widdhin yinhabu. ^{i}nhabo, riğeʿ el-bōš. riğeʿ el-bōš.	64 he went off the horse, fixed its belt, and put it properly, and took the sword and rode and went off. Where did he go? He followed them, followed [and caught up with] the enemy that wanted to loot. [He] looted them, the sheep returned. The sheep returned.
69 fazʿat[8] hā-n-nās, hā-r-reʿyān kulla ygūl, "ʾana rağğaʿto." haḏāk yegūl, "ʾana rağğaʿto."	69 The people gathered, these shepherds, all of them said, "I brought them back," that one says, "I brought them back."
72 qāl-ilhin, "mīn illi rağğaʿ el-bōš? wēn ʿānt el-xēl," yaʿani, al-ʿānt tabaʿ el-xēl, wēn-hu.	72 He [the coffee man] said to them, "Who is the one who brought back the sheep? Where are the horses' bag parts?" That is, the bag parts laid on the horses, where are they?
75 bī baḷāṭa, maḥṭūṭ ʿalēha hēka. ešber šeber ʿala l-baḷāṭa u-illi ḥaṭṭ-ha, ešber šeber ʿala l-baḷāṭa šibru.	75 There is a rock, and they are on it like that. He had [put] a hand span on this rock, and he who put his hand span—his hand span was on this rock.
78 haḏōl ʿala ha-l-baḷāṭa, kān illi yrağğeʿ al-bōš (š-) tšabar šaber damm ʿala l-baḷāṭa. "illi yīği šibro ʿalē huwwa-lli rağğaʿ el-bōš." haḏāka yiğību, haḏāka, haḏāka, haḏāka ygūl, "ʾana." haḏāka ygūl "ʾana." kullam.	78 those on the rock—whoever brought back the sheep left a blood hand span on the rock.. "The one whose hand span is on it, is the one who brought back the sheep." They tried like that, that one, that one, that one said, "I [brought them back]," that one says, "I," all of them.

84 mīn ḏaḷḷ? huwwa l-ğallāl alli bya'mel el-'ahwe. la 'imel b'īd 'an il-bēt.	84 There remained only the dung man who was making coffee. He stayed not far from the tent.
86 qāḷat-ḷo, "yā 'abūya, mā radd ba'ed al-ğallāl, mā šabar šiber."	86 She said to him, "O father, no one has remained except the coffee man; he has not tried the hand span."
88 qāḷ-ḷha, "hāḏa btā' radd bōš?" gāḷat-ḷo, "nšūf."	88 He said to her, "Is this one [capable of] bringing back the sheep?" She said to him, "[Bring him forth and] let us see."
90 nāda 'alē, 'ağa, ta'a š-šiber. 'īdo, b-'īdo šabar šiber damm. gāḷ-ḷo, "ğatak binti. lā ğaza wa-lā wafe."	90 He called him, he came, gave his hand span. [It was] his hand; he had put the blood hand span with his hand. He said to him, "My daughter has come to you [she is yours], with no remuneration or good faith promises [for dowry from you]."
93 'ağat binto, wa-'inno, la-ḥatta, ya'alam aḷḷa kam sine u-hu ydawwer warā(ha), u-xaḏa u-riğe'. 'imel lo 'ers, 'imel lo kull 'iši u-ğawwazha. 'āy, al-ḥamdo-li-ḷḷā.	93 His daughter came [became his], and until when, Allah knows how many years passed while he was looking for her. He took her [for wife], and returned [to his own home]. He [the emīr] made the wedding for him, made everything for him, and he married her. Aye, praise Allah.

Commentary

The informant, Ṯalğe Mūsa, told me the story twice, once in 1980 and again in 2015. The first version, which is not provided here, was told in Arabic but written down in Hebrew. I translated it with the help of other people who were present at the narrative event, while trying to preserve the vivid narrator's style, which contained many dialogues.

The second version, which I am giving here, was also recorded in Arabic and translated accurately into English.

In the story, the daughter, in her appeal to her mother, calls the singer *'abed.* In Arabic, that word has two meanings: slave and black because many Bedouin slaves were brought from Sudan. It seemed that in the course of his wanderings the hero's face became black because of the sun's heat, and the daughter mistakes him for a black slave. In the hero's reply in the short *qaṣīda* that he sings, both meanings are expressed: "I am Allah's slave, not a slave of people."

Qaṣīda (قصيدة) is a figurative poem that has ancient roots. It commonly contains at least seven verses, but usually the *qaṣā'id* (قصائد) are much longer. Each verse consists of two parts: the first hemistich is called "front" (*ṣader*), and the second hemistich is called "back" (*'ağuz*). The *qaṣīda* is a song of praise, in which the poet glorifies his tribe and mocks his enemies, but the first part is often devoted to matters of the heart (*nasīb*). The poet describes a meeting of lovers from two tribes. Their acquaintance does not last long and ends in their separation because one of the tribes migrates to another place. The poet describes the sorrow of the lover who is forced to part from his beloved.

The short *qaṣīda* that appears here as part of the story is actually a small section of a much longer *qaṣīda*. Three lines in the poem—"I died for her lips which have tattoos. / Her hair is spread on her forehead, / It is equal to the moon in beauty."—were taken from an old *qaṣīda* from the thirteenth century CE about a cultural hero named Xalaf ibn Dāʿiǧa.

The first two lines of the *qaṣīda* glorify the beauty of the girl's appearance: the spread of her hair and the tattoo spots around her lips, her chin, and her forehead. Bedouin women used to tattoo these parts of their faces, and many of the older Bedouin women I met during my research had blue tattoo marks there. The tattoo marks (*wašem*), in the forms of dots, flowers, lines, swords, fish, birds, and other images, were made by gypsies using needles when the girls were young.[9] In this *qaṣīda*, the girl's hair is likened to a white crescent moon (*ġurra*, a white stain on the horse's forehead).

The opening line of the *qaṣīda* says, "Am I a slave from the slaves of the Mawāli?" The word *Al-Mawāli* (الموالي) has several meanings. One of them refers to the *ḏimmis*, *ɜahl al-ḏimma* أهل الذمة (protégés). This is a (derogatory) name given to non-Arab Muslims, mainly of Persian origin, in the first centuries of the establishment of Islam. It was used for anyone who wanted to convert to Islam and join an Arab tribe as a protégé. The Mawāli lived mainly in the former Sassanid Empire, that is, Iraq and Iran. They suffered discrimination from the authorities and were forced to pay additional taxes. This led to feelings of deprivation and frequent rebellions, which later helped the Abbasid regime to gain control. Following the rise of the Abbasid dynasty, the condition of the Mawāli was improved, and they were integrated as senior officials in the administration and in the clerical work of the caliphate. In modern times, Mawāli is the name of a Bedouin tribe.

The wandering singer, who travels from one tribe to another, accompanying himself with the *rabāba* (rebab), was once a familiar figure in the Bedouin traditional life. The narrator's cousin heard, as a child, such a singer and even told me some of his stories, which she kept in her memory.

The *rabāba* (ربابة) is a violin with one string. Its resonance box is made of a rectangular wooden frame measuring about twenty centimeters by thirty centimeters and is coated on both sides with sheepskin. Copper studs and thread bind the taut skin on both sides of the frame. The skin is pierced by a few holes at its four corners. The instrument's neck is made of a simple wooden rod that passes through the resonance box and peeps out at the other end. At its upper end, there is a metal wedge for stretching the string, which crosses a small bridge that sits atop the skin and is connected to the hole at the end of the rod. The arch is made of a bent branch, and the strings are made of horsehair.

Players hold the instrument diagonally with their knees crossed. To change the string length, they press their fingertips on the upper part of the string. Before playing, players adjust the string to the required tension with the peg and heat the sound box on both sides over the fire to stretch the skins. The instrument produces a continuous rising and falling sound. The sound scale is quite limited. The *rabāba* is used both as an accompaniment to singing and as an independent instrument. In the first case, musicians play the poem verse by verse, with each verse separated from the next by a musical fragment. The lyrics are slow with trills, and the singers draw out the last syllable in every verse.

The tradition of playing the *rabāba* is disappearing in the north of Israel. It is still played mainly by the elders. In the 1980s, I met two musicians from the ʿArab el-Mazārīb tribe in Bēt Zarzīr. One of them maintained a tradition that had passed through his family, and even his son followed his footsteps. The other learned to play the instrument following contact with Bedouin tribes in southern Jordan, while serving as a soldier in the Arab Legion. Some elders of the ʿArab el-Ḥuğērāt tribe, and probably elders of other tribes, also have *rabābas*.

The hero in the story sings, as mentioned, a *qaṣīda*, but he does not accompany himself on the *rabāba*, He presents himself as a *dallāl*—a coffee server. The stem of the term is the word *dalla*, a large copper pitcher (*dallat el-qahwa*) in which large quantities of coffee are brewed for guests. Serving coffee to a guest has been a common practice in Bedouin culture for hundreds of years. The guest is served bitter black coffee without sugar in a small porcelain cup (*finğān*). It is customary to serve three cups of coffee, according to the common saying "*wāḥed la-s-sēf u-wāḥed la-l-ḍēf u-wāḥed lal-kēf*"—one [cup] for the sword, and one for the guest, and one for the pleasure [of the guest]. The first cup is called the peace cup. A guest who has a quarrel with the host, such as a conflict over land or grazing, refuses to sip it until they find a solution to the conflict. The second cup is called the cup of requests. If a guest has a request from the host, for example, he wishes to marry the host's daughter to his son, he refuses to sip it until the host has fulfilled his request. In his book, Ashkenazi gives a poetic description of such a negotiation. The guests refuse to drink coffee, while the host is afraid to commit himself in advance and agree to their request, so he asks his wife to bring his newborn baby, and he pulls out his knife and announces that he is going to slaughter his son in honor of his guests. The guests calm him down and agree to drink his coffee and continue the negotiation later.[10] The drinking of the third cup is regarded not as a duty but as a pleasure. Another formulation of the above proverb expresses this: "*el-'uwla la-ḍ-ḍēf u-l-tānieh la-s-sēf u-l-tālet—hēf*"—the first [cup] for the guest and the second for the sword [the guest's bravery] and the third—extra [unnecessary].

The story reflects many characteristics and customs of the Bedouin culture, such as tattoo marks, qaṣā'id (قـصـائـد) singing and coffee serving. At the end of the story another cultural characteristic appears. The emīr says, "You have received my daughter without reward and without obligation": *lā ğaza we-lā wafa* (لا جزا ولا وفا). His words combine two expressions. The first expression, "without reward," is derived from the Qur'ān, the Sūrah of Man, "We want from you neither reward nor gratitude" (sūrah 76, 9). The other expression, "without duty," is derived from Bedouin law. When people are attempting to reconcile two sides of a vendetta by means of a *ṣulḥa* (الصلحة—making peace between enemies), they appoint two functionaries. The first, *wakīl el-dafa*, makes sure that the injured party does not take revenge before the *ṣulḥa* takes place, and the other one, *wakīl el-wafa*, makes sure that the other side keeps his promise. Here it means that the father marries his daughter to the hero who saved the flock without any obligation on the hero's part. A Muslim woman explained to me that the phrase *lā ğaza we-lā wafa* (ولا وفا لا جزا) is used when a man marries his daughter and does not ask the bridegroom for a dowry either before or after the wedding (*wafa* means "faithfulness, keeping one's word").

The earliest version contains some details missing in the later version:

1. The conversation between the hero and his father, a conversation the girl's father eavesdrops on. In this conversation, the son informs his father about his intention to marry the emīr's daughter. Therefore, the emīr decides to migrate with his tribe to another place.

2. The narrator's explanation that the girl does not identify the hero and treats him as a slave because he has been exposed to the sun and his face has tanned.

3. The manner in which the hero presents himself as a wandering singer and accompanies his song with a *rabāba*.

4. The reason given for the absence of the tribesmen when enemies attack their tents: the tribe members are themselves engaged in an attack on members of another tribe.

5. The explanation of the horse's reverse riding style: the desire not to arouse suspicion among the women who remain in the encampment (in the later version, another, less convincing explanation is given—the hero's desire for the emīr's daughter to speak to him, which has already happened).

6. The hero's behavior after the battle: his impersonating a stranger who raises questions in front of the emīr about where the horses' bridles are. (Although in the later version the hero is the one who raises the question about the missing bridles, he claims later that he was away from home while the emīr and his men were looking for the hero who imprinted his hand on the rock. It is the girl who turns to her father to see if the hand of the coffee server also fits the mark.)

7. The removal of the rock from the hidden bridles, which only the hero is able to perform.

I tend to think that the earlier version is truer to the original story, as the narrator heard it in her youth. The early version clearly shows that the girl identifies the hero as her lover immediately after he sings his song and that they both work together to consummate their love at the right time. Under normal circumstances, the emīr would not have married his daughter to her lover if he had identified him. The young man's victory in battle causes the emīr to declare his desire to give the hero his daughter, and he is faithful to his word even when he realizes that the hero (the impostor) is a black slave. At the end of the story, when the real hero appears without disguise and the emīr's daughter convinces her father to examine his hand as well, the emīr is ready to give his daughter to the hero who has saved the tribe, whatever the color of his skin. When it becomes clear to the emīr that his son-in-law is not a slave but a man of a high rank—the son of another emīr—he is happy about it, and the way is paved for the couple's marriage with the father's full blessing (a similar situation appears at the end of the story "Between the Sun and the Moon"). This is also implied by the emīr's words to his son-in-law, "You received my daughter without reward and without obligation," which means that he does not ask the groom for a dowry.

The *ġazu* (robbery of another tribe) mentioned in the story also appears in other stories. Such raids gradually diminished toward the end of the Ottoman period and disappeared completely with the beginning of the British Mandate in the region (1917).

The motif of marking places and objects with a fingerprint stained with blood also appears in other stories. The story also reflects the attitude toward people with mental illness in Bedouin society, as those whose actions should not be interfered with. The hero pretends to be mentally ill by riding backward on his horse.

The story is familiar in various formats throughout the Bedouin culture in the Land of Israel, as well as in the south of Israel and Jordan.

In his book *Parable, Story and Legend in Bedouin Tents*, Sasson Bar-Zvi presents two versions of the story. The first version, "The Story of Ḥalaf," is the more familiar version of the story and presumably originated in one of the Bedouin tribes in Jordan.[11] Ḥalaf is described as a famous tribal leader who used to go on raids robbing other tribes. In one of these raids on a southern tribe, he arrives at the *maḍāfa* (guests' tent) of the attacked tribe. The chief's daughter scolds him for daring to rob the hospitality tent. Ḥalaf is hurt by her words but is impressed by her beauty and her cleverness, and he stops his men from looting the tent. The girl is impressed by his manners and his ability to control his men and falls in love with him, and he, too, falls in love with her. One day he wears the best of his clothes, but he wears a servant's clothes over them, blackens his face with soot, and reaches the tent of his enemy, the girl's father.

Peeping out of the women's section, the girl recognizes him immediately. The host, in contrast to what is customary, asks his guest to identify himself, on the pretext that it is wartime and no one can be trusted. The girl, who fears for her lover's fate if his identity is revealed, turns to her father and says to him, "Father, we are ashamed to ask the guest his name. Don't you see that this is a slave of the masters' slaves?" When he hears the words, anger rises in Ḥalaf's heart. He takes off his wretched clothes, rinses his face, and turning to the girl, who is behind the curtain in the women's section, he says to her in poetic verse:

> Have fear of Allah, Oh daughter of love,
> While saying: 'this is a slave of the masters' slaves.'
> I am Allah's slave, not a slave of people,
> I'm Ḥalaf, I will not hide my face.

Right afterward, he turns to the audience and informs them that he has not come as an enemy but as someone who seeks their relationship by marriage. In the course of his speech, an alarm is sounded: enemies are raiding the tribe from the north. Ḥalaf turns to the sheikh with a well-known saying—"My brother and I against my cousin, and I and my cousin against the stranger" (*'ana w-'axūy 'ala ibn 'ammi, u-'ana u-ibn 'ammi 'ala l-ġarīb*)—and offers his help in destroying the enemy. The meaning of the proverb is that internal rivalry is extinguished when there is a need to join forces and fight a common enemy. After the battle, which ends with the victory of Ḥalaf and the sheikh and the restoring of the stolen property, the sheikh marries his daughter to Ḥalaf.

This version has recently been produced in a television series made for the month of Ramadan by a film company in one of the Gulf States. Ḥalaf is known as a thirteenth-century Bedouin hero. Ido Cohen of Yavneh gave me another version of the story, told by Abdo Mūsa (1927–77), a famous Gypsy narrator and *rabāba* player in Jordan. In the *qaṣīda* included in his version, the singer compares the white color of his beloved's teeth to sweet sugar and silver coins and her forehead to the luster of the moon.

Some of the motifs contained in these formulas seem to have been incorporated into the Bedouin story as told by Ṯalǧe Mūsa: the romantic encounter, the impersonation of a black slave, the hero's assistance to the sheikh during the battle, the return of the stolen property, and the marriage of the hero and his beloved. In addition, a short *qaṣīda*, close in its spirit to the *qaṣīda* of Ḥalaf, appears here: a turning to the lover, a description of her beauty, and a denial of his inferior origin.

The second version, "The Sheikh Maslaṭ el-Ğarba," which appears in the same book, describes the Ḥweiṭāt tribes and their neighbors, Bedouin tribes from Jordan.[12] The sheikh Maslaṭ el-Ğarba raids a neighboring tribe. In his absence, members of the tribe expel a guest who has arrived at the sheikh's tent. On his return, the sheikh cuts off the heads of the three men who expelled his guest and goes into exile. He finds shelter in the tent camp of Waṭbān ad-Dawiš. One day, Waṭbān ad-Dawiš, the sheikh of that place sets out on a robbery raid. Maslaṭ el-Ğarba, who found refuge in his home and did not tell his name to his host, accompanies him on the robbery. Waṭbān ad-Dawiš's daughter, who does not know who Maslaṭ el-Ğarba is, mocks him by thinking him a simple man. He does not respond to her mockery, but one night he sneaks into her tent, touches her with his staff, and wakes her. The girl recognizes him and says, "You are our new neighbor. Leave immediately, lest you be crushed to pieces." The next day footprints leading to the girl's tent are revealed. Her father, who suspects her of adultery with a strange man, commands she be sold as a slave. The sheikh Maslaṭ el-Ğarba asks to buy her. The two members of the tribe who were ordered to sell the girl insult him: "This is not for men like you, o dog!" Maslaṭ el-Ğarba pulls out his sword, kills both of them, puts the girl on his horse, and flees for shelter with a neighboring tribe. It turns out that the sheikh with whom he found shelter is the girl's cousin and fiancé, but the latter gives him shelter and does not let the pursuers hurt him. One day, the chief of the tribe leaves with Waṭbān ad-Dawiš on a robbery raid. Unaware of this, the sheikh Maslaṭ remains in the encampment. Meanwhile, in the absence of the tribe's fighters, enemies come and steal the tribe's flocks and horses. The girl comes out of the tent, stares at the sheikh, and says nothing. The sheikh tells her, "Girl, untie my horse." He mounts his mare, pursues the enemies, attacks them, manages to retrieve the lost herds, and even takes the mares and weapons of the attackers. He brings the flocks back to their owners. He takes the loot—the enemies' mares and their weapons—and divides it into two: half of the horses he ties to Waṭbān's tent and the other half near the tent of the girl's uncle. When the fighters return from the robbery and discover what has happened, Waṭbān, the girl's father and her cousin, the man who gave him shelter, decide to hand the girl over to Maslaṭ, and he marries her.

This seems to be one of the stories about the Bedouin poet and fighter Ğalʿūd ibn Haḏāl and his love affair with a woman from an opponent tribe, the ʿArab el-Ğarba tribe. In this version, we find other elements that appear in Ṯalğe Mūsa's story, such as the hero's departure for battle in the absence of the tribesmen, his success in returning the stolen property, and his scorn for his enemies' mares and their weapons. In this case, the young woman encourages the protagonist to go into battle not through words but through a merely hinting gaze.

Another version of the story is presented in Mordekhai Yanai's book *Why Did the Earth Laugh? Bedouins Narrate*.[13] The story is named after the heroine Ḏuwāba (hair plait). In this version, the sheikh's son falls in love with a girl who asks him to draw water from a well for her. He asks her for her name, but she only waves one of her hair plaits and goes away. The sheikh's son searches for her and eventually finds her in the ʿAzana tribe. It turns out that she is the tribe sheikh's daughter. The hero disguises himself and offers his service as a *ḥaššāš* (a man who cuts grass for cattle). When the sheikh is not present, he removes his disguise; pours himself a cup of coffee from the sheikh's pitcher (which is permissible only for the sheikh himself and his coffee server); takes the *rabāba*, the Bedouin violin; and sings a song to the sheikh's daughter, who is listening to him behind the tent cloth:

Woe to me, said *el-ḥaššāš* at the end of the night,
My life has passed, and what else will happen to me?
How beautiful were the days when people sat together
And set fire with the camels' dung,
The camels whose reins are yellow, red, and black.
The camels who lie down in El-Dakta and grow up in El-Tash.
Even the flies did not approach the *'ūd* [oud] musicians,
And did not violate the joy.

Upon the sheikh's return, his daughter tells him about the deeds of the *ḥaššāš*. The sheikh's bodyguard pulls out his sword and waits for a sign from his master to hit the young man, but the sheikh ponders the young man's singing and understands that something else is hidden behind his arrogant behavior. He invites him to tell his story. When he finds out that the young man's origins are noble and that he wants to marry his daughter, he calls his daughter and, after he receives her consent, marries her to the sheikh's son.

In this version the coffee server also appears, not as the hero but as one of the sheikh's people.

A similar story is found in Jihād Aḥmad Dakkur's book *Galilee Stories* (ḥakāya el-ğalīl دكور، جهاد أحمد).[14] This story brings together elements from the story of Ḥalaf and the story of the *ḥaššāš* quoted above.

Ṯalğe Mūsa's story thus derives its materials from many versions that have been told throughout the entire area. Their roots are as early as the thirteenth century, but to these roots are added characteristics typical of Bedouin tales, such as unusual physical strength and bloody handprints that mark the hiding place.

Notes

1. *eš-šābb, ya'ani, biḥibbha, widdu iyyāha, widdu iyyāha, ya'ani, bint ḥalāl, miš ġaṣbin 'anha. hī bitḥibbu, bas abūha bidduš*: "The boy, that is, he loved her, he wanted her is, wanted her, that is, a decent girl, not forcing her. She loves him, but her father does not want." This is the core of love stories around the world: A boy loves a girl; she loves him; but her father does not allow their union. The narrator stresses that the boy wants a legitimate relationship, without forcing her—this attitude may reflect a modern viewpoint in the Galilee Bedouin community.

2. *lā fī byūt, wa-lā fī 'arab*: "There were neither tents nor Bedouins." Normally a nominal negation is expressed in these Bedouin dialects by the negative particle *mā/mū*. In double negation ("neither *A* nor *B*"), the negative word *lā* is used (*lā* usually negates imperative verbs or answers a yes-no question). The narrator could have used the structure *mā bī . . . wa-lā bī*, too. In addition, note the sedentary word form *fī* instead of Bedouin *bī/bū* (cf. chap. 4, note 1).

3. *qāl-la, "di n'ēt," qāl-la "hū lli-biddha nī'a*: "He said to her [to himself], 'Well, I've gone far.' He said [to himself], 'This distance is what this [search] requires.'" The narrator expresses the wanderer's thoughts. *di* is a discourse marker, an exclamation, similar to English *well*. (Cf. Barthélemy, *Dictionnaire arabe-français*, 260.) The verb *n'ēt* and its verbal noun *nī'a* refer to the distance of the journey which he had to undertake to find the girl.

4. The poetry lines are probably only a part of a longer poem (*qaṣīda*). They follow the structure of traditional Bedouin poetry (cf. Sowayan, *Nabati Poetry*; Henkin, *Negev Arabic*). Such poems use vocabulary that does not belong to the everyday Bedouin speech and is passed on orally from one narrator to another among tribes and generations. The texts undergo many changes over the years, and at present the poets/narrators do not always know the exact meaning of the words. Here, too, one of the lines is repeated with some changes, and the syntactic structure is not entirely clear.

5. *qa'ad 'endhen hā-(z)-z'ēne*: "This vagabond stayed with her." In Arabic, verbs of movement take not only a basic, literal meaning (e.g., *qa'ad*, "to sit down") but also an abstract meaning (e.g., *qa'ad*, "stayed in a place for a prolonged time," also "he was awake/woke up"; cf. chap. 10, story 10b). Cf. *qām*, "get up, stand up" and "begin to do something."

6. The word *z'ēne* also exists in other dialects and Literary Arabic. *z'ēne* is derived from the root *ḏ'n*, "move, go away, leave." This meaning has also developed to include camels' trekking, sheep's roaming, and humans' wandering about. Cf. the adjective *wanderer*, which is *za'īn* in, for example, Negev Bedouin Arabic (cf. Shawarbah, *Grammar of Negev Arabic*, 380). The pattern *z'ēne* could be a diminutive feminine form of the latter, although the meaning of the word in this context is not diminutive. (In MSA, *ḏa'īna* is a woman traveling on a camel sedan; cf. Wehr, *Dictionary of Modern Written Arabic*, 581.) Apparently, the exact meaning of this word is not entirely clear to the narrator.

7. *bōš* in Bedouin dialects refers to small animals such as sheep, which Bedouins used to keep. Barthélemy, *Dictionnaire arabe-français*, 62. (In MSA, the noun *bawš*, pl. *awbāš*, means "mob, rabble"; cf. Wehr, *Dictionary of Modern Written Arabic*, 82.) *ṭarš* in these folktales means a herd of sheep, cattle. The word *ṭarš* is characteristic of Syrian dialects groups, including Galilee Bedouin ones (cf. Barthélemy, *Dictionnaire arabe-français*, 69, 475).

8. *faz'at hā-n-nās*: "The people gathered." *faza'* means "be alarmed, fear" in LA and MSA. Wehr, *Dictionary of Modern Written Arabic*, 711. In the Galilee Bedouin dialects, it means "get excited, be alarmed, be shocked," as well as "call for help" and "come to help." That is to say, when learning about some danger or a shocking event in the community (the tribe), all the people (the men) are summoned for help. Note that the verb for a (singular) group is in the s.f. person. This feature is known from Classical Arabic times and is still found to some extent in various dialects.

9. Ashkenazi, *Bedouins in the Land of Israel*, 144.
10. Ashkenazi, 67.
11. Bar-Zvi, *Fable, Story and Legend in Arab Tents*, 21–22.
12. Bar-Zvi, 15–17.
13. Yanai, *Why Did the Earth Laugh? Bedouins Narrate*, 143–47.
14. Dakkur, *Galilee Stories*, 287.

12. The Old Man and the Girl, the Old Woman and the Young Man

NARRATOR: ʿĒide Xalīl Mrisāt

TRIBE: *ʿArab el-Mrēsāt*

IFA 17417 August 7, 1983

1 marra kān wāḥad[1] māriǧ[2] min balad. uhū nāfid, šāf wāḥad xityār māxeḏ bint ṣabiyya; hū xityār, ʿağūz, hi ṣabiyye bint ʿešrīn. u-šāf wāḥad . . . šāf wiḥda ʿağūz māxḏa kamān šābb iben ʿešrīn. u-lamma šāf inno yegūl "ye ʿōnt-aḷḷa, šlōn xityār māxeḏ ṣabiyye bint ʿešrīn, u-xityāra māxḏa šābb iben ʿešrīn." ā, winno yegūl, "šlōn hāḏa, yā ʿōnt-aḷḷa, šlōn hāḏa ṭayyib, tamm?"[3]	1 Once there was one passing through a village. As he was going out, he saw an old man having taken a young girl [in marriage]. He was an old man, she—a girl of twenty. And he saw one . . . he saw an old woman having taken a young man, of twenty. And when he saw [this] (lo) he says, "How is this, o, Allah's help, how has an old man taken a girl of twenty, and a married old woman having taken a young man of twenty?" Yes, and he says, "How has this, well, come about?"
11 gām ğē b-el-lēl u-humma nāimīn. šāl aṣ-ṣabiyye men ʿind es-šābb . . . e . . . šāl aṣ-ṣabiyye men ʿind el-xityār u-ḥaṭṭa ʿind aš-šābb. u-šāl al-xetyāra men ʿind as-šābb u ḥaṭṭa ʿind el-xityār.	11 He went in the night, when they were sleeping, took the girl from the young man . . . took the girl from the old man and put her at the young man's [place]. He took the old woman from the young man and put her at the old man's [place].
16 'aṣ-ṣubḥ, ḥass aš-šābb daḥḥag ᵉbḥadde, liga ha-ṣ-ṣabiyye. lamma šāf inno l-xityāra ḥawwalat ṣabiyye enbaṣaṭ u-kayyaf. ğa, yaʿani ittafag hū wiyyāha u-ʿāšam ʿāyše[4] saʿīde.	16 In the morning, this young man looked next to him, he found this young girl. When he saw that the old woman had become a young girl, he was happy and glad, that is, he and the girl agreed [between themselves] and they lived a happy life.

21 u-lamma fattaḥ al-xetyār aṣ-ṣobḥ, lige al-xetyāra w-ygūl, "yā ʿōnt aḷḷa,	21 And when the old man woke up in the morning, he found the old woman and said, "O, Gold's help,
23 mīn ǧāb li ha-l-xityāra l-mhabūle?" kamān hī daḥḥagat tgūl-lo "minnēn ǧīt inte? ?aḷḷa yāxḏak." u-hī tgul-lo "mnēn ǧīt inta" u-hū ygūl-la "mnēn ǧīti inti?"	23 who brought me this crazy old woman?" She, too, looked and said to him, "Where did you come from? May Allah take you!" She says to him, "Where did you come from?" and he says, "Where did you come from?"
27 u-gāmat titwallaʿ aṭ-ṭōše bēnhom xaḏōhom ʿal-ʿaṣfuriyye, u-šallaḥum baʿaḏhum, mātam. wa-š-šābb wa-š-šābba ʿāšam ʿīše saʿīde u-haniyye.	27 There began a quarrel between them, they took them to prison, they quarreled and beat each other [with some weapon], and died. And the young man and the young woman lived a happy and good life.

Commentary

This short story can be attributed to the tales-of-fate group (ATU 930–949). Like the story of the king's daughter imprisoned in the tower, in which the king tries to change the fate of his daughter, the hero in this story seeks to change the fate of two couples. Although the task does succeed, the results for one of the couples are disastrous.

In the ancient Jewish Midrash Bereshit (Genesis) Rabba, there is an amusing story in which a Roman lady asks Rabbi Yose (Jose) Ben Halafta (second century CE) various questions about God's actions. Among other things, she asks him what God has been dealing with since he completed the creation of the world. Rabbi Yose replies, "Matching couples for marriage: the daughter of one person to another, the wife of one person and another." The Roman lady wonders at this, "Is this the art of God? Even I can do that."

Here is the story:

> She asked R. Yosi, "In how many days did God create the world?" "In six," he answered. "And since then," she asked, "what has God been doing?" "Matching couples for marriage: the daughter of one person to another, the wife of one person and another," responded R. Yosi. "Is this the art of God?" she said dismissively. "Even I can do that. I have many slaves, both male and female. In no time at all, I can match them for marriage." To which R. Yose countered, "Though this may be an easy thing for you to do, for God it is as difficult as splitting the Red Sea."
>
> Whereupon, he took his leave. The next day she lined up a thousand male and a thousand female slaves and said, "This slave would marry that handmaid and this handmaid would marry that slave." She paired them off in one night. The morning after, her estate resembled a battlefield. One slave had his head bashed in, another had lost an eye, while a third hobbled because of a broken leg. No one seemed to want his or her assigned mate. She asked them, "What happened to you?" This one said, "I don't want her!" and that one said, "I don't want him!" Quickly, she summoned R. Yose and acknowledged. "Your God is unique, and your Torah is true, pleasing and praiseworthy. You spoke wisely." (Bereshit Rabba 68, 4)

As in the Bedouin story, the lady's experience of pairing couples leads to disastrous consequences. Both stories reflect the belief that marriage is determined by God and that man cannot intervene in his actions. God decrees the fate of his creatures. Attempts to correct God's actions violate the natural order of the world. In the Bedouin story, human intervention is beneficial to one of the couples, and the couple, as the Midrash says, "broke into song"—that is, lived in harmony—but at the same time the intervention causes the death of the other couple.

It is also possible to relate to the story as social criticism of a phenomenon in the Bedouin society of marrying a young bride to an old man because of financial considerations while ignoring the girl's wishes.

On one of my visits to Mūsa Diab, a Bedouin tracker from the ʿArab el-Ḥuğērāt tribe, who set up his tent not far from Yodfat, I heard from him a story that illuminated the previous story from a slightly different angle. The story was told in Hebrew, and at the time I did not have a sound recorder. Here is the story as I wrote it down a few days after he had told it to me:

> There was once an old man who wanted to remarry after his wife's death. His big son heard this and wanted to make his father content. He went and bought, as was the custom of those days, a young bride and married her to his old father.
>
> A day came and a day went by, and the old man died, and the young widow returned to her parents' house and soon married another husband and went with him to his place of residence. It was not long before the woman brought a son into the world. The son grew up and went out to graze the flocks together with his fellow boys.
>
> One day they went out to draw water from the well. This well was deep, and they used each time to lower one of them into the well to draw water for the rest.
>
> They lowered the boy down into the well, and a stone fell on his head and he fell into the well, like Yusuf (Joseph) our prophet.
>
> When he fell, he cried out in fear, "Oh, my brother, my brother!"
>
> By Allah's will, at that time the eldest son of that old man [the woman's first husband] passed by. He heard his cries and pulled him out of the well. He looked at him and saw that he resembled him in his features. He said to himself: Maybe this is really my brother?
>
> He brought him to his parents' house and met the boy's mother, the woman whom he had married to his old father.
>
> He said to them, "Your son is my brother. I want to take him with me."
>
> The husband said to him, "No, he is not your father's son, he is my son!"
>
> He told them: "Let us go to the sheikh and he will decide on our case." In those days, the sheikh was a judge and arbitrator in all matters of the tribe.
>
> The sheikh listened to their claims and said to them, "Leave the boy in my hands, and tomorrow I will inform you of my trial."
>
> The sheikh summoned the boy and said to him, "I want you to sneak into someone's pen tonight and steal a lamb from there and bring it to me without anyone watching you."
>
> He said to him, "Yes, sir."
>
> The boy went in the middle of the night, sneaked into the pen, took out a lamb, and brought it to the sheikh without anyone observing his actions.
>
> The next day the owner of the herd awoke and discovered the theft. The shepherd followed the footprints and discovered that they led to the sheikh's tent.

He came before the sheikh and said to him, "So-and-so happened to me: A lamb was stolen from my herd. I followed the thief, and the footprints led to your tent. Would you give your protection to thieves?" The sheikh said to him: "And the thief, how is he?"

He said to him, "Sir, whoever took the lamb from my flock came from an old back and a young belly."

He said to him, "Why, oh, so-and-so?"

The shepherd replied, "I followed him, and saw that the footprints are changing; sometimes he steps on the heel first like the elders, and sometimes on the toes like the young."

The sheikh said to him, "Allah with you, here is the lamb, take it and go back to your house in peace."

The sheikh turned to the people standing in front of him and said to them, "Your ears hear, this boy comes from an old back and a young belly, and he is really his brother, his father's son!"

The eldest son gave his protection to his brother and took him to his home.

The same story with very slight differences appears in Rosenhouse's paper "An Arabic Story and Its Linguistic Analysis."[5]

In this story, the subject of marriage between an old man and a young woman emerges between the lines. There is no attempt to criticize the marriage. The narrator includes it as a fact, and, indirectly, the story reflects the legitimacy that Bedouin society has given to this kind of marriage. As is customary in patriarchal societies, the woman is perceived as property, and the son acquires her with cash as a gesture to his old father. On the other hand, when the question of the son's origins arises, the matter is brought before the sheikh for a legal hearing. The older brother fought the new husband for his right to adopt the boy. The woman's opinion about the identity of her son is ignored.

Notes

1. Like many other stories in this book, this story refers to unnamed protagonists. There is "someone" who causes the events that occur to the other protagonists in the story. This person is neither Allah (he does not foresee the results) nor a human (he has immense magical power). This feature of the Arabic Bedouin stories gives the listener a picture without irrelevant details that do not interest the narrator.

2. The word *māriǧ*, "passing by," can also be pronounced *mārig*. The affricate consonant is due to the high vowel *i* preceding the voiced stop *g* (< an unvoiced *q*). In many Bedouin dialects, including the Galilee, the reflex of *q* can be *g*, *ǧ*, or even *q* (the latter reflects the LA/MSA system; cf. Rosenhouse, *Bedouin Arabic Dialects*, 62–63). In other Bedouin dialects (e.g., the Negev, Israel), *q* is pronounced only as *g*, and in others, in the Arabian Peninsula, it can be *ǧ*, *d^y^*, or *ž*. Some of the dialects use only one form of the consonant (*g* or *ǧ*), while others use phonetically conditioned allophones as found in this Galilean story. Such allophones may indicate a transitional stage of the dialect speakers, while some other dialects use only the affricate allophone *ǧ*. Generally, Arabic dialects tend to mix all available allophones due to interdialectal and bilingual contacts and communication options. Note this feature also in the other folktales in this volume.

3. *šlōn hāḏa, ṭayyib, tamm?*: "How has this, well, come about?' *tamm* is a verb meaning "to end, finish, complete, come about." Here the narrator asks how this situation happened. In the spontaneous speech of the narrators, articulation, word order, and word form do not

always keep the expected sequence or speech rhythm. Here the word *tayyib* (a hedging expression) appears between the subject (*hāḏa*) and the predicate (or verb, *tamm*). We present the narrators' actual text, without correcting it (except in the English translation).

4. *u-'āšam 'ayše sa'īde*: "And they lived a happy life." The syntactic feature cognate/absolute accusative (e.g., "to live a life," "to dream a dream") occurs at the end of the story, using the verbal noun *'ayše* for the structure. The word *'ayše*, "living, life," is pronounced at the end of the story with word-final *ʒimāla*, as sedentary speakers might pronounce it (cf. MSA *'īša*; Wehr, *Dictionary of Modern Written Arabic*, 662; the section "Diverse Criteria for the Classification of Arabic Dialects and Bedouin Dialects" in the chapter on Bedouin Arabic dialects at the end of this book).

5. Rosenhouse, "Arabic Story and Its Linguistic Analysis," 62–83. A different analysis of the same story appears in Rosenhouse, "Whose Child Is He?" That narrator was Abu Ibrahim from the *'Arab el-Ġrifāt* tribe (Beit Zarzīr).

13. The Girl and Her Brother Who Became a Deer

NARRATOR: Ṯalǧe Mūsa

TRIBE: *'Arab el-Ḥuǧērāt*

IFA 15232 February 5, 1982

1 bī hanāk hā-l-ʿarab, hāy al-'amīr, ʿindo hā-l-walad u-hā-l-bint. mātat 'ummhen. ḍaḷḷat—'aǧa, ǧawwaz 'abūha, 'abūhin tǧawwaz, 'abu hā-l-iwlād.[1] yōm, mart 'abūhen, šū biddha tsāwi bihin? tuṭrudhen.[2]	1 There is that Bedouin tribe, this emīr, he has a son and a daughter. Their mother died. There remained. . . . He went, her father married—their father married, the children's father. One day, their father's wife, what does she want to do with them? To drive them away.
7 xaḷḷathin tann hinne nāimīn, u-gāḷat la-l-ʿarab, "yā mā-nḥīl, yā l-ʿarab." raḥlat al-ʿarab kullayātha, ḥammalat ʿala ha-ǧ-ǧmāl u-raḥlat al-ʿarab kulla. w-al-uwlād ḍaḷḷu nāimīn, al-walad w-al-bint. hāḏ mā gāmum ba-l-lēl.	7 She left them alone until they were asleep and said to the Bedouins, "O, we're roaming, o Bedouins." The Bedouins went away, all of them, loaded on the camels and all the Bedouins went off, and the children remained asleep, the boy and the girl. This, they did not get up in the night.
13 'aṣ-ṣubḥ[3] gāmum ha-l-uwlād, fišš ʿarab, fišš 'iši ṣafanu gaʿadam. yōmin ʾgʿadam šū gāḷat-lo? gāḷat-lo, "yā xūya, wēn widdna rrūḥ?" gāḷ-ḷa, "yā xayya, widdna nugḏub hā-d-darb u-nimši."	13 [In] the morning, these children got up—no Bedouins, nothing. They froze in their place thinking, and remained sitting [for a while]. When they were sitting, what did she say to him? She said to him, "O my brother, where shall we go?" He said to her, "O my sister, we will take this road and go."
18 u-humma māšīn ba-d-darb, mātam min aǧ-ǧūʿ w-al-ʿaṭaš. māšīn, ǧam[4] ʿala hā-l-ḥarrāṯ.[5]	18 As they were walking along the way, they died of hunger and thirst. Walking, they came to a plowman.

21 gāḷu-lo, "yā ʿammi, mā mʿāk lugmat xubz?" gāḷ-ḷhin "ᵉmbaḷa," yeḥaruṯ,[6] ḥarrāṯ. ʾanṭāhin šaqfat xubz, rġīf xubz. kalō.	21 They said to him, "O uncle, haven't you got a piece of bread?" He said to them, "Certainly." He was plowing, a plowman. He gave them a slice of bread, a bread loaf. They ate it.
25 widdhin yišrabu. ğamma ʿa-l-ḥarrāṯ aṯ-ṯāni. gāḷ-ḷo, "ʾamma mā mʿāk mayy?" gāḷ-ḷhin, "lā, waḷḷa, yā ʿammi."[7] ʿala-aṯ-ṯāliṯ, gāḷu-ḷo, gāḷ-ḷo "lā, waḷḷa, giddāmak al-ʿēn, giddāmak."	25 They wanted to drink. They came to the second plowman and said to him, "Don't you have water with you?" He said to them, "No, by Allah, my boy." [They met] the third one, they said to him, he said to him [to the boy], "No, by Allah. Further on there is a spring, further on."
30 ʾağa ʿa hā-l-ḥarrāṯ, wāğib, gāḷ-ḷhā, "guddāmač[8] al-ʿēn, bas alli yišrab min al-ʿēn, bū sabeʿ ʿyūn. all-yišrab min al-ʿēn, ʿēn al-ġuzlān, yeṣīr ġazāl. w-alli yišrab mayyt ʿēn al-ḥamīr yeṣīr ᵉḥmār, w-alli yišrab mayyt ʿēn al-ğmāl, yeṣīr ğimal. u-man ʿēn a. aḏ-ḏīb, min ʿēn al-waḥaš, min ha-l-ʿuyūn, kulla al-ʿuyūn, kull wāḥad ilu ʿēn." "wēn al-ʿēn alli nišrab minna?" gāḷ, "ğiddām, ğiddām, išrabu."	30 He came to the plowman, and this one said, "In front of you there is the spring, but he who drinks from the spring—there are seven springs. He who drinks from the spring, the deer spring, becomes a deer. He who drinks water from the donkeys' spring, becomes a donkey, and he who drinks the water of the camels' spring, becomes a camel, and from the spring of wolves, and from the wild animals', from these springs, all these springs, each [animal] has a spring." "Where is the spring from which we can drink?" He said, "In front [of you], further forward; drink."
41 haḏōla, mn-al-ʿaṭaš, al-walad, ʾaxūha, mn-al-ʿaṭaš, gad-ma mayyit min al-ʿaṭaš,	41 Those (children), due to their thirst—the boy, her brother, due to the thirst, being dead from how thirsty he was,
43 ʾawwal mā ġabb min (b)taʿat al-ġuzlān, min-ʿēn al-ġuzlān hu-šireb.	43 he gobbled first from that of the deer. He drank from the spring of the deer.
45 mā xallaṣ šireb, walla hu ġazāl. gāḷat-ḷo, "yā-axuy, še-widdak asāwi bak?" gāḷ, "ʾani ʿāref, yā-xti?" yunṭuq, bas hū ġazāl.	45 He just finished drinking, and lo, he was a deer. She said to him, "O my brother, what shall I do with you?" He said, "What do I know, sister?" He speaks but he is a deer.
48 mišyat hī wiyyā. mišyat, mišyat, mišyat, ağum, ğam ʿala hā-l-ʿarab. ʿal-hā-l-ʿarab, naṣṣo hā-l-bēt, bēt al-ʾamīr. ʾakbar bēt bi-hā-l-ʿarab—bēt al-ʾamīr, ʾakbar bēt.	48 She went with him, went, went, went, they came to those Bedouins. To those Bedouins [their area]. He put it up, this tent, the emīr's tent [house]. The biggest house in this Bedouin tribe [was]—the emīr's house. The biggest house.

53 ʾağum ʿala hā-l bēt. ʿawāyid al-ʿarab mā yisʾalūn, yaʿani, as-sāyir alla baʿad talatt-iyyām. bēš rāyeḥ u-b-ēš ğāy. baʿad hā-t-talatt-iyyām gāḷ la-marto, al-ʾamīr mā ʿindūš wlād. mā ʿandu wlād šēle.

53 They came to this house. Bedouin habits are that they do not ask any passer-by [anything] but only after three days. What he was going for and why he was coming. After these three days, he said to his wife, the emīr did not have children. [He] did not have any children at all.

58 gāḷ-ḷha," ʾasʾalīha, hī ḥurma, mā titğawwaz?" ʾasʾalatha, gāḷat-ḷa, "mā tizawwağīn?" gāḷat-ela "waḷḷa, ağ-ğōz sitra.[9] ʾamma ʾana, lli widdi ʾāxḏo, ʾašarreṭ ʿalē šarṭ."

58 He said to her, "Ask her, she is a woman, does she not [want to] marry?" She asked her, said to her, "Will you not marry?" She said to her, "By Allah, a husband is security. But I, the one I will take [marry] I have a condition for it [on him]."

63 gāḷ-ḷha, "šū aš-šarṭ?" gāḷat-ḷo, "(y)dīr bālo ʿala ʾaxūya. ʾaxūya maskīn, widdi (y)iḍaḷḷ ʿindi. ʾalli (y)idīr bālo ʿala axūya, ʾāxḏo."

63 She said to her, "What is the condition?" She said to him [her], "[That] he will look after my brother. My brother is poor, I want him to stay with me. He who will take care of my brother, I'll take him [for husband]."

67 gāl al-ʾamīr, "ʾāxuḏha, lēš lā." ʿizam al-ʿarab u-sinnt aḷḷa wa-rasūlo, u-tizawwağ hāḏ-al-bint. ḍaḷḷ axūha b-ḥaddhin.

67 The emīr said, "I'll take her, why not." He invited the Bedouins and [according to] Allah's decrees and his Prophet, and he married this girl. Her brother remained [near] them.

71 yōm min al-iyyām, gāḷat al-ʿarab "ağa mōsam al-ḥağğ." ʾal-amīr gāḷ, "widdna nerū(ḥ)-ʿa-l-ḥağğ." gabuḷ kānum yerūḥūn ʿa-ğmāl, yirkabūn ʿağ-ğmāl[10] wi-(y)rūḥūn. gaddēš yuguʿdūn? sitt-ᵘšhur.

71 One day, the Bedouins said, "It is the pilgrimage season." The emīr said, "We want to go to the pilgrimage." In the past they used to go on camels, ride camels and go. How much would they stay? Six months.

76 hū "mara ʾani-igūm ʾani rāyi(ḥ)" gāḷ, "ʾani awaddiʿ marati." šū daššar marato? daššarha ḥuble. ʾuxt al-walad ḥiblat.

76 He [said], "Woman, I'll get up and I go." He said, "I'll part with my wife." How did he leave his wife? He left her pregnant. The boy's sister got pregnant.

79 gāḷ-ḷa, "baḷḷa, yā mara, dīri bāleč hīn ʿalēha, ʿala hā-l-fagīra, hīyye—dīri baleč ʿalēha, taṭʿamīnha u-tizgīnha u-in ğābat diīri bāleč ʿalēhum."

79 He said to her, "By Allah, wife, look after her here, the poor one, she—look after her, feed her and make her drink, and if she gives birth, look after them."

83 gāḷat-lo, "ʾanta twaṣṣīni yā-(a)mīr? ʾana ʾadīr bāli ʾakṯar min al-lāzim ʿalēha." gāḷ-ḷa, "ṭayyeb."

83 She said to him, "Are you giving me orders [telling me what to do], oh, emīr? I'll look after her more than necessary." He said to her, "Good."

86 siḥab ḥālo[11] hā-l-ʾamīr, ḥaṭṭ ʿala hā-ğ-ğimal, umaʿā hā-n-nās, ʿala l-ḥağğ, u-miša ʿa-l-ḥağğ. hū miša ʿa-l-ḥağğ, šharēn-talāṯa, ʾaḷḷāhu ʾaʿlam.

86 He went off, this emīr, loaded on the camel and with him [were] these men, to the pilgrimage and went to the pilgrimage. He went to the pilgrimage two months, three—Allah knows.

90 'al-mara gʿadat[12] . . . ǧa šaharha, yaʿani ǧa waqt tabaʿa ǧābet. ḍarritha, ʿārfa bū bīr hīn, ʿārfa b-hāḍa l-maḥall bū bīr.

94 gāḷat ilha, "yā ḍurrti, widdna nenaggl-al-bēt[13] bāker ^{i}tǧībīn,[14] u-yrawweḥ al-'amīr. hāḍa l-bēt barḍo mū zēn. widdna nungul al-bēt, widdna nungul al-bēt—dār zēn, dār zēna, mišān yīǧi l-'amīr u-tsallem ʿalē an-nās, min al-ḥaǧǧ."

100 (gāḷat-lo) gāḷat-ilha "ṭayyeb." haḏīč siḥbat ḥālha, haḏīč mā tiʿraf bū bīr b-hāḏa l-maḥall. ǧābat ḥaṣīra, min hā-š-šikel, ġaṭṭat bāb al-bīr b-ḥaṣīre u-riḥlam.

104 'al-bēt—čam wāḥad? hāḏi wiḥda, ṯintēn, ṯalāṯe, yaʿani ṯalāṯ maḥallāt al-bēt, ṯalāṯ ʿumdān. gāḷat-ilha "ṭayyeb." saḥbat ḥālha u-ḥaṭṭatu.

108 ṣārat al-mara ^{a}tgāsi, widdha tǧīb, gāḷat-ilha, "ḥabībti, mā widdeč ^{i}tǧībīn hīn, biddek ^{i}tǧībi b-il-'ōḍa hān,[15] b-il-maḥall hāḏ, bi-l-bēt hīn. hīn adfā-leč u-aḥsan-leč u-ʿādlič nār." gāḷat-ilha "ṭayyeb."

114 ḥaṭṭatha ʿala l-ḥaṣīre ʿa-bāb al-bīr, ḥaṭṭatha u-gaʿʿadatha.

116 haftat al-ḥaṣīre b-galb al-bīr, wagʿat b-al-bīr. yōm wagʿat b-al-bīr, ġaṭṭato, al-bīr, ḥaṭṭat ʿalē ḥadīda u-ġaṭṭato u-rāḥḥalat al-bēt, ʿawd raǧǧaʿato 'abel ma čān.

120 'al-mara ǧābat, šū ǧābat? ǧābat walad. 'axūha šāyifhe yōminha dabbat b-al-bīr. dabbatha b-al-bīr, ḥaṭṭatha b-al-bīr. ṣār 'axūha yerūḥ la-ʿindha, sār yerū(ḥ) ʿala l-ʿarab yišḥad, ṣār yišḥad ʿind al-ʿarab akel u-yerūḥ yewaddi l-uxto l-al-bīr.

90 The woman remained. Her month [time] came, that is, the time of her giving birth came. Her fellow wife knew that there was here a pit.

94 She said to her, "Oh, my fellow-wife, we will move the tent. Tomorrow [soon] you will have a child, and the emīr will come back home. This tent is also not good. We will move the tent, [to] a good house, good house, so that [when] the emīr comes, and the people will [come to] greet him, [after his return] from the pilgrimage."

100 She said to her, "All right." That one [co-wife] went [away], she [the girl] did not know that there was a pit at that place. She brought that straw mat, of this kind, covered the opening of the pit with the mat and they moved.

104 A tent—how many [rooms in it]? This is one, two, three, that is, three spaces [rooms] in the tent, three stick-poles [hold them]. She said to her, "All right." She went and put it.

108 The woman began to be in labor, she had to give birth. She said to her, "My dear, you would not want to give birth here, you need to give birth in this room here, in this place, in this room. Here it is warmer for you and better for you and there you will have fire [to keep you warm]." She said to her, "All right."

114 She put her on the mat at the opening of the pit, put her and made her sit down.

116 The mat fell inside the pit, and she fell in the pit. When she fell into the pit, she covered it, put on it an iron [cover], covered it and took the tent, took it back to the place [where it had been] before.

120 The woman gave birth. What did she have? She had a boy. Her brother saw her when she fell, she threw her to the pit, put her in the pit. Her brother began going to her, he began going to the Bedouins, going begging for food, he began asking for food, and would go and bring, for his sister, to the pit.

127 šū ygūl-la? ygūḷ-ḷa, "'axūč al-maskīn, saḥabū ʿala s-sakkīn, ʿa-drūb aṣ-ṣalāṭīn." yaʿani, l-ġawwāya, wāḥad ⁱmʿā barūda yšūf hā-l-ġazāl widdo ygawwṣo. kān yinhazim. yiṣīr ygūḷ "'axūč al-maskīn, yaʿani w-ana rāyiḥ ğāy ʿalēč, 'axūč al-maskīn, saḥabū ʿala sakkīn," yaʿani yisḥabū ta-yiḏbaḥūnu. w-hī tgūḷ-ḷo, "šnū widdi ʿalēk, ya-xūya, 'ana b-al-bīr." yisḥab ḥālo yugʿud hāḏa.

127 What did he say to her? He said to her, "Your poor brother, they dragged him to the knife, on the ways of the sultans." That is, the hunters, one who has a rifle, sees this deer and wants to shoot him. He was running away. He began saying, "Your poor brother, that is, while I am going to you, your poor brother, they dragged him to the knife," to kill him. And she says to him, "What shall I do for you, o my brother, I'm in the pit." He goes away and sits, that one [the deer].

137 wāḥ(ad) yōm, rawwaḥ al-'amīr. šu rāḥat hī? rāḥat tğīb hā-č-čibš, ġanam, u-biḥšat b-hā-l-'arḏ. ba-l-awwal ğābat hā-č-čabš, ḥaṭṭato u-labbasato, u-čaffanato, u-nādat ʿala l-ʿarab,

137 One day, the emīr came home. Where did she go? She went to take this ram, lamb, and dug in the ground. At first, she brought this ram, put it and dressed it and shrouded it, and called the Bedouins.

142 gāḷat-ilhom, "mart al-'amīr mātat. taʿālam istaʾeğram wa-'eḥemlūha ta-nrūḥ nugburha."

142 She said to them, "The emīr's wife has died, come and win [a good religious deed] and carry her so that we'll go to bury her."

145 mā ʿirfam ᵃšnū bī, mā-hū al-mara, mamnūʿ ar-rāğil yšūfha. msakkar kull ši. ḥimlam hā-l-hāḏa u-rāḥam biḥšam hā-l-gabur u-ḥaṭṭam al-mara bīha. miš al-mara—rās al-ġanam. al-ġanam ḥaṭṭūha maḥall al-mara. al-mara b-al-bīr, mā tidri ši.

145 They did not know what was in it, for a woman—a man is not allowed to see her. Everything is sealed [the shrouds]. They carried that thing and went, dug the grave and put the woman in it. Not the woman—the [one] lamb. They put the lamb instead of the woman. The woman was in the hole, did not know anything.

151 rawwaḥ hāḏa al-'amīr min al-ḥağğ. gāḷ-ḷha, "yā flāne, ani māni šāyif wēn ᵉflānu." gālat-lo, "waḷḷa, yā l-'amīr, flāne aʿṭatak ʿomerha."[16] gāḷ-(ḷ)ha, "lah, lah, lah, lah, maskīna, in-ša-aḷḷa, yaʿni, gumti b-wāğibha, yaʿani, čaffantīha u-ḥtarasti ʿalēha u-gumti, yaʿni, dirti bāleč ʿalēha?"

151 This emīr came home from the pilgrimage. He said to her, "O woman, I don't see where so-and-so is." She said to him, "By Allah, Emīr, so-and-so gave you her years [lifetime]." He said to her, "Oh, no, no, no, no, the poor one, Allah willing [I hope] that is, you took care of the necessary for her, that is, you shrouded her and took care of her and looked after her?"

158 gāḷat-ḷo, "akṯar min al-lāzem, miṯel ma widdak u-ziyāde." haḏāk al-ġazāl ğāʿed ʿind hā-n-nās. an-nās tīği ʿand al-'amīr u-tsallem ʿalēh. ʿawāyid al-ʿarab, ği, trūḥ tsallem, w-al-ġazāl ğāʿid.

158 She said to him, "More than the obligation, as you want and more." That deer was sitting near the people. The people came to the emīr and greeted him, the habits of the Bedouins are to come and greet [after the pilgrim returns from the pilgrimage]. And the deer was sitting.

163 šū ğāyib mʿā? yeğīb goṭṭtēn, tīn yābes, yaʿani, goṭṭēn u-zbīb, u-tamer u-ši.	163 What did he bring with him? He brought goṭṭen, dried figs, that is [to say], dried figs, and raisins and dates, and other things.
165 yinṭī. ygūḷ-ḷo "xuḏ kul" hāḏ yākul, al-ġazāl, w-iyḥuṭṭhin b-idēh. wēn yiḏaḷḷ rāyeḥ? yurkuḏ la-ʿind uxto. yiṭʿamha iyyāhen.	165 He gives it, says to him [to the deer], "Take, eat." That one eats, the deer, and puts them in his hands. Where does he go? He runs to his sister, gives them to her, to eat them.
169 yōm u-hū ğāʿed, gām hū min aṣ-ṣubḥ, hā-l-'amīr, ta-yṣalli, waḷḷa hā-l-ġazāl mnaṣṣeb, seḥab ḥālo, u-ḏaḷḷ ᵉmġarrib.	169 One day, as he was sitting, getting up in the morning, that emīr, to pray, there was this deer standing, and went off and went to the west.
173 qāl, "hā-l-ġazāl, māni ʿāref wēn yrūḥ. kull yōm, kull yōm, afqud hā-l-ġazāl, mā-(a)lgāh. widdi aʿrif wēn yrūḥ hā-l-ġazāl, wēn yrūḥ b-hā-n-nahār. hāḏa min aṣ-ṣubḥ yiḥuṭṭ u-yišrab kubbāyet šāy w-yākul u-hā-l—yāxuḏ al-aklayāt ⁱmʿā, yiḥuṭṭhin b-idēh w-yḏaḷḷ ⁱmġarrib."	173 He said, "This deer, I don't know where it goes. Every day, every day I look for it and do not find him. I want to know where this deer is going, where it goes at daytime. This one, in the morning it puts and drinks a cup of tea and eats, and this—it takes the food kinds with him, puts them in its hands and goes to the west."
180 gāḷ, "waḷḷāhi, ġēr 'alḥago. 'amši šwayye šwayy u-alḥago, 'ašūf wēn yrūḥ, al-ġazāl." siḥab ḥālo hāḏ u-hā-l-'amīr; hā-l-ġazāl ğiddāmo, u-hū warā, šwayye šwayy, u-hū mū šāyfo.[17] yimši šwayye šwayye, šwayy, tanno ğe ʿa-bāb al-bīr.	180 He said, "By Allah, I will follow it. I'll go little by little [quietly quietly] and follow him, will see where it goes, this deer." It went off, this [deer] and the emīr, the deer in front of him and he is after it, slowly, slowly, and it [the deer] does not see him [the emīr]. He goes quietly, quietly, quietly until it came to the opening of the pit.
186 yinṭi la-'oxto w-iygul la, "axūč al-maskīn, saḥabū ʿala s-sakkīn, ʿa-drūb aṣ-ṣalāṭīn."	186 It gives to its sister and says to her, "Your poor brother, they dragged him to the knife, on the ways of the sultans."
189 mā daḥḥag ʿalē(a) w-unno b-gaḷbo. wunno al-mara ğāʿde w-al-walad mẓaḷbaṭ b-ḥaḏenha. ğāʿad yirḏaʿ minha u-hī b-qāʿ al-bīr. gāḷ, "hū-'anti hīn?" gāḷat-lo, "'ani hīn."	189 He looked at him, and lo—she was in it [in the pit]. And lo—there was the woman sitting, and the child naked in her lap, sitting suckling from her and she is inside the pit. He said, "Is it you that are here?" She said to him, "I am here."
194 seḥab ḥālo ʿāwad ʿala l-ʿarab. gāḷ-(ḷ)hin, "mīn yeḥibb al-'amīr?" gāḷu, "šū as-sīre yā-(a)mīr?"	194 He [the emīr] went away, returned to the Bedouins. He said to them, "Who loves the emīr?" They said, "What is the matter, oh, emīr?"

197 gāl-ilhum, "taʿālam ʿa-l-bīr, taʿālam, ilḥagūni ǧāy, bū wāḥad wāǧeʿ b-al-bīr, ilḥagūni ǧāy, wāḥad wugaʿ b-al-bīr, ilḥagūni ǧāy, ilḥagūni ǧāy."	197 He said to them, "Come to the well, come follow me this way, there is one who fell into the well, follow me this way, someone fell into the well, follow me here, follow me here."
201 liḥgat al-ʿarab winnha marto. gāḷu-ḷa, "yā flāne, wēn, mā-gulti mātat. šnū-lli gabarnā?" gāḷat-ḷo . . . saḥbat ḥālo . . . u-ǧat — rāḥat al-ʿarab aṭlaʿat ʾal-mara, hī u-ʾibinha.	201 The Bedouins followed and there [was] his wife. They said to her [the other wife], "Oh, so-and-so, where, did you not say that she died? What did we bury?" She said—she went away, came. . . . The Bedouins went, took out the wife, her and her son.
206 rāḥ beḥaš ʿala l-ġaname, u-ʾaṭlaʿha u-gāḷ-(ḷ)hin, "mīn yeḥibb al-ʾamīr u-yǧīb-lo ḥamlet ḥaṭab u-šwayyet nār?" widdi yiḥriǧhe, yiḥriǧ marto.	206 He went and dug [out] the sheep, and took it out and said to them, "Who loves the emīr and will bring for him a load of wood and some fire?" He wanted to burn his wife.
210 saḥab ḥālo, ʾaḥrag marto, gaʿad hū u-marato ǧ-ǧadīde w-el-ġazāl wa-staladḏu u-qaʿadu. u-hāḏi xallṣat.	210 He went, burned his wife, and remained, he and his new wife and the deer, and enjoyed [life] and remained. And this is finished.
213 (wa-ḥna ʿamilna killa ba-š-šuġul, fišš waqt e-nuqʿud. nuqʿud nuṣṣ sēʿa, wēn-ma biddna nōkol, wēnma widna nitxarraf.)	213 (And we did all this at work, there is no time to sit [idle]. We sit half an hour, whenever we want to eat, whenever we want to talk.)

Commentary

The story of the brother and the sister belongs to the international narrative type ATU 450, "Little Brother and Little Sister." The international type is described as follows: A little brother and little sister run away from their home because of their cruel stepmother or because their parents want to eat them. Despite his sister's warning, the brother drinks water from an enchanted spring or an animal's track (motif D555.1, "Transformation by drinking from animal's track") and is transformed into a deer. The children live together in the forest until a prince finds them. The sister hides in a tree, but the prince tricks her into coming down. She marries the prince, and they take the animal brother with them (motif P253.2, "Sister faithful to persecuted brother").

The prince is absent when their child is born. Another bride (often the daughter of the bad woman [stepmother, witch]) takes the place of the sister (motif K1911.1.2, "False bride takes true bride's place when child is born"). The sister is thrown into the water, transformed into a bird, or swallowed by a fish. She returns at night to suckle her child and to look after her brother the deer. A servant overhears the conversation between the animal brother and the sister and informs the prince. The false bride and her mother are punished.

In some variants, the false bride and her mother want to kill the animal brother because they fear that the truth will be discovered. The cook saves him.

The story is known in different versions throughout Europe, Russia, Turkey, Armenia, the Middle East, North Africa, Iran, India, and Japan. Its best-known version is the one in the Brothers Grimm book, "Little Brother and Little Sister."[18] One of the earliest versions of the story is the seventeenth-century Italian version of Ninnillo and Nennella, which is in Giambattista Basile's book *Pentamerone*, a collection of Neapolitan folk tales.[19] In this version, the enchanted spring does not appear and the brother does not become a deer. Pirates kidnap the sister. Later on, their ship sinks, and she is swallowed by a large fish. She calls for her brother's help, and he, with the help of a kindhearted prince, extracts her safely from the bowels of the fish.

In IFA there are several interesting parallels to this story from Yemen, Tunis, and Morocco.[20]

The Bedouin story parallels the main lines of the international narrative type yet differs from it in several significant points, some of which stem from the Bedouin Muslim background: The stepmother causes the children to leave their home, but she does not appear again later on in the story. The rivalry is not between the sister and the stepmother but between her and the emīr's senior wife. The older woman wants to kill her young rival. The opportunity falls into her hands when the emīr is away from home for a long time on a journey to Mecca to fulfill the *ḥağğ*, the Islamic pilgrimage. The punishment of the senior woman at the end of the story is death by fire.

The brother becomes a deer after drinking water from an enchanted spring, while his sister refrains from drinking despite her thirst. Those who feed them bread and warn them against drinking water from the enchanted springs are a few plowmen (or shepherds) the children meet by chance on their way. The two children remain faithful to each other: the sister remains faithful to her brother even after he becomes a deer, and the brother, later in the story, feeds his sister in the pit, despite the danger posed by the hunters.

The situation that opens the story, the abandonment of children because of the migration of members of the tribe, appears in many Bedouin stories that I collected in the Galilee. Sometimes the abandonment is unintentional due to lack of attention, and sometimes, as in this case, it is the planned action of a stepmother who wants to get rid of the children. Moving about was a typical situation for Bedouin tribes living in the desert, whose range of migration was extensive, but not for the northern Bedouin tribes, who are now permanently sedentarized and who even at the beginning of the twentieth century did not migrate more than a few dozen kilometers. This strengthens the hypothesis that this story (and perhaps other stories) has been passed on from mother to daughter for generations and reflects the lifestyles of past generations. It is interesting to note that the order to move from one place to another is given by the emīr's wife, and not by the emīr himself, which attests to the high status of the emīr's wife in the hierarchy of the tribe. Later on in the story, this is also the case with the emīr's second wife, who during her husband's absence manages the affairs of the tribe and decides to move from place to place.

In his book *The Bedouins in the Land of Israel*, Tovia Ashkenazi writes, "The Bedouin woman in the north of Arabia is free, lives with the members of the camp and participates in their entire lives, and in matters of marriage she is not subject to coercion. It is not so with the semi-Bedouin who is forced to marry."[21]

The two children arrive at the emīr's tent, which is the largest tent of the tribe. The dimensions of the tent depend on the number of pillars supporting it.[22] Later, the emīr's tent is described as having three pillars, indicating wealth and status.

As is customary in Bedouin hospitality, guests can stay with their host for three days and a third of a day, and during this period, they are not asked their reason for coming, the identity of their tribe, or their plans for the future. After three days of hospitality, guests are expected to leave or, alternatively, to tell their host the purpose of their visit. The Arabic adage *Al-ḍēf—talat iyam u-tult*, "the guest [may stay with the host] three days and a third," summarizes this custom.

The emīr does not address the girl directly with a marriage proposal but does so through his senior wife. In part, he does this to examine his senior wife's response to her husband's marriage with another woman. Her consent to the mediation is seen as her agreement to his having a second wife. In other stories in which there is a similar situation, the emīr turns to the girl through his mother. The girl's positive answer to the marriage proposal is "Marriage [a husband] is a protection" (*al- ǧōz sitra*). In Bedouin patriarchal society, a woman is always under the protection of a man. She usually moves from her father's custody to her husband's protection, but here, it is different, for the young girl is in a situation where she must act alone after her brother has lost his human form.

Two Islamic religious elements that appear in the story are the *ḥaǧǧ*, pilgrimage to Mecca, and the *zakāt*, giving of charity. The emīr goes on a pilgrimage to Mecca, and the deer wanders among the tribespeople and begs for food for his sister. *Ḥaǧǧ* and *zakāt* are considered two of the Five Pillars of Islam ('arkān al-islām al-khamsa), the five central commandments of Islam.

Preparing the body of a dead woman for burial, as the narrator explains, is done by the women. The emīr's wife takes advantage of this practice to carry out her evil intent: to bury a sheep's carcass and declare that it is the body of her rival. The brother's transformation into a deer appears both in the Grimm version and in our story. Maria Tatar, in her book *The Annotated Brothers Grimm*, gives a psychological interpretation of the story.[23] The relationship between brother and sister is perceived as a metaphor for humanity's animal and spiritual duality. The brother represents the instinctive male side, and the sister, the rational female side. The brother is unable to control the urge to drink from the enchanted spring despite his sister's warnings. Therefore, he is "punished" and becomes a real animal. The sister, who is perceived as the spiritual element, casts her patronage over him.

However, the story also contains another type of metamorphosis, which is related to God's relationship with humans. At the beginning of the story, in the Brothers Grimm version, the falling rain is a metaphor for tears, which God casts down on the fate of the children: "And when it rained, the little sister said: God, our hearts are crying together!"

In the Neapolitan version of Basile, the heroine is kidnapped by pirates, and God's intervention is explicitly stated, punishment for sinners and saving for the innocent. The motif of swallowing by fish also appears in the Portuguese version, as well as in the Judeo-Tunisian version found in the IFA (7562). The fish and burial at sea, which is a kind of baptism, are of course reminiscent of the story of the prophet Jonah. These are distinctly Christian motifs, related to the return to the womb and the metamorphosis of swallowing, which Bruno Bettelheim discusses extensively.[24] God's intervention in these versions is connected to water, and the rescue of the heroine, like the rescue of Jonah, is brought about by divine salvation. In the Bedouin story, Allah is clearly present. The name of Allah is mentioned ten times in the story. First of all, in the context of an oath: "No, by Allah, there is a spring, further on," says the plowman. The emīr makes his wife swear in the name of Allah to guard his young wife. The woman swears to Allah when she tells of the death of her rival. Secondly, the name of Allah appears in the context of marriage: "He invited the Bedouins [according to] Allah's decrees and his Prophet, and he married this girl." In the passage of time, the narrator also mentions the name of Allah: "Two months, three—Allah knows." This is not surprising. The narrator is a religious woman who made a pilgrimage to Mecca, fasts in Ramadan, and observes prayers.[25]

Allah is revealed in the story not only by mentions of his name but also in the context of food. At the beginning of the story, we find what the folklorists call "a wondrous agent," those plowmen who provide bread to the children and warn them about the enchanted springs. Later, there is a reference to the Muslim custom, according to which one who returns from pilgrimage brings gifts to relatives. Many of the pilgrims to Mecca bring water from the holy waters of the Zamzam Well. In our story, the emīr brings with him dried figs, almonds, and raisins. He gives the food to the enchanted deer, and the deer passes it on to his sister, who is imprisoned in the pit.

Ostensibly, there is no magical motif here, just a simple transfer, but the food is not an ordinary food. It is a divine food, in the sense that it is brought from Mecca, meaning the source of supreme sanctity, and it rolls through the emīr and the deer to the bottom of the pit, to the lowest place, to support the woman trapped there.

The motif of the pit, by the way, is clearly related to the motif of swallowing by a whale, or the sister's magical death and her burial at sea. The girl's entrance to the pit is a kind of burial, and it is even emphasized by the woman's pseudo-burial in which the sheep is buried. So we can say that here there are two lines of metamorphosis, which I call the horizontal line and the vertical line. The horizontal line is related to the relationship between the protagonists and is symbolized first and foremost in the metamorphosis of a man into a deer and in a pseudo-burial—swallowing in a pit. The second line is the vertical line—the intervention of Allah in the plot—which is expressed in the basic food, bread, that the children receive at the beginning of the story, and in dried figs and raisins from Mecca later on. The tracing of the food given to the deer leads the emīr to discover his wife who has been dropped into the pit. Here the brother plays an active role. If at the beginning of the story the sister is the one who takes care of her brother, at the end of the story, the brother is the one who takes care of and nourishes his sister.

Notes

1. Spontaneous speech is known to be full of incomplete utterances, hesitations, and errors with or without corrections. This feature occurs many times in this story (and in other stories) right from its beginning; for example, the saying verbs *gāḷ-ḷo/gāḷ-ḷa* and others are sometimes used erroneously, and incorrect vowels occur for various pronouns.

2. Note again the conciseness of Bedouin narration in the beginning of this story: the narrator presents all the family history (the father, his children, his dead wife, and the new wife) in short sentences, comprising just twenty-seven words.

3. Time expressions (adverbials) in Arabic (and in Hebrew) can be expressed with time nouns (e.g., hour, day, morning) with or without prepositions to indicate their meaning and syntactic role. For example, see here *'aṣ-ṣubḥ gāmum hā-l-uwlād*, "[In] the morning, these children got up," without the preposition *in*. This adverbial structure has expanded in many colloquial Arabic dialects.

4. The verb *ǧamma*, "they came," is the Galilee Bedouin form of the verb *ǧa*, "to come," which in Galilean sedentary Arabic is pronounced *'aǧa/'iǧa*, as in *'ákal*, "eat," and *'áxad/'áxaḏ*, "take" (cf. chap. 6, note 6). In some Galilee Bedouin dialects, the suffix of the verb in the third m.pl. is *-m*, thus *ǧam* (*mātam*), while in short verbs (having only one syllable, such as *ǧa*) it is geminated to *ǧamma*, as here, which makes the verb form bisyllabic.

5. *mātam min al-ǧū' w-al-'aṭaš. māšīn ǧamma 'ala hā-l-ḥarrāṯ*: "They died of hunger and thirst. Walking, they came to a plowman." The past tense verb forms *mātam* and *ǧamma* take the third m.pl. suffixes *am/amma*, which are the typical Galilee Bedouin forms. Certain Bedouin dialects in Syria and Jordan use similar suffixes with *-m*, but in the Galilee Bedouin tribes these forms seem to have expanded. With the spreading effect of nearby sedentary dialects, these suffixes are gradually exchanged into the sedentary (rural/urban) *-u* (without the *-m* for m.pl. or *-n* for f.pl.), as with *mātu*, "they died." The narrators sometime mix these Bedouin and sedentary forms.

6. The parallel of the Bedouin *y(e)'ḥáruṯ* in sedentary dialects is *yáḥruṯ/yúḥruṯ*. An inserted helping vowel breaks the cluster of the first and second root consonants, *ḥr*. This vowel shortens, or even deletes, the vowel of the imperfect prefix *ye-/yu-* and moves the word stress to the helping vowel, thus differentiating the Bedouin from the sedentary system. (Cf. *gaháwa syndrome* in point 6 of the section "Diverse Criteria for the Classification of Arabic Dialects and Bedouin Dialects," in the chapter on Bedouin dialects at the end of this book.)

7. *gāḷu-ḷo, "'amma mā m'āk mayy?" gāḷ-ḷhin, "lā, waḷḷa, yā 'ammi"*: "[They] said to him, 'Don't you have water with you?' He said to them, 'No, by Allah, my boy.'" Note the address form, which is the same as in the children's addressing the first plowman and in the second plowman's answer: both use the same address word, literally "O [my] uncle." This is not a mistake but a typical address manner in both Bedouin and sedentary speakers. That is to say, the child uses the same address word as the parents (or other kin members) do. A father will answer a girl addressing him by saying "O my father" (not "my daughter"). With certain differences due to seniority (age), social authority, kinship (first degree or more distant), or pragmatic implications, this is valid also for strangers' discourse. (See more details on such "reverse kinship terms" in Henkin, *Negev Arabic*, 192–217; Henkin, "Come, O Your Mother.")

8. *gāḷ-ḷha, "guddāmač al-'ēn . . . gāḷ, "giddām, ǧiddām, išrabu"*: "He said to her, 'In front of you there is the spring.' . . . he said, 'In front [of you], further forward; drink.'" Cf. chapter 12, note 2. *k* is another consonant that shows a dialectal mixture of phonetic systems. In the Galilee Bedouin dialects, using *k* (apparently) depends on non-front vowels. The process is activated near the front vowels, e.g., *ek* > *eč*, *ik* > *ič*, but usually not with the back

vowels, *a, o, u*. In spite of this, this form ends with *-ač* instead of *-ak*. See also the phrase *min-čud-ma huwwa mu'tazz bih* (story 1, first sentence), where *čud-mā* is derived from *gadd-mā* < *qadr-mā* (i.e., <*q* and not <*k*). In spite of the various phonetic rules that seem to function (or to have functioned) in these dialects, the listeners understand what is said and do not get confused by the (erroneous) varieties. This example reveals a high level of phonetic mixture in the Bedouin narrator's speech (and the importance of redundancy features in speech).

9. *"waḷḷa, ağ-ğōz sitra. 'amma 'ana lli widdi 'āxḏo, 'ašarreṭ 'alē šarṭ"*: "'By Allah, a husband is security. But I, the one I will take [marry] I have a condition for it [on him].'" In contrast with Arab sedentary girls/women, this Bedouin woman is free to marry whom she wants and is not forced to marry against her will. (Cf. chap. 4, note 5.) This attitude may be rare and due to her specific (independent) social situation.

10. *gabuḷ kānum yerūḥūn 'a-ğmāl, yirkabūn ağ-ğmāl w-irūḥūn*. Note the suffix of the imperfect verb form with *-ūn* in contrast with *-am*, seen above. Certain Galilee Bedouin tribes use the ending with *-ūn*, which is conservative, since it is used in LA/MSA, while other tribes use the ending *-am* for the imperfect as well, and not only for the past tense (cf. Rosenhouse, *Bedouin Arabic Dialects*, 91–92). Bedouin speakers, such as the narrators, often mix these forms—again because of dialect mixtures in the region.

11. *siḥab ḥālo hā-l-'amīr, ḥaṭṭ 'ala hā-ğ-ğimal, . . . u-miša 'a-l-ḥağğ*: "He went off, this emīr, loaded on the camel . . . and went to the pilgrimage." The past tense verb *miša* takes the CiCaC pattern, which is typical of Galilee Bedouin dialects (cf. the section "Morphology" in our chapter on Bedouin dialects at the end of this book), whereas verbs where C1 or C2 is a pharyngeal or laryngeal tend to the CaCaC pattern. Still, *siḥab* keeps the *i* of nonpharyngeal roots, perhaps by assimilation to the pattern of most of the nonpharyngeal roots.

12. *'al-mara g'adat*: "The woman remained." Cf. chapter 11, note 5.

13. The verb pattern basically has the vowel *e* in the last syllable (*nenaggel*), but it is deleted in *widdna nenaggl-al-bēt* because of the following context (junction), which begins with a vowel.

14. Here the 2f.sg. *t-* is assimilated to the following voiced affricate, *ğ*. As there is no gemination of *ğ*, it seems that *t* is completely elided. Consonant elisions also occur in other consonantal sequences, which yield assimilation in nearby consonants. Cf. note 15 immediately below.

15. *"ḥabībti, mā widdeč ⁱtğībīn hīn, biddek ⁱtğībi b-il-'ōḏa hān, b-il-maḥall hāḏ, bi-l-bēt hīn. hīn 'adfa-leč u-'aḥsan-leč u-'adlič nār."* This long sentence includes three cases of code mixing, with the first two being *widdeč* (Bedouin) versus *biddek* (sedentary) and *hīn* (Bedouin) versus *hān* (sedentary). The third one is *u-adlič*, which seems to be the Modern Hebrew word *'adlik* (< Hebrew spelling *'adliq*) with *k* > *č*. The phonetic rule in note 8, above, seems to function even for a word borrowed from another language.

16. *flāne a'ṭatak 'omerha*: "So-and-so gave you her years." This is a polite announcing of a person's death. The woman's years of life, which she should have had, go to the emīr's life expectancy. The audience naturally understands this phrase.

17. Bedouin *mū* < *mā* + *hū*. For the present (time) and nonverbal negation, sedentary speakers use *muš* ~ *miš*, with the correlative particle, *š*, suffixed to the negative particle. As we see in this example, Galilee Bedouins usually do not use this *š*. Galilee Bedouin negation of past and imperfect tenses applies the negative particle *mā*, "not," for all personal pronouns. Many sedentary dialects in Israel (and other regions of the Levant) use the correlative negation particle, *š*, suffixed to the verb, as in *mā šafōš*, "he did not see him."

18. Grimm *The Original Folk and Fairy Tales of the Brothers Grimm*, story 11.

19. Basile, *Stories from the Pentamerone*, tale 30.

20. Yemen: 4698, 7074, 12075; Tunis: 7562; Morocco: 6277.

21. Ashkenazi, *Bedouins in the Land of Israel*, 65.

22. Ashkenazi, 125.

23. Tatar, *Annotated Brothers Grimm*, 41, 44.

24. Bettelheim, *Uses of Enchantment.*

25. Allah is omnipresent in Muslims' speech; see Piamenta, *Islam in Everyday Arabic Speech.*

14. Do Good and Throw It into the Sea

NARRATOR: Nūra Ḥalīfa

TRIBE: *'Arab el-'Arāmša*

IFA 14075, recorded in Hebrew 1985

Text

One day, there was a small family—*'ašīreh* [the Bedouin term for the tribe]. And they passed [from one place to another]. There was a case of murder between them, and they went from one *'ašīreh* to another. They had only one child, and both parents died.

This boy was hired as a shepherd, and someone came, an old man, and said to him: "They take you only for the food [that is, they rent your services only for food and clothing]. Think about the future! Don't work only for the food and the clothes that they give you. Every year, you should get a goat!"

He grew up, he was ten years old, and he said to them, "Either you give me [for] a year, in addition to food and clothes, a goat, or I cancel [the agreement], go from this place and leave the *'ašīreh*!"

They needed him. They took the boy and gave him a goat every year, until he had ten [goats]. They saw that this boy is progressing, and they did not like it. They thought he was impudent. They were jealous of him. They said, "We shall show him."

He felt that they hated him, so he moved from this place, from this tribe. They frightened him.

[He abandoned the first tribe in which he found shelter and went to another tribe, where] he entered into certain neighborhood, into the house of a neighbor [a woman] and all day long he would graze her goats and cattle. She did not feel sorry for him in spite of the fact that he did all the tasks, taking the goats to the pasture and milking them. He did everything he could for this woman, but she did not take pity on him, did not clean [wash] him, did not make his clothes, she did not give him food, and if he was sick, she did not look after him.

He said, "Oh my Allah, one day I'll take revenge, I'll take revenge on this girl!"

One day he came to the spring, and a beautiful girl came, to fill her jar with water.

She asked him, "Why do you look like that, are you alone? Is there no one who cares for you?"

She saw him with his dirty hair and his torn clothes. She asked him, "Why is it that no one sews your clothes?"

He said to her, "I have no one. I have no mother, no father, no family."

Then she said to him, "Go and get married!"

He said to her, "Who would like to marry me? Nobody!"

She said to him, "I will be the first one that would marry you!"

He did not think [he did not believe she meant what she was saying].

The first day, the second day, she asked him, "Why did you not come to my father and ask for my hand?"

He asked about this girl, and the girl was the daughter of *Šēx el-ʿašīreh* [the daughter of the tribal head]. He did not dream of having such a girl, he did not believe it, and every time she came to the water, to take water, she would come and talk with this boy.

He went to the elders and said to them, "Go and ask this girl [from her father]."

They said to him, "You look like that, and you think of girls who are the daughters of rich and respected people? She will not want you, they'll kill you!"

So he said, "Please try, maybe Allah will help me and bring her to my hand!"

He went to other elders and they said to him, "We are going to talk on your behalf, but if we fail and she does not want you, we are going to kill you!"

He went with an anxious heart and was afraid of what was going to happen. When he came to this house, they honored him with coffee, with dinner, with everything, and they asked for the girl.

Then he asked if the girl agreed, and the girl came without her father calling her, saying to him, "Yes, Father, I agree [to marry him]!"

So the two elders looked at each other, from where did the boy have money he could give to her father, buying the girl?

They told him, "We'll see another week, we're coming, and we'll pay the child! [We will give him one more week, and then he should bring the money.]"

The child became pale with fear when he heard that they wanted money. Therefore, they started talking to him quietly, "From where do you have money to buy the girl?"

The girl said, "I do not want anything from him. Bring two more [witnesses], and we'll make the engagement."

And her father agreed to make the celebration [the wedding] at his own expense. He asked him what is his work and how many goats or camels he has.

He said to him, "I have ten goats."

He said, "It's a lot, do you have a house?"

He said to him, "I have a small tent."

He said, "OK, that's enough."

Then after one more week, they finished it all. The girl was engaged to this child, and her father said to her: "Keep [good relations with] your neighbors, keep your husband's secrets, and guard his money and do whatever you can to help people, even if they are not good, help them . . . I want one thing: what you saw in this house, keep doing it in your house."

The girl, her father gave her many camels, many sheep, lots of goats. He made them rich. And people were startled that he lived in this house, in the neighborhood.

The neighbor, one day she tried, she could not [apparently she had trouble working and needed help]. . . . His wife went and helped her. She helped her every morning. When she finished her work, she went to her house, milking the goats for her, preparing the cheese, souring the milk. She did everything for her.

This boy, this man, he got mad at it. He wanted to put an end to that. He did not want the girl to go and help her. He wanted to take revenge on her [it can be understood that her neighbor was the woman for whom the boy had previously worked as a day laborer].

He said to her, "I do not want to fight with you, but one thing, if I'm dear to you, stop going to this woman, stop helping her."

She said to him, "I want to help her. That is what I learned in my parents' house, to help, to help as much as possible."

He said to her, "But she's not worth it."

She said to him: "[Although] she is not worth it, this is what I learned: do good and throw it into the sea!"

He thought in his heart, OK, I'll show you, how you get back from the sea what you throw!

One day he took the gold, which her father had given her, her two bracelets, and threw them into the sea.

Then came the holiday of the sacrifice, which is called *'id el-aḍḥa,* and he said to her, "Let's go to your parents."

He was waiting for her to go and look for it, to wear it, and if she asked where it was, he would say to her, "Go and bring it from the sea. You said that what you had done for this woman would come to you back from the sea." [It can be understood from this that the holiday has not yet arrived and that the husband is only planning and imagining the future exchange.]

He went one day with his friend and saw fish for sale.

He said, "Here are fish. Let us buy some."

His friend bought three, and he bought three.

And she [his wife] opens the fish, and she sees that one of them is a big fish, maybe more than a pound, and has a big belly. She thought that perhaps this fish swallowed something from the sea. She said, "I'll leave it to the end."

She opened the first and second [fish] and cleaned them. Then she opened the third one and saw inside it her handkerchief with the bracelets. Allah, from where did they come? The fish came from the sea, and my bracelets, how did they get there? She began to think and did not tell her husband. She hid them and washed them and returned them to their place.

And then the holiday came, and her husband tells her: "Let's go to your parents."

He was waiting for her words. So she got dressed and wore her bracelets. And he just wanted to look at her hands and say, "Why do not you wear this?" And he looked at her hands, at her hands—she had the bracelets.

He said to her, "From where did you get this? I threw them into the sea!"

She said to him, "Into the sea?"

He said to her, "Yes."

She said to him, "From the sea. I got them from the three fish which you brought. I found them in the belly of one of them."

She asked him, "Why did you throw them there?"

"Because if you ask me where they are, I would tell you: you said, do good and throw it into the sea. Bring them from the sea! I see that they really came to you from the sea!"

And that's the story. He believed it was worth helping. As much as you can help—help!

Commentary

The story was originally told in broken Hebrew and was written as it was recorded on the tape.

The motif of a ring or another treasure lost to its owner, and brought back by a fish that swallowed it, N211.1, "Lost ring found in fish. (Polycrates)," is familiar from many folktales. It is included in the narrative type ATU 736A, "The Ring of Polycrates," in the group of "Fate Stories." Polycrates, according to a story cited by Herodotus, was the ruler of the island of Samos and had many successes on the battlefield. His ally, the Egyptian king Amasis II, feared that his success would arouse the jealousy of the gods and advised him to throw a precious object into the sea to harm himself and soothe the wrath of the gods. Polycrates threw a precious ring into the sea, but a fisherman who came to the court brought him a fish, and in the fish's gut was the ring that had been thrown into the sea. In the wake of this incident, Amasis canceled his alliance with Polycrates, and shortly afterward Polycrates fell captive and was executed.

In another account that is included in this narrative type, the outline of the plot is somewhat different: a rich, arrogant woman who is disturbed by the sight of a beggar hurls her ring into the sea and says, "Just as I cannot see this ring again, so can I never become a poor woman." But the ring comes back to her in a fish she buys, and shortly afterward she loses her property and becomes poor.

Although the Bedouin story has a different character, it somewhat corresponds to the stories described above. The hero of the story, who has emerged from poverty and become a wealthy man because a sheikh enriched him, is unwilling to treat the poor with the same generosity. He does not understand that success involves a proper ethical approach to those around him, and to prevent his wife from behaving generously, he throws her jewelry into the sea.

At the core of the story lies the proverb quoted by the hero's wife, "Do good and throw it into the sea" (*'e'mal mlīḥ wa-'irmīh fi l-baḥer*). It can be said that this proverb is the Arabic equivalent of the Hebrew verse "Cast thy bread upon the waters: for thou shalt find it after many days" (Ecclesiastes 11:1). Sometimes the Arab proverb is used in a negative sense, to refer to doing useless good, but the story aims to show the correctness of the proverb in the positive sense. At the end of the story, the husband acknowledges the justice of his wife and the truth of the saying: "I would tell you: you said, do good and throw it into the sea. Bring them from the sea! I see that they really came to you from the sea!" The narrator adds the moral of the story: "He believed it was worth helping."

There are several Hebrew stories based on the verse "Cast thy bread upon the waters: for thou shalt find it after many days," in which the verse is interpreted literally (a man gives bread to a fish and is rewarded). One of the most well-known stories of this type appears in the second version of the book *Alpha Beta De Ben Sira*, a Midrash from the tenth century, first printed in Constantinople in 1519. In this story, a man commands his son: "Throw your bread in the water and you will find it at the end of time." The son obeys his father's command literally and throws bread into the river. One fish grows and fattens from the bread and begins devouring all the fish around it. The fish complain to a whale, and the whale orders the fish to bring the bread thrower to him. The fish swallows the young man and brings him to the whale. The whale hears the boy's explanations and vomits him back to land, after teaching him the animals' languages. Later in the story, the young man catches a crow's chick. The chick's father calls to the boy in the language of the crows and asks him to release his son, and in exchange he tells the boy about the treasure that King Solomon stored there. The young man releases the crow, finds the treasure, and gets rich.

In the Bedouin tale, we can find many Bedouin lifestyles and customs. At the beginning of the story, the family abandons its tribe because of a bloody conflict and finds refuge with a neighboring tribe. Ashkenazi writes about this in his book: "A Bedouin whose enemies harass him for murder, injustice, women's affairs, etc. would come to one of the most important members of the foreign tribe or to one of the effendis, or one of the sheikhs of the village, requesting asylum and protection."[1] Such a man is then called *Daxīl* (someone who take refuge with someone else) and becomes a member of the tribe, and the tribe protects him from his enemies.

Later in the story, we hear about the sad condition of the hero, who is an orphan. Ashkenazi explains that "an orphan from father and mother—especially from the father—has a bad status among the Bedouin neighborhoods. Over time an orphan would become a slave and the orphaned girl a maid servant of their guardians."[2] An Arabic proverb says, "On the head of the orphan, the barber learns his profession (*al-ḥallāq bit'allam yiḥliq 'ala rās el-yatīm*)." The saying means "Woe to the poor." The orphan is in the lowest social status.

In the story, the hero meets his future wife near the fountain. The fountain, or water pit, serves as a meeting place for young people and gives them an opportunity to develop romantic relationships. Later on, the engagement customs are described: A delegation of elders goes to the father to offer him the match, and after coffee and dinner, the elders speak in the name of the groom. After receiving the father's agreement in principle, the groom discusses the dowry sum with the bride's father. Two details in our story indicate that the tale reflects desert Bedouin traditions: First, no one forces the bride to marry; she has the privilege of choosing her groom. (In the northern tribes like the narrator's, maybe because they adopted the sedentary rural custom of their neighbors, the daughter is as a slave to her father, and he marries her to whom he wishes.) Second, the dowry is given up. In the desert tribes, it is not customary to give a dowry; the groom gives only a small symbolic gift to the bride's parents. Here in Israel, as is the custom in the Arab villages, the groom pays *ṣyāg*—a dowry to the father of the bride. The girl does not take part in the negotiations, since the women do not sit with the men in the guest section of the tent, but she eavesdrops over the curtain separating the women's section from the men's section, and at the right moment, she lets her voice be heard. "And the girl came without her father calling her, saying to him: 'Yes, Father, I agree!'"

The bride receives bracelets from her father. Ashkenazi says, "The Bedouin customarily adorn themselves with silver bracelets (*asawira*). On each hand there are three bracelets, and the more bracelets she has—the better."[3] The Bedouin keeps the bracelets in a *sanduk* (box).

Beyond the fact that the story is rooted in the Bedouin culture, it can be called a feminine story because it deals with the relationship between men and women and the Bedouin woman's struggle for her place in the tribe. The hero of the story descends from a family of refugees, asylum seekers in a foreign tribe, and grows up as an orphan on the margins of society. He must feel inferior, compared to the privileged bride who consents to marry him, and he despises the generosity she brings with her from her parents' home. (One should remember that the command of charity, giving to the poor, is one of the Five Pillars of Islam.) The husband tries to impose his authority on her by force, and he casts her property into the sea so that one day he will be able to hurl insults at her and humiliate her. He turns his need for revenge from his former employer toward his wife, who has dared to help the woman.

The woman is forced to suffer her husband's blunt behavior. The patriarchal environment in which she lives demands absolute obedience on her side. An Arab proverb says, "May Allah protect me from a woman who behaves like a man" (*'a'ūḏu bi-l-lāh min al-mar'a alli titṣarraf zayy ar-rāǧil*).

The story expresses the hidden wish of women in the Bedouin society to be respected and valued by their husbands. The wondrous event of the fish returning her jewelry symbolizes the woman's victory in the contest. It is not for nothing that the story ends with words she puts in her husband's mouth, "I see that they really came to you from the sea!" and in the narrator's words (or conclusion), "And that's the story. He believed it was worth helping. As much as you can help—help!"

Notes

1. Ashkenazi, *The Bedouins in the Land of Israel*, 186.
2. Ashkenazi, 78.
3. Ashkenazi, 143.

15. The Transposed Heads

NARRATOR: Ṯarwa Yāsīn

TRIBE: *ʿArab el-Ḥaǧāǧra*

April 17, 1984

1 bī hā-l-ixwān aṯ-ṯnēn.[1] haḏ̣ōl hā-l-ixwān aṯ-ṯnēn, haḏ̣ōl ha-l-ixwān aṯ-ṯnēn ^{e}mǧawwazīn. gāʿdīn taḥt malla. ǧāʿdīn taḥt hā-l-malla. gāmat ǧat ʿalēhum hā-l-ḥamāma. kātalam maʿa—ǧāʿdīn yōklam. tʿaššam. yōm-innam[2] tʿaššam, ixtilfam. kātalam. hasāʿa ǧā . . . ǧamma kātalam. aṯ-ṯnēn, aṯ-ṯnēn gaṭṭaʿam rūs baʿaḏ̣. kull wāḥad ḏ̣arab aṯ-ṯāni, giṭaʿ^{a} rāso.	1 There were these two brothers. These two brothers. These two brothers [were] married. They were sitting under an oak tree. They were sitting under this oak. There came to them this pigeon. They quarreled—they were sitting to eat. [They] had dinner, when they had dinner, they argued—fought [with each other]. Now, there came . . . they fought. The two, the two cut off each other's head. Each one hit the other and cut off his head.
10 gāḷam, ʾarbaʿ, xamest-iyyām, sitt-iyyām ʿando, u-niswānhum ʿindhom yeʿayyṭan. kull min ḥāṭṭa rās ǧōzha ʿindo u-yeʿayyṭan.	10 They said, four, five days, six days [passed] and their wives were by them, crying. Each one put the head of her husband near him and cried.
14 aǧat al.e. margat ʿalēhum hā-l-ḥamāma, margat ʿalēhen. gāḷan. ^{i}txarrafan maʿ baʿaḏ̣hen al-ḥamāmāt. gāḷat-ilha, "tiʿerfi, ḥamāma," gāḷat-^{i}lha: "ta-dgūli." gāḷat-^{i}lha, "law-inhom hassāʿa račban, kull min ḥāṭṭa rāso ʿalē, hā-s-sāʿa yigūmu. yigfum ʿa-l-ʿāda wi-yṣīram yṭības, miṯel-mā llī kānam ʾawwal."	14 There came the . . .There came by the pigeon, came by them. They said . . . they spoke with one another, the pigeons. She said to her, "You know, pigeon," she said, "Well, speak." She said to her, "If they put now, each one of them, puts together back his head on him, they will now get up as usual, and will become, and heal, as they had been before."

22 hinne iṣannaṭan ʿalē, ʿala-al-ḥamāma, al-ḥamāma rāčba minhen fōg, ʿa-l-malla. gāḷat ilha, “sāmʿa, wulli, xayya, sāmʿa? tismaʿi l-ḥamāma čēf ⁱtgūḷ?”

26 raddat, ʿādat ʿalēhin al-ḥači. gāḷat-ⁱlhin, “wuliyye ḥamāma,” gāḷat-ⁱlha, “hasāʿa-šnu tgūli, yā ḥamāma” gālat ilha, “law-innhen hāssa, halla, hā-n-niswān hunne rāčba rūshem, hā-s-sāʿ yigūmu, yṣīram al-ʿāda, mitel-mā čānam ’awwal.”

32 gāman, gāman. ḥaṭṭan ar-rūs, min farḥithen wa-ʿağalithen ğat al-ḥurma al-’awwala, mart al-ᵉkbīr, ḥaṭṭat rās ğōzha ʿala-ğiṯṯet silfha, u-rās silfha ʿa-ğiṯṯet ğōzha. hazzam, subḥāno wa-ʿizzo wa-ğalālo, miṯel mā čānam ’awwal u-’aḥsan kamān.

39 gāḷat-ⁱlha, al-ḥamāmāt fōgen. qāḷat-ⁱlha “ṭayyeb, yā ḥamāma, al-mastōra hāy min farḥitha rakkabat rās ğōzha ʿala silfha, u-rās silfha ʿala ğasad ğōzha, al-wiḥda tilḥag al-ğiṯṯa willa tilḥag ar-rās?” gāḷat-ilha, “la’, tilḥag ağ-ğiṯṯa.”

45 gāḷat-ⁱlha, “lā, yā mastūra,” gāḷat-ⁱlha: “ⁱmbala, tilḥag ağ-ğiṯṯa.” gāḷat-ⁱlha, “ṭayyeb, šū, eḥči baʿad marra” gāḷat-ilha “ana aguḷ-ḷeč tilḥag rāso. tilḥag ar-rās.” gāḷat-ⁱlha, “la’, tilḥag ağ-ğaṯṯa.”

50 haḏīka xaḏat e . . . rās silifha u-haḏīk xaḏat rās silifha. kull min ’axḏat, nihağat ʿala l-ğeṯṯa.

22 They [were] listening to it, to the pigeon—the pigeons were perching above them, on the oak tree. She said to her, “Do you hear? O, sister, do you hear? Do you hear what the pigeon is saying?”

26 She repeated for them this talk, she said to them, “O, pigeon,” she said to her, “now, what are you saying, o pigeon?” She said to her, “If they now, these women, put together their heads, they will get up, will become as they had been in the beginning.”

32 They [the women] got up, they got up. They put the heads together. Due to their joy and the speed, the first woman, the elder’s wife, put the head of her husband on the body of her brother-in-law, and the head of her brother-in-law on her husband’s body. They moved, praise Allah, his greatness and power and glory. [They were] as before, and even better.

39 She said to her, the pigeons above them, she said to her, “All right, o pigeon, this lady, because of her joy she put back her husband’s head on her brother-in-law’s body and the head of her brother-in-law on her husband’s body; will the one join the body or will she join the head?” She said to her, “No, she will join the body.”

45 She said to her, “No, lady,” she said to her. “But yes, she will join the body.” She said to her, “All right, what? Say again.” She said to her, “I am telling you, she will join his head. She will join his head.” She said to her, “No, she will join the body.”

50 This one took . . . eriup
. . . the head of her brother-in-law and this took the head of her brother-in-law. Each one took, and went off by the body.

53 ğat yām hin ğāʿdāt, winna tgūḷ-ḷa "la', lāzem in wiḥda tilḥag ar-rās. tilḥag ar-rās, tilḥag ar-rās." gāḷat -^{i}lha: "yā xayya, widna nalḥag ar-rās. 'ani 'alḥag rās ğōzi u-inti telḥagi rās ğōzek." gāman, haḏīč xaḏat silfha u-haḏīč xaḏat—ʿāwadat ʿa-silfha. ʿāšan.	53 One day when they were sitting, and she said to her, "No. Each one has to join the head. She has to join the head. She has to join the head." She said to her, "O, sister, we will join the head. I'll join my husband's head and you will join your husband's [head]." They got up, that one took her brother-in-law, and that one took, and went back to her brother-in-law. They lived (settled).
60 gāḷat-^{i}lhin, ḥekat imʿāhem al-ḥamāma, gāḷat-luhum, "lēš? ʿalāmkam?[3] šnū[4] xlāfkam?"	60 She told them, the pigeon spoke with them [the brothers], she said to them, "Why? What for did you? What was your quarrel [about]?"
63 gāḷ-ḷa,"walla, šnū xlāfna, xlāfna šē[5] basīṭ. yaʿani, l-exwān mā tithāwaš? titkātal al-exwān. mā bī. u-'eḥna tkātalna u-hēča ṣār bina. w-al-ḥamdu-li-ḷḷā al-ʿumer mā rāḥ, al-ʿumer ḏaḷḷ hōn."	63 He said to her, "By Allah, what was our quarrel, our quarrel was [over] a simple thing. That is, don't brothers quarrel? They quarrel. And we quarreled and this [is what] happened to us. And thank Allah [our] lifetime has not left [us], [our] lifetime has remained here."

Commentary

"The Transposed Heads" describes how the heads of two brothers are severed under violent circumstances. Then the two are brought back to life when their heads are attached to their bodies, but inadvertently each of the heads is connected to the wrong body.

This motif, E34, "Resuscitation with misplaced head. In restoration of several persons simultaneously through reassembling of members, the heads are placed on the wrong bodies. Sometimes the damage is repaired, sometimes not," appears in some old Indian tales. The great Indian epic Mahābhārata, which dates back to the fourth century BCE and more or less crystallized about eight hundred years later, tells about Jamadagni, who was married to a woman named Renuka and who ordered his sons to execute her. One of them obeyed the order and decapitated her. Later Jamadagni agreed to fulfill his son's wish and bring his mother back to life. According to a later version of the story, Renuka found refuge with a woman from a low caste called Yellamma, and the son of Jamadagni cut off the heads of both of them with his sword. Later, when he brought them to life, he mistakenly put Renuka's head on Yellamma's body and Yellamma's head on Renuka's body.

Although there is some resemblance between the stories, it seems that the Bedouin story is genetically related to another Indian story, taken from a collection of stories called *Kathasaritsagara* (Ocean of Stories). This work from the eleventh century CE includes hundreds of stories and was originally written in rhyme.

One of the best-known parts of *Ocean of Stories* is the Vittala story, featuring a vampire demon in a corpse. The file contains twenty-five stories told by the demon who resides in a corpse, which the king carries on his shoulder. Each of the stories ends with a riddle, which the king has to solve.

One of these riddles, which later formed the basis for Thomas Mann's book *The Transposed Heads*, tells about a young woman who married a young launderer. One day the launderer and his wife, accompanied by the bride's brother, went to visit her parents' home. On their way, they passed a great temple of Kali, the goddess of death. The groom entered the temple, and suddenly a fatal thought came to his mind: "People tend to bring the goddess bloody gifts; would it be not proper for me to sacrifice the noblest sacrifice of myself?" The young launderer tied his hair to the rope of the bell, and, holding the sword that was in the temple, he decapitated himself. His dead body dropped to the floor, and the bell, announcing the offering of a gift to the goddess, rang as the rope stretched under the weight of the decapitated head attached to it. When the husband lingered, his brother-in-law entered the temple to find out what had happened to him. When he saw the groom's severed head, he understood what had happened. He became agitated, behaved like his brother-in-law, and sacrificed himself to the goddess with the sword. For a long time, the girl was waiting for her brother and her husband to return, and as they tarried, she also entered the temple. At the sight of the two dead men lying on the ground, she was horrified. "Woe to me! What happened here? I'm lost forever!" In desperation, she fell to the ground and mourned her two loved ones, who had been plundered from the land of life so suddenly. "What's the point of my life without them?" she thought. "I'd better kill myself!" She picked up lattices of an *asuka* wood and shaped them into a choke loop. But as she tightened the loop around her neck, the voice of the goddess Kali was heard from heaven: "My daughter, do not act in haste. I am pleased with the courage you display despite your youth. Throw away that noose! Attach the heads of your husband and brother to their bodies, and by my grace, they will rise up again alive!" When the young woman heard the goddess's words, she let go of the rope and ran happily to the bodies of her brother and husband. But in her haste to bring them back to life, she did not realize that she was attaching the heads to the wrong bodies. And so it happened that she, by the will of fate, attached her brother's head to the body of her husband, and her husband's head to the body of her brother. The two came back to life and stood up. After they fell down before the goddess and thanked her for her kindness, the two men and the girl left the temple, thinking of the miracle that had happened to them. But suddenly the girl noticed her mistake and stood still, stunned and lost for advice.

At this point the story ends, and the demon in the body of a dead man poses the riddle: "Which of the two is the true husband of the girl?"

The king, who listened to the story attentively, replies, "The body to which the head is attached is the husband, the head is the main thing, and the body only goes after the head!"[6]

The king's answer to the demon is identical to the conclusion reached by the two women at the end of the Bedouin story. First, each of them preferred to stick to her husband's body, but at the end, each realized that she had to cling to her husband's head.

The narrator calls the story "Smart Muḥammad and Smart Ḥusen." In Bedouin folklore, these names belong to popular heroes, famed for their cleverness. However, in the course of the story, the narrator no longer mentions the names of the two brothers or ascribes them any unusual cleverness. On the contrary, they are described as hot-blooded people who resort to violence because of a controversy and kill each other.

The two pigeons here play the role of the goddess in the Indian story. The two widows understand their speech. The motif of birds or animals that transmit messages to humans is familiar from many stories, both in the Muslim culture and in the Jewish culture space. In the Bible, Noah sends from the ark two birds, a raven and a dove, to find out whether the water has abated from the face of the earth. The first time, the dove finds no rest for the sole of her foot, but after seven more days, Noah sends her away again, and this time she brings the desired message: "And the dove came in to him in the evening; and, lo, in her mouth was an olive leaf pluckt off: so Noah knew that the waters were abated from off the earth" (Genesis 8:11). In fact, the dove motif is much older and appears already in the story of Utnapishtim, Noah's Sumerian-Akkadian character, in the Gilgamesh tales. In this version of the story, the hero sends three birds: a dove, a swallow, and a raven. The first two birds return to him, while the raven does not. The motif of the olive leaf does not exist there at all, and it is the raven that gives the hero the hint that the water has abated.

The Babylonian Talmud tells of Rav Ilish, a friend of Rabbi Nachman Bar Ya'akov, who lived in the second half of the third century CE in the city of Nehardea in Babylon (a city that was located between the Euphrates and the Tigris). I provide parts of the story here:

> One day when Rav 'Ilish was in captivity, he had with him one man who knew the language of the birds. A raven came and called to him. Rav 'Ilish said to the man who knew the birds' language, "What does the raven say?" He said to him, "The raven said, "Ilish, run away! 'Ilish, run away!'" Rav 'Ilish said: "The raven is a liar and should not be trusted." Meanwhile a dove came and called. He said to him, "What did it say?" He said to him, "'Ilish, run away! 'Ilish, run away!" Rav 'Ilish said, "The assembly of Israel to the dove is likened, a miracle is happening to me." He stood up and fled, and the man who interpreted the bird's language joined him. Rav 'Ilish crossed the river in peace, and that person—they found him and killed him. (Babylon Talmud, Gittin 45a)

In this story, we already hear about talking birds, whose words are interpreted explicitly to the hero by a person who is familiar with the language of the birds.

The motif of the pigeons that reveal to the hero a secret related to miraculous healing is common in various cultural spaces. For example, El-Shamy writes: "Overheard conversation of birds (turtledoves, pigeon) reveals that some of their own organs are the only medicine to cure hero: they are caught and killed for the cure."[7]

This motif also appears in another Bedouin story that I wrote down, "The Prince and His Two Wives." But here, in the brothers' story, the pigeons play an active role in the plot. Once the heads have been replaced, they negotiate among themselves about the philosophical (and practical) question of whom the women are supposed to adhere to, the head or the body. At first, the women seem to behave as the first pigeon thought, but in the end, they change their minds and follow the opinion of the second pigeon. The dispute is decided, but the pigeon is not satisfied with this and wants to know the reason for the quarrel, and she turns to the husbands to ask, "Why? . . . What was your quarrel [about]?"

The narrator does not explain why the women changed their decision. However, it can be assumed that at first the women clung each to her husband's body because of a reluctance to maintain relationships with a body that does not belong to the husband but to his brother, a deed that may be interpreted as treachery. But later they realize that the head is the main thing and that actually having a relationship with the husband's original body may be interpreted by the husband's head as betrayal.

The sentence, "[They were] as before, and even better," is a metatext in which the narrator expresses her opinion on what happened. It is possible that in her words there is some hidden unrealized erotic fantasy.

It seems that the titles "Smart Muḥammad" and "Smart Ḥusen" are more suitable for the pigeons than for the two brothers. Unlike the two brothers, the pigeons conduct a cultural debate without violence, and together they study the reasons for the women's change of mind.

The two sisters-in-law are described in the story as taking initiative and bringing their husbands back to life. Even the decision of to whom they should stick is theirs to make. The two men, even after their return to life, do not take an active part in the plot, and we are told nothing about their attitude toward their wives' choice. The husbands thank Allah, and not the pigeons, for the miracle that happened to them (as the girl in the Indian story thanks the goddess): "And thank Allah [our] lifetime has not left [us], [our] lifetime has remained here."

It seems that the women submissively accept the event that causes their husbands' death. In any case, only the husbands explicitly relate to the event, but they do so briefly in response to the pigeon's question: "By Allah, what was our quarrel, our quarrel was [over] a simple thing. That is, don't brothers quarrel? They quarrel. And we quarreled and this [is what] happened to us."

We see, then, how a magic story based on an imaginary event wanders from one cultural space to another, and in every cultural space it fulfills various functions in the context in which it is told. In the Indian culture, it is a riddle story in a sequence of similar stories that present various aspects of traditional Indian thinking. In the Bedouin narrative space, it seems to convey a message about violence and its consequences. The pigeons express to some extent the feelings of women in a distinctly patriarchal society who attempt to balance the hasty male character and to maintain the integrity of the family.

Notes

1. *bī hā-l-ixwān aṯ-ṯnēn*: "There were these two brothers." For *bī*, see chapter 4, note 1, and chapter 11, note 2. Note that more than half the stories in this collection begin with this particle on its own or with some other introductory element, such as the demonstrative particle *hāḏa* (literally "this"), and a conjugated form of *kān*, "to be." These are opening particles characteristic of Galilee Bedouin narratives. (For other presentative openings in the Negev, see Henkin, *Negev Arabic*, section 7.4, esp. p. 137–38.)

2. Galilee Bedouin dialects have time adverb forms that do not exist in sedentary dialects. The word *yōm-innam*, “when,” includes three elements: *yōm* (“the day when”), *inn* (“that”), and *-am* (3m.pl. bound pronominal suffix). The latter changes according to the required person. Cf. other particles with similar structures, such as *inn-winno, winna* (< *wa-inn-o*), “lo,” to express a surprising fact or something similar (on –inn, cf. Owens, “Historical Linguistics”).

3. *'alāmkam?*: “Why are you?” This interrogative particle is composed of three elements: *'ala* (“on, about”), *mā* (“what”), and *kam* (masculine 2m.pl.). The word is also used without the suffixed bound pronoun: *'alā-mā*, “What for? Why?” Sedentary dialects in Israel do not have this word.

4. *šnū*, the Bedouin form of the interrogative particle “what,” is also used in Bedouin dialects outside Israel, but *šū* is used in sedentary dialects in Israel. Both these forms apparently derive from (*’ayy*) *šay’in hū~ huwwa* (literally “which thing [is] it”). In Bedouin dialects the word can be *šnūwwa*, with a lengthened bound pronoun (< *šnū* + *huwwa*).

5. *xlāfna šē basīṭ*: “Our quarrel was [over] a simple thing.” The word for “something, thing” is *’iši* in sedentary dialects (< *šay’*, “thing”) and is sometimes shortened to *šī* (cf. note 4, above). But since the vowel systems of Bedouin Arabic dialects are not entirely stable and the vowel *i* appears as *ē*. In many cases, it is very hard to decide by ear which vowel is uttered. This speech feature occurs in many tales in this collection.

6. Penzer, *Ocean of Story*, 6:204–8.

7. El-Shamy, *Types of the Folktale*, 1044, B517§.

16. The Son Who Obeyed His Mother

NARRATOR: Zaid ʿAli Muḥammad Saʿadi

TRIBE: *'Arab el-Sa'adiyya*
IFA 13713 October 1, 1981

Text

Once there was a widow and she had a son. The son grew up. When he was about twenty to twenty-five, he asked his mother to buy him a horse and a rifle. So she bought them for him. Every day he goes hunting and he brings rabbits, partridges, gazelles, and everything.

And one day he went hunting, and he hunted a lot, and on his way back he found wheat [seeds]—that's a little pile next to ants. So he took it.

His mother took the gazelles and saw the wheat in it, in the sack. He put them in a sack.

Then she asked him, "Where did you get this wheat?"

He said to her, "I found it, like that, near an ants' house."

Then she said to him, "It's not good, *ḥarām* [forbidden]—you know what *ḥarām* is?—*ḥarām*, you have to give them the wheat back, they worked hard to get this food, they eat it in the rain. Go and give it back."

He went and returned the wheat to the ants.

On the second day, he went, he hunted whatever he hunted, and on his way back, he found a goat. He took it, and when his mother saw the goat, she asked him, "Where did you get this?"

He said to her, "I found it like this near the . . . tied to a tree."

So she said to him, "Go return it. It belongs to a"—I don't know the name in Hebrew—we call it *ğinn* [demon].

He went back and returned the goat.

On the third day, he hunted too, and on his way back, he found gold near the river. He took the gold.

She said, "Where did you get the gold from?"

He told her, "I found it near the river."

Then she said to him, "This is an angel, an angel. He went down to bathe in the river. Go and give it back."

So this time he got mad at her.

He told her: "Every time I bring something to the house, you say to me, 'Go and give it back.' I'm going to give it back and I will not come back to you!"

She loved him very much. Now he went to give them [the gold] back and he left. And he went to the city. He saw a large building that was built of heads of people. One more head was missing. This building only lacked one more head.

Then he went in and said, "What is this?"

They told him that whoever entered here had to meet three tests. If he succeeds, he will marry the beauty queen, the most beautiful [girl] in the world at the time.

So he said, "OK." He did not . . . he could not go back, only to continue. So he said, "OK."

He went to the first test. They mixed barley and wheat and salt and sugar and that. They made him a big pile of all this. And they asked him to separate them. For example, the salt—to do one pile. The barley—one pile. The wheat—one pile. Sugar also. In one night. And it was difficult for him—what, you saw how much.

When he returned the wheat to the ants, the ants did not forget it, and then they all came and helped him. Do you know how many ants there are in the world? All the ants in the world, because he gave it back to them, he made them a favor, they all came and helped him, and they separated the seeds, and he succeeded in the first test.

Well, on the second test, they put a pigeon. A pigeon under the blanket, and he had to know what was underneath. Then the angel came and told him, because he had returned the gold to the angel, and the angel had not forgotten it. Then he came and told him that there was a pigeon under the blanket. So he said to them, "Pigeon!" And so he succeeded in the second test.

On the third test, they let him eat meat, and this meat—he should know what sort of meat it is? Of animals, of birds, of what? And they gave him a gazelle, gazelle, meat of gazelle. Then he did not know what it was. The *ǧinn* came and said to him, "This is gazelle meat!" Then he said, "The meat of a gazelle!" And so, he succeeded in all the tests, in the three tests, and got her [the princess].

And now he went back to his mother. His mother, because she loved him very much, she kept crying about him. That's why she now does not see.

Then he comes and knocks on the door. "Mom, Mom, it's me!"

Then she did not answer him. She thought it was the children, because the children kept coming and knocking on her door, saying, "Your son is coming, your son is coming!" And they lie, lie about it. That's the way they laugh at her, those little children.

In the end, she gets up, and he sees that she's blind, she does not see. Then he had a handkerchief, and then he put it on her eyes, and then she, his mother, started to see again, and then she saw him.

Well, she asked him, she said to him, "From where is this pretty girl you have?"

He said to her, "This is my wife."

Then she kissed her and that, and held her, and the story was over.

Commentary

The story "The Son Who Obeyed His Mother" was recorded in Hebrew from a young Bedouin, about seventeen years old, who had heard the story from his grandmother, Ṯalǧe Ibrahīm Diāb Ġadīr, from the ʿArab el-Ḥuǧērāt tribe.

This story is a deteriorated version of the narrative type ATU 851, "The Princess Who Cannot Solve the Riddle." According to the description of the international type, a princess is destined to marry someone who presents her a puzzle that she cannot solve. The hero of the story, who in many cases is a simple man, presents the princess a riddle based on personal events that happened to him (motif H565, "Riddle propounded from chance experience. On the way to the riddle trial, a youth sees things that give him a clue for his riddles"). The princess (in some versions) disguises herself and visits the hero at night to discover the solution to the riddle. The hero shares the solution with her but preserves some object from her clothing as proof that he has identified her (motifs H81.2, "Clandestine visit of princess to hero betrayed by token"; H117, "Identification by cut garment. Garment is cut and fragment taken as token"). The next day, when he comes to the palace, the princess solves the riddle but allows the hero to pose another riddle. He poses her the riddle, the solution of which is related to her visit in the previous evening, and she prefers to marry him instead of solving it. Different versions present different riddles.

It is interesting to compare our story to the Egyptian version from El-Shamy's book *Folktales of Egypt*, titled "The Man Who Put His Mother over His Shoulder and Rode His Father."[1] In this version, the hero first turns to his mother, asking her to be liable for the return of a rifle he borrowed from a neighbor, and later asks his father to be liable for the return of a horse he borrowed from another neighbor. He goes hunting, and during the hunt, he shoots a gazelle, but she dies before he can approach her and slaughter her according to the laws of religion, and therefore its flesh is *ḥarām*, meaning that eating it is forbidden. But immediately afterward, he cuts off the belly of the gazelle, takes out the living fetus, and slaughters it, and therefore the fetus is considered *ḥalāl*, meaning pure and legally (by religious laws) edible. In his thirst, with one hand he scrapes the sweat from his horse's skin into the palm of his other hand and drinks it.

When he enters the princess's palace, he is put to the riddles trial, although he is aware that if the princess solves his riddle, he will be executed by her father.

The hero poses this riddle to the princess: "What about somebody who put his mother over his shoulder, rode his father, ate the pure out of the profane, and drank water that came neither from heaven nor from earth?"

The princess fails to answer the riddle and turns to cunning ways. She finds out where the young man is living, goes disguised to the house where he lives, and asks the landlady to introduce her to the hero as her daughter. The two converse, and the disguised princess asks him to tell her the solution to the riddle. The hero is ready to do so if she stays in his room one night. As she sleeps, he chops off part of her braid.

The next day when he arrives at the palace, the princess answers the riddle. Her father wants to kill him, but the hero asks permission to pose another riddle: "A bird left its nest, with a stranger to rest. / When it came back, one wing it did lack." Hearing the riddle, the princess is silent. She admits that she heard the solution to the first riddle from the hero himself, and she agrees to marry him.

In a Jewish version from Yemen (IFA 245), the hero sells his father and mother and asks the princess to say who sold his father and mother and drank water not from the earth nor from heaven. In another Jewish version from Yemen (IFA 3445), which is very similar to the Egyptian version, a newborn that was removed from its mother's womb also appears.

This idea of a riddle based on personal experiences known only to the hero himself and solved by the riddle solver's deceit is ancient, and it appears in the Bible in the story of Samson and Delilah. Samson slays a lion on his way to Timnath, and some days later, he extracts honey from a beehive he finds in the dead body of the lion. On the basis of these experiences, he poses the Philistines a riddle: "Out of the eater came forth meat, and out of the strong came forth sweetness" (Judges 14:14). The Philistines solve the riddle by deceit. They get the solution from Samson's wife. It is possible to view the lion's corpse as an unclean thing that contains pure food (honey), like the dead gazelle in the Egyptian version of the story, which is considered forbidden food because it was not ritually slaughtered but which contains within it a newborn animal that can be slaughtered properly and therefore be considered *ḥalāl*, or pure.

The Bedouin story mentions the rifle and the horse, but they do not play any role in the riddles presented below. In this case, the princess has posed the riddles, and the hero is supposed to answer them; otherwise he will be beheaded and his skull will complete the skull building, which stands next to the princess's palace. However, just as the personal events the hero has undergone in the Egyptian version serve as raw materials for the riddle, so too, in parallel, do the experiences of the hero of the Bedouin story help him solve the riddles.

As in the Egyptian version, the Bedouin story begins with the hero's relationship with his mother. Later, the terms *ḥarām* and *ḥalāl* appear in a different context, in the mother's advice to her son.

But the uniqueness of the Bedouin story lies in its moral perception. Anyone who behaves honestly and generously will end up being rewarded, and this principle, according to the story, is universal, valid not only in the human world but also in other worlds. In the animal world, the grateful ants reciprocate; in the demonic world, the genie does; and in the divine world, it is the angel that helps him solve the third riddle.

The three riddles that the princess poses to the hero are all related to food: food from the plant world, seeds; food from the birds' world, pigeon; and food from the animal world, gazelle. The hero is required to use all his senses to solve the riddles. In the first riddle, he uses sight, the power to separate different types of seeds, which is like the separation of good and evil. In the second riddle, it is the tactile sense—recognition of what is invisible, the inner essence. And in the third case, it is the sense of taste, the recognition of food according to its taste and therefore recognition of things that have been transformed, exposing the changing essence of things.

The whole story circles around the mother-son relationship. It begins with a mother who supports her son as he is growing up and gives him both financial and moral guidance. The son revolts against what he perceives to be overly self-righteous, but he obeys her instructions even when he does not agree with them, and ultimately, it is this obedience that enables him to solve the riddles, to escape death, and to win the princess's hand. At the end of the story, the hero, who internalized the lessons he learned from his mother, rewards his mother and cures her from her blindness. His moral behavior is accentuated by the bad behavior of the neighborhood children, who abuse and mock the blind mother.

Note

1. El-Shamy, *Folktales of Egypt*, 81–86, 257–58.

17. The Silent Princess and Smart Mḥammad

NARRATOR: Ṯarwa Yāsīn

TRIBE: *ʿArab el-Ḥaǧāǧra*
IFA 17393 April 18, 1984

1 hāḏa, bī hā-l-ezlima, lē ṯalaṯ iwlād. ṣāram . . . rāḥ minhom ač-čebīr, ḥammal ʿala hā-l-baġla u-rāḥ yebīʿ—yebīʿ ᵉgmāš m-maṣar. hēna, maṣar, bī hā-l-malak ʿindo binet. binto mā teḥki.	1 There was this man. He had three children/ boys. They became . . . the eldest went from them, packed on the mule and went to sell—sell cloth [material] in Cairo. Now, Cairo, there was in it a king who had a daughter. His daughter does not speak.
6 gām—ğa ʿala hā-l-xetyār, ʿendo ḥōš yeḥoṭṭha hā-l-duwāb ʾalli l–al-ġarīb. ḥaṭṭ hā-l-faras u-bāt ʿendo. gāḷ-ḷo, "yā-būy," gāḷ-ḷo, "naʿam." gāḷ-ḷo, "šnū hā-r-rūs hāḏ-alli mdaḥdara?"	6 He [the boy] went to an old man who had a courtyard, where he kept the riding animals of the strangers [foreign people]. He put the horse and spent the night at his place. He said to him, "O father." He said to him, "Yes." He said to him, "What are these rolling heads?"
11 gāḷ-ḷo, "walla, hāy, bint al-malak mā taḥči. u-ʾabūha gāḷ-ḷhom ʾalli yeḥaččīha, ʾanṭī al-mamlaka w-ʾanṭī al-bint." gāḷ-ḷo, "waḷḷāhi ġār arūḥ."	11 He said to him, "By Allah, these, the princess does not speak and her father said to them, that whoever makes her speak I'll give him the kingdom and I'll give him the girl." He said to him, "By Allah, I will [certainly] go [there]."
15 gāḷ-ḷo, "yā-būya, šābb u-ma tistāhal al-mōt, u-ḥarām, u-xiyāna ʿalēk, tinḏabiḥ. u-ḥači, mi-hi rāiḥa taḥči maʿāk."	15 He said to him, "O son [boy], [you are] young and do not deserve to die. A shame [if you die] and treachery on you, you will get butchered. And [as to] speaking—she will not speak with you."

19 gāḷ-ḷo, "wēn, yā šāṭer. waḷḷa ġēr arūḥ." gāḷ-ḷo, "dīr bālak ʿala hā-l-hdūm u-ʿala hal-baġla ʿindak, wa-ʾani wid(i) arūḥ ʿalēha." rāḥ.	19 He said to him, "Wherefor, o clever [man]?" He said to him, "By Allah, I must go." He said to him, "Take care of these clothes and the mule at your place, and I will go to her." He went.
23 ḥaṭṭ ʿalē ḥaras. yišūfha inha taḥči walla mā taḥči. ḥaṭṭ ʿalēha ḥaras. mā ḥakat. aṣ-ṣubeḥ xaḏā hā-l-ğallād, giṭaʿ rāso. mā xaḏūš, ramā.	23 He put a guard on him. To see her if she speaks or does not speak. He put a guard on her. She did not speak. In the morning, the hangman took him, and cut his head off. He did not take it, threw it.
27 ġābat sina, sintēn, ṯalāṯa, ğa ʾaxū, gāḷ, "waḷḷa, hāḏ-axūya staġna maṣer, hassa imʿā li-mwāl u-ʾiši." rāḥ. yōman rāḥ gāḷ-ḷo "waḷḷa, hāḏ alḥag axūy." liḥeğ.	27 This [issue] remained unknown a year, two years, three years. His brother came, he said, "By Allah, this brother of mine has become rich in Egypt, has now property [and money] etc." He went. When he went, he said, "By Allah, I'll follow [and join] my brother." He followed [him].
31 daḥḥag, yaʿani šāf hāy el-ebġaḷa, ʿerifha. gāḷ, "hāy, bġaḷt axūy." liga ha-l-xityār, gāḷ-ḷo, "yā ʿammi, hāḏ-al-bġaḷa la-mīn?" gāl-lo, "hāḏi l-ibġaḷa, ğat—ṣāḥiba, hēna, u-fāt, u-ʿendīna bint al-malak mā taḥči, u-ḥaṭṭam ġār arūḥ, ugult u-nihēt, lā trūḥ, lā trūḥ, mā raḏa, gāḷ, "widd-arūḥ."	31 He saw, that is, he saw that mule, and recognized it. He said, "This is my brother's mule." He met the old man. He said to him, "This mule—whose is it?" He said to him, "This mule came—her owner—here, and he entered—and at our place, the princess does not talk, and he swore that he must go. And I said and warned, 'Don't go, don't go.' He did not agree; he said, 'I must go.'"
39 gāḷ-ḷo, "waḷḷa, ani-(a)ḥsan min axūya? waḷḷa, ġēr arūḥ." "yā-būya, lā trūḥ, ya šēn, an-nāḥā, la trūḥ, yā waḷḷa ġēr etmūt." hā-s-sāʿa rāḥ. yām ma-rāḥ, alli—miṯel mā ṣār (maʾ) axū, ṣār ʿalē—iḏbaḥū. bi-š-šaros.	39 He said to him, "By Allah, am I better than my brother? By Allah, I must go." "O, son, don't go, o bad, the place [is bad], don't go, or else you will [surely] die." Now, he went. When he went, that—as happened to his brother, happened to him—they killed him. With malice.
45 ḏaḷḷ axūhum az-zġayyir. (ha-s)sā gāḷ-ḷ-abū, gāḷ-ḷo, "yā-būya," gāḷ-ḷo, "yā-būya,"[1] gāḷ-ḷo, "waḷḷa, widd-alḥag ʾaxwāni." gāḷ-ḷo, "tilḥag ʾaxwānak, yā-būya, txaḷḷa iyyāna la-ḥālna, ʾana w-immak."	45 Their young brother remained. Now, he said to his father, he said, "O father." He said to him, "O father." He said to him, "By Allah, I want to join my brothers." He said to him, "You'll join your brothers, son, you will leave us alone, me and your mother?"
50 gāḷ-ḷo, "waḷḷa, ʿalēkam ʾaḷḷa. waddi (arūḥ)." ḥammal ʿala hā-bġalto, ḥaṭṭ baʿadha ğ-ğibla bančo šāf.[2] hū miše.	50 He said to him, "By Allah, Allah [is] with you [goodbye], I must [go]." He loaded his mule and took the direction of Mecca [south] as the best point [for the journey] that he saw. He went.

53 ǧa ʿala, ʿala hā-l-bīr, bīr ṃayy. liga hā-l-bīr hā-ṭ-ṭrīš, hā-l-^{i}bnādamīn, hā-l-ḥarīm, hā- š-šyūx, hā-l-ḥayy, kullha tistanna widdha mayy ta-tišrab.

53 He came to this well, water well. He found [around the well] flocks of sheep, people, women, old men, all these [living] animals, all waiting, wanting water to drink.

57 u-bīha ḥūt mā yizgī. ḥāmi l-mayye ʿalē. ḥāṭṭ ʿala rkāba . . . ǧāʿid bal-mayy, ḥāṭṭ ʿala rkāba ṯ-ṯnēn niswān ^{a}ṯnēn, waḥda samra, u-weḥda bēḏa. gāḷ-hū, gāḷ-ḷo, “mīn aḥsan, yā šāṭr-^{i}mḥimmad, as-samra walla l-bēḏa?”[3]

57 In it was a ḥūt [a monster], not letting people drink. He was keeping its water. He had put on his knees. . . . He was sitting in the water, put on his two knees two women, a swarthy one and a white one. He said to him, “Who is more beautiful/better, o Smart Mḥammad, the swarthy or the white one?”

63 gāḷ-ḷo, “waḷḷa, ʾalli yḥebbo gaḷbak, law-an yekūn ʿabd aswad.” gāḷ-ḷo, “inta ḥačēt aṣ-ṣaḥīḥ. yaḷḷa, inšil b-al-mayy.”

63 He said to him, “By Allah, whichever your heart likes, even if it’s a black slave.” He said to him, “You spoke right. Come on, draw up the water.”

66 ṣār yinšil u-yizgi hā-l-. hāl-eṭ-ṭrīš hā-lli ḥawalē, kullha šerbat, hā-l-ibnādamīn, hā-l-mawāšīn, kullo šereb.

66 He started drawing water [up] and making drink these . . . herds around him, all of them drank, the people, these herds, everybody drank.

69 ṣāram kull min yirkab ʿalē yḥibbo, ybūso. gāḷ-ḷo, “ʾani—ʾinta rāye(ḥ) ʿala l-blād (hā)ḏīče, wa-hunāka widdak taḏḏāyig. ʾani widd-anṭīk sabeʿ ʾaškāl, u-haḏōl as-sabeʿ farağ lēk. hāḏa minhen ṭēr u-minhen rīšt an-namla, u-minhen sakkīnet bōlāḏ, u-minhen baṭṭīxa.” w-unṭāh. aṭ-ṭer ḥaṭṭa b-ʿubbo, mā ḥada yšūfo. waḷḷa, w-al-iġrāḏ alli mʿā, ḥaṭṭhin bi-ğyābo u-qaʿad.

69 They started, each one that was riding past him, [started] kissing him. He [the ḥūt] said to him, “You are going to that country, and there you will suffer. I will give you seven things, and these seven [magical objects] are your salvation [help]. One of them is a bird, and another is an ant’s feather, and another is a steel knife, and [one] of them a steel watermelon.” He gave [them to] him. The bird he put in his lap, so no one would see it, by Allah, and the things which he had, he put in his pockets and stayed.

79 s-sāʿa gāḷ-ḷo, fāt. gāḷ-ḷo, “yā-būy, haḏōla li-bġāl, haḏōla, la-d-dawāb haḏōla la-xwāni?” gaḷ-ḷo, “ʾā waḷḷa.” gāḷ-ḷo, “haḏōla-xwāni?” gāḷ-ḷo, “hā, waḷḷa, haḏōl homme, taʿāl tanni awarrīk rūshon.” ssa warrā rūshom, ṣār yʿayyaṭ ʿalēhom, gāḷ-ḷo, “lēš tibči?” gāḷ-ḷo, “waḷḷāhi, ġēr arūḥ. hiyya mīta walla mīttēn? mīta wiḥda widd-amūt. t-afūt, ʿand bint hal-malak wa” . . . fāt.

79 Now he said to him, he entered [Cairo]. He said to him, “O father, those mules, those, the animals there are my brothers’ [mules]?” He said to him, “Yes, by Allah.” He said to him, “Are these my brothers?” He said to him, “Aye, by Allah, these are them. Come and I’ll show you their heads.” Now he showed him their heads. He began to cry for them. He said to him, “Why are you crying?” He said to him, “By Allah, I must go. Is it one death or two? For one death I’d die [sacrifice myself]. I will go, to that king’s daughter and . . .” He entered.

89 ḥāčīha min hēn, xarrifha min hēn, mā rḏat ta-trodd.[4] geḏab ha-l-^{i}frēx u-ṭayyaro. ṭayyaro, wuga(ʿ) ʿindhen b-al-ḥāl. ṣār yxarrifha. xarrifha, xarrifha. gāḷ-ḷha, gāḷ-ḷha,	89 He talked to her here, told her from there—she did not agree to answer. He took that little bird and let it fly. He let it fly, it alighted near them at once. He began telling her. Tell her, tell, he said to her, said to her,
94 gāḷ-ḷha, "mā widdeč tiḥči?" gāḷ-ḷo . . . mā ḥačat. ṣār aṭ-ṭēr ygūḷ, ygūḷ, yā . . . ṣār yxarrifhum aṭ-ṭēr. yāmin ṣār yxarrifhum, gāḷ-ḷum, "yā ʿarīs, yā ʿarūs, la-mīn ^{e}tkūn?" gāḷ-ḷo, "^{e}tkūn . . . la-l-xaššāb." gāḷ-ḷo, "la'. 'an-agūl la', "gāḷ-ḷo, "la-ʿādi la-l-imṣalli." gāḷ-ḷo, "la'."	94 said to her, "Don't you want to talk?" She said to him. . . . She did not speak. The bird began to say; it, the bird, began telling them. When it started telling them, it said to them, "O bridegroom, o bride, who will she belong to?" He said to him, "She will be for the carpenter." He said to him, "No, I'm saying no." He said to him, "Then to the praying man." He said to him, "No."
101 winha tgūḷ-ḷo, "lā', mu-hu hēč." gāḷ-ḷa, "la-ʿād, ešlōn?" wunha tgūḷ-ḷo, "lōla l-xaššāb mā ṣār ağ-ğeṯṯe, u-lōla l-^{e}mṣalli, mā dabbat ar-rūḥ." gāḷat-ḷo, "ḥičat," al-ḥurrās, 'al-ḥurrās, "ḥičat," al-ḥurrās, "ḥičat bintak, yā malak, ḥičat bintak, yā malak." mā ṣaddag.	101 And suddenly she says to him, "No, not like this." He said to her, "Then how?" And suddenly she says to him, "But for the carpenter, there would not have been the body and but for the praying man, the spirit would not have entered." She said to him. The guards, "She spoke!" The guards, "Your daughter has talked, o King. Your daughter has talked, King." He did not believe.
108 gāḷ, "ṯāni lēla widdi- baʿad 'aḥuṭṭ ṯāni ḥaras ʿalē." gaʿad, yxarref biha, yxarref biha, mā truddo. radd xarrafhom. gāḷ-ḷhum, "bī hā-ṯ-ṯalaṯ-ezlām, u-hā-ṯ-ṯalāṯa tiğğār. wāḥad imʿā zēt, wāḥad imʿā xām, u-wāḥad imʿā, še-isem-hā—gāḷ-ḷo,	108 He said, "[On the] next night I want to put another guard on her." He sat telling her, telling her, she did not answer him. It again talked to them. It said to them, "There [were] these three men, and these three [were] merchants. One had with him oil, one had [cloth] materials with him, one had—what's its name"—he said to him.
114 gāḷ-ḷo, "gām ğāb xaššāb, faṣṣal hā-l-xšaba, ʿamelha miṯel bani'ādam wa-rās wa-'idēn, wa-kull ši bēha.	114 He said, "He brought a carpenter, he carved this piece of wood, made it like a human, and the head and hands and body and everything in her.
117 "u-'ağa l-xayyāṭ, ʿimel lēha badla. sattar ʿalēha. ʿemel ʿalēha, sattar ʿalēha. u-intam nimtam. u-'ağa al-imṣalli, ṣalla wa-ddaʿa la-ṛabbo, innha idubb bīha r-rūḥ wa-ṣṣīr ibnādama tiḥči wa-tḥačēna wa-tgūl lēna ṣabāḥ al-xēr.	117 "[Then] the tailor came and made her a suit [of clothes]. He covered her [bare body, for chastity], hid her [body]. And you were asleep. And the praying man came and prayed to his Allah that he would put spirit in her and she would become a female human, talk and speak to us, and say to us good morning.

123 "mā xallaṣ alla hal-birze-lla winnha hā-š-šābba alli sibḥān alla mā xliǧha. 'ā. xtilfam ʿalēha." gāḷ-ḷa, "ṭayyeb, yā ʿarīs, yā ʿarūs, la-mīn etkūn?"	123 "He hardly finished that form of hers, and lo, there was this girl who—praise the Lord that has created her. Yes. They argued about her". He said to her, "Well, o bridegroom, o bride, whose will she be?"
127 gāḷat . . . huwwa gāḷ, "'ana (a)gūḷ la-l-xaššāb. w-inta, yā ṭēr?" gāḷ, "ana-gūḷ la-l-xayyāṭ." winha tgūḷ, "la', al-xayyāṭ labbasha l-badla, w-al-xaššāb faṣṣalha, w-al-imṣalli tmanā-lha dabbat ar-rūḥ fīha." 'ā. ḥičat. "ḥičat bintak yā malak, ḥičat bintak yā malak." hā-s-saʿ ṣaddag.	127 And she said . . . he said, "I am saying to the carpenter, and you, Bird?" He said, "I say—to the tailor," and lo she says, "No, the tailor dressed her the suit, and the carpenter made her form, and the praying man wished for the spirit to get into her." Yes. She spoke. "Your daughter has spoken, o King, your daughter has spoken, o King." Now he believed [him].
134 yōminno ṣaddag, gāḷ-ḷo, "widdi 'armi ʿalēk miʿiǧza." "šnū ddak" . . . ṣār yʿayyeṭ ʿabinno ġarīb ib-il-blād. gāḷ-ḷo, "lēš?"	134 When he believed, he said to him, "I want to give you [to do] a wonder [puzzle]." "What do you want?" He began to cry because he was foreign in the country. He said to him, "Why?"
138 gāḷ-ḷo, "widdi 'armi, 'akawwem, 'aǧīb kull ši 'alli timši ʿalē sičče wa-f-ad-dār, bakawwmo b-hā-l-maḥall,	138 He said to him, "I want to give, to collect, bring everything that [people on] the road and at home walk on, pile it up in this place,
141 "wa-ṣ-ṣubeḥ yeṣabbeḥ kull ḥabba la-ḥālo." hāḏa l-malak.	141 "and as morning rises, everything will be on its own." This [said] the king.
143 hāḏa ṣār yegūḷ, "ṭayyib, 'ani mnēn widdi aǧīb? mnēn widdi aǧīb? mnēn widdi aǧīb?" gāḷ-ḷo ṭ-ṭēr, "mʿāk rīšt an-namla. iḥeriǧ rīšt an-namla ḥatta tiǧmaʿ ʿalē kullha. farrig lak, kull ǧins la-ḥāl."	143 This [man] started to say, "Well, I—where from shall I bring [it]? Where from shall I bring [it]? Where from shall I bring [it]?" The bird said to him, "You have the ant's feather. Burn the ant's feather [that it] will collect all of it for him. It will separate them for you to stacks, every kind on its own."
148 'ā. giḏab, ḥarrag haḏīk rīšt an-namla, fziʿat ʿalēha, ḥarragat, farragat ʿa-ha-l-mazraʿāt kullha. gāḷ-ḷo, "ṭayyib:." aṣ-ṣubaḥ ǧa, liga kull ši m-maṭraḥo laḥāl. kull šī laḥāl, yamma mḥarrak tifrīg.	148 Yes. He burned, burned that ant's feather. They all [the ants] rushed, they moved, separated all the fields into separate stacks. He said to him, "Good." Morning came, he found everything in its place on its own. Everything was in its place separately, exactly arranged [moved aside] by separating [them into stacks].
153 assa ʿāwad gāḷ-ḷo, "waddi baʿad 'armi ʿalēk maʿaǧza ṯāniya." gāḷ-ḷo. "šnū?" gāḷ-ḷo, "widdi aǧīb lak baṭṭīxat bālāḏ. widdak tifligha." yitḥayyar, "ṭayyib, bēš ašugg lak baṭṭīxat bālāḏ? 'al-bālāḏ yinfalig?"	153 Now, he [the king] again said to him, "I want also to charge you with another wonder [puzzle]." He said to him, "What [is it]?" He said, "I want to bring you a steel watermelon. You must split it [in half]." He became perplexed. "With what shall I split a steel watermelon? Can steel be split?"

159 gāḷ-ḷo ṭ-ṭēr, "maʿāk as-sakkīna." aṭ-ṭēr yifaṭṭen bī, gāḷ-ḷo, "as-sikkīne mʿāk. fligha." giḏab, ṭāl-as-sikkīn min ʿubbo, u-filagha. ḥazzaqha. gāḷ-ḷo . . .	159 The bird said to him, "You have the knife." The bird reminded him and said to him, "The knife is with you. Split it." He took, took out the knife from his lap and split it. He pierced it. Said to him. . . .
163 ğa, liga al-baṭṭīxa maflūga. gāḷ-ḷo, "mnēn ğibt hal-asliḥa ḏi?" gāḷ-ḷo, "'aḷḷa baʿaṯ-li, 'aḷḷa baʿaṯ-li." gāḷ-ḷo, "ṭayyib, hāy, hāy binti lēk, binti lēk, lā ğiza walā wafa." xaḷaṣ.	163 He [the King] came, found the watermelon split [open]. He said to him, "Where did you bring these weapons from?" He said to him, "Allah has sent [them to] me, Allah has sent [them to] me." He said to him, "Well this, this my daughter is for you [as wife], my daughter is for you without any dowry and no obligation." Finished [that's it].

Commentary

The story by Ṯarwa Yāsīn, "The Silent Princess and Smart Mḥammad," also belongs to the international narrative type ATU 851, "The Princess Who Cannot Solve the Riddle," but contains elements associated with another narrative type, AT 945, "Luck and Intelligence." The motif of making the princess talk appears in the second part of this narrative type: a mute princess is offered in marriage to whoever can make her speak (motif H343, "Suitor test: bringing dumb princess to speak"). While the princess is present, a shepherd tells his dog (or a picture) of a carpenter who carved a wooden girl, a tailor who sewed clothes for her, and a clergyman who animated the figure. He asks the dog (or the picture) who the girl is supposed to marry and gives an answer that the princess does not like. The princess breaks her silence, and the suitor wins her. El-Shamy suggests that this section should be transformed into a separate international narrative, AT 572, "Bringing the Dumb Princess to Speak by Telling a Story That Ends with a Riddle" (motif Z16, "Tales ending with a question"). He claims that such stories are very common in Islamic culture.[5] In the IFA, there are several Jewish parallels from Kurdistan, Iran, and Iraq.[6]

The Bedouin story describes the journey three brothers make to Egypt to cause a mute princess to speak. Two of them fail in the mission. Their heads are cut off and added to the pile of heads of previous suitors (motif S110.3, "Princess builds tower of skulls of unsuccessful suitors"). On his way to the princess, the third brother, Smart Mḥammad, volunteers to go down to the well, where there is a *ḥāmi* (guarding ogre) with two women sitting on his knees, one of whom is white and the other black. The monster asks him which one is more beautiful, and the hero replies: "By Allah, whichever your heart likes, even if it's a black slave!" This motif appears in other Bedouin stories that I have collected (see chap. 6, "The King's Wife and the Poor Man"). The correct answer entitles the hero to a gift. In this case, the monster gives him seven objects, which are supposed to rescue him in states of distress, but the narrator lists only three of them: a speaking bird, an ant "feather," and a magical steel knife. (The narrator mentions a fourth object—a watermelon—but in fact, as the story goes, the steel watermelon that the hero must split is not given to him by the monster but is presented as a challenge by the king, and the hero uses the magical knife to fulfill the task assigned to him.) The hero meets the princess, and the speaking bird tells him, in the presence of the mute princess, a story about a carpenter, a tailor, and an oil seller. The three set guard duty. The carpenter, in his turn, carves a wooden doll. The tailor, who replaces the carpenter in his turn, discovers the doll and dresses her with clothes. The oil seller, on his guard duty, prays to Allah to breathe life into her body, and she becomes a flesh-and-blood girl. The three disagree over whom the girl belongs to. The bird ends its story with a question: "O bridegroom, o bride, whose will she be?" The hero replies that she belongs to the carpenter. The speaking bird claims that she belongs to the tailor. The princess intervenes in the argument and announces that both of them are wrong. The girl belongs to the one who breathed life into her body (or all three—the narrator's wording is not clear). In this way the younger brother succeeds in making the princess talk.

The story is told in a slightly confused way. The narrator first presents the argument and the princess's response, and only then remembers that the listeners have not yet heard the bird's story and completes the blanks. As in a previous story, thanks to the good deed the hero made on his way to the princess—showing a value judgment that does not depend on the color of the girls' skin—the monster gives him the speaking bird, which will help him make the princess speak. The king is not satisfied with this, and he has yet another task for the hero: to sort out a pile of seeds and separate them into its components. This is the same task the princess imposed on the hero in the previous story (chap. 16), but here it comes from the king. The hero uses the second gift he received from the monster, the ant's "feather," to summon ants to assist him in sorting the seeds. As a result of his success, the king gives him another task: to cut a steel watermelon. At the advice of the bird, he uses the third gift from the monster, a magical steel knife, to split the watermelon. In return, the king gives his daughter to the hero.

This story is less sophisticated than the previous one, but it is based on a similar idea: a person is rewarded for behaving in the proper way. The story is not about any kindness granted by the hero to the ants. He gets all the gifts from the monster. The mother figure is also absent from this story.

Noteworthy is the sentence the king says to the suitor at the end of the story: "My daughter is for you without any dowry and no obligation" (*hai binti lēk lā ğiza walā wafa*). The expression *lā ğiza walā wafa* comes from the Qur'ān, and it means that there is no expectation of reward. In the language of the Qur'ān: "We feed you for the sake of Allah alone; we wish for neither reward nor gratitude from you" (sūrah 76, 8). The connection is not accidental. The Sūrah of Man (*sūrat al-insān*) in the Qur'ān deals with the reward expected for a person who does good deeds and distributes his bread to the poor, the orphan, and the prisoner, with no expectation of reward.[7]

Notes

1. *gāḷ-ḷ-abū, gāḷ-ḷo: "yā-būya", gāḷ-ḷo: "yā-būya"*: "He said to his father, he said, 'O father.' he said to him, 'O father.'" Regarding this "reverse kinship" address form, cf. chapter 13, note 7. Note the difference between the father's answer to his son and the old man's previous answers to the young men who were not his offspring. As noted, this dialogue does

not mention the speakers' personal names. The listener is supposed to follow the story and understand who says what.

2. *ḥaṭṭ ba'adha ǧ-ǧible bančo šāf*: "[He] took the direction of Mecca [south] as the best point [strong—for the journey] that he saw." *ǧible* (or *qibla* in LA/MSA) is the direction of Mecca, the holy city for Muslims. This direction is usually the south or east for Bedouin wanderers in the Arabian Peninsula. *banč* (*bunk* in LA/MSA) is the best and strongest part of something, such as life or springtime. This sentence seems to mean that he got courage after taking the direction of Mecca as his basic point of reference for the way.

3. *gāḷ-ḷo, "mīn 'aḥsan, yā šāṭr-ᵊmḥimmad, as-samra walla l-bēḏ̣a?" gaḷ-ḷo, "walla, 'alli yḥebbo gaḷbak, law-an yekūn 'abd aswad"*: "He said to him, 'Who is more beautiful/better, o Smart Mḥammad, the swarthy or the white one?' He said to him, 'By Allah, whichever your heart likes, even if it's a black slave.'" The need to choose between a white girl and a swarthy girl reflects the distinction between black-skinned and white-skinned people. The former were usually slaves in the Arab (including Bedouin) communities and belonged to tribes that were not esteemed highly in those communities Yet the correct answer to this tricky question advocates both equality between girls of the two human groups and the importance of true love, which Bedouin poetry has exalted since classical pre-Islamic times.

4. *ḥāčīha min hēn, xarrifha min hēn, mā rḏ̣at ta-trodd*: "He talked to her here, told her from there—she did not agree to answer." The narrator uses the imperative form (*ḥāčīha . . . xarrifha*) referring to an action in the past. This is a special Bedouin speech structure, found in narratives from many Arab Bedouin dialects and in this volume. This "narrative imperative" is used to emphasize the importance of the action. See Blanc, "Arabic Dialects of the Negev Bedouins"; Palva, "Descriptive Imperative of Narrative Style."

5. El-Shamy, *Folktales of Egypt*, 249.

6. Iraqi Kurdistan: 11413; Iranian Kurdistan: 4478, 6941, 6948; Iran: 7156; Iraq: 3321.

7. See also the end of "The Coffee Server," in chapter 11.

18. The Two Notes (Smart Ḥasan)

NARRATOR: Maḥmūd Muḥamad Mrisāt

TRIBE: *ʿArab el-Mrēsāt*

IFA 17418 August 7, 1982

1 el-xurrrāfiyye ʾesemha, ʾeḥna ngul-la š-šāṭer ḥasan. ʾassa[1] yegūlūn ʾanno čān bō malek ʿendo bent. bint waḥīde. yaʿani mā bō ġēre.[2] lā walad wala banāt. assa ʾal-malik yeḥibb bintu, yaʿani miṯel ma yeḥibb nafso.	1 The story, we name it "Smart Ḥasan." Now, they say that there was a king who had a daughter. One daughter. That is, there was no one except her, no son nor daughters. Now the king loved his daughter, that is, he loved her as he loved himself.
7 ṭabʿan čān yehimmo inno yeǧawwazūnhe ʾumara. ʾassa ǧamma ʾumara min ǧamīʿ al-ᵉblād tanno yexuṭbūn bint al-malek. assa kull marra yiǧi la-ʿindha wāḥad ʾamīr, kānat turufḍo, mā tigbalo.	7 Naturally, he wanted that princes would marry her. Now there came princes from all the country to betroth the king's daughter. Now, each one, an emīr, came to her—she refused him, did not accept him.
13 assa ʾabūha, lamman turfuḍ al-ʾamīr, kān yizʿal, lainno yehimmo inno tāxaḏ ʾamīr. miš muhimm ʾayya ʾamīr, miš muhimm, al-muhimm inno tāxoḏ ʾamīr. ʾiǧa ʾawwal ʾamīr—ravḍato (=rafḍato), ʾiǧa ṯ-ṯāni—rafḍato, ʾiǧa ṯ-ṯāliṯ—rafḍato.	13 Now, her father, when she refused an emīr, he would be angry/sad, because he wanted her to take an emīr [as husband]. It did not matter which emīr, any emīr—not important—it was important that she would take an emīr [as husband]. The first emīr came—she refused him, the second came—she refused him, the third came—she refused him.
19 assa taḏāyig ʾakṯar u-ʾakṯar. ʿeref b-il-ʾāxer inno binto widdha wāḥad ismo Ḥasan, u-hāḏa Ḥasan miš ʾamīr—min ʿāmmat aš-šaʿab, basīṭ ǧiddan.	19 Now, he got more and more irritated. He finally knew that his daughter wanted one whose name was Ḥasan, and this Ḥasan was not an emīr—[he was] from the simple folk, very simple.

23 ʾassa ṣār yifakker ʾinno yibʿid binto al-ʾamīre ʿan Ḥasan u-yibʿid Ḥasan ʿen binto. ʾassa ʾiḏa widdo yibʿid Ḥasan widda tizʿal binto, u-ʾiḏa ziʿlat binto, yeʾaṯṯer ʿalē nafasniyyan, yizʿal hū.

23 Now, he began thinking that he wanted to distance his daughter the princess from Ḥasan and distance Ḥasan from his daughter. Now, if he wanted to distance Ḥasan, his daughter would be angry/sad, and if his daughter were angry/sad, that would affect her psycho-logically, he would be angry/sad [too].

28 ʾessa kān ʿindo wazīr, musāʿad la-l-malik. hāḏa l-wazīr čān ḏaki ğiddan u-ṯaʿ^{a}lab, xaddāʿ gāḷ-ḷo, "daššer hāḏ ^{a}l-xurrāfiyye ʿalayy [al-wazīr]. ʾarčen ʿalay u-ʾan(a)-adabber-lak al-xurrāfiyye šlōn ʾinta widdak." gāḷ-ḷo, "dabber-li al-xurrāfiyye bas ^{e}b-šarṭ waḥīd, ʾinno tibʿed Ḥasan ʿen binti, u-binti (t)ḏaḷḷ mabṣūṭa, mā tizʿal."

28 Now, he had a minister (wazīr) assistant to the king. This wazīr was very smart and a fox, cheater. He said to him, "Leave this story [issue] to me," said the wazīr. "Rely on me and I will arrange this story, as you wish." He said to him, "Arrange for me the issue [story] but on one condition that you distance Ḥasan from my daughter and my daughter will remain happy, will not be sad."

37 gāḷ-ḷo, "lā yehimma(k)", gāḷ-ḷo, "ʾana ʿendi ṭarīga." gāḷ-ḷo, "kīf? eḥči ta-(a)šūf "gāḷ-ḷo, "ʾe . . . ^{e}nğīb Ḥasan u-ngūḷ-ḷo inno ʾal-malik wāfag yaʿṭīk binto—^{e}b-šarṭ wāḥad. ʾiḏa twaffi hāḏa š-šarṭ, tāxaḏ bint al-malek." gāḷ-ḷo, "šū hāḏa š-šarṭ?" ʾal-malik gāḷ-ḷo, "šū hāḏa š-šarṭ?"

37 He said to him, "No, do not worry." He said to him, "I have a way." He said to him, "How? Speak so I will see [understand]." He said to him, "We will bring Ḥasan and tell him, that the king agrees to give you his daughter, on one condition. If you fulfill this condition, you will take the king's daughter." He [the king] said to him, "What is this condition?" The king said to him, "What is this condition?"

44 gāḷ-ḷo, "esmaʿ, iḥna nğīb wurugtēn, nuktub ʿalēhen, ʿala wriga nuktub "mōt"

44 He said to him, "Listen, we will bring two pieces of paper, we will write on them—on one piece of paper 'death'

46 u-ʿala l-wriga ṯ-ṯāni nuktub "ḥayā" wa-ngūḷ-ḷo, "ʾesmaʿ yā Ḥasan, al-malik manṭīk binto iḏa tuṭleʿ al-wriga alli maktūb ʿalēha "ḥayā(h)." sāʿte, ʾinta tāxuḏ (bint) al-ʾamīr."

46 "and on the second piece of paper we will write 'life.' And we will say to him, 'Listen, o Ḥasan, the king gives you his daughter if you take out a piece of paper on which is written "life." Then you will take the king's daughter.'"

51 gāḷ-ḷo, "ṭayyib, ^{e}šlōn ʾinta widdak taʿṭī al-waragtēn? balči tiṭlaʿ b-ʾīdo al-wurega alli biha "ḥayā." maʿnāto hīna bū ʾamal čeṯīr inno huwa yāxuḏ al-ʾamīra—hāḏa illi ʾana mā widdi iyyā." gāḷ-ḷo, "wala yehimmak.

51 He said to him, "Good, how will you give him the two pieces of paper? He may succeed and draw the paper on which 'life' is written. It means that there is great hope [chance] here that he will take [marry] the princess—this is what I do not want." He said to him, "Don't worry.

57 “’iḥna ngūḷ-ḷo hīn maktūb “mōt” u-”ḥayā.” bas ’eḥna lamma ᵉnǧību, nuktub ʿala ṯ-ṯintēn mōt—ʿa-hāḏi “mōt” u-ʿala hāḏi “mōt.” u-b-hāḏi ṭ-ṭarīga ’ani wriga ma tiṭlaʿ b-’īdu hī maktūb ʿalēha “mōt.”

57 “We will tell him here it is written ‘death’ and ‘life,’ but we, when we bring him, we will write on the two papers—on this ‘death’ and on this ‘death.’ And this way, whichever note comes to his hand, it will be written on it ‘death.’”

62 gāḷ-ḷo, “lak tislam, ’inte . . . ’inta l-wazīr al-’amīn ’alli mumkin ’arčin ʿalēk.” wāfag al-malik w-anḅaṣaṭ u-tarayyaḥ.

62 He said to him, “Be well. You are the loyal wazīr, on whom I can depend.” The king agreed and was happy and relaxed.

66 ’essa ṯāni yōm ʿezam kull ’aṣḥābu ’ahal al-madīne. ʿezamhum ʿa-l-ḥafle u-ʿezam Ḥasan. assa mīn ʿeref b-al-ḥīle? al-’amīre, bint al-malik. beʿṯat, e-ʿirfat min—fī ʿendha ǧāsūs čān sāmeʿ ’al-xādem, simeʿ al-xurrāfiyye, al-ḥīle bēn al-’amīr—bēn al-wazīr w-al-malik,

66 Now the next day he invited all his friends, the people of the town. He invited them to a feast and invited also Ḥasan. Now, who knew this mean scheme [contrivance]? The princess, the king’s daughter. She sent—knew from—she had a spy who had heard the servant, heard the story, the contrivance between the emīr—between the wazīr and the king.

73 rāḥ gāḷ ḷ-al-’amīra. al-’amīra biʿṯat xabar ᵉl-Ḥasan. gāḷat-ḷo, “’al-guṣṣa kaḏa, kaḏa, kaḏa.” fahhamatu šū (wid)d-yeṣīr u-ḥaḏḏaratu inno mā yiǧī ʿa-l-ḥafle. ’assa hiyya nāmat mabṣūṭa inno Ḥasan miš rāyiḥ yiǧiʸ ʿa-l-ḥafla.

73 He [the spy] went and told the princess and the princess sent the message to Ḥasan. She said to him, “The story is so and so and so.” She explained what would be and warned him not to come to the feast. Now she slept, happy that Ḥasan was not going to come to the feast.

79 ’iǧa mawʿid al-ḥafle, kull a š-šaʿab kān ḥāḏir, al-wazīr mistanne, al-malak yistanne, w-al-’amīra mabṣūṭa. ʿa-l-waʿad, walla ǧāy Ḥasan. bidūn xōf. kull aš-šaʿab wuga(f) u-šāf u-stanna šu beṣīr. ’al-malik ’enḅaṣaṭ. ’al-wazīr kayyaf. gām gāḷ, “hassa binxaḷḷaṣ men Ḥasan.”

79 The time of the feast came, all the people were ready, the wazīr was waiting, the king was waiting, and the princess was happy. Following the promise, lo Ḥasan came. Without fear. All the people stood and looked and waited for what would happen. The king was happy. The wazīr was celebrating. He said, “Now we’ll get rid of Ḥasan.”

86 wigaf al-malik giddām aš-šaʿab u-xeṭab xiṭāb. gāḷ-ḷhum, “’ismaʿam yā šaʿab, ’ani malik ʿādel, ʿādel ʿala kull aš-šaʿab. ’ani ʿindi l-’amīra l-waḥīde alli ’aʿazz min nafsi. ’ani mwāfig ’aʿṭīha l-Ḥasan, alli hū min ʿāmmat aš-šaʿab, ’ani miš mitkabber, bas ʿindi šarṭ inno Ḥasan yiṭlaʿ—hēna bū wrugtēn—wāḥ(i)da maktūb ʿalēha “mōt” u-waḥda maktūb ʿalēha “ḥayā.”

86 The king stood up in front of the people and gave a speech. “Listen, o people, I am a just king, just for all the people, and I have the one princess who is dearest for me—more than myself. I agree to give her to Ḥasan, who is from the simple people, I am not arrogant/haughty. But I have a condition—that Ḥasan will take out—here there are two pieces of paper—on one is written ‘death’ and on one is written ‘life.’

96 ’iḏa Ḥasan itḷa‘ l-wriga lli maktūb ‘alēha “mōt,” widna nuqutlo. huwwa kital ḥālo b-’īdo. ’iḏa maktūb ‘alēha “ḥayā” ma‘nāto ’anṭī al-’amīra.”	96 “If Ḥasan takes out the paper on which is written ‘death,’ we will kill him. He kills himself with his own hand. If it is written ‘life’ on it, it means that I will give him the princess.”
100 gāḷū-ḷo, “bra, maẓbūṭ.” hassa, gām ’al-malik u-’a‘ṭa al-Ḥasan al-waraga. gāḷ-ḷo, “ṣ-ṣabar, yā Ḥasan.” Ḥasan gām u-xaḏa waraga duġri bela‘ha u-gāḷ-la-š-ša‘ab, ē . . . gāḷ-ḷa-š-ša‘ab, “’ani bela‘t woraga. niftaḥ aṯ-ṯāni. ’iḏa maktūb ‘alēha “mōt” me‘nāto ’ani bela‘t “ḥayā,” w-ani xaḏēt ḥayā.”	100 They said to him, “Bravo, correct.” Now, the king got up and gave Ḥasan the piece of paper. He said to him, “Endurance, Ḥasan.” Ḥasan got up and took a piece of paper and directly swallowed it, and said to the people, er . . . he said to the people, “I’ve swallowed a piece of paper. Let’s open the other one. If ‘death’ is written on it, it means that I swallowed ‘life’ and I have taken life.”
108 ’al-malek ’ertebak, wereṭ,[3] w-al-wazīr irtibkam, ‘irfam inno Ḥasan ’a‘ẓam minhom u-’a‘gal minhom u-’ašṭar minhom. ṭab‘an, al-wurogtēn maktūb ‘alēhen “mōt.” bila‘ wargat al-ḥayā, gāl-lhom, “iftaḥam u-šūfam šū maktūb ‘ala l-weraga.”	108 The king got embarrassed, was trapped [in a dilemma], and the wazīr, they got embarrassed. They knew that Ḥasan was greater than they were, and cleverer than they, and smarter than they were. Naturally, the two pieces of paper had “death” written on them. He swallowed the “life” and said to them, “Open and see what is written on the piece of paper.”
115 fitḥam, enġibram yiftaḥum al-weraga, ligam maktūb ‘alēha “mōt.” ’assa aš-ša‘ab kullayāto wigaf’ ṣār yeṣaffeg inno “Ḥasan huwwa l-malek, Ḥasan huwwa l-malek, Ḥasan huwwa l-malek.”[4]	115 They opened [it], had to open the piece of paper and found “death” written on it. Now all the people stood up and applauded that “Ḥasan is the king, Ḥasan is the king, Ḥasan is the king.”
121 gāḷ al-malek, gāḷ l-al-wazīr, “’inta ma tista’ahil ^{i}tkūn wazīr, ’inta lāzim ^{i}nmawtak, ’inta xaddā‘”, u-Ḥasan xaḏa bint al-malik u-ṣār huwwa l-wazīr ‘end al-malek. uxaḏā la-niyo. hāḏa hū.	121 The king said to the wazīr, “You do not deserve to be a wazīr, you should be put to death. You are a cheater.” And Ḥasan took the king’s daughter [for wife] and became the wazīr at the king’s place, and took his goal [wish]. That is it [the tale is ended].

Commentary

Smart Ḥasan (*Šāṭer Ḥasan*) is a popular hero in the Arab culture space. He is described as a simple man who knows how to deal with the upper class and overcome them with the power of his mind and his cunning. In this sense, he fulfills the people’s hidden wish to live in a society in which a simple man also has the potential to attain a dignified status thanks to his talents and virtues. The figure of Smart Ḥasan is so well known in the Arab culture that even hotels and business companies adorn themselves with his name.[5] One version of the story is included in a reader of Arab schools in Israel.

The narrator tells the story amazingly. He creates tension in his listeners' hearts and leads them slowly in the plot, using various narrative tricks. After the introduction to the plot, he emphasizes how each of the three heroes, the king, the vizier, and the princess, are pleased with what is about to happen, each for his or her own reasons. He even bothers to quote to us, as an omniscient narrator, a brief conversation between the king and the vizier just before Ḥasan arrives to the trial. The vizier says to the king, "Now we'll get rid of Ḥasan."

When Ḥasan comes to the trial contrary to the princess's expectations, the tension reaches its peak. The narrator emphasizes once again how much the king and the vizier are satisfied with the way things are handled and lets us, the listeners, understand, without actually telling it, how the princess feels at that moment, knowing that her world will soon be ruined and her beloved executed. To intensify the tension, he puts in the king's mouth a righteous speech:

> Listen, o people, I am a just king, just for all the people, and I have the one princess who is dearest for me—more than myself. I agree to give her to Ḥasan, who is from the simple people. . . . Here there are two pieces of paper—on one is written "death" and on one is written "life." If Ḥasan takes out the paper on which it is written "death," we will kill him. He kills himself with his own hand. If it is written "life" on it, it means that I will give him the princess.

The king boasts that he does not discriminate between high-ranking people and commoners: as far as he is concerned, what is important, as it were, is not social status but courage. He emphasizes in his speech that if Ḥasan dies, it will be because he has killed himself with his own hands, meaning that the king will not harm him but the hand of fate will.

When Ḥasan swallows the paper, the king and vizier's conspiracy falls back on them like a boomerang. After such a speech, the king cannot retract his words. The king expected that Ḥasan would determine his fate with his own hands, and exactly the opposite happens: he himself determines his own daughter's fate with his failed trick. At this point, the narrator emphasizes the embarrassment of the king and the vizier, which contrasts the exaltation they felt a moment before: "The king got embarrassed, was trapped [in a dilemma], and the vizier, they got embarrassed."

The reversal of the king's relationship to the vizier and the appointment of Ḥasan to vizier complete the narrative symmetry of the story, which ends with Ḥasan's marriage to the princess.

From the king's speech, as quoted by the narrator, another thing arises: The king is bound by a code of ethics whose essence is the absence of discrimination between commoners and high-ranking people. He takes advantage of his position to emphasize this and to magnify himself to the people. In the Bedouin society, the king (or his realist successor, the sheikh) is described, not as an omnipotent ruler, but as the first among equals, as someone who is in the best interest of the people. Righteousness, justice, and courage are values admired by the Bedouins, and the king is obliged to them like everyone else.

In the Egyptian cultural space, many stories are told about *El-Šāṭer* Ḥasan. The name appears in Egyptian versions of Snow White (ATU 709) and Cinderella (ATU 510A). It is also the name of the hero in a story in Ḥasan El-Shamy's book *Folktales of Egypt*, "The Man Who Put His Mother over His Shoulder and Rode His Father."[6] This is a charming version of the narrative type ATU 851, "The Princess Who Cannot Solve the Riddle" (see chap. 17, "The Silent Princess and Smart Mḥammad"), which somewhat resembles our story. Smart Mḥammad, a commoner, is put to the test of a princess; he has to pose her a riddle that she cannot solve. If she does not find the solution, the hero will marry her, but if she can solve his riddle, he will be executed. Here the princess herself uses a ploy to find the solution, but her ploy fails. The hero manages to reveal her intentions, uses his cleverness to thwart them, and marries her.

It is interesting to note that there are several Jewish versions that relate the story to Maimonides's wisdom. According to these versions, the enemies of Maimonides conspire against him and libel him with the accusation that he intends to harm the king. They suggest that the king examine him in a trial by ordeal.[7] The king puts Maimonides to the test: The enemies of Maimonides write "death" on the two chits. Maimonides swallows one of them and is saved.

The story is known from several sources, mainly on religious sites on the internet. It seems to me that it corresponds with one of the episodes in the story of "Maimonides and the Study of Medicine."[8] Tamar Alexander-Friser presents this story in her book *The Story of a Beloved and a Half: The Folktale of Sephardi Jews*, as a joke about the wisdom of a Jewish rabbi who is indicted by the Inquisition and is required to choose between two chits, one of which is "guilty" and the other "innocent." The inquisitor writes "guilty" on both chits, and the rabbi swallows the chit he chooses.

According to Alexander-Friser, this is an international story motif, which is applied here to the Conversos in Spain, and reflects a historical situation in which the kings of Spain gave the Jews a choice between deportation and conversion to Christianity. She also says that among the members of the Sephardi-Jewish group, this story is attributed to Maimonides as part of his praises.[9]

Notes

1. In any language, narrative style includes many elements named discourse markers. These elements may be full words, combined words, parts of words, or even nonverbal hums, and they serve many linguistic, semantic, and pragmatic functions. Discourse markers also abound in Galilee Arabic dialects. Note the word *now* (< *as-sāʿa*, "the hour, time"), pronounced as *'assa*, *'essa*, or even shortened to *ssa*, *sa*. Its occurrence rate fluctuates among speakers. *'essāʿa* is used when the narrator pauses or hesitates for planning or saying an utterance. Many examples occur in this story and others (e.g., see chaps. 10, 15, 28, 30, 32, 38, 40 [story A], 44).

2. *bint waḥīde. ya'ani, ya'ani, mā bō ġēre . . . ṭab'an kān yehimmo inno yeǧwwzūnhe 'umara*: "One daughter. That is, there was no one except her, no son nor daughters. . . . Naturally, he wanted that princes would marry her." Note the use of *-e* in 3f.sg. bound pronouns, such as *ġēre*, "besides her," and *yeǧawwazūnhe*, "they will marry her off," and in the adjective *waḥīde*, "single f.sg." This final *e* vowel for the personal f.sg. suffix is not expected in Galilee Bedouin dialects, but it exists in some Syrian Bedouin dialects (cf. Cantineau, "Études sur quelques parlers de nomades arabes d'Orient"; Bettini, *Contes Féminins de la Haute Jézireh Syrienne*). For *waḥīde*, it may reflect a case of local sedentary interference.

This *'imāla* (so named in LA works) is the rising (or, literally, tilting) of a short or long *-a* > *e/i*, within a word or at its end, in front nonlaryngeal, nonpharyngeal environments, as in *'amīre* (sedentary) versus *'amīra* (Galilee Bedouin), "princess," and the above examples. Many Bedouin dialects (including Galilee Bedouins) do not use *'imāla*. Still, this feature appears in many tales in this collection.

3. LA/MSA Arabic has basically two methods to express the passive (compared to the active verb forms): (1) in the "internal passive," vowels change and turn the active form into a passive one; (2) two verb measures, namely measure V and measure VII, are used for passive and reflexive (and middle) forms. The sedentary Arabic dialects of Israel have completely lost form 1, leaving only measures V and VII for the passive. (Some other dialects have innovated new measures.) Bedouin dialects have usually preserved method 1 to some extent, as we see in a few examples in this collection. One example is the form *wereṭ*, "he [the king] got . . . trapped [in a dilemma]" (cf. *twarraṭ* [measure V], "get confused, mixed up"). See Chapter on Galilee Bedouin dialects and Table 10 there.)

4. Chapter 2, note 2 refers to repeated rhetorical questions. Repeated utterances are a feature of spontaneous narratives in the Galilee Bedouin stories, and generally in Arabic narratives. Repetition has also other functions, such as allowing speakers time to organize the following sentence or their thoughts if distracted by an external factor, to emphasize an idea or fact, to give the sentence a new meaning by using another intonation pattern, or to correct a "slip of the tongue" (speech error, incorrect word pronunciation). In this story we refer to the repetition of the crowd's shouting in joy, "Ḥasan is the king." Because of their discursive function, in this book we do not delete such repetitions.

5. For example, Shāter Hassan Palace in Tripoli, Lebanon; Al Shāter Hassan Restaurant in Al Dhafrah, Abu Dhabi; and Shāter Hassan—Arab Fast Food in ʻAqaba, Jordan.

6. El-Shamy, *Folktales of Egypt*, 81–86, 257–58.

7. An ancient judicial practice by which the guilt or innocence of the accused was determined by their being subjected to a painful, or at least an unpleasant, and usually dangerous experience. The test was one of life or death. It was a legal system, when there were no witnesses, similar to that described in the Torah (Numbers 5:11–31).

8. Ben-Amos, *Folktales of the Jews*, 1:55–61.

9. Alexander-Friser, *The Story of a Beloved and a Half: The Folktale of Sephardi Jews*.

19. The Kidnapped Bride

NARRATOR: Ṣabḥa ʿAbūd

TRIBE: *ʿArab el-Ḥuğērāt*

IFA 13260 March 1980

1 bū wāḥad walad,[1] ʿind abūh, iben ʾamīr, iben malak. iben malak. u-bū (b)ḥadde ğār. ğāro, ʾamīr. aywā, huwwa ibn el-malak yiḥibb bint ğāro. hī yaʿani, ṣāḥibto. aywa, yōm, abūha winno ygūl daḥḥag winno hiyye maṭlūba la-wāḥad ṯāni, miṯel yaʿani lli ṭālibha la-mīn u-nāzil hū . . . hiyye. ṃ-ṃaṣar, alli ṭālibha.	1 There was a young man, at his father's, an emīr's son, a prince. A prince. And he had a neighbor, his neighbor [was] an emīr. Yes. He, the prince, loved his neighbor's daughter. She, that is, was his girlfriend. Yes. One day, her father looked and she was asked for [in marriage] by another one, like, that is, who asked for her from him and he was living . . . she . . . from Egypt/Cairo, the one who was asking for her.
9 ğē yōm abūha, hadd u-raḥal, raḥal ʿa-ṃaṣr^{a}. abūha w-al-walden, gāḷ l-al-walad. hīn al-walad maraḍ, maraḍ min zaʿalo ʿalēhe. zaʿal inno hi ṣāḥibto u-widdo yiğawwazhe, u-kēf-hī nihğet u-mā gāḷat-lo.	9 A day came, her father pulled down [the tent] and went off—went off to Egypt. Her father and the children. Someone said to the young man. Now, the boy got ill, he got ill because of his sorrow about her. He was sad because she was his girlfriend and he wanted to marry her, and how did she go away and did not tell him?
15 aywa, ği abū gāḷ-ḷo, "ya abūy, inta mrīḍ, widdi āxḏak ʿa-d-daktōr." gāḷ-ḷo, "mā widdi arū(ḥ) ʿa-d-daktōr," hāḏa l-walad. aywa. šū b^{i}dd-yisāwi? lā yākul wa-lā yišrab, hā-l-walad, hu zaʿalān ʿalēhe. šū widdo ysāwi,	15 Yes. His father came and said to him, "O son, you are ill, I will take you to the doctor." He said to him, "I don't want to go to the doctor," that young man [said]. Yes. What does he want to do? He does not eat nor drink, that young man, he is sorry for her. What does he want to do?
21 gaḏab abū muʿiḏḏo, xatyāra, ğāra lo, ʾumm . . .	21 His father, his guide/preacher, took an old woman, his neighbor, mother . . .

23 sitte l-al-walad. gāḷ-ḷha, “rūḥi, ḥkī-li mʿā, lēš, xaḷḷo, yinṭīk sirro, mā lo. hū zaʿalān u-mrīḏ̣, u-šnū widd . . . hū mrīḏ̣, tanni (y) āxḏo ʿa-d-daktōr. mū mrīḏ̣—ygūḷ-ḷi šnū widdo.”

23 grandmother of the boy. He said to her, “Go talk with him, why; let him give you his secret, what is the matter with him—that he is sad and ill—and what does he want, so that I can take him to the doctor. [If he is] not ill—let him tell me what he wants.”

28 šnū gāḷ-ḷa-l-xityāra, gāḷ-iḷha, “’ani, ’ani miš ᵉmrīḏ̣, bas ’ani, ’ani widdi iyyāha, ṣāḥibti, hiyye-nni raḥlat, axaḏha abūha u-raḥlat ʿa-maṣᵒr, w-ani zaʿalān ʿalē, wa-’ani min zaʿali in mā xaḏ̣ētha ’ani ’amūt.” hāḏ̣a l-walad.

28 What did he tell the old woman, he told her, “I, I am not ill, but I, I want her, my girlfriend, she that went off, her father took her and she went to Egypt, and I’m sad about this, and because I’m sad that I did not marry her, I’ll die.” This boy [said].

34 gāḷat-ḷo, “šnū nsāwi,” gāḷ-ḷha, “yanṭīni abūya iḏa wuddo iyyāni u-’aṭīb, yanṭīni, yanṭīni malyōn ḏahab, wu-’ani widdi alḥagha.” gāḷ-ḷo abu . . .

34 She said to him, “What shall we do?” He said to her, “Let my father give me—if he wants me, and that I’ll get well—let him give me, give me million gold, and I’ll go and follow [look for] her.” His father said to him . . .

38 rāḥat al-xityyyāra gāḷat el-abū. gāḷat-lo, “ibnak, huwwa yeḥibb al-bint, u-widdo iyyāha, u-kinnak widdak ibnak, tištari, tanṭī malyōn lēra ḏ̣ahab, u-hū (wid)d-yilḥagha.” gāḷ-ḷha “ṭayyib,” g̣aḏ̣ab anṭāha malyōn lēra, anṭā gāḷ-ḷo “elḥag” . . .

38 She, the old woman, went and said to his father, she told him, “Your son, he loves the girl, and wants her. And if you want your son, you’ll buy—give him a million lira gold, and he will follow [look for] her.” He said to her, “Well.” He took and gave her a million lira, he gave him and said to him, “Follow [her].”

45 malli hā-l-xurǧ ḏahab, maše, rakab ᵃḥṣāno u-maše, ʿala ṃaṣar. waṣlin yaʿani, ṃaṣer.

45 He filled the bags and went, he rode his horse and went, to Egypt. And they reached, that is, Egypt.

48 huwwa yesīr ma(ʿ)-hā-ṭ-ṭarīg, tagrīban yaʿani ta-ṣār gurb ṃaṣar. garrab, bi ’awwal bēt, gāḷ-ḷa, iyyāh, ǧa winna ’awwal bēt . . . bēt ᵉzġīr, xušše,

48 He went along the way, that is, approximately, until he was near Cairo. He approached, there was the first house, he said to her—it—he came and lo—the first house, a small house, a hut.

52 ǧa hā-l-xetyāra, gāḷ-ḷa, “mā tbayytīni, yā xatyāra?” gāḷat-ḷo, “la’, iḥna wāḥad ġarīb, mā nbayyto.” rāḥ hāḏ̣a, widdo iyyā, šnū widdo ysāwi? aǧa, ġāb ᵉšwayye u-rāḥ, ǧāb ilha xames līrāt ḏahab. gāḷ-ḷha, “tfaḏ̣ḏ̣ali, bas bayytīni hā-l-lēle.” šū hāḏ̣a, kayyafat, gāḷat-ḷo, “’ahlan wa-sahlan, yā ’ebni.” šū, wa-rāḥat ištarat-lo ʿašin, wa-ʿaššato, wa-ṣār yerūḥ yīǧi ʿalēha.

52 He came to this old woman and said to her, “Won’t you let me stay here for the night, o old woman?” She said to him, “No, we do not lodge a stranger.” He went, he wanted it, what will he do? He came, disappeared for a little while and went, brought her five gold liras and said to her, “Please [take it], just lodge me tonight.” What’s this, she was glad, and said to him, “Welcome, my son.” What, she went and bought for him dinner, and gave him dinner, and he began to go and come to her.

61 gāḷat ḷo—gāḷ-^{i}lha, “mā teʿarfīn ^{e}flān, ʿendo bent u-aǧa la-hīn.” gāḷat-ḷo, “al-lēle widdo yiǧawwaz - yenṭīha abūha, yenṭīha la-wāḥad ṯāni.” gāḷ-ḷha, “ṣaḥī(ḥ)?” gāḷat-ḷo, “ṣaḥīḥ.”

61 She said to him—He said to her, “Don’t you know a certain person? He has a daughter and has come here?” She said to him, “Tonight he will marry—her father will marry her off to someone else.” He said to her, “Really?” She said to him, “Really.”

66 huwwa, bū xātam min xātem el-bint mʿā, maʿ el-walad, u-maḥrama min (ʿen)dīha, mʿa-l-walad. gāḷ-ḷha, “ṭayyib, mā tigdarīn, yā sitti, u-hāḏ̣an kamān uxra . . . uxra mīt lēra ḏahab,” la-l-xatyāra. “u-trūḥīn inti . . . tanṭīn hāḏ̣a l-xātam u-tanṭīn hā-l-maḥrama u-tgūlī-la

66 He—there was a ring of the girl with him, with the boy, and a handkerchief from her, with the boy. He said to her, “Good, won’t you, my grandma, and this is again . . . a hundred gold lira, to the old woman, and you’ll go to her . . . give her this ring and give her this handkerchief and say to her

73 ṣāḥbeč huwa bi-l-manṭaga. u-gūlī-lhe tanṭīni ^{e}hdūmha.”

73 [that] your friend, he is in the area and say to her she will give me her clothes.”

75 hiya maṣmūdi, ta-tiǧawwaz, lēletha mā-titǧawwaz, aywa, šū hā-li, gāḷ-ḷa “gūlī-lha, tanṭīni, šū, s’alīhe, šū widdi asāwi. wa-s’ali šnū (wi)ddi asāwi.”

75 She [the girl] was sitting on the “stage” [kept apart], that night she was going to get married, yes, he said to her, “Tell her, she will give me, what, ask her what I should do; and ask what I should do.”

79 rāḥat hāḏ̣i ʿandhe, gāḷat-ilha, sallamat ʿalēha u-”yā binti,” uxaḏat, dazzet il-hadiyye mʿāha [$_{H}$matanáH$_{H}$] u-gāḷat-ilha, “hāḏ̣a l-xātam mā teʿarfīn la-mīn?” daḥḥagat, ʿarfato. gāḷat-ilha.”mnīn hāḏ̣?” gāḷat-ilha, “ṣāḥbo hēn.” bēna, yaʿani, bēna baʿaḏ̣hen.

79 She went to her, and said to her, greeted her, and “O my daughter” and took, brought the gift with her [gift—Hebrew] and said to her, “This ring, don’t you know whose it is?” She looked—recognized it. She said to her, “Where is this from?” She said to her, “Its owner is here,” [the talk was] between her, that is, between the two of them.

86 al-xityāra, gāḷat-ilha, “u-ygūl-li, šnū wideš issāwīn, oʿa, (a)waddīha ʿande al-ʿēn.” gāḷat-ilha, “ṭayyib, tigdarīn inti, tāxḏīn hāḏ-al-malābis min ʿendi, u-tlabsīnu libs bint u-dgulīn hāḏ̣i binti, u-ǧibīno la-ʿendi.”

86 The old woman said to her, “And he tells me what you want to do, careful, I will deliver it to him, near the [water] spring.” . . . She told her, “Good, you can take these clothes from me and dress him in these girl’s clothes, and say this is my daughter, bring him to me.”

92 gāḷat-ilha “šukran laki.” xaḏat min awāʿīha, min awāʿe l-ʿarūs, u-rāḥat lo u-labbasato miṯel bint u-ǧat maʿ al-xityāra. gāḷan al-banāt, en-niswān, gāḷan, “hāḏ̣i mīn, mīn hāḏ̣i.” gāḷat-ilhin, “binti” u-fātat ʿindhe,

92 She said to her, “Thank you.” She took from her clothes, from the bride’s clothes, and went to him and dressed him like a girl and came with the old woman. They said, the girls and the women, “This one, who is she, who is this?” She said to them, “My daughter,” and went in to her

98 u-ḥabḥabathe, u-sallamat ʿalēha u-gʿadat ʿindha. gāḷat-ilha, "u-šnū widdna nsāwi, šnū widda niʿemal,"	98 and she kissed her and greeted her and sat next to her and said to her, "And what shall we do, what shall we do?"
101 yitxarrafu b-al-lēl. gāḷat-ilha, gāḷat-ilha "fiš ṭarīg alli āxḏeč u-aṭlaʿ"	101 They were talking in the night. She said to her [the boy in the girl's clothes], she said to her, "There is no way I can take you and get out."
103 gāḷat-ilha, "šū hāḏ." u-mʿā maṣāri, u-lōla mʿā maṣāri ma waṣalhe. aywa. šū hāḏa ʿimel, hāḏi hī b-gaṣer, u-bāb-el-gaṣer msakker ʿalēha u-mā tigdar taṭlaʿ. gāḷat ilha, "ṭayyib."	103 She said to her, "What is this?" And he had money, and unless he had money, he would not have reached her. Yes. What did this [man] do? This one, [she was] in the palace, and the palace gate [was] closed on her and she could not go out. She said to her, "OK."
108 šū hāḏa ʿimal? bū dukkāne. yaʿani, bū [$_{H}$ḥanút$_{H}$] gbāl dār, gbāl el-gaṣer alli tibāʿ^{a} ǧōzha. šū sāwa hāḏ? uxra anṭa mīt lēra la-ṣāḥb al-hāḏ, ṣāḥb al-dukkāne. gāḷ-ḷo, "widdi aʿmal, min taḥt al-'arḍ,"	108 What did he do? There was a shop, that is, there is a ($_{H}$ḥanút$_{H}$) shop in front of the house, in front of the palace which belonged to her husband. What did this one do? Another hundred liras he gave to the owner of that, the shop owner. He said to him, "I want to do, from under the ground."
113 ǧāb nās tibḥaš lo min taḥt al-'arḍ u-tinfeḏ ʿa-l-bēt tibaḥḥa, mi(n) šān widdo yiǧībhe. rāh ǧāb ʿummāl u-ǧāb anṭāhum maṣāri, antˁāhum kūll-šī, u-ṣāram yibḥašūn lo.	113 He brought men to excavate for him under the ground and penetrate her house, so he could take her. He went and brought workers and gave them money, gave them everything, and they started to dig for him.
118 sawwā-lo ṭarīg min taḥt al-'arḍ, min al-bēt—min al-dukkāne alli . . . u-maššа ṭarīg alli yaṭlaʿ ʿala bētha. haḏāka mā yaʿlam, al-ǧōz ta-le . . . ṣāhibto.	118 He made for him a road [that went] under the ground from the house—from the shop which . . . and he made a road that would go up to her house. This, the husband of his girlfriend did not know [it].
122 aywa gaḏab . . . ʿandinma maša ṭ-ṭarīg, ṣār yfūt ʿindha u-yerūḥ yīǧi. aywa,	122 Yes. He took . . . when the road was ready, he started going into her [room] and coming [back]. Yes.
124 ʿandinma xaḷḷaṣ hēk gāḷ-ḷha, "yalla." ǧābhe, labbasha, libsat awāʿīha u-ṭalʿat min al-taḥt al-'arḍ, u-ṭalʿat ʿa-d-dukkāne, u-rāḥ ǧāb taksi, stakrā, u-rakkabha ba-t-taksi, u-rawwaḥ, rawwa(ḥ) ʿand abūh . . .	124 When it was finished like that, he said to her, "Let's go." He brought her, dressed her, she put on her clothes and went out from under the ground and [they] went out at the shop. And he went and brought a taxi, rented one, and put her in the taxi and went back home, went to his father.

128 [šū b-at-taksi, bal-faras![2] . . . miš taksi!][3] [la:, mu-hu, yiṭlaḥ-ḥa mí-l-balad, alla yiṭlaḥ-ḥa mí-l-balad, ʿala-l-minṭaga. at-tnēn mā yirkabūn ʿa-l-faras. humma tnēn. xaḏāha u-nihay] (= u-nihağ)[4]	128 (What, by taxi? By horse!—Not taxi!) (No, for he took her out, taking her from the town, he did take her out from the town, to the area. Two cannot ride a horse. They were two. He took her and went off.)
134 hāḏa ğōzha rāḥ ʿa-l-gaṣer tabaʿo, "'e, wē(n)-rāḥet?" ṣār yidawwer, "'aḷḷa, 'aḷḷa wēn rāḥet?" hū ma yiʿarif inno min taḥt al-arḏ ⁱṭlaʿat, yīği ʿala l-maḥall, dārha—msakkara, mīn axaḏhe?	134 This, her husband went to his palace, "Where did she go?" He began looking for her, "O, Allah, Allah, where did she go?" He does not know that she went out by the way under the ground. He came to the place, her house—it was closed. Who has taken her?
139 u-hiyye libsat hīč, ġamġamat wağeha, rakbat ba-t-taksi, 'axaḏha bi-t-taksi. u-hu ṣār ydawwir. hū miṯil mağnūn, ğōzhe. xaḏāha u-nihağ ba-t-taksi, la-ʿand abūh.	139 She was dressed like that, hid her face, rode the taxi, he took her by taxi. And he started searching. He was like a madman, her husband. He took her and went off in the taxi, to his father.
144 abūh gāḷ-ḷo, "yā 'aḷḷa, ğibthe," gāḷ-ḷo, "ğibthe." sawwā-lo ʿers, sawwā-lo ḥafle,	144 His father said to him, "O Allah, you brought her." He said to him, "I brought her." He prepared a wedding for him, made a feast in his honor,
146 alli 'ibno baʿed mā čān widdo ymūt, u-'aḷḷa 'aḥyā. hāḏa hu.	146 [for] that his son after he had wanted to die, Allah has revived him. That is it.

Commentary

This short story illustrates the customs and lifestyles of Bedouin society. At the center of the story is the kidnapping of the bride on the eve of her wedding by her first lover.

The kidnapping of a bride by her lover with her full consent is known in Arabic as *xatīfah*. Tovia Ashkenazi in his book "The Bedouins in the Land of Israel"[5] writes as follows:

> It happens that a Bedouin would kidnap a girl and run away with her to a secret place before negotiating with her parents and without paying the dowry. For the most part, the kidnapping is because of the will of the abducted woman, because her parents refuse to marry her to the kidnapper. The reason for the refusal is usually because the kidnapper cannot afford to pay the dowry as required, or because the girl's parents seek to give her to a relative, since according to the Bedouin tradition, he has the precedence. Only rarely would the girl be abducted against her will. And there is always a third party—usually an old Bedouin female confidant, who helps the lovers escape.

The story does not explicitly state that the girl's parents preferred a relative to the king's son, but it is clear from the continuation of the story that the girl had a friendly relationship with the hero and knew him well before she was expelled by her parents to Egypt.

The story describes two old women. The first mediates between the prince and his father, explaining to the king the nature of his son's sickness, the love sickness, receiving the money the son needs to realize his plans, and bringing it to the king's son.

The second old woman in the story, who lives in Egypt, helps him make contact with his beloved, pass on his ring, and get her women's clothes for the disguise that will allow him to reach her. Egypt is perceived by the narrator as a small village, where everyone is familiar with the others. At the hero's first encounter with the old woman, she refuses to let him into her house on the pretext that she does not accommodate strangers in her house, but after giving her a generous financial gift, she softens and is ready to help him. This episode also occurs in other Bedouin stories.

The hero arrives at his beloved's place disguised in woman's clothes. A similar episode is found in a Jewish story "The Two Brothers," which was told by a Kurdish Jew.[6]

The story reflects some Bedouin wedding practices. The bride in the story sits on top of a raised platform, known as *Masmūda*. The bride and groom sit in separate tents. The bride's tent is for women only, so the hero has to dress up as a woman. Since he is a stranger, the old woman introduces him as her daughter, and thus the hero manages to reach his beloved, talk to her, and obtain her consent to the abduction. This motif is well known as motif K1321.2, "Man disguised as woman abducts princess," and is part of the narrative type ATU 516 "Faithful John."

For the purpose of the kidnapping, the hero digs a secret tunnel that leads to her husband's house. This is also a familiar motif from other folktales, motif K1344, "Tunnel entrance to guarded maiden's chamber." This motif also appears in *Pentamerone*, the literary work of the Italian author Giambattista Basile, written in the early seventeen century, where the hero drives away his beloved through a crystal tunnel.[7]

At the end of the story the hero drives away his beloved in a hired taxi. This is, of course, a modern feature that has entered the story in recent decades. The folktale is constantly changing during its delivery, and the narrator adapts it to the changing reality.

Notes

1. The subject of this story is the love of a couple whose marriage is thwarted by the girl's father. The lad's perseverance wins in the end: he finds the girl (who had been married off to another man in the meantime), and they elope to the lad's father's place and get married there. Such love stories are not unknown in Bedouin tribes, but the manner of taking the woman from her husband's house is exceptionally modern.

2. Narration is a social event, where the narrator tells the story to an audience, whether a single listener or a larger audience. The narrator's oratory skill makes the story lively and affective with the use of pauses, repetitions, rhetorical questions, and intonation patterns, which highlight the main points or peaks and their resolution. In this tale, there is an example of a side dialogue between the narrator and the listener about the use of a taxi rather than a horse for the escape.

3. In the dialogue, the narrator explains the act of using a taxi instead of a horse by saying that two cannot ride a horse, implying this solution for this problem, when they need to be in a hurry. Thus, the modern vehicle is included and used in the traditional story. This

mixture of old and modern elements in a tale (whether based on a real or imaginary event) occurs in many folktales collected and published in the twentieth century.

4. The verb (*xaḏāha u-*) *nihay*, "and went off," is pronounced with the semivowel *y*, though the verb is usually pronounced as *nihağ*. Words have a formal phonological form of pronunciation, but in spontaneous speech, many phonetic changes may occur. Here, an affricate speech sound (*ğ*) is pronounced as a semivowel. Some other phonetic changes may occur sometimes before a pause.

5. Ashkenazi, *The Bedouins in the Land of Israel*, 110.

6. Shilo, *Lishana Deni*, 26–43.

7. Basile, *Stories from the Pentamerone*, story 12, The Three Sisters (Petrosinella).

20. The Prince and His Two Wives

NARRATOR: Ṣabḥa ʿAbūd

TRIBE: *ʿArab el-Ḥuğērāt*

IFA 12721 December 8, 1979

Text

There was a king's daughter who wanted to get married. She was selective and did not want to marry, except to *farrās* [literally: horseman, a strong man], a brave and courageous man who would know how to rule her. What did she do? She dressed in a man's clothes—a sword on her hip and a rifle on her shoulder—and she built her tent in Wādi Ġana (Cana), on the road. Every man who passed the road, she would go into battle with him. She said: "The first man who would prevail over me, I'll be his wife."

Many men passed by, warriors and fighters, but none of them could overcome the disguised princess. One by one, they had to surrender to her, and she took them prisoner and closed them in her tent.

And in a neighboring country lived at that time a blind king with three sons. One day the king convened his sons and commanded them, "Go and look for a medicine that will restore the light of my eyes!"

The three sons set out on their father's orders, and each chose a different path. The two senior brothers wandered for many days but could not find a remedy. And the third, the youngest son, what happened to him? The third son chose the path that passed by the tent of the disguised princess. When he got there on his horse, the princess went out to greet him.

"Welcome!" she said to him. "Be my guest and come in the shadow of my tent."

The prince accepted her invitation, got off his horse, and entered her tent. She served him all sorts of pastry and gave him coffee.

The prince ate and drank. He was sure that he is talking with a man. When he was about to leave, the princess invited him to fight her. For a long time, the two "men" fought, and the prince did his best to evade her sword. In the end, the prince had the upper hand; he hit the princess with his sword and cut off the tip of her finger with his sword.

When the princess realized that her rival had overcome her, she returned her sword to her sheath and invited him back into her tent.

She said to him, "Sit down again, my champion, and rest."

And the princess, what did she do? She gathered all the prisoners who were in her tent, sat them down with the prince, and ordered them to tell, each in his turn, the story of his life. Among the princess's captives was a tall, powerful black.

He said, "I was a slave of a certain king. One day the king died. His brother wanted to marry his brother's widow, but she refused and decided to flee for her life. I helped her, I put the king's widow on a horse, and set out with her. We rode and rode until we were tired and sat down to rest in a forest, and the king's widow was pregnant from her dead husband.

"When I realized that we were alone in the forest, I turned to her and asked her to be my wife. 'A slave and a son of a slave,' she replied. 'How dare you ask me such a thing!' And immediately she hit me on my head with a club until I fell to the ground. When I awoke from my fainting, I realized that the queen had given birth to a son, and her powers had not yet returned. I immediately took a knife and stuck it in her heart, and I did not pity her son and killed him too." The black finished his story, and the disguised princess said to him, "Slave and son of slaves, you have convicted yourself with your own words!" She pulled a sword out of her sheath and decapitated him.

The princess freed all the other captives, only she and the prince remained in the tent. The king's daughter took off her costume and confessed to him that she was a woman. She told him her story.

"My champion," she said to him, "you overcame me in battle, and it is the will of Allah that I will be your wife!"

The prince said, "I am ready to marry you, but first I have to finish what I have begun and find a remedy for my father's sickness."

She said to him, "Go, and may Allah be with you, and I will wait for you here until you return safely."

The prince parted with her, got on his horse, and continued on his way. He rode and rode and came into a city. Next to the city, there was a large spring, which supplied drinking water to the city's residents. The prince came to the place of the spring and sat down to rest on its bank, and now what did he see? A pretty girl sits by the spring, tears streaming down her cheeks.

The prince asked her: "Why are you crying, and Allah has blessed you with beauty and grace that no one has?"

The girl answered: "I am a princess and I came here by the command of my father, the king. This spring that supplies drinking water to our city belongs to certain *ḥūt* [a water ogre]. Every year the *ḥūt* comes and demands for himself the daughter of a king, and the people of the city have no choice but to submit to his will, or else the *ḥūt* will stop the waters of the spring, and all the people of the city will die in thirst. And you, it would be better for you to flee from here before the *ḥūt* comes and kills you!"

The prince said, "I will not go away from here and I will not leave you to your fate."

The *ḥūt* came to the spring, and the king's son went into battle with him. They fought for a long time, and at last, he decapitated him.

The princess returned to her father's home. The king was happy to see her safe and well.

He asked her, "Who saved you from the *ḥūt*?"

She said, "So-and-so, I sat by the spring, and I cried bitterly for my fate, and behold, a handsome and courageous young man came and fought with the *ḥūt* and saved me."

The king commanded to bring the young man before him and said to him, "You have saved my daughter from a cruel fate, and I would like to marry her to you."

The Prince thanked him for his kindness and asked his help in finding a cure for his father's illness.

The king turned to his advisers, and they brought him the desired medicine.

The prince took the king's daughter and the medicine, thanked the king for his favors, and set off. He returned to the first princess, who was waiting for him in her tent, and from there he went to his father's house with his two wives.

When he arrived at his town, he gave the medicine to his father. The king took just a pinch of it and his sight came back to him. And what was the first thing he had seen? Two handsome and good-looking maidens. His two daughters-in-law, the wives of his youngest son.

The king lusted for their beauty and said to himself, "I will kill my son and take his wives to myself."

The king sent to his two sons and ordered them to kill their younger brother.

His sons said to him, "Father, this is the way you repay your son, who risked his life for you and healed your blindness?"

The king said, "It is none of your business: take your brother, blind him, put him in a coffin, and throw him into the sea."

The sons did as their father commanded. They blinded their brother, put him in a coffin, and threw him into the sea.

For a long time, the coffin floated on the water. A fisherman who passed by saw the coffin, pulled it out, and put it in his boat. When he arrived at the beach, he opened the coffin and found, to his surprise, a blind man. He pitied the blind man, fed him, and let him drink, and allowed him to walk around in his orchard.

The blind prince sat in the fisherman's grove, inhaling the scent of its fruit, and listened to the birdsong among the trees. Suddenly two pigeons landed on the tree under which the prince sat, and began to talk.

"This blind man, who sits under the tree, if he takes feathers that fell from our wings, burns them, and sprinkles the ashes on his eyes, he will be healed and get back his sight."

The prince groped around and gathered the feathers scattered on the ground. He took the feathers and gave them to the fisherman and asked him to burn them and bring him the ashes.

The fisherman did as he asked, and the prince scattered the ashes on his eyes, and at once his sight was restored.

And what had happened in the meantime in his father's palace? The old king wanted to marry his brides, but they refused.

"Let's have a war." They said to him, "If you overcome us in battle, we will be your wives, and if we overcome you, you will lose your head!"

Now, the king's son who was cured of his blindness entered the fisherman's house and saw tears streaming down his eyes.

"My benefactor," he said to him, "why should you cry?"

The fisherman replied, "The king is about to fight his brides, and therefore he is enlisting all the young people of the state, and my son is also called to the flag, and I fear that he will die in battle."

The prince said to him, "Don't worry, I will go to the army instead of him."

The prince put a sword on his thigh and went to the king's palace, and when he arrived there, he drew his sword out of its sheath and decapitated his father.

After his father's death, the young prince ascended to the throne. His two wives came back to him, and he ruled them and the entire kingdom for many, many years.

Commentary

The narrator told her story in Arabic. Since I did not have a tape recorder with me, I wrote it down in chapter headings and later phrased it in Hebrew. At the same time, I was careful to remain as faithful as possible to the details of the story, as provided by the informant, and to the manner of her narrative.

The location of the plot in Wādi Cana, next to the narrator's place of residence, is undoubtedly an addition of her own initiative. The Bedouin listeners to the story chuckled at this attempt to place the story in their immediate surroundings, and the narrator did not mention the place again. The location of the story in places that are familiar to the audience is a common phenomenon in folk narrative. Such landmarks also appear in other Bedouin stories that I recorded.

The storyteller heard the story as a child from a professional storyteller who used to travel among the Bedouin tribes and tell stories and songs, accompanying himself on the *rabāba*, a single-stringed Bedouin violin. As far as she remembers, the storyteller came from Syria, but she does not remember his name.

The story sounds like a combination of several separate stories, yet it has a homogeneous plot. The motif of a woman disguised in man's clothing and going into battle is familiar from many folktales. The international narrative type ATU 884, "The Forsaken Fiancée: Service as Menial," opens with motif K1837, "A woman disguised in man's clothes."

The story of the blind king who sends his sons to bring medicine to cure his blindness is known as the international narrative type ATU 551, "Water of Life" (previously, "The Sons on a Quest for a Wonderful Remedy for Their Father"). Here is its main outline: A sick king can only be healed by a wonderful remedy (motif H1324, "Quest for marvelous remedy")—water of life, rejuvenating apples, phoenix bird, or something similar. Whoever brings it will inherit the kingdom. His three sons go on a quest. The two elder haughty ones are diverted from their goal.

The youngest is single-minded and friendly toward old men (dwarf, eagle) who show him the way and give advice. With their help, he reaches a magic castle that opens only for one hour. He appeases the animal guards (dragon, etc.) and finds everyone else asleep. He locates the fountain of life (golden apple tree) and takes the remedy. He sleeps with a beautiful woman (princess) and leaves his name (identification token) with her. When he leaves the castle, it closes (sinks). On his way back, he rejuvenates (releases) the helpful old men and receives magic objects in return. At home, his unsuccessful brothers secretly exchange a common (poisoned) remedy for his healing one. They give it to the king, and he recovers. These brothers slander the youngest, and the king orders him to be killed. With the help of his magic objects, he is able to escape this sentence. Meanwhile, the beautiful woman in the magic castle has given birth to a boy and has discovered the name of the intruder. She arrives at the head of an army and demands the father of her son. The haughty brothers pretend it is they. They accompany her, riding beside the golden cloth (path) that the princess has spread, but they find that the gate at its end is closed. The youngest brother appears in rags, rides down the middle of the golden cloth toward the castle (is recognized by his tokens), and the gate opens for him. He marries the woman and becomes the ruler of the kingdom. The old king learns what really happened.

This type of storytelling is familiar from across Europe, North Africa, and Asia. It often appears as part of a combination of other narrative types, including the narrative type ATU 300, "The Dragon-Slayer," as is the case in the Bedouin story. A young man arrives in a city, where once a year the villagers are forced to give the dragon a virgin girl. In that year, fate falls on the king's daughter to be handed over to the dragon. The young man fights the dragon, kills him, and wins the princess's hand. This episode is found in other stories that I have recorded among Bedouin tribes in the north of the country.

In the IFA archives, there are eight Jewish versions of the story, narrated by immigrants from Morocco, Iraqi Kurdistan, and Yemen.[1]

The episode of the slave, recounting his exploits and confessing his actions, is reminiscent of similar episodes in many stories from *Arabian Nights*. So is the search for a magical remedy. In the story "Tale of Kamar Al-Zaman," the king's son says to the princess, "I will go round about all lands and will seek for what may heal thee."[2] In the story "Tale of Harun Al-Rashid and Abu Ḥasan, the Merchant of Oman," we hear about an amulet that heals the king's daughter from her malady.[3]

It is possible that the professional storyteller from whom the narrator heard the story knew the *Arabian Nights* tales and incorporated passages from them in his stories, yet the story is imbued with the stamp of Bedouin storytelling.

Ṣabḥa's story is a typical adolescence folktale, whose plot somewhat resembles the plot of the story "Between the Sun and the Moon," in chapter 1. Here, too, we are dealing with a young man and two girls, who eventually become his wives, and here too there is a confrontation between the older generation and the younger generation. But the plotlines in this story are completely different. The narrator begins her story with a female figure, a king's daughter who wishes to marry a courageous and brave man. This is an unusual opening: a king's daughter who rebels against her parents' authority and seeks to find her groom in her own way. We have already encountered a somewhat similar situation in the story "The Son Who Obeyed His Mother," in chapter 16. In that story, a princess chooses her groom by posing riddles to her suitors, but she does so in consultation with her father, the king. However, here the heroine leaves her home disguised in man's clothes and tests, not the wisdom of her suitors, but their physical strength. In fact, these are not suitors but passersby, who have the misfortune to meet her. The princess fights many men, subdues them, and takes them captive. She builds a kind of male harem and controls the captives' fate.

This is a story of reverse control, in which the princess plays the male role, but her true desire is to marry "a courageous and brave man who will know how to rule her." In other words, she does not wish to control her future husband but to accept his authority as is customary in the Bedouin patriarchal society, but she wants her husband to be a man who will "prove himself," a man who will give her family strength and economic stability.

The heroine chooses an unusual way to achieve her goal: disguising herself as a man. Tova Rosén, in her book *Hunting Gazelles: Reading Gender in Medieval Hebrew Literature*, discusses the subject of Transvestia (cross-dressing) as disturbance of the putative order and devotes a whole chapter to it.[4]

Discussing the subject of gender symbolism in dress in Arab-Muslim culture, she quotes from Bouhdiba's book *Sexuality in Islam*: "In the theological system itself, compliance with clothing regulations is formulated as a religious command. In order to fulfill Allah's intentions, therefore, the man must 'realize his masculinity', and the woman is obligated to 'accept her femininity'—and this will be done by wearing the 'right' clothes for each of them. Wearing the clothing of the opposite sex constitutes a 'severe violating of order, the source of evil and anarchy'."[5]

It is interesting to note that the motif of the maid who is disguised in man's clothing and is going into battle is known from the Spanish-Jewish romance "The Warrior Maiden" (La Doncella Guerrera). This romance begins with a father who has no sons and is called to serve in the army. His daughter wears a man's clothes and goes to battle in his place. In our story, there is a similar motif: the hero goes to battle instead of the fisherman's son.

The story "The Promises of the Three Sisters"[6] is an Egyptian version of the story "The Golden Children," which I will discuss in chapter 36. In the Egyptian story, a girl goes on a quest for her brother who disappeared. She disguises herself as a man and thus manages to conduct herself in the male world. But once she finds him, she removes the costume, and the brother takes the initiative, rides the horse, and puts his sister behind him. In other words, she retains the "natural" place that is expected of her in the patriarchal society in which she lives. This is also the case in our story. Once the girl has achieved her goal and found the man she was looking for, she returns to wearing a woman's clothes and subordinates herself to the hero's will.

The story of the princess who wears a man's clothes and competes with men somewhat resembles the story of Atalanta in the Greek mythology. Here are the main lines of that story.

According to the *Bibliotheca of Pseudo-Apollodorus*,[7] Atalanta is the daughter of Iasus, son of Lycurgus, and Clymene. King Iasus wants a son; when Atalanta is born, he leaves her on a mountaintop to die. Some stories say that a she-bear suckles and cares for Atalanta until hunters find and raise her, and she learns to fight and hunt as a bear would. Having grown up in the wilderness, Atalanta becomes a fierce hunter. She takes an oath of virginity to the goddess Artemis. After the Calydonian boar hunt, Atalanta is rediscovered by her father. He wants her to be married, but Atalanta, uninterested in marriage, agrees to marry only if her suitors can outrun her in a footrace. Those who lose will be killed. The king agrees, and many young men die in the attempt until Hippomenes comes along. Hippomenes has asked the goddess Aphrodite for help, and she has given him three golden apples to slow Atalanta down. The apples are irresistible, so every time Atalanta gets ahead of Hippomenes, he rolls an apple ahead of her, and she runs after it. In this way, Hippomenes wins the footrace and comes to marry Atalanta.

But in the Bedouin story, the heroine takes once more an active male role, and together with the prince's second wife, the two rebel against the king, the prince's father. They declare war and recruit an army. The episode of a princess who presides over an army appears in the description of the international type ATU 551, "Water of Life," but the one who ultimately wins the battle is the prince himself.

At the beginning of the Bedouin story, the narrator presents the heroine and her actions, and then she goes on to describe the hero's story. The younger brother leaves his home on a mission to find a cure for his father's blindness (motif D1505.1, "Herbs restore sight"). Here there is a common motif in folktales: the younger brother who succeeds where his older brothers fail. On his way to search for the remedy, he comes across the princess, who is disguised as a man, and here, too, he succeeds where others have failed. He manages to win the princess and cut off the tip of her finger.

This scene in which the little finger is cut off is very interesting. It seems that the narrator wishes to emphasize that even a woman whose finger has been cut is worthy of admiration and marriage to a prince. Perhaps this is the narrator's reference to herself, for she herself lost half of her pinkie in unclear circumstances.

After the princess was defeated in the battle with the prince, she gathers all the captives who were in her tent and asks each of them to tell his story. In fact, we hear only the story of the black slave. The slave tells the story of his mistress, the king's widow, who refuses to marry her brother-in-law after her husband's death. According to the usual practice in Bedouin society, the brother-in-law is obligated to marry his brother's widow if she has no offspring.[8] A similar situation appears in the story "The Emīr's Daughter Who Flew to Switzerland" (chap. 35), where the younger brother marries the fiancée of his older brother.

The woman refuses to marry her brother-in-law, and the slave helps her run away from the palace in the middle of the night. In the forest, while the woman is at the mercy of the slave, he demands that she marry him, even though she is in advanced pregnancy. The widow does not agree, and she attacks the slave, but after she gives birth, he takes advantage of her exhaustion and kills her and her son.

After the princess hears the story, she punishes the slave and cuts off his head. Such an episode, which is integrated as a side story in the main story, is very common in the stories of the *Arabian Nights*. Here it serves as an anticipation story to the episode in which the prince punishes his father later on. The slave punishes the king's widow for not obeying his demands and murders her, and the princess avenges the widow by killing him.

The princess removes her costume and reveals herself to the prince as a woman. She wants to marry him, but he aspires to complete his mission first of all. During his journey, he encounters another princess, who was abandoned at the mercy of a *ǧinn*, after this *ǧinn* had threatened to shut down the spring that supplied drinking water to the city, and demanded a virgin girl every year (motif B11.10, "Sacrifice of a human being to dragon"). This is a familiar motif from other Bedouin stories. The struggle with the dragon and the rescue of the king's daughter also appear in a Judeo-Kurdish version of the story (IFA 2783).

The encounter with the *ǧinn* symbolizes another stage in the hero's adolescence: at the beginning of the story, he goes out to the wide world at his father's command, obeying the authority of his parents. In the battle with the princess, he appears as a man who is wise enough to cope with life circumstances on his way, but he is still passive. He does not initiate the confrontation. When he saves the princess from the *ǧinn*, he is revealed for the first time as an active hero. Despite the warnings of the princess, he does not refrain from the encounter: "I will not go away from here and I will not leave you to your fate." When he returns to his father's house, he behaves once again as a passive hero. When, following his father's command, his brothers put him in a coffin and throw him into the sea, he does not revolt against his fate (or at least we hear nothing about it). Only after the fisherman saves him and houses him in his home does he resume the initiative. Unlike his blind father, who sent his sons to find a cure for his blindness, our hero cures himself of blindness with his own hands.

At the end of the story, the hero completes the process of growing up by killing his father and seizing the throne.

In the international narrative type, the hero's brothers are the ones who harass the younger brother and steal the medicine, while the king punishes the brothers and hands his throne to the young son. In our story, it is precisely the king who harasses his son despite his brother's protests and forces them to blind him and throw him into the sea. The brothers are described here as people who remain in the circle of obedience to the authority of the father. Just as at the beginning of the story they did not discover enough initiative and failed in their mission to bring the remedy, so now they are trying to protest, but ultimately succumb to their father.

Ṣabḥa's story revolves around the oedipal axis. The father lusts for his daughters-in-law and orders his son to be killed, and the son fights him, kills him, and takes his place. Sigmund Freud coined the term "Oedipus complex" in 1899. He called it the "Oedipus complex" after Oedipus, the hero of a Greek tragedy. According to the Greek mythology, King Laius, Oedipus's father, was told a prophecy that his son would end up killing his father, marrying his mother, and inheriting his place. Laius tried to kill his son, but the boy survived and, as a young man, unconsciously fulfilled the prophecy: killed his father and married his mother. When his eyes opened to the truth, Oedipus blinded himself with his own hands.

In his writings, Freud attributes to every man a primal sexual desire for his mother and murderous jealousy toward his father. These are childhood feelings that most people succeed in conquering and overcoming, but in pathological cases, they continue to manifest themselves even in adulthood. He claims that in childhood the boy perceives the father as a sexual competitor for his mother's grace. The child wants his father to die so he can take his place, but eventually he has to accept his father's place in the family and give up his sexual love for his mother. He overcomes the complex by shifting his sexual feelings to girls of his age.

In the Bedouin story, the father is the one who develops jealousy toward his son, wants to marry his brides, and orders the blinding of his son. The son and his wives take the initiative, which eventually leads to the father's being punished for his unusual desires and his death. This is similar to what happened in the beginning of the story to the black slave, who was also punished for his improper actions. During his adolescence, the hero experienced the trauma of blindness, like his father at the beginning of the story. At the end of the story, he completes his adolescence process in the overt oedipal act and decapitates his father.

The hero's two wives rebel against the father, who wants to inherit the place of his son, and declare war on him, but it is the hero who wins the battle and overcomes his father, just as at the beginning of the story he won his wife who was disguised as a man. The struggle for control runs through the whole story. The heroine longs for a man who will be strong enough to impose authority on her and control her. The queen's brother-in-law wants to control his brother's widow and inherit his place. The slave also seeks to control the queen, who fled, and the hero's father wants to control his daughters-in-law and kill his son.

The story thus presents a series of relationships between a father and his sons, between brothers and sisters, between a man and his wives, and between a king and his daughters-in-law. The father sends his sons to the world and gives them his blessing, but he wants to continue controlling them. When the younger son becomes overly independent, the father commands his other sons to kill him, and they obey him, thereby violating the required brotherhood. The hero follows the circumstances. When attacked by a girl, he fights back and overcomes her. When he meets a girl in distress, he acts according to a knightly code and endangers his life for her. As for the two women, the first woman takes an active initiative to obtain a husband to her liking. The second woman, at least in the beginning of the story, is a passive figure who does not rebel against her father's decision to sacrifice her to the *ḥūt* for the kingdom's economic interests. Later she joins the first woman, and together they take the initiative and rebel against the king. The king's widow in the story of the slave is also an active figure. She flees from her brother-in-law and fights the slave, who wishes to desecrate her honor.

On the other hand, the male characters in the story, except for the hero, are mostly passive. The first king, the hero's father, expects someone to cure his blindness and takes no initiative by himself. The second king, the father of the young woman who was handed over to the *ḥūt*, does nothing to save her. The king wants to enlist the fisherman's son into the army, and the worried fisherman sheds tears and shares the hero's concern but takes no action to prevent it. Maybe he expects the hero to go to battle instead of his son, although this is not explicitly stated.

As is customary in many folktales, the moral principle of reward and punishment is at the center of the story. The slave who murders the helpless woman and the king who tries to murder his son are punished and killed. The hero who saves a helpless woman and the fisherman who gives protection to the hero benefit: the hero wins the princess's hand and succeeds in bringing the medicine to cure his father's blindness, and the fisherman saves his son from military service.

The different characters in the story reflect one another, or pose a mirror to other characters. The slave and the king are both motivated by envy and greed. The active women reflect each other.

This story, though in some respects it matches versions recorded in other cultural spaces, is unusual in its plot. Like other Bedouin stories collected from women, it expresses the hidden wishes of women to gain respect and esteem in the patriarchal society in which they live.

Notes

1. Morocco: 8205; Iraqi Kurdistan: 2783, 5263, 10125; Yemen: 64, 65, 6573, 14061. In the version from Morocco, the younger son brings his brother and father back to life on the advice of two birds. Kurdish version 2783 also includes the story of the struggle against the dragon and the rescue of the king's daughter.

2. Burton, *Arabian Nights*, night 194.

3. Burton, night 951.

4. Rosén, *Hunting Gazelles: Reading Gender in Medieval Hebrew Literature*, 231–44.

5. Rosén, 233.

6. El-Shamy, *Folktales of Egypt*, 63–72, 254–56.

7. The *Bibliotheca*, also known as the *Bibliotheca of Pseudo-Apollodorus*, is a compendium of Greek myths and heroic legends, arranged in three books, generally dated to the first or second century CE. The author was traditionally thought to be Apollodorus of Athens, but that attribution is now regarded as false, and so *Pseudo-* was added to Apollodorus.

8. Ashkenazi, *Bedouins in the Land of Israel*, 75.

21. In the Family

A. Between a Brother and His Sister

NARRATOR: Ṯarwa Yāsīn

TRIBE: *ʿArab el-Ḥağāğra*

IFA 17397 April 18, 1984

1 kān yā mā kān yā samʿīn al-kalām,[1] hēna,[2] bī ʾaš-šāṭr-imḥammad. ʾaš-šāṭr-imḥammad huwwa w-uxto, laḥālhin. mātat ʾummo, māt ʾabū. ḍaḷḷam humma ^{u}wlād ^{u}zgār, rubu[3] ʿind al-ʿarab. fa-ṣāru šabāb.	1 Once upon a time, oh listeners of the talk, there was here Smart Muhammad. Smart Muhammad, he and his sister were alone. His mother died, his father died. They remained small children, and were brought up at the Bedouins'. They became youths.
7 ʾağat ʾoxto, xaṭbat la. lamman xaṭbat lo, ğawwazato, šarat lo hā-l-faras, ʿemlat lo hā-d-dār, ʿemlat lo hā-l-bēt, kbīr, hēk, u-geʿdat hī wiyyāh. baʿadēn, rūḥ yōm, taʿāl yā yōm,[4] ʾağat mart axūha, ṣārat miš ^{e}mlīḥa ʾila. ṣārat titkātal hū wiyyā(ha), "taʿamal hēk," "taʿamal hēk."	7 His sister came, betrothed him [to a woman]. When she betrothed him, married him off, she bought him this mare, made for him this house, made for him a house, big, like this, and stayed with him. Afterward, day in, day out, her brother's wife became unpleasant with her, she started quarreling with him, "She does this, she does that."
14 yōm min al-iyyām (xawā) xawātha gāḷat-ḷo "ʾoxtak taʿamal hēk hēk, biddha tuktilni." gaḏbat ʾoxto, gaḏab ʾoxto, xaḏāha, xaḏa ʾoxto, waddāha ʿād a xāḷa, beʿīd, beʿīd. ričeb hū wiyyāha ʿala hā-n-nāga u-rāḥam.	14 One day, her sister-in-law (she pretended to be her a good sister-in-law) told him. "Your sister does this and this, she wants to kill me." She took her—he took his sister, took her, took his sister, brought her again to her maternal uncle's place, very, very far away. He rode with her on this she-camel and they went off.
20 bātu lēla lēltēn ʿa-ṭ-ṭurg, ʿa-d-darb, ta-wiṣlum dār xāla, u-rawwaḥ daššarha ʿend al-xāḷ.	20 They spent a night or two on the way, the way, until they reached her maternal uncle's home. He went back home and left her with the uncle.

23 yōm la-yōm, yōm la-yōm.[5] nām—ṣārat al-ḥikāya maʿā(h)a miš ᵉmlīḥa. ḏeʿef;[6] rāḥ. gāḷ, "hāḏi ʾoxti, taddaʿi ʿalayya, (wid)di arūḥ ʿind ʾoxti." rā(ḥ) ʿind oxto, šū ligāha b-ḥāla mlīḥa, b-ḥāla zēna, b-ḥāla yaʿani ʾiši-ʾiši.

23 A day follows a day, a day follows a day. He stayed—the story with her became unpleasant. He got poor, and. went. He said, "This is my sister, [she] is putting the curse on me. I will go to my sister's [to check it]." He went to his sister, what [state], he found her in a good state, in a good state, that is, in a wonderful state.

29 daḥḥagat, šāfato, gāḷat, "ī, waḷḷa, haḏāk ʾaxūya, š-šāṭr-imḥammad. lēš ʾaxūya hēč?" gāḷ-ḷa, "yā xayya, waḷḷa, fagarna, bas mā ḏaḷḷaš ᵉmʿāna—mā ḏaḷḷeš ʿandīna māl."

29 She looked and saw him, and said, "O, by Allah, that is my brother, Smart Muhammad. Why is my brother like that?" He said to her, "O my sister, by Allah, we got poor, but there remained nothing with us—no money remained with us."

34 ʾağa, ṣārt taḥṭuf (<taʿṭuf) ʿalē, ta-banat-lo ṯāni, ʿammarat-lo u-ğawwazato mara ṯāniya, ṣār ʿindo wlād, ṣār ʿindo riziq, ṣār ʿindo xēr, ṣār ʿindo ḥumra, ṣār ʿindo ʾiši-ʾiši. riğʿat al-ḥāl hī hī. ṣār ʾaḥsan wāḥad min gaboḷ.

34 He came, she started pitying him. So she built for him again, constructed for him and married him off to a second wife, he had children, he had livelihood, it started being good [state], he got having a wife, started being a wonderful state. The state became as before. He became better [in a better state] than before.

40 yōm gāḷ-(ḷ)ha, "yā xayya, widna rrūh ʿa-blādna." gāḷat-ḷo, "lā, yā-xūya, hāyya[7] blādna hēna, aḥsan lēna." ḏaḷḷat, ḏaḷḷat bi-blādha. hī wiyyāh, w-axūha, u-mart axūha, kullhin.

40 One day he said to her, "O sister, we'll go back to our country." She said to him, "No, my brother, this is our country here, it's better for us." She remained, remained in her country. She with him, her brother, and her brother's wife, and all of them.

45 ʾā. yōmanna ḏaḷḷat. ḏaḷḷat. gāḷat-ḷo—rāḥ ğōzha, xiṭar, sāfar mišwār ᵃbʿīd, gāḷ-(ḷ)ha. waṣṣa ʾommo, gāḷ-ḷo "dīri bāleč ʿala ḥamda. dīri bāleč ʿal-ʿēle hēn u-ʿala l-uwlād" u-ṣār.

45 Yes. When she remained, remained, she said to him—her husband had gone, went on a journey, traveled [on] a distant journey, he said to her—he ordered his mother, said to her, "Look after Ḥamda, look after the wife here and the children," and went.

50 hiyya ʾommo, mā teʿarif ʾoxto—ma teʿarif ʾaxūha, illi ğārha. qām ğa qāḷ-ḷha, qāḷ-ḷen tannen yukutlanna. qāḷat-enhen—gāḷ-ḷehen, "wēn tukutlan ʾoxti? ʾani mā-ni ʾaxūha u-ğārha. tukutlan-ha, ʾani ḏaḷḷ minha, kafīlha ta-yīği zalmatha, ʿa-d-dār."

50 She, his mother, did not know she was his sister—she [the mother] did not know that he was her brother, the one who was her neighbor. He went and told her—they [the husband's mother and sister] said they would kill her. She told that they—he [her brother] said to them "How will you kill my sister? I am her brother and her neighbor. Will you kill her? I remain for her, her protector, until her husband [man] comes home."

57 rawwaḥ. gāḷat-ḷo, gāḷat-ḷo, "'ommak, 'oxtak widdhan yukutlanni." gāḷ-(ḷ)ha "la'." nuṣab-lēha bēt ṯāni la-ḥālha, u-gaʿʿadha, u-'ummo, 'uxto u-'abū la-ḥālhin be-ddār, bēt la-ḥālhin. kull min ḍaḷḷ ʿinda.	57 He [her husband] came home, she told him, said to him, "Your mother and your sister want to kill me." He said to her, "No. [That will not be]." He put up for her another house, on her own, and settled her [there] and his mother and sister and his father alone in the house—a house for themselves. Everyone remained at his [own] place.

B. Between a Bride and Her Mother-in-Law

NARRATOR: Maryam Šatwah
TRIBE: *ʿArab el-Ḥuǧērāt*
IFA 18981 August 1982

Text

There was a married man. His mother [was] with him. This one—his wife had found fault with her mother-in-law.

"My dear, my daughter-in-law [the old woman says to her son's wife], shall I wash for you, clean for you?"

"No, I do not want your mother! Your mother—you must keep her away from me!"

The man came, stood up, put his mother on the donkey.

Then he said to his wife, "Come on, woman, put food for her."

She went, she brought camel dung—Allah forbid—donkey urine—forgive me, the listeners. She filled the jug for her. Goat dung—[as] dried figs. Cow dung—[as] bread. The oil—donkey urine, forgive me, the listeners. This one [the wife] came and filled the bags and held it out.

He went, put her [his mother] there. She fasts and prays. He went, put her next to the rock [in a deserted place], and here come angels. He put her there and returned.

And now angels come to her, "What is this, ma'am?"

She said, "It is oil, *inšallah* [by Allah's will]!"

"And that's what?"

"This is bread, by Allah's will!"

"And this?"

"These are dried figs, by Allah's will, please, dear [guests], please come in."

"By Allah's will, you will not say anything unless a pound of gold falls from your mouth!"

She fasts, she prays. Thus, for two months [after] he left his mother by the rock, and a spring of water came out—she can purify herself and pray. This one [his mother]—she was hungry, she wanted to eat. She went and searched, and here [she found] cow dung and goat droppings, and the oil is donkey urine.

She said, "From where do I get food, oh my Lord?"

Allah sent her. She began to eat.

He [her son] said, "This is a long separation from my mother. I want to go and see her—is she alive or dead?" This man, he thought that she has dried figs and oil in which she dips her bread and eats. This one went, rode the donkey and went, and here is his mother, and she has a sack full of gold in her hand. As she prepares herself for praying and prays and speaks, and then a golden coin falls from her mouth.

He came to his mother, he begins to kiss her from here and from there, a gold pound falls from her mouth.

He said, "Come on, Mama, let's go."

This one came, put his mother on the donkey's back, and returned.

Those—the neighbors [said], "The mother of so-and-so returns, the mother of so-and-so returns! Let us go and visit her."

This one goes to see her, that one goes, that one goes. She just speaks, and there is a gold pound falling from her mouth, she just speaks, and there is a gold pound falling from her mouth.

This one [his wife] came, forcing her husband: "Take my mother instead of your mother" [put my mother where your mother was].

He put her on the donkey. He prepared for her oil and real bread and dried figs—the bags are so full! He mounted her on the donkey, put her in his mother's place, and came back.

Two or three days, those who came to the old woman came to her. They came to her.

[She said to them,] "What do you want? Get out of here! I have nothing! Get out of here! I have nothing!"

They said, "O old woman, by Allah's will, thou shalt not speak unless you fart! Thou shalt not speak unless you fart!"

This one, a week, two weeks, a month, Allah knows [how long].

She [his wife] said, "Come on, go see my mother." He went, rode the donkey, and went to see his mother-in-law.

"Hello, my mother-in-law, how are you?" And there comes a fart.

He took her on the donkey and returned home.

"Here comes my mother, my mother comes!"

She sat down, offered her the bed, and her mother sat down. Greeting her and nothing but fart.

Commentary

The narrative type ATU 480D*, "Tales of Kind and Unkind Girls," deals with a group of stories in which an unkind girl (woman, neighbor) seeks to win the same reward a kind girl wins but is punished for her selfishness. The reward received by the kind girl may take various forms, including gold coins that fall from her mouth: motif D1454.2, "Treasure falls from mouth."

The two stories reflect the shaky relationship between a woman and her sister-in-law and between a mother-in-law and her daughter-in-law.

In the first story, "Between a Brother and His Sister," the basic confrontation is between the hero's wife and her sister-in-law. An orphaned brother and sister reach adulthood. The sister (who is probably the elder one, although this fact is not explicitly mentioned in the text) makes sure to marry her brother off, build him a house, and give him a horse. This is a reversal of roles, since in Bedouin society a man, usually a brother, is responsible for finding a husband for an unmarried girl. In this respect, "Between a Brother and His Sister" is a feminist story that enhances the place and role of women in society. The sister lives in the same house she gave her brother, along with her sister-in-law. As in the second story, "Between a Bride and Her Mother-in-Law," the hero's wife is the complainant and the initiator of the expulsion of her rival from the house. Following the expulsion of the sister, the couple is punished and their economic situation deteriorates. The husband leaves his wife and wanders to the place of his sister's exile. This time, too, the sister treats him generously, builds a house for him, and brings him a new wife.

The sister's husband goes on a journey and entrusts his wife, the hero's sister, with his mother. The mother-in-law and the sister-in-law harass her and want to kill her, but her brother comes to her aid and protects her. The hero thus rewards his sister for her past favors. When the husband returns from his journey and hears about the course of events, he builds a separate house for his wife and children. By doing so, he separates her from his relatives and prevents the continuation of the conflict.

In her work *The Bedouin Woman: Changes and Transformations since the Establishment of the State up to the Present*, Safa Abu Rabiʿa, a Bedouin woman of the Negev, writes:

> The woman maintains contact and loyalty to her original family. Over the years she gives birth, the children grow up, and she becomes more and more a part of her new family. However, in times of conflict, her husband's family still sees her as a stranger—a member of her original family.
>
> Part of the general approach in Bedouin society emphasizes marriage as a link between two groups rather than between two individuals. The accepted norm is this: a bride should play the role of daughter, as she often replaces her. She must help her mother-in-law in the house, ease her physical work, and allow her to rest. The bride has to bake, gather wood, cook, wash, and bring water. If the family is seminomadic, she sometimes has to graze the herd and reap the harvest.
>
> The bride usually lives with her husband in a tent or a hut next to her husband's parents, or she lives with her widowed mother-in-law. If she lives with her mother-in-law and her husband, they help each other during the day in joint activity; only at night do they separate, so that the bride's absorption into the husband's family is fraught with conflict. The common theme in these conflicts is the bride's desire to have a home of her own and to have economic independence.
>
> Bedouin women still maintain a norm of obedience to the mother-in-law, but since the bride lives in changing social conditions that are contrary to this norm, she tries to create a behavior that will fit her new situation without changing the norm on which she grew up. The economic base changed following the transition to permanent settlements and, as a result, to hired jobs, and so forth; this change has affected relations between brides and sisters-in-law.[8]

In the second story, "Between a Bride and Her Mother-in-Law," the mother and mother-in-law of the hero take the place of the girls in the international narrative type, but the idea is the same: anyone who treats others with generosity and kindness is rewarded, while those who behave selfishly and evil-heartedly are punished.

The mother-in-law, who was exiled to a desolate place, receives a gift in which a golden coin drops from her mouth with every word. The wife demands that her husband take her mother to the same place he brought her mother-in-law, but the mother, unlike the mother-in-law, acts selfishly, and her punishment is passing gas with every word that comes out of her mouth. In Bedouin and Arab culture, a public fart is considered a blatant violation of the rules of politeness.

In the book *Seed of Pomegranate: The Woman in Arab Folktales*, Joram Meron gives a version of the story "The Blind Mother-in-Law" recorded from Ḥamda Qāsem Ġrifāt, who is from the ʿArab-ʿAyadāt tribe and resides in Bēt Zarzīr.[9] This version is very close to the first Bedouin story above. To the blind and paralyzed mother of the hero who was abandoned in the cave, two angels arrive, one named Winter and the other Summer. To their question "Who is better, old woman, Summer or Winter?" she replies, "Were it not summer, winter would not come, and were it not winter, summer would not come. We use during summer the good things of winter. In winter the *mulukhiyya* [a sort of food plant] grows, and everything that is a vegetable grows, and in the winter, everything grows, *ʿilt* [chicory] and *xubbēza* [*malva*, "mallow," an abundant food plant]; everything grows in winter, and in summer everything grows, both of them are equally beautiful." In response, the angels wish that a pound of gold will fall from her mouth with every word and that she will return to the days of her youth, will be cured of her blindness and paralysis, "and will return to being beautiful and comely as a sixteen-year-old." Later, the husband brings his mother-in-law to the cave. She treats the angels who come to visit her disparagingly. As for their question of which is better, she replies, "Allah will curse you, and curse the summer and the winter, one is worse than the other, at summer the heat eats us, and in winter the cold eats us." In response, the angels wish she will become blind and paralyzed. At the end of the story, the hero abandons his wife and, on his mother's advice, marries a better girl.

In the story "The Bride and Her Mother-in-Law" in the same book, Meron quotes a folk saying of the narrator Xalīl Mḥammad Maḥmūd of Yāmā (a Muslim village in the Sharon region in the central part of Israel). Maḥmūd says, "A mother-in-law never loves the daughter-in-law, and if she does, *Iblīs* [Satan] will burst into heaven" (*ʿumur mā ḥamā ḥabbat kinneh, u-ʾiḏa ḥabbat el-kinneh ʾiblīs biṭīḥ lal-ğanna*).[10]

The two stories thus reflect in different ways the complex relationship between a woman and her husband's relatives in the Bedouin society. They emphasize the need to mitigate the rivalry as much as possible through physical separation, and at the same time, they also reflect the state of the husband, who is torn between his obligations toward his wife and those toward his mother or sister. As in many folktales, the issue of reward and punishment is also emphasized here: those who behave in a proper manner are rewarded, while those who behave in an inappropriate manner are punished.

Notes

1. *kān yā mā kān yā sām'īn al-kalām* ("Once upon a time, oh listeners of the talk") is a traditional opening formula for a narrative, equivalent to the English "Once upon a time." Note the added address to the listeners. Traditional Arabic folktale openings mention Allah and his blessing, addressing the audience, or a "disclaimer" about the reality or truth value of the forthcoming story. In this collection, few narrators use any kind of formal opening. They often begin the tale by mentioning a protagonist's existence and location. Here, these directly follow the formal opening.

2. After the opening, the narrator says *hēna*, "here," as a discourse marker (cf. chap. 18, note 1).

3. *rubu*, "were raised, educated," is an internal passive form (cf. chap. 18, note 3 and the chapter on Beoduin dialects below in this volume).

4. *rūḥ yōm, ta'āl yā yōm*, lit.: "Go, day—come, oh day," is another frequent vocative formula in Arabic folk stories, implying the passage of time between events. This formula has a sequence of two verbs in the "narrative imperative," which alternates with past-tense verbs in Bedouin dialects (cf. chap. 17, note 4).

5. *yōm la-yōm, yōm la-yōm*, "A day follows a day, a day follows a day," is another expression of the passage of time in a different linguistic structure, including repetition as a rhetorical device.

6. *ḏe'ef*: literally "he got thin" as well as "he weakened," and metaphorically, "became poor." Many narrative elements in the Bedouin tales describe facts in one word, which should be understood within the context.

7. The form *hāyya* apparently derives from *hā hiyya*, "this [is] it [f.sg.]." Note that in the narratives in this book, various demonstrative pronouns (and other structures) are not used by sedentary speakers.

8. Abu Rabiʿa, *Bedouin Woman*, chapter 2.

9. Meron, Shehadi, and Masarwi, *Seed of Pomegranate*, 314–23.

10. Meron, Shehadi, and Masarwi, 89.

22. The Replaced Bride

NARRATOR: Maryam Muṣṭafa Ṭabbāš

TRIBE: *’Arab Ḥilf-Ṭabbāš*

IFA 15229 August 8, 1982

1 ’esemha ^{e}ğbēna. ^{e}ğbēna.[1] ’aywa. bī hnāk hā-l-bint, yaʿani, ḥurra, bēḏ̣a, tiʿeref, u-bī [$_{H}$ša’xor$_{H}$], ’aswad, haḏōl ğirān, ḥadd baʿaḍhum el-baʿaḍ. haḏōla bī ʿirs [teʿeref al-ʿir^{i}s? fanṭaziyya?] rāḥan ʿalēha, [$_{H}$ḥatuna$_{H}$] u-rāḥan.	1 Her name [is] Ğbēneh. Ğbēneh. Yes. There was this girl, that is, free [not a slave], white. You know. And there is ($_{H}$ša’xor$_{H}$) black, black. These were neighbors, one near the other. Those—there is a wedding. (Do you know [what is] a wedding? “Fantasy?”) They went to it, ($_{H}$ḥatuna$_{H}$) wedding, and they went.
7 hāy al-samra, al-ʿabda[2] hāy, as-sōda[3] biddha tiḏbaḥ al . . . haḏīč ’ā, yaʿani, hī zaʿalāna minha, ġairān(a). biddha tiḏbaḥha. hāḏi rāḥan hi wiyyāha ʿala-ʿirs, yaʿani, miš ^{e}bʿīd ^{e}kṯīr, miš ^{e}bʿīd, yaʿani, min ta-le . . . ’oranim [faḏ̣li zay abū.] rāḥan.	7 This, the swarthy one, this slave, the black one, wants to kill the . . . That. Yes, that is [she was] angry with her, envious. She wants to kill her. This—they went, she with her, to the wedding, that is, not very far, not far, that is, from to . . . Oranim [a college name, near Tivʿon]. (Fadli is as his father.) They went.
14 ṭaššan u-rāḥan ʿala hā-l-ʿir^{e}s. hīne hāy, lammen hen wiṣlan, gabuḷ-mā wiṣlan ʿa-l-ʿir^{e}s, bī wādi, teʿeref hā-l-wādi? bī mayye, ’aywa. gāḷat-lēha, “yā, inneč hā-s-sāʿa tanṭīni ^{e}hdūmeč, uwāʿīč, u-tlabsīni iyyāhen,” haḏīč ʿalēha šī fuḏ̣ḏ̣a yaʿani, ḏahab, fuḏ̣ḏ̣a—yaʿani, ṯōb ʿirs, “yā ’inni ’aḏbaḥeč.” hiyye ’agdar minha, ’akbar minha.	14 They went, got out and went to that wedding. Here, this when they reached, before they had reached the wedding, there is a *wādi* [small spring]—(Do you know [what is a] *wādi*? There is water [in it], yes.) She said to her, “Either you now give me your clothes, your clothes, and dress me with them,” that one had on her some silver, that is gold, silver—that is wedding clothes—“or I will kill you.” She [was] stronger than her, bigger than her.

23 gāḷat-ḷēha “la’, xuḏi hdūmi.” hāy šilḥat
ᵉhdūmha, (ʿ)ṭatha
25 l-al-bint az-zēna, u-rāḥat—bī mišḥara.
[tiʿarif al-faḥame?] ġaṭṭatha b-ha-l-wādi,
ġaṭṭastaha b-hā-l-waḥal, xaḷḷatha ʿabde
sōda. u-haḏīk xaḏat ᵉhdūma z-zēna,
u-libsat—u-libsat—u-labbasatha awāʿi
l-bint al-mazyūna, u-rāḥan ʿa-l-ʿers.

23 She said to her, “No, take my clothes.”
This took off her clothes and gave them
25 to the pretty girl, and went—there is a
coal-making place [from wood]. (Do you
know the coal-making place?) She covered
her, in the *wādi*, covered her with mud,
and made her like a slave. And that one
took the pretty one’s clothes and put them
on, and she dressed her the pretty girl’s
clothes, and they went to the wedding.

31 rāḥan ʿala hā-l-ʿers. gabuḷ-ma waṣlan al-ʿers—mā bī ʿers. fiš ʿers. mā fī. lifan ʿala bēt wāḥad ’amīr. ʿindo ḥalāl, ʿindo wazz [tiʿerif al-wazz?] rāḥan, ligum hā-l-hāḏa, fātan; wēn widdan yefūtan? lifan ᵉb-ğinb al-ʿarab. giʿdan, b-iši maṭraḥ, gālt lēha ugʿud. ḍabb al-lēl, ḍabb al-lēl hīča, fātan ʿind ’ummo, ’ummo la-l-walad. fātan ʿind ’ummo, geʿedan ʿendīha,

31 They went to the wedding. Before they had reached the wedding [place]—there is no wedding. No wedding. Nothing. They turned to the house of an emīr. He had property [cattle], he had geese. (Do you know [what are] geese?) They went, found this, entered. Where should they enter? They turned to the side of the Bedouins and sat down, at some place. She said to her, “Sit.” The night came, the night came like that, they entered his mother’s part [of the tent], the young man’s mother. They entered his mother’s [part], and sat down by her [i.e., stayed there].

40 daḥḥag ʿalēha, šāf hā-l-al-ʿağiyya hā-z-zēna, zēna, zayyena, lamma tġassil, zēna haḏīča. gāḷ-ḷa, “yā hala la-l-bint.” hī hayya l-ʿabde, kull mā widdha hā-l-bint hāy tegūl-la, ta-tġassil, tegūl-lēha, “lā tġassli wağheč.” lā taxaḷḷaṣ, te’admī-lha bi-l-waḥal.

40 He looked at her, saw this pretty girl, pretty, she was pretty when she washed, that one was pretty. He said to her, “Welcome, o girl”—she, this slave. Whenever the girl wanted to wash, she said to her, “Don’t wash your face,” [she should] not get rid, color her with mud.

47 gāḷ-ḷa, “mā te’axḏīni, yā bint?” ʿan haḏīč as-samra, yaʿani, lābs(e) ’awāʿi. gāḷat-ḷo, “’ā, lēš lā.” haḏīč al-bint az-zēna, wa-l-min al-saʿāda kānat māš ġērha ʿind ’ahalha, gadd-mā hum gardīnha u-taʿbānīn ʿalēha u-masʿada.

47 He said to her, “Won’t you take me [for husband], o girl?” About the black one, that is, she was wearing [fancy] clothes. She said to him, “Yes, why not.” This good girl, and for whose happiness there was nothing else except her for her parents, how much they kept her and troubled around her for her happiness.

53 gāḷat-lo, “sarreḥ hā-l-bint hāy b-al-wazz.” serḥat b-al-wazz. hāḏi kull an-nahār čef tiʿemal? tfūt ʿind hā-l-wādi, titḥammam, u-terxi šaʿarha, u-mazyūna. tirğaʿ. hāḏ al-wazz baṭṭal yirʿa, u-titmarğaḥ. al-ḥabel ⁱmʿāh(a), tiʿemal hā-l-marğīḥa b-hā-l-zatūn, u-hā-l-wazz yidaḥḥiğ ʿalēha.

53 She said to him, “Let this girl be the geese girl.” She was a geese girl. This one, what did she do every day? She would go into the spring, wash herself, let her hair go free and [would be] beautiful. She returns [to the geese]. These geese stopped feeding, and she would swing [on a swing]. She had the rope with her, would make the swing on the olive tree, and the geese would look at her.

61 ᵉtguḷ-ḷo, "'erʿa, yā wazz," "itgūḷ-ḷi wuliyya čēf widdi 'arʿa wa-l-zēna ğiddāmi tihtazz?" ṣār yōm, al-yōm al-wazz xereb. baṭṭal. gāḷ-ḷēha, "lēš al-wazz rāʿīt, yā rāʿi?" gāḷat-ḷo, "mā baʿaraf." gāḷ "ṭayyib."

61 She would say to it [the gander], "[Go] feed, o gander"—"A lady says to me how should I feed, when the pretty one in front of me is swaying" [the gander's line of poetry]. A day came and the gander got ill. It stopped [feeding]. He said to her, "Why is the gander not feeding, o shepherd?" She said to him, "I don't know." He said, "All right."

67 hāḏa mā ḥiča. yōm rikeb al-faras tabaʿto u-rāḥ la-ğ-ğibal, bi-lā mā ḥada yišūf, lēš al-wazz mā yarʿa. gāḷat-ḷo, "mā yarʿa." hī me tadri bo.

67 This [man] did not talk. One day he rode his mare and went to the hill, without anyone seeing him, [to check] why the gander was not feeding. She said to him, "It does not feed." She did not know about him [following her].

71 hāḏa rāḥ libad-ⁱlha, txabba, u-'ağat hā-l-bint, šilḥat hā-l-uwāʿi, u-tġassalat u-mā-šā-'aḷḷa ʿalēha

71 This one went, watched out for her, hid, and the girl came, took off her clothes and washed and how nice she was

74 u-tḥammamat u-ṣārat titmarğaḥ. ᵉšnū bent—tafreṭ al-ʿagol. terğaʿ. hāḏa 'awwal yōm, ṯāni yōm—ʿeref inn hā-l-bint mazyūa, hāy. mā sa'alha. mā sa'alha šēle.

74 and bathed, and started swinging. What a girl—she boggles the mind. She returns [later]. This is on the first day, the second day—he knew that this girl was beautiful. This [girl]. He did not ask her. He did not ask her at all.

78 ʿāwad le-'ommo, gāḷ-lēha, "hāy l-bint alli sārḥa maʿ al-ġanam—hāy zēna, all-maʿ-al-wazz, u-hāy alli māxeḏha 'ani—ʿabde." gāḷat, "'ani mā 'aʿref, hāḏa šuġlak, mū šuġli." gāḷ-ḷa, "hāy zēna, hāy al-bint." rāḥ ʿa-l-medīna, rāḥ ğāb ilha hdūm, uwāʿi, ğāb ilha xayyāṭ hāḏi, ḥaṭṭha ʿindo

78 He went back to his mother and said to her, "This girl who goes with the sheep—this [girl] is pretty, the one with the geese, and the one I have taken is a slave" His mother says to him, "I don't know, this is your business, not my business." He said to her, "This [girl] is pretty, this girl." He went to town, went and brought for her clothes and a tailor for it, and he put them with him.

86 liḥeğ al-bint. ʿāwad liḥeğha ʿa-l-marʿa. xaḷḷāha tannha tḥammamat u-xaḷḷaṣat ulibsat hāy-il-awāʿi, uḏaḷḷat gabuḷ mā dahhanat ḥāla –
haḏīč gāḷat-ḷa "'iḏa trawwḥi ʿa-l-bēt gabeḷ m-inti mdahhna ḥāleč 'ani 'aḏbaḥeč" gabuḷ-mā dihanat ḥālha, ʿindma widdo yerawwiḥ, aṭ-ṭarš.

86 He followed the girl. He again followed her to the pasture. He let her until she had bathed and finished and put on her clothes and remained before she smeared herself—that one had told her, "If you come home before you have smeared yourself, I'll kill you." Before she had smeared herself, when the herd was about to return home.

94 g̣aḅuḷ-mā widdha tfūt ʿa-l-wād tdahhen ḥālha b-al-waḥal, b-al-hāḏa, gāḷ-ḷaha, “stanni.” gāḷat-ḷo “lāʾ.” gāḷ-ḷaha, “bagṭaʿ rāsek b-as-six. stanni.” ^{i}stannat. gāḷ-ḷaha, “taʿāli, ʾuguʿdi hīna.” gaʿadat hīna, xarrafat.	94 Before she had wanted to go into the spring and smear herself with the mud, with that, he said to her, “Wait.” She said to him, “No.” He said to her, “I’ll cut your head off with the skewer. Wait.” She waited. He said to her, “Come, sit here.” She sat here and spoke.
100 gāḷ-ḷaha, “wallāhi, txarrfīni šnū as-sibab, ʾinti mnēn u-šlōn inti ğīti.”	100 He told her, “By Allah, tell me what is the reason, where from are you and how did you come.”
102 gāḷat-ḷo, “ʾani ruḥet ʿal-ʿerʿs u-ğīna winna tikḏib ʿalayya, mā bī ʿirs, widda tiḏbaḥni. u-gāḷat-ḷi ʾiḏa mā tilbasi ^{e}hdūmi u-teʿṭīni ehdūmeč, ʾani widdi ʾaḏbaḥeč. wu-dahnatni b-al-waḥal, wu-b-il-waḥal mišḥara, hāḏa l-aswad, u-xaḏat ^{e}hdūmi. w-ani mā astağri agūḷ—tiḏbaḥni.”	102 She told him, “I went to a wedding and we came, and suddenly [I found out that] she was lying and there was no wedding, she wanted to kill me. And she said to me that if you do not wear my clothes and give me your clothes, I will kill you. And she smeared me with mud and with that black mud [of coal] and took my clothes and I have not dared to tell—she will kill me.”
109 gāḷ-ḷaha, “mā-ʿalēš.” rawwaḥ g̣aḅuḷha, wa-l-^{i}wāʿe ʿend ʾummo, gāl-lēha, lamma yāxuḏ al-bint hāy, “yā yumma,” u-xawāto “rā(ḥ) ʿād ta-tḥammam wa-tilabbas al-awāʿi hāy,” labbasat al-awāʿi hāy,	109 He said to her, “Never mind.” He went back home before her, and the clothes at his mother’s, he said to her– when he took this girl—“O mother,” and [to] his sisters, [that] she would again bathe and put on these clothes. She [the mother] dressed her these clothes.
115 gāḷ-ḷēha, “taʿāli,” la-haḏīč, “bilḷa, yā, taʿāli,” xaḏāha la-ʿa-l-ġād. bas teʿerfu, gaṭaʿ rāsha. gaḷab hā, ğāb al-mazyūna, ʿeged ʿegādo ʿal-bint al-mazyūna u-xaḏāha. u-hā xuḷāset mā ṣārat ʿalē. ʾesemha ğbēne.	115 He said to her, “Come,” to that one [the slave girl]. “Come on, by God, oh, come.” He took her there [far away]. As soon as she knew it [the matter], he cut her head off. He turned [became]. . . . He brought the pretty [one], married the pretty girl legally and took her [for wife]. And this is the summary of what happened to her. Her name is Ğbēneh.

Commentary

This story belongs to the narrative type AT 533, “The Speaking Horsehead,” or, as it is more commonly known, “The Goose Girl.” A princess is sent to her fiancé, a prince of a neighboring country. Her mother orders a maidservant to accompany her, and gives her a small rag with some drops of her mother’s blood to protect her, and sends a speaking horse to take care of her.

When during the journey the princess loses her mother’s charm, the waiting maid gains control of the princess, forces her to change clothes and roles, and makes her swear an oath of secrecy.

The prince unwittingly marries the maidservant, and the real princess is employed as a goose girl. When the false wife orders the horse to be killed, the princess persuades a farmhand to hang the horse head on the wall by the gate where she passes daily. Every day she greets the horse head with a formula, and it answers regretting the injury that is being done to her.

When she speaks a magic formula to make the hat of a goose boy fly away (to keep an obtrusive goose boy away from her), he complains to the king. Thereupon the old king starts observing her and finally makes her tell her life story to a stove (her dog). The truth comes to light, the real bride marries the prince, and the maidservant is punished (she unwittingly declares her own judgment).[4]

This narrative type is known throughout Europe, Russia, and the Caucasus, Kurdistan, Jordan, and Israel, as well as in Morocco, Egypt, East Africa, Yemen, China, and India.

The two Bedouin versions I have collected (of which I here present only one) preserve the main story lines. In the version by Maryam Muṣṭafa Ṭabbāš from the ʿArab Ḥilf-Ṭabbāš tribe, it is a black woman neighbor who forces the heroine to hand over her clothes and jewelry. On the threat of death, she also forces the heroine to blacken her face with coal and soil her clothes with mud. They arrive at the emīr's house, where, at the request of the black girl, the heroine is sent to graze geese. In the pasture, she bathes herself, and her beauty is revealed. The geese stop eating because they are occupied in looking at the heroine's beauty. The emīr's son follows her and compels her to tell her story, and he later marries her.

Goose raising has not taken place in Israel and its neighboring countries for hundreds of years. It seems that the fairy tale of Maryam Muṣṭafa, a member of the ʿArab Ḥilf-Ṭabbāš tribe, drew this motif from European parallels. The tribe of Ḥilf-Ṭabbāš originally began with a family that fled the southern (Negev) tribe of ʿArab el-Hozayyel. It is possible, therefore, that the motif of goose raising stems from a southern tradition that was influenced by European tales.

In the second story, from Warda Hawāš of ʿArab el-Mazārīb, the neighbor is an ugly married black slave. The maidservant arrives at a pool of water and sees the face of a beautiful bride sitting in a raised place above the pool. She mistakenly thinks this is her own image. The bride's fiancé raises her up on a camel on her way to a wedding. The black girl stabs a magical needle into the bride's head, and she turns into a bird. The black girl puts on her clothes, whitens her face with chalk, and takes her place on the wedding camel. The groom mistakenly believes that this is his intended bride. The real bride, in the form of a bird, repeatedly causes the wedding dishes to burn. The groom lurches for her, grabs her, and pulls the magical needle out of her head. The bride returns to her human form and tells him her story. The groom commands that the slave be burned.

Bushnaq gives an Arabic version of the story from Israel, "Jubeinah and the Slave."[5] In this version, the mother places a bead of blue glass on the neck of Jubeinah (her daughter). On the way, a Nubian slave tries to force her to descend from the camel, but the magical bead sends her away. Later the heroine loses the bead, and it falls into the water. In the absence of the bead, the slave succeeds in overcoming the heroine and taking her place. Jubeinah has to be a shepherd. The king's son discovers the deceit, burns the slave, and marries Jubeinah.

In the IFA archives, there are many versions of the story. In the Yemenite version (IFA 5111), the heroes of the story are the son of a king and a slave who takes his place.

Three Muslim versions from Kafar Qaraʿ (IFA 23131), from ʿIbellīn (IFA 24273), and from Dēr al-Asad (IFA 24011), as well as a Druze version from Dāliyat al-Karmel (IFA 23987), are very similar to the version in Bushnaq's book. The magical object is a blue glass bead, an object known in Arab folklore as a lucky object, or a magical ring that tells the distant mother what is happening with her daughter. Only when the bead is lost does the slave vanquish the heroine. In the continuation of the story, the heroine asks birds, as they pass over her, to give regards to her mother.

The story thus emphasizes the special bond between the mother and her daughter. The departure of the daughter from her parents' home to the home of her prospective husband involves the severing or weakening of this connection, symbolized by the bead, which even after falling into the water continues to call the mother, although its strength weakens. Marriage is one of the major rites of passage in life. A girl leaves her parents' home and moves to her husband's house, and this is not an easy process for her. The story symbolizes the girl's fear of her future life. She is in an ambivalent state: on the one hand, she wants to get married as an important phase in her maturity, and on the other hand, she fears the unknown future. The story expresses the girl's secret wish that someone else will take her place. When she is in the pasture, her thoughts turn not to the slave who takes her place but to the mother who has remained behind. But in the end the truth comes to light. The bride is married to her intended groom, and the social order is restored.

Notes

1. Personal names in Arabic have meanings from the general (dialect) vocabulary. Bedouin names, in particular female names, are not always related to Islamic personalities' names. This girl's name is the diminutive of the word *ǧibna*, "cream cheese," so named because of her fair skin. The color white is a favorite of Bedouins (and Arabs, generally), as it expresses cleanliness, purity. Other proper names may have the diminutive form (e.g., for girls, *Grē'a*, "small pumpkin," and *Ḥmēda*, "small praised one"; for boys, *Ḥsēn*, "a small good one"). Bedouin dialects often use diminutive forms to express love (caritative function), in addition to diminution (e.g., *bnayyāti*, "my little daughters"). The girl's name in this tale ends with *-e* or *-a*: *-e* with *imāla* and *-a* without it. On *imāla* see the chapter on Bedouin dialects in this volume.

2. In terms of social class, Bedouins distinguish between "pure" Bedouins and "others." People with dark skin often originated in African areas. Migrant Bedouins (partly light-skinned people) came mostly in groups and joined a stronger tribal framework (cf. Medzini's chapter, "Bedouin Tribes in the Galilee," this volume). Still, "real Bedouins" often look down on them and call them *'abīd*, "slaves," even if they are organized in a tribe (cf. tale 11). This is the background for the swarthy girl's behavior toward the white one, and the emīr's behavior toward the girls. On Negev Bedouins, see Henkin, *Negev Arabic*, 30–40, esp. 37.

3. As noted in note 2 above, Arabs (and Bedouins) appreciate light-colored women (*bēḏa*, "white f.sg."), but not swarthy ones (*samra*, "dark brown, brownish f.sg.," or *sōda*

"black f.sg."). (Cf. chap. 6, note 4). However, color distribution and definition in the Bedouin society are neither exactly as in sedentary Arab communities nor as in the Western color system (cf. Blanc, "Story of a Blue Wolf"; Borg, "Linguistic and Ethnographic Observations"; Henkin, *Negev Arabic*). Some of these color systems reveal a rich hue variation, while other "main colors" (according to the main Western system) are entirely missing or take different meanings.

4. Uther, *The Types of International Folktales*, 1:312.

5. Bushnaq, *Arab Folktales*, 206–8.

23. The Dangerous Night-Watch

A. Šāṭer Ḥasan and His Nine Brothers

NARRATOR: Unknown

TRIBE: *ʿArab el-Sawāʿed ca. 1982*

1 waḥḥdam ʾaḷḷa.[1] kān fi gadīm al-zamān hā-l-ğibīlet hā-l-ʿarab. u-bēn aš-šēx ʿandīhum, wa-š-šēx hāḏa tibaʿhom, ʿendo min al-ʿiyāl ʿašara.[2] kullayāthom[3] rakkābīn xēl, yrūḥūn ʿa-l-ġazu,[4] wiğībūnu.[5] ʾāxer wāḥad bīhim az-zġayyer, ʿomro xamestaʿsar sine.	1 Say: Allah is one. There was once upon a time this Bedouin tribe. And among their sheikh and this, their sheikh, had ten children. All of them were horse riders, they would go to loot, to hunt and bring it [their gains]. The last one of them, the small one, his age was fifteen years.
8 wulla gāʿdīn bi-n-nhār, yōm min ḏāt al-ʾayyām, ṣādom ġuzlān, wallaʿom nār, gʿadam yeġaddūn. gāḷ-ḷom, "yā ʾexwāni, ṭayyib, lē ʾabūna mā yğawwizkam? šū, ʾani widdi ʾadğawwaz." hāḏa z-zġayyar.	8 Lo they were sitting one day, on a day among days, they had hunted deer, made fire, and sat down to have lunch. He said to them, "O my brothers, well, why does our father not marry you [off]? What, I want to marry"—This young one.
13 gāḷam, "hū mū rāḏi yğawwizna, u-aḥna miš rā(y)ḥīn naṭlub minno." gāḷ-ḷhim, "ʾana lli ʾaṭlub minno; ʾaṭlub minno ağ-ğawāz." gāḷu-ḷo, "ta-nšūf, yaḷḷa." baʿad al-ġada, ağ-ğmāʿa seḥbam ḥālhom ḏaḷḷom ᵉmrawwḥīn.	13 They said, "He does not want to marry us off, and we are not going to ask [it from] him." He said to them, "I will [be the one who will] ask him. I'll ask him about marriage." They said to him, "We'll see. Let's." After lunch, the group went off going home.
19 rawwaḥam ʿand ʾabūhum hināka, inğammaʿam, baʿad mā ḥaṭṭam ʿaša w-inbiṣṭam ba-hā-s-sahra. ʾaṯnāʾ as-sahra, gāḷ-ḷo, "yā būy, hāḏim ixwāni ṣāram xityāriyya,	19 They went home to their father there. They gathered up, and they had set the dinner [table] and enjoyed the evening meeting. During the meeting he said to him, "O my father, these my brothers have become old.

24 'akbar wāḥad ṣār ʿišrīn sina, 'aw 'akbar. 'ani widdi 'ağawwaz. lē mā adğawwaz?"

24 "The oldest one among them is already twenty [years old] or more. I want to marry. Why won't I marry?"

27 'abūhum ʿaṣabi—malʿūn wāldēn—gāḷ-ḷhom, "ismaʿam, 'ani ḥālif yemīn. intam ʿašara ^{a}min 'umm w-ábu;[6] mā ağawwizkam ġēr tanni 'algā-lkam ʿašra min 'umn w-ábu.[7] ʿašar banāt." 'ā, al-ʿiyāl tfarʿaṭam u-zeʿalam—šaġla ṣaʿba. ala wēn widdom yilgūn?

27 Their father was nervous—curse his parents—he said to them, "Listen [all], I have sworn that you are ten from one mother and father. I will not marry you off unless I find another ten from [one] mother and father. Ten girls." Yes. The children were baffled and sad—a difficult case. For, where will they find?

34 rāḥam ʿalá-mmhom[8] gāḷu-ḷha, "yā yumma, sāwī-lna zāde zuwwāde,[9] w-aḥna widdna nhiğğ"[10] bi-s-sirr. ṭayyeb, sāwat–ilhom zuwwāde u-ʿabbam el-xrēğe, min sukkar min šāy, min ^{e}ghawa, min ğamīʿo, xubz alli ykaffīhum ğumʿa-ğumʿatēn. siḥbam ḥālum b-hā-l-lēl u-mišam.

34 They went to their mother and said to her, "O mother, prepare for us provisions and we will be off. In secret." All right, she made for them provisions, and they loaded the horse bags—with sugar, tea, coffee, everything, bread that will suffice them for a week or two. They went off at night and went.

42 kull wāḥad ilu zuwwādtu, maši; sēfu, dirʿu, rumḥo u-kull ši. yaʿani, il-tāmm.

42 Each one had his provisions, going. his sword, his shield, his spear, and everything. That is, [a] complete [set].

44 'aṣ-ṣubaḥ—tiṣbaḥ ʿal-xēr—'abūhum mā yilāgi al-iʿyāl. wa-lā liga ḥada f-al-bēt. "wēn al-ʿiyāl?" gāḷat-ḷo, "al-ʿiyāl tsahhalam, zeʿlam minnk u-fallam."

44 In the morning—good morning to you—their father does not find the boys. Neither does he find any of them at home. "Where are the boys?" She said to him, "The children parted [left courteously]. They were angry because of you and took off."

48 mišyam ʿa-l-wağeh sabaʿ-ṯamant-iyyām, u-hum māšīn, haḏōl. blād ^{i}tšīlhom, blād ^{e}tḥuṭṭom.

48 They went straight on [for] seven, eight days, and they were going, those [men]. A country pulls them, a country expels them.

51 yōm nizlam ʿala maṭraḥ, miṯel mā tgūḷ, čōl, u-xeḷṣat minhom al-mayy. čēf widdhom yesāwūn? blād ḥamās. faggadam winn hā-l-bustān giddāmhum.

51 One day, they reached a place, as you say, a desert, and their water was finished. How will they do? A fierce country. They were looking around, and lo, that garden [was] in front of them.

55 bustān ḥaḏar, u-ʿan-dāyer mšarraṭ u-ḥaḏar. gāḷ-ḷuhum hāḏa, 'axūhum al-čebīr, gāḷ-ḷhum, "hāḏa bū mayy. yaḷḷa unṣub." naṣabu l-bustān, ğamma ʿa-l-bustān, ğamma ʿala-l-bustān, mšarraṭ ʿal-dāyir, u-hā-l-bawwāba ʿalē . . . u-msakkar.

55 A green garden, and around it fences and green. He said to them, their eldest brother, he said to them, "This—it has water. Let's make an effort [strain ourselves]." They made an effort to [reach] the garden, they came to the garden, came to the garden—fenced all around and a gate on it . . . and it's closed.

61 xaḷḷaʿam al-bawwāba, hadōl al-ğemāʿa, u-fātam. fātam ğowwa, fawwatam al-xēl, šū hāḏa miyy, ʿal–al-naʿar, al-ʿelu. fātat al-xēl ʿa-z-zarad, daggam as-sīwān, gaʿadom, kaʾinna hā-(r) māš bi-nugṣud. hiyya ʿīša-ʿīša, mā bī minna, hāḏi.	61 They dismantled the gate, that group, and entered. They went inside, brought the horses in, what water—the river—the top [best]. The horses entered on the chains, they struck the pegs [to which they tied horses], they sat down, as if it [there] was nothing [else] they wanted. It was a super life—nowhere like it, this one.
68 gāḷ-ḷhum axūhum ač-čebīr, kull yōm yerūhūn yeṣīdūn ġuzlān, ṯalaṯ(a)-arbaʿa, yāklūn laḥem ġuzlān. gāḷ-ḷhum, "aḥna hīn bi-blād čōl, u-yimkin bī ġazu, yimkin yiği ḥada yiḏbaḥna, yeġazīna, yāxḏ al-xēl minnīna; kull lēle as-sahra ʿala l-wāḥad minkam."	68 Their oldest brother said to them, every day they went hunting deer, three, four, and ate deer meat. He said to them, "We are here in a desert land and looting may be here. Maybe someone will come to kill us, plunder us, take the horses from us. Each night, watching is the duty of one of you."
75 ṭayyeb. sihe̊r ʾawwal lēle al-kebīr bīhum. ṯāni lēle—aṯ-ṯāni, aṯ-ṯāliṯ, ar-rābiʿ ta-l-ʾāxer.	75 Well, the oldest one stayed awake the first night. The second night—the second [brother], the third, the fourth, until the last one.
78 ʾāxer lēle, ṭilʿat ʿala z-zġīr, aš-šāṭer ḥasan. gaʿad yishar, fitaḥ al-^{i}ktāb gaʿad yigrā-bo̧, wa-š-šamʿadān maḏwi ğiddamo. ğat nismet hawa, haffat aš-šamaʿdān, ṭafato. en-nār maʿa axū al-čebīr, w-ixwāto nāimīn.	78 On the last night, it [the turn] was on the young one, Šāṭer Ḥasan. He was sitting keeping watch, opened a book and sat reading it, and the candle was giving light in front of him. A wind came, blew at the candle, and put it out. The fire is with his oldest brother, and his brothers are asleep.
84 staʾnaf ʿa-nafso inno yiğʿidhom yāxeḏ nār minhom. gām ṭalaʿ hāḏa ʿa-l-bustān, u-ṣār yemašši. ḥaṭṭ hā-s-sēf b-ğenbo, hāy miše b-al-bustān, hāy. bustān wāsiʿ, wāsiʿ, sabʿa̧-ṯmāniat-idlūmet ʾarḏ. ʿašer dlūmet ʾarḏ. min ğamīʿ al-fuwāki(h) bū.	84 He did not want to wake them to take fire from them. He got up, went out to the garden, and began walking. He put the sword at his side. This one walked in the garden, this one. A wide garden, wide, a ground of seven, eight dunam [a measure of land area], ten dunam ground. There were [in it] all the fruits.
90 hū māši, mā ḥiss willa hā-r-raṣād[11] ṭalʿat ʿalē min ġād, hī ṭilʿat. "yā sittār, yā . . . šū hāḏ?" xawwaḷ ʿalē gāḷ-ḷo, "barḏak, yā šāṭer ḥasan." illa itʿida iyyā ʿalē, gāḏab šeğīb, ğē b-wağho šeğīb, yaʿalam aḷḷa gadd-ʾē zlima.	90 He was walking, he felt that this *raṣād* [a demon that guards properties and treasures] appeared in front of him, from there, appeared to him. "Oh, Protector [Allah], oh . . . what is this?" It turned to him and said to him, "Stand where you are, oh Šāṭer Ḥasan." If he attacked him—it had a murderous shape, its face got a frightening [murderous] form, Allah knows what a person it was.

96 sa'alo "lima, yā šāṭer ḥasan, li-ma tiʿamel-ši." ğa min ʿēno widdo yiʿmal wağho šeğīb ṯāni, zett ḥālo ʿalē nafsi ṯāni, šagg rāso. gāḷ-ḷo, "zēd, yā šāṭer ḥasan," gāḷ-ḷo, "'immi mā ʿallmatni 'azēd," li'anni, yaʿani, iḏa-mā 'azēd—yiṭīb.	96 It asked him, "Why, o Šāṭer Ḥasan, why do you do a thing?" It seemed that it wanted to have again murderous form, he [Šāṭer Ḥasan] threw himself at it again, and cut his head off. It said to him, "Add [repeat], o Šāṭer Ḥasan." He said to it, "My mother did not teach me to add." For if I add, it will recover.
102 ṭāḥ min—ṭāḥ ᵉmdaḥdel, daḥdal gadd el-ğimal. ʿāwed rāḥ la-ʿand uxwito. hū - ğā ʿendhom, sta'naf ʿala nifso, xāf minhom, ʿal(a)-mā ğadd.	102 It fell from, fell rolling off—rolled like a camel. He returned to his brothers. He went to them—began to think about himself. He was afraid of them, because of what had happened.
106 ṣār mwağğih hīki gbālo, miṯil ma tgūl ʿalē, miṯel ḥazzūr, hēč twaqqed, willa basbūset nār tbasbes.	106 He began looking thus in front of him, as you say, above, like Hazzūr [the mountain's name] burning like that, and lo—there was a small firelight gleaming.
109 gāḷ, "waḷḷa, ġēr arūḥ[12] ağīb nār li." rikab hā-l-faras, ričeb, sakkar al-bawwāba u-nṭalaq. an-nār itwağğid ib-hā-l-lēl—imši, imši, imši, beʿīd hā, ā, tanno weṣal(h)e.	109 He said, "By Allah, I must go and bring me fire." He rode this mare, closed the gate, and took off. The fire gleams in the night—[he] went, went, went—it was far away, yes, until he reached it.
114 wiṣel hināk winnha maġġāra, u-hā-l-maġġāra līha ṭāga, u-min-aṭ-ṭāga basbūset an-nār tḏaww(i), tšōf. xēr. rbaṭ al-faras, u-ḥaṭṭ čitfo bi-hā-l-bāb gām, "yāḷḷa, aḥ, yā 'aḷḷa"—willa hū fitḥo.	114 He arrived there and it was a cave, and this cave had a niche, and from the niche the small firelight was gleaming, was seen. Good. He tied the mare and put his shoulder at the door, said, "Let's go, oh, oh Allah," and lo he opened it.
119 fāt winno ʿale-kullin arebʿīn zʿara ʿa-l-mizʿar. nāimīn kull min ʿala-txato, u-hā-ṭ-ṭāwle min dūnem b-il-dār yammhum b-al-maġġāra. kull—kull ğāt ˡl-wāḥad. ʿalē ha-l-rizz u-ʿalē al-laḥam, u-ʿalē kull šī.	119 He went in and lo, [there were] forty scary brigands, in the brigands' place, sleeping, each one in his bed, and this table beside them, in the house, directly near them, in the cave. Each—each plate had rice and meat and everything on it.
125 ğe hāḏa, meran ʿala kull ğāt, xaḏa xašūga, xašūga, u-fāt bēnhum u-nām. ḥaṭṭ sēfo bēn ᵉsyūfhum, u-rumḥo bēn-ᵉrmāḥḥum.[13] u-fāt bēnhum u-nām. sakkar al-bāb.	125 This one came, tried from each plate, took a spoonful, a spoonful [from each], and entered between them and slept. He put his sword among their swords and his spear among their spears and went between them and slept. He had closed the door.

130 gaʿad hā—bī wāḥad alli yishar ʿalēhum, qaʿad hā-r-riğāl, ʿadd ağ-ğimāʿa u-zād-lo wāḥad. ʿadd al-bisātīr (ʿadd $_{H}$ze mispar$_{H}$) ʿadd al-rmāḥ, as-syūf—zād lo xēl.

130 He woke up—there was one who kept watch over them, this man got up, counted the group, and had an additional one [one too many]. He counted the shoes (*ʿadd* is a number), counted the spears, the swords, a horse was added.

135 eih?! gāḷ, "ʾaʿidd l-al-ğimāʿa," tūgaʿ-lo miʿza, gāḷ-ḷum,"bēnna wāḥed—bēnna wāḥed ġarīb." naṭṭ al-gāʾid gāḷ-ḷo, "ismaʿ, elli bēnna—ʾiḏa inta alli fitaḥt al-bāb u-futt—ʾinta tkūn ʿagīd ʿalēna. u-ʾiḏa-mā ʾinta fāit waqt el-fitaḥna l-bāb, hāy di tiftaḥ, walla la-nefaṣfiṣ ʾilḥāmak ʿan-iʿḏ̣āmak."

135 Eh? He said, "I count the group," a goat appeared to him [a new member appeared in the count], he said to them, "There is one among us—among us there is a stranger." The leader got up and said to him, "Listen, he who is among us—if you opened the door and entered, you will be our leader. And if you entered when we opened the door, this which is opened, by Allah, we will grate your flesh off your bones."

143 hāḏ gāḷ, "lā, ʾani fitaḥt al-bāb." "iḥna arbeʿīn wāḥad alla wāḥad ta-niftaḥa, u-arbʿīn wāḥad alli wāḥad ta-nsakker." ḥaččaču hā-l-walad . . . winno rāḥ ftaḥ al-bāb, ʿāwad sakkaru, gaḷū-ḷo, "inta ʾaxūna bi-ʿahed-aḷḷa w-al-xāin yuxūno ʾaḷḷah.[14]

143 That one said, "No, I opened the door." "We are forty but one to open it, and forty but one who close it." They challenged the boy . . . lo, he went and opened the door, and then closed it again. They said to him, "You are our brother in Allah's covenant, and the traitor—Allah will betray him.

149 ʿahed. "ʾinta ʿagīd ʿalēna, u-widna naḥčī-lak hāy-l-^{i}ḥčāya. ʾeḥna, fī ʿalēna gōm, al-malek al-^{i}flān. u-al-malek hāḏa, gōm aḥna w-iyyāh, u-baddna nrūḥ nğīb, nisrug al-xazīna tabaʿo." "ṭayyeb, yaḷḷa." rikbum al-xēl. taʿaššam haḏōl ağ-ğimāʿa, ʿala innahum. taʿaššam, rikbam xēlhum, wa-syūfhum.

149 Oath. "You are our leader, and we want to tell you this story. We have an enemy, the king so-and-so. And this king, we are enemies with him and we want to go and bring, steal his treasury, treasury pack." "Good, let's [go]." They rode the horses, they had dinner, that group, yes, they had dinner, rode their horses, [with] their swords.

157 ʿād haḏōl xaḏam liyāli, mišam walaw.[15] weṣlam ʿa-l-madīna, weṣlam, al-gaṣer—al-malak ʿa-l-ğanb al-ġar(b)i. gāḷu-ḷo "hāḏa l-gaṣer."

157 Again, those, it took them nights, they went, anyway. They reached the town, reached the palace—the king was on the west side. They said to him, "This is the palace."

161 gāḷ, "ṭayyib, xaḷḷīkam hōn taḥat, ʾani widdi ʾaṭlaʿ. ʾunṭūni kull wāḥad ḥaṣu, ʾintu, mi-šān kull mā-ʾan azaṭṭ ḥaṣwa, yiṭlaʿ wāḥad ʾašayyil min al-xazna." xazna kmād, u-mī hum yinhabūn. gāḷum "zēn."

161 He said, "Good, you stay here below, I want to go up. Give me each one a pebble, you [each one]. Each time I throw down a pebble, one will come up, I'll take from the treasury, a treasury pack, so that they will not loot. They said, "Good."

167 gaḏab—kull wāḥad ʾinṭā ḥaṣu. ṭayyib, ʾinṭā ḥaṣu. ḥaṭṭhen b-ǧēbto u-gaʿad. ṭalaʿ hāḏa ʿala fōg, ʿa-l-gaṣar. fāt ʿala, fitḥ ʿala—miṯel ma tgūḷ—ʿa-l-ʾōḏa hāḏi, willa bīha bint, subḥān al-xāliq,[16] nāima ʿala-hā-t-taxet. gāḷ, "hāḏāki[17] tkūn naṣīb ʾaxūya li-čbīr."

167 He took—each one gave him a pebble. OK, he gave him a pebble. He put them in his pocket and started. He went up high, to the palace. He enters, opens the—as you say—this room, and lo, there is a girl in it—praise the creator [Allah]—asleep on the bed. He said, "This will be the lot of my oldest brother."

174 fitaḥ al-ʾōḏa ṯ-ṯānyi, ǧawwa, fīha bint ʾahamm minha. "hīyya naṣīb ʾaxūya ṯ-ṯāni." wiṯ-ṯāliṯ, wi-r-rābe[aʿ],

174 He opened the second room; inside, there was a girl more precious than her [the first girl]. "She is the lot of my second brother," and the third, the fourth,

177 la-l-ʿašara. la-l-ʿašar. al-ʿāšre, msāwī-lha abūha taxat mirtfeʿ u-ḥāṭṭa ʿala wiǧha, mġaṭṭēto b-šaʿar. gāḷ, "ʾaḷḷāh, naṣībi. činnē[18] ʿabde!"

177 until the tenth. The tenth. The tenth [girl], her father made for her a high bed, and she put her hair, covering her face with it. He said, "By Allah, this is my lot. She could be a (black) slave!"

181 gāl hīčiḏa b-šaʿarha fadwaten taʿha. gāḷ, "fadētek min ḥaẓẓi u-naṣībi." giḏab xātemha, gāmu min iṣbaʿeha, u-gām xātemo u-ḥaṭṭo bi-ṣbaʿha. uxaḏa xātemha.

181 He said so because of her hair, for her safety. He said, "I liberate you from my luck and fate." He took her ring, took it off her finger, and took his ring and put it on her finger. And he took her ring.

186 riqeb ha-r-riǧāl min taḥat et-taxat, mīš mistaǧriye tugʿod, tgūl, "ʾani ʾāxer ʾōḏa, mnēn fāt hāḏ?" saḥab ḥālo u-ḏaḷḷ ṭāleʿ, gāḷ uhū rāǧeʿ. "waḷḷāhi, ġēr aḏbaḥḥom kullayātom."

186 She was watching this man from under the bed, not daring to get up, and said [to herself], "I am the last room, where did this man enter from?" He took off and continued to go out, he said [to himself[as he was going back, "By Allah, I must kill them all."

191 ṭalaʿ hāḏa la-fōq ʿa-s-sāḥa, ṣār yirmi ḥaṣwa. u-ba-l-ḥaṣwa ṭalaʿ wāḥad, šaqq rāso. ṭalaʿ al-ṯāni—šaqq rāso. kull mā yirmi ḥaṣwe—yišuqq rāso. yirmī—gāḷ, "ʾaḏbaḥḥom kullayātom. ʾaktilhom." xallaṣam ar-riǧǧāl.

191 He went high up to the courtyard and started throwing a pebble. With the pebble one [man] went up, he cut off his head. The second one came up—he cut his head off. Whenever he threw a pebble—he cut his head off and threw him. He said, "I'll butcher all of them. I'll kill them." The men ended.

197 saḥab ḥālo, hawwid ʿala fraso, rikabha, w-al-xēl ḏaḷḷat mrabbaṭa, hī b-xēr. zaʿal ʿal- . . . ḏaḷḷo[19] mrawwiḥ ʿala ʾuxwuto. (a)ssa ʾawwal an-nahār, miṯel mā tgūḷ, geʿadam aǧ-ǧmāʿa, šāfum aš-šōfa hāḏi, "wallak, šū s-sīre yā-xi, ṭayyib, igʿedni, šū ʾenta?" gāḷ-ḷhum, "waḷḷa staʾnaft ʿa-nafsi agʿadkum, u-hāḏ illi ṣār maʿi."

197 He took off, went down onto his mare, rode her, and the horses remained tied, they were all right. He went on, going back home to his brothers. Now, at the early morning, as you say, the group woke up, they saw this sight. "By Allah, what is this issue, o brother? OK, you [could have] wakened me for you, what are you [thinking]?" He said to them, "By Allah, I did not want to wake you, and this is what happened to me."

206 ṭayyib. yirǧaʿ marǧūʿna l-al-malak. al-malak, aṣ-ṣubeḥ—tiṣbaḥom alla bi-l-xēr—gaʿadan al-banāt. ʾeh. kull yōm al-banāt yrūḥan la-ʿand ʾabūhen, yugʿuden. yerūḥen la-ʿando ysāwin-lo ghawa, ysāwin lo šāy.

206 All right. Let's return to the king. The king in the morning—have [pl.] only a good morning—the girls woke up. Eh. Every day the girls go to their father, sit [with him]. They [would] go to him, make coffee for him, make tea for him.

212 hā-l-yōm mā staǧran yiṭlaʿan ʿa-l-bāb min ʾāxer ʾōḏa, waḥḥalan min az-zeʿarān, alli-nḏabaḥam kullaha. hāḏi l-ʿoqōba alli-. bēno u-bēnum maḥall. mā-widdo ʿād^{a} yifham. wēn rākibhom, hāḏ-aš-ši? w-aǧa hīna ar-riǧǧāl—šū sāwa?

212 That day add they did not dare go out the door from the last room, they were agitated because of the rogues, all of whom were butchered. This punishment which. . . . Between him [the king] and them [the girls] there is a space. He [the king] does want, again, to understand: Where is the rider of this thing? And this man came here, what did he do?

218 ǧat waḥde minhen, az-zġayra ʿād, gāḷat-ḷo, "yā-ba, ʾana šufto hāḏa z-zalame wagten fāt, u-hāḏa xātemto, xātamo. u-xaḏa xātemi." qāḷ-ḷa, "taʿāli, ʾanti tʿarfīno." minšān šāfato, hi ta^{ʿa}rfo. "ʾeṭlaʿi." nāda l-imnādi ʿa-l-medīna, ṣārat ^{e}tmurr min taḥt al-gaṣur, "ʾalli widdo—sāwa hēč šaġle, u-ḏibaḥ ha-z-zʿarān hāḏi, al-malak widdo yaʿṭī banāto, yinṭī bint min banāto."

218 One of them [the girls] came, the young one again, she said to him [the king], "O father, I saw this man when he entered and this is his ring. And he took my ring." He said to her, "Come, you will recognize him." Because she saw him, she would recognize him. "Come up." The announcer [herald] went round [and] called the town [people]. They started passing below the palace. "Who wants—has done this thing, and butchered these rogues, the king wants to give him his daughters, that is, will give him one of his daughters."

228 ṣārat taṭalla^{ʿa} hī lo, taṭallaʿ šū fāyit. hāḏi ǧāʿada ʿala l-balkōn, fōq, gāḷat-ḷo, "māš, margat ad-dinya kulla, mā ḏaḷḷ ḥada." aǧ-ǧewād, alli hāḏa—mā ši.

228 She began to look for him, look at who was passing. This [girl] was sitting on the balcony up high, and said to him [to the king], "Nothing. Everybody has passed, no one has remained." The noble horse—this which—[there is nobody].

232 gāḷat-ḷo baʿdēn yaʿani, "widdna naʿref mīn hāḏ illi sāwa hāy aš-šaġle."

232 She said to him afterward, that is, "We want to know who it is who did this thing."

234 ǧe wāḥad, rāʿi, miṯel ma tgūl, hēčeḏa, yisraḥ ba-n-nhār b-aǧ-ǧbāl, yešūf hā nās ba-l-bistān hāḏa. gāḷ-ḷo, "yā malek ez-zmān, bī nās bi-l-bistān tebaʿak," [el-bistān hāḏa marṣūd.—hāḏ ar-raṣād alli-ketlu]—gāḷ-ḷo, "ġād yeǧūz bū sukkān hināk, humm-alli sāwum hāḏ."

234 A person came, a shepherd, as you say, like that, he herds in the mountains during the day, he saw men in that orchard. He said to him, "O king of this time, there are people in your orchard." That orchard was haunted—that *raṣād* [demon] whom he had killed. He said to him, "There, maybe there are people living there, and they are those that did it."

241 kān-le hā-l-wufūd, qāl, ğat-la. ṯalāṯ-'arbaʿ xayyāle, ğnūd w-as-syūf maʿāhom. gāḷ-ḷom, “la txāfum, rūḥam.” rāḥam hadōl. wagten wiṣlam hunāk, šū yišūfūn? . . . “'ei? šū widdna naʿmel?” fiʿlan fāt al-xēl ğawwa, u-hā-z-zinn [šnū hā-l-ʿiyāl, šnū widdak iyyāh.]

241 He had these delegates, came to . . . three, four cavalrymen, soldiers, and their swords with them. He said to them, “Do not be afraid, go.” These [soldiers] went. When they reached there, what do they see? . . . “Eh? What should we do?” In fact, the horses entered and these boys (What are these boys? What do you want?).

248 “'as-salāma ʿalēkam”—“ʿalēkam as-salām.” gāḷ aš-šēx, “tu'mur. al-malak ṭālibkam, maṭlūbīn la-ʿand al-malek. u-hassa, ḥālan.

248 “Good day to you”—“And good day to you.” The old man said, “Command [us]. The king wants you; you are wanted at the king’s. And now, at once.

252 'iḏa taʿmalūn, tfaḏḏalam maʿāna.” gāḷ-ḷu “lā, waḷḷāhi, lēš . . .” libsam 'awāʿīhum, ʿaddadam ʿaddethum, u-ğum, māšīn.

252 “If you do, please come with us.” He said to him, “No, by Allah, why . . .” They put on their clothes, prepared their tools, and came, going.

256 hāy, limman wiṣlam hināk, ṭilʿam a-ğmāʿa taḥt 'el-gaṣor, wa-ḏāk mā (tā-) titġayyir . . . al-bint šāfato, ḥaṭṭat—tiffāḥa maʿāha, ḏirbato mi(n)-yad, gāḷ—šammā, ḥaṭṭa (b-ğēbo) (gāḷ . . .).

256 This one, when they came there, the group went out under the palace, and that one does not change. . . . The girl saw him, put—she had an apple with her, threw it from [her] hand. He said—he smelled it, put it [in his pocket and said].

261 gaʿadam haḏān esbūʿ. 'eḥtefal bīhom, tgūl, 'abṣar šū msāwīno. “'ahlan wa-sahlan”—u-sāwa ḥafla, ṭawīla ʿarīḏa.

261 Those stayed a week. [The king] celebrated them, you’d say, who knows what they have done. “Welcome,” and he made a great feast [long and wide].

264 haḏolāk mā yidrūn, wala sōlaf la-'ixwito. “šū s-sīre?” gāḷ-ḷo, “yā ḥaḏart al-malak, ʿani š-šāṭer ḥasan,” gāḷ-ḷo, “ʿani ṣārat emʿāya šaġle. u-'ani ḏabaḥtom u-hāḏ-alli ṣār. wa-l-raṣād alli b-al-bustān, 'ani kitalto kamān, haḏāk al-bustān xalaṣ, trūḥūn alē.”

264 Those did not know [why], and he had not told his brothers. “What is the issue?” He said to him, “O your Highness, the King, I am Šāṭer Ḥasan.” He said to him, “I, a thing happened to me. And I butchered them and this is what happened. And the *raṣād* [demon] that was in the orchard, I killed him, too. That orchard is free, you [can] go there .”

271 al-bustān hū la-l-malk hāḏa. mā ḥada yifūt ʿalē. gāḷ li-hāḏ ar-riğğāl, gāḷ-ḷo, “šū b-tu'mor?” gāḷ-ḷo, “'eḥna ʿašar xūt min 'umm w-abu. widdna ʿašar banāt min 'umm wa-abu.” gāḷ-ḷo, “ʿandi.” gāḷ-ḷo, “mā-ʿaṭītha.”

271 The orchard was the king’s property. No one entered it. He said to this man, he said to him, “What do you want [order]?” He said to him, “We are ten brothers of one mother and one father. We want ten girls from a mother and father.” He said to him, “I have [them].” He said to him, “I am giving them to you.”

277 ǧāb al-xaṭīb, ʿagad tabaʿ– ʿagad ʿagādāto kull wāḥad ʿa-l-waḥde. ač-čšebīr ʿa-č-čebīre, wi-z-zġayra—la-zġayyir. ʾisimha sitt ḥisin, az-zġayra. ǧawwazhum, u-gʿadam ʿando la-middet yaʿani šahar-šharēn, gāḷu-ḷo, "yā ʿammi, al-^{i}blād ištāgat la-ʾah^{e}lha, tismaḥ-^{i}lna widdna nrawweḥ."

277 He brought the preacher, made the marriage [ceremony], for each one of them on his own. The oldest [brother] with the oldest [girl] and the youngest [girl] for the youngest [brother]. Her name was Sitt Ḥisin, the young one. They got married, stayed at his place for, that is, a month, two months. They said to him, "O uncle, the country is missing its people. Please, we wish to go home."

285 gāḷ, "ʾē. tismaḥ-^{i}lna tanṭīna banāt ʿamm, banāt alli maʿāna, ʾiḏa mā tismaḥ ʾaḷḷa yxaḷḷīhom." gāḷ, "lā, yā-būya, mintāk alf yā banāt al-ʾimm? ʾaḷḷa yesahhel ʿalēk."

285 He said . . . "Allow us, give us our brides with us. If you do not allow, Allah be with them." He said, "No, o my son, have I given you a thousand or one mother's daughters? Goodbye [lit.: may Allah help you]."

290 šadd lin ^{i}l-kull minhin faras u-ʿabbā la xurǧ ḏahab u-mašša kull wāḥda mʿāha ʿabd, gaḷḷaṭhin, ygaḷṭūnhin la l-^{e}ḥdūd, miṯel mā tgūl. mišam haḏōl, min hā-l-ʿabdūle, gisem ʿāwad, ḏ̣aḷḷam, ʿabd, ʿabd wāḥad. ḏ̣aḷḷ-ḷhem masʿūd.

290 He bridled for all of them a mare and filled the horse bags with gold, and with each one [girl] he made a slave go with her [as] an escort for them, to accompany them to the borders, as you say. These went, from the slaves, went to the border. A part of them returned, they remained [with] one slave, one slave remained with them. Masʿūd remained with [for] them.

296 masʿūd ǧi l-dag (=ḏāk) mafāriǧ ṭurg. digar hināk. ^{a}fṭin ^{a}hināk. gāḷ ḷ-masʿūd "lēš digart? šnū?" gāḷ-ḷa, "ʾabūy, hāḏa darb al-ḥarīǧ, u-hāḏa darb al-ġarīǧ, u-hāḏa darb in-sadd-mā-radd. hāḏi ṯalaṯ ṭurug.

296 Masʿūd came to that road junction. He stopped and thought there. He said to Masʿūd, "Why have you stopped and thought? What [is there]?" He said, "O my son, this is the road that burns, this road is the road that drowns, and this road is the road you do not return from. These are three roads.

302 ʾayya ṭarīg widdak ʾafūt imʿāk? miš ʿārif ʾani. hāḏa hī aṭ-ṭarīg ʾin-sadd-mā-radd u-alli yrūḥ mā yʿāwid. u-hāḏa darb il-ġarīǧ yiġarag alli yrūḥ. widdak bū hunāk mūta, mā ydallī. u-hāḏ ad-darb ʾin-sadd-mā-radd."

302 "Which road do you want me to enter with you? I do not know. This road 'if enter you do not return' and he who goes will not return. And this road drowns the one who takes it, there is death there, it pulls [you] down. And this road is 'the road you do not return from.'"

308 gāḷ-ḷo, "yalla, yā darb ʾin-sadd-mā-radd. ʾimši." mašam haḏōl aǧ-ǧemāʿa. aš-šāṭer Ḥasan taʾaxxar ʿanhom šwayye, maša, qaffam ʿanno činno l-ǧadwal hičiḏa. laḥag, wagtinno laḥag, ṭallaʿ, māš ḥada.

308 He said to him, "Get on, [take] the road you do not return from. Go." They went, this group. Šāṭer Ḥasan got delayed a little from them, they disappeared from him; perhaps the schedule was like that. He was catching up with them—he looked—there was no one.

314 winn hā l-gaṣōr, ğiddāmo, bas al-gaṣar. lā hū l-al-ʼarḏ, wa-lā hū wēn. ʼē? šū hāḏ? twaggad, wanna s-sitt ḥisin fōg, ʻando, barra. gāḷat-ḷo hīč hīč, “taʻāl.” ʻāwad ta-ʻāwad hāḏa r-riğğāl, ʻindo faras. u-ribaṭ ha-l-faras b-maṭraḥ hīč u-ʻāwad.

314 And lo, that palace [is] in front of him. Only the palace. It was neither on the ground nor where. Eh? What is this? He was looking and lo, Sitt Ḥisin [is] above, at his place, outside. She said to him like this, “Come.” He returned, this man returned. He had a mare. And he tied the mare at that place and returned.

320 wa-ʻāwad yesalsel ʻalēha. ṭaḷḷ hīč igbālha, gāḷat-ḷo, “hāḏa ḥūt, u-haḏōla ixwānak alli rṣadum, kullum ⁱḥğār sōda. yirušš ʻalēhom trāb, yiğilbūn ᵉḥğār sōda, humma w-al-xēl w-al-marākib alli . . .

320 He came back and climbed up to her. He appeared in front of her, she said to him, “This is a *ḥūt* and those are your brothers whom he transformed, all of them are black stones. He sprays on them earth and they turn to black rocks, they and their horses and the loads which . . .

325 u-hāḏa-al-ḥağāğīr kullha bnādamin, marṣūde, raṣadat.”

325 “and these stones are all bewitched people. They were bewitched.”

327 gāḷ-ḷa, “ṭayyeb, isʼalī wagtin hu yīği ʻalēč, gūli-lo, ʼinta ḥāṭiṭni hīna, u-widdi-rūḥak, a(ta)salla-(a)ni wiyyā.” ʻarrfīni rūḥu wēn.” al-ḥūt hāḏa rūḥu mī hī b-ğismo, ğisem wēḥda ġēro, ğasad ġēro.

327 He said to her, “All right, ask him when he comes to you, tell him, ‘you have put me here, and I want your soul, to go and have fun, I with it.’ Let me know where its soul is.” This *ḥūt*, his soul is not in his body, [it is] in the body of someone else, in someone else’s body.

332 hāḏa rawwaḥ, al-ḥūt, gāḷat-ḷo, “ʼinta ḥāṭṭnī, law inne trūḥ tdawwer al e . . . tdawwar al-ḥāyiṭ, al-bēš teḥuṭṭ, al-e . . . kaḏa, w-ente rūḥak, ʼatasalla ani wiyyāha.” gāḷ-ḷa, “rūḥi b-al-makensa.” gaḏbat al-makensa u-ṣārat teṣannaʻha u-telabbesha u-thandesha. “šū hāḏ?” ṣār yiḏḥak, gāḷ-ḷa,” ʼaḷḷa yixreb bēteč, mā ʼagaḷḷ ʻagleč. gult-leč rūḥi bal-mečnase.”

332 This came home, the *ḥūt*, she said, “You have put me here [alone] . . . and that when you go to look at the wall, whatever you put, like that, and your soul, I [can] play with it [then].” He said to her, “My soul is in the broom.” She took the broom and started decorating it, dressing it up, and playing with it. “What is this?” He started laughing. He said to her, “May Allah ruin your house, how small your brain is. I told you my soul is in the broom.”

341 gāḷat-ḷo, “ʼilla šnū—taḏḥak ʻalayy?” gāḷ-ḷha, “rūḥi min ğawwa sabʻa-bḥūr, bi-baṭen xanzīra ğarba be-bistān es-sitt ᵉbdūr, bistān abūha. xanzīre ğarba. rūḥi hnāk. barra.”

341 She said to him, “But what? Are you laughing at me?” He said to her, “My soul is inside seven seas in the belly of a mangy sow [she-swine] in the orchard of Sitt ᵉBdūr, her father’s orchard. Mangy she-swine. My soul is there. Outside.”

346 hāḏe rādd ʻa-l-bistān—raṣad. ṯāni yōm ṭallaʻ ʻalēha, gāḷat,

346 This one [the *ḥūt*] went to the orchard, watched [guarded] it. The next day, he [Šāṭer Ḥasan] went up to her. She

348 “bīği, ğawwa sabaʻ bḥūr” šū biddo ygaṭʻo hāḏ. saḥab ḥālo u-ḏaḷḷo mšarrig[20] nefad ʻa-darb tāli, ʼimši, ʼimši, ta-ʼawwal baḥar.

348 said, “It is inside seven seas.” What does he need [to do] to cross it? He went off and continued going to the east, he went on another road, went and went, until the first sea.

352 ʿindma waṣel ʾawwal baḥar, dār al-faras hināk la-ʿād tirʿa ʿa-l-marʿa, walla sidra, šnū, fayyitha mraʾa mġalṭāt. ğey taḥt as-sidra u-nām. gāḷ yatarayyaḥ šwayy.

352 When he reached the first sea, he turned the mare there, to graze in the pasture, and lo, there was a jujube tree. What, its shade is a misleading sight [showing black and white]. He went under the jujube tree and slept. He said [to himself] he would rest a little.

357 hū nāyem, mā ḥass winn-al-ʿaṣāfīr fōg as-sidra yizarreq (=yezaqzeq) "zzzz," gaʿ^{a} maʿavīs.[21] daḥḥag hīč willa hā-l-ḥayy(a) ṭālʿa b-sabaʿ rūs. ṭālʿa ʿala l-makūt (=magūd), ʿa-l-tall. sāḥba, ṭālʿa rūsa, fēga-la.[22]

357 As he was sleeping, suddenly he felt the birds [chicks] above the jujube tree chirping ("zzzzz"), totally upset. He looked like that, and lo, there was this snake coming out with seven heads. [It was] going out to the raised place, the mound, going, lifting its heads, alert to them.

363 gaḏab hāḏa r-riğğāl s-sēf, ʾal- as-sēf, tināwal as-sēf winno hū yšūf ʾinna mā bī ḥada. [ḏāyig, hā?] gām gaṭʿo hā, ʿāwad ḥaṭṭ rāso nām.

363 This man took the sword, the sword, took the sword, and lo, he sees that there is no one [heeding]. (Suspenseful/thrilling, isn't it?) He got up and cut it [the heads] and went back to sleep.

367 šwayye, ḥabībi, walla šūḥa[23] ğāya, ʾummhan. gāḷat, "yā bayyē, hāḏa (i)lli kull sine yākel walādi, walla ġēr ʾafaqqeṣ ʿuyūno." ʾaḷḷa sibḥāno w-taʿāla naṭṭaghin.

367 After a little while, my dear, by Allah, [there] came a bird of prey, Šūḥa, their mother. She said, "O my [o my father], this is [the one] who every year eats my children. By Allah, I must rip out his eyes." Allah, may he be praised and elated, made them [the chicks] speak.

371 gālam, "yā yimma, hāḏa huwwe-lli gtalu al-ḥayye, alli šaggā li." bi-gudret-iḷḷā naṭṭ(a)gat. twakkadat čānat hā-l-ḥayya, winha š-šams ṭālʿa ʿalē. fardat el.-ḥālha wulla wugfat ʿalē fayya, tanno gaʿad. wagtinno gaʿad, "la ʾilāh ʾilla ḷḷā,"

371 They said, "O mother, this is the one who killed the snake, who cut it [its heads] for me." By Allah's power they spoke. She made sure it was a snake, and lo, the sun was rising [and shining] on him [the hero]. She unfolded herself [her wings] and stood above him, to shade him, until he got up. When he got up, "No Allah but Allah."

377 gāḷat-ḷo, "ʾuṭḷub w-itmanna, yā šāṭer ḥasan." gāḷ-ḷa, "ʾaṭlub widdi tgaṭṭʿīni sabʿa-bḥūr." gāḷat-ḷo, "ḥāḏer, šnū widdak ḥāḏer.

377 She said to him, "Ask and wish, o Šāṭer Ḥasan" [and you will get it]. He said to her, "I want you to make me cross seven seas." She said to him, "Yes, sir. Whatever you want—is set [for you].

381 "bas bū dūnak, bū šilʿet ġanam. ğīb li xarūf, tiḏbaḥo we-tgaṭṭʿo sabʿa gṭāʿ u-tḥuṭṭo ğiddāmak u-tirkab ʿalayy. kull mā giṭaʿet baḥar tanṭīni giṭʿa, w-in rāḥat giṭʿa minnak ruḥna b-il-bḥūr ʾana wiyyāk."

381 "But on that side of you, there is a herd of sheep. Bring me a sheep, butcher it and cut it into seven pieces and put it in front of you and ride my back. Whenever I cross a sea, you'll give me a piece, and if a piece gets lost from you, we will be in the sea, me and you."

386 giḏab hāḏa, ǧāb al-xarūf, ḏibḥo, ugaṭṭāʿo sabaʿ gṭāʿ u-ḥaṭṭhen u-ǧa. ʿṭāha ʾawwal giṭʿa u-rāḥam. kull mā giṭʿat baḥar—yanṭīha giṭʿa, kull mā giṭʿat baḥar yinṭīha giṭʿa, la-ʾāxer baḥar. widdo yiṭūl al-giṭʿa—wagʿat min ʾīdo. willa ʿindo ba-s-sēf, yguṣṣ min faxḏo l-yamīn giṭʿat laḥam, laḥam ilha. bilʿatha winha māklitha.

386 He caught, this man, brought a sheep, butchered it and cut it into seven pieces and put them and came. He gave her the first piece and they went. Whenever she crossed a sea—he would give her a piece, whenever she crossed a sea—he would give her a piece until the last piece. He wanted to hand her the piece—it fell from him. Lo, he had the sword, and cut from his right thigh a piece of flesh, meat for her. She swallowed it and ate it.

395 (ʾulti-llo) wiṣel ʿād hināk, qālat, ḥawwalet ʿa-š-šaṭṭ, gāḷat-ḷo "ʾin ǧēt, šāṭer ḥasan, ʾimeš ʾawwal ta-nhawwid." walla ʾaʿarağ. geṭlat-la, ḥaṭṭat-lo iyyāha ʿala maṭraḥ mā kānat, lizgatha willa hi miṯel mā hi. gāḷat-ḷo, "ssa hī hāḏi mdīnt es-sitt ᵉbdūr, u-ʾani ʾayyi wagtin tiḏāyag ʾakūn ʿandak. bas taḥriğ hā-r-rīšāt." ʿaṭato rīšāt.

395 (I told him) He reached there, she said, she turned to the shore. She said to him that "you have come, "Šāṭer Ḥasan, go as soon as we alight." And lo, he was lame. She threw it up [his slice of flesh], put it back to the place where it had been, and stuck it on, and lo, it was as it had been. She said to him, "Now, this is the town of Sitt Bdūr, and I—any time you are in trouble, I will be with you. But burn these feathers." She gave him feathers.

403 zēn. saḥab ḥālo u-ḏaḷḷ ṭāleʿ ʿala l-medīna. wagtin weṣil hināk, ǧanb al-medīna, winna bēt xityāra hināk.

403 Well. He went off and continued going up to the town. When he reached there, at the side of the town, there was the house of an old woman there.

406 fāt ʿalēha. gāḷat-ḷo, "yā yumma, wēn fāyet ʿalayya. dūnak ʾiyyāni, xityāra u-ʿāǧze, dūnak al-medīna muzayyna w-al-medīna, ʾagūḷ-ḷak, yā bīha all-yibčō ʿal-hāḏa, widdha trūḥ as-sitt ᵉbdūr."

406 He went in, to her. She said to him, "O son, wherefore are you coming to me? Not me, I am an old woman and crippled, on that side of you—the town is decorated, and the town, I'm telling you, in it there are those who are weeping [mourning] for this [is because], she will go, Sitt Bdūr."

411 gāḷ-ḷa, "wēn ⁱtrūḥ?" gāḷat-ḷo, "widdhom yāxḏūna la-l-ḥūt. al-yōm ad-dōr ʿalēha." gāḷ-ḷha, "ṭayyeb, ʾester ʿanna. wēnta yāxḏūna?" gāḷat-ḷo, "bāčir." bāčir.

411 He said to her, "Where will she go?" She said to him, "They will take her to the *ḥūt*. Today it is her turn." He said to her, "Good. [May Allah] protect her. When will they take her?" She said, "Tomorrow." Tomorrow.

416 ṯāni yōm, ṣalla ʿala s-sitt ᵉbdōr, u-xaḏa l-ǧider bḥata mʿāha, ʾalla yāxḏūna l-al-ḥūt. wa-ṭalaʿam, miṯel mā tgūl, ʿala rās el-tōm, hā-t-tōm, hā-l-en-nās, u-ḥaṭṭam as-sitt ᵉbdūr hināk.

416 The next day, he prayed for Sitt Bdūr and took a pot of porridge with him, [he went with] those who were taking her to the *ḥūt*. And they went out, as you say, at the head of the group, the group, the people, and they put Sitt Bdūr there.

421 u-ğītak hā-d-dunya mʿazzqa men-ʿend ad-dār. ʿala r-rāṣd al-mayy ʿalēhum may, mesakkar mayy, ʾalla mā yeğibū-lo l-ʿarūs. kull sine, kull šahar kān yifallit al-mayy.	421 And all the people came flowing from the house to the guard of the water. They had the water closed down, the water, unless they bring him the girl [bride]. Every year, every month he used to stop [chase away] the water.
426 gaḏab hāḏa r-riğāl, huwwa rāği. gāḷat-ḷo, "yā walad, xiyāne ʿa-šabābak, essa yīği l-ḥūt, ʾana—ʾamer ʾaḷḷa mfalltīni l-al-ḥūt, w-inte?" gāl-lha, "miṯel mā yeṣīr ʿalēk(i), yeṣīr ʿalayy. miš rāḥ adaššrek."	426 This man grabbed, and he was hoping [praying for good]. She said to him, "O boy, pity on your youth. Soon the *ḥūt* will come. I—Allah's decree will save me about the *ḥūt*, and you?" He said to her, "As [whatever] happens to you, will happen to me. I am not going to leave you."
432 sēfo maʿa-ğanbo, waddaru, u-gaʿad ḥaddha, irtika ʿa-ğanbha. lākin šū, hāyya tḥinn ʿalā. šwayy, šwayy, wenn al-ḥūt ğāy. nām hāḏa ṣ-ṣāleḥ. mā ḥass(h)a willa tibki. mā hiyye tistiğeri tiğeʿedo. ḥassa all-mā waqqadu men zaʿfara. fazz. anzabaṭam ba-hāyy el-ḥīn-(h)ā.	432 His sword was at his side, he hid it and sat down near her, leaned on her side. But what—she was having pity on him. Slowly, slowly [gradually], and lo, the *ḥūt* was coming. He slept, that good man. He did not feel, except [when] she wept. She did not dare wake him up. He was awaked by her stream [of tears]. He got up. They arranged themselves at this time.
439 gāl-la š-šāṭer ḥasan, "šū ğābak min blād el-naʿīm la-blād ağ-ğaḥīm?" gāl-lo, "ğābni ʾaḷḷa wa-n-naṣīb. ḏēf ʿandak. walaw." gāḷ-lo, "šū, aḏ-ḏēf yugʿud ʿand al-ḥarīm? mamnūʿ^{a}"	439 He said [to] Šāṭer Ḥasan, "What has brought you from the land of paradise to the land of hell?" He said to him, "Allah and fate has brought me. Guest at your [place]. So what! [Isn't it OK?]" He said to him, "What, a guest sits next to the women? It's not allowed!"
444 hāḏa gāl-lo, "hassa ʾadabbrak." ḏaḷḷo mdawwer ʿala ğidir al-^{i}bḥate. ḥaṭṭ rāsa u-gaʿad yišrab-bō lamma hū yisḥab ḥālo yimsak hā-s-sēf u-yišugg rāso. gāl, winno rāso midaḥder. "falliṭni yā šāṭer ḥasan." gāl-la, "ʾahlan wa-sahlan." wāwe.	444 This one said to him, "Now [soon] I'll trick you." He continued looking for the porridge pot. He put his head and sat down to drink in [from] it. When [at this time] he [Šāṭer Ḥasan] took himself, got hold of the sword and cut off his [the *ḥūt*'s] head. [He said] and lo, his head rolled off. "Save me, Šāṭer Ḥasan." "Welcome." Jackal!
450 rāḥat. hāyyi ṣārat ^{i}tzaġrid min ġād, ʾaḷḷa ^{a}frağha ʿalēha w-al-mayya hawwadat serīʿan, yā sīdna w-ʾahalha, masākīn, nāmam ʿala wuğūhhum čabi, min zaʿalhom ʿalēha. "wēlak, rāḥat ʿalēha."	450 It went [it came to be]. This [girl] began ululating from there, for Allah had freed her and the water flowed down quickly, o sir, and her folks, poor ones, were asleep leaning on their faces because of their sorrow for her [thinking] "Woe on her, she is lost."

456 hī saḥbat ḥālha u-ḏaḷḷat ^{e}mrawwḥa ʿalē yā tanno wṣil hāḏ al-bald– al-medīna, widdo yemayyil ʿa-l-xityāra. gālat lo, "wēn? waḷḷa mā-daššrak min hīn la-nāyif. minnak lissa wa-(i)nnak gaḷbi, yā 'abu ṣāleḥ,"[24] gālat lo, "la-nšūf, 'ana ğet-lak." ʿağabo. meša ʿād mʿāha ʿand abūha,

456 She took off and continued going home to him until he reached the edge of the country—the town, he wanted to turn off to the old woman's [house]. She said to him, "Where? By Allah, I won't leave you from now on. I am part of you and you are my heart, o Abu Ṣāleḥ." She said to him, "Let's see, I have come to you [I am yours]." He liked it. He went again with her to her father's [home].

464 daggat ʿala l-bawwāb(a) hunāk, "mīn?" min az-zaʿal u-l-hāḏ, gālu-la, gālat-lom, "taḥammalet, ana s-sitt ^{e}bdūr." fazzam yerukḏūn exwetha, le-hān, fetḥam al-bāb u-šāfam hināk, winno aš- šābb. "'ahalan, 'ahalan, 'ahalan," ṣāram yeḥabbibūhum.

464 She knocked at the door there. "Who [is it]?" out of their sorrow and all that, they said to her. She said to them, "I have survived [passed the test]. I am Sitt Bdūr." Her brothers, they started running [in a frenzy] to [the door] there, opened the door and saw [them] there, and lo, [there was] the boy. "Welcome, welcome, welcome"—they started kissing them.

471 gālat-ilhom, "hāḏa lli 'ingaḏni; ḏibaḥ al-ḥūt.w-intam hīna blād hāḏi bnādamīn? šū btinfaʿu? w-ana nsībe. w-hāḏa miš rā(ḥ)-'adaššro ʿala kull ḥāl." gāl, "'inta ʿala ḥsābna." ğāb al-xaṭīb ʿagad-lo ʿgādo ʿalēha u-ğawwazo, la(h)a, u-hū gaʿad ^{e}b-maḥall, fāhem, yā sīdna.

471 She said to them, "This is the one who saved me, killed the *ḥūt*, and you here, this country, are these human beings? Of what use are you? And I am his relative [family member by marriage]. This one, I am not going to leave him in any case." He [her father] said, "You are on our account." He brought the preacher, married him legally to her, and he stayed in some place. Do you understand, o sir?

478 rāḥat al-midda, šahar, ^{e}šharēn, ṯalaṯ-arbaʿt-^{i}šhir, kānat (ti)twaxxam, hāḏi. gālat lo, "āx, yā šāṭer ḥasan, law-yṣīr-li kūz rummān min bistān 'abūy." gāl-la, "wēn bistān abūč? dallīni ʿalē, 'anī hū." gālat-lo, "mā-gdar adillīk, hāḏa-l-bistān marṣūd." hāḏa ziʿel min hā-r-riğāl,[25] u-ma fʿil ygūl lo ʿan al-bistān.

478 The period went by—a month, two months, three, four months. She became yearning, this one. She said to him, "O Šāṭer Ḥasan, if [only] I had a pomegranate from my father's orchard." He said to her, "Where is your father's garden? Guide me to it. Which is it?" She said to him, "I cannot lead you to it, the orchard has a *ḥūt* in it." This man [Šāṭer Ḥasan] was angry with the man [the woman] and [that she] did not want to tell him about the orchard.

486 saḥab ḥālo, ṭulaʿ ʿala hā-l-medīne, yisyal bayyāʿ al-fiğel, gāl-lo, "yā ʿammi, bistān el-malek 'inta taʿarif wēn hiyye?" gāl-lo, "yā ʿammi, kīst al-fiğel bi-taʿrīfe hiyye."

486 He went off, went up into the town, asked a radish seller, said to him, "O uncle, the king's orchard—do you know where it is?" He said to him, "O uncle, a pack of radish costs a taʿrīfe [a cheap coin during the Ottoman period]."

491 gāl-lo, "yā ʿammi, hāt li fiğel." gāl-lo, "minnak wa-rūḥ." mā fʿil yedillo.	491 He said to him, "O uncle, give me radish." He said, "[The orchard is] from you [away from your direction] and go [away]." He did not want to guide him.
493 rāḥ ğiddāmo šwayye willa šaḥḥāt, nūri. gāl-lo, "bistān al-malek wēno?" gāl-lo, "waḷḷa dāyer tann-ašḥad tanni aʿīš." gāl-lo, "wēš yā ʿammi, xuḏ hāḏ-le-. u-dallīni ʿa l-bistān." gāl-lo, "(i)smaʿ, ʾadallak ʿa-bistān al-malak min beʿīd, awaṣṣif-lak ʾiyyā. min beʿīd." gāl-lo, "bas waṣṣaf-li ʾiyyā, wēnu, waṣṣaf li ʾiyyā."	493 He went on forward a little, and lo, a beggar, a gypsy. He said to him, "The king's orchard—where is it?" He said to him, "By Allah, I'm going round begging so that I can live." He said to him, "What, o uncle, take this . . . and guide me to the orchard." He said to him, "Listen, I will guide you to the king's orchard from afar, I'll describe it to you. From afar." He said to him, "Only describe it to me, where it is, describe it to me."
502 lima waṣṣaf-lo ʾiyyā ṭalʿam ʿala ğibal hīk, waṣṣaf-lo ʾiyya, wēn, wann hunāk yaʿmal yewaṣṣif. bistān ḥaḏar, hāy hīn, al-mayya bī, šiğariyye. gāl-lo, "ṭayyib, maʿa s-salāma, tfaḏḏal, hāyy sāʿati."	502 When he described it to him, they went up a mountain, like that, he described it to him where [it was], and lo, there [he was] doing, describing: a green orchard, that here, the water is in it, many trees. He said to him, "Good, goodbye, please, this is my watch [as a payment]."
507 saḥab ḥālo, rāḥ aš-šaḥḥāt, u-huwwa ğāk rāye(ḥ) ʿala hīki. šadd ʿala hā-l-faras, ḥaṭṭ sēfo b-ğanbo, u-ḥaṭṭ hā-l-xurğ u-ğāy. ʾisḥab, ʾisḥab, ta-wiṣel. waṣel hināka—al-bistān msakkar. fitaḥ el-bāb, fawwat al-faras, u-fāt. dawwar, hā-lli fāt, ʾimši, šū hā-l-rummān, aṣ-ṣabbār, at-tuffāḥ –	507 He went off, the beggar went, he went going to this [place]. He bridled the mare, put the sword at his side and put the horse bag, and came. He went and went off, until he arrived. He arrived there—the orchard was closed. He opened the gate and brought the mare inside and entered. He went around, the one who entered, was going, what [good quality had] these pomegranates, the [prickly pear] cactus, the apples—
514 ʾimši aš-ši, mkawwam kull šī. ar-rummān, kūz ar-rummān hā—gadd el-baṭṭīx. šū hāḏa, giṭaʿ kuzēn rummān, ḥaṭṭhin ^{i}b-hā-l-xurğ, ṣār sāḥeb hā-l-faras u-ṭāleʿ barra.	514 he went, everything was piled up. The pomegranates, a pomegranate [had] the size of a watermelon. What is this? He cut two pomegranates, put them in the horse bag, and began going out, leading the mare and going out.
519 mā ḥass willa l-wuhīf ğāy warā. daššar al-faras dallha ġād, rubbaṭ ʿa-ğanb al-bāb, saḥab hā-s-sēf, u-gaṣṣa. [mā widdha tinfud hīč, lamma hū inhabid. bas aguḷ-ḷak, ta-tra.] gāḷat-ḷo, "ṯnē, yā š-šāṭer ḥasan," gāḷ-ḷa, "ʾimmi mā ʿallamatni ʾaḏaḷḷ."	519 He could not help but feel the *wuhīf* [a monster similar to a ḥūt] coming after him. He left the mare, led it tied to the side of the gate, took this sword and cut it [its head off]. (It did not want to go out [die] like that, when it was being destroyed [crushed]. But I'm telling you, you will see.) It said to him, "Repeat [do it again], o Šāṭer Ḥasan." He said to it, "My mother did not teach me to continue [remain like that]."

526 ḏaḷḷ wāgef ʿinda tā xaḷḷṣat, giḏab hā-s-sēf biʿaǧǧa waḷḷa hā-lli bi-baṭenha ginīna, miṯel mā tgūl marṭabān hīč. giḏab hāḏa aṭlaʿ al-marṭabān bi-gaḷba ʿaṣfūr, ṣāfir. laflafo bi-hā-l-maḥrama, ḥaṭṭo b-ǧēbo, gāḷ, "hāḏa alli dāyer ʿalē ʾani. widdi ʾaḥyi uxuwti."

526 He remained standing next to it until it ended [died], [then] he took the sword and slit it open, and lo, in its stomach was a bottle, as you say, a jar, like that. He took that, took out the jar in which there was a bird, whistling. He wrapped it in this handkerchief and put it in his pocket and said, "This is what I'm looking for, me. I want to revive my brothers."

533 saḥab ḥālo iǧǧāsim hā. rā(ḥ) ʿalēha. xaḏa lēha kūzēn rummān. rumāhin ihnāk, wagtin šāfato hāy inhiblat. "yā wēlak," mā šāfato wagtin rāḥ. "wēnta raḥt? kēf-in ṣār bak?"

533 He went off to share them with her. He went to her. He took for her two pomegranates—two pomegranates. He threw them to her there. When she saw him, she got crazy. "Oh, woe to you." She did not seen him go. "When did you go? How was it with you?"

538 hāḏlāki gāl-la, "ʾintam bnādamīn hīn b-hā-l-iblād? intam faṭāyis. haḏīk ḏibaḥta, xalli ʾabūki yirūḥ."

538 This man said to her, "Are you people here in this country? You are carcasses. This, I killed it [the *wuhīf*], let your father go [to see]."

541 rāḥ. gaʿad šharēn-ṯalāṯa ʿind(h)a, gāḷ-ḷa, "yumma, dīri bālek ʿindi, ʾin xaḷḷafti walad—tilḥagīni.

541 He went. He stayed two, three months with her. He said to her, "O mum [girl], pay attention to me. If you give birth to a boy—join me.

544 ʾin xaḷḷafti bint, ʾaḷḷa ysahhel ʿalēki.—ʾani mrawwiḥ." "yā zēn, yā šēn." ʿāšat u-mātat, ʿāšat ʿalē. ʿāšat, uxayyaṭat ʾawāʿīha l-uʾawāʿīh.

544 "If you give birth to a girl—goodbye [Allah help you]. I am returning home." "Oh good, oh bad" [cries of dismay]. She lived and died for him. She sewed her clothes onto his.

548 giḏab hāḏa b-al-lēl, fakk ʾawāʿīha u-siḥab ḥālo u-rāḥ. maḥtafiz ʿa-rīšāt hāḏi. rā(ḥ) ʿala rāʿi ġanam, ištara xarūf gaṭṭaʿo, sabʿa gṭāʿ, iḥtarag ar-rīšāt, willa hī ǧāya.

548 At night he took, untied her clothes and went off and was gone. He was saving these feathers. He went to the sheep shepherd, bought a sheep, cut it into seven pieces, burned the feathers, and lo—it [the Šūḥa] is coming.

552 lā tinsāha, ʿād inṭāha hū, inṭāha rīšāt, gāḷ-ḷa, "in ǧibti walad, bas tiḥirǧīn ar-rīšāt hāḏen, tiǧūn ʿalayya, tiǧūn ʿa-š-šaṭṭ, tīǧi aš-šūḥa ʿalēkam, tgaṭṭaʿkam ʿalayya laʿandi. ʾani min ġād, min sabʿe bḥūr."

552 Do not forget her, he did not forget her [his wife], he gave her, gave her feathers and said to her, "If you give birth to a boy, only burn these feathers and you will come to me, you will come to the shore. The Šūḥa bird will come to you, will make you cross [the seven seas] to me. I am from there, from [beyond] seven seas."

557 ğat al-šūḥa, rakkbatu gaṭṭaʿatu, liga al-faras hinā̄k, šū mhabbla min an-naṣḥ. baʿad hā wa-l-insa u-kull ši, ʾağa ta-l . . . wagtinno wiṣel ⁱhnāk ʿa-s-sūr ta-l-gaṣer, ṭall (h)aḏāk min fōg, gāḷ, "daxīlak, yā šāṭer ḥasan, ʾani b-wağhak."	557 The Šūḥa bird came, made him ride her, and brought him over, he found the mare there—how fattened [it was] with the fat [plenty of food] there. After this and the woman and everything he came to the. . . . When he arrived there, to the palace wall, he [the *ḥūt*] appeared from above and said, "Please, o Šāṭer Ḥasan, I am at your mercy."
563 gāḷ-ḷo, "šnū daxīli min ğins as-salām? ʾanṭīni bil-ʾawwal (ʾa)gawwaman al-bnādamīn hāy, ʾanṭīk rūḥak.	563 He said to him, "What, my protection is a kind of greeting? Give me first [that with which] I will revive these people, I'll give you your soul.
566 hāḏi hi rūḥak bi-ğēbi." ʾī, gāḷ-ḷo, "xuḏ, hāḏ-aš-šwāl," zaṭṭ le-šwāl min fōg. gāḷ-ḷo, "xuḏ hāḏa š-šwāl rušš ʿale, hāḏa l-ḥğār as-sōd—kulla bnādamīn. hāḏi tgūm."	566 "This, your soul, is in my pocket." Ei? He said to him, "Take this bag." He threw the bag from above and said to him, "Take this bag, spray [it] on it. These black stones—are all people. These will rise."
571 giḏab min hā-šwāl, ṣār yāxeḏ min hā-š-šwāl u-yerušš. hāḏa mešarrig, hāḏa meġarrib, wunna gāmat hā-d-dinya kulla ṭayyiba, "la ʾilāha ʾilla ḷḷāh," ʾuxuwtu gāmam, miṯel mā hum, maʿ xēlhum u-ğmāl, wa-l . . . ʾei! gāl-lo, "hawwid li as-sitt ḥisin." hawwadat as-sitt ḥisin, hawwad-lo ʾiyyāha.	571 He took from the bag, started taking from the bag and spraying it—this to the east, that to the west, and lo, all these people got up, all of them safe and sound. "No Allah except Allah." His brothers got up, as they had been, with their horses and camels and . . . ei! He said to him, "Get Sitt Ḥisin down to me." Sitt Ḥisin came down to him, it [the *ḥūt*] lowered her to him.
579 gaḏab hāḏa r-riğāl, ḥaṭṭa ʿale ḥağar, baḷāṭa, ğāb ḥağar u-feġaso. win figsat rāḥat rūḥo. saḥbam ḥālhom u-ḏaḷḷam mrawwḥīn. rawwaḥom hinā̄k ligam al-š-šēx al-gebīla haḏāka, aṯ-ṯāni, wāḥad, ḥāčim al-ğebīle.	579 This man took and put it [the jar] on a stone, a rock, and brought a stone and crushed it. And his soul was crushed [the *ḥūt* died]. They went off and continued going home. They went home. There they found that tribe's sheikh, that other one, the tribe ruler.
585 wagten rāḥam walādu, ʾabū, nazzlū ʿan-al-ḥukum, "u-mutna, ši-xbār(h)um, u-šnū ḥālek, ᵉmnihtadi ʿalē."	585 When his children went [away], his father, they removed him from the rule. "We died—how they are [doing = what is their news]—and how you are, that we will know [be guided]."
588 ʾummu w-abū, ʾummhum w-ʾabūhum. bass ʾinn wiṣlam ʿal-iblād hinā̄k, u-šāfhum, ğam ʿala ʾabū, ʾummhum, ʾinhum miʿānyīn min gadd mā yibčūn.	588 His mother and father, their mother and father. As soon as they [the brothers] arrived at that country, and saw, came to his father, [and] their mother, [they saw] that they were suffering from how much they had been weeping.

593 ’inṭāhum hāḏa maḥramto, aš-šāṭer ḥasan. bas massaḥam ʿyūnum winnhum ṭayyibīn, mā bīhom ši. u-gāmat al-ḥaflāt, u-r-raqṣ u-l-ġanāni,	593 He gave them his handkerchief, Šāṭer Ḥasan. As soon as they wiped their eyes—lo, they were healthy, had nothing [no problem] at all. And they made celebrations, and dancing and songs.
597 hī, gaʿadam aǧ-ǧemāʿa, ʿāwad as-silim (ʿ)al-ḥukum, miṯil mā kān.	597 She . . . they, the group sat down [settled] and peace [came back] on the control [of the tribe and everything] got back as it had been.
599 yirǆaʿ marǧūʿna la-marto hadīč. ǧābat walad. hā-l-wulēd wāʿi, miṯel mā tgūl, wald as-sālfa yikbar. wagtinno čiber, ǧat, gāḷat-ḷo, “ismaʿ, iḥna nrū(ḥ) ʿa-būk.” gāḷ-ḷa—šāyif widdha tšūfo—gāḷ-ḷa, “wēn ’abūy?” gāḷat-ḷo, “’abūk min ǧawwa sabaʿ bḥūr, gaṭaʿ sabaʿ bḥūr.”	599 We return now to that wife of his. She had [gave birth to] a boy. The little boy was clever, as you say—the child of a story grows up. When he grew up, she said to him, “Listen, we are going to your father.” He said to her, “I see you want to see him.” He said to her, “Where is my father?” She said to him, “Your father is inside seven seas, he crossed seven seas.”
606 gaʿadat, xaḏat al-welēd u-rāḥat ʿala š-šaṭṭ, xaḏat hā-r-rīšāt, ḥarragathen walla š-šwāḥ ǧāye. ʿa-ṯalāṯ–’arbaʿ. hāy, imʿāha laḥam, kull mā giṭʿan baḥar, tlahhimha giṭʿa.	606 She stayed, took the little boy, and went to the shore. She took the feathers, burned them and lo, the šwāḥ [Šūḥa bird] was coming at three, four [minutes]. This [woman] had meat with her, whenever they crossed a sea, she fed it a piece.
611 gāḷat-iḷha, “hadīč madīnt aš-šāṭer ḥasan, yaḷḷa, tsahhalam.” ʿindmā wiṣlam ⁱhnāk, ʿa-l-medīne, waṣlat hāḏi uḏaḷḷat tisyal tanna wiṣlat la-ʿand ’abūha, ʿand ǧōza. taʿārafam haḏōl aǧ-ǧmāʿa. u-ʿāwadam miṯl-mā kān. u-hāḏi xurrāfti.	611 It said to her, “This is Šāṭer Ḥasan’s town. Come on, Allah help you.” When they reached there, the town, she reached and continued asking until she reached her father’s, her husband’s [place]. They got acquainted, that group, and they got back as it had been. And this is my story.

B. Seven Brides for Seven Brothers

NARRATOR: Ṣabḥa ʿAbūd
TRIBE: *ʿArab el-Ḥuǧērāt*
IFA 17407 November 27, 1980

Text

There was one who had seven sons and they are his sons. They said to him, “We want to marry seven sisters.”

Their father said to them, “From where shall I bring you seven sisters? Go search.”

They rode their horses and went to look for [seven sisters], and they are going on their way. They walked, walked like that in the *wādi* [an arroyo, a dry streambed]. They had a tent. They built the tent and settled on the ground.

One day—each one guarded every night, guarded them and the horses. The smallest [the youngest] arose at night [and saw that] the light [fire] was out.

When the light was out, he said, "What, shall I awake them in the night? It's a shame to awake my brothers and ask them about matches."

He looked eastward and westward in the night, and behold, a small light. He rose, he walked, walked, walked, walked—the light [was] far away. When he arrived—and behold, the light comes from a cave and at the [entrance to the] cave a round rock [a stone closes the cave's entrance]—forty [men are needed] to remove it and forty to close it. Allah helped him. He removed the stone and went in and lay among them. As he lay among them at night, they wanted to go out to rob, they left the house open, he began to eat, he ate a little from each plate and lay among them.

When they awoke, one said, "Something is missing in my plate." "And me, too—something is missing in my plate." "By Allah, who is this? Who is this among us? Show yourself—Allah will be with you and protect you. We will not betray you. Get out!"

He stepped forward; he said to them, "It's me."

He said to them, "Come on, let's set out and search [for something] to steal, let's go to the king's treasury to rob it."—This is [what] he [said].

Good.

They walked at night. He walked ahead of them. When he went ahead of them, he said to them, "I have with me forty stones [pebbles], every time I throw a stone, one [of you] will come out."

He entered the rooms, and in the first room [there is] a maiden, and in the second [room] a maiden, and in the seven rooms—in each room [there is] a maiden. The smallest one . . . he looked and here in the room where this maiden is, and above her head a snake about to bite her. He got up, killed the snake, and stamped his hand with blood on the door of the room, meaning that he put his hand on the door of the maiden's room. And every time he threw a stone one [of the bandits] came out and he killed him, removed his head, killed him. [He killed them] the forty. The girl—he took her ring, he took from the young girl over whose head he killed the snake, he took the ring and gave her his ring, and he got up and killed the forty men.

The king rose in the morning: What is it in his house? Forty [dead] people? Terror! Who, who, who? They began to search. There is someone [who killed those people]! Every time someone came [to the country], they brought him, they said: "Who?"

She said—the girl, "I know him" [I can recognize him].

"Who, who, who?"

Every time someone came, she would stand by the palace and look.

He said to her, "Who?"

She said, "Bring more, bring more."

What, there is no one left. She said to them, "Look around the city."

No one. They brought his brothers. They told her: "We found these by the city."

She said to them, "No, bring more."

They said [to the six brothers], "Don't you have more brothers?"

She said to them, "Look for [their brother]."

They found their brother.

She said to them, "This one!"

They brought him. When they brought him, she recognized him. They brought him. They put him with her, and they [all the brothers] sat with the king.

He said to him, "Your Honor, the king, we are seven brothers and we want seven sisters."

He said to them, "I have seven daughters."

He gave to each one [of them] one [daughter]. They stayed with him for one month.

They said to him, "Now we want to go back, to go [ride] to our father."

By Allah, they went. Each one rode a mare and each one his spouse with him. As they walked along the way, the young man's spouse forgot something at home.

She said to him, "I want to go back and fetch it."

He said to her, "No, I'll go back to fetch it."

He said to them, "Well, wait for me here"—this one, the young man.

When they waited for him, they did not feel that the girl who was sitting with them got up [and walked away]. A cloud came, grabbed the girl, and took her. When it took her, the lad [the youngest brother] came and said to them, "Where is the girl?"

They said to him, "A cloud came and snatched her."

He [the youngest brother] said to them, "Well, what shall we do?"

He said to them, "You stay here, I'll go to look for her."

He went. As he walked, walked, he came to the sea. He looked, and behold, a girl [mermaid].

She said to him, "Turn that stone upside down and enter under the earth and come to me."

He got up, he turned the stone and reached her.

She said, "What are you looking for?"

He said to her, "A cloud came and took my bride."

She said to him, "Well, do you have a horse?"

He said to her, "Yes."

She said to him: "Go, try, see [if] the mare jumps over the sea."

He went, he tried, he trained her. She got up and jumped over it.

She said to him, "Jump over the second sea, when you jump over the second sea, enter a house in which there are a black horse and a white horse, kiss the black horse from here and from here [from both sides] and tell him [to let you in]. You will find the girl hanging by her head's hair." The *ḥūt* [ogre] took her.

He got up, came to the horse, kissed him, and said, "Come on, let me in."

He came to the girl, cut her hair [released her from her hanging] and put her behind him on the horse and crossed the water.

The *ḥūt* jumped and found no one. He chased him from behind, from behind. He came to his brothers, they rode the horses, she and them, and he returned to his mother and father and held a wedding and married her.

Commentary

The two stories cited above are local oikotypes of the international narrative type ATU 304, "The Dangerous Night-Watch." Here is the outline of the story.

Together with his brothers (companions), a youth (the youngest of three brothers, hunter, prince, soldier, etc.) has various hunting adventures, or he defeats dragons (wild animals, monsters) during one (three) night-watch(es) in the forest (at his father's grave). While the youth fights, his fire (light) goes out (the youth loses his way, is tempted away by a bird). He (stops time and) meets giants (robbers, supernatural beings), whom he impresses by shooting tricks (motif F661.1, "Skillful marksman shoots meat from giant's hands") or by his extraordinary physical strength.

The giants go to plunder a castle (town) or to carry off a princess, and take the youth with them. The youth shoots a watchdog (rooster), enters the castle first, calls the giants and, as they enter, cuts off their heads one at a time (motif K912, "Robbers' (giants') heads cut off one by one as they enter house"). Often, he cuts off their tongues (heads, other parts of the body), which he takes away as trophies (motif H83, "Rescue tokens. Proof that hero has succeeded in rescue").

In the castle, the youth comes to a room where a princess lies sleeping (motif N711.2, "Hero finds maiden in [magic] castle"). He looks at her (falls in love, kisses her, rapes her) and, before leaving, takes a souvenir (jewelry, handkerchief, shoes, etc.), which later becomes a token (motifs H105.1, "Dragon-tongue proof. Dragon slayer cuts out the tongues and uses them later to prove his identity as slayer"; H81.1.1, "Hero takes token from sleeping princess"; see ATU 300, "The Dragon-Slayer"). Then he returns with a burning log (lets time resume) and kindles the fire again.

An impostor pretends that he has killed the giants and claims the (pregnant) princess for his wife. The princess refuses to marry him. She sets up (is made to live in) an inn where guests need not pay anything if they tell a tale (life-history, news). (Accompanied by his brothers and mother) the youth stops at this inn, proves his identity by means of his tale and the tokens, and marries the princess. The impostor is punished.

The narrative type is known from Europe and North Africa, and from Turkey, Armenia, Syria, Israel, and Mongolia. One version of the story is included in the Grimm Brothers Collection (1815, story 111) under the name "The Skillful Huntsman." In the IFA there are Jewish versions from Iraqi Kurdistan, Morocco, and Yemen.[26] The suspension of the course of time by the protagonist and the extension of the night until the completion of his missions, which is mentioned in the description of the international narrative type, appear in all the Jewish-Yemenite versions of the story in the IFA but not in the Bedouin versions.

I recorded three versions of the story in three different tribes. Two of them (one from ʿArab el-Ḥuğērāt and one from the ʿArab Ḥilf-Ṭabbāš tribe) are similar in most details, so only the version by Ṣabḥa ʿAbūd, from the ʿArab el-Ḥuğērāt tribe, is reproduced above. In her version, there are seven brothers and the hero fights robbers, while in the version by Maryam Muṣṭafa Ṭabbāš from ʿArab Ḥilf-Ṭabbāš, there are three brothers, and instead of forty robbers, there are forty *ġūls*.

Ṣabḥa ʿAbūd's version is more complex and contains another episode that is not found in Maryam Muṣṭafa Ṭabbāš's version—the kidnapping of the bride by a *ḥūt* (ogre) and her rescue. This scene further emphasizes the helplessness of the older brothers in contrast to the heroism and resourcefulness of the younger brother.

The motif found here of identification by the print of a palm smeared with blood has been discussed already in the story "The Coffee Server" (chap. 11). The motif of a woman who lives in the sea and helps the hero also appears in "The Golden Children," to be discussed in chapter 36.

The version "Šāṭer Ḥasan and His Nine Brothers" was recorded from a male narrator of the ʿArab el-Sawāʿed tribe. Despite the confused language of the narrator and the ambiguity of the content, that version is extremely rich in popular motifs. Below is a description of the main lines of the plot:

An Arab sheikh has ten sons. The boys want to marry, but their father is willing to let them wed only if he finds for them ten sisters from the same mother and same father. The boys leave the house and go on a search. They reach a locked orchard full of fruit, enter it, and build a tent there. Every night, one of the brothers is on guard. When it is the younger brother's turn, his lamp dies out. He goes out to look for fire and encounters a demon (*al-Raṣād*) (motif N571, "Devil (demon) as guardian of treasure"). The demon is constantly changing its shape. The younger brother, known as Clever Ḥasan, fights the demon and beheads him. A moment before his death, the demon turns to him with the words, "Add [repeat], o *Šāṭer* (Clever) Ḥasan," and the hero answers, "My mother did not teach me to add. For if I add, it will recover."

As in other Bedouin stories that I recorded, the demon asks the hero to hit him once more, but the hero refuses because another blow may restore the demon's strength (motif C742, "Taboo: striking monster twice. Though monster begs that hero strike him again, hero refuses. Monster would otherwise revive," motif E11.1. "Second blow resuscitates. First kills." Later, as in the previous two versions, the youngest brother arrives at a robbers' cave, and after he shows them his strength by opening the huge door blocking the mouth of the cave, they appoint him as their leader. The hero rides along with the robbers to the king's palace, which they intend to rob. He climbs first into the palace and asks the robbers to give him forty pebbles. He throws out one pebble at a time to signal to the next robber to climb up. When each robber reaches the top of the palace, he decapitates him, and thus he manages to kill all the robbers. In the palace, he finds ten sleeping princesses in ten rooms. He exchanges rings with the most beautiful princess lying on a raised bed in the last room, and then he returns to his brothers.

The king wants to know who killed the robbers. He seats his young daughter in the palace balcony and orders men to pass before her so she can identify the hero. A similar episode appears in Ṣabḥa ʿAbūd's version, but here it is described in much more detail. Eventually, the hero and his brothers arrive at the palace, and the princess recognizes the younger brother and throws him an apple. Throwing an apple as a sign of recognition is a familiar motif that appears in folktales in many cultural spaces: motif H316, "Suitor test: apple thrown indicates princess' choice (often golden apple)."

The king marries his ten daughters to the brothers. The hero and his brothers return to their country together with their brides. One of the slaves accompanying the convoy draws the hero's attention to three possibilities in front of him at a crossroads: "the road of fire," on which travelers may be burned with fire; "the road of water," where travelers are likely to drown; and "the road 'if-enter-you-do-not-return' and he who goes will not return." (ʾin-sadd-mā-radd u-alli yrūḥ mā yʿāwid). The motif of choice between three different paths at a crossroads is familiar from many folktales, especially from Russian folktales and folktales of other Slavic peoples, as well as from the Indian and Turkish culture space: motif N122.0.1, "The choice of roads. At parting of three roads there are equivocal inscriptions telling what will happen if each is chosen. Brothers each choose a different road."

In this story, the hero chooses "the road that prevents passage and return," but his brothers' choices are not clear. In any case, as in Ṣabḥa ʿAbūd's version, the protagonist is delayed, and in the meantime, his bride, Sitt Ḥisin, is abducted by a *ḥūt*. In addition, the *ḥūt* turns his brothers into stones. The hero arrives at the palace and meets his bride. She explains to him what has happened, and the hero asks her to find out where the *ḥūt* hides his soul. Initially, the *ḥūt* tells Sitt Ḥisin that his soul is hidden in the broom. In response, she dresses up and decorates the broom. The *ḥūt* laughs at her innocence and reveals the truth: his soul is in a wild boar that dwells in the orchard of El-Sitt Bdūr, beyond the seven seas. She reveals this to her husband, and he goes on a journey to obtain the soul of the *ḥūt*.

This motif of a monster whose soul is outside his body and is located in a remote place is known in the Slavic and the Indian culture spaces, as well as in other cultural spaces: motif E710.1, "Ferocious animal guardian of separable soul of ogress"; E711.1, "Soul in egg"; E715.1, "Separable soul in bird"; E713, "Soul hidden in a series of coverings." This motif is combined with several others. Usually the soul will be hidden in an egg, in a duck, in a well, in a church, or a similar series.

In fact, this is an ancient motif that appears in an ancient Egyptian story from the period of the Nineteenth Dynasty (1293–1185 BCE), "The Story of Two Brothers," in which one of the brothers hides his soul on a distant acacia tree.[27] The motif is repeated in various Indian stories,[28] as well as in the *Arabian Nights*. In the latter, a princess is kidnapped by a demon, and her beloved comes to save her. She tells him that one cannot kill the demon without first finding his soul.

The demon has told her the secret of his soul: "What time I was born, the astrologers predicted that I should lose my soul at the hands of the son of a king of mankind. So, I took it and set it in the crop of a sparrow and shut up the bird in a box. The box I set in a casket, and enclosing this in seven other caskets and seven chests, laid the whole in a alabastrine coffer, which I buried within the marge of yon earth-circling sea; for that these parts are far from the world of men and none of them can win hither."[29]

Later in the story, the prince manages to find the soul of the demon hidden in a bird, and when he strangles the bird, the demon dies. It should also be noted that the description of the kidnapping of the princess by the demon in the story from the *Arabian Nights* resembles the description of the kidnapping in Ṣabḥa ʿAbūd's version. "Presently, before I could be ware, a something as it were a cloud swooped down on me and snatching me up from amongst my handmaids, soared aloft with me betwixt heaven and earth."[30]

The motif of the demon that first leads the girl astray and informs her that his soul is in the broom is found in one of the most common Russian stories, "Koschei the Deathless." Koschei is a demonic figure capable of changing its shape and wearing many shapes, including that of a cloud.

In the Bedouin story, during the quest for the soul of the *ḥūt*, the hero undergoes a series of adventures. First, he comes to a seashore, where he kills a snake with seven heads, and then he falls asleep in the shade of a jujube tree. A giant bird (*Šūḥa*) suspects him of stalking her nestlings and devouring them in her absence, and she intends to peck out his eyes, but the nestlings explain to her that it was the sleeping hero who saved them from the seven-headed snake.

As a result, the *Šūḥa* protects him from the hot sun by shading him with her wings. When the hero wakes up, she thanks him for killing the snake and asks him where he is going. Clever Ḥasan tells her about his desire to cross the seven seas, and the *Šūḥa* carries him there on her back. On the way, he feeds her with pieces of meat, but when one of the pieces accidentally falls into the sea, he continues to feed her with a piece of meat he cuts from his thigh.

When they succeed in crossing the last sea and land on earth, the *Šūḥa* finds out what has happened. She vomits the piece of thigh meat she has swallowed, puts it on the hero's thigh, and heals it. Many of the details in this story were told in an unclear way and with many missing portions, but it was possible to reconstruct the narrator's intention on the basis of other versions of the story. Such stories about a legendary bird carrying the hero on its back after he has saved its nestlings from the snake are known from the Turkish cultural space, where the bird is called *Zümrüdü ü Anka*, or simply *anka*. A Turkish version of the story appears in Ignaz Kúnos's book.[31] It seems that the roots of this story are in the ancient Iranian tradition, where the bird is called *Simorg*.

In our story, the *ḥūt* hides his soul in the body of a wild boar, but later in the story, the hero finds the soul of the *ḥūt* in the form of a bird fluttering in a jar inside the body of a large bird, and the wild boar is not mentioned at all. The hero takes the *ḥūt*'s soul, and when he encounters him, he crushes the soul, kills the ogre, and revives his brothers, their wives, and all the other people that had been petrified.

Before that, he saves another princess from the hands of another *ḥūt*, who has dammed the waters of the spring and does not allow the city's inhabitants to drink unless they bring him a virgin girl every month. The hero kills the *ḥūt* and marries the girl. This episode appears in many of the Bedouin stories I have collected. I discuss it in detail later, in chapter 31, "The Sickle Hand." At the end of the story, Clever Ḥasan rescues his parents from a ruler who had removed his father from his rule. His parents were blinded, and he restores their vision by passing his handkerchief over their eyes, but this part of the story is not clear. At the end of the story, the second princess arrives on the back of the *Šūḥa* bird with her child and joins her husband and his first wife.

The story reflects several Bedouin customs and ways of life: Clever Ḥasan arrives at the *ḥūt*'s palace, where he meets his kidnapped wife. When the *ḥūt* returns from his journey and finds the hero sitting with the young woman, he treats him according to the best traditions of the Bedouins and does not devour him. On the contrary, he follows the rules of Bedouin hospitality, which determine that anyone who comes into an enemy's tent should be under the host's protection and that no one is allowed to hurt such a person who remains in the enemy's tent. On the other hand, the *ḥūt* admonishes the hero and is annoyed because the hero has broken the customary taboo and entered the women's section in the owner's absence, which is considered a blatant violation of the rules of modesty: "He said to him, 'What, the guest sits next to the women? It's not allowed!'"

Later in the story, when the hero's second wife becomes pregnant, she asks her husband to obtain special foods for her. The phenomenon of a pregnant woman who desires a special food and asks her husband to obtain it is known in many cultures. When the narrator describes the wife's desire, he uses the Arabic word *tetwaḥḥem*, which usually means "to be in heat," but here it indicates the uncontrollable craving of the pregnant woman for a special food. In the story, the husband embarks on a journey to acquire the desired fruit.

Clearly this is a story about adolescence, in which the younger brother rises in power and wisdom over the older brothers. In Jewish-Yemenite versions that are found in the IFA, sibling rivalry occurs and older brothers attempt to harass their younger brother (who is sometimes presented as the son of another woman). On the other hand, the Bedouin versions that I collected describe cooperation among the brothers. The younger brother finds a bride for himself, and, at the same time, he finds brides for his brothers.

The snake that threatens the princess destined to become the hero's bride and, afterward, the bride's abduction by a demonic creature on the eve of her marriage are motifs connected with the transition period related to married life. This transition abounds with the couple's apprehension toward and fears about the new situation and unfamiliar state they are entering into, and these fears manifest themselves in many stories (for further discussion, see chap. 39, "Personal Narratives about Meetings with Ġūls"). In the Jewish culture space, the motif of the snake that threatens to kill the bride on the eve of her marriage is known from the legend of Rabbi Akiba's daughter:

> Rabbi Akiba had a daughter. The Chaldeans [astrologers] said to him: "The day that she enters the *chuppah*, a snake bites her and she dies." He worried about it [the prophecy] a lot. That day she took the hairpin and stuck it in a crack in the wall. It happened that it [the hairpin] landed in the eye of a snake. In the morning when she took it, the [dead] serpent was dragged after it. Her father said to her, "What have you done?" She said to him: "In the evening a poor man came and called at the doorway, and everyone was preoccupied with the meal, and no one could hear him. I got up, took the plate that you gave me, and gave it to him." He said to her, "You have done a *mitzvah*!" Rabbi Akiba went out and interpreted, "Righteousness delivers from death" (Proverbs 10:2)—and not [just] from an unsuspected death, but from death itself. (Babylonian Talmud, Shabbat 156:2)

Notes

1. As noted in chapter 21, note 1, one of the opening formulas in a Bedouin discourse—narrative or other—mentions the name of Allah in a short prayer or blessing. The formula in this story is short, mentioning only Allah's unity. However, monotheism is a basic element of Islam and suffices here. This formula is typical also in Bedouin court discussions, when one of the people involved (plaintiff, witness, etc.) begins to present his or her argument. Frequent formulas are the *basmala* (*b-ism al-lāhi al-raḥmān al-raḥīm*, "in the name of Allah the merciful and mercy giving"), which also begins written texts, or *ṣalli 'ala n-nabiy ṣalla al-lāhu 'alayhi wa-sallama*, "pray on the Prophet, may Allah pray for him and give him peace." In general, these nonreligious texts are deeply immersed in Islamic beliefs and habits. This is evident in the noted formulas. Their beliefs and worldview are also sometimes presented in narrators' comments. (On these formulas, see, e.g., Stewart, *Texts in Sinai Bedouin Law*, parts 1, 2; Piamenta, *Muslim Conception of God*).

2. Word order is part of syntax, and language speakers know how and when to use the various speech elements. However, in spontaneous speech, many hesitations, repetitions, and

speech errors occur. Listeners usually understand the utterance, in spite of such problems, by using contextual and vocal cues (e.g., intonation). However, when written, such a text looks somewhat hectic. In this volume, we usually do not change or delete these errors, but in the translation, we replace intonation and pauses with punctuation marks and more proper English or add some explanations in brackets.

The following examples demonstrate this aspect of spontaneous speech very clearly: *kān fi gadīm al-zamān hā-l-ğibīlet hā-l-'arab. u-bēn aš-šēx 'andīhum, wa-š-šēx hāḏa tiba'hom, 'endo min al-'iyāl 'ašara*: "There was once upon a time this Bedouin tribe. And among their sheikh and this, their sheikh, had ten children."

Note that Arabic dialects and LA/MSA do not usually use the definite article and demonstrative pronoun before a construct noun as in *hā-l-ğibīlet hā-l-'arab*, "this Bedouin tribe" (*-t* in *ğibīlet* marks the construct phrase). The first *hā-l* is, then, redundant. Such a structure suggests that the speaker began speaking while thinking of a definite noun but at the last moment changed it to the construct structure (*ğibīlet hā-l-'arab*, "the tribe of Bedouins") and thus the first *hā-l* was not deleted. The final phrase in this example, "he had ten children" is, literally, "he has of the children—ten."

3. For *kullayāthom*, "all of them," the basic form *kull*, "all" + *hom*, "(of) them," could have sufficed to express the meaning. The additional syllables, *-ayāt-*, make *kull* plural, to stress the fact that he is speaking about "all and every one" of these people.

4. The sentence *kullayāthom rakkābīn xēl, yrūḥūn 'a-l-ġazu*, "all of them [were] horse riders, they would go to loot," presents several Bedouin masculine activities and traits.

5. *'a-l-ġazu*, "looting attack," was a well-known activity of Bedouin warriors before their sedentarization.

6. The stress mark on the vowel (á) in *'ašra min 'umm w-ábu . . . rāḥam 'alá-mmhom* ("ten from one mother and father . . . they went to their mother") shows the difference between the two occurrences of the word *'umm*, "mother."

7. *'ašra min 'umm w-ábu*: "ten from [one] mother and father." *wa-'ábu* > *w-ábu*, "and father," which loses the first glottal stop *'* of the noun after the conjunction *wa-*. Sedentary dialects do not have such changing word-stress cases, and this utterance there would be *'ála-úm*(m)*hom*; the Bedouin word-stress rule tends to disappear, however, because of sedentary effects.

8. In the utterance *rāḥam 'alá-mmhom, 'ála-* > *'alá*. This stress pattern occurs in Galilee Bedouin speech, Negev Bedouins (Henkin, *Negev Arabic*, 44–45), and elsewhere.

9. *yā yumma, sāwī-lna zāde zuwwāde, w-aḥna widdna nhiğğ. bi-s-sirr*: "O mother, prepare for us provisions and we will be off. In secret." This sentence, too, has several typical Bedouin forms, the first of which is the address *yumma* < *yā 'umm*(*i*) (or *yā imma* elsewhere), "o mother."

The words *zāde zuwwāde*, "sufficient provisions" for the route, (in a morphophonetic wordplay) are based on the same root (*zwd*). The first word is the noun for "food." The second noun is in the pattern CaCCāC, which usually augments meanings in Arabic. Note that the vowel in the first syllable is *u*, assimilated to the following *w* (elsewhere also *zawwāde*).

10. *widdna nhiğğ*: "we will be off." For *widdna*, cf. chapter 4, note 2. The root *hğğ*, "to leave, emigrate," is used also in Syrian dialects (cf. Barthélemy, *Dictionnaire arabe-français*, 863).

11. This and other stories in the volume involve imaginary monsters originating in the Arabic literature, mainly the *ḥūt*, *ġūl*, and *raṣād*. See al-Rawi, "Arabic Ghoul." Their characteristics differ, but they participate in many Arabic folktales. They are big and strong, have magical powers, and can be fatal for humans. The stories in this collection sometimes present them as not very clever or fast. More of their features follow: The *ḥūt*, *ġūl*, and *raṣād* keep

watch over gardens; they often live in a cave, sometimes in a castle (palace). Sometimes they do human works such as raising sheep and shepherding them. A *ġūl/a* can be male or female and can have children, and the *ġūla* takes good care of her offspring. A *ġūl* can be killed by very strong or cunning humans. As they cannot swim, a *ġūl* can drown and die in a river or a sea. Other Bedouin tribes (outside the Galilee) know about them, and their stories emphasize various additional features. Women narrate different stories about them than men do, and the demons' personalities differ between male and female narrators. Cf. Marom, "Bedouin Dialect of the Women," "Fisherman and the Wishing Ring," "Samḥa, the She-Camel," "World of the Monsters," and their references; Lebling, *Legends of the Fire Spirits*, and its references.

12. *gāl, "waḷḷa, ġēr arūḥ ağīb nār li"*: "He said, 'By Allah, I must go and bring me fire.'" The word *ġēr* (LA/MSA *ġayr*) means basically "another, different," as in chapter 18, note 2, for example. This meaning has expanded over time in the Galilee Bedouin dialects to mean *'ġēr arūḥ*, "[if I do] something other than go" and then to "I [will/shall/must] do [this] i.e. go."

13. *u-rumḥo bēn-ᵉrmāḥḥum*: "and his spear among their spears." When ', *ḥ*, or *h* (laryngeal/ pharyngeal phonemes) at the end of a word is suffixed by a bound pronoun beginning with *h*, the preceding phonemes and pronoun phonemes assimilate and change into *ḥ*, as in *ᵉrmāḥḥum* (< *ᵉrmāḥ* + *hum*), *maḥḥa* < *ma'ha*, "with her." This process exists in many other sedentary and Bedouin Arabic dialects in Israel.

14. *inta 'axūna bi-'ahed-aḷḷa w-al-xāyin yixūno 'aḷḷah* ("You are our brother in Allah's covenant, and a traitor—Allah will betray him") is another formula in these stories, and it reveals agreement and loyalty creation among partners and friends. Note Allah's presence in this phrase: Allah watches over partners' behavior (cf. chap. 4, note 3).

15. *mišam walaw*: "They went anyway." The word *walaw* (< *wa* + *law*; lit. "and + if" in a hypothetical condition sentence) has changed in time to indicate various discourse functions, mainly meaning "so what?" In other words, it means that something is unimportant, that a person does not care for something that another person does, says, or wants to do. This word is known in many dialects (for Jerusalem, cf. Piamenta, *Use of Tenses, Aspects, and Moods*, 565–67).

16. *bīha bint, subḥān al-xāliq*: "In it [lies] a girl—praise the creator [Allah]—]." When praising something or someone, as here, the speaker does not forget to refer to the Creator, who is behind everything in the world (cf. Piamenta, *Muslim Conception of God*, 22). Such praising expressions are frequent in daily speech since they also protect one against the evil eye.

17. The Galilee Bedouin narratives reveal morphophonetic variations of words, some of which reflect phonetic processes. The demonstrative pronoun *hāḏāki* ("that f.sg.") is a variety of the more usual and widespread *hāḏāk* ("that one"). *hāḏāki* derives from *hāḏāk* (m.sg.) + suffixed f. bound pronoun *hi*, with deleted *h*.

18. In *činna 'abde!* ("She may be a slave f.sg.!"), *činna* derives from the prepositional conjunction *ka* ("like") + *inn* ("that") + *a* (suffixed bound pronoun), with *č* instead of *k* (*kinna*) because of the adjacent high vowel *i*, after the deletion of *a* (< *ka-*) and the following glottal stop of *'inn-*. The meaning of činn- developed in time to "perhaps, apparently."

19. The added *-o* (the bound 3m.sg. suffix) in *ḍaḷḷo* is apparently syntactically redundant. In this book we found only eight such forms, while there were more than one hundred other forms of the verb *ḍaḷḷ*, in 3m.sg. and other persons, with the following participle (or without it), the past and imperfect tenses, but without a suffixed pronoun as in *ḍaḷḷo.* It therefore seems that the use of this *-o* in *ḍaḷḷo* (marking 3m.sg.) is due to rhythmical-phonetic factors, assimilating the monosyllabic verb form to the other bisyllabic forms of the conjugated verb (in any tense or mood). Henkin says that *ḍaḷḷa* is the usual form at least in the Negev Bedouin dialects. Henkin, personal communication, 2020. But she did not refer to other persons

with this verb. Deeper research is needed to reveal whether the rate of this form in the Galilee Bedouin dialects and the Negev dialects is the same or similar.

20. The verb *ḍaḷḷ* means "to continue, remain in the same state." It can serve as a free verb or as an auxiliary verb, governing a participle verb as here. The structure exists also in sedentary dialects (e.g., in Jerusalem; cf. Piamenta, *Use of Tenses, Aspects, and Moods*, 118).

21. The Bedouin expression *gā'(a) ma'avīs* probably derives from the words for "totally upset." *gā'* < qāʿ, "bottom of, lowest part of." Wehr, Dictionary of Modern Written Arabic, 797. *ma'avīs*, pl. of *ma'vūs*. Cf. Barthélemy, Dictionnaire arabe-français, 537, *'fs* "écraser d'un seul fois, ou en piétinant," in other words, become humiliated, crushed, or stamped by feet because of rage or excitement.

22. Apparently, *fēga-la* is a casual (shortened) form of *fā'iqa-laha*, "[it was] awake/alerted by them [the chicks]."

23. *šūḥa* is the name of a large bird of prey (cf. Barthélemy, 415). This bird is also mentioned elsewhere in this volume.

24. *yā 'abu ṣāleḥ*, "O Abu Ṣāleḥ," is calling to a revered (holy) person, "the father of good qualities/virtue." It is not a personal name of a protagonist in the story but a nickname for a righteous person. *Ṣāleḥ* is, however, also a personal name in Arabic.

25. *hāḏa zi'el min hā-r-riğāl*: "This man [Šāṭer Ḥasan] was angry with the man [the woman]." The word *riğāl*, "man," serves also to indicate a protagonist, a person in general, not specifically a male person, not even necessarily a human. Here it refers to the wife.

26. Iraqi Kurdistan: 3328; Morocco: 5183; Yemen: 60, 1355, 6173.

27. Maspero, *Popular Stories of Ancient Egypt*, 10–11.

28. Penzer, *Ocean of Story*, 1:131.

29. Burton, *Arabian Nights*, night 669.

30. Burton, night 668.

31. Kúnos, *Forty Four Turkish Fairy Tales*, 77–86.

24. My Mother Slew Me; My Father Ate Me

A. The Green Bird

NARRATOR: Ḥalīma Ḥasan Slimān

TRIBE: *ʿArab el-Zbēdāt*

IFA 17429 September 2, 1982

Note: The beginning is missing from the recording. The mother of two children, a boy and a girl, died. A woman wooed their father to marry her. The children begged the father to marry her, and he did.

1 yā būya—ǧawwaz—[hāy tugʿud, hāy tugʿud.][1] wāḥad mitǧawwaz. gāl, "hāy tḥinn ʿalēna, tḥinn ʿalēna;" xaṭab lēha u-xaḏāha. hī hāḏi ḥaṭṭat, ḥaṭṭathu(m). mū widha tuṭʿimhum. mawwatathum . . . [ʾa, hī al-ḥurma t-ṯāniya;[2] ʿārif hū.] ssā ʿīd,	1 "O father"—he married. (This [woman] is sitting.) A married man. He said, "This [woman] takes pity on us, takes pity on us." He betrothed her and married her. She opposed them [the children of his first wife]. [She] does not want to feed them, and "killed" them [wanted them to die].—(Yes, she is the second wife. He [the listener] knows.) Now, a holiday (came),
9 gāḷat lo, "lā tiḏbaḥ al-ⁱbgara. ⁱḏbaḥḥa. haḏōla yišrabum ḥalīb u-haḏōla mā yāklum ʾakel u-ǧāʿeda ʾakubb al-ʾakel u-mā baʿraf čēf inha."	9 she said to him, "Do not butcher the cow. Butcher it. Those drink milk, and these [her children] do not eat food and I keep throwing away food, and I don't know how it is that . . ."
13 hiyya ġallabat al-ⁱḫčāye. yōm-an hēča, ǧā la-hā-l-ⁱbgara u-ḏibaḥḥa. ṣārum hīč bačum, "yā būya lā tiḏbaḥ ᵃbgaretna. yā būya, lā tahawwidna."	13 She blew up the matter. When [it was] like that, he came to the cow and butchered it. They [the first wife's children] began, cried, "O father, do not kill our cow. O father, do not lower us [from our status]."
17 gāḷ-ḷēhum, "yā būya, xaḷas, widd(i)-aḏbaḥḥa." ḏibaḥ hā-l-ⁱbgara –	17 He said to them, "O son, that is it, I will butcher it." He butchered the cow.
19 w-hā-al-ʿeǧān ṣārum mīt bāčum. "ē, kēf insāwi, kēf neʿamal?" gāḷum, "lā." mā kalom.	19 And these children began crying [in sorrow], "Oh, how shall we do? How shall we do?" They said, "No" [they will not eat their cow]. They did not eat [it].

22 ʿāwad yōm ğam ʿalēha ḍyūf. gāḷat-ḷo, gāḷ-ḷēhu, “widdna niḏbaḥ lēhum ḏebīḥa.” ḏbaḥum hā-ḏ-ḏebīḥa.	22 Again, there came guests to her. She said to him, said to him, “We will butcher for them a sacrifice animal.” They butchered this sacrifice animal.
25 yōm ğābum aḏ-ḏebīḥa, ṣārat tākel hāḏi min hēn, u-hāḏi min hēn—waddarat al-lḥamāt.	25 When they brought the sacrificed animal [home], she began to eat from this [piece] and that, from here and from there, and hid the meat pieces.
28 “’e, kīf ᵉnsāwi?” wa-ḍ-ḍyūf b-il-bēt. gām ğāb . . . ğābaṭ, gḏabat wāḥad min al-ʿiğān ᵉḏbaḥato, ḥaṭṭato bi-ha-l-ğider ʿa-n-nār, u-waddarat rāso, kalo.	28 “E, what shall we do?” And the guests were [already] in the house. She brought, she took one of the children and butchered him, put him in the pot on the fire, and hid his head; they ate.
32 yōminnom kalum, ’uxto hnāk titfarrağ, lē ’uxt ᵉzġayre. gāmat ⁱgḏabat, lammat hāḏi l-ⁱʿḏām, lammathin u-ḥaṭṭathin b-waʿā u-rāḥat ⁱdmalathin.	32 When they were eating, his sister was there, looking. He had a young sister. She went and gathered those bones, she gathered them and put them in a utensil, and went and buried them.
36 yōm ⁱdmalathin b-ha-l-’areḍ, rāḥat iyyām u-ğat iyyām, yōm gāḷat, “ġēr ’arūḥ ’aṭillaʿ ʿala hā-l-ⁱʿḏāmāt, alli kēf ṣār bīhen.”	36 When she had buried them in the ground, days came and went, one day she said, “I must go and look at these bones, [see] what has become of them.”
40 yōm-inha rāḥat, ⁱftaḥat, yōm-inha ṭaragha hīč, winna ṭēr xaḏar[3] yefirr, hīč, min hā-l-’arḍ. ’aywa.	40 When she went, opened [it], then it hit her like that, lo—a big green bird flies away like that from the ground. Yes.
43 hī, mart abū gāʿda, mart ’abūha ğāʿeda hīn, miṯel mā tgūl hā-n-niswān ğāʿadīn miṯel hīn.	43 She, his father’s wife was sitting, her father’s wife was sitting here, as you say, like these women [who are] sitting here.
46 ṣār yeṣīḥ hā, “’ana ṭ-ṭēr l-axḏar, mart abūy ḏibḥatni, w-abūya kal min laḥmi, u-xayyti al-ḥanūn, la ḥanna l-lāha ʿalayha, ḥaṭṭat ʿaḏmāti bēn erxāmāti.”[yaʿani, dmalathin bal-balāṭ.]	46 This [bird] started shouting, “I am the green bird, my father’s wife killed me, and my father ate of my flesh, and my loving/merciful sister—may Allah have mercy on her—put my bones between marbles.” That is, buried them in the rock.
51 “wē, ṣīḥ, yā ṭēr, ṣīḥ.” gāil, “mā baṣīḥ ġēr tannha haḏīč al-mara tiftaḥ ᵉtommha” ʿen mart abūh.	51 “O bird, shout, o bird, shout.” He said, “I will not cry unless she, this woman, opens her mouth.” [This was] about his father’s wife.
54 yōminha ftaḥat ᵉtummha, dallāha girḏet ’ubar b-ḥal’iha. “ṣīḥ, yā ṭēr, ṣīḥ” gāl, “ġār tann haḏīč ʿād hiyya tiftaḥ ferğha.” ftaḥat ferğha winnha šnū hā-l-māl ḥāṭṭa-hā l-ferğha.	54 When she opened her mouth, he slid a bundle of needles to her throat. “Shout, o bird, shout.” He said, “[I will not stop shouting] unless this [woman] opens her dress.” She opened her dress neckline and lo—how much money she had put in it.
59 u-gāma(t) ʿād hi xaḏat al-māl u-xarrafathum “hīč hīč ṣār u-fitaḥt ar-ragga u-ṭār hā-ṭ-ṭēr.” u-ṭaḥt,	59 And she got up and took the money and told them, “This and this happened. And I opened the dry ground, and this bird flew away.” And she fell [died].

62 (w)inno 'and-mā mātat mart abū, hawwad hā-ṭ-ṭēr, u-gām, ligat es-sʿarāt b-ʿenogru, glaʿathen, winno 'axūha, winno 'axūha—lā ġayyaro z-zmān. u-hāḏa (hū).	62 When his father's wife died, [lo] the bird alighted [in the house] and got up. She [the sister] found some hairs in his "round root" [white spot on top of his head], she plucked them out, and lo, there was her brother—there was her brother—time did not change him. And this is it.

B. The Yellow Cow

NARRATOR: Maryam Šatwah
TRIBE: *'Arab el-Ḥuğērāt*
IFA 17430, September 1985

Text

There was a man with a son and a daughter. Their mother was dead. They have a stepmother. This one is their stepmother, and they graze the yellow cow to drink its milk, to milk it.

This one [the stepmother], every day she sifts the bran [*nkhaleh*—the waste that remains in the sieve] and kneads it and brings it to the children who graze the cow, so that they will eat bran, brings them with her daughter [her own daughter] and returns home.

They fed the cow with the [bran] bread and said to her, "Oh, our cow, manure us [shit for us] dried figs and bread!"

The cow manured [shit] for them dried figs and bread. They ate. Their arms, their faces became like that [full from satiation]!

On one day of the days [one day], her mother (the mother had a daughter of her own) said to her, "Take, bring them [the bran bread] and don't come back, stay with them. Let us see, I bring them bran, and their face is red and white, and I knead the dough and bake it, and they are not thin. Stay with them and see what happens."

This one, she went, brought them two breads made of bran.

These, they are hungry—bran, how can one eat bran?

They fed the cow with the two breads and said to her, "Oh, our cow shit for us dried figs and bread."

They ate until they were satisfied.

She took two dried figs and put them in her lap. The children did not see.

They said to her, "Do not say that [do not tell your mother]!"

She said, "No."

She took two dried figs and put them at her breast.

They returned in the evening.

"Oh, have not you seen anything?"

She took the two dried figs from her breast and gave them to her mother. What sort of dried figs! From the good red ones!

She said, "Ahh!"

[Next morning, the mother] she got up ill, she got up ill. "Akh, akh!"

Her husband said to her, "Come on, go to the doctor."

This one, she went to the doctor. She, she has nothing. She returned.

"Oh, what did he tell you?"

"He said to me, 'Eat a yellow cow—you will recuperate.'"

These people wanted to catch the cow.

The children said to the cow: "O our cow, do not stop, do not stop!"

And [the cow] flew [ran] like a spark [at lightning speed], the cow, and she flew like a spark.

They returned to the children and began to beat them to death.

They said, "O our cow, stop, stop!"

She stopped.

"O our cow, don't be slaughtered by sickles, by knives, by skewers!"

She did not want to be slaughtered. They went to the children. They beat them.

"O our cow, be slaughtered, be slaughtered."

She was slaughtered.

They said to her, "Do not let them skin you!"

They went to the children, they beat them.

"O our cow, let them skin you, let them skin you."

They stripped her skin and cut her, put [her meat] on the fire.

"O our cow, do not be cooked, do not be cooked!"

They put the meat on fire from morning to afternoon. Each piece of wood [they found, they put] under the pot. It was not cooked. Cold water. The fire is burning, and the water is cold. They went to the children—the two at home. Their father went to the children, he beat them.

They said to her, "Be cooked, be cooked, o our cow, be cooked."

The cow quickly was cooked. She ate it.

Then the children became like sticks of firewood [very thin].

Commentary

I recorded two versions of the story in two different tribes. These two stories can be attributed to the narrative type ATU 720, "The Juniper Tree," or in its previous name, "My Mother Slew Me; My Father Ate Me." Here are the main lines of the plot: A childless couple wishes for a child. A boy is born, but his mother dies. The little boy is slain by his cruel stepmother, who closes the lid of an apple chest on him. She cooks him and serves him to his father, who eats him unwittingly.

The boy's sister gathers up his bones and buries them under a juniper tree. A bird comes forth and sings about what has happened. It brings presents to the father and the sister and drops a millstone on the stepmother, killing her. The boy is resuscitated.[4]

Parallels of the story are familiar from all over Europe, Syria, Jordan, Israel, the Persian Gulf countries, North Africa, Ethiopia, Iran, India, and Southeast Asia. Jewish versions are also known.

The two Bedouin versions begin with a father's marriage to another woman after the death of his first wife. His children from his first wife have a yellow cow. The stepmother feeds her stepchildren with bran. The children give the bran to the cow, and the cow provides them with dried figs (or raisins and almonds). The stepmother sends her own daughter to investigate the children's deeds, and she tells her mother about the cow's deeds. The mother pretends to be ill and claims that she must eat the meat of the cow. The father slaughters the cow. The story from the ʿArab el-Ḥuǧērāt tribe ends at this point.

In the story from the ʿArab el-Zbēdāt tribe ("The Green Bird"), this section is presented briefly. Although the cow is mentioned, there is no reference to its magical properties, and the reason for the stepmother's desire to get rid of it is not explained. After killing the cow, the mother slaughters her stepson and feeds her husband with his flesh. The dead boy's sister buries his bones. A green bird rises from the grave and publicizes what has happened. The bird punishes the stepmother. It fills her throat with needles, and she dies. The sister tears hair out of the bird's head, and the bird turns out to be her resurrected brother. This part of the story matches the description of the international narrative type.

In her wide-ranging book *Negev Arabic*, Roni Henkin, a linguist who studies Arab dialects spoken by Bedouin tribes in the Negev, gives ten stories she recorded in the course of her fieldwork, including five stories that were recorded from Bedouin women in the Negev. One of the stories, "The Yellow Cow,"[5] is identical in most details to the first story I recorded in the ʿArab el-Ḥuǧērāt tribe. At the end of the story, after the cow is slaughtered and its meat cooked and served to the household, the stepmother and her children find out that the meat is bitter, and they cannot eat it. They serve it to the orphans, who do not feel any bitterness and enjoy eating it. The children collect the bones and the skin, bury the remains in the *wādi*, and continue to visit the place, but the stepmother's discriminatory treatment of them continues. It seems that burying the cow does not help to improve their situation.

In a version recorded in Yanūḥ-Ǧat, a Druze village in the Galilee (IFA 24101), the story begins with the children's biological mother, who asks her husband before her death to cut her hand, wrap it in a cloth, and punish her children with it if it should be necessary. The father marries a new wife, who finds a pretext to hurt her stepchildren and replaces the mother's hand with a wooden hand. The children are fed with the cow's milk. The stepmother slaughters the boy and feeds his flesh to her husband and his guests. The boy's sister buries his bones. From the grave, a green tree grows, and a green bird lands on it and sings about what has happened. The father is told about it and dies of pangs of conscience, and the stepmother goes mad.

Another Druze version recorded in Bēt Ǧan (IFA 22660) also opens with the mother's request before her death to punish her children with her severed hand "because a mother's hand is not painful, only teaches." The father is married to another woman. The daughter has a yellow cow that provides her with raisins and almonds instead of the bran bread given her by her stepmother. The stepmother's daughter reveals to her mother the secret of the stepdaughter. At this point, the story develops in a different direction from the previous one and contains many motifs from ATU 533, "The Speaking Horsehead."

In a Jewish version of the story from Iraqi Kurdistan (IFA 10124), the sister, on the advice of the Prophet Elijah, buries the bones of her brother after he is slaughtered by his stepmother. A huge watermelon grows from the grave, and inside it, the daughter finds her resurrected brother. The brother sings a song to his father and asks him to close his eyes, and then he drops needles into his throat and kills him. He does the same to his stepmother. It is interesting to note that in this version, as in one of the Druze versions, the father is also punished even though he was not a partner to the mother's actions. In an Arabic version recorded by Muhawi and Kanaana from a Muslim Arab woman in the village of ʿArabeh in the Galilee, both the father and the mother are punished by needles that the bird drops into their throats.[6] Then the bird turns out to be the brother, who has returned to life. An almost-identical Arab Muslim version from the Rāmallah area is mentioned in Schmidt and Kahale's book.[7] Another Muslim version of the story was recorded in the Upper Galilee in 2010 and is posted on Perez's Hebrew website.[8] This version is a combination of two story types, ATU 510, "Cinderella," and ATU 720, "The Juniper Tree."

Bushnaq provides an Egyptian version of the story.[9] This version is almost identical to the version from Muhawi and Kanaana, and here too both the father and the mother are punished. El-Shamy gives another Egyptian version, which is also identical in most of its details to the previous stories.[10] El-Shamy's version is particularly complete. The brother who became a bird sings his song to three craftsmen: a seller of needles, a seller of poisons, and a seller of candies. He drops the needles he has received in exchange for his song into his stepmother's throat and kills her. He puts the poison into his father's mouth and the candy in his sister's mouth.

As can be seen, in the Muslim and Druze versions of the story, unlike the European versions, both father and stepmother are punished. In the two Bedouin versions I collected, the father prefers the stepmother to his children. In the first story, he beats them to force them to give up the cow and allow it to be slaughtered. In the second story, he slaughters the cow at the request of his wife, despite the cries of the children and their pleas not to slaughter the cow. It seems that the father's sin is neglecting his children and handing them over to the stepmother's care, and in many versions, it is emphasized that the father does not wonder about the disappearance of his son and does not seek him.

The story of the yellow cow sometimes appears as an independent story, but it seems that it is an inseparable part of the Middle Eastern versions of the international type.

Like the narrative type ATU 450, "Little Brother and Little Sister," discussed in chapter 13, "The Girl and Her Brother Who Became a Deer," this story also emphasizes the relationship between the brother and the sister. In some of the versions, the brother cannot resist his childlike urges and lets the stepmother tempt him by grabbing him and abducting him to slaughter him, while his sister plays the role of the "responsible adult" and does her best to prevent the slaughter of her brother. This difference between a brother and a sister is also expressed in the narrative type of "Little Brother and Little Sister."

It seems that the yellow cow fulfills the role of an alternative mother. First, it provides the children with her milk, and later, it provides them with additional foods.

Hagar Salamon has examined Ethiopian versions of the story, in which the cow is called "*lameh bora*" (the cow bora, meaning a cow that has a white mark on its forehead).[11] Before her death, the mother turns to the cow and sings to her: "*Lamyeh bora, lamyeh bora, liğyochaen adera*" ("My cow bora, my cow bora, my children are in your hands—*adera*"). The word *adera* describes a kind of strong commitment, a divine obligation that must be fulfilled if someone undertakes it.

In one of the Ethiopian versions, the cow is not slaughtered. To be sure that her husband does slaughter the cow, the stepmother climbs a rock to see better. However, just as the knife is lifted toward the cow bora, the mother stumbles, falls from the rock, and dies on the spot. The cow and the children are saved, and they stay in their home.

In the Freudian interpretation, the stepmother seems to represent the negative aspect of biological motherhood, and in the Jungian interpretation, she matches the "shadow archetype," the inferior and undesirable aspect of personality that people repress because they are unwilling to admit to it.

Tamar Alexander, in her commentary on the Judeo-Yemenite version of the Cinderella story (ATU 510), writes: "In the Freudian interpretation, the stepmother represents the negative aspect of the mother's image. The prohibition and guilt of negative feelings toward the mother, who is also the object of love, create the split between the 'good mother' and the 'bad mother.' The former belongs to the past. So she is dead, and her place in the house is taken by the bad mother. In the Jungian interpretation, the stepmother represents the 'shadow figure,' the negative aspects of motherhood. These aspects are expressed in the story through the stepmother's abuse of the heroine."[12]

This interpretation also fits our story.

In many folktales, the stepmother is portrayed as someone who harasses the father's children and gives precedence to her own children. In most stories, the father plays almost no part in the family drama. He is briefly mentioned at the beginning of the story or is completely absent. In these stories, however, his responsibility for the rift in his family is emphasized. The father does not function as the head of the family, and he lets his new wife do as she pleases. In the story from the ʿArab el-Zbēdāt tribe, this situation is emphasized in a metatext statement by the narrator: "She blew up the matter."

Thus, the story criticizes the poor functioning of the father, and it is not by coincidence that he is punished for this, like the murdering mother.

The subject of cannibalism is prominent in the story. Motif G61, "Relative's flesh eaten unwittingly," is an ancient motif and already appears in Greek mythology. One myth tells of two brothers, Atreus and Thyestes. After Atreus learns that his wife has betrayed him with his brother, he kills Thyestes's sons, cooks them, and hands Thyestes his children's flesh to eat. Afterward, he presents him with their hands and feet, which have not been cooked.

In the Bedouin stories, the *ġūla* is often portrayed as a cannibalistic creature. In the *Saṭūra* story (ATU 315A, "The Cannibal Sister"), discussed in chapter 31, it is a human being, born with cannibal traits and turned into a *ġūla*, but in this story the situation is completely different. The father eating his son does so unknowingly. It is the stepmother who slaughters his son and cooks him. In many versions, the stepmother is portrayed as having been possessed by a frenzy of eating. She prepares food for her husband, tastes it, and then consumes it completely, and, to mislead the household, she cooks her stepchild instead of the eaten meat. In the Bedouin version, she first slaughters the children's cow, and in Schmidt's version, she eats the meat of an animal that has been killed in a hunt and has been brought to her by her husband. In the Egyptian version provided by

El-Shamy, the father sends his son to bring a fish to his wife so that she will cook it. The son loses the fish on his way home and tells his stepmother about it, and she slaughters him and cooks him instead of the fish. In this case, the motive is not the fear of the husband's expected wrath, for the guilt lies with his own son. The woman only exploits the situation to hurt her stepchild. The entire story revolves around the constant tension between the woman and her stepchildren.

In the story from the ʿArab el-Zbēdāt tribe, the father marries the second wife out of concern for his children. He believes that she will replace the biological mother: "This [woman] takes pity on us, takes pity on us." But soon it turns out that it was a mistake, or in the words of the narrator, "She opposed them [the children of his first wife]. [She] does not want to feed them, and 'killed' them [wanted them to die]." She wants to destroy any trace of the presence of the first wife. It can be said that, symbolically, she wants the descendants of the father from his first wife to disappear and be assimilated back into his body.

A Judeo-Español romance that I recorded from Tamar Marciano in Jerusalem, who heard it during her childhood in Morocco, tells of a husband who comes home and asks his son, "Who was here when I was gone?"[13] The son replies, "Mother's lover." She gets angry, slaughters her son, cooks him, and serves his meat to her husband to eat. While the father eats from the flesh of his son, the son's tongue turns to him and says, "Father, do not eat me, I am your flesh." The mother is punished and executed. In this case, she punishes her own son for revealing her secret to her husband.

Many psychologists have pointed out the close connection between eating and sex. There is another hint in the Bedouin story that points to this connection. The son, in the shape of the green bird, punishes his stepmother for her actions by inserting needles into her mouth and money into her vagina.

Notes

1. These first two lines reflect the fact that the narrator is not narrating the story as yet. We have not deleted this sentence because it is in the recording.

2. This story includes motifs found in other folktales. The stepmother is similar to a *ġūla*: she hates her husband's children, eats in a disorderly manner, cooks a child, and serves it to the guests to eat; she is very impure and greedy. She finally dies when the green bird thrusts needles into her throat in revenge. The boy's sister collects his bones and buries them, until he is revived as a green bird. He gets back his human form after his sister plucks poisonous elements from his head (cf. chap. 28, "Snow White").

3. The color green is *xáḏ̣ar* in Bedouin dialects instead of *'áxḏ̣ar* found in sedentary dialects (on color see chap. 6, note 4; chap. 23, note 8). Such a change in certain color names and other words was named *gaháwa syndrome*. Blanc, "Arabic Dialects of the Negev Bedouins." This process refers to words with the syllabic pattern $C_1vC_2C_3v(C)$, including verbs (cf. Bedouin *ye'áref*/sedentary *yi'rif*, "he knows") and nouns (*gaháwah*, *gháwa*, *qahwa*, *'ahwe*). In the Galilee Bedouin dialects, this process involves vowel and stress shifting to the new second syllable and deletion of the first syllable (*'a*). Thus *'áxḏ̣ar* > *'axáḏ̣ar*, "green," (e.g., in the Negev) and *xáḏ̣ar* (in the Galilee); *'áḥmar* > *ḥámar*, "red"; *'á'rağ* > (*'á*)*'árağ*, "lame, limping"; etc.

4. Uther, *The Types of International Folktales*, 1:389.

5. Henkin, *Negev Arabic*, 350–57.

6. Muhawi and Kanaana, *Speak, Bird, Speak Again*, 98–102.

7. Schmidt and Kahale, 1: 187–89.

8. Perez, Arab Versions of Cinderella stories, story no. 38, "The Green Bird," in Perez's website, 2000 [in Hebrew] http://folkmasa.org/masa/a03740.htm.

9. Bushnaq, *Arab Folktales*, 150–52.

10. El-Shamy, *Tales Arab Women Tell*, 289–92.

11. Salamon, "Lameh Bora," 232.

12. Alexander, "Haninat-Allah," 124–48.

13. You can listen to the romance sung in Ladino on Perez's website: Perez, Ladino Song Treasure, song no. 2833 "Ay Arribita arribita," in Perez's website, 2015 [in Hebrew and Ladino] http://folkmasa.org/avshir/shirp.php?mishtane=2833, Record: http://folkmasa.org/avshir/2833.mp3.

25. The Boy, the Uncle, and the Lover

NARRATOR: Ṣabḥa ʿAbūd

TRIBE: *ʿArab el-Ḥuğērāt*

IFA 18178 March 1982

1 haḏ̣āk wāḥad, bū walad. ʾummo mayyte u-ʾabū mayyet. hāḏ̣a hīn al-walad, walad ᵉzġīr. ʾabū mayyet u-ʾummo mayyte. hīn, ʿendo xāḷ—ʾax-ummo. ʾaiwa, gaʿadam, xāḷo—ʾax-ummo.	1 That one, there was a boy. His mother is dead, his father is dead. This boy here is a young boy. His father is dead, and his mother is dead. Here—he has a maternal uncle—his mother's brother. Yes, they lived [literally: sat], his maternal uncle—his mother's brother.
6 hīn, hāḏ̣a xāḷa, maskīn, ʿando wlād u-mā ʿando maṣāri. kull yōm, yāxoḏ hā-l-ᵉḥmār, yegalle(ʿ) ḥaṭab, gaṛāmi, u-yerūḥ yāxuḏhen, u-yebiḥḥen wi-yeğīb ʾačel la-wlāda.	6 Now, his maternal uncle is poor, he has children, and has not got money. Every day he takes the donkey, cuts wood, tree logs, and goes and takes them and sells them and brings food for his children.
11 hiyye marto, ke(n)-ṣāḥba wāḥad. mṣāḥba wāḥad. al-xetyār yinhağ u-hiyya (ḏ̣)ḏ̣aḷḷ yiği ʿandha ṣāḥeba. kull mā yiği ʿandha ṣāḥeba. yōm rağğaʿ ʿindha. gāḷat-lo, "šū (wi)dna netġadde?" gāḷ-(ḷ)ha, "šū (wi)ddna netġadde?" gāḷat-lo, "yaḷḷa ta-niḏbaḥḥa, ğāğa."	11 She, his wife, has a boyfriend. She had some boyfriend. The old man goes and she remains [at home]. Her friend comes to her. Whenever, her friend comes to her. One day he comes to her. She said to him, "What shall we have for lunch?" He said to her, "Let us butcher her, a hen."
18 hāḏ el-walad gāḷ-ḷo "yā xāḷi," la-ṣ-ṣobḥ, "waddīni mʿāk, widdi arūḥ ⁱmʿāk, yā xāli, ʿa-l-ḥaṭab." hāḏ̣a l-walad rāḥ ⁱmʿa xāḷo u-mayyal ʿa-hā-l-bīr u-m.. mayyal yiṣayyed ʿaṣāfīr. mayyil ṣēd ʿaṣāfīr, ṣād ʿaṣfūr. ṣād ʿaṣfūr. rawwaḥ.	18 This boy said to him, "O uncle," in the morning, "take me with you, I want to go with you, o uncle, to the woods." This boy went with his uncle and turned to this water well, turned and went to hunt birds. He turned and went to hunt birds—he hunted a bird. He went back home.

24 winno ğat tḥuṭṭ ʾačel lia u-la-ṣāḥibha. ṭagg ʿa-l-bāb al-walad, waddarato. waddarato ʿa-ḏaher al-ᵉxzāna. ʾaywa, ğe al-maġrib xāḷo, ḥaṭṭ(a) al-ᵉḥmār al-walad ʿaše, beʿad ʿād el-ʿaše ʿan al-ᵉḥmār. w-al-ᵉḥmār yešanhek.

24 And there she was putting food for herself and her friend. He knocked on the door. She hid it. She hid it on top of the cupboard. Yes. He came at sundown, his uncle, the boy put the supper for his donkey. After supper, the donkey started braying.

30 gāḷ-ḷo, “ʾagūḷ-ḷak, yā xāḷi, lēš al-ᵉḥmār yešanhek?”[1] gāḷ-ḷo “ʾā wi, yā walad.” gāḷ-ḷo, “bū ğāğe mḥammara all(i) sawatha ʿa-ḏahr al-ᵉxzāne.” gāḷ-ḷa, “ṣaḥīḥ?” gāḷat-ḷo “ī, ʾā waḷḷa yā zalame, ʾinta titʿab, u-ḏibaḥt ha-ğ-ğāğa. mišān tōkel.” gāḷ-ḷha, “yaḷḷa, ḥāṭṭīha, ta-nōkel.” ğābatha u-kelum.

30 He said to him, “I’ll tell you, o my uncle, why the donkey is braying.” He said to him, “What, boy?” He said to him, “There is a roasted chicken she has prepared on top of the cupboard.” He said to her, “Is it right?” She said to him, “Yes, by Allah, man, you are getting tired [all day long] and I killed this chicken for you to eat.” He said to her, “Well, then bring it forth, so we eat it.” She brought it and they ate them.

38 waḷḷa, aṣ-ṣobḥ ʿāwad miša aṣ-ṣobḥ. ʿandinma miša, rāḥ al-walad gāḷ-ḷo, “(wi)ddi arūḥ maʿāk, yā xāḷi.” mayyal al-walad yeṣayyid ʿaṣāfīr, ṣād hā-l-ʿaṣfūr u-libad. zī ʾawwal miṯel mā gaddim.

38 By Allah, in the morning, again he went in the morning. When he went, the boy went and said to him, “I want to go with you, o my uncle.” The boy turned to hunt birds. He caught this bird and hid, as in the first time, as it was before.

43 gāḷat-ḷo “šū-(wi)ddna, šū-(wi)ddna nitġadde.” gāḷ-ḷha ṣāḥibha “taḏbaḥīn ğōz zġālīl.” ḏibḥat zġālīl. ğē el-walad ʿandinma ğeʿadam widdum yāklūn, iğa al-walad yidugg ʿala l-bāb. dagg el-walad ʿa-l-bāb, waddarathin. kullayāthin ʿa-ḏahr al-ᵉxzāne.

43 She said to him, “What shall we eat for lunch?” He said to her, her friend, “Butcher for us a pair of chicks.” She butchered chicks. The boy came when they were sitting down, were about to eat. The boy came, knocked on the door. The boy knocked on the door, and she hid them. All of them on top of the cupboard.

50 [yiğiē l . . .] maʿa-l-maġrib. baʿad al-ʿaša wann-el-ᵉḥmār ṣār yešanhek. gāḷ-ḷo, “mā-lak yā walad?” gāḷ-ḷo, “bū zaġālīl maḥṭūṭāt ʿa-ḏahr al-ᵉxzāne. tanni nğīb-ilna nākulhen, bibaṭṭel al-ᵉhmār yešanhek.” gāḷ-ḷa, “ḥurma, ṣaḥīḥ?” gāḷat . . . kalōhom. gāḷat-lo, “walḷḷa yā zalame, ʾinta titʿab u-besawwi-lak tōkel.” kalūhen.

50 He [her husband] came with sundown. After dinner, lo—the donkey began to bray. He said to him, “What is the matter with you, boy?” He said to him, “There are chicks put away on top of the cupboard. Until we bring them for us to eat them, the donkey will stop braying.” He said to her, “O woman, is that right?” She said. . . . They ate them. She said to him, “By Allah, man you are getting tired [all day long] and I made it for you to eat.” They ate them.

59 aṣ-ṣubḥ oxra miṯel. ğē aṣ-ṣāḥeb. ḏibḥat lo baṭṭa. ğē al-walad. alli . . . hū ḏibeḥha u-maʿaṭūha u-gaḷatha u-widdhom yāklūha, dagg ʿala-l-bāb ğāy. waddarathen.

59 Next morning, again another example [like it]. The friend came and she killed for him a goose. The boy came. That . . . he killed it, they plucked its feathers, and she roasted and they wanted to eat it, the boy knocked on the door, coming. She hid it.

64 ǧē al-maġrib al-xatyār, gāḷ-ḷa, “yā xāḷi, walak, ʿandak al-ᵉḥmar?” gāḷ-ḷo, “bū baṭṭa ʿala l-ᵉxzāne.” gāḷ-ḷo “ṭayyeb, yā ḥurma, ṣaḥīḥ hēk?” gāḷat. ǧabūha, kalūha. ʾaywa . . . walla . . .

64 The old man came in the evening and said to him, “O my uncle, why, have you got the donkey?” He said to him, “There is a goose on top of the cupboard.” He said to him, “Well, o woman, is it right like that?” She said. . . . They brought it, ate it. Yes . . . by Allah. . . .

69 aṣ-ṣobḥ ʾağa ʿandha ṣāḥibha, yamm ṣaʿaq al-walad, u-ṣāḥibha ʿandha, mā žari yiṭlaʿ az-zalame. wēn waddarato? waddarato bū ʿandha, birmīl, birmīl ⁱkbīr u-bū ṭaḥīn. waddarat az-alima b-barmīl aṭ-ṭaḥīn, la-yešūf al-walad.

69 In the morning, her friend came to her, and at that time the boy shouted, while her friend was with her. He, the man, did not dare to come out. Where did she hide him? She hid him in this barrel, a big barrel with flour. She hid the man in the barrel, so that the boy would not see [him].

75 walla, ağa el-maġrib, ḥaṭṭ al-ʿaša la-l-ᵉḥmār u-baʿad al-ᵉḥmār, al-ʿaša. ṣār al-ᵉḥmār yešanheč. gāḷ-ḷo, “mā li-l-ᵉḥmār, yā walad?” gāḷ-ḷo “widdo yeḥammi dist mayy ta-yiġli u-yinḥaṭṭ ab-gaḷb barmīl aṭ-ṭḥīn, u-baṭṭaḷḷ al-ᵉḥmār yešanheč.”

75 By Allah, in the evening, he put the dinner for the donkey. After the donkey—the dinner, the donkey began braying. He said to him, “What is the problem with the donkey, o boy?” He said to him, “It wants water to boil and be poured in the flour barrel, and then the donkey will stop braying.”

81 gāḷ, “ṣēḥ hā?” gāḷ “gūmi, yā ḥurma, ḥammi dist mayy u- ḥaṭṭi b-gaḷba.” gāmat al-ḥurma, ḥimlat dist mayy ta-yeġli, waddarato b-gaḷb al-bermīl, wanna z-zlima b-gaḷbo, wunno wāğeʿ wunno mayyet.

81 He said, “Is that right.” He said, “Get up, o woman, boil a cauldron of water and pour it in it.” The woman got up, heated a cauldron with water until it boiled, and poured it in the barrel, and there was the man in it, and lo—he fell out, and lo—he was dead.

87 ṣār al-xetyār yegūḷ, “bayyē, xarrabt bēti, bayyē,” w-iyṣayyeḥ u-yibki, u-šnū hāḏa xatyār, u-ṣār yiḏrabo, maʿa finğān mn-al-xōf. gāḷ-ḷo, “yā xāḷi, yā xāḷi, lā txāf, lā txāf.” gāḷ-ḷo, “bayyē, ḏibeḥt,[2] xarrabt bēti.” al-xatyār ṣār yeḏārib, fa-rənnto[3] ṣārat min šān yemūt, lēš lā.

87 The old man started saying, “Oh my, you have destroyed my house, oh my,” and he was shouting and crying. And what this old man, he started hitting him, with a coffee cup, because of his fear. He [the boy] said to him, “O my uncle, don’t be afraid, don’t be afraid, don’t be afraid.” He said to him, “Oh my, I am killed, you have destroyed my house.” The old man started trembling and his screaming began because he would die. Why not [fear it].

94 ʾaği hā-l-walad, ğāb hā-l-ᵉḥmār,[4] ğāb hā-l-zalame, laḥḥago ʿal-l-ᵉḥmār, ḥabbal ʿalē,

94 The boy came, brought the donkey, brought the man, attached him to the donkey, and tied him with a rope.

97 yōman hīn, hanāk miṯel yaʿani, bū biyāder, gaḅuḷ, gamḥ, yḥaṭṭūn ʿa-l-biyāder, u-ḥaṭṭ hāl-^{e}ḥmār ʿa-l-bēder, wa-hā-l-zalame ʿalē, ē . . . mayyet.	97 When here . . . there, like, that is . . . there [were] threshing floors, in the past, wheat, they used to put it on the threshing floor—and he let the donkey to the threshing floor, and the man on him . . . er . . . dead.
101 ṣāḥeb al-bēder yegūḷ-ḷak "hē . . . walad, walak, gīm al-^{e}ḥmār,"—z-zalame mayyet—haḏāk wūḷi libad el-walad? waḷḷa libad, yaʿani, ḥadd al-bēdar. ğa ṣāḥeb al-bēdar, ğāb al-maḏrūb ugāḷ yuḏrub hā-l-zalame u-hū ʿala-l-^{e}ḥmār.	101 The threshing floor owner was saying [to you], "He, boy, oh, get the donkey away"—the man was dead—this one [the boy], where did the boy hide? He hid, that is to say, near the threshing floor. The owner of the threshing floor came, brought a stick, and wanted to hit the man while he was on the donkey.
107 wagaʿ az-zalama, hū mayyit. ṣaʿaq al-walad, "yā bayyē, ḏibḥu ʾabūy, yā bayyē, ḏibḥu ʾabūy." gāḷ-ḷo, "yā walad, lā txāf, lā txāf, lā txāf, lā txāf, yā walad, lā txāf.." ʿobṭo, u-ḏammo, u-xaḏam az-zalame, rāḥam gubrō.	107 The man fell, and [he was] dead. The boy started shouting, "Oh, my father, they killed my father, oh, my father, they killed my father." He said to him, "O boy, don't be afraid, don't be afraid, don't be afraid, don't be afraid, o boy, don't be afraid." He hugged him and embraced him, and they went and buried him.
113 gubrō u-ḥammalō-lo sabʿ-^{e}ğmāl gamḥ u-siḥab hā-ğ-ğammāl bihin u-rawwaḥ, ʿala bēt al-xatyār. u-l-xityār baʿade yeḏāreb ʿala siğāno. ʾaywa, waḷḷa, gaʿadom. ṣārom.	113 They buried him, and they loaded for him seven camels with flour and brought—the camel driver brought them and went home, to the old man's home. The old man was still shaking, on his legs. Yes, by Allah. They sat down they were. . . .
118 bāt ağ-ğemmāl, gām b-al-lēl, hāḏa al-walad, b-al-lēl, rāḥ yeğīb hā-ṭ-ṭaḥīn, u-xarraʾa(t), ḥaṭṭ ʿalē ḥarīra, ḥaṭṭa hēč, u-ḥaṭṭo, u-ḥaṭṭo be-banṭalōn al-e-ğammāl.	118 The camel driver spent the night [slept] there. In the night, the boy got up, at night, went and brought flour and heated it and poured hot soup on it and put it like that, and put it in the camel driver's trousers.
122 gām ağ-ğammāl b-al-lēl, ḥass, ḥass hāl-ṣafarmo wunno mayye. gām ağ-ğammāl b-al-lēl winno minhazem, minhazem minno. minhazem. daššar ağ-ğmāl u-daššar hā. ʾağa, ğe ʿala l-xetyār gāḷ-ḷo, "čēf yā xāḷi, hāḏ ʾani ğibt lak gamḥ, u-ğibt lak ^{e}ğmāl, u-ʾana ġnītak. muš ^{i}mlīḥ hēk?" gāḷ-ḷo, "mlīḥ."	122 The camel driver got up at night and felt his trousers and lo—[it was full of] water. The camel driver ran away, ran away from him, left the camels, and left that. He [the boy] came to the old man [his uncle] and said to him, "O my uncle, I brought flour for you, and brought you camels and made you rich. Isn't it good like that?" He said, "[It's] good."

Commentary

The story is known as the narrative type ATU 1358C, "Trickster Discovers Adultery: Food Goes to Husband instead of Lover." Uther gives a detailed description of the type:

> A traveler (a student, soldier, etc.) asks for food and lodging, so a housewife gives him plain food and tells him to sleep in the haystack. He sees her (through the window) feasting in the company of her lover. When the husband comes home unexpectedly, he tells the traveler he would invite him in if he could offer him decent food. When the wife pretends that there is no food in the house, the traveler (with the help of a bird or a magical implement) pretends to use magic to produce the (hidden) food leftover from the feast. He uses pretended magic a second time to raise the devil (actually the hidden lover) and chase him away. The lover and the wife or the host give the traveler a generous reward. Often the husband buys the magic object from him.[5]

In the Bedouin story, the child plays the role of the trickster, who reveals the lover. He claims to interpret the donkey's braying as a means to reveal the hidden food. At the end of the story, the child causes the death of the lover and manages to get rid of the corpse with a trick: he accuses another person, who has no connection to the heroes of the story, of killing the lover. Fearing that the trickster will accuse him of manslaughter, this person pays him hush money. Later, using another trick, the child causes the camel driver to flee the house and thus steals his property. This part of the story is found in a close narrative type, ATU 1535, "The Rich and the Poor Farmer." It is also found in the Grimm brothers' *Märchen*[6] and in a story from Hans Christian Andersen, "Little Claus and Big Claus," where the hero's adversary tries to kill him but hits the hero's dead grandmother and is later is charged with her murder.

The hero of the Bedouin story is an orphaned child who was adopted by his uncle. In this position, he cannot turn directly to his uncle and accuse the uncle's wife of adultery. He therefore uses various tricks to keep the lover out of the house without his uncle's knowledge. Three times, he manages to rob the lover of his meal and leave it for his uncle, but that is not enough to get rid of the lover. The fourth time, he takes a more severe step: by interpreting the donkey's braying, he causes the uncle to order his wife to pour boiling water into the flour barrel. Forced to do what he asks of her, the woman murders her lover with her own hands. It seems that throughout the story the landlord does not suspect that the slain man is his wife's lover, and he takes responsibility for his death, as he himself has given his wife an explicit order to pour boiling water into a barrel.

Adultery is considered a serious offense among the Bedouins. When a man exposes his wife's adultery, he is supposed to kill both her lover and her. The boy is not eager to destroy the family unit with whom he has taken shelter. He finds a creative way of killing the lover and punishing the woman for her actions, but he does all this without revealing her secret to the betrayed husband.

Later he finds a creative way to remove the corpse and, by the way, enrich his uncle. Not only does the owner of the threshing floor pay the child hush money, a seven-camel load of wheat, but he is forced to flee from the house and leave his camels behind, after the child uses another trick and makes him think he has made a mess in his pants. The owner of the barn prefers to abandon his camels and flee rather than lose his honor and be shown publicly as someone who has no control over his needs.

The story was told by a woman. It seems that it offers a creative way to deal with adultery, by a path that will not necessarily harm the adulteress and her lover or expose the husband's disgrace to the public. The boy solves the problem peacefully, preserving the integrity of the family, preventing the woman from being killed, and, at the same time, causing her to be punished. The responsibility lies with the donkey and the child's interpretation of its braying, and not with the adult members of the household.

In a story that Abraham Ben-Shahar shares in his book *From the Arabic Folklore*, entitled "The Murder of the Bedouin in the Negev," a young man tries to sneak into a girl's tent in the dead of night because he believes she is in love with him.[7] The girl resists, and the boy flees. However, the girl chases him and takes his *kafiyyah* (square cotton headkerchief). The next day, the girl tells her story to her five brothers, and, with the help of the *kafiyyah*, they identify him. Afterward, they murder the young man. At their trial, the judge asks them, "Is it true that the victim only touched the girl's foot?" They reply, "Even if he did not touch her, and we would have seen him nearby in a close place that would have roused our doubts, we would have killed him too!"

In another story, "Murder on the Grounds of Family Honor," Ben-Shahar writes about a young rural woman who falls in love with a distant relative and maintains a relationship with him after he promises to marry her.[8] The act is publicized, and the girl's family quickly marries the couple but finds in their actions a flaw and a violation of their honor. The man is forced to leave his village with his young wife. Nine years later, the woman's brothers come to sue for their insult. They demand three things: first, financial compensation; second, a marriage between his sister and one of them; and third, permission for prenuptial relations between the man and the sister before the wedding, so that she will not be a virgin at her wedding, thus wiping out their shame. The husband agrees to the first two conditions but not to the third. Afterward, during a visit to a wedding ceremony, the husband and wife stay at the brothers' home. Taking advantage of the opportunity, the brothers throw a grenade into the couple's room. The husband is killed and the woman is injured. Thus, the brothers obtain their revenge.

It seems that these stories illustrate the attitude of Arab society to adultery or loss of virginity before marriage. On the other hand, the Bedouin story related above offers a creative way to solve the problem without hurting the people involved.

Notes

1. The verb *šanhak* combines the root *nahaq* and *šahaq*, all meaning "to bray [like a donkey]." These three verbs exist in the sedentary dialects in Israel, but in the Bedouin tales of this collection, we find only the combined variety.

2. *ḏibeḥt*, "I am killed, butchered," is another example of internal passive verb forms. Internal passive verb forms exist in LA/MSA but are lost in sedentary dialects, whereas Bedouin dialects have partly retained them, though they are rather rare (cf. chap. 18, note 3). In the active past tense conjugation, the form would be, for example, *ḏabaḥt* or *ḏebaḥt*, "I slew."

3. In *fa-rənto*, "and his sound, scream," *fa-* is the coordinating particle ("and"), like *wa-*. Its use is rather limited and does not occur often in the colloquial Arabic dialects. The root *rnn* (in *rənto*) occurs in MSA.

4. In *'ağī hā-l-walad, ğāb hā-l-ᵉḥmār*, "This boy came and brought this donkey," note the verb form *'ağī* instead of *'ağa* for the narrative imperative (instead of *ta'āl*, the imperative form of this verb). Cf. chapter 17, note 4.

5. Uther, *The Types of International Folktales*, 2:162.

6. Grimm, *The Original Folk and Fairy Tales of the Brothers Grimm*, story 61.

7. Ben-Shahar, *From the Arabic Folklore*, 231–34.

8. Ben-Shahar, 235–37.

26. The Inheritance Case

NARRATOR: Ḥasan Maḥmūd Swēṭāt

TRIBE: *ʿArab el-Saʿadiyya*

IFA 17423 September 2, 1982

1 kān fī wāḥad, u-xaḷḷaf ṯalṯ-^{i}wlād. aṯ-ṯalṯ-^{i}wlād haḏōl, ṭabʿan kān ʿando weld u-ʾarzāg—min baʿad mā yemūt al-ʾinsān, uwlādo biddhen innhen yitwarraṯu, walla lāʾ? biddhon yitgāsamu al-xuṣūṣ, al-māl aw al-ʾarḏ u-yefarrgu ʿala baʿaḏhen.[1]	1 There was one, and he had three children. These three children, naturally he had children and property—after he dies, a person, his children want to inherit, isn't it? They want to split the things, the money or the ground, and split them between them.
7 gabuḷ-mā māt, gāḷ, ʿala-waǧeh mā-biddo yemūt, gāḷ, "mḥemmad yāraṯ,[2] u-mḥemmad yāraṯ u-mḥemmad mā yāraṯ." mā sammā, lā gāḷ ^{a}ḥsēn wa-la ʿali wa-la (ʾe)sḥāg. ḥaka, tā-l-gāḷ "mḥemmad yāraṯ, u-mḥemmad yāraṯ u-mḥemmad mā yāraṯ." gāḷ hāḏa flān mā yāraṯ. ʾisḥāg aw ḥasan aw ʿali mā yāraṯ—gāḷ "mḥemmad yāraṯ u-mḥemmad mā yāraṯ."	7 Before he died, he said, just when he was about to die, he said, "Muḥammad will inherit, Muḥammad will inherit, and Muḥammad will not inherit." He did not name, did not say Ḥusēn, not ʿAli, not Isḥāq. He spoke, he said, "Muḥammad will inherit, Muḥammad will inherit, and Muḥammad will not inherit." He said this person would not inherit. Isḥāq or Ḥasan or ʿAli. He said, "Muḥammad will inherit, and Muḥammad will not inherit."
16 widdhin yeʿarfu mīn mḥammad alli mā yāraṯ. kīf biddhin yeʿamalu? al-ʿarab fī ʿindha šarʿ, al-bedu. biddhin yeʿarafu mīn alli mā yāraṯ. muškila hāy. gāḷu, bi-rrū(ḥ)[3] ʿala š-šarʿ. siḥbu ḥālhin hā-ṯ-ṯalāṯa u-hum rāyiḥīn ʿala š-šarʿ.	16 They want to know which is Muḥammad who is not going to inherit, how [what] should they do? The Bedouins have, they have law, the Bedouins. They want to know who will inherit. This is a problem. They said they would go to the law [court]. They set out these three and they were going to the law [Bedouin court].

22 wa-hinna ba-ṭ-ṭarīg, lagu g^{y}amal, waṣfu kaḏa kaḏa kaḏa. ğimal, 'aṯar ğimal. (h)umma lagum al-'aṯar tabaʿo, mā šāfum ağ-ğimal. 'amma 'ağu, gāḷu, wāḥad gāḷ, "ağ-ğimal waṣfu kaḏa," wāḥad gāḷ, "ağ-ğimal waṣfu kaḏa." wāḥad gāḷ, "ağ-ğimal waṣfu kaḏa."	22 While [they are] on their way, they come across a camel, whose features were such, such, and such. A camel, a camel's footsteps. They found its footsteps, did not see the camel. But they said, one [of them] said, "The camel, its features are such." One [of them] said, "The camel, its features are such." One [of them] said, "The camel, its features are such."
29 lagāhum ṣāḥb-al-ğimal, gāḷ-ḷhum, "mā šuftū-li ağ-ğimal?" gāḷ-ḷo wāḥad, "waḷḷa, ğimalak 'azʿar—mā 'ilo ḏēl?" gāḷ-ḷo, "'ā, waḷḷa." naṭṭ aṯ-ṯāni gāḷ-ḷo, "ğimalak mḥammal tam^{u}r?" gāḷ-ḷo, "'a, waḷḷa, ğamali mḥammal tamar." naṭṭ aṯ-ṯāliṯ, gāḷ-ḷo, " ğimalak ʿawar?"	29 The camel's owner met them and said to them, "Haven't you seen [for me] the camel?" One [of them] said to him, "By Allah, is your camel tailless, it does not have a tail?" He said to him, "Yes, by Allah." The second one jumped and said to him, "By Allah, is your camel carrying dates?" He said to him, "Yes, by Allah. My camel is carrying dates." The third one jumped and said, "Is your camel blind in one eye?"
36 gāḷ-ḷo, "'a. wēn ğimali?" gāḷu-ḷo, "mā šifnā." gāḷ- ḷo, "lā', 'inta 'axaḏt al-ğimal." "'axaḏt ağ-ğimal"—"mā šift ağ-ğimal" "'inta 'axaḏt ağ-ğimal"—"mā šift ağ-ğimal." gāḷu-ḷo, "yaḷḷa, ihna rāyiḥīn ʿa-š-šarʿ, wa-'inta taʿāl, rūḥ maʿāna ʿala-š-šarʿ." gāḷ-ḷēhum "zēn." siḥbu ḥālum kullayāthom u-rāyiḥīn ʿala-š-šarʿ.	36 He said to him, "Yes, where is my camel?" They said to him, "By Allah, we haven't seen it." He said to him, "No, you have taken the camel." "You took the camel"—"I didn't see the camel"—"You took the camel"—"I didn't see the camel." They said to him, "Come on, we are going to the court, and you come, go with us to court." He said to them, "Good." They took off, all of them, going to court.
44 lifam ğamma ʿala bēt aš-šarʿ, u-gaʿdam. ṭabʿan min baʿad ma gaṛṛbam, sa'alhum al-mʿazzeb. 'aḷḷa yaʿalam, innu min baʿad sāʿa, 'amma hū, ʿind al-bedu, yuguʿdam ṯlaṯ-iyyam u-ṯulṯ an-nhār tann-yisyal al-bēt šnū ṭalabak.	44 They turned and came to the house of the court [judge] and sat down. Naturally, after they had approached, the host [house owner] asked them. Allah knows, if [it was] after an hour. However, it is [a habit] with the Bedouins, they sit three days and a third day until the house asks what is your request.
50 min baʿad mā gaʿadam se'alam, "šū ṭalabak, šnū ṭalabkam." gāḷu-ḷo, "iḥna, 'abūna bī warā erzāg ketīr. w-eḥna xwān. u-'abūna gabeḷ-mā māt gāḷ "mḥammad yāraṯ, u-mḥammad yāraṯ, u-mḥammad mā yāraṯ." u-kullayātna widna naḥfaz (w)uṣīt 'abūne, 'amma m-iḥna ʿārfīn ukamān kullayātna widna niʿeref, mīn el-mḥammad alli mā yāraṯ."	50 After they had sat [down for a while], he asked them, "What is your [singular] request, what are your [plural] requests?" They said to him, "We, our father, there is after him much property and we are brothers. And our father, before he had died, said, "Muḥammad will inherit, Muḥammad will inherit, and Muḥammad will not inherit. And all of us want to keep our father's will. However, we do not know and also all of us want to know, who is Muḥammad, who is not going to inherit."

59 gāḷ-ḷo, "'inte," gāḷ-ḷo, "'ani marrēt ʿalēhum, u-tlagēt 'ana wiyyāhum u-mḏayyeʿ ğamali, u-sa'althum ʿan igʸ-gʸamal. wāḥad gāḷ-ḷi gʸmalak 'azʿar, wāḥad gāḷ-ḷi gʸmalak mḥammal tamᵒr, wāḥad gāḷ-ḷi, ğimalak aʿawar. qilt-illom "hāḏ 'intam alli 'axaḏtam ğamali," u-humma qālu li, "mā 'axaḏna ğimalak, u-ğīna la-ʿandak."	59 He said to him, "You." He said to him, "I passed by them and I met with them and I have lost my camel. I asked them about the camel. One said to me your camel is tailless; one said your camel is carrying dates; one said to me, your camel is blind in one eye. I said to them, 'It is you who have taken my camel,' and they said to me, 'We haven't taken your camel, come with us to you [to the judge].'"
68 ğē, gaʿad, u-hū yamm gāḷ-ḷahum, "'intam šuftam ağ-ğimal?" gāḷ-ḷo, "lā, mā šufna ağ-ğimal." gāḷ-ḷo, "inta, šnū ʿarrafak inna ağ-ğimal mḥammal tamᵒr?"	68 He [the judge] came, sat down exactly next to them, and said to them, "Have you seen the camel?" They said to him, "No, we haven't seen the camel." He said to him, "You, what let you know that the camel was carrying dates?"
72 gāḷ-ḷo, "la'inna al-ğimal, ad-dibbān yeḥibb al-ḥala, w-ad-dibbān yibbaʿ[4] ʿala aṯar al-ğimal. hāḏa dalāyil 'inno marr ğimal u-kamān 'iḏa yikūn damm 'iben -'ādam w-ad-dibbān yešimm rīḥto, bīği, aw yešumm rēḥ aṭ-ṭēr—yīği, 'aᵉ?."	72 He said to him, "Because a camel, a fly loves sweet, and the fly follows the camel's traces. This is the proof that a camel went by. In addition, if there is human blood and the fly smells its smell, it comes, or if it smells the smell of a bird—it comes. Eh?"
78 hassaʿ gāḷ-ḷo, "mā bikūn, miš maʿagūl inno l-ğimal kān mayyit, lā'. 'aṯar ğimal. maʿnāto inno hāḏ al-ğimal daššar 'aṯar warā alli baṯṯ al-ḥilu. lainnum kān la'ēna al-ğamal mayyit."	78 Now he said to him, "It does not happen, it is not logical that the camel was dead, no. Camel's traces mean that this camel left behind itself [signs] that disseminate the sweet. Because [otherwise] we would find the camel dead."
83 gāḷ-ḷo, "inta, šū ʿarrafak innu al-ğimal azʿar, mā ilu ḏēl?" gāḷ-ḷo, "la'inno ligēt al-baʿar tabaʿ ağ-ğimal, waqt-il-kāin yuḏrob al-baʿar, mā yesarb sarb wāḥad, yunṯur ḥabba hanāk u-ḥabba hanāk. hāḏa ḏēl ağ-ğimal gaṣīr. yunṯur al-baʿar tabaʿa."	83 He [the judge] said to him, "You, what made you know that the camel was tailless?" He said to him, "Because I found the camel's droppings, when it drops the droppings, it does not do it in a straight row. It scatters it: a piece there and a piece there. This, a camel's tail is short, and it scatters its droppings."
90 gāḷ-ḷo, "inta šū ʿarrafak inno ğ-ğimal ʿawar?" gāḷ-ḷo, "la'anna ağ-ğimal, min nāḥiyet ʿēn al-yemīn ʿeddet maḥallāt, kān yedūs ʿala šōk alli muš lāzem yedūs ʿalē. u-hā ḥaywān,	90 He said to him, "You, what made you know that the camel is blind in one eye?" He said to him, "Because the camel, from the side of the right eye, in several places was treading on thorns on which it was not necessary to tread. This is an animal,
95 al-ḥaywān yeʿarif inno hāy, hāy elli yedūs ʿalē bdāl mā yīği ʿala ḥadd al-ḥağar yidūs ʿala ṭaraf al-ḥağar. yaʿani, muš šāyif, aw itbaḥtar ib-ḥağar aw itbaḥtar bi-'iši mū lāzim itbaḥtar bī."	95 "and the animal knows that on which it treads instead of going on the edge of a stone, it treads at the side of the stone. That is, it cannot see, or it bumps at a stone or hits something, which is not necessary to bump against."

100 gāḷ-ḷo, "rūḥ dawwer inta ʿala ğmalak." ʾassa iḥna qunna (=qulna) inno [$_{H}$lakaḥ$_{H}$] bi-ğ-ğamal, alli lāgāhum, u-gāḷ-ḷo, "ʾenta ᵉtṣeḥḥ-ʾetrūḥ ᵉtdawwer ʿala ğimalak tannak tirgaʿ. hadōl al-ğimāʿa mā ʾaxadō-lak al-ğimal tabaʿak. ʿala ḥasab al-ʾaṯar w-al-farğ alli ʿindhom ʿerfam inno ğmelak waṣfo min kaḏa u-kaḏa." [child weeping]

100 He said to him, "Go look for your camel." Now, we said that he ($_{H}$lakaḥ$_{H}$) took the camel, [the man] who had met them; and [the judge] said to him, "You will rightly go and look for your camel until you return. That group did not take your camel from you. According to the traces and the differences, which they had, they knew that your camel's characteristics were such and such." [child weeping]

109 ʾassa u-hinne māšīn . . . ʾassa wa-hinne māšīn, wuṣlu la-bēt aš-šarʿ, la-ʿind al-gāḏi hāḏa, dār aš-šarʿ.

109 Now, as they were going . . . now as they were going, they reached the judge's home, to this judge, the judge's house.

112 ʾağa min baʿad-mā gaʿado wa-ḥaṭṭam ilhem el-ʾakel [šāyef], kān al-ⁱmaʿzzeb, hū al-gāḏi, kān b(e)rrīt al-bēt, b(e)rrīt al-bāb. ʾağa wāḥad minnīham, gāḷ, "waḷḷāhi, ⁱmʿazzibna iben ḥarām." wāḥad minnīhum gāḷ, "al-laḥam hāḏ laḥam kalb alli dāro ʿind al-ⁱmʿazzib." wāḥad gāḷ, "waḷḷāhi, al-ⁱmʿazzbe"—yōminno šamm rīḥt az-zād—"z-zād miš ᵉnḏīf."

112 He [the judge] came after they had sat down, and they had put food for them. See, the host, who was the judge, he was outside the house, outside the door. One of them said, "By Allah, our host is a bastard [illegitimate son]." One of them said, "This meat is the meat of a dog whose house is at the host's place." One said, "By Allah, the hostess—when he smelled the odor of the food—the food is not clean [it is impure]."

122 hāḏ-al-gāḏi itʿağğab, "šū hadōl ağ-ğimāʿa ğāyīn yitgāḏam ʿandi

122 This judge was surprised. "What are this group coming to let me judge them

124 wa-l-maʿlūmāt hāy kullayātha tabaʿhom?" gāḷ, "gabuḷ la ʾafūt ʾašraʿ ʿalīham, widdi ʾarūḥ ʾašūf inno hāy il-ʾašyā ṣaḥīḥa ʾaw la."

124 "while they have all this information?" He said, "Before I enter to judge them, I will go and see if these things are true or not."

128 rāḥ gāḷ la-martu, gāḷ-elha "taʿāli. ʾinti ʾeḥči al-maḏbūṭ. ʾinti naḏīfe walla m-inti neḏīfe? ʾeḥči al-maḏbūṭ." gāḷat-lo, "waḷḷāhi, ʾani bī ʿālayya al-ʿāda." fa-šū al-āda? [$_{H}$vezet$_{H}$ (<$_{H}$/veset/$_{H}$)]. "u-ʾana miš ᵉnḏīfe." yaʿani, ṭabxat az-zād u-hiyye miš ᵉnḏīfe. [šāyef?] ṭayyeb.

128 He went and said to his wife, "Come. You—tell [me] the truth. Are you clean or not clean? Say the truth." She said to him, "By Allah, I have the period." (Do you know what a period is? $_{H}$veset$_{H}$ [menstruation].) "And I am not clean." That is, she cooked the food while she was not clean. See? Good.

135 rāḥ la-l-rāʿi. gāḷ-ḷo, "ʾinta, aḏ-ḏebīḥa alli ḏabaḥta la-hadōl an-nās, aḏ-ḏebīḥa lli ḏebaḥta la-hadōl an-nās, ʾinta ḏibaḥt—ṣaḥīḥ inno čalb alli ḏibaḥto? waḷḷāhi, ʾiḏā mā teḥči al-maḏbūṭ, inni rāsak ġēr ʾagṭaʿ(a)."

135 He went to the shepherd. He said to him, "You, the butchered animal which you killed for those people, the butchered animal which you killed for those people, you butchered—is it correct that it was a dog which you butchered? By Allah, if you do not tell the truth, your head—I will cut it off."

141 gāḷ-ḷo, “waḷḷāhi, yā gāḍi, ’ana ṣaḥīḥ rāʿi, we-’ani ’aḥčīk b-al-maḍbūṭ. waḷḷāhi, ’inni, ’ani mā ḏibaḥt līhom čalb. ’amma ’ani, kānat ʿindīne čalbe, w-ač-čalbe kānat wālde, u-xalag hāḏ al-xarūf min baṭan ’emmo, u-šufto raḍaʿ min ak-kalbe. reḍaʿ min ak-kalbe. ’assa hinne, wāḥad minnīhum gāḷ inno ḏebaḥ lēna kalb,$[_{H}az_{H}]$ minšān al-xarūf reḍaʿ min al-čalba, gāl kān(a) hū maḍbūṭ.”

141 He said to him, “By Allah, o judge, I am really a shepherd, and I am telling you the truth. By Allah, I, I have not butchered for them a dog. But I, we had [at our place] a bitch and the bitch had given birth, and this sheep was born from the belly of its mother, and I saw it sucking with the bitch. It sucked [milk] of the bitch. Now they, one of them said that he had butchered a dog for us, $(_{H}az_{H})$ then since the sheep sucked with the bitch, he said, it was correct.”

151 rāḥ la-’ummo. gāiḷ-ḷa, “waḷḷāhi, ’iḏā mā tiḥki al-maḍbūṭ, ġēr b-as-sēf, ’agṭaʿ rāseč. ’ani ʿirift inni ’ani ’iben ḥarām u-saḥīḥ inni ’ani ’iben ḥarām, ġēr ʾtgulī-li hassa mīn ’abūy. bī nās illi gāḷat li inni ’ani ’iben ḥarām. widdeč ᵉtgūlī-li mīn ’abūy.” gāḷat-ḷo, “waḷḷāhi, ’ani ’aguḷ-ḷak al-maḍbūṭ. ’abūk čānat ʿindo rzāg u-’arāḍi četīra, u-čān makrūp. wa-’abūk mā čān yiğī uwlād.

151 He went to his mother, saying to her, “By Allah, if you do not tell the truth, with this sword, I will cut your head. I have learned to know that I am an illegitimate son and it’s true that I am an illegitimate son. You must tell me now who is my father. There are some people, who told me that I am an illegitimate son. You will [must] tell me who my father is.” She said to him, “By Allah, I am telling you the truth. Your father had property and many lands, and he was sad. And your father could not have children.

161 u-kān bī ʿindīna ḥarrāṯ, u-bi-ttifāgit ’abūk ʿala šān mā yiğī wulād, ’ani raḥet (w)ufakt ʿala l-’arzāg, w-al-māl alli kān ʿendo, u-ruḥet ʿind al-ḥarrāṯ, nemt lēla, u-’inta ’ibn al-ḥarrāṯ” ē? hā ʿiref gāḷ, “kalāmhom haḏōla kullayāthom maḍbūṭ.”

161 “And there was near us a farmer, and in agreement by your father because he did not have children, I went and agreed for the property and the money that he had, and went to the farmer, slept one night, and you are the farmer’s son.” (Eh?) He knew, he said [to himself], “The speech of all of them [what all of them had said] was correct.”

168 riğeʿ la-ʿindham u-humma yāklam, min baʿad ma ’akalam u-kull ši—’ā, mā-rāḥ, sa’alha. gāḷ-aḷhem, “’ani—gaḷū-ḷi ’inti—m-inti lli miš neḍīfa. ’iḥči l- maḍbūṭ, inno miš neḍīfa walla neḍīfa. gāḷat-ḷo “waḷḷāhi, ’ani, ʿalayy al-ʿāda . . . ʿalayya l-ʿāda” . . . hā?[5]

168 He went back to them and they were eating, after they had eaten and everything (yes, he went and asked them). He said to them, “I—they said to me—you—you are who is not clean. Tell the truth whether [you are] not clean or clean.” She said to him, “By Allah, I have the period . . . I have the period. The period $(_{H}vezed_{H} < {}_{H}veset_{H})$ . . .” This?

175 rāḥ gaʿad huwwa wiyyāhom. gāḷ-ilhum, “šū, ’intam, ’abūkom gāḷ, meḥimmad yāraṯ,” hū al-gāḍi, ’assa widdo yeḥill maškiletam, u-ʿerif inno humma ṣādgīn b-illi gāḷo. u-rāḥ ḥaggag u-liga kull ši maḍbūṭ.

175 He went and sat with them. He said to them, “What, you [pl.], your father said Muḥammad will inherit”—he, the judge—now he wants to solve their problem, and he knew that they were saying the truth in what they said. He had gone and investigated, and found that everything was right [true].

181 gāḷ-ilhom "'abūkom gāḷ mḥammad yāraṯ u-mḥammad yāraṯ u-mḥammad mā yaāraṯ, gāḷ -'abūkom?" gāḷum "'ā." gāḷ-ilham "ṭayyib, rūḥam uguʿdam b-al-bēt haḏ̣āk alli gbāḷum. u-taʿālam ʿandi wāḥad wāḥad." yiǧūz yōm, kānat maʿāhum al-misāfe yiǧūz yōmēn, yiǧūz ṯalāṯa.	181 He said to them, "Did your father say Muḥammad will inherit and Muḥammad will inherit and Muḥammad will not inherit—your father said [so]?" They said, "Yes." He said to them, "Good, go sit in that house there, which is in front of them, and come to me one by one." It could be a day, the distance was for them two days, it could be three [days].
188 yōm assa 'aǧam, 'aǧa ʿindo 'awwal wāḥad. gāḷ-ḷo, "smaʿ, 'inta widdak ašhad lak, 'agūḷ 'inta alli tāraṯ, mā widdi 'aḥarmak min māl 'abūk. 'amma hū widdi minnak ṭalab wāḥad—tāxaḏ hā-l-mankūš u-hā-ṭ-ṭūriyye, u-trūḥ tibḥaš ʿala gabar 'abūk wu-(t)ǧīb li rāso. u-'ani 'amḏ̣ī-lak 'innak inta alli tāraṯ."	188 Now they came, he went to him, the first one. He said to him, "Listen, you want me to testify for you, I will say that you inherit, I don't want to exclude you from your father's money. But I want from you one request—take this pickax and this hoe, and go dig your father's grave and bring me his head and I will sign for you that you are the one that inherits."
196 gāḷ-ḷo, "'aʿiḏḏ b-iḷḷā min šarr aš-šayṭān ar-raǧīm, kīf widdi 'arūḥ 'abḥaš w-aǧīb lak rās-'abūya? ʿumrak lā tamḏ̣ī-li. 'ana, waḷḷa, rās abūya mā-ni ǧāyīb lak 'iyyā." gāḷ-ḷo, "ṭayyib, rūḥ (u)-waddi aṯ-ṯāni."	196 He said to him, "I seek refuge in Allah from the accursed Satan—how shall I go and dig and bring you my father's head? You will never sign for me. I, by Allah, my father's head—I am not bringing it to you." He said to him, "OK, go and send me the second [one]."
202 ǧē aṯ-ṯāni. xarrafo nafs al-xurrāfa. gāḷ-ḷo, "'ani 'amḏ̣ī-lak bas innak ^{i}trūḥ tǧīb li rās 'abūk."	202 The second [brother] came. He [the judge] told him the same thing. He said to him, "I will sign for you, but you will go and bring me your father's head."
205 gāḷ-ḷo, "ʿaḏḏ bi-ḷḷā, 'ani—miš mumkin; 'inn māt 'abuya. kīf 'aǧīb lak rās 'abūy? ʿumrak lā tumḏ̣i."	205 He said to him, "[Asking] Allah's protection, I cannot. My father has died, how will I bring you my father's head? You will never sign this."
208 ǧē aṯ-ṯāliṯ. gāḷ-ḷo, "widdak bas rāso walla 'aǧīb lak 'abūya kullayāto?" gāḷ-ḷo, "lā, lā (t)ǧīb li (i)yyā kullayāto wa-lā (t) ǧīb li bas rāso. xaḷḷī nāyem b-g̣abṛo,"	208 The third one came. He said to him, "Do you want only my father's head or shall I bring you all of him?" He said to him, "No, don't bring me all of him, and do not bring me only his head—let him lie in his grave."
212 nāda ʿalēham kullayātom. gāḷ-ḷo, "kullhum yāraṯam mḥimmad u-mḥimmad yāraṯu, 'inta alli widdak ^{i}tǧīb rās 'abūk, 'inta alli mā tāraṯ." wa-hāḏa hu.	212 He called all of them. He said to him, "They will all inherit, Muḥammad and Muḥammad will inherit. You, who want to bring your father's head—you are the one who will not inherit." And that is it.

Commentary

The story of the three brothers who want to know to which of them their father has left his inheritance is known in Europe, the Middle East, North and East Africa, and South and East Asia. Its origins are ancient. Thompson associates it with two close narrative types: AT 655A, "The Strayed Camel and the Clever Deductions," and AT 655, "The Wise Brothers."[6] It is possible, with a great deal of justice, to combine them, as Uther does, into one narrative type: ATU 655, "The Wise Brothers."[7] The following is a description of the narrative type in his book:

A father leaves his wealth to his three sons. One of them steals diamonds (pieces of gold) that had been willed to all three brothers in his will. In order to settle the case, they consult a wise man. On their way, they see tracks of an animal and make the following deductions: It was a camel (horse, pack animal), it was one-eyed (grass is eaten on one side of the road only) [motif J1661.1.1]. "Deduction: the one-eyed camel. A she-camel has passed, blind in one eye; on the one side she carries wine and on the other vinegar; two men lead her, one a heathen and the other a Jew. Solution: She is recognized as a she-camel by the footprints; she is blind because she feeds on only one side of the road; the wine dropping down has soaked into the earth; the vinegar makes bubbles; the heathen is not so careful in his manners as is the Jew." It was lame (because of its tracks); it was carrying oil or honey, etc. (drops are seen on the ground); it had no tail (dung on a heap instead of being spread by the tail), etc. When they meet the owner of the lost animal, he overhears their remarks, takes them for thieves, and brings them to the judge. They explain their observations to the judge and are absolved. When they are invited for dinner (by the judge), they say the meat is dogmeat, the wine (bread) smells like a corpse, and their host is a bastard.

On investigation, all their statements are found to be true. The animal had been suckled by a bitch [motif F647.5.1] ("Marvelous sensitiveness: meat is dog's flesh. Animal has been suckled by a dog"); the wine (corn) had grown on a cemetery, smells like a corpse [F647.1] ("Marvelous sensitiveness: meat (wine) tastes of corpse. Has been near grave"); and the mother (of the judge) confesses her adultery.

In some variants, the judge tells the story of the noblest act (cf. ATU 976, "Which Was the Noblest Act?") in order to settle the dispute of the inheritance, based on his reaction, he declares the youngest to be the thief. Or the brothers are asked to shoot their father's corpse so their behavior will disclose the real son and heir. In other versions, the judge enforces another test of paternity or he pronounces another of Solomon's judgments.[7]

The first part of the story—the tracking of the camel—is known to us from the regular printed version of the Babylonian Talmud. It appears in tractate Sanhedrin, and it tells of two Jews who were captured on Mount Carmel:

> Our Rabbis taught: It once happened that two men [Jews] were taken captive on Mount Carmel, and their captor was walking behind them.
>
> One of them said to the other, "The camel walking in front of us is blind in one eye, and is laden with two barrels, one of wine, and the other of oil, and of the two men leading it, one is a Jew, and the other a heathen." Their captor said to them, "Ye stiff-necked people, whence do ye know this?" They replied, "Because the camel is eating of the herbs before

it only on the side where it can see, but not on the other, where it cannot see. It is laden with two barrels, one of wine and the other of oil: because wine drips and is absorbed [into the earth], whilst oil drips and remains [on the surface]. And of the two men leading it, one is a Jew, and the other a heathen: because a heathen obeys the call of Nature in the roadway, whilst a Jew turns aside." He hastened after them, and found that it was as they had said. So he went and kissed them on the head, brought them into his house, and prepared a great feast for them. He danced [with joy] before them and exclaimed, "Blessed be He who made choice of Abraham's seed and imparted to them of His wisdom, and wherever they go they become princes to their masters!" Then he liberated them, and they went home in peace. (Babylonian Talmud, Sanhedrin 104:1–2)

Rashi's commentary, which is attached to the text, states: "And those Jews said about their captor's face that it resembles the face of a famous king: 'his face was *ashkenaq* of a king that brought him to the world by act of adultery.'" The word *ashkenak*, as Steinsaltz points out in his commentary to the Babylonian Talmud, is probably a distortion of the word *ishkania* in ancient French, meaning "a stunt person, an exchange." Rashi refers here to another part of the story that is not found in the regular patterns (as does Rabbi Natan Ben Yechiel, a contemporary of Rashi, in his dictionary). Steinsaltz presents the missing passage according to the Munich manuscript (1342), which states:

And he would dance before them. They said to him: It seems to us that our master has the same face as a certain king. He [the king] went and asked his mother. He said to her, it had better if you confess, and if not, I'll give an order to kill you. She said to him, on her wedding her husband went out and one who resembled a king came upon her, and she became pregnant from him.

He brought them meat. When they smelled it, they said to him, this meat has the taste of a dog; he [the shepherd] had one sheep, and it died, and the kid sucked from a bitch breast. He brought them wine. They said to him, this wine has a taste of a corpse. He went to his mother and said to her: it had better if you confess, and if not, I'll give an order to kill you. She said to him, this wine came from a grapevine that grew on your father's grave. He stood and kissed them respectfully. [The continuation is identical to the end of the previous text.]

Another version, which preceded the Munich manuscript by a century, is located in the Cairo Genizah, but because of the state of the page, only a small part of the addition can be identified. In these two manuscripts, the passage is presented as an addition in the margins of the text. In the Green manuscript from 1703 that is kept in the National Library of Israel, the addition was integrated in the text.[8]

Another complete version of the story is presented in Midrash Eichah Zuta (Buber edition, version A), a Midrash that was apparently written at the end of the Geonim period, around the tenth century CE. In this version, several details are presented that are not included in the Talmudic story: When the Jewish prisoners arrive in Rome, they tell their captor that they can smell the pot of stew in Kfar Hanania in Judea. The captor does not believe them, but a man who has descended from a ship sailing from the Land of Israel to Rome in one day, because of the strong wind, confirms their words. After the meal prepared by the captor's mother for her son, he goes out dancing, and then one of the prisoners says to his friend:

> "His mother prostituted herself with a dancer who was a singer and became pregnant from him!" When the man heard these things, he took the sword in his hand, and went to his mother and told her all the things that the captives had told me: "Truly they told me [the truth], because I have already checked their words. If you do not tell me who is my father, I will kill you!" She said to him, "Son, do not kill me, and I will tell you the truth." Once your father brought a singer and he was also a dancer and he had a pleasant voice, and your father could not have children [could not inseminate] and as I saw him I had sexual intercourse with him and became pregnant from him and gave birth to you. Did I act wrongly by bringing an offspring [posterity] to your father?" When he heard what she had done, he said: "I have brought to me [to my house] someone who tells my condemnation to people." He commanded them [he freed them] and said to them, "Get out in peace from here. It is not worth that people like you would serve me." He gave them all kinds of provisions and supplies and accompanied them to the road until they left him, and he returned to his house, and so he calmed down. (Midrash Eichah Zuta [Buber edition, version A], chap. a)

Amir Lerner argues that both parts of the story are ancient, from the fifth century CE and perhaps earlier.[9] However, the evidence we have for them merging into one plot is not earlier than the tenth century CE. Isaac Aboab da Fonseca was one of the sages of Spain at the beginning of the fifteenth century. In his book *Menorat HaMa'or*, the complete text of the story is presented exactly as it was presented in the Munich manuscript.[10] A comprehensive discussion of the Jewish versions of the story appears in Dan Ben-Amos's book *Folktales of the Jews*.[11]

In the IFA archives, there are many parallels to the story.[12] In one of the Iraqi versions (IFA 1938), in addition to the camel episode, there is another episode: the brothers encounter a woman's footsteps and conclude that she is in advanced pregnancy (because of the depth of her footprints), that she carries a four-year-old child on one arm (one of her footprints is more immersed), and that she quarreled with her husband and fled from her home (because her footprints indicate that she occasionally turned to see if she was being pursued). At the end of the story, the judge states that one of the brothers is a bastard and therefore is not entitled to an inheritance. The explanation for the identification is that this brother has managed to discover that the judge is a bastard and a bastard knows other bastards. In a Jewish version from Turkey (IFA 3491), the judge determines his ruling on the basis of the reactions of the three brothers to the story "Which Was the Noblest Act?," which I mentioned at the beginning of the discussion. The story of the pregnant woman and the story the judge tells the brothers also appear in the Jewish version of Iraqi Kurdistan (IFA 5115). In this version, the judge does not know how to rule in the case of the brothers, one of whom stole from the others. The judge's wife is the one who tells them the story and concludes that the thief is the brother who favors the robber. A Judeo-Persian version (IFA 10204) of the story is particularly complex and complicated, intertwined with literary motifs taken from the Iranian poet Nizami's book *Seven Princesses* and other sources. In the story "The Manager of Synagogue Affairs and the Messenger," a story of the Kurdish Jews of Zakho in Iraq, guests from Jerusalem are hosted by the manager of synagogue affairs in the Istanbul community.[13] During the meal, the messengers reveal hidden things about their host: the wine served to them is the wine of dead man, the meat is dog flesh, and the owner is a bastard. The host checks the charges and finds that the lamb served to the guests was not slaughtered following kosher rules but was bought from an Arab seller (Muslims may eat Jewish slaughter, but not vice versa); the wine was taken from a barrel containing a dead mouse; and the host's mother brought him into the world after having a relationship with a Christian neighbor. Following the revelations, the host hastens to send away the emissaries and forbids them to return to Istanbul. This is an example of the integration of part of a folktale into a legend, presented as a real story.

The third-century Chinese book *The Proverbs of Ancient Morality*, which is an adaptation of Indian Buddhist composition, contains a part parallel to the first part of the Bedouin story. It tells of two students who walk along the road and correctly decipher the footprints left by an elephant. They discover that the elephant was blind in her right eye, carried a female elephant in her womb, and carried a woman on her back, who also had a female fetus in her womb.[14] A parallel to the second part of the story appears in *Ocean of Story*, in the eighth story of the Vittala stories (featuring a vampire demon that dwells in a corpse), already mentioned in chapter 15, "The Transposed Heads." Three sons of a Brahmin are going to a trial in front of the king. During the meal served to them by the king, one of them refrains from tasting the rice on the grounds that it smells of burned corpses. It turns out that the rice grew near a cremation site. The second brother is disgusted by the woman who serves the meal. He claims that she smells of goats. It turns out that she sucked goat's milk in her childhood. The third son feels pain from a hair that lies beneath the seven mattresses on which he sleeps.[15]

In the Islamic culture space, the complete story appears at the beginning of the ninth century in a book by Ibn Hišām (died in the second quarter of the ninth century CE), and in the late ninth century, it is in the works of historians Al-Ṭabari (died in 923 CE) and Al-Mas'ūdi (died in 956 CE). From there it wanders on to other Islamic works.[16] Ibn Hišām presents the story's chain of transmission from one generation to the next. According to him, the earliest link in this chain is Ibn 'Abbās, the cousin of the prophet Muḥammad, who is considered one of the great scholars of early Islam. According to the Islamic tradition, this sage was a central figure in the collection and transmission of these types of materials, such as *Isra'iliyyāt* (Stories of the Children of Israel) and *The Stories of the Prophets* (قصص الانبياء), and was nourished, among other things, from Jewish and Christian informants, although this does not necessarily indicate Jewish sources for the story.[17] The matter of the inheritance, which was absent from the ancient Jewish texts, appears in Ibn Hišām's version.

The heroes of the story are the four sons of Nizār ibn Ma'ād ibn 'Adnān: Eyād, Mudar, Rabī'a, and Anmār, whom the Islamic genealogical tradition of the Middle Ages identified as the offspring of Išmael and the fathers of the northern tribes. Nizār gives Eyād a slave girl with gray hair, and also his clothes and his stick. To Mudar he gives the tent with the red tent cloth and his golden ring. Rabī'a receives his horse, his spear, and his flag, and Anmār receives his donkey. In addition, he hands each of them a sealed jar and sends them to a wise judge named Alaklamas ibn Ammar (king of Nağrān in Yemen, known as Afaa Nağrān, meaning the ruler of Nağrān). The brothers set off, and on their way to the judge, they encounter puzzling phenomena: First they see a dog that has a small puppy sucking its breasts. The puppy barks, and the dog is silent. Then they reach a pile of glittering dung. Later they see three thick trees held tight, one standing, the second bent to the left, and the third bent to the right. On the tree bent to the right stands a bird, and so on the tree bent to the left. The two birds change their places for a while, and then each returns to its first place. Neither of them sits on the middle tree. The brothers continue on their way and see two old men wrestling with each other, each holding the other's beard. The brothers order Anmār, the younger brother, to separate the warriors, but when he tries to do so, the old people beat him, and he leaves them alone. This is also the case with Rabīʿa. When the third brother approaches them, they fall apart, flee—each in a different direction—and disappear. Later on, the episode of the camel's footprints and its owner is told. When they come to the judge, they explain how they discovered that the camel that had lost its way was blind in one eye, had a chopped tail, and was lame in one leg, and the judge acquits them of theft and sends the camel owner away. The judge explains to the brothers what they saw. He explains the sight of the dog and the puppy: "Behold, the days come, the ignorant shall speak, the wise shall hold his tongue." Regarding the matter of the trees and the birds, he says: "The days will come, the rich will give to the rich, and the indigent who stays between them, they will not give him anything." To explain the pile of glittering dung, he says, "Here are the days to come, the slaves and the crowd will rise, noblemen and dignitaries will be humiliated." These descriptions appear to be related to descriptions of the Day of Judgment in the Qur'ān. When the brothers tell him the story of the old elders, he looks at Mudar and says to him, "Well done, a tree bearing fruit you are." He rises from his seat and gives his place to Mudar, and then he turns to the other brothers and says, "These elders were two devils who wanted to try you, in order to know who is superior among the sons. And you Mudar are the finest, you have the righteous reading today and the great place for tomorrow. By his virtue you will escape doom and attain closeness [to Allah or heaven]." According to tradition, Mudar was the first branch of the Arab family tree, from which Qurayš, the Prophet Muḥammad's tribe, was to grow.

Later on, the judge hears the brothers talking about the lamb, which grew on a dog's breasts; the wine produced from a grapevine planted on a grave; and the fact that the judge is not his father's legal son. The judge investigates the matter, and it turns out that the lamb was indeed sucked by a bitch, the vine was planted on a child's grave (or in other versions, the grave of the judge's father), and his mother became pregnant with her brother-in-law, who raped her in his drunkenness. At the end of the story, the judge explains to the brothers the meaning of the division of the inheritance, "The tent and the ring for Mudar, who will rule you, and the clothes and the slave with the gray hair to Eyād, and he will revive you. The horse and the spear and the flag for Rabīʿa, he will fight for you. You will come under his banner on the day of battle. Anmār is the owner of the donkey. You will load heavy burden on him, because the man who will serve people in this world—he gave him the donkey."

The judge opens the sealed jars that the four brothers brought:

> He opened Eyād's jar and found nails clippings in it. He said, "Eyād, take the slaves that he had." Then he opened Mudar's jar and found a piece of gold and a piece of silver. He said to him, "Mudar, take all the gold and the silver that he left behind." Then he opened Rabīʿa's jar and found a piece of horseshoe, and said to him, "Take the male horses. All the horses and the mules and the donkeys are yours." Then he opened Anmār's jar and found a hoof in it, and said to him: "Anmār, you will have the camel and the cattle."[18]

In an Ethiopian Jewish version, which was recorded by the researcher Dr. Jacques Faitelovitz in the 1930s, there is a similar scene, in which the brothers encounter unusual sights on their way and receive an explanation from the judge.[19] In this story, before his death the father divides all his property, his cattle, and his money among his five children, all of whom bear the name Negusiyeh ("my king" in the Amharic language), and a moment before his death, he says: "I curse my son, Negusiyeh!" The five sons bring the father to burial and intend to hold the memorial service, *tazkar*, as it is known in Amharic, without which the soul of the dead cannot enter heaven but must remain in a dark place. One of the sons suddenly says, "Our father said before his death that he curses his son Negusiyeh. We are all called Negusiyeh, and we do not know who he meant. How can we then hold the memorial service together?" The brothers decide to go out and ask the advice of a wise man who lives in a remote village. On their way, they see a monkey holding a rosary and murmuring to himself, a strong horse whose skin is covered with boils, and a big bird swimming in the lake, trying to capture with its open beak the raindrops from the sky. The brothers come to the village, where there are three sages. The first sage, who is very old looking, with a gray beard and hunched back, sends them to his older brother. The older brother seems much younger than his brother, but he too cannot judge between them, so he directs them to his older brother. The older brother looks even younger than his two brothers, his beard is black, his skin is smooth, and his age marks are not visible on his face. The five brothers tell him about the strange scenes they saw on their way and also wonder about the differences between the host and his two younger brothers. The old man answers their questions and explains:

> The monkey holding a rosary is a metaphor for a stupid ignorant man who has risen to greatness and has become rich. He does not know the ancient language of prayers, the Geʿez language, but he holds a rosary in his hand and mumbles to himself to impress those around him. The horse covered with boils is a metaphor for a strong man who came from a good family, but his luck did not work for him and he lost his possessions, so all his friends moved away from him as if he were infected with boils. The bird that swims in the lake that is filled with water and opens its beak to swallow the raindrops is a metaphor for the dignitaries and eminent peoples who are not satisfied with the great wealth they have and covet the pennies of others, poorer than themselves. They do not know how to give anything, they just take. As for our appearance, I will explain to you: my younger brother had married a bad woman who is like a stinging wasp; she does not leave him for a moment and harasses him all the time, so he grew old prematurely. My second brother, who seems less old, has a wife who is like the wild bee; it has many virtues but also disadvantages. It gives honey but also knows how to sting, so he has grown less old than his younger brother. But I did not age at all because I have a wife like *tauzama*—the noble

> cultural bee—who produces excellent honey and never stings. She respects me so much that once when she woke up and was about to get up for the day, she found my head on her hair. In order not to disturb me in my sleep, my wife preferred to cut her hair with scissors and leave it under my head, so I would not wake up. She is always diligent in her work and she has no complaints against me, so I won and did not age like my other brothers.[20]

Later on, he explains the curse of their father: "The curse is for the one who claimed that the ceremony should not be conducted without first finding out who was cursed. Four of you asked to hold the ceremony so that the soul of your father could go up to heaven. They thought of his goodness and forgot the curse, while he prevented the ceremony and led you all the way to here, so it was he who drew your father's curse upon himself."[21]

It is interesting to note that in the Babylonian Talmud a story with a motif similar to this is included in Ibn Hišām's story—the motif of the jars, which the father bequeathed his sons. In this story, Rabbi Bana'ah plays the role of the judge: "A certain man [when on his deathbed] said, I leave a barrel of dust to one of my sons, a barrel of bones to another, and a barrel of fluff to the third. They could not make out what he meant, so they consulted R. Bana'ah. He said to them: Have you any land? We have, they replied. Have you cattle? Yes. Have you cushions? Again, the answer was in the affirmative. If so, said R. Bana'ah, that is what your father meant" (Babylonian Talmud, Bava Batra 58:1).

In her book *The Bedouin Arabic Dialects*, Judith Rosenhouse records two Bedouin versions of the story from the ʿArab el-ʿArāmša tribe on the Lebanese border and from the ʿArab el-ʿUmariyya tribe in Ibtin.[22] In both versions, only the story of the inheritance appears, and both the episode of the camel and the episode of the meal given to the brothers are missing. In the ʿArāmša version, the judge asks a young shepherd to look at the brothers and determine which one is Muḥammad, who will not inherit, and the girl points at one of them. It seems that here the intention is that the appointment of the heir will be done by testing or by female intuition.

In the ʿUmariyya version, the judge rules that the brother who agreed to violate his father's honor (desecrate their father's body) and was willing to bring not only the bones of the father but also the dirt below him does not deserve to have a part in the inheritance.

This episode appears in another Talmudic story about Rabbi Bana'ah, who sends the heirs to knock at their father's grave. The real heir refuses to do so. Here is the story:

> A certain man heard his wife say to her daughter: Why do you not observe more secrecy in your amours? I have ten children, and only one is from your father. When [the man was] on his deathbed, he said, I leave all my property to one son. They had no idea which of them he meant, so they consulted R. Bana'ah. He said to them, Go and knock at the grave of your father, until he gets up and tells you which one of you [he has made his heir]. So they all went to do so. The one who was really his son, however, did not go. R. Bana'ah thereupon said, "All the estate belongs to this one." (Babylonian Talmud, Bava Batra 58:1)

The first part of our story (the camel's marks) appears in a Bedouin version from the ʿArab el-Šibli tribe (IFA 9432). In another Bedouin version, recorded from an Arab watchman, whose precise source is unclear (IFA 9942), the father gives his sons three sealed jars. After his death, it turns out that one jar contains earth; the second, bones;

and the third, gold. The wise judge explains to the brothers that the father intended the owner of the earth jar to inherit the land, the owner of the bone jar to inherit the flocks, and the owner of the gold jar to inherit his money.

The Bedouin version discussed here is very similar in most details to the description of the international narrative type ATU 655. The story begins with the inheritance affair, "Muḥammad will inherit, Muḥammad will inherit, and Muḥammad will not inherit." Later on appear the camel episode and the episode of the brothers' talk about the food served to them and the bastard judge. The story ends with the statement that only the brothers who refused to desecrate their dead father will receive the inheritance.

When one looks at the Bedouin version I recorded, several elements are visible. The story opens with a riddle that seems to have no logical solution. The three brothers have the same name, and it is impossible to tell which one the father referred to when he said that Muḥammad would not inherit. The three brothers have sharp thinking. On the basis of traces they find on the way, they figure out what the camel looks like and what the nature of its burden is. Later on, they discover with their unusual sensory sensitivity the origin of the food served to them and the host's family background—the fact that he is a bastard. In the first part of the story, they play an intellectual game, competing with one another for their wisdom, but this entangles them in a quarrel with the camel owner. Later, their unusual sensory sensitivity entangles them with the judge (in some versions, the judge hastens to get rid of them so as not to spread his disgrace).

The judge is also described as a wise man, but his wisdom is based, not on intellectual competence or unusual sensitivity, but on deep psychological understanding and knowledge of the human soul. The story compares external wisdom based on intellect and perception of the senses with inner wisdom based on emotion and morality.

This comparison is a *leitmotif* in all versions of the story in different cultural spaces. The fact that all the brothers have far-reaching intelligence does not imply anything about their character or morality. The judge reveals the father's deep familiarity with his sons and the reason that led him to deprive one of them of his inheritance. We meet here a popular statement about the importance of emotion and heart in a person's life: wisdom and intellect have no meaning if the person who is endowed with them is morally flawed.

Moreover, the story relates to a multigenerational relationship, fathers versus sons. The younger generation, represented here by the inheriting sons, seems to boast of its intellectual skills and see them as the essence of everything, while the older generation, the father and the judge, operates on the basis of years of experience. They are the ones who can decipher the greatest mystery of all—the human soul. The story in its various versions thus compares the wisdom of the old to that of the young and encourages listeners to appreciate the wisdom and experience of the adult generation and give them the respect they deserve.

Another thing that stands out less in the Bedouin version I recorded, and more in the other versions, is the distinction between symbolic riddles, in which a puzzling scene or action is interpreted as a metaphor for human behavior, and real riddles, which are based on logical reasoning.

In some of the versions of the story in different cultural spaces, the narrator makes use of symbolic puzzles, which attract the attention of the listener, to give him insights into various aspects of life. The narrator deals with the place of a good woman in her husband's life and the conduct of the world as a means to criticize negative phenomena in society and to educate listeners about moral values and justice.

Notes

1. This story, with its overwhelming quantity of sedentary features, could serve to demonstrate the effect of sedentary dialects on Galilee Bedouin dialects. These features occur next to genuine parallel Bedouin features. This picture demonstrates the gradual loss of Bedouin features in the speech of these communities. This trend has been growing since the beginning of the twentieth century, and even more so since the establishment of Israel. The following table shows examples of this process in verbs, bound pronouns, and particles based on phrases in this collection.

Phrase in the text	"Pure Bedouin"	Translation
uwlādo biddhon innhen	*'iyālo widdhom innhom*	His children want that they
widhin ye'arfu	*widdhom ye'arfam*	They want to know
gāḷu, "bi-nrū(ḥ)-'ala"	*gāḷam, "nrū(ḥ) 'ala"*	They said, "We'll go to . . ."
mā bikūn	*mā ykūn*	It does/will not happen
miš ma'agūl	*mū ma'agūl*	It is not logical
u-'ana miš ᵉnḍīfe	*u-'ana mā-ni / mū nḍīfa*	And I am not clean [f.]

2. Typical Bedouin lexical items occur in the story in addition to sedentary ones. For example, consider *yārat̠*, "[he] will inherit"; *zēn*, "good"; *'az'ar*, "tailless"; *hassa'/hassa/assa*, "now"; *al-ᶦma'zzeb*, "the host"; *yōminno*, "when [he]"; *ġēr*, "must [in other environments it can mean: only, other]."

3. The verb *bi-rrūḥ 'ala* shows a phonetic feature: the *n* that would appear in *bi-nrūḥ* is assimilated to the following *r*. Such assimilation is not typical of sedentary dialects.

4. As in note 3, in *w-ad-dibbān yibba' 'ala at̠ar al-ğimal*, "and the fly follows the camel's traces," the form *yibba'* reveals assimilation *t* > *b* in the verb *yitba'*, "follow" (< root *tbʿ*).

5. This story deals with a serious problem for the brothers, the judge, his wife, and his mother. These are emotional, religious, and social issues for all of them—and the narrator conveys their difficulties and excitement by much use of L(left)-dislocation, such as in *waḷḷāhi, 'ani bī 'alayya al-'āda*, "by Allah, I have the period" (lit.: "by Allah, I—there is on me the period"). After the oath formula, the woman begins with the 1sg pronoun. She continues with "there is on me," implying something that is beyond her power to change. The brothers use a similar structure: *'a'iḏḏ bi-ḷḷā min šarr aš-šayṭān ar-rağīm . . . 'ana, waḷḷa, rās 'abūya māni ğāyib lak 'iyyā*, "I seek refuge in Allah from the accursed Satan'. . . . I, by Allah, my father's head—I am not bringing it to you." After the religious phrase that reflects a Koranic phrase (Q.16:98), he commits himself, using "I," and then dares to refuse the judge. Although the story is narrated in a restrained manner, such structures reflect the involved emotional depth (cf. chap. 30, note 5).

6. Thompson, *The Folktale*, 231.

7. Uther, *Types of International Folktales*, 361–62.

8. Lerner, "Construction," 15.

9. Lerner, 9–55.

10. Aboab da Fonseca, *Menorat HaMa'or*, 660.

11. Ben-Amos, *Folktales of the Jews*, 1:315–23.

12. Yemen: 1357, 1577, 10302, 12328; Iraq: 1730, 1938, 7439, 8047, 12001; Turkey: 3491, 12711; Iraqi Kurdistan: 5115; Morocco: 5179, 9553; Afghanistan: 9432; Iran: 10204; Druze version: 1507; Bedouin versions: 9494, 9942.

13. Shilo, *Lishana Deni*, 108–11.

14. Lerner, "Construction," 29.

15. Penzer, Ocean of Story, 6:217–20.

16. Lerner, "Construction," 32–34.

17. Lerner, 37–38.

18. Lerner, 40–47.

19. Faitelovitz, *Stories of Beta Yisrael*, 15.

20. Faitelovitz, 17–18.

21. Faitelovitz, 18.

22. Rosenhouse, *Bedouin Arabic Dialects*, 226–29.

PART II · Stories about Ġūls and Demons

27. The Giant

NARRATOR: Warda Hawāš

TRIBE: *ʿArab el-Mazārīb*
IFA 17420 March 11, 1982

1 hāḏi, min hēn la-hēn, čānam ṯalāṯ šibāb. hassa šnū hāḏ-al-šibāb? wāḥad ’iḥsan min wāḥad. yaʿani gabaḏayāt. yōm gāḷum "widdna nrūḥ ʿala l-waʿar. nšumm al-hawa, nṭūš, yaʿani nšūf ad-dinya." rāḥam. u-humma māšīn daḥḥagam willa l-ġanam, šnū al-ġanam[1] kull ^{i}nʿaǧa, illi yšūfha mā yiṣaddeg inha rābiya ba-l-^{i}blād alli humma biha. taʿaǧǧabam. gāḷam, "wēn hāy al-ġanam rābiya?"	1 This—from here thereto, there were three young men. Now, what young men? Each one is more handsome than the other. That is, [they were] strong guys. One day they said, "We wish to go to the wild terrain, take a walk, get around, that is, see the world." They went [off], and as they were going, they saw sheep—what sheep! Each ewe, if anyone sees it, he will not believe that it has grown in the country in which they were. They wondered and said, "Where has this sheep been raised?"
11 gāḷam, "waḷḷāhi, la-nimši wara hā-l-ġanam nšūf wān rāyḥa, wu-nrūḥ ^{e}nšūf al-ġanam, wēn ^{e}ṣḥāba hāya, b-el-waʿar." hassa sḥabam ḥālum u-rāḥam, humma māšīn, gāmum, ǧam ʿala šnū muġġāra, yaʿani muġġāra ʿalēha—bala zuġra b-ad-dār—gadd hā-d-dār u-’akbar. hassa daḥḥagam gām(a)t al-ġanam fātat fatḥ al-maġġāra.	11 They said, "By Allah, let's go after this sheep to see where it is going, and we'll walk and see the sheep, where its owners [are] in the wild area." They took themselves and went. As they were walking, they came to—what a cave; that is a cave, on which—without disrespect for this house—like this house and [but] bigger. Now, they looked [and saw] the sheep entered the opening of the cave.
20 gām tabaʿha ṣāḥibha—šnu ṣāḥibha! ṭūlo—ṭūl ʿamud el-kahraba, yaʿani ṯnēnum u-zāwid, ’akṯar.	20 After it followed its owner—what an owner! His height—you'd say, is the height of an electricity pole, that is, two of them and more [higher].

23 hassa, hū lē ʿēn weḥda hēna b-ṣubāḥo. hē^{i}ke ʿēno. hassa lamm-enno šāfū, mā ḏaḷḷ ^{a}b-rāsam ḥatta-l-ʿagel, min al-xōf minno. essa humma gabaḏayāt ʿāddīn ḥālhom, yaʿani, mā humma ḥayaḷḷa.[2]

23 Now he, he had a single eye in his forehead. His eye was like this. Now when they saw him, their brain did not remain in their head because of the fear from him. Now they were strong men, considered themselves—not somebody unimportant [feeble].

28 ʾimma gāḷ-ḷēhum "yā mīt marḥaba bikam, ṣār liyya waḷḷa zimān ʾani ma šufet" e . . .[yaʿani simač ba-n-nisba lē], "min šikelkam. yā ʾahla u-sahla bikam." "waḷḷa," gāḷu-ḷo, "tfaḏḏalam, yā ʿammi, yā zēn, yā šēn"[3] gāḷ-ḷhom: "minkam warākam.[4] tfaḏḏalam ʿendi ʿala-al-maġġāra."

28 But he said to them, "Oh, a hundred welcomes to you, it's been long since I saw, er . . . (that is, fish in relation to him) of your form. Oh, a hundred welcome to you." "By Allah," they said to him, "please, o uncle, by good or bad" [beseeching their freedom]. He said to them, "From you and behind you [anywhere round you—no escape]. Please [go] to my place, the cave."

36 fātam. hēka sāqam. wāḥad nāṣeḥ, wāḥad mitwasseṭ be-n-naṣāḥa, wāḥad ḏaʿīf. hā-s-sāʿa, lamma fātam kān ifakkar šū bisāwi bi-nazlāʾ. gām ǧāb ʾakbar čabeš gām ^{i}ḏbaḥo lēhom gāl-lhom, "itʿaššam, kulam." hā-s-sāʿa, ʿindmā kalam, hu mā riḏa yākel maʿāhom. "kul maʿāna:" huwwa ygūl, "ʾani mā widdi ʾākel."

36 They entered. Like that he led them. One [of them was] fat, one was medium fat, and one was thin. Now, when they entered, he was thinking what to do with his guests. He got up and brought the biggest ram, killed it for them, and said to them, "Have dinner, eat." Now when they were eating, he did not want to eat with them. "Eat with us." He says, "I don't want to eat."

44 ʿindma kalam u-šibʿam, gām, giḏabhum ʿasʿashum wāḥad wāḥad, gām ǧe la-n-nāṣeḥ. gām gāḷ-ḷo "inta al-lēle widdi atʿašša ʿalēk." "yā zēn, yā šēn" gāḷ-ḷo, "minnak warāk. al-lēla ana widd(i)-āklak."

44 When they ate and got satiated, he got up, caught them, and touched them one by one, and came to the fat one. He said to him, "Tonight, I want to have dinner on you [have you for dinner]." "Oh good, oh bad." "From you and behind you [no escape]. Tonight, I will eat you."

50 gḏabo, bī ʿindo si^{a}x miṯel ma ʿindna hināk, masūra yaʿani, šakku bi-hā-l-si^{a}x u-wallaʿ an-nār ʿendu u-ḥaṭṭo ʿala ha-n-nār, ṣār yegaḷḷeb bī. u-hū ṭayyeb bas yerīxo, yeṣayyeḥ. šalwaṭo ʿala hā-n-nār, šiwā u-kalā.

50 He caught him, he had a skewer, like ours there, a pipe, that is, he stuck the man to this skewer and lit the fire on him and put him on the fire, and started turning him, as he was being cooked [prepared], but he was softening him [his flesh], he was shouting. He roasted him on the fire, roasted him and ate him.

56 hā-s-sāʿa ṯāni yōm, ṯāliṯ yōm, yinaṣṣeḥ haḏlāk. ṣāram yimʿasam.[5] ṣāram yeḥissam mā yenṣaḥam. kull yōm yiḏbaḥ ^{i}lhum ^{i}nʿaǧa, kull yōm yiḏbaḥ ^{i}lhum ^{i}nʿaǧa, mū-hum dāizīn yinṣaḥam. yōm gāḷ la-l-mutwassiṭ hāḏ b-al-naṣāḥa, gāḷ-ḷo, "mā-ni yalli ʾāklak ʾinta al-yōm, gabeḷ la tixlaṣ min marra, tmūt."

56 Now, the second day, the third day, he was getting those [two men] fat. They started to get crushed [pressed with fear], to feel [that they did] not get fat. Every day he would kill for them an ewe, every day he would kill for them an ewe—they were not getting fat. One day he said to this medium-fat one, said to him, "I'm going to eat you today, before you end entirely, [and] die."

64 giḏabo, šakko b-as-si^{a}x, šiwā u-kalā, kamān. ḏaḷḷ mīn? ḏaḷḷ hāḏa ḏ-ḏaʿīf, yā ḥarām, yigarges.[6] kull yōm yiḏbaḥ lō w-iġaḏḏi bī, u-tanno yanṣaḥ, u-bidūn fāyida. yōm, gāḷ—šnū gāḷ, gāḷ-ḷo, "ba'īs, 'inta, miš ġādi tanṣaḥ, widdi 'āklak, nṣiḥet willa 'ağʿalak 'inšaḷḷa mā tinṣaḥ."

64 He seized him, stuck him on the skewer, roasted him, and ate him, too. Who remained? This thin one, oh what a pity! [lit.: what a sin!]. He was gnawing his teeth [with fear]. Every day he would kill for him an ewe and feed it to him, so that he may get fat, with no benefit. One day he said, what did he say? He said to him, "Unlucky you, thin one, you will not get fat, I'll eat you whether you are fat or by Allah's will, I'll make [it that] you do not get fat."

71 hāḏa mā ḏaḷḷ—yā baṭṭal yigdar yigaf ʿala 'ağrē min al-xōf. gāḷ, "mā-ni yā alli xaḷḷi hā-l-ʿimlāq tam-inno yinām wa-(a) sāwi bī šaġla yaʿani, mā twaffi hīč." ğā, xaḷḷā tanno nām, hassa lama ynām mā tġammaḏ ʿēno, l-il-ʿimlāg.

71 This one did not remain—or he stopped being able to stand on his feet for fear. He said, "I must be the one that will leave this giant until he sleeps and I'll do to him a thing—it [his wish] will not be fulfilled like that." He came, waited until he, the giant slept, now when he is asleep his eye does not shut.

77 qām ğā, ḥamma sarīṭ ḥadīd, hāḏ-all-yišwīhum bī, ḥammā tanno ṣār ḥamar. ğa xaḷḷā nāim, 'ā, ḥammā ʿa-n-nār. gām ğāb hā-š-šarīṭ hāḏa šakko b-ʿēno, ḥarraq ʿēno [yā bayyē!] 'ā. ḥarraq ʿēno hāḏa, b-ṣubāḥo.

77 He got up, heated a piece of iron [rod], that which he would roast them with, heated it until it became red. He let him sleep. Yes, he heated it on the fire. He brought that piece [of iron], stuck it in his eye, burned his eye (oh my!), yes, this [man] burned his eye, in his forehead.

83 dabb aṣ-ṣōt, hāḏa, ṣār yeṣarrex, hāḏ hū mī yšūf. huwwa enʿema. hassa hāḏ huwa l-ḏaʿīf ṣār yewadder bēn-el-ġanam, yurkuḏ warā min hēna yetwadder bēn-el-ġanam. gāḷ-ḷo, "ʿandak, wēn ^{i}trūḥ mā-ni 'ageḏbak."

83 The voice trailed [spread around]—this one—he started shouting, this one did not see. He was blinded. This weak one began to hide between the sheep. He [the giant] was running after him from here he was hiding between the sheep. He said to him, "Stop, where will you go? I'm certainly going to catch you."

89 bāb al-muġġāra mā yiftaḥ. bī ^{i}ʿrāg yaʿani ʿala bāb al-muġġāra. gad wāğib hā-d-dār. bas yigūl-lo bi-četfo hēč hāḏ al-ʿimlāg yiftaḥo. 'iḏa mā yiftaḥo l-ʿimlāg, al-bāb mā yinfatiḥ. yaʿani hāḏa frēx yaʿani bin-nisba li-bani-ādam. 'ā. hassa ğuwwa, čēf widdo bi-yiṭlaʿ hāḏa ḏ-ḏaʿīf?

89 The cave door did not open. There was a big rock, that is, on the cave door, of the size necessary for this apartment. However, he would say to him, with his shoulder this giant would open it. If the giant did not open it, the door would not get open. That is, it's a chick, [this man] that is, relative to humans [to the giant]. Yes, now, inside, how would he get out, this thin/weak man?

96 yidawwir ʿalē b-al-ġanam, bas hū mā yešūf, yitwaddar. yōm gāḷ, "'ā, mā-li 'alla 'ağīb ğild al-xarūf," hāḏa l-čabeš alli inḏibaḥ awwal yom lamma astāḏāfhum. "u-'albaso u-m(in)-šān 'aḥammi ḥāli, yaʿani." hā-l-ġanam maḥbūsa ṯalaṯt iyyām, arbaʿt iyyām, ğuwwa, mā tuṭlaʿ. mātat min ağ-ğūʿ^{a}, widda tākel.

96 He was looking for him in the sheep, but he did not see, he was hiding. One day he said, "Yes, I have only to bring the skin of the sheep," the ram that was killed on the first day when he hosted them. "And I'll wear it, to keep myself warm, that is." These sheep were locked in three days, four days, inside. They were dying of hunger, they wanted to eat.

104 fātet barr, el-ġanam. elli wa. hīn, yōm gāl, "la-aʿraf lahin. lāčin 'agḏabhin wiḥda wiḥda, mišān aʿarif—mišān 'aguḏbo." 'imma hīn ṭelʿat al-ġanam, ṣār yeʿasʿes bihin, 'awwal wiḥda, ṯāni wiḥda ^{i}ṭlaʿan.

104 The sheep missed the outside [where they had their food]. (That which . . .) Here, one day he said, "I'll know them. But I'll seize them one by one, to know—to catch him." But here the sheep went out, he started touching them, first one, second one, went out.

110 gām ğā dōro huwwa, assa huwwa libes farwet al-xarūf, ač-čabeš, u-ḥaṭṭ al-^{i}grūn wa-r-rās ʿala rāso. gḏabo yeʿasʿes bīh hīča, lamma gḏabo grūno gām fāṭen, gāḷ, "bayye," mezaṭ ʿalē minno, nifad.

110 His turn came, now he put on [dressed in] the fur of the sheep, the ram, and put the horns and the head on his head. He seized him, started touching him like that. When he took hold of his horns he recalled and said, "Oh my—" he slipped away from him, escaped.

115 gāl, "bayye, hāḏ-al-čabeš alli zimān ḏibaḥto, nifadet." mā ḏaḷḷ-ḷo b-rāso 'alla ṣār yeṣarrex ʿa-ṭūl ḥiṣṣo. gām ğe hāḏa z-zlima ḏ-ḏaʿīf, kaḥaš al-ġanam, seḥab ḥālo u-rawwaḥ ʿa-halo.

115 He said, "Oh my, that is the ram that I killed a long time ago, I lost [have become empty-handed, failed]." Nothing remained in his brain [the giant could not do anything] but start shouting in full voice. He came, this weak man, gathered up the sheep and went off, and went back home to his family.

120 hasaa, huwwa u-mrawweḥ, šnū yegūḷ-ḷo az-zlima—al-ʿimlāg hāḏa? yegūḷ-ḷo, "ṭab, ʿimet, min šān 'aḷḷa, xaḷḷī-li bas 'ačam min nʿağa, naʿīš minne." gāḷ-ḷo, "waḷḷa, wa-'aḷḷa, mā ʿād ^{e}tšūf el-ḥayā."

120 Now, while he was walking back home, what did that man, the giant, say to him? He said to him, "Well, I've been blinded; for Allah's sake, leave for me a few sheep to live on." He said to him, "By Allah, you will not see life anymore."

126 al-muhimm, xaḏa n-nʿağāt u-rawwaḥ. lamma rawwaḥ, rawwa(ḥ) ʿala balado, ġāib yīği arbaʿt-ušhur. lamma rawwaḥ, gāḷu-ḷo, "mnīn hā-l-ġanam hāya? ġanam ʿağība hadīč hī, nāṣḥa." gāḷ-ḷhom, "hīč-hīč al-guṣṣa." gāḷu-ḷo, "maʿāya al-xurrāfiyya čiḏba. mū ṣaḥīḥ."

126 In short, he took the sheep and went home. When he went home, went to his town, he was away about four months. When he went back home, they said to him, "Where are these sheep from? [They are] strange sheep, being fat sheep." He said to them "The story is so-and-so." They said to him, "I think this story is a lie, not true."

133 gāḷ-ḷum, "taʿālam ta-(a)warrikam 'iyyā b-al-muṭraḥ al-flāni." fzaʿat hā-l-ʿarab, 'iši ʿağīb, yaʿani. (h)im (y)rūḥam išūfū. u-lamma rāḥam, 'alli mātam 'akṯar min a(lli)-ḍaḷḷam māšīn, bas šāfū—min šōfto, yaʿani, ʿa-gadd mī hī rahība. al-muhimm, lamma šāfū ṣaddagu al-xurrāfiyya. xilṣat al-ḥaddūṯa.[7]	133 He said to them, "Come with me, I'll show him to you in the certain place." The Bedouins called out [cried out]—it [was] a strange thing, that is. They went to see, and when they went, those who died were more than those who remained walking, because of his looks, that is, so horrible it was. In short, when they saw him, they believed the story. The story has ended.

Commentary

The one-eyed giant story is a fine example of Hellenistic cultural influence on all peoples of the Middle East. The story is a transmigration of the tale of the war of Odysseus and his men against the Cyclops Polyphēmos. The narrative type ATU 1137, "The Blinded Ogre (Polyphemus, Tefegös)," is found in Europe, Asia, and North Africa.

In Greek mythology, the Cyclopes are described as having the form of a man with only one eye. Odysseus's war against the Cyclops Polyphēmos, Poseidon's son, is described by Homer in the ninth chapter of the *Odyssey*[8] and in Hesiod's *Theogony* (The birth of the gods), eighth–seventh century BCE.

In those sources, the Cyclops is not explicitly described as a giant, and yet his dimensions can be inferred from the description of his club in the *Odyssey*: "Beside one of the sheep pens lay a huge pole / Of green olive which the Cyclops had cut / To use as a walking stick when dry. Looking at it / We guessed it was about as large as the mast / Of a black ship, a twenty-oared, broad-beamed / Freighter that crosses the wide gulfs. / That's how long and thick it looked."[9] See also the description of the stone that blocked the opening of the cave: "Unable to budge the enormous stone He had set in place to block the entrance."[10]

It is interesting to compare the Bedouin story to the story in the *Odyssey*. The Cyclopes on Odysseus's journey live on an island, while the Bedouin story describes a land voyage conducted by three Bedouin. Odysseus and his friends are caught on the Cyclopes' island by chance during his wandering, forced on him by Poseidon, the sea god, while the heroes of this Bedouin story, depicted as mighty men ("strong guys"), set out on purpose to explore the world.

In the *Odyssey*, Odysseus and his men first see the Cyclopes' fat sheep. "We got to the cave quickly. He was out, Tending his flocks in the rich pastureland."[11] They enter his cave intending to rob him of cheese and lambs, but then they decide to wait for him. In our story as well, the protagonists first encounter the herd of sheep. They are indeed very frightened by the sight of the giant who comes out of the cave, but he welcomes them cordially and invites them to a meal according to the prime Bedouin custom. He slaughters the largest sheep for them and makes them an evening meal. He says to them, "Oh, a hundred welcomes to you, it's been long since I saw . . . [fish in relation to him] of your form. Oh, a hundred welcome to you."

In the *Odyssey* story, Odysseus and his men hide with fear at the back of the cave. When the Cyclops discovers them, Odysseus tries to beseech him and even expects to receive gifts from him as is customary: "Now we are here, suppliants at your knees, Hoping you will be generous to us And give us the gifts that are due to strangers."[12] But the Cyclops does not treat them as guests, and, after a brief exchange of words, he smashes the skulls of two of Odysseus's men and eats them as they are, without cooking them.

In this Bedouin story, the cannibalistic character of the giant is revealed only at the end of a hearty meal. After his guests have eaten, he picks the fattest of the three, skews him, roasts him on the fire, and then eats him. In the succeeding days, he tries to fatten the remaining two, slaughtering sheep for them in the hope that they will eat and put on more weight, so he can enjoy more of their meat. This motif of feeding the intended victim is repeated in many Bedouin tales.

After Odysseus gives wine to the Cyclops and makes sure he is drunk and has fallen asleep, he sticks a hot skewer into his eye and blinds him. Odysseus prepares the skewer from a piece of wood he has broken off from the huge Cyclops's club. In the Bedouin story, the hero blinds the giant with a white-hot iron wire. The wine element is completely absent from the Bedouin version, which is not surprising, since the story is told in a society that forbids drinking wine.

Odysseus and his friends manage to escape from the cave by tying the rams in threes, side by side, and the men tie themselves under the ram in the center so that the long wool of the rams will cover them (motif K603, "Escape under ram's belly. By hiding under the belly of a ram the hero escapes under the legs of the blind ogre"). In the Bedouin version, the hero uses a similar trick: he wraps himself in the skin of the sheep slaughtered by the giant as he prepared the meal at the beginning of the story (motif K521.1, "Escape by dressing in animal [bird, human] skin").

In both cases, the giant's suspicion arises. In Odysseus's story, the Cyclops notices that the ram who carries Odysseus is moving in an unusual way:

> My poor ram, why are you leaving the cave / Last of all? You've never lagged behind before. / You were always the first to reach the soft grass / With your big steps, first to reach the river, / First to want to go back to the yard / At evening. Now you're last of all. Are you sad / About your master's eye? A bad man blinded me, / Him and his nasty friends, getting me drunk, / Noman—but he's not out of trouble yet![13]

But he does not realize that the reason for the unusual movement is the weight of Odysseus's body, which clings to the ram's belly. Instead, he attributes the ram's slowness to its grief for the loss of its master's eye.

In the Bedouin story, the giant gropes the ram and wonders how the slaughtered lamb has been revived: "When he took hold of his horns he recalled and said, 'Oh my. . . . That is the ram that I killed a long time ago.'" In both cases, the stupidity of the giant prevents him from understanding what is happening.

At the end of the story, Odysseus takes the sheep to his ship. He communicates with the Cyclops from a distance and mocks him. The angry giant throws a large rock in an attempt to sink the ship. In our story, too, the hero robs the giant's flocks, but the blind giant does not try to fight him. Instead, he begs the hero to leave him some sheep so he can revive his soul.

It is interesting to note that this description corresponds to the description of the Cyclops Polyphemus in the work *Aeneid*, written by Virgil (70–19 BCE). Virgil relates how Aeneas and his friends reach the island of the Cyclops and meet a Greek man from the city of Ithaca, who was one of Odysseus's men and was abandoned on the island. He tells them about the encounter between Odysseus and Polyphemus. Virgil describes the Cyclops as a lonely, miserable creature whose only friends are the sheep and the rams of his herd.[14]

In the last episode of the Bedouin story, the hero returns to his country after a four-month journey and encounters skepticism from his listeners when he describes his experiences. He leads them to the cave to see the giant with their own eyes, and many of those who go with him die of fear because of the terrible sight of the giant. This scene further emphasizes the heroism and courage of our hero, who unlike them managed to deal with the giant and be saved.

In another version of the story I recorded in the ʿArab el-Sawāʿed tribe, the protagonists are three brothers who hire themselves as shepherds to an old man for a salary of ten Talian (Italian coin). Later it turns out that the old man is a *ḥūt*. The *ḥūt* devours the hero's two brothers, while he escapes, covered in the skin of a ram that he slaughtered. The monster's blindness is not mentioned at all.

In 1910, the German researcher Hans Schmidt wrote down a version reminiscent of the Bedouin story in many details. The story was told by Abu Ibrahim in the Arab village of Bīr Zēt near Rāmallah.[15] This story also includes three heroes who embark with the intent to rob: one is a Bedouin, the second a city dweller, and the third a *fellah* (a peasant farmer). They can see the shepherd from afar but cannot find a suitable occasion for robbing him of a sheep, as planned. Eventually, they arrive at the shepherd's cave in the evening. The shepherd welcomes them as honored guests, spreads out a rug for them, and invites them to sit down. Then he honors them with bread and meat, but it soon becomes clear to them that this is human meat, and they stop eating. They understand that their host is a *ġūl*. The *ġūl* takes his meal and then, as dessert, takes the urban hero, slaughters him, roasts him on a fire, and eats him. He ties the other two with their hands behind their backs. Soon he kills the *fellah*, too, and devours him. The remaining hero seeks refuge at the back of the cave and discovers a young woman hanging by her hair from the ceiling. He learns that this woman went out to collect herbs with her friend. The two fell into the hands of the *ġūl*. One of them was slaughtered by him, and that was the source of the meat the *ġūl* offered to his guests. The Bedouin manages to release the woman, and she helps him untie his bound hands. On the advice of the woman, the hero waits until the *ġūl* falls asleep, and then he pokes a burning stick into his eye and blinds him. The protagonist, described by the narrator as "the brother of Shamma" (Shamma is a cultural heroine in the Palestinian Arab folk narrative), slaughters a young ram, removes its skin, and wraps it around his body. The giant stands at the entrance to the cave, with his hands feels the rams going out to pasture, and examines the ram's head with his fingers but does not recognize the hero hiding underneath. After he manages to escape from the cave, the hero taunts the blind *ġūl* and mocks him. The *ġūl* is filled with rage and dies of anger. After the death of the *ġūl*, the hero returns to the cave, releases the woman, marries her, and returns home safely. At the end of the story, the narrator wishes that anyone who sets out on a journey will return home safely, as rich as the hero of the story.

As in the Bedouin story, here there are three heroes, but in the Bedouin story all three are Bedouin, differing only in size, and the hero who lives was the thinnest of them. In the story from Bīr Zēt, the three heroes represent the three classes in the Arab society: urban, peasant, and Bedouin. The hero who remains alive is the Bedouin, which emphasizes the superiority of the Bedouin over the city dweller and peasant in the eyes of the narrator and perhaps also attests to the Bedouin origin of the story. The woman who appears in the story turns it into a novella, full of motifs found in other stories about *ġūls*: eating human flesh, hanging a girl by her hair, and dying of anger.

The image of a giant cannibal *ġūl* who has two eyes is familiar in Arabic literature from the stories of the *Arabian Nights*. In the third journey of Sindbad's wandering in the seas, the *ġūl* is described as a huge black monster that dwells inside a castle on a deserted island and that captures Sindbad and his friends.[16] He feeds the group and then chooses the fattest among them, throws him down, kills him by stepping on his neck, roasts him on coals like kebab, and finally swallows him. This description is reminiscent of the choice of the victim in the first Bedouin story. There, too, the giant first devours the fattest of the three. Unlike the stories mentioned above, Sindbad and his friends are not imprisoned in a cave or a castle but on an island where they have no escape from the *ġūl*. In the *ġūl*'s absence, they build a boat, and then, when he returns to the castle and falls asleep, they blind him with iron skewers, which they have heated with fire. As in the story of Odysseus, the blind *ġūl* calls his friends and they pursue Sindbad and his friends. Some of Sindbad's friends drown in the sea or die from the rocks thrown at them by the other *ġūls*, and in the end only three, Sindbad and two of his friends, are saved. The story of the sheep and the escape by means of hiding under a ram's belly or by a skin covering are not mentioned at all in Sindbad's story.

In another story from *Arabian Nights*, "The Story of Prince Sayf al-Mulūk and the Princess Badīʿat al-ğamāl," the hero fights with a *ġūl* who has blinded his friends with poisoned milk. The hero serves him wine, and after he becomes drunk, he blinds the *ġūl*'s eyes with hot skewers and then slays him with his sword.[17]

The two versions, the Bedouin version and the one from Bīr Zēt, are much closer to the ancient Hellenic story than to the *Arabian Nights*, although the *Arabian Nights* have a distinct Arab imprint and are an inseparable part of the Muslim culture.

In one of the stories I heard from Muḥammad Ibrahim, of the ʿArab el-Ḥuğērāt tribe, the Hellenistic escape motif appears: hiding under the belly of a ram or a goat. I wrote down this story in Hebrew, and here it is:

> One day a group of Bedouins went out to steal goats from the shepherd of a neighboring tribe who used to house his goats in a large cave. When the thieves came to the shepherd's cave, they realized that he was sleeping near the mouth of the cave. The thieves sought a trick how to steal the goats without waking the shepherd, and then they discovered that the cave had another opening in the ceiling. The thieves took a rope and lowered one of their members through the opening in the ceiling. The thief began tying the goats one

by one with the rope in his hand. Each time he signaled to his friends outside, and they would pull and raise the goat and roll back the rope. With the goats in the cave was the shepherd's donkey. Because of the darkness in the cave, the thief accidentally tied the rope to the donkey's neck and motioned to his friends to pull the rope. As they began to pull the rope, the donkey began to shake. The shepherd woke up, and the thieves, fearing that they would be caught, abandoned their friend in the cave and ran away. The shepherd realized that a thief had penetrated his cave and was hiding among the goats. The cunning thief took advantage of the fact that among the goats there was also a billy goat. He was hanged under the billy goat's belly, and its long hair, extending nearly to the ground, hid him from the shepherd, and left the cave unharmed [at that time the Bedouin did not shear billy goats' hair].

When the thief saw that the shepherd was still busy looking for him inside the cave, while his goats were walking out of the cave, he grabbed thirty of them and fled to his tribal camp. When he arrived there with all the goats, he found his friends sitting in his father's house, mourning his death. None of them believed that he would be able to get out alive from the shepherd's hands.

Although the story is a realistic act, as it were, without giants and *ġūls*, some of the motifs we saw in previous stories recur, such as stealing the herd being a motive for the actions of the hero and his friends.

The Odysseus story has an interesting humorous motif. When the Cyclopes ask Odysseus his name, Odysseus replies, "Noman is my name, Noman do they call me—my mother and my father, and all my friends too."[18] When Polyphemus's friends hear his cries in the middle of the night and ask him who has attacked him, he replies, "Noman," and they conclude that no enemy has attacked him but rather a disease sent to him by the gods.

In the first Bedouin story, the humorous motif appears in the description of the giant who touches the skin of the ram that he himself slaughtered, without realizing that the hero is hidden beneath it. In Muḥammad Ibrahim's realistic story, the humoristic point is connected to the thief, who mistakenly ties the rope to the donkey's neck, causing it to bray and allowing the shepherd to understand what is happening and block the door. Adding a humorous episode to the story is a familiar storytellers' trick, which slightly relaxes the narrative tension at the climax. We encounter this trick again and again in written literature and the theater.

Notes

1. As in *šnū al-ġanam*, "What sheep!" the interrogative *šnū* ("what") is used by the Bedouins to mean "how great" a thing is by grammaticalization to an exclamation particle. Such processes exist in many languages, including Arabic. See also below in this story *šnū ṣāḥibha!* ("What an owner!"). The word *šnū* is not used in sedentary dialects in Israel, where it is *šū*.

2. Seen here in *mā humma ḥayaḷḷa*, "they (are) not somebody unimportant," the word *ḥayaḷḷa* derives from *ḥayyā 'aḷḷa*, "Allah has blessed [it]"—in other words, "May Allah bless [it]"—said when one does not want to give exact details or does not know details about someone or something. This expression is frequent in Arabic dialects, not only in Galilee Bedouin dialects in Israel and the Palestinian Authority.

3. *yā zēn yā šēn*, "Oh good, oh bad," is an exact Bedouin exclamation of alarm, fear, and begging for help, when someone is in severe trouble. The translation adapts it to English, to some extent. For similar examples, see chapter 23, story A. *zēn* means "good" in Bedouin dialects ("beauty" in LA; cf. Wehr, *Dictionary of Modern Written Arabic*, 390). *šēn* is "disgrace, shame," in LA/MSA (Wehr, 499) and in the Levant (Barthélemy, *Dictionnaire arabe-français*, 421).

4. *minkom warākam*, "from you [ahead of you] and behind you," is a threat meaning "I am both in front of you and behind you—you cannot escape."

5. In LA, *ma'asa* is a transitive verb ("to squash, press someone/something"). Here in *ṣāram yim'asam*, it is used as an intransitive verb: they themselves began to be pressed or press each other.

6. *yigarges* is a Bedouin four-radical vocabulary item, apparently derived from the three-radical root *grš/qrš*, which is used in Syria, meaning "gnaw one's teeth on a hard object, bite" (cf. Barthélemy, *Dictionnaire arabe-français*, 647). The phonetic transfer of *š-s* occurs also in other words in Arabic dialects (e.g., *šağara/sağara*, "tree," and *šarīṭ/sarīṭ* "iron bar" in this story) and other articulation-wise close consonants.

7. *ṣaddagu al-xurrāfiyya. xilṣat al-ḥaddūṯa* "They believed the story. The story has ended"—Arabic has several narration types with different names. The Bedouins' stories distinguish *xurrāfiyya*, which means a folktale, derived from xarraf, "to talk, tell," and *ḥaddūṯa*, derived from the root *ḥdṯ*, "to speak, tell" (cf. LA *'uḥdūṯa*, "a small story"; Barthélemy, *Dictionnaire arabe-français*, 147). In general, Bedouin women's folktales involve imaginary creatures, and men tell stories and legends (*guṣṣa/giṣṣa*, "story") about Bedouin tribal and historical heroes. Henkin, *Negev Arabic*, 99-102. Linguistic structural features also distinguish female from male tales/stories (cf. Rosenhouse, "A Comparative Analysis of Stories Narrated by Bedouin and Sedentary Male and Female Speakers").

8. Homer, *The Essential Odyssey*, pp. 64–77, 9:103–551.

9. Homer, p. 70, 9:313–19.

10. Homer, p. 70, 9:297–8.

11. Homer, p. 67, 9:207–8.

12. Homer, p. 69, 9:258–60.

13. Homer, p. 74, 9:445–53.

14. Virgil, *Aeneid*, Book 3.

15. Schmidt and Kahle, 1918, 1:228–39.

16. Burton, *Arabian Nights*, nights 546–50.

17. Burton, nights 772–73.

18. Homer, *The Essential Odyssey*, p. 72, 9:364–365.

28. Frēṭ Rummān (Snow White)

NARRATOR: Zehiyya Ġrifāt

TRIBE: *ʿArab el-Ġrifāt*

IFA 17413 September 11, 1982

1 nxarref ʾaw nenām, yā sāmʿīn al-kalām.[1]	1 Shall we tell or sleep, o listeners of the speech?
2 alla hā-l-mara mā tiḥbal wala tğīb. u-ğōzha yištaġal. yōm ʾaġa biyyāʿ, "rummān l-al-ḥabal, rummān l-al-ḥabal." ʾaġat hāḏi, ʾaxḏat kūz rummān.	2 There was this woman, who did not get pregnant and did not have a child. And her husband was working. One day, a peddler came: "Pomegranates for pregnancy, pomegranates for pregnancy." This [woman] came, took a pomegranate.
6 kalat hā-kūz-al-rummān, gāḷat, "yā ṛaḇḇʷi,[2] subḥānak wa-taʿāla, ʿizztak u-karāmtak u-ğalāltak, taṭʿimni bint ʾaw walad miṯel ḥabbet hā-r-rummān—ḥamra miṯelha u-mlīḥa." subḥāno b-gidirto u-b-ğalālto, u-min baʿad ʿišrīn sana ğābat hā-l-bint.	6 She ate the pomegranate and said, "O my Allah, your praise and greatness, with your power and generosity, and greatness, give me a daughter or a son like this grain of pomegranate—red like it and pretty." Praise Allah, in his power and sublimity, and after twenty years [of barrenness], she had this girl.
13 gāmat sammatha "Frēṭ Rummān." u-hāḏ-al-bint hī Freṭ Rummān, gadd miṯel mā hiyya šalabiyya u-mlīḥa. gaddēš ⁱtgūl mlīḥa mlīḥa. ṣārat ⁱtgūl al-nās, ṣārat ⁱtgūl "Frēṭ Rummān ʾaḥsan min ʾummha." ʿād hī al-mara ġārat šwayye, ṣārat innha tġār šwoyye, tizʿal ʾanna bintha tṣīr ʾaḥsan minha.	13 She named her Pomegranate Grain. And this girl, Pomegranate Grain, how pretty and beautiful [she was]. As much as you say—pretty pretty [very pretty]. People started saying, "Pomegranate Grain is prettier than her mother." This woman was jealous a little, she began being jealous a little, angry that her daughter would be prettier than her.

20 ṣār ’abūha yeḥibb al-bint ’akṯar min ’ummha. ta-tguḷ-ḷo, “lēš tḥibb al-bint ’akṯar minne^{y}?” yegūḷ-ḷa, “ā. hiyya ’aḥsan minneč.”	20 Her father began to love the daughter more than her mother. She would say to him, “Why do you love the girl more than me?” He would say to her, “Yes . . . she is prettier than you are.”
24 ṣārat ^{e}tgūḷ la-li-nǧūm, “yā nǧūm, man ’aḥsan, ’ana walla Frēṭ Rummān?” tgūḷ-ḷa, “Frēṭ Rummān.” “gumaṛ, gumaṛ, mīn ’aḥsan, ’ana wella Frēṭ Rummān?”yegūḷ-ḷa, “Frēṭ Rummān.” “yā ʿarab, mīn ’ahsan, ’ana wella Frēṭ Rummān?” yegūḷ-ḷa, “Frēṭ Rummān.” ʿa-kull saʿalat kull ’azmaʿa(t).	24 She started saying to the stars, “O stars, who is prettier—me or Pomegranate Grain?” They [the stars] would say to her, “Pomegranate Grain.” “O moon, moon, who is prettier—me or Pomegranate Grain?” It would say to her, “Pomegranate Grain.” “O Bedouins, who is prettier, me or Pomegranate Grain?” It would say to her, “Pomegranate Grain.” Everyone she asked, all [the people] agreed [gave her the same answer].
31 ṣārat “’ani mā l(i), widdi ’aḏbaḥḥa. wa-’afaḏḏal.” gāl(a)t-ilha, ʿemlat zāda zuwwāda, gāl(a)t ilha, “yā imma, ba-nrūḥ ’ani wiyyāki ʿala la-xawāḷ.” gāḷat-ḷa, “lā, mā nrūh, imma, ’ani mā arūḥ ’aʿref ʿand xawāli, mā ’aʿrefhom.” hāḏi “lā, ’anṭēna ʿand al-xawāḷ, widd ’aʿarrfek ʿala-l-xawāḷ.”	31 She began, “I don’t have [a choice], I must kill her and I will be better.” She said to her, made provisions, and said to her, “O child, we are going, I with you, to the maternal uncles’.” She said to her, “No, we will not go, Mom, I will not go to [get to] know my uncles, I don’t know them.” This [her mother said], “No, let us [go] to the uncles, you and I, I want to get you acquainted with your uncles.”
38 gāmat ’axḏat al-bint bēn ^{i}ǧbāl, bēn widyān, mā biha ġār ^{i}ḏbāʿa w-al-ġuwaḷ u-kull ši. mā ta-ḏaḷḷ al-lēl, ġābat aš-šams wa-d-dinya ʿatma, fišš^{i} gamar, wa-widdha tnām.	38 She took the girl among hills, among valleys, in which there were nothing but wolves and *ġūls* and everything [like those]. Until they remained [in the] night, the sun set and the world [was] dark, no moon, and she wanted to sleep.
43 gālt-^{e}la, “wēn, mā-’ana ḥāṭṭa šʿari bi-šʿarek, ’alla lḥami bi-lḥamek, ’awāʿī b-awāʿīk, u-ḏrāʿek taḥt rāsi u-ḏrāʿi taḥt rāsek.” mi hī tirkin ʿalēha al-bint—ṣabiyye ṣārat.[3]	43 She said to her, “Where, I will put my hair in your hair, my flesh in your flesh, my clothes in your clothes, and your arm under my head and my arm under your head.” She does not trust her, the girl—she became a maiden.
48 gāḷ(a)t ilha, “’ā.” xayyaṭat ^{i}lha aṯ-ṯōb bi-ṯōbha, u-rāḥat ḥaṭṭat ^{i}ḏrāʿha taḥt rāsa u-nāmat. ḥarām ʿala-l-bint, min at-taʿab w-al-ǧūʿ min al-’ihāna, ġiflat.	48 She said to her, “Yes.” She sewed her dress with her dress, and put her arm under her head and slept. Pity [shame] on the girl, for [because of] the difficulties and hunger and the humiliation, she fell asleep.
52 al-mara mā ġiflat. al-mara maʿāha mōs. gaṭʿat aṯ-ṯōb tibaḥḥa, u-giṭʿat aš-šaʿar, u-ʿāwadat tābat ʿa-l-bēt, u-ḏaḷḷat al-bint nāima. al-bint ḏaḷḷat nāima, ta-ṭilʿat aš-šams ʿalēha, ḥimat. ’iz(a) gāmat aš-šams, giʿadat.	52 The woman did not sleep. She had a knife, she cut her dress and cut her hair and went back home, and the girl remained asleep. The girl remained asleep until the sun rose on her, she got warm. When the sun rose, she woke up.

57 mā gʿadat—mā ḥawleha ḥāda. "yāmma, yāmma, yāmma," mā fīš ḥada ḥawalēha, alla ha-l-ġūḷa ali gāḷat lēha, "sm-aḷḷa ʿalēki,[4] yumma, yā Frēṭ Rummān." ṭallat ʿalēha—miš ʾommha. gāḷat-^{i}lha, "sm-aḷḷa ʿalēki, yumma, yā Frēṭ Rummān, ʿalēk(i) ʾaḷḷa w-ʾamān ʾaḷḷa, w-al-xāyin yexūno ʾaḷḷa.

57 She woke up—no one near [around] her. "Mommy, Mommy, Mommy"—nobody there around her, except this *Ġūla*, who said to her, "Allah's blessing on you, child, Pomegranate Grain." She looked at her—[she was] not her mother. She said to her, "Allah's blessing on you, child, Pomegranate Grain. Allah is on you and Allah's security, and the traitor, Allah will betray him.

65 minnēn ğīti hēna, min bāb al-naʿīm la-bāb el-ğaḥīm?"[5] gāḷat-ḷa, "ğābatni al-gisma wa-n-naṣīb." xaḏatha al-ġūḷa, ḥaṭṭatha l-ġūḷa sārḥa b-ġuzlān. ḥaṭṭatha ta-hiyya b-al-ġuzlān u-rawwaḥathan ʿa-l-mġāra. mġāra al-ʿādi, mġāra tabʿat al-maʿza. u-fawwatat hā-l-ġuzlān u-fawwatatha.

65 "Wherefrom did you come here, from the door of paradise to the door of hell?" She said to her, "Fate and lot brought me." The *Ġūla* took her, made her to herd the deer. She made her so she would be with the deer and led them home to the cave. A usual cave, a cave of the sheep. And [the *Ġūla*] made the deer enter and made her enter.

72 ḥammamatha u-labbasatha u-gāḷt-^{i}lha, "ʾenti binti be-ʿahad aḷḷa, u-l-xāyin yixūno ʾaḷḷa. hāy zemān ʾadawwer ʿalēki, yā Frēṭ Rummān." hāḏ-al-ġūḷa fawwatatha b-al-ġuzlān, yaʿani, ṣārat kull yom al-ġūḷa trawweḥ bal-ġuzlān tgūl, "^{e}Frēṭ Rummān, iftaḥi al-bāb la-l-ġuzlān." tiftaḥ-ilha ^{e}Frēṭ Rummān al-bāb la-l-ġuzlān.

72 She bathed her and dressed her and said to her, "You are my daughter in Allah's covenant, and the traitor Allah will betray him. It has been long since I began looking for you, o Pomegranate Grain." This *ġūla* made her bring in the deer, that is, the *Ġūla* began every day to bring the deer home, saying, "Pomegranate Grain, open the door for the deer." Pomegranate Grain would open the door for the deer.

80 fawwatatha ʿa-l-maġāra ğawwa, ʿan(d)a bī dūr, ʿinda. fawwatata ʿa-l-mġāra ğawwa. gāḷat ilha, "hāḏa l-bāb—iftaḥī, u-hāḏa l-bāb—iftaḥī, hāḏi l-ḥanafiyya—ftaḥīha, u-hāḏa ḥanafiyya—tiftaḥīha, bas yā yumma, lā tiftaḥi al-^{i}msakkarāt."

80 She made her enter the cave [inside]. She had apartments [rooms]. She made her enter inside the cave. She said to her, "This door, open it, and this door—open it, and this faucet [tap], open it, and this faucet, open it, but o child, do not open the closed ones."

86 wa-ʿaṭata mafatīḥ la-l-maḥall kullayāto, al-ġūḷa. lammin ʾağat al-bint, ṣārat tġīb al-ġūḷa, ṣārat tiftaḥ al-maḥallāt alli gāḷat "lā tiftaḥīhum." fitḥat ʾawwal ḥanafiyya u-ġaṭṭat iṣbaḥḥa wunno kullo ḏahab. ʾaṣbaḥ eṣbaʿha kullo ḏahab ʿa-l-laḥam.

86 And she gave her keys to all the place, the *Ġūla*. When the girl came, the *Ġūla* began to stay out [with the deer], she [the girl] started opening the places which she had told her "do not open them." She opened the first tap and dipped her finger, and lo, it was all gold. All her finger became gold on the flesh.

92 wu-tgīm ^{e}tgīm . . . ^{e}tgīm eḏ-ḏahab mā yezūl aḏ-ḏahab ʿan el-laḥam. ṯāni maḥall winno bī banāt ṯintēn, mʿallagāt min šaʿarhen. mā ḥakathen, ʾā. sakkarat el-bāb u-laflafat eṣbaḥḥa.

92 And she [tried to] take off, take off . . . take off the gold—it did not get off the flesh. The second place—lo, there were two girls, hanging on their hair. She did not speak to them. Yes. She closed the door and bandaged her finger.

97 “Frēṭ Rummān, ’iftaḥi al-bāb la-l-ġuzlān—be-greināthen eḥṣaibāt u-be-derrāthen ḥleibāt. Frēṭ Rummān, ’iftaḥi al-bāb la-l-ġuzlān—be-greināthen eḥṣaibāt u-be-derrāthen ḥleibāt.”	97 “Pomegranate Grain, open the door for the deer—with their little bountiful horns and in their udders there is [much] milk. Pomegranate Grain, open the door for the deer—with their little bountiful horns there is [much] milk and in their udders there is much milk.”
102 tiftaḥ al-bāb willa mlflafa eṣbaḥḥa Freṭ Rummān. lamman nādata, “lēš yā ḥabībti, eṣbaʿek mlaflafa?” gāḷat -lēha, “ʾinğiraḥt.” al-ġūḷa ʿirfat. lamminna ağata gāḷat ilha, “hāti ’ašūfo ani” gāḷat ilha, gāḷt ilha, “lā, biwğaʿni.” gāḷat ilha, “yimma, ’ana mā-gult-lek ’innek mā tiftaḥi al-bāb? miš muhimm.” gadd-mi hiyya ġālia ʿalēha.	102 She opened the door and lo—Pomegranate Grain’s finger was bandaged. When she called her, “Why, my dear, is your finger bandaged?” She said to her, “I was wounded.” The *Ġūla* knew [it]. When she came to her, she said to her, “Let me see it, [let me].” She said to her, said to her, “No, it hurts.” She said to her, “Child, didn’t I tell you not to open the door? Never mind [it’s not important].” [See] how precious [beloved] she [the girl] was for her [the *Ġūla*].
110 yōm winna hā-l-bayyā(ʿ)-al-amšūṭ, ’a-l-bukal, l-al-mitēin, ’awwal marra yīği hnāk bayyāʿ ʿala ḥmār. ṭelʿat ʿalē Frēṭ Rummān. min kuṯr aḏ-ḏahab alli ṣār bī ʿindha starxaṣat al-ḏahab waxaḏat mušoṭ biyya.	110 One day, lo—there came this peddler of combs, groceries for two hundred, [it was] the first time a peddler comes there on a donkey. Pomegranate Grain went out to him. Since she had a large quantity of gold, she considered it cheap and bought combs with gold.
115 gāḷ-ḷa l-biyyā(ʿ), “’inti, bī ’ins hān?” gāḷat lo, “intibih, hā ’ani, Frēṭ Rummān.” gāḷ-ḷa, “Frēṭ Rummān ʿandīna kānt bī u-’ummha waddatha u-warhafatha.” gāḷat lo, “’ani Frēṭ Rummān. ’ammi hā hnāk?” gāḷ-ḷa,“’ā.” gāḷat-lo, “widdi ’awaddī-la maʿāk hā-l-amāna, šwayyet ḏahab la-’ummi.”	115 He said, “Are there people here?” She said, “Look, here I am, Pomegranate Grain.” He said, “Pomegranate Grain was at our place and her mother sent her [away] and got rid of her.” She said to him, “I am Pomegranate Grain. Is my mother there?” He said to her, “Yes.” She said to him, “I want to give her with you this [present] in trust, some gold for my mother.”
122 gāḷ-ḷaha, “ṭayyib. yaḷḷa, ’aʿṭīha.” xaḏat-lo kull iḏ-ḏahab, ḥaṭṭathen bi-ḏarf wa-’aʿṭathen ’amāna l-al-biyyāʿ.	122 He said to her, “Good, go on, I’ll give it to her.” She took for him all the gold, put it in an envelope, and gave it in trust to the salesman.
125 ’ummha baʿadha mā - mā zaʿlāna minha keṯīr, bas biddha tmawwitha, ba-nāy. “’ana ḥaṭṭatha b-al-bādiya u-hiyya baʿadha ṭayyiba? ’ana bamawwitha. tʿāwid tirğaʿ ʿalayya bukra, hāḏi.”	125 Her mother was still very angry with her; but she wanted to kill her, from the distance. “I put her in the desert and she is still well [healthy]? I will kill her. [If not—] she will come back to me again tomorrow [in the future], this one.”

130 ǧat, ǧābat ilha mišṭ. māḥḥa samm u-mā ḥada. waddato maʿa l-biyyāʿ “ka-’amāna lā-ḥad yiftaḥa ’alla binti. lamma tiṣal tiftaḥo u-tmaššaṭ al-bint šaʿarha.”

130 She brought for her a comb. With her [there was] poison, and no one [knew]. She gave it over to the peddler, “As a trust—no one shall open it except my daughter. When you reach [her] she will open it and the girl will comb her hair.”

134 hāḏa l-bayyāʿ ṣār yidūr hā-n-nās b-al-ḏahab alli ʿaṭato Frēṭ Rummān. rāḥ ʿala Frēṭ Rummān. gāḷ-ḷha “hāḏa l-’amāna min ’ummeč.” gāḷat-ḷo, “’e, hāḏi lā, hā, ’aḷḷāhu taʿāla, mā baddi (i)yyā . . .”

134 This peddler began going round the people with the gold that Pomegranate Grain had given him. He went to Pomegranate Grain and said to her, “This is in trust from your mother.” She said to him, “Er, this, no, this—Great Allah, I don’t want it.” . . .

139 ġallat mayya ʿala n-nār u-ġassalat rāsha u-maššaṭat. ’awwal nāḥa tkassaru sinnēn b-rāsha; ṯāni nāḥa ḥaṭṭat ’edēha, miṯel haḏāka, ṯāni nāḥa, ṯāliṯ marra—mātat Frēṭ Rummān.

139 She boiled water on the fire and washed her head and combed [it]. The first stroke—two [comb] teeth broke in her head; the second stroke—she put her hands like that, the second time—[with] the third stroke Pomegranate Grain died.

143 ǧat al-ġūḷa min ġād “^{e}Frēṭ Rummān, ’iftaḥi al-bāb la-l-ġuzlān. ^{e}Frēṭ Rumān, ’iftaḥi al-bāb la-l-ġuzlān.” mā fitḥat al-bāb. gāḷat “’in ligētha nāima ʿalēha ’aḷḷa u-’amān ’aḷḷa. wa-’in ligētha ṭayyiba wallāhi ġēr ’ākolha, la-Frēṭ Rummān.”

143 The *Ġūla* came from there [outside]: “Pomegranate Grain, open the door for the deer, Pomegranate Grain, open the door for the deer.” She did not open the door. She said, “If I find her sleeping—Allah is with her and Allah’s security, and if I find her healthy, by Allah, I will [definitely] eat her, Pomegranate Grain.”

149 raḥat, fatḥat al-bāb willa Frēṭ Rummān (mayyita). “yā ḥabībti, yā Frēṭ Rummān, yā Frēṭ Rummān”—mā trudd Frēṭ Rummān.

149 She went, opened the door, and lo—Pomegranate Grain [was dead]. “Oh my dear, oh Pomegranate Grain, oh Pomegranate Grain.” She did not answer, Pomegranate Grain.

152 ǧābat hī bi-ǧmal al-hawa. “haddi ǧmal el-hawa, waddi aḥuṭṭ ʿalēk Frēṭ Rummān.” hadda ǧmal el-hawa, ḥaṭṭat ʿalē busoṭ, ḥaṭṭat al-fist^{y}ān, labbasat Frēṭ Rummān min ’aġla al-xām, min ’aġla (a) ǧ-ǧnās.

152 She brought the Air Camel “Alight, Air Camel, I will deliver, put on you Pomegranate Grain.” The Air Camel descended, she put on it carpets, put on her the dress, dressed Pomegranate Grain with the most expensive linen material, the most expensive kinds.

157 aḏ-ḏahab alli ḥaṭṭat ʿala Frēṭ Rummān bigiyyima l-insān šēla. ’abl-ma ṭār ǧmal el-hawa min ġād, rāḥat la-ǧmal el-hawa, gāḷat-lo, “’amāna b-xāṭr-ʿalēk, yā ǧmal el-hawa.

157 The gold that she put on Pomegranate Grain, one cannot assess its value at all. Before the Air Camel flew away from there, she went to it and said to it, “[A] trust upon your honor, o Air Camel.

161 lā thaddi ’alla ’iḏa gālū-lak “b-ḥayāt alli ʿalēk, haddi,” la Frēṭ Rummān. gaḷlab hāḏa taḥat Freṭ Rummān, ʿala b-Frēṭ Rummān, saḥib ḥālo.

161 “Do not alight except if they say to you, ‘Upon the life of that which is on you, alight’—[that is] Pomegranate Grain. It turned round, under Pomegranate Grain, raised Pomegranate Grain, and went off.

165 willa hū mārig ʿala malʿab fitbōl, u-maʿāham wāḥad fagīr ʿaglo kebīr. u-hāḏa ygūḷ-ḷo, "walāk, haddi yā ğmal el-hawa," mā hadda; u-hāḏa yegūḷ-ḷo, "walāk haddi yā ğmal el-hawa," mā hada; u-haḏāk yeguḷ-ḷo, "walāk, haddi yā ğmal el-hawa,"

165 Lo, it was passing above a football ground [field], and with them [those who played there] there was a poor one, with a big brain. One said to him, "O you, alight, o Air Camel." It did not alight. And this one said to him, "O you, alight, o Air Camel." It did not alight. And that one said to him, "O you, o Air Camel." It did not alight.

171 mā ḥada yehaddo. baʿadēn nāda ʿalē al-fagīr, "be-ḥayāt alli ʿalēk, tehaddi, yā ğmal el-hawa." . . . hadda ğmal el-hawa.

171 No one made it alight. Afterward, the poor [man] called it, "Upon the life of that which is on you, alight, o Air Camel." The Air Camel alighted.

174 lammen hadda, xaḏa hāḏa, gāḷ-ḷam "'intam al-māl temannētam, u-'ana bāxuḏ hāḏi l-bint w-axaḷḷi 'immi tġassilha u-nidfinha." xaḏam aḏ-ḏahab, xaḏam al-maṣāri, xaḏam al-bsāṭ, xaḏam al-suğod, šālha u-rāḥ

174 When it alighted, this one took and said to them, "You wanted the money and I will take this girl and will let my mother wash her and we will bury her." They took the gold, took the money, took the carpets, and the small carpets, he carried her, and went.

180 xaḏāha gāḷ-ḷa, "yā yumma." gāḷat-lo, "yā yumma." gāḷ-ḷa, "'aġli mayyāt, xaḷḷi yumma, ta-ġassli hā-l-bint, 'ana lagetha ʿala ğmal el-hawa, miyyta, ġasslīha w-nidfinha."

180 [he] took her and said to her, "O mother." She said, "O son." He said to her, "Boil water, Mother, let's wash this girl. I found her on the Air Camel, dead. Wash her and we will bury her."

185 gāḷat, "ā, yumma. 'aġli l-mayya, 'aġsilha, w-nidfinha kamān." rāḥat ġallat al-mayya, u-faršat meramiyya taḥtīha, u-ṣārat tġassilha.

185 She said to him, "Yes, o son. I will boil water and wash her and we will also bury her." She went and boiled the water, brushed salvia beneath her, and began to wash her.

189 ṣārat tġassilha ʿa-šān yidifnūha, mā yigbirūha bidūn mā yġasslu. ṣārat al-mara wa-tġassilha ^{a}tgūm ^{e}thizz rāsa, winna fī arbaʿ–xams ^{e}snān ^{e}b-rāsha.

189 She began to wash her so that they would bury her, they do not bury without washing [the dead]. The woman began washing her, take and move her head and lo, there were four, five [comb] teeth in her head.

193 gilʿat 'awwal-wāḥad, gālat "'ax," ṯāni wāḥad—"^{e}mlabbe." ṯāliṯ wāḥad gāmat gāḷat "'ašhad 'an lā ilāh illa ḷḷāh u-mḥammad rasūl (Aḷḷāh)." lammin gāḷat hīč, al-xityāra gāḷat-ḷa, yaʿani . . . "hāy kānat miyyta u-halla ḏi fāqt." . . .

193 She plucked out one, she said, "Ach [ouch]," another one—"at your service [to Allah]." With the third one she got up and said, "I testify that there is no Allah but Allah, and Muḥammad is the Messenger [of Allah]." When she said this, the old woman said to her, that is . . . "This one was dead and now this [one] woke up [has revived]."

199 ğābat-la 'awāʿi, al-'aṣabīḥ, u-geʿedat, u-ğābat-la 'awāʿi, u-labbasatha, ğābat-la 'awāʿi, el-ḥawāiğ, u-laflafatha[6] u-ḥammamatha min gabel labbasatha, u-gaʿʿadatha u-zaʿʿaratha, willa hiyya Frēṭ Rummān. mā tigdar thuṭṭha fī hā-l-'anwār.

199 She brought her clothes, the morning clothes, she got up, and she dressed her the things, and wrapped her, and bathed her before she dressed her, and made her get up and fluffed her hair—and lo, she was Pomegranate Grain. She [or: you] could not put her in the [day]light.

205 ṣārat il-mara timnaʿha tiṭlaʿ bēn an-nās, ʾabṣar mā tiṭlaʿ ʿa-l-nās . . . min xōf mā wāḥad yišūfha fi ṭ-ṭirīg u-yāxuḏha la-ʾilo.	205 The woman began stopping her from going out among people, lest she would go to people . . . lest someone would see her on the way and would take her for himself.
208 yōm, al-^{i}xtiyāra rāḥat ʿala-l-mayya u-ʾağat hayya, ṭalʿat hiyya, widha trūḥ ʿala-l-mayya . . .[7]	208 One day, the old woman went to the water [well] and this one went out, she wanted to go to the water.
211 yōm šāfha ʾibn el-malak. rawwaḥ la-ʾimmo u-ʾabūh, gāḷ-ḷhum, "widdi ʾuxt al-walad al-fagīr." gāḷu-ḷo, "mā ʿindo xawāt." gāḷ-ḷhum, "baṭībeš ġēr mā ʾāxoḏ hāy al-bint."	211 One day the king's son saw her. He went home to his mother and father and said to them, "I want the poor boy's sister [to marry her]. They told him, "He does not have any sisters." He said to them, "I will not be well [healthy] unless I marry this girl."
216 rāḥu l-al-xityāra u-gāḷu-lha. gāḷat-ilhum "hāy mart ibni, ^{i}ḥkāyitha kaḏa kaḏa, miš binti." gāḷu-ḷha, "widna iyyāha, wa-law b-guwwa." al-xityāra xaḏat al-bint u-rāḥat la-ʿend ʾibn il-malek. xarrafū bi-giṣṣitha min al-ʾawwal la-l-ʾāxer.	216 They went to the old woman and said to her. She told them, "She is my son's bride, not his sister, not my daughter." They said to her, "We want her, even if by force." The old woman took the girl and went to the prince. They told him her story from the beginning to the end.
222 ṣār ʾibn al-malk widdo yfūt ʿind al-bint. gāḷu-ḷo, "ʾaḷḷa baʿaṯha l-al-fagīr, ʾinta ʾamīr, ḥarām tāxoḏha. ʾinta ʾayya bint widdak ʾiyyāha tāxoḏha." gāḷ, "ʾā."	222 The prince wanted to enter to the girl. They told him, "God sent her to the poor man, you are emīr, shame if you take her. You can take any girl you like." He said, "Yes."
226 ʾağa ʾaʿṭa l-al-fagīr xamsīn ġaname, xamsīn ʿanza, u-ʿaṭāha-l-māl, u-zaff Frēṭ Rummān u-waddāha la-l-fagīr. u-hāḏi l-xurrāfe—mlīḥa willa mī mlīḥa?	226 He gave the poor man fifty sheep and fifty goats and he gave her the money and married Pomegranate Grain off and gave her to the poor man. And this is the story—[is it] nice or not nice?

Commentary

The narrative type ATU 709, "Snow White," is one of the most familiar narrative types in the world. It appears throughout Europe, from the Scandinavian countries to the southern countries, Bulgaria, Greece, Italy, and Spain. It is known in North and East Africa and all over Asia, from Turkey to China, including the Middle East, Iran, Kurdistan, Iraq, Syria, Lebanon, Israel, and Saudi Arabia. In the IFA archives, there are parallels from Morocco and Yemen.

The description of the narrative type in Uther's *The Types of International Folktales*[8] is based mainly on the version recorded by the Grimm brothers: Snow White has skin white as snow and lips red as blood. A magic mirror tells her stepmother that Snow White is more beautiful than she is. The jealous stepmother orders a hunter to kill Snow White, but he substitutes an animal's heart and saves her.

Snow White goes to a house belonging to dwarfs (robbers), who adopt Snow White as their sister. The stepmother now attempts to kill her by means of poisoned lace, a poisoned comb, and a poisoned apple. The dwarfs succeed in reviving the maiden from the first two poisonings but fail with the third. They lay her in a glass coffin.

A prince resuscitates her and marries her. The stepmother is made to dance herself to death in red-hot shoes.

The four Bedouin parallels I recorded in three tribes—ʿArab el-Ġrifāt, ʿArab el-Ḥuǧērāt, and ʿArab el-Ḥaǧāǧra—differ in many details from this description. Only one version is presented here, the story as told by Zehiyya Ġrifāt from ʿArab el-Ġrifāt, but the three other versions are referred to: the version of ʿAliyah Muḥammad Ḥreb (version B), that of Šatwah Muḥammad (version C)—both from ʿArab el-Ḥuǧērāt—and the one of Ṭarwa Yāsīn from ʿArab el-Ḥaǧāǧra (version D).

In all the Bedouin versions, the mother is not a stepmother but the biological mother. A barren woman eats a "pregnancy pomegranate" she bought from a traveling peddler. She asks Allah for a daughter or a son "red and good." She gives birth to a daughter, and she calls her by the name of *Frēṭ Rummān* (Pomegranate Grain), as she is a "white and beautiful" child (version A and C), or she calls her by the name of *Ǧbēnah* (version D). Version B narrates that she sews in the doorway of her tent on a snowy day. Her finger is pierced by a needle, and her blood is dripping, and she asks for a girl "red as blood and white as snow." The father prefers his daughter to his wife because she is more beautiful than her mother. The mother asks the stars, the moon or the sun, and the tribe people which of them is more beautiful, and they all reply that her daughter is more beautiful than she is (motifs D1311.6.1, "Moon (stars) answers questions"; D1311.6.3, "Sun answers questions").

The mother wants to get rid of her daughter. She takes her to a deserted place on the pretext of visiting relatives the daughter does not know. Night falls, and they stay to sleep in the woods (or in a cave). The daughter asks her mother to tie their hair together and link their garments together by sewing. After the heroine falls asleep, the mother unties their hair, separates her garment from her daughter's, and abandons her. In the morning, a *ġūla* (or a *ġūl*) appears and takes the heroine under her protection. They live together in a cave with many rooms (or in a ruined city whose inhabitants have been eaten by the *ġūl*). The *ġūla* goes out every day to graze gazelles (or the *ġūla* goes out to fetch a cow to eat it) while the heroine is shut in the cave.

The *ġūla* gives the heroine the keys to all the rooms (or the *ġūl* gives her the keys to all the houses in the city) but forbids her to open a certain room (or three rooms or three houses in the city) and a certain tap. The heroine violates the prohibition: she opens the door of the room or the door of the forbidden house (version B) and discovers two girls hanging by their hair or a girl hanging from her eyelids (version C). She opens the forbidden tap, from which gold flows (or she opens the two rooms, or the other forbidden houses, and in one of them she finds two black horses and in the other a pool with gold water). She closes the room or the forbidden house, but she does not succeed in removing gold stuck to her finger. She wraps a cloth around her finger to hide the gold. The *ġūla* returns home and discovers that the heroine has broken the prohibition. She scolds her for not obeying but does not harm her.

A peddler sells the heroine a comb. She pays him in gold and even sends gold to her mother through him (or beggars, who have come to the heroine's home, inform her mother of her whereabouts). The mother sends a poisonous comb intended for her daughter with the peddler (or with one of the beggars, or she disguises herself as a peddler of combs). The heroine combs her hair, or the *ġūla* herself combs the girl's hair unwittingly with the poisonous comb. The teeth of the comb pierce her head, and she dies.

The *ġūla* dresses Frēṭ Rummān in expensive clothes (or immerses her in the waters of the Golden Pool) and places her with carpets and silver and gold treasures on the back of the "Air Camel"—a giant bird. She has the bird vow that it will not descend from the sky unless it is told, "Go down in the name of what you are carrying on your back." The Air Camel takes off, and no one succeeds in convincing it to alight except for a poor boy (or "the old woman's son" or the heroine's mother). The villagers loot the carpets, the treasures, and the clothes, and the poor boy (or the mother) is left with the naked body. He asks his mother to prepare her for burial.

During the preparations for the burial, the boy's mother (or the heroine's mother) discovers the poisoned teeth of the comb and pulls them out of her head. Frēṭ Rummān is revived. The king's son sees her and falls in love with her. He wants to marry her, but the poor man's mother convinces him that the heroine is for her son. The king's son pays the expenses of the wedding and the bride, and the heroine marries the poor boy (or the king gives the old woman the dowry and marries the heroine himself, or the mother reveals herself to her daughter and the heroine stays with her).

Bruno Bettelheim dedicates an entire chapter in his book *The Uses of Enchantment: The Meaning and Importance of Fairy Tales* to Snow White.[9] He claims that the story deals with the oedipal difficulties of children and their parents. The story encourages children who hear it to believe that they are able to find their way out of oedipal difficulties, and at the same time it warns parents of the consequences, which may be disastrous, if they let themselves get into these difficulties.

> Fairy tales do not tell why a parent may be unable to enjoy his child's growing up and surpassing him but becomes jealous of the child. We do not know why the queen in "Snow White" cannot age gracefully and gain satisfaction from vicariously enjoying her daughter's blooming into a lovely girl, but something must have happened in her past to make her vulnerable so that she hates the child she should love. How the sequence of the generations can account for a parent's fear of his child is illustrated in the cycle of myths of which the story of Oedipus is the central part.[10]
>
> Only an acceptance of the child as a child—neither as a competitor nor as a sexual love object—permits good relations between parents and children, and between the siblings.[11]
>
> Death [of the heroine] is rather a symbol that this person is wished away—just as the oedipal child does not really wish to see his parent-competitor die, but simply wants him removed from the child's way of winning his other parent's complete attention.[12]

Bettelheim's interpretation implies that the young girl projects her jealousy onto her mother: "If a child cannot permit himself to feel his jealousy of a parent (this is very threatening to his security), he projects his feelings onto this parent. Then 'I am jealous of all the advantages and prerogatives of Mother' turns into the wishful thought: 'Mother is jealous of me.' The feeling of inferiority is defensively turned into a feeling of superiority."[13]

What of all this can be found in the Bedouin versions of the story? The first, obvious feature is that the mother in all the Bedouin versions is not a stepmother but the biological mother. In fact, in the first version of the story, as published by the Brothers Grimm, it was indeed the actual mother, and only in versions published in later editions was the mother converted into a stepmother. In a Gaelic version, "Gold-Tree and Silver-Tree," given by Joseph Jacobs in his book *Celtic Fairy Tales*,[14] and in an Italian version, "Beautiful Venice" (Bella Venezia), given by Italo Calvino in *Italian Folktales*,[15] the mother is also the real mother.

The motive for the daughter's exclusion from the house in all the Bedouin versions is the mother's jealousy of her daughter's beauty: "This woman was jealous a little, she began being jealous a little, angry that her daughter would be prettier than her" (version A); or "How is it that Ǧbēneh, my daughter, is more beautiful than I am and more handsome than I am?" (version D). But what is more interesting in the Bedouin versions is the father's attitude toward the heroine. In the European versions, the father plays no part in the story. He is only mentioned in the background at the beginning of the story. On the other hand, in the Bedouin versions, the father's behavior is the primary cause of the mother's jealousy. In version A, it is said: "The father began to love the daughter more than her mother." In version D: "She went and asked her husband, 'Who is more beautiful, me or Ǧbēneh?' He said to her: 'Ǧbēneh.'" And in version B: "Every day her father comes and says, 'I wish, my Lord, that you will give me a bride like her!'"

It is quite possible that these remarks imply a forbidden relationship between father and daughter, and in this case, it is possible to explain the mother's desire to send her daughter away from the house not only as an act of jealousy but as an attempt to protect her from the danger of incest.

In *Seed of Pomegranate: The Woman in Arab Folktales*, Meron provides a version of the story "Frēṭ Rummān" that was heard from Ḥamda Qāsem Ġrifāt, a member of the ʿArab ʿIyadāt tribe and a resident of Bēt Zarzīr.[16] In this version, the father, looking at his beautiful daughter, says, "By Allah, my daughter, your mother had born you and did not bear another except you. I want to marry you [to someone], Pomegranate Grain. Come on, grow up so I can marry [another woman] in exchange for you." This means the husband wants to marry his daughter to another man in what is called in Arabic *badal*, exchange marriage, where the father offers his daughter for a daughter from the bridegroom's family. The mother is afraid that her husband will have another wife besides her (Muslim law allows polygamous families with up to four wives), and therefore she abandons the child in a distant place. It is interesting to note that the storyteller comments in parenthetical terms, "The women, in their stupidity, they believe," meaning that the husband only jokes and does not mean what he says but that his wife believes he means it seriously.

The image of the *ġūla* in the stories is complex, multifaceted, and ambivalent. In Bedouin and Islamic culture, the *ġūla* is usually perceived as a negative demonic character that harms people and seeks to devour them. These qualities are not absent from the descriptions of the *ġūla* in the corpus of the stories here. The heroine's initial encounter with the *ġūla* is characterized by the young girl's fear of her: "She said to her: 'No, you are *ġūla*! You want to devour me!" In the forbidden room opened by the heroine, she discovers a girl hanging by her hair, who pleads with her not to release her, lest the *ġūla* devour both of them.

At some point in the story, when the heroine fails to open the door, the *ġūla* says: "If I find her asleep, Allah and Allah's protection on her, and if I find her alive [awake], by Allah, I will eat her—I will eat Frēṭ Rummān!" In version B, when the narrator describes the *ġūl*'s place of residence, she says, "This *ġūl* ate the whole city. He is [living] in the city, and the city is desolate: there is no one else in the city."

Nevertheless, the ambivalent character of the *ġūla* is expressed in the story at the moment of the encounter between Frēṭ Rummān and the *ġūla.* The *ġūla* says to the frightened girl, "The name of Allah is upon you, my daughter, Frēṭ Rummān. Allah and Allah's protection are with you. The one who will betray you, Allah will betray him. From where did you come to me? From the paradise doorway to hell's doorway." On the one hand, she assures her of her patronage, but, in the same breath, she describes her future life with her as a passage from the doorway of heaven to the doorway of hell. She demands absolute obedience.

However, in all versions, the *ġūla* treats the heroine with kind and loving care. At a certain point in the story, the *ġūla* puts the heroine to a test by handing over the keys to the rooms or the houses of the city while forbidding her to open certain rooms and a specific tap. The heroine violates the prohibition, but when it is revealed to the *ġūla*, she does not punish her. When the narrator, quoting the *ġūla*'s response, says: "She told her, 'I told you not to open the door! Never mind,'" she adds an interpretation of her own, "Because she was dear to her." In version B, the *ġūla* says, "By Allah, why should I not immerse the whole of you in the pool and you will come out decorated [gilt] with gold. You are so afraid."

When the *ġūla* discovers the heroine's death, she responds with an emotional outburst: "Oh my love, oh Frēṭ Rummān, oh Frēṭ Rummān, oh Frēṭ Rummān!" In version B, the *ġūl* sheds tears of sorrow: "The *ġūl* came, saw that she was dead, he began to cry, he wept, he sobbed. . . . He continued to cry until he calmed down." In folktales, an externalized expression of emotions is not common. In this case, the triple repetition of words intensifies the emotional expression and transmits it to the listener.

At the moment of leave-taking, the *ġūla* takes care to dress the heroine in silk and gold clothes and load treasures on the camel, and the *ġūla*, in version B, dips her in the golden pool water.

Bettelheim claims, quite rightly, that Snow White's story is a classic adolescence story. Every stage of the heroine's life—her childhood at her parents' home, her life with the dwarfs (or with the *ġūla*), and her marriage—symbolizes a stage in her psychic development, from little girl to grown-up girl, and from grown-up girl to woman. The magical sleep symbolizes the transition from one stage to another.[17] In the Brothers Grimm's version, the dwarfs play a passive role. There is a clear division of labor: the dwarfs spend their days working in the mines, while Snow White runs the household, prepares their meals, and makes their beds. In the Bedouin stories, the *ġūla* is portrayed as an alternative mother. It is a female figure who has occupations outside the home, bringing meat or grazing deer (motif G249.1, "Witches drive herds of deer"), but the heroine participates in the household. She milks the gazelles that have returned from the pasture or helps prepare food for a meal. The heroine learns how to perform housework from the *ġūla* and thus prepares herself for marriage (according to the patriarchal worldview prevailing in Bedouin culture), but she also undergoes emotional changes. In the world of the *ġūla*, she encounters a complex reality. The *ġūla* is not a stereotypical figure dripping with sweetness. She has cruel sides, and she has maternal sides. The incident of the forbidden room illustrates this the most. The *ġūla* puts the heroine on trial. She forbids her to enter but places the keys in her hand. As expected, the young girl violates the prohibition and succumbs to her curiosity. Now she has to pay the price. She makes every effort to hide what has happened, but the *ġūla* does not let her. She forces her to expose her bandaged finger and admit her actions. In version B, the girl lays the blame for her pretended injury on the *satura* (a sort of rigid sickle for chopping branches) and other housewares, but she is ultimately forced to take responsibility for her actions. The *ġūla* does not punish her but acts as an educational figure. She accepts the fact that the heroine, being a young girl, has not resisted temptation and has yielded to curiosity, but she insists that the girl should stand behind her actions and not falsify her misbehavior.

During her stay at the *ġūla*'s house, the girl is exposed to the complexity of life. She learns that life does not go smoothly. She has to face various challenges that prepare her for her future life as a married woman.

It appears that the three older feminine figures in the story, the mother, the *ġūla*, and the old woman who brings her back to life, all symbolize the archetype of the mother figure in its different aspects. Of particular interest is version D, in which the heroine returns to her mother's home. Initially, the girl denies her and defies her: "No. I was raised by a *ġūla*! You are not my mother, she is my mother." But in the end, she reconciles herself to reality and remains in her mother's house.

The forbidden-room motif, C611, "Forbidden chamber. Person allowed to enter all chambers of house except one," is familiar from many tales in the entire area of the Indo-European culture space. It appears, among other places, in the *Arabian Nights* in the story "The Porter and the Three Ladies of Baghdad."[18]

Notes

1. In these Bedouin folk stories, *nxarref 'aw nenām, yā sām'īn al-kalām* ("Shall we tell or sleep, o listeners of the speech?") is a shortened rhymed opening formula in the form of a rhetorical question. The answer is usually positive, and the rhetorical question has become a formal formula. Cf. chapter 21, note 1.

2. In *yā ṛaḅḅ^{w}i*, "O my Allah," the small upper ^{w} marks the labialization of *b*. This feature occurs in certain Bedouin dialects, but rather rarely in the Galilee Bedouins' speech. Other labialization occurrences involve, for example, emphatic *ṃ*, as in *'uṃṃ^{w}i*.

3. *mī hī tirkin 'alēha al-bint—ṣabiyye ṣārat*: "She does not trust her, the girl—she became a maiden." The Bedouin narrator adds a wise observation: the girl has become a teenager who can ask questions and criticize even her mother. The first sentence has the imperfect verb form, which is the habitual present tense, and the next sentence has a verb in the past tense. Nominal and verbal sentence types change in Arabic freely, without any grammatical limitation. Note that the second sentence explains the cause for the first sentence without an explicit conjunction particle (i.e., this is an asyndetic structure), as is frequent in Arabic, including Galilee Bedouin dialects.

4. *ṣṃ-aḷḷa 'alēki, yumma, yā Frēṭ Rummān, ᵃ'alēk(i) 'aḷḷa w-'amān 'aḷḷa, w-al-xāyin yexūno 'aḷḷa*: "Allah's name [blessing] on you, child, Pomegranate Grain. Allah is on you and Allah's security, and the traitor, Allah will betray him." These are three important formulas in the Muslim everyday vocabulary. Cf. Piamenta, *Islam in Everyday Arabic Speech, Muslim Conception of God*; chap. 4, note 3; chap. 23, story A, note 1.

5. The narrative formula *minnēn ǧīti hēna, min bāb al-na'īm la-bāb el-ǧaḥīm?* ("Wherefrom did you come here, from the door of paradise to the door of hell?") occurs in the folktales not only because of narrative tradition but because it is related to daily (human) Muslim belief attested in the notions of paradise and hell. See below in this story the customs of preparing the dead for burial and Pomegranate Grain's behavior when she is revived (she says the *šahāda*, the testimony that declares the belief that Allah is one and his messenger is the Prophet Muḥammad).

6. *u-laflafatha*: "and [she] wrapped her." Four-radical roots are not new to Bedouin dialects—they exist in LA/MSA and other Arabic dialects, too. There are other such verbs in these folktales. Note that one of the implications of reduplicating a two-consonant root (here, **lf > lff > lflf*) is stressing the action by adding power and depth to it: the old woman wrapped her up meticulously and well.

7. The quality of the recording was impossible to understand toward the end, and therefore a part of it is omitted here, but the text from line 211 onward is what could be properly perceived.

8. Uther, *The Types of International Folktales*, 1:383.

9. Bettelheim, *Uses of Enchantment*, 194–213.

10. Bettelheim, 195.

11. Bettelheim, 198–99.

12. Bettelheim, 196.

13. Bettelheim, 204.

14. Jacobs, *Celtic Fairy Tales*, 97–101.

15. Calvino, *Italian Folktales*, 739.

16. Meron, Shehadi, and Masarwi, *Seed of Pomegranate*, 296–313.

17. Bettelheim, *Uses of Enchantment*, 214.

18. Burton, *Arabian Nights*, night 16.

29. The Man Who Delivered a Daughter

NARRATOR: Ṯarwa Yāsīn

TRIBE: *'Arab el-Ḥağāğra*
IFA 18484 April 18, 1984

1 gām—'āya—tiğawwaz u-mā bixallef. gaʿadat maʿā marato sabʿ-^{e}snīn, sabaʿ sanawāt. hassa lamminno mā xaḷḷaf, marag hā-t-tāğer, bayyā ʿ rommān, ^{e}ngūḷ-ḷo ḥna mḥammel, ḥammel hā-r-rommān, “rommān l-al-bēʿ, rommān l-al-bēʿ.”	1 There was—yes—he married and did not beget children. She stayed with him, his wife, seven years. Seven years. Now, when he did not beget children, this peddler went by, a pomegranate seller, we call him the carrier, carrying pomegranates, “Pomegranates for sale, pomegranates for sale.”
7 'aštara, (a)štarat marato kūz rommān. kūz wāḥad. 'aklat minno filga, u-ḏabbat minno filga. rāḥat teğīb mayy, tmalle mayye ʿa-d-duwāb. 'ağa ğōzha min aš-šuġul, ydawwer ʿa-xub^{u}z, ligāha miš xābza.[1] 'ağa gāḷ “baḷḷa mā hēn,” ēš liga,[2] filget ar-rummān, kalāha. kala l-rummāna.	7 His wife bought a pomegranate, one pomegranate. She ate from it a half, and hid from it a half. She went to bring water, fill water for the animals. Her husband came from work, looked for bread, found that she had not baked bread. He said, “By Allah, there is nothing here,” what did he find? He found the half of the pomegranate. He ate it. Ate it. He ate the pomegranate.
15 hassa lamminno kalāha, gāḷat-lo, dawwarat ʿalēha, mā ligatha. gāḷat-lo, “ṭayyeb, lā šeft li r-rummāne,” gāḷ-ḷa, “waḷḷa, kalētha. kalētha” daʿat ʿalē, gāḷat-lo, “rētak iğat txaḷḷef min rižlak bint u-tsammīha frēṭ rummān.”	15 Now when he ate it, she said to him—she was looking for it, and did not find it. She said to him, “Well, haven't you seen the pomegranate [by chance]?” He said to her, “By Allah, I've eaten it, I've eaten it.” She cursed him and said, “May you deliver from your foot a girl and call her Pomegranate Grain (Frēṭ rummān).”

21 hassa, subḥāno ʼaḷḷa simaʻ minha,[3] ʼaḷḷa ṭʻamhum min riǧlo bint. hassa lamminno . . . e . . . sāwa . . . daššaro, u-naggaḷo miṭraḥ ṯāni beʻīd, ḏaḷḷ . . . b-al-^{i}mrāḥ. ḏaḷḷ, lamminno ḏaḷḷ . . . aǧa—ʼaǧat ʻalē šalyet hā-l-ġozlān, šalyet hā-l-ġuzlān aǧat ʻalē.	21 Now Allah, praise him, heard it from her. He gave them a girl from his leg. Now, when, er, he did. . . . He left him, and moved him to a very distant place, he remained . . . in that pasture place. He remained, when he remained, there came to him a deer herd, a deer herd came to him.
28 ʼaǧat ʻalē šalyet al-ġozlān, ligat hā-z-zalama yeṣīḥ, gāḷan lo, "mā-lak ^{e}(t)ṣīḥ?" gāḷ-ḷhen, "iǧri tōǧaʻni." rāḥan, dawwaran hā-l-ḥāle hīč, dawwaran ginniyya, ksaranha u-šgaḥan iǧro. hū māt u-ligan bīha bint . . .	28 The deer herd came to him [and] found this man shouting. They said to him, "Why are you shouting?" He said to them, "My leg hurts." They went, searched [what to do in] this case, like that, searched for a bottle, broke it and cut open his leg. He died, and they found in it a girl.
34 maʻan hā-l-vetrin (< fetran) hā-l-rāʼi b-enha mā tinǧe hā-l-zalama ugḏbanha, laffanha be-šarāyiṭ u-ḥaṭṭanha u-rabbanha, u-kull yōm waḥda tarḏaḥḥa. kull yōm waḥda tarḏaḥḥa, minnīhen, min ibzāza. kull yōm, kull yōm, kull yōm.	34 Together, this—they agreed on this opinion, that they could not save this man, and [they] took her and wrapped her in rags, and put her and raised her and every day one of them would suckle her, every day one of them would suckle her from her udders, every day, every day, every day.
40 rabat al-bint, ṣārat hā-l-bint, halgēt gadd al-bint hāy, akbar, akbar maʻāhin. yirūḥan yirʻan miṯel hēk, (t)rūḥ miḥḥin.	40 The girl grew up. This girl became now like this girl, bigger, bigger, with them. They would go to pasture like that with them. She would go with them.
43 yām min ḏāt al-ayyām wirdat šalyet hā-l-ġozlān ʻala hāl-ʻēn. ʻēn māyy. yammen wardet šalyet hā-l-ġozlān ʻala hā-l-ʻēn, ʼaǧa rāʻi, walad miṯel hēč, miṯel hā-l-uwlād haḏōl.[4]	43 One day, the deer herd went to drink water at the spring, water spring. When the deer herd came, there came this shepherd, a boy like that, like these boys there.
48 šāfha, u-hī mdalǧa tišrab.[5] ʼaǧa ǧāb ṯōbu	48 He saw her, as she was spilling water while drinking. He took his garment
50 u-ġaṭṭāha. gāḷat-lo, "ʼostor" ʻala mā šaqqā-lha. gāḷ-ḷha "mastōra." laffha l-aš-šābb gāḷ-ḷa, "yalla yā xayya, tšūf raḥal maʻi." xaḏāha, rāḥ ilha.	50 and covered her. She said to him, "Protect!" for what he tore for her [his garment]. He said, "You are covered [hidden, protected]." The young man wrapped her and said to her, "Come on, girl [lit.: little sister], see [agree to] the travel with me." He took her, went for her.
54 liḥǧan l-ġozlān alli rabbanha liḥǧanha, rāḥan ^{i}mʻāha. lamman hāḏan rāḥan ^{i}mʻāha gāḷ, "widdi ʼaʻmal lēha ʻers w-aǧawwazha, w-aʻmal leha hāl-ḥafla, w-asāwi." šāfha ʼabū, gāḷ-ḷo, "yā-(a)būya, mnēn ǧib^{e}t al-bin^{e}t hāy?" gāḷ-ḷo, "ʼani, ʼabūya, ligētha maʻa l-ġozlān." haḏōlāk xaḏō-lak al-ġozlān ^{e}mʻāha.	54 The deer who raised her joined her, went with her. When those went with her, he said, "I want to make a wedding for her and marry her and I'll make her this party and I'll do." His father saw her, and said to him, "O my son, where did you bring this girl from?" He said to him, "I, Father, found her with the deer." Those—they took the deer with her.

62 yāmin ǧābha, gāḷ-ḷo “hayya widna nāxḏa ʿalēk ʿarūs.” ʿimel lo hāl-ḥafla, čebīra, ʿemel lo hā-l-fanṭaziyya, sawā-lo hā-l-ʿeres, u-ḏabaḥ ġanam, ʿezam hā-l-iblād ḥawalē, uǧawwazo, ʾaxaḏha, ʾaxaḏ frēṭ rummān.	62 When he brought her, he said to him, “This one, we will take her as bride for you.” He prepared this party, a big one, he made for him a *fanṭaziyya* [a big party], he made for him the wedding, he butchered sheep, invited all the country around him, and married her to him. He took her [as wife], he took Frēṭ Rummān.
68 yāmenno xaḏāha, kān(a)t al-gisma, ḏaḷḷan al-ġozlān ʿindha. ḏaḷḷan al-ġozlān ʿindha. hassa, lamma ḏaḷḷan al-ġozlān ʿindha yegūl-(l)hin, “ṭayyeb rūḥan irʿan, rūḥan irʿan, ṭuššan[6] b-halli-wēred ʾali ṣār.” yegūl-(l)hin.	68 When he took her, it was [by] fate, the deer remained with her. The deer remained with her. Now, when the deer remained with her, he said to them, “Well, go graze, go to graze, spread out in the valley that was [there],” he said to them.
74 yegūlan-lo, “laʾ, ʾeḥna mā ndaššer bintna. hāy bintna, nḏaḷḷ ^{aʿ}indha.” u-xaḏa al-bint, u-rabba al-ġozlān ^{i}mʿāha. hāy, xaḷḷaṣtha.	74 They said to him, “No, we will not leave our daughter. This is our daughter, and she is dear to us.” And he took the girl and raised the deer with her. This, I’ve finished it.

Commentary

The story from Ṯarwa Yāsīn about the man who gave birth to a daughter corresponds to a large extent to the stories of Frēṭ Rummān (Snow White), although this is a different narrative type. The story begins in a way similar to the version of Snow White told by Zehiyya Ġrifāt: A barren woman buys a “pregnancy pomegranate” from a peddler (motif T511.1.1, “Conception from eating apple”), but she eats only half of it, and the other half is eaten by her husband. As a result, the husband becomes pregnant (motif T578, “Pregnant man”). The woman abandons the husband to his fate, and after a while he gives birth to a daughter out of his leg (motif T581.12, “Man gives birth to a daughter; woman gives birth to a son”).[7] The husband dies, and a herd of deer adopts the baby and raises her until she reaches maturity. The girl gets the name Frēṭ Rummān (Pomegranate Grain). A prince finds her in the field and marries her. The deer continue to accompany the girl even after her marriage.

The story is unknown in Europe. Thompson offers a similar narrative type, AT 705 (ATU 705A), “Born from a Fish (Fruit),” in which a man becomes pregnant after eating a magic fish or magic fruit designed for his wife. The man gives birth to a daughter from his knee. Birds take the baby and raise it. A prince finds her and marries her (motif N711, “King [prince] finds maiden in woods [tree] and marries her”). This type of story is mainly found in the Scandinavian countries, but it also occurs in Russia and southern Europe. El-Shamy, in his book *Types of the Folktale in the Arab World*, defines a secondary type ATU 705A§, “Born from Pregnant Man, Raised by Bird (Animal).”[8] He claims that this narrative type is common in Muslim culture, from Iraq, Kuwait, and Bahrain to Sudan, Egypt, and North Africa, and also appears in Syria, Jordan, and Israel. Many Jewish parallels are found in the IFA.[9] The reader can find a detailed discussion of the Hebrew versions in Dan Ben-Amos’s book *Folktales of the Jews*.[10]

As in Frēṭ Rummān's story, here, too, the motive of jealousy is evident. The woman punishes her husband for depriving her of the possibility of conceiving (curses him), and he is left in a desolate place. The abandoning of the husband to his fate is tantamount to the abandoning of the daughter who will be born to her husband. The gazelles play the role of the dwarfs in the European versions of Snow White and the role of the *ġūla* in the Bedouin versions. In one of the Bedouin versions of Snow White, the *ġūla* shepherds a herd of gazelles, and the heroine's role is to milk the gazelles upon their return from the pasture. Here the tables are turned, and the gazelles take care of the heroine. At the end of the story, the heroine finds her mate, and the herd continues to live with her.

Notes

1. The sentence *ligāha miš xābza*, "he found that she had not baked [bread]" (with the literal translation "he-found-her not having-baked" indicates the perfect tense, or in other words, a resultative function. This structure is used here instead of a subordinate clause, such as "he found that she had not baked [bread]." This use of the present participle verb form exists also in other Arabic dialects (cf. Piamenta, *Use of Tenses, Aspects, and Moods*; Henkin, *Negev Arabic*).

2. *ēš liga, filget ar-rummān, kalāha*: See chapter 2, note 2, about the use of rhetorical questions.

3. *subḥāno 'aḷḷa sima' minha, 'aḷḷa tʿamhum min riğlo bint*: "Allah, praise Him, heard it from her, Allah blessed them, gave them a girl from his leg." These (Bedouin) folk stories with their fantastic, unrealistic events do not contrast with the anchored Islamic culture, including Allah's role in human life (cf. Piamenta, "Linguistic System of Bedouin Manners," *Muslim Conception of God*; also chap. 28, note 4, above).

4. In *hā-l-uwlād hadōl*, note the short demonstrative *hā* before the noun and the longer demonstrative form *hadōl* following the noun. This pattern of double demonstrative pronouns is very frequent in many Bedouin dialects, and in this book.

5. *šāfha, u-hi mdalğa tišrab*: "He saw her, as she was spilling water while drinking." To describe a state, Arabic uses the present participle and the imperfect tense. The present participle expresses an ongoing action in verbs of movement (e.g., *go, run*), and a (resultative) action in the present perfect in other (dynamic) verbs (e.g., *eat, write*; see note 1 above). *mdalğa* is here in a circumstantial clause, with the fixed structure [*u* + personal pronoun subject + present participle predicate]. *mdalğa* is a present participle form for a state, while *tišrab* is in the imperfect. Because of its semantic trait group it cannot be here in the present participle to express a state.

6. The word *wēred* (< *wārid*) may mean "a place descending to the water source," as the present participle of the root *wrd*, "to go to the water spring to fetch water." The vowel *ē* is somewhat curious in this word, for "internal *'imāla*" (vowel raising within a word) is rare in Bedouin dialects. See the chapter on Bedouin dialects at the end of this book. *'imāla* is generally not usual in the Galilee Bedouin dialects (cf. chap. 18, note 2). Word final *'imāla* is frequent in Negev Bedouin dialects. (Cf. Henkin, *Negev Arabic*; Shawarbah, *Grammar of Negev Arabic*. Also, cf. chapter on Bedouin dialects, section 1, note 4.)

7. Ben-Amos, *Folktales of the Jews*, 3:474.

8. El-Shamy, *Types of the Folktale in the Arab World*, 374.

9. Samaritan version (recorded in Arabic): 1841; Egypt: 7234; Morocco: 6760, 6855; Yemen: 5139, 5452.

10. Ben-Amos, *Folktales of the Jews*, 3:467.

30. The Girl and Her Seven Brothers

NARRATOR: Maryam Muṣṭafa Ṭabbāš

TRIBE: *ʿArab Ḥilf-Ṭabbāš*

IFA 15230 August 8, 1982

1 bī hnāk, hā-l-ʿarab, u-nāzla ʿarab, maṯal yaʿani, biduw, čānat byūt gaboḷ. hēna bī waḥda līha sabeʿ uwlād. mā lha banāt. hāy čānat yaʿani widdha . . . ʿend . . . neḥna ngūl ḥubla, iḥna mengūḷ-ḷēha, yaʿani, widdha txaḷḷef. haḏol-al-awlād, widdhom bint.	1 There was this Arab tribe, and it was living, that is, Bedouins, there were tents [camel-hair housing] in the past. Now there was one [woman] who had seven children. She did not have a daughter. This [woman] had to [give birth], that is, we call her pregnant, that is, she had to deliver [the child]. Those boys [children] wanted a girl [sister].
8 [ʾaḥna gaboḷ mā čānat ᵉsbiṭarāt u-ġēro, yaʿani. hāḏa walla ʿindhin, yisāwīn, hīč gāʿde, dāye txaḷḷi . . . txaḷḷef al-mara ʿind hā-n-nisāwīn ʿindha ad-dāye alli tiqṭaʿ aṣ-ṣorra u-teʿmal.]	8 (In the past there were no hospitals etc., that is. By Allah, this, they did it, a midwife was helping . . . helping the woman deliver. With the women, the midwife would cut the placenta and do [various things].)
13 gāḷu-ḷa, "ʾiḏa ğibti binet, ḥuṭṭi-(l)na mrā" [ʾēš ⁱngul ⁱmrā—ᵉmrāy, yaʿani, ʾā.] "ʿa-ḏahar el-bēt, fōq. u-ḥuṭṭi-(l)na, yaʿani, makḥale" m-šān kaḥḥalam. ʾē, ʾelo ʿalāma. w-ⁱnhağam, rāḥum.	13 They said to her, "If you have a daughter, put for us a mirror (we say *mrā*, mirror, that is, yes) on top of the house, above. And put for us a kohl jar," because they [used to] paint [the face] with kohl. Yes, that was a sign for it. And they went off, went away.
18 rāḥum. hāye, xaḷḷafat binet. hīna haḏōḷa, gāḷat la-n-niswān "tigdaran tḥuṭṭan li al-makḥala wa-li-mrā ʿala ḏahar al-bēt, mi-šān al-uwlād." al-uwlād rāḥam yilʿabum, yedawwrum aṣ-ṣēd, šibāb, miš ᵉṣġār.	18 Went away. This [woman] had a daughter. Now, she said to the women, "Can you put for me the kohl jar and the mirror on top of the house, for the children." The children were playing [amusing themselves], hunting animals, they were young men, not small ones.

24 ’ā, rāḥam hadọ̄la, daḥḥagum winno mā bī maḥṭūṭ—maḥṭūṭ sēf. [tiʿerif es-sēf.] ḥaṭṭan as-sēf. gāḷ-ḷehin, “’idạ ğibti walad ḥuṭṭ(i) as-sēf.” hādạn n-niswān, yaʿani, min ġašāšīthin min . . . ḥaṭṭan as-sēf.

24 Yes, they went, those boys, looked and lo—there was not put out [the kohl jar]—a sword was placed there. (Do you know the sword?) They put a sword. He [the son] said to them, “If you have a boy, put the sword [on the rooftop].” These women, that is, because of their deception . . . they put the sword.

30 dạḷḷum al-uwlād, ligum as-sēf, ʿāwadum. siḥbum ḥālhum, dạḷḷum nāhğīn ʿala blād yaʿani beʿīda, beʿīda. ’ay yaʿani, mitẹl hēna w-al-ʿaffūla, ’abʿad min al-ʿaffūla,[1] metẹl ğinīn, ’aḷḷa ’aʿlam.[2]

30 The children remained, found the sword, went back. They went off, continued going to a distant, very distant country, that is, like [from] here to ʿAfula, farther than ʿAfula, like Ğenin, Allah knows.

36 rāḥum min hēna, hāya dạḷḷum ta ligum maṭraḥ, geʿdum. suwwāḥ, u-geʿdum. ṣāram yāklum, yišrabum, yeğībum, yegīmam, yiḥuṭṭum,[3] laḥaddin-mā kibrat al-bint. kibrat al-bint. šnū sammatha ummha? wdīʿa. ’ā, wudīʿa.

36 They went from here, they continued [going] until they found a place and settled. As tourists, they settled there. They started eating and drinking, establishing and leaving [e.g., work], until the girl grew up. The girl grew up. What did her mother call her? Wdīʿa [i.e., Trust, Charge]. Yes, Wdīʿa.

42 kibrat al-bint ṣārat ^{i}trūḥ maʿa l-banāt ʿa-l-midrasa, ʿala l-hawa, yeguḷan lēha, “’eḥna lēna xwān, w-’inti mā leč axwān.” ’ummha, hiyya baṭṭalat yaʿani ^{e}txaḷḷef. “’eḥna lēna (^{e})xwān, ’inti mā leč axwān.” hiyya trawwe(ḥ)[4] ʿala-immha tʿayyaṭ, tibči, tguḷ-ḷēha, “’ani mā li axwān.”

42 The girl grew up, began to go to school with the girls, to journeys. They said to her, “We have brothers, and you don’t have brothers.” Her mother stopped having children, that is to say. “We have brothers, and you don’t have brothers.” She would go home to her mother, crying, weeping, saying to her, “I haven’t got brothers.”

49 gāḷat-ḷēha, “’inti lēč exwān sabʿa,[5] bas ’ani, exwāneč ma ’aʿref wē(r)-rāḥu.”[6]

49 She said to her, “You, you have seven brothers, but I, your brothers—I don’t know where to they went.”

52 hīna čibrat, ṣārat bint ḥawālay yaʿani ʿašara, ṭnaʿšar sina, xamasṭaʿšar sina, mā bayyan exwāna. hāy al-bint, yōm, ḥaṭṭat al-fiker ’alla-nna trūḥ ^{e}tdawwer exwāna, min-ḥālha. hāy mišat ^{i}b-hā-al-xaḷa,

52 Now she grew up and became ten, twelve, fifteen years old—her brothers did not appear. This girl, one day, had the idea that she would go to look for her brothers on her own. This [one] went in the open area.

57 ʿimlat xubez, grāṣ, [’iḥna činna niʿmalu b-an-nār], tiʿemal. min wāḥad šeʿīr, u-gamḥ, u-kursanna u-ʿadas u-fūl, yaʿani, ʿemlu minha ṭaḥīn, kullu. ʿemalat kull wāḥad wāḥad.

57 She made bread loaves (we would make it on the fire). She did. [She made bread] of barley, wheat, ervil [plant], lentils, and beans [fava beans]. That is, they made flour of them, all of them—she made one [loaf] of each [plant].

62 hāy ṣārat titḥačči[7] mʿā-hā-d-darb u-hī rāyiḥa maši hīč. hāy, ʿilem ʾaḷḷa, es-sāʿa mišat yōmin hī bō, ba-l-lēl ^{e}tnām. mā tidri, yaʿani. dawwarat yōm, ʾaḷḷa ǧābha ʿala hā-l-gaṣ^{o}r alli hum bī, uxwānha, ʿala hā-l-maṭraḥ. dār.

62 She began talking with this road while she was walking like that. This [one], Allah knows, she walked during the day and slept at night. She did not know, that is. She was searching [during the] day. Allah brought her to the palace in which they [lived], her brothers, [she came to] to this place. A house.

68 hā-l-maḥall, fātat ^{i}b-hā-l-maḥall, mā bī ḥada. ligat kull šī maḥṭūṭ ^{i}b-ā-l-maḥall, b-hā-l—ʿalam ʾaḷḷa, ^{a}xzāna, ʿalam ʾaḷḷa ʾēš. ligat. hāy gʿadat kalat minno ligat bī . . . al-bisse . . . [šnū tgūl-la al-goṭṭa hāy, bisse, ʾaḥna ngūl-lo.] ligat hā-l-bisse u-gʿadat.

68 This place, she entered this place. No one there. She found everything placed in its place in this—Allah knows—cupboard, Allah knows what. She found. This one ate from it, she found in it . . . the cat. (What do you say to this cat? Cat, we call it.) She found this cat and stayed.

75 ʿimlat hā-l-ʿaša. ʿirfet inno hāy ed-d-dār maskūna

75 She prepared dinner. She knew that this house was lived in [by ǧinn or humans].

77 u-mā biha, yaʿani, nisa. ʿimlat hā-l-ʾakel u-stannato, u-txabbat. txabbat wara l-^{e}xzāna, wara ʿalam ʾaḷḷa ʾēš.

77 and that there were no women there, that is to say. She made the food and waited for him. She hid behind the cupboard, behind Allah knows what.

80 ʾaǧa wāḥad, widdo ysāwi ʾakel. al-ʿaṣar widdhon yīǧi man yoṭbux. ǧē liga hā-ṭ-ṭabīx maṭbūx u-mġaṭṭa. dawwar, laṭṭaš, yēn ilaxxam—mā bī ḥada. mā bī ḥayy. gaddam al-bissa tākel ^{i}mn-aṭ-ṭabīx, yišūfha tmūt, yšūfha masmūm, ʾaw lā. kalat. u-nāmat. mā bīha šiy.

80 There came one [man], wanted to make food. In the afternoon they want a man to come to cook. He came, found this food cooked and covered. He searched, beating around, clumsily/ confused—there was no one. No living [person]. He offered the cat a portion of the food, to see whether she would die, whether it was poisoned or not. She ate and went to sleep. She had nothing [wrong].

87 ʾaǧam axwāno kullhum. ʾas-sitta-barra, hū ǧē ta-yaṭbax, ligom, gāḷom ta-yaġaddum. kalum men hā-ṭ-ṭabīx, u-širbum mayya u-ʿalam ʾaḷḷa šnū ʿimlum, gāḷum, "ta-ngūm ^{e}ndawwar." dawwarum ʿalēha—mā bī.

87 All his brothers came. The six were outside, he came to cook it, and they found, they said [that] they will have dinner. They ate from this food and drank water and Allah knows what they did. They said, "Let's get up, begin to search." They searched for her—[there was] no one.

93 gāḷ-ḷa, "yā lli sawēti l-ʾakel, ʿalēč ʾaḷḷa u-ʾamān ʾaḷḷa, w-al-xāyin yexūno ʾaḷḷa. bas ʾaṭlaʿi, šnū ʾanti, w-ʾenta, ǧinn walla ʾins walla šnū dīnak?" ṭallaʿat winha ʿaǧiyya miṯel at-toffāḥa.[8]

93 He said to her "O, one (f.) who made the food, Allah's security is on you, and the traitor, Allah will betray him. Just come out, what are you, and you: a ǧinn or human, or what is your religion?" She appeared and lo—[she was] a girl like an apple [perfect and beautiful].

98 lamman ʾaṭlaʿat ʿalēham, giʿedet ʿendīhom, gāḷu-ḷa, “šnū ʾismeč u-mnēn ʾinti u-mnēn ğīti?” xarrafathom. gāḷat-iḷhom, “ʾani mḏayʿa axwāni, uxwāni sabʿa gaddīkom.”

98 When she appeared to them, she sat with them, they said to her, “What is your name, and where from are you, and where did you come from?” She told them, said to them, “I have lost my brothers, my brothers are seven, like you.”

103 gāḷ-ḷha “šnu ismeč?” gāḷat lo, “ʾismi wdīʿa, ʾummi ḥāṭṭa, ḥāṭṭa ʾummi, gāḷat la-n-niswān “ḥuṭṭi al-mikḥala w-al-ʾmrā,” u-hinne ḥaṭṭāt liha s-sēf. ʾas-sēf ʾinha ğābat walad, yaʿani.”

103 He said to her, “What is your name?” She said to him, “My name is Wdīʿa [Trust, Charge], my mother gave it, my mother said to the women, ‘Put the kohl jar and the mirror,’ and they put the sword for her. The sword that she had a boy, that is.”

108 ʿābaṭōha, bawwasōha, gāḷo-ḷha, “ʾaḥna xwāneč.” itʿārafam u-ḏaḷḷom, ʾgʿadom. ʾaḷḷa ʾaʿlam, šahar, ʾagaḷḷ, ʾakṯar. widdom yerağʿūha, hiyya trūḥ tirğaʿ hiyya wiyyāhom ʿa-l-bēt.

108 They hugged her and kissed her: “We are your brothers.” They introduced themselves and continued to sit [live] there, Allah knows, a month, less or more. They wanted to take her back, she should go and return home, she with them.

113 gaḇoḷ-mā riğaʿat ʿa-l-bēt, ğāʿda[9] tkannes.[10] tkannes b-al-bēt, timsaḥ, ligat ḥabbet ḥommoṣ min ha-š-šikel, gḏabatha, kalatha. ligatha, mā-š ġērha.[11]

113 Before she returned home, she was sweeping [the dust]. She was sweeping the house, washing [the floor] she found a hummus [chickpea] grain like this, she took it, ate it. She found it—there was nothing except it.

117 hāy al-bissa gāḷat-ḷēha, “ʾanṭīni min-alli kalētī u-ʾaḷḷāhu yaʿlam. ʾanṭīni min hā-llī kalētī.” gāḷat-ḷēha, “mā bī, ḥabbet ḥummuṣ ligētha w-an(i)-akannes. mā bī.” gāḷat-ḷēha, “ʾanṭīni iyyāha, ʾaḥsan mā ʾarōḥ ʾakobb leč mayya b-an-nār.” “mā bī.” [hīna l-ʿarab gaḇuḷ, mā ʿindha nār, šaḥḥāṭa, mā ʿendīha, yaʿani,

117 This cat said to her, “Give me of that which you ate, and Allah will know. Give me of that which you ate.” She said to her, “There is nothing. I found a chickpea grain, I found it while I was sweeping, there is nothing.” She said to her, “Give it to me, or I’ll pour water in the fire.” “There is nothing.” (Now, the Arabs [Bedouins] in the past did not have fire, a match, they did not have, that is,

125 ʾaw gaddāḥa, ʾaw ʾiši. nār, etḥuṭṭ ḥaṭab ba-n-nār, gurmiyyāt, wu-txaḷḷīha ba-ha, maḏrūb b-an-nār ʿa-kull an-nhār.] mā ʿindha ḥada.

125 or a lighter or anything. Fire—they would put [throw] a log of wood in the fire, a log, and let it [be] in the fire all day long.) There was no one with her.

129 hīn ġafalat al-bint, rāḥat ḥaṭṭat mayye bi-hā-n-nār. hāy daḥḥagat, lōḥat hā-š-šabāb, xaḏat sāwat ʾakel la-xwānha—(nār) mā bī. daḥḥagat, wigfat, winn bī—miṯel ʿarab al-kaʿabiyye, [tiʿerif ʿarab al-kaʿabiyye, la-ġād.] daḥḥagat šāfat nitfet duxxāne, ʾaḷḷa ʾaʿlam, fōga nitfet nār.

129 Now the girl did not pay attention [fell asleep]. It [the cat] went and poured water [urinated] in the fire. This one looked, this silly youthful [girl], and made food for her brothers—there was not [any fire]. She looked, stood up, and there was—like the Kaʿabiyya Bedouins (do you know the ʿArab al-Kaʿabiyya [a Bedouin village], there [that direction]). She looked and saw a little smoke, Allah knows, above some fire.

136 hāy el-ʿaṣar, as-sāʿa arbaʿa, maʿa s-sāʿa hīk—walla ta-rāiḥa. turkuḏ. rāḥat daḥḥagat winnha hā-l-ġōḷa ğāʿada. ğat hā-l-ġōḷa, ğat hā tiğruš. [tiʿerif anta tiğruš ʾēš? tiğruš gamaḥ, la-tsāwi ṭabīx.] hāy gāḷat-ḷēha "as-salāma ʿalēč."

136 This afternoon, four o'clock, with the hour thus—by Allah, she is going, running. She went and saw—lo, there was this *ġūla* sitting. This *ġūla* began grinding. (Do you know what is "grinding"? Grinding wheat, to make cooked food.) This one said to her, "Peace on you [Hello]!"

142 gāḷat-ḷēha, "ʿalēč as-salāma. lamma salāmeč ġalab kalāmeč l-axaḷḷi wḥūš al-barr tismaʿ tağrīš ʿaḏāmeč." ta-tākilha, yaʿani. "š-widdeč?"[12] gāḷat,"widdi nitfet nār."

142 She said to her, "On you peace. If your greeting had not preceded your words, I would have let the wild animals hear the sound of your bones being ground." That is, she would have eaten her. "What do you want?" She said to her, "I need some fire."

147 gāḷat-ḷēha, "ṭayyib." eš-šū ʿāmla al-ġūḷa? ʿāmla šwayyet selīğa, burġul,

147 She said to her, "Good." And what had the *Ġūla* done? She had made some "*selīğa*," wheat groats [burghul].

149 [tiʿerfum al-burġul intom? ʾā.] ʿāmlīto baʿado xaḏar, yaʿani, b-ṣāʿita čānam, ʿāmlito, ḥāṭṭīten. gāḷat-ḷēha, "xuḏī-leč ešwayyet hā-l-burġul, selīğe." ğābat tāklo.

149 (Do you [pl.] know burghul? Yes.) She had done it, it was still a little fresh [green], that is, they were in her grain measure, she had prepared them and put them. She said to her, "Take some of these wheat groats, *selīğe*." She brought for her to eat it.

154 [inkūn ṭari nāklo iḥna, ʾawwal mā yekūn, (ʿ)an-nār.] gāḷat-ḷēha "lā." gāḷat-ḷēha, "embaḷa" ḥaṭṭat hi lēha b-ğēbitha, u-bgarat[13] ğēbitha min hēn. bgaraṭhe le-nift^{s}a, b-laḥasa. mišat.

154 (We are [used to] eating it fresh when it first appears [young vegetable], [roasted] on fire.) She said to her, "No." She said to her, "But of course [you will]." She gave her in her pocket, and ripped her pocket from here. She ripped it to a small hole [like a blister] in a lick [very quickly]. She went [away].

159 al-ʿağiyya rāḥat turkuḏ u-hā-l hinne yehurran warāha. ḏaḷḷat min bāb bēt al-gūḷa la-bāb bētha. hāḏi yōm al-ʿaṣar mišat b-ʾāṯārhen. mā gāḷat hī la-xwānha, ʿimlat ʿaša, u-gʿadat.

159 The girl began running, and they [the groats] fell [rolling down] behind her. This [thing] continued from the *ġūla*'s house door to her house door. This one [the *ġūla*], in the afternoon one day, she followed the fallen groats. She [the girl] did not tell her brothers, made supper, and sat down.

164 ğamma xwānha aṣ-ṣubeḥ, rāḥam ʿa-l-ʿamal, ištaġalam. ʾağat la-ʿindha aṣ-ṣubeḥ ṯāni yōm, winnha ğāyya. winnha ğāyya. humma xwānha kāinīn kātlīn ğōzha, l-al-ġōḷa, kātlīn ğōzha,

164 Her brothers got up in the morning and went to work; they worked. She [the *ġūla*] came to her in the morning next day and lo, she came [to her]. There she came. Her brothers had killed her husband, the *ġūla*'s husband.

169 ǧāibīn rāso u-ḥāṭṭīno b-saḥḥāb, kartōna, ʾaḷḷa ʾaʿlam, yilʿabom ʿalē.	169 They had brought its head and put it in a box, a cardboard, Allah knows, amusing themselves with it.
171 hāḏi ʾağat min hēn, giʿdat ʿind hā-l-bint, txarrafat hī w-al-bint ab-ṣafāt, innha, yaʿani, šikel ḥilu, miš šikel waḥš. giʿdat hī wiyyāha, gāḷat-ḷēha, "ʿaṭīni mišṭ, tanni ʾamaššeṭ rāsi min ʿandeč."	171 This, she came from here, sat down with the girl, spoke [chatted], she and the girl. She and the girl spoke nicely, that is, in a sweet manner, not a coarse manner. She sat with her and said to her, "Give me a comb to comb my head at your place [home]."
176 fa-rāḥat. gāḷat-lēha l-bissa, "nṭīni ʾarawwaḥ ʾağīb lēha al-mišṭ." gāḷat-ḷēha, "ʾağīb lēk rās al-šēx b-il-guffa." [e. gāḷat-ḷēha—mā gāḷat hēk al-bint.] ǧābato, gāḷat-lēha, "ǧībī," gāḷat-lēha al-ġōḷa, gāḷat lēha, "hātī." hāy šālat illi ʿindha, u-mata daḥḥagat ʿalēha, ʿirfato.	176 She went, and the cat said to her, "Let me go and bring her the comb." She [the cat] said to her (the *ġūla*), "I'll bring you the old man's head in the box." (Er . . . she said to her—the girl did not say that.) She [the cat] brought it The *ġūla* said to her, "Bring it." This [cat] carried it to her. When she looked at it, she recognized it [him].
183 hāy sāʿatin-mā ṭlaʿat hā-l-ġōḷa min ʿind hā-l-ʿaṣ°r, šū ʿimlat? ḥaṭṭat, daggat lēha mismār samm wa-mismār damm ʿala l-ʿatabe. u-ʾaḷḷa yaʿlam. ṭilʿat al-bint, daggan hā-l-masāmīr, ḍaḷḷat ʿala l-bāb. ʿādim ixwānha min hā-l-ʿamal, ligum hā-d-dār m(e)ʿattma, ligum mā fī šī ṣāyer, ligum, ligum ʾuxthum.	183 This one [the *ġūla*] when she went away [left the girl] in the afternoon, what did she do? She put, knocked for her a poison nail and a blood nail on the door lintel. And Allah knows. The girl came out and they [the nails] knocked [nailed] her and she remained at the door. Her brothers coming back from work found the house dark, found there was nothing [ready], found—found their sister.
191 Šū widhum yiʿmalum? gāḷum, "hāy ʾuxtna, mā nigdar nḥuṭṭha b-al-ʾarḍ nidmelha. hāy ʾalla nḥuṭṭha maʿa ǧmal el-hawa."	191 What shall they do? They said, "This is our sister, we cannot put [bury] her in the ground and bury her. This, we can only put her with the Air Camel."
195 [hāḏa xurrāfa, yaʿlam ʾaḷḷa fi šlōn. u-rabbna yigdar ʿa-kull šī.	195 (This is a legend, Allah knows how, and our Lord can [how to] do everything.
197 (ǧmal al-hawa miṯel ʿaṣfūr. ʾaywa.] haḏōḷa, ʾaḷḷa yaʿlam, ǧābum hāl-maḥārim ḥarīr, ǧābum h(e)dūm ḥarīr, u-ǧābum labbasum ʾoxthom u-maʿa mšayt ʾaḷḷa ʾağa ǧmal al-hawa [yaʿlam ʾaḷḷa ṣ-ṣaḥīḥ, ʾaḷḷāhu ʾaʿlam.]	197 (The Air Camel is like a bird. Yes.) They, Allah knows, brought silk kerchiefs, brought silk clothes, and brought and dressed their sister, and with Allah's will the Air Camel came (Allah knows the truth, Allah knows best).
203 ḥaṭṭōha, gāḷū-ḷo, "rūḥ; ʾalli ygūḷ-ḷak 'haddi,' lā thaddi, ʾalla ġēr ʾalli ygūḷ-ḷak 'b-ḥayāt alli inta šāyil, ithaddi."	203 They put her [on it] and said to it, "Go. He who says to you alight, do not alight. Only that one who says to you, 'By the life of the one you are carrying, alight,' then you will alight."

206 rāḥ. hāḏa ṭār. ʾan-nās tiʿirfo. gāḷum, "ʾalla-n šāyif ši mbayyen ʿalē, haddi, haddi," mā hadda. bī xetyār, sāriḥ maʿa šwayye ṭarš. gāḷ-ḷo, "b-ḥayāt ʾalli b-aḏharak, thaddi." hadda, daḥḥag, winnha hā-l-bint. "lā widdi ʾāxaḏha. lā, essa ʾağīb ʾağār, ʾāwīha, ḥarām, hīč barra."	206 It went, this one flew [away]. People knew it, they said, "There is something seen on it, alight, alight." It did not alight. There was this old man, shepherding with some sheep. He said to it, "By the life of that on your back, alight." It alighted. He looked and lo, there was this girl. "I need to take her. No, now I'll get a good [religious] deed [in heaven]. I will bury her. Shame on it, [her being] like that, out in the open."
213 ʿendo xetyāra, hū mā ʿendo, (mā) xaḷḷaf, mā lo lā walad wa-lā bint. xaḏāha hā-l-xetyār ʿa-hā-l-xetyāra, gāḷ-ḷeha, "taʿāli, šlōn hā-š-šābba mā (a)ḥsanha, u-ḥarām, ta-nʾāwīha, ʾaḥsan, b-al-ʾarḏ." gāḷat-ḷo, "yaḷḷa." hāy geʿadat tḥammemha, ta-tḥammemha, hāy giʿadat etsāwī-lha hīč, tmasseḥ b-ʾidēha, tġassilhen, winn hā-l-mismār. ʾawwal wāḥad šalato—šilgat al-bint. ṯāni wāḥad—šilgat al-bint—ṭābat al-bint.	213 He had an old woman [wife], he did not have any offspring, neither a boy nor a girl. He took her to the old woman and said to her, "Come, how pretty this young girl is, and shame [that she is dead], we will bury her, better [to do this], in the ground." She said to him, "Let's [do it]." She began to wash her, to wash her. She sat down doing for her like that, wiping her hands, washing them, and lo, there was the nail. The first one she pulled out—the girl hiccupped. The second one—the girl hiccupped and got well.
224 geʿedat ʿindīhom ʾalla ʾaʿlam čam yōm, ṣaḥḥat, u-xaḷḷōha. hā, te-tfakker, "hā, ʾinti šāifa, čēf, imnēn, ğīti, mnēn, mnēn?" xarrafathum b-al-ḥagīga. ḏaḷḷat ʿindhum hā-l-bint.	224 She stayed with them, Allah knows how many days. She got well and they left her [with them]. That, she [the old woman] was thinking, "You see, how, where from did you come, where from, where from?" She told them the truth. This girl remained with them.
229 lamman ḏaḷḷat ʿindīhom hā-l-bint, hāḏa, yōm, šāfha ibn al-ʾamīr. ṭalabha. ṭalabha min ʿandīhom, ʾaḷḷa ʾaʿlam, xaḏāha. xaḏāha, yaʿlam ʾaḷḷa, sina—ʾakṯar, ʾagaḷḷ—xaḷḷafat walad.	229 When this girl remained with them, one day, the emīr's son saw her. He asked for her [to marry her]. He asked for her from them [their permission to marry her]. Allah knows best, he married her. He married her, Allah knows, a year—more, less—she had a boy.
234 xaḷḷafat hā-l-walad, u-ḏaḷḷat. yōm, mīn istaġaššat minnīha? e, maṯalan, min ar-raḥmān, kamān, hī, ğanniyye waḥde [hīč, ʾēš itkūn—mā baʿraf]. xaḷḷat lēha yōm mata hā-l-walad ṣār yaʿani miṯel hāḏa hēč, hāy al-ġōḷa, nifxat ʿalēha winnha ḥamāma.	234 She had this boy and remained [there]. One day, who wanted to trick [cheat] her, er, for instance, from the Merciful [Allah]? She, a female ğinnie (like that. What she is I don't know). She let her one day, when this boy became like that one [a boy in the audience], this *ġūla* blew on her and there she [the girl] became a dove.
241 b-as-sima ṭāyira. hāḏi trūḥ itḥūm itḥūm etgūḷ-ḷēha "mī(n) yaʿarf al-ʿaği."	241 in the sky, flying. She would go and fly round and round and say to her, "Who knows [how to care for] the little boy?"

243 yeguḷ-ḷa "yā raff el-ḥamām, mā šufti 'ummi?" etgūḷ-ḷo, "'ummak maʿa r-raff ʿa-t-telāli u-tibči ʿalēk u-ʿala sabaʿ xelāli" [ʿa-sabe ʿaxwān]. [ʿalam 'aḷḷa l-ḥadīṯ kullo, kullo hu xurrāf b-al-hawa . . . kullu mayya ġē(r)]	243 He would say to her, "O dove flock, haven't you seen my mother?" She would say to him, "Your mother is with the dove flock on the hills and crying for you and for seven paternal uncles" (about seven brothers). (Allah knows—all the story is a legend in the wind—all of it is water only.)
249 hāḏi yōm min ḏāt al-'iyyam, 'aḷḷa ʿalam, ğe ğōzha, mā 'aʿlam kēf, ʿimel lēha širke, lammanha, ṣādha, yaʿlam 'aḷḷa aš-širke, alli ʿimel bīha.	249 One day, Allah knows, her husband came, I do not know how, he made for her a trick, they gathered her, he caught [hunted] her. Allah knows the trick that he made with her.
253 xaḏōha ʿala-š-šēx. bī š(y)ūx, yaʿani (t)dāwi ta-ḥğūb, tiʿmal 'aḷḷa, min al-qor'ān min ġēro, 'aḷḷa yaʿalam.	253 They took her to the sheikh. There are sheikhs, that is, who heal with charms [amulets]. They do things from Allah, from the Qur'ān, from elsewhere—Allah knows.
256 ṣāram yiʿmalū-la min hēn min hēn u-ṣaḥḥat u-ṣārat hā-l-bint alli šlōnha. xarrafatum gāḷat ilhum "mā 'aḏa(l)ni ʿindak hēn, ġēr adaššrak w-adaššer uwlādak, iben-ax wa-, w-arūḥ 'adawwer axwāni ṯāni marra."	256 They started doing [things] to her from here and from here and she got well and became the girl that [how] she was. She spoke to them and said to them, "I will not remain here with you, I must leave you and leave your children, his brother's son, and I will go to look for my brothers again [a second time]."
262 haḏōla rāḥam min hēna, ričbat ʿa-l-xēl, ['aḷḷa 'aʿlam, gaḅuḷ mā čānat sayyārāt—xēl], rāḥat i(t)dawwer ʿa-l-xēḷ ʿala axwānha, ṭāliba xwānha. ligum axwānha, gāḷu-lhom ʿannīha,[14] xaḏōha, ğābum axwānha lēha.	262 Those went from here. She rode the horse. (Allah knows, in the past, there were no cars, [but] horses.) She went on horseback to look for her brothers, searching her brothers. They found her brothers, said to them about her, took them, and brought her brothers to her.
268 u-tʿarrafat hī wiyyāhom u-rāḥam ʿind 'ahalha, u-hāḏi xurrāfti u-ṭārat ʿalēk.	268 And they got acquainted with them and went to her family. And this is my story, and [it] has flown unto you.

Commentary

The story "The Girl and Her Seven Brothers," from Maryam Muṣṭafa Ṭabbāš, also largely corresponds with the Snow White stories. Although the story belongs to another narrative type, ATU 451, "The Maiden Who Seeks Her Brothers," the section about the dead heroine being carried on the Air Camel (a huge mythical bird) largely coincides with what appears in some Bedouin versions of "Snow White."

The Bedouin version is very close to the description of the second of the three forms of the international narrative type:[15] A girl finds her brother in a remote place and keeps house for them. They tell her to take care of the cat (dog), watch the fire, and be careful of the demonic neighbor (ogre, witch). Once, however, since she forgets to divide her food with the cat, it puts out the fire. After the girl asks the neighbor for help, the ogre comes regularly to suck her blood. When the brothers discover this, they kill the ogre. The girl gathers flowers (herbs) from the grave of the ogre. Her brothers eat them, and they are changed into oxen (sheep, birds). The episode of disenchantment is less important.

This narrative type is common throughout Europe and Asia and is known throughout the Muslim culture space, from Iraq, Kuwait, and Bahrain to Sudan, Egypt, and North Africa. It also appears in Syria, Jordan, and Israel.

The Bedouin story has a similar plot: The seven sons of a pregnant woman ask their mother to place a mirror with makeup on the tent pole if a sister is born or to place a sword in case of another brother's birth. The mother gives birth to a daughter, who is called Wdīʿa, but women who envy the mother place a sword on the tent pole to symbolize the birth of a son. The disappointed brothers, who see the sign, decide to leave the house and settle far away. When the daughter becomes mature, she discovers the existence of the brothers and goes to look for them. She arrives at the brothers' house. The brothers are absent at the time, and there is only a cat. The heroine is preparing a meal for her brothers. When they return, she introduces herself as their sister and continues to live with them. The heroine finds a chickpea and eats it without sharing it with the cat. The cat takes revenge and extinguishes the fire in the stove. The heroine steps out to look for fire and arrives at a *ġūla*'s house. The *ġūla* gives her fire but follows her and discovers her dwelling place. When the brothers are not at home, the *ġūla* comes, and the heroine welcomes her. The *ġūla* asks for a comb to take the lice from the heroine's hair. The heroine asks the cat to bring a comb, but, instead, the cat brings the decapitated head of the *ġūla*'s husband, who was killed by the heroine's brothers. In revenge, the *ġūla* leaves a poisoned nail on the threshold of the house. It seems that the heroine steps on it and sinks into a magical sleep (the text is not clear about what exactly kills the heroine). Her brothers load her onto the Air Camel's back, and it flies with her into the sky. An old shepherd causes the Air Camel to descend. He carries the heroine's body to his home. His wife prepares her for burial, but after she pulls the poisoned nail out of her leg, the heroine comes back to life. The emīr's son marries her, and she has a child, but a female *ǧinn* blows on her and turns her into a dove (it is not clear if the female *ǧinn* and the *ġūla* are the same figure). Her husband grabs the dove and manages to restore her human image. The heroine finds her brothers and returns to her family.

In this story, the heroine leaves the house of her own volition, but an act of deception, which is based on envy, necessitates her leaving. The birth of a daughter after the birth of seven sons undermines family stability. According to various Druze parallels (IFA 24002, IFA 24104), the father threatens his family and announces that if he has a daughter, he will kill his seven sons, and as a result, the brothers flee from the house. In a different Druze version (IFA 22662), the heroine is known as the "Who-Sends-Away-the-Seven" (*meṭalqat al-sabʿah*), and the explanation is that the brothers themselves threatened their mother that if she gives birth to a daughter, they will leave the house. On the other hand, in another Bedouin version from Bēt Zarzīr (IFA 24270), which is almost identical in its details to the Bedouin story above, the brothers want a sister and ask the mother to hang as a sign a mirror and cosmetics. But the women surrounding the mother deceive her and place the symbol that indicates the birth of a son.

Meron presents a version of this story by Bahiyya Yūsuf Maḥamīd from the village of Muʿāwiyeh, an Arab village in Ramot Menashe (a geographical region in northern Israel).[16] In this version, the sister finds her lost brothers when a loaf of bread rolls in front of her and thus indicates the way. After she arrives at her brothers' house, she manages their household. The fire is extinguished, and the heroine, looking for fire, arrives at a *ġūla*'s house. She takes the meat cooked by the *ġūla*, slaughters the *ġūla*'s son, cooks him, and puts him in the pot. The *ġūla* finds out that she ate the flesh of her son. She dresses up as a shoe peddler and sells seven pairs of shoes to the heroine. As soon as her brothers put on their shoes, they become oxen, and that is the end of the story. Among the Arabic versions I have examined, this is the only one that includes the episode of the brothers turning into oxen, which is part of the description of the international narrative type.

Another version, which appears in the same book, taken from Rubah Nagībeh Ḥamūd from Bēt Ǧan, lacks the first part of the search of the brothers.[17] Following a rolling loaf of bread, the heroine arrives at the house of the *ġūla*, and the *ġūla* adopts her as a daughter. Contrary to the instructions of the *ġūla*, the heroine does not share a grain of beans with the cat, and the latter extinguishes the fire. In her search for fire, she arrives at the house of another *ġūla*. This *ġūla* gives her fire but follows her to the house of the first *ġūla* and tries to devour her. The first *ġūla* manages to kill the second *ġūla*, but a drop of her blood that has become a thorn stabs the girl, and she dies. The *ġūla* puts her coffin on a camel and orders the camel not to kneel unless it is told the phrase: "By the life of whom you carry on your back, kneel down." An old woman in a village says the right words. The camel kneels, and the old woman brings the girl back to life, after she has removed the magic thorn from her leg. The girl marries the boy who called the old woman to stop the camel. This episode of the story appears in the various Bedouin versions of "Frēṭ Rummān" (Snow White), discussed earlier (in chap. 28). This is an exceptional case, in which a "good" *ġūla* fights an "evil" *ġūla* and defeats her.

The search for the brothers is part of the heroine's process of growing up and leaving the house. Neighbors accuse her of indirectly causing the exile of her brothers, and she takes on the task of locating them and bringing them home. When she finds them, she becomes their housemaker, and like the heroine in the Snow White stories, she acquires skills that will help her in the future when she gets married. She also copes with various difficulties. In this respect, the brothers' demand to fulfill a certain condition, to share her food with the cat, is not significantly different from the *ġūla*'s demand in Frēṭ Rummān not to open the forbidden room. Violation of the prohibition leads to many difficulties. The brothers play the same role as do the dwarfs in the European versions of "Snow White" or the maternal *ġūla* in the Bedouin stories.

In version B of the Bedouin Snow White story, to hide the truth about the circumstances that lead the heroine to wound her finger, she accuses the scythe of hurting her. The scythe says, "Not me, by Allah, it is not me," and immediately afterward a puzzling phrase appears: "The scythe said: **The cat left nothing to him**." It may happen that the narrator inserted there by mistake a motif taken from the story "The Sister and Her

Seven Brothers" and meant to say that the scythe revealed the truth, because it refused to take the blame upon itself, just as here the cat took revenge on the heroine for not sharing her meal. What is important is that the heroine, while she is in the brothers' home, learns from her experience how important it is to observe the instructions given to her and to share her food with others (hospitality and charity are values of great importance in Bedouin culture), just as her duplicate in the Snow White stories learns the importance of telling the truth and taking responsibility.

Notes

1. *be'īda. ay ya'ani, miṯel hēna w-al-'affūla, ab'ad min al-'affūla, meṯel ǧinīn*: "Distant . . . that is, like [from] here to Afula, farther than Afula, like Ǧenin." Afula and Ǧenin are towns not very far from the narrator's location, though the way looked very long for people who had to walk or ride a horse in the past. The narrator brings the story closer to real life with the place names. See this tendency also in other stories in this volume (e.g., Acre and Baṭṭōf Valley in chap. 10).

2. In this story alone, the expression *'alam 'aḷḷa* (literally "Allah knows" or "Allah [is the one who] knows [the truth]") is repeated twenty-one times in this form or its variants: *'ilem 'aḷḷa, 'aḷḷāhu ya'lam, ya'lam 'aḷḷa, 'aḷḷa 'a''a)lam, 'aḷḷāhu 'a'lam*. This phrase is used when the speaker is not certain of something, for Allah's supreme knowledge is among the features that Muslims refer to in such cases. This phrase has many variants about Allah's knowledge in many other dialects (e.g., Piamenta, *Islam in Everyday Arabic Speech*, p. 10, section 0.5.2.3, and p. 185–186, section 6.8). This expression has here a verbal sentence structure with *'ilem* and *ya'lam*, and a nominal sentence structure with *'a'(a)lam*, a superlative adjective. The past tense (*'ilem*) in this phrase reflects one of the functions of this tense in LA: implying the certainty of the action (cf. Wright, *Grammar of the Arabic Language*, 2:2). This is another example of the inseparable part of the relationship between man and Allah in Muslim life (Piamenta, *Islam in Everyday Arabic Speech, Muslim Conception of God*).

Note: Henkin suggests that *'álam* derives from *ya'álam* (i.e., in the *gaháwa* syndrome), with a deleted first syllable. Henkin, personal communication.

3. *u-gi'dum. ṣārum yāklum, yišrabum, yeǧībum, yegīmam, yiḥuṭṭum*: "And they sat down, [they] started to eat, drink, bring [import], put up [ventures], place down." This sequence of verbs very succinctly describes human life. This sequence is asyndetic (without conjunctive particles), even before the last member of the sequence. Each part of the sequence ends with a rising intonation, indicating continuation.

4. *hiyya trawwe(ḥ) 'ala-immha*: "She goes back home to her mother." In these Bedouin dialects, the sequence *ḥ* + *'* ends in deletion of the *ḥ*, as in *trawwe* + *'ala*. Similarly, a sequence of *'* or *ḥ* + *h* usually creates geminated *ḥ*, as in *ma'hum* > *maḥḥum*, "with them" (cf. chap. 24, note 8). This process also exists in sedentary dialects in the Galilee and elsewhere.

5. *'inti lēč exwān sab'a, bas 'ani exwāneč mā 'a'ref wē(r)-rāḥu*: "You, you have seven brothers, but I, your brothers, I don't know where to they went." In Arabic discourse, not only in these folktales, left dislocation sentences are very common (cf. chap. 27, note 4). That is to say, the pronominal particle (*you*, *I*, etc.) occurs as the first element in the sentence, and the rest of the sentence takes the ordinary word order.

6. The verb form *rāḥu*, "they went," instead of Bedouin *rāḥam*/*rāḥum*, demonstrates sedentary impact on Bedouin speech. Note also the deletion of *n* of *wēn* and its assimilation to *r* before *rāḥu* in *bas 'ani exwāneč mā 'a'ref wē(r)-rāḥu*. Assimilation occurs also in sedentary dialects in Israel.

7. The Arabic verb (root: *ḥčy*) means "speak to" in CA and LA, but also "imitate" in LA (not CA).

8. *'ağiyya miṯel at-toffāḥa*: "a girl like an apple." Perfect beauty is described here as a beautiful apple. Cf. *'abu xalīl mabṣūṭ min hā-l-walad. walad tiffāḥa, u-'adīb*: "Abu Xalil [was] satisfied with the boy. The boy [was like] a [sweet] apple, and polite" (chap. 1).

9. Note the interchangeability of *ğ/g* in *ğā'da*, which occurs not only in this narrator's speech.

10. *ğā'da tkannes*: "sweeping [the floor]." Literally, *ğā'da* means "sitting (f. sg.)," but it is also used as a stative verb (in Israel and other Arabic dialects), when governing an imperfect verb as here.

11. *mā-š ġērha*: "there is nothing except it." The negative particle *mā-š* occurs without */fī ~ bī/*, "there is." This structure is known elsewhere (cf. Al-Barghuthi, *Dictionary of Colloquial Palestinian Arabic Dialects*), including Negev Bedouin dialects, but in this collection it is rare.

12. *š-widdeč?*: "What do you want?' Here the interrogative particle that is usually *šnū* is shortened to *š*. (Cf. chap. 15, note 4.)

13. The root *bgr* here means "cut," as in LA/MSA (cf. Wehr, *Dictionary of Modern Written Arabic*, 68), but not in sedentary dialects in Israel. This verb may demonstrate Bedouin conservative use of this lexical item.

14. In *gāḷu-ḷhom 'annīha* ("they told them about her"), *'an*, like *min* ("from") in *minnīha* ("from her"), is lengthened with the suffixed pronoun. This feature is common neither to all the pronouns nor to all the prepositions nor all the sedentary dialects in Israel, but it occurs in various other Bedouin and sedentary dialects.

15. Uther, *The Types of International Folktales*, 267.

16. Meron, Shehadi, and Masarwi, *Seed of Pomegranate*, 178–84.

17. Meron, Shehadi, and Masarwi, 344–51.

31. The Sickle Hand

NARRATOR: Ṯalǧe Mūsa

TRIBE: *'Arab el-Ḥuǧērāt*
IFA 15231, March 9, 1985

1 bī hnāk hā-l-ʿarab u-nāzle. yōm hā-l-'amīr ʿendo sabʿ-iwlād, mā ʿindū-š banāt. yōm marato rāiḥa ʿala l-ḥaṭab u-maʿaha ṣāṭōra gāḷat-ḷi, "yā rabbi, yā ḥabīb, hā ṭanṭīha bint, wa-law innha 'īda ṣāṭōra." rabbna naṭaq ʿala lsānha, 'anṭāha hā-l-bint, 'īda ṣāṭōra.	1 There was this Bedouin [tribe] living [somewhere]. One day—the emīr had seven children [boys]; he did not have any [daughters] girls. One day his wife was going to cut wood and had a cleaver knife in her hand. She said to him [Allah], "O my Allah, my dear, please give me a daughter, even if her hand will be a cleaver knife." Our Lord spoke on her tongue and gave her a girl, with a cleaver-knife hand.
8 yōm hā-l-bint ᵉtlaffiʿha b-hā-l-lēl u-tnāwilha. 'aṣ-ṣubḥ yeṣabbeḥ ʿendhen aǧ-ǧmāl wu-l-bagar nāyim, yeṣabbiḥ wāḥad b-kull yōm mayyite. šū gāl al-'amīr? gāḷ-ḷhum, "yā ǧmāʿa, mīn yākul hā-l-bagar? widdna nšūf mīn illi kull yōm yifūt b-hā-ǧmāl, yōm ǧimal, yōm nāga, yōm e. bgara. widna nšūf."	8 In the daytime, the girl, she [the mother] would put her in diapers and at night she would give her [things]. In the morning the sleeping camels and cattle would get up and one [of them] would be dead every day. What did the emīr say? He said to them, "O men, who eats the cattle? We want to see who it is that every day goes into these camels one day a camel, one day a she-camel, one day er . . . a cow. We want to see."
16 šū gāl al-uwlād? gāḷu, "widdna nurbuṭ. kull wāḥad, 'iḥna sabʿ-ewlād, kull wāḥad yurbuṭ yōm." 'awwal wāḥad, ač-čebīr, rabaṭ.	16 What did the boys say? They said, "We will sit in ambush. Each one, we are seven boys, each one will keep watch one day." The first one, the eldest, watched.

20 mā šāf-š 'iši. gāmat b-al-lēl, '^{e}tgūm, tākul al-^{e}bgara, tfūt b-baṭenha, tākul al-xawāṣ tabaʿha we-trūḥ il-ğidir al-liben, u-ğidir-al-liben tabaʿha hā-l-gadde, tannha trūḥ ^{e}tlaffeʿ ḥāle u-tnām maḥallhe. 'aṯ-ṯāni, 'aṯ-ṯāleṯ, kull yōm min hā-š-šikel. kull yōm, kull yōm, ta-ṣāram sitte.

20 He did not see anything. She gets up in the night, eats the cow, enters her belly, ate her intestines [internal organs], and goes to the milk bowl, and her milk bowl is like this [big], until she goes, puts on her nappies and sleeps in her place. The second, the third, every day like that. Every day, every day, until the sixth [boy].

28 Yōm, az-zġayyir ismo š-šāṭer ^{i}mḥimmad. gāḷ-ḷa, "yā yimma," gāḷat-ḷo, "yā yimma." gāḷ-ḷa, "yā yimma, ḥoṭṭī-lī kīs naylon, wa-ʿalgī-li (i)yyā fōg rāsi. mallī-li (i)yyā mayy, wa-ʿalgī-li yyā fōg rāsi." gāḷat-ḷo, "la-wēš, yā yimma?" gāḷ-ḷa, "widdi 'ashar, mi(n) šān gabuḷ-mā 'aġfa, gabuḷ-ma tiġmaḍ ʿaini, tungoṭ ʿalayy al-mayy, 'agʿod."

28 One day, the young one, his name is Smart Mohammed, he said to her, "O mother." She said to him, "O son." He said to her, "Put for me a nylon bag and hang it for me above my head. Fill it with water and hang it above my head." She said to him, "Why, o son?" He said to her, "I want to stay awake so that before I fall asleep, before my eye closes, a drop of water will drip on me—I'll wake up."

37 ḥaṭṭat lo hāy hā-l-kīs, fōg rāsa, kīs hā-l-mayy, an-naylon, u gādḥa b-al-'ibre. gadd hū ṣār yunguṭ hā. kull yaʿani hā-, ṣār yinaggeṭ ʿalē mayy. daḥḥag winn hā-l-bint, fātat, gāmat min-hā-š-šiyyāle, hā-š-šiyyāle, fa-gāmat ḥāle, u-gāmat al-lfāʿ tabaʿha, u-gāmat ta-tadxal hā-l-^{e}bgara. u-hū ydaḥḥeğ ʿalēha. fātat . . . min wara. 'aklat al-lubb galbha kullu, ṭalʿat u-rāḥat ʿa-l-gidr-il-liban, laḥsato, u-laffat ḥālha u-nāmat.

37 She put for him this bag, above his head, the water bag, the nylon, and made in it a hole with a needle. Thus, it started to drip, this one, every, that is . . . began dripping water on him. He looked and lo, that girl, entered—got up from this crib, this crib, stood up and took off her diapers, and entered a cow. And he was watching her. She entered . . . from the back. She ate all her center, inside, came out, went to the milk bowl, licked it, and covered herself [with nappies] and went to sleep.

48 'aṣ-ṣubḥ gāmam, gāḷū-ḷu, "šnū, yā šāṭr ^{i}mḥammad, šuft da ši?" gāḷ-ḷum, "šift." gāḷum, "šnū šift?" gāḷ-ḷhum, "hāḏi 'uxti^{i}, alli b-aš-šiyyāle." hāḏi 'uxto ġūḷa. gāḷat-ḷo, ta-nnin šāfū . . . gāḷat-ḷo 'ummo, "yā wēlak mn-'aḷḷa, mā li ġēr hā-l-bint, mā ʿamitto (=ʿamidto), mā ḥinēto, šift wa-l-ḥinēto ta 'ağetna hā-l-ʿağiyya. čēf ġūḷa?"

48 In the morning they got up, said to him, "What, Smart Mohammed, did you see anything?" He said to them, "I saw." They said, "What did you see?" He said to them, "It is my sister, who is in the crib." That sister [of his] was a *ġūla*. She said to him, that they saw . . . his mother said to him, "Oh woe to you from Allah, I haven't got [any other] girl besides this girl, how much I wanted [aimed at] it, prayed [emotionally] for it, until this girl came to us. How is she a *ġūla*?"

57 gāḷ-ḷha, "ġūḷa." gāḷat-ḷo (=gāḷ-ḷa), "yā yumma, hād̠ 'ani, mī wara gām bala gūḷa. 'ani šuft ešū šāfu ʿeyūni. rāḥat u-kalat ğider hā-l-laban u-ğat, u-laffaʿat ḥāla u-ğat." šū ṣār yegūḷ 'abū, gāḷ-ḷo, "rūḥ min hēn, hiğğ:, hiğğe minnē, min hēn." gāḷ-ḷo, "ṭayyīb, yā yumma, ḥoṭṭī-li zāde zuwwāde." saḥab ḥāl, ḥaṭṭat lo hād̠a, zāda zuwwād(a), u-miše.

57 He said to her, "(She is) a *Ġūla*. [S]he said to her, "O mother, it [was] me [was] behind, [who] got up without a *ġūla*. I saw what my eyes saw. She went and ate this pot of milk and went, covered herself with nappies and came [back]." What did his father begin to say to him? He said to him, "Go away from here, be off, be off from me, from here." He said, "Well, o mother, put for me some provisions, he put it on the mare, I will be off." He went—she put it for him, some food, and he went away.

66 'ad̠int ar-rāwi, sitt—sabeʿt-iyyām, hū māši. miše ği hā-l-balad. ʿarab. ği ʿala hā-l-ʿarab. win hā-l-xatyāra ʿindhe šwayyet miʿze. fāt ʿala hā-l-xetyāra. gāḷ-ḷa, "marḥaba yā—yā xatyāra,"

66 With the narrator's permission—six, seven days he was going. He went and came to a village, Bedouins. He came to this Bedouin tribe. Lo, there was this old woman, who had a few goats. He entered this old woman's [place]. He said to her, "Good day, o—o old woman."

71 gāḷat-ḷo "ahlan." gāḷ-ḷa, "ma tbaytīni al-lēle?" gāḷat-ḷo, "mnēn al-maṭraḥ yā ḥabībi? mā ʿendi maṭraḥ. dūnak[1] hād̠a min ḥāli. winni šāif min hā-l-ʿarab kullha—ğāy tbāt ʿendi. dūnak bēt al-'amīr, dūnak bēt eflān. dūnak bēt eflān—tāxed̠ etbāt ʿendi. bāt lahem, mā maʿi matraḥ ʿendi."

71 She said to him, "Welcome." He said to her, "Wouldn't you let me stay at your home this night [sleep here]?" She said to him, "Where from the space, my dear? I do not have place. Do not take this, because of my situation. And I see from all these Bedouins you are coming to sleep at my place. Is the emīr's place beneath you[r honor], is this person's place beneath you, is this person's place beneath you—[that you] stick to sleep at my place. Stay the night with them—I haven't got place here."

79 gāḷ-ḷa, "hād̠a xud̠i xamas lirāt. u-bayytīni al-lēle." bayyatato. gāmat aṣ-ṣubḥ ta-tḥaleb al-meʿza, meʿzāha, winn hā-l-meʿza ḥelban damm, (may—) ḥalīb ḥamar. gāḷ-ḷa, "lēš yā yumma, yā xetyāra, ḥalīb meʿzāki hēk?"

79 He said to her, "Here, take five liras, and let me sleep here tonight." She let him stay the night there. She got up in the morning to milk the goats, her goats. And lo, the goats' milk was blood, [water] red milk. He said to her, "Why, o mother, o old woman, is your goats' milk like that?"

85 gāḷat-ḷo, "yā yomma, mā ši (hiy)ye terʿa, tākl et-trāb il-meʿaza, mā yerʿan yāklan trāb hā-l-meʿza." gāḷ-(ḷ)ha, "lēš?" gāḷat-ḷo, "yā yomma, hād̠-an-nāḥa, al-man mayya—ḥāmīha ḥūt. u-hād̠i hī, yā-ḥabībi, ḥāmīha sabeʿ.

85 She said to him, "O son, they do not graze, the goats eat the earth; they do not graze, they eat the earth." He said to her, "Why?" She said to him, "O son, this direction which is from the water—the *ḥūt* guards over it; and this, o my dear, a lion guards it.

91 u-hāḏi, yā yomma, ḥāmīha ḥayya, sabeʿ rūs. u-hāḏa bī hā, yumma, bas alli narʿa bīha. dōlak hiyya min-kutr at-triš̌š(e) ^{e}trāb."

91 "And this, o son, the snake guards it—[a snake] with seven heads. And this is it, son, only where we can graze. These, because of the large number of the herds, is soil [earth]."

95 gāḷat-ḷo, "xaḷḷi-dd-ʾasraḥ liki, mā twaḏ̣fīni rāʿi ʿandeč?" gāḷat-ḷo, "embaḷe." gāḷ-ḷa, "ʾawadd, fīni arʿā, kull yōm ʾanṭīč līra." gāḷat-ḷo, "ṭayyeb, yā ḥabībi."

95 She said to him [he said to her], "Let me herd for you, won't you appoint me shepherd for you?" She said to him, "Certainly." He said to her, "I want for me to be as a shepherd every day, I'll give you a pound." She said, "Good, o my dear."

100 hāḏa maš baʿad w-ʾiḏa fāt ʿala l-maġġara dawwar hīč, liga gaṭʿat hā-s-sēf, hā-l-gadde ḥadīda, ṣār yesimm biha w-isāwi bīha. ği ʿala s-sabʿa. [sbūʿa, nta-ʿārf as-sbūʿa]. ğe ʿala hā-s-sabʿa winn hā-s-sabʿa gāʿda tğīb.

100 This [man] did not go far, and lo, he entered the cave. He wandered around like that, and found a piece of this sword, iron, such iron. He started swinging it [forcefully] and doing [things] with it. He came to the lioness (lions, you know lions). He went to this lioness, and lo, she was giving birth.

106 gāḷat-ḷo, "wēn ğāy ʾinte?" gāḷ-(ḷ)ha, "min ^{e}blād ġarībe u-ġašīm(e), u-mā-na ʿāref wēn an-nās terʿan." gāḷat-ḷo, "taʿāl sāʿidni^{y}, ğāʿada ʾağīb-ʾan(i), ğe sāʿidni, ʿa-tann ʾanṭīk wāḥad ^{e}mn-iwlādi. ʾawwal walad ^{i}mn-iwlādi ʾanṭīk ʾiyyā." gāḷ-(ḷ)a, "ṭayyib."

106 She said to him, "Where—are you coming (from)?" He said to her, "From a strange and gross country and I don't know where people make [their sheep] graze." She said to him, "Come help me, I'm delivering now, come help me, and I'll give you one of my children. The first born of my children, I'll give it to you." He said to her, "All right."

113 hāḏa gaʿad yeğayyibha wi-yšiddha, wi-hi nāima wi-tğīb, ʾassa bdi $_{H}$simān$_{H}$ hū, ʾawwal wāḥad ḥaṭṭ al-yad ad-damm; aṯ-ṯāni ḥaṭṭo b-ʿobbo. raddat ğābat ʾaṯ-ṯāni ḥaṭṭa-lha ʾiyyā, aṯ-ṯāleṯ ḥaṭṭa bʿobbo, ḥaṭṭa b-ʿobbo ṯnēn.

113 This [man] went to deliver her, and squeeze her, and she was lying [down] giving birth, now he made a HsimanH [sign], the firstborn, he put the blood on its hand; the second one he put in his lap. She again gave birth, the second one he put it to her, the third one—he put two in his lap. He put two in his lap.

119 u-xaḷḷaṣ, entahat ta-ʾinha tarayyḥat u-saḥab ḥālo u-rāḥ imʿa ṯ-ṯnēn. gāḷat-ḷo, "ʾerʿa, yā šāṭr ^{i}mḥimmad, xaḷḷik terʿa," gāḷ-ḷa, "ʾa-mā tanṭīni wāḥad?" gāḷat-ḷo, "waḷḷa, yā mḥimmad, yā šāṭr ^{i}mḥimmad, ḥada yenṭi banā, yaʿani, ḥada yanṭi wlādo? yaṭ-lak (=ğat-lak) ḥada yenṭī banā?"

119 And [it] ended—she finished and rested. And he went off with the two. She said to him, "Graze, o Smart Mohammed, I allow you to [let the goats] graze." He said to her, "Are you not going to give me one [cub]?" She said to him, "By Allah, o Mohammad, Smart Mohammad, would anyone give his children away? That is, would one give away his children? Did it occur to you that one would give his children?"

127 gāḷ, "baḷḷa, bas widd-ʾarʿa," gāḷat-ḷo, "ʾerʿa, ʾerʿa." hāḏa ṣār yerʿa. ṣārat hā-l-ʿarab ^{e}tgūl, "čēf aš-šāṭer ^{e}mḥemmad yerʿa b-arḏ hā-s-sabʿa, u-s-sabʿa—ʿalāma, kinnha mayyte. ʾabṣar ʿalāma, ʾabṣar ʿalāma." ṣārat ^{i}tgūm.	127 He said, "By Allah, I only want them to graze." She said to him, "Graze, graze." He started to let the goats graze [there]. The Bedouins started saying, "How does Smart Mohamad graze in the lioness's land? And the lioness—why? Maybe she is dead. . . . How, why, how, why." They got up [and they began coming there to graze].
133 ṣār ar-rabīʿ ʿāli, šū widdo yerūḥ? widdo yerū(ḥ) ʿād ʿala-l-ḥayya. gāḷ-ḷa, "ya-imma, mā ʿandeč ḥašūše?" gāḷat-ḷo, "embaḷa, yumma, ʿendi." gāḷ-ḷa, "ʾanṭīni ḥašūše."	133 The spring grass got high; where does he want to go? He wants to go now to the snake. He said to her, "O mother, don't you have a sickle?" She said to him, "Certainly, son, I have." He said to her, "Give me a sickle."
138 hāḏa kull yōm ʿa-ḏ-ḏuhūr yugʿod yḥišš. yeḥišše b-al-ḥašīš. yesawwi kull kōm gadd bāb hā-d-dār. tanno sāwa sabʿ-^{e}kwām. sabʿ-^{e}kwām kānum, sāwa sabʿ-^{e}kwām.	138 This [man] every day at noontime he would cut, cut the grass, doing every day [stacks] as big as the house door. Until he made seven stacks. They were seven stacks. He made seven stacks.
143 gāḷ, "al-yōm widdna nišʿal ʿala-l-ḥayye." hā-s-sēf bi-ʾīdo. ǧat al-ḥayye, turkuḏ ʿalē, šāfato min beʿīd, turkuḏ. ʾawwal kōm nifxat ʿalē, ṭayyarato. aṯ-ṯāni—nifxato, ṭayyarato; aṯ-ṯāliṯ—nifxato—ṭayyarato; al-xāmis, la-s-sādis, as-sābiʿ mā gidrat.	143 He said, "Today I want to set fire to the snake." He had the sword in his hand. The snake came running to him—it saw him from afar, [and came] running. The first stack it blew at it, and made it fly [disperse]. The second one—it blew at it and blew it away. The third—it blew at it and blew it away. The fifth, the sixth—[but] the seventh it could not.
150 tiʿebat. tunfux b-as-sabiʿ rūs, ṣārat timši maʿ(a)hem gadd-ma hiyya w-turkuḏ, lihṯat. lamminnha tiʿebat wa-huwwe giṭaʿ rāse. giṭaʿ rāse min sabeʿ (e) rūs. gāḷam al-ʿarab, "yā māt ala (m), ʾirʿam ʿād." ṣārat hā-l-ʿarab tirʿa ʿind hā-s-sabʿe u-tirʿa ʿind al-ḥayya, b-arḏ al-ḥayya.	150 It got tired, blowing with the seven heads. It began walking with them, as much as it was running, it panted heavily. When it got tired—he cut its head off. He cut its head, of the seven heads. The Bedouins said, "Oh, it died, then, graze, then." The Bedouins started grazing their goats at the lioness's place and graze at the snake's place, at the snake's land.
158 ǧē, gāḷum hā-l-banāt tibči. gāḷu-ḷo. "mā lha, leš, yā yumma, hā-l-banāt kullha tibči^{i}?" gāḷat-ḷo, "yā yumma, widddum yiftaḥūn al-mayya al-yōm, u-kull mā widdum yiftaḥūn al-mayye yḥuṭṭūn-lo bint, l-al-ḥūt, ʿala bāb hā-l-ʿēn, minšān yiftaḥ ^{i}lhom al-mayy al-yōm, yimallum al-biyāra, u-kull sina yinṭū-lo bint."	158 He came, they said, the girls are crying. They said to him [he said to her]. "What's the matter? Why, Mother, are all these girls crying?" She said to him, "O son, they want to open the water today. Whenever they want to open the water, they put for him a girl, for the *ḥūt*, at the opening of the spring in order that it will open the water for them today [and] they will fill the wells, and every year they give him a girl."

167 gāḷ-ḷa, "wēnta widdhom yinṭūn(h)a?" gāḷ-ḷa, "wēnta widdhom yinṭūn(h)a?" gāḷat-ḷo, "yinṭūnha—bāčir

167 He said to her, "When will they give her [to him]?" He said to her, "When will they give her to him?" She said to him, "They will give her—tomorrow

170 biddhin yinṭūha." gāḷ-ḷa, "ṭayyib, bāčir—bāčir." seḥab ḥālo rā(ḥ) ʿala l-bēt ḥatta maʿ-al-miġrib maʿa l-bint labbasōha u-waddōha ʿala hā-l-bāb hā-l-ʿēn u-ḥaṭṭōha ʿa-bāb al-ʿēn u-daššarūha.

170 "they will give her." He said to her, "Well, tomorrow—tomorrow." He went off to the house until, at sunset time, the girl—they dressed her and brought her to the opening of the spring and put her there, and left her.

176 ğe ʿala-al-bint, gāḷ-ḷa, "mā-leč, yā bent?" gāḷat, "daxxalak b-waǧhak, lā tiği la-hēn." gāḷ-ḷa, "lēš?" gāḷat-ḷo, "b-astanna la-yīği al-hūt, ʾassa b-yīği yāxoḏni." gāḷ-ḷa, "wēn hū al-ḥūt?" gāḷat-ḷo, "ʾessa yīği." gāḷ-ḷha, "lā txāfi. ʾēmta waṣṣal mā yīği bas ʾugʿudi xarrfī, u-lā txāfi ." gāḷat-ḷo, "ṭayyib." "haḏāk as-sēf ᵉmʿā.

176 He came to the girl and said to her, "What is the matter, o girl?" She said, "I beg you, upon your honor, do not come here." He said to her, "Why?" She said to him, "I'm waiting for the *ḥūt* to come; it is coming soon to take me." He said to her, "Where is the *ḥūt*?" She said to him, "It is coming soon." He said to her, "Do not be afraid, when it arrives as soon as it comes, just sit and talk to him and do not be afraid." She said to him, "Good." That sword was with him.

185 mā fāt ʿalēha widdo yxarrefha, u-gām hū yeʾoṣṣ rāso. mā ʾaṣṣ rāso, gāḷ-ḷo, "ṯanni," gāḷ-ḷo, "ʾummi mā ʿallamatni," gāḷ-ḷha, "taʿāli ğāy," ʾağat. min hā-d-damm hā-l-ḥūt ḥaṭṭ ʾīdo hīč ʿala šiber damm u-ḥaṭṭ ʿala ṯōbha. gāḷ-ḷa, "rawwḥi ʿind-abūč yeden."

185 As soon as it came to her, it wanted to talk with her, he got up and cut its head off. When he cut his head off, it said to him, "Do it again." He said to it, "My mother did not teach me [that]." He said to her, "Come here." She came. From the blood, of the *ḥūt*, he put his hand like this at a hand measure of blood and put it on her dress. He said to her, "Go home to your father with the hand [sign]."

192 rawwaḥat hāḏi—hinne ṣāran lē ṣārat al-ʿarab yegūlan lē, yegūlan lē, ta wiṣlat ad-dār. u-saḥab ḥālo u-rāḥ hū nām ʿind al-xetyāra.

192 She went back home. They began, "Why?" The Bedouins started to say, "Why?"—the Bedouins started to say, "Why?" until she came home. He went off and slept at the old woman's place.

196 gāḷ-iḷha, rawwaḥat, ṣārat al-ʿarab itgūl "yē, bint al-ʾamīr ⁱmrawwḥa, bint al-ʾamīr ⁱmrawwḥa, gām yigṭaʿ el-mayya, mā yiftaḥ el-mayya." gāḷat-ilhum, "wāḥad yē (=ğē), min al-ʿarab, ḏibaḥo, ḏibaḥ al-ḥūt, u-rawwaḥ, u-šiber, šiber dimm ʿala ṯōbi, u-mā-(a)dri."

196 He said to her, she went home, the Bedouins started to say, "Oh, the emīr's daughter has come home, the emīr's daughter has come home; it will stop the water, it will not open the water." She said to them, "Someone came, from the Bedouins, killed it, killed the *ḥūt* and went home. And the hand measure, blood hand measure, [is] on my dress. And I do not know [him]."

203 rāḥat, rāḥat al-ʿarab tufgud, winn al-ḥūt mayyit, tmaddad. saḥab ḥālo, rawwaḥ ʿind ʾommo, nām.

203 The Bedouins went, they went to check, and lo—the *ḥūt* was dead, sprawled. He [the hero] went home to his mother [the old woman], and slept.

206 as-sbāʿa kibran, ṣāran ^{e}kbār, yilʿaban. gāḷ-lha, "yā yumma, widdi ʾarūḥ ʾaṭill hassa ʿād ʿind immi u-ʾabūya, widd ʾaṭoll ʿa-l-ʿarab." gāḷat-ḷo, "yā yumma, yā ḥabībi, lā trūḥ"

206 The lions [cubs] grew up, they became big, and were playing. He said to her, "O mother, I want to go and have a look now, then, [go] to my mother and father. I want to see the Bedouin [tribe]." She said to him, "O son, o my dear, don't go."

211 gāḷ-ḷa, "ʾimma, widdi ʾaṭull ʿala ʾummi u-ʾabūya, widd ʾašūf al-ʿarab, šnū ṣār bīhen." ḥaṭṭa ʿala hā-l-faras u-seḥab ḥālo u-miša.

211 He said to her, "Mother, I want to see my mother and father, I want to see the Bedouins [the tribe], what has happened to them." He put [his stuff] on the mare and took off and went.

215 gāḷ-ḷha, "yā yimma, hāḏa kōm ram^{o}l, u-hāḏa kōm tam^{o}r. ʾin činnan as-sbaʿa yilʿaban, yāklan min at-tam^{o}r—daššrīhen, w-ʾin čānan yiǧan, yilʿaban ʿala r-ram^{o}l, yilʿaban b-ar-ram^{o}l, falltīhen." gāḷat-ḷo, "ṭayeb." siḥbat ḥāla hāḏi^{j} u-rāḥat.

215 He said to her, "O mother, this is a heap of sand, and this is a heap of dates. If the lions play, eat from the dates—leave them alone, and if they come, play on the sand, play with the sand—let them go [free]." She said to him, "All right." She took off and went.

222 rāḥ ha-z-zlima, miše, miše, miše, hū rāyiḥ ʿala ʿandhom, yōminno miša b-il-ʾawwal čān rāmi sabaʿ ḥabbāt tam^{o}r. ʿa-ǧanb al-baḥra. ʿa-šaṭṭ hā-l-baḥra ṭālʿa, ṣāran ʿāliya. ǧē ʿala hā-l-ʿarab, ʿala dār ʾahalo, winha byūt xarāb, winha ġēr hiyya—ʾoxto.

222 This man went, went, went, went—he was going to them. When he went in the beginning, he had thrown seven date pips, at the side of a lake, at the shore of the lake, they had grown, became high. He came to the Bedouin village, to his parents' house, and lo—they were destructed houses and lo—[there was] only her, his sister.

229 gāḷat-ḷo, "marḥaba, marḥaba, ǧīt, yā-xūya?" gāḷ-ḷha, "ǧīt." walla, hiyya u-čalb baʿad, ʾismo dirbās. gāḷat-ḷo, "ǧīt." geʿedat ʿindo

229 She said to him, "Hello, hello, have you come, my brother?" He said to her, "I've come." By Allah, [it was] her and a dog, named Dirbās. She said to him, "You have come." She sat with him.

233 gāḷat-ḷo," farasak ʿala- ʿa-ṯalāṯa wulla arbaʿa?" gāḷ-ḷa, "ʿa-ṯalāṯe." šilxat iǧerha. ǧoʿāna, widdha taʾakul, turkuḏ wara dīč. dīč, ʿala l-ḥēṭān, widda tāklo. gāḷat-ḷo, "farasak ʿala ṯalāṯa ʾaw ʿala ṯintēn?" gāḷ-ḷa, "ʿa-ṯintēn." šilxat aṯ-ṯāniya. gāḷat ḷo, "ʿala wiḥda willa ʿa-ṯintēn?" gāḷ-ḷa, "ʿa wiḥda." šilxato. "w-as-sāg?" gāḷ-(ḷ)ha, "mā-š."

233 She said to him "Is your mare on—on three or four?" He said to her "On three." She tore off its leg. She was hungry, wanted to eat, [she had been] running, running after a cock, a cock on the walls, she wanted to eat it. She said to him, "Your mare is on three or two?" He said to her, "On two." She tore off the second [leg]. She said to him, "On one leg or on two?" He said to her, "On one." She tore it off. "And the leg?" He said to her, "There is none."

242 gāḷ-ḷha, “xayya, widd-ašrab. widd-ašrab ’ani, mayyit ani min al-ʿaṭaš.” gāḷ-la, “widdi mayya mkaṛḅaḷa u-mġaṛḅaḷa.” hāḏa bū ġuṛḅāḷ hīč ʿuyūno zġār. gaḷ-ḷa, “widdi mayya mkaṛḅaḷa u-mġaṛḅaḷa.”

242 He said to her, “Little sister, I want to drink. I want to drink. I am dying of thirst.” He said to her, “I want sieved and sifted water [through a coarse and a thin sieve].” That is, there is a sieve, whose holes are small. He said, “I want sieved and sifted water.”

248 gāḷat-ḷo, “widd(i)-’aṛubṭak b-al-ḥabel, la trūḥ tinhazim.” gāḷ-ḷha, “’ana wēn widdi ’anhazim?” wēn-mā ligam bī mištāl ḥaddīni (=ḥaddīno). “’urubṭīni.” gāḷat-ḷo “yalla yā dirbās,” l-ač-čalb, “yalla ’iḏa bašrab wiyyāk ʿala l-bīr, malli.”

248 She said to him, “I’ll tie you with a rope, so you do not go and run away.” He said to her, “Where shall I run away to?” Where they met there was a plant nearby [near him]. “Tie me.” She said to it, “Come on, o Dirbās,” to the dog, “let’s, if I drink with you at the well, [you] fill [it up].”

255 hī mišyat ʿala hā-l-bīr u-hū ʿindo ʿāmūd. ribaṭ ba-l-ʿāmūd, ribaṭ hā-l-ḥabel b-al-ʿāmūd ʿašān ^{i}tčinn (=^{i}tḏinn) hū b-il-ḥabel bʿado. u-ğaʿad hāḏa yurkuḍ. ṣ-ṣāṭōra gāḷat, “yišrab willa mā yišrab, widd ’arūḥ ’āklo.” siḥabt ḥālha u-rāḥat—mā ligat ġēr hā-l-ʿāmūd. daḥḥagat hīn, daḥḥagat hīn, daḥḥagat hīč, wēno? meṯl al-ʿaṣfūr.

255 She went to the well. There was a column near him. She tied him to the column. He tied the rope to the column, so that she would think that he was still with the rope. He began to run. The Cleaver-Knife Hand said, “Whether he drinks or not, I want to go and eat him.” She took off and went [back]—and did not find [anything] but that column. She looked here, she looked there, looked thus, where is he? Like a bird [flown].

264 gāḷat-ḷo, “dirbās, ’urkuḍ, liyya (a)ğ-ğiṯṯa u-lak ar-rās.” ’iḏa tanṭi a-č-čalb ar-rās, u-lihe l-ğiṯṯe, ač-čebīr. gāḷat, “’urkuḍ ta-nurkuḍ warā. ’urkuḍ.” saḥab ḥālo hāḏ u-rāḥam yerukḍūn, yerukḍūn, u-wiṣlam, willa hū ʿala—’ağa ʿa-šaṭṭ al-baḥra.

264 She said to it, “O Dirbās, run; for me the body, for you the head” [to eat]. If she gives the dog the head, and she [will get]—the body, the big [part]. She said, “Run, let’s run after him. Run.” He took off this one, and they went running, running and they arrived, and lo—he [was] on—he came to the lakeshore.

271 maša ta-l-baḥra, ṭallaʿ ʿala hā-lla . . . hāḏan, al-kilāyāt, tamor. ʿala hā-n-naxḷāt u-ṭalaʿ. ’awwal naxḷa ṣārat– mā ’īda ṣāṭūra, gaʿadat tagṭaʿ bīha.

271 He went to the lake, went up the . . . these kidneys [fruit] . . . dates. He climbed the palm trees and went up. The first palm she began—why, her hand was a cleaver knife, she began cutting with it.

275 gaṭʿat waḥda, integal ʿaṯ-ṯāni, ʿaṯ-ṯālṯe, ʿa-r-rābʿe, ḏaḷḷ ʿa-l-xāmse. as-sādsa, waḷḷa, mā daḥḥag winna as-sbāʿa ğāyyāt.

275 It cut one, he went over to the second [palm tree], the third one, the fourth one, he remained on the fifth, the sixth—by Allah, he saw—lo, there were the lions coming.

279 ’ummin čānat, u-marran, ṭallaqathen ’ummo. wann hī ğayyāt hī uxra. ḏāt al-ḥadd, winnhen gḏabanha wu-šgafanha ṯ-ṯintēn, hiyya wa-č-čalb. šū ’a-ṣaxār.[2]

279 Their mother [the old woman] was, and they passed—she let them go free, his mother. Lo, they came at last [at the last moment]. At once [simultaneously, like one] they caught her and tore her, the two [of them], her and the dog. What turmoil [uproar]!

284 gāḷ-ḷa, “yā ḥabībāti, ğītan b(h)-ā-nāi.” saḥab ḥālo, gaʿad hāḏ̣, tarayyaḥ. gāḷ, “waḷḷāhi, ġēr ’āxoḏ minha ^{i}lsānha. ġēr ’aguṣṣ ^{i}lsānha w-’aḥuṭṭo b-ğēbi. w-’amši.” ḥaṭṭ ʿala hā-l. māši, hassa ṣāran ṯalāṯe.

284 He said to them, “My darlings, you have come [at] this distance!” He went and sat down to rest. He said, “By Allah, I’ll only take her tongue from her. I’ll just cut her tongue and put it in my pocket, and will go.” He put it on . . . and went. They were three now.

290 u-hū māši^{y} winn hā-l-gaffāla, ğimāl ^{i}mʿāh. gāḷu-ḷo, “yā walad, yā šāṭr ^{i}mḥammad” gāḷ-ḷhum, “naʿam.” gāḷu-ḷo, “’iḥzir šnū ḥmūl ^{e}ğmālna. ’in ḥezart, nanṭīk al-ğmāl wi-ḥmūlha. wa-(’i)n mā ḥazart, nāxḏ as-sbāʿa (a)lli mʿāk” gāḷ-ḷhum, “ṭayyib.”

290 While he was walking, this caravan came, with camels. They said to him, “O boy, o Smart Mohammad.” He said to them, “Yes.” They said to him, “Guess what the load of our camels is. If you guess [right], we will give you the camels and their load, and if you do not guess, we will take the lions that are with you.” He said to them, “All right.”

297 hāḏa ṣār yeḥazor, yeḥazor, mā ḥizrī-š. gāḷu-ḷo, “yaḷḷa, inta mā ḥezart, xuḏ as-sbāʿa,” gāḷ-ḷhum. baʿadēn gāḷu-ḷo, “yaḷḷa, mā dāimak nifadt, mā nifadtam.”

297 This [man] started to guess and guess—he did not guess [right]. They said to him, “Well, you did not guess.” “Take the lions,” he said to them. Afterward they said to him, “Well, as long as you lost, you lost them.”

302 xaḏam hā-s-sbāʿa u-hā-ğ-ğmāl saḥabum ḥālhom rawwaḥam. huwwa gaʿad u-ṣār yibči ʿala hā-s-sbāʿa.

302 They took the lions and the camels and went off going home. He sat down and began to cry because of the lions.

305 wanna hiyya tgūḷ-ḷo, “gūḷ ṣammag, ṣammāg,” lisānha, alli b-ğēbo. “’agūḷ-ḷak ṣammāg, walla, ṣammāg hāḏ.” saḥab ḥālo yegūḷ-ḷum, “stannam, hē, ’agūḷ-ḷak ṣammāg.” gāḷu-ḷo, “ḥezart, taʿāl, yaḷḷa.” xaḏa ğ-ğmāl u-xaḏa as-sbāʿa, u-rawwa(ḥ) ʿind al-xetyāra.

305 Lo, she said to him, “Say sumac, sumac,” her tongue, which was in his pocket. “I’m telling you, sumac, by Allah, it is sumac.” He went off saying to them, “Wait, ho, I’m telling you: sumac.” They said to him, “You have guessed [right]. Come, then.” He took the camels and took the lions and went back home to the old woman’s place.

312 hāḏa hā-l-xetyāra, geʿedat hā-l-ʿarab ^{e}tdawwer—weṣal al-xetyāra. al-ʿarab bidda (t)ddawwer mīn alli kital al—as-sabeʿ, kital al-ḥayya, u-kital al-ḥūt, u-ğāyeb as-sabʿe. widdum yidawwrūn ʿalē.

312 Now this old woman—the Bedouins were searching—he reached the old woman’s [place]. The Bedouin wanted to look for whoever killed the lion and killed the snake and killed the ḥūt and brought the lions. They wanted to look for him.

318 ṣāram al-balad, nāda-lem, nādam al-ʿarab, “al-yōm kull wāḥad ʿind al-’amīr.” ṣār-la sabʿat iyyām, hāḏa, nās ^{i}ddawwer, ğeh. šū ’aḥad gāḷ?

318 They began, the village, called out for them, they announced, the Bedouins, “Today everyone will come to the emīr.” It was seven days, and the people were looking for him. He came. What did one [man] say?

322 gāḷ, “baʿad bū wāḥad ʿind al-xatyāra, rāʿi hā-l-xatyāra, hā-r-rāʿi ll-ʿind al-xatyāra. ğībū ta-nšūfo.” šnū gāḷ wāḥad, yaʿani, miṯel ṣāleḥ?

322 He said, “There is still one at the old woman’s, the shepherd of the old woman—that shepherd at the old woman’s place. Bring him so we will see him.” What did someone say, someone like Ṣāleḥ?

326 gāḷ, "yā šaḥaḏa maʿa rkibto, yā maʿa, miṯel ᵉḥnēni." gāḷ, "yuktelu lana, ğību." mā ḏaḷḷ min-el ʿarab ġēr huwwa. widdna nšūfo." ğābu hāḏ. geʿad. gaʿad hunāk, hū gaʿad yifsawa.	326 He said, "He begs, this [one], with [on] his knee, like a beggar [imploring for charity]." He said, "They will kill us [if anyone thinks that]. Bring him. No one has remained among the Bedouins except him. We want to see him." They brought this one. He sat down. He sat there, he sat [and] broke wind.
331 gāḷu-ḷo," taʿāl ta-rri ğāy yā r-rāʿi" gāḷ-ḷum, "hāḏ 'ani ğāʿed." ğābū-lo aš-šēnta gāḷu-ḷo, "gūḷ hīč." gāḷ hīč.	331 They said to him, "Come here to see, this way, o shepherd." He said to them, "I'm sitting." They brought him the thing [the dress] and said to him, "Do like this." He did like this. [The announcer called out, said, "The emīr says that all]
334 inn hā-l-ʿarab tākul u-tišrab sabʿet iyyām min čīs al-'amīr u-tiʿmal ʿurs la-š-šāṭr ⁱmḥimmad."	334 "The Bedouins will eat and drink seven days from the emīr's pocket, and will make a wedding for Smart Mohammed."
337 hāḏa ğē siḥbam ḥālum u-ğe hāḏa al-'amīr, ṣār yuṭbux u-yiṭʿam u-ysāwi, ğābum hā-l-. aš-šāṭr ⁱmḥammḥad, gāḷu-ḷo "yaḷḷa, rūḥu, yiḥammimū, (i)ġasslū, widdna niğawwzū bint al-'amīr." sāwū lo ʿirs u-ğawwazō[3] u-gaʿad u-nbasaṭ hū w-al-xityāra 'ummo. hāḏi xurrāfti, xaḷḷṣat.	337 Thus, he came, they went off, and this emīr came and began to cook and taste and prepare. They brought this . . . Smart Mohammad and said to him, "Come on, go and they will bathe him, wash him. We want to marry him to the emīr's daughter." They made him a wedding and married him off and he stayed [there] and was happy, he and the old woman, his mother. This is my story, [which] ended.

Commentary

The narrative type ATU 315A, "The Cannibal Sister," is known in many cultural spaces. Most folklore scholars believe that it originated in India, although Bascom suggests that it first appeared in Africa.[4] This narrative type contains the following elements: A woman (queen) who has only sons gives birth to a daughter. The girl first devours the animals, then her brothers and parents, and finally the inhabitants of the village (city) (motifs G30, "Person becomes cannibal"; G33, "Child born as cannibal"). Only one brother escapes. (Or: At a king's court every night, someone devours horses. The elder princes who keep watch fail, but the youngest shoots the monster. He recognizes his baby sister as the cannibal because one of her fingers has been shot off. The youth is driven away [as a liar] or flees [sometimes together with his mother or elder sister].)

The youth marries, gives his wife a life token, leaves his dogs (young lions, panther) behind, and returns home. He finds everything devastated. His sister devours his horse and threatens to devour him, too. While she is sharpening her teeth, the youth must play an instrument to prove he is still there. A mouse takes his place, and he flees. The youth escapes and climbs three trees in succession, which his sister gnaws down (motif R251, "Flight on a tree, which ogre tries to cut down"). Warned by the life token, his dogs come to save him and kill the cannibal sister (motif B524.1.2, "Dogs rescue fleeing master from tree refuge"). When examining the five versions collected in four different tribes, one can see that most of the international motifs appear in them, with the addition of various elements.

In the Bedouin versions, a mother who has no daughters wishes to have a daughter, even if she has a cleaver-knife-shaped hand (*ṣāṭōra*. a type of rigid sickle used for chopping branches). Her request is answered, and she gives birth to a daughter whose hand has a *saṭūra* shape and calls her Saṭūra (or Swatira). The daughter leaves her cradle nightly and devours goats (cows). Her brothers try to find out who kills sheep and cattle but fall asleep on their watch. The younger brother prevents his eyes from shutting by using a waterskin that drips water on him and discovers that his sister is the one who slaughters the household animals. He tries to convince his parents that the culprit is his sister, but he is denounced as a liar and expelled from the house. On his way, near a pool of water, he eats dates he has brought with him and throws the pits beside the pool.

He works as a hired shepherd with an old woman in another village, helps a lioness to give birth, and receives (or takes away from her) two cubs, which he raises. After he helps a hyena to give birth, as well, she allows him to graze his sheep in her territory. He fights a seven-headed snake and kills it, enabling the villagers to graze there. He fights a *ḥūt* (water monster) that prevents the villagers from drinking water unless they hand over a girl (princess) every year. He kills the monster and sends the princess to her father (motif R111.1.1, "Rescue of princess from ogre").

The emīr wishes to marry his daughter to the hero who saved her. A black slave pretends to be the one who killed the monster, but the fraud is revealed. The hero is identified by the mark of his hand, which he had dipped in the monster's blood before touching the princess's garment, and the king gives her to him in marriage.

The hero intends to return to his birthplace and orders the old woman (or his wife) to release the lions he raised if they alter their normal behavior. He returns to his birthplace and discovers that all the people of the village (town) have been eaten by his cannibal sister, except for a rooster she is trying to chase. His sister welcomes him. She asks how he came to the village, and the hero replies that he came riding on his horse. The sister devours the horse leg after leg. She then plans to devour her brother, but he manages to deceive her and flee from the village. His sister chases him (with her dog). He reaches the pool and climbs one of the palm trees (three or seven) that have grown from the pits he threw during his first flight. His sister cuts down the trees one by one, and the hero skips to another tree each time. His trained lions alter their behavior. The old woman (or his wife) releases them, and, rushing to the aid of their master, they tear the cannibal sister and her dog to pieces (or fight her underwater in the pool). The hero cuts off her tongue (or her head) and takes it with him.

Merchants who meet him on his way seek to get his trained lions. They suggest that he guess the contents of the sacks their camels are carrying. If he guesses correctly, he will get the camels and their load, and if he does not guess correctly, he will have to hand over the lions. He fails in his first two attempts, and then the tongue of his cannibal sister (or her head or drops of blood that fell on the ground when she was killed) whispers to him that the load is sumac powder (a spice made from the fruits of the sumac

[*Rohus coriaria*]). The hero guesses correctly, receives the camels and their load from the merchants, and returns home.

The version I recorded from Ṯalǧe Mūsa of the ʿArab el-Ḥuǧērāt tribe is the most complete of all the versions I have written down and contains many details that are not included in other versions. Among them is the narration of the trick by which the hero manages to escape from the *ġūla*-sister. He asks her to draw water in a sieve and a strainer, and while the *ġūla* tries in vain to fulfill his wish, he flees. As shown below, this motif of pumping water in a sieve (motif H1023.2, "Task: carrying water in a sieve") appears again and again in the group of "The Children and the Ogre" stories, as one of the ways by which the heroes deceive *ġūls*.

The version by Ṣabḥa ʿAbūd, of the same tribe, includes most of the details of the plot. In the description of the hero's war with the *ḥūt*, there are additional details that do not appear in Ṯalǧe's version. On the other hand, the episode involving the merchants and the wager over the contents of their load does not appear at all.

In the version from the ʿArab el-Ḥaǧāǧra tribe, the hero helps two lionesses give birth and takes a cub from each of them. The description of the protagonist's visit to his sister, Saṭūra, does not appear. There is a description of the pursuit. The cutting of trees by the cannibal sister is also lacking in this version. The struggle with the lions takes place at the pool. The merchandise carried by the merchants' camels is oak wood. The hero cuts off the head of the *ġūla* and carries it with him, but the description of the help he receives from the *ġūla*'s tongue (or head) is absent. Nor does the story include the protagonist's battle with the *ḥūt* or his marriage with the emīr's daughter.

The version of Zaid ʿAli Muḥammad from the ʿArab el-Saʿadiyya tribe differs slightly from the previous versions in its opening. Each of the three brothers reveals in his turn the cannibalistic nature of their sister, and their father expels all three from the house. The eldest of the brothers is destined to be the hero of the plot afterward. In this version, the sister is described not as having a hand in the shape of a sickle but as having iron teeth. The lions later in the story belong to the landlady who hired him as a shepherd, and he did not get them as a result of helping the lioness deliver her cubs. In this version, the struggle against the *ḥūt*, the marriage of the hero to the emīr's daughter, and his winning the wager with the merchants are absent. The two lions in this version have names: *Sinsāl* and *Riāḥ*. The first name means "chain" and perhaps alludes to the chain by which the lion is tied or to his brave bond with the hero. The second name, *Riāḥ*, is the plural form of *rīḥ*, "wind," and may be related to the lion's speed when it hurries to help its master.

The fifth version, told by Zehiyya of the ʿArab el-Ġrifāt tribe, is unique and significantly different from all other versions. It will be discussed later.

The Indian scholar Ramanujan gives an Indian parallel to the story of the cannibal sister in his book *A Flowering Tree and Other Oral Tales from India.*[5] In many details, this parallel is close to the Bedouin versions I recorded. The hero escapes from his family after he finds that his cannibal sister has been devouring people. He wins the princess, having won a pit-jumping competition. He adopts a tiger cub and a lion cub. He returns to his parents' house and asks his wife to release the tiger and lion if they show signs of distress. He arrives at the village and discovers that his cannibal sister has devoured all the inhabitants. His sister devours his horse leg after leg. The hero escapes and finds shelter on a tree. The tiger and the lion come to his aid and tear the cannibal sister to shreds. It is interesting to note that the unique motif of the horse being devoured (motif G312.7, "Ogress devours horses") leg after leg and the sister's repeated question, "How many legs does your horse have?" appear in this version in a form very similar to that in the Bedouin versions.

In his comments on the story, Ramanujan emphasizes that the perception of the younger sister as a cannibal is the projection of the murderous emotions felt by the older brother toward his sister:

> Here the younger sibling, the newcomer to the family, is seen as a predator, a destroyer of the very family she is born into, and therefore fit only to be destroyed. As in all such cases, projection of the older child's own murderous feelings is never absent. Furthermore, the tale explores the fear of the evil child, the "bad seed" (a favorite motif of horror movies), or of the psychotic or grasping relative who devours and savages an entire extended family—which depends for its existence on the limits placed on any one person's use of others' attention and resources. Such tales also more than hint at the fear and hatred of the strange new child who supplants the older child in the affection of the parents. The tale, of course, is told from the point of view of the triumphant savior, the older child, the survivor.[6]

The episode of the hero who finds refuge in a tree and is rescued by his dogs or other animals he has raised is discussed at length in Bascom's book.[7] He provides many African parallels to this episode in the story. In the IFA archives, there are four Jewish parallels to the story of the cannibal sister; two of them were recorded from Jewish narrators from Kurdistan, one from a Jewish-Moroccan narrator, and one from a Jewish-Yemenite narrator.[8] In the IFA archives, there are also two Muslim parallels. One of them (IFA 23974), as told by Ṭaha Yūnes Ḥayāt, from the village of Ğdeidi in the Galilee, is almost identical to the Bedouin versions I recorded, and the hero's name is Šāṭer (Clever) Ḥasan.

In Ṭaha Yūnes Ḥayāt's story, when the hero leaves the house, he is already a married man and a father. He visits his family's home and meets his cannibal sister as she is chasing the only rooster left in the village. The sister devours the hero's horse leg after leg, and Ḥasan flees after he leads his sister astray: he goes up to the attic as if to pray and leaves there a pitcher of dripping water. It can be understood from this that the sister believes he is busy with purification washing, to which every Muslim is obligated before prayer. The hero escapes, and the cannibal sister chases him. He climbs palm trees that have grown from the pits he threw on his way to her (in this version, the dates are presented as a miracle: trees that have rapidly grown in the short time that has passed since he made his way to the *ġūla*). The lions come to his aid and rip the *ġūla* to shreds. Later, the hero meets merchants, who wager the contents of their sacks. A drop of blood, left over from the *ġūla*, whispers the correct answer—*sumac*—to him, and he wins the bet. It should be noted that at this point in the story the narrator explains: "The drop of blood on the stone did not give her brother up to others," that is, family loyalty precedes everything else, and the cannibal sister, even though she tried to devour her brother, stands beside him after her death.

In another Muslim version told by Rasem Amāra from Kafr Kanna (IFA 24175), the story opens with an Arab prince who has married a new wife after the death of his first wife, the mother of his three children. The new woman gives birth to a cannibal daughter. The continuation is very similar to the previous story. The hero uses the same trick of bathing before prayer to deceive his cannibal sister. He escapes and climbs three palm trees, which the *ġūla* cuts down one by one. At this point, a lion comes to his aid and fights the *ġūla* in the waters of the nearby river. The story about the hero's encounter with the lioness and the adoption of the lion's cubs does not appear here. During the encounter with the merchants, the sister takes her head out of the water just before her death and tells the hero the correct answer: *sumac*. What is interesting in this version is the attribution of the cannibal daughter to another mother, and not to the hero's mother. From a psychological point of view, the daughter who comes from another mother threatens the integrity of the family when she takes the place of the brothers in their father's heart.

Sumac (*Rhus coriaria*) is a deciduous tree growing in the forest of the northern mountains of Israel and the Carmel, as well as in the hills of Judea and Samaria. The word *sumac* apparently originated in Syrian Aramaic, and from there it spread to other languages. It is derived from the root *smk*, "blush, redden." The name derives from the red color of the fruit. In the Mishna and the Talmud, the plant was called *og* (*ogha* in Aramaic). Then, it served as a food plant, from which spices were produced for seasoning salads and dishes. *Og* powder is also one of the components of the *za'atar* (hyssop) spice mixture. The *og* was previously used to produce color, primarily in tannery. Tannin, produced from the *og* plant, was used to tan the skins while processing them. The *og* also has many medical uses. Documents in the Cairo Genizah have revealed that the trade in sumac was common in the eleventh and twelfth centuries along the shores of Lebanon, Israel, and Egypt. Its use continued until the early twentieth century, and in some Arab communities, it is still used. The mention of merchant caravans carrying sumac in Bedouin stories confirms the antiquity of the stories.

An unusual Muslim version of the story is presented in Hanauer's book *Folk-lore of the Holy Land: Moslem, Christian and Jewish*.[9] A barren woman turns to a beetle and asks for a child: "I want a child, even though she be only a girl and as black as a beetle." She gets what she has wished for, and the beetle to whom she turned becomes her daughter and is given the name Khûnûfseh, "beetle." But later on, it turns out that the daughter is a *ġūla* in a woman's disguise. Soon the *ġūla* devours her mother, her mother's husband, and all the family. A wise old man manages to kill the *ġūla* with his dagger and removes from her belly all the family members safe and sound. The constant repetition of the ever-growing list of all the devoured people with their utensils—four loaves and the *kumis* (fermented milk products) jar, the man behind the plow and his pair of oxen, the baker with the kneading basin and the dough, the old woman and her spinning wheel—indicates that this is a fairy tale for children. At the end of the story, the moral is told: Do not sit on the threshold of the house in the evening for fear of demons, and do not talk to any living creature, except for a person, without pointing to it.

In their book, Muhawi and Kanaana give a version told by a Muslim narrator from the village of ʿArrāba in the Galilee.[10] This version is identical in most respects to the Bedouin versions. At the beginning of the story, it is said that the mother has wished for a daughter, even if she was a *ġūla*. The sickle hand is mentioned only later. When the *ġūla* chases her brother and reaches the palm tree, she turns her hand into a sickle and tries to cut the tree. In this version, the two lions are called *Šawaḥ* and *lawaḥ*. The authors explain that *Šawaḥ* and *lawaḥ* are the plural form of wooden boards and that, according to popular belief, wooden boards provide immunity from *ġūls*.

In his book *Seed of Pomegranate*, Joram Meron gives a short version that was told by Sāmi Yūsuf Šḥāde, a Christian Arab from Shefarʿam.[11] Here the story begins with a king who has married his son to a barren woman. The woman asks Allah for a daughter, "even if this daughter would have a dagger hand and a sickle," and her request is fulfilled. Later, the woman also gives birth to a son (unlike the other versions, in which the daughter is born last). The continuation is similar, but without the episode of the adoption of lions. The cannibal sister devours all the village people and the animals except a blind rooster. Her brother comes to visit her after many years. She devours his horse leg after leg. The brother pulls out his sword and cuts off her head. Thus the story ends.

To a great extent, the sickle-hand story expresses the fear of brothers regarding the addition of a new daughter to the family, a daughter who captures the parents' attention and "deprives" the brothers of their status in the family. This fear is expressed in the perception of the new baby as a demonic creature that threatens the integrity of the family or, in the language of the tale, "devours" all the members of the family, except the hero.

A *Ġūla* as a cannibal creature appears again and again in Bedouin stories, but in this instance, the *ġūla* is of human origin. Cannibalism is a well-known social phenomenon in human societies. In addition to the phenomenon of cannibalism in times of famine, which is also mentioned in the Bible and known from many sources, the phenomenon of ritual cannibalism among certain tribes in New Guinea is also known, and stories about cannibalism within the family are familiar to us from Greek mythology. For one example, see the story about the brothers Atreus and Thyestes discussed in chapter 24, "My Mother Slew Me; My Father Ate Me."

Another story from Greek mythology is the story of King Tereus, who craved Philomela, his wife's younger sister. Tereus rapes Philomela, cuts her tongue so she cannot tell anyone what he has done to her, and locks her in an isolated hut. Philomela embroiders her story in the form of an illustration on a carpet, which she sends to her sister, Procne. Procne understands what has happened and releases her sister. She kills her son by Tereus, Itys (or Itylos), boils him, and serves him as a meal to her husband. After he has finished his meal, the sisters present Tereus with the severed head of his son, and he realizes what has been done. Intending to kill the sisters, he snatches up an axe and pursues them,. They flee but are almost overtaken by Tereus. In desperation, they pray to the gods to be turned into birds to escape Tereus's rage and vengeance. The gods transform Procne into a swallow, Philomela into a nightingale, and Tereus into a hoopoe. In these two mythological stories, cannibalism is not an intentional act but one of revenge, but it is always linked to a struggle involving the parental generation and has implications for their children.

The versions I recorded in the ʿArab el-Ḥuğērāt, from Ṯalğe Mūsa and Ṣabḥa ʿAbūd, include the protagonist's battle with the *ḥūt*. This episode is known as an independent narrative type, ATU 300, "The Dragon-Slayer," which is common throughout Europe and Asia. In the Middle East, it is known in Syria, Lebanon, Iraq, Jordan, and Israel, as well as in Egypt and North Africa. In many cases, the episode of a battle with the dragon and rescue of the girl is integrated into other narrative types, such as an Arabic story called "Gazelle," which was recorded in a village near Rāmallah and appears in Muhawi and Kanaana's book.[12]

The word *ḥūt* in literary Arabic refers to a whale, and this is also the meaning of the word in the *Arabian Nights*. In spoken Arabic in Israel, the name is given to a water monster that controls a spring or other water source and prevents the residents from drinking water (motif B11.7.1, "Dragon controls water-supply"). The *ḥūt* demands a virgin girl (a king's daughter) as a condition for allowing the city's inhabitants to draw water (motif B11.10, "Sacrifice of human being to dragon"). The hero rescues the maiden in distress, kills the dragon, and marries the girl.

In Greek mythology, we find a story about the rescue of a young woman from a dragon. Perseus, one of the heroes of Greek mythology, is best known as the slayer of the Gorgon Medusa, a fearsome monster, and as the rescuer of the Ethiopian princess Andromeda. Perseus stays in Ethiopia (or according to other versions in Egypt or in Jaffa), ruled by King Cepheus and Queen Cassiopeia. Cassiopeia, vain and proud of her own beauty, awakens the anger of the sea god Poseidon with her boasting. Poseidon sends a sea monster that kills many people and animals. The oracle of Apollo predicts that Poseidon's anger will not expire unless the king offers his daughter Andromeda to the monster. Andromeda is tied to a cliff by the beach. Perseus finds her, kills the monster, frees Andromeda, and marries her.

In the folktales of the Assyrian community living in Iraq, *Lilisa*, the Mesopotamian Lilith, appears as a monster who keeps water from the inhabitants and is slaughtered by the national hero Katini Gabra, but in this story there is no mention of the rescue of a maiden in distress.[13]

The best-known stories about a hero who rescues a maiden in distress from a dragon are those around Saint George, who lived at the end of the third century CE and is considered the most important saint in Orthodox Christianity. Aviad Kleinberg, in his book *Brother Ginepro's Pork Leg*, claims that the struggle with the dragon was associated with the image of Georgius in an illustrated eleventh-century book that described the story of the saint's suffering.[14] In this book appeared a painting of the dragon, probably as a symbolic expression of the devil, torturing the saint. One of Satan's names is "the primordial serpent," or "dragon," in Greek and Latin. And so he writes: "At first the dragon was only a symbol of the martyr's struggle, gradually he began to have his own life and become an independent creature. . . . In 1245 he was first mentioned by Bartholomew of Trent, not as a symbol, but as a real monster, and a few years later it appears in all its features and lineaments in *The Golden Legend* (*Legenda Aurea*) of Jacobus da Varagine (the thirteenth century)."[15]

The stories of Saint George's struggle with the dragon were thus spread in Christianity from the thirteenth century onward, but their roots are more ancient. No reliable historical sources tell the story of Saint George's life. According to tradition, he was born into a Christian family at the end of the third century. His father was from the Cappadocia province and served as an army officer. His mother was from Lod, and after his father was killed in the war, his mother returned to her hometown with her son and educated him herself. According to the legend, Saint George, or Georgius in Latin, rescued the inhabitants of the Libyan city of Silene, who suffered from the thrust of a dragon living in a nearby swamp. The dragon captured Sabra, the princess of the city, and was about to devour her, but then Saint George appeared on his horse, fought the dragon, and killed it, and afterward he married the princess. Saint George joined the Roman army as an officer. In 302, Emperor Diocletian decreed that every Christian soldier in the army should be arrested. Saint George was commanded to take part in suppressing Christians but instead confessed to being a Christian himself and criticized the emperor's decision. The emperor ordered his death by torture for treason. The body of Saint George was brought to Lod, where he was buried as a martyr.

The Christian inhabitants of the Land of Israel call Saint George Mar Jaris, and the story of his struggle with the dragon is told to this day. It also illustrates many of their churches. James Edward Hanauer gives the story in his book *Tales Told in Palestine*.[16]

It is interesting to compare the princess's behavior as described in *The Golden Legend*, by Jacobus da Varagine, with the behavior of the Bedouin princesses in the two stories cited above.

> At this moment blessed George happened to be passing by and, seeing the maiden in tears, asked her why she wept. She answered: "Good youth, mount your horse quickly and flee, or you will die as I am to die." George responded: "Lady, fear not; but tell me, what are all these people waiting to see?" The damsel: "I see, good youth, that you have a great heart, but do you want to die with me? Get away speedily!" George: "I will not leave here until you tell me the reason for this." When she had told him all, he said: "Don't be afraid, child! I am going to help you in the name of Christ!" She spoke: "Brave knight, make haste to save yourself; if not, you will die with me. It is enough that I die alone, for you cannot set me free and you would perish with me." While they were talking, the dragon reared his head out of the lake. Trembling, the maiden cried: "Away, sweet lord, away with all speed!" But George, mounting his horse and arming himself with the sign of the cross, set bravely upon the approaching dragon and, commending himself to God, brandished his lance, dealt the beast a grievous wound, and forced him to the ground. Then he called to the maiden: "Have no fear, child! Throw your girdle around the dragon's neck! Don't hesitate!" When she had done this, the dragon rose and followed her like a little dog on a leash.[17]

In the version by Ṯalǧe Mūsa, the description is rather minimalist:

> He came to the girl and said to her, "What is the matter, o girl?" She said, "I beg you, upon your honor, do not come here." He said to her, "Why?" She said to him, "I'm waiting for the *ḥūt* to come; it is coming soon to take me." He said to her, "Where is the *ḥūt*?" She said to him, "It is coming soon." He said to her, "Do not be afraid, when it arrives as soon as it comes, just sit and talk to him and do not be afraid." She said to him, "Good." That sword was with him. As soon as it came to her, it wanted to talk with her, he got up and cut its head off.

In the version by Ṣabḥa ʿAbūd from the same tribe, there is a similar description, but here the princess does not seem to be worried about the hero's fate. The creature guarding the water source is described as a genie. It seems that the genie wants to play with the king's daughter, that is, to have intercourse with her:

> They had a *wādi*. This valley opened [that is, flowed with water] every ten [years]. This valley has a genie and every ten years it opens once and [the genie] takes a girl from the tribe. It was the king's daughter's turn. He [the hero] went to the *wādi*, he wants to drink. He passed by the *wādi* and said to her: "You, what are you doing?" She said to him: "This valley is of our people, of the king, and the *wādi* [stream] does not open unless this genie takes a girl." He said to her: "Well, you sit on the side of the *wādi* and talk to him, and I will wait for him here." She said to him, "Good." When he sat down, this genie came out, he wants to play with her. That boy [hero] was waiting for him [lurking for him] with a sword, waiting for him while he spoke to her. He got up, hit him, and took off his head and immediately [its head] fell into the water.

The hero takes advantage of the distraction of the genie, who is trying to play with the princess, and kills him. But in the previous section of this episode, the protagonist fights with a *ḥūt* rather than a genie. In this case, the battle with the *ḥūt* is not related to the presence of a princess, but the hero needs the presence of a female figure who will give him the energy needed to wage his war against the *ḥūt*:

> By Allah, one day he went again to the mountain where the *ḥūt* is. He took the sword with him and went there. He said to it, "I [call] you for war!"—he said it to the *ḥūt*. He said to him, "Come on." He fought with the *ḥūt*, he fought with it. He said, "I'm tired," said this *ḥūt* to the boy [young man] when he was tired. He said to him, "I rest, and you rest." They sat down to rest. The boy, leaning back, sat down to rest. He said, "Oh, who will give me a sip of fresh food, and a tasty drink, and a kiss from a girl's cheek?" That is, a girl to kiss, and a sip of food to eat and water to drink. And immediately he felt the old woman bring him her daughter and bring him a pitcher of water and bring him food, and here the daughter over his head. She said to him: "Please." He drank and amused himself with her and said to the *ḥūt*: "Come on, come out, I'm not tired, I've become a hero now." It said to him, "I want to rest." He said to it, "No, go to war!" He went out to it, fought with it, killed the *ḥūt*.

In this case too, it seems that the encounter of the hero with the daughter of the old woman has an erotic nature, expressed by the verb "to amuse himself." Later in the story, the hero also marries the old woman's daughter.

Kleinberg, in his commentary to the Saint George legend, writes:

> On the one hand, therefore, the dragon does not represent forces as terrible and utterly negative as in the mythical epic; On the other hand, he does not represent a threat to the sexuality of the maiden as in fairy tales. Jacobus uses the princess almost casually. As soon as the dragon is defeated, he forgets her completely. Not only does she not marry our hero, who is supposed to symbolize a restrained sexuality that replaces the unbridled and threatening sexuality of the monster, the narrator does not even assign her the role of an asexual companion to the hero. She simply disappears.[18]

The version told to me by Zehiyya Ġrifāt, of the ʿArab el-Ġrifāt tribe, is very different from any other version I recorded. The beginning of the story is similar to the opening of the other versions: A barren mother gives birth to a daughter after nine sons. The mother calls her daughter Saṭūra, although there is no explanation for the name. The daughter comes out of her cradle and devours goats. The nine brothers go out in turn to guard the flock, but they fall asleep on guard duty. The ninth brother, the youngest, uses the trick of a dripping leather bag to keep his vigilance, and he discovers the deeds of his cannibal sister. The other brothers believe the younger brother's claims and want to kill her, but the mother is unwilling to believe them. Three of the brothers flee for their lives. The cannibal sister devours two of the six brothers who remain at home. The four surviving brothers try again to convince the mother that their sister is a cannibal, but to no avail. The four join the three who fled earlier. All seven find shelter on a high mountain, where a man-eating snake is located. The cannibal sister, who also has magical powers, curses them, and as a result of her curse, they become shoes (!) with the ability to speak. The sister devours her parents, and then by the force of her magic reaches the top of the mountain. At this point, the informant's story is not clear. The brothers who turned into shoes turn to Allah and ask for his help. Allah hits their sister with a sword and turns the shoes back to human beings. In the process, the narrator relates that after the blow, a bird flies from the place. The cannibal sister says the *Šahāda* ("I testify: there is no Allah but Allah, and Muḥammad is the messenger of Allah"). It seems that the younger brother is the only one who has not been harmed by his sister's magical powers and remains in his human form: the narrator describes how the cannibal regrets her deeds and asks Allah to revive the two brothers who were devoured by her and turn the shoes back into human beings. She says, "My Sovereign, my Beloved, I have eaten my brothers, revive the two who died, and the shoes will become human beings!"

Her request is fulfilled, and all the brothers return to life. At this stage, the cannibal sister provides an excuse for her deeds: she was chosen to be a tool of Allah's will and to kill all her family members because her father had murdered his sister with a skewer. The brothers ask their sister to revive their father and mother, but she refuses, claiming that her mother was also a partner to the murder of her aunt. At the request of the brothers, the *ġūla* kills the man-eating serpent, although at first she claims that this is the role of the younger brother, who is called "Šāṭer Ḥasan" (Clever Ḥasan) here for the first time. It is interesting to note that to kill the snake the sister masquerades as a man and wears her brother's clothes. In patriarchal Bedouin society, the killing of wild animals, *ġūls*, and dragons is a role intended for men. This is also the case in one of the previous stories discussed above, "The Prince and His Two Wives" (chap. 20): The heroine also wears a man's clothes when she challenges men who stumble upon her path.

Later, an Arab king intends to harm the brothers, and the *ġūla* turns them and herself into pigeons. It's likely that the previous mention of a flying pigeon, when the brothers turned back to humans, relates to this episode. In any case, the cannibal sister and her brother fly as pigeons to their relatives' village. The relatives try to chase the pigeons away from the *burġul* (crushed oats or similar grain with husks removed), which is meant for the chickens, but the pigeons reply to them in human language: "The property is our family property, so we have the right to eat it." At the request of the *ġūla*, the brothers return to being human and tell their relatives what has happened to them, and at this point the story ends.

There is no mention of the heroic deeds of the younger brother. His role in the story is limited to finding out the true nature of his sister at the beginning of the story and the casual remark of the sister that he, Šāṭer Ḥasan, was supposed to hit the snake, although the sister performs the actual killing of the snake. In fact, the cannibal sister, and not the younger brother, is the central figure in the story. She was chosen by Allah to punish her parents for the murder of her aunt, but later, by Allah's will, she brings her brothers back to life and saves them from the hand of a king who seeks to kill them.

Despite the great difference between Zehiyya's version and all the other versions, in terms of its psychological significance, it expresses the same idea of rivalry and jealousy between brothers. The younger sister who was born last is perceived as a threat to her older siblings because she is preferred by their mother. In a short Bedouin story, a mother is asked which of her children she loves the most, and she replies: "The young one until he grows up, the sick one until he is cured, and he who left the house until he returns" (*s'alam 'umm, "mīn tḥibīn min kull wlādeč akṯar?" ğāwabat, "az-zġīr ḥatta yikbar, w-al-marīḍ ḥatta yišfa w-al-ġā'ib ḥatta y'ūd*"). In other words, the preference for one child over the other is a changing matter depending on the circumstances. This short story seems to correspond with the story of the cannibal sister through the theme of sibling rivalry.

In versions other than Zehiyya's, the threat is removed by eliminating the unwanted sister. Here the conflict is resolved peacefully. It is precisely the sister, who is perceived as a threat, who helps her brothers and saves them from the dangers that lie ahead. The Bedouin proverb says: "I and my brother against my cousin, and I and my cousin against the stranger" (*'ana w-'axūy 'ala ibn 'ammi, u-'ana u-ibn 'ammi 'ala l-ġarīb*). The internal rivalry between the family members is canceled when the family members must join forces to fight a common enemy. The other versions of the story hint that the cannibal sister helps her brother with her magical forces in his fight against strangers, but this only occurs after her death, when her tongue (or her blood) reveals to him the contents of the goods hidden from the eye in the merchants' bags.

The story also corresponds to some extent with the story of Joseph. There, too, the story begins with the older brothers' jealousy toward their younger brother, due to their father's preference, a jealousy that leads them to sell him as a slave; and later the younger brother is the one who saves his brothers.

But in Zehiyya's story there is another psychological element: intergenerational rivalry. The sister kills her parents and takes their place as head of the family. This is a clear case of what Freud calls the Electra complex: the daughter murders her mother and her father and takes their place. The harm to the brothers is conceived as punishment for the parents' sin: the parents harmed their relative, and the sons must endure the consequences. The narrator attributes to the sister the proverb "Fathers ate sour, and the sons' teeth are dulled" (*il-ⁱkbār btōkel ḥāmeḍ, w-isnān il-ⁱzġār tidras*), which is identical to the biblical proverb "In those days they shall say no more, The fathers have eaten sour grapes, and the children's teeth are set on edge" (Jeremiah 31:29 [28]; also Ezekiel 18:2).

Notes

1. *dūnak hāḏa min ḥāli . . . dūnak bēt al-'amīr, dūnak bēt ᵉflān. dūnak bēt ᵉflān—tāxeḏ ᵉtbāt 'endi*: "Do not take this, because of my situation. . . . Is the emīr's place beneath you[r honor], is this person's place beneath you, is this person's place beneath you—[that you] stick to sleep at my place." The word *dūn* is "without," negating an option. Its meaning developed in Galilee Bedouin dialects to drive away any evil event. Here it implies something like "below, beneath"—in other words, "are the other places less appropriate for you than my place?"

2. The interjection (vocative) structure *šū 'a-ṣāxār!* begins with the word *what* as it is in sedentary dialects in Israel. The main word, *ṣāxār,* is apparently the Bedouin form of the root *šxr* in Levant sedentary dialects, meaning "snort, be at one's last gasp." Barthélemy, *Dictionnaire arabe-français*, 381. Bedouin dialects are well known for their profuse use of pharyngealized speech sounds (cf. *ṣṃ-aḷḷa 'alēki*, chap. 28, note 4). In addition, */s~š/*, */s~ṣ/*, */ḥ~x/*, and similar interchanges occur in various Arabic dialects, though not frequently.

3. *widdna niğawwzū bint al-'amīr. sāwū lo 'irs u-ğawwazō*: "'We want to marry him to the emīr's daughter.' They made him a wedding and married him off." Three verbs here end in different vowels: in *niğğawwzū*, the final vowel marks the direct object 3m.sg. suffixed to the verb. In *sāwū* (*lo*), *ū* is the lengthened 3m.pl. verb form, which replaces the ending *-am*/*um* of the Galilee dialects, a phonetic lengthening of the vowel before the indirect object *lo*. However, in *ğawwazō*, the final *ō* vowel indicates a 3m.sg. form ("he married him off"). This suggests the narrator's mixture of the persons (sg. and pl.) is due to the small difference between the vowels *ū*, *ō*.

4. Bascom, *African Folktales*, 155–56.
5. Ramanujan, *Flowering Tree*, 26-27.
6. Ramanujan, 234.
7. Bascom, *African Folktales*, 155–95.
8. Turkish Kurdistan: 18095; Iranian Kurdistan: 7426; Morocco: 14138; Yemen: 7186.
9. Hanauer, *Folk-lore of the Holy Land*, 196–98.
10. Muhawi and Kanaana, *Speak, Bird, Speak Again*, 94–98.
11. Meron, Shehadi, and Masarwi, *Seed of Pomegranate*, 214–20.
12. Muhawi and Kanaana, *Speak, Bird, Speak Again*, 150–59.
13. Shilo, *Lishana Deni*, 149–65; 197–204.
14. Kleinberg, *Brother Ginepro's Pork Leg*, 349–63.
15. Kleinberg, 357.
16. Hanauer, *Folk-lore of the Holy Land*, 56–57.
17. Jacobus de Voragine, *The Golden Legend: Readings on the Saints*, 239.
18. Kleinberg, *Brother Ginepro's Pork Leg*, 362.

32. Bells Sound

A. Ğbēna and the Jujube Tree

NARRATOR: Zehiyya Ġrifāt

TRIBE: *ʿArab el-Ġrifāt*

IFA 17412 September 11, 1982

1 kān yā mā kān, nxarref walla nnām—nxarref. yā sāmʿīn al-kalām—nxarref walla nnām.[1]	1 Once upon a time, there was—shall we tell or go to sleep? We will tell. O listeners of the speech—shall we tell or go to sleep?
4 hēna mā-bī ʾalla hā-l-ʾamīr, u-ʿarabo. lamman al-ʾamīr u-ʿarabo, ʿendo l-bent al-wiḥda, ʾesemha ğbēna. ʾal-bint, bēn sabaʿ exwa. u-garāyibha biddhen[2] ʾiyyāha.	4 There was there this emīr and his Bedouin tribe. The emīr and his tribe, he had the single daughter, her name was Ğbēna. The girl was [one] among seven brothers. Her relatives wanted her [for wife].
9 lamma hōn fī dōm [dōm, yaʿani miṯel ma tgūḷ ē—ğōz, ʾeḥna, bi-blādna]. yiğu al-banāt, tigūl lē, "yā ʾabu ğbēna, xaḷḷi ğbēna trūḥ maʿāna ʿa-d-dōm." yigūl lēha "gūli la-ʾaxūha, gūli l-ʾomma." tanno xaḏum ʿalēha, rāḥat maʿāhen.	9 When, there is jujube (jujube, that is, as you say, [means] nuts, we [say], in this country). The girls come and say to him, "Ğbēna's father, let Ğbēna go with us to the jujube." He says, "Tell her brother, tell her mother" [to get their permission], until they got it [the permission], she went with them.
15 lamman rāḥat al-banāt, al-banāt widdhen yiwaherfūha le-ğbēna, widdhen yukutlūha la-ğbēna.	15 When the girls went, the girls wanted to get rid of Ğbēna, wanted to kill Ğbēna.
18 yōm rāḥat al-bent. lamma rāḥat al-bent, gālat "mīn tiṭlaʿ ʿa-š-šağara, ʿa-d-dōm? ğbēna, anti ʾiṭlaʿi, anti tiṣlaḥi tiṭlaʿi," bint el-ʾamīr. bint ʾamīr tiṭlaʿ ʿala fōq?	18 One day, the girl went. When the girl went, she [one of the other girls] said, "Who will climb up the tree, for the jujube? Ğbēna, you climb up, you are fit to climb." An emīr's daughter; an emīr's daughter would climb high up?

23 ṭalʿat winnha tekutt ᵉlhen. lā xaḷḷū lā ḥayya, lā xaḷḷu ḥerbā, lā xaḷḷu ḥartūn, lā xaḷḷu defḍaʿa, lā xaḷḷu ʾiši ʾalla ḥaṭṭūha b-al-ʿallīğa tabaʿat ğbēna, ba-ṣ-ṣandūg tabaʿa ğbēna. wa-ḥaṭṭam ᵉšwayya ʿa-wağeh al-ʿallīğe tabaḥḥa.	23 She climbed up and started picking for them. They did not leave no snake, no chameleon, no lizard, no frog, nothing but put them in Ğbēna's bag, in the box of Ğbēna. And they put a few [jujube nuts] at the top of her bag.
29 wēn rāḥan? ṣāran mitel mā tgūl nuṣṣ aṭ-ṭarīg ʿan šaʿab gāḷu "biddna nšūf mīn dōmha ʾaḥsan. w-in ṣār ad-dōm, wa-nšūf mīn ykūn dōmha, ykūn aḥsan" hā ʿemlan ta farraġu al-ḥayya ta-al-li-ğbēna.[3] kull ed-dōm hin tabaḥḥan[4] ġār [i]ğbēna.[5] al-ḥayya min hōn, al-qurqaʿa min hōn, al- . . . kull il-ḥarāṯīn min hōn. al-ḥerbāy min hōn.	29 Where did they go? They began, as you say, in the middle of the way, from Shaʿab [a village], they said, "We want to see whose jujube nuts are better [than the rest's]. If the jujube nuts are—and we'll see whose nuts are the best." This they made until they emptied the snake of Ğbēna, all their nuts, [all the girls did this] except Ğbēna. The snake from here, the croaking noise from here, all the lizards from here, the chameleons from here.
38 hōn ṣārat tibki. lamma ṣārat tibki, "ʾanṭūni kull[i] waḥde ḥad, ḥafne, tanni ʾamalli ʾani ʿalliğti wa-ʾarūḥ maʿā(ken)." gāḷan, "lā, ʾiḥna ğibnāki hōn ʿašān al-ġūḷ yākleč." ʿāwadat ʿa-d-dōm la-ḥālha, ğḅʷēna. lamma ʿādat ʿa-d-dōm, ṭalʿat ʿa-š-šağara fōq. wanna ğāy hā-l-ġūḷ.	38 She began to cry. When she began to cry, [she said,] "Give me each one—one [nut], a handful, so that I can fill up my bag and go with you." They said, "No, we brought you here so that the *ġūl* will eat you." She returned to the jujube tree alone, Ğbēna. When she returned to the jujube, she climbed high up on the tree. And lo, the *ġūl* is coming.
45 ʾağāha l-ġūḷ. gāḷ-ḷa, "ḥawli[i], walla ʾağrušak min kull il-ʾağrāš." gāḷat-ḷo, "ʾağrušak min kull il-ʾağrāš"—min-ʿawd la-ʿawd. lamma naṭṭat min ʿōd la-ʿōd, gāḷat-ḷo, "mā ʾanzal ʿan aš-šağara alla mā tuṭraḥ al-ʾimān ʿalayya."	45 The *ġūl* came to her. He said to her, "Get down, or I'll crush you more than all the crushings." She said to him, "I'll crush you from all the crushings"—from branch to branch. When she jumped from branch to branch, she said to him, "I will not get off the tree unless you grant me security."
51 gāḷ-ḷa, "ʾinzali, ʿalēk ʾaḷḷa w-ʾamān ʾaḷḷa, w-alli yuxūneč yixūno ʾaḷḷa." nizlat.	51 He said, "Get down, you have Allah's security, and whoever betrays you, Allah will betray him." She went down.
53 gāḷ-ḷa, "šnū tḥibbi, ʾaḥuṭṭeč ʾibre b-ğībi, walla ʾanfux ʿalēk ʿand ahlek?" gāḷat-ḷo, "lā, ʾanfux ʿalayya ʿand ʾahali, wa-ʾasbug al-banāt, u-ʾani, šayyin ʿend ʾabūya wa-ʾagdar ʿalē, ʾanṭīk iyyā."	53 He said to her, "What would you like, shall I put you as a needle in my pocket or blow on you [and get you] to your family?" She said to him, "No, blow me to my family, and I'll come before the girls and I—anything at my father's [place] and I can—I'll give it to you."

58 hāḏa mallāha l-aš-šanṭa tabaḥḥa dōm. u-nafax ʿalēha wunnha sabgat al-banāt wunha b-dār abūha. ġūḷ, hāḏa. gāḷ-ḷaha, "b-šarṭ awaṣleč. 'aḥsan badla la-'abūč alli mʿallaga badlat al-mamlaka tinṭīni 'iyyāha wa-t-tāǧ.

58 This one filled up her bag with jujube nuts and blew on her and lo, she preceded the girls and was at her father's house. [He was] a *ġūl* this one [he can do such things]. He said to her, "I'll get you home on condition: the best suit of your father's, which is hanging, the state suit, you'll give it to me, and the crown.

64 u-'iḏa mā tanṭīni 'iyyāha, law ḥīnin baʿadēn ġēr 'āxuḏ wa-'atǧawwaz 'ana mara liyya." gāḷat-ḷo, "ṭayyeb. wēnta tiǧi?" gāḷ-ḷa, "yōm al-ḥadd 'aǧīk"

64 "And if you do not give them to me, even if it is sometime afterward, I must take and marry [you. You will be], wife to me." She said to him, "Good, when will you come?" He said to her, "Sunday I'll come to you."

68 gāḷat-ḷo, "ṭayyeb, zēn." 'aǧa, xaḷḷa ḥālo šaḥḥād, huwwa, al-ġūḷ, yišḥad, "'anṭīni xubza, 'anṭīni 'iše." 'aǧa la-ʿand ᵉǧbēna, "'aḷḷah yanṭīki, tanṭīni, trazgīni," ḥaṭṭat lo xubza ʿala hā-l-muknasa, nāwalato 'iyyāha, gāḷat-ḷo "tnāwal." maḥarha. gāḷ-ḷha, "yīk,"—ġūḷ, hēk ᵉbtākol.

68 She said to him, "Good, OK." He went, made himself a beggar. He, the *ġūl*, was begging, "Give me bread, give me something." He came to Ǧbēna: "Allah will give you, give me, provide [food] for me." She put a slice of bread on the broom, handed it to him, and said to him, "Take it." He ate it away and said to her, "Yeek" (—*ġūl*—this is how they eat).

76 ṣārat ᵉǧbēna torǧof. ṣārat ᵉtṣayyeḥ, haḏōl 'aǧu, nahhaǧu hā-z-zalama.

76 Ǧbēna began to tremble, she began to shout; those [people] came and drove that man away.

78 yōm-inno nāzel az-zalama, bī miʿza tirʿan miṯel mā tgūḷ ʿa-l-ǧabal, maṯal ǧabal hāḏa, hāl el-ⁱbyūt hā l-fōg. rāḥ l-al-rāʿi.

78 One day, when the man went down, there are sheep grazing, as you say, on the hill, like this hill here, this with the houses above. He went to the shepherd.

82 gāḷ ḷ-ar-rāʿi, "mā rāyak tāxoḏ mīt līrat ḏahab tanṭīni badeltak, anṭīk 'iyyā, lo 'aʿmal ḥāli ʿammāl u-biddi 'aṣīr 'arkab ʿa-l-ʿarab, mišān ᵉǧbēna tarkab al-ʿalūl, ʿammāl. u-xarref bōᵘ-bīʿu—"mīn yištari hā-l-ʿalūl? mīn ymalli ḏāno yāxḏo.""

82 He said to the shepherd, "What do you say [think], you'll get a hundred gold liras, and give me your suit of clothes, I'll give it to you. If I pretend to be a bull, and I want to ride to these Bedouins, so that Ǧbēna will ride the bull. And you'll tell about it and sell it. "Who will buy the bull? Whoever fills its ears, will take it."

88 hāḏa al-rāʿi rāḥ, saḥab hā-l-ʿalūl, man manāxar hā-l-fatḥa, "mīn yemalli 'iḏān al-ʿalūl naxāḷa yāxḏo." hadīk ᵉtnaxxeḷ aṭ-ṭḥīn, hadīk ᵉtnaxxeḷ aṭ-ṭḥēnāt, hadīk ᵉtrūḥ ᵉtmalle lo nxāḷa—wi-ykibbo be-ḏān el-ʿalūl—fišše yintali.

88 This shepherd went, took the bull from the opening of its nostrils. "Who will fill the ears of the bull with bran will take it." This woman sieves flour, that sieves other crushed cereals, and this [one] goes to fill it with bran, and he pours it in the bull's ears, it does not fill up.

94 gāḷ-ḷa, ʾabūha, "rūḥi, balki yintali ḏān al-ʿalūl u-nšaḷḷa nğībo; ṭallaʿi mā ʾašlaba hā-l-bagar." rāḥat ^{e}ğbēna, ḥaṭṭat hā-l-gadde, gāmat ntalat ḏān el-ʿalūl. huwwe ġūḷ, miš ʿalūl, ġūḷ.

94 He said to her, her father, "Go, maybe the bull's ears will be filled and we'll enjoy and bring it; look how beautiful this bull [cattle] is." Ğbēna went and put this much [very little] and the bull's ear was filled up—it was not a bull, a *Ġūl.*

99 lammanna ḥaṭṭatha, ṭileʿ l-ʿalūl, ğābō. mā widdo yugḏub ^{e}ğbēna wi-yiʾaṯṯir bīha.

99 When she put it, the bull came, he brought it [to her father]. Indeed, he wanted to catch Ğbēna and affect her.

101 lammanna ḥaṭṭat lo, widdo yulguṭ, hā ṣārat ʿēnē ḥamra-ḥamra, tigādaḥ ʿalēha, ṣārat ^{e}tṣayyeḥ. ṣār yiʿedar (ba) ʾabūha ʿalē, gāḷ, "taʿālam xuḏam al-ʿalūl, mā widdi l-ʿalūl."

101 When she put it [the bran], he wanted to catch [her]. These, his eyes, became very red, burning at her. She started shouting. Her father began to apologize for it, he said, "Come, take the bull, I do not want it."

106 ʿāwad rāḥ l-ar-rāʿi kamān. gāḷ-ḷo, "bū widdo yeṣīr ʿur^{u}s ʿind el-ʿarab." [u-kānat al-ʿarab tirkab ʿa-ğmāl gabuḷ, miš ^{e}b-ṭayyārāt, ʾā, ʿa-ğmāl.] gāḷ-ḷo, "ʾinta lāzem ^{e}tgūḷ"—la-hāḏa l-ḥamal ḥdāğa tabaʿo. [ʿandak al-bāb . . .] gāḷ-ḷo, "xaḷḷa l-^{e}ḥdāğa ḏahab, all-al-a- magwad tabaʿo ḏahab, alla kull ši ʾilo ḏahab, al-busṭ ḏahab ḥaṭṭa ʿala l-ğamal."

106 He went again to the shepherd. He said to him, "There is—there will be a wedding by the Bedouin." (The Bedouins used to ride on camels in the past, not airplanes. Yes, on camels.) He said to him, "You must say—to that one who carried its [the camel's] sedan chair (Mind the door . . .). He said to him, "Let the camel's sedan chair be of gold, its leading rein gold, everything it has—with gold, the carpets with gold—put them on the camel."

115 "šū tiʿamal?" gāḷ-ḷo, "ʾana mustaʿidd ğamali yrūḥ b-il-fārda, bass mā tirkab ʿalē ġār bint al-ʾamīr." gāḷ-ḷha: "ṭayyeb." ğā hu, rikbat ʿalē. lamman rikbat ʿalē, wuṣlam ʾahal al-ʿarūs. kullham nizlam ʿan iğ-ğimal (illa ğbēna).

115 "What are you doing?" He said to him, "I am willing to let my camel go on the convoy [the camels and people accompanying the bride], but no one will ride on it except the emīr's daughter." He said to her [him], "Good." He came and she rode on it. When she rode on it, they reached the bride's family. Everybody got off the camels (except Ğbēna).

121 yuḏurbam ağ-ğamal ʿala ʾīdo, ygūḷ, "ʾāx ʾīdi." yuḏurbam ağ-ğamal ʿa-rāso, "ʾāx rāsi." yā wēn, kēf mā ʿimlam ba-ğ-ğamal (y)iğurr. sabʿet-iyyām, sabaʿ layāli u-hum nāṭrīn hā-ğ-ğamal.

121 They hit the camel on its hand, it says "Ouch, my hand"; they hit the camel on its head, "Ouch, my head." Where—whatever they do to the camel, it is irritated. Seven days and seven nights, they kept watching the camel.

126 yōm, ḥaṭṭam ba-ğ-ğirba, ğūb mayya ta-yenaggeṭ ʿalēham mišān yeḥissam, ʿalē xōf lā yāxaḏha wa-yeṭīr. ṣārat yōm nāmam, ṭār biha.

126 One day, they put the waterskin, the water can, so it drips on them so they feel [it], it feared lest [they fall asleep and] it [the camel] would take her and fly [away]. It happened one day [that] they slept—he flew [away] with her.

130 yigūḷ-ḷa, "šū šāifa ma(n)-ġād bā-t-taḥtiyya?" itguḷ-ḷo, "gadd ar-rġīf." "u-šū šāifa?" "gadd aṣ-ṣaḥan" "u-šū šāifa?" "gadd al-lēra." "šū šāifa?" "gadd at-taʿrīfa" "šū šāifa?" "mā-ašūf 'iši." ssa waṣṣalha la-l-gaṣer tabaʿo.

130 He [the camel-*ġūl*] said to her, "What do you see there at the bottom?" She says, "The size of a bread loaf." "And what do you see?" "The size of a plate." "And what do you see?" "The size of a līra [a pound coin]." "What do you see?" "The size of a small change coin." "What do you see?" "I don't see anything." Now he brought her to his castle.

136 gāḷ-ḷa, "hassa widd(i) 'atgaḏḏa bīki ḥasāyeb. hassa 'ani widdi 'atǧawwaz." hāyya ʿala kīs 'iben ʿammha. hū da (wi)ddo (yā)xḏa. gāḷat "'ana bēn 'idēk, mahma taʿmal, 'ani gablāne. al-ḥagg ʿalayya 'ani, miš ʿalēk."

136 He said to her, "Now I want to settle up things with you. Now I want to marry." She was on the account of [betrothed to] her cousin. He wanted to take [marry] her. She said, "I am [standing] before you [at your mercy]. Whatever you do, I accept. The blame is on me, not on you."

142 xaḏāha, ǧawwazha al-ġūḷ, u-ṣār yerū(ḥ) ʿa-ṣ-ṣēd, yeǧīb ʿa-ǧanbo hāḏa šaǧara, ʿa-ǧanbo hāḏa bagara.[6] u-yeraww(ḥ)ʿalēha ḥaṭab gaṣer, xames ṭawābeg, sitt ṭawābeg, 'aḷḷāhu 'aʿlam.

142 He took her, the *ġūl* married her and began to go to hunt, and bring on one side this tree, and on his other side a cow. He would bring her firewood for the palace, five or six floors, Allah knows [how many].

147 hōn awlād ʿammha l-al-bent, hāy kānat maxṭūba la-'iben ʿammha, ṣār warāha, ṣār yaʿani miṯel maǧnūn, dār b-al-ⁱblād. yōm, wunno gāʿed taḥt hā-l-gaṣer. ṭallat ʿalē ʿerfato. dallat-lo šaʿarha, u-ṭlaʿato.

147 Now, the girl's cousins, she was betrothed to her cousin, he began looking for her, he became, that is to say, like mad, he was roaming the country. One day, lo, he was sitting beneath the palace. She looked at him, recognized him. She lowered to him her hair and lifted him up.

153 gāḷat-ḷo, "kēf widdi 'asawwi bīk 'ani, hāssa? hāssa yīǧi yāklak, hāḏa l-ġūḷ." gāḷat-ḷo, "ib-gudret 'aḷḷa, yā ṛaḅḅʷi, sibḥānak wa-taʿāla, 'anfux ʿalē 'ibra b-dīdi, u-mahma saḥt (=ḥassat?) inno (wi)ddo (=widdo) yākul, 'aṭelʿo, tanno widdo, yiʿamil, tanno yiǧi mawʿed al-ġūḷ, t(a)-itelʿo 'ibre, 'aġazzo b-ṣadri." ṛaḅḅna, subḥāno wa-taʿāla, ʿemilha bīha. ['ad-dinya kānat gaboḷ ʿa-l-baraka.]

153 She said to him, "What shall I do with you, now? Now the *ġūl* will come and eat you." She said to him, "With Allah's power, o my Lord, you are praised and exalted, breath on him [to make him] a brooch in my breast. Whenever he wants to eat, I'll take him out as much as he wants to do, until the *ġūl*'s time comes, so I'll take him as a brooch and attach it to my breast." Our Lord, he is praised and exalted, did it for her. (The world [life] was previously with [Allah's] blessing.)

163 'aǧa l-ġūḷ min ġād gāḷ-ḷa, "rīḥet 'ins, ma-(a)dri min al-yām m-adri mn-ams, m-adri min mā sāfr-aš-šams." gāḷat-ḷo, "mnēn al-'ins wa-l-ǧins bi-dyālak? 'ani ḥaṭṭēt bi-l-blād 'ins u-ǧins? mā ḥaṭṭēt bi-l-ⁱblād 'ins wa-ǧins."

163 The *ġūl* came from there, and said to her, "The smell of a human, I don't know if it's from today, I don't know [if it's] from yesterday, I don't know if it is from where the sun went." She said to him, "Where from is this human and *ǧinn* of yours? Have I put on earth the human and the *ǧinn*? I have not put the human and *ǧinn* on earth."

169 niʿam, gāḷ "'anṭīni l-ibra (a)lli fīgi (=fīki), kūd agḷaʿ aš-šōka alli b-riğli. widdi 'aglaʿ aš-šōka, mā daggatni aš-šōka." gāḷat-ḷo, "'ibre tfūt b-iğrak? 'abra mā bitfūt ib-'iğrak, 'inta ġūḷ.

169 Yes. He said, "Give me the brooch which is on you. I may take out a thorn that is in my foot. I want to take out a thorn, indeed, the thorn has pricked me." She said to him, "A needle goes into your foot? A needle does not enter your foot, you are a *ġūl*.

174 mā bitfūt al-'ibra b-'iğrak." gāḷ-ḷa, "'ani mā widdi 'alla hadīk." ʿiref 'innu l-'ins bīha, b-al-'ibra. gāḷat-ḷa, "mū mumkin, hāḏ al-'ibre—'ana 'aṭarrez bīha, 'axayyeṭ bīha, mā 'anṭīk iyyāha."

174 "A needle will not enter your foot." He said to her, "I don't want anything but that one." He knew that the human was in it, in the needle. She said to him, "Impossible. This needle, I embroider with it, I sew with it, I will not give it to you."

179 zaʿal. 'azgato ḥamer, u-nām. lamma nām al-ġūḷ, ṭalʿat iben ʿamma, ṭaʿmato, zgato, u-geʿdat wiyyā w-inbasṭat. w-al-ġūḷ nām.

179 He was angry. She gave him wine to drink, and he slept. When he slept, she took out her cousin [bridegroom], fed him, let him drink, and sat with him and was happy. And the *ġūl* was sleeping.

183 lamman yegūḷ-ḷa, widdo yerūḥ beʿīd, yegūḷ-ḷa zat ḥawālay gaṣr al-ġūḷ. lamman yegūḷ-ḷa "widdi 'arūḥ egrayyib" maʿnāto yerūḥ beʿīd al-ġūḷ.

183 When he says to her that he wants to go far away, he says [that he was] near [around] the *ġūl*'s palace. When he says to her, "I want to go somewhere nearby," it means he is going far, the *ġūl*.

187 yōm gāḷ-ḷa, "'ana widdi 'aḥawwel al-bēt 'aḥāfiḏ. 'inti ġēr xāwi l-banān ḥawāl-al-bēt." gāḷat-ḷo, "'ā." ʿirfat, rāyeḥ beʿīd hiyya.

187 One day he said to her, "I want to go round the house to keep watch. You just 'turn your fingers' around the house." She said to him, "Yes." She knew he was going far away, she [knew].

191 gāḷat ḷo, "hassa widdak titrawwaḥ, 'inta. widdna nrawweḥ 'ana w-iyyāk, ninhazam." xaḏat dazāzīn 'obar, fa-xaḏat almāz-lē, xaḏat dazāzīn al-kuḥla, xaḏat al-misk, ma xaḷḷat ši, al-ḥenna, kull 'iši xaḏato, neheğet hī w-iben ʿammha.

191 She said to him, "Now you need to go home, you. We will go home, you and I, we will run away." She took dozens of needles, and took diamonds of his, took dozens of eye color [tins], took the musk, she did not leave anything—she took everything—the henna [dye], everything—she took it, and ran away, she and her cousin [bridegroom].

197 'aža l-ġūḷ, mā-hū gāḷ-ḷa, "dalli šʿūrek dalli, ğāk min as-sahel taʿbān. dalli šʿūrek dalli, 'ağāk min as-sahel taʿbān." fīš ḥada. gāḷ, "'in ligēta nāima, ʿalēha 'aḷḷa w-'amān 'aḷḷa, 'in ligēta rāiḥa, waḷḷa, wēn mā rāḥat ġēr 'ākulha."

197 The *ġūl* came and said to her, "Let down your hairs, he has come to you from the valley, tired. Let down your hairs, he has come to you from the valley, tired." Nobody there. He said, "If I find her asleep, Allah is upon her and Allah's security. If I find her gone, by Allah, wherever she has gone—I will definitely eat her."

203 ṣārat—liḥagha. lāgia—hiya tğurr b-al-bēt, mī hiyye ḥāmītha. gāyiḷ-ḷa. dīr "bubb bubb" gūḷ "bubb bubb" 'a xaḏāha l-ⁱbduwi u-rāḥat. "bubb bubb" xaḏāha l-ⁱbduwi u-rāḥat. ʿiref huwwa, an 'ağa wāḥad 'axaḏha. lamman ʿeref, ṭallaʿat winn(e) warāha.	203 She began [to go]—he followed her. He found her—she was irritated in the house, she did not keep it [well]. He said to her, "Do 'bubb bubb, say 'bubb bubb.'" The Bedouin took her and she went [saying] "bubb bubb," the Bedouin took her and she went [saying]. He knew that someone came and took her. When he knew it, she looked and lo—he was behind her.
210 ramat lo l-mišṭ. rāḥ ᵉtmaššaṭ w-iktaḥal yilḥagha. ramat lo dazzīnt 'obar, rāḥ ḥaṭṭha b-al-bēt tabaʿo u-liḥagha. ramat lo dazzīnt al-mosk—rāḥ ḥaṭṭa b-al-bēt, u-lḥagha.	210 She threw a comb at him. He went and combed [himself] and put the eye color and followed her. She threw at him a dozen needles, he went and put them in his house and followed her. She threw at him a dozen of musk [tins]—he went and put them in the house and followed her.
215 ḏaḷḷ ʿinda waragatēn, waragat baḥar nīli u-waraga, wargit damm. warigtēn ad-damm. ramat-lo wargit ad-damm. leqqha. maʿā ğero, huwwa. maʿā kalb ᵉżġīr. lamma laqqha, baʿadēn ramat lo l-warga z-zarga. laqqet al-waraga z-zarga.	215 There remained with her two sheets of paper—a blue paper and a blood paper; two blood papers. She threw at him the blood paper. He licked it. He had a puppy—he had a small dog with him. When he licked it, afterward she threw at him the blue paper. It [the dog] licked the blue paper.
221 "leggi yā kalb tanni 'aluqq maʿāk, leggi yā kalb tanni 'aluqq maʿāk," tanno mā ḥassat al-kalba mātat, u-hū māt. ṭallaʿat warāha—fiš ḥada. rağaʿat ʿalē, ligat al-al-ġūl mayyit, al-kalba mayta. rā hī-xurrāftak xilsat assa. mlīḥa walla mā mlīḥa?	221 "Lick, o dog, until I lick it with you; lick, o dog, until I lick it with you." Until she did not feel but that the dog [bitch] died, and he [the *ġūl*] died. She looked backward—there was no one. She went back to him—found the *ġūl* dead and the dog [bitch] dead. This is your story, [it has] ended now. [Is it] good or not good?

B. The Ğinn and the Girl in Dog Clothes

NARRATOR: Ṣabḥa ʿAbūd
TRIBE: *ʿArab el-Ḥuğērāt*
IFA 12720 November 1979

Text

There were once seven brothers, and they had one sister. Every day the brothers would go hunting and return at evening, and their sister would stay home and prepare food for them.

One day, while she was busy preparing the food, a beggar knocked on her door and asked her for some bread. The girl felt sorry for him and handed him a pita, but the beggar, instead of taking it, began to walk back. The girl moved toward him and handed him the pita, and once again, the beggar stepped back. She moves toward him, and he steps back. She moves forward, and he continues to step back. This continued until they both left the house. When they were a little away from the doorway, the beggar grabbed her, put her on his shoulder, and left.

The brothers returned home and did not find their sister. They began to look for her. They searched, they searched, and could not find [her].

And the beggar who had kidnapped the girl was nothing more than a disguised *ğinn* who lived in a castle in a faraway village, where he had brought the girl.

The elder brother went out to look for his sister. For many days, he wandered the roads and searched until one day he came near the *ğinn*'s house. His sister saw him through the window and beckoned to him with her hand, and when her brother recognized her, she said to him, "Come in the evening and save me from the *ğinn*!"

The brother sat and waited for the arrival of the *ğinn*. At night, the *ğinn* appeared on horseback. The older brother came out to meet him and said, "You kidnapped my sister. Let us fight over her!"

The *ğinn* heard his words. He blew on him: "Fooh! Fooh!" and the brother turned into stone.

After a while, the second brother arrived, and his fate was no different from that of his older brother—the *ğinn* blew on him and turned him into stone.

This was also the fate of the other four brothers—all of them became stone in their attempt to free their sister.

And one day the younger brother arrived. When he got there, his sister told him, "All your brothers have turned to stone in their attempt to free me. It's better to get out of here secretly and not fight the *ğinn* face to face."

The young man agreed. He mounted her on his horse and they ran away.

When the *ğinn* returned home, he realized that the young woman had fled. The *ğinn* had a big dog. He began to pursue the two with the dog. Soon he was close to them and almost reached them, but the girl did not lose her courage. While she was in the *ğinn*'s house, she had also learned the *ğinns*' ways.

The girl blew, "Fooh, Fooh!" and immediately a wide, deep lake opened between them and the *ğinn*. But the *ğinn* and the dog, who were thirsty, drank the water to the fullest. The lake dried up completely, and the distance between them was diminishing again.

The girl blew again, "Fooh!" and an iron fence appeared between them and the *ğinn*, but the *ğinn* said something to his dog and immediately the dog gnawed a hole in the fence. The *ğinn* and his dog went through the hole and continued the chase.

When the girl realized that she would not be able to save them, she turned to her brother and said, "Run away for your soul, and I will stay here and delay the *ğinn*."

The brother obeyed her, left the place, and fled on his horse.

The *ğinn* came, cast a spell on the girl, and turned her into a dog. The girl started walking like a dog and wearing a dog's cloth [fur]. Nothing set her apart from the appearance of a dog, except that she could speak human language.

The dog began to wander on the roads. She went from place to place until one day she came to a small village, like Kawkab (a nearby Arab village). She came to the house of an old woman. The old woman took pity on her and threw her a piece of bread. She ate the bread and settled in the old woman's garden. The old woman had an orchard, like the avocado orchard here [the narrator told her story near the avocado orchard of kibbutz Yodfat, and when she reached this point in her story, she pointed at it], and inside the orchard there was a spring. When no one would see, the girl would shed the dog clothes from over her. Then she returned to the orchard and dressed again as a bitch.

This orchard belonged to the king, and one day, the king's son came and saw the girl—how she dressed in dog clothes. The prince followed her until they reached the old woman's house. Now, while the girl was bathing in the spring water in the orchard, she would take off her rings, and the king's son took one of them.

The king's son went to his mother, handed her the ring, and said to her, "Go to the village and find the old woman and bring me her dog."

His mother went and came to the old woman's house and asked for the dog.

The old woman said to her, "The dog is not mine. I cannot give it to you."

The mother brought a gold lump and handed it to the old woman. Then, the old woman handed her the dog, and the mother took the dog and brought it to her son.

The king's son told his mother, "I will marry this bitch."

They set a date for the wedding and on the appointed day, all the guests were gathered. The king's son came in fancy clothes, and then they brought the dog.

When the guests saw that the bride was a bitch, they began to laugh: "The king's son marries a bitch! The king's son marries a bitch!"

But the king's son did not care at all. At night, the king's son took seven rods. He came to the dog and said, "Come on, take off your dog's clothes and turn into a girl!"

The dog replied with barking, "Ruff! Ruff!"

The young man began beating the dog with the rods very hard until a beautiful girl emerged from the skin. Anyone who saw the king's daughter-in-law said, "What a beauty!"

And some of those who saw her and heard the story went and married bitches and on the wedding night began to beat them, but all they got was dog bites.

Remark

The story was told in Arabic but written down in Hebrew, as it was translated by some listeners who were present while the narrator told her story.

Commentary

I recorded the story "Bell Sound" in four versions in three tribes, two versions in the ʿArab el-Ḥuğērāt tribe, one in ʿArab el-Ġrifāt, and one in ʿArab el-Naʿīm. Only two appear here.

Here is a summary of the story: The heroine is a girl named Ğbēnah (cheese), Dann Ğaras (bell sound), or Ġada (gentle), names that indicate skin as white as cheese, or a crystal-clear voice. The girl goes out with her friends to pick the fruit of the hawthorn or the jujube. She climbs the tree and picks fruits for all of them. Her friends fill her sack or basket with stones, or with reptiles, instead of fruit. On their way back, the girl discovers the deception and returns to the tree to pick more fruit. A *ġūl*, a *ǧinn*, or a *māred* (giant demon) forces her to descend from the tree. He fills her basket with fruit and blows on her a magical breath, which brings her home before the other girls. In exchange, he demands that the girl give him valuables from her father's house (this part of the story is missing in Ṣabḥa ʿAbūd's version).

Later in the story, the demon appears in the girl's house disguised as a beggar or an old man and asks for fire or a piece of bread (sometimes on a bread shovel, to avoid direct contact). The girl turns him down, or she hands him a burning coal on a bread shovel.

The demon leaves, or he takes the burning coal from her, or he steps back and makes her leave the house, and as soon as they get away from the house, he kidnaps her.

Or alternatively, he disguises himself as a camel purchased by the heroine's father. The heroine keeps close to the camel, and every time they beat the camel, the girl yells, "You beat me!" Her relatives abandon her, and the demon kidnaps her (in the version that was recorded in the ʿArab Al-Naʿīm tribe, this episode appears after the episode of the girl's rescue).

Afterward, the versions split in different directions. In Zehiyya Ġrifāt's version, the girl's cousin, who is engaged to her, goes out to look for her. He reaches the *ǧinn*'s palace, climbs up, and reaches her by using her long plait like a ladder. The girl turns him into a needle to hide him from the *ǧinn*. In the *ǧinn*'s absence, the heroine escapes with her lover. The *ǧinn* pursues them, but they succeed in poisoning him.

In the version from Ṯalǧe Mūsa of the ʿArab el-Ḥuǧērāt tribe, the *ǧinn* brings the heroine to his cave, where she discovers two other girls. After learning to read the demon's magical book, she uses it to open the cave. A camel herder comes to the place. He enters the cave and hides, and when the demon falls asleep, he leaves his hiding place and kills the *ǧinn*. The camel herder and the girls take the property of the dead demon. They buy horses, and the girls, disguised as men, go out with the shepherd to look for their family members. A similar episode appears in chap. 32 "The Girls and the Ġūla," to be discussed later on.

The girls in disguise arrive at the house of the shepherd's father. The shepherd reveals their identity to his father, and the father wants to marry one of them. The heroine and the other girls refuse and ask the shepherd to return them to the place where he found them. In the end, the shepherd marries the three daughters, but the shepherd's father continues to harass them. He sneaks into the bed of one of them, pretending to be his son. At the end of the story, the son discovers his father's actions and executes him by burning him. This oedipal act expresses the harsh attitude of Bedouin society toward incest in the family.

In this part of the story, we hear about an intimate detail in polygamous families where a husband has more than one wife. The husband is supposed to visit each of his wives in turn, and every woman knows when it is her turn to have intercourse with her husband. This matter of arranging visits has been hinted at in the Bible: "And Reuben went in the days of wheat harvest, and found mandrakes in the field, and brought them unto his mother Leah. Then Rachel said to Leah, Give me, I pray thee, of thy son's mandrakes. And she said unto her, Is it a small matter that thou hast taken my husband?

And wouldest thou take away my son's mandrakes also? And Rachel said, Therefore he shall lie with thee to night for thy son's mandrakes" (Genesis 30:14–15).

Leah acquires from Rachel, her sister, the right to sleep with Jacob not according to her queue but in return for the mandrake, found by her son Reuben, which was probably considered a talisman of pregnancy.

In the version recorded from Basma Khalīl Sawāʿed of the ʿArab el-Naʿīm tribe, the girl's brother and her engaged cousin go out to look for her. She hides them in the palace, and in the absence of the *ğinn*, they escape. The *ğinn* masquerades as a camel and captures her again. He turns her into a bitch, and she walks about the sultan's court, occasionally removing the dog's clothes. The sultan's son sees her and decides to marry her. After the wedding, the heroine returns to her human form. Trying to imitate the sultan's son, the vizier's son marries a dog. The dog bites him, and he dies.

In the version by Ṣabḥa ʿAbūd of the ʿArab el-Ḥuğērāt tribe, the demon turns the girl into a dog. The king's son, who sees her in her human form, marries her. After the wedding, he beats her, and she returns to her human image. Other people try to imitate him and marry bitches and are bitten by them.

The four versions show considerable variation, each focusing on different motifs, yet each of them is a story in itself. Muhawi and Kanaana believe that this is a conglomerate of different stories that deal with separation and reunification.[7] In their view, this simple framework may develop into a more complex story, using motifs taken from other stories. El-Shamy defines a subtype of ATU 533, "The Speaking Horsehead (The Geese Girl,)" called AT 533A§, "Beautiful Maiden in Hideous Disguise. She Is Detected by the Prince."[8] Indeed, some of the motifs in the versions I collected enable them to be included in this subtype. However, I think there is room to set apart this story as an independent type, which will include the three episodes: (a) a girl picks fruit and meets the demon; (b) the demon impersonates a camel and kidnaps the girl; (c) the demon turns the girl into a bitch, and the king's son marries her.

In the book *Seed of Pomegranate: The Woman in Arab Folktales*, there is another version of "The Pomegranate Seed," which was taken from Ḥamda Qāsem Ġrifāt, a member of the ʿArab el-ʿIyadāt tribe and a resident of Bēt Zarzīr (a Bedouin village).[9] This version begins in a very similar way to the Bedouin version of "Snow White," but later it develops in the direction of the subtype "Beautiful Maiden in Hideous Disguise" as described by El-Shamy.

In Hanauer's book *Folk-lore of the Holy Land*, there is a similar version of the story, which was told by a Christian Arab woman from Bethlehem at the beginning of the twentieth century.[10] In Hanauer's version, the heroine is called Iğbeyneh because she is as white and lovely as cream cheese (*ğibneh* in Arabic). The story begins with an episode of gathering the fruit of the hawthorn. Iğbeyneh goes out with her cousins to pick fruit. They replace the fruit she picks up with rotten fruit and abandon her in the forest. A *ġūl* adopts her as his daughter, brings her to his home on the top of a high mountain, and makes her shepherd over his sheep. The heroine's pigeons, which remain in the dovecote at her home, fly out to find her. Her father and brother follow the pigeons and locate her. They plunder the *ġūl*'s treasures and bring the heroine back to her home. The *ġūl* dies of grief. The heroine's cousins are burned at the stake as punishment for their behavior.

In the version of a Muslim Arab woman from a village near Rāmallah in the book *Speak, Bird, Speak Again*, the girl is called Ğbēne.[11] Her friends envy her for her beauty. They go out with her to pick the fruit of the *dōm* (jujube), and they abandon her on the tree. A horseman, riding a mare, passes by, takes her off the tree, and brings her to his home. Ğbēne paints her face to camouflage her beauty. Considered a servant, she is sent out to graze the emīr's herds of sheep and camels. In the pasture, she tells the birds about her misfortune. The sheep and camels weep with her and stop grazing. The emīr's son tries to find out why the animals become thinner. He follows her and hears her words. He forces her to tell him her story and remove the color from her face. After her beauty is revealed, he marries her.

In the IFA, there are several parallels:

1. A Muslim Arabic version from Shefarʿam (IFA 23153): Ğbēne goes out with her friends to pick jujube fruit. Her friends replace her fruit with stones. She returns to pick new fruit and is kidnapped by a *ġūl*, who brings her to his cave. She sees a grape seller passing by the cave, and she calls for help. The grape seller calls her brothers, who come and rescue her. Pretending to be a beggar, the *ġūl* tries to abduct her once again, but her brothers kill him.

2. A Muslim Arabic version from Buʿēneh (IFA 23632): After becoming pregnant, a woman gives birth to a bitch. The bitch steals fruit from the king's garden. The king's son follows her and sees her removing the dog's clothes and turning into a beautiful girl. Despite his parents' resistance, he marries the bitch and burns her dog's cover, and she becomes a beautiful girl. The vizier's son envies him and marries a dog too. He beats the dog in an attempt to turn it into a girl, and the dog devours him.

3. A Druze version from ʿUsifiyeh (IFA 24001): A girl asks her mother to give her pita. The wind blows the bread out of her hand, and the girl runs after it and reaches the cave of a giant wolf, who adopts her as his daughter. A goose warns the girl the wolf is going to devour her when she gets fat. As a result, she stops eating and loses weight daily. The wolf soothes her, and the girl threatens the goose, saying that she will slaughter her on her wedding day with the prince. The goose grows thin, and the king's son, who tries to understand why she is thin, comes to the wolf's cave. He falls in love with the girl and asks his mother to marry him to her. The mother does this despite her reservations about her son marrying the wolf's daughter (it seems that the narrator was not familiar with the details of the story and missed a passage in which, before his death, the wolf suggests that the girl remove his skin and wrap herself in it). After the wedding, the mother asks her daughter-in-law to go up to the roof. Her cover falls, and all the villagers are amazed at her beauty. At the girl's request, the prince slaughters the goose.

4. A Christian Arab version (IFA 24138): A girl named Ğbēneh goes out with her friends to pick acorns. They fill her sack with stones. She comes back to pick up more acorns. A *ġūl* catches her and brings her to his cave. Her brother

> kills the *ġūl* and brings her home. Later, the heroine marries the king's son. A black slave takes her place and forces her to become a geese guard. The geese cease grazing. The king's son discovers the deceit, and the impostor bride is punished. In this version, the connection to the narrative type AT 533, "The Speaking Horsehead (The Goose Girl)," is conspicuous.

Most of these versions start with a scene of jealousy. Friends or cousins are envious of the heroine because of her beauty or her status as an emīr's daughter, and they try to get rid of her. In Zehiyya's version, the girls want to kill the heroine and say to her explicitly: "We brought you here in order that the *ġūl* will eat you."

Like Joseph in the Qur'ān, the heroine internalizes the need to be modest and refrain from emphasizing her beauty, so as not to arouse people's envy. In many versions, she initiates an action designed to camouflage her beauty: she paints her face black or covers it with the skin of an animal. This is a story of adolescence, in which the girl finds shelter in the home of a certain demon, where she learns to function as a housewife, or a shepherd until the completion of her training, and her marriage. The stay in a demon's home is repeated in many Bedouin stories, such as "Frēṭ Rummān" (Snow White) or "The Goat, the Kid, and the Ġūla" (see chap. 42). Bettelheim describes this period in the heroine's life as latency, prior to her sexual maturity.[12]

As we have seen, many of the versions begin with the gathering of wild fruits. The trees mentioned are hawthorn, jujube, and oak.

The fruit of the common hawthorn (*Crataegus aronia*) are reminiscent of small apples. The fruit is used to cook jam, and it is picked and sold in Middle Eastern markets. In Arab folk medicine in northern Israel, hawthorn fruits are used to treat diarrhea, sore throat, internal bleeding, dizziness, spasms, high blood pressure, atherosclerosis, and heart disease. An alcoholic marinade made of flowers is used as a remedy for insomnia, menopause, anxiety, and irritability.

The fruits of Christ's thorn jujube (*Ziziphus spina-christi*) are also eaten, although they are not that tasty. The Bedouin used to pick the fruits, dry them, and, during the winter, prepare from them a thick dough for making bread.[13] The jujube is a thorny evergreen tree of Sudanese origin. It is mentioned in the Mishna (Kilayim 1:4), and it is assumed that the name refers to a cultured species of jujube that was cultivated as a fruit tree. In Arabic, the tree has various names: *sidr*, *dōm*, and in Sinai *nabek*. According to Christian tradition, the crown of thorns of Christ was prepared from the jujube branches. In the Muslim tradition, the tree is known as the dwelling place of spirits and demons.[14]

The fruits of the common oak (*Quercus calliprinos*) and the Mount Tabor oak (*Quercus ithaburensis*) are edible after cooking and roasting and are also used to prepare delicacies. They, too, have various medical uses.

In Zehiyya's story, the *ġūl* tries to impersonate a bull, but the heroine recognizes him as a *ġūl* because of his red eyes. Later, he impersonates the camel that carries the bride to the wedding ceremony. Underlying the narrative at this point is one of the wedding customs: bringing the bride on a camel decorated with rugs and gold ornaments. Even though the family tries to guard the daughter, who is stuck to the camel, the *ġūl* succeeds in kidnapping her and flying off with her. As the *ġūl* rises up in the sky, he asks her how the earth looks from above, and the heroine replies that its shape is like a large loaf of bread, then as a saucer, then as a coin, and finally the earth disappears completely from her eyes. This motif is familiar from Persian folktales and other sources.

The heroine lets down her hair so that the *ġūl* (and later her fiancé) can climb up to her. This motif, F848.1, "Girl's long hair as ladder into tower," is included in Rapunzel's story, AT 310, "The Maiden in the Tower."

In Zehiyya's version, the *ġūl*, who suspects that the heroine has turned her beloved into a needle inserted into her cloth, asks her to hand him the needle to remove a thorn from his foot. The girl refuses, claiming that a *ġūl*'s skin is impervious to needles. I did not find this trait attributed to a *ġūl* in other Bedouin stories. In contrast, the heroine's use of some magic is known from other tales. It seems that during her stay at the *ġūl*'s house, the heroine acquired various magical powers. In Ṯalǧe Mūsa's version, the heroine learns to read the *ġūl*'s magical book, which enables her to open the cave where she is imprisoned.

The heroine escapes with her lover. When the *ġūl* returns home, he calls to the heroine to let down her hair so that he can go up to her, but since she does not answer, he says: "If I find her asleep, she is under the protection of Allah; if I find that she has gone—by Allah, wherever she goes, I'll eat her!" A similar statement is uttered in one of the versions of "Snow White." Although the *ġūl* gave her his protection, it was contingent on absolute obedience.

Ṯalǧe Mūsa's version ends with the escape of the heroine and the other girls who were in the *ġūl*'s house, dressed as men. The father of the hero who saved them wants to marry one of them, and they refuse. This episode seems an unnecessary addition to the story. It emphasizes the dependence of unmarried women on a man who offers them his protection. When the hero wishes to go on a looting journey (*ġazu*) and leave them behind, they insist that he stay with them.

In the story of Basma Khalil Sawāʿed from the ʿArab el-Naʿīm tribe, the demon is called *māred* (literally: "giant" in Arabic). This is a demonic figure familiar from the *Arabian Nights*. This version, too, includes the motif of long hair as a ladder, and the heroine performs various magical feats to escape from the demon.

Basma's story abounds in descriptions of the Bedouin wedding ceremony and the musical instruments accompanying it. The bride, seated in a palanquin carried on a decorated camel, is led to the bridegroom's house in a parade known as *zaffa*. In the 1980s, I had the opportunity to see such a parade near the Bedouin village of Dmeideh, where the palanquin was resting on the back of a horse. Musicians and singers accompanied the parade. The singing that accompanies the celebrating people on the way to and at the wedding ceremony is called *ḥaddāyeh* (singing for the camels). In the wedding itself, a singer or a pair of singers improvise rhymes, in which they greet and praise the dignitaries of the tribe who are invited to the wedding ceremony. Such ceremonies are held to this day.

The story also mentions the *miǧwez*, one of the musical instruments accompanying the ceremony and the dancing. The *miǧwez* and the *yarġūl* are simple clarinets, which are prepared from common reed (*Phragmites australis*), a perennial herb that grows in moist habitats throughout the country. The instruments have mouthpieces with reeds that vibrate and create the sound. Both are common instruments in all Galilee tribes.

The *miğwez* is made of a pair of flutes identical in shape and length. Each of them has six holes. The two mouthpieces produce sounds of a different pitch, one high and the other somewhat lower, determined by the length of the reeds. In the high-sounding mouthpiece, the reed is about 26 mm long, while in the lower-sounding mouthpiece the reed is about 28 mm long. The difference between the two flutes creates a rich sound that gives the impression of several instruments playing at the same time. The length of the tool is between 33 and 35 cm, and the mouthpieces are between 50 and 60 mm long. The distance between the holes is 15–21 mm, and the distance of the last hole from the end of the instrument is between 78 and 87 mm. The linkage points between the parts of each flute and between the two flutes are reinforced with wax. The wax stabilizes the instrument, preventing the movement of its parts, and may also increase the resonance. In northern India, there is an instrument called *zummāra* made of hollow eagle bones. In the past, some Bedouin musicians used to build *miğwez* from hollow eagle bones, and to this day, one Bedouin player still uses this technique. The instrument is made from the ulna bones of eagle wings. In the south of the country, the instrument is called *magrūn*. The name given to the mouthpiece is *bint*, meaning a girl, whereas the first link in which the mouthpiece is fixed is called *ʿazwa*—an old woman (Malka, 1996).[15] According to ʿĪd el-Tori, a member of a southern tribe, musicians used to prepare the *yarġūl* from the hollow thigh bones of an eagle.[16]

The *yarġūl* is also built of two flutes joined by wires and reinforced with beeswax. The shorter flute is made up of two reeds, one of which is stuck in the other, with six holes in the upper part. The left flute is almost twice as long as the right flute. It is built in the same way as the right flute, but it has another part that can be dismantled. The left flute, which has no holes, produces a lower, constant droning sound, which is used as an accompaniment. Both pipes have mouthpieces that can be dismantled, which are also made of common reed. Their outer openings are sealed, and the airflow enters the pipes through the openings of the reeds. The dimensions of the *yarġūl* vary from place to place. In the ʿArab el-Ḥuğērāt, ʿArab el-Mazārīb, and ʿArab el-Ğawamīs tribes, the instruments are large, while in the ʿArab el-Nuğeidāt tribe and among the Bedouin tribes of Wādi Ḥamām, as well as in the Arab villages of Buʿēna and Rāma, the instruments are smaller.

The instruments are often decorated with geometric patterns engraved on the pipes, and sometimes with glass beads and necklaces embedded in the wax. The dismantled parts are attached to the instrument body with wires.

The player first blows into the mouthpieces and adjusts the reeds to the desired flexibility by carefully bending them. Sometimes the player inserts a hair under the reed to raise the opening. After adjusting the sound and putting the mouthpieces together, the player inserts the mouthpieces deep into the mouth so that they are not visible. The player inflates the cheeks and blows a constant stream of air into the instrument while breathing through the nose. The result is a continuous sound, similar to the sound of bagpipes. The oral cavity is used as a "bag" for storing the air. The holes provide a rich, nonstop sound. The player usually covers the pair of parallel holes in both flutes at once, but one can vary the playing by covering one of the holes in the pair. The melody produced in the right flute of the *yarġūl* is accompanied by the low monotonous sound of the left flute (the drone). A good player can keep playing for three hours without a break.

The *miǧwez* and the *yarġūl* are used as accompaniments for singing, especially for dancing at weddings and celebrations. The number of musicians who control them well is not great, but the instruments are quite common. The music repertoire is mostly shared by the Bedouins and the *fallaḥīn* (farmers). Bedouins sometimes hire Arab musicians for their weddings. The *yarġūl* players usually play *miǧwez* and the *miǧwez* players play *yarġūl*.[17]

Another instrument mentioned in the story is the coffee mortar (*meǧna*). Some researchers claim that the folk singing is called *mēǧana*, because of the sounds and the rhythms that emerge from it during the grinding. The coffee mortar is also called *mahbaš*, or *mahbaǧ*, or *ǧurn*, and is used to grind roasted coffee beans. The coffee mortar is not a musical instrument in the usual sense, but the Bedouins, who are sensitive to rhythm, play it and produce complicated rhythms. The mortar is built of a single wooden unit that resembles a straight-walled jar about 40 cm high, with deep niches that increase its resonance. The vessel rim is coated with metal, and the whole vessel is decorated with copper buttons, geometrical shapes, and sometimes even letters that are carved in the wood. The length of the pestle is about 60 cm. Its lower end is rounded, and its upper edge is decorated with grooves.[18]

The pestle, *'īd el-ǧurn*, is held with a limp hand at about a third of its height. The percussion sounds are a mixture of the muffled grinding created by the edge of the pestle as it hits the bottom of the mortar and the "hollower" accompaniment produced by the free swing of the pestle against the edge of the mortar. The position of the hand holding the lower part of the pestle allows its rapid vibration, thus improving the ability to produce the sounds. The instrument is common, and almost every adult Bedouin knows how to play it.[19]

Reeds are used in Bedouin culture not only for making musical instruments or mats. In one of the episodes of the story, the heroine wraps reeds around her leg to prevent the *ġūl* from hurting her: "She went and brought some reeds and wrapped them around her leg." This episode is reminiscent of an ancient Roman usage of reeds. When a child's arm or leg was broken, they would wrap the fracture with split reeds. The healing ceremony was accompanied with the utterance of magic spells and the passing of three reeds over the child's mouth, which were tossed into the river.

Notes

1. *kān yā mā kān, nxarref walla nnām—nxarref. yā sām'īn al-kalām—nxarref walla nnām* is the well-known opening formula of Arabic (Bedouin) folktales (cf. chap. 1, note 2; chap. 21, note 1). Here, the listener completes the missing rhyme, yā sāmʿīn al-kalām, "o listeners of the speech," first, and the narrator repeats it.

2. The narrator mixes Bedouin and many sedentary features in her narration, as in *u-garāyebha biddhen 'iyyāha* ("and her relatives want her [for wife]"), with Bedouin *g* in *garāyebha* and sedentary *b-* in *biddhen* for Bedouin *widdhen*. Cf. other examples with phonetic aspects of pronunciation in chapter 12, note 2; chapter 13, note 8; chapter 27, note 2.

3. The narrator's utterances are sometimes not clear. Such disfluency occurs in dialogue exchanges between speakers as well as when she hesitates, stutters, or repeats parts of words until she finds the correct expression. For such disfluency cases, we add explanatory words in brackets.

4. Note *tabaḥḥan* (< *taba'han*). For this process (*'h* > *ḥḥ*), see chapter 24, note 8; chapter 31, note 4.

5. *kull ed-dōm hīn tabaḥḥan ġār ʿĞbēna*: "All the jujube here was theirs, except ʿĞbēna." The preposition *ġayr*(*a*), "other, except, but for," of LA/MSA is often pronounced in the colloquial dialects as *ġēr* or *ġār* by deletion of one vowel of a two-vowel structure (diphthong), making it a single vowel (monophthong). (On monophthongization in Arabic dialects, see Philippa, Philippa, and Roeleveld, "Monophthongization.") Cf. ġār in chapters 23, 35 (story D), and 38 (story B). In the other stories, only *ġēr* appears. *ġār* occurs also in Negev Bedouin dialects (e.g., Shawarbah, *Grammar of Negev Arabic*) and Sinai (Yong, "Bedouin Dialects," 99; Marom, "Bedouin Dialect of the Women").

In the Galilee Bedouin dialects, *ġār/ġēr* has acquired a few other meanings, such as "only, just, must, necessarily." Similar trends exist also in other dialects (not necessarily Bedouin ones). In this collection (and in Marom, "Bedouin Dialect of the Women"), we find *ġār* only in women's speech, while *ġēr* is used by both men and women. The small number of occurrences of *ġār* (eight) compared to several scores of *ġēr* may imply that it is either a dying or developing allomorph (cf. chap. 23, note 12).

6. *yeğīb 'a-ğanbo hāḏa sağara, 'a-ğanbo hāḏa bagara*: "He used to bring on this side a tree, and on his other side a cow." Note the rhyme in this phrase. His great power is described positively: he could carry in one hand a tree and in the other a cow, each of which is very heavy for ordinary people. Moreover, he keeps his word and does not touch the girl before she agrees to it. This *ġūl* does not live in a cave like other *ġūls* encountered in most of the above folktales: he has a well-maintained castle or palace. However, he also does not lose his *ġūl*ish nature, and he swears in his rage that if the girl leaves him, he is going to eat her.

7. Muhawi and Kanaana, *Speak, Bird, Speak Again*, 343.

8. El-Shamy, *Types of the Folktale*, 294–97.

9. Meron, Shehadi, and Masarwi, *Seed of Pomegranate*, 296–313.

10. Hanauer, *Folk-lore of the Holy Land*, 214–17.

11. Muhawi and Kanaana, *Speak, Bird, Speak Again*, 122–25.

12. Bettelheim, *Uses of Enchantment*, 194–213.

13. Crowfoot and Baldensperger, *From Cedar to Hyssop*, 113.

14. Crowfoot and Baldensperger, 113.

15. Malka, *Animal Kingdom.*

16. In Malka's book *The Animal Kingdom*, there is a yearning song from a mother to her son, translated into Hebrew, written by ʿĪd el-Ṭūri, who learned it from his mother. The song ends with the words "My dearest went eastward, and he has four braids / Who will bring me message from him / He, who has a flute made of eagle wings."

17. Perez, "Musical Instruments of the Bedouins in Northeren Israel," 27.

18. Perez, 24.

19. Perez, 24.

33. The Golden Palm Tree

NARRATOR: Unknown

TRIBE: *ʿArab el-Neʿēm ca. 1982*

1 bū hā-l-malek ᵃhnāk. ʾessa hā-l-malak mā yiǧī wᵃlād. ʿendo bayyāra ġarbi dāro. ʿando nxaḷa, laha l-warag ʾabyaḍ. rāḥat ⁱmrato, ġarrabat hī wiyyā ʿala l-bayyāra la-l-ġād. ʾassa ṭabbat hā ǧuwwa l-bayyāra, gāḷat, "yā ṛaḅḅi, yā ḥabībi, ʾalla tibrīni w-tiǧīni bint ʾaw walad hā-lli huwwa. inni l-aǧīb leč, l-an-nxaḷa, mayye min mayyet derdakān, mayye ḏahab, w-akuttha ʿalēč."	1 There is this king there. Now, this king does not have children. He had an orchard to the west of his house. He had a palm tree, which had white leaves. His wife went westward, she with him, to the orchard there. Now she entered inside the orchard and said [prayed], "O my Lord, o my love, please free me [of sins, problems] and bring me a girl or a boy, whichever. I will bring—for this palm tree—water from the water of Derdakan, gold water, and I will pour it on you [the tree]."
11 ʾaḷḷa nṭāha. ǧābat bint. ssa lamman wa(ʿ)yat el-bint, min-wuʿiyat al-bint,[1] ṣārat trū(ḥ) ʿe-l-madarasa, l-bint. kull yōm tumrug min hāḏ, hā-l- . . . hā-n-nxaḷa. tgūḷ-ḷa, "gūḷi l-ummeč tōfi ᵃndēreč[2] ʾaxēr mā (a)gṣof ᵉʿmēreč." kull yōm, kull yōm tgūḷ-ḷha, hā-l-ʿaǧiyya tinse. tinse la-ʿaǧiyya.	11 Allah gave her. She had a daughter. Now when the girl became a person [came of age] she began to go to school. Every day she used to pass by this . . . palm tree. It would say to her, "Tell your mother to keep her vow, or I will shorten [cut] your years [life]." Every day, every day it would say it to her—this girl would forget it. The girl would forget it.
19 yōm, gāḷat-iḷha, "ḥuṭṭi ḥaṣwāt ⁱb-ǧēbteč." ḥaṭṭat ḥaṣwāt ⁱb-ǧēbitha. ṯāni yōm, ʾummha tġassl-al-ʾawāʿi, daqqanha al-ḥaṣwāt b-īdhe. gāḷat-ⁱlha, "yā yuṃṃa, lēš hēč ⁱtḥuṭṭīn ḥaṣwāt be-ǧersāyteč?"	19 One day, it said to her, "Put pebbles in your pocket." She put pebbles in her pocket. The next day, her mother was washing her clothes, and they pricked her hand. She said to her, "O child, why do you put like that, pebbles in your sweater?"

24 gāḷat-^{i}lha, “yā yumma, bō nxaḷa ʿala hā-d-darb, kull yōm tgūl li woffi ^{a}ndēreč ʾaxēr mā-(a)gṣef ^{eʿ}mēreč.” ^{a}fṭant hassa. gāḷat-ilha, “yā waḷḷāhi, yā yuṃṃa, ḥallan n-nadrāt, yaḷḷa.” sāwat ilha zāde zuwwāde, u-gāḷat-^{i}lha, “rūhi.”

24 She said to her, “O mother, there is a palm tree on the way, every day it says to me to keep your vows or I will cut your lifetime.” She now recalled it. She said to her, “By Allah, child, the time of [fulfilling] the vows has come, come on.” She made for her provisions and said to her, “Go.”

30 ʾa, mišyat hā-l-bint mʿa hā-l-darb, wāʿiye ṣār(a)t al-bint, tnaḥšar sine. mašat ^{i}mʿ-hā-d-darb, u-linha ġōḷa ʿa-d-darb, tiğriš sukkar ʿa-ğ-ğarūše u-rādda dyūdha l-wara. ğat al-ʿağiyya, lihemat lehemat sukkar u-mn-al-sukkar all b-al-ğarūša, u-baʿadha nitfe min-^{e}dyūdha.

30 Yes, she went this girl on the way; she had become of age, the girl, twelve years old. She went on this way, and lo, [there was] a *ġūla* on the way, grinding sugar on a grinder and putting her breasts onto [her] back. The girl came, ate, ate from the sugar and afterward a little from her breast.

37 gāḷat, “mīn alli reḏaʿ ʿann ^{i}bzāzi ṣār ʾaʿazz min awlādi.” gāḷat-^{i}lha, “ʾani.” gāḷat-^{i}lha, “wṣelti. šnū waddeč, yā binti^{y}?”

37 She said, “Who sucked from my breasts has become dearer [to me] than my children.” She said, “I.” She said to her, “You have come to your aim. What do you want, my daughter?”

41 gāḷat lēha, “widdi mayye min mayyet derdakān, mallat hā-l-ibrīg hāḏ.” gāḷat-^{i}lha, “ṭayyib. hassa yīğūn uwlādi, ʾarebʿīn wāḥad. widdhum yāklūnič.” nefḥat ʿalēha wannha rġīf xubz, ḥaṭṭatha taḥt al-xubz kullu.

41 She said to her, “I want water from the water of Derdakan, to fill [filled] this can.” She said to her, “Good. Soon my children will come, forty [of them]. These will want to eat you.” She blew on her and lo, she is a bread loaf. She put [hid] her under all the bread.

47 šwayye ğam ulādha, ṣāram yigūlūn, “nīna, mīno ğa ʿalēč? rīḥtič ʾens.” “al-ʾens li biya (a)nnkam, yamma,

47 A little [while] later her children came, they started saying, “Mom, who has come to you? Your smell is that of a human [person].” “The human who is in me—you are, o child,

50 ʾana mā ʿindi ʾins, mā ḥad yīği ʿalayya, mā ḥad.” gāḷū-ḷha, “turī hā-ḷḷi ʿandeč, ʿalē ʾaḷḷa w-amān ʾaḷḷa.”

50 “I have no human with me, no one comes to me, no one.” They said to her, “Show that [one] who is with you, Allah and Allah’s security is on him.”

53 nafḥat ʿalēha wa-la-nnha banādma. nafḥat ʿalēha la-nnha banādma. ḥičat, gāḷat, “ʾanṭūn al-ʾimān.” ʾanṭūha l-ʾimān. gāḷu-lha, “ʿalēh ʾaḷḷa w-amān ʾaḷḷa, walli yexūn, yexūn ʾaḷḷa.”[3] ʾassa nafḥat ʿalēha wa-lannha banādme.[4]

53 She blew on her and lo, she was a human female. She blew on her and lo, she was a human female. She talked and said, “Give me the security.” They said to her, “Allah is on him and Allah’s security, and whoever betrays [it], betrays Allah.” Now, she blew on her and lo, she was a human female.

59 gāḷat-ilhum, "man widdo yāxiḏhe, u-yāxḏ al-'ebrīg hāḏ ymalli mayy min mayyet derdakān?" haḏāk yegūḷ "'ani." haḏāk yegūḷ "'ani." haḏāka . . . bū wāḥad minhum, ʿarağ, riğil weḥda, gāḷ-(l)hum, "'ani lli 'āxḏa, wala wāḥad."

59 She said to them, "Who wants to take her and take this can and fill it from the Derdakan water?" This one said, "I." That one says, "I." That one. . . . There was one of them, a lame one, with one leg. He said to them, "I will be [the one] who takes her, no one [else]."

65 yalla, ḏibḥat lum hā-ḏ-ḏabīḥa u-šaggafatha arbaʿa šgāf. kull-mā . . . irkabha ba-ḏharo, kull-mā yiltafet ^{a}ʿalēha, tinṭī šiğfe, šiğiftēn, kull mā yiltafet ʿa-čān tinṭī šigfe, šigiftēn.

65 Well, she prepared for them this butchered meat, and cut it to four pieces. Whenever . . . he loaded her on his back, whenever he turned to her, she would give him a piece, two pieces. Whenever he turned, she would give him a piece, two pieces.

70 lamman wuṣal ^{i}hnāk, gāḷ-ḷha, "dūneč,[5] fūti. hāḏi hīn, hīna baniādmīn. hīn baniādmīn. u-lamman ^{i}tfūtīn, yiṣīrūn yigūlūn "ġarīb, ġarīb, ġarīb, ġarīb."

70 When he arrived there, he said to her, "Pay attention. Enter. These here are [human] people. Here [are] humans. And when you enter, they will start saying, "Stranger, stranger, stranger, stranger."

74 lā truddīn. wa-la tiltafti, wa-l-in iltafatti wa-ḥačēti min alli ruḥti. 'asḥač." qāḷat-ḷo, "lā'."

74 Do not answer them and do not turn, and if you turn and talk [you will return to] where you went [set out]. Pay attention [be clear about this]." She said to him, "No. [I will not talk or turn]."

77 'assa rāḥet, fātet bēn hā-l-'awādim hā-lli, mā ltaftat. huwa yegūl "ġarīb, ġarīb, ġarīb, ġarīb" mā ltaftet, fātat ʿala hā-l-mayy, ʿala hā-l-bīr, mallat al-berīğ, ġaṭṭ ḥanṣarhe.

77 Now she went, entered among these people, who. . . . She did not turn. He said, "Stranger, stranger, stranger, stranger." She did not turn. She entered to the water, to the well, filled the can, [and] her pinkie [smallest] finger got wet with the water.

82 gāḷ-ḷha, "la yeġaṭṭ ḥanṣar min īdēč" ġaṭṭ ḥanṣarha ba-l-bīr. mallat al-berīğ mayya wa-ʿāwadat ʿala hāḏa lli xaḏāha. rakkabha[6] wa-ʿāwad ʿala-mmo. lamman ʿāwad ʿala-mmo, mīn addi yiwaddīha ʿād? waddāha wāḥad min ixwito hadōlāk. 'arkabha u-xaḏāha la-halhe.

82 He had said to her, "Do not let the smallest finger of your hand immerse [with water]." Her pinkie finger got wet in the well. She filled the can with water and returned to that one who had taken her. He put her on his back and returned to his mother. When he returned to his mother, who again would deliver her back? One of those brothers of his took her. He put her [on his back] and took her to her family [parents].

89 'assa lamman ḥawwalha hnāk, ʿind 'ahalha, (h)u mā xaḷḷa ḥada yešūfha. ḥaṭṭētu u-fātat ʿala hā-l-bēt. 'īdha, eṣbaʿeha kullo ḏahab. xaḏat al-berīğ, hī w-'ummha, u-rāḥat kattato ʿala hā-n-nxaḷa. 'an-nxaḷa ^{e}gḷabet tibriğ ḏahab aṣfar ^{e}šlōn.

89 Now, when he put her there, at her parents' [place], he did not let anyone see her. She put him and entered the house. Her hand, her finger, was all gold. She took the can, she and her mother, and went poured it on the palm tree. The palm tree turned shining/glistening—and what yellow-gold!

96 ʾassa, gām ṣāḥb el-bīr fagad al-berīǧ al-mayy, ^{e}ʿerif inno xanṣarha ġaṭṭ bi-l-mayy. ḥaṭṭ šwayye ḏahab ʿala dābba u-dār ^{a}b-hā-l-madīna. ṣār yegūḷ, "bayyāʿ xawātem, bayyāʿ ʾasāwir, bayyāʿ."	96 Now, the well owner was looking for the water can. He knew that her pinkie had immersed in the water. He put a little gold on a riding animal and drove around in the town. He began saying, "Selling rings, selling bracelets, salesman."
101 šarat hā-d-dinya minno, ṣāḥ enn ʿalēhinna, sās widdo yeʿaref mīn hōn, mīn hōn kān (a)l-mayy. maʿeṣba ṣbāʿha. ǧat ta-tištari xātam. gāḷ-ḷa, "yā binti, ḥilli uṣubʿeč, lēš meʿaṣbīto?" mā raḏiyat.	101 Everyone bought from him, he shouted at them, for he wanted to know who here, who here from whom the water was. Her finger was bandaged. She came to buy a ring. He said to her, "O my daughter, take off the binding, why are you bandaging it?" She did not agree.
106 gadd-mā ḥāwal—ḥallato. ʾabūha w-umha ǧāʿadīn. hassa daššar al . . . daššar al-dābba alli hī ʿalēha ḏahab, u-ḥaṭṭha ʿa-čatfo min bēnhum, u-šalafha u-farr b-aǧ-ǧaww. rāḥat.	106 Since he tried so much—she took it off. Her father and mother were sitting [watching]. Now he left the . . . left the animal on which there was the gold, and put her on his shoulder from among them and took her and flew in the air. She was gone.
111 ṣarrxu "bint al-malak rāḥat, bint al-malak rāḥat" ḏāt al . . . ʾabat, rāḥat, xaḏāha b-al-ǧaww, xaḏāha u-rāḥ. ṣarraxum ʾabūha šwayya u-sektam.	111 They screamed, "The king's daughter is gone, the king's daughter is gone." . . . She refused, she was gone, he took her in the air; he took her and went [off]. They shouted, her father, a little and became silent.
115 ʾassa rāḥ xaḏāha ʿind ʾummo, hāḏa ṣāḥb al-mayy. lēš mā hū ġūḷ? b-ism-iḷḷā ar-raḥmān, hū ġūḷ, hū ǧanne, hū šnū mā-(a)dri. ḥaṭṭa ʿind ummo.	115 Now he went and took her to his mother's, this owner of the water. Why, he was a *ġūl*? In the name of Allah the Merciful, he was a *ġūl*, he was a *ǧinn*, he was—I don't know what. He placed her at his mother's.
119 ʾummo līha xawāt, widden yāklanha. gāḷat-ilha, "yā binti, rūhi hātī-li al-ġirbāḷ, min ʿind-uxti ^{i}hnāka, ḥaddna."	119 His mother had sisters, they wanted to eat her. She said to her, "O my daughter, go and bring for me the sieve, from my sister there, near us."
122 rāḥat teǧīb ^{i}lha l-ġerbāḷ. ʾessa hū lāgāha. gāḷ-ḷha, "dūneč, ʾessa lamma tāxḏi al-ġirbāḷ, ḥuṭṭī ʿa-l-bāb. ʾessa xāḷteč ^{e}tkūn ^{e}tsenn ^{e}snānha, mišān tākleč. ḥuṭṭi b-al-mismār, wa-l-ġirbāḷ ʿa-su^{w} al-bāb, tanāwalī u-ḏaḷḷi ṭāḷʿa wu-l-mismār yeṣīr yeḥāčīhen." xaḏat u-rāḥat.	122 She went to bring her the sieve. Now he met her. He said to her, "Pay attention. Now when you take the sieve, put it at the door. Now your aunt is sharpening her teeth, to eat you. Put it in the nail and the sieve [the sieve on the nail] at the door, take it [the sieve] and continue [and] go out, and the nail will begin to talk to them." She took [it] and went.

129 miṯel-mā ʿallamha sāwat. ʾassa al-mismār ṣār yigūḷ-ḷha, “yaḷḷa yā ʿammti widdi ʾarūḥ, yaḷḷa yā ʿammti,” w-hī tsenn asnānha mišān ta . . . rāḥat, xaḏat al-ġirbāḷ u-rāḥat. hāḏi ʾummo tebahwalat, yaʿani, čēf mā kalatha kulhe hāḏi? gāḷat, “ʾā, walla hāḏ̣a flān alli sāwa fī al . . .”

129 As he had taught her, she did. Now the nail began saying to her, “Come on, o my aunt, I want to go, come on, o my aunt.” And she was sharpening her teeth to eat her. She went, took the sieve and went. This mother of his got bewildered, that is, how was it that she [her sister] had not eaten this one [the girl] entirely? She said [to herself], “Oh, by Allah, it is this person who made this with the. . . .”

136 ᵉtğīb ᵉlha ʿadīlet ġasīl, fātḥā. widdha tġassilha. tgūḷ-ḷha, “gūḷi-lha ʾani mā-ʿārf aġassil ġēr ⁱb-ʾōḏ̣a lhā, l-imsakkar ʿaleyy.” assa (t)ğībe leya, tḥoṭṭa b-ʾōḏ̣a tesakkar ʿalēha. yīği (Hsam laH) b-ism ⁱḷḷā ar-raḥmān ar-raḥīm, činno ğān, yumrug ʿala hā-l-ġasīl b-sāʿ yiġassalo.

136 She brought for her a box of laundry, light colored. She wanted her to launder it. She [he] said to her, “Tell her I cannot launder except in a room which has been closed on me.” Now she brings her, puts her in a room, and shuts it on her. He comes, (Hsam laH) puts for her, in the name of Allah the Merciful and Ever Merciful, maybe he is a *ğinn*, he passes on the laundry quickly, washes it

143 u-yirušš ᵉrīḥa u-brinği, u-yeʿabbī be-lʿadīle u-tiže tqūḷ-ḷha, “yā ʿammti, taʿāli xaḏi al-ġasīl.” tiği tebahwal, “yā bayyē, hāḏ̣a flān, čēf widha tsāwi?”

143 and [he] sprays [good] scent on it, first class, and fills the laundry box up (with the laundry) and she come and says to her, “O my aunt, come and take this laundry.” She [the aunt] comes, bewildered. “Oh my! This person, how will she do [how can she overcome that person]?”

147 hāḏ̣a ʿindo ʾuxt biğawwezhe. lammanna di-teğawwezha ṣārat. ē- gāḷ-ḷha, “dūneč, hassa, widdan yeragṣanneč, bēnhin, u-widdhin yegaḏbanneč, yešallḥanneč, yāklanneč. ʾamma gūḷī-lhen ʾani mā ʿārf ʾarguṣ ġēr ⁱtkūn ṣīniyya malyāne ṣaffa. ʾahuṭṭha ʿa-rāsi wu-ʾarguṣ.

147 This one, he had a sister who was going to get married. When she got married, she became. . . . He said to her [to the king’s daughter], “Take care, now, they want to make you dance, among them, and they want to seize you and undress you and eat you. But say to them, ‘I cannot dance unless I have a *ṣiniyya* [tray] full of money; I put it on my head and dance.’

155 bas dūri dōrtēn wa-nʿafīha ʿād ṣaffa ʿalēhin, ʿa-hāḏi šway, ʿa-hāḏi šway, wa-ṭlaʿi ʿa-l-bāb, ʾana ʾastannāč ʿa-l-bāb, ʾawaddīč la-haleč.”

155 “But turn around twice and sprinkle the money on them, on this a little, on that a little, and go out by the door and I’ll be waiting for you at the door, I will take you to your parents.”

159 hassa, ʿamilt el-mā ʿallamha, sāwat. nāfat ʿalēhen aṣ-ṣaffa, nhazmat ʿa-l-bāb, u-lāgāha ʿa-l-bāb, ᵉrkabha u-waddāha la-halha.

159 Now, she did what he had taught her, she did. She sprayed them with the money and ran away to the door, and he met her at the door, took her and brought her to her parents.

163 ’assa gabuḷ lā-wuṣal, liḥgato waḥda minha—’ummo, xālto lli liḥegat. liḥegat xāḷto. ’essa bas šāfha warā, ramāha u-linna bistān, b-ism-iḷ-ḷāh ar-raḥmān ar-raḥīm. bistān.	163 Now, before he had arrived, one of them chased him—his mother, his aunt was who chased him. Now as soon as he saw her behind him, he threw her [the girl], and lo, she was a garden, in the name of Allah the All Merciful the Ever Merciful. A garden.
168 fātat min fōgiyyo, gāḷat-lo, “yā bistanǧi,” gāḷ-ḷha, “naʿam.” gāḷat-lo, “mā fāt min hīna wāḥad mrakkib bint?” gāḷ-ḷha, “mā šufto.” hāḏi gaḷṭat ᵉl-ġād ᵉšwayya u-riǧʿet.	168 She entered and stood on it and said to him, “O gardener.” He said to her, “Yes.” She said to him, “Has not passed here anyone carrying a girl?” He said to her, “I did not see him.” This one [the woman] stayed there a little and went back.
173 riǧʿat, liḥegat ummu. wakkad unno (=inno) ’ummu warā. ḥassa bō ba, u-hawwadha min ⁱḏharo winna ṭaḥūne, b-ism-iḷḷāh ar-raḥmān ar-raḥīm.	173 She went back, his mother chased [him]. He was sure that his mother was behind him. Now he felt that [she] was [with him]—and he dropped her [the girl] off his back, and lo, she was a mill, in the name of Allah the All Merciful the Ever Merciful.
177’assa gāḷat-lo, “yā barrāq, mā šuft hā-l-walad min hōn birkab waḥada fāyit?” gāḷ-ḷha, “lā’, mā šufthe.” hassa dašš hāḏ, waddāha la-halhe. ’arrban (=qarrban) ’arkabha, ḥawwalha b-al-baranda, wa-halha ǧawwa mū hum šāyifīnhe.	177 Now, she [the mother] said to him, “O shining one [handsome], haven’t you seen this boy, carrying a girl, pass from here?” He said to her, “No, I haven’t seen him.” Now this [one] took a look and delivered her to her parents. They approached. He made her ride on him, he conveyed her onto the balcony, and her family, inside, did not see her.
183 fitḥat al-bāb ufātat ʿalēhum. ḏāharam ʿalēha, u-ṣāram yebawwsūnha, u-ṣāram. ʿezam hā-l-madīna, sāwa-la ḥafla, u-hāḏi ḥkāyti ḥakētha u-ʿindkam ḥaṭṭētha.	183 She opened the door and entered to them. They stormed her and began kissing her, and became . . . they went down to the town, he [her father] invited the town, made a party for her. And this is my story that I told, and placed it with you.

Commentary

“The Golden Palm Tree” is an unusual story. Neither in Israel nor in neighboring Arab countries have I found parallel stories. It seems to me that it can be associated with the narrative type ATU 425, “The Search for the Lost Husband,” especially for the subtype ATU 425B, “Son of the Witch,” or in its previous name in Thompson’s book, “The Disenchanted Husband: The Witch’s Tasks.”[7]

Here are some of the characteristics of the narrative type:

A young woman marries a supernatural bridegroom: (1) She is given to her bridegroom because of a present she has asked her father to bring back from a journey. (2)

The bridegroom performs a set of difficult tasks. (3) She pulls up an herb and discovers the bridegroom's subterranean castle (a wind carries her there). (4) she finds him in another way. The bridegroom is the son of a witch (ogress) or he is (during the day) an animal.

Main part: The young woman breaks the bridegroom's prohibition, and he goes away. (Before he leaves, he gives her a token, e.g., ring, feather.) (In iron shoes) She sets out to find him.

The bride comes to the house of her bridegroom's mother, a witch, who swears by her son's name not to devour her. The witch imposes difficult tasks on the young woman, which she performs (with the help of her bridegroom): to sort a large quantity of grain, to fill mattresses with the feathers of all kinds of birds, to wash the black wool white and the white black, to sweep a house but leave it unswept, etc.

The young woman is sent on a dangerous journey to bring a casket from the sister of the witch.. Having passed obstacles (with advice of her bridegroom) and obtained the casket, she is forbidden to open it. When the bride acts against the prohibition, her husband helps her.

At the wedding of the bridegroom and the witch's daughter, the young woman has to hold ten burning candles (torches). Her bridegroom saves her from being burned.

The young woman remarries her bridegroom, or both escape by a magic (transformation) flight.[8]

The Bedouin story differs in many details from the description of the narrative type. It seems that this is a declined version of the story, since the owner of the well who kidnaps the girl and brings her to the kingdom of demons, and later helps her fulfill the tasks his mother imposes on her and escapes with her back to her home, is not presented in the story as the intended bridegroom. When he returns to her parents' home, he does so secretly and then disappears from the stage; therefore, it is not clear why he kidnapped her to begin with and brought her to the demons' land.

The story begins, like many other Bedouin stories I have recorded, with a barren woman asking for progeny and making a vow. This is a familiar motif from many cultural spaces. In this case, the vow is to bring *Derdakan* water, magical gold water, and to water a certain palm. After the mother gives birth to a daughter, the fulfillment of the vow is imposed on the daughter, and she sets out to do it.

This seems to be an adolescence story. The journey to obtain the golden water will bring the heroine together with her future bridegroom. A hint of this is found in the enigmatic words of the palm tree: "Tell your mother to keep her vow, or I will shorten [cut] your years [life]." This motif appears in many folk tales: M341.1.1, "Prophecy: death on wedding day." There is also a narrative type called AT 934B, "The Youth to Die on His Wedding Day." The motif appears in Jewish folktales. The most famous of these is the story of Rabbi Akiba's daughter, referred to extensively in chapter 23, "The Dangerous Night-Watch." It also appears in "A Soul for a Soul," in which the father is informed that his son will die on the night of his wedding.[9]

The couple's transition to unfamiliar married life is often accompanied by fears and anxieties. In *Anna Karenina*, Tolstoy gives this a literary expression, as he describes the feelings of Kitty, the young bride, on the eve of her marriage with Levin, her favorite: "She could neither think nor wish apart from her life with this man; but this new life had not yet begun, and she could not even picture it to herself clearly. There was only anticipation—terror and joy at the new and uncertain. And now behold: this anticipation, and uncertainty, and remorse for renouncing her former life—all this was coming to an end, and something new would begin. This something new could not help but be frightening due to its uncertainty."[10]

In this Bedouin story, these fears are expressed in the death prophecy threatening the groom or bride. That the daughter forgets to deliver the words to her mother is another expression of her fear of the future. This may very well be interpreted as an act of repression: the girl is afraid of growing up, a process that will force her to leave her home and move to her bridegroom's house. The palm tree needs a trick to convey the message to her mother. It asks her to perform an act the girl considers meaningless—placing gravel into her pocket—and the girl does as it says. Only when the mother asks her daughter to explain the meaning of the stones does the girl remember the palm tree, hand the stones over to her mother, and tell her about the tree.

The mother imposes on the daughter the fulfillment of her vow. She is the one who encourages her to embark on a journey that will lead her to meet her favorite. The *Derdakan* waters may be perceived here as symbolic of life: water that can restore the heroine to life and prevent the fulfillment of the palm tree's prophecy (motif E80, "Water of Life. Resuscitation by water").

On her way, the heroine is assisted by supernatural helpers, a family of *ġūla*s. She sucks the *ġūla*'s breast milk and eats from her food and, as a result, receives her patronage. An almost identical episode appears in another Bedouin story, "The Wicked Old Woman," to be discussed in chapter 36. There, too, a hero sucks from the *ġūla*'s breasts and eats the sugar made by the *ġūla*; and there, too, the *ġūla* turns the hero into an object to hide him from her children's eyes, and only after they give her their vow of protection does she return him to his human form. The *ġūla* functions here as an alternative mother. This motif appears in many Bedouin tales, as well.

The *ġūla*'s sons compete with one another to help the heroine reach the well of the golden water: This one said, "I." That one says, "I." That one . . . There was one of them, a lame one, with one leg. He said to them, "I will be the one who takes her, no one [else]."

This episode is reminiscent of a similar description in "*Ma'aseh Yerushalmi*," "The Story of the Jerusalemite" (a medieval story attributed to Abraham Maimon, Maimonides's son, but most likely written later). In this story, the demons compete among themselves to see who can transmit the hero to his home in the shortest time. The last demon, "lame and blinded by one eye," is chosen for the role after he announces that he could do so in one day. In "*Ma'aseh Yerushalmi*," too, there is a marriage between a man and demon (in this case, the human hero marries a demon's daughter), and there, too, appears a city of demons.

The heroine reaches the well of gold water and draws from it, but while she does so, her finger is covered with gold, and she cannot remove it. To hide the gold, the heroine dresses her finger. A similar motif appears in the Bedouin version of "Snow White": she violates the order not to open a forbidden room. Her finger is covered with gold, and she dresses it to hide the gold coating.

Later the demon succeeds in finding and kidnapping her. This episode has already been encountered in other Bedouin tales. The demon carries her with him to a city of demons, and there she has to confront the mother of the demon who kidnapped her. The demon's mother assigns various tasks, and with the demon's help, the heroine executes them successfully. This episode in the story likely reflects the actual coping of each bride in the Bedouin society with her mother-in-law. In the chapter "In the Family" (chap. 21), stories dealing with the relationship between a bride and her husband's relatives are discussed extensively.

At the end of the story, the demon and the girl escape the city of demons and return to her parents' home. In the course of their escape, the demon conceals himself and the girl from his persecuting relatives, and he first turns himself into a gardener and the heroine into a garden and later turns himself into a guard and the heroine into a flour mill. This is not explicitly stated, but it can be deduced from the text.

The Bedouin story does not end as expected with the heroine's marriage to the demon that saved her. As already stated, it seems that the narrator did not remember the story well enough and thus dropped the conclusion from it.

A study of a Jewish-Spanish tale, "The Camel Prince," recorded by Tamar Alexander from Rivka Cohen-Ariel (IFA 12744), can shed light on some unclear points in this story. The storyteller, who spoke Ladino, Hebrew, and Arabic, was born in Jerusalem to a Jewish-Sephardic family from Monastir (Yugoslavia). She heard her stories from her family and neighbors in the old city of Jerusalem. It is not clear whether she heard this particular story from Arab neighbors or drew it from her Jewish-Sephardic sources. At the beginning of the story, the king's daughter marries a camel. On the wedding night, the camel becomes a handsome prince, but during the day, he returns to the camel figure. The prince warns his young wife not to reveal his secret. A neighboring king declares war on the kingdom of the bride's father. The prince joins his brother-in-law and fights wonderfully on the battlefield. Teased by her sisters, the heroine exposes her husband's secret. As a result, the prince disappears, and the heroine searches for him. In the end, she finds him in a city of demons. The queen of demons wants to marry the prince to her daughter. As in this story, she sends the heroine to bring a sieve from her sister and later to bring other objects. The prince helps her and prevents the queen's sisters from hurting her. On the wedding evening, the heroine dances with candles, and at certain moment she throws the candles at the demonic bride. The heroine and her lover take advantage of the uproar and flee. The queen of demons hunts them. In the course of their flight, the prince turns himself into the ground and his wife into a farmer with a plow, and, in this way, they deceive the queen:

> The queen approached them. The prince turned himself into a plot of land and the princess into a farmer with a horse and a plow. Comes the queen and asks the farmer, "Hello, have not you seen a man and a girl who just passed by here?" And the farmer answers, "Oh, how many acres I have plowed today, how much I have sown, how many acres I will

> manage to plow till evening!" The queen becomes furious. "What do I have to do with your land? Answer my question!" However, the farmer continues and says, "How many acres have I plowed, how many acres have I sown! . . ." In vain, the queen inquires of him. The princess so confuses the queen that she cannot speak out of anger and turns back.[11]

Later, the prince turns himself into an oven and his lover into the baker, and for the third time, he turns himself into a mosque and his wife into a muezzin calling the believer to pray (which may perhaps indicate the Muslim source of the story). It is possible to assume that in the Bedouin story, too, the demon and the heroine's flight ended in the couple's marriage, which gave meaning to the abduction and closed the circle, but the narrator did not remember the end. The groom, who was described at the beginning of the story as a demonic figure, appears toward the end as a loving husband who helps his young wife return to their common home and protects her from the conspiracies of his abusive relatives. The story thus conveys a reassuring message to the teenaged girl who is anxious about her marriage with a stranger (i.e., not of her family circle) and what awaits her at his parents' home.

Notes

1. *lamman wa(')yat el-bint, mn-(w)u'iyat al-bint*: "when the girl became a person [could perceive, was attentive]." The root of *w'y* in *wa(')yat*/*(w)u'iyat* in the past tense forms means "perceive, be aware of, be attentive." The sentence means "when the girl could judge for herself what was happening around her." The narrator repeats the sentence, but the pronunciation of her words is not identical: both *lamman* (*lamma* + *an*) and *mn-* (< *min*) mean "when" but derive from different words. The vowel of the verbs *wa(')yat* and *(w)u'iyat* can have different vowels, as noted in the notes on the vowel system and in the chapter on Bedouin dialects toward the back of the book.

2. *gūḷi l-ummeč tōfi ^{a}ndēreč 'axēr ma-(a)gṣof ^{e}'mēreč*: "Tell your mother to keep her vow, or I will shorten [cut] your years [life]." The narrator mixes indirect speech, *tōfi*, "that she will fulfill [the vow]," with *^{a}ndēreč*, "your little vow." The rhyme in this text indicates its importance—as noted already elsewhere. Note: *^{e}ndēr* is *naḏr* and *^{e}'mēr* is *'omr* in LA/MSA. These forms are in the diminutive pattern in the Bedouin dialect. Bedouin speakers often use the diminutive (cf. the chapter on Bedouin dialects; Rosenhouse, *Bedouin Arabic Dialects*, 23–24; Henkin, *Negev Arabic*, among other Arabic dialects).

3. "*'alēh 'aḷḷa w-amān 'aḷḷa, walli yexūn, yexūn 'aḷḷa*": The slogan for assuring one's safety in a new and uncertain environment. This slogan has occurred in several other stories in this volume. Here the phrase *walli yexūn* is not *walli yexūno*. The latter means that the traitor himself is betraying Allah if he betrays the covenant with his friends.

4. *wa-lannha banādme*: "and lo she was a human female" (also *banādma*). This is a further development of the masculine form *ibenādam*, "the son of man [Adam]," a human, also found in plural as *bani'ādam* and *bani'ādmīn*.

5. Here *dūneč* implies "pay attention so that [this thing] will not harm you," but cf. chapter 31, note 1.

6. *rakkabha wa-'āwad 'alá-mmo*: "He put her on his back and returned to his mother." The word *'umm*/*'imm*/*'amm*, "mother," in *'ala-mmo* loses the first vowel, and only the *mm-* remains with the bound pronoun suffix. This may reflect the process *'ála* + *'ímmo* / *'ála* + *'ámmo* > *'ála-mmo* > *'alá-mmo* (cf. chap. 23, note 8).

7. In their book, Muhawi and Kanaana present a story that was recorded from a Christian narrator from Gaza and is associated with the narrative type ATU 425B but has no resemblance to our story. Muhawi and Kanaana, *Speak, Bird, Speak Again*, 244–48, 362–63. El-Shamy mentions in his book three stories belonging to this type from Egypt, Syria, and Iraq. El-Shamy, *Types of the Folktale*, 202–3.

8. Uther, *The Types of International Folktales*, 250–1.

9. Bin Gorion, *Mimekor Yisrael*, 207–9.

10. Tolstoy, *Anna Karenina*, 415–16.

11. IFA 12744. p. 8.

34. The Children and the Ogre

THE GROUP OF STORIES 300–399 in the narrative type index is called "Supernatural Adversaries." The stories presented below are various versions of the narrative type ATU 327, "The Children and the Ogre." This type refers to a cycle of related tales. It combines episodes from the types 327A, 327B, and 327C and often mixes with other narrative types. Nevertheless, the stories presented here can be divided into three distinct groups:

A. "The Girls and the Ġūla"—three stories belonging to the subtype ATU 327A, "Hansel and Gretel," of which I provide only one representative version.
B. "Grēʿa, Ḥmēda, and Ḥdaydūn"—five stories belonging to the subtype ATU 327C, "The Devil (Witch) Carries the Hero Home in a Sack." Here, too, one story represents the group.
C. "Nuṣṣ-Nṣēṣ"—three stories belonging to a close narrative type ATU 328, "The Boy Steals the Ogre's Treasure." Here, also, one story is a representative of the group.

See these stories below, followed by the commentary.

A. The Girls and the Ġūla

NARRATOR: Warda Hawāš
TRIBE: *ʿArab el-Mazārīb*
IFA 18171 March 11, 1982

1 hāḏa, bī ʿarab. ʿindīhum ᵉğmāl. wēn mā yilgam ē . . . yaʿani maṭraḥ bī rebīᵉʿ, yirḥalam ʿalē. yōm, yāxḏom aǧ-ǧmāl, gaṭīʿ aǧ-ǧmāl w-iyrūḥan. yerūḥan mīn hinna, yirūḥan arbaʿ ʿağiyyāt. [laʾ, sitt ʿağiyyāt, sitta.] ʿağiyya binnīhen—bī šēx ʿandīhum yibga kebīr, ʿarab, biduw. fa-ʿindīhum šēx.[1]	1 This—there are Bedouins. They have camels. Wherever they find . . . that is, place where there is grass, they wander thereto. One day, they take the camels, the herd of camels and go. They go from here. Four girls go. (No, six girls. Six.) A girl among them—they have a sheikh, there, old, Arab, Bedouins. And they have a sheikh.
9 gāḷam ḷēhum, "widna narḥal." bī ʿindīhum ğmāl, wu-ğmāl maʿa l-banāt	9 They said to them, "We want to set out." They have camels, and the camels are with the girls.
11 yirūḥan yisraḥan. ğam hā-l-ġwaḷa šnū ygūḷam? ygūḷam, "widdna narḥal." ˈṭṭuḷḷ ʿalēhen waḥde ʾesemha Grēʿa. tgūḷ-ḷēhun "hā-l-ʿarab baʿadha hēna" gāḷat lēha "hā-l-ʿarab mġasslīn u-mištaġlīn u-ʿammi mšāyiš bēnhum." [u-šnū ʿammi mišāyiš bēnum? ʿammi yugʿud bēnhum.]	11 They go herding [them]. These *ġūls* came, what did they say? They say, "We want to set out." There looks at them one [girl] whose name is Grēʿa. She says to them, "The Bedouins are still here." She said to her, "These Bedouins are laundering and working, and my paternal uncle is staying among them." (What does it mean "my paternal uncle is staying among them"? My uncle is staying among them.)
19 gāḷan lēha, "ṭayyeb." kull sāʿa u-hī ṭālʿa. ġābat aš-šames, baʿadēn hā, wiḥde maʿāhen, Ğbēna [–ʾā, ʾisma ğbēna, ṣaḥīḥ.]	19 They [the girls] said to her, "Good." Every hour she looked. The sun went down, afterward, this, one among them, Ğbēna (yes, her name was Ğbēna, right).
23 šnū gāḷat lēhen? ġābat aš-šams u-mā rawwaḥan. daḥḥagan ʿa-l-ʿarab wann al-arab rāḥla. al-ʿarab rāḥla—mā raḥlan warāha. rawwaḥan	23 What did she say to them? The sun set and they did not get back home. They looked at the Bedouins' [place], and lo, the Bedouins had gone away. The Bedouins had gone away. They did not go after them, they went back home.
27 yōminhin rāḥan, rawwaḥan. wiḥda, kull minhin, ligat gurṣ min biʿīd ʿan-nār. mā yefḥarūha, kull wiḥda ḥaṭṭat ʾummahāt(h)in, ḥāṭṭāt bīha xubez mišān yāklan—ġēr ᵉGrēʿa. Grēʿa mā ligat ši. gāḷat b-an-nār hīč, gāḷat b-an-nār hīč, mā ligat ši.	27 When they went, went home. One, each one among them found a loaf far from the fire. They dug it out. Each one, their mothers had put in it bread for them to eat—except Grēʿa. Grēʿa did not find anything. She looked at the fire like this, looked at the fire like this, [but] did not find anything.
34 hāḏlāka, ligat kull wiḥda gurṣ xubez hīč, b-an-nār. u-kull min hiyya ʿindīha ē ğūz mayya. uṭʿamanha la-Grēʿa. gāḷan, "yaḷḷa, ta-nna nirkab hā-ğ-ğmāl u-nḏaḷḷ ᵃnahğīn." daḥḥagan b-al-lēl hunāk yā—daḥḥagan ʿala ḏahr hā-ğ- ğibal, winnhā bī nār. gāḷan, "hā, haḏāk ʾahlana." rāḥan.	34 Those, each one found a loaf of bread like that, in the fire. And each from here, she had a pair of water [cans]. They fed Grēʿa. And said, "Come on, let's ride these camels and go on going." They looked at the night there—oh—they looked at the top of the mountain, and lo, there was fire, they said, "This, that is our family [tribe]." They went.

41 yōminn raḥlan, winnha ġōḷa. yōminha(n) raḥlan, winnha ġōḷa. yōminha daḥḥagat winnha bī (a) hā-l-banāt ğāyāt ʿalēha. rāsha hīč. gāmat taḏuḅḅ as-HseʿarH (=aš-šaʿar) winnhin ʿād ^{i}tnādi hīč, "'ahlan u-sahlan, 'ahlan u-sahlan, 'ahlan u-sahlan, tfaḍḍalan fūtan, fūtan," tanna fātan. fawwatathin.

41 When they went, lo, it was a *Ġūla*. When they went, lo, there was a *ġūla*. When she looked and lo, there were these girls coming to her. Her head was like this [disheveled]. She arranged the hair and lo—she called them thus, "Welcome, welcome, welcome, please come in, come in." Until they entered, she let them in.

49 ʿād[2] yōminnha gāḷat, fātan ʿalēha, winnha tgūl, "widčan tāklan?" gāḷat lēha, "ṭayyib. 'ā, widdna nākel." haḏāka šū maʿāhen — maʿāhen laḥam [laḥam—tiʿeraf al-laḥam?] ē . . . u-maʿāhen xubez, ḥāṭṭāthin kull wiḥda hīč . . .

49 Then when she said, they came in to her, she said, "Do you want to eat?" She said to her, "Good, yes. We want to eat." Those, what did they have with them? They had meat (meat—do you know [what is] meat?) er . . . and they had bread. They [the mothers] had put for each of them like that.

55 ğat hiyya [tiʿeraf al-gaṃeḷ šin dīnu?] ḥaṭṭat min hēn gaṃuḷ . . . u-min ^{i}dyūdha ḥaṭṭat ḥalīb, u-sawat liha l-^{i}bḥata. hiyya gūḷa, ^{i}gʿadat yōminha sāwat lēhen u-ğābat lēhen xawašīr. ʿād^{i} haḏīča,[3] al-^{i}Grēʿa, hāḏi ṣārat tāčel. šnū gāḷan lēha, hī gāḷan,"lā tākli, min^{i} 'ōkli (lā) tākli." hiyya ğawwadat-le 'akel.

55 She came (do you know lice, what they are? [lit.: What is their religion?]), she put lice from here [. . .] and from her breasts milk and made for her "porridge." She was a *ġūla*. Then she did for them and brought them offal [bad food]. Then this, Grēʿa, began to eat. What did they say to her? They said, "Don't eat, from this food [don't] eat." She liked the food [found it good].

63 hinna wēn, bḥašan ğūra, kull wiḥda, mā kalan minno, 'ā. bḥašat kulli wiḥda ğūra, u-kalat hāḏa alli ʿinda, kalatha u-šibʿat, yaʿani. 'ā. hinna [–'a, Grēʿa.] hinna la', mā kalan. ḥaṭṭan kull wiḥda bḥašan ğūra hīč, uwi-dmalan.

63 They, where, they dug a hole, each one, they did not eat of it, yes. . . . Each one dug a hole and ate that which she had, she ate it and was satiated, that is. Yes, they (Grēʿa [ate]), they—not, they did not eat, they put—each one—dug a hole like that and buried [the *ġūla*'s food].

69 gāḷat lēha, "yā ḥabibti, yā taʿāli, yā ʿād." 'ā, kalan min alli ğābanna maʿāhen. baʿadēn, 'ā, "kalētan, yā ḥabībti?" gālat, "la'." winna tgūl lēhan, haḏīča, ta-lli Grēʿa, tgūḷ-ḷa, "waḷḷa, mā kalan." wannha tgūḷ "lā, kalēna xāḷti. hā, šnū bī šū māčlito?"

69 She said to her, "O my dear, oh, come, come, then." They ate from what they had brought with them. Afterward, yes, "Have you eaten, my dear?" She said, "No." And she said to her, that Grēʿa, she says to her, "By Allah, they did not eat." Lo, she says, "No, we ate, Auntie. This, what is there [left anything] that we did not eat?"

76 gāḷan lēha aṣ-ṣubeḥ, gāḷan lēha "widdna nišrab" gāḷat-lēha, "ṭayyeb, šnū widdeč, wa-mayya mā ʿindīna." gāḷat-lēha, "'eḥna mayya—mayya 'eḥna mayy mā nišrab min hēn, mayya rāḥ ^{i}tğībi b-al-ġirbāḷ." [teʿref šū yaʿni ġirbāḷ?— ġirbāḷ u-kirbāḷ, yaʿani—'aywā].

76 They said to her in the morning, they said to her [to the *ġūla*], "We want to drink." She said to her, "Good, what do you want, as we have not got water with us?" She said to her, "We water—water we do not—do not drink from here, water you will bring in the sieve. (Do you know what a sieve is? That is, *ġirbāḷ* and *kirbāḷ*. Yes.)

83 hawwadat ʿal-hā-l-qenn, xaḏat hā-l-kirbāḷ u-xaḏat hā-l-ġirbāḷ, sāyiba—al-ġirbāḷ mā twaddi bī mayya? . . . gāḷat- lēha, “ġad taǧībi ḥabel u-tḥuṭṭi bī ǧalla mi-šān noxbez ʿalē” gāḷat lēha, “yā yumma, yā yumma, inšaḷḷa tiǧībi-lna ǧalla [hāḏa min ḅugaṛ] u-wa-tǧībī b-al-ḥabel, u-nišrab mayya ann-naṣli-bā.”	83 She went down to this coop, took the *kirbāl* and took the *ġirbāl* leaving it—will the sieve bring water? . . . She said to her, “There, you will bring a rope and put in it dung so we can bake on it.” She said to her, “O mother, o mother, I hope you will bring us dung (this is from cattle) and bring it with the rope, and we will drink water that we will roast with.”
91 rāḥat hadīč. ʾi! šū ḏaḷḷat—gūḷi taǧi—taṣīr titḥaṭṭ ʿalēa . . . b-il-waḥal—titḥuṭṭ bi-l-mayya, šū bī mayya? hin hadlāka, yirkaban ʿala l-xēl, wa-ḏaḷḷan nāhǧāt. (gūḷi . . .) ʾā, ʿala-^{a}ǧmāl. račban u-ḏaḷḷan nāhǧāt.	91 This one [the *ġūla*] went away. E! What remained—say she will come—she begins to put [water] on it . . . in the mud—she will put it in the water—what water is there [in the sieve]? They, those [girls], they rode the horses and continued fleeing. (Say. . . .) Yes, on the camels, they rode and continued fleeing.
97 hadīča, winnha tgūḷ, rawwaḥat mā ligat ḥada, ʾā, ʾal-ġōḷa. “čēf widdi ʾasāwi, čēf widdi ʾasāwi?” gāmat liḥǧathen. widdha tilḥaghen ṣārat. winnha nāfša kapišha (<qabiḏha) hīč, warāhin,	97 This one [the ġūla], lo, she says, she went back home and found no one [there]. Yes, the *ġūla*. “How shall I do? How shall I do?” She went and followed them. She wanted to chase them. Lo, she gathered her fist like that, after them,
102 “rūb yā ḥalībi, rūb, wa-ʿaǧǧid lēhen ba-rkūb, ʿaǧǧid lēhen ba-rkābhen.” hadīča ḏaḷḷat, ^{e}Grēʿa, gadd mā kalat. baʿadēn ʿāwadat, yā ḥabībti, yōmenha—yōmenha ʿaggad—ʿaggad lēha ba-rkābha, baṭṭalat ṣārat timši. ḥaṭṭan ʿala ǧanba ḥaǧar u-daššaranha.	102 “Curdle, o my milk, curdle, and tie up their knees, tie up their knees [for them].” That one stayed, Grēʿa, [because] she had eaten [so much]. Afterward, she returned, oh my dear. When—when it curdled—curdled her in her knees, she stopped being able to walk. They [the girls] put a stone at her side and left her.
109 ṣār(a)t ^{e}tgūḷ, “yā ṛaḅḅ^{w}i, yilgan xēr, yā yā ṛaḅḅ^{w}i, yilgan māl, yā ṛaḅḅ^{w}i, yilgan šnū”	109 She began to say, “O my Lord, let them find good; o my Lord, let them find money, my Lord, let them find whatever.”
112 baʿadēn, ē. waḥade ʾisemha šmēsa, ʾisemha Ǧbēna [. . .] u-gāmat hāḏi daggat waḥda šōka. ʿigib-ma daggatha šōka, [činne tḥoṭṭ šwayy.]	112 Afterward er . . . one, her name [was] Šmēsa. Her name [was] Ǧbēna. [. . .] And she, a thorn pricked her. Because the thorn pricked her (maybe she could put a little [something]).
116 yōminnha ʿād hi daggatha š-šōka, hadīča, yōminha ričbat ʿala-l-ḥaǧar. ričbat ʿa-l-ḥaǧar, ṣārat ʿala la-[$_{H}$ṣōf$_{H}$], ^{a}Grēʿa.	116 When, again, the thorn pricked her, this one, when she sat on the stone, sat on the stone, Grēʿa became near the ($_{H}$ṣōf$_{H}$) end [nearly died].

120 haḏīča, ʿād, yōminnha ʿād daggatha š-šōka, liḥgata, mā gidrat timši, l-ⁱšmēsa. lā— ᵉǦbēna. wu-Šmēsa, winha tgūḷ-(ḷ)ā, "tiʿerfi?" gāḷat lēha, "'imma, ʿayyāni," winnha šnū 'agūḷ-(ḷ)ha, "yā yumma, daggatni šōka w-'ana 'astanna bīč, mišān ᵃṭṭullaʿ-li 'iyyāha." gāḷat lēha, "ṭayyeb, taʿāli ta-naglaʿha lēč."	120 That one, then, when the thorn pricked her, she caught up with her, she could not walk, Šmēsa. No, Ǧbēna. And Šmēsa, she said to her, "Do you know?" She said to her, "Mother, [I am] ill, " and lo—what I'll tell her, "O mother, a thorn pricked me and I am waiting for you, so you will pluck it out for me." She [the *gūla*] said to her, "Good, come so that I'll take it out for you."
128 ḍaḷḷat lēha hāḏi winnha tgūḷ lēha, "uguʿdi, tann-'afallīč." nāmat, mā xaḷḷatha tnām ʿala l-ḥağar. [. . .] baʿadēn, 'assa gāḷat lēha, "yōminneč ᵉtnāmi, šlōn ᵉʿyūneč?" gāḷat lēha, "yōminni 'anām, ʿeyūni ḥumor, u-yōminni 'agʿud, ʿuyūni bīḍ." gāḷat lēha, "ṭayyeb."	128 She stayed [for her], this one, and lo, she says to her, "Sit down, so I will delouse you [take out the lice for you]." She lay down, she [the girl] let her lie on the stone. [. . .] Afterward, now she said to her, "When you are asleep, how are your eyes?" She said to her, "When I sleep, my eyes are red, and when I get up, my eyes are white." She said to her, "Good."
135 nawwamatha. xaḷḷatha tannha nāmat ⁱšnū. gāḷat lēhan, gāḷat lēhan haḏlāka, kān nāhğāt, "ⁱšnū ⁱstanēatan? stannēnāni b-al-maṭraḥ al-flāni. 'ani 'alḥagčin. 'ani 'aʿmal ʿalēha ḥīla w-'alḥagčan."	135 She lulled her to sleep. She let her until she slept well [and how]. She said to them, those were running away. "What were you waiting [for]? Wait for me at the certain place. I will catch up with you. I'm doing a trick on her and I'll catch up with you."
140 xaḷḷatha tannha nāmat yamm, yamm, hī siḥḥer rāsa,[4] ḥaṭṭ(at) taḥta ḥağar, u-tilḥaghen. mā ḥassat (al-ġūḷa) wanna mā bī ḥada. "u-reytin[5] yilgan māl, u-reyitin yilgan ḏahab, u-reyitin yilgan xēr, u-reyitin m-adri šnū yilgan barūdi, yilgan m-adri šnū"	140 She let her until she fell sleep completely, completely, her head was dizzy [under a spell]; she put a stone under it and [went] following them. She [the *ġūla*] did not feel but that there was no one [there]. [She cursed them:] "I wish [to see] they will find money, I wish they will find gold, I wish they will find good, I wish I don't know, they will find a rifle, they will find I don't know what."
147 baʿadēn hi gāḷat lēha, "walla hāy kull tistadʿī-lna hiyya. 'amma 'eḥna, šadd, bsāʿ." ligan xēl, ričban, dasššaran aǧ-ǧmāl, ā, rāčbīn al-xēl, 'ā, ʿāwadan ligan māl, (mallan) al-xurᵘǧ ḏahab u-min kull 'iši, w-ⁱnhağan.	147 Afterward, she told her, "By Allah, this one wishes everything for us. But we [let us be] strong, fast!" They found horses, they rode them, left the camels, riding the horses. Yes, then they found money, [filled] the horses' side bags with gold and everything, and fled.
153 ʿāwadat ʿala Grēʿa, ṣārt ta- fa-kalatha, u-haḏlāka ligan 'ahalhin, u-mā ʿirfanhum, baʿadēn ʿād hi, tanni ʿirfam. u-hāḏi xurrāfti.	153 She [the *ġūla*] returned to Grēʿa, began and ate her up. And those found their family, and they did not recognize them, [but] afterward, again, they recognized them. And this is my tale.

Commentary

I collected three versions of the narrative type ATU 327A, "Hansel and Gretel," of which I provide only one that was recorded in the ʿArab el-Mazārīb tribe.

Here is the type description according to Uther:[6] A (poor) father (persuaded by the stepmother) abandons his children (a boy and a girl) in the forest. Twice the children find their way back home, following scattered pebbles. On the third night, birds eat the scattered peas (bread crumbs). The children come to a gingerbread house, which belongs to a witch (ogress). She takes them into her house. The boy is fattened, while the girl must do housework. The witch asks the boy to show his finger to test how fat he is, but he shows her a bone (stick). When the witch wants to cook the boy, the sister deceives her by feigning ignorance and pushes her into the oven (the witch's son finds out that his mother has been killed and pursues the children). The children escape, carrying the witch's treasure with them. Birds and beasts (angels) help them across water. They return home.

Despite the many differences between the Bedouin versions of the story and the description presented above, the Bedouin versions contain many components of this description. A group of girls (six or three) is engaged in grazing camels or sheep outside the campgrounds. When they return to the settlement, they discover that their tribe has set off on a nomadic journey. They dig into the remains of the campfires and find loaves of bread (or they slaughter kids from the herd), except for one of them called Grēʿa (which means "round pumpkin" and serves as a nickname for baldness), who cannot find bread in her parents' fireplace. They come to a *ġūla*'s cave, and she invites them to stay at her house and offers them food. The food prepared by the *ġūla* is a dish called *baxtah* (a porridge made of rice, milk, and sugar), which the *ġūla* makes with milk from her breasts and lice from her hair. The girls, except for Grēʿa, do not taste the *ġūla*'s food but pour it into a hole in the ground. The girls mislead the *ġūla*, asking her to bring them water drawn in the sieve and a strainer, and in her absence, they escape. The *ġūla* chases them uttering a magic spell, which causes her food to curdle in Grēʿa's knees. Grēʿa who ate from the *ġūla*'s food, lags behind the other girls, and the *ġūla* captures her and devours her. The *ġūla* wishes the girls to encounter silver treasures in the hope that this will delay them so she can catch them. One of the girls, who is named Šmēsa (meaning "a small sun," a name that indicates beauty), is delayed by a thorn stuck in her leg. The *ġūla* catches her, but the girl deceives her. She says to her that she waited for her deliberately to help her remove the thorn from her foot, and after the *ġūla* does what she wants, she offers to allow her to delouse her. Then she lulls her to sleep and escapes. The *ġūla* once again wishes the girls to find gold and rifles in the hope of delaying them. The girls collect the treasures without pausing and escape riding horses they found while disguised in men's clothes. They reach the tribal encampment. At first, they are not recognized, but in the end, the parents identify them, and the girls share the treasures with them.

One version of the story was told by Warda Hawwāš of the ʿArab el-Mazārīb tribe, in the village Bēt Zarzīr. Two additional versions were recorded in the ʿArab el-Ḥuğērāt tribe. In the ʿArab el-Mazārīb version, the girls are camel drivers, while in the ʿArab el-Ḥuğērāt versions they shepherd sheep. In all cases, the fate of the herd is not told. In the ʿArab el-Ḥuğērāt versions, the *ġūla*'s neighborhood is described as a seven-room palace, with each room inside another. The *ġūla* lives in the innermost room, and the girls, before their flight, lock all the doors so that the *ġūla* will have to break through door after door to get out of the palace, enabling them to escape. In one version, one of the girls found an iron horseshoe. The role of the horseshoe is unclear. This detail may have been inserted by mistake from the story of Ḥdaydūn, in which a horseshoe plays a central role.

As we shall see below, the girls' story is combined with a close narrative type, ATU 327C, "The Devil (Witch) Carries the Hero Home in a Sack."

The most striking feature in all the narrative types of "The Children and the Ogre" is the subject of food. Reference to food appears in a large number of folktales, both in the Bedouin cultural space and in other cultural spaces, but in "The Children and the Ogre" tales, food occupies a central place. In the European version of the story, hunger is what drives parents to abandon their children in the forest. The children mark their way by dropping bread crumbs, which is a kind of food; the witch's house is made of bread, which the children are tempted to eat, and the witch treats the children as food. She fattens them and intends to eat them.

The Bedouin versions of the story are also characterized by a special emphasis on the subject of food. The abandoned girls look for food and find loaves of bread in the remains of the fires, or they slaughter kids from the herd to calm their hunger. A typical Bedouin food, *baxtah*, is served at the *ġūla*'s house. The *ġūla* uses milk from her breasts and lice from her hair to prepare the dish. Later, it turns out that the food is spellbound, and the *ġūla* uses it to delay the girls in their escape. In another attempt to stop them, the *ġūla* (see the Ḥdaydūn stories below) wishes them to find a "*wādi* of sweets, halva and baklava," and be tempted by them.

Why does food play such an important role in this folktale type? Quite probably, it is connected with the fact that the stories are typical adolescence stories. In the life of a young child, food has a central place. In Bettelheim's view, the story symbolizes the anxieties of children who are required to overcome and refine their "gluttonous" primitive desires.[7] The bread house in "Hansel and Gretel" represents an existence based on gluttony and primitive satisfaction of needs. The children succumb to temptation and surrender to their unrestrained desire for food. At the same time, the witch's house symbolizes the mother who feeds her children from her body. The children rebelled against the actual mother, who imposed various restrictions on them, and yearned for an ideal mother who would not force them to do anything. They must go through this phase of restraining their desires and adapting themselves to the rules of society as part of their growing up.

In the Bedouin versions of the story, the message becomes even more acute. Grēʿa, the ugly girl, represents the consequences of irresponsible and unrestrained actions. Initially, she does not fulfill her role as someone who is meant to be aware of what is happening in the tribe and to warn her friends that the tribe intends to move on. Afterward, she is tempted to eat from the *ġūla*'s food and thus allows it to stop her in her flight. When her friends hide her, covering her with a stone slab, she exposes herself by breaking wind (see the Ḥdaydūn stories below), and as a result she is revealed and devoured by the *ġūla*.

The other girls, on the other hand, resist temptation and do not taste the *ġūla*'s food. Even when one of them is forced to linger because of a thorn stuck in her leg and risks encountering the *ġūla* who persecutes her, she is able to cope with it, and unlike Grēʿa, she finds a way to lull the *ġūla* and continue her flight. Later, when the *ġūla* tries to lure the girls to halt by scattering treasures and foods in their path, they act responsibly, taking advantage of the objects they find to aid them in escape. They are not tempted to stop. On their way to their parents' home, they disguise themselves as men to reduce the risk of being exposed to sexual assault on the road, without a man to sponsor them. Only after they have come to know that their parents have not deliberately abandoned them do they remove the men's clothing and identify themselves as the lost daughters.

In a Druze version that Salmān Falāh wrote down (IFA 1031), seven girls are deliberately abandoned by their father. The first time, they return home thanks to flakes of straw they disperse on their way, but the second time they lose their way and arrive at the house of the *ġūla*, who schemes to devour them. By means of a trick, they succeed in shoving the *ġūla* and her daughter into the oven and gathering all their treasures. Later they disguise themselves in men's clothing and move from village to village riding horses and using the *ġūla*'s gold to buy groceries. At last, they return to their village, identify themselves to their old father, and tell him their story. The father kills the girls' stepmother. This version is very close to the European versions of the story.

The bread house, according to Bettelheim, symbolizes the image of the mother. The Bedouin versions express the same idea: the *ġūla*'s food is made of milk she took from her breasts and lice from her hair. In the versions quoted above, nothing is said about the fate of the *ġūla*, but in the Ḥdaydūn stories, she explodes and dies in anger and frustration. Bettelheim emphasizes that as a grown-up figure, she cannot be forgiven for her cannibalistic desires and is punished. The European versions emphasize the cooperation between the brother and the sister in their efforts to overcome the dangers on their way. This is also evident in the Bedouin versions. The girls do not denounce Grēʿa after her failure to realize that the tribe intends to move on. Later, they try to convince her not to be tempted to eat the *ġūla*'s food. When she cannot continue to travel, they make sure to hide her under a stone slab. Finally, they take care of each other during the escape. When one of them must stop because of the thorn stuck in her leg and the other girls worry about her, she says to them, "Wait for me in a certain place, I will deceive her and catch up with you."

This group of stories thus emphasizes the coping of young children with the anxiety of abandonment, their overcoming gluttonous tendencies, and their resisting various temptations. Simultaneously, the children adapt to the laws of society around them, as well as cooperate among themselves as part of their integration into the life of their age group.

B. Grēʿa, Ḥmēda, and Ḥdaydūn

NARRATOR: Maryam Muṣṭafa Ṭabbāš
TRIBE: *ʿArab Ḥilf-Ṭabbāš*
August 8, 1982

1 u-hāyya Ḥdaydūn, šikel ṯani. hāyya Ḥdaydūn, kāna bī kamān ʿarab, u-ʿindo mart abū. u-bī bēn ğīrānhum ʿağiyyāt yilʿabam. rāḥam yilʿabum b-al-waʿar yaʿani, yilʿabum. ᵉzġār, miš ᵉkbār ᵉkṯīr, meṯal, ʾakbar min hāḏa šwoyye. haḏōl rāḥam yilʿabum.	1 And this Ḥdaydūn [is] something else. This Ḥdaydūn, there was also a Bedouin tribe, and his father's wife [stepmother]. And among their neighbors there were girls playing. They went to play in the scrubland. That is, they were young, playing, not very big, like, [they were] somewhat older than this [child]. These [children] went playing.
8 al-ʿarab ʿugubhum hīka tinsāhum u-tarḥal, w-il-ʿarab kānat tirḥal min maṭraḥ l-maṭraḥ. haḏāla ʿāwadam ʿa-d-dūr—mā ligam ḥada—ḏaḷḷ al-maṭraḥ. mā fī ḥada. ʾēš widhum yeʿamalum? šū (wi)dhom yeʿmalum?	8 The Bedouin after them forgot them and roamed away, and the Bedouin used to roam from one place to another place. These returned to their homes—they did not find anyone—[only] the place remained. There is no one. What will they do? What will they do?
14 ḏaḷḷam nihğum, mišam maʿa hā-d-darb, biddak ᵉtgūl, ḥaṭṭum hā-l-ğibel, ʾaḷḷa ʾaʿlam, hū šimāl, al-ğibel, mā baʿraf, ʾayy šimāl, ʿala šfa-ʿamur, ʿala wādi šfa-ʿamur, ʾaḷḷa ʾaʿlam.	14 They went on off, walked with this road, you'd say, they took to the mountain, Allah knows, it is north, the mountain, I don't know, that is, north—to Šfaʿamr [Shefarʿam], to the valley of Šfaʿamr, Allah knows [best].
19 ḏaḷḷum māšīn. haḏōla lamman hum mišum, mā ligum . . . e . . . mā ligum ḥada. rāḥum winna hāy al-ġūḷa ğāʿeda. hā-l-ġūḷa winnha ğāʿeda.	19 They continued walking. When they went, they did not find . . . e . . . did not find anyone. They went and lo, this *ġūla* is sitting. Lo, this ġūla is sitting.
23 gāḷat-lem lammin šāfathum, gāḷat ilhum, "ʾahlan u-sahlan bi-ʿyāl ʾaxūya. ahlan wa-sahlan." čā(f) widdha—fātam ʿalēha. "ʾani ʿammetkum, u-ʾani tiğawwazet zimān u-ʾani mā adri wēn"—gūḷa.	23 She said to them when she saw them, she said to them, "Welcome, my brother's children. Welcome." What does she want. . . . They entered her place. "I am your paternal aunt and I got married a long time ago and I don't know where." *Ġūla.*
29 fātam ʿind hā-l-gūḷa, gʿadum, huwwa hāḏa Ḥdaydūn, wa-l-banāt aṯ-ṯintēn. waḥda Grēʿa, ʾaywa, u-waḥda Ḥmēde. ʾaywa, Ḥmēda u-Grēʿa.[8] ᵉgʿadum ʿindhe.	29 They entered this *ġūla*'s [place], sat down, he, this Ḥdaydūn and the two girls. One was [named] Grēʿa, and one was [named] Ḥmēda. Yes, Ḥmēda and Grēʿa. They stayed at her [place].

34 hāḏam ʿimlat ilum ʿaša. ʿimlat ilhum ḥalīb, yaʿani, miš yaʿani ʿaša maḏbūṭ, ḥayaḷḷa, ʾaywa . . . ʿimlat lēhum, huwwa mā kalē. ʾaywā . . . [ʾaywā, ʾinta teʿarifha.] ʾaywā . . . haḏāk yā(ʿre)f ʿemel ^{e}Ḥdaydūn. huwa mā kale.	34 These, she made for them dinner. She made for them milk, that is to say, not really a dinner, just so, yes . . . she made for them—he did not eat. Yes. (Yes, you know it). Yes. That [one] knew [to] do, Ḥdaydūn. He did not eat.
40 hiyya gāmat b-al-lēl, daḥḥagat ʿalēhem, widdha tākel ʾā lēham, gām, daḥḥag fīha. en-natīǧa, aṣ-ṣuboh nihǧam. hiyya gālat lehum	40 She got up at night, looked at them, she wanted to eat [some] of them. He got up, looked at her. In short, in the morning they ran away. She said to them,
44 "yā ḥalībi rūb, rūb, ʿaǧǧid lehum ar-rkūb." hāḏi hinne l-banāt, ʾargaban, min al-xōf, ʾargaban. ʾawwal weḥda liḥgitha—kalata. mišyat aṯ-ṯāniya, ṣārat tgūl, "yā shala, šuggi wi-blaʿīne, yā shala, šuggi wi-blaʿīne," ḏaḷḷ ʾuṣbaʿ min ʾaṣābʿ al-bint aṯ-ṯāniya rafʿatu fawqa b-il-ʾarḍ.	44 "O my milk, curdle, curdle, stiffen their knees [paralyze them]." These here girls froze, with fear, they froze. The first one she caught up with—she ate her. The second one went, and began to say, "O plateau, break up and swallow me, o plateau, break up and swallow me." [Only] a finger of her [the second girl's] fingers remained, she had lifted it up, above the ground.
51 ḏaḷḷ huwwa. huwwa čāf widdo ysāwi, maʿāh ḥadīda meṯel daḥḥāǧa, meṯel ʿaǧal. hī b-ḥaǧo, (y)imši, mū mistanna hāyā. yiḏaḷḷ māši. hāḏa siḥab ḥālo, ^{i}trakha warā, mā—tmallaṣ minha.	51 [Only] he remained. He—how would he do? He had this metal, something like a [turning] wheel, like a wheel. It is with him [it is his]. He goes, he does not wait, this [boy]. He continues to go. This one [Ḥdaydūn] took off, left her behind him—why, he slipped away from her, he got away from her.
56 ^{e}tmallaṣ minha, gāḷat, "ʾaḷḷa yiblāk, yā Ḥdaydūn, baḥar ḥāyif lāyiṭ,[9] mā bī yigūm ġār illi yfūt."	56 He escaped from her. She said, "[May] Allah try [test, torment] you, o Ḥdaydūn, [in] a stormy, noisy [reaching and killing] sea, of which no one will get out except he who enters it [i.e., only the one who enters it can survive]."
59 daḥḥag willa hā-l-baḥar. hāḏa bi-gudret ʾaḷḷa, daḥḥag al-ḥadīda gad ǧa l-baḥ . . . al-baḥar. baḥar—miš baḥar, yaʿani, ʿala-l-ʿāda, wādi, marag ʿalēha, nifad.	59 He looked, and lo—[there was] a sea. This, with Allah's power, he looked at this iron [wheel] how much the sea came. Sea—it was not a sea, that is, as usual, [it was] a *wādi* [a canyon]. He passed on it [the wheel]—he got away.
63 hāḏa nifad, ṭalaʿ ʿa-l-gaṣor. bī bi-hā-l-gaṣor xāli, xārib, mā ḥawalē ḥada. wēn e . . . wennha ǧāto kamān ġūḷa. hāḏa nifad.	63 This one got away, went up to the castle—empty, destroyed castle, no one around him. And lo . . . lo, there came to him another *ġūla*. This one got away.
66 lēha ḥmāra. kull yōm yrūḥ yirkab ʿa-la-ḥmāra, yetāʿib ʿa-hā-l-^{e}ḥmāra, trūḥ ta-turkuḍ—we-yinhazem.	66 She has a she-ass. Every day he goes riding on the she-ass, making her tired, the she-ass. She [the *ġūla*] goes running [to catch him] and he runs away.

69 yōm xarrab al-baṭṭīx. gāḷat-lo, "yā, Ḥdaydūn, mā tru(ḥ) ʿa-la-l-baṭṭīx, ta-nğīb ^{i}lna baṭṭīxa?"	69 One day the watermelons got stale. She said to him, "O Ḥdaydūn, won't you go to the watermelon [field] and we'll bring us a watermelon?"
72 gāḷ-ḷa, "yā hala, rūḥi-nti." hī rāḥat el-ḥāla, hū rāḥ la-ḥāl. kala hu, hā-l-uwlād, hā-r-reʿyān, hā-l-nās, kalam u-liʿebum, mā-ša-aḷḷa ʿalēha. daḥḥag winnha ğāya min gād.	72 He said, "Welcome, you go." She went on her own, he went on his own. He ate and the children and the shepherds and these people, they ate and played, with no problem [on them]. He looked and lo, she [was] coming from there [from a distance].
77 fī baṭṭīxa 'akbar min bani 'ādam, bī hā-l-xurrāf, bī baṭṭīxa čebīra hīča, baḥašha min ğawwa, aywa, u-fāt bīha, u-sakkaram ʿalē. ḥaṭṭum as-skāra ʿalē u-daššaram. ğat hāy, daḥḥagat hiyya hā-l-baṭṭīxa, šālatha.	77 There is a watermelon, bigger than human people. There is this story. There is a big watermelon, like that. He dug in it from the inside, yes, and entered it, and they closed it on him. They put the lid on it and left [him]. She came, saw this watermelon, and took it.
83 ṣāyir inaġġez bīha. yinaġġez bīha, dugʿod b-'ibre, b-'iši, naġġaz bīhe, tā-b- dubara (ʿa-ḏahara), la-hān, rumatha, daḥḥagat ʿa-hā-l-baṭṭīxa	83 He started pricking her, pricking her with a needle, with something, he pricked her, at her back side [the back], to here. She threw it, looked at the watermelon
87 gāḷat-lēha, "dān, dān, dānek, yā hā-l-baṭṭīxa, miṯil dān ^{e}Ḥdaydān . . . dān, dān, dānek, yā hā-l-baṭṭīxa, miṯil dān ^{e}Ḥdaydān." ^{e}Ḥdaydān, ḏāno mitbayynan min-al-baṭṭīxa. ḏāno mbayyne minhe.	87 and said to it, "Ear, ear, your ear, o watermelon, [is] like [that of] Ḥdaydūn. Ear, ear, your ear, o watermelon, [is] like [that of] Ḥdaydūn." Ḥdaydūn, his ears protrude from the watermelon. His ears [are] visible from it.
92 hī mī ʿārfi $_{H}$'oto$_{H}$. hāḏa saḥib ḥāl. daššarha u-ṭalaʿ min al-baṭṭīxa, fāt ʿa l-gaṣer, mā tigdar tewuffo.	92 She did not recognize ($_{H}$'oto$_{H}$) him. This [one, Ḥdaydūn] took off. . . . He left her and got out from the watermelon, entered the castle, [and there] she could not harm him.
95 yōm bī ʿeres. gāḷat-lo, "yāḷḷa, Ḥdaydūn, taʿ-(n)rū (ḥ)-ʿa-l-ʿeres." gāḷ-ḷa, "yaḷḷa 'anti rūḥi, 'ani mā-rūḥ." huwwa rāḥ, wiṣel gaboḷha. kala, u-dibač, u-liʿeb, u-ʿimlem hā-l-fanṭaziyya,	95 One day, there was a wedding. She said to him, "Let us, Ḥdaydūn, let us go to the wedding." He said to her, "Well, you go, I am not going." He went, and arrived before her. He ate and danced and played and they made a fanṭaziyya
100 u-hiyye daḥḥag ʿalēha 'inna tākel maʿ ač-člāb—maʿ mi(n) yezittu la-ʿaḏam, yezittu l-ʿeḏām. daḥḥag ʿalēha winnha tākel, čalbe ʿarğa, ʿāmle ḥālha, u-tākel [maʿ] al-ʿeḏām, maʿ ač-člāb.	100 and she—he looked at her, she was eating with the dogs—with whom they threw bones to, they threw the bones. He looked at her and she was eating [like] a lame dog, pretending, and she was eating [with] the bones, with the dogs.

105 giḏab hāḏa l-ʿaḏem, nigafha hēn, winna dammha yesīl. hāy ṣārat tišrab min dammha. tgūḷ-ḷēhum, "ʾaḷḷa yiṭʿamku, yā ʾahal al-ʿirs, aṭʿamtūni laḥam wa-dibs" u-hī mā šāfato, mā ḏāgato.

105 He took this bone, threw it at her, and lo, her blood [was] flowing. This one started drinking from her [own] blood. She says to them, "Allah may feed you, o family of the wedding, you fed me meat and honey." And she did not [even] see it, did not taste it.

110 hiyya rawwaḥat, u-hū rawwaḥ gabuḷha. gāḷat-lo, "ʾani ruḥet la-l-ʿires, w-enta mā roḥt." gāḷ-ḷēha, "hāy-ʾani roḥt gableč u-ḏarabteč b-il-ʿaḏum, fašaḥteč u-šufteč ʾakalti, čalbe maʿ ač-člāb." čē widdha tiʿmal, tiḏbaḥo tāklo—mi hi ʿārfa.

110 She went back home, and he went back home before her. She said to him, "I went to the wedding and you did not go." He said to her, "I went before you and hit you with the bone, hit you, and saw you were eating, a bitch with the dogs." What can she do, kill him, eat him. She did not know [how to do it].

116 hāḏa yōm, ḥaṭṭat lo dibeg ʿa-la-ḥmār. dibg ʿa-la-ḥmāra, dabbag ʿala ḏhar al-ᵉḥmāra, ričeb al-ⁱḥmāra. ǧa tann-i(y)ḥawwel—mā gidar. ᵉgḏabato. gḏabato,

116 This, one day she put [for] him glue on the donkey. Glue on the she-ass. He was glued to the back of the she-ass. He was riding the she-ass. He wanted to get off—and could not. She caught him. She caught him,

121 gāḷat-lo, "čēf widdak ʾasāwīk? šlōn baʿmal bīk? ʾiḏa widd ʾāklak, mā tišbiʿni." ʿindīha bint. gāḷ-ḷēha, "yā hala, ʾagūl-leč, xuḏīni, u-ḥuṭṭi, hātī-li guṭṭēn, ḥūṭṭī-li wa-ṭaʿmīni guṭṭēn, tanni ʾanṣaḥ, wa-ḏbaḥīni."

121 and said to him, "How will I do with you? How shall I do with you? If I eat you, you will not get me satiated." She had a daughter. He said to her, "I'll tell you—take me and put, give me dried figs, and put for me and feed me dried figs, so that I will get fat and you will kill me."

127 ḏaḷḷat tištari guṭṭēn wa-tḥuṭṭ-lo. yōm gāḷat-lo, "ʾani, ʾinta—widd(i) aḏbaḥak hassa," gāḷ-ḷa, "ʾinti rūḥi, eʿezmi garāybič w-al-bint tiḏbaḥni. ʾanṭīha hiyya sikkīna, u-hī tiḏbaḥni."

127 She continued buying dried figs for him and giving him. One day she said to him, "I—you—I want to butcher you now." He said to her, "You go and invite your relatives and the girl will kill me. Give her a knife. She will kill me."

132 hiyya rāḥat min hēn, gaḏab al-bint, ḏibaḥḥa, u-gaṭṭaḥḥa (=u-gaṭaʿha), ḥaṭṭ ʿalēha b-al-ğider [tiʿeref al-ğider] ʿala hā-n-nār, ṭabax ʿalēha, mā-ša-aḷḷa,[10] ḥaṭṭha, u-gaṭṭaʿha, u-libes ⁱhdūmha. ğam ʿa-l-bint, ʿimel ḥālo l-bint, u-rāḥ. ʾağat hī, lamlamat garāyibha, u-ğat ʿala hā-l-mā-ša-aḷḷa, ḥaṭṭ lēham, u-kalam u-šibʿum, mā-ša-aḷḷa.

132 She went from here, he caught the girl and killed her, and cut her up, put her in the cauldron (you know [what is] the cauldron) on this fire, he cooked her, nicely [lit.: as Allah wants]—he put her and cut her up, and put on her clothes. They came to the girl, he pretended to be the girl, and went. She (the *Ġūla*) came, gathered her relatives, and came to the—whatever [lit.: what Allah wants]—he had put for them, and they ate and were satiated, nicely [lit.: as Allah wants].

141 fāt winno ʿa-l-gaṣor. gāḷ-ḷēha, gāḷ, "hāyni alli ḏibaḥt ⁱbnaytič u-kalētīha." ē, šu-(wid)dha tiʿemal? mā ʿād tigdar tiʿemal bī ʾayyat, fgaʿat—winnha meyyte. u-hāḏa xurrāfti ṭārat ʿalēk.	141 He entered and lo, [he was] in the castle. He said to her, "Here I am, I killed your daughter and you ate her." E . . . what will she do? She could not do with him anything; she burst, and was dead. And this, my story, flew to you.

Commentary

The second group, the Ḥdaydūn story group, belongs to another subtype of "The Children and the Ogre" stories: ATU 327C, "The Devil (Witch) Carries the Hero Home in a Sack." The following is a description of the narrative type according to Uther:[11] A witch (ogre) entices a boy (conceived by magic, Thumbling) into her bag and carries him away (from his home). By deceiving the witch (putting stones, thrones, mud, etc., in his place), the boy is able to escape twice from the bag. The third time, the witch carries him to her home. He is to be killed by the witch's daughter. The boy tricks the daughter (by making her show him how he should prepare to be killed; motif G526, "Ogre deceived by feigned ignorance of hero. Hero must be shown how to get into oven [or the like]. Ogre shows him and permits himself to be burnt"), throws her into a pot (burns her in the oven) and serves her as a meal to her family (motif G61, "Relative's flesh eaten unwittingly"). He taunts the witch, kills her, and returns home (sometimes with the witch's treasure).

I collected five versions of the story in three different tribes, of which I provide here only one: "Grēʿa, Ḥmēda, and Ḥdaydūn," recorded in the ʿArab el-Ṭabbāš tribe. Ḥdaydūn's stories begin in a very similar way to the stories of the girls and the *ġūla*, with one difference: the hero, Ḥdaydūn, is one of a group of abandoned children, who have reached the *ġūla*'s house. He escapes with the girls from there. As in the stories of the girls and the *ġūla*, here too Grēʿa, the bald girl, eats from the *ġūla*'s food, and the *ġūla* devours her. Ḥdaydūn finds a horseshoe or another magical object made of iron that fulfills his wishes. He wishes to have a magical palace "from the earth to the sky" appear before him, and he finds refuge there. The hero's name derives from *ḥadīd*, حديد, "iron" in Arabic.

From now on, we no longer hear about the fate of the girls, and Ḥdaydūn becomes the main hero. He has an ambivalent relationship with the *ġūla*. She invites him to three food-related events: visiting a wedding banquet, picking from fig trees, and gathering watermelons from the field. Ḥdaydūn refuses her suggestions but hastens to the three events before her arrival. At the wedding, he recognizes the *ġūla* in the form of a bitch, sniffing at the edges of the wedding. He throws a bone at her and wounds her. The *ġūla* thinks she obtained good food, and when she returns from the wedding, she mocks Ḥdaydūn for not answering her invitation and not coming to the wedding, but he retorts that what she thought of as rice and honey was nothing but her own blood as he threw a bone at her forehead. In the next scene, he arrives in the fig orchard before her, climbs one of the trees, and throws feces at her instead of figs. The *ġūla* eats the feces, and when she returns to her home, she mocks him for not coming with her to pick figs, but he mocks her in return and replies that she has eaten feces instead of figs. In the third scene, he arrives at the watermelon field before she does, eats watermelon, and then hides in one of the watermelons (which indicates his tiny size, like Tom Thumb in the European versions). The *ġūla* takes the watermelon with her in the edge of her robe, and Ḥdaydūn takes advantage of it to stab her in her back with the tool in his possession. The *ġūla* thinks the sensations come from fleabites and drops the watermelon. The hero jumps out of the watermelon, says the magic words, and comes to his palace safely while mocking the *ġūla*.

Later on in the plot, Ḥdaydūn taunts the *ġūla* by riding her donkey (or her donkey foal) and does not allow it to graze. The *ġūla* smears the donkey's back with glue. Ḥdaydūn cannot get off its back, and she catches him. She puts Ḥdaydūn in a sack and fattens him with food. She asks her daughter to slaughter Ḥdaydūn and cook him, while she herself goes to invite relatives to the party. Ḥdaydūn deceives the *ġūla*'s daughter and persuades her to let him show her how to slaughter. The foolish daughter takes him out of the sack and hands him the knife, and he slaughters her, cooks her flesh, and then wears her clothes and pretends to be the *ġūla*'s daughter. He serves the daughter's flesh to the *ġūla* and her relatives and leaves the place. Then he calls to her from the top of the palace and announces that she has eaten her daughter's meat. The *ġūla* explodes out of anger and frustration and dies.

The Bedouin versions are therefore different from the European versions in the long supplement preceding the inserting of the hero into the sac. Later, the stories contain the main plotlines, as they appear in the description of the narrative type. Instead of the double escape from the sack, there is a section dealing with the provocation by Ḥdaydūn, who rides the *ġūla*'s mare. In addition, we find here the motif G82, "Cannibal fattens victim," which does not belong to this narrative type but is known from the previous narrative type ATU 327A, "Hansel and Gretel."

The story of Ḥdaydūn is one of the most popular stories in the Bedouin cultural space and in Arab culture in general. The five stories I wrote down were recorded in three different tribes. The differences between the various versions are marginal, and the story is told almost identically in different tribes.

The story of Maryam Muṣṭafa Ṭabbāš from the ʿArab el-Ṭabbāš tribe opens with the abandonment of the children who are preoccupied with a game. In another version, they go to bathe in the river, and in the third version, they go to pick hawthorn fruit. The narrator moves the plot to her immediate surroundings, north of Shefarʿam. The *ġūla* presents herself to the children as a relative. In addition to Ḥdaydūn, two girls appear in the plot, Grēʿa the bald and Ḥmēda, meaning "cute" (derived from *aḥmad*, "praised"). Their names indicate ugliness versus beauty and hint at the girls' character. Grēʿa is caught by the *ġūla* and devoured, whereas her friend Ḥmēda makes a magical statement: "O plateau, break up and swallow me." She is swallowed up in the ground and thus is saved. From now on, she no longer appears in the narrative.

A beautiful and special version of the story, which was taken from Naḏmiyya ʿAzzām from Ğish (الجش), appears in Jihad Ahmad Dakkur's book *Galilee Stories*.[12] This version tells about three brothers: Ḥdaydūn, who has a house of iron (from *ḥadīd*, حديد "iron"); Manichlān (منيخلان), who has a house in the form of a sieve (from *munchul* منخل "a flour sieve"); and Qaṣibān (قصيبان), who has a house made of reeds (from *qaṣab* قصب "reed"). A *ġūla* destroys the homes of and devours two of the brothers, but she fails to destroy Ḥdaydūn's iron house. A similar motif is found in Arabic versions of the story

"The Wolf and the Kids," in which the hyena succeeds in devouring two of the kids while the third kid manages to trick him.[13]

In two of the Bedouin versions I recorded, in the fig tree scene, the *ġūla* asks Ḥdaydūn to wipe his buttocks and throw her, which seems unlikely. Perhaps the rhyme was originally in the form that appears in the ʿArab el-ʿArāmša version: "The one who rides the fig tree, let down your basket, and give me" (*yā illi rākib b-al-tīneh, nish saliltak wa-ʿaṭīni*). However, in the versions that appear in the ʿArab el-Ḥuǧērāt tribe, the rhyme has been changed and has another form: "O the one who rides the fig tree, wipe your buttocks and give me!" (*ya illi ʿa-l-tīneh, masseḥ ṭīzak wa-ʿaʼṭīni*). In the version of Naḏmiyya ʿAzzam, Ḥdaydūn spits on the figs and urinates on them before he gives them to the *ġūla*. The *ġūla* thinks the liquids covering the figs are a sweet dew. Later in her version, in the watermelon scene, the hero eats the watermelon interior and urinates into it, and the *ġūla* comes and drinks from it. In an additional scene that does not appear in the Bedouin versions I have recorded, the *ġūla* invites Ḥdaydūn to gather firewood with her. Ḥdaydūn hides himself in the load and pricks the *ġūla* while she carries the load to her house. The *ġūla* catches him and wants to eat him, but Ḥdaydūn tricks her and finally throws her into the oven, and she is burned.

Ḥdaydūn finds a piece of iron "like a wheel." In other versions, it is an iron horseshoe. Bronze horseshoes are known to us from archaeological excavations at the Etruscan tomb in Italy from the fourth century BCE. Written testimonies on the use of horseshoes appear in Roman writings from the first century CE. Magical properties of rejecting demons have been attributed to iron, and in Europe, it is customary to hang an iron horseshoe with seven holes on the door of the house as an object that blesses the house and removes evil spirits from it. Hence, the practice spread throughout the world. In Tibet, meteoric iron was used, and magical properties were attributed to it as a material that had fallen from the sky.

In the Christian legenda, there is a legend about a saint named Dunstan, who was the archbishop of Canterbury in the tenth century. According to the legend, the saint was a blacksmith in his youth. One day the devil came to his smithy and asked him to shoe his hooves. Dunstan, who identified him as the devil, nailed the horseshoes to the feet of Satan himself and caused him great pain. In exchange for removing the horseshoes, he compelled the devil to promise that he would never enter a house with an iron horseshoe on its door. Thus, the saint became a patron of goldsmiths.[14]

Hanauer provides a detailed version of Ḥdaydūn's story.[15] The hero is called Uhdeydûn,[16] which he claims is a nickname for a blacksmith *haddad*.

In Maryam Muṣṭafa's version, the *ġūla* curses Ḥdaydūn and wishes him to drown in a sea that has no way out, but through the medium of his piece of iron, Ḥdaydūn splits the enchanted sea (or stream) and escapes. Later, he lives in a ruined palace and confronts another *ġūla*. In the version recorded in Basmat Ṭabʿūn, the magic object takes the form of the reins of a mare, which, when thrown, lead to the appearance of a palace "from earth to heaven." The hero has control of the magical palace, and it obeys his orders, or as the narrator says, "Wherever you are, when I say to you: 'Stand up!'—stand up; wherever you are, when I tell you: 'Lower down'—lower yourself down. This is what the lips and tongue asked for and, behold, he is in the palace."

In this version, the girls throw stones at the *ġūla*, and one of them hits her forehead and kills her. The girls take the *ġūla*'s horse and flee. Afterward, Ḥdaydūn confronts the *ġūla*, and although this is not explicitly stated, it is possible to understand that another *ġūla* is meant. In Ṯalǧe Mūsa's version, the enchanted object is a ring that is rubbed while uttering the words "Ring, *shubek lubbek*!"[18] which makes a demon appear to fulfill the hero's desire and build him a palace.

In the version from Ibrahīm ʿAli, a member of the tribe of ʿArab el-Ḥuǧērāt, the children arrive at the site of the *ġūla* with the help of a dog. They turn to it with the words "O dog, guide us, on the way to our family," and the dog guides them on their way. Here, too, the magical artifact through which Ḥdaydūn gets to the palace is iron. In this version, the *ġūla* commands her daughter: "Well, Mom [Daughter], slaughter him and put his testicles in the window." Later, when the hero slaughters the *ġūla*'s daughter, he puts her buttocks in the window. In all the other versions I recorded, this matter is only hinted at. It is reasonable to assume that the narrators were ashamed to mention explicitly the removal of the genital organs, when telling the story to a male researcher who is not a member of a tribe. In Ṯalǧe Mūsa's version, the *ġūla* inserts the children into a sack, but they release themselves and fill it with stones. This motif, G441, "Ogre carries victim in bag (basket)," appears in the description of the narrative type in Uther's book.

In this version, there is a significant change: the *ġūla* does not devour Grēʿa, the girl she caught, but adopts her for a daughter. It is not clear from the continuation whether the hero slaughters the adopted daughter of the *ġūla* or her biological daughter. However, adoption of the girl in this case is certainly unusual—precisely because the ugly and gritty daughter is the one adopted by the *ġūla*. It has already been shown, in the story of Frēṭ Rummān, how a *ġūla* adopts the abandoned girl. In the story "The Goat, the Kid, and the Ġūla" (chap. 42), the *ġūla* adopts the kid of her neighbor the goat after it provokes her and rides her donkey. In the present case, however, it appears that the *ġūla* adopts the "evil" and ugly girl to turn her into a *ġūla*. However, even in this case, the *ġūla* appears to represent, in psychological interpretation, an alternate mother willing to adopt the girl as she is, in contrast to the biological mother who restrains and inhibits her daughter's negative behavior. On this matter, see the broader analysis presented in the discussion of "The Goat, the Kid, and the Ġūla" (chap. 42). It should also be noted that in Maryam Muṣṭafa Ṭabbāš's version, one of the heroines is called Ḥmēda, whereas in the fifth version I recorded, that of Warda Hawwāš, this is the name the narrator gives to the *ġūla*'s daughter. This version, however, is rather incomplete and does not include the introduction with the story of the girls. The pattern of the events in the story is distorted, and it is clear that the narrator does not remember the story properly.

To attach Ḥdaydūn to the donkey's back, the *ġūla* uses a glue produced from the resin of the mastic tree (*Pistacia lentiscus*). Today, that resin is used as a raw material for the epoxy adhesive industry. The plant is mentioned in ancient Jewish sources as a sort of spice *mastica*: "It is forbidden to chew *mastici* on Shabbat" (Tosefta, Shabbat 12:8). It is mentioned in the books of Rabbi Assaf Harofeh (sixth century) and by Maimonides. The spice *mastika* was known mainly by Eastern Jewish communities and by the Jews of North Africa. The Jews of Morocco called it *mastaka* and chewed it just like chewing gum. The Jews of Libya used to add it to an almond drink called *rozetta*. As a medicinal plant, it is used mainly to treat gynecological problems, such as to heal a hemorrhage from the uterus, strengthen the uterus during pregnancy, calm contractions during pregnancy, and the like. Today, the *mastica* spice is produced in an area called *Masticuchuria* (the gum villages) in the southwest of the island of Chios in Greece. The *mastica* is used, among other things, to prepare oriental dishes such as Turkish delight and gum ice cream.

The *dibs*, one of the foods served at the wedding according to the *ġūla*, is grape honey (or honey extracted from other fruits), a sweetened dish made from boiled grape juice. The *dibs* was known in the Land of Israel even before the Arab conquest in the seventh century. In Arabic literature of the Middle Ages, the name *dibs* was given to all types of fruit honey but primarily to date honey. Today it refers to grape honey or carob honey. Unlike wine, grape honey is permissible for consumption by Muslims.

In Ḥdaydūn's stories, too, food plays a central role. Beyond the reference to food at the beginning of the story, discussed earlier, the confrontation between the hero and the *ġūla* revolves around food matters, whether it is a wedding meal, a fig tree, or a watermelon. In addition to her cannibalistic qualities, the *ġūla* also runs a household with domestic animals and consumes vegetables and fruits as humans do. When she fattens the hero, she feeds him with figs and meat (candies and apples in a different version).

In contrast to the previous group of stories, which focuses on the girls' escape from the *ġūla*'s house and their return to their parents' house, the stories of Ḥdaydūn present an active hero who repeatedly challenges the *ġūla* and ultimately brings her to her death. This closely matches the structure of the patriarchal Bedouin society, in which the girls are expected to behave passively, for example escaping from the *ġūla*'s house, while the masculine model, shown to boys, is the protagonist who fights demonic forces and defeats them.

The *ġūla*'s request to cut off the hero's testicles is an act of castration. The hero, in turn, replies to her in the same way, and cuts off the buttocks of the *ġūla*'s daughter.

In his teachings, Freud coined the term "castration complex." André Green, one of the most important psychoanalysts in contemporary France, discusses this concept in detail in his book *The Castration Complex* (Le complexe de castration). Among his comments, he says the following:

> The Latin word for sex (sexe), derived from the Latin root *secare*, which means section. The name thus bears the traces of a section that separates the two sexes and sends us to primitive mythic androgynism. But the section, the castration, is also the one that separates the penis from the body. . . . In its narrow sense, castration is the prevention of procreation. . . . What Freud describes as the castration complex is a completely new discovery. It is a mental creation born of the development of infantile sexuality, of the desire it evokes and its implications on the child's imagination. Sometimes it is preceded by a threat expressed by the mother or by one of her substitutes (governesses, nannies) to deter the child and cause him to give up the auto-erotic pleasure. However, even if the source of the menace is women, the execution of the punishment is attributed to men: the father, the doctor, and so on.[17]

Green hints here at the story from Plato's *Symposium*, which states that humans did not come into the world as separate creatures but as an intersex creature: "The primeval man was round, his back and sides forming a circle; and he had four hands and four feet, one head with two faces, looking opposite ways, set on a round neck and precisely alike; also four ears, two privy members."[19]

Zeus decided to cut these creatures in half to weaken them, and thus he formed males and females: "He spoke and cut men in two, like a sorb-apple, which is halved for pickling, or as you might divide an egg with a hair. . . . After the division, the two parts of man, each desiring his other half, came together, and throwing their arms about one another, entwined in mutual embraces, longing to grow into one, they were on the point of dying from hunger and self-neglect, because they did not like to do anything apart."[20]

From the Greek mythology, the story also appeared in Midrashic literature: "Rabbi Yirmiyahu Ben Elazar said, When God created the first man, he created him as Androgynus, as it is written: 'male and female created he them'" (Genesis 1:2); and "Rabbi Shmuel Bar Nachman said: When God created Adam, two faces he created him, and he sawed him and made him two backs—a back here and a back here" (Genesis Rabbah [Vilna] 8:1).

The reference to genitals, the wiping of the buttocks, flatulence, and the like in the Ḥdaydūn stories, as well as the tiny dimensions of the hero, may hint that the story was designated for very young children.

C. Nuṣṣ-ᵉNṣēṣ

NARRATOR: Ṯalǧe Mūsa
TRIBE: *'Arab el-Ḥuǧērāt*
IFA 15231 April 15, 1980

1 bī hināka hā-l-'amīr. hā-l-'amīr fī ʿando niswān ṯintēn. haḏōl an-niswān, mā kānūš yiḥbalu, yaʿani. yōm maraq wāḥad maʿa ṭ-ṭarīq, qāḷ "tuffāḥ l-al-ḥabal." 'aža l-'amīr, šara ḥabbtēn, ṯalaṯ ḥabbat. 'anṭa la-marato, la-waḥad(a) alli-biḥibbha, 'anṭāha ḥabbtēn, haḏīk 'anṭāha noṣṣ—nuṣṣ ḥabbe.	1 There was there this emīr. He had two wives. Those wives did not get pregnant. One day, someone passed by on the street, he called out, "Apples for pregnancy." The emīr came, bought two apples, three. He gave his wife, the one he loved, two apples, and that [other] one [he] gave one—a half, half an apple.
9 yōm ḥiblu haḏōl, ǧābat hāḏīk wlād eṯnēn, u-hāy ǧābat nuṣṣ, nuṣṣ walad, nuṣṣ-ᵉnṣēṣ,[21] yaʿani zġayyar, nuṣṣ-ᵉnṣṣēṣ. haḏōl ṣāru yerūḥu ʿala ṣ-ṣayd w-al-ganaṣ. šū yaʿani aṣ-ṣṣayd w-al-ganaṣ? yerūḥu ʿala l-ġuzlān.	9 When they got pregnant, this one had two children and this one had half, half a child, half of small half (Nuṣṣ [E]nṣēṣ) that is, a small one, half of halves. Those began to go hunting and setting traps. What does hunting and setting traps mean? They went for the deer.

15 kull yōm yerūḥu yeṣayyadu ġuzlān. hinne yerūḥu ma yeğībūš, hū yeğīb. šū, mā ʿindūš yaʿani barūda wa-la ʾiši. hū ʿindo yaʿani xašab, yuḏurbu hēk. ^{i}nqūl-lo iḥna miqḥāf. yuḏurbu yeğīb al-ġazāl u-yīği. y(i)inṭi la-ʾabū šwayye.

15 Every day they went hunting deer. They went and did not get [any], he would bring [hunted deer]. What, he did not have a gun or anything—he had a wooden stick, he would throw it like that—we call it *miqḥāf.* He would throw it, and bring the deer and come [back]. He would give some of it to his father.

21 yeṣīru y(e)qūlū-lhin ʿād, "ṭayyib, lēš nuṣṣ ^{e}nṣāṣ yeğīb ġuzlān u-ʾintam mā tğībūn?" yegūlū-lo, "nuṣṣ enṣāṣ yerū(ḥ) ʿala-maṭraḥ, ʾiḥna mrū(ḥ) ʿala maṭraḥ."

21 They started saying to them, then, "Well, why Nuṣṣ-^{e}Nṣēṣ brings deer and you do not bring?" They would say to them, "Nuṣṣ-^{e}Nṣēṣ goes to [some] place, we go to a [different] place."

25 yōm ittifgam imʿa baʿaḏhum, aṯ-ṯnēn, innin yōxḏum nuṣṣ-^{e}nṣēṣ yiḏbaḥū. gāḷu-ḷo, "taʿāl, yā nuṣṣ-^{e}nṣēṣ, yaḷḷa nrūḥ iḥna w-ʾiyyak ʿala ṣ-ṣēd w-al-ganaṣ beʿīd. šnū yeʿarif al- ġuzlān ihnāk? qwām, gadd-mā bū l-ġuzlān, ssa nrūḥ ʾiḥna w-iyyāk wi-nğīb." gāḷ-ḷhin "yaḷḷa."

25 One day, they agreed between themselves, the two of them, to take Nuṣṣ-^{e}Nṣēṣ to kill him. They said to him, "Come, Nuṣṣ-^{e}Nṣēṣ, let's go we and you to hunt far away, what do the deer know there? [There are] loads, the quantity of deer. We will go with you and bring [deer]." He said to them, "Let us."

32 hū šnū rāčib? rāčib yaʿani miṯel e . . . ḥmār . . . yaʿani miš faras. humma rākbīn xēl. hū rākib ^{a}ḥmār. ṣār mišyu mišyu mišyu ʿa-maṭraḥ beʿīd beʿīd. maṭraḥ beʿīd, gaḷō-ḷo, "widdna nugʿod nerayyaḥ hīn." gaʿadam yrayyaḥūn haḏōl.

32 He—what did he ride? He was riding that is, like . . . a donkey, that is, not a mare. They were riding horses. He was riding a donkey. They began going, going, going, to a very, very far place. A far place. They said to him, "We want to sit and rest here." They sat down to rest.

38 gāḷu-ḷo, "teʿarif, ʾessa widdna b-il-ʾawwal nākol u-baʿadēn ^{i}nrūḥ, hā-l-izgan al-xēl. "dawwarna ʿa-bīr" mi(n)-šān yizgam al-xēl." gāḷ-ḷum, "ṭayyib." alli humma rāyḥīn, ğamma ʿala hā-l . . . ğamma ʿala hā-l-bīr,

38 They said to him, "You know, now we want first to eat, and afterward we will go to let the horses drink. We were looking for a well," to let the horses drink. He said to them, "All right." As they were going, they came to a . . . came to a well.

44 gāḷū-lo, "mīn widdo yinzal yiğīb, e . . . yimalle mayya l-al-xēl?"

44 They said to him, "Who wants to go down and bring . . . er . . . fill water for the horses?"

46 gāḷu-ḷo, "ʾiḥna." "ʾani." haḏāk yigul "ʾana." haḏāk yigūl "ʾana." gāl-lhum nuṣṣ -^{e}nṣēṣ, "la, ʾani." gāḷu-ḷo, "taʿāl m-innak zġayyer, nigdar nhawwdak ʿa-l-bīr u-nṭalʿak b-ʿašer sāʿa." gāḷ-ḷhum, "ṭayyeb." hawwadō, lammin hawwadō, ʾazgu l-xēl u-širbam humma, u-(y)xallūnu f-nuṣṣ al-bīr, u-gaṭʿam al-ḥabel fōgo.

46 They said to him, "We do." "I do." That one said, "Me." That one said, "Me."—Nuṣṣ-^{e}Nṣēṣ said to them, "No, I will." They said to him, "You come, you are smaller, we can lower you to the well and bring you out easily, in a part of an hour." He said to them, "Good." They lowered him. When they lowered him, they let the horses drink and they drank and left him in the middle of the well, and cut the rope above him.

55 wēn ʿāwadna ʿa-l-bīr taḥat. u-hū māši, ḏaḷḷo māši f-al-bīr, yōmēn, ṯalāṯa, yaʿalem ʾaḷḷa, haḏākam rawwaḥu. gālam, "wēn rāḥ al-nuṣṣ-ᵉnṣēṣ? gālum, "mā-ḥna ʿārfīn wēn rāḥ." ṣārat ʾimmo maskīne ʿalē, tibči.

55 Where we return to the well below. He was walking, he remained walking two days, three, Allah knows [how many]. Those went back home. They said, "Where did Nuṣṣ-ᵉNṣēṣ go?" They said, "We do not know, where he went." His poor mother began weeping for him.

61 u-hī mārğe hnāk, gaffāle, yaʿani gaffālt eğmāl, ğammāle, mʿa hā-l-ğmāl. mergam ʿala hā-l-bīr, widdhin yišrabu, willa hā-l-zalame bīh. gāḷ-ḷhum, "ʾaṭilʿūni" gāḷu, "šnū ʾinte, yaʿani, ğins walla . . . ğinn walla ʾins, walla šnū dīnak?"

61 There was a caravan going there, that is, a caravan of camels, camel herders, with those camels. They passed by that well. They wanted to drink. And lo—there was a man in it. He said to them, "Take me out." They said "What are you, a ğinn or a human? Ğinn or a man? Or what is your faith?"

68 gāḷ-ḷhum, "la', ʾana ʾins, ʾaxyar al-ʾins. ʾaṭalʿūni." ʾaṭlaʿō. yōmin ʾaṭlaʿo saḥab ḥālo yiṭlaʿū u-gaʿad. ʾanṭū šwayye, kala, tarayya(ḥ) šwayye, u-gaʿad yaʿani yōmēn ṯalāṯa ʿand(h)in, gāḷ-ḷhin, "widdi ʾarawwa(ḥ) ʿend ʾummei." rawwaḥ

68 He said to them, "No, I am a man, the best of men. Take me out." They took him out. When they took him out, he went and sat down. They gave him a little, he ate, rested a little and sat, that is, two, three days with them. He said to them, "I want to go back home to my mother." He went back home.

74 yōmin rawwa(ḥ) ʿend ʾommo, gāḷu-lo, "ṭayyib, šū (wi)ddna nsāwī bī, widdna nʿāwid niḏbaḥo ʾoxra marra. wēn (wid)dna-rrūḥ, hāḏa ʿāwad ği."

74 When he came home to his mother, they said to him, "Well, what shall we do with him, we want to kill him again. Where shall we go? That one has come back."

78 gāḷū-lo, "ʾtiʿerif," gāḷ-ḷ(h)um "naʿam." gāḷū-ḷo, "(wi)ddak trūḥ, widdna nrūḥ, bū ġūḷa, b-al-maġġāra, b-ağ-ğibal haḏāk, widdak trūḥ (t)ğīb-ilna lḥāfe. tigdar etrūḥ?" gāḷ-ḷhin "ʾağībo."

78 They said to him, "You know." He said to them, "Yes." They said to him, "You will go, we will go; there is a *Ġūla*, in the cave in that mountain. You will go to bring us her blanket. Can you go?" He said to them, "I'll bring it."

83 rāḥ hāḏa ba-n-nahār ʿalēha, liga, fāt ʿa-l-maġġāra, mā ligāš ḥada. ğāb al-ʾubar. al-ʾubar yaʿani [$_{H}$maʾxat$_{H}$.][22] ḥaṭṭ kull al-[$_{H}$mazroʾnim$_{H}$],[23] kullo ġazzo ʾubar, u-ḥaṭṭo.

83 This one went to her in the daytime, he found, he entered the cave and did not find anyone [there]. He brought the needles. Needles, that is ($_{H}$maxat$_{H}$) needle. [He] put [them in] all the ($_{H}$mazronim$_{H}$) [mattresses], all of them, stuck them with needles, and put it [like that].

88 b-al-lēl ğat ᵃtnām hiyya, ṣār kullo yġuzzha hōn u-hōn u-hōn, gāḷat, "ġēr azuṭṭo barra. yimkin bū barāġīṯ."

88 In the night she came to sleep. All of it began pricking her here and here and here. She said, "I will just throw it out. Maybe there are ticks in it."

91 [taʿarif al-baraġīṯ ʾinte? baraġīṯ hāy min [$_{H}$ʾadaʾma$_{H}$], ḥamra hīč, kamān hōn, isāwi hīč.] gāḷat "malyān baraġīṯ, widd(i) ʾadaššro barra." ʿāwad ṯāni b-al-lēl, ğe ʿalēha b-al-lēl, xaḏa l-lḥāf.	91 (Do you know what ticks are? They are from the ($_{H}$ʾadaʾma$_{H}$) ground, red like that, also here, it does like that.) She said, "It is full of ticks, I want to leave it outside." He returned again at night, came to her at night, and took the blanket.
96 gāḷu-ḷo "baʿad widdna," gāḷu-ḷo (=gāḷ-ḷhum) "šū?" gāḷu-ḷo, "widdna ğāğāt—widdna trūḥ ^{i}tğīb-^{i}lna ğāğāt."	96 They said to him, "We still want [more]." They said to him [he said to them], "What?" They said to him, "We want hens, we want you to go and bring for us hens."
99 rāḥ ^{i}b-hā-l-lēl. fāt ʿala ha-l-xumm, sarag aǧ-ǧāǧāt ḍaḷḷ ad-dīk. ad-dīk yeṣīḥ, šnū yegūḷ? yegūḷ "ki-ki-hīk, nuṣṣ-^{e}nṣēṣ b-al-xumm, yiḏbaḥ wi-yilumm." yaʿanu, hū maʿā sikkīne, yiḏbaḥ wi-yiḥuṭṭ b-aš-šwāl." wa-d-dīk yeṣīḥ.	99 He went at night, entered the hen's coop, and stole the hens. There remained the cock. The cock was crying, what did it say? It said, "Ki-ki-hīk, Nuṣṣ-^{e}Nṣēṣ is in the coop, killing and gathering." That is, he has a knife, and he kills them and gathers them in the sack. And the cock was calling out.
105 tgūḷ-ḷo, "lā, wēnak, wēn noṣṣ-^{e}nṣēṣ." ʾaxaḏ aǧ-ǧāǧāt u-rāḥ. wa-xaḏa l-lḥāf, yǧīb lḥāfa u-rāḥ.	105 She said to him, "No, where are you, and where is Nuṣṣ-^{e}Nṣēṣ!" He had taken the hens and gone. And he had taken the blanket. [He] brought her blanket and went [away].
108 ʾā, gāḷu-ḷo, "widdak ^{e}tǧīb alla hī, hiyya b-ḥālha." gāḷ-ḷhum, "ṭayyib. ʾanṭūni ḥmār čebīr hīč, tanna . . . aǧība ʿalē" gāḷu-ḷo, "ṭayyeb."	108 Yes, they said to him, "You will bring her, she herself." He said to them, "Good. Give me a large donkey, like that, so that . . . I will [be able to] bring her on it." They said to him, "Good."
112 ʾanṭā hēk ^{e}ḥmār hēč, ʿāli šwayye, rāḥ ǧāb hā-ṣ-ṣaḥāḥīr, [$_{H}$ʾargazim$_{H}$] al-boksāt, min al- hā-l-gaddi, ṣaḥāḥīr, u-rāḥ ǧāb bīha min kull el-aġrāḍ, miṯil dukkāne. ḥaṭṭa b-ha-l-ṣaḥāḥīr, u-rā(ḥ) ʿalēha.	112 He gave him a donkey like that, a little high, he went and brought those boxes, ($_{H}$ʾargazim$_{H}$) boxes, boxes from the . . . like this [size], boxes, and went brought in it all the things, like a shop. He put them in the boxes and went to her.
117 gāḷat-lo, "šnū mʿāk?" gāḷ-ḷa, "waḷḷa, bayyāʿ." gāḷat-ḷo, "tanni-ašūf šū mʿāk, widd(i) ʾaštari." gāḷ-ḷa, "taʿāli," ṣārat taštari. gāḷ-ḷa, "ʾinti ʾugʿudi b-gaḷb aṣ-ṣaḥḥāra, ʾugʿudi ʾanti b-gaḷb aṣ-ṣaḥḥāra u-dawwri šnū bo." gāḷ-ilha, "ʾugʿudi b-gaḷb aṣ-ṣaḥḥāra."	117 She said to him, "What have you got with you?" He said to her, "By Allah, [I am] a peddler." She said to him, "I want to see what you have, I want to buy." He said to her, "Come." She began to buy. He said to her, "You, sit inside this box; sit you inside the box and look for what is in it." He said to her, "Sit in the box."
124 yōm gaʿadat b-gaḷb aṣ-ṣaḥḥāra, ḥaṭṭa u-hiyya gʿadat etnaggi, sakkar ʿalēha. sakkar ʿalēha u-sāg al-^{e}ḥmār u-miše. gāḷ, "il- hāḏi al-ġūḷa alli šuftūha. šū baʿed?" gāḷū-ḷo, "ṭayyib."	124 When she sat inside the box, he put her and she was sitting sorting [the things], he closed it on her. He closed it on her, and drove the donkey and went [off]. He said to them, "This is the *Ġūla* whom you saw. What next?" They said to him, "Good."

129 baʿad al-ʾamīr, hadōl ʾwlādo, yaʿani. gāḷū-ḷo, "ṭayyib hāḏa sāwa kull ʾiši u-šnū nsāwī bo?" gāḷ-ḷhen ʾabū, "hāḏa xaḷaṣ, hū ʾibniʸ, u-ʾintu uwlādi, w-ʾana, xaḷaṣ, hāḏa hū, xaḷḷaṣna."	129 Afterward the emīr, these were his children, that is. They said to him, "All right, this one did everything and what shall we do with him?" His [their] father said to them, "That is it. He is my son, and you are my children, and I—enough, that is it. We have finished."

Commentary

The third group, the Nuṣṣ-Nṣēṣ stories, belongs to a narrative type close to "The Children and the Ogre" group: ATU 328, "The Boy Steals the Ogre's Treasure."[24] Here is a description of the narrative type according to Uther.

An introduction only appears in some versions: three (twelve, thirteen, thirty, etc.) brothers arrive at the house of an ogre (devil). He would kill them in the night, but the smart youngest brother saves them by exchanging their caps with those of the ogre's daughters. The brothers take service at the king's court.

The jealous brothers claim that the youngest can steal the ogre's treasures: magic horse, bedspread, carpet, parrot (lamp, sword, silver or golden poultry, musical instruments, etc.). Using tricks, the youth gets these objects. At last, the brothers claim that the youngest can kidnap the ogre himself. In disguise, the youth tells the ogre that the thief died and persuades him to lie down in the coffin to measure it. The youth nails up the coffin, traps the ogre, and is given a princess as his wife.

In some variants, the youth sets out to steal from the ogre to take revenge for former ill-treatment or to help a friendly king. In some variants, mainly from northern and northwestern Europe and the Americas, the protagonist is female.

In the three Bedouin versions I have recorded, the opening differs from the description of the narrative type. In the version of Ṯalǧe Mūsa from the ʿArab el-Ḥuǧērāt tribe, an emīr buys pregnancy apples for his two wives (motif T511.1.1, "Conception from eating apple"). He gives two apples to his beloved wife and half an apple to his second wife. The first woman gives birth to two sons, while the other wife gives birth to a "half child," meaning a tiny child who receives the name Nuṣṣ-Nṣēṣ (Half-Tiny Half).

In the version that I recorded in the ʿArab el-Saʿadiyya, it is the woman who buys the pregnancy apple. In her absence, her husband eats half of the apple. The woman eats the other half and brings into the world a tiny child. The woman's husband has two brothers. Each of her sisters-in-law also gives birth to a child.

In the version by Ṯarwa Yāsīn from the ʿArab el-Ḥaǧāǧra tribe, the sheikh is married to two women, one of whom has seven sons and the other of whom has one. The second woman's son is called *Šāṭer* (Clever) Muḥammad, but he calls himself Nuṣṣ-Nṣēṣ. In this version, no pregnancy apples are mentioned, but from the continuation of the story, it is clear that he is also a tiny hero.

Nuṣṣ-Nṣēṣ goes out with his brother (or cousins) to hunt or rob. The brothers are riding horses while Nuṣṣ-Nṣēṣ is riding a donkey or a kid. Nuṣṣ-Nṣēṣ excels in hunting and brings in plentiful game, while his brothers return empty-handed, despite the fact that they are armed with guns, while Nuṣṣ-Nṣēṣ's weapon, according to one of the versions, is a *makhaf* (an agricultural tool—sort of a stick used for threshing the grain).

Nuṣṣ-Nṣēṣ awakens the envy of his brothers (or cousins). According to Ṯalğe Mūsa's version, they plot to kill him. They invite him to hunt with them, and they reach a well. Nuṣṣ-Nṣēṣ volunteers to go down, tied to the rope, into the well. His brothers take advantage of his state and cut the rope halfway down. Nuṣṣ-Nṣēṣ falls into the well and remains there until a caravan of camels arrives, and the caravan people pull him out. His brothers return home without him and claim that they know nothing of his fate.

This passage of the story, of course, awakes the association with the story of Joseph (*Yūsuf* in Arabic), to which the Qur'ān devotes a whole chapter—the twelfth *sūrah*. The Qur'ān says that Joseph's brothers plan to murder him, but at the suggestion of one of them, they decide to throw him into a pit instead, as they assume that a passing caravan will remove him from the pit and take him. Jacob does not want Joseph to accompany them, but they answer him: "O our father! Why do you not trust us with Yusuf, when we are indeed his well-wishers?" (Qur'ān, 12:11).

When they are in the field, they carry out their plot and throw Joseph into the pit, and a caravan indeed arrives; the person in charge of drawing water discovers Joseph in the pit and gets him out.

The episode of cutting the rope when the hero goes down the well is repeated in many folktales. An Arab proverb summarizes this issue of treachery and deception: "Brought him to the middle of the well and cut the rope" (*axadū la-noṣṣ il-bīr wa-qaṭaʻa fi-l-ḥabel*).

Further on in the story, the brothers, by sending him on various missions, try to bring about Nuṣṣ-Nṣēṣ's death. They tell him initially to bring the *ġūla*'s bedding, then her chickens, and finally the *ġūla* herself. Nuṣṣ-Nṣēṣ successfully performs all tasks. At the end of the story, the father intervenes and prevents his sons from continuing to challenge him: "Enough, he is my son, and you are my sons, and from now on—we are done!" We are not told what happens to the *ġūla*.

In the story from the ʿArab el-Saʿadiyya tribe, the scene of the throwing into the pit does not appear, but the envy of the brothers is expressed later on. When the hero proposes to capture the *ġūla*, the brothers accuse him of a false boast: "Go! All the lies you lied, and you are still lying!" In this version, Nuṣṣ-Nṣēṣ leads the group of boys from the beginning, and the initiative to steal the *ġūla*'s property is his own. It seems from the course of the story that he bets with his cousins on which one of them is the bravest, and he wins the bet. Later on, Nuṣṣ-Nṣēṣ's mother also boasts to her sisters-in-law: "My son, half a child, is a hero more than your children!"

The narrator also emphasizes that the robbery of the *ġūla*'s properties is not a robbery for its own sake, because the *ġūla* stole the items from people: "She stole them from the people, ate people and took the best of the houses, takes it and puts it in her own house—a *ġūla*!" As we have seen in the description of the international type, there is an attempt to rationalize the robberies of the hero by the harm that the ogre inflicted on him in the past.

In Ṯarwa Yāsīn's version, the brothers' jealousy is not emphasized. On the contrary, when the protagonist urges his brothers to escape while he himself remains in the *ġūla*'s house to confront her, they respond: "How can we leave you, and you are under our protection? How can we leave you?" In this case, the mutual responsibility between the brothers stands out. Nevertheless, here, too, the superiority of the younger, small-sized brother is emphasized again. He is the one who protects his brothers from the *ġūla*, guards them at night from her intrigues, and remains behind to fight her during their escape. This part parallels the opening scene, as it appears in the description of the international narrative type mentioned earlier. When the brothers try to escape, they realize that the *ġūla* has devoured the legs of two of the horses, leaving each horse with only one leg. This description echoes the scene of the eating of the mare legs by the cannibal sister in the story of Saṭūra, discussed in chapter 31, "The Sickle Hand." Later in the story appear motifs from Ḥdaydūn's tales. The *ġūla* captures the hero and wants to devour him. He convinces her that she must fatten him first. At a certain point, the hero steals the *ġūla*'s bedding and goes away. The *ġūla* chases him and reaches the tribe, but the hero takes advantage of her stupidity and causes her death. In a comparison of the three versions cited above, it is clear that in all of them, two aspects are emphasized in one way or another: (1) the father's bias toward his wives, and (2) competition and jealousy between brothers (or cousins).

The father's bias toward his wives is explicitly stated in Ṯalǧe Mūsa's version: "He gave the woman whom he loved two apples, and to the other he gave half an apple." In Ṯarwa Yāsīn's version, this is only hinted at. One of the women has seven sons, while the other has only one child, which elevates the honor of the first woman in her husband's eyes, since in Bedouin society a woman is measured by her ability to bear children. The second wife's son does not receive a horse but rather rides a kid. In the story from the ʿArab el-Saʿadiyya, we are told, not about two wives of the same husband, but of a woman and her two sisters-in-law. But there is a hidden competition between them, which is expressed in the words of the hero's mother: "My son, one half, is a hero more than your children!"

As for competition and jealousy between brothers or cousins, in Ṯalǧe Mūsa's story, the conflict almost ends in murder. In the story from the ʿArab el-Saʿadiyya, the cousins accuse the hero of a false boast. In Ṯarwa Yāsīn's story, the brothers fail in their hunt and plead with the protagonist, who has successfully hunted a lot of game, to share it with them.

The stories thus reflect Joseph's story: preference and envy in the parents' generation finds their expression in that of the children, as well. The stories express both the struggle of the rejected woman for her place and status in the family and the younger brother's struggle for his place among his contemporaries. Like many of the children's stories, these stories encourage the younger brother in the family to stand up to his brothers, hold his own, and make his way in the world, but at the same time, the stories contain a hidden criticism of parents who discriminate against one of their children.

In the IFA archives, there are two versions recorded from Muslim narrators in the north of Israel.[25] "The Young Woman and the Demon," told by Ǧamīla Tīti of the village of Biʿena (a Christian village between Dēr al-Asad and Maǧd al-Krūm), is particularly interesting. The hero is not a tiny hero but rather a heroine. The beginning of the story is reminiscent of the story of the three girls and the *ġūla*: A stepmother demands that her husband expel his daughters from his first wife. He leaves them in a distant place. The girls buy chickens in the village. The young girl's hen casts diamond eggs every day. Her sisters envy her, and they throw the hen into the pit where a *ġūl* lives. The younger daughter descends into the pit with a rope, but her sisters cut the rope, and she stays at the *ġūl*'s house. Hiding in the *ġūl*'s house, in his absence, she cleans the house. The *ġūl* discovers this and realizes that someone has lodged in his house. "If you're small, you'll be like my daughter, and if you're big, you'll be like my sister," he says. The *ġūl* adopts her as a daughter and takes care of her. Seven pigeons visit her and warn her that the *ġūl* intends to eat her. The emīr's son follows the pigeons and discovers the girl in the *ġūl*'s house. He marries her with the *ġūl*'s consent.

The continuation of the story contains motifs from "Frēṭ Rummān" (Snow White) and all the subtypes of "The Children and the Ogre." Here, too, the story opens with the jealousy of a stepmother toward her husband's daughters and continues in the second generation with envy among the girls.

The other Muslim version (IFA 24262), as told by Ẓarīfa Ḥamsa from Kafr Kanna, opens with three sisters-in-law, only two of whom have children. The barren sister-in-law buys a pregnancy apple, but her husband eats half of it. She gives birth to a tiny child, Nuṣṣ-Nṣēṣ, or as she says, "She gave birth to half a child: he has one eye, one leg, one hand, so they called him half a child," meaning that the narrator thinks of him not as a tiny or small child but as a child with half his limbs missing. The boy goes hunting with his cousins. His cousins are wealthy, and each of them has a horse, while Nuṣṣ-Nṣēṣ, coming from a poor family, rides a kid. The cousins have rifles, but the hero has only a *muqlaʿa* (slingshot).[26] With his slingshot, he manages to hunt deer, but his cousins plunder his game, hand it over to their mothers for cooking, and throw the remains near the hero's house. Nuṣṣ-Nṣēṣ complains to his family that his cousins are beating him and plundering his game, but no one believes him. His father follows the boys and finds out that his cousins are beating him. The son and the father eat the game meat and throw the remains in front of the cousins' homes.

This arouses the cousins' jealousy, and they throw the hero into a deep well and inform his father that he is dead. Nuṣṣ-Nṣēṣ manages to get out of the well and tells his father what has happened. At this stage of the story, a *ġūla* appears in the village, pretending to be a relative of the hero's father. Nuṣṣ-Nṣēṣ is sent with his cousins to bring her food. The *ġūla* welcomes them and prepares them *maftūl* (crushed oats or similar grain that has had its husks removed, with flour and chicken meat). She invites them to stay at her house so she can devour them. Nuṣṣ-Nṣēṣ refuses to go to bed and asks the *ġūla* repeatedly to prepare food for him until dawn comes. All three flee. Nuṣṣ-Nṣēṣ then goes on to rob the *ġūla*'s chickens, and he finally manages to catch the *ġūla* herself and burn her.

This version is identical in most of its items to the Bedouin versions I have collected. Here, too, the envy characterizing the mothers' generation reaches the generation of the sons. The small-sized young son is eventually recognized and honored.

In the IFA archives, there are also four Druze versions of the story.[27] In the version of ʿAfāf Šxīdam from the Druze village ʿIsfiya from ʿAfāf Šxīdam (IFA 24000), there are seven brothers. The youngest of them is Nuṣṣ-Nṣēṣ, who rides a rooster. The older brothers despise the young brother for his tiny body. They enter a *ġūla*'s house. The hero guards his brothers and prevents the *ġūla* from devouring them. They run away, and the *ġūla* chases them. They try to cross the sea. The *ġūla* lays nails in the sea floor, delaying the horses. Nuṣṣ-Nṣēṣ rescues his six brothers and himself on the back of his rooster. Nuṣṣ-Nṣēṣ disguises himself as a candy peddler, and he manages to put the *ġūla* in a box and burn it.

The version of Aštiāq Naṣr-el-dīn from Dāliyat El Karmel (IFA 24003) is mostly identical to the previous version, but it is more detailed. It begins with a man who bought his wives three pregnancy apples but ate half an apple so that only half is left for his third wife. Here, too, the hero rescues his brothers from the *ġūla*, steals her property, imprisons her in a closed cart, and burns her. In another version from the same village, recorded from Hadiyya Ḥaddād (IFA 24004), motifs from the narrative type "Hansel and Gretel" appear. A poor father decides to abandon his seven children in the forest. The younger brother, Nuṣṣ-Nṣēṣ, marks the road with pebbles and is able to return home in the moonlight. The next time, he marks the road with crumbs of pita bread, but the birds eat them. The children arrive at the house of a *ġūl* and his wife. The *ġūl*'s wife hides them from her husband, and they escape in the morning. The *ġūl* follows them with magical shoes ("leap-forward boots"), but eventually he falls asleep, and the brothers take off his shoes and use them to return home.

Notes

1. The narrator's real-life communication features include theatrical performance with modulated voice between loud and tense and low and secretive; melodic intonation going up and down; volatile speech rate, from slow to very fast and incomprehensible. Her pronunciation is not always clear. She omits words, hesitates, and utters syllables as fillers. In this story there are some interactions with listeners by addresses to them, laughing with them, getting advice about the story line, and other methods. These features make it difficult to transmit her story in coherent and faithful English translation. Because of these features, the translation includes bracketed elucidations or three dots indicating omitted words. We note this here because these features seem to be overflowing in this tale.

2. The word *'ād* is a frequently occurring discourse particle with several meanings. Its original meaning is the verb "to return, come back." It has fossilized and grammaticalized and is used here to mean "again" or "then" in various contexts.

3. Demonstrative pronoun forms abound in Arabic. See Fischer, *Die demonstrative Bildungen der neuarabischen Dialekte*; Vicente, "Demonstratives." Notes on their various short or longer forms in the Galilee Bedouin dialects appear in chapters 6, 8, 12, 15, 21, 23, 39, and 41. In this story we find the form *hadīča*, "that f.sg.," repeated several times. Note that the narrator uses this form also when referring to the *ġūla*, instead of the noun *ġūla* itself.

4. The root of the verb *siḥḥer rāsa*, "her head was dizzy," is found in Barthélemy as *šḥr*. Barthélemy, *Dictionnaire arabe-français*, 336–80. This word may also be read as the passive of *saḥḥar*, "to bewitch, cast a spell on." As noted in chapter 31, note 2, *s/š* may be exchanged between Arabic dialects.

5. *u-reytin yilgan māl*: "I wish they will find money." *reytin* literally means "I saw them [the girls]," implying her wish to see them get something, because that would delay their fleeing and help her in catching up with them. Past tense verbs often occur in LA/MSA and Arabic dialects for wishes, which are considered as if they have already come true (cf. Wright,

Grammar of the Arabic Language, 2:2). The suffix *-in* refers to 3f.pl. “them.” Another wish form is *yā rēyt*/*yā-rēt* with an optional suffix (cf. Barthélemy, *Dictionnaire arabe-français*, 303; in LA/MSA: *layta*). *yā rēt* is more frequent than *u-reytin*. See also in this story the jussive form *yilgan* (+ the prayer *yā ṛaḅḅ*^{w}*i*) for wishes.

6. Uther, *Types of International Folktales*, 212.

7. Bettelheim, *Uses of Enchantment*.

8. The two girls’ names, Grēʿa and Ḥmēda, have the diminutive forms of the nouns *gar'a* (< “a thump, knock”; also “squash, marrow”) and *ḥamda* (< “a praising”). The boy’s name, Ḥdaydūn, has another diminutive pattern that derives from the form *ḥadd*, “sharp, clever,” and *ḥadīd*, “iron.” The ending *-ūn* is apparently a residue of Western Aramaic substrate influence on dialects of the Levant region at large. Neishtadt, “Lexical Component,” 293. These children’s names qualify and reflect their characteristics.

9. *baḥar ḥāyif lāyiṭ, mā bī yigūm ġār illi yfūt*: “[May] Allah try [test, torment] you, o Ḥdaydūn, [in] a stormy, noisy [reaching and killing] sea, of which no one will get out except he who enters it [i.e., only the one who enters it can survive].” The *Ġūla*’s curse is said in a nearly poetic rhythm. *ḥāyif*, *lāyiṭ*, and *yizgul* are found in Al-Barghuthi’s *Dictionary of Colloquial Palestinian Arabic Dialects* but not in Galilee sedentary dialects.

10. *mā-ša-(a)ḷḷa*: literally, “what Allah wanted”—in other words, by Allah’s decree. In colloquial speech, it is a positive discourse marker meaning “whatever, however,” derived from an admiring interjection.

11. Uther, *Types of International Folktales*, 214.

12. Dakkur, *Galilee Stories*, 617–19.

13. Bushnaq, *Arab Folktales*, 233–34.

14. In an earlier version of the legend, the saint holds the devil’s nose with white-hot pincers. The story is common in English folklore and has even been given poetic form in a pair of rhymes:

“St. Dunstan, as the story goes,
Once pull’d the devil by the nose
With red-hot tongs, which made him roar,
That he was heard three miles or more.”

See Hone, *The Every-Day Book*, vol. 1, 671.

15. Hanauer, *Folk-lore of the Holy Land*, 217–21.

16. Uhdey-dûn is Ḥdaydūn according to the modern transcription of the name in this volume. Hanauer probably did not hear the name properly and did not know how to transcribe it correctly. The name derives from the root /ḥdd/, “iron.” In this name, it is the diminutive form of /ḥadīd/, “iron,” plus an ending /*-ūn*/, apparently a (neo-)Aramaic suffix, which occurs in various words in Galilee dialects.

17. Green, *Le complexe de castration*, 9.

18. The phrase appears in the *Arabian Nights*. Burton, *Arabian Nights*, vol. 6, night 618. Burton does not bring the original words in Arabic, but its literal meaning is “Ask and it shall be given to thee.”

19. Plato, *The Dialogues of Plato, vol 1* (*Symposium*), 559.

20. Plato, 560–561.

21. The narrator explains why the boy is named Nuṣṣ-^{e}Nṣēṣ: because his mother had eaten only half a “pregnancy apple,” he was born very small, the size of half a child. Or, rather a “quarter child”: *nuṣṣ* is “half,” and ^{e}*nṣēṣ* is “small half,” that is, in the diminutive. In LA/MSA, “half” is *niṣf*/*nuṣf* and its plural is *ʾanṣāf*. But in the dialects /*f*/ is assimilated to the

preceding /*ṣ*/. (The long vowel of ^{e}*nṣēṣ* could also have been derived from the plural *'anṣāf,* "halves," with *f* > *ṣ* + *'imāla* of *ā* > *ē*, on which see chap. 18, note 2; chap. 29, note 6.)

22. *al-'ubar ya'ani maxát. ḥaṭṭ kull al-mazronim*: "The needles, that is needle [$_H$*maxát*$_H$] [He] put [them in] all the mattresses [$_H$mazronim$_H$]." The narrator uses Hebrew words to explain what she means to the listener, but uses the singular form in Hebrew instead of the plural that should be according to the Arabic word. Note that she places the accent on the second syllable of *maxát*, though in Modern Hebrew the first syllable is accented, i.e., *máxat.*

23. *mizraním*, "mattresses," is here pronounced as *mazroním*, with *a* instead of *i* and o instead of *a*.

24. Uther, *Types of International Folktales*, 216.

25. IFA 23633, 24262.

26. The slingshot is a very ancient weapon. Slingshots were found in the tomb of Tutankhamun from 1325 BCE. Bedouin shepherds use this tool to this day. The slingshot is made of a long woven yarn (70–100 cm) expanded in its central part. The shooter places a stone in the middle of the strip, folds it in half, and turns the slug several times in the air. It is mainly used to prod and direct the herd.

27. IFA 24000, 24003, 24004, 24230.

35. The Emīr's Daughter Who Flew to Switzerland

NARRATOR: Zehiyya Ġrifāt

TRIBE: *ʿArab el-Ġrifāt*

IFA 17410 September 11, 1982

1 kān zalama ʿandu ṯalaṯ awlād. hā-ṯ-ṯal(a)ṯ-awlād yitʿallamu ba-l-madrasa. yaʿani xaḷḷaṣat maʿahum, rāḥu ʿa-l-ǧāmʿa. lamma rāḥu ʿa-ǧ-ǧāmʿa ḥaṭṭam ab-balad, miṯel-mā tgūḷ, tal-ʾabīb. lamma rāḥu ʿa-l-balad, ṣāru yitʿallamu. fīha ʾamīr.	1 There was a man who had three sons (children). The three children were studying at school. That is, they finished school and went to the university. When they went to the university, they moved to a town, as you would say, Tel Aviv. When they went to the town, they began studying. In it there was an emīr.
8 al-ʾamīr ʿando bint mamnūʿ wāḥad ḏiker yešūfha. wa-ʿalēha ḥaras. lamman tiṭlaʿ al-bint barra, mamnūʿ yibarraḥ ḥad b-al-madīna. kullha tfūt ǧawwa u-tisakkar ʿalēha.	8 The emīr had a daughter, and no one, male, was allowed to see her. And she had guards [guarding her]. When she was going out, it was not allowed for anyone in the town to leave it [home]. Everyone would go inside [their homes] and close themselves in them.
13 yōm haḏōla mā yiʿlamūš mā bī. homma. hassa humma ṯalaṯ ixwān b-al-bēt, dār ʾōḍa wāḥda istakrūha, kull lēle rāḥ ḥad yewaddī-lham ʾakel min al-mdīna. lamman hāḏa rāḥ ʿa-l-mdīna yōm. ʾaǧa ʿa-l-kbīr bī ad-dōr.	13 One day—these did not know what there was. They, now, the three brothers in the house, [it was] a one-room apartment that they had rented. Every night one [of them] would go to bring them food from the town. When this one went to town one day, it was the turn of the elder one.

20 yitʿallamum. lamman at-tnēn az-zġār ḏallu b-al-bēt wa-l-walad al-kbīr rāḥ ʿa-l-mdīna, yitʿallamum. hū ṣāyiḥ, an-nāṭūr, mamnūʿ at-taǧawwul uhum qāʿdīn b-al-bēt. lamman ṭalaʿ al-walad, šāf bint al-malak. ṭālʿa hī wa-l-banāt ṣaffa, ʾarbaʿ wa-ʿašrīn bint maʿāha wa-l-ḥaras min barritha.

20 They were studying. When the two younger ones remained at home and the oldest went to town, they were studying. The guard was announcing curfew while they were sitting at home. When the boy went out, he saw the king's daughter. She was going out with the girls in a line, twenty-four girls with her and the guards around her [them].

29 lammin šāf, hū, bint al-malak šāfato. bint al-malak widdha l-walad w-al-walad ṣār widdo bint al-malak. lammin šāfha rawwaḥ.

29 When he saw the girl, the king's daughter saw him. The kings' daughter wanted the boy and the boy wanted [became amorous with] the king's daughter. When he saw her, he went home.

33 gāḷ-ḷa . . . ʾaxaḏ al-ʾakla u- rawwaḥ. gāḷ-ḷo, "kīf atmannā-lak inte, ya-(a)xūy?" al-zġīr l-axū at-tāni. gāḷ -ḷo, "ʾatmannā-lak tṣīr taktōr."

33 He said to her. . . . He took the food and went home. He said to him, "What shall I wish for you, o brother?" The young one to the second [brother]. He said to him, "I wish for you to become a doctor."

38 gāḷ -ḷo, "ʾinta, šū titmanā-li?" gāḷ-ḷo, "tṣīr moḥāmi." ǧa al-walad al-kbīr alli nizel ʿa-l-balad gāḷ-ḷom, "šū titmannū-li ʾantom?" gāḷ-ḷo, "tmannū-li ʾinni ʾāxaḏ bint al-malak."

38 He said to him, "You, what do you wish for me?" He said to him, "That you'll become a lawyer." The eldest boy who went to town came, said to them, "What do you wish for me, you [two]?" He said to him [them], "Wish for me that I'll marry the king's daughter."

44 Hōna, fī ʿa-l-bāb ḥaras; wāḥad—lāzim. kull wāḥad ġarīb ḥaṭṭū-lo ḥaras. simʿum. ḏirbum li-l-malak. b-al-[$_{H}$maxšír$_{H}$][1] aža l-malak fi-l-ʿaskar ṭawwagū oxra min wara. ʾaxḏum at-talāta.

44 Now, there was guard, one. Must [be—it was obligatory]. Every foreigner, they assigned guards to him. They heard [it]. They called the king—with the (HmaxšírH) [tool, phone]. The king came with the soldiers, surrounded them from the back. They took the three.

50 lamman axḏum at-talāta, ṭilʿat bint al-malak. gāḷat bint al-malak, al-walad widda iyyā. ḥaṭṭūhum ba-ṭ-ṭayyāra waddūhum ʿa-swēsra

50 When they took the three [brothers], the king's daughter came out. The king's daughter said, the boy—she wanted him. They put them in an airplane and sent them to Switzerland.

54 lamman waddūhum ʿa-swēsra. aže b-as-sāʿa ṭnaʿaš ba-l-lēl. bint al-malak liḥgathen ʿa-l-maṭār. rikbat u-rikbat maʿāhom. wala widha abūha wala axūha wala ḥada—hāḏa widha al-walad. rākbīn at-talāta aṭ-ṭayyāra u-bint al-malak ar-rābʿa.

54 When they took them to Switzerland, it came [to be] twelve at night. The king's daughter followed them to the airport. She traveled—and traveled with them. She wanted neither her father nor her brother nor anyone—she wanted the boy. The three [of them] traveled in the airplane and the king's daughter [was] the fourth one.

61 ḥaṭṭūhum b-al-maṭār hināka, be-ṭayyārt en-naham, mā fiš hunāka byūt.	61 They put them [down] in the airport there, in the airplane of hunger—There, there are no houses.
64 ğāʿam hāḏōla, widdom yāklom. rāḥ al-ʿarīs wa-ʾaxū al-waṣṭāni rāḥam yeğību min swēsra ʾakel, mn-il-balad.	64 They were hungry—they wanted to eat. The bridegroom and his middle brother went—they went to bring food from Switzerland, food from the town.
68 lamman waṣalam hināka, mamnūʿ at-tağawwul ba-l-lēl, fatḥam b-as-sūg bal-lēl—fiš ḥada. lamman fiš ḥada—xalaʿu al-bāb min al-maxzan u-ṭaqqu ʾakel minnu u-riğʿam.	68 When they got there, [there was] curfew for the night. They opened [and went into] the market in the night—there was no body. As there was no one, they broke open the door of the storehouse, and took food from it and went back.
74 (lam)ma riğʿam al-ḥaras, gawwaṣu ʿala-ṯ-ṯnēn, mātu aṯ-ṯnēn ʿa-l-maḥall. šu ḏaḷḷat hi? ḏaḷḷat hī wa-l-ʾax az-zġīr, ʾazġar wāḥad bīham.	74 When the guards returned, they shot at the two. The two died on the spot. How did she remain? She remained and the young brother, the youngest of them.
79 ʾaṣ-ṣubḥ—nuṣbiḥ ʾani (wi)yyāk ^{a}b-xēr—marr nāṭūr yinādi, "mīn fāged azlām ^{a}ṯnēn b-(h)a-l-balad, hāḏinna inketlu, māto, katalaham al-ḥaras, u-ba-s-sāʿa ṭnaʿaš ^{i}mmawāthen.	79 In the morning—let us hope you and I [we] get up well in the morning—the guard passed by calling out, "Who has lost two people in the town? They were killed, they died, the guard killed them, and at twelve o'clock they died."
85 hāḏa ʿiref axwato ṭalʿam min al-balad, wardīn henna, henna rāiḥīn min as-swēsra ʿa-l-balad. lamma rāḥ ^{a}ʿalēn, ʿaraf al-^{i}wlād u-riğ^{ʿa}. gāḷ-ḷa, "šu widdna iḥna?" gāḷat-ḷo, "wala ʾiše."	85 This [boy] knew that his brothers went out from town, and they went [down] here, here from Switzerland to town. When he went to them, he recognized the boys and returned. He said to her, "What do we want [to do now]?" She said to him, "Nothing."
91 winna gāḷam "wēn widna nrūḥ?" gāḷam idawwru ʿa-bēt bi-swīsra. lā ʾakel wa-la šarb.	91 And then they said, "Where shall we go?" They said [decided] they would look for a house in Switzerland. [They had] no food and nothing to drink.
94 ṭayyib, hōn ṣār an-naṭūr ynādi, "mīn yefūt ʿa-ha-l-bēt, aṭ-ṭāleʿ minno rabḥān w-al-fāit ʿalē ḥasrān. mīn yefūt yugʿod b-ha-l-bēt . . . alli fāyit ʿale ḥasrān, aṭ-ṭāleʿ minno rabḥān." gāḷat "waḷḷa, nfūt ʿalē hā-l-marra." fātam ʿalē.	94 Well, here the guard began calling out, "Who will enter this house, the one who comes out of it is a winner, and the one who enters it is a loser. Who [is the one who] sits in this house . . . whoever comes into it is a loser, the one who goes out is a winner." She said, "By Allah, we'll take it [enter to live in it] this time." They entered it.
101 ğārthom teṭallʿa ʿalē, tgūl-lēha, "yā-xti, la tfūtu ʿa-hā-l-bēt, hāḏa l-bēt yā mā mawwat ʿēlāt. miš mumkin ʿēle fātat ʿalē ṭilʿat sālma.	101 Their [female] neighbor looked at him, and said to her, "O my sister, do not go into this house. This house—how many families it has already killed. It is not possible that a family that entered it came out of it intact [alive].

105 kullam yemūtam. yā-xti, lā titgallabi as-sabḥān ʿalēki." gāḷat-la, "'ani mittakla ʿala 'aḷḷa. ġēr aḷḷa mā-ni mittākla ʿala ḥad."	105 "All of them die. O my sister, do not turn the Lord against you." She said to her, "I am depending on Allah. Except him I am not depending on anyone."
109 hāḏ-al-bint titḥayyek, ʿa-ṣ-ṣinnāra. mallat al- ağ-ğarra mayya u-ḏaḷḷat ʾtḥayyek a-ṣ- ṣinnāra. al-bint kīna tkāseb, 'abṣar šnū maʿāha. mallat ağ-ğarra mayya u-gaʿdat hināka, gaʿadat ʿa-s-sāʿa ṭnaʿaš ba-l-lēl.	109 This girl was knitting with one needle. She filled the jug with water and continued knitting with the needle. The girl was maybe waiting to gain [something], who knows what was with her [what she was thinking about]. She filled the jug with water and was sitting there, sitting there until twelve at night.
116 ʿa-s-sāʿa ṭnaʿaš ba-l-lēl, walla ğāye ḥayya, afʿa min al-'afāʿ(i). ā ğaʿdat tlugg lugg lugg b-hā-ğ-ğarra ta širbat al-mayya b-al-ğarra kollayātha. hāḏa lamma šāfatha, ḥaṭṭat ha-s-samm kulla ba-ğ-ğarra. [hāḏa samm al-ḥayya alli yiktil bani 'ādam. alli yišrabum min al-ğarra u-hī mi yiḥsabūha yišrab uhū mayyit.]	116 At midnight, lo, there came a snake, a great snake of snakes, it started licking lick-lick-lick from this jug until it drank all the water in the jug. This, when she saw it, it put the venom, all of it, in the jug. (This venom of the snake is what kills people. Those who drink from the jug and it is not what they think [it is], he drinks and he is dead.)
125 ʿala yōmēn ṯalāṯa 'anna mā tišrab min al-ğarra. al-bint ḏakiyya ṭalʿat innha. lamminna l-mara šāfat al-ḥayya gāḷat, "hāḏ alli tmawwit al-bani 'ādamīn. kīf niʿemal bīha?"	125 For the two or three days that she does not drink from the jug, the girl turned out [to be] clever. When the woman saw the snake she said, "This is what kills the people. How shall we do [deal] with it?"
130 gʿadato tanna ʿādat al-ḥayya assa gʿadat al-zalama. gāḷat-ḷo, "šūf hāḏi l-hayya alli tmawwet al-ʿēlāt." miš ḥayya, ġūḷ hiya, ġūḷ. gāḷ-ḷa, "ṭayyib."	130 She woke him up, until the snake returned. Now she woke the man up and said to him, "Look, this is the snake that kills the families." It [was] not a snake, [it was] a *ġūl*, a *ġūl*. He [the boy] said to her, "Good."
135 walla, ʿayyinha ta fātat ʿala-bāb al-maġġāra u-fātat ʿalēha ğawwa. lamman fātat ʿalēha, winna, u-sakkarat warāha al-bāb. b-gidret 'aḷḷa ġallaq ʿalēha l-bāb. b-ṣaxara ġallaq ʿalēha.	135 By Allah, he watched it, until it entered the doorway of the cave and entered inside. When it entered it [the cave], and closed behind it the door. By Allah's power, he closed the door on it [the snake]. With a rock, he locked the door on it.
141 rāḥ ʿala l-ḥaddād, gāḷ-ḷo, "widdak tiʿmal li sēf bulād, widdak tiʿemal-li barūda mā bī 'aḥsan, mā fīna 'aḥsan minha ba-d-dinya, u-widdak tiʿemal-li balṭa alli 'aguṣṣ rāsa, mā bī 'aḥsan minha ba-d-dinya. ḥarža." gāḷ-ḷo, "ṭayyib." "fa-'asʿa l-maġrib tekūn xāḷṣāt. gaddēš ḥagghin widdak 'anṭīk iyyā." gāḷ-ḷo, "ṭayyib."	141 He went to the smith and said to him, "You will make for me an iron sword, you will make for me a gun that there is no[thing] better than it, there is no[thing] better than it in the world, and you will make for me an axe with which I will cut its head, and an axe [that] there is no better [than it] in the world. A [critically] dangerous axe." He said to him, "Good." "And make efforts to make them ready for dusk. As much as you want me to pay for them, I'll give you." He said to him, "Good."

151 hāḏ-an-nās aṣ-ṣubh tiǧī, ṭabʿan an-nās ṭayyibīn hāḏ—alli b-al-bēt, šū ʿāmlin hāḏan b-al-bēt u-ḏ̣aḷḷam ṭayybīn? kīf hem ʿāmlīn u-ḏ̣aḷḷam u-humma ṭayyibīn? fa-kānat, yaʿani, ligata yaʿani ʿaḏ̣īma, hāḏi.

151 Now people saw that when morning came, of course these people were alive—those in the house—what were those in the house doing that they were alive? How did they do and remained alive? It was, that is, they thought this was a miracle.

157 lamminna ligat hā-l-masʾala min hā-š-šekel, az-zalama gām naʿam libad līha maʿāha libad ḥadd-il-bāb u-stanna ḥatta z-zalama tṣal-lah, u-hi tlugg, u-gām u-ḏ̣rubha ba-s-sīx.

157 When the issue turned out this way, the man got up, yes, and hid with it, ambushed it by the door and waited until the man [i.e., the snake] reached him, and it was licking, and he struck it with the iron sword [iron prong].

163 gāḷat-ḷo, "ṯanni." gāḷ-ḷa, "ʾammi mā ʿallamatni ʾanni ʾaṯanna." ʿāwad yuḏ̣rubha ṯāni marra. gāḷat-ḷo, "stanna, lā tuḏ̣rubni w-tiktilni. bī maʿāya ṯalaṯ ʿalāmāt, hāḏi tisʿad bīhen."

163 It said to him, "Hit me again." He said to it, "My mother did not teach me to repeat." He again hit it. It said to him, "Wait, don't hit me and kill me. I have three signs, which will help you [make you happy]."

169 gāḷat-ḷo, "hāḏi l-ʿalāmāt, iglaʿ ṯalaṯ šaʿrāt min hēn." galaʿ-la ṯalaṯ šaʿrāt min hanāk, min fōg. gāḷat-ḷo, "ʾoglaʿ ṯalaṯ šaʿrāt alli sferāt min ḏ̣ahari, min warā." galaʿ ṯalaṯ šaʿrāt min warā.

169 It said to him, "These signs—pluck three hairs from here"—he plucked three hair strands from there, from above. It said to him, "Pluck three hair strands [coarse ones] from my back, from my back." He plucked three hairs from the back.

175 gāḷat-ḷo, "ʾal-bēt ʾalli ʾani bī, bī ǧarrat ḏahab ha-l-gaddi. uʿūd-ʿayinni lamman ʾafūt ʿalē, baṣṣar bē wēn b-aḥuṭṭ rāsi, bī ǧarrat ḏahab. u-bī- u-ʿendi bistān kullo ḏahab—rummān u-lamūn u-burdgān—kullo ḏahab. u-ē wakīl ḥūt." gāḷ-(ḷ)ha, "ṭayyeb."

175 It said to him, "The house where I am in, there is in it a gold jug like this [this big]. Stay and look at me when I enter it [the cave]. Observe where I put my head—there is a gold jug. And there is—I have a garden all of which is [of] gold—pomegranate and lemon and oranges—all of it is gold. And a *ḥūt* [is] guarding it." He said to it, "Good."

183 hāḏa ḏibaḥḥa. "ṯāni hiyya l-mara." gāḷat-ḷo, "ḏī ḥaṭṭ al-mara ʿindak, dīr bālak ʿalēha, hāḏi l-mara ʿala šān rāḥu ixwānak aṯ-ṯnēn. enta, ʿaqebak el-mara. hāḏi l-mara, dīr bālak ʿalēha.

183 This [man] killed it. "Secondly, [it] is the woman," it said to him. "This, he placed the woman with you. Pay attention to her. This woman is because your two brothers died. You, your reward is the woman. This woman, take care of her.

189 bī ḥūt. iḏa ḥāl bīk, ʾawwal mā tanṭī ʾawwal šaʿara. ʾawwal šaʿara,

189 "There is a *ḥūt*. If it obstructs you, the first thing you will give him is the first hair strand.

191 yirmi-ʿalāk el-ʾamān, al-ḥūt." lamman ḏibaḥḥa, fāt warāha ʿa-l-maǧǧāra.

191 "It will give you his protection, the *ḥūt*." When he killed it, he entered the cave after it.

194 lamman fātat gāḷat-ḷo "'iḥriq aš-šaʿara awwal ši, ʿa-šān ma tisakkar ʿalēk aṣ-ṣuxra." aḥraq aš-šaʿra, mā sakkarat aṣ-ṣaxara fa-ḏaḷḷat aṣ-ṣaxara maftūḥa.

194 When he entered, it said to him, "Burn the first hair strand so that the rock will not close on you." He burned the hair and the rock did not close on him, but remained open.

199 lamman ḏaḷḷat aṣ-ṣaxara maftūḥa, assa rāḥ ǧāb aš-šuful, u-ǧāb ṯāni ta-l-al-balad, u-ǧāb ṯāni—al-winš, tīǧi yaʿani sitta tōn, sabʿa tōn, aḷḷāhu 'aʿlam.

199 When it remained open, now he went and brought a *šufel* [power shovel] and brought again [he went] to the town, and brought a winch, it reaches six or seven tons, Allah knows [how much].

204 ḥaṭṭūha ba-s-sayyāra wa-l-kull al-balad ṣārat tġanni u- . . . u-la-hā-l-walad. gadd-mā nbaṣaṭ-lo alli katal-la al- ḥayye hāḏi. fātam ʿala l-makān tabaḥḥa—winna š-šiǧar aḏ-ḏahab, gidd-al-ǧarra alli barra, hāḏi, ǧarra ḏahab. ǧā, u-'axaḏaha.

204 They put it [the snake] in the car and all the town began to sing and . . . for this boy, so much they were happy that he had killed this snake. They entered its place [the cave] and lo, the gold tree—the size of the jug [was] the size of this jug outside, this gold jug. He came and took it.

211 gāḷ, "widdi aʿraf hā-l-bistān hāḏa wēn." fāt b-aṭ-ṭāga alli hī, min al-ḥayye, tabaʿet al-ḥayye, al-ġūḷa, wanna l-bastān, min ǧamīʿ al-'aškāl bī, u-bī ḥūt.

211 He said, "I want to know, this garden—where it is." He entered in the niche which it is—from the snake, belonged to the snake, the *ġūla*, and lo—the garden—it had all the kinds and there was a *ḥūt* [in it].

216 wanna (a)al-ḥūt ʿendo banāt ṯintēn. ʿando banāt ṯintēn, u-šū banāt hin! zayy min a-l-ġuzlān bi-t-tikmīl. maʿallagāt min wēn? min šaʿarhan. lamman maʿallagāt min šaʿarhan, gāḷ-(ḷ)an, "šū hāḏa?"

216 And lo, the *ḥūt* had two girls with it. He had two girls and what girls they were! Like deer in their perfection. They were hanging—by what? By their hair. As they were hanging by their hair, he said to them, "What is this?"

222 gāḷan, "anta nāyim? assa yāklak al-ḥūt, hāḏa. kēf widdna niʿmal bīk, inta? ḥillna min šaʿarna." ḥallhin min šaʿarhen

222 They said, "Are you sleeping? The *ḥūt* will come now and eat you. How shall we do with you? Untie us from our hair." He untied them

226 gāḷ-ḷhen, "walla, mā ʿalēkun šarr alla min šaʿarkan" aḥrag aš-šaʿara alli aʿṭātu al-ḥayya.

226 and said to them, "By Allah, no harm will come on you except because of your hair." He burned the hair, which the snake had given him.

229 lamman 'aḥrag aš-šaʿra, al-ḥūt gāḷ-ḷo, "waḷḷāhi, lōla ma ramēt 'alli ramēta ʿalayya, wal-'aḏbaḥak wa-'anne min 'aḷḷa šū sawēt. wa-asakker ʿalēk aṣ-ṣaxra. lākin inta hassa inta ṣurt 'ebni. hāḏ as-sāʿa, 'ani baʿad ʿalē saʿtēn widdi 'amūt, ʿala-inta aḥragt aš-šaʿra hāḏi.

229 When he burned the hair, the *ḥūt* said to him, "By Allah, if you had not thrust at me what you have thrust at me, by Allah, I would have killed you, and that is from Allah what you did. And I would have closed the rock [cave door] on you. However, you have now become my son. This hour—I—after two more hours, I will die, because you burned on me this hair.

237 bas ʾani, widdi amūt, ʾani. hādi r-rummān, al-limūn-hā, al-limūn hāda—dahab, hāda l-burdgān—dahab, hāda l-krefūta—dahab, u-hāda l-šağara l-yābsa—taḥtha ğarrat māl. l-šağara l-yābsa bas tegīm ğarrat al-māl min taḥtha—tetmir. hāda kullo šuġlo dahab."	237 "But, I will die, I. This pomegranate, this lemon, this lemon—is gold. This orange—is gold, this grapefruit is gold, and this dry tree—under it there is a money jug. The dry tree—as soon as you just take out the money jug from under it, it will bear fruit. All of this produces gold."
245 u-bī gaṣur hināka. lammanna l-ḥūt mayyit. gāḷ, "kīf widdi aʿmal bīku w-intu ṭayyibīn, ʾani, ʿandi ʿarūs la-ʾaxūya, w-assa ʿandi duburha.[2] hassa talāta ʿandi. kīf aʿmal bīku, ʾani?" gālu-lo, "aḥna ma nʿarif."	245 And there was there a castle. When the *ḥūt* was dead. He said, "How shall I do with you and you are well [alive]? Me, I have my brother's bride and now I have her followers. Now I have three. Well, what shall I do with you?" They said to him, "We do not know."
252 ḥaṭṭhin ba-l-bēt at-talāta. gaʿadam ba-gaṣar al-ḥūt, tabaʿ-al-ḥūt.	252 He put them in the house, the three [of them]. They lived in the *ḥūt*'s castle, which was of the *ḥūt*.
255 lamma gaʿadam b-al-gaṣar, ṭallaʿat al-ʾawwaliyya, bint el-ʾamīr, walla tnēn, al-wazir—ʿamma—u-ʾabūha. wēn ham masākīn, ʿārfāthom.	255 When they lived in the castle, the first [of them], the emīr's daughter, looked [out], and lo, [there were] two—the minister, her uncle, and her father. And lo, they were poor; she recognized them.
260 ḥālathom txawwef, al-ʿāda hiyya zayy aš-šaḥḥād. mā tigdar tufṣul ʿalē. gāḷat, "hāda abūya wa-l-wazīr ʾani ʿārfitom, miš ʿārfitom, ʿārfitom, miš ʿārfitom."	260 Their condition was frightening [terrible], in all, [it was] like a beggar. She could not decide about it. She said, "This is my father and the minister. I know them—do not know them, know them—do not know them."
265 baʿadēn gāḷ-ḷo, "ʿal-ʾē dāyir" el-banāt hadlāki, "yā ʿammi, into." gāḷ-ḷha, "ʾana ʿād aʿteqed wāḥade minko . . . ʾana binti kānat ʿala hā-š-šekel, u-rāḥat ʿala—nizlat wa-l-ḥaras maʿāha, u-bē talt-ewlād yitʿallamo ʿendīna. u-šāifa wāḥad minham,	265 Afterward he [she] said to him, "What are you looking for"—those girls—"o my uncle, you [two]?" He said to her, "I think [that] one of you . . . I, my daughter was of this form [similar], and she went to—she went down with the guards with her, and there were three boys studying at our place. And she saw one of them.
272 u-xadūha ʿala swēsera, u-smeʿtom mdabbaḥīn, u-l-bint u-wāḥad ṭayyibīn." gāḷat-ḷo, "ʾani hā bintak hōn."	272 "And she was taken to Switzerland, and I heard that they were killed and the girl and one of them are alive." She said to him, "I am this, your daughter, here."
276 gām yʿabbeṭ ʿalēha yebawwesha, u-ṣār yibki. u-gāmat rāḥat ġassalato, labbasato, u-ʿeged el-ʿaged ʿa-l-bent,	276 He began hugging and kissing her, and started weeping. And she went and washed him and gave him [clean] clothes and he married the girl off.
280 gāḷat-ḷo, "laḥadd halla mā tğawwazt. w-alli widdi iyyā māt u-hāda ʾaxū." ʿegad al-ʿaged ʿala ʾaxū.	280 She said to him, "Up to now, I have not married. The one I wanted is dead, and this is his brother." He married her to his brother.

283 ʿeged al-ʿaged, gāḷ al-ʾaxu, "ʾana mā ʾagbal yeʿaged al-ʿaged ʿalēk inti la-ḥālek, widdi hāḏan aṯ-ṯintēn maʿāk(i)." haḏ(o)lāk aṯ-ṯalaṯ niswāno.	283 [When] he was marrying her off, the brother said, "I will not accept to marry only you alone. I want these two with you." Those three—his wives.
288 gāḷat-ḷo, "ani mwāfga, u-tʿīšan kull ḥayāton be-hanā, u-b-hā-r-rizga hāḏi."	288 She said to him, "I agree. And you will live all your lives in pleasure, with this livelihood."
291 ʿegad ʿigādo u-wa-ğawwazha,[3] u-ʾabūha rakkabo hā-ṭ-ṭayyāra hāḏam, waddō ʿala blādo. u-hāḏi xurrāfti u-nʿabber ʿebre fā.	291 He married her, and her father—they took him and put him on an airplane and took him to his country. And this is my story, and I teach you a lesson with it.

Commentary

Folktales, when they are transmitted orally from generation to generation, undergo a metamorphosis. Often, the narrators match the stories to their audience and change certain details in the course of the plot while preserving the basic pattern of the story. The changes reflect, among other influences, the changing environment caused by accelerated modernization in the twentieth century. The changes are expressed in two ways: first, the narrators often transfer the setting to places close to the dwellings of their audience or to cities and countries known to them by name; second, they insert into the plot modern tools and objects familiar to them from everyday life. In the stories from Ṣabḥa ʿAbūd of the ʿArab el-Ḥuğērāt tribe, for example, the plots take place in Wādi Ghana and Shefarʿam, places close to her home. In another instance, the hero goes on a journey to Egypt, which is perceived by the narrator as a small village where everyone knows one another, as in her own village. In one of her stories, the hero escapes with his beloved in a taxi, and when the wondering researcher asks her whether they might not have escaped on horseback, she explains to him that they were in a great hurry.

In Zehiyya's story, these changes are so striking that when Rafael Patai published this story in his book *Arab Folktales from Palestine and Israel*, he called it "Ġūls in Switzerland," (Patai, 1998, 183), a title that highlights the extraordinary contrast between the demonic creatures appearing in the plot and its location in a peaceful European state, a symbol of the modern West.[4]

Indeed, the plot is full of modern features. It begins in a big city: "They moved to a town, as you would say, Tel-Aviv." The three brothers, the protagonists of the plot, study at the university and dream of becoming doctors or lawyers. The guards use walkie-talkies to report the brothers' deeds to the king (the narrator used the general Hebrew word *maxšír*, a tool, that could be any sort of two-way radio). The king exiles the three boys, sending them to Switzerland on a plane, and the king's daughter hastens her horse to the airport and joins them as a stowaway. In Switzerland, which the narrator perceives as a city and not as a country, curfew is imposed, and armed guards shoot curfew violators. At some point, the hero uses heavy mechanical tools: a bulldozer, a winch, and a truck. At the end of the story, the heroine's father returns from Switzerland to his country by plane.

Such changes are not only characteristic of our times. Thus, for example, in many of the tales collected by the Grimm brothers in the early nineteenth century, one of the weapons used by the heroes is the rifle, a tool invented three hundred years earlier. Today, such a thing seems entirely natural to us, but it is reasonable to assume that at the time, when the rifle was integrated into folktales as a conventional weapon, it was perceived as an extraordinary change.

Patai believes that the combination of modern and traditional elements in this story conveys a hidden message concerning the coping of Arab society with the modern world in Israel.[5] He argues that the story extols the importance of tradition and emphasizes the concept that the tools and inventions of the modern world must be used wisely. People should not adopt the lifestyle and customs of the Western world. It is an interesting creative interpretation that relies on several prominent elements in the story, such as the helplessness of heroes in defending themselves against modern weapons (guns) as opposed to their resourcefulness in dealing with demonic creatures. As is the case with psychological interpretations, it is difficult to assess how much this interpretation is anchored in the subconscious minds of the narrator and her listeners. Patai himself states explicitly that this idea is not expressed on the visible level of the story. It was revealed to him in course of an interpretive analysis.

Examining the less modern aspects of the story reveals a dense network of traditional motifs that are also known from other Bedouin stories: The older brother, on seeing the princess with her twenty-four-person entourage, falls in love with her at first sight. The princess is engaged in a distinctly feminine work, knitting, using a *ṣunnāra* (single knitting needle). A serpent poisons water in a jar. The *ġūl* asks the hero to beat him again, and the hero refuses to do so. The hero removes three scales from the snake, struggles with the ogre, and saves the two girls whom the ogre had hung by their hair.

Two of these motifs are particularly interesting and should be dealt with in detail. According to popular belief, a snake usually enters houses and sips water, milk, or other fluids (motif B765.6.1, "Snake drinks milk"). In the Mishna, there is a detailed discussion of the factors that may contaminate a drink for consumption if it is touched by various animals: "Rabban Gamliel says: Even the snake because it vomits" (Para 9:3). A further discussion of this issue is found in "The Shepherd and the Snake" (see chap. 41). In addition, in the *Arabian Nights*, in the story of Prince Sayf al-Mulūk and the Princess Badīʿat al-Ǧamāl, we are told about a *ġūl* who blinds people by giving them poisoned milk.[6]

In *Parables of King Solomon*, a collection of stories apparently composed at the end of the fifteenth century,[7] there is a description very similar to that of the Bedouin story. It tells of a snake who sips wine from the pitcher and vomits his venom into it. The story is about a woman who betrays her husband with a bandit while the couple are on their way to her parents' house. The woman and the robber join forces and tie the husband to a tree. At certain point, they lie down and sleep together, and this is what the story says: "Then the bandit came to sleep with the girl, and he took the jar and put it near his head and slept, and now a snake came and drank from the wine and vomited deadly poison inside it. As the bandit woke from his sleep, he took the jar and drank and died."[8] After the bandit's death, the woman releases the husband. They arrive at the house of the woman's parents. The husband tells what happened, and as a result, the father kills his daughter.

The second motif that appears in many folktales in the Muslim culture is the prohibition of repeated beating of the ogre, motif C742, "Taboo: striking monster twice. Though monster begs that hero strike him again, hero refuses. Monster would otherwise revive." This motif appears also in the *Arabian Nights*, in the continuation of the story of Prince Sayf al-Mulūk and the Princess Badīʿat al-Ğamāl. The hero describes how he kills the *ġūl* who tried to blind him with poisoned milk: "Coming up to him I smote him with the sword a single stroke across his waist and he fell in twain. Then he screamed and cried out to me, 'O man, as thou desire to slay me, strike me a second stroke.' Accordingly, I was about to smite him another cut; but he who had directed me to the niche and the scymitar said, 'Smite him not a second time, for then he will not die, but will live and destroy us.'"[9]

It is interesting to note that a similar motif also appears in Celtic cultures: motif E11.1, "Second blow resuscitates. First kills." In the first branch of the Mabinogion, the Welsh national epic, Arawn, king of the otherworld, asks King Pwyll to fight Hafgan, his enemy, and says to him: "And you must give him only one blow— he will not survive it. And although he asks you to give him another, you must not, however much he begs you. Because no matter how many more blows I gave him, the next day he was fighting against me as well as before."[10]

In "Ġūls in Switzerland," the princess is described as an active figure. First, she flees her father's house on horseback to join her lover and sneaks onto an airplane. Later, she stays awake at night, identifies the snake-*ġūl*, warns the younger brother of the *ġūl*'s intentions, and even arms herself, although she does not take an active part in the battle between the hero and the *ġūl*. At the end of the story, she takes care of her father, bathes him, and dresses him. When the younger brother declares his intention to marry not only her but also the two young women whom he saved from the ogre, she gives her consent and even blesses her bridegroom and the two young women: "I agree. And you will live all your lives in pleasure, with this livelihood." However, after identifying the snake-*ġūl*, she disappears from the stage of the plot, and the promoter of the plot is the younger brother. At the end of the story, after taking care of her father and agreeing to the triple marriage, she no longer plays an active role. Her father is the one who arranges her marriage with the younger brother, in accordance with the social code accepted in Muslim society.

Therefore, this is a story of women's empowerment, in which the woman initiates moves, rejects her father's authority, and escapes from the house. On the other hand, she is aware of her limitations as a woman in the patriarchal society in which she lives, and she eventually lets her father marry her to a man, while it is not at all clear whether she is in love with him. She says to her father, "I have not married yet, and the one I wanted to marry is dead, and this is his brother." In other words, she emphasizes the fact that she kept her virginity and female innocence and gives tacit approval to her father's decision to marry her to the younger brother.

Notes

1. *ḍirbum li-l-malak. b-il-maxšīr*. In Arabic, "to call on the phone" is *ḍarab talafōn* (literally "hit a telephone"). Modern conditions enable communication by a phone or a similar

tool. Here, the narrator uses the Hebrew word *maxšīr*, "instrument, tool," semantically as a vague term for the telephone.

2. *'andi 'arūs la-'axūya, w-assa 'andi duburha*: "Me, I have my brother's bride and now I have her followers." The word *followers* is not usually used in sedentary dialects or Literary Arabic in this sense, but the root means (among other meanings) to "be at the back, follow."

3. *'egad 'igādo u-wa-ğawwazha*: Marriage is first legalized by a religion official, who "ties the knot" (literal translation, based on an old custom), after which the marriage is formal and can be celebrated. Wherever marriage is described in this collection, the narrator mentions this official symbol of the legal union.

4. Patai, *Arab Folktales*, 183.

5. Patai, 187–96.

6. Burton, *Arabian Nights*, night 972.

7. Yassif, *Hebrew Collection of Tales*, 240.

8. Jellinek, *Bet Hamidrash*, 4:146.

9. Burton, *Arabian Nights*, night 972. A detailed discussion of this theme is found in Al-Rawi, "Arabic Ghoul and Its Western Transformation," 296.

10. Davies, "The Mabinogion," 4.

36. The Golden Children

A. The Three Siblings and the Talking Birds

NARRATOR: Ḥalīma Ḥasan Slimān

TRIBE: *ʿArab el-Zbēdāt*

IFA 17404 September 2, 1982

1 marra kān bī weḥda . . . malik. ʿindo t̠alat̠ niswān, čān ǧawwaz ʾinno maʿa t̠alāt̠a. ʾassa marra bī wāḥad rāḥ yidǧawwaz wiḥda. ʾessa hā-l-wiḥda ṣārat, xaḷḷafat ʾawwal marra. ʾassa tiʿeraf niswān el-malek at̠-t̠alāt̠a mā, šū-smo, kānen ḥāgdāt ʿalēha liʾannha ǧābat. (ʾ)a-ʾulli ǧābat walad.[1]	1 Once there was one… a king. He had three wives, he had married the three. Now, once there was a man who went and married one [woman]. Now, this one became—had a child the first time. Now, you know the three king's wives—what is its name—they were envious of her, because she had had a child. The one who had a child.
9 ǧat wiḥda dāya, bidda el-walad, xad̠at el-walad min taḥt ʾummo u-ḥaṭṭat bidālo biss, qaṭṭ yaʿani. u-ʾawwal marra ǧābat walad. xad̠am bidālo u-ḥaṭṭum qaṭṭ. xad̠am u-rāḥam waddō ʿend wāḥad—ē šū ʾismo—^{i}štaġal ǧanāyni.	9 A midwife came, she looked for the child, and took the child from under his mother and put instead of him a cat, that is, a cat. The first time she had a child. They put instead of him a cat, they took and went and gave him to one—a, what's his name—working as a gardener.
15 xad̠a al-walad, rabbā. sammā ʿazz ad-dīn. ʾassa, t̠āni marra ḥiblat al-mara, kamān d̠ī hī mart-al-malak. ǧābat kamān walad. ʾassa lammin ǧābat al-walad kamān duwat ad-dāya—yeḥagdan niswān al-malik al-ʾūlinyyāt,[2] ḥagdan ʿalēha u-ḥagdan al-walad uḥaṭṭan taḥtiyya kalb.	15 He took the child and brought him up. He called him ʿIzz ad-dīn [Religion Pride]. Now, a second time the woman got pregnant, and again this was that king's wife. She had again a boy. Now when she had the boy, also now the midwife treated [her]—the king's first wives were envious of her and of the boy, and [took the child and] put instead of him a dog.

22 ’essa gām—baʿadēn itḥiyyar el-malak, gāḷ, “kulla yōm hī ğābit li sāʿa biss, sāʿa kalib.” ’assa ṯāni dōr—ṯāliṯ dōr, ’akam marra ğābat binet. xaḏam al-bint u-ḥaṭṭu bidālha ḥağar, ʿašān yigūlu l-al-malik ’inha ğābat ḥağar. ’assa lamminna, lamma hīč šāf al-malik inno marto mā txaḷḷif—ğābat sāʿa biss, sāʿa kalb, sāʿa ḥağar, rāḥ ṭaḷḷagha. gāḷ, “xaḷḷīha tištaġaḷ b-al-maṭbax.”

22 Now, the king got perplexed and said, “Every day she has given birth to me—once a cat, once a dog.” Now, the second time; the third time the woman gave birth to a girl. They took the girl and put instead of her a stone, so that they could say to the king that she had given birth to a stone. Now, when the king saw that his wife did not give birth to a child—she had once a cat, once a dog, and once a stone—he went and divorced her. He said, “Let her work in the kitchen.”

32 ’essa kibrum al-ⁱwlād, haḏōl alli rabbāhum l-ğanāyni, ʿiyālha. samma wāḥad ʿizz-ad-dīn, wāḥad yiḥya-d-dīn w-al-bint sammāha ḍaw el-qamar. ḍaw el-qamar. ’assa kibrat al-bint hāy u-xwānha kibrum ʿand ağ-ğinēyni. ’abūhum yaʿani wāḥad ištaġal ğinēini. miš ’abūhum al-ḥagīgi—’abūhum al-ḥagīgi al-malak.

32 Now, the children grew up, those whom the gardener brought up, her children. He named one ʿIzz-ad-dīn [Religion Pride], one—Yiḥya-d-dīn [Let-Live-the-Religion], and the girl he named Ḍaww el-Qamar [Moonlight]. Ḍaww el-Qamar. Now, these children grew up . . . now, this girl grew up and her brothers at the gardener’s. Their father was one who worked as a gardener. He was not their real father—their real father was the king.

40 ’assa kibrum. kibrum u-ṣāram šibāb. ’assa yōm ğat wiḥda ʿala hāy al-binet, ḍaw el-qamar, ğat hāy il-mara alli xaḏat al-uwlād u-ḥaṭṭathum ʿind haḏāk ağ-ğinēyni, ad-dāya, yaʿani. gat (sic!) ḥaṭṭathum, ’essa u-ḥaṭṭat al-walad hināk.

40 Now they grew up, they grew up and became youths. One day, there came one [woman] to visit them, this girl, Ḍaww el-Qamar, there came to them this woman who took the children and put them at the gardener’s, the midwife, that is. She came and put them, now, she put the children there.

46 ’assa gā(ḷ)t lēha, “’inti mkayyfa, bas ’ēš xasseč ? xasseč mrāt ed-dunya.”

46 Now, she said to her, “You are having a good life, but what are you missing? You need the world’s mirror.”

48 mrāt ad-dunya hāy zayy at-tel(e)viziōn.[3] tšūf-noṣṣ ad-dunya biha. gāḷat-lēhu (=lēha), “u-mnēn ağīb hāy?” gāḷat-ilha, “tiqṭaʿi sabaʿ bḥūra. ’assa widdeč tğībīhen.”

48 This half-world mirror is like television. You see half the world with it. She said to her, “And where shall I bring it from?” She said to her, “You will cross seven seas. Now you will get them.”

53 ’assa ’ağu n-niswān ligūha tibki. “lēš tibki?” widdha ⁱmrāt nuṣṣ ad-dinya. ’assa rāḥat, gālan-la, “ṭayyib, mnīn (y)inṭi?” gāḷat la, “tiqṭaʿi sabʿa bḥūr. ’iqṭaʿu sabʿa bḥūra.”

53 Now, the women [the brothers] came and found her crying. “Why are you crying?” She wants the half-world mirror. Now she went [and told her brothers]. They said to her, “Good, where are you [getting it] from?” She said to her [them], “You [f.sg.] will cross seven seas. Cross [2m.pl.] seven seas.”

58 ’essa rāḥum, dawwaram hīk ’issa ligum waḥda ṣabiyye wāgfa, u-hī bint sāḥera, hāy al-bint. hāk hiyya. (’e)ssa gāḷū-lha, ’essa gāḷū-lha, “tismaḥi tgūlī-lna wēn mrāt nuṣṣ ad-dinya nelāgīha?” gāḷat-ilhum, “’ā. mrāt nuṣṣ ad-dinya maʿa ’umm^{w}i. ’essa, mrāt nuṣṣ ad-dinya”—’ummha sāḥira—“’assa ’iḏa tāxḏūn hā-l-mišeṭ tabaʿt al-bint min ’ummha, tinṭīkum mrāt nuṣṣ ad-dinya.”

68 ’assa gāḷt-ilhom “ṭayyib.” gāḷū-lha “ṭayyib.” xaḏum al-mišeṭ min ’ummha-al-sāḥira u-’anṭūha l-al-binet, bint al-sāḥira, u-xaḏum . . . ’anṭatum mrāt nuṣṣ ad-dinya u-riğʿum la-’uxthum.

73 ’anṭūha mrāt nuṣṣ ad-dinya. ’assa lamman ’anṭūha ’iyyāha kayyafat ʿalēha, šāfat kull ’iši zayy television, šāfat kull ’iši.

77 ’essa marra ṯāniya, ’ağa ʿalēhum ’axūha. ğat hā-l- il-mara alli qālt-^{i}lha ʿan mrāt nuṣṣ ad-dinya. gāḷat-^{i}lha, “šāifa inte mkayyefa u-ʿāiša, ’ēš xāssek? ^{i}šğara u-ʿalēha ʿaṣfārēn.” w-al-ʿaṣfurēn tiḥkan kill ’iši. ’assa—š(ū) ’ismo—’assa rāḥam a-saraw nuṣṣ ad-dinya, ʿa-l-ʿaṣfurēn. saraw ʿa-l-ʿaṣfurēn.

85 ’assa rāḥam yidawwrum, ’assa u-gāmam mišyam mišyam giṭʿam sabaʿ bḥūra ḥawālē. ’assa ligum hanāka binet hāy-as-sāḥira, bint as-sāḥira. gāḷt-ilhum . . . gāḷū-lha, “widna wēn al- al-ʿaṣfurēn, al-bilbil w-al-^{i}šğara.”

91 gāḷat-ilhum, “’ā, hīn hiyye, ʿind a-l-ġūl.” sāʿadatum yiṣlu-lo, la-el-ġūl. ’essa, al-ġūl gāḷ-^{i}lhum, “’aʿṭīkum ’iyyāhin alla tğībū-li fāṭma, fāṭma al-’amīra.” ’assa gāḷu-lha “ṭayyib.” gāḷū-lo, “ṭayyib. mnēn nğībha hāy?”

58 Now they went, they were looking for it like that. Now, they met a girl standing, and she was a sorceress’s daughter, this girl. This she is. Now, they said to her, “Please tell us, where we shall find the half-world mirror.” She said to them, “Yes, the half-world mirror is with my mother. The half-world mirror.” Her mother was a sorceress. “Now, if you take this girl’s comb from her mother, she will give you the half-world mirror.”

68 Now, she said to them, “Good.” They said to her, “Good.” They took the comb from her sorceress mother and gave it to the daughter, the sorceress’s daughter, and took . . . she gave them the half-world mirror and went back to their sister.

73 They gave her the half-world mirror. Now when they gave it to her, she was very happy with it, she saw everything like television, she saw everything.

77 Now a second time her brother came to them. That woman who told her about the half-world mirror came to her. She said to her, “I see you are having fun and living. What do you need? A tree with two birds on it.” And the birds tell everything. Now, what’s his name—they went and walked half the world [looking for] the two birds. They walked [looking] for the two birds.

85 Now, they were looking for [them], they walked and walked and crossed seven seas all around. Now, they met there that sorceress’s daughter, the sorceress’s daughter. She said to them. . . They said to her, “We want where the two birds are, the nightingale and the tree.”

91 She said to them, “Yes, it’s here, at the *ġūl*’s.” She helped them reach the *ġūl*. Now, the *ġūl* said to them, “I will give them to you only if you bring me the Princess Faṭma.” Now, they said to her, “Good.” They said to him, “Good, where from shall we bring her?”

97 gāḷ-ilhum, "al-muhimm tdabbrū-li 'iyyāha. taḥt al-baḥar, b-gāʿ al-baḥar hī sākna." fa-gāḷam "ṭayyeb."	97 He said to them, "[What] is important [is] that you will arrange her for me. Under the sea, at the bottom of the sea, she is living." They said to him, "Good."
100 'assa rāḥam la-hāḏi bint as-sāḥira u-gāmam hināka ligūha u-gālt-ilhom, "ṭayyeb, taʿālu warāya."	100 Now they went to this sorceress's daughter and they met her there and she said to them, "Good, come behind me."
103 gāḷat-ilhom, "lā (t)daḥḥgum warākum. 'iḏa (t)daḥḥgum warākum teṣīrum ḥağar yābes." gāḷ-(ḷ)ha "ṭayyeb."	103 She said to them, "Do not look back. If you look back, you will become a dry stone." They said to her, "Good."
106 mišyum warāha, gāmum ligum gaṣar kebīr, biyyu[4] xadam u-hāḏa. ṣārum yenādum "yā fāṭma, yā fāṭma" 'assa ğatt, raddat ʿalēhum fāṭma. fāṭma ṭilʿat—waḥda tiğannen.	106 They walked after her, and found a big palace, in which there were slaves and this [and that]. They started calling out "O Faṭma, o Faṭma." Now, she said, Faṭma answered them. Fatma came out—one who makes you crazy.
111 fāṭma. gāḷat-^{i}lhom martēn. gāḷ-ḷa, "yā fāṭma." ʿa-šān tridd ʿalēhum. nizlat fāṭma, waḥda tiğannen, yaʿni ḥilwa, kṯīr.	111 Faṭma. She said to them twice. He said to her, "O Faṭma," so that she would answer them. Faṭma went down, Faṭma, one who makes you crazy, that is, very pretty.
114 'essa, lamma šāfūha hīč gālum, "xiyāna, 'essa al-ġūḷ yākilha." gāḷū-lha, "niʿmal minnek timṯāl, xašab, u-nẓabbṭo u-ngūl 'inneč 'inti hiyya." gālt-ilhom, "ṭayyib." 'assa ʿamlom minnīha timṯāl xašab, u-riğʿat hiyye la-gaṣerha u-xaḏam at-timṯāl maʿahom. yaʿani ka-'annha hiyya. xaḏūha ʿala l-ġūḷ.	114 Now, when they saw her like that, they said, "Treachery [we have been cheated]. Now, the *ġūl* will devour her." They said to her, "We will make a sculpture of you, of wood, and arrange it and we will say it is you." She said to them, "OK." Now, they made a sculpture of wood of her, and she returned to her palace and they took the sculpture with them, that is, as if it was she. They took her to the *ġūl*.
122 lamma rāḥum ʿa-l-ġūḷ 'assa gāḷū-lo, "ğibnā-lak fāṭma el-'amīra." gāḷ-ilhom,"wēnha?" gāḷū-lo. "hāḏ(i)-hiyya."	122 When they went to the *ġūl*, they said to him, "We brought you the Princess Faṭma." He said to them, "Where is she?" They said to him, "This is her."
125 'assa hī xašab. 'essa gām š-'ismo, gāḷū-lo, "'inṭīna b-il-'awwal ^{i}š-šğara w-il-ʿaṣfurīn u-naʿṭīk fāṭma l-'amīra."	125 Now, it was of wood. Now, he got up, what's his name, they said to him, "Give us first the tree and the two birds and we will give you the Princess Faṭma."
128 gāḷ-ilhom, "ṭayyib." ʿinṭāhum al-ʿaṣfurēn w-al-^{i}šğera, u-zattum al-binet, hāy il-'amīra ʿalēhum, u-inhazmum—u-xaḏum al-ʿaṣfurīn w-inhizmom.	128 He said to them, "OK." He gave them the two birds and the tree, and they threw the girl, this princess, to them and ran away—and took the two birds and ran away.

132 riǧʿom la-ʾoxthom. fa-kayyafat ʾoxthom lamma šāfathim, mā ʿād riǧʿat lēha ad-dāya. al-ʿaṣfurīn. gāmam garraram—maʿāhum mrāt ad-dinya, mrāt ad-dinya hāy, u-maʿāhum al-ʿaṣfurīn, yiʿmalum ḥafla kibīra. ʿizmum al-malik. ʾessa al-malik mīn hū? ʾabūhum.	132 They returned to their sister. Their sister was very happy when she saw them. The midwife did not return to her anymore. The two birds—they decided—were with them, and this half-world mirror, and they had the two birds—they will make a big party. They invited the king. Now, the king, who was he? Their father.
139 ʾassa ʿizmum hāḏa, u-gām ṣāram al-ʿaṣfurīn yġannan. ṣāram yegūlan wāḥad yegūl la-ṣāḥbo, aṯ-ṯāni, al-ʿaṣfūr aṯ-ṯāni, "yā abū-ṣayyāḥ, tōkol ğazar? yā abū-ṣayyāḥ, tōkol ğazar?" aṯ-ṯāni gāḷ-ḷo, "gaḷbi min hā-d-dīr(a)-infağar. mart-il-malak mā ğābt qiṭṭin wa-la kalbin wala ḥağar. ğābat ʿizz ad-dīn, yiḥya d-dīn wa-ḍaw el-qamar."[5]	139 Now, they invited this and the birds began to sing. They started to say—one said to its friend, the other bird, "O Abu Ṣayyah [Yeller] bird, are you eating carrots? O Abu Ṣayyah, are you eating carrots?" The other one said to it, "My heart has broken from this house. The king's wife did not give birth to a cat neither to a dog nor to a stone. She gave birth to ʿIzz-ad-dīn, Yiḥya-d-dīn, and Ḍaww el-Qamar."
148 ʾessa gām, lamma hīč samaʿ il-malik, gāḷ-ḷēhum, "ʿīdum" gāmam ʿalēha kamān dōr. "yā abū-ṣayyāḥ, tōkol ğazar? gaḷbi min hā-d-dīr(a)-infağar. mart–il-malak lā ğābt qiṭṭin wa-lā kalbin wala ḥağar. ğābat ʿizz ad-dīn, yiḥya d-dīn, ḍaw el-qamar."	148 What did he [do], the king, when he heard this? He said to them, "Repeat this." They did it another turn. "O Abu Ṣayyah, are you eating carrots?" "My heart has broken from this house. The king's wife did not give birth to a cat, neither to a dog nor to a stone. She gave birth to ʿIzz-ad-dīn, Yiḥya-d-dīn, and Ḍaww el-Qamar."
154 al-malek simaʿ hīk (=hēk), rāḥ gām gāḷ, ğat marto illi šaġġalha b-al-maṭbax, lli ğābat ṯalaṯ uwlād. ğābha, ṣār yiguḷ-ḷēha, "ʾinti ʾassa marti."	154 The king heard this and went and said, his wife came, whom he had employed in the kitchen, who had given birth to three children, came. He brought her, and began telling her, "You are now my wife."
158 u-xaḏa n-niswān aṯ-ṯalāṯe illi kānan yāxḏum al-binit w-al-walad u-yḥuṭṭum hināk we-yḥuṭṭṭum hināk al-kalb wu—l-biss u-l-ḥağar. ṣār yeʾūl l-an-nās, "ʾalli yeḥibb ʾaḷḷa yeğīb ḥaṭab u-yeḥriʾehin eṯ-ṯalaṯ nisāwīin." (ʾa)ssa, u-riğʿat al-mara lli ʾummhum u-riğeʿum al-uwlād suʿada wu-kayyafu.	158 He took his three wives, who had taken the girl and the boy[s] and had put them and put there a dog and a cat and a stone. He started saying to the people, "He who loves Allah will bring firewood and burn them," the three wives. Now the woman returned, who was their mother, and the children returned [and were] happy and enjoyed [it].

B. The Wicked Old Woman

NARRATOR: Warda Hawāš
TRIBE: *ʿArab el-Mazārīb*
March 11, 1982

1 hāḏa bī ᵉzlima. xaḏa, xaḏa wiḥda. ʿinda sabaʿ banāt ʿamm. gāḷat-lo, "mā tāxḏ haḏīča?" "txaḷḷif li walad u-bint, wāḥad gumar, wāḥad šams." gāḷat-lo, widda tesammīm wāḥad gumar, wāḥad šams, ṯneinhom mazyūnīn, miṯel gumar, miṯl aš-šams. al-binet—(mā haḏōla)—xaḷḷafat wāḥad gumar, wāḥad šams.	1 There is a man. He took [a wife], takes one. He had seven female cousins. She [one of them] said to him, "Won't you take that one [for wife]?" "She will bear for him a boy and a girl, one Gumar [Moon] and one Shams [Sun]." She said to him—she wanted to name them, one Gumar and one Shams. Both of them are beautiful like the sun and the moon. The girl [woman] delivered (not those) delivered one Gumar and one Shams.
10 ᵃyōm-innha xaḷḷafathem, gāḷat lēha banāt ᵃʿammo, gāḷan lēha—"taʿāli, yā ʿağūz," [bī ʿağūz, xityāra],[6] gāḷat-lēha, "nanṭīč ḏahab, nanṭīč māl, u-bass-in ğābat hāḏi ʿiyāl ⁱtnēn, binet u-walad, ʾinti ʾisergīhum, wa-ḥuṭṭi čläb taḥtīha, ʿegeb mā tğīb."	10 When she delivered them, her [female] cousins said to her, they said to her, "Come, o old woman." (There was an old woman, an old woman) she said to her, "We will give you gold, we will give you money, and if she, this one, delivers two children, a girl and a boy, you steal them for us and put dogs instead of them, as soon as she delivers them."
17 ḥiblat hāḏi u-ğābat, ğābat . . . binet u-walad. ğā binnīhum šames, u-ğā binnīhum gumar. u-mazyūniīn.	17 She got pregnant and gave birth to a girl and a boy. Between them was Shams and Gumar. And [they were] beautiful.
20 [$_{H}$ʾaz$_{H}$] [yōm ʾagʿadat, yōm hā ğābathum, mā čānat bī ʿindīha yaʿani miṯel hīč, ʾitğīb b-al-bēt].	20 ($_{H}$ʾaz$_{H}$) Now then (when she was—when this [one] delivered them, it was not with her, that is, like this [as now]—she gave birth at home).
23 yōm-innha ğat, sriganhum, srigan al-ⁱwlād u-ḥaṭṭat el-klāb. winna tgul-lo "yī, illa mā-guḷ-ḷak, ʾalla martak ğāiba klāb."	23 When she [the midwife] came, they stole them, stole the children, and she put the dogs. And lo—she says to him (to the husband), "Oh, I must say to you, that your wife gave birth to dogs."
27 wēn kabbanham? ḥaṭṭanham b-ṣandūg, ḥaṭṭanhom b-al-baḥar. yōmin ḥaṭṭanhom b-al -baḥar yiği sammāč, b-al-mihna, wēn? min ᵉbḥēra.	27 Where did they throw them? They put them in a box, put them in the sea. When they put them in the sea, there came a fisherman, in this profession (where?) from the sea.
31 gḏubatha, gāḷ, "šnū hā-l-saḥḥāra?" yōminno ğābha, hā-s-seḥḥāra u-ligam, winno ygūḷ, "ʾassa mā widdi ʾawaddīha . . . widdi ʾahdīha l-al-malak."	31 She [he] took it. He said, "What is this box?" When he brought it, this box, and [he] found [them], he says, "Now I will surely want to give it away, I will give it as a present to the king."

36 yōminno hadāha l-al-malak, yōminno daḥḥag, hāḏa min ğān, ʾaḷḷa widdo yiʿayyišhom, yaʿani, hū-mā ṭār, ṭār. gaʿadam čam yōm ʿenda . . . qablam yaʿani, ṣaḥṣaḥam nitfa u-ḥaṭṭom u-gaṣṣaram ʿalē min haḏōla, banāt ᵃʿammo, mišān daššarhin u-xaḏa min ġēr.

36 When he presented it to the king, when he saw that this is from Allah's angels, Allah wanted to keep them alive. That is, he did fly, fly [the angel]. They stayed a few days with him. . . . They got, that is, recovered a little, and he put them and restricted them from those king's cousins. They were not allowed to get near the children. [They were jealous] because he [the king] had left them and took [a wife] from another [family].

44 ḥasan, ğa as-sammāk, ğābha, gāḷ, "šnū widdi hāy ṣiḥḥa, mā widdi biha māl, ʾahdīha l-al-malak. yiʿimlū li ṣiḥḥa." la-mīn hadāha? hadāha l-al-malak.

44 Well, this fisherman came, he took it [the box] and said, "What do I want this box, I don't want money for it, I'll give it [as gift] to the king. They will do for me [a] good [thing]." Whom did he present it to? He gave it as present to the king.

49 yōminn hidāha l-al-malak, daḥḥag winnhum walad u-bint. gāranā(m). šāfathum ʿağūz a-saw, ʿağūzt a-saw tiʿerifo. šnū ğābat u-šnū waddat. widda tisrughum. "ʾaḷḷa yā ğidda taʿāl, ʾaḷḷa yā yumma taʿāl, ʾaḷḷa taʿāl"—tanna xaḏatom. ričbat ʿala l-ⁱḥmār, ṣārt ti-tbīʿ mlabbas. [taʿarif šū l-ⁱmlabbas?]

49 When he gave it to the king, he looked and saw a boy and a girl. They were similar. The Old Woman of Evil saw them. The Old Woman of Evil recognized them—what she had brought and what she had given away. She wanted to steal them. "O Allah, o granddaughter, just come, child, come, just come"—until she caught them. She rode the donkey; she began selling candy. (Do you know what [is] candy?)

57 yōm ʿanṭatum ᵉmlabbas, "taʿālum, taʿālam, taʿālam," ḥaṭṭathum b-xurğ al-ḥmār. wi-srigathom. wēn ⁱsrigathum? ḥaṭṭathum ib-ḥerš, alli tākilhum hā-ḏ-ḏbāʿ. yōminnam yibčam—tṣīr tišti ʿalēhom ad-dinya. u-yōm-ʾinnham yilʿabam . . . ʾad-dinya (t)ṣīr zēna. ʾad-dinya (t)ṣīr zēna. ğat ʿalēhum.

57 When she gave them candy, [she said,] "Come, come, come." She put them in the side basket of the donkey. And she stole them. Where did she steal them? She put them in a wood, so that hyenas would eat them. When they cried it began raining on them, and when they were playing it was good, it [the weather] was good for them. It came on them.

65 šnū bīhum sōda, ṭayar čebīr, yirūḥ—yiğīb lēhum ʾačel, yeṭʿemhum. winha tgūḷ, "čēf widdna nsāwi? widdna dīma nḏaḷḷ ᵉhēk?" kibru ta-l-ʿağiyya haḏī(m), al-wal(a)d ṣār čebīr šwoyye. "čēf widdna nsāwi?" winha tgūḷ, winha tgūḷ al-ʿağiyya, al-ʿağiyya winha tgūḷ, "ʾani agūḷ, yā ṛaḅḅʷi, yā ṛaḅḅʷi, yikūn lēna ḅēt, hēna, gaṣaṛ." tagrīb ḅi-ṛaḅḅna simeʿ minha, winnhum ğāʿadīn b-gaṣar. [kā(i)na kulla xurrāfe.]

65 There was for them a black, big bird, going and bringing food for them, feed them. Lo, she [the girl] says, "How shall we do? Shall we always be like that?" They grew up, this girl, and the boy grew up a little, "How shall we do?" Lo, she says, the girl says, the girl says, "I am saying, my Lord, we shall have a house, here, a castle." It seems our Lord heard from her, and lo, they were sitting in a castle (all this is a story/legend).

76 yōm w-hinne gʿadam bal-gaṣar, gāḷat al-xetyāra hāḏa, ʿağūz as-saw, gāḷat, “widdi ʾarūḥ ʿa-hā-l-muṭraḥ alli čānum bī, alli zaṭṭētum bī, widd(i) ʾarūḥ ʾašūfo.” daḥḥagat b-al-ḥorš winno hā-l-gaṣar. ʾaḥsan minno mā bī.

76 One day, when they were sitting in the palace, this old woman, the Old Woman of Evil, said [to herself], “I want to go to this place where they were, where I threw them; I want to go to see it.” She looked at the wood and there was this palace—there is no [palace] more beautiful than it.

82 šāfato.”taʿāl, yā yumma, mīn hāḏi, mīn hāḏi, taʿāli, taʿāli, taʿāli.” šnū ʾesemha l-ʿağiyya. haḏāka ʾismo gumar. hī ʿārfa šnū (ʾa)sāmīhom, humma mū hum ʿārfīn šnū (ʾa)sāmīhom, hā-l-ʿiğān. hiyya l-xatyāra ʿārfa šnū (ʾa)sāmīhum. “ʾešnū ismeč?” “mā baʿraf mā ʾiši.” al-walad mā ʿarf ʾiši. ğat hāḏihi ʿalēhum, gāḷat lēha, widda trūḥ tiqtel-axūha.

82 She saw it. “Come [m.sg.], child, who is this, who is this, come [f.sg.], come [f.], come [f.].” What is this girl’s name? (Šmēsa is her name, of the girl.) His name is Gumar, she knows their names, they do not know their names, those children, She, the old woman knows their names. “What is your [f.] name?” “I do not know anything.” The boy did not know anything. She came to them, said to her, she wanted to kill her brother.

92 gāḷat lēha, “(a)lla mā ʾagūḷ-ḷeč, ʿalāmeč hēna tanneč hēna ḏaḷḷeč ğāʿeda, xalli yeğīb leč—ē, yerūḥ yeğīb-leč minn. e. min mayyt as-sbāʿ, tišrabʷi, lā, rūḥi ğībi min a(d)-danāden” gāḷat hi, “ğib-^{i}lna danāden, danāden wi-ğrās” gāḷat lēha, “(wēn) danāden w-ğrās hāḏi?” “hāḏi, ʿind bīr as-sbāʿ, ʿind bīr as-sbāʿ, bīr as-sbāʿ, ^{i}hnāka agūḷ-ḷak bī gaṣar la-wāḥad, all(i) yšūfo b-il-muṭraḥ addi ^{i}hnāk, yiḏbaḥo.” ʾimši, ʾimši, ʾimši,

92 She said to her, “But I am telling you, why [are] you here, that you are sitting here. Let him bring you—let him go and bring you from, e . . . from the lion’s water, you will drink. No. Go bring from the buzzing [things].” She said, “Bring [m.sg.] for us buzzing things, buzzing and bells.” She [had] said to her, “(Where are] these buzzing and bells?” “These [are] by the lions’ well, the lions’ well. There, I’m telling you, there is a palace of one, whom he sees in that place there, he kills.” Go, go, go [the boy went],

103 liga ġōḷa giddāmo. lamminno ğāʿada . . . laʾ, ğa ʿala, ğa ʿala—ʿala ḥūt. šaʿar ʿuyūnu, w-ʾaḏāfro b-al-ʾarḏ. gaṣgaṣ ʾaḏāfro u-gaṣgaṣ addye (ʾidē), u-gaṣgaṣ—činne mā gaṣgaṣ, u-gāḷ-ḷo, “ā, dazzatak al-essawīra, ʿağūzt as-saw?” gāḷ-ḷiha, “ʾā.” gāḷ-ḷo, “ʾā” gāḷ-ḷo, “widdak trū(ḥ) ʿala wiḥda, sitt tağriš sukkar, ḥāṭṭa bizzha warāha, ē . . . tiğriš sukkar. ē. ʾerḏaʿ min dī^{e}dha, taʿāl warāha, ʾarḏaʿ min dī^{e}dha u-ʾelham min es-sukkar.”

103 he met a *ġūla* in front of him, while [she was] sitting. . . . No, he came to—he came to a *ḥūt*. The hair of his eyes and his finger nails reached the ground. He cut his finger nails and cut his hands [the nails], whatever he cut. And he said to him, “Ah, the Essawīra sent you, the Old Woman of Evil?” He said to him, “Yes.” He said to him, “You have to go to one [f.], a lady grinding sugar, she has put her breasts behind her, e . . . she is grinding sugar. e . . . suck from her breasts, come from her back, suck from her breasts and eat from the sugar.”

116 gāḷat-lo hāḏi. laham. laham ^{e}mn-el-sukkar u-riḏaʿ min dī^{e}dha. winnha tgūḷ-ḷo, "'ā, lawinnak, lawinnak mā lihamt e. laḥaste min aḏ-ḏīrra u-lihamte min as-sukkar ğiddāmi, tanni ġār axaḷḷak ^{a}tmūt."

116 She said to him (he had sucked from her breasts, eaten from the sugar), and lo, she says to him, "Ah, if you hadn't, if you hadn't eaten e . . . licked from the abundance and eaten from the sugar in front of me, I would just let you die."

122 gāḷ-ḷo, gāḷ-ḷo, "dazzatak hiyya," winna tgūḷ-ḷo la-l–ʿaġi, "dazzatak ʿağūzt as-saw," čēn hu, hī ʿārfā. winnha tgūl, "ṭayyib, taʿāl," liha sabeʿ-^{iʿ}yāl, ʿindīhom sabeʿ ʿiyāl, ṭayyeb, ḥilew, ḥwate, ġwaḷa.

122 He said to him—he said to him, "She sent you." And lo, she said to him, to the boy—"The Old Woman of Evil sent you," possibly, she knew [it]. Lo, she says, "Good, come." She had seven children, they had seven children. Well, nice, *ḥūts*, *ġūls*.

118 winnha tgūḷ-ḷo, "wēn widdi 'arūḥ bīk? waḷḷa ġēr . . . wala 'imši msāwa bihim. ğābat—sawato, fff—niffaḥat ʿalē we-'inno 'ebra. ḥaṭṭata b-ṣaderha.

118 Lo, she said to him, "Where shall I take you? By Allah, just . . . and I will not go to appease them." She brought—she did "fff"—she blew on him and lo, he was a needle. She put it in her breast.

122 ğa 'ebenha 'az-zaġīr, winno yegūl, "rīḥet 'ins, ma-(a)dri ğens, ma-(a)dri huwwa 'al-yōm willa min 'ams [marra tāni] rīḥet ğins walla 'ins, rīḥet ben'ādam, walla hū čiḏeb wala min ^{e}mbārḥ ^{a}mā min ğa ʿalēk." winna tgūḷ-ḷo, "mā-bī ḥada."

122 Her young son came and lo, he says, "Smell of a man, I don't know smell of a *ğinnie*, I don't know if it is [from] today or from yesterday." ("Another time" [the listener asks her to repeat it:]) "The smell of a *ğinnie* or a man, smell of a human, or is it a lie, or since yesterday nobody has come to you." Lo, she says, "There is no one."

129 ʿāwad ğa aṯ-ṯāni, winnhum al-kull. ʿāwad ğa wāḥad winnhu yiʿuruğ, 'iğro maksūra. winno yugūḷ-ḷīha, "waḏḏarī walla aḏbaḥeč" winnha tgūḷ-ḷo,"li-tannkam ^{a}tgūlam ʿalēč 'aḷḷa, ʿalē 'aḷḷa w-amān aḷḷa w-al-xāyin yexūn . . ." hāḏi gāḷ -(ḷ)ha kullayāthom.

129 Then the second [son] came too, and lo, they were all [there]. Then one of them came, and he was lame, his leg was broken, and he says to her, "Then, show him, or I'll kill you." Lo, she says, "Until you say, 'Allah is [watching] on you, and on him, and Allah's security [is for you] and the traitor will betray [Alllah, and will be revenged]. . . .'" This—all of them said.

136 yōmin gāḷō-lha, gāḷat lēhum, "ṭayyib, hāḏ-huwwa." gḏabato, winno hā-š-šābb alli miṯel mā-kē(n)š. winno ygūḷ "'inta 'axūna bi-ʿahd 'aḷḷa w-al-xāyin yexūno 'aḷḷa." ṣār 'axūhin.

136 When they said [it] to her, she said to them, "Good, this is him." She took him, and he was this boy, like whom there is no one. And lo, he says, "You are our brother in Allah's covenant, and a traitor—Allah will revenge [betray] him." He became their brother.

141 gāḷat-lo, "yā-xūya, dazzatak al-xatyāra" winno yugūḷ-ḷēha,[7] "yā yumma, widdi. widdi . . . widdi danāden u-ğrās." gāḷ-ḷo, "'ā, hāḏi danāden u-ğaras, hāḏi maṭraḥḥa beʿīd u-maṭraḥḥa xaṭar." ^{i}nhāyto, rāḥam ğābu-lo.

141 She said to him, "O brother, the old woman sent you." And he says to her, "O mother, I want . . . want . . . want buzzing and bells." He [she] said to him, "These are buzzing and bells, these—their place is far and their place is dangerous." In short, they went and brought it for him.

147 rāḥ huwwa u-axū b-al-'awwal, gāḷ-ḷo—rāḥ. hāḏi ʿağūzt as-saw gāḷat lēha, "en ğāb leč?" ḏaḷḷat titxarraf inṭa iyyāha, čēf mā hāḏa ğāb la danāden u-ğa.	147 He went with his brother, at first, he said to him—he went. That Old Woman of Evil said to her [to the boy's sister], "Did he brings it to you?"—she continued to talk with her, did he give it to her, how he did bring her the buzzing things and came [back].
151 ^{i}nhāyto rāḥ hū w-axū, rāḥ ^{a}rčib ʿa-l-ḏahro, ġad 'a ṣāb ʿa-l-fōq, rāḥ ğābha ʿand malak, wa-l-malak hāḏa šagīhom; alli yigaʿ hināk yigṭaʿ ^{a}rgobto, wa-ʿarğo.	151 In the end, he went with his brother, he rode on his back, there, until he reached the top [height]. He went and brought it [the request] to the king. And this king made them miserable; he who comes there [by chance], he cuts his neck and root [original family].
156 šnū yirmi? yirmi ʿalē miʿiğza. [tiʿerif al-miʿiğza? hinne ʿalē b-al-miʿenā anno tiʿerif hīč, hīč, hīč, hīč. in ʿirifha—hāḏ huwwa yenṭī, w-an mā ʿerefha—yigṭaʿ ergobto.] hīč, ^{i}nhāyto, ḏaḷḷ warā u-ğiddāmo, u-yāxḏu wi-yğību, ta-mi ānno xaḏāhu. tā min ğāb—ğat al-danāden u-ğrās, šağara kebīra.	156 What does he ask? He asks him a riddle. (Do you know what a riddle is? It is that, its meaning is that you know thus and thus and thus and thus. If he knows it—then he gives him, and if he does not know—he cuts his neck.) Thus, in the end, he remained before and behind him and took and gave [i.e., answered all the riddles] until he took it. He brought—the buzzing and bells, [and] a big tree.
164 šālha—hāḏa al-ḥūt ač-čebīr 'alli 'āxar wāḥad. šālha, u-šālo u-rāḥ. ğābha, umā gāḷ-ḷo, "'essa in ğat ʿağūzt as-saw, widdi 'agṭaʿ rgubuta."	164 He carried it, this big *ḥūt*, the last [youngest] one, carried it. He carried it and went. He brought it, but he said to him, "Now if the Old Woman of Evil comes, I want to cut her neck."
168 ğat ʿağūzt as-saw, ^{i}twaḏḏar lēha—mīn, twaḏḏar lēha?	168 The Old Woman of Evil came, he hid for her—who, did he hide from her [from the old woman]?
170 'axūhā-l-čebīr. gāḷ-ḷo, gāḷ-ḷo, "taʿāl," yām-innha ğat winnha tgūḷ-ḷa, "yā ğidda, yā ğidti, ğāb ileč danāden u-ğrās?" gāḷat ḷēha, "'ā."	170 Her [the girl's] big brother. He said to him, he said to him, "Come." When she came, she said to her, "O granddaughter, o my granddaughter, did he bring for you the buzzings and bells?" She said to her, "Yes."
174 yōminha hazzata ṣārat ġēr 'ağrās u-ġēr al-ġanāni u-ġēr, yaʿani ka'annu rizz. yōminha ğāya, yōminna ğat ʿağūzt as-saw gāḷ-ḷēha, "taʿāli ğāy, 'ašūf, yaḷḷa." gaṣṣha min ^{a}rgubitha, u-qitalha, u-hāḏa xurrāfti.	174 When she shook it, there began the bells and the songs, that is, like rice [rice scattered in a happy wedding]. When she came, when the Old Woman of Evil came to them, he said, "Come this way, [let me] see, come on." He cut her neck and killed her, and this is my story.

C. The Emīr and the Slave

NARRATOR: Unknown

TRIBE: *ʿArab el-Saʿadiyya*

IFA 17421 September 2, 1982

1 hāḏa bī h(i)nāk hā-l-ʼamīr. marto lā tiḥbal wa-lā tǧīb, mā txaḷḷef. [fāhem inte?] marto mā txaḷḷef. hāḏa, ǧat hā-l-iyyām wu-rāḥat hā-l-iyyām, ǧat marto, ǧē ʿalēha, ḥilmat b-al-ḥilim, b-al-ḥilim, inno ǧāy ʿalēha wāḥad, yigayyiḷ-ḷēha, "iḏbaḥi xarūf," u-mā tākul minno. "u-ḥuṭṭī bi-manāṣef ṯnēn, [yigūḷ-ḷak], min hā-l-ᵃkbār, u-rūḥi ḥaṭṭī b-muṭraḥ xaḷa, mā fī ḥada."	1 This—there is this emīr. His wife neither gets pregnant nor bears a child. (Do you understand?) His wife does not bear children. Now, days came and days went [time passed]. His wife came, there came to her, she dreamed a dream, there came to her one, saying to her, "Kill a sheep [sacrifice animal]," and she should not eat from it. "Put it in two large trays and go and put it in a deserted place, where no one is there."
10 hāḏi ḏibḥat hā-ḏ-ḏebīḥa u-ḥaṭṭatha b-al-manāṣif u-fōgha—taḥtīha—rizz, u-fōgha laḥam. fī ʿendīhum ʿabed, [$_H$šaxor$_H$]. gāḷat-lo, "šīl hāḏa ʿala rāsak u-rūḥ ḥuṭṭo bi-muṭraḥ beʿīd beʿīd." rāḥ, bī ʿabraha hēč. ḥaṭṭo u-gaʿad bi-ǧanbo.	10 This [woman] killed the sacrifice animal, and put it in the trays, and above it—below it rice, and above it meat. They had a slave, ($_H$šaxor$_H$) black. She said to him, "Carry this on your head and put it in a very, very far place." He went. There was a storax tree like that, he put it [down] and sat at its side.
16 ʼaǧa wāḥad, šwoyye, šwoyye, šwoyye, w-hū gāʿed, wu-lenn hā-ṭ-ṭyūr ᵉṯnēn ᵉkbār, yaxwu ʿala hā-l-lagan. kalam, kalam, kalam, kalam ta-šibʿu.[8] gāḷ-ḷa, "šnū ʼinta titmanna la-hāḏi alli ʼaṭʿamatna?	16 There came one—slowly, slowly, while he was sitting, and lo, these two big birds, plunging onto the big bowls. They ate, ate, ate, ate, until they were satiated. It [one bird] said to it [the other bird], "What are you wishing for that one [woman] who has fed us?"
22 [mīn alli gāl? aṭ-ṭyūr ḥakam baʿaḏ] gāḷ-ḷo, "ʼana ʼatmanna ʿala ʼaḷḷa yibʿaṯ-ⁱlha ġuḷām,"[9] walad, yaʿani. gāḷ-ḷo, "w-ʼinte?" gāḷ-ḷo, "ʼana ʼatmannā-la mahma ṭalab min ṛaḅḅna yuṣil." u-ṭār.	22 (Who was that who talked? The birds were talking together.) It said to it, "I am wishing that Allah will give them a boy." A child, that is to say. It said to it, "And you?" It said to it, "I wish that whatever he asks from our Lord, it will be fulfilled [by Allah]." And it flew away [both birds].
27 ʼaǧa z-zalama, ḥaṭṭa, al-lagan, ʿala rāso u-rawwaḥ. gāḷat-lo, "šnū šift?" gāḷ-ḷēha, "waḷḷāhi, mā šift ši."[10] "mā šift ši, mā ḥad yeʿalā?" gāḷ-ḷa, "kabbētu," gāḷ-ḷa, "kabbētu u-rawwaḥt."	27 The man came, put the bowl on his head, and went home. She said to him, "What have you seen?" He said to her, "By Allah, I haven't seen anything." "Haven't you seen anything, no one coming up?" He said, "I dumped it." He said, "I dumped it [all the food out] and came home."

32 hāḏa, yōm min al-ʾiyyām, al-mara ḥeblat. ʾā, ǧābat. ǧābat walad. baʿadha mā xaḷḷafat, ṣārat il-mara biddha[11] tǧīb, mā kānat ^{i}trū(ḥ) ʿala ṣ-ṣbīṭārāt u-hā-š-šī—ba-l-bēt.

32 Now, one day of the days, the woman got pregnant. Yes, she gave birth. She had a boy. Until then she had not had a child. This woman was about to deliver [the child]. She did not go to hospitals and such a thing [she gave birth] at home.

37 hāḏa ǧeh, bas simaʿ ʿal-mart sīdo widdha txaḷḷef, waḷḷa rāḥ ʿala xetyāra yeǧīb-ilha lwān, mi-šān teǧayyib ilha. gāḷ-ḷēha, "šū bīč ba-s-serr?"[12] gāḷat-lo, "bīr mā bī gāʿ." gāḷ-ḷēha, "xuḏi hāḏa, sitte-ḏhabāt, u-alli tǧību ǧībi li ʾiyyā min baʿad,

37 This [slave] came, as soon as he heard that his master's wife was having a child, he went to an old woman, bringing her things [as payment], in order to deliver her. He said to her, "How is a secret with you?" She said to him, "A well without a bottom." He said to her, "Take this, six gold [coins] and whatever she [the wife] delivers bring me,

44 wara l-bēt, yaʿani, min wara r-rwāg, min wara r-rwāg, u-ʾana ʾanṭīki ǧaru zġayyūr."[13]

44 behind, that is, behind the porch, behind the porch, and I will give you a tiny pup."

47 hāḏa ǧat ʿād al- hiyya, al-dāye,[14] ad-dinya ʿatma u-lēl, xaḷḷafat al-ḥurma, tnāwalat al-ʿiyyil, zarragatu min wara ar-rawāg. ʾanṭāha ǧaru zġayyūr ^{i}bʿadu ʿanhum.

47 This, this midwife came, it was dark, and night. The woman gave birth. She [the midwife] took the baby, smuggled it behind the porch. He gave her a tiny pup, and distanced it from them [the house people].

52 "ǧābat—ǧābat, ǧābat mart al-emīr, ǧābat mart al-emīr, ǧābat." inhazam. ^{i}nhaǧat al-xetyāra min ġād. nāda al-hā-ʾaššīr, "taʿāli, ʾišrabi finǧān ^{e}ghawa, wa-ʿād tigḏebī-leč." ġayūr.

52 "She has delivered! She has delivered! The emīr's wife has delivered! The emīr's wife has delivered!" He [the slave] fled. The old woman [midwife] went away from there. He [the emīr] called for her, signaled [the husband], "Come, drink a cup of coffee, and again you will get [something] for you [a payment]." [He was] zealous.

57 ǧet hāḏi, geʿadat, gaḷ-ḷēha "šnū ʾaḷḷa baʿaṯ?" ṣārat tibči. "ʾē, yā—(ʾa)mīr, yā rētni mā ǧīt, yā-l-ʾamīr, yā rētni mā ǧīt, yē." gāḷ-ḷēha, "gūḷi." gāḷat-lo, "xaḷḷafat ǧeru." gāḷ-ḷha, "ǧeru—ǧeru. mā-ʿalēš. ǧeru—muš mehimm." ʿaṭāha maṣāri u-rawwaḥat.

57 This [woman] came, he said to her, "What has Allah sent [us]?" She began to cry, "O emīr, I wish I hadn't come, o emīr, I wish I hadn't come." He said to her, "Say!" She said to him, "She had a pup." He said to her, "A pup—a pup! Never mind. A pup—it is not important." He gave her money and she went home.

64 Al-az-zalame čān ʿind al-ʿabed, xaḏa al-walad u-xaḏa al-marbiya, ḥaṭṭo hunāk u-xaḷḷā. šwayye, šwayye, šwayye, šwayye, kiber el-walad. ṣār ʾiben sitt-^{i}snīn, sabʿ-^{e}snīn, fgado—

64 The man [the child] was with the slave, he took the child and took the nanny, he put him there and left him. Slowly, slowly, slowly, slowly, the child grew up, he became six to seven years old. He [the emīr] looked for him [the slave]—

69 mā yilgum al-ʿabd. ḥaṭṭ al-walad ʿala ktūfu, w-iǧāk, minhizem. hāḏa wiṣel la-ʿind al-maṭraḥ, ʿaṭšam.

69 they did not find the slave. He put the child on his shoulders and went, ran away. This, he reached a place, and they were thirsty.

72 gāḷ, "ddi-'ašūf 'iḏa al-walad hū ṣaḥīḥ, mehme yuṭlub min ṛaḅḅi, ta-yaʿṭī willa lā." gāḷ-ḷo, "yā walad, gūḷ, yā ṛaḅḅi, tibʿaṯ-^{i}lna mayya nišrab." gāḷ il-walad iz-zġayyur "yā ṛaḅḅi, tibʿaṯ ^{i}lna mayya nišrab" willa hā-n-nabʿa maftūḥa giddāmo. gāḷ, "kayyafet."

72 He said [to himself], "I want to see if the child is truly, whatever he asks from my Lord, he will give him, or not." He said to him, "O child, say 'O my Lord, send us water [so we can] drink.'" And lo, the small child said, "O my Lord, send us water [so we can] drink." And there was a spring [of water] open in front of him. He said, "I am happy."

79 xaḏa al-walad u-ṭār. ṭār, ṭār la-ʿind wādi ǧāri, u-nizel. gāḷ-ḷo, "yā walad," gāḷ-ḷo, "ā." gāḷ-ḷo, "gūḷ, yā ṛaḅḅi, tibʿaṯ-^{i}lna dār čebīra, gaṣur ʿāli, u-bīha kull ši." ṭalab, w-innha mawǧūde. ṭalaʿ ʿalē u-gaʿad bu hū w-al-walad.

79 He took the boy and flew. He flew, and flew, to a *wādi*, with flowing water [spring; the *wādi* is often dry] and alighted there. He said to him, "O boy." He said to him, "Yes." He said to him, "Say, 'O my Lord, send us a big house, a high palace with everything in it.'" He asked, and lo—it was there. He went up to it and sat [settled] in it, he and the child.

85 kayyaf. kull hāḏa an-nahār kayyaf u-yōminnu widdo yuṭlub 'akel, ygūḷ l-al-walad inno yuṭlub 'akel—kull šī mawǧūd.

85 He was happy. All the day he was having fun, and when he wanted to ask for food, he would say to the boy to ask for food—everything was there.

89 hāḏ al-ʿarab alli b-ḥadd a hā-l-mayye, tʿaǧǧabat, "mīn hāḏa z-zalame, 'aǧa yōm, u-ṣār ʿindu bēt, u-gaʿad, mnū giʿed?" 'aǧu ʿazamū.

89 These Bedouins who were living near that water [spring] were wondering, "Who is this man? He came one day, and had a house and he settled [there]. Who settled [there]?" They came and invited him.

92 yāminnom ʿezamō, rā(ḥ) ʿalēhom, sāwū-lo hā-l-ʿaša, u-teʿašša wu-nbasaṭ u-rawwaḥ. gām hū u-rawwaḥ, 'aǧa ʿ alā—ʿa-bēto, gaʿad 'esbūʿ ^{e}zemān, u-ʿizamhum.

92 When they invited him, he went to them. They prepared for him a dinner and he had dinner and enjoyed [it], and went home. When he went home, came to—to his house, he waited a week's time and invited them [to him].

97 ǧamma. lamma hum ǧamma, mā fī b-al-bēt mara, mā fī hā-l-bēt ḥada[15] [šāyif kēf?] mā bī ḥada hā-l-bēt. 'aǧa šwoyye, šwoyye, gaʿad—min ġād msakkar al-bāb. yifūt wi-ysakkar al-bāb. ǧāb lak ^{i}šnū hā-ṭ-ṭawlāt, laḥām, ruzz, kull 'iši bī. fawākeh. kalat hā-n-nās w-inbasṭat.

97 They came. When they came—there is no woman in the house, no one in this house (Do you see how [it was]?) There is no one in this house. He came, slowly, slowly, he sat—from there the door is closed. He [the host] enters and closes the door. He brought for you—what—these tables, meat, rice, there was everything. Fruit. These people ate and enjoyed [themselves].

104 xaḏa l-^{i}brīg u-ba- barra, fa’at (=fāt) wāḥad ḏ̣yūf. wāḥad min aḏ̣-ḏ̣yūf fitaḥ al-bāb, u- ṭall minha le-ʿağiy, liga l-ʿağiyy gāʿed. ʿabaṭo u-ğābo. gāḷ-ḷo, “mnīn lak hāḏ al-walad?” gāḷ-ḷo, “’ibni.” gāḷ-ḷo, “lā.” gāḷ-ḷo, “’ibni.”

104 He took the jug and—[went] outside. One guest, one of the guests opened the door, and the boy appeared in it—he found the boy, sitting. He hugged him and brought him [out]. He said to him [to the slave], “Where have you got this boy from?” He said to him, “My son.” He said to him, “No.” He said to him, “My son.”

110 gāḷ-ḷo, “lā. gūl-li mnīn lak hāḏ al-walad. ’inta ’asmar, hū ’abyaḏ̣. waḷḷa mā gu(l) t mīn hāḏa l-walad, ’alla ġēr agṭaʿ ʿengak šēle šēle. “yā mīr, yā mīr.” gāḷ-ḷo, “fiš xaḷāṣ.” gaḏ̣ab hā-le. . . .

110 He said to him, “No. Tell me where from you have this boy. You are swarthy [black], he is white. By Allah, if you do not tell me who this boy is, I will cut your neck entirely.” “O emīr, o emīr.” He said to him, “No rescue [for you].” He took the. . . .

115 gāḷ-ḷo, “hāḏa ’amro kiḏa, kiḏa, kiḏa, kiḏa, ’inno ’ana ’axaḏto min ʿinda—ta-lo yaḷḷa. “yā walad,” l-al-walad az-zġīr, gāḷ-ḷo, “mā lak?”

115 He said to him, “This, his story [issue] is this, this, this, this; I took him from—and so on.” “O boy,” to the young boy; he said to him, “What is it [the matter] with you?”

119 gāḷ-ḷo, “gūḷ, yā ṛaḅḅi, ’abūya al-ʿabd yiṣbiḥ baġaḷ u-’arkabo.” winno baġaḷ, rikbo. wu-yḏ̣aḷḷo māši. ḏ̣aḷḷam māšīn la-bēt ’abū.

119 He said to him, “Say, ‘O my Lord, this my black father will become a mule and I will ride him.’” Lo—he was a mule and he was riding him. They kept walking. They went to his father’s house.

123 ’abū haḏāk, ’ab al-kalb, al-kalb ğāʿed giddāmo. gāḷ-ḷo, “yā aš hā, yā zalame? min hāḏa?” “’ebni.” gāḷ-ḷo, “’ibnak kalb?” gāḷ-ḷo, “’ā, ’ismo ġassān. hāḏa ġassān ’ibni.” madd ʿalē š-šēx,

123 That, his father, the dog’s father, the dog was sitting in front of him. He said to him, “Oh what is this, o man? Who is this?” “My son.” He said to him, “Your son is a dog?” He said, “Yes, his name is Ġassān. This is Ġassān, my son.” The old man [sheikh] stretched himself and said to him,

128 “ušutt! ’ebze’ (ez) ’ibnak, we šū ’aḷḷa laʿab ʿalēk al-’agwa.” yōminn nihağ ʿala-mmo, gāḷ-ḷo, “gūḷ-ḷi, ’inta gut li ’ani mxaḷḷef kalb, wēn al-kalbe, wēn ’ummo, min alli ğayyabato?”

128 “Šū (driving the dog away)! I spit if [this is] your son. And what a trick Allah has played on you, the strongest [one].” When he turned to his mother, he said to him, “Tell me. You told me you have fathered a dog. Where is the bitch, where is his mother? Who has delivered him [the midwife]?”

133 hāḏa lli ğāy ʿa-ğanbo, gāḷ-ḷo, “gūḷ, yā walad, yā ṛaḅḅi, ’abūya yuṣbiḥ al-ʿabd miṯel mā hū” winno miṯel mā hū, al-walad—az-zalama al-xetyār. “hā, al-ʿabd ^{e}sʿīd, ’ahla u-sahla”

133 He came to his [the boy’s] side and said to the boy, “Say, o boy, ‘O my Lord, that my father will become black [slave] as he is.’” Lo, he is as he is, the boy—the man, the old man [the slave]. “Ha! The slave Saʿīd, welcome, welcome.”

138 (aš-šēx lāgāh), “’ahla u-sahla, waḷḷa wēn čāyin?” gāḷ-ḷo, “waḷḷa, čint ^{e}b-matraḥ u-mā-dri wēn, u-hassa ğīt.”

138 The sheikh [the dog’s father] met him [and greeted] him. “Welcome, welcome; by Allah, where have you been?” He said to him, “By Allah, I was in a place and I don’t know where, and now I have come.”

141 gāḷ-ḷo, "ad-dāye lli ğayyabat martak, xaḷḷīha trūḥ tiği hassa la-hēn." gāḷ-ḷo, "rūḥ, yā ʿabd, yaḷḷa rūḥ ᵉmʿā ʾoxra wāḥad." rāḥum ğābum ad-dāya u-ğat.	141 He [the sheikh] said to him, "The midwife who delivered your wife, let her come here now." He [the emir] said, "Go, o slave, go with another one." They went, brought the midwife and she came.
145 "ʾugʿudi. čīf al-mara hāy ğābat čalb?." ṣārat tibči, "yā (a)mīr, dxalak." gāḷ-ḷēha, "ʾani ğīt b-as-salāme. ʾiḏa ta-tgūli mīn hāḏa, hā ʾani ʿafēt ʿannek. w-ʾiḏa mā gulti šnū as-sīre, ʾalla ġēr hassa agṭaʿ rāsek ʾinti w-ʾiyyā."	145 "Sit down. How did this woman deliver a dog?" She began to cry, "O emīr, I beg your protection." He said to her, "I've come in peace. If you tell me who this is, I will forgive you, and if you do not tell the story, I will now cut your head off, you and his."
151 gāḷat-lo, "ʾani, ʾalla hāḏa-lli ğa ʿalēha, ʿaṭāni maṣāri u-ʿaṭēto el-walad, u-ʿaṭēto el-walad, w-al-walad hāḏa ʾanṭāni ač-čalb ḥaṭṭēto ʿend al-mara, ṣār ʾebenha, wa-dxalak, yā mīr, hāḏa alli sār maʿāya."	151 She said to him, "I, this one who came to her [me] and gave me money and I gave him the child and this boy gave me the dog and I put it with the woman, it became her son. And I beg your protection, o emīr. This is what happened with me."
156 al-walad mahma yuṭlub min ṛaḅḅu, ssa yigaḷḷo. gāḷ-ḷo, "ʾā." gāḷ-ḷo, "yā walad, gūḷ, "yā ṛaḅḅi, al-xityāra tṣīr čalbe, w-al-ʿabd yiḏaḷḷ baġaḷ." mā xiḷṣat—u-gāḷ-ḷo, u-hāḏi xurrāfti ṣārat ʿalēk.	156 The boy, whatever he asks from his Lord [he gets it]—now he tells him—he says to him, "Yes." He says to him, "O boy, say, 'My Lord, the old woman will become a bitch and the slave will remain a mule.'" It's finished—and he said to him. And this, my story, has passed on to you.

Commentary

This story belongs to the international narrative type ATU 707, "The Three Golden Children." I recorded three versions of the story, one from the ʿArab el-Zbēdāt tribe, one from the ʿArab el-Mazārīb tribe, and one from ʿArab el-Saʿadiyya tribe.

Here is a description of the narrative type in Uther's book:[16] Three girls boast that if they marry the king they will have triplets with golden hair, a chain around the neck, and a star on the forehead. The king overhears the youngest and marries her. When she gives birth to three marvelous children, the elder sisters substitute animals (dogs) (motif K2115, "Animal-birth slander. A woman is accused of having given birth to animals. Her children are put out of the way and animals substituted"). She is imprisoned (banished); her children are exposed but are rescued by a miller (fisherman). When they have grown up, the eldest son sets out to find his father, to seek a speaking bird, a singing tree, or the water of life. He and his brother both fail and are transformed into marble columns. The sister, with the help of an old woman, succeeds in rescuing them and in bringing back the magic objects. The attention of the king is drawn to the children and the magic objects. The bird of truth reveals the whole story. The children and their mother are restored; the sisters are punished.

This narrative type first appeared in print in Europe in the early sixteenth century in Giovanni Francesco Strápárola's book *The Facetious Nights* (Italian: *Le Piacevoli Notti*). Strápárola was a writer and poet who lived in Venice. *The Facetious Nights* is built as a group of stories integrated into a frame story, similar to the one Giovanni Boccaccio used in his fourteenth-century work *The Decameron*. Many of the stories in Strápárola's book are adaptations of folktales. The third story, told on the fourth night, is called "Ancilotto, King of Provino." In this story the king marries a girl who has boasted that she would give the king two sons and a daughter, each with golden hair, a gold star on the forehead, and a gold necklace around the neck. The queen indeed gives birth to the promised children, but the king's mother, in consultation with the midwife and the queen's sisters, exchange the children with three puppies, with a black star on their foreheads and a stain that looks like a necklace on their necks. As a result, the king throws his wife in prison.

The three children are placed in a box and thrown into the river. A miller finds the box, saves the children, and raises them. The miller finds that every time their hair is cut off, gold coins fall from it. The king's mother is told that the children are alive, and she sends the midwife to lure the younger sister to send her brothers on a dangerous search for the dancing water, the apple of the sweet song, and the talking bird. In the course of their search, the brothers become stone statues. Their sister follows them, rescues them, and brings the magical objects back with her. The talking bird tells the king what has happened. The king brings his children back home, releases his wife from prison, and sentences his mother, his sisters-in-law, and the midwife to death by fire.

Later versions of the story, such as the Italian version of the late nineteenth century written down by the folklorist Thomas Frederick Crane and the Russian version from Alexander Afanasyev in the middle of the nineteenth century, were probably influenced by Strápárola's version. However, it seems that this is not a story of European origin, as Thompson thought at the time, but rather a story of Asian origin.

The Bedouin versions I have written down can be seen to be very different from one another, yet they maintain the main lines of the international type. In all the Bedouin versions, the opening about the three boastful sisters is missing.

The story of Ḥalīma Ḥasan Slimān, a member of the tribe of ʿArab el-Zbēdāt, begins with the jealousy of the king's three barren wives toward the new woman he has married, after she turns out to be a prolific mother. In consultation with the midwife, they exchange her first child with a dog, the second with a cat, and the third with a stone. The children who were replaced are given to the gardener. The king punishes his wife. He expels her and makes her a kitchen slave. The midwife induces the young daughter to send her brothers on a search for the "half-world mirror." The brothers manage to obtain the magical object with the help of the "sorceress's daughter." The second time, the midwife tempts the daughter to send her brothers to look for the tree with talking birds. This time the sorceress's daughter sends them to a *ġūl* who keeps the object. The *ġūl* asks them to bring him the princess Faṭma, who lives below sea level. The sorceress's daughter warns them they might be turned to stone: "She said to them, 'Do not look back. If you look back, you will become a dry stone.'" However, unlike what happens in the ancient Italian version, the brothers are careful and do not turn to stone. They cheat the *ġūl*, hand him a wooden statue of the princess, and get the singing birds from him. In course of a banquet, in which the king also takes part, the birds tell what has happened. The king returns his wife and children to the palace and orders the burning of his other three wives and the midwife.

The story of Warda Hawwāš of the ʿArab el-Mazārīb tribe begins with a simple man who prefers another woman to his seven cousins, thereby arousing their jealousy. The woman brings into the world a handsome son and daughter, whose names are Moon and Sun. The cousins bribe the "Old Woman of Evil"[17] to replace the two children with dogs. It seems that she is the midwife, but this is not explicitly stated in the story. They put the twins in a box, which they place in the sea. A fisherman finds the box and brings it to the king. The king raises the twins, but the Old Woman of Evil snatches them and abandons them in the forest. At this point in the story, it becomes evident that the two children have miraculous properties: when they cry, it rains, and when they are happy, the weather becomes clear. A magical bird provides food for the children. The girl asks Allah to send them a palace, and her request is fulfilled. The Old Woman of Evil appears in the palace, tempting the girl to send her brother to bring her a magical object, "the tree of buzzings and bells." The brother sets off and arrives at the palace of a *ḥūt* (water ogre). He cuts the *ḥūt*'s claws and hair, and as a token of gratefulness for that service, the *ḥūt* sends him to a *ġūla* who has breasts on her back. The brother sucks on her breasts, and the *ġūla* does not hurt him. On the contrary, she hides him from her seven children, all of whom are *ḥūts* and *ġūls*. After they give the brother their protection, they go with him to an ogre, whose nature is not interpreted. The ogre poses to the hero some riddles, and after he answers them, he receives the tree of cymbals and bells, and the largest *ḥūt* of the *ġūla*'s sons helps him carry the tree home. When the magical tree is shaken, it makes sounds of cymbals and bells like those heard at a wedding: "When she shook it, there began the bells and the songs, that is, like rice [rice scattered in a happy wedding]." The *ḥūt* that brought the tree kills the Old Woman of Evil. At this point, the story ends abruptly. It can be assumed that the tree of the cymbals and bells was supposed to reveal to the king in some way the story of the brothers and bring about their reunion. Nothing is related regarding the fates of the brothers' parents and the seven daughters of the father's uncle.

The story recorded in the ʿArab el-Saʿadiyya tribe opens with a barren emīr's wife, who realizes in her dream that she must sacrifice a sheep and place it in a desolate location. The woman fulfills what is required of her in the dream. She slaughters a sheep and sends her slave to place it in a desolate location. Two birds eat the offering and wish for the mother to have a son, whose wishes will be fulfilled by Allah. The slave does not tell his mistress about the blessings of the birds. When the child is born, the slave bribes the midwife to replace him with a dog. The emīr raises the dog as if it were his son. The slave escapes with the child. He uses the child's miraculous qualities to build a palace for both of them and provide them with food. The slave invites an emīr with his tribe to a dinner. One of them finds the child, and the emīr interrogates the slave. The slave has to reveal his secret. The emīr tells the child to ask Allah to turn the slave into a mule.

He rides the mule with the child and brings him to his father's house, where, at the boy's request, the slave returns to his human form. The emīr, the child's father, investigates the slave and the midwife. When the deception becomes apparent, the king asks his son to ask Allah to turn the slave into a mule and the midwife into a bitch.

In all the stories, two characteristics stand out. First, the motif of jealousy. In the European versions, this is the envy of the sisters. In the Bedouin versions, this is the envy of the emīr's other women. In the second story, the seven cousins are the jealous ones. As is well known, in Muslim (and Bedouin) society, the marriage of cousins is quite common, as is the custom of *badal*—a marriage of exchange—in which a brother and sister marry a sister and brother from another family. The cousins expect the hero to marry one of them, and when that does not happen, they want to punish the bride. In the third story, the slave is jealous of his mistress and decides to benefit from his knowledge about the special qualities of the child and to abduct him.

The second characteristic emphasized in the stories is the motif of pride or bragging. The European stories begin with the boast of the three sisters. In the Bedouin stories, pride takes a different form. The midwife, who works on behalf of the king's wives, or the hero's cousins, is afraid that the truth will be revealed and tries to bring about the death of the brother or brothers. However, she is so sure of herself and of her ability to succeed in her plot that she challenges fate and sends the brothers to get the very things that will reveal her secret. So, too, is the slave who is far from the emīr's reach and who seemingly should not be afraid of revealing the secret. He is not satisfied with the fact that the child provides him with food and a place to live but wants to brag about his wealth in front of his neighbors, the tribe members, and it is precisely this boast that leads to the discovery of the secret.

The stories thus express criticism of two indecent human traits, jealousy and pride, and show how people with these qualities are punished.

The stories' heroes have opposite properties. They put their trust in Allah, and Allah helps them and fulfills their wishes. The second story describes the children's influence on the weather: "When they cried it began raining on them, and when they were playing it was good, it [the weather] was good for them." Afterward, the sister's wishes are fulfilled, and Allah gives them a palace. In the course of his search for the miraculous object, the brother reveals an attitude of generosity toward the *ḥūt*. He cuts off its hair and clips its long fingernails, and the *ḥūt* responds accordingly and helps him. In the third story, the child is described as one whose wishes are fulfilled by Allah, and Allah provides the slave water, food, and accommodation. The boy behaves innocently. He does not wonder that he is white and his father is black (the word *slave* in Arabic has both meanings: slave and black). However, the emīr, who has revealed the slave's secret, uses this trait later to turn the slave into a mule and the midwife into a dog.

The story is very common throughout the Muslim world, in North Africa, Israel, Syria, Lebanon, Iraq, Kuwait, and Iran, as well as in sub-Saharan Africa. In the Sudanese parallels, as in the first Bedouin story, the cause of contention is jealousy among the other wives of the children's father. El-Shamy notes fourteen parallels in the Egyptian archive of stories, almost all of which were told by women.[18] One of them is presented in his book.[19] Like the European versions, the Egyptian version he gives begins with the boasting of the three sisters. The king secretly listens to their nocturnal conversation. The older sister brags and says she can bake a cake that will feed the king's whole army, and the other sister promises to be able to weave a rug that all his army can sit on. The king marries the elder sister, but when he demands the fulfillment of the promise, she replies, "Night talk is covered with butter; it melts when the sun rises." The same happens with the other sister. The third sister fulfills her promise to give birth to twins, whose hair is gold and silver, and to call the children Sitt el-Ḥusn (Mistress of Beauty) and Šāṭer (Smart) Muḥammad.

With the help of the midwife, the sisters replace the children with a puppy and a kitten, and the twins are placed in a box and thrown into the river. A fisherman finds the box among the reeds. When he opens it, he discovers the twins, each sucking the other's finger. A motif that we met in one of the Bedouin stories follows: When the girl cries, it rains, and when she smiles, the sun shines. The brother goes out to get three wonderful objects for his sister: the dancing bamboo, the singing water, and the talking lark. In his last attempt, he fails and turns to stone. His sister comes to his aid wearing a man's clothes. At the end of the story, the king is invited to the twins' palace. He comes with the dog and the cat, which he thought to be his sons (similar to what happens in the third Bedouin story). The talking lark exposes the deception, and the king orders the midwife and the sisters to be burned. At the end of the story, the narrator remarks, "The tale shows how a brother must be kind to his sister and look after her, no matter what; and the sister more so!"[20] El-Shamy, in his preface to the story, comments: "Two major sentiments underlie the plot of this tale: affection between brother and sister and conflict among sisters over the same man; these sentiments are highly pervasive and stable in Middle Eastern cultures. The story also expresses hostility between female children and their maternal aunts, which is a product of conflict among the sisters. (i.e., the children's mothers)."[21]

It is interesting to note that some of the motifs that characterize the Muslim stories are also found in Celtic traditions. The end of the first branch of the Mabinogion, the Welsh national epic from the tenth century, tells the story of Rhiannon, the wife of Pwyll, King of Wales, whose son is abducted by a mysterious entity when six women employed to look after the mother fall asleep. The women kill puppies, smear the woman's face and hands with their blood, and accuse her of murdering the newborn baby. The king believes them and punishes the queen. She will have to sit at the gate of the courtyard, tell every passerby her story, and carry on her back anyone who asks. The golden-haired boy arrives at the palace of one of the king's friends, is raised by him, and after a few years is returned to his parents.

Several versions of the story were recorded in Israel. The Arabic version, which was recorded by Muhawi and Kanaana in the village of ʿArrāba in the Galilee, is very similar in general to the Egyptian version.[22] The nightingale's retort helps to clarify the meaning of the question posed by one of the birds in the Bedouin story: "What did one of them say to the other bird? Abu Ṣayyāḥ ['the yeller'] would you eat carrot?" In the Arabic version, there is only one nightingale. Before dinner at the home of the brothers, to which the king is invited, the nightingale asks the brothers to serve a dish of carrots with the rest of the food. During the meal, they turn to the nightingale and say, "Little nightingale, come and eat." And the nightingale says to them, "No, by Allah! Little Nightingale the Crier does not eat carrots, o you stupid people of this city! You bulls and donkeys! In all your life have you ever heard that a daughter-in-law of the king's household would give birth to a dog, a cat, and a stone?"

The king hears this and commands the midwife to be brought before him. He extracts the story from her and punishes her and the queen's sisters.

Muhawi and Kanaana point out in their analysis that the first concern of the three sisters at the beginning of the story is not only the need for food but also primarily the desire to marry husbands who will satisfy their economic needs. A woman has no firm social status unless she has married and brought children into the world. The daughter, who saves her two brothers who became stone and returns home with them, is a model for the ideal woman, who knows how to cope with dangers, unite her family, and achieve what she wants without losing her individual identity.[23]

Muhawi and Kanaana discuss the Arabic versions of the story and its sources in detail in their book, *Speak, Bird, Speak Again*.[2224] The story is also included among the tales of *Arabian Nights* in the third volume of *Supplemental Nights* that Burton added to his translation.[25] There are other versions in Bushnaq's book and in Schmidt and Kahle's book.[26]

In a Yemenite Jewish version taken by Nissim Benjamin Gamlieli from Zehava Sarah Jaridi (IFA 11593), the children are replaced by a grinding stone and a pestle. At the end of the story, the king's mother gives the talking bird poisoned peas and says to her, "Wonder of wonders, how does a bird pick up peas?" The bird does not taste the poisoned peas but replies: "Wonder of wonders, how does a woman give birth to a grinding stone and a pestle?" and the truth comes out. As in the stories from the Galilee, the astonishment about a bird that eats a carrot or peas is answered with a parallel astonishment: how a woman gives birth to dogs and cats or grinding stones. In this version, the brothers suck from the breasts of an *afreeta* (genie), just as in the Bedouin version of Warda Hawwāš. Sucking the *ġūla*'s milk and eating her food, like signing a covenant with bread and salt, makes the heroes part of her family, thus giving them her protection. In the Yemenite version, it is said: "Her mother's mercy overcame her looking at these children, and she said: 'What is your request, silly children? You're saved!'" and the narrator explains that once they have sucked her breasts, they are considered her children. This is also the case in another Yemenite Jewish version, written down by Elisheva Schoenfeld from Yefet Froy (IFA 40).

In another version told to Elisheva Schoenfeld by Mamo Damari, a native of Tunisia (IFA 42), a childless king and queen adopt a black slave. After a while, the queen dreams of an old man, who announces that she will have a child of her own, whose requests will all be fulfilled. The older queen is indeed pregnant and brings a son to the world. The slave threatens the midwife, forcing her to replace the infant with a dog. The slave takes the child and brings him to America, where he uses the child's virtues to build a palace and accumulate assets. After some time, he marries a woman, but he hides the kidnapped child from her. One day, the woman discovers the boy, who has grown up to be a handsome lad, and marvels at his beauty. She thinks to herself, "If I were not married, I would like to marry this lad." The woman forces her husband to reveal his secret.

The young man hears this and immediately makes a wish that the slave will become a donkey. He marries the woman and returns to his country with the donkey. There he meets his father, the king, who invites him to a feast. The king's son asks his father to take his mother out of the henhouse in which she has been locked up for bringing a dog into the world instead of a child. During the meal, the prince turns the donkey back to his human form and forces him to confess his deeds. The king executes the slave. He apologizes to the queen for the way he treated her and returns her to her former status. This story largely corresponds to the third Bedouin story. It is interesting to note that here the prince plays an active role in the plot.

In the IFA archives, there are other Jewish versions from Yemen, Turkey, Morocco, Turkish Kurdistan, and Iraqi Kurdistan.[27]

In the Egyptian version described above, the girl goes on a journey disguised in man's clothes and thus manages to conduct herself in a masculine world. However, when she returns home with her brother, she removes the disguise, and then her brother takes the initiative, rides the horse, and puts his sister behind him. It seems that she reestablishes her "natural" place, as expected from her in the patriarchal society in which she lives.

Ostensibly, the girl could have given up the services of the talking nightingale and directly revealed her identity to the king, but a woman has no voice in society. For her story to be accepted as true, she needs an objective witness who will denounce the stupidity of the king and the people around him.

Notes

1. This story is narrated by a seventeen-year-old narrator. Her speech rate is generally quicker than that of others. As with other narrators, she often exchanges Bedouin *ṯ*, *ḏ̣* and *č* to sedentary *t*, *ḍ*, and *k*.

2. *'ūliniyyāt*, f.pl. of "the first," has a curious form: in MSA (LA) the m.sg. form is *'awwal*, and in various dialects it can be *'awwalāni*. In MSA (LA) the f.sg. is *'ūlā*, and in the dialects we heard also *'awwala* or *'awwalāniyya*. The form *'ūliniyyāt* seems to combine both these patterns and add the sane f.pl. suffix *āt* to the word.

3. The narrating girl uses modern notions and terms for old ones—for example, she compares "the half-world mirror" to television, using the borrowed (foreign) word.

4. *biyyu* Note the form of *bī*, "in it," with the suffixed 3m.sg. personal pronoun with geminated y. This form did not occur elsewhere in these folktales. This seems to be influenced by similar forms in sedentary dialects.

5. *yā abū-ṣayyāḥ, tōkol ğazar? gaḷbi min hā-d-dīr(a)-infağar. mart–il-malak lā ğābat qiṭṭin wa-lā kalbin wala ḥağar. ğābat 'izz ad-dīn, yiḥya d-dīn, ḏ̣aww el-qamar*: "O Abu Ṣayyah [Yeller], are you eating carrots? " "My heart has broken from this house [area]. The king's wife did not give birth to a cat, neither to a dog nor to a stone. She gave birth to ʿIzz-ad-Dīn, Yiḥya-d-Dīn, and Ḏ̣aww el-Qamar. " This repeated rhymed birds' duet makes the punch line of the story. It resolves the problem for the king and the children. (Repetition often occurs in folktales, as noted in, e.g., chap. 18, note 4.) This rhyme also clarifies why the girl is named, Ḏ̣aww el-Qamar, "moonlight," which implies beauty, not religious elements, as the boys' names do, and why the *ḥağar*, "stone," was chosen when she was born; these words end with the syllable /*-ar*/, which rhymes with Arabic *ğazar*, "carrots," in the birds' duet.

6. *'ağūz as-saw*, the nickname "the Old Woman of Evil," contains two elements for discussion: the world *'ağūz*, "old woman," is used in LA for women, without a separate

masculine form for an old man or a feminine suffix for the women. However, in these Bedouin tales we find the form *'ağūz* used for both masculine and feminine persons, but for females, the suffix is sometimes added, thus *'ağūzt as-saw*. The word *saw* is related to the (LA) word *sayyi'*, "bad," which is not usually used in the colloquial dialects. "Evil" in LA is *sū'*; but the form *saw* occurs also in other Bedouin dialects. Marom, "Bedouin Dialect of the Women"; Lebling, *Legends of the Fire Spirits.*

7. The verb form in *winno yugūḷ-ḷīha* gets an infixed epenthetic vowel *u* in the first syllable, reflecting assimilation to the following *ū* of the verb pattern. This vowel is not frequent as an epenthetic in the Galilee Bedouin dialects, though it occurs also in sedentary urban and rural dialects of the Galilee. See Palva, *Lower Galilean Arabic.*

8. More features of non-Bedouin dialects occur in this story. For example, the Bedouin 3m.pl. suffix, *am/um*, is exchanged sometimes with the sedentary *-u* pl. suffix, as in *yaxwu 'ala ha-l-lagan. kalam, kalam, kalam, kalam ta-šib'u*, "They plunge on this big bowl. [They] ate, ate, ate, ate, until they were satiated."

9. This tale, like several others in this collection, presents all the (normal and magical) events as emanating from Allah, yielding them legitimacy based on religion. Typical expressions in this story include "What do you wish Allah will grant her?" "What has Allah sent us?" and "By Allah."

10. *mā šift ši*: "I did not see anything." The negative particle in these dialects can be with or without the correlative particle *ši*, but here the word is used in its original full meaning. (Cf. note 3 directly below.)

11. *ṣārat il-mara biddha tğīb*, "The woman began to be in the state that she was going to give birth," uses sedentary *biddha* instead of Bedouin *widdha*. Note the use of the Bedouin *widd-* for a prolonged action (cf. the discussion on it, p.XXX).

12. Keeping secrets is an important feature in human life and society, well known to the Bedouins. Henkin mentions the rhymed formula *as-sirr 'indikiy fī bīr?*: "Is a secret [as] in a well with you?" (so that it cannot be revealed). Henkin, "Narrative Styles of Palestinian Bedouin Adults and Children," 74.

13. Instead of *zġayyūr*, "small, very small," Bedouin dialects usually say *zġayyir*, a diminutive pattern of sedentary *zġīr* (Elihay, 2005, 612) and LA/MSA *ṣağīr*, "small" (*Wehr, Dictionary of Modern Written Arabic*, 516). *zġayyūr* is used also (at least) in Galilee sedentary dialects and elsewhere in the country. Al-Barghuthi, *Dictionary of Colloquial Palestinian Arabic Dialects.*

14. The *dāya*, "midwife," had an important role in women's lives in the past, before hospitals were built (in Israel and elsewhere). This tale presents some customs related to midwives. For her services, she got a very generous reward, particularly if the infant was a boy.

15. In the sentence *mā fi hā-l-bēt ḥada*, "In it [there is] no one," *fi* means literally "in" (not "there is," as in *fī*). Bedouin negation hardly uses the sedentary correlative *-š* (*mā fīš*, "there is not," occurs only once in this book, in the story "Frēṭ Rummān" [chap. 28], compared with thirteen occurrences of *mā fi*).

16. Uther, *Types of International Folktales*, 1:381–82.

17. The same nickname is given to the heroine of a story given by Joram Meron in the book *Seed of Pomegranate*. Meron, Shehadi, and Masarwi, *Seed of Pomegranate*, 144. However, that story has no resemblance to the Bedouin story.

18. El-Shamy, *Folktales of Egypt*, 255.

19. El-Shamy, 63–72.

20. Muhawi and Kanaana, *Speak, Bird, Speak Again*, 102.

21. El-Shamy, *Folktales of Egypt*, 63.

22. El-Shamy, 63.

23. Muhawi and Kanaana, 111.

24. Muhawi and Kanaana, 337–40.

25. Burton, *Supplemental Nights*, vol 3, night 667 in the story "The Two Sisters Who Envied Their Cadette." In this volume he discusses versions of the story from all over Europe.

26. Bushnaq, *Arab Folktales*, 89–94; Schmidt and Kahle, *Volkserzählungen aus Palästina*, 1:168–79.

27. Yemen: 12076, 15765; Turkey: 5998, 16563, 21263; Morocco: 5705, 6852, 11329, 11781, 14884, 16390; Kurdish Kurdistan: 18093; Iraqi Kurdistan: 2029, 5369, 5915, 6026, 8870, 9348, 10719, 14493, 14785, 16708; Israel—Druze: 22667.

37. The Ġūla, the Mallow Gatherer, and His Daughter

NARRATOR: ʿĀlia Muḥammad Ḥrēb

TRIBE: *ʿArab el-Ḥuǧērāt*

IFA 13252 June 3, 1980

1 hāḏa, b-al-xubbēz, kull yōm yerūḥ yeḥawweš xubbēza u-yerūḥ yebīʿo w-iǧīb la-banāto ʾakel. kull yōm yerūḥ yeḥawweš ^{i}lhen. kull yōm yerūḥ yeḥawweš w-ibīʿ.	1 This [man] [he is] in the mallow, every day he goes to gather mallow, sells it, and brings food for his daughters. Every day he goes gathering for them. Every day he goes gathering and selling.
6 yōm min al-iyyām ǧāy ʿa-ḏaher hā-l-maġġāra. ṭilaʿ ʿa-ḏaher hā-l-maġġāra yiḥawweš ʿa-l-maġġāra. ṭālʿa ʿalē hā-l-mara. gāḷit-lo, "ʿ yā ḥabībi, ^{e}nta tḥawwiš xubbēz; ʾani mā-n-uxtak[1] u-rḥal la-ʿandi." ǧāy rāḥ-el(a). gāḷ la-marto, hadd u-rāḥel, ǧāy māxeḏ banāto u-rāḥam. kull yōm i(t)ssāwī-lo rizz u-laḥam. kull yōm teṭʿimhom. u-kull yōm.	6 One day of the days, he comes to the top of this cave. He climbed to the top of the cave to gather [mallow] above the cave. A woman comes out of the cave to him. She said to him, "O my dear, you are gathering mallow. I—I am verily your sister, come [move away] to me [my place]." He came moving. He told his wife, took [their things] and moved, came and took his daughters and they went. Every day she made rice and meat for him. Every day she fed them and every day.
15 yōm min ^{a}zāt hā-l-ʾiyyām, rāyiḥ ta. ǧāya tishar ʿandīhom. gāḷit-lo, "ya-xūya, čalb niba(ḥ) ʿalayya." gām ḏabḥ-ač-čalb. rāiḥa māčla č-čalb. yōm, ṯāni lēla ḏi rāiḥa tishar. gāḷit-lo, "al-bgara daḥḥagat ʿalayya" ḏabḥ-al-^{i}bgara.	15 One day of the days he goes . . . she comes to spend the evening with them. She said to him, "O my brother, a dog barked at me." He took and slayed the dog. She went and ate the dog. Another day, at night she came to spend time [with them]. She said to him, "The cow looked at me." He slayed the cow.

21 gālit-lo marto, “widdna nhidd u-narḥal, widdna nhiǧǧ. hāḏi ’oxtak hī ġūḷa.” gāiḷ-lha, “’isma‘an, hāḏi ’oxti” gāḷit-lo, “ġūḷa” gāiḷ-ḷa, “’oxti.” gāiḷ-ḷa. . . .

21 His wife said to him, “We must break camp and move away. This sister of yours is a *ġūla*.” He said to her “Listen [pl.], this is my sister.” She said to him, “A *ġūla*.” He says to her, “My sister.” He said to her. . . .

25 ’iǧa yōm, šāila banātha u-hāǧǧa. gāḷit-ilha, “yā ‘amma, widdna (n)rūḥ ’aġassil hā-l-‘aǧiyyāt, ṣabbaḥan zārbāt. widdna rrūḥ nġassil ‘a-l-‘ēn.” bū ‘ēn, bi‘īda, bi‘īda, ǧāyya tgūl al-banāt “ḏ̣ubban ǧalla, ḏ̣ubban kōm ǧalle, u-mā” . . . dāirāt hā-n-nār u-minhazmāt.

25 One day, she took her daughters and left. She said to her, “O aunt, we must go to wash these girls. They got up in the morning [flowing] wet. We will go to wash at the spring.” There was a spring far, far away. She went speeding up the girls, “Gather dung, gather a pile of dung and do not. . . .” They made a fire and ran off.

32 mistaṭ^{u}wlīthin[2]—lāḥǧa ‘a-ha-l-‘ēn. mistaṭ^{u}wlīthin—ǧāya l-abu l-xubbēz, gāḷit-lo, “yā bayyē, ’aḷḷa, mnēn widdi ’āklak? hāǧǧan” gāiḷ-ḷa, “kulīna min liḥaiti lli-mā raddeit ‘a-bnayti . . . ‘a-mrāyti” māklīto. u-lāḥǧato kud ǧāya ‘alē ha-l-‘ēn, mī lāiga ġēr hā-n-nār.

32 She [the *ġūla*] thought they were gone too long [and not coming back]—she followed to the spring. She [the *ġūla*] thought they were gone too long. She came to the mallow picker and said to him, “O my father . . . Allah, from where shall I eat you? They have fled. ” He says to her, “Eat me from my beard, which did not answer to my little daughter . . . my little wife.” She ate him. And she followed—almost came to the spring—[and] did not find there [anything] but the fire.

39 ǧāyāt hāḏan fāitāt ‘ala ‘arab. dāxlāt ‘a-hā-l-‘arab u-fāitāt ‘a-hā-l-‘arab u-mxarrfāt ‘an guṣṣatin. u-ǧā‘dāt ‘ind hā-l-bēt hā-l-’amīr. yāklan u-yišraban u-yištaġlan ‘end hā-l-’amīr.

39 These [the woman and daughters] came to a Bedouin tribe, entered the tribe, and told their story. They stayed at the emīr’s tent, eating, drinking, and working at the emīr’s place.

44 yōm min hā-l-’iyyām, ‘ind(h)a bint zēna, semha frēṭ rummān, ṭālibha l-ibno.

44 One day of the days, she had a pretty daughter, whose name was Frēṭ Rummān [Pomegranate Seed], and he [the emīr] asked her [the woman’s] permission to marry [the girl] to his son.

46 hāḏ-al-ġūḷa (t)ddawwer ‘alēhen. sam‘āna[3] hā-l-ġūḷa widdha titǧawwaz frēṭ rummān. ǧāya hā-l-ġūla, msāwiya ḥāla mara u-ǧāya ‘a-hā-l-‘irs. ‘irs ^{e}frēṭ rummān.

46 This *ġūla* was searching for them. The *ġūla* heard that Frēṭ Rummān was going to be married. This *ġūla* came, made herself [pretended to be] a woman and came to the wedding, Frēṭ Rummān’s wedding.

51 ǧāya hā-n-niswān rāiḥa ta(t)ġadda hiyya wa-l-‘arūs. ḏ̣āḷḷa hiyya w-al-‘arūs. “rūḥi yā xityāra, rūḥi yā mara, kuli,” gāḷat-ilhin “la, widd(i)-’aḏ̣aḷḷ ‘end al-‘arūs.”

51 Those women come, going to have lunch, she and the bride. She remained with the bride. “Go, old woman, go, woman, eat.” She said to them, “No, I will stay at the bride’s place.”

56 baʿad mi- hen^{e} ʿād ğannāt, mšālḥa al-ʿarūs ʾawāʿīha, lābsa ʾawāʿi l-ʿarūs, fāḥra l-il-ʿarūs ğūra, u-lābsa ʾawāʿe l-ʿarūs, damla l-ʿarūs ba-ğ-ğōra. u-ḥāṭṭa lagun. u-čāfya lagun u-dāmli.	56 After they had gone, she took off the [bride's] clothes, put on [herself] the bride's clothes, dug for the bride a pit, and wearing the bride's clothes, she put the bride in the pit and put a bowl and covered the bowl [with various things] and put [it].
61 ğa el-maġrib ^{e}lḥam hin, mī hī, hiyye—hiyye mi hiyye, yaʿani. ṯāni yōm—mī hiyya. mistaxišš min hā l-ġūḷa. rāḥlin āʿdin al-ʿarab u-rāḥlīn al-ʿarab min hā-l-bēt al-ʿers, yōmēn-ṯalāṯa, rāḥlīn.	61 In the evening [the bridegroom] came and approached her—isn't she, is she—her—not her, that is. On the second day [he decided]—it was not her. He was afraid [thinking unto himself] from that *ġūla*. They were roaming, the Bedouin were staying and roaming, the Bedouin, from the house of the wedding, [where they stayed] two days—three [days], [afterward] they were roaming.
66 hāḏi ba-ğ-ğōra taḥt al-ʾarḍ, ṣārat da (=widdha)-tmūt. ʿandīhum muhra tākul ḥabb al-fihem. baʿad mā hum rāḥlīn, trū(ḥ) ʿa-ha-l-bēt tifḥar, tifḥar, tifḥar, tṣīr ʾiğirha tulṭum b-hā-l-lagun.	66 This [girl] in the pit under the ground became, almost died. They had a mare who ate the grains of understanding [was exceptionally clever]. After they went roaming, she went to the house, dug, dug, dug—her foot started kicking [bumping at] this bowl.
71 yrūḥūn yeğību l-muhra—tʿāwid. yrūḥūn yeğību l-muhra—tʿāwid. kinhin yešūfam al-muhra šnū be(t)rīd he. rāyḥīn fāḥrīn al- al-lagun rāyḥīn fāḥrīn al-lagun ʾalla hī taḥt al-lagun. frēṭ rummāan. ṣārat tāli rūḥ, ḏāble.	71 They went to bring the mare back—she would return [to the wedding place]. They went to bring the mare back—she would return [there]. They started looking—what the mare wanted, they went and dug the bowl under which she was. Frēṭ Rummān. She was almost a ghost, wilted [almost dead].
77 ğābūha, dāwūha, gāḷit-ilhum hīč hīč. ğāy il-ʾamīr, gāiḷ, "ʾilli yeḥibb al-ʾamīr, yeğīb ḥaṭab." ṣāira hā-n-nās alli hāḏi trūḥ, hāḏi teğīb ḥamla ṯintēn, ta-nnum ^{i}šnū mxaḷḷīn hā-l-ḥaṭab—ʾaʿla m(i)n-ad-dār.	77 They brought her [out], healed her, she told them so-and-so [had happened]. The emīr came and said, "He who loves the emīr will bring firewood." Those people began going. These brought two [loads], until [how much] they let the wood—made it [the pile] higher than the house.
82 wa-l-ġūḷa min hā-ğ-ğumla tḥaṭṭeb. gāiḷīn-^{i}lha, "ʾiṭlaʿi min fōg, min fōg, min fōg" tannum mxaḷḷīna ṭālʿa ʿa-l-ʾāxer, dāirīn hā-n-nār u m(w)allʿa hā-l-ġūḷa. u-mḥarūg al-ġūḷa w-al-^{i}ḥṭibāt, wa-frēṭ rummān māxeḏha bin-ʿamma. ḥikāyti ḥakēt wa-ʿa-brahīm ramēt.	82 And the *ġūla* was among those who cut the wood. They said to her, "Go up, up, up," until they got her gone up to the end [of the pile of wood], [then] they put fire and burned the *ġūla*. And the *ġūla* and the wood were burned. And Frēṭ Rummān, her bridegroom married her. I have told my story, and have thrown it to Ibrahim.

Commentary

The tale of the mallow gatherer and the *ġūla* is one of the most common stories among Bedouin tribes in the Galilee. I recorded four versions in three different tribes. An additional version, which I recorded in the ʿArab el-Ḥuǧērāt tribe, is part of a longer story, "The Two Brothers and the *Ġūla*," discussed in the next chapter (story 38).

In terms of narrative type, the story of the mallow gatherer and the *ġūla* belongs to the narrative complex ATU 327, "The Children and the Ogre," but it does not appear with the details of the complex in Uther's book.

Hasan El-Shamy defines it as a subtype, AT 327H§, "Foolish Husband Ignores His Wife's Advice and Leads Her and the Children to Ogress. He Is Devoured."[4] This type of story is unique to the Muslim cultural space. It is known all over the Middle East, Jordan, Syria, Israel, the Gulf States, Saudi Arabia and Sudan, as well as North Africa, Egypt, Tunisia, Morocco, and Algeria.

The following are the main story lines: A poor Bedouin who makes his living from collecting mallow plants meets a *ġūla*, who presents herself as his sister or his relative. She gives him food and invites him to come and live near her place of residence with his family. He accepts her offer despite his wife's objections. The *ġūla* tries to devour the hero's children. His wife manages to escape with her children, but her husband is caught. At the end of the story, the *ġūla* asks him, "Where do I start eating you?" And he replies with a rhyme—"Eat me from my beard, for I have not listened to my wife, and eat me from my testicles (or my ears) for not having listened to my daughters!" or in another version, "Allah is on my beard for I did not obey my wife"—and the *ġūla* devours him.

In four of the versions I recorded, the hero of the plot is a poor man who supports his family by selling mallow (*Malva nicaeensis*), which he collects. In one of the versions, he is also called Abu El-Xubbēz, "the mallow picker." Collecting mallow leaves and selling them as a source of livelihood testify to the poor economic state of the hero's family.

Grace Crowfoot and Louis Baldensperger write in their book *From Cedar to Hyssop: A Study in the Folklore of Plants in Palestine*:

> Among the wild greens that have to be cooked to be palatable by far the most important is the *Khubbezi*; it is abundant everywhere and known to everyone as a wholesome vegetable. It is best when cooked in layers with rice in between, *Khubbezi maklubi*, or *Shakhtura* as it is called. This way of cooking greens in layers is very like a recipe given in a 16th century cookery book for "A Sallet of Mallows." "Seethe them tender . . . over coals with butter and vinegar . . . and put in grated bread and sugar between every lay." Mallows indeed have been esteemed since the days of the Ancient Romans and earlier still, and they were the commonest pot and salad herb throughout the Middle Ages.
>
> But the Mallow to be really nice should be eaten young and this she laments in verse to her cousin the bean, for the bean is allowed to bear flower and fruit while her leaves are cut off early.
>
> "O my cousin, O bean pod,
> They pulled me up by the root, they will not let me grow tall"
>
> *Ya ibn ʿammi, ya qren el-ful* (lit. horn of the bean)
> *Qalaʿuni bi shurshi ma khalluni aṭul.*

Yet in famine years, even the old plants, disdained in time of plenty, are valued, seeing they are able to support life for a time. Two pictures come to mind, one of a poor old woman up above Amman, groping half blindly about, cutting off old plants all covered with dust, flowers, fruit and all, sure of a supper, however unsavoury; and the other of a woman who might have been her sister in age and poverty, in a bit of waste land in the heart of Constantinople, near Santa Sophia itself, gathering equally dusty plants into her kerchief. Such sights were multiplied in Palestine in the war years [World War I], so they tell. As in the book of Job, "For want and famine they were solitary, fleeing into the wilderness . . . who cut up mallows by the bushes for their meat." (Job 30, 3–4 [R.V. has "salt wart" instead of mallow].)

No wonder the poor sing to the mallow:

"O Mallow in the valleys,
Smiling like ladies;
O Mallow. I will raise thee banners
In the years of famine."

(*Ya Khubbezi fil wadat*
Bitbussim zey el sittat
Ya Khubbezi aqimlik rayat
Fi senat el ghalyat).

Like most Arab poetry, even this simple little verse requires some explanation. One might think that the first lines praised the smiling faces of the little pink flowers; not so, the allusion is to the veins on the leaves which look like the wrinkles caused by smiling. The third line of the verse speaks of the '*rāya*' to be raised for the Khubbēzi. The *rāya*, or white flag, is a 'banner' of love. Whenever you see one over a house in a village, you may know it as a sign of thanksgiving. There was once a boy at Artās who fell and injured his hand and it was long in healing; indeed at one time amputation was feared. But after treatment with salt he recovered and his parents set up a white flag before the door of the house, saying, "We raise a banner to our Lord" (*Ninqim rāyi li Rabbna*).

Again, in another case a child was sick unto death in Bethlehem, lying in the hospital, at a time of feasting. The people of his Ḥamūle (clan) in Artās would not feast but waited for news of the child. Then one day they saw his family returning from the hospital with the white flag carried before them, and they knew their prayers were heard and the child [was] saved. Then they hasted and killed the kid and made their feast.

So in the verse the white flags are promised to the Khubbezi as a sign of the gratitude of the poor.[5]

In Egyptian versions of the story, instead of the mallow there appears another plant, common purslane (*Portulaca oleracea*), which is also mentioned in the Talmud as a food plant (Babylonian Talmud, Rosh HaShana 26:2).

The hero of the story meets a *ġūla*, who presents herself to him in three of the versions as his sister and in one version as his aunt. In the Egyptian version of the story, the *ġūla* presents herself as the hero's sister.[6] In his interpretation of the story, El-Shamy argues, and I agree with him on this point, that the *ġūla* symbolizes the real sister of the hero and that the story describes the conflict between a woman and her sister-in-law. However, it can be said that the *ġūla* is perceived by the hero as an imaginary reflection of his actual wife, who, in contrast to his actual wife, does not force him to seek a livelihood (as is evident in the Egyptian version) but respects him and provides him with food without his having to bother to work. The husband is portrayed in all the versions of the story as someone who refuses to listen to his wife. The refusal to listen to a woman's advice has roots in Muslim religious literature. The Prophet Muḥammad is quoted as saying: "Look for their advice but do the opposite."[7] The story highlights the sharp contrast between the wise woman and her foolish husband. The woman does not accept the husband's words literally, but rather disagrees with them. Later in the story, she is portrayed as a resourceful woman who manages to extricate herself and her children from the *ġūla*'s schemes. This is in contrast to her naive husband, whose trust in the *ġūla* costs him his life. The family does not fall apart after the husband's death. The woman manages to survive with her children even without him. In the first version I brought, she also manages to marry her daughter to an emīr's son. In the Egyptian version, she inherits the *ġūla*'s treasures and moves to her home with her children.

The domestic animals that appear in the different versions of the story, a dog, a rooster, a cow, and a horse, are shown to be more sensitive than the husband is. Using their natural senses, they identify the imaginary sister as a *ġūla* and prevent her from carrying out her scheme. However, the foolish husband kills them at the *ġūla*'s request, thus allowing her a foothold in his house.

The hero's wife uses a series of maneuvers to save herself and her children from the *ġūla*. In one version, she uses inflated intestines to make sounds during the night and give the impression that the household has not yet gone to bed. She then initiates a step that will enable her to leave the house without arousing the suspicion of the *ġūla*: she soils the children to create the impression that they wet themselves at night and must be taken to bathe in the spring or in the river. The *ġūla* suspects her intentions and follows from afar, whether by means of a rope she has tied to the woman's foot or by the smoke rising from the fire kindled to dry the laundry. The wise woman uses another trick to delay the *ġūla* and escape: she cuts the rope by burning it and ties it to a stone (or tree in another version) or alternatively raises a bonfire with damp branches that produce a lot of smoke, giving the impression that she and her children are still nearby.

In some versions, the story does not end with the death of the husband. The *ġūla* continues to harass the woman and her children. In the version of 'Aliya Muḥammad Ḥrēb of the 'Arab el-Ḥuǧērāt tribe, the woman and her children get shelter in the emīr's house, and the emīr engages one of the daughters to his son. The *ġūla*, who hears about the marriage, disguises herself as a woman and stays with the bride. While left alone with the bride, the *ġūla* imprisons her in a pit, puts on her clothes, and pretends to be her. This motif of impersonation and taking the real bride's place recurs in other Bedouin stories I have collected. The emīr's son suspects her of being a *ġūla* but does nothing. The one who saves the bride is the mare, described by the narrator as one who has received "special pills of brains." At the end of the story, the *ġūla* is burned at the stake, after she foolishly brings the twigs to the bonfire and responds to the requests of those around her to climb up with the twigs to the top of the pile. This episode is repeated in other Bedouin stories, as well.

In the version of Ḥusein ʿAli Ḥusein of the same tribe, the woman finds refuge with a camel caravan. The camel driver releases a crazy camel, which attacks the *ġūla* and prevents her from fulfilling her nefarious intentions.

In the version cited in Muhawi and Kanaana's book, the *ġūla* turns herself into a dog and tries to enter the house of the woman and her daughter.[8] The woman pours boiling oil on her head, and the *ġūla* dies. She then invites all her relatives to loot the *ġūla*'s food treasures. Here, too, the importance of food in the plot is emphasized. In Muhawi and Kanaana's comments to the story, they mention another version that they recorded but did not include in their book. In that version, the *ġūla* appears in the form of a cow. The woman recognizes the demonic character of the cow by her laughter, and she flees with her children, while the husband is devoured by the *ġūla*.[9] A similar version was told by a Muslim narrator, Kāmel Ṭaha Yūnes, from the village of Ǧdeida in the north of Israel (IFA 24009). In this version, the hero, called Abu-Shalil, collects mallow and chicory. The hero is devoured by the *ġūla*, but his wife manages to trick her; she invites her to sit on a rug beneath which is a deep hole. The *ġūla* sits on the carpet and falls into the pit. Later on, the village *muxtār* and his men come and burn her.

A Syrian version of the story appears in a recent collection of Syrian refugee stories published on the internet: "Moḥammad aš-šāṭer and His Sister, the Ogre."[10] This version is identical in most details to the Bedouin versions I have collected, but it is rich in other motifs: The *ġūla* gives the hero's daughters magical milk, which is supposed to curdle in their knees and prevent their escape, but the mother takes her daughters on her horse far beyond the range of the magic. A similar motif appears in one of the Bedouin versions of the story "Ḥdaydūn and Grēʿa," in which the *ġūla* manages to prevent the escape of one of the heroines and devours her. Another motif is eating the hero's camel. Each time, the *ġūla* eats one leg of the camel and asks the hero how many legs it has, and he responds accordingly: three legs, two legs, one leg. This motif, G312.7, "Ogress devours horses," which apparently originated in India, appears in the group of Bedouin stories about the cannibal sister. The devoured animal there is a mare and not a camel. The name of the hero, Clever Ḥasan, is identical to the hero's name in the story of Faṭma ʿAbdallah, "The Two Brothers and the *Ġūla*," discussed in the next chapter. In both cases, the name is ironic because the protagonist is not really clever.

Another Syrian version abounding with rhymes appears in Bushnaq's book.[11] In this version, too, the story ends with the husband's being devoured by the *ġūla*.

Meron collected a full version of the story from Khalil Abu Yassin from Yamma (a Muslim village in the "Triangle" area in the Sharon). The story is entitled "Bsetān's Wife and the *Ġūla*." In this version, the hero and his wife, like Ruth the Moabite, collect wheat and barley leftovers in the field after the harvest. The verb *itbaʿar* in Arabic refers to the act of gathering, and the noun *buʿʿār* is used for the poor who usually gather in the fields, especially after the end of the olive harvest.[12] The story ends with the husband being devoured by the *ġūla* and the *ġūla* being killed by the woman, using boiling oil spilled on her head, as in the version of Muhawi and Kanaana.

In a Jewish version from Morocco, told to Haya Bar-Yitzhak by Farcha Haputa (IFA 16445), the hero and his family arrive at the house of a *ġūla* who has seven sons. The woman's daughters are forced to serve the *ġūla*, clean her teeth, delouse her, and so forth.

The *ġūla* is plotting to devour the girls. During the night, the hero's wife exchanges the headgears of her daughters with the headgears of the *ġūla*'s sons, and the *ġūla* devours her sons instead of the girls. The woman runs away, and the *ġūla* devours her husband. Later on, the *ġūla* falls into the river and drowns, and the woman and her children acquire her property. Exchanging head coverings is a motif known from other versions of the narrative type ATU 327.

The story is thus a distinctly feminine story, emphasizing the husband's need to consider his wife's opinion and act according to her advice. The rhymed answer at the end of the story further emphasizes the importance of listening to the counsels of the woman and the children. It appears in three of the versions I gathered, as well as in parallel versions from neighboring countries. El-Shamy added in his book a separate motif that describes this episode, J229.16.5.1§, "Captive man to ogress: who is captured by the monster turns to her and says, 'Devour me beginning with my little ears (beard) which did not heed my wife's fears (advice),'"[13] This rhyme further illustrates the hidden message in the story.

Notes

1. *'ani mā-n-uxtak*: "I am verily your sister." The stories are full of words that are glued together (amalgamated) because of high speech rate, and often some parts of the words are deleted in the process. Here, the *-n-* stands for *'ani*. This process can occur in all types of words and phonemes in the sequence (e.g., *'alāmkam*, "why-what-you [pl.]"; cf. chap. 15, note 3). Usually, the unstressed parts of the word are deleted or shortened if a long vowel is involved. Note the many examples of such "condensed" utterances in this volume.

2. The verb *mistaṭuwlīthin*, "She [the ġūla] thought they were gone too long," develops the root *ṭāl*, "was long" (cf. *ṭawīl*, "long [m.sg.]"), with the meaning "feeling/thinking (something)" of the tenth verb measure with the prefix *ist-*, as in *istaṭāl*. The accusative bound pronoun *-hin* is attached to the verb, thus yielding this very complex meaning in one word.

3. The pattern in *sam'āna* (with *-ān*[*a*] suffixed to the root) is an adjectival pattern usually used to denote personal states (e.g., hungry, thirsty, tired), but it is rather rare for this meaning of "listening, hearing, as a continuous state." For sedentary dialects and the use of this form for the name Simeon, cf. Barthélemy, *Dictionnaire arabe-français*, 358.

4. El-Shamy, *Types of the Folktale in the Arab World*, 166–68.

5. Crowfoot and Baldensperger, *From Cedar to Hyssop*, 32–34.

6. El-Shamy, *Tales Arab Women Tell*, 199–207.

7. El-Shamy, 387, com. 482.

8. Muhawi and Kanaana, *Speak, Bird, Speak Again*, 234–37.

9. Muhawi and Kanaana, 363.

10. Abu Risha, *Timeless Tales*.

11. Bushnaq, *Arab Folktales*, 137–41.

12. Meron, Shehadi, and Masarwi, *Seed of Pomegranate*, 103–11.

13. El-Shamy, *Types of the Folktale in the Arab World*, 166.

38. The Two Brothers and the Ġūla

NARRATOR: Ṯalğe Mūsa

TRIBE: *ʿArab el-Ḥuğērāt*

IFA 17403 February 2, 1982

1 fī hnāk hā-l-uwlād aṯ-ṯnēn. hāḏa ʾabūhin mitğawwez, hā-l-ⁱwlād sayyabhen hēk, l-ᵉṯnēn, ʾismam ḥasan wa-ḥsēn. yōm w-himme māšīn ʾağu ʿala basātīn et-tīn, qaʿadu yōklo. ⁱṭṭaḷḷaʿu willa hā-l-ġūḷe sārḥa b-al-ʿanzāt. šāfathim.	1 There are there two boys. These, their father married and left the boys on their own like that, the two. Their names [are] Ḥasan and Ḥusein. One day when they were walking, they came to fig-tree orchards. They sat down to eat. They looked and lo, this *ġūla* was herding the goats. She saw them.
8 gāḷat-ⁱlhin, "wān rāyḥīn, yōmma, ʾana ʾimmkum." ʾağu, šū biʿarref al-iwlād ʾinno ʾimmhum ġūḷa willa miš ġūḷa? ʾağu yurukḏu la-ʿindha. ṣāru yxarrfu baʿaḏhin, gāḷū-ḷu, "ġūḷe." haḏāk yequḷ-ḷo "lāʾ." wāḥad minhom ᵉšwayye, mağnūn ᵉšwayy, wāḥad minhin mlīḥ.	8 She said to them, "Where are you going, o my child? I am your mother." What do the children know if their mother is a *ġūla* or not a *ġūla*? They came running to her. They started talking with each other, they said, "(She is a) *ġūla*." That one says to him, "No." One of them [is] a little crazy [and] one of them [is] good [in the head].
15 ṭayyeb w-ağa gāḷ-ḷo, l-al-walad, qāḷ-ḷo, "wallak, hāy ġūḷe." qāḷ-ḷo, "lāʾ, miš ġūḷe." saḥabam ḥālum, u-rāḥum maʿha. ʾağu ʿindha ulliˡ fawwatathum ʿindha l-il-mġāra. gālat ilhum, "tisraḥu li b-hā-l-ʿanzāt, yā yamma?" qālu la, "ʾā."	15 Good, and he came and said to him, to the boy, he said to him, "Woe on you, she is a *ġūla*." He said to him, "No, she is not a *ġūla*." They took off and went with her. They came to her and she [who] let them into the cave [her place]. She said to them, "Will you herd for me the goats, o child?" They said to her, "Yes."

21 haḏōl l-^{i}wlād, kull yōm yrūḥu yisraḥu. yōm qāḷu “walla, sibnā, ḏī, widna nōkol saxal min hā-l-ʿanzāt. widna naḏbaḥ saxal nōklu.”

21 Those boys, every day they would go to herd [the goats]. One day they said, “By Allah, let us leave her. We want to eat a kid of these goats. We want to kill a kid to eat it.”

25 ḏabaḥa saxel wa-kalō. ʾakalu minno šwayy. wēn ḥaṭṭū? ḥaṭṭū ʿa-ḏ̣ahr hā-l-xarrūbe. bī xarrūbe, ḥaṭṭū ʿa-ḏ̣ahr al-xarrūbe. kull yōm, yīğu yōklu minno šwayy.

25 He killed a kid and they ate. They ate a little of it. Where did they put it? They put it on top of the carob tree. There was a carob tree, [so] they put it on top of the carob tree. Every day they would come and eat of it a little.

30 ʾağat kull yōm teʿiddhin, hā-l-ʿanzāt. tlāqīhin rāyiḥ minhin. kull ʾesbūʿ, kull ğimʿa[2] yaʿani, yōklu saxal. qāḷat-^{i}lhum baʿadēn, “biddi haḏōl al-^{u}wlād, biddhin yōklu ʿanzāt. biddi ʾaqūḷ–^{i}ḷhin illi mā yākulu l-ʿanzāt.”

30 She came every day to count them, the goats. She found that some were missing of them. Every week, every week, that is, they would eat a kid. She said to them, afterward, “I want these children—they want to eat goats. I want to tell them not to eat the goats.”

36 ^{i}b-hā-li-mġāra bī barāġīṯ. bī hāḏa hēke zġīr, ^{e}zġīr, hēk yōkel, yaʿani berġūṯ huwwa min el-ʾarḏ̣, min el-[$_{H}$ʾadama$_{H}$]. hāḏa [$_{H}$ʾadama$_{H}$] qabel, el-yōm fīš minno. šū ṣār el-walad yuqūl-lha? xāf. gāḷ-ḷa, “yamma ḥaṭṭīni bi-s-salle, fōq.” qāḷat-ḷo, “lēš, yamma?” gāḷ-ḷa, “el-barāġīṯ ʾaklatni. ḥaṭṭīni bi-s-salle wa-ʿalqīni.”

36 In this cave, there were ticks. There is, this small [bug] like that, small, like that eating, that is, a tick is from the ground, from ($_{H}$Adama$_{H}$) ground. This ($_{H}$Adama$_{H}$) ground, [was] before, today there is nothing of it. What did the boy begin to say to her? He was afraid. He said to her, “O mother, put me in a basket above.” She said to him, “Why, my child?” He said to her, “The ticks have eaten me. Put me in the basket and hang me up.”

45 hāḏa ṣār. nawwamat wāḥad fōq w-istannat, wāḥad ḥadda hī. twalleʿ hā-n-nār b-il-mġāra b-al-lēl u-tqarreb annha tōkl el-walad. ken haḏāk ṣār hēk “eḥ-eḥ . . . eḥ”

45 This happened [she did it]. She put one above to sleep, and was waiting—one [was] near her [to fall asleep]. She made fire in the cave in the night and approached to eat the child. That one went like that: “Eḥ eḥ-eḥ . . . eḥ.”

50 qālt-lo, “nām, yā yamma.” qāḷ-ḷa, “kīf ʾanām, kīf ʾanām u-baṭni xāli (min ṭaʾām) widdi ʾākul ğāğe min hāḏi as-smān.” yaʿni min al-^{i}čbīrāt.

50 She said to him, “Sleep, child.” He said to her, “How shall I sleep, how shall I sleep, and my belly is empty [of food]? I want to eat a chicken, of the fat chickens.” That is, of the big ones.

54 (wid)da-trūḥ hāy ba-l-lēl hāy, tiḏbaḥ hā-ğ-ğāğe u-tšalweṭ-lo yyāha. u-ḏi tqul-lo, “xuḏ yā yamma, kul u-nām.” hī di-trūḥ ta-tōkol haḏāk-al-walad. ti(t)qarrab ʿalē. yṣīr (y)itnaḥnaḥ w-iqūḷ, “kīf ʾanām, u-kīf ʾanām u-qalbi xāli min aṭ-ṭ(a)ʿām?” tqūḷ-ḷo, “nām, nām.”

54 This one goes and kills the chicken and roasts it for him, and she tells him, “Take, o child, eat and sleep.” She wants to go and eat that child. She approaches him. He begins to groan and say, “How shall I sleep and how shall I sleep and my belly [is] empty of food?” She said to him, “Sleep, sleep!”

61 yōm šāfha, qāḷ-ḷa, “walak, hāḏi ġūḷe, widda tākulna, widdna neh^{e}zim.” šū ṣār bitʿadd il-ʿanzāt? taqūḷ-ḷha—yeqūḷ-ḷa, “wān rāyḥāt al-ʿanzāt?” yeqūḷ-ḷha, “’ana, ’ana ’aqūḷ ḷ-axūye, hū yeʿiddhen, ’ana-(a)qūḷ-ḷo ^{e}ṯnēn-^{e}ṯnēn,” yaʿani ṣār ḏābiḥ ṯintēn. hū yeqūḷ-ḷa “la’, truddiš .” yeqūḷ-ḷa, “^{e}ṯnēn-^{e}ṯnēn” yeqūḷ-ḷa “truddeš. ^{e}ṯnēn-^{e}ṯnēn.” fišš, yaʿani ṣāram ḏābḥīn ^{e}ṯnēn.	61 When he saw her, he said to him, “Woe to you, this is a *ġūla*, she wants to eat us, we must run away.” What happened [when] she counted the goats? She says to him, “Where do the goats go?” He says to her, “I, I tell my brother, he counts them. I tell him two-two [by pairs],” that is, he butchered two. He says to him, “No, do not answer.” He says to him, “Two-two.” He says to him, “Do not answer two-two.” Nothing. That is, they had butchered two.
70 yōm qāḷ-ḷo, qāḷ-ḷo “biddna ni-nihzim.” qāḷ-ḷo, “yaḷḷa.” haḏōl sarahu bi-hā-l-ʿanzāt, w-inhazamu. inhazamu, ’aǧu ʿa šaṭṭ hāl-baḥar. šū ṣār(u) yiʿamalu b-aṭ-ṭīn, bi-t-trāb? niʿemal hēk, uwlād yiʿmalam hēk miṯel qadāḥ, yaʿani, hēk, kāsāt yiʿmalu, kubbayāt, u-’iši min hā-llē-hā.	70 One day, he said to him, “We shall run away.” He said to him, “Let’s.” Those went to herd these goats and ran away. They ran away, and came to the shore of this sea. What did they begin to do in the mud, in the ground? We do like that, children do like this, cups, such cups they do, glasses and such [things].
77 willa hī ǧāye min ġād, el-ġūle, turkuḍ. qālat-^{i}lhin,”nhazamtem, widd(i) ’ākulku” qāḷu, “šū biddna nsāwī-lha?” qāḷ-ḷo, “^{a}ssa bindibbha b-il-baḥer haḏāka.” qāḷ-ḷo, “šū biddna bindibbha b-il-baḥar?”	77 Lo, she, the *ġūla*, came from there [the distance] running. She said to them, “You ran away, I will eat you.” They said, “What shall we do to her?” He said, “We shall throw her now to that sea.” He said to him, “What [how] shall we throw her to the sea?”
82 ’aǧat, tmāsakat hī wiyyāhin, hī w-il-^{i}wlād. ṣār ydizzha ʿala l-qadāhi, šū yeqūl-la? yeqūl-la “ibiʿdi ʿan il-qadāḥi, ibiʿdi ʿan il-qadāḥi,” tannhin qarrabūha aṯ-ṯnēn yidizzu biha, ta-zattūha b-il-baḥar. yōm zattūha b-il-baḥar, šū qālat-^{i}lhin? qālat-^{i}lhin, “ṭallʿūni u-banṭīku alli bi-l-kwār. ṭallʿūni u-banṭīku lli ʿandi ṭāḥūni. [yaʿani ṭaḥūni, illi biṣammdu ʿalēha.] ^{i}ṭallʿūni, banṭīku-lli b-iš-šwāl.”	82 She came and began to grapple with them—she and the boys. He began pushing her to the cups [of sand], and what does he say? He says to her, “Get away from the cups, get away from the cups,” until they drew her near [the sea] these two, and pushed her until they threw her into the sea. When they threw her to the sea, what did she say to them? She said to them, “Get me out and I’ll give you what is in the cupboards. Get me out and I will give you the mill I have.” (That is a mill, in which they grind [wheat].) “Get me out and I’ll give you what there is in the bags.”

92 qāḷu-ḷha, “mūti w-il-kull ^{i}lna, mūti.” hāy mātat. wān riǧʿu? riǧʿu ʿa-l-^{i}mġāra. wāḥad minhen, el-walad hāḏa l-ʿāqel, li-mlīḥ, ’axaḏ, malla hā-š-šwāl maṣāri u-ḏahab. haḏāk el-maǧnūn šwayye, ḥiml aṭ-ṭaḥūni. [tiʿrif aṭ-ṭaḥūne alli biṣimmdu ʿalē?] ḥiml aṭ-ṭāḥūna, ḥaṭṭ waḥade hōn u-waḥade hōn, ḥāmelhom u-miši. u-’axaḏ bāb-šaqfet xašabe hī hā-l-qaddi, u-’axaḏ ^{e}šwayyet fūl.	92 They said to her, “Die and all [of it] is ours, die.” This one died. Where did they return? They returned to the cave. One of them, this smart boy, the good [one], took, filled the bags with money and gold. That, the somewhat-crazy one carried the mill (you know the mill which they grind with?). He carried the mill, put one here and one here, carried them and went. He took a door, a piece of wood, of this size, and took some fava beans.
102 qā-ḷo, “walak, lawēš, šu biddak bīhin?” qāḷ-ḷo, “biddi ’ākul, mayyit ’ani min aǧ-ǧū^{a}ʿ.	102 He said to him, “O you, what for, what do you want [to do] with them?” He said to him, “I want to eat, I’m dying of hunger.”
105 mišyu haḏōl, mišyu mišyu miṯil mā tqūl ʿala-l-baṭṭōf, fī b-il-baṭṭōf saǧara. saǧara b-il-baṭṭōf min tiḥitha. qaʿadu ʿala hā-s-saǧara haḏōl u-qaʿadu wulla hum buqūḷu, “’aǧat ǧēš u-suwwāḥ, yaʿani, xēm, ’aǧat al-ġazzāy, ’essa tiġzīna.” ’essa ’aǧa ʿas-saǧara.	105 These went, went, and went, as you say, to the Baṭṭōf [Valley]. There is in the Baṭṭōf a tree. A tree in the Baṭṭōf under which [to sit]. They sat at [the shade of] this tree. They sat at this tree, and sat, and lo, they say, “A group [of army] and travelers is coming, that is a camp. The raiders came. They will loot us now.” Now, he came to the tree.
112 haḏāk ṭileʿ, qāḷ-ḷak “’āxuḏ-lak hā-ṭ-ṭaḥūne?” qāḷ-ḷo, “šū biddna ba-ṭ-ṭaḥūne (i) nno nōxoḏha?” qāḷ-ḷo, “xuḏ hā-ṭ-ṭaḥūne, šū biddak fīna, iṭlaʿ fōq.” ’aṭlaʿo.	112 That one climbed up and said to him, “Shall I take [for you] the mill?” He said to him, “What do we need the mill for, that we shall take it?” He said to him, “Take this mill, what do you want with it? Climb up.” He lifted it.
116 qāḷ-ḷo, “’aṭlaʿ el-fulāt.” ’aṭlaʿ el-fulāt, u-’aṭlaʿ el-bāb. ḥaṭṭha la-ṭ-ṭaḥūni. ḥaṭṭ ha-l-bāb min hā-š-šikel ʿala hā-l-ʿudānāt hēk, u-ḥaṭṭ hā-ṭ-ṭaḥūne ʿalēhen.	116 He said to him, “Take up the fava beans.” He lifted the broad beans and the door. He put it for the mill—he put it this way on the branches—and put the door and put the mill on them.
120 u-’aǧu min eš-šams we-l-ḥamm, ’aǧu nās illi maʿhin al-xēl, u-maʿhin il-hāḏa, qaʿadu taḥt eš-šaǧara. we-šū hāḏ ṣār yesāwi? hū min fōq, u-qāʿed yešuxx ʿalēhin. qāḷu, “kiš, ʿaṣfūr, kiš, ʿaṣfūr” u-hinne miš šāifīno. “kiš, ʿaṣfūr, kiš, ʿaṣfūr” u-yešixx ʿalēhen,	120 They [the group] came from the sun and the heat. People came with them, people who had horses and had this, and they sat under the tree. What did this start to do? He [was from] above, and sitting pissing on them. They said, “Shoo, bird, shoo, bird,” and they did not see him. “Shoo, bird, shoo, bird,” and he was pissing on them.
127 “kiš, ʿaṣfūr,” tannhen yerūḥu la-ġād, yesāwu la-ġād šwoyy.	127 “Shoo, bird,” so that they will go away there, move a little away.

129 misek, ḥaṭṭ aṭ-ṭaḥūne, ṣār yeḥuṭṭṭ fūl u-yiṣmid. qāḷ-ḷu, "habbat as-sama. habbat as-sama, habbat" inhazamu. illi daššar faraso, illi daššar sayyārto, illi daššar maṣriyyāto, taḥtīha, ta ǧaw nādaw, qāḷu, "habbat as-sama. habbat." inhazamu. hadōl inhazamu.

129 He took, put the mill, began putting in the broad beans and grinding it. They said, "The sky has fallen. The sky has fallen, it has fallen." They ran away. One left his mare, one left his car, [another] one left his money, under it [the tree]. Then they came and called, they said, "The sky has fallen, has fallen." They ran away. Those ran away.

136 gāḷ-ḷo, "šūf, hiyyāna d̲i nefʿat aṭ-ṭaḥūn(e)." nizlu had̲lāk, rikbu, kull wāḥad faras, u-ḥaṭṭ hā-ṭ-ṭaḥūn ʿal-ǧanb min hōn u-ǧanb min hōn. wu-rikeb al-faras u-miši. gāḷ-ḷo, "badāl-mā nimši ʿa-iǧirna, hiyyāna ḥaṣalna ʿala xēl, faras." had̲lāk inhazamu.

136 He said to him, "See, here the mill has been of use." They climbed down, rode, each one [of them] a mare, and put the mill on one side here and one side there. They rode the mare and went [off]. He said to him, "Instead of walking on foot, here we have won horses—a mare." Those ran off.

143 u-hinne māšīn bi-hā-ṭ-ṭarīq, 'aǧat ʿalēhin hāna, lāqathin hā-l-mara. qāḷat-ḷo, "tarkibni warāk, yā ʿammi?" had̲āk el-ʿāqel bidduš yerakkebha. šū el-maǧnūn qāḷ-ḷo? qāḷ-ḷha, "taʿāli, 'irkabi maʿāy."

143 While they were going on this road, there came to them here a woman, met them. She said to him, "Will you let me ride behind you, o [my] uncle?" That smart one did not want to let her ride [with him]. What did the crazy one say to him? He said to her, "Come on, ride with me."

148 yōm-mā rikbat maʿā, ṣārat 'iǧrēha tǧirr b-il-'arḍ, ġūḷe! ṣārat 'iǧrēha taḥfir b-il-'arḍ. yuḏrub el-faras, yuḏrub el-faras—btiġdarš timši—hiyye tiḥfir 'iǧrēha b-il-'arḍ. ḥatta ġazzathen b-il-'arḍ.

148 When she rode with him, her feet began to dig in the ground. [She was a] *ġūla*! Her feet began to dig in the ground. He hit the mare, hit the mare—she could not walk—she stuck her feet on the ground, till she stuck them in the ground.

153 iltafat ʿalēha hād̲a-l-walad, willa hī ġūḷe. qāḷ-ḷo, "šū biddna nsāwi?" qāḷ-ḷo, "ġūḷe."qāḷ-ḷa, "'uqʿudi, biddna nitrayyaḥ. biddna ninzal nitrayyaḥ." qāḷat-lo, ā." qāḷat-lo, "'intu wēn rāyḥīn?" qāḷ, "'iḥna maʿāki, wēn biddek trūḥi, 'iḥna biddna nrūḥ maʿek." qāḷat-lo, "yaḷḷa."

153 He turned to her, this boy, and lo, she was a *ġūla.* He said to him, "What shall we do?" He said to him, "[She is a] *Ġūla.*" He said to her, "Sit [down], we want to rest. We want to get off and rest." She said to him, "Yes." She said to him, "You, where are you going?" He said, "We are with you, where you want to go, we will go with you." She said to him, "Let us [go]."

160 rāḥat. yōmin rāḥat, hū wiyyāha mišyat, 'aǧat ʿala hā-l-ᵊmġāra. qāḷat-ⁱlhin, "biddna nbāt hōn." qāḷu-ḷa, "'a, minbāt. yaḷḷa ǧībī-lna, biddna nōkel." rāḥat hāy ⁱ(t) ddawwer hēk ʿala hā-l-ziyād, ʿala l-'akel, u-hād̲lāk rikbu l-xēl u-(i)nhazmu.

160 She went. When she went, she went with them, and she came to that cave. She said to them, "We will spend the night here." They said to her, "Yes, we will spend the night. Come on, bring for us, we want to eat." This [woman] went to look for provisions (food [for them]), and those [two] rode the horses and ran off.

166 liḥaqathen. liḥaqathen—miskat el-mağnūn. qāḷat-lo, "wēn biddak ᵉtrūḥ essa?" qāḷ-ḷa, "muš 'ana, 'imeski 'axūy. muš timiskīni 'ana, 'ana mā qulteš 'iši ʿannek, 'imiski 'axūy." qāḷat-lo, "ṭayyeb." daššarato. rāḥat turkuḏ wara 'axū.

166 She ran after them. She ran after them and caught the crazy one. She said to him, "Where do you want to go now?" He said to her, "Not me, catch my brother, do not catch me—I did not say to him anything about you. Catch my brother." She said to him, "OK." She left him. She went running after his brother.

173 'ağat yōmin-mā miskato, 'ağat ʿala hā-l-zalame. yōminna 'ağat ʿala hā-l-zalame, willa hā-l-zalame qāʿed yibaqqel, yibaqqel xubbēze. qāḷat-lo, "šū bitsāwi?" qāḷ-ḷa, "ʿād 'abaqqel xubbēze."

173 She came—when she did not catch him—she came upon this man. When she came to this man, and he was picking, picking mallow. She said to him, "What are you doing?" He said to her, "I'm picking mallow."

178 qāḷat-lo, "tabaqqel xubbēze?" qāḷat-lo "w-inta šū biddak fīhen?" qāḷ-ḷa, "barūḥ abīʿhen bi-ʿakka, bağīb-li šwayyet malfūf la-wlādi, šwayyet lamūn. u-šwayyet 'iši la-hā-l-uwlād." qāḷat-lo, la-baqqāl el-xubbēze. qāḷat-lo, "mā šufet ez-alame illi maraq min hōn?" qāḷ-ḷa, "quddāmek, yā ʿamme, quddāmek." rāḥat hadīk mā liḥqatōš.

178 She said to him, "Picking mallow?" She said to him, "What do you want [to do] with them?" He said to her, "I go and sell them in Acre [Akko]. I bring for me some cabbage for my children, some lemons, and something for these children." She said to him, to the mallow picker, she said to him, "Haven't you seen the man who passed from here?" He said to her, "In front of you [farther ahead], o aunt, in front of you." This one went, and did not catch him.

187 rāḥ hadāk, riğʿat lo. qāḷat lo, "'ani 'uxtak, miš dāyer bālak ᵃtğawwazet. 'inti yōm-mā ⁱxliqet walā kunet mitğawwze. ğawwazni 'abūy w-'ana zġīr, u-teʿarifnīš, xayya. w-'ana 'axūk, 'oxtak. wēn xayya bētak?" qāḷ-ḷa,"hiyyāha hān, xayta."

187 This one went. She returned to him. She said to him, "I am your sister. You do not remember I got married. You, when you were born, I was married. My father married me off when I was young, and you do not know me, young brother. I am your brother, your sister. Where is your home, young brother?" He said, "Here it is, little sister."

193 saḥbat ḥāla u-riğʿat maʿ ez-zalame hāḏ ʿala hā-l-bēt. yōm riğʿat ʿala hā-l-bēt ṭallaʿat ʿalēha marato, qāḷat-lo, "walak, hāy ġūḷe, minnēn ğibtha u-ğīt?" gāḷ-ḷa, "wēlek, 'esekti. hāy 'uxti, mitğawwze w-'ana zġīr."

193 She took off and returned with the man to that house. When she returned to that house, his wife looked at her and said to him, "Woe unto you, this is a *ġūla*, where from did you bring her and come [with her]?" He said to her, "Woe unto you, shut up, this is my sister. She was married when I was little."

199 qāḷat-lo, "kīf 'oxtak?" qāḷ-ḷa, "'oxti, (ag)ul-lak, hāy rikbat maʿāy, u-'ağat la-ʿindi u-kānat tedawwer ʿalayy."

199 She said to him, "How [is she] your sister?" He said, "She is my sister; I am telling you, this rode with me and came to me and was looking for me."

202 qāḷat-lo, "'ā." hāy, xaḷḷat el-lēl ta-ṣārt ed-dinya lēl, yaʿani ta-l-lēl baʿado, ta-ṣārt ed-dinya lēl. hāy ṣārat teṭallaʿ hēk, wu-ʿ^{e}yūnha ḥumor-ḥumor. bidda tūkulhen.	202 She said to him, "Yes." This one [the wife], let the night, until it became night, and the night was still . . . until it became night. She began to look and her eyes were red-red. She wanted to eat them.
206 šū ṣārat ta-taqūḷ-ḷha el-mara? el-mara ʿirfatha ġūḷe. ʿindha banāt ṯintēn. rāḥat ṭabxat marqat al-ʿadas, ʿimlat marqat ʿadas, ṭabxat šōraba, [${}_{H}$marak$_{H}$], uḥaṭṭat ʿala l-banāt, kabbat ʿalēhin.	206 What did the woman begin to say to her? The woman knew her to be a *ġūla*. She had two daughters. She went and cooked lentil (${}_{H}$marak$_{H}$) soup, made lentil soup, cooked (${}_{H}$marak$_{H}$) soup, and put on the girls—spilt it on them.
211 qāḷat, "šū, el-banāt šaxxāt b-'awāʿīhin. biddi 'arūḥ 'aġassilhin ʿa-l-ʿēn," qāḷ-ḷha "wēnek?" qāḷat-lo, "ta-xaḷḷīk 'inta w-'uxtak. tann-arūḥ 'aġassīlhin ʿa-l-ʿēn w-'arğaʿ." hī 'axaḏat[3] el-banāt wa-ğatak hazīmi. haḏīki istannat, istannat—ma-fišš.	211 She said, "The girls wetted [pissed on] their clothes. I will go to wash them at the [water] spring." He said to her, "Where [are you going]?" She said to him, "I will leave you with your sister, I will wash them at the spring and come back." She took the girls and took off fleeing. This [one] was waiting, waiting—nothing. [They did not return.]
218 qāḷat-lo, "stanna ʿal-ʿēn. minnēn biddi 'ākl ak ʿād ^{i}stanēti?" qāḷ-ḷa, "kulīni min lḥayti, illi mā ṭāwaʿet šōr ^{e}mrayti." yaʿani mā ṭāwaʿteš marati šū mā qāḷat li. naṭšato. qāḷ-ḷha, "kulīni min ^{i}dayyti, illi mā ṭāwaʿet šōr bnayti." naṭšato w-aklato.	218 She said to him, "Wait at the spring. From where shall I begin to eat you, so, you waited?" He said to her, "Eat me from my beard, because I did not obey my little wife's advice." That is, I did not obey what my wife said to me. She plucked it. He said to her, "Eat me from my hand that did not obey my daughter's advice." She tore it off and ate him.
224 'aklat hā-l-zalame u-liḥqat, biddha tilḥaq hā-l-banāt haḏlāk. mā liḥqateš. hāy el-xurrāfiyye xaḷḷṣat.	224 She ate this man and followed—she wanted to catch those girls. She did not catch them. This story has ended.

Commentary

I recorded two versions of the story, which deals with two brothers who are abandoned by their father. One of the brothers is called Clever Ḥasan. His brother, Ḥusein, is described as the opposite and is presented by the two narrators as "a bit crazy," or as someone "whose mind is wrong." The brothers meet a *ġūla*, who has a herd of goats. The *ġūla* invites them to graze her herd. The two boys occasionally slaughter a kid and eat it. The *ġūla* suspects their deeds. The brothers deceive her and flee. The *ġūla* chases them and tries to devour them, but the brothers deceive her again, eventually succeeding in drowning her (or burning her in a fire) and winning her possessions.

The story as presented here belongs to the narrative-type cycle ATU 327, "The Children and the Ogre," a cycle of related types that deal with the struggle between children and an ogre, a struggle that ends with the children overcoming the monster and killing it. The most common subtype is ATU 327A, "Hänsel und Gretel," which appears in the Grimm brothers' collection.[4]

The complex of ATU 327 consists of many subtypes whose boundaries are not sufficiently defined. Episodes of one subtype are often combined with episodes of other subtypes. For example, the motif of the fool (or the lunatic) appears in the subtype ATU 327G, "The Brothers at the Witch's House."

Ṯalǧe Mūsa's version is actually a combination of three different stories. The first part begins with the abandonment of the brothers by their father following his marriage to a new wife. The brothers, in search of food, arrive at a fig orchard, where they meet a *ġūla* who has goats. The *ġūla* presents herself as the brothers' relative: "Where are you going, o my child? I am your mother." The brothers argue over whether she is indeed a *ġūla*. The fool seems to believe the *ġūla*'s words, while his brother tries to dissuade him. In any case, the *ġūla* takes both of them to her cave and employs them as shepherds, but apparently, she does not take care of them and does not give them food. They feed on the goats they take from the herd. The *ġūla* suspects their deeds and decides to devour them before they kill the whole flock.

At this point in the story, another episode is integrated, one that is part of the narrative type ATU 327B, "The Brothers and the Ogre." The *ġūla* tries to devour the children in their sleep, but they wake up and claim that they suffer from insomnia because of their hunger. The *ġūla* cooks chickens hoping to cause them to sleep, and, thus, the night passes and she is not able to get them. This episode appears in other Bedouin stories, which belong to the circle of the narrative type of the children and the ogre.

The narrator resumes the main line of the story: the *ġūla* counts her goats and finds that some of them are missing. The text at this point is not clear, but it seems that the boys succeed in tricking her (the second version I collected describes the trick more clearly). The boys escape to the seashore, and the *ġūla* follows them. The boys convince the *ġūla* to get closer and closer to the sea, and finally they drown her. The *ġūla* tries to convince them not to kill her and promises to give them her treasures—millstones and sacks of grains—which she has in her closets, but the brothers are not tempted. They drown the *ġūla* and inherit her treasures.

The second version ends at this point, but Ṯalǧe's story has two additional parts. After the death of the *ġūla*, the clever boy takes the gold and silver treasures of the *ġūla*, while his foolish brother takes the door of the *ġūla*'s house, her millstones, and the bean grains found in her house. The clever brother does not understand why he needs these things, but his brother replies that he is hungry and wants to eat the beans. The two go on their way to Bet-Netofa (Baṭṭōf) Valley. They climb a tree for fear that robbers will harm them, and they lift the door, the millstones, and the beans with them. At midday, robbers come to rest under the tree. The foolish brother urinates on them from the top of the tree, and they think a bird is peeing on them and try to drive it away. Then the fool grinds the beans with a mill. The robbers think this is an unusual phenomenon, a rain of beans falling from the sky, and flee for their lives. The two brothers take the robbers' horses and property and continue on their way. The foolish brother defies his clever brother: "Have you seen? These millstones helped us!" It is not clear from the story what the door's role is. It seems that the door serves here only as a point of support to lay the millstones on or to hide them from the robbers. The cry of the robbers—"The sky has fallen, the sky has fallen!"—is also not fully clear.

In his anthology *Italian Folktales*, the Italian writer Italo Calvino gives a Sicilian story called "Giufà, Pull the Door after You!"[5] Giufà is the Italian parallel of the Arab trickster Ǧuḥā (جحا). This story illuminates some of the puzzling episodes in Ṯalǧe's story. In the Italian story, the mother asks her foolish son, Giufà, to pull the door when he gets out of the house. The fool understands the order literally, pulls the door from its hinges, and carries it with him. Later in the story, the mother and son find refuge in a tree. Robbers sit to rest under the tree. Giufà urinates on them, and the robbers think it is raining. Later, he shits on them. The robbers wonder if this is manna falling from the sky or bird feces. Finally, the fool throws the door at them. The robbers flee for their lives, and the mother and son get their treasures. The mother, who fears that her stupid son will reveal the treasury's secret to the authorities and that it will be taken away from them, uses a trick. She casts raisins and dried figs from the roof. Giufà thinks it is a rain of fruit. Later, Giufà tells the local judge about the treasure. The judge asks him when it happened, and he replies that it happened on the day raisins and dried figs rained from the sky. The judge thinks that these are nonsense stories and does not bother to investigate, and so the treasure remains in the mother's possession.

This story may explain the role of the door in our story. It seems that in the original version of the Bedouin story, the fool also threw the door on the robbers, hence their cry of horror, "The sky has fallen, the sky has fallen!" The rain of beans that the fool casts on the robbers might be related to the mother's trick in the Sicilian story. This episode is known from other stories of simpletons in different cultural spaces and is part of the narrative type ATU 1653, "The Robbers under the Tree."

The two stories demonstrate how even stupid acts can prove useful. The ludicrous figure of the foolish brother is suddenly revealed in a different light, overshadowing the clever brother's wisdom.

The third part of Ṯalǧe's story is also a story that can stand on its own and that, in fact, is glued to the previous two sections. This is the narrative type AT 327H§, "Foolish Husband Ignores His Wife's Advice and Leads Her and the Children to Ogress. He Is Devoured" (see the discussion in the previous chapter). In this part of the story, the two brothers meet another *ġūla*, in the form of a woman. The foolish brother puts her on his horse, and then, as the narrator says, "Her legs began to dig in the ground. [She was a] *Ġūla*! Her feet began to dig in the ground. He hit the mare, hit the mare—she could not walk—she stuck her feet on the ground, till she stuck them in the ground. He turned to her, this boy, and lo, she was a *ġūla*." This description of the *ġūla* disguised as a woman appears in two memorates (personal stories) and is presented as an event that happened in reality. See detailed discussion in the next chapter, "Personal Narratives about Meetings with *Ġūl*s."

During the *ġūla*'s chase of the two boys, the foolish brother persuades the *ġūla* to pursue his brother. She tries to catch the clever brother, but she fails. At this point in the story, the two brothers leave the stage, and the continuation deals with another man the *ġūla* encounters on her way. This man is displayed as a married man with children. The artificial seam between this part of the story and the previous part is obvious.

In the second Bedouin version, recorded from Faṭma ʿAbdallah, the dominant character is that of the foolish brother. At the beginning of the story, he slaughters all the *ġūla*'s goats except the billy goat. The brother's stupidity is expressed by the fact that he throws carobs from the top of the tree and expects that the goats will leave him a few, which, of course, does not happen. The hero takes revenge on the goats for their behavior. He does not slaughter the billy goat only because a few of the carobs remain stuck between his horns, and to him, it seems as if the goat has obeyed his expectation. Next, the foolish brother deceives the *ġūla* with the only billy goat that is still alive. Later, the *ġūla* chases the two brothers. They invite her to remove the baked bread from the earthen stove and take the opportunity to burn and kill her. This version has no additional parts.

In both versions of the story, the subject of food is repeatedly emphasized. At the beginning of the first story, the abandoned boys search for food in a fig orchard. Later, they slaughter a goat to calm their hunger. The hungry children ask for a "fat big hen" at night. Before her death, the *ġūla* tries to convince the two brothers not to drown her, promising them the treasures of food stored in her house. The foolish brother takes beans from the house of the *ġūla*. The same is true of the second version—the children slaughter the *ġūla*'s goats and at the end of the story prepare bread for themselves. The intensive preoccupation with food is not unique to these stories but appears in all the subtypes of the narrative type ATU 327. One of the motifs, which is also found in other stories, is motif G610.4§, "Stealing from ogre because of hunger (to avoid starvation)."

Notes

1. *ulli* is a curious form of the word. It could be perceived as *u* + *lli*, "and that/which," or simply as an impaired pronunciation of *illi*, "which."

2. In *kull esbūʿ, kull ğemʿa*, the word for "week" is repeated in its two lexical forms: *ʾesbūʿ/ʾusbūʿ*, (in LA/MSA) derived from *sabʿ*, "seven (days)," and *ğemʿa* (LA/MSA *ğumʿa*), derived from *ğmʿ*, "to meet, gather together." These synonymous words are used also in the sedentary colloquial dialects in Israel and elsewhere.

3. This narrator, like the others, mixes MSA/LA and sedentary dialects' speech sounds with Bedouin ones; thus, *q* ~ *g* occur interchangeably (see the chapter on Bedouin dialects, section "Phonology/Phonetics," at the end of this book). The 3m.pl. bound pronoun of the Bedouin and rural dialects is often exchanged between the final consonants *m* ~ *n*. In addition, the sedentary form *ʾaxaḏ* appears instead of the Bedouin form xaḏa (see chap. 6, note 2). In spite of these mixtures, she is clearly a native speaker of Galilee Bedouin Arabic.

4. Grimm, *The Original Folk and Fairy Tales of the Brothers Grimm*, story 15.

5. Calvino, *Italian Folktales*, 684–86, story 190.

39. Personal Narratives about Meetings with Ġūls

A. The Young Man and the Ġūla

NARRATOR: ʾUmm Mūsa Mizʿil

TRIBE: *ʿArab el-ʿArāmša*
Recorder: Yehuda Katz 1980

1 bū hīna wiḥda. wāḥed rāyiḥ, widdo yiksi^{y}[1] il-bint ʿammo, yaʿani rāyeḥ yiksi, widdo yğahhiz-^{i}lha, balad yiqūlū-lha ʾumm ^{i}ğbēl, hāḏi b-lubnān. čānat gabuḷ ʿala dōr al-inglīz, itrūḥ an-nās u-tiği ʿa-baʿaḍha, yaʿani, yaʿani mā bēnhom šayy.	1 There is one [f.]. Someone [m.] is going, he wants to buy dowry stuff for his bride [lit.: f. cousin], that is, he is going to buy, wants to buy [prepare the household stuff] for her. A town, called ʿUmm ^{i}Ğbēl. This is in Lebanon. It was previously, at the time of the English [British Mandate], people would go and come to one another, that is, there was nothing between them [no border].
8 rāḥ hāḏa kisa l-bint ʿammo u-šayyal há-l-faras[2] u-ḥaṭṭhā-ğ-ğhāz ^{i}b-hā-l-xurğ, yqūlū-lo xurğ hāḏa, min hōn ʾēna, u-min-hōn ʾēna, u-ḥaṭṭhin u-mila. u-hāḏan[3] al-banāt al-ʿazzābiyyāt, yaʿani, iwaṣṣannu, ʾalli twaṣṣi ʿa-ṭayyār, ʾalli twasṣṣi ʿa-maḥrama, ʾalli twasṣṣi ʿala badla.	8 This one went, prepared the dowry for his bride and took this mare and put the stuff in the side bag—it is called side bag, this [thing]. From here to here, and from here to here, and he put them and filled [the side bags]. And these unmarried girls, that is, they ask him—she who asks him for a shawl, she who asks him for a headkerchief, she who asks him for a suit of clothes.
15 ğāb ^{i}l-kull šinen wiḥda waṣṣato u-ğa, ta-ṣār miṯel ma tgūl yaʿani ʿinn-ʾumm-ğbēl, yaʿani yiği min hīna u-šlemo, winn hā-l-ʿağūz al-xityāra gāʿda ʿala hā-ḏēl hā-ṭ-ṭarīg winnha tgūl-lo, "yā mīt ʾahla wa-sahla yā ḥbaybi, ğīt be-s-salāma?" gāḷ-ḷha, "walla, yā sitti, ğīt."	15 He brought everything to each one as she requested him and came [back], until he was as you would say, that is, near ʿUmm ^{i}Ğbēl. That is, it is from here and Shlomi [a Jewish town]. And lo, this old, old woman, sitting at the side of the road, and lo, she says him, "Oh a hundred welcomes, my grandson, have you come in peace [safely]?" He said to her, "By Allah, my lady [grandmother], I have come."

22 gāḷat-lo, "n-ša-ḷḷa ğibt ^{i}l-ḥabbābtak[4] ṯōb?" yigūḷū-ḷo ṯōb. gāḷ-ḷha, "walla, yā ḥbayba, nsi^{e}t, ^{i}nsitič, yā ḥabbāba, mā ğīti b-bāli^{y}. 'inti wēn nāzla?" gāḷat-lo, "yā wēli, mā tʿarifni wēn nāzla?" gāḷ-ḷha, "m-inti b-ʿarabna ta-ḥēt (a)ʿarfič wēn." gāḷat-lo, "ṭayyeb, yalla yā ḥabbāba, ġēr hā-l-marra. ʿugub mā tehanna[5] wu-tiğawwaz ^{i}dğīb-li." gāḷ-ḷha, "'ahla wa-sahla b-liḥitič,[6] yā sitti^{y}."

22 She said to him, "I hope [if Allah will] you have brought your grandmother a robe?" It is called a robe. He said to her, "By Allah, my lady, I forgot, I forgot you, o grandma, I did not remember you. Where do you live?" She said to him, "Oh my, you don't know where I live?" He said to her, "You are not in our tribe so that I will know where." She said to him, "Well, come on, my grandson, just this time. After you get happy and marry, you will bring for me." He said to her, "Welcome, in your honor, o my lady."

32 hīna gāḷat-lo, "irčib ʿād iḥbayyibtak, mā bha timši sittak w-inta rākb ál-faras." ašnuw ʿēnt al-xurğ, kullha gmāš ğāyibha l-al-banāt w-il-ʿarūsa u-luwwa w-il-xawāto, yaʿani ^{i}l-kull-al-ʿēla wu-l-el-ʿağiyyāt kullhen.

32 Here she said to him, "Let your grandma ride, your grandma cannot walk while you are riding the mare." What beauty the side bag—all [the best] material he was bringing for the girls and the bride and for him and his sisters, that is, all the family and all the girls.

38 hēna arkabha, yaʿani miša min hēna u-bētna hāḏa, hāḏa l-bēt hāḏa. daḥḥag yaʿani hēk min taḥat, el-taḥat, wēr-riğlēha tgušš aš-šōk, ^{i}tgušš al-^{e}ḥğara, ^{i}tgušš, yā laṭīf, winn ^{i}šnū ʿuyūnha tegādaḥ nār.

38 Here, he put her on the mare, that is, he went from here, and our house was this, this [very] house. He looked, that is like that, from below, below [the mare] and her legs were tearing out the thorns, picking out the stones, tearing, o Kind [Allah], and behold her eyes were glowing like fire.

44 gāl, "bayye!"[7] b-gaḷbo hāḏ, mā stağra yḥači, gāḷ, "bayyē! hāḏi ta-tākulni, 'ā, yā gaḷbi, yā ḥazīn, čē-dd-asāwi?" gāmat hī, 'ağasato inno yaʿani ṣār heč^{i} u-hēč (y) ilaffat, u-gāmat ḏabbat ḥālha, gatt-lo, "wīli, ʿalāmak yā ḥabbāba? ʿalāmak yā ḥabbāba hēč tilaffat ġād u-ğāy?"

44 He said, "O my [little father]"—in his heart [to himself], he did not dare speak. He said, "O my [little father]! This will eat me, o my heart, o poor [one], how will I manage [what shall I do]?" She felt that he was, that is, like this and that, turning around. She gathered herself up [got back her human form] and said to him, "Oh my, why, my grandson, why my grandson, are you turning round here and there [lit: there and back here]?"

51 gāḷ-ḷha, "walla, ya ḥabbāba, čēfič ^{i}ḥzām al-faras karb, widd araxxī šwayya." hāḏa, b-īdo mūs, eṭlaʿo ʿa-s-sakt min ğēbto u-waṭṭa hēč. gatt-lo, "lēš waṭṭet, yā ḥabbāba?" gāḷ-ḷha, "yā ḥabbāba, mā-dd[8] araxx-^{i}ḥzām[9] al-faras." giḏab hā-s-sīx u-gām yuzluf hā-l-^{i}ḥzām. lumma zilef hā-l-^{i}ḥzām, gām yunġuz hā-lfaras u-gāmat hā-lfaras tirbiʿ.

51 He said to her, "By Allah, o grandma, for your convenience, the mare's buckle is too stretched, I want to loosen it a bit." This [man], he had a knife in his hand, he had taken it quietly out of his pocket, and bent down like this. She said to him, "Why have you bent down, o grandson?" He said to her, "O grandma, for I want to loosen the mare's buckle." He took the knife and cut the buckle [in a fast move]. When he cut the buckle, he pricked the mare, and it began to gallop.

60 wugʿat hiyya u-wigaʿ al-xurğ u-wugʿat al-baḏāyaʿ kulha u-ḏaḷḷ māḷeṭ huwa wa-l-faras.	60 She [the *ġūla*] fell and the side bag fell, and all the merchandise, and he continued escaping, he and the mare.
63 lummin ʿād wigʿat gāḷat-lo, "bayyē, ruḥt! mā-sawētha b-liḥiti^{y}, mḥarram ʿalēk. law inni zigaṭṭak ġēr afaṣfiṣ ^{i}lḥāmak ʿin ^{i}ʿḍāmak u-yiğīk."	63 When she fell down, she said to him, "O my father, you have gone away! You have hurt my dignity, you are not allowed [to do it]! If I catch you, I'll peel your flesh off your bones and you will know!"
67 tixarsan hāḏa mn-aḏ-ḏalla. ğa ʿa-l-ahalo^{u}, u-gbāl yaʿani ʾahalo miṯl al-kubbāniyya, u-gām yiṭīr mʿa-hā-d-darb, rāḥ. wiṣal ʿalēhom.	67 He became spellbound for fear. He came to his family. And before, that is, his family, like the kibbutz, he "flew" on this way, he went. He reached them.
71 lummin wiṣal, mī ğāʿda tunṭur han-nās, gāḷam, "haḏāku ğa, haḏāku ğa, haḏāku ğa." weṣal. lummin wiṣal, gāḷ-ḷo, "bayyē, ʿalāmak, yā mēma, hičiḏa?" gāḷ-ilhom, "usuktam, izgūni mayya u-xaḷḷūn-arayyaḥ."	71 When he arrived, the people had been sitting waiting [watching for him], they said, "That is he coming, that is he coming, that is he coming." He arrived. When he arrived, they said to him, "O my [father], why are you, o son, like that?" He said to them, "Shut up, let me drink water and let me rest."
77 ğābō-lo mayya, šrib u-faǧǧo-lo hā-l-^{i}gyās, yaʿani ḥaṣīra, u-gāḷū-ḷo, "ogʿod, sōlifna, ʿalāmak aš-ṣār"—ʾummo, u-xawāto, banāt ʿammo, garabāto.	77 They brought water for him, he drank, and they stretched out for him a mat, that is, a mat [to lie on], and said to him, "Sit down, tell us, why are you [like that], what happened"—his mother, his cousins, his female relatives.
81 gāḷ-ḷhin, "ʻal-ʾamur bēḷa bēḷa." gāḷaḷ-ḷo, "bāṭel ʿalēna, yā mēm, milīḥ alli ʾaḷḷa sallamak, yā yumma, wēn yā-yumma hāḏi ṣārat imʿāk hā-s-sālfe?"	81 He said to them, "The thing is so-and-so." They said to him, "The evil [will come] on us, o son; [it is] good that God has saved you, o son. Where, son, did this happen to you, this story?"
85 gāḷ-ḷhin, "b-hutt ^{i}ġnām." hāḏi hutt ^{i}ġnām hīč tiği, ḥawēla zirʿīn—beʿadha l-al-yōm. gāḷō-ḷo, "ṭayyeb." ed-dinya ṣārat ta-l-en-nhār, yaʿani ḥawāla s-sāʿa xamsa. mā-ʿād imʿāhum yrūḥūn yxummūn wi-yʿawdūn.	85 He said to them, "At hutt ^{i}ġnām." This hutt ^{i}ġnām is like that, here, [near] about Zirʾīn—it is still [there] until today. They said to him, "Good." The day was coming to its end, that is, [it was] about five o'clock. They did not have [time] to go and search and come back.
91 gāḷam, "la-ṣ-ṣubeḥ." ʾaṣ-ṣubeḥ, nāmam, u-rikab ğiddāmhom ʿa-l-faras u-tšarragam, winnha šnuwwa nāṯrīto, ašnū hā-l-baḏāyeʿ gāṣṣīto, kull hīč šigfa mšarišrīto, kullo ḥarīr ^{i}mšarišrīto ʿa-rūs al-billān, ʿa-rūs al-waʿr, ʿa-rūs al-^{i}ḥğara, ʿa-rūs há-š-ši. hāḏa dūn(kam) rāḥam, ligōha mšaggfīto kullo.	91 They said, "In the morning [we will go there]." In the morning, they [had] slept, and he rode in front of them on the mare and they rode to the east. And behold—how she had dispersed it, how she had cut the merchandise into pieces, everything like this, in disorder, all of it, the silk, was disordered on top of the thistles, on top of the barren land plants, on top of the rocks, on top of this thing. This, begging your pardon, they went and found it having been cut, all of it.

99 dawwaram ḥawāla ʾarḏen ṣārat hā-l-miʿraka, dawwaram laṭṭašam, dawwaram mā ligam. hāḏi ġūḷa. rāḥat. u-gām ʿād ʿāwad, ǧa wi-ʿāwad ṯāni ǧumʿa rāḥ, kisa min ǧidīd, u-ʿāwad ǧāb kisa wu-tiǧawwaz u-gaʿad.	99 They searched around the ground, which was as if a battle had been there. They went round, searched, did not find [her]—this [was] a *ġūla*. She had gone. He got up and went again, came and returned on the other week and went again and bought the dowry stuff anew and brought [it] and provided [the dowry] and married and settled down [lived well afterward].

B. The Ġūla Who Posed as a Tribe Member

NARRATOR: Unknown
TRIBE: *ʿArab el-ʿArāmša*
IFA 17427 ca. 1980

Text

My father told me that one of our family went out to Bint-Ǧbēl [the second-largest city in the southern Lebanese province of Nabatieh, near the border with Israel], where he wanted to buy wedding presents to the bride. These [presents] are for the bride. We have no city other than Bint-Ǧbēl, and Bint-Ǧbēl is far away.

He had a mare. This mare was of the noble horses. My father also heard from my grandfather that his uncle had gone out to buy wedding presents in Bint-Ǧbēl, his name was Aḥmad El-Xalīfah. When he bought the presents in the market of Bint-Ǧbēl, and came near Marǧ El-Basal valley, where there is a cave called the cave of Ǧil ʿAnim. This cave of Ǧil ʿAnim is known for having a *ġūla*, and this *ġūla*, who lived in Ǧil ʿAnim, was called Imm ʿOmar. And among the Arabs [the tribe], there was an old woman, whose name was Imm ʿOmar. He came to his grandfather and asked [if the tribe intends to wander to another place]. When he asked him, he said, "We want to wander."

He said, "Where do you want to wander?"

He said to him, "By Allah, we want to wander to another place."

Here [now], when this one went, bought in the market, and came back, he did not find the people.

When he did not find the people, he came to the cave of Imm ʿOmar, and there she says to him, "Aḥmed, take me with you. The people abandoned me here."

He said to her, "Where, Imm ʿOmar? They abandoned you here and no one took you?"

She said to him, "By Allah, they left me. Take me with you on the horse and bring me home."

When he put her behind the mare, the mare was a noble mare. He looked at her, and her feet were dragging on the ground.

When he found her dragging on the ground, he said to her, "Go back a bit, oh Imm ʿOmar, back."

He left her until she went [moved] back a little, and he went [moved] striking the mare saddle with the knife. He cut it. When he cut it, he lay on the horse's neck and beat it with two whips. When she was hit twice by a whip, the mare jumped. When the mare jumped, she threw her under her [with the wedding presents].

When she threw her behind, she said to him, "In the morning you will come and find your clothes sewn."

Here [now], he went to look for the people, he returned to the people.

In the morning, they said to him, "Where are the wedding clothes, Aḥmed?"

He said to them, "Silence! By Allah, I came to the cave of Ğil 'Anim and I thought that Imm 'Omar is there [but it was] the *ġūla* of Ğil 'Anim who came out. She rode behind me on the mare, and I cut off the horse's bands and the wedding presents I had all fell down with her."

They went in the morning to see it—a lie or a truth. They found them torn, every piece of this size. She tore them up and put them on the rocky top.

And that is what happened.

C. The Groom and the Ġūla

NARRATOR: Warda Hawāš
TRIBE: *'Arab el- Mazārīb*
IFA 18173 March 11, 1982

Text

There was a man. He went to buy [wedding] gifts for his bride. He bought for her, for example, from Nazareth. As he returned, he returned along the rocky terrain. It was evening. A woman was sitting next to the street [road].

She said to him, "Come, I have no one, and I want to come back with you."

He said to her, "OK, come on, ride [with me]."

He rode. The mare, there are two bags on it from here and from here [on both sides], two sacks. The sacks are full of clothes for the bride. She rode behind him on the mare. He looked at her, and [it will be] a long time before he reaches the Arabs [his tribe]. He looked at her, and here she says, "*Hish* [Stop the horse]!"

Her head is like that and her feet are dragging on the ground [that is, she grew in size].

He said, "What shall I do with it?" He said to her, "Move back a little, so I'll see you." He had a *šabriyyeh* [knife]. He cut off the mare's saddle and moved forward until he sat on the mare's neck, and unhooked the mare's saddle and fled.

The next day she said to him, "What, you are safe and sound? By Allah, I'll slaughter you!"

This is a *ġūla*. The next day he came to the place at daytime, and the bride's clothes were torn. Torn on the trees, in the forest.

He said, "Enough, I will not go into this place anymore."

He returned to the bride and said to her, "[I did as you wish.] I bought for you."

And he went. He came back again. He went with the people. He dared not go back alone.

D. The Ġūla in the Waterhole

NARRATOR: Ibrahim ʻAli
TRIBE: *ʻArab el-Ḥuǧērāt*
IFA 13248 July 1980

Text

This happened to Diāb Ibrahīm, the grandfather of Diāb ʻAli, my neighbor.

In springtime, it is customary at night to take the cows to graze. One night, Diāb went out with the herd of cows to pasture, armed with his rifle. His intention was to spread the herd over the ground and let the cows graze until morning. He himself intended to return to his tent to sleep.

As he approached with the cows to the rock-hewn cistern, known as Ǧorn Baʻabur [near Yodfat], he arranged them in a row so that they would not crowd by the trough. Suddenly he felt his hair bristling and the rifle was about to fall out of his hands. Even the cows approaching the pit seemed uneasy.

Diāb went to the edge of the pit and suddenly noticed the image of a baby with long hair peering out of the water. It was a *ġūla*, and Diāb, though he was a strong man, he was almost out of breath. He fell ill and did not recover until three days later. No one knew what had happened to him, and only three days later he told his family about what had happened to him at the well.

E. Abu Xiḏ̣ᵉr and the Ġūla

NARRATOR: Nūra Ḥalīfa
TRIBE: *ʻArab el-ʻArāmša*
Recorder: Naomi Raies
IFA 17425 August 1980

1 bidd(i)-ʼaḥkī-lkam goṣṣa, ḥakā-lna iyyāha xatyār ismo abu xiḏ̣ᵉr, ʼaḷḷa yarḥamo, tuwuffa gabel ḥawēla ṯaman ᵉsnīn, ṣār. ḥakā-lna guṣṣa ʿan wādiʸ.[10] w-al-wādi da ʼesmo wādi nafx. [$_H$ha-yóm$_H$] ṣār ⁱb-maḥall b-lubnān, u-garya lubnāniyya.	1 I will tell you a story, which an old man called Abu Xiḏ̣ᵉr told us, Allah have mercy on his soul, he died about eight years ago, it happened. He told us a story about a *wādi*. And this *wādi* was named Nafx. ($_H$hayom$_H$) Today, it is in a place in Lebanon, a Lebanese village.
8 u-rawwaḥ bi-l-lēl as-sāʿa ṭnaʿaš bi-l-lēl. wu-dinya gumar.	8 And he was going home at twelve o'clock in the night. And there was moonlight [in the world around].

10 ḥatta ʿa gūm rāyiḥ b-il-lēl, fāt ib-ha-l-wādi, giṭaʿ hā-l-gāṭeʿᵃ ḥatta ṣār b-il-gāteʿᵃ ṯ-ṯāni.	10 Until he went in the night, entered this *wādi*, crossed that side [bank] until he was on the other side [bank]. He
13 daḥḥag warā wu-lenn hā-z-zlima, hū ḥass hā-tḥissa hunāk, ta-ḥatta giṭaʿ hunāk, mā ṣār yeḥisso hināk. winno hunāk hā-z-zlima, māši. lumman šāfo māši, bitḥaṣṣin.[11] mā intifaḍ, u-gām hā-z-zlima gaʿad, lamma ṣār (yimāl). daḥḥag ʿalē, yaʿan(i), zēn, gaʿad.	13 looked behind him, and lo, there was a man. He felt that feeling there, until he crossed there, he did not begin to feel that he was there. Lo, there was there that man, walking. When he saw him walking, he braced himself, he did not tremble, and this man sat down, when he began . . . he looked at him, that is, well—he sat down.
20 lumman gaʿad, gāḷ-ḷo, "ilḥag ta-ḥatta-rrawwaḥ 'ana wiyyāk." gāḷ-ḷo, "lēš, yā bu xaḏar, widdak ᵉddaxxen sigāra?" daḥḥag ʿalē willa hū gāʿad ᵉmġāra, wu-ha-l-mġāra di tilmaʿ miṯl-al-dxān wullʿa nār. gāḷ-ḷo, "'aywa, widd(i)-adaxxen sikāra, elḥagni ta-ḥatta-rrawwweḥ[12] siwa."	20 When he sat down, he said to him, "Join [me] so that we will go home, me with you." He said to him, "Why, o Abu Xiḏᵉr, do you want to smoke a cigarette?" He looked at him, and lo, he was sitting at a cave, and this cave was illuminated [shining] like black smoke, lit by fire. He said to him, "Yes, I want to smoke a cigarette. Join me so that we will go home together."
27 gām hā-l-xityār all-ismo (a)bu xiḏᵉr, gaʿad u-liff[13] sikāra. maʿā mā laff as-sikāra, madd 'īdo, gāḷ-ḷo, "xuḏ wallʿā" ʿaṭāʰ u-wallaʿ-lo s-sikāra. mā ḥaṭṭ as-sikāra b-a(l)-ʿeḏmo[14] hēk, gāḷ-ḷo, "mā bawallʿā" madd 'īdo mi-l-gāṭeʿᵃ lē u-gāḷ-ḷo, "xuḏ waḷḷa, wallaʿ li iyyāha." gāḷ, "wallaʿ lo s-sikāra" wu-(y)gūḷ, subḥān aḷḷāh, u-yimkin māleṭ.	27 This old man, whose name is Abu Xiḏᵉr, sat down and folded [prepared] a cigarette. While he folded the cigarette, he reached out his hand and said to him, "Take, light it for us." He gave it to him and he lit him the cigarette. He did not put the cigarette in his mouth like that, he said to him, "I don't [cannot] light it." He stretched his hand from the other bank and said to him, "Take, light it, light it for me." He said, he lit the cigarette for him, and said, "Praise Allah," and maybe fled.
36 rawwaḥ al-xetyār b-haḏīka as-sāʿa maša al-xāyif ḥatta wuṣal ʿa-l-bēt, mātᵃ min al-xōf.	36 The old man went home at this time, he went frightened, until he reached home, he was dying with fear.
39 gāḷ,"kīf, yā 'aḷḷa, yā 'anni mā nğannēt, kīf mā ṣār ʿalāyy, kī(f) lō mā ṣār ʿalayy ḥādṯa min hā-š-šikel." yōm, al-yōm, aṣbaḥ al-ṣobḥ, wu-ṯāni yōm rāḥ yesōlef ᵉb-hā-l-ʿarab wēš ṣār ⁱmʿā.	39 He said, "How, o Allah, I did not go mad, how what happened to me, how if what happened to me, an event of this kind." A day, the day, morning came, and the next day he went and told in the Bedouin tribe what had happened to him.

44 selef-lo wāḥad min ʿalma-šaʿab, lamman simaʿ sālfet abu xaḏar anna silef alli ēš ṣār ^{i}mʿā, gāḷ-ḷo, "waḷḷa, 'ani kint yōm hināk, s-sāʿa sabʿa (u-nuṣṣ), ḥawāla s-sāʿa sabʿa, u-d-dinya hēk tagrīban, 'awwal aš-šetwiyya, š-šams ^{e}tġāb badri. waḷḷa mišēt hināk, mā ḥassēt alla hā-l-bint ^{i}btibki. (a)fatteš ḥawalay, fōq, taḥat, ta-ḥatta timši, ta-ḥatta (a)šūf hā-l-mṣayyabe, mā lak tišūf f-hā l-wād.

44 One from ʿAlma-Šaʿab [a village] told him, when he heard Abu Xaḏ^{e}r's story, that he told what had happened to him, he said to him, "By Allah, I was there one day, the time was seven (and a half), about seven o'clock, and it was approximately like this, the beginning of winter, the sun was setting early. By Allah, I walked there, and lo, I felt that this girl was crying. I looked around me, up, down, until she would go, to see this afflicted [girl]—You can't see [anything] in this *wādi*.

54 "wēn ya ʿammti,[15] ṣirti tḥuṭṭ hā-l- . . ." winna tigūḷ-ḷak, "daxīlak, 'ani, bint, kint ʿarūs el-ṣāḥb aḥabb u-aḥibbni, u- u-bū nās, seḥrūni u- u-arrṣūni (='arrṣūni)[16] taḥt al-'arḍ magbūra." gāḷ-ḷha, "ṭayyeb, wēš asāwī-lek 'ani?"

54 "Where, o my aunt, did you put it[?]" And lo, she says [to you], "I am at your mercy, I am a girl, I was a bride to a friend whom I loved and he loved me, and there were people who bewitched me and confined [squeezed] me under the ground, buried." He said to her, "Well, what shall I do for you?"

60 gāḷat-lo, "taʿāl ež-žumʿa ž-žāya, tiği miṯel hāssa, u-taʿadd ṯalaṯ marr(āt): taʿadd ṯalāṯa, u-tiqfiz ʿaniyye sabaʿ marrāt. ^{i}b-hāḏa sabaʿ marrāt, 'iḏa mā tʿadd, iḏa gedirt u-nizaʿt (=nižaḥt?) as-sabaʿ marrāt qefizt min fōgi,

60 She said to him, "Come next week, come at about this time and count three [time . . .] count up to three and jump over me seven times. In this seven times if you do not count, if you can and succeed the seven times jumping above me,

66 'ani raḥ-'aṭīb u-'aṭlaʿ. 'amma-ni rāḥ abayyen ʿala šikel šī min ḏahab." mā gāḷat-ḷo 'ēš hī, gāḷat-lo "rāḥ abayyen šī min ḏahab." rāḥ hāḏa sbūʿ^{a}, e.

66 "I will heal and get out. But I am going to appear in the form of something of gold." She did not tell him what she was, she said to him, "I will appear a thing of gold." This [man] went for a week, e. . . .

70 ṯāni yōm žumʿa ža la-ʿandha. ʿala hā-l-maḥall mā daḥḥag 'illa ṣūret hā-l-xarūf min ḏahab mumaddad ʿa-hā-l-talla. ʿadd waʿadd nizal ʿadd fōga, ʿa-d-dōra ṯ-ṯālta, r-rābʿa, l-xāmes—taʿab u-wugaʿ ʿalēha. limma wugaʿ ʿalēha, 'íxtifa.[17] 'ixtifa hā-ḏ-ḏahab. rawwaḥ.

70 Next Friday he came to her. To this place. He did not see [anything] except a picture of a sheep of gold, spread on this hill. He counted, "One," and jumped above it [the picture]. On the third, fourth, fifth turn—he got tired and fell on it. When he fell on it, it disappeared. This gold disappeared. He went home.

77 šū lli bū . . . walla bū wāḥad ygūḷ-ḷo, "wuḷḷa, ṣārat ^{i}mʿāya sālfa min hā-š-šikel, wa-'addēt—ʿaddēt w-ani galbi gāsi, mā-xāf, ʿaddēt ṯalaṯ marrāt, u-fazzēt min fōgha sabaʿ marrāt

77 What is there . . . by Allah, there was one [man] who said to him, "By Allah, a thing of this kind happened to me and I counted, I counted, and my heart is strong, I [he] was not afraid. I counted three times and jumped above her seven times,

82 wulla ṭālᵃʿa bint rākba ʿa-faras uṣīla, ʿarūs b-ism-iḷḷa,[18] bas-hiya u-ḏahaba, w-al-bint di kānat masḥūra saḥrīna sāḥrāt, u-rābṭīnha b-ar-rabṭ taḥt al-ʾarḍ, ʾamma miš hā-l-maḥall ʾamma maḥall ṯāni."	82 and lo, there came out a girl riding a noble horse, a bride, in Allah's name [as beautiful as Allah's prettiest creature], only she and her gold. This girl was bewitched, witches had bewitched her, and tied her under the ground, but not in this place, in another place."

Commentary

In addition to the rich repertoire of fairy tales of *ǧinnies*, *ġūls*, and other demonic creatures, the Bedouins have stories (as in other cultural spaces) that are memorates (personal stories) according to their folkloristic definition. That is, there are events that the narrator claims to have experienced directly or to have happened to someone he knows.

Although these stories are presented as real events that took place and are interspersed with names of people, places, and time markers, they attest to the social and cultural characteristics of the studied society and often contain supernatural elements known to us from the genre of fairy tales.

The stories I have brought here are typical examples of this type of story.

The first three stories about the encounter between the *ġūla* and the groom were recorded in two tribes far from each other. Two of them were written down in the ʿArab el-ʿArāmša tribe in the north of Israel, on the Lebanese border, and the third one in the ʿArab el-Mazārīb tribe in the Bedouin village of Bēt Zarzīr in the Jezreel Valley. Nevertheless, the stories are almost identical in content: A bridegroom goes out to buy engagement gifts for his bride. On his way, he comes upon a *ġūla* pretending to be a human creature (or a woman from his tribe), and she asks him to put her on his mare. During the ride, he finds out that she is a *ġūla*. When he finds that her legs are dragging on the ground (that is, the *ġūla* has changed its dimensions and grown in size), he throws her off his horse. The next day he returns to the scene and finds the clothes torn to pieces.

This description of the *ġūla*, who changes her dimensions while riding on the horse, until her feet are dragging on the ground, has already been encountered in the story "The Two Brothers and the *Ġūla*" (chap. 38): "Her feet began to dig in the ground. *Ġūla*! Her feet began to dig in the ground. He hit the mare, hit the mare—she could not walk [the *ġūla* dragged her feet in the ground until they were dug in]."

The first version, "The Young Man and the *Ġūla*," was written down by Yehuda Katz from ʿUmm Mūsa Miz'il, from the tribe of ʿArab el-ʿArāmša.[19] This version is almost identical to the version I recorded in the same tribe. The narrator in the first version noted that the story takes place "during the British time," that is, during the British Mandate (1917–48). The hero meets a *ġūla* who masquerades as an old woman from his tribe. The description of the *ġūla*'s return to her demonic shape is almost the same: "He looked, from the top down, and then her feet tear the thorns, uproot the stones, uproot, oh Allah Almighty, and behold her eyes are burning with fire." After the hero throws the *ġūla* off his horse, she curses him, "Woe to you, you have run away, you have hurt my beard (that is to say, my honor). Damn you, if I catch you, I'll pluck your flesh off your bones!" The location of the encounter with the *ġūla* is near the cave of ʻAnim, (Ğil ʻAnim in the Bedouin version I recorded).

After it becomes clear to the bridegroom that all the clothes he brought with him have been vandalized by the *ġūla*, he goes on another shopping trip, which ends peacefully, "and he married and lived."

In a person's life cycle, there are transition periods: birth, maturation, marriage, and death. These periods are also called liminal periods (threshold periods, from the Latin word *limen*, for threshold). They are accompanied by rites marking the change in the status of the participants. According to the theories of Arnold Van Gennep and Victor Turner, the liminal state is characterized by lack of clarity. It has risks and uncertainty, and therefore a liminal period is a time prone to misfortune. For example, in many cultural spaces, there are popular beliefs about demons abhorrent to the newborn, and therefore the newborn must be protected during the first week or month of life. Marriage ceremonies are also characterized by the couple's fear of the new and unfamiliar situation into which they enter. There are many stories about the death of one of the spouses on the wedding night and the like. It seems that the event described in the stories cited above relates to this fear and expresses it.

Desolate places, especially pits and caves, are seen as the dwelling place of various demonic creatures. In every geographical area, there are usually defined and well-known places notorious among the local inhabitants as hiding places of one demon or another.

The story of Ibrahīm ʻAli of the tribe of ʿArab el-Ḥuğērāt illustrates this very well. The story was told to me in broken Hebrew. I rephrased it in standard Hebrew and put it down in writing. It therefore reflects the content of the story alone and not the language of the narrator.

The last story, recorded in the ʿArab el-ʿArāmša tribe, also takes place in a cave. It begins as a natural encounter between one passerby and another late at night, but soon demonic elements are added. The hero sees a man in a cave "glowing like a flame." He asks the hero to roll him a cigarette. The hero gives him the cigarette, but the owner of the cave does not succeed in lighting it and asks the hero to light it for him. He stretches his hand with the cigarette from the other bank of the *wādi*, and the hero lights the cigarette. As in the story of the groom, the narrator's interlocutor is identified as a demonic figure according to his unreasonably large dimensions.

The storyteller who narrates the first hero's encounter with the demon describes how, during a meeting she attended, she heard an additional story about an encounter with demons that occurred on the same site as the first story. In that story, the narrator encounters a magical bride buried beneath the ground, who cannot be released. She assures him that if he can free her through a magical ritual, she will reward him with a gold object. The narrator tries his hand but fails. He tells his story to one of his acquaintances, and his interlocutor tells him that he himself had a similar case but somewhere else. Unlike the failed interlocutor, he was able to perform the ceremony to the fullest and release the bride imprisoned by the chains of magic.

In this case, too, the story is related to a figure in a liminal stage—a bride who is enchanted on the eve of her marriage.

Notes

1. *widdo yiksī^y il-bint 'ammo*: "he wants to buy dowry for his female cousin." It was customary that the bridegroom (and his family) provide gifts for the bride, mainly clothes, which will start the new family household. The verb *kisa* is basically "dress up, cover"; here it means "to cover her needs in clothes." Note that there are several verbs used for this goal, such as *ğahhaz*, which originally means "to prepare, equip."

2. *kisa l-bint 'ammo u-šayyal há-l-faras*: lit: "he provided for his bride and loaded [carried the things] on this mare"—note the stress mark of *há-l-faras*, "this mare." This narrator often uses the features of *gaháwa* syndrome (see chap. 24, note 3; chapter on Bedouin dialects, section 1, point 5).

3. The demonstrative pronoun "f.pl. these" in *u-hāḏ̣an al-banāt*, "and these girls," is peculiar. The narrator adds the plural feminine suffix *-n* to the singular form, making it plural feminine. This *n*, however, is a suffix usually used in verb conjugations, and not with nominal declensions. Demonstrative pronouns have many forms in different dialects, however, and the one noted here is rare. See also below in the text the example *haḏ̣āku ğa*, derived from *haḏ̣āku* < *haḏ̣āk* + *u* (< *huwwa*).

4. *"walla, yā ḥbāyba, nsī^{e}t, insītič yā ḥabbāba"*: "'By Allah, o grandma, I forgot, forgot you, o grandma.'" He is not her grandson, and she is not his grandmother, but age difference between them dictates these address forms in the Arabic-speaking society. Note that the form for *grandmother* can be in the diminutive pattern (with *y* inserted), *ḥbāyba*, or without it (but with geminated *b*), *ḥabbāba*. Henkin names this address form a "reversed kinship term," among other kinship terms, such as *yāba* for one's son or daughter, if the speaker is male, and *yumma* for a male or female child, if the speaker is female. Henkin, *Negev Arabic*, "Come, O Your Mother." Older male and female speakers address younger persons like that (cf. chap. 13, note 7; chap. 17, note 1).

5. The form *tehanna* ("you will get happy, satisfied" is in the imperfect of measure V. This measure in the Galilee Bedouin dialects is without the prefix *-t* (which is *tithanna* in sedentary dialects, as well as in MSA/LA).

6. The word *liḥitič* literally means "your (f.sg.) beard," though this female *ġūla* does not have a beard. Here, this beard expresses respect to someone with (who might have) a beard—in other words, someone adult, rather old, experienced, and wise. The old are traditionally respected for being wiser than young people in the Middle East.

7. *gāḷ, "bayyē!"*: "He said, "Father! [Oh my!]" This cry derives from a call for help by one's father. The diminutive form *bayyē* instead of *abūy* reflects here emotional alarm or surprise rather than just the usual diminutive meaning.

8. *mā-dd-araxx-^{i}ḥzām ál-faras*: "I want to make the mare's buckle a little looser." The particle *mā* at the beginning of this sentence is here a stress marker for the following utterance: "I mean, after all, indeed," in contrast with anything previous. It also stresses the fact that this issue has already been mentioned. A similar example is *mā sawwētha b-liḥitī^y!*: "indeed, you harmed my dignity." This role of *mā* is known and occurs also in sedentary dialects, such as Jerusalem. Piamenta, *Use of Tenses, Aspects, and Moods.*

9. The geminated *-dd-* in *mā-dd-araxx-^{i}ḥzām ál-faras* is what remained from *widdi*, "I want," shortened because of the fast (and casual) speech rate. Similarly, *araxx-^{i}ḥzām* derives from *araxxi-^{i}ḥzām*, where the full verb form includes a final *i*, which is elided here because of speech rate and casual speech.

10. Note the additional small ^{y} at the end of the word *wādi.* (Cf. *wādi* in the following utterance: *w-al-wādi da*, "and this *wādi*.") The short ^{y}, called a pausal form, usually marks the ending of a phrase or a sentence when it occurs at the end of a prosodic phrase. Pausal

forms exist in other Arabic dialects and in different forms, such as vowel change (*a re > i*) or suffixed glottalization (cf., e.g., Blanc, *Studies in the North Palestinian Arabic*, "Arabic Dialects"; Hoberman, "Pausal Forms"; Watson and Bellem, "Glottalisation and Neutralization"; Zubi, "Pausal Forms"). Some pausal forms have been noted for the Bedouin dialects of the Galilee (Rosenhouse, *Bedouin Arabic Dialects*). The stories in this book have additional examples of pausal forms, though not many, and not all of them are marked.

11. *bitxāṣṣin*: "You would brace yourself, keep strong." The narrator mixes the pronunciation of various sounds sometimes: for example, pronouncing *x* as *ḥ* (in *bitḥāṣṣin*, written in the text) and emphatic consonants as nonemphatic.

12. *ta-ḥatta-rrawwaḥ 'ana wiyyāk*: "until we go home, me and you." This is another assimilation feature, which takes place often in various forms (e.g., chap. 6, note 2; chap. 23, note 3; chap. 13, note 14; chap. 30, note 6; chap. 34, story C, note 20; chap. 36, story B, note 7). Here, the prefix of the first-person plural of the imperfect verb form is assimilated to the first root consonant (here: *nr > rr*). See also *widdak* ^{e}*ddaxxen*? ("Do you want to smoke?") in the following utterance, where ^{e}*tdaxxen* > ^{e}*ddaxxen*.

13. *u-liff sikāra*: "and he folded a cigarette." In the past, people used to roll slices of tobacco leaves in a piece of paper to make a cigarette by themselves. Note the consonant *k* for *g* in "cigarette." Note that *liff* can be the narrative imperative, an imperative form used for the past tense (cf. chap. 22, note 2).

14. *'eḏmo*, "mouth," is *'iṯmo* in other dialects.

15. The address "my paternal aunt" is used here to a woman who is presumably young but more aged than the speaker, even when she is not a real family member. See more on address forms in chapter 17, note 1.

16. *u-arrṣūni* seems to be a form of MSA/LA *qarraṣūni* (*qrs*, "squeeze, pinch, cut"), though in Bedouin dialects the regular parallel of LA *q* is *g*/*ğ*, while ' is its urban variant. Here even the ' of *'arrṣūni* is omitted, leaving only the vowel as a trace. Further study is necessary to see if this form reflects sedentarization effects or is an idiolectal feature.

17. The first-syllable stress in *íxtifa* (measure VIII) is typical of Bedouin dialects and does not occur in Levant sedentary dialects, where the second syllable is stressed in this pattern, thus *ixtáfa*, "he/it hid/was hidden." This stress pattern is apparently dying out in the Galilee Bedouin dialects. (On stress, see the chapter about Bedouin dialects, point 8.)

18. *'arūs b-ismi-llā*: "a bride, in Allah's name." The phrase *b-ismi-llā* usually begins a speech or written text by (religious) Muslims. This phrase, which follows the description ("a bride") here, aims at praising the girl—beauty and good qualities, which exist together because of Allah's grace. This implies that she is pure and good, as well as pretty, according to the faith notions.

19. The story was included in Rosenhouse and Katz, *Texts in the Dialects of Bedouins in Israel*, 40–43.

40. The Old Woman and the Ḥūt

NARRATOR: Ṯalǧe Mūsa

TRIBE: *ʿArab el-Ḥuǧērāt*

IFA 17400 February 5, 1982

1 bī hā-l-ixtyāra ʿ^{i}nda hā-l-binet. hāy hā-l-ixtiyāra ʿindha bint, mā ʿindha ʾiši tōkel. ʿindīha ǧiǧāt. al-ǧiǧāt kull yōm bibīḍu. kull arba(ʿ)-xamest-iyyām bitḥuṭṭhin bi-hā-l-qubʿa u-bitrūḥ twaddīhen ʿala n-nāṣre, tbīʿen.	1 There is this old woman who has a daughter. This old woman has a daughter, she does not have anything to eat. She has hens. The hens lay eggs every day. Every four, five days she puts them in the hat and goes to deliver them to Nazareth and sell them.
7 šū btištri? ^{e}btištri zahra, tištri malfūf, ḥāmeḍ, tištri ʿašān yōklu hī u-bintha. kūsa. yōm min ḏāt el-ʾayyām, u-hī ǧāya, aštat[1] ʿalēha ad-dinya u-ġābat aš-šames.	7 What does she buy? She buys cauliflower, she buys cucumber, lemon, she buys in order that they eat, she and her daughter. Squash [zucchini]. One day [of these days] while she was coming [back], it began to rain on her, and the sun disappeared.
11 qālat, "wallāhi, biddīš ʾabāt hōn, biddi ʾarawweḥ." ṣārat ad-dinya tišti ʿalēha, tišti kṯīr, ^{i}kṯīr, ṣārat ad-dinya lēl. ʾa- šāfat hī mġāra. qālat "wallāhi, haḏik il-mġāra ḏāwiya hī, yimkin ḥarrāṯīn mwal(l)ʿīn bīha nār, ʾaw reʿyān mwal(l)ʿīn nār min as-saqʿa ʿalēna." mā mayyalat, willa hā-l-ḥūt, mwalleʿ hā-n-nār u-qāʿed. ʿindo ḥṣān	11 She said, "By Allah, I don't want to spend the night here, I want to go back home." It began to rain on her, rain much, much, and it became night. She saw a cave. She said, "By Allah, this cave is lit up—maybe there are plowmen having lit a fire in it or shepherds having made fire because of the cold on us." She has hardly turned away from the road, and lo, there was this *ḥūt*, having lit a fire, and sitting. He had a horse.

20 qām qāl-la, "'ahlan, ʿağūz, 'ahlan, 'ahlan, ʿağūz, ğīti?" qālat-lo, "ā." qālat-lo, difyat ʿād,	20 He got up and said to her, "Welcome, old woman, welcome, welcome, old woman, you came?" She said to him, "Yes." She said to him—she warmed [herself] already.
23 qāl-la, "daffi, daffi ʿād," difyat. qālat lo "biddi arawweḥ." qāl-la, "wēn ⁱtrawwḥi? essa bidda turquṣ."	23 He told her, "Warm [yourself], warm [yourself] then." She warmed herself and said to him, "I want to go home." He said to her, "Where will you go? Now she wants to dance."
26 qāl-la, "šū hāḏa-lli b-il-qubbaʿa?" qālat lo, "yā bnayya, haḏōl, ya ḥabībi, haḏōl la-binti. ʿindi hā-l-binet, u-biddi (i)yyā, 'asāwī-la, nōkel, 'ana wiyyā hā-l-binet, mā ilnāš ḥada, biddna nōkel." qāl-la, "ṭayyeb." misek b-hā-l-nōbe, bhā-l-msalle, ṣār yōxoḏ, yoġroz fīhen, hā-yaʿamilhin b-ḥabel hēk.	26 He said to her, "What is this which is in the hat?" She said to him, "O son, those, my dear, those are for my daughter. I have a daughter, and I want her, I make for her to eat, we eat, I with this daughter, we do not have anyone, we want to eat." He said to her, "Good." He took one by one, with this needle, and began holding and making holes in them, putting them by a string [a rope] like that.
34 iz-zahrāt w-il-fiğlāt w-il-malfūfāt ʿimilhen hēk wa-ḥaṭṭha, rabaṭhen ʿalēha hōn. qāl-la, "yalla, qūm azraʿ hēk, qūm 'urqoṣ, ʿağūz, ʿād, 'azraʿ ṭīzak bistān. yalla qūm 'urqoṣ, ʿād 'azraʿ ṭīzak bistān."[2]	34 The cauliflowers and the radishes and the cucumbers, he made them like that and put them, tied them on her here. He said to her, "Come on, get up, sow like that, get up, dance, get up and dance, old man, again I will plant a garden on your behind. Come on, get up and dance, again, I will plant a garden on your behind."
40 qālat-lo, "yā bnayya, 'ana ʿağūz, ⁱxtiyāra." qāl-la, "'ē, yā, biddak tqūm turquṣ, inta ʿağūz—lāzim yurquṣ al-ʿağūz." qālat lo, "ṭayyeb, yā ḥabībi, biddi 'arūḥ hēk ta- la-[$_{H}$bet- šimúš$_{H}$] nitfi."	40 She said to him, "No, my son, I am an old woman, an old woman." He said to her, "Oh, well, you will get up and dance, you are an old woman—an old woman should dance." She said to him, "Well, my dear, I want to go like that, to the ($_{H}$bet- šimúš$_{H}$) toilet, a little."
45 fātat ʿala hā-l-ⁱmġāra ğuwwa. ʿindo hā-l-ⁱḥṣān. qaṭʿat hā-l-ḥabel min hā-l-ⁱḥsān, w-inhazam l-ⁱḥsān, daššar il-ʿağūz w-inhazam. liḥaq al-ⁱḥsān yurkuḏ. qāl-(l) ha, "dīnak ʿağūz, dīnak ʿağūz, dīnak ʿağūz,"	45 She entered the cave, inside. He had a horse. She cut the rope of this horse, and the horse ran away. He left the old woman and ran away. He followed the horse running. He said to her, "[Curse] your religion, old woman [=go to hell], [curse] your religion, old woman, [curse] your religion, old woman."
51 liḥq al-ʿağūz u-rāḥ yurkuḏ. haḏīk, ḥimlat al-xurğ—bī maʿā xurğ māl. maṣāri. ḥimlat nuṣṣ al-xurğ il-māl u-'ağatak mrawwḥa b-hā-l-lēl ʿa hā-l-balad.	51 He left the old woman and went running. This one, she took the saddlebag—he had a money saddlebag—money. She took half the saddlebag and went home in the night to this village.

56 qāl-laha, “šū inti ismek ʿād?” qālat-lo, “fēn axra” qāl-lha, “u-bintek?” qālat lo, “fēn anām.”[3] misek hāḏa ʿala hā-l-e . . . rāḥ ^{e}l-eḥṣān minno. šū biddo ysāwi? biddo yirğaʿ, ydawwer ʿala l-^{i}xtiyāra. biddo yiḏbaḥ, biddo yōkol al-xityāra, yiḏbaḥḥa (=yiḏbaḥha).	56 He [had] said to her, “What is your name, then?” She said to him, “Where-Shall-I-Shit.” He said to her, “And your daughter?” She said to him, “Where-Shall-I-Sleep.” He took this to. . . . The horse went away from him. What would he do? He must go back, look for the old woman. He wants to kill, he wants to eat the old woman, kill her.
63 ṣār yisyal ^{i}b-hā-l-balad, yiʿemal ḥālo maskīn, miṯel šaḥḥāḏ. qāl, “fēn axra, fēn anām.” yiqūlū-lo “rūḥ šuxx barra bi-ṣ-ṣab^{e}r, rūḥ šuxx bi-ṣ-ṣab^{e}r, u-taʿāl nām bi-ṭ-ṭabābīn.” hī sāmiʿto, tsakker ʿa-ḥālhe al-bāb. “fēn axra, fēn anām, fēn axra, fēn anām”—mā-fiš.	63 He started asking in the village, making himself poor, like a beggar. He said, “Where-Shall-I-Shit, Where-Shall-I-Sleep.” They would say to him, “Go urinate outside, where the cactus is, go urinate at the cactus, and sleep in the [big] stone ovens.” She hears him, closes the door on herself [locks herself in]. [He continues calling,] “Where-Shall-I-Shit, Where-Shall-I-Sleep. Where-Shall-I-Shit, Where-Shall-I-Sleep”—nothing.
70 yōm, ʿāwad riğaʿ ʿala hā-l-ʿēn. qaʿad, misek ʾīdo, madd ʾīdo hēk. qāl, “mā ʿağūz, mā nābak[4] ʿağūz, wa-lā ḥeṣān nābak, wa-lā ʿağūz nābak, wa-lā ğazar nābak. hā.” qaṭaʿ ʾīdo willa hū qāṭ^{e}ʿha. xalṣat. hiyye nitfe, hāy zġīre.	70 One day, he went back to this spring. He sat down, took hold of his hand, stretched his hand like that, and said, “Not an old woman—not an old woman replaced you, neither a horse, nor an old woman, or carrots. Ha.” He cut his hand, and lo—he has cut it. [It is] finished. It is small [story]. This is small.

Commentary

The story of the encounter between the old woman and the ogre resembles the previous group of stories. Although this is not a personal story or a memorate, here too the encounter of a man with a demonic creature is at the center of the story.

An old woman returning late from the market with a basket full of vegetables is making her way in the middle of the night. Hoping for shelter from the pouring rain, she heads for a bright cave. To her dismay, it turns out that she has arrived at the cave of a *ḥūt* (demonic ogre). At first, he welcomes her with a greeting and invites her to sit by the fire and warm herself, but as soon as she asks to leave, he begins to abuse her. He takes the vegetables she bought, threads them on a string, creates a kind of necklace, which he ties to her body, and demands that she begin to dance.

The old woman finds an excuse to reject his demand. She requests a brief respite from the *ḥūt* to relieve herself, enters the cave, and releases the ogre's horse. The *ḥūt* follows his fleeing horse and leaves the old woman, who takes advantage of the opportunity and flees with a bag full of money.

The *ḥūt* curses her. He plans to take his revenge on her when the day comes, and as he pursues the horse, he tries to find out what her name is. The old woman replies,

"Where-Shall-I-Shit." He asks her daughter's name, and she replies, "Where-Shall-I-Sleep."

In the next scene, the *ḥūt* tries to locate the dwelling place of the old woman and her daughter. Pretending to be a beggar, he enters the village and calls out, "Where-Shall-I-Shit! Where-Shall-I-Sleep!" He seems to interpret the old woman's answers to his questions during the chase as real names for herself and her daughter. The villagers understand from his cries that he is looking for a place to relieve himself and a place to sleep. They answer accordingly: "Go urinate outside, where the cactus is, go urinate at the cactus, and sleep in the [big] stone ovens [*tabūns*, large baking ovens made of clay, which are about the size of a human being]."

The disappointed *ḥūt*, unable to locate the old woman and her daughter, punishes his own hand and cuts it off, and this is the end of the story.

It seems that the story's purpose is to demonstrate the stupidity of the *ḥūt* and to praise the wisdom of the old woman, who tricks him.

The narrator uses the word *ḥūt*, which refers to a demonic creature, usually identified as an ogre, that lives in springs or water sources. The *ḥūt* appears in many Bedouin stories as one who dams up the water and demands that the people of the city hand over a virgin girl if they wish to receive any. The narrators do not always make a clear distinction between *ḥūt*, *ġūl*, and *ǧinnie*. The description in the current story is much more suitable for a *ġūl* than for a *ḥūt*. In many stories, *ġūls* are characterized as stupid creatures that can be outsmarted in different ways: children who ask the *ġūla* to pump water in the sieve, and escape while she is trying to do as they ask; a boy who, after asking the *ġūla*'s daughter to release his fetters so he can show her the right way to slaughter him, takes advantage of it to slaughter her; and so on.

In the story presented above, the heroine uses some tricks. Initially, she finds an excuse to reject the ogre's request, on the pretext that she must first relieve herself. The ogre releases her for a moment, and she uses the opportunity and releases his horse, forcing him to go after the animal and let her go. The maintenance of a household with a herd of sheep, cows, chickens, or horses is also characteristic of descriptions of *ġūls* in the stories. Running off to her village, the old woman carries a sack of money. It seems that in addition to releasing the horse, she also exploits the ogre's lack of supervision to rob him of his treasures, since she is a destitute woman, as noted at the beginning of the story.

When the ogre tries to find out the names of the heroine and her daughter, the heroine gives him fictitious ones. This episode is somewhat reminiscent of the trick Odysseus uses in the Cyclopes' cave. When the Cyclops asks him for his name, he replies, "Noman is my name. They call me Noman—My mother, my father, and all my friends, too."[5] The Cyclops believes that this is Odysseus's real name. Later on, when he calls the other Cyclopes, his brothers, for help and is asked who attacked him, he replies, "Nobody," and therefore his brothers do not come to his aid.

The pseudonyms given by the heroine are connected to her first trick, when she was looking for an excuse to enter the cave and released the horse. The ogre does not make the obvious link and thus demonstrates his stupidity even more.

At the end of the story, the ogre punishes his hand. He reproaches it with words, as if it were another creature, and cuts it off. This foolish act once again underscores the stupidity of the ogre and serves as a proper ending to the tale. It is interesting to note that this motif of punishing a particular part of the body also appears in stories in the indigenous cultural space of North American Indians.[6]

Despite the linguistic design that is not always clear, the story is full of humoristic descriptions that probably amused the narrator's young listeners, yet the story contains hidden messages of resourcefulness and ingenuity, as well as a warning against going out in the middle of the night and entering caves.

Notes

1. *aštat 'alēha ad-dinya*: "it rained on her" (literally: "the world rained on her"). For "to rain," sedentary dialects in Israel use *šattat* (same root, different verb measure).

2. The *ḥūt* was addressing her in the masculine person. This narrator apparently aimed to present the *ḥūt* as someone who does not speak grammatically and is not eloquent. Or maybe he did not perceive that she was a woman, because Arabic *'aǧūz* refers to both male and female old people.

3. The names the old woman gives the *ḥūt* for her and her daughter are intentionally not real personal names but interrogative sentences that rouse listeners' responses. These names are used to humorously mock the *ḥūt*. This story further presents the *ḥūt* as a foolish, uncivilized creature who does not understand human language properly.

4. The verb in *mā nābak 'aǧūz* means in LA and Colloquial Arabic "to represent, take the place of"—in other words, "not an old woman represents you and takes your role." This recurs in the following sentences, referring to the horse or "even a carrot."

5. Homer, The Essential *Odyssey*, p. 72, lines 9:364–5.

6. Radin, *Trickster*, 135.

PART III · Animal Stories

41. The Man and the Wounded Snake

A. The Snake Story

NARRATOR: ʻABDALLAH ASʻAD ŠIBLI

TRIBE: *ʻArab eš-Šibli*
Recorder: Judith Rosenhouse 1980

1 ʼasʻad widdu yyāha,[1] widdu minni ʼaḥaddiṯkum ʻala ḥayya.[2] teʻarfīn šū al-ḥayya? wāḥad rāʻi, hū yirʻa barra. fī ʻendo kēf,[3] yaʻani, šubbāba hāy, yikayyef ʻalēha. kull-yōm yiği ʻa-hal-maṭraḥ hāḏ, u-yigef ʻalēha u-yeṣīr yilʻab ʻala hā-š-šibbāba u-yekayyef.	1 Asʻad [his son] wants it—he wants me to tell you about the snake. (Do you [f.sg., addressing the researcher] know what is a snake?) A shepherd, he was grazing outside [in an empty place]. He had a flute (*kēf*). That is, this flute (*šubbāba*), he had fun with it. Every day he would come to this place, stand on it, and start playing the flute and enjoying it.
8 ʼessa tuṭlaʻ hā-l-ḥayya, tṣīr turguṣ, al-ḥayya tṣīr turguṣ guddāmo. muš ʼawwal marra, ṯāni marra, ṯāliṯ marra, ṣārat kull-yōm termī-lo lēra.[4] gaʻad ᵊsnīn ṭawīla u-huwwa hāḏa. kull yōm yiği ʻa-hā-l-maṭraḥ yilʻab ta-hāḏ-aṣ-ṣēra u-hiyya tiṭlaʻ tergeṣ.	8 Now this snake would come out and begin dancing, the snake started dancing in front of him. Not the first time, the second time, the third time, it began every day throwing a lira to him. He remained long years like that. Every day he would come to this place, play the flute until this thing [happened] and it would come out and dance.
15 yōm min al-ʼiyyām gāḷ, "widd-ʼarūḥ ʼaḥiğğ." ṣār ʻendo maṣāri, gāḷ, "ʼarūḥ ʼana ʻand (el-xityār) ʼarūḥ ʼatfarrağ ʻala blād as-soʻodiyya.	15 One day [of the days] he said [to himself], "I want to go to make a pilgrimage." Money accumulated with him, he said, "I'll go, to [the old man] I'll go and look at the land of Saudia [Saudi Arabia]."

19 ṭayyib. ʾağa la-ʾebnu gaḷ-ḷo, sallem[5] ʿala kēfa. gaḷ-ḷo, "haḏ aš-šebbāba w-haḏōl al-ʿanzāt, w-asraḥ bihen u-dīr bālak. ʾamma ʾin ğīt ʿa-l-maṭraḥ el-ᵉflāni u-ṣurt tilʿab aš-šubbāba u-ʾağat hā-l-ḥayya ʿalēk alli turguṣ, ʾowʿak tuḏurba. ʾowʿak tuḏurba. leʾanno ʾana kill ha-l-ʿamar ʾana w-ʾiyyāha ʾoxwān, ʾowʿak ʾin teṣība."

19 Well. He came to his son and said to him— he handed him his fun [the flute]. He said to him, "This is the flute and these are the goats, graze them and pay attention. But if you come to a certain place and begin playing the flute and this snake which dances comes to you, mind you do not hit it. Mind you do not hit it. Because I—all my life I am [like] brothers with it. Take care you do not harm it."

28 hāḏ ʾaxīna b-iḷḷa[6] rāḥ u-ṣār yilʿab ʿa-š-šebbāba u-ṣārat al-ḥayya turguṣ giddāmo, yaʿani miṯel ʾabū. ṣārat kill-yōm tirmī-lo lēra. yōm min el-ʾayyām, men ṭamaʿo, gāḷ, "ṭayyib, ʾeḥna lēš ma niktil hāḏ-al-ḥayya,[7] niṭūl hā-l-maṣriyyāt[8] ʾila mīt marra bi-baṭna."

28 This, our brother in faith [i.e., his son], went and began playing the flute and the snake began dancing in front of him, that is to say, like his father. It began throwing a lira every day to him. One day [of the days], out of his greed, he said, "Well, we—why don't we kill this snake and take the money [coins] which is a hundred times [more] in its belly?"

35 teʿeraf, ar-rāʿi maʿā ʿaṣa, al-ʿaṣa maʿā, saḥib hā-l-ʿaṣa, xaḷḷāha lamma widda tfūt u-rāḥ laʿaṭša. lamma lṭiša, kiṭaʿ ḏēla. ʾassa al-ḥayya, ʾiḏa mā-trūḥ mādeta lā tmūt. haḏīk ᵉtḥuṭṭ al-ğurḥ ᵉb-ʾuṯma, ⁱtḏaḷḷ msakkra ʿalē ta-yuxtum.

35 You know, a shepherd has a stick—the stick is with him. He took this stick, left it [the snake until] when it was going to enter [its place], and he hit it. When he hit it, he cut its tail. Now a snake, if its abdomen does not go [is not entirely wounded], it does not die. This one puts the wound in its mouth and remains closing on it until it heals.

41 min-šān ʾēš? min šān tiblaʿ la-d-damm mā yefūta. hāḏi rāḥat ḥaṭṭat ḏēla b-ʾuṯma u-sakkarat ʿalē. ʾeddēš nāmat? mudda ṭawīla.

41 What for? In order that it may swallow the blood that is going out. This [snake] went and put its tail in its mouth and closed on it. How long did it lie [like that]? A long time.

45 ʾaxīna b-iḷḷa mā-hu ʿiref ḥālan ʾinno ʾaḏāha la-l-ḥayya, ṣār yibʿed ʿan ar-rağel. baʿad ma ṭābat, šāfat min hī hiyyi, u-rāḥat . . . geddām ha-š-šōka, u-nāmat geddām ha-š-šōka.

45 Our faith brother knew at once [of course] that he had injured the snake, and began avoiding the animal [lit.: the man]. After it had healed, it was looking from where it was and went . . . in front of this thorn, and lay in front of this thorn.

50 ʾessa xaṭar o-hi qarṣato. qarṣato—māt maṭraḥo. baʿad yōmēn—ṯalāṯa diryam ʾahalo, rāḥam dawwaram ʿalē, wuždū.

50 Now he [the son] went away [made a journey] and it bit him. It bit him—he died on the spot. After two days—three days his family knew [he was missing], they went and looked for him—[they] found him.

53 rawwaḥ huwwa. baʿad ma rawwaḥ hū min al-ḥağğ gāḷ, "wēn ^{e}flān?" gālū-lo, "waḷḷa, flān māt." "wēn māt?" gālū-lo, "b-al-muṭraḥ al-^{e}flāni." yaʿani maʿnāto ğamb ğabal aṭ-ṭōr. gāḷ, "'ā." ʿerefo.[9]	53 He came back home. He returned home. After he had come home from the pilgrimage, he said, "Where is so-and-so?" They said to him, "By Allah, so-and-so has died." "Where did he die?" They said to him, "At the certain place." That is, it means, near Mount Tabor. He said, "Ah." He knew it.
58 'assa ʿiref 'inno l-ḥayya hanāk. gāḷ, "'ibni ḍarab al-ḥayya w-al-ḥayya 'aḏato girṣa." baʿad-ma sallamam ʿalē hā-n-nās yōmēn-ṯalāṯa, 'arbaʿa, ğumʿa-ğumʿatēn, rāḥ ʿala hā-l-ğabal miṯel mā kān 'awwal u-ṣār yilʿab ʿa-š-šubbāba.	58 He knew now that the snake was there. He said, "My son injured the snake, and the snake injured him with a bite." After they had greeted him, these people, for two days, three, four, a week, two weeks, he went to that mountain as it had been in the beginning, and started playing the flute.
64 ṭallat min bēn hā-l-^{e}ḥğāra ʿalē, gāḷat-lo, "'inet m-int rāyeḥ tinsā-li alli 'ana garaṣto wa-'ana m-āni rāyḥa 'ansāk. w-'aḷḷa ysahhel ʿalīna."	64 It [the snake] peeked at him from among the stones and said to him, "You are not going to forget that I bit him, and I am not going to forget you. And goodbye to you [may Allah ease our parting]."

B. The Shepherd and the Snake

NARRATOR: Nūra Ḥalīfa
TRIBE: *ʿArab el-ʿArāmša*
Recorder: Naomi Raies
IFA 14076 October 1981

Text

One day—there was a man. He had a few goats, and every morning he went on a donkey and took the goats about three kilometers in the forest—to graze the goats.

And there he is . . . he . . . every morning when he comes out of the house and reaches the pasture, he begins to play [the flute]. And there he is sitting under the tree and plays. And next to the tree there was a pile of stones.

Suddenly he saw something, getting out of the stones, and he saw a snake come out and begin to dance. After about half an hour of playing, he got tired, and at the end, the snake threw him a gold lira from its mouth. The snake went back to its place, and he [the shepherd] went home.

And the second day he went especially to play the flute, so that the snake would give him a gold lira. And as he thought, each time the snake came out and gave him a gold lira, and so it went [continued] day after day, all his life till he got older.

And one day he took his son and taught him how to play the flute and told him: "This snake—you go to this place and do such and such and the snake throws you a gold lira, from which I was living, and from this you will live."

This boy went on the first day to play for the snake.

The snake came out and said, "You're new to me!"

He says to him, "I am the son of the man who used to play for you."

And at the end it threw him—after it danced for him—a gold lira.

For some time [after a while], one day he was greedy, and he said, "I'll kill it and I'll take all the gold within [it]." So after it threw him a gold lira pound—as it [the snake] came into the pile, he gave it [a blow] with a stone and cut half of it.

The snake did not die, and from its pain, it came up to the man and bit him, and the child died.

On this morning, the man does not feel well. He heard the dog wailing and did not feel well at home; he—whatever he eats it is [like] sticks in his throat, and he is thirsty. He—the way he puts on the shoes he reverses the sides, and he did not feel well. And tears come to his eyes and he feels bad, and his heart tells him: "Something happened!" So he slept and dreamed that something happened. He saw a dead man at night, and in the morning, he said, "My child, something happened to him. He died in this place where I used to play [the flute]." And just as he thought, as his heart said, so he went and found him. He brought the boy, they buried him.

After a year, he went back—he needed something to live. He went and began to play the flute. For ten days, every day he does it for an hour, an hour and a half.

After ten days, the snake came out, and told him, "I'm no more. . . ." It threw him three [liras] after he played; it did not dance, only heard, stood and heard him. In the end, it threw him three pounds of gold.

And after throwing him this, it says to him, "I cannot . . . I do not want you to come again. You may remember your child and kill me, or I remember your child's situation and I'll sting you, and here it is where we part."

He [the shepherd] tells it: "What happened is dead [what is done is done], and we start again. The child was guilty, and I forgive you."

So every day he would come and play for it, and the snake danced for him till the old man died. That's the story.

The recorder: "Does this story have a title?"
Informant: "A Shepherd Plays the Flute."[10]
The recorder: "And the snake has a name?"
Informant: "Black snake."

Remark

This version was told in Hebrew and was recorded by Naomi Raies. The narrator's knowledge of the Hebrew language is flawed, but the story itself is complex and rich in detail.

Commentary

The story is known as the international type AT 285D, "Snake Refuses Reconciliation" (in Uther's index, this narrative type is included as a part of the narrative type ATU

285A, "The Man and the Wounded Snake"). According to the description in Thompson's book,[11] a snake gets milk and in return gives gold from its tail (motif B103.0.4.1, "Grateful snake gives gold piece daily"). The man's son wants all the gold at once and cuts off the snake's tail. The snake bites the boy. The hero of the story tries to give the snake milk again, but they cannot be reconciled, for each has injuries that cannot be forgotten.

The story has ancient roots. Pliny the Elder, who lived in the first century CE and was a Roman author, naturalist, and natural philosopher, put in his book *Natural History*, in the name of a Greek historian named Phylarchus (third century BCE), a story from Egypt about a she-viper that used to eat at the table of a certain man. One of her offspring bit the owner's son, and when the she-viper heard of it, she realized that her son was to blame. She killed him and never returned to the man's home.[12]

Among the stories of the *Panchatantra*, a collection of Indian stories from the third century BCE, also known as *Kalīla and Dimna*, there is a story about a Brahmin who sees a snake coming out of an anthill in his field and identifies it as the God guarding the field. He brings him a saucer of milk as homage. When he returns to the field the next day, he finds a gold coin in the saucer. From that day on, he takes care to bring the snake a milk offering and receives a coin from him daily. One day, the Brahmin's son replaces his father. The son decides to kill the snake to take the entire treasure. He hits the snake's head with a club, but the snake escapes injury, bites the young man, and kills him. The Brahmin returns home and hears about his son's death.

According to popular belief, snakes feed on milk (motif B765.6.1, "Snake drinks milk") and dance to the sounds of a flute (motif ‡B767.2, "Snakes enjoy music"). The motif of a snake drinking milk and other beverages is also found in the Talmud: "Rabbi Shimon said: I saw a snake drinking sauce in Tsidan" (Babylonian Talmud, Chulin 39b). In the Bedouin story, the provision of milk is replaced by flute playing.

The first version was written down by Rosenhouse and was taken from ʻAbdallah Asʻad Shibli of the ʻArab el-Shibli tribe on Mount Tabor.[13] In this version, the shepherd entrusts his secret to his son while he goes on a *ḥaǧǧ* pilgrimage. It seems that the image of the father who observes the commandments of his religion is presented as an antithesis to the character of the greedy son. The son is referred to as "our brother of faith." He hits the snake and cuts its tail. At this point in the story, the narrator inserts a popular belief about the behavior of a wounded snake: "Now a snake, if its abdomen does not go [is not entirely wounded], it does not die. This one puts the wound in its mouth and remains closing on it until it heals. What for? In order that it may swallow the blood that is going out [which he loses]." The narrator places the event "near Mount Tabor," in his own place of residence. The story also describes one of the customs of the *ḥaǧǧ*. When the father has fulfilled the *ḥaǧǧ* commandment, he is crowned as a *Ḥāǧǧ*. His friends come to congratulate him: "They had greeted him, these people, for two days, three, four, a week, two weeks." Only after the celebrations are over does he reunite with the snake. The snake comes out of its hiding place and says, "You are not going to forget that I bit him, and I am not going to forget you. And goodbye to you [may Allah ease our parting]."

The story is common in Arab culture and is known in Israel, Syria, Lebanon, Iraq, Egypt, and other countries. The story is the source of the Arab proverb "You shall not forget your son, and I shall not forget my tail" (*inta ma tinsa Shalabi* [the son's name] *u-ana ma ansa ḏanabi*). Or in another formulation, "Do not cheer with joy and do not let out a sigh, you will not forget your son, and I will not forget my tail" (*La tqūl ye-lēli wa-la tqūl yu-wēli. Inta ma tinsa waladak u-ana ma ansa ḏeily*).

These two proverbs appear in a Bedouin version of the story, "The Friendship between the Old Man and the Snake," from the Negev, which Sasson Bar-Zvi includes in his book *Fable, Story and Legend in Arab Tents*.[14]

In the IFA archives, there is a Muslim version that is identical to our story in most of its details. It was recorded from Maḥmūd Titi of Biʿena, near Karmiel (IFA 24263). In this version, the Bedouin shepherd introduces the snake to his son and warns him not to harm it. After three days, the son decides to kill the snake and equips himself with a large stick. The son does not succeed in hitting the snake because the latter bites him to death. When the herd comes home without the shepherd, the father understands that his son is not alive. He goes to the cave with his wife and realizes that he was not wrong. There is no further mention of the snake or a dialogue between him and the father after the son's death. The narrator sums up the moral of the story with the words "Greed is harmful and not helpful."

Gruenwald includes in his book a particularly interesting Judeo-Spanish version in which the flute is replaced by a tambourine.[15] The son cuts off the snake's tail. However, the snake does not kill him but spits on his face. This spitting causes the son's face to be distorted, and it remains in this form until the day of his death. From a member of the ʿArab el-ʿArāmša tribe, I heard a similar story about the distortion of a man's face following an injury caused by demons.

The second story, "The Shepherd and the Snake," denounces the traits of greed and ingratitude. Contrary to most of the familiar versions of the story, this version ends in an optimistic manner. The old man forgives the snake and does not blame him for his son's death: "What happened is dead [what is done is done], and we start again. The child was guilty, and I forgive you." The narrator uses here a common Arab proverb, "What has passed is dead" (*illi fāt māt*), which replaces the proverb that appears in the other versions.

Both the snake and the flute are considered in psychology to be symbols of the penis or, in this case, symbols of seduction.

The narrator's description of the old man's sorrow is touching:

> On this morning, the man does not feel well. He heard the dog wailing and did not feel well at home. And tears come to his eyes and he feels bad, and his heart tells him: "Something happened!" So he slept and dreamed that something happened.

The dog's wailing foretells the disaster. This belief has a real basis. Dogs are very sensitive to events in human life, and there are many stories about it. The narrator brings into her story an element of a dream. Bedouins attribute deep meaning to dreams. In another of the same narrator's stories, that of the girl who fell into a well (chap. 3), she describes her heroine's dream following the death of her son, an element that does not appear in other versions of that story. (See also the discussion about dreams in chap. 1, "Between the Sun and the Moon.")

The shepherd's flute mentioned in the story is called *šubbābah*. It is still quite common among the Bedouin shepherds and the Arab *fallāḥīn*. The flute is open from both sides and has five holes. They used to prepare it from common reed (*Phragmites australis*) or a hollow stalk of Spanish oyster thistle (*Scolymus hispanicus*), whose natural air space was widened with a pointed wooden stick, and holes were drilled into it using white-hot iron. Nowadays, it is prepared from a metal or plastic pipe.

According to musicians' testimony, a copper pipe is best suited for creating a flute. I did not see the shepherds' flutes made of common reed or a stalk, but a Bedouin from the ʿArab el-Ḥuǧērāt tribe testified to me that he had learned to play the flute made of Spanish oyster thistle stalk. The length of the instrument is 42–44 cm, and the diameter of the holes ranges between 6 and 10 mm. The distance between them is 25–35 mm, and the distance between the lower hole and the edge of the flute is between 62 and 86 mm.

The flute is held tilted downward. Its tip rests on the lips, and the player blows into it with pursed lips. Another way of playing is to hold the flute vertically and press its entrance open against the palate. The range of sounds is quite wide. By regulating the intensity of the exhalation, one can get two scales at different heights. There are musicians who accompany their playing with a hum. Usually the sounds are not clear, and the playing sounds hoarse, but from instruments of high quality, one can produce cleaner sounds.

As stated above, the *šubbābah* is very common among shepherds—Bedouins and peasants alike. The melodies are also common, and the influence of the Arab village is evident. The most common melodies are the *ẓarīf aṭ-ṭūl* ("The Lad with the Fine Height"), *šimāliyya* ("The Northern One"), *marǧiyyeh* (from *marǧ*, "valley"), *ganaṣ* (hunting songs), and *ʿatabi* (slow tunes with continuous and curly sounds). All these melodies are adapted to many different texts. The *šubbābah* is used as a musical instrument in everyday life. It can sometimes be heard at weddings and celebrations.[16]

Jewish sources mention flutes made from common reed. For example, it is said that "the flute in the Temple was [made of] reed and it came from the days of Moses. Once they covered it with gold, and its sound was not pleasant as it was. They took the gold cover off and its sound became pleasant as it was before" (Tosefta, Arachin 2:3).

Greek mythology tells of the nymph *Syrinx*, who was pursued by the amorous god Pan. She ran to a river's edge and asked for assistance from the river nymphs. In answer, she was transformed into hollow water reeds that made a haunting sound when the god's frustrated breath blew across them. Pan cut the reeds to fashion the first set of panpipes, which were thenceforth known as *syrinx*. The word *syringe* was derived from this word.

Notes

1. *ʾasʿad widdu yyāha*: "Asʿad wants it." In Arabic, inanimate objects (e.g., "thing") are often expressed in the feminine gender. Here, too, the general, inanimate notion of "something" is referred to in the 3f.sg. suffixed pronoun *–ha*.

2. The snake has a feminine word form (see its feminine suffix, *-a*) and therefore is referred to as a feminine entity, whatever its biological sex. Some other animals also take the f. suffix without reflecting their biological sex (e.g., *ḥamāma*, "dove"; *naḥla*, "bee"). In such nouns, the parallel form that lacks the suffix is not the m. animal but a group of that kind.

Still, certain other nouns do not take the f. suffix and are common to both f. and m. genders (e.g., *'ağūz*, "old man/woman").

3. *kēf, ya'ani, šubbāba—kēf* in colloquial Arabic means "fun, joy, enjoyment" and here probably also "hobby." This form is apparently derived from the word *how?*, which in various dialects is *kēf, čēf* (in various Bedouin dialects) or *kīf/čīf*. This verb form in measure II *kayyaf*, "take pleasure, have fun, enjoy something," probably derives from this noun (cf. Barthélemy, *Dictionnaire arabe-français*, 735).

4. lēra: "lira." The word *lira* originates from Latin *libra*. This is a money coin used during the British Mandate in Palestine and later on in Israel until 1980. It was the currency of Italy, Malta, San Marino, and the Vatican City until the euro replaced it in 2002. It is still used in Turkey, Syria, and Lebanon at varying rates.

5. *sallem 'ala kēfa*: "he handed him his flute." The verb here is actually an imperative—this is another example of the narrative imperative, which occurs only in Bedouin Arabic dialects (cf. chap. 17, note 4; chap. 39, story E, note 4; Palva, "Descriptive Imperative").

6. The expression *'axīna b-iḷḷa*, "our brother in Allah [faith]," refers to a person who belongs to the speaker's faith group—whatever it is—and whose name is not known or not mentioned for some other reason. Another expression for such unnamed persons is *ar-rağel ~ ar-rağul*, literally "the man," as in this story.

7. Note that in some demonstrative pronouns, such as *hāḏa, hāḏ*, emphasis (velarization) occurs with forms with low vowels, like *a*, and not with other vowels, such as *haḏōl*, "these," or *hāḏi*, "this [f.sg.]." Such emphasis is characteristic of numerous Bedouin Arabic dialects. For more examples of demonstrative pronouns, see chapter 8 note 3, chapter 39, note 3.

8. *hā-l-maṣriyyāt*: "the money [coins]." Money has several names in Arabic. The word discussed here is the sane f.pl. form of *maṣri* (i.e., Egyptian [money from Egypt]), with the suffixed *-āt* after the glide phoneme *y*. However, the word is often used in the broken plural form *maṣāri*, meaning just "money," with no reference to any specific country or coin.

9. *gāḷ, "'ā." 'erefo*: "He said, 'Ah.' He knew it." The m.sg. suffixed pronoun *-o* refers to the place discussed (and what had happened there), not to the man's son who died by the snake bite. This point relates to the way this Bedouin speaker refers to the question at hand.

10. Usually, informants do not give titles to their tales unless they are asked to do so. The title given by the informant is a casual name, so we changed the title to "The Shepherd and the Snake."

11. Thompson, *Motif-Index of Folk Literature*, vol. 1, 376.

12. Pliny, *Natural History*, 10:96.

13. Rosenhouse and Katz, *Texts in the Dialects of Bedouins in Israel*, 24–27.

14. Bar-Zvi, *Fable, Story and Legend*, 59–60.

15. Gruenwald, *Tales, Songs & Folkways*, 58–59.

16. Perez, "Musical Instruments of the Bedouin Tribes."

42. The Goat, the Kid, and the Ġūla

NARRATOR: Maḥmūd Muḥammad Mrisāt

TRIBE: *ʿArab el-Mrēsāt*
IFA 17419 August 7, 1982

1 marra kān bū ġūḷa, sākne b-maġāra. w-al-ġūḷa ʿindha ḥmāra. u-hassa b-maġāra ṯāniye, sākna ʿanz u-ʿindha saxaḷ ᵉzġayyer, ʾebenha. hassa, kull yōm al-ᵉḥmāra twaddi—al-ġūḷa twaddi al-ᵉḥmāra ʿala l-marʿa, yaʿani, ʿa-šān terʿa. (e)ssa, as-saxaḷ kamān yerʿa, yigḏab ʿala l-ᵉḥmāra yirkab ʿalēha[1] u-kull an-nahār yilʿab ʿalēha, mā yxaḷḷīha tākol.	1 Once there was a *ġūla,* [she was] living in a cave. And the *ġūla* had a she-ass. And now, in another cave, [there] lived a goat and she had a small kid, her son. Now, every day the she-ass would bring—the *ġūla* would bring the she-ass to the pasture, that is, so that she will graze. Now, the kid was also grazing, he grabbed the she-ass, and rode on her, and every day he would play on her, [and] would not let her eat.
10 essa kull yōm. kull yōm. ṣārat al-ᵉḥmāra trawweḥ bala ʾačel, ğaʿāne. ʾessa ṣārat taḏʿaf. tdaḥḥeğ al-ġūḷa, tdaḥḥeğ ʿala l-ᵉḥmāra—al-ᵉḥmāra taḏʿaf. šū ṣārat ᵉtfakkir, qāḷat,"bō ḥada yirkab ʿala l-ᵉḥmāra u-mā yexaḷḷīha tākol."	10 Now, [this was] every day, every day. The she-ass began to go home without food, hungry. Now, she started to get thin. The *ġūla* was looking, looking at the she-ass—the she-ass was thinning. What did she begin to think? She said, "There is someone who rides the she-ass and does not let her eat."
16 rāḥat ğābat dibg u-ḥaṭṭat ʿala hā-l-ᵉḥmāra. ʾassa, rāḥ hā-s-saxaḷ yirkab u-min aṣ-ṣubḥ la-l-muġrib hū yirkab ʿalēha, mā yexaḷḷīha tākul. (e)ssa, rawwaḥ—al-muġrib widdo yrawwiḥ,	16 She went and brought glue and put on the she-ass. Now, this kid went and rode. And from morning to dusk, he was riding her and did not let her eat. Now, he wanted to go home—

21 yeḥawwil yerawweḥ, mā gidir yehawwed. ḏaḷḷo mlazzeg[2] ʿala l-ᵉḥmāra. rawwaḥat al-ᵉḥmāra ʿend al-ġūḷa, hū rākeb ʿalēhi.	21 at dusk he wants to go home, tries to go home—could not get off [the she-ass]. He remained glued to the she-ass. The she-ass went home to the *ġūla*, with him riding on her.
25 gaḏbato al-ġūḷa, ḥaṭṭato ʿindha b-al-bēt. ṣārat teṭaʿmī(h). kiber. ṣārat ʾummo (t)dawwer ʿalē. ḏaḷḷat ᵉddawwer ʿalē, tīži ḥawāl-al-maġāra tḥāḏḏī u-tnādī. simeʿ ṣōtha, ṭelaʿ yorkoḏ la-ʿindhe.	25 The *ġūla* took him, put him in her home, and began to feed him. He grew up. His mother began to look for him. She continued looking for him, came around the cave trying to smuggle/steal him and calling him. He heard her voice and went out running to her.
30 ṭilʿat al-ġūḷa, šāfat al-ʿanz. (e)ssa, ṣāran hāḏīn yikāwanan. al-ʿanz ta-tāxoḏ ʾibinha u-trawweḥ, w-al-ġūḷa mā widdhe. (ʾe)ssa l-ʿanz tuḏrub al-ġūḷa bi-grūnhe.	30 The *ġūla* came out and saw the goat. Now, these began fighting. The goat to take her son and go home, and the *ġūla* does not want it. Now, the goat hits the *ġūla* with her horns.
34 (ʾe)ssa, al-ġūḷa tḥuṭṭ ᵉgrūn min ʿūdān—tkasserhen; tḥuṭṭ ᵉgrūn men ḥağar—tkasserhen; tḥuṭṭ ᵉgrūn men xašab—ᵉtkasserhen; ʾāxar ši ḏarbatha b-baṭenha, be-(ma)ʿedatha u-mātat, u-xaḏat al-ʿanz ʾibenha u-rawwaḥat.	34 Now, the *ġūla* put on horns of sticks—she [the goat] broke them; she put horns of stone—she broke them; she put horns of wood—she broke them. In the end she [the goat] hit her in her (the *ġūla* 's) belly, her stomach, and she died. And the goat took her son and went back home.

Commentary

I recorded this short story, along with another story, from Maḥmūd Muḥammad Mrēsāt of the tribe of ʿArab el-Mrēsāt, a small tribe whose members settled in a village unrecognized by the Israeli government near the Bedouin village of Salāmeh and the Jewish settlement Lotem.

The story belongs to the international type ATU 123, "The Wolf and the Kids." A wolf comes while a mother goat is away, hoping to eat her kids (kid). When they do not open the door, the wolf changes his voice and colors his paws with flour. The children believe that it is their mother, and they open the door. The wolf eats the kids (all except one). The youngest kid hides in a clock. The mother returns and takes revenge on the wolf. She finds him asleep, cuts her children out of his belly, and fills it with stones. Or she challenges him to a fight, which she wins. Or she invites him to her house, where he falls into a pit of hot coals.

The story is an ancient one, and one of its versions appears in the Greek book of fables by Aesop (fifth century BCE). In Aesop's version, the kid manages to outsmart a wolf by asking him to play the flute while he dances. The shepherd hears the music, pursues the wolf, and saves the kid.[3] In an anonymous fable collection written in Latin in the fourth century CE and attributed to the author Romulus, there is a partial version containing the first part of the story of the goat and the kids. A goat goes out to pasture and warns the kid left in the house not to open the door to wild animals. A wolf tries to enter the house by imitating the goat's voice, but the kid does not trust him and says to him, "Your voice is like my mother's voice, but you are an impostor who is trying to ensnare me, drink my blood, and eat my flesh."

Another version of the story appears in the twelfth-century book of fables by Marie de France, written in France.[4] The story in its more familiar version appears in Grimm's collection.[5] It is known throughout Europe, Turkey, North Africa, and the Middle East.

The reader will find a comprehensive discussion of the various versions of the story and its historical development and an analysis of the motifs appearing in it in a monograph written by Kristin Goldberg.[6]

In the Bedouin version, a *ġūla* plays the role of the wolf. The kid teases the *ġūla*, rides on her donkey, and does not allow the donkey to graze. By smearing glue on the donkey's back, the *ġūla* captures the kid. The mother comes to the kid's aid, fights the *ġūla*, and kills her.

The episode in which the kid teases the *ġūla* is unique to the Bedouin version and does not appear in the sedentary Arab and Druze versions recorded in Israel. An identical episode appears in one of the stories about Nuṣṣ-ᵉNṣēṣ, the Bedouin "Tom Thumb." On the other hand, the part in which the wolf (or *ġūla*) breaks into the goat's house is missing in the Bedouin narrative.

Ravit Raufman, in her article dealing with versions of the story that were recorded in the Druze villages of Dāliyat al-Karmel and Bēt Ǧan and in which the *ġūla* also replaces the wolf, analyzes the psychological significance of the story.[7] According to her, both the goat and the *ġūla* represent maternal figures. And so she writes:

> The *ġūla* is a familiar figure in Druze, Bedouin and Arab folklore in general. The confrontation between the goat and the *ġūla* in the Druze versions of the type "The Wolf and the Kids" does not stem from gender characteristics, as in the case of the confrontation between the female goat and the male wolf. Instead, the conflict is characterized by a polarization between the natural animalistic creature (the goat) and the supernatural creature (the *ġūla*). Psychoanalytic evidence shows that these versions illustrate the fact that the mother makes room in the arena not to the father image, who is perceived as dangerous, but to another mother's image. During the absence of the mother, the children are busy preserving her picture in their memory. By dealing with the image of the *ġūla*, they form a picture of the mother's image in their inner world. The purpose of this image is to be able to provide them with a distinction between the world of reality (goat) and fantasy (*ġūla*), between regressive and more developed thinking processes, between an inner mother who is part of their body, and a mother with a subjective existence of her own, one that can go and return. From the kids' point of view, such a mother, who leaves the shared psychic space and has her own needs, may be perceived as hostile and dangerous, not because she is really "bad," but because in her absence the little kids are exposed to all the threats in the world, and her leaving is connected with the sensation of fear and negative feelings.

Indeed, in the Bedouin story, the *ġūla* plays in some way the role of an alternate mother. She does not harm the kid she has captured, but rather feeds and raises him as a mother, with all that this implies. At the beginning of the story, neighborly relations are hinted at between the goat and the *ġūla*. They both live in nearby caves. However, what has begun as an act of mischief by the kid turns into a daily provocation. It seems that the kid, as it is commonly said of young children, tries to "check boundaries," as part of his development process.

Bruno Bettelheim, in his book *The Uses of Enchantment*,[8] claims that all children of preschool age sometimes feel the need to split the image of one parent into two images, one with good character and the other with threatening character. He believes that children cannot comprehend the fact that the same person has pleasant and unpleasant aspects at the same time. This feature is reflected in the story. The mother who imposes discipline and boundaries is perceived as a *ġūla*, a demonic figure. At the end of the story, the good figure defeats the demonic figure and kills it.

The father figure does not appear at all in the story or in the parallel versions from all over the world. In his discussion of the Egyptian version of the story, El-Shamy emphasizes the centrality of the mother in early childhood.[8] The father figure occupies a place in stories intended for older children.

The motif of the *ġūla* putting artificial wooden or stone horns on her head to fight the goat appears in the Druze versions of the story. It is interesting to note that in two of the Druze versions (IFA 23978, 24007), the *ġūla* refuses to fight with the goat on the pretext that she has no horns and the battle is unfair. The goat prepares for her horns made of dough, and, of course, she breaks them during their battle.

Muhawi and Kanaana bring an Arabic version of the story, which was recorded in the village of ʿArrāba in the north of Israel.[9] In this version, the goat fights against a hyena that is attacking her kids. In a Lebanese version that appears in Bushnaq's book, the enemy is also a hyena.[10] In this version, the mother does not appear at all. The story is of three kids. Two of them are devoured by the hyena, while the third manages to trick him, to smash him with his horns and take out of his belly his two brothers who have been swallowed alive.

Notes

1. *hū rākeb ʿalēhi*: "he is riding on it [her]." This narrator sometimes uses the suffixed personal pronoun of the 3f.sg. with the vowel *-i* or *e* instead of the expected *a*. It is interesting to find these suffixed forms in Galilee Bedouin dialects, though such forms were reported in some Syrian Bedouin dialects about eighty years ago, and fifty years before these recordings (see Cantineau, "Études sur quelques parlers de nomades arabes d'Orient"). This feature might be attributed to the assimilation of this suffix to the vowel changes of word final *'imāla* (cf. chap. 18, note 1; chap. 29, note 6). Word final *'imāla* exists in the Negev (cf. Henkin, *Negev Arabic*; Shawarbah, *Grammar of Negev Arabic*), but there it is usually higher (*-i*, *iy*), though *-e* also occurs in some tribes there. Local sedentary *'imāla* does not affect personal pronouns, and therefore it is not a likely explanation. In MSA/LA, however, *-hi*, as a bound suffixed pronoun, occurs when the genitive (possessive) case is syntactically required. Still, in the Bedouin dialects, MSA/LA forms are not frequent.

2. *ḍaḷḷo mlazzeg*: "it/he remained glued." Cf. chap. 23, story A, page 209, note 19 about *ḍaḷḷo*.

3. Aesop's Fables, fable 97.

4. Martin, *Fables of Marie de France*, 231–34.

5. Grimm, *The Original Folk and Fairy Tales of the Brothers Grimm*, story 5.

6. Goldberg, "Wolf and the Kids," 277–91.
7. Raufman, "Teaching Folklore," 613.
8. Bettelheim, *The Uses of Enchantment*, 69.
9. El-Shamy, *Tales Arab Women Tell*, 63–69.
10. Muhawi and Kanaana, *Speak, Bird, Speak Again*, 281–83.
11. Bushnaq, *Arab Folktales*, 233–34.

43. The Lion Who Wanted to Know Man's Nature

NARRATOR: Zidān ʻAli Muṣṭafa

TRIBE: *'Arab el-Sawā ʻed*

IFA 13258 July 1979

1 fī sabeʿ sāken ᵉb-wādi. fī sabeʿ sāken ᵉb-wādi. u-teʿeraf ʼilo ʼiben ᵉzġīr, es-sabaʿ. qāḷ-ḷo, ʼabū, es-sabeʿ le-kbīr bigūḷ la-ʼebno, bigūḷ la-ʼebno, "dir bālak min al-baniʼādam. baniʼādam gawe kṯīr, gawe kṯīr u-bixawwef."[1]	1 There is a lion living in a wādi [valley]. There is a lion living in a valley. And, you know, he has a young son, the lion. He said to him, the big lion says to his son, "Beware of man. Man is very strong, very strong, and frightening."
7 qāḷ-ḷo, "šū hāḏa baniʼādam? šū, ʼana baddi ʼarūḥ ʼašūf baniʼādam, u-baddi ʼašūf kull gudrat banaʼādam." gāḷ-ḷo, "mā tigdar ʿala baneʼādam. ẓālem."	7 He said to him, "What is this man? What? I want to go and see a man, and I want to see all the power of this man." He says to him, "You cannot overcome a man. [He is] unjust/unfair/evil."
11 nizel ʿala hā-l-wādi hēk u-rabaṭ ʿala hā-ṭ-ṭarīq. šwayy winn hā-ǧ-ǧamal, kbīr, ǧāy. fakkaro baneʼādam, gāḷ-ḷo, "taʿāl, bidd(i) ʼašūfak mīn ʼinta." gāḷ-ḷo "ʼana ǧamal." gāḷ-ḷo, "mā šuft li hāḏa l-baniʼādam wēn rāḥ?" gāḷ-ḷo, "walla, ʼana minhazem minno. ʼana minihzim minno. hāḏa ʼiši yxawwif."	11 He went to this valley like that, and ambushed on this way. Shortly, and lo, there is a camel, a big one, coming. He thought it was a man. He said to him, "Come [here], I want to see who you are." He said to him, "I am a camel." He said to him, "Did you not see [for me] a man, where did he go?" He said to him, "By Allah, I am running away from him, I am running away from him. He is a frightening thing."
19 šwayy winn hā-l-bagara minhazma. saʼala, gāḷat-lo, "ʼana minhazma minno. ẓālem, buqtil hāḏ."	19 Shortly, lo, there came a cow running away. He asked her and she said, "I am running away from him. He is evil/ unjust/unfair. He kills [is a killer]."

22 šwayy winno xityār wunna nāfed ydawwer ʿala ğmāl.	22 Shortly [after that], lo, an old man was going around, looking for camels.
24 gāḷ-ḷo, "'inti bani'ādam?" gāḷ-ḷo, "'ani bani'ādam."	24 He said to him, "Are you a man?" He said, "I am a man."
26 gāḷ-ḷo, "baddi atḥārab 'ana wiyyāk. badd(i) nitkātal." gāḷ-ḷo . . . gāḷ-ḷo, "mā ğibt ʿidde maʿāy. tistanna hīn tanni 'aṣal ağīb 'iši lli beḥārbak w-'akātlak? stannāni hōna." gāḷ-ḷo,"ṭayyib, rūḥ, bastanāk."	26 He said to him, "I want to fight with you, I want us to fight." He said to him, "I did not bring tools with me. Will you wait here for me, until I go and bring something to fight you with and I will fight with you? Wait for me here." He said to him, "Good, go, I will wait for you."
32 gāḷ-ḷo, "miš 'amīn minnak. baddi 'arabṭak. biddi 'arabṭak ⁱb-ḥabel ʿala sağara, 'arabṭak ⁱb-ḥabel ʿa-sağara tanni 'arğaʿ'" gāḷ-ḷo, "rboṭni"—miš xāyif hāḏa, 'ibnu-li-s-sabeʿa. rabaṭo ʿala hā-s-sğara, ʿala - u-makkano.	32 He said to him, "I am not secure about you [I do not trust you]. I will tie you. I will tie you with a rope to this tree. I'll tie you with a rope to this tree until I come back." He said to him, "Tie me." He was not afraid, this lion's son. He tied him to this tree, to . . . and fastened it.
38 rāḥ hāḏa l-ⁱxtiyār, ğāb dist mayy, ṭonğara kbīre, ḥaṭṭa ʿala n-nār, ṣārat tiġli, tiġli, ta-tfūr, ṣār yitnāwal ṭāse hēk ᵉkbīra, w-idīr ʿalē. hū marbūṭ. gāḷ-ḷo, "fallitni." gāḷ-ḷo "lā', xallīk marbūṭ." yidīr mayy suxne w-idīrha ʿalē.	38 This old man went, brought a big cauldron, brought a pot of water, put it on the fire. It began to boil, boil, until it boiled. He started taking a large pot and spilled it on him. He was tied. He said to him, "Let me go." He said to him, "No, stay tied." He splashed hot water and put it on him.
44 yiṣrax ta-tswā (=tšwā), katt šaʿaro. u-fallato, gāḷ-ḷo, "rūḥ la-'abūk." rāḥ hāḏa 'ibnu le-s-sabeʿ, rāḥ, winn ḥālto hēk, hāḏa l-walad, 'ibn es-sabaʿ, ḥāla txawwaf.	44 He was shouting [shrieking] until he was roasted, his hair fell out. He let him go and said to him, "Go to your father." He went, this lion's son, went. And his condition [was] like that, this child, the lion's son, a frightening state.
49 gāḷ-ḷo, "kīf bane'ādam?" gāḷ-ḷo, "bane'ādam, fišš 'agdar minno	49 He said to him, "How is man?" He said to him, "Man, there is none mightier
51 ġēr 'aḷḷa." hāya ḥkāyatna ḥakēnāha wa-ʿandak rumēnāha.	51 "than [he is] except Allah." This is our story [which] we have told, and to you we have thrown it.

Commentary

The narrator is a member of the tribe of ʿArab el-Sawāʿed who at the time the story was recorded lived far from his tribe, on a leased plot of land near Yodfat. He had heard the story in his tribe as a child.

The story of the encounter between man and lion belongs to the narrative type ATU 157A, "The Lion Searches for Man." A young lion is warned by his parents to stay away from men. He asks other large animals if they are men. They answer that they are only the ill-treated servants of man. He meets a man and is scornful of him, but the man tricks him into entering a cage and leaves him to starve, or the man tricks the lion into placing his claws in a tree crack, where he is trapped.

In the Bedouin version, the man succeeds in deceiving the lion with a different trick. He ties him to a tree on the pretext that he fears that the lion will not wait for him to bring his weapons, and as soon as the lion is tied, he pours boiling water on him, causing him severe burns.

The story is very ancient, and one of its versions appears already in ancient Egyptian texts from the fourteenth century BCE, where it is integrated into a framework story: the monkey Tut, the messenger of the gods, tells Tafnut, the daughter of the sun god, stories to appease her. One of the stories is about a lion who meets a group of animals that have been injured by man. The lion brags and says that he will succeed in defeating man. The god of fate wants to punish him for his pride and teach him a lesson. On his way, the lion encounters a mouse and almost tramples him, but releases him after the mouse assures him that one day he will save him from death. Later on, the lion falls into the hunters' trap and is tied by ropes. His acquaintance, the mouse, comes to help him and gnaws at his fetters. He then hides in the lion's fur, and the two escape together into the desert.[2]

Haim Schwarzbaum discusses the story in detail in his book *From the Source of Israel and Ishmael: The Folkloristic Aspects of Judaism and Islam*.[3] According to Schwarzbaum, the Egyptian story combines two narrative types: ATU 157A, "The Lion Searches for Man," and ATU 75, "The Help of the Weak," a mouse helping the lion to free itself from a trap into which he has fallen.

In 1483 a Latin book of fables by Mayno de' Mayneri, *Dialogus Creaturarum*, was published in Sweden. The book includes 122 fables, one of which is the story of the encounter between a lion and a man. In the *Arabian Nights*, the story appears at great length:[4] Fearful of lions, a pair of peacocks escapes to a deserted island. A frightened duck arrives on the island, warning them against humans. She tells them that, in her dream, she saw the shape of a human being and heard a voice calling out to her: "O thou duck, beware of the son of Adam and be not imposed on by his words nor by that he may suggest to thee; for he aboundeth in wiles and guiles." She later tells them that she met a lion cub who had a similar dream. The lion cub decides to go and deal with the man. On his way, he meets a donkey, a horse, and a camel that warn him against man. Finally, the lion meets an old carpenter but does not understand that it is a human being in front of him. The carpenter tells him that he is on his way to the tiger, who invited him to build a house for him as a shelter from man. The young lion demands that the carpenter also prepare a house for him. The carpenter builds a cage and convinces the lion to enter it. After he enters the cage, the carpenter informs him that he is the creature called man. He throws the cage with the lion inside it into a pit and burns it. Then the peacock invites the duck to stay with her, and the gazelle joins them. At a certain point in time, people come to the island. The gazelle and the peacocks escape, but the duck is caught. At the end of the story, the peacock and the gazelle mourn the loss of the duck and warn each other against man and his cunning. According to the peacock, the duck was punished for not praising Allah and his actions sufficiently.

In Brothers Grimm's book, there is a story entitled "The Wolf and the Man."[5] Here the wolf plays the role of the lion. The fox warns the wolf against man's cunning. The wolf brags and says that if he meets a man, he will attack him. He goes out with the fox to look for a man. First, they meet an old man, and the fox explains to him, "It was a man." Then they meet a little boy, and the fox tells him that the child is "just about to be a man." Finally, they meet a hunter, who shoots the wolf with his rifle and stabs him with his dagger. The wolf escapes and tells the fox figuratively how the man blew into a stick on his shoulder and tossed at him something that tickled him like hail and how he pulled a shiny rib out of his body and stabbed him until he nearly killed him. To which the fox replies, "See what a braggart you are. You throw your hatchet so far that you cannot get it back again."

In his book *Folktales of Egypt*, El-Shamy includes an Egyptian version of the story, "Son of Adam and the Lion," which was recorded from an informant who heard the story in his youth as a *nuktah*—humoristic story.[6] A mouse warns the lion about the Son-of-Adam. The lion goes to meet the Son-of-Adam and is surprised by the unimpressive appearance of a farmer. He invites him for a confrontation, but the farmer claims that his power is not with him and he must bring it from his home. As in the Bedouin story, the farmer demands that the lion allow him to tie him to make sure he does not run away. The lion agrees. After the farmer ties him, he beats him with a leash until he bleeds and leaves him tied to the tree. Later in the story, the lion asks the mouse to gnaw the rope. After the lion is released, he follows the man and tries to break into his home. The farmer asks his wife to boil water, and, as soon as the water is boiling, he shouts to his wife: "Faṭma, pour the water!" The lion is badly burned, and it flees. A few days later, the farmer leaves for the field, where the lion awaits him with all his relatives. The farmer escapes them and climbs a palm tree. The lions climb on one another's backs in an attempt to build a tower of lions and reach the top of the tree. At the bottom of the tower stands the lion who had been injured twice by the farmer. The upper lion almost manages to reach him, but then the farmer yells, "Faṭma, pour the water!" The lion at the bottom of the tower panics and flees "with its tail between its teeth," and the whole tower collapses.

A Jewish version recorded from an informant from Iraqi Kurdistan (IFA 22686) is reminiscent of the Egyptian story I mentioned above: The lion was first caught in the tree after the woodcutters yelled, "Moses, release the *kleen* [peg]!" Later the lion comes with his friends to Moshe's house, and they build a tower of lions to reach the second floor. Moshe cries, "Release the kleen!" The lion at the bottom is frightened and runs away, and the whole tower collapses. The narrator considers the story as a parable of the deterrent power of the State of Israel, which proved itself during the Six-Day War but faded over time.

In a Muslim version recorded from Samīra 'Awad Ada of Ṭamra in the Lower Galilee (IFA 24267), a young lion hears his father repeating again and again: "Allah, remove from us the evil of men!" The young lion wonders about his father's words. He goes to look for man. On his way, he encounters a donkey, a horse, an ox, and a camel, who warn him against man, and finally he meets the man, who asks the lion to allow him to bring his weapons. The man convinces the young lion to let him tie him to a tree to make sure he does not leave. After the lion has been tied, the man hits him hard. The young lion returns to his father, and next time, when he hears the lion's comments about the Son-of-Adam, he answers after him, "Amen."

In the IFA archives, there are other Jewish versions of the story. In a version from Iraq that was recorded from Manasseh Mashled, "Who Is the Worst of All Creatures?" (IFA 1130), a mouse helps a lion free himself from a net. At the beginning of the story, the lion denigrates humans as despicable creatures and praises the mice, which cause damage to man. A skeptical lion decides to check his words. He goes to look for men. On his way, he encounters a donkey, a camel, and a cow, who tell him about the cruelty and strength of men. Finally, he meets a man and challenges him. The man asks the lion to allow him to bring his weapons, and similar to what is happening in this story, he ties the lion to the tree and leaves to bring a gun to kill him. The description is very similar to that of the Bedouin story:

> Before he left, the man turned to the lion and said, "How can I really know that you will wait for my return and you will not run away like all the animals that escape from man?"
>
> "A lion like me will not run away!" roared the lion.
>
> "I cannot believe you unless you let me tie you to a tree," said the man.
>
> "Tie me as you wish," agreed the lion.
>
> The man took thick ropes, tied the lion to the tree, and went home to fetch a rifle.

But in contrast to what happens at the end of the Bedouin story, when the man goes to bring his weapons, a mouse comes up to the place and says to the lion, "You look powerful, but you do not have a brain. How can you be such a fool to trust the man, don't you understand that he went to get a gun and will come back to kill you?" The mouse gnaws the ropes and releases the lion. The story ends with these words: "To this day the lion has not yet decided in what man passes animal: in his cruelty or in his cunning?" Like the ancient Egyptian story, this version unites the two narrative types mentioned above.

Another version from Persian Kurdistan (IFA 5206) resembles that of the *Arabian Nights*, but instead of a young lion, there is a young elephant.

On the internet, there is a video in which an Ethiopian Jewish young girl by the name of Yubi Tsuma tells a charming story she heard from her mother as a child.[7] This story corresponds to some extent with the Bedouin tale. A lion turns to the king and asks to marry his daughter. The king agrees, but on condition that he shave his mane, cut his claws, and uproot his teeth, so as not to frighten the princess. After the lion fulfills his demands, the king mocks him and says, "To marry my princess? Tell me what kind of king I am, that I will give the princess to such a cat?" The lion gets annoyed and tries to roar and frighten, but in the absence of mane, claws, and teeth, he can do nothing.

The narrator concludes her story with a moral: "So the moral for someone like me, who immigrated to Israel as a child and did so much, cut her nails, smoothed her hair, lost her accent, tried to speak Israeli slang, pushed. Everything I considered Israeli, I tried it in order to be accepted by the Israeli society. However, the bottom line is, nothing really helps. Stay the way you are and who you are. Who we are, a very strong community with strong teeth, with a mane, with proper fingernails."

Several aspects are apparent in the story about the meeting between the lion's son and man. First, the story reflects man's primeval fear of beasts of prey. Man appears in almost all versions as "the Son of Adam," that is, as representing the human race as a whole, not as a particular person. In order to overcome predators, a man must turn to cunning and use his intellectual skills.

Second, the story warns against boasting and disrespect. The young lion sins the sin of pride, initiates an unnecessary encounter with man, and is punished. There is also a general statement about the relationship between an older and younger generation. The older lion, who is experienced, tries to educate his son and prevent him from the unnecessary encounter with his human enemy. The son is not willing to learn from past experience and learns to respect mankind by the hard way.

Finally, we must note the storytellers' varied use of the story to convey moral. The moral varies according to the circumstances in which the story is told. It may be an educational moral, as in the Bedouin story—respect for the experience attained by older generations. It can be a religious moral—presenting the defeat of the lion and the duck as punishment for lack of modesty or heresy toward the Creator, as in the version from the *Arabian Nights*. It can also be a parable regarding status and acceptance in society, as in the young Ethiopian woman's story.

Notes

1. *qāḷ-ḷo, 'abū, el-sabe' le-kbīr bigūl la-'ebno, . . . 'ana baddi 'arūḥ 'ašūf baṇi'ādam*: "He said to him, the big lion says to his son . . . 'I want to go and see a man.'" These sentences show several types of sedentary and Bedouin dialects' features mixed as follows: sedentary *qāl* versus Bedouin *gāḷ*, "he said" (*q* versus *g*); sedentary *bigūl* versus Bedouin *yigūl*, "he says"; sedentary *baddi* versus Bedouin *widdi*, "I want" (*ba-* versus *wi-*); sedentary *'ašūf* versus Bedouin *'adaḥḥeğ* "that I [will] see." Note that the stories in this volume were recorded about forty years ago. At present, the rate of such code mixing is even higher.

2. Spiegelberg, *Der Ägyptische Mythus vom Sonnenauge*, 42–47.

3. Schwarzbaum, *From the Source of Israel and Ishmael*, 274–80.

4. Burton, *Arabian Nights*, nights 146–47.

5. Grimm, *The Original Folk and Fairy Tales of the Brothers Grimm*, story 72.

6. El-Shamy, *Folktales of Egypt*, 190–92, 290–91.

7. Yehuda Atseva, "The Lion and the Princess," 5:07, 2010, https://www.youtube.com/watch?v=rv1TrEcleb4.

44. The Two Hunters

NARRATOR: Ḥasan Maḥmūd Swēṭāt

TRIBE: *'Arab el-Sa'adiyya*

IFA 17424 September 2, 1982

1 Ṯnēn ^{a}ṣḥāb, kull wāḥad min ʿašīra. ʾaḷḷa ʿalīm. ḥakum la-baʿaḏ̣ inno "lāzem ʾiḥna nimši duġri maʿa baʿaḏ̣ b-al-gaḷub u-ba-al-niyya u-b-al-ʿageḷ, u-b-al-gaʿda u-b-al-gōma u-ba-kull^{a} mišwār." limma rāḥum ʿala ṣ-ṣēd w-al-ganaṣ,[1] hāḏam lamma yirūḥam ʿala ṣ-ṣēd w-al-ganaṣ bi-yiġību šahar šaharēn.	1 [There were] two friends, each from a [different] tribe. Allah knows [which]. They said to each other that "we must be honest with each other in our heart and intentions and our mind, and when sitting down and getting up and in any journey." When they went hunting, these [men], when they go hunting, they are gone [away] for a month, two months.
9 xaḏam kull wāḥad zuwwāda, yaʿani. tiʿraf zuwwāda bitkaffi yōmēn—ṯalāṯa, kull wāḥad. zuwwāda, ʾakel, yaʿani. mišyu be-hā-ṭ-ṭarīq, ǧāʿo, ǧāʿo. ḥaṭṭo hā-l-barūdāt, u-gaʿado, ʾakalo. ʿala ḥadd bīr. bīr, šita. ǧābum tanaka u-nšalum mayya u-ʾakalum,[2] ʾakalum min zuwwādet wāḥad at-tinēn. ʾakalu, širbu u-gāmu[3]	9 They took each his provisions, that is, you know, provisions suffice for two, three days for each. Provisions [are] food, that is. They went on the way, they became hungry, they became hungry. They laid down the rifles and sat down and ate at the edge of the well. Well, [of] rain [water]. They brought a can and raised water [from the well] and ate. They ate from the provisions of one of the two. They ate, drank, and got up.
18 mišyu. . . . mešyu, mešyu, mešyu, mešyu, ǧāʿu. gāḷ-ḷo, "yaḷḷa niftaḥ zawwādtak" gāḷ-ḷo, "lāʾ, ta-nkammel zuwwādtak u-baʿadēn niftaḥ zuwwwādti."	18 They went. . . . They went, went, went, went, [and] became hungry. He said to him, "Come on, let's open your provisions." He said to him, "No, we'll continue [and finish] your provisions and afterward we will open my provision."

23 ʾakalo al-zāidīn, mā ḏaḷḷ maʿā. wāḥad minhum xaḷḷaṣ zuwwādto, ʾakalūha aṯ-ṯinēn—mar(r)tēn, ^{e}tġaddu w-^{e}tʿaššu. hum bātu ḥadd, ḥadd al-bīr, l-aṣ-ṣuboḥ ḥadd hā-l-xarāba. aṣ-ṣuboḥ mišu, mišu bakkīr, min al-arbaʿa, min aṯ-ṯalāṯa, mišu. ʾemši, ʾemši, ʾemši, ğāʿo. [widdom yāklu.]

23 They ate [his] provision, it did not remain [no food remained] with him. One of them finished his provisions. They ate it, both of them, twice, they ate lunch and dinner. They went and slept near—near the well, until morning, near the ruins. In the morning, they went early, from four, from three, went, went, went, went, and got hungry. [They want to eat.]

30 gāḷ-ḷo, "ʾeftaḥ ziwwādtak, yā flān, yā ʾaxūy,"—mā mitxāwi humme, miš ʾexwe, kull min ʿašīre, mā mitxāwi, yaʿani, zayy ʾexwa. gāḷ-ḷo, "ʾiftaḥ zewwādtak, widdna nōkel." gāḷ-ḷo, "lā, ʾanta xaḷḷaṣet zawwādtak, ʾana min ziwwādti mā widdi ʾaṭaʿmīk."

30 He said to him, "Open your provisions, o man, o my brother," for they were like brothers. They were not brothers—each was from a [different] tribe, he was like a brother, that is. Like brothers. He said to him, "Open your provisions, we want to eat." He said to him, "No, you finished your provisions; I do not want to feed you from my provisions."

37 "yā šēn, yā zēn, xāf min ʾaḷḷa, fiš dakākīn, fiš sūq, fiš mudun ništri, fiš ʿarab nišḥad, fiš mudun nišḥad, mā min zēd yeḥāfiẓ." gāḷ-ḷo, "tmūt, ṣāyibna, mā xuṣṣni bīk."

37 "Oh, bad! Oh, good! Fear Allah! There are no shops, there is no market, there are no towns to buy [in], there are no Bedouins to beg [for food], there are no towns to beg [in], there is no food to preserve [me]." He said to him, "You'll die. Leave us [me] alone, I do not want [need] you."

42 ʾakal, ḥaṭṭ tabaʿāto hōn, ḥoḏno, ʾakal u-nhazam. daššaro. hāḏa min-al-ğūʿ^{a}, maskīn, ṣafren[4] u-nām ba-l-ğūʿ^{a}. mā bī yimši. nām. ḏaḷḷ nāyim ta-ġābat aš-šams,

42 He ate, put his belongings here, in his lap, ate and went off. He left him. This [one] with hunger, the poor man, he fainted and lay in hunger. He did not have the power to go. He lay [slept]. He remained lying [asleep] until the sun set.

46 ṣārat ad-dinya lēl. mn-aġ-ğūʿ^{a} mā yigdar yimši. u-hāḏa axū, daššaro, ṣāḥbo. daššaro hāḏa. nīyto salīma, maskīn. ʿando d-dinya duġri hēk, haḏāk ʿando ḥerfāt, bas be-lsāno yiḥki, miš maḏmūn

46 It became night. From his hunger he could not walk. And that one, his brother, had left him, his friend. This [one] left him. His aim was [always] righteous, the poor man. With him the world is straight [honest] like that. That one [his friend], he had tricks, only his tongue was talking [not talking from his heart or soul], he was not to be trusted.

51 hāḏa nām bi-l-lēl, daḥḥag, id-dinya bard, b-il-lēl ṣārat bard. miši šwayya, winno bī mġāra, ʿa-ğ-ğabal hāḏ, fāt b-al-mġāra, nām. lamma nām winna ğāya wḥūš, wḥūš al-barr, ḏīb [taʿraf al-ḏīb, min al-ḥayawanāt ḏīb] ḏīb, wa-ḥsēni u-ḏabeʿ. [ʾā, ḥsēni ṯaʿlab].

51 This one slept at night, looked: it was cold, at night it became cold. He went a little, and lo, there was a cave, on that mountain. He entered the cave and lay down. When he was lying—lo, there came wild animals, wild animals: a wolf—you know what a wolf is from [among] animals—a wolf, and a fox and a hyena. (Yes, fox, fox.)

58 kamān hadōla ṣḥāb. ḏaḷḷam yižtamʿam b-il-^{i}mġāra hāy. ṣḥāb . . . hadōla gʿadam yitxarrafom. huwwa maskīn, min xōfo fāt, hēk fī zexōv, hēk fī zexōv, hēk fī zexōv, fāt fī, min xōf mā yāklū, xāf minnin, yaʿani. ʾā, xāf minnin, yiṣannat ʿalēhin.	58 Those, too, are friends. They continued to meet in this cave. Friends . . . those sat [down] talking. He, the poor, he entered because of his fear, like that, there were burrows, like that, burrows, like that, burrows like that, because of his fear, he entered [a burrow]. Because of his fear, lest they eat him. He was afraid of them, that is . . . yes, he was afraid of them, he was listening to them.
65 ṣāru yitxarrafu. gāḷ-ḷo, "ʾinta, kēf yā-bū ḥasan? šabʿān willa ğoʿān?" qāl-lo, "waḷḷāhi, šabʿān." Abu Ḥasan—l-^{e}ḥsēni.	65 They started talking. He said to him, "You, how [are you], o Abu Ḥasan? Satiated or hungry?" He said to him, "By Allah, satiated." Abu Ḥasan—the fox.
68 gāḷ-ḷo," w-ʾenta, yā ḏabeʿ, yā Abu serḥān?" ʾaḏ-ḏabeʿ ismo Abu Serḥān. "šū ʾinta, yā ʾabu serḥān?" gāḷ-ḷo, "waḷḷāhi, kamān ʾani šabʿān, liqēt ğamal u-ʾakalt min ağ-ğamal u-šbiʿet" mīn ḏaḷḷ? ʾaḏ-ḏīb.	68 He said to him, "And you, o hyena, o Abu Serḥān?" (The hyena's name is Abu Serḥān.) "What are you, Abu Serḥān?" He said to him, "By Allah, I too am satiated. I came across a camel and ate of the camel and became satiated." Who remained? The wolf.
73 gāḷ-ḷo, "w-ʾanta yā ba-ḏ-ḏīb? šū, ğaʿān?" gāḷ-ḷo, "lā waḷḷa, xayya, kamān ʾana ğīt ʿala šalyet ġanam w-ar-rāʿi daššar al-ġanamāt u-daššar li waḥade yamm ʾakalta u-šbiʿet u-ḏaḷḷ ğāy warāy."	73 He said, to him, "And you, o Abu-Ḏīb? What, hungry?" He said to him, "No, by Allah, brother. I too went to a sheep herd and the shepherd left the sheep and left for me one, and I ate it and got satiated, and he was following me."
78 gāḷ, "ḥamduḷḷa, kullna šabʿānīn." gāḷu la-baʿaḏ. fa-huwwa yiṣannat ʿalēhen yiṭṭallaʿ ʿalēhen. ʾanbiṣaṭ, gāḷ, "law ğūʿānīn ʾassa yedawwru hōn hōn biddhen yidawwrūn, ʿād, mā ydawwrū yōklū." ʿiml-^{e}ḥsāb, yaʿani.	78 He said, "Thank Allah, we are all satiated." They said to each other. And he was listening to them—looking at them. He was happy, he said, "If they had been hungry now, they [would] search here and here, they [would] want to search, again, they look for [food], they would look for it, to eat." He made this calculation, that is.
84 hāḏa, ṭalaʿ an-nahār hēk, ṣār sāʿa ṯalāṯa-ṯintēn, ṭaššu bi-hā-l-waʿar hadōl al-wuḥūš. taṭlaʿan šē. fārāt, fīrān, firān. fīrān—min hā-z-zuḥuf. ṣāran yiṭlaʿan waḥade waḥade. kull-waḥade ḥāmle līra ḏahab, min ğuwwa, ḏi, min al-^{i}mġāra, min ğuwwa ḏi, kinez.	84 This [one], the day came like that, it became three, two o'clock, they dispersed [went each his way] in the rugged region, those wild animals. They come out . . . a thing—mice, mice, mice, mice—from these burrows. They began to come out, one by one, each one carrying a gold pound [lira] from inside, from the cave, from the inside, this, a treasure.
91 yiğībum yekawwemum ʿala—fī ḅaḷāṭa hēk, ʿala hā-l-ḅaḷāṭa.	91 They bring it, and heap them onto—there is a rock there, on this rock.

93 yiğībum yikawwemum, yiğībum yikawwemum ta-ṣār kōm hēk. ʾā, al-. al-^{i}wḥūš itxarrafen w-hinne yitxarrafan b-as-sahra maʿa baʿaḏ.

93 They bring them and heap them, bring them and heap them like this. Yes, the . . . the wild animals spoke with each other, when they spoke in the night meeting with each other.

97 ʾabu Ḥasan gāḷ-ḷēhen, "b-aṣ-ṣubeḥ yegūmen fārāt, yilʿabu bi-hā-ḏ-ḏahabāt, eššū byišawbu, yā-bu-ḥasan, u-yā ʾabu ḏ-ḏēb u-yā ʾabu serḥān yexarrfum la-baʿaḏ. yeʿmalūhen kōm hēk, u-yiğum yeṭaššūhen yilʿabum bīhen. wi-yeruddum yiḥuṭṭūhen maṭraḥ mā kānen." xarrafu bēn baʿaḏhen; hū yisannat. ḏaḷḷat ^{e}b-bālo.

97 Abu Ḥasan said to them, "In the morning mice will get up, play with this gold pieces, what—they heat up, o Abu fox, and o Abu wolf, and o Abu Serḥān, they tell each other. They make a heap like this and come and disperse them and play with them. And they take them back and put them in the place they had been." They talked among themselves; he was listening. It remained in his head.

106 lamman el-fārāt ṭilʿo ṣ-ṣubeḥ ta-ẓahar ḏaww šwiyye, ṣār fī, yaʿani, ʾawwal en-nahār, nafs al-ʾiši ṣāran yiṭallʿan aḏ-ḏahab w-iykawwmen. gāḷ, "law yuḏrubhen ʿaẓma waḥade, yuḏrubhen bi-ʿaẓme, be-ḥadd, ḏarab ʾiši, yōxeḏ eḏ-ḏahab kullo." hāḏa xarrafu l-wuḥūš b-il-lēl.

106 When the mice came out in the morning, until light appeared a little, it began to be, that is, the beginning of the day—just the same thing [happened]: they started taking out the gold [pieces] and heap them. He said, "If he hit them—one bone, he would hit them with a bone, near, [if] he hit something, he would take all the gold." The wild animals said this in the night.

114 hāḏa xaḷḷāhen ta-ʿemlen kōm hēk, gaḏab hā-l-ʿaẓma u-ḏrabha ʿalēhen. ʾassa ḏaḷḷat aḏ-ḏahabāt mkawwamāt.

114 This one [the man] let them until they made a heap like that, he took this bone and threw it at them [the mice]. Now, the gold pieces remained heaped.

117 ğābhen, ḏabban, ḥaṭṭhen fi l-maḥrame, ṣarren, xabbāhen be-ʿobbo, u-mša. mā ḥadāš yidri ġēr ʾaḷḷa.

117 He brought them, gathered them, put them in the handkerchief, wrapped them up and hid them in his lap and went. No one knows [about it] except Allah.

120 ʿād yitḥārem ʿa-minno ^{i}trayyaḥ, u-hāḏa yitnaššaṭ, u-ʾinno liga kinez u-ʾiši, naššaṭ ^{a}šwayy, ṣār yimši.

120 Then he avoided doing anything since he had rested. This one [the man] got more energetic for [since] he found a treasure and things, he was revived a little, he began to walk.

123 ṣār yimši, yimši, yimši, daḥḥag winn bī balad, zayy—zayy balad el-ḥilef haḏīk. qāl, "balki ʾalgi wāḥad yeṭaʿmīni, ʾatnaššaṭ ^{a}šwayy kamān, balki ʾaštri min dukkān, ʾiši^{y}."

123 He began to walk, walk, walk, he looked and lo, there was a village, like—like that Ḥilf village. He said [to himself], "Maybe I will find someone who can feed me and I'll also refresh myself a little, maybe I'll buy from a shop, something."

128 ʾağa hāḏa fī l-dakākīn, u-fī byūt u-fī kull ʾiši. dakkān. štara u-ʾakal u-šireb, šū ṣār. ṣaḥḥto mnīḥa. aḏ-ḏahabāt ib-ʿibbo, mā ḥada, yaʿani, yiʿelam, ġēr ʾaḷḷa.

128 This [man] came—there were shops and there were houses and everything. A shop. He bought and ate and drank, [that is] what happened. His health was good [again]. The gold pieces were in his lap, nobody, that is, knew [about them] except Allah.

132 rāḥ hāḏa, rawwa(ḥ)-ʿa-balado. šira ʾareḏ, o-ʿammar gaṣ^{a}r, [šāyef?] u-ʿammar gaṣ^{a}r, u-fetaḥ dakākīn min aḏ-ḏahab, u-fitaḥ kull ʾiši u-ʿimel, yaʿani, ʾiši mašārī^{ʿi}, maṣāne^{ʿa}, u-ʾiši, yaʿani šū, ṣār huwwa zayy ʾafandi. zayy ʾafandi.

132 He went, this one, returned to his town. He bought lands, and built [for himself] a castle ([do you] see?) and built a castle, and opened shops with the gold, and opened everything and did, that is, some projects, factories and such things, He became like an effendi, like an effendi [rich and respected].

138 ṣār yaʿani b-al-mižtamaʿāt, yeʿezmū, ṣārat ʾilo kilma, hū mlīḥ, ʾinsāni, mā-qulna mā gabuḷ, gabuḷ, u-niyyto masallme, mā yiʿmal ši [$_H$beʿayot$_H$].

138 He began [to be], that is, in meetings, was invited, he had a word [a say], he [was] good, humane, as we said before, before, and his intention peaceful, he did not do any ($_H$beʾayot$_H$) problems.

142 bas wēn, el- . . . xagāni, ma-lūš ṣīṭ, yaʿani, ʾinno kbīr, yaʿani bēk, ʾaw, ʾaw, mā-lūš, yaʿani, ṣīṭ. [$_H$maʿamad$_H$], bixaḷḷi el-wāḥad kbīr, u-ʾilo ṣīṭ. yiʿmalo ḥtifālāt, yiʿmalo žtimāʿāt, yiʿmalo ʾiši yiʿezmo. ṣār yerūḥ. yōm ʿemlo. gadd-mā tʿarrafum bī, yaʿani, b-al-wazāra u-ba-l-hāda fa-yaʿani, ǧam al-wazāra, li-mlūk—ʿendom antixābāt.

142 But where, the—xagāni [monarch, ruler], he did not have reputation. That is, he was big, that was, like a *bēk* [bey], or he did not have reputation, ($_H$maʿamad$_H$) status which makes a person great, and has reputation. They make parties, make meetings, they make things—they invite him. He began to go [to attend them]. One day they made. . . . The more they got to know him, that is, in the ministry and this, and that is, the ministers came, the kings—they had elections.

151 ʿandom antixābāt—raʾʾāṣo, ṭalaʿ malek. šūf kēf, ʾaḷḷa hēk biddo. naʿam. ṭalaʿ malek. lamman ṭalaʿ malek, ṣār malek ʾessa, al-ḥukum b-īdo, xazāin aḏ-ḏahab b-īdo, kull ʾiši ṣār b-īdo.

151 They had elections—they made him the head, he became a king. Look how—Allah wanted it like this. Yes. He became a king. He became king, now, the government was in his hand, the reign is in his hand, the gold treasuries are in his hand, everything became in his hands.

156 yōm min ḏāt al-ʾiyyām, ṭalaʿu—hāḏa—[ʿā-.d—ʿala dōr gabeḷ, b-el-ḥanṭūr, yaʿani, el-ḥanṭūr ʿala ḥṣān, b-imši be-š-šāreʿ, kān mitwalli ^{i}mlūk, b-il-ḥanṭūr.] . . . ʿā hāḏa māši, ʿando l-wezara min hōn u-min hōn,

156 One day, they went out—this—[in the old time, the past], in a carriage, that is, a carriage with a horse. He walked in the street, he was befriending kings, in the carriage. . . . Yes, this [one] was walking, with him the ministers from here and here [both sides],

162 hū gāʿed, malik, mištaġal w-an-nās, b-aṭ-ṭarīq, kullha titmannā-lo, ta ḥatta winno mārig ʿala ha-l-ʿattāle, ḥāmlīn . . . ḥāmlīn e-kyās u-iši, taʿref, yaʿani, al-malek bimurr ʿala kull ʾiši, min fagīr min ġani, men mlīḥ, men ʿāṭel, men nūri men—min malek, min fagīr, yigūl-lak, yaʿani, min ġani, men fagīr, yimurr ʿala kull ʾiše.

162 he was sitting, a king, working, and the people on the way, all were saluting him [wishing well to him] until he passed those porters, carrying . . . carrying bags and things, you know. That is, the king passes on [inspects] everything, from poor and rich, the good and the bad, the gypsy and the—the king, the poor, he says to you, that is, from rich and poor, he passes by everything.

170 winno rfīgo, alli daššaro, mā ġaddā maʿo, u-humma šabāb u-humma ṭālʿīn, u-ḥām ʿalē l-ʿaqel. rafīgo. u-hinne sxām ʿala l-ʿattāla, ʿala ḍaharo, wi-ynāḥaṭ.	170 Lo, there was his friend, who had deserted him, did not let him have lunch with him, when they were young and were going out, and his brain was hot on him [he was furious]. His friend. And they, soot [was] on the porters, on his back, and he was groaning.
174 gāḷ-ḷo, "wālak yā kalb," ḥēṯ as-sāmʿīn, "taʿāl la-hōn," ṣār yiṭallaʿ ʿalē "lā, yā malik az-zamān, ʾana mā ʿamilteš ʾiše." gāḷ-ḷo, "lā, ʿamilet. ʾirmi hā-l-kīs min ʿala ḍaharak."u-ḍrabo b-il-korbāğ.	174 He said to him, "Woe to you, o dog"—asking the listeners' pardon. "Come here." He began looking at him. "No, o king of the time, I did not do anything." He said to him, "No, you did. Drop that bag from your back." And he hit him with the whip.
179 al-malik yuḍrobeš?! ṣārat kull an-nās tiṭṭallaʿ—kīf al-malek ḍrabo la-hāḏa. [ʾahlan wa-sahlan. . .] ḍrabo b-al-korbāğ gāḷu-ḷo, "lēš," yaʿani, gāḷu-lo al-wuzara, gāḷū-lo, "al-ʿafu yā malek ez-zemān, al-malak mā yeḥmaq yuḍrob aš-šaʿab."	179 A king does not hit! Everybody began looking—how the king hit that one. (Welcome, welcome [to new guests].) He hit him with the whip. They said to him, "Why?" That is, the ministers said to him, they said to him, "Pardon, o king of the time, a king does not get furious and hit the people."
185 gāḷ, "ʾā . . . "taḏakkar. "lamman gaʿadna ʿand al-muṭraḥ al-^{a}flāni, ʿand al-bīr al-^{e}flāni, mā ṭaʿamētni min zuwwādtak?" . . . "ʾinta? ʾinta, yā rafīgi, ʾinta, yā ḥabībi, daxīlak" ṣār yibawwis b-ʾidē, yibawwis b-ʾidē, yibawwso, "daxīlak, yā ḥabībi, yā-xūya,"	185 He [the king] said, "Ah." He recalled. "When we sat at the certain place near the certain well, you did not feed me from your provision?" . . . "You? You, o my friend, you, o my dear, I beg your protection." He began to kiss his hand, to kiss his hand, to kiss him. "Please, my dear, my brother."
192 gāḷ-ḷā, "mā-nn ğibtak as-salāma. ʾinta lamma kānat maʿāk ziwwāda, ṭaʿamētak ziwwādti, w-ʾanta mā ṭaʿamētni zawwādtak."	192 He said to him, "It was indeed I who brought you peace. You, when you had provision with you, I let you eat my provision, and you did not let me eat your provision."
196 "eššū waṣṣalak la-(h)āy ad-darağa?" gāḷ-ḷo, "ʾalli ʾaḷḷa maʿā mā binxāf ʿalē. ʾani ʿendi raḥma, u-mā ẓalamet ḥada, wa-l-ḥamde-li-ḷḷā, ʾaḷḷa rafaʿni, wa-ʿemel li darağa. [ʿend ʾaḷḷa ʿemlu darağa. kamān al-malak miš basīṭ. ʾā. kamān b-ad-dinya w-al-ʾāxra mnīḥ.]	196 "And what has made you reach this status?" He said to him, "He who Allah is with him, we do not fear [worry] for him. I have pity and I have not exploited anyone, and thank Allah, Allah has lifted me and made for me status." (With Allah they did the status. In addition, a king is not a simple [thing]. Yes. Both in this world and in the hereafter it is good.)

203 “eššū waṣṣalak we-šu mā waṣṣalak?” gāḷ-ḷo, “hāḏi ʿamali al-^{i}mlīḥ alli waṣṣalni. ’ar-raḥma mlīḥa, u-’imši duġri ʿend ’aḷḷa, beʿaṭīk.” gāḷ-ḷo, “ṭayyib, ’ani šū—tiḏbaḥni, tuslaḥni, mā-ʿād ’adaššrak, biddi ’arūḥ maʿāk.” ’axaḏo,

203 “What made you reach [this status] and what did not?” He said to him, “These—my good deed is what made me reach it. Pity is good, and if you go honestly with Allah, he will give you.” He said to him, “Well, I—what—if you kill me or forgive me, I will not leave you again; I want to go with you.” He took him.

209 gāḷ-ḷo, “taʿāl ’ixdim bi-hā-l-bēt, w-’aḥna hunāka, kannes-li hā-[$_{H}$s-salon$_{H}$], u-teʿmal lēna finǧāl gahwa, ’iši, u-xādim ’ōxḏak.” rāḥ maʿo.

209 He said to him, “Come, work in this house, we are there, sweep the ($_{H}$s-salon$_{H}$) guests’ hall for me, and make a cup of coffee for us, something, and I will take you [as] servant.” He went with him.

213 lamman gaʿadu hēk u-faḏḏ lak,[5] yaʿani, hā-d-dīwān, hā daxxal ʿind al-malek u-’iši, baʿad maʿa rfīgo, gaḷbo ḥann aʿalē.

213 When they were sitting like this and he stayed, that is, in the guests’ hall, this one entered to the king, etc.—still he was with his friend, his heart pitied him.

217 gāḷ-ḷo, “taʿ ta-’agūḷ-ḷak. ’ana kunt hēk hēk lamman daššartni, u-fotet b-al-^{i}mġāra alli hī moṭraḥ mā daššartni, lgīt ^{e}mġāra u-futet bīha, u-’aǧu wḥūš u-txarrafu guddāmi hēk hēk u-ṭilʿu fārāt u-ǧābu ḏahab u-kawwamū u-’ana ḏarabthen be-ʿaẓma, ’axaḏt eḏ-ḏahab u-’aḷḷa subḥāno wa-taʿāla nešal biyya w-waṣṣalt la-hā-d-daraǧe.”

217 He said to him, “Come, I’ll tell you. I was like this and that when you left me and I entered the cave which is in the place where you left me, I found a cave and entered it. And there came wild animals and talked in front of me so-and-so, and mice came out and brought gold and heaped it and I hit them with a bone. I took the gold and Allah the praised and exalted lifted me and I reached this status.”

226 gāḷ, “’ā, waḷḷa, ’ani barūḥ wa-’aʿmal min hā-š-šikel o . . . o-balki ’aṣīr zayyak.” hā, lamma ʿindo l-makān illi kānu bī, hū wiyyā. duġri la-ʿando. rāḥ, ṭallaʿ hēk hēk, willa l-^{i}mġāra zayy-mā waṣṣafo rafīgo, waṣṣaf lo. fāt ʿala hā-l-^{e}mġāra. d-dunya l-muġrib, hēk, yaʿani, baʿad eḏ-ḏoher, ’a.

226 He said, “A, by Allah, I will go and do like this and . . . and maybe I will become like you.” This [one], as he had the place where they had been, he with him—directly thereto [he went]. He looked this way, that way, and lo, there was the cave as his friend had described it, described it to him. He entered the cave. It was dusk, like this [time], that is afternoon, yes.

234 fāt hā-l-muġāra wenno ǧāy ’abo ḥasan, u-ḏ-ḏabeʿ, hāḏa lli ngūl-lo ’abu serḥān, huwwa wa-ḏ-ḏīb, u-gaʿado. šū hāḏa yīǧi yḏibb ḥālo, ʿala bāb hā-l-^{e}mġāra hāḏa yiǧi, yigaʿ. hāḏa yiǧi, yigaʿ. hū baʿaḏhen min-baʿaḏ.

234 He entered the cave—and lo, [there] came Abu Ḥasan and the hyena, whom we call Abu Serḥān, he and the wolf, and they sat down. What [how] this one comes, straightens himself, at the entrance of this cave, this one comes, collapses. This one comes, collapses. He [they were talking to] each other.

240 “’āx, yā xayya, ’ana ǧūʿān” ’abu ḥasan yegūl, “’āx, yā xayya, ’abu serḥān, ’ana ǧūʿān.

240 “Ah, my little brother, I am hungry.” Abu Ḥasan says, “Ah, my little brother, Abu Serḥān, I am hungry.”

243 aḏ-ḏīb yegūl, "'āx, yā xūy, 'abu sirḥān, 'ana ğāʿān. šū, li, mā 'akalet ṣār li yōmēn, we-šū hā š-šanānīr. [aš-šanānīr yaʿani l-ḥažel.] eš-šū aš-šanānīr. 'al-ġewwāya, kull mā 'ağe ʿala š-šanānīr, yiġzūn al-ġewwāya, u-yōxḏūnen hōn, u-mā 'ākul 'iši."	243 The wolf says, "Ah, o little brother, Abu Serḥān, I am hungry. What—I have not eaten for two days now, and what—these partridges—[The partridges, that is partridges] what partridges. The hunters [criminals], whenever I come to the partridges, the hunters attack and take them here, and I do not eat anything."
250 'abu sirḥān gāḷ, "šū, ğīt ʿala hā-ğ-ğmāl, gaṭīʿ^{a}, u-šū hā-l-ḥīrān az-zġār, warā 'immahāthin. biddi 'ōkel wāḥad minnīhen, mā xaḷḷūni. gawwaṣūni waġadi."	250 'Abu Serḥān said, "What, I came upon these camels, a herd, and what, these young camels [hiding] behind their mothers. I want to eat one of them, they did not allow me, they shot at me, [to] my misery/misfortune."
255 'abu ḏīb gāḷ, "šū, 'ağīt ʿala ha-n-nʿāğāt, ṣāḥibhen mistaʿizz bihen, wāgif u-hā-l-bārūd maʿā. kull mā 'agarreb bīhen, yiṭoxxni 'ana b-al-bārūd. mā 'akalt, waḷḷa, bas ṣār li yōmēn."	255 Abu Ḏīb said, "What, I came to these sheep. Their owner holds them dear, standing with this rifle with him. Whenever I approach them, he shoots at me with the rifle. I have not eaten, by Allah, only—this [has been] two days."
260 gāḷ-ḷo, "waḷḷāhi, yā 'abu ḥasan, 'inta 'axaff minnēna šwayy, dawwer ^{i}b-hā-l-^{i}mġāra balki 'aḷḷa yilqā lak ʿaẓma ḏālla warāna gabuḷ, 'iši." gām nišag ar-rīḥa, ṣār yimxaṭ lēha. šū. gāḷ, "ligēt." gāḷu, "šū ligēt?" gāḷ, "zalama kbīr, hēk." kull wāḥad 'axaḏ šaqfe. māt, rāḥ. hā. salāmitkam wi-tʿīšam.	260 He said to him, "By Allah, o Abu Ḥasan, you are somewhat nimbler than we [are], go round in this cave, Allah will make you find a bone that has remained after us, previously, something." He got up, sniffed the smell, and began wiping his nose for it. "What?" He said, "I've found." They said, "What did you find?" He said, "A big man—like this." Each one took a piece. He died, died. This. . . . Peace to you, and may you live.

Commentary

The story belongs to the narrative type ATU 613, "The Two Travelers (Truth and Falsehood)." Here are the main lines of the plot:

Two men (travelers, brothers, tailor and cobbler) argue (wager) about whether truth or falsehood (justice or injustice, whose religion) is more powerful. They call on animals and people they meet to act as judges. The loser (the one who stands for the truth) is robbed and blinded, or the wicked man shares his bread with his hungry companion only if he will let his eyes be put out. The blind man spends the night in (under) a tree, where he overhears secrets of birds (other animals, devils, ogres, witches). By means of this knowledge, he is able to restore his sight, to cure sickness (of the princess, king) to end drought, etc. He is rewarded (marries the princess). His companion, intending to acquire the same wealth, imitates him. He goes to the same tree (sometimes also blinded), but the birds (devils) think it was he who betrayed their secrets and tear him to pieces.[6]

The Bedouin version preserves some of the episodes mentioned. Quite similar versions are known from Iraq, Kurdistan, and other countries.[7] The story is familiar from Europe and Asia, including the Mediterranean and Arab countries.

Most versions include three animals: a lion, a wolf, and a fox. In the Bedouin story, a hyena appears instead of a lion.[8] The hyena, the wolf, and the fox are well known to the Bedouins in the north of Israel, while the lion is known to them only by name, since lions have been extinct in the Land of Israel since the tenth century. In a Judeo-Kurdish version recorded in new Aramaic, a bear replaces the lion.[9] The fox (ṯaʻlab) and the hyena (ḏ̣abeʻ) appear in the story by their local names, Abu el-Ḥusain and Abu Sirḥān.

A similar story, in which the hero hears secrets that he is not supposed to hear and afterward uses them, is already found in the Babylonian Talmud. This version follows:

> It is related that a certain pious man gave a *denar* to a poor man on the eve of New Year in a year of drought, and his wife scolded him, and he went and passed the night in the cemetery, and he heard two spirits conversing with one another. Said one to her companion: My dear, come and let us wander about the world and let us hear from behind the curtain [that screens the Divine Presence] what suffering is coming on the world. Said her companion to her, I am not able [to do it], because I am buried in a matting of reeds [and not in a linen shroud]. But do you go, and whatever you hear tell me. So the other went and wandered about and returned. Said her companion to her: My dear, what have you heard from behind the curtain? She replied: I heard that whoever sows after the first rainfall will have his crop smitten by hail. So the man went and did not sow till after the second rainfall with the result that everyone else's crop was smitten and his was not smitten. The next year he again went and passed the night in the cemetery and heard the two spirits conversing with one another. Said one to her companion: Come and let us wander about the world and hear from behind the curtain what punishment is coming upon the world. Said the other to her: My dear, did I not tell you that I am not able because I am buried in a matting of reeds? But do you go, and whatever you hear, come and tell me. So the other one went and wandered about the world and returned. She said to her: My dear, what have you heard from behind the curtain? She replied: I heard that whoever sows after the later rain will have his crop smitten with blight. So the man went and sowed after the first rain with the result that everyone else's crop was blighted and his was not blighted. Said his wife to him: How is it that last year everyone else's crop was smitten and yours was not smitten, and this year everyone else's crop is blighted and yours is not blighted? So he related to her all his experiences. The story goes that shortly afterwards a quarrel broke out between the wife of that pious man and the mother of the child, and the former said to the latter, Come and I will show you your daughter buried in a matting of reeds. The next year the man again went and spent the night in the cemetery and heard those conversing together. One said: My dear, come and let us wander about the world and hear from behind the curtain what suffering is coming upon the world. Said the other: My dear, leave me alone; our conversation has already been heard among the living. (Babylonian Talmud, Brachot 18:2)

The Bedouin story expresses a moral perception of reward and punishment. A person who betrays his friend and abandons him to death will be punished with the same punishment as his friend. The hero is saved from death and rises to greatness, while his traitor friend goes from bad to worse until he reaches the lowest point and is eventually killed in his attempt to imitate the hero's actions. The motif of a foolish imitation appears in a large number of folktales all over the world.

Notes

1. The narrator of this story mixes non-Bedouin and Bedouin linguistic features. The many native Bedouin and non-Bedouin lexical items are interwoven to form a new blend of what may now be named a "Modern Galilee Bedouin dialect (in Israel)." The narrator also uses two Hebrew words, which suggests contact with native Hebrew speakers (at work?). Such code mixing deserves a separate study; however, it is beyond the present framework.

2. *ǧābum . . . u-nšalum . . . u-'akalum . . . 'akalu, širbu u-gāmu, mišyu*: The verb forms mix the Bedouin suffix *-um* and non-Bedouin, (local) sedentary *-u*. The story presents some other variations for 3m.pl. verb forms.

3. Repetitions of certain phrases, for stressing a point or allowing the speaker to formulate the utterance, also occur here, as in various other tales in this book.

4. As a summary of this collection, we note that the vocabulary of Galilee Bedouin dialects includes local sedentary elements and MSA. The vocabulary may derive of LA origins, which are used in MSA, or it may be related to some other sedentary or Bedouin spoken dialects. In any case, current Galilee Bedouin dialects combine old and modern vocabulary. These Bedouin dialects are considered conservative in their phonological and syntactic aspects. In this volume, we have found words that do not occur in Levant sedentary dialects but occur in MSA, which makes their vocabulary conservative. Moreover, there are Bedouin lexemes that do not occur in either sedentary dialects or LA/MSA. The following Galilee Bedouin examples (from this story) are compared with MSA (Wehr, *Dictionary of Modern Written Arabic*) and sedentary dialects (Barthélemy, *Dictionnaire arabe-français*):

daḥḥag: "he looked." Cf. *ḥaddaq(a)*, Wehr, for LA/MSA; Barthélemy, 148, who writes that it is a "literary word."

ḥerfāt: "tricks [pl.]." MSA: *ḥirfa*, "craft, trade, profession"; Barthélemy: "cunning, trick"; pl. not noted. The meaning here is semantically more general or vague than in MSA and Barthelemy's work, referring to things that are not honest.

nišal: "take out, draw (water) [semantically neutral]." Wehr: "extract, take out"; Barthélemy: "snatch, steal" (negative meaning).

ṭaššu: "they dispersed." Elihay, *The Olive Tree Dictionary*: 605, "roam, ramble"; Barthélemy: "break, make noise."

zexōv < zoxōf: "(animal) burrows." Cf. Wehr: zaḥafa, "crawl, creep (animal)"; Barthélemy and Elihay: zaḥaf, "crawl (animal, young child)" but no "animal burrows."

fārāt: "mice." In addition to fīrān. (The latter is in Wehr, 692; Barthélemy, 625; Elihay, 124.)

mitxāwi: "fraternizing, behaving like a brother" (measure VI). It occurs also in Barthélemy, 223; but Elihay, 206, gives only measure II. In MSA (Wehr) this notion is *muta'āxi*.

šalyet (*ġanam*): "a (sheep) herd." Found in the Negev (Henkin, personal communication, 2020), but found neither in Wehr nor in Barthélemy. For this word, f. Hebrew *šilyah*, "placenta"; in Freytag 1833, 447, Latin *šaliyyah*, "frustum carnis; morsel of flesh/meat." A semantic change of this word may be assumed.

daššar: "(he) left someone alone." In Barthélemy, 240; but not in MSA (Wehr); Elihay, 103, writes only *dāšer*, "abandoned" (measure I).

ṣafren: "(he) fainted." Exists in the dialects (Barthélemy, 420) but with *safrene*, a somewhat different meaning,

ḏalḷat ᵉb-bālo: "(it) [f.] remained in his mind, he remembered." Not in MSA. A similar phrase occurs in Barthélemy, 70 (*rāḥ/mā baqā b-bālo*, "[it] did not remain in his mind [he did not remember]"); and in Negev Bedouin dialects (Henkin, personal communication, 2020).

5. *u-faḏḏ-lak*: "he remained (for you, to you)." The preposition *-lak*, "for you," is here an example of the Arabic ethical dative. This structure adds an "easy" colloquial flavor to the verb, without changing its meaning. This structure occurs frequently in this collection and many Arabic dialects in, for example, *ǧāb lak*, "he brought (for you)"; *aǧāk*, "he came (to you)"; *ǧāy-lak*, "he has come/is coming (to you)." Thus, it is not a specific Bedouin feature.

6. Uter, *The Types of International Folktales*, 1:353.

7. See especially Turkish Kurdistan: IFA 7433; as well as Tunis: 654; Iraq: 3076; Iranian Kurdistan: 3702, 3877, 3896, 22441; Morocco: 3937, 6111, 14572; Yemen: 5002, 14053; and Egypt: 7009.

8. Similarly, in the version written by Rachel Lasri from her neighbor who was born in Turkish Kurdistan (IFA 7433), the animals are also a lion, a wolf, and a fox. In this version, the plot is much more complicated and includes additional elements known from the international type of story.

9. Shilo, *Lishana Deni*, 138–47.

Epilogue

STORIES ARE MIRRORS, MIRRORS that reflect the customs, lifestyles, and worldviews of the society in which the stories were told. However, it would be a mistake to treat them as textbooks. Stories are not intended to document the history or customs of specific human societies. Stories are *works of art*. They have a completely different role.

Ostensibly, folktales are simple works that cannot compete with complex literary works. Their plots are short, and their protagonists rarely reveal their thoughts and feelings to us. Their main concern is narrating external acts and descriptions.

"From where did you come to me? From the paradise doorway to hell's doorway," says the *ġūla* to Frēṭ Rummān, the Bedouin Snow White, as the *ġūla* takes care of her and brings her home. The narrator does not explain the enigmatic sentence to us. She lets it arouse our curiosity and resonate within us. What did the heroine think when she heard this statement? How did she feel? We are not given an answer. But it is precisely this reticence that imparts to folktales their power. In this respect, folktales are reminiscent of Old Testament stories, many of which were transmitted for hundreds of years in an oral tradition before they were written down. "And Abraham took the wood of the burnt offering and laid it upon Isaac his son; and he took the fire in his hand, and a knife; and they went both of them together" (Genesis 22:6). This is how the biblical writer describes Abraham and Isaac's walk to the place of sacrifice. In the single word *together*, the narrator is able to express an entire world of emotions, the feelings of a father and son marching together, but each one immersed in his own thoughts, in his own world. What does each protagonist feel? This the narrator does not reveal. It leaves us listeners to put ourselves in their place and imagine what is happening in their hearts.

Such are the Bedouin stories we present in our book. These are oral stories, stories told by mothers to their children, through which the children were given insights and values that shaped their world. The messages hidden in these stories were not expressed aloud. They were beyond the words and the plot, at the unconscious level, and those readers who listen to them with their inner ear hear in them the beauty and the joy, the sadness and the pain, the love and the compassion that fill their world.

However, the value of this book is not limited to the narrative aspect. As we said in the foreword, its uniqueness lies in the combination of folkloristic research on the one hand and linguistic research on the other. The linguistic side is as important as the narrative side because it complements the folkloristic aspect and enables us to offer a fuller and more comprehensive picture of the discussed culture. On the other hand, these folktales provide an invaluable and necessary source for the linguistic analysis, enabling the researcher to learn the speakers' language as it is used spontaneously in real life, with all its devices and pragmatic means of communication.

The narrators' texts reflect their dialects as well as their linguistic, psycholinguistic, and sociolinguistic background. These folktales are an excellent material for linguistic studies of the dialects of the Bedouin residents of the Galilee. The Bedouin tribes immigrated to this region from many geographical directions, with their different origins and tales, and thus their traditional language habits also vary. Some studies have already described their dialects, but the current tales complement and expand the past range of their described dialectal features with many examples produced in spontaneous, natural running speech. Examples from the tales refer readers to the specific language features and to a few effects of other Arabic varieties and Hebrew, the dominant language in Israel, found in their speech. For the interested reader, whether a professional linguist or not, a relatively detailed linguistic chapter provides a structural survey of these dialects.

Another aspect to complete the wide scope of the picture presented here is the historical-demographical one, as expressed in Medzini's comprehensive chapter, which describes the history of the Bedouin tribes and their settlement in the Galilee up to the present.

In our book, we tried to open a window to the world of the Bedouin tribes living in the Galilee region of Israel. Our hope is that through this acquaintance, readers will also gain understanding and appreciation of the Bedouin culture in our country.

We choose to finish our book with the same words that appear at the end of the first chapter, which are largely valid in relation to all the stories:

> The good storyteller succeeds in maintaining a certain ambiguity. Just as in a dream, there are unmistakably fundamental, enigmatic elements, and the heroes must interpret their dreams; thus, in a good story, things are not so cut and dried.
>
> The plot of the story has a convoluted course, and we, the listeners, do not know everything. We must fill in the gaps using our imagination.
>
> This is true in stories as in real life—where we also must decode signs and interpret them throughout the course of our lives. This is a source of pain and sadness but also a source of beauty and excitement in dreams, in stories, and in reality.

Bedouin Dialects in the North of Israel

Judith Rosenhouse

1. The Arabic Language, Arabic-Speaking Bedouins, and Arabic Dialects

The name Bedouin derives from the root BDW and is linked to the word *bādiyah*—an open, empty terrain, denoting the desert. Bedouins are thus the desert dwellers—nomads whose existence relied mainly on livestock, usually camels on the one hand and sheep or goats on the other. Nomads lived in the Middle East and in other areas of the world long before the Christian era. Today, too, there are nomadic tribes in many places, such as Siberia and Mongolia, in addition to the Bedouins in the Middle East.[1] Several millennia ago, the humans were gatherers and hunters. Along history, many became sedentary farmers, living in a fixed place. Civilizations developed in many regions all over the world. But we focus here on the Galilee area, in a small country in the larger region of the Levant in the Middle East. Urbanization and the passage to a sedentary lifestyle existed also in that region, as well as in others of the Middle East and the Arabian Peninsula. Even in early periods, nomadic tribes and rural and urban populations lived side by side in these geographical areas. The Prophet Muhammad himself (ca. 570–632 CE) grew up in a Bedouin tribe in the desert, but during his adult life, he was active in the towns Mecca and Medina.

The Arabic language, which is a relatively young Semitic language, began to develop in the Arabian Peninsula. The oldest written evidence in this language is more than two thousand years old. At present, the number of native speakers of Arabic is higher than three hundred million people, and it is now the fifth language in the world in this respect. Immigrants who are native speakers of Arabic are living all over the world. In the Middle East and Africa, there are twenty-six states in which Arabic is the formal language. In many of them, it is the only official language. Because of the number and spread of its speakers around the world, the importance of the Arabic language has been growing.

Linguists, including Arab linguists, have been studying the Arabic language and its dialects at least since about the eighth century CE. During the millennia of its existence, the Arabic language has undergone many changes. This process is not unique to Arabic. Every language develops and changes in time. For example, native English speakers typically neither speak Shakespeare's language nor write it. Native speakers of Hebrew in Israel, similarly, need to learn the Hebrew Bible as a separate subject because its Hebrew structures and vocabulary are very different from Modern (Israeli) Hebrew. The political, technological, and cultural changes that occurred all over the world during the twentieth century have also accelerated the linguistic changes in Arabic.

The linguistic features of high-dispersion languages vary among their speakers, along with the changing living environments that yield human social developments in time.

These factors create linguistic dialects, which distinguish (at least) between social, communal, faith, and geographical groups. Arabic today has numerous dialects, and the Galilee Bedouin dialects in the north of Israel constitute a small group of the larger class of Bedouin dialects. Additional factors that affect dialects relate to foreign languages and dialects. Speakers of these dialects/languages have increased contact with Arabic dialects' speakers, in particular since the twentieth century.

A basic distinction in Arabic is between the *fuṣḥā* (فصحى), the Literary Arabic (LA), which is also considered the Classical Arabic (ClA), and *the ʿāmmiyyah* (عامية), the general, daily colloquial Arabic (CA).[2] Although all the dialects are part of one language, they themselves differ in many of their linguistic structures. LA also differs from Modern Standard Arabic (MSA), its modern variety used in the written media that developed mainly after the eighteenth century.

Since the twentieth century, the modern urban culture and the expansion of schooling systems for Arabic-speaking children have been causing both MSA and CA to affect each other in different manners and rates. Literate native speakers of Arabic are now assumed to know both of them—the mother tongue, which is the local colloquial dialect, and MSA, according to his or her education and literacy. Indeed, the Israeli schooling system has yielded considerable cultural and linguistic changes in the Bedouin dialects.[3]

Researchers who visited the Bedouins in previous centuries gathered information about the history of Bedouin tribes, their customs, and their language while befriending them. Researchers heard stories about the tribes' important events, legends, and customs—all of which were passed down to their narrators from their ancestors. This manner of oral culture existed in the Middle East and the Arabian Peninsula even before the beginning of Islam (and the Christian era). Such material about the Bedouins was collected by researchers and published in books and papers since the Middle Ages and the Renaissance and later. Some of these publications contain maps describing the living areas of the various tribes.

Such research was conducted in the Arabian Peninsula and North Africa, as well as in the Negev and the North of Israel. For example, Bergsträsser published maps of the Sham (الشام) area, which includes the area of current Syria, Lebanon, Jordan, and Israel.[4] Bauer described sedentary and nomadic dialects in the area of Palestine (as called at that time), distinguishing between them.[5] Oppenheimer surveyed the Bedouin tribes in Palestine, Jordan, and Sinai and Hedjaz.[6] Other volumes of his book study other Bedouin tribes in the Middle East. Cantineau studied the dialects of many Bedouin tribes, mainly in Syria, Jordan, and the edge of Palestine.[7] Al-ʿĀref described in Arabic the Negev Bedouins near Be'er Sheva' (*Bīr as-Sabaʿ*, in colloquial Arabic).[8] Later on, Blanc, Henkin, and Shawarbah described dialects of several tribes of Negev Bedouins.[9] A few publications also studied the Bedouins in the north of Israel.[10] Some of these works include folktales and songs, which were written down (or in later years, recorded on tape recorders) as heard from local tribal narrators, poets, and singers.[11] These materials appeared in Arabic or in various phonetic transcription systems, with translations into the author's language, which was then mainly German, French, or English. Some Bedouin material appeared also in Hebrew after the establishment of the State of Israel.[12]

In the rest of this chapter, we describe some features of Arabic in general and the Galilee Bedouin dialects (in northern Israel) in particular. These features include phonetic, morphological, syntactic, and lexical aspects.

2. Phonology/Phonetics

Phonology is the language part that examines the pronunciation and components of a language's speech sounds and their changes in time and place. The most well-known speech units are the consonants and the vowels. When discussing dialects, we mainly refer to the spoken features and not written language conventions (i.e., not LA/MSA).

When speaking, people use several body parts in a united communication system. This system begins in the brain, which transmits the speaker's wish to express him—or herself. The brain activates the muscles that operate the speech organs, namely, diaphragm, lungs, vocal folds (cords), throat, tongue, lips, and nose. The airflow in the vocal tract, combined with the movement of the uvula, the tongue, and the lips, creates speech sounds and the speech elements of the language-dependent system. Listeners of that language perceive the vocal utterance through the ears. In the inner ear, the mechanical wave vibrations are transformed to electrochemical pulses and pass to the brain, which processes the signals, and the listener "understands" them.

The speech organs produce consonants by shaping or blocking the pulmonary airflow in the vocal tract in various manners. Speech sounds vary in their manner of pronunciation, in the locus of pronunciation, and in voicing (vocal cord usage). Vowels do not use total airflow blocking. Vowels differ by tongue shape and its position (upward, downward, forward, backward), mouth opening form, and rate (very open versus slightly open versus closed) and lip use (opening, raising, stretching, contracting, and protruding). Consonants differ between languages, but usually their number is larger than that of vowels. A fully blocked airflow creates stop consonants. The stops can be unvoiced (*t*, *k*, *p*), if the vocal folds are not vibrating during the airflow. Vocal fold vibration, with airflow blocking, creates voiced stops (e.g., *b*, *g*, *d*); using the nasal passage creates (voiced) nasal consonants and vowels (e.g., *m*, *n*, *ã*, respectively). Production manners include, for example, stops (*t*, *k*, *p*); fricatives (*f*, *s*, *x*, *š*); laterals (*l*); nasals (*m*, *n*); and affricates (*č*, *ğ*). Consonant locus (production place) may be described from the throat to the lips: glottal, pharyngeal, uvular, velar, palatal, alveolar, dental, labiodental, labial, bilabial.

Literary Arabic and Arabic dialects also use "emphasis" or pharyngealization, which does not occur in various other languages. Pharyngealization (also velarization) occurs when the throat area is contracted and the tongue root is pushed back. This feature distinguishes regular speech sounds from those produced in the same locus but with this "emphasis" and is marked with a dot beneath the "usual" letter (e.g., *ṣ, ṭ, ḷ, ṃ*).

Literary Arabic speech sounds include laryngeal consonants (*h*, ʾ); pharyngeals (*ḥ*, ʿ); uvular (*q*); velar (*k, x, ġ*); postalveolar (*š, ǧ*); alveolar (*s, z, r*); dental (*t, d, n, ṯ, ḏ*); labiodental (*f*); and bilabial (*b, m*). In modern Arabic dialects, including Bedouin ones, some of these speech sounds are produced in different manners, and some have disappeared from the list. Thus, the speech sounds in LA *q, k, ǧ* may appear in the Galilee Bedouin dialects as *g* ~ *ž, č, ž*, respectively. The first speech sound, *q*, is usually voiced in the Galilee Bedouin dialects to *g* or *ǧ*. The latter appears in the environment of a front vowel (*e, i*) but may occur as *q* in formal or elevated style. The second consonant, *k*, appears as *č*, mostly where *k* follows the same rule (i.e., in the environment of an *e*, *i*), but not only there. *ǧ* is usual for the Bedouin (and MSA) speech sound, but *ž* occurs, too, apparently because of its use in neighboring sedentary Arabic dialects. As noted above, a few emphatics (*ḍ, ḏ̣, ṣ, ṭ*) occur already in LA/MSA. Other emphatic consonants (e.g., *ḅ, ḷ, g̣, ṃ, ṇ, ṛ*) characterize Bedouin Arabic dialects, since such emphatics do not occur (and are not marked in writing) in LA/MSA and sedentary dialects.

The LA/MSA Arabic vowels are three pairs of short and long vowels, namely, *i, ī, a, ā, u, ū*. In the current Arabic dialects, including the Galilee Bedouin ones, one can add the vowels *e, ē, o, ō*. The short vowels *e, o* are usually used instead of *i, u* in unstressed syllables. To break up consonantal clusters (sequences) in a word and in juncture (between words), the short vowels *a, e, ə, i, o, u* occur as epenthetic (with various allophones) in the Galilee Bedouin and sedentary speech.

However, in many Bedouin (and certain sedentary) dialects, the speakers mix vowels in casual speech, so that the intervowel differences are not always phonemic.[13] The stories in this volume contain many examples of such fluctuation (e.g., *ʿindo* ~ *ʿendo* ~ *ʿando*, "he has, with him"; *šeber* ~ *šaber* ~ *šiber*, "hand span"; *gāḷ-ḷu* ~ *gāl-lo*, "he said to him"). Even in personal names, we find such variations, including, for example, Muḥammad, Moḥammed, Moḥammad, Mḥimmad, the Prophet's name when referring to the Prophet himself or to people named after him. Blanc wrote about Negev Bedouin vowels that they have "partial non-contrast"—in other words, that they are hardly phonemic.[14]

3. Morphology

Morphology in linguistics is the field that studies word forms. Arabic has features that are common to other Semitic languages, and other features that are unique to Arabic. We mention here only a few features shared by LA/MSA and the dialects (with certain differences between them):

3.1. The "root + pattern" system reflects the combination of the consonantal root (e.g., *k-t-b*) and the pattern created by added vowels (e.g. *a* in LA/ MSA *kataba* and colloquial *katab*, "he wrote") or added syllables (e.g., MSA and dialects *maktab*, "office").

TABLE 1. Singular, dual, and plural forms in LA/MSA and Galilee Bedouin dialects

Gloss	LA/MSA	Galilee Bedouin
(One) day	**yawm**	**yōm**
(Two) days	**yawmāni**	**yōmēn**
(Many) days	**'ayyām**	**'iyyām**

TABLE 2. Comparison of dual and plural verb forms in LA and Galilee Bedouin

Gloss/person	LA ("wrote")	LA ("will write")	Galilee Bedouin ("wrote")	Galilee Bedouin ("will write")
They (3m.)	**katabā**	**yaktubāni**	**ketbam, kitbam**	**yukutbam, yukutbūn**
They (3f.)	**katabatā**	**taktubāni**	**ketban, kitban**	**yukutban**
They (m.pl.)	**katabū**	**yaktubūna**	**ketbam, kitbam**	**yukutbam, yukutbūn**
They (f.pl.)	**katabna**	**yaktubna**	**ketban, kitban**	**yukutban**
You (2m.) wrote	**katabtumā**	**taktubāni**	**ketabtum, kitabtam**	**tukutbam, tukutbūn**
You (2f.) wrote	**katabtumā**	**taktubāni**	**ketabtan, kitabtan**	**tukutban**
You (m.pl.)	**katabtum**	**taktubūna**	**ketabtum, kitabtam**	**tukutbam, tukutbūn**
You (f.pl.)	**katabtunna**	**taktubna**	**ketabtan, kitabtan**	**tukutban**

TABLE 3. Some verb forms and measures in Literary Arabic and Galilee Bedouin

Gloss (3m.sg. & 3f.sg.)	Literary Arabic form		Galilee Bedouin form	
	Past	imperfect	Past	imperfect
he wrote	**kataba**	**yaktubu**[15]	**kitab ~ ketab**	**yuktub**
he plowed	**ḥaraṯa**	**yaḥruṯu**	**ḥaraṯ**	**yeḥaruṯ**
he ate	**'akala**	**ya'kulu**	**kala**	**yākel ~ yokel**
he came	**ǧā'a**	**yaǧī'u**	**'aǧa, ǧe**	**yiǧi**
he looked at	**ḥaddaqa naḏ̣ara**	**yuḥaddiqu yanḏ̣uru**	**daḥḥag**	**yedaḥḥeg**
she asked	**sa'alat**		**'as'alat**	
she dared	**'iǧtara'at**	**taǧtari'u**	**istaǧrat**	**tastaǧri**

3.2. The Arabic number system has three categories: singular, dual, and plural in the nouns (in LA/MSA, also in verb conjugations, pronouns, and adjectives). In the colloquial dialects, including the Galilee Bedouin ones, only a few residues of dual nouns are used (dual verbs and adjectives are referred to by the pl. or sg. f. forms). Table 1 presents a few examples of these forms in MSA and Galilee Bedouin dialects. Tables 2 and 3 compare verb forms in MSA and Bedouin Galilee dialects.

3.3. The plural patterns of nouns are divided into two groups:

A. "Sane plural," where a suffix is added to the singular form, with different suffixes for masculine and feminine nouns, such as *m'allem—m'allmīn*, "male teacher—male teachers"; *m'allma—m'allmāt*, "female teacher—female teachers"; *'anza—'anzāt*, **"**goat—goats."
B. "Broken plural," which refers to various patterns that differ from the sg. pattern. The pl. forms involve changes in vowel(s) or syllable structure(s) of the sg. noun, as in *bēt—byūt*, "house, tent—houses, tents"; *ğimal—ğmāl*, "camel—camels"; *ġazāl—ġuzlān*, "a deer—pl. deer"; *maxlūq—maxālīq*, "a creature—pl. creatures."

3.4. Abundant verb measures and conjugations, referring to verb patterns (i.e., measures), tenses, and persons. Table 3 above presents a few examples of this system in LA and the Galilee Bedouin dialects.

Verb measures have fixed patterns. In the Galilee Bedouin dialects, nine patterns are used (**measure IX** is not used at all), and some of them are more frequent than others. (In this list, C= consonant and v = vowel.)

Measure I, the basic pattern, has two varieties: CaCaC/CeCaC, for example, *ḥaraṯ*, "he plowed"; *ketab*, "he wrote": and CiCiC *širib*, "he drank." (Note the vowel in the second syllable.)

Measure II has a geminated root consonant, thus CvCCvC, e.g., *kammal*, "completed."

Measure III has a long vowel instead of the gemination, thus CvvCvC, e.g., *fāraq*, "part with someone".

Measure IV has a prefixed *'a-*, thus *'aštat*, "(it) rained."; "*anṭa*" he gave"**.**

Measure V has a prefixed *t-* and a geminate vowel (like measure II), e.g., *tmallaṣ*, "he got away"; *tkassar*, "it broke". This measure is used for passive or reflective actions.

Measure VI has the *t-* prefix and a long vowel (like measure III), e.g., *t'āraf*, "he got acquainted with".

Measure VII has the prefix *in-*, as in *inkatal*, "he was killed," or *infağar*, "he/it exploded," and is used for passive and reflexive actions.

Measure VIII has an infixed *t-*, thus, for example, *intagal*, "he moved (to a new place)."

Measure X has *(i)st-* as prefix, as in *istakra*, "he hired (something)."

The verbs are conjugated for tenses (perfect, imperfect) and moods (indicative, imperative, subjunctive, and jussive), and they have active and passive participle forms. Verb conjugations have different forms for person, gender, and number.

3.5. Definite/indefinite nouns. Nouns in an utterance can be definite (refer to specific objects) or indefinite (refer to nonspecific objects). In Arabic, the consonant *l* of the definite article *al-* is changed in LA/MSA to the first consonant of the following word when it is one of the following consonants: *d, ḍ, z, ḏ, ḏ̣, s, ṣ, š, t, ṭ, r, l, n*. In colloquial dialects, including Bedouin ones, additional consonants may be added to this list (e.g., *ğ*). But in spontaneous speech this rule is not always kept. Note that in Bedouin dialects, the vowel that precedes the definite *-l* is usually *a*, yielding the form *al-*, not *el-* or *il-*, as in various sedentary speakers' dialects.

4. Syntax

Syntax refers to utterances, such as sentences, which are usually longer than a single word, and to sentence parts. Arabic and its dialects have nominal and verbal sentences. Nominal sentences do not have a conjugated verb as predicate. See for instance:

4.1. al-ʿağiyy guwiy, "The boy (is) strong."

4.2. az-zlima hina, "The man is here."

4.3. huwwa gāʿed ġād,[16] "He is sitting there."

4.4. hiyya fi-d-dār, "She is in the house."

In verbal sentences, the predicate is a verb form in the past tense, the imperfect tense, or the imperative mood. The verb can follow the subject or precede it (in various conditions), e.g.,

4.5. gāmat al-ḥurma "Got up the woman. (= The woman got up.)"

4.6. al-ḥurma gāmat, "The woman got up. (= The woman got up.)"

The number category governs singular and plural verb and participle forms according to the number of the head noun. See:

4.7. huwwa gāʿed, "He is sitting."

4.8. humma gāʿdīn, "They are sitting."

4.9. al-ʿağiyya gāʿda, "The girl is sitting,"

4.10. al-ʿağiyyāt gāʿdāt, "The girls are sitting."

However, a special agreement rule in Arabic refers to plural inanimate, animal, or group nouns as a feminine (singular) noun. Thus:

4.11. ğat 'iyyām, rāḥat 'iyyām, "Days came, days went = "day in, day out."

In the Bedouin dialects, this latter rule is effective very frequently, probably more than in sedentary dialects.

Syntactic rules are used to form agreement between the predicate and the subject or the nominal complements. Thus, the gender category governs different verb and adjective endings as, for example,

4.12. al-ʿağiyy al-guwiyy rāḥ, "The strong boy went."

4.13. al-ʿağiyya al-guwiyya rāḥat, "The strong girl went."

4.14. an-nās rāḥu = an-nās rāḥat, "The people went."

4.15. an-niswān rāḥān, "The women went."

The definiteness marker *al-* (among its other functions) thus distinguishes between adjectives complementing nouns (governed by nouns) and between predicative adjectives. Compare the following examples:

4.16. al-ʿağiyy al-guwiyy rāḥ. "The strong boy went."

4.17. al-ʿağiyy guwiyy. "The boy (is) strong."

Most of these morphological and syntactic structures are similar in LA and colloquial dialects, including Bedouin ones.

5. Diverse Criteria for the Classification of Arabic Dialects and Bedouin Dialects

The classification of dialects to groups involves various factors:

- Geography—Eastern versus Western dialects. The transition between them is found roughly in Egypt,[17] where it is not a line but a "transfer zone" with mixed features.

- Demography—There are differences between the sedentary speakers' speech in urban centers and rural areas and between them and the nomadic speakers' speech.
- Faith community, religion—Muslims, Christians, Druze, and Jews, with their various sects (Shi'ite and Sunni Muslims, Greek Orthodox and Catholic Christians, etc.) have their (more or less distinctive) Arabic dialects.
- Gender—As in dialects of other languages, there are differences between the manner of speech of women and that of men.[18]
- Education—Literacy (i.e., LA and MSA) affects speakers' communication manner according to their different educational levels, which are acquired at school.

The groups of Bedouin dialects have differences reflecting the above factors:

1. Eastern and Western dialects differ, but they are often more similar to one another than to local, geographically closer sedentary dialects.
2. Nomadic dialects differ from sedentarized Bedouin dialects.
3. Bedouin dialects (both nomadic and sedentarized) vary among themselves, often reflecting their speakers' way of life. For example, differences exist between camel herder tribes and seminomadic sheep- and goat-herding tribes.

However, many of the (nomadic) Bedouin tribes have already settled down or are in the state of transfer to sedentarization.[19] The sedentarization trend has been increasing because of the number and types of links between Bedouin and sedentary speakers, affecting Bedouin dialects.[20]

An important distinction between sedentary and Bedouin dialects is that the latter are relatively more conservative. Bedouin traditions and customs also reveal this trait.[21] Here are a few linguistic features considered either conservative in the Bedouin dialects or specific to them, as compared with sedentary dialects:

1. The LA/MSA consonant *q* is voiced in Bedouin dialects (in Israel and elsewhere) to *g*, *ğ*, whereas it is usually the glottal stop **'** in the sedentary urban dialects and *k*, *q* in rural dialects. Yet certain rural and urban speakers (mainly men) use *g* for this consonant in some words, as it is considered more virile (probably following a romantic Bedouin image). This classification is very rough because cases have been noted that even members of one urban family use **'**, *g*, *k*, *q* by sociolinguistic accommodation. Register raising and sedentary influence are among the factors that affect and change the Galilee Bedouin dialects.[22] This instability or fluctuation reflects undergoing phonetic processes in these Bedouin dialects, sometimes due to speakers' lack of clear awareness of the rules of *q*, *g*, *ğ* use in their own dialect.
2. LA/MSA *k* is pronounced as affricated *č* by Galilee Bedouin speakers, usually when it is adjacent to the front vowels *i* and *e*. Other dialects (e.g., Negev

and Sinai Bedouins) never affricate *k*. However, various sedentary rural Galilee dialects also use this allophone (*č*).

3. Bedouins generally retain the emphatic consonants *ḍ*, *ḏ̣*, *ṣ*, *ṭ* and pharyngealization (e.g., *ḅ*, *ḷ*, *g̣*, *ṃ*, *ṇ*, *ṛ*), and they pronounce them forcefully. (Various sedentary speakers, however, often pronounce even the MSA emphatics weakly.)

4. The *'imāla* ("inclination, tilting" in Arabic) rule (cf. chap. 18, note 2; chap. 29, note 6) changes the low (short or long) vowel *a* to a (short or long) *e* or *i* in many sedentary dialects. This *'imāla* occurs word internally or word finally, usually in nouns, participles, and adjectives and sometimes in suffixed pronouns. In the Galilee Bedouin dialects, only word-final *'imāla* practically occurs.

5. Note that in Bedouin dialects, *e* or *i* may change to *a* near pharyngeal, laryngeal, or uvular consonants. (This tendency is not related to *'imāla*.)

6. Bedouin dialects usually retain the *gaháwa* syndrome. This word pattern exists neither in sedentary dialects nor in MSA. This pattern involves stress shifts in words with the pattern CvCCVC (e.g., *gáhwa(h)*) so that CvCCVC > CvCvCVC > CCvCVC, for example, *qáhwah* (LA/MSA) = *gaháwa* (Negev Bedouin) > *gháwa* (Galilee Bedouin) "coffee"; *yáḥruṯu* (LA/MSA) = *yúḥruṯ* (sedentary) = *y*[e]*ḥáruṯ* (Galilee Bedouin) "he plows, will plow."

7. Another typical Bedouin feature is the rise of a low vowel to the high *i*; in other words, *a* > *i*, even in the CvCCVC pattern. This feature takes place when the adjacent consonants are not emphatic or pharyngealized, as in sedentary *ġáname* = Bedouin *ġanáma* > *ġnáma* > *ġníma*, "ewe."

8. A similar phonetic process related to word patterns in Bedouin dialects is the deletion of a weak first syllable when the stress shifts to the second syllable of the word, as in *'áḥmar* > *'aḥámar* > *ḥámar*, "red m.sg." Table 4 summarizes these features with a few Bedouin and sedentary examples.

9. A stress difference between Bedouin and sedentary dialects in the Galilee and elsewhere involves the definite article + noun, as well as some verb patterns (measures VII and VIII), which have the same syllable structure (CVCCVCV) as the *gaháwa* syndrome (e.g., Bedouin *ál-ǧimal* versus sedentary *al-ǧámal*; Bedouin *ínbaṣaṭṭ* versus sedentary *inbáṣaṭ*, "he was satisfied, happy"; Bedouin *íḥtaram* versus sedentary *iḥtáram*, "he respected," as shown in table 4.

10. Bedouins use diminutive patterns very often, both for nouns and adjectives. These patterns are used not only for diminution but also as hypocoristic (caritative, to express liking). Sedentary speakers use such forms at a much

TABLE 4. Stress differences between Galilee Bedouin and sedentary dialects

Gloss	Bedouins	Sedentary
(One) onion	**bṣála**	**báṣale**
Sheep, f., ewe	**ġníma**	**ġáname**
He knows	**yeʿáref**	**yéʿraf**
Red m.sg.	**ḥámar**	**ʼáḥmar**
The camel	**ál-ğímal**	**al-ğámal**
The king	**ál-malek**	**al-málek**
He was satisfied, happy	**ínbaṣaṭ**	**inbáṣaṭ**
He respected	**íḥtaram**	**iḥtáram**
He moved (to a new place)	**éntagal**	**intáqal, intaɔal**

TABLE 5. Diminutive patterns in Bedouin and sedentary dialects

Gloss	Bedouins	Sedentary
Short	**gṣayyir**	**qaṣīr**
Dog	**klēb**	**kalb**
Shepherd	**rwēʿi**	**rāʿi**
O my sister	**yā-xayta**	**yā-xti**
O mother	**yā mʷēma**	**yā-mma**

smaller rate. In addition, not all diminutive patterns of Bedouin speakers occur in sedentary speakers' speech. Table 5 demonstrates this issue.

11. In verb conjugations, the Bedouin dialects, unlike sedentary dialects but like LA/MSA, retain morphological distinctions between second and third person masculine and feminine genders, in both singular and plural persons. See examples in table 1.

6. Galilee Bedouin Dialects in the Twentieth Century, and Their Contacts with Hebrew and Other Languages

This section focuses on the Bedouin dialects in Israel compared to sedentary dialects there. Bedouin and sedentary speakers accommodate their dialects to one another in different traits. These processes are asymmetric, however.[23] Usually, the Bedouins are those who adopt sedentary dialect features, which the Bedouins consider more prestigious than their own. The sedentary speakers, on the other hand, do not acquire Bedouin dialects; they do not even know them passively—they do not understand them.[24] Therefore, an ideal picture of Bedouin dialectal features does not reflect the real current state of the dialects. We should remember that the recordings in this collection are from the 1980s, that is to say, about forty years ago, or more than a generation ago. Since then, these "foreign" influences on Bedouin dialects have accumulated and become stronger, more numerous, and more effective. We discuss some of these features below.

6.1. Phonology

6.1.1. Consonants

Table 6 below presents a few comparisons between LA, Galilee sedentary, and Galilee Bedouin consonants. The phonetic symbols (letters) in brackets reflect possible pronunciation manners, which are not the main or the only pronunciation manner of these consonants—they do not always occur in the respective dialect. That is to say, both sedentary and Bedouin dialects use certain common consonants, which are not the "traditional" (LA) pronunciation manner. Speakers' accommodation to another dialect is marked by the bracketed symbol. Sedentary features of consonants are often mixed in the Bedouin dialect, often by the younger generations but also by older Bedouin speakers, as these folktales show. It has not yet been studied whether, in the Galilee, the rate of such mixtures (also considered code mixing) differs between these age groups. In any case, listeners do not usually pay attention to speakers' pronunciation of words with, for example, *ğ* or *ž*, or with *i* or *a* in *ğamal*, *žamal*, *ğimal*, "camel," or *ṯ* or *t* in *ṯnēn* and *tnēn*, "two." They can understand the meaning of the word, given its root, pattern, and context, whatever the original speech community. For example, see *ğā'da/gā'da*, "sitting, remaining," in which *ğ and* g interchange in several narrators' speech.

TABLE 6. Some LA/MSA, sedentary, and Bedouin consonants in the Galilee

LA/MSA	Sedentary	Bedouin
ğ	**ğ, ž**	**ğ (ž,)**
q	**', q, k, ğ**	**g, ğ (', q, k)**
k	**k (č)**	**k, č**
ḍ	**ḏ̣, ḍ**	**ḏ̣ (ḍ)**
ḏ̣	**ḏ̣, ẓ (ḏ̣)**	**ḏ̣ (ẓ)**
ḏ	**z, d (ḏ)**	**ḏ (z, d)**
ṯ	**t (ṯ)**	**ṯ (t)**

6.1.2. Word Stress

The main word-stress rule in the Galilee Bedouin dialects is that the last long syllable in the word is stressed—search for it from the end of the word backward. A long syllable has three to five elements (i.e., consonants and vowels). The syllables include a short or a long vowel and one or two consonants. The syllable patterns are CVV, CVC, CVCC, CVVC, CCVCC (C= consonant, V= vowel). There may be consonant clusters (i.e., two or three consonants without a vowel separating them), depending on the morphological pattern.

TABLE 7. Stressed syllables in various words in Galilee Bedouin dialects

Pattern	Galilee Bedouin dialects	Gloss
CV	**ǧa**	He came
CVV	**lā**	No
CVCC	**nimt**	You slept m.sg.
CVVC	**gāḷ**	He said
CCVCC	**šribt**	I drank
CVCVC	**ġánam**	Sheep (group, herd)
CVCVCV	**ḥéṣado**	He harvested it
CVCVCV	**mífḥama**	Coal-making place

The second rule is that in words that do not have a long syllable, the main stress is on the first syllable of the word. Table 7 shows examples of these patterns. These rules are similar to those of the local sedentary dialects.

Note, however, that the *gaháwa* syndrome is an exception to the above rule and is unique to Bedouin dialects, not only in the Galilee, as discussed above, section 5, points 6 and 7 and table 4.

6.2. Morphology

As noted above, morphology refers to nouns, verbs, adjectives, and other word forms. Here, we limit ourselves to pronouns and verb forms because nouns are too numerous to deal with in this chapter.

6.2.1. Free pronouns and verb conjugation affixes

The free personal pronouns (e.g., *I*, *he*) in Galilee Bedouin dialects differ from those of the sedentary dialects and LA/MSA to some extent. Their differences lie in the gender and number categories. Like LA/MSA, Bedouin dialects retain the distinction between masculine and feminine persons in the singular (*you*, *he/she*) and plural (*you*, *they*) paradigms of pronouns and verb conjugations. This feature demonstrates the Bedouin dialects' conservative nature. Sedentary dialects in Israel have, in contrast, lost this

TABLE 8. Free personal pronouns in Galilee Bedouin, LA/MSA, and sedentary dialects

Gloss	Galilee Bedouin	LA/MSA	Galilee sedentary
I	**'ani**	**'anā**	**'ana**
You m.sg.	**'inta**	**'anta**	**'inta**
You f.sg.	**'inti**	**'anti**	**'inti**
He	**hū, huwwa**	**huwa**	**huwwe, hū**
She	**hī, hiyya**	**hiya**	**hiyye, hī**
We	**'iḥna**	**naḥnu**	**'iḥna, niḥna**
You m.pl.	**'intam**	**'antum**	**'intu**

TABLE 8. ***(continued)***

Gloss	Galilee Bedouin	LA/MSA	Galilee sedentary
You f.pl.	**'intan**	**'antunna**	**'intu**
You dual m.	**'intam**	**'antumā**	**'intu**
You dual f.	**'intan**	**'antumā**	**'intu**
They m.pl.	**humma, hum**	**hum**	**humme, hum**
They f.pl.	**hinna, hin**	**hunna**	**humme, hum (hinne)**

distinction for second and third person in the plural.[25] Table 8 compares the pronouns of Galilee Bedouin dialects with LA/MSA and sedentary dialects. Note that specific forms of sedentary Galilee dialects are presented here only in brackets.

Verb conjugations of the past and imperfect tenses vary between the Bedouin and sedentary dialects and LA. Suffixes mark the person and number categories in the verb forms for the past and imperfect tenses. Table 9 below compares the Galilee Bedouin forms with LA/MSA. (Cf. table 2 for additional forms.)

Note that the conjugation forms shown in tables 2 and 9 reveal that some verb suffixes in the second and third pl. persons of the past and imperfect conjugations vary between different Galilee Bedouin dialects.[26] In one group, the bound personal suffix in the past tense of the 3m.pl. form ends with *–am*, and in the other it ends with *-um*. In the 2f.pl. and 3f.pl. feminine past tense, the suffix is *-tan* and *–an*, respectively. In the imperfect,

TABLE 9. Verb conjugation in Galilee Bedouin and LA/MSA ("write")

Gloss	LA/MSA past	LA/MSA imperfect	Galilee Bedouin past	Galilee Bedouin imperfect
I	**katabtu**	**'aktubu**	**ketabt, kitabt**	**'aktub**
We	**katabnā**	**naktubu**	**ketabna, kitabna**	**nuktub**
You (m.sg.)	**katabta**	**taktubu**	**ketabt, kitabt**	**tuktub, tiktub**
You (f.sg.)	**katabti**	**taktubīna**	**ketabti, kitabti**	**tukutbi**
You (2, m.)	**katabtumā**	**taktubāni**	**ketabtum, kitabtam**	**tukutbam, tukutbūn**
You (2, f.)	**katabtumā**	**taktubāni**	**ketabtan, kitabtan**	**tukutban**
You (m.pl.)	**katabtum**	**taktubūna**	**ketabtum, kitabtam**	**tukutbam, tukutbūn**
You (f.pl.)	**katabtunna**	**taktubna**	**ketabtan, kitabtan**	**tukutban**
They (2, m.)	**katabā**	**yaktubāni**	**ketabum, kitabam, kitbam**	**yukutbam, yukutbūn**
They (2, f.)	**katabatā**	**taktubāni**	**ketban, kitban**	**yukutban**
They (m.pl.)	**katabū**	**taktubūna**	**ketbom, kitbam**	**yukutbam, yukutbūn**
They (f.pl.)	**katabna**	**yaktubna**	**ketban, kitban**	**yukutban**

TABLE 10. Examples of verb patterns in measure I in Galilee Bedouin and sedentary dialects and LA

Gloss	Galilee Bedouin past—imperfect	Sedentary past—imperfect	LA/MSA past—imperfect
Look for	**figid—yufgod**	**feqed—yefqad**	**faqada—yafqidu**
Descend	**nizal—yinzil**	**nizil—yinzil**	**nazala—yanzilu**
Take	**xaḏa—yāxeḏ, yōxeḏ**	**'axad—yōxod**	**'axaḏa—ya'xuḏu**
Kill, butcher	**ḏebaḥ—yiḏbaḥ**	**ḏabaḥ—yiḏbaḥ**	**ḏabaḥa—yaḏbaḥu**
Have pity	**šfig—yešfeg**	**šefeq—yešfaq**	**šafiqa—yašfiqu**

the 3m.pl. suffix is *-um* in one group, and in the other it is *-ūn*, which is like the LA/MSA suffix. Furthermore, feminine forms vary between *-i* and *-īn* in the 2f.sg. of the imperfect tense of these two groups.

Verb measure I patterns reveal differences between the dialects and LA/MSA in the vowel array in each verb. A few examples are given in table 10, where the vowels in the first and second syllables reflect the different patterns. Pattern variations follow to some extent the consonant types, so that "back" consonants (pharyngeal, laryngeal, pharyngealized, etc.) tend to attract the low vowel *a* (and sometimes *e*) in the Bedouin dialects. The front consonants, on the other hand, tend to use the higher vowel *i* or *e* (e.g., *miša* versus sedentary *miši*). Forms such as *ye'áref*, "he knows" (cf. sedentary *yé'raf*) reflect the *gaháwa* syndrome effect.

A few verb forms are typical of Bedouin dialects in the Galilee and many other dialects. See Bedouin *kála*, "he ate" (sedentary *'ákal*), and *xáḏa* (sedentary *'áxaḏ* ~ *'áxad*); Bedouin *yigaf*, "he is standing" (past: *wigaf*, "he stood") versus sedentary *yu'af*; but Bedouin *yibas* and sedentary *yības*, "it dries out" (past, both: *yibes*, "it dried out").

Note that in some cases, the same root has a different meaning in different dialects or varieties. Thus, Galilee Bedouin *figad—yufgod*, "look for," means in sedentary dialects *fiqed-yefqad*, "lose, be lost,"[27] and in LA/MSA it means "fail to find, lose," and LA/MSA *tafaqqada* (measure V) means "miss, be lacking."[28]

6.3. Syntax

Most of the rules in the Arabic dialects and LA/MSA are similar, since they belong to the same language. Therefore, only a few distinctive structures are discussed here. We presented above (Morphology) the basic categories of nouns and verbs. Table 11 below summarizes three distinctive structures: modal forms, negation, and existential patterns.

The "modes" slots in table 11 show the modes for the three language varieties by three verb forms (subjunctive, jussive, imperative). Note that morphologically, the modal forms are the same in the Bedouin and sedentary dialects, because sedentary speakers who use the prefix *b-* with the imperfect form omit it in the modal forms.

"Negation" uses negative particles followed by a verb or a nominal element (noun or adjective), and the negative particles vary between LA/MSA and the two dialect groups. For negation, Bedouin and sedentary speakers usually use *mā* or lā.[29] *mā/lā . . . wa-lā*

TABLE 11. Negation, modal structures, and existential elements in Galilee Bedouin dialects, LA, and Galilee sedentary dialects

Structure	Galilee Bedouins	LA/MSA[30]	Galilee sedentary
Modes			
Subjunctive	**yirkab**	**yarkaba**	**yirkab**
Jussive	**yirkab**	**yarkab**	**yirkab**
Imperative	**'irkab**	**'irkab**	**'irkab**
Negation	**mā** + [verb] (past/ imperfect) (+/- **š**) **lā** + verb (imperfect) in 2 person means also negated imperative. **mā/lā… wa-lā…**+ past/ imperfect (no **-š**) **mū, mī, mu-hu** + nominal element	**mā** + [verb] past **lā** + [verb] (all modes except past) **lam** + jussive **lan** + subjunctive **laysa** + nominal accusative element	**mā** + [verb] + (past / imperfect) (+/-) **š** **lā** + verb (all modes) +/- **š** **mā/lā . . . wa-lā** + past/imperfect (no **-š**) **muš, miš** + nominal element
Existential expressions "There is/are"	**bī, bū (fī)**	**yūğadu, hunāka, ṯamma**	**fī (bī)**

(neither… nor) are used in both Bedouin and sedentary dialects with past or imperfect verb forms.

The existential expressions are similar in the Bedouin and sedentary dialects, and both differ from the LA/MSA expressions. All of the existential expressions are predicates and require a nominal element as subject. For negation, Bedouins usually use *mā bi*/*mā bū* or *biš*. In the Galilee Bedouin tales, we often find *bī*/*bū zlima*, "there is a man" as the opening sentence. Some speakers prefer *bī*, while others (sometimes from other tribes) use *bū*. The form *fī* is mainly sedentary but is also used sometimes by Galilee Bedouins because Bedouins have been acquiring sedentary dialectal features. Likewise, *bī* may sometimes be used by sedentary speakers.[30] The suffixed *š* of *biš* is used mainly by sedentary speakers but sometimes also by Bedouins.

6.4. Vocabulary

In addition to the phonological and grammatical features described above, every speech group develops a vocabulary to serve its communication needs. The Bedouin and sedentary speakers' different lifestyles have thus affected and changed their respective lexicons. In the past, Bedouins had many terms that distinguished various colors, ages, kinds, and health conditions of camels, goats, sheep, and horses. They also discerned the variegated desert landscapes, kinds of hills, soil, water sources, animals, plants, etc. They noted their specific activities and objects, which were essential for life in the desert, such as tent parts and structures, tools, and equipment for survival, bread baking, coffee making, weapon types to protect their properties or loot others' properties, etc.[31]

Sedentary groups had only part of these fine distinctions—they did not need them and had other distinctions for other objects and notions. However, the Bedouins have gradually adopted the sedentary and urban lifestyle. Already Ibn Khaldun described this process in his fourteenth-century book *Prolegomena to History.*[32] This process continues to shape their vocabulary wherever they settle down. In the last two centuries, this process seems to have become faster and deeper. Words that are not relevant for daily life anymore go out of use while new terms for novel notions come onstage. In the Galilee, camel herding has totally stopped, and even the sheep herds have dwindled considerably in the twentieth century; therefore, the terminology pertaining to these vocations is hardly used at present, and the younger generations hardly know it. These linguistic processes are not unique for Galilee Bedouins; they exist also in other Bedouin and sedentary communities.

An example of this process of vocabulary change in speakers of various generations in Israel can be found in the study of a small part of the vocabulary in forty-six native speakers of Arabic from the Galilee, the "Triangle" area and Jerusalem area.[33] These participants were not Bedouin, but the process is practically the same. The study checked 120 words, 30 words from each of four works published in the twentieth century: Schmidt and Kahle, Meron and Kabha, Havelová, and Geva-Kleinberger.[34] Not one among the participants recognized or used all 120 words; they used only some of the items on the lists.[35] Published texts (e.g., in Rosenhouse's *Bedouin Arabic Dialects*) and the folktales published in this collection can reveal the effect of local sedentary dialects and LA on the Galilee Bedouins.[36] The Bedouins acquire many daily lexical items of sedentary or LA origin. An example of a very frequent lexical item is sedentary *bidd-* and Galilee Bedouin *widd-*, "want, need, will (do)." This lexical item derives from *bi-wudd*, "in (the) wish (of)." In the Bedouin Galilee texts, we find it also grammaticalized to indicate a lengthened action (see, e.g., *ṣārat il-mara biddha tğīb*, "the woman became in the state that she was going to give birth," chap. 36, story C, above).

The difference between these "foreign" and "original" words is often expressed in the pronunciation of the former, which differs from the traditional Bedouin phonetic system. The speakers also self-translate sedentary items by repeating the same word in their Bedouin dialect. Table 12 presents a few sedentary and LA words found in Bedouin speakers' texts.[37]

The use of such "foreign" lexical items during the recording sessions may be partly due to the fact that foreign listeners (the researcher, the recording person, etc.) were present. Clearly, sedentary and LA effects were there even about forty years ago, and this tendency has certainly solidified in the meantime.

The alternating use of two languages or dialects in the same utterance is called code switching (CS). CS appears when both the speaker and the listener know these language systems, the mother tongue and the second/other language. Therefore, CS is to be expected when a Bedouin speaks to a sedentary person, but not the other way around. CS can appear in syllables (morphemes within words), full-scale words, phrases, clauses, or complete sentences. A study of the speech of college students from four Arabic-speaking communities in Israel (Muslims, Christians, Druze, and Bedouins) has found interesting facts. In that study, CS rates (in percent) were higher in the Druze and Bedouin students

TABLE 12. Examples of sedentary, Bedouin, and MSA lexical items used by Galilee Bedouin narrators

Dialect/ Gloss	MSA	Bedouin	Sedentary
Now	**al-'āna**	**hassa**	**essa**
Good	**ǧayyid, ṭayyib**	**zēn**	**ṭayyeb**
Mouth	**fam**	**ṯumm**	**tumm**
So, thus	**hākaḏa**	**hīč**	**hēk**
These	**hā'ulā'i**	**haḏōl**	**haḏōli**
Why	**limāḏa**	**lē? ʿalāma?**	**lēš?**
How much?	**kam**	**gaddē?**	**'addēš?**
Like that	**kaḏālik**	**miṯel, zayy**	**mitel, zayy hēk**
By	**bi-wāsiṭat, ʿan ṭarīq**	**bi-**	**bi-wāsṭat**
Must	**ḥatman, wāǧib, ʿalayhi**	**ǧēr**	**lāzim, ḥatman**
During	**xilāla, ṭūla**	**fī, (time expression)**	**xilāl, ṭūl**
Talk	**ḥadīṯ**	**ḥači**	**ḥadīṯ, ḥaki**
That	**'an**	**'inno**	**'enno**
When	**lammā, ʿindamā**	**lammenno**	**lamma, ʿindama**

TABLE 13. Hebrew effects on the speech of Galilee Bedouin speakers of Arabic

Words from Rosenhouse	Gloss	Words from Brand	Gloss
dirá	Apartment	**pašút**	Simple
al-mišta'ra	The police	**'aḥúz**	Percent
maḥát[41]	Needle	**('áwwal) moʿed**	(1st) Appointment time
markódet[42]	Trap	**(ṣirna) nešaḥzér**	(We began) to reconstruct
bdikót	Checkups (at the doctor's)	**lo holéx li (bi-hāḏa)**	I do not succeed (Lit.: it doesn't go for me [in it])

TABLE 14. Hebrew words found in texts in this volume

Hebrew word	Gloss	Hebrew word	Gloss
histakél	He looked	**ḥatuná**	Wedding
'af 'aḥád lo 'ba	No one came	**ze**	This (m.sg.)
ḥódeš	Month	**mispár**	Number
yištú	They (will) drink	**beʿayót**	Problems
kafé	Coffee	**'adamá**	Soil, ground
bét šimúš	Water closet	**maxšír**	Tool, instrument
nehené	(He) is enjoying	**'argazím**	Boxes
yavaním (<'avaním)	Stones	**mazroním (<mizroním)**	Mattresses
matanà	Gift	**maráq**	Soup
ḥanút	Shop	**maʿamád**	Status

TABLE 15. Words from other languages in colloquial Galilee Arabic speech

Gloss	Words from Rosenhouse	Gloss	Words from Brand	Gloss	Word in this collection
Cement	**batōn**	Maximum	**maksimum**	Boxes	**boksāt**[43]
Bulldozer	**bildōzer**	Makeup	**meykap**	Telephone	**telefōn**
Blouse	**blūz**	Action	**akšen**	Million	**malyōn**
Balcony	**baránda**	Bye-bye	**bay-bay**	Switzerland	**swísra**
Gas	**gaz**	Course	**kurs**	Power shovel	**aš-šuful**
Stockings	**kalsāt**	Goal	**gól**	Winch	**al-winš**
Semester	**simístar**	Sport-elegant (fashion)	**sport-elegant**	Ton	**ton**

than in Christian and Muslim ones and that the CS rate in the Bedouin speakers was lower than in the Druze speakers.[38] We may assume that these results reflect stronger links between Hebrew speakers and those speakers. Similarly, Hebrew words were found in the Arabic narrations.[39] Such borrowed items exist also in the present collection. Table 13 demonstrates this point with a few examples from Rosenhouse and Brand.[40] Table 14 lists such Hebrew words found in these folktales. In addition, words derived from European languages (which usually derive via Hebrew after the establishment of Israel) occur in the Galilee Bedouin Arabic speech (cf. examples in table 15). Words from European languages were, however, few in the present volume, neglecting words absorbed into Arabic in earlier centuries.

7. The Future of Bedouin Dialects

Languages and their dialects keep changing all the time. The changes are inevitable because no one speaks exactly like his or her parents, siblings, children, friends, or others. Nowadays, many changes occur in languages over the world because of contact among cultures and peoples, and these can be materialized mostly because of the advanced technology of communication media and means.

In particular, languages with few speakers display these changes, which may lead to their dwindling and extinction. Linguistic studies examine and try to document many such languages before they are lost forever. Even when the older generation is still alive, younger generations stop using the home language and may cease to understand it. This process develops in most of immigrants' communities: immigrants still use their mother tongue among themselves; their children use it less, mixing it with the local languages or dialects; and their grandchildren hardly know the immigrants' mother tongue. Such a process is gradually happening also in the Arabic dialects, including among Bedouins, who are not immigrants: many of their features change because of LA/MSA, foreign dialects, and neighboring languages. Already in the fourteenth century, Ibn Khaldun described similar processes of Bedouins' sedentarization.[44] The question arises now as to which future is to be expected for the Galilee Bedouin dialects.

For the time being, Bedouin dialects are still in use in many Bedouin tribes (communities) all over the Middle East and North Africa, including the Galilee. However, they keep changing at a growing pace. They seem to be gradually losing their unique features by *koinéization* and *leveling* and the use of more general, more prevalent, and prestigious forms of nearby urban or rural dialects.[45] It may happen that they will lose their Bedouin traits or that their Bedouin features will be undiscernibly mixed with non-Bedouin features.[46]

This picture may be similar to the development of dialects in the hilly central region of the country (now in the Palestinian Authority), which is mainly rural but may have absorbed Bedouin elements. The speech sounds *č* and *g* ~ *ǧ* are sometimes used there in parallel to the consonants *k*, *q*, respectively. But some dialects of the rural central region of Israel use *č* and *ǧ* all the time, for words in which *k*, *q* are used in other dialects.[47]

Several generations of Bedouins settled down in the Galilee and in other regions of current Israel and became sedentary again and again over time (cf. Medzini's chapter, below), which gradually changed Bedouin and sedentary dialects.[48] So far, we noted phonetic features, but vocabulary elements are the first to be lost in Bedouin dialects (and elsewhere), because of contact with the close sedentary communities and the ever-changing nature and terminology of material objects, tools, and fashions.

Linguists are usually of the opinion that grammar (morphology and syntax) develops in languages more slowly than phonology and vocabulary. This conservative tendency is obvious in the Bedouin dialects presented in this volume.

We should note that in the recorded texts, a few laryngeal and pharyngealized phonemes sometimes sound weaker than generally usual in Bedouin dialects. This phenomenon should not be considered to reflect, for example, Modern Hebrew influence on the studied Galilee speech, because weakened production of these phonemes is also found in other Arabic dialects (not only in Israel).

The processes in the Galilee Bedouin features following other linguistic influences were not unexpected, since studies of second/other language learners' speech showed a variety of changes in manner of speech.[49]

In sum, there are numerous Bedouin dialects in the Arabic-speaking world. Bedouins in Israel differ according to their origins: the Galilee Bedouins came from Syria or Jordan, but also from elsewhere (cf. Medzini's chapter below), whereas the Negev Bedouins came mainly from Hedjaz in the western Arabian Peninsula, via southern Jordan. In line with their different origins within the Arabian Peninsula, current Bedouin dialects reflect their development along different lines.

Here, I reviewed some phonological, morphological, syntactical, and lexical features of the Galilee Bedouin dialects, while briefly mentioning other Bedouin dialects. The processes that occur in Bedouin dialects are similar to processes in many other languages and dialects all over the world. The unique features of Bedouin Galilee dialects lie in the domains of the linguistic changes in their local environment. From a linguistic point of view, the texts in this volume exhibit the complexity of the Galilee Bedouin dialects as they were in the 1980s, while probably pointing at further future developments.

Notes

1. Harrison, *When Languages Die.*

2. This phenomenon, which has been named *diglossia*, refers to the distinction between the formal written and read language variety and the language spoken in everyday life. Krumbacher was the linguist who coined this term in a paper that discussed Modern Greek versus Classical Greek, *Das Problem der Modern Griechishen Schriftsprache.* After him, Marçais used it for Arabic in "La diglossie arabe," but its main spread followed Ferguson's paper entitled "Diglossia."

3. See Ben-David and Barkai, *Bedouins*, 197–203.

4. Bergsträsser, *Sprachatlas von Syrien und Palästina.*

5. Bauer, *Das palästinensische Arabisch.*

6. Oppenheimer, *Die Beduinen*, vol. 2.

7. Cantineau, "Études sur quelques parlers de nomades arabes d'Orient."

8. Al-ʿĀref, *Bedouin Tribes.*

9. Blanc, "Arabic Dialects"; Henkin, *Negev Arabic*; Shawarbah, *Grammar of Negev Arabic.*

10. Ashkenazi, *Tribus semi-nomades de la Palestine du nord*; Rosenhouse, *Bedouin Arabic Dialects*; Ben-David and Barkai, *Bedouins.* Behnsdtedt and Geva-Kleinberger, *Dialects of Galilee.*

11. For example, for the Negev, Bailey, *Bedouin Poetry*; for the Sinai Peninsula, Stewart, *Texts in Sinai Bedouin Law*, parts 1, 2.

12. For example, Piamenta, "Linguistic System"; Rosenhouse, 1980; Bar-Zvi, *Fable, Story and Legend*; Etkin, *On a Cup of Coffee.*

13. *Phoneme* is the term for a speech sound within a language system. It is the smallest speech unit with a distinctive meaning. Thus, *s* and *b* (in, e.g., *sad* and *bad*) are different phonemes; the vowels *i* and *e* (in, e.g., *bit* and *bet*) are also different phonemes. Their differences are phonemic.

14. Blanc, "Arabic Dialects," 116.

15. Case endings do not exist in the colloquial dialects but do exist in LA and MSA, as marked by the vowel *a* or *u* at the end of the verb forms.

16. By *conjugated verb*, we mean a verb in the past or the imperfect tense. The participle is not considered a tense in Arabic.

17. Behnstedt, Peter, and Manfred Woidich, *Arabische Dialektgeographie.*

18. Rosenhouse, "Arabic Story"; "Comparative Analysis"; Henkin, *Negev Arabic.*

19. Rosenhouse, *Bedouin Arabic Dialects.*

20. Ben-David and Barkai, *Bedouins.*

21. Ben-David and Barkai.

22. Cf. Henkin, "Diachronic and Synchronic Accommodation"; *Negev Arabic.*

23. Henkin. "Hebrew and Arabic in Asymmetric Contact."

24. Rosenhouse, *Bedouin Arabic Dialects.*

25. In addition, LA/MSA dual pronouns and verb forms have been lost in all Bedouin and sedentary dialects.

26. Cf. Rosenhouse, *Bedouin Arabic Dialects.*

27. Barthélemy, *Dictionnaire arabe-français*, 615.

28. Wehr, *Dictionary of Modern Written Arabic*, 722.

29. I have not found a form like *bu-š* or *bū-š* for negation.

30. Negev dialects use this prefix as a rule.

31. Note that *lam* and *lan* exist only in LA/MSA (not in Bedouin and sedentary dialects).

32. See Harrison, *When Languages Die*, for a discussion of such linguistic distinctions and the prospects for language death in nomadic groups in Central Asia.

33. Ibn Khaldun, *Muqaddimah.*

34. Rosenhouse, "Vocabulary Changes."

35. Schmidt and Kahle, 1918; Meron and Kabha, *Tales of the Wadi*; Havelová, "Arabic Dialects of Nazareth"; Geva-Kleinberger, *Die arabischen Stadtdialekte von Haifa in der ersten Hälfte des zwanzigsten Jahrhunderts.*

36. That study also revealed gender, age, and dialect differences among the participants.

37. The texts in both this book and Rosenhouse, *Bedouin Arabic Dialects*, were recorded during about the same years.

38. Rosenhouse, *Bedouin Arabic Dialects.*

39. Brand, "Arabic-Hebrew Codeswitching."

40. Rosenhouse, *Bedouin Arabic Dialects.*

41. Rosenhouse; Brand, "Arabic-Hebrew Codeswitching."

42. *Sic*, though the word stress in correct Hebrew is *máḥat.*

43. *Sic*, though the correct Hebrew form is *malkódet.*

44. The Arabic f.pl. suffix is attached to a foreign word, implying its integration in colloquial Arabic.

45. Ibn Khaldun, *Muqaddimah.*

46. Cf. Ferguson, "Diglossia"; Blanc, 1968; Ferguson, 1959b; Henkin, *Negev Arabic.*

47. Sedentary dialects may themselves change by Bedouinization processes, as happened in Iraqi "gelet dialects" centuries ago. Cf. Blanc, *Communal Dialects in Baghdad*; Abu Haidar, "Bedouinization."

48. Cf. Schmidt and Kahle, 1918; *Volkserzählungen aus Palästina.*

49. An opposite force of Bedouinization seems to draw urban/rural speakers to use a few Bedouin (mainly phonetic) features because of their virile and romantic prestige (cf. Abu Haidar, "Bedouinization").

50. For example, Chang, "First Language Phonetic Drift."

Bedouin Tribes in the Galilee: Historical and Settlement Background

Arnon Medzini

Introduction

A researcher who seeks to trace the history of the Bedouin tribes discovers that in the absence of proper historical documentation or certificates, myths and interests in the past and in the present are all mixed together. History, as it is known to the various tribes, is remembered in the memory of the elders of the tribes, and, with the help of stories and songs, it is also imprinted in the consciousness of the younger members of the tribe.

In many cases, we are dealing with conceptual images more than objective reality, and those who study the Bedouins can only accept the description of the tribes' origins and their genealogy as it is told, because of the absence of orderly historical documentation.[1]

All the tribes make efforts to attribute themselves to the "pure" Bedouin tribes—the "real Arabs" from the Arabian Peninsula (even if history has to be rewritten). Despite the distance of the generations, there will always be a story that offers excuses to the severing of the connection from the original tribe. It will always find proof that the connection to the "mother tribe" still exists.[2]

The Bedouins in the Land of Israel also attribute their origin to the Arab tribes in the Arabian Peninsula. They regard the Arabian Peninsula as their homeland and the cradle of their culture, and they look upon their heritage as an inseparable part of Arab culture.

The Bedouin tribes in the Galilee, like those in the Negev, developed from the same desert culture that characterizes all the Bedouins in the Middle East. They originated in the Arabian Peninsula or from nomadic groups that came into contact with the Bedouins of the Arabian Peninsula and were influenced by them. Because of repeated droughts, population density, tribal wars, or intertribal conflicts, they were forced to leave their natural habitat. However, the migration of the Bedouin tribes out of their homeland and their contact with other cultures throughout history did not change their heritage, nor did they blur their identity. They knew how to differentiate themselves from peasant or urban culture. In general, Bedouin culture should be treated as one culture, and the differences between the tribes in Israel and the Bedouin tribes in the Middle East derive solely from the differences in location and the influence of the environment and the modern state.[3]

According to Ben-David, it is difficult to define the Bedouins in Israel as a separate entity from Arab society. The reason for this is that over the years, the Bedouins have lost some of the characteristics that characterized them in the past and have become more like other Arabs in the State of Israel. At the same time, the attempt to talk about a "former Bedouin" is misleading and does not fit reality. Despite the changes that have taken place and continue to influence Bedouin society, the members of this society still have "Bedouin characteristics," in the sense that "a Bedouin remains a Bedouin."

According to Ben David, there are physical, historical, social, and political differences between the Bedouins in the Galilee and the Bedouins in the Negev. The Bedouins in the Negev live in a desert environment, while in the Galilee they live in a temperate, relatively wet environment. This fact is significant and has an impact on tribes' size, strength, and character. It also creates differences in the methods of economic management. Bedouin in the Negev raised sheep and goats under desert conditions. To overcome changes in grazing conditions every year or every few years following years of drought, migration was necessary. On the other hand, the Bedouins in the Galilee did not suffer from instability in rainfall but lacked rights for using grazing land. These areas are almost entirely state property or are in the possession of the Arab villages that existed in the Galilee before the Bedouins immigrated to the Land of Israel.

The Bedouins of the Galilee were significantly affected by the rural-agricultural environment, and much more than the Negev Bedouins, because of the geographical, social, and economic proximity between the culture of the *fellāḥīn* and Bedouin culture. This proximity also directly affected the transition process from nomadic to seminomadic and from seminomadic to permanent settlement. The Bedouins of the Galilee tend to describe the nomadic way of life in the past as a way of life similar to that of the Bedouins of the Negev, because in their eyes the Bedouins of the Negev are "more Bedouin," "more nomadic," "more authentic."

In the Galilee, the interaction between the two cultures changed from a state of cooperation to conflict, as both cultures competed for the same land and water resources. This geographical proximity also had an impact on the relations between the Bedouins and the state. It seems that the presence of the Bedouins of the Galilee in a rural environment that differed in its culture and political approach to the state, and their military and political weakness due to the fact that they were small and fragmented tribes, forced them to come closer to the state and identify with it more closely than the Bedouins of the Negev.

As mentioned above, the tribes of the Negev and Galilee also differ in their relations to the state. Ownership of the land still constitutes the central issue in the difficult relationship between the state and the Bedouins in the Negev, as opposed to the question of civil rights that is more troubling to the Bedouins in the Galilee. This also has a direct link to the scope of illegal construction, a central issue that in recent years has shaped the relationship between the Bedouins and the state.

The "diaspora communities" outside the recognized and planned Bedouin towns in the Negev are growing because of disagreement with state institutions over the ownership of the land. Some eighty thousand people in the Bedouin communities in the Negev are waiting for a resolution. On the other hand, the phenomenon of spontaneous illegal construction in the Galilee has almost disappeared, and according to the Israel Land Administration data from 2005, only about 100 families still live in unrecognized villages (table 3).

On the subject of relations with the state, there is little difference between the State of Israel and other countries in the Middle East. Every regime in the Middle East had its own reasons for interfering with the way of life of the Bedouin tribes. However, when we examine the attitudes of the various authorities and regimes to the Bedouins throughout history, it seems that they all had similar goals: to restrict migration, to settle down the Bedouins, to control the bedouism, and to stop the tribal wars and the harassment of the permanent agricultural settlements. Efforts were also made to stop Bedouin control of commercial routes. The methods used to achieve these goals were different and varied.[4]

Bedouin Infiltration into the Galilee

The infiltration of Bedouin tribes into the Galilee began at the time of the Arab conquest in the seventh century CE and proceeded continuously until the twentieth century. The migration processes of the tribes were related to local factors of the areas of origin, such as tribal wars, blood conflicts, droughts, and others. The weak or defeated tribes were forced to leave their original habitat and migrate to mountainous areas in the north of Israel.[5]

More than half of the Bedouin tribes in the Galilee have come to the region over the past three hundred years from the Syrian desert, especially from the Hauran and Golan Heights, from western Iraq and northern Jordan.[6] According to Ben David, the tribes moved mainly on two axes: The first one ranged from the Syrian desert to the west, to the Sea of Galilee, which made the various groups settle in the Bēt She'an Valley and the Jezreel Valley.[7] Bēt Zarzir, Kaʿabiyya, and others are located on this axis. The second axis included the Golan Heights and the Ḥula Valley, which were adequate for the economic needs of the Bedouins in terms of grazing areas and security, since these areas had large vacant areas relative to other parts of the country (see Map 1).[8]

According to Gideon Golani, the infiltration of the Bedouins into the Galilee was mainly to uninhabited areas or rural areas, which were characterized by low population density.[9] Empty or semi-empty areas from settlements were found in the Galilee in several places:

- The swamps: Jezre'el Valley, Zevulun Valley, Bēt She'an Valley, and the Ḥula Valley. These areas were not used by the fellāḥīn, but they constituted good areas for grazing, and as a result, relatively large Bedouin tribes converged on them.
- The natural forest areas: the Alonim hills of Shfarʿam and Mount Kamūn. In these areas, only small plots of agricultural land can be found, but these areas are excellent for grazing.

- Rocky areas, especially areas covered with limestone, such as the Alonim-Shfarʿam hills. These areas could not be cultivated, and therefore no villages were established on them. On the other hand, it was possible to find there grazing areas for herds (map 2).

In the Galilee, certain tribes found the Ḥula Valley to be a suitable place for migration and settlement, such as the ʿArab el-Sawāed and Krād-el-Xait tribes, and part of the ʿArab el-Hēb and the Ġawārna, who settled in the Ḥula swamps. At the beginning of the twentieth century, the Ġawārna tribe resided in the Ḥula Valley. This tribe settled in twelve villages, the main one being Halita, the seat of the tribal leader. The tribe immigrated to the region in the second half of the eighteenth century from Umm el-Faḥm. They related the origin of their name to their presence in the area of *Al-Ġōr* (or *Al-Ġawr*) in the Jordan Valley. It should be noted, however, that the name al-Ġawārna was originally given to residents of different ethnic and geographic origins and referred to residents who had lived in the area in the past as well as to deserters and slaves from the Egyptian army and others. The tribe members largely maintained a rural lifestyle alongside the preservation of the Bedouin tradition.[10] According to the British census of 1931, the tribe was settled in thirty-four villages and was counted as rural rather than as a nomadic population.[11]

In the Bēt She'an Valley, four tribes—el-Bašātwah, el-Bawatiyya, el-Ġazawiya, and el-Tikur (the largest and most powerful of the tribes in the area)—tended their tents. In the northern part of the valley was a faction of the Bani Ṣaqr tribe, most of which concentrated on the eastern side of the Jordan River. The tribes that lived in the valley maintained flocks of sheep and cattle but also engaged in agriculture and traded with much of their crops.[12]

From the north came Turkmans, Horanis, Bosniaks (Muslims from Bosnia), and the Bedouin tribe of Al-Shqirat, who settled in the Haifa area. The tribes of ʿArab el-ʿArāmša, ʿArab el-Šamaliyya and ʿArab el-Hēb entered the Upper Galilee from the north through the crossing valleys.[13]

In his study, Falah (1990: 400) notes that about half of the Bedouin population in the Galilee in the nineteenth century originates in non-Bedouin population groups: Turkmān, Kurdish, tribes from the Maghreb and North Africa, a tribe of Gypsy origin, and fellāḥīn who adopted a nomadic lifestyle.[14]

A detailed British mapping of the Land of Israel from 1880 (PEF) notes sixty-seven Bedouin tribes in the territory of Mandatory Palestine.[15]

An analysis of the British census data in 1931 shows that the number of Bedouin tribes that have penetrated arid or semiarid regions is small and that the number of those entering rain-fed areas is large. On the other hand, tribes that have penetrated arid or semiarid regions have larger populations. In the rainy and inhabited areas, small tribes or tribal fragments squeezed into areas between existing settlements.[16]

Bedouins in the Galilee at the End of the Ottoman period

Ottoman rule in the region lasted four hundred years (1516–1917). Ostensibly, the Ottomans maintained a regime of law and administration, but this power could not subdue the Bedouins. They were equipped with firearms, and their great advantage was familiarity with and control of the desert. Therefore, the Ottoman regime succeeded in bringing the Bedouins under its authority only for short periods.

The Bedouins were known as the enemies of any powerful government, which, by its very nature and essence, was a barrier to their freedom and independence. Strong rule also tended to threaten one of their more important sources of livelihood, robbery and raid. Therefore, in every form of government, the Bedouins have always fought to maintain their autonomy.[17]

Shortly after the Ottoman conquest, Ottoman enemies in Europe and Persia began to fight the Bedouins until they were forced to withdraw their forces from the Arab provinces to participate in other wars. Thus, some of the Ottoman forces were also withdrawn from the Land of Israel, and, as a result, their military strength weakened. This caused Palestine to gradually come under Bedouin rule. Bedouin strengthening was also enabled by the flow of large quantities of weapons into their hands: weapons from European merchants and Ottoman soldiers and commanders were stolen from army warehouses and sold to the Bedouins. When the authorities tried to respond forcibly to Bedouin riots, they failed because of their lack of sophistication and smaller number of fighters.

The Crimean War (1853–56) contributed to the weakening of the Ottoman rule. The Land of Israel remained without military protection, and this enabled the Bedouins to expand their incursions into Israel. Other tribes penetrated from the eastern side of the Jordan. For example, the tribe of ʿArab el-Ṣaqr penetrated Kafr Kanna, took over the Jezreel Valley, and robbed the flocks of sheep and cattle in the valley that belonged to the inhabitants of Nazareth, Daburiya, and other nearby villages. Only after the end of the Crimean War and the return of the army to Israel did the Ottomans renew their harsh policy toward the Bedouin tribes. But the Bedouin tribal organization operated as a kind of military unit: they knew the country better, and their easy mobility with horses and camels enabled them to retreat to the rear of the desert, which made them invincible against both the villagers and the authorities. In addition, the Bedouins had large quantities of firearms—weapons that were generally superior to those of the Ottoman army.

The infiltration of Bedouin tribes into the Galilee was a result of the depletion of the population in the Galilee, due to the policies of the various rulers and the incessant wars that severely affected the rural population. The Bedouins settled in the low-population areas: in the valleys that were swamps—the Jezreel, Bēt She'an, and Zevulun Valleys. Others preferred to settle in low-populated areas such as Mount Meron and the Alonim-Šfarʿam hills. These tribes exploited their power to carry out raids on the agricultural areas and on the road convoys, undermining the regular life throughout the country and not only at the edge of the desert.[18]

The Bedouin tribes took control of the Galilee and other areas of the country. They engaged in robbery and looting during periods of separation between them and the government and ensured the security of the inhabitants during the periods in which they operated in the service of the Ottomans. During these periods, they made a living from collecting taxes or, more precisely, from collecting "protection fees." For example, Ashkenazi notes that until the British occupation in 1918, the collection of protection fees was a significant economic source for the tribes of ʿArab el-Hēb and ʿArab el-Ḥamdīn.[19]

In his study, Sa'id Kozali notes that the Ottoman authorities had to pay the tribal leaders who sat along the road to ensure the safety of pilgrim convoys on their way from Syria to Mecca.[20] The payment was intended to prevent the Bedouins from attacking and looting the convoys, but despite the payment, the Bedouins always found pretexts and justifications for their attacks. The Ottoman authorities tried to find a solution to the problem by building small fortresses along the way, which were also robbed by the Bedouins. Another strategy was to appoint important sheikhs who would defend the convoys themselves in exchange for land estates, payment, and other benefits. These sheikhs identified the weakness of the regime, and instead of carrying out the task assigned to them, they themselves became the leaders of the bandits. At the same time, the weakness of the government caused the growth of Bedouin families who had attained the status of rulers within the country, and the government had no choice but to recognize their rule.[21] The Ottomans appointed Bedouin sheikhs for high administrative posts, and they were given the rank of district governor. The most prominent of these sheikhs were members of the tribe of Terahai, who were concentrated in the Carmel region including Ğenin and the Jezreel Valley. Thaher al-Omar, from the Zidane tribe, ruled the northern part of Israel from the 1830s until the mid-1870s. In the nineteenth century, Sheikh Aqil al-Hassi was prominent in the Hanadi tribe, which took over large areas of the Galilee. Aqil's family came to the Land of Israel with the Egyptian conquest of Ibrahim Pasha (1830–1840).

The Bedouin takeover left destruction and ruins in the Galilee, and not only for its agriculture. Convoy robbery and the loss of road security devastated the entire economy. The important roads in the north of the country were ruled by the Bedouins. For example, the route from Tiberias to the Jordan Valley, to Nazareth, and to Nablus was ruled by the tribe of ʿArab el-Zikr. The Bedouins exploited their power and control over the roads to rob convoys and take road taxes. They were rewarded both as guides and as convoy guards and camels, and by leading convoys of their own.[22]

In the early nineteenth century, the country was in a state of great turmoil. The Bedouins exploited this and spread to various parts of the country, including the Galilee, the Jordan Valley, and the Jezreel Valley.[23] The impoverished villages that remained lived under the protection of the Bedouin tribes in the area of Nazareth and the Jezreel Valley. The two great tribes that wandered in this area were the children of Zikr and ʿArab el-Ṣbēḥ. These tribes forced the fellāḥīn to pay them a sponsorship tax (*khawa*). Nazareth and the neighboring villages also paid a considerable sum of money in the hope that they would not be robbed and that the Bedouin would allow herds to graze freely in the valley fields. In travelers' literature from the beginning of the nineteenth century, the Jezreel Valley is described as an area empty of peasants' settlements and as an area that serves as pasture for Bedouin herders. The Bēt She'an Valley is also described as very thinly populated. The sparse agricultural settlements had left significant grazing areas for the Bedouins. The few residents who survived in the Valley paid a guarantee tax to the Bedouins to insure themselves against their attacks.[24]

The influence of the Bedouins on the rural-agricultural population, on the state of agriculture, and on the nondevelopment of the area was crucial. The backward policies of the government caused the instability of the agricultural population in the area, and the peasants were forced to abandon their villages because of the frequent raids of the

Bedouins and their flocks' penetration into their grain fields.[25] Arieh Bitan-Buttenwieser describes the situation very well:

> The most influential factor in the eastern Galilee during the nineteenth century was undoubtedly the Bedouin tribes, whose influence on the rural population, on the state of agriculture, on the development of the region, in fact, on its lack of development, was decisive. It has more significance than the influence of natural factors, such as land and water, and confirms the results of the failed policies of the Ottoman government. Their frequent raids into the villages and the raising of their flocks on the farmers' fields of grain forced the villagers to frequently abandon their villages and wander away from them. The villagers were unable to take care of the minimum required for their existence and certainly not improve the economic situation.[26]

Around the middle of the nineteenth century, there were raids by Bedouin tribes, Beni Saqr, ʿArab el-Ṣaqr, and ʿArab el-Ṣbēḥ, across the Jordan River. But they did not try to settle.

By the second half of the nineteenth century, the northern part of the country was a wild and deserted area. The Ottoman rule neglected the area, and the Bedouins roamed there without restriction. Bedouin tribes across the eastern Jordan River used to infiltrate into the north of Israel, mainly through the Jordan Valley and the Bēt She'an Valley, to steal and rob.

In an attempt to gain control of the Bedouin tribes, the Ottoman government published the Land Law in 1858 and the Taboo Law in 1861. These laws defined the types of land and the right to ownership and regulated the issue of tax collection. Among other things, the law states that all arable land, which for three consecutive years has not been cultivated and remains desolate, loses private rights over it and is transferred to the state.

Some of the Bedouins, especially those who were far from the cities and villages, did not register ownership of the land. Others did not want to pay taxes or feared their sons would be enlisted into the army. Thus, they were forced to become tenants, and most of their lands were registered in the names of mukhtars, effendis, and land dealers.[27] Through this law, the state confiscated the lands of the Jezreel Valley from the tribe of Beni Ṣaqr. In the end of the second half of the nineteenth century, the security situation in Israel improved, but this improvement was far from satisfactory. The tribe of ʿArab el-Ṣaqr was expelled from the Galilee toward the Jordan River, but in 1877 the tribe reconquered the area between Tiberias and Bēt She'an.[28]

Only toward the end of the nineteenth century did the security situation improve, which contributed to the gradual submission of the Bedouin tribes, mainly because of the reforms introduced to restrict Bedouins' migration freedom. The immediate result of the reforms was that many of the Bedouin tribes had to start paying taxes to the treasury of the Ottoman regime.[29] The power of the Bedouin tribes was weakening. Restraining them stopped many robberies; the raids on the settlements diminished, and the yoke of the sponsorship tax, which the Bedouins demanded, was removed from the fellāḥīn. Thus, in the description of Oliphant in 1883, the Jezreel Valley is already described as an exemplary agricultural area of the local fellāḥīn villages.[30]

The Ottomans understood that the only way to restrain the Bedouin tribes was to settle them in permanent settlements and to change the nomadic way of life, as they had already successfully done in the Anatolia region of Turkey. These attempts generally failed not only because of the resistance to give up the nomadic way of life but also because in their settlement attempts, the authorities failed to protect the settlers from strong tribes. The Bedouin tribes, which were gradually crushed by the Ottomans, were also forced to accept the need to find alternative sources of employment, including the transition to being hired workers. Many of them worked in the Jewish *moshavot* (settlements), and some of them were employed as guards, whose function was to protect the crops from thieves who in many cases were their friends.[31]

However, toward the end of the Ottoman rule, with the outbreak of the First World War, the Ruwāla tribe, whose living areas extended between the Damascus basin and the northern border of Saudi Arabia, invaded the Galilee. This invasion, made possible by the weakness of the Turkish government, caused the destruction of agriculture in the north of the country. The residents of the villages were weak and could not defend themselves against the invaders, and the government did not provide them with protection; the Bedouin invaders even returned to collect protection money from the new peasants.[32]

Mazarib claims that at the end of the Ottoman rule, there were in the Galilee forty-seven tribes, of whom only four tribes numbered more than six hundred people and the whole Bedouin population in the Galilee numbered about thirty thousand.[33]

Bedouins in the Galilee during the British Mandate

At the end of the First World War, and in the framework of the San Remo Accords of April 1920, the Allies formally granted a mandate to France for Syria and Lebanon and Britain for Palestine, Transjordan, and Iraq. In 1920, Israel's northern political border was established between the British and the French authorities. In this context, it is important to remember that the Bedouins by nature do not recognize state borders but recognize grazing areas. The Bedouins view political borders as an arbitrary buffer, contrary to their needs. The political framework is unacceptable to them, since their connection is directed only to a tribal organization. For the Bedouins, the state is a factor imposed on them, and at this stage it was impossible to cooperate with it honestly.[34]

The Bedouin tribes, who were greatly strengthened militarily by the seizure of weapon depots abandoned by the disintegrating Turkish army, did not realize that their military might was not suited to dealing with modern armies. An example of this is an attempt led by the Bedouin tribe of ʿArab el-Ġazawiyya to conquer Zemah in April 1920.[35] Prior to the assault, several Bedouin meetings were held on both sides of the Jordan, and it was decided which tribes would take part in the mission, how many riders each tribe would have, and how they would share the wealth of the colonies and their women.

This is described in the history of the Haganah:[36] "The next morning on Saturday morning, April 24, 1920, the attackers stormed Zemach—[they were] arranged in rows, rows extending several kilometers. . . . At the head were the riders and after them foot-soldiers. . . . The Indian army, fortified behind the railway station and a battery of protective excavations. . . . The attackers dispersed in panic, and the Indian cavalry, together with the Jewish defenders, charged the fugitives."[37]

In the northernmost section of the Galilee, called the "finger of the Galilee," bordered by Lebanon to the north and the Golan Heights to the east, the Bedouin tribes rebelled against the French rule and Christian villages. The tribe of ʿArab el-Faḍl, headed by Emīr Maḥmūd al-Faʿūr, was quite prominent in the revolt against the regime. Other tribes also joined the revolt, such as the ʿArab el-Hēb and ʿArab el-Krād.[38] The revolt, although not directed specifically against Jewish settlements, caused regional insecurity and ultimately the abandonment of the Jewish settlements. Israelis are familiar with the rebellion mainly from the skirmish at Tel Hai, where the small force of Jewish fighters were vanquished by Arabs. It took the French a few months to manage all of Syria, the Ḥula Valley, and its finger of the Galilee. In the meantime, the political negotiations between England and France continued over the delineation of the borders, and in December 1920, the agreement was signed in San Remo, according to which the entire area was under British rule.

The infiltrations of the Bedouin tribes into the Galilee also took place during the British Mandate period, but they gradually diminished as the government stabilized. In 1917, the Ruwāla tribe invaded the Syrian Desert. Armed with English weapons, they tried to collect a protection tax from the settlements in the Galilee. The residents of the *moshavot* (settlements) also paid them this tax.[39] In 1920, families from the Beni-Xāled tribe entered the Galilee and reached as far as Bēt-Gan and Yavniel, and in 1924 they again penetrated the Galilee. From northern Jordan, families from the Beni-Ḥasan tribe reached Nahalal in the Jezreel Valley, and in 1927, families from the Beni-Ṣaqr tribe entered the Galilee. It was cold, and they returned and invaded again in 1932. The last infiltration of a Bedouin tribe into the Galilee took place in 1934.

The British and French governments were harassed by the raids of the Bedouins and their flocks' grazing on the villagers' cultivated land, sometimes accompanied by an even more aggressive aspect, such as robbery or demands for payment for protection of the villages and weak Bedouin tribes. The authorities also feared that the Bedouins would cross the new political borders established in the area.[40]

The political borders established in the north began to restrict the migration of several tribes. The borders crossed the migratory areas of tribes such as ʿArab el-ʿArāmša and ʿArab el-Ḥamdūn on the Lebanese border. In the east, along the Jordan River, the historical migrations of the Arab tribes of el-Ṣaqr, ʿArab el-Ġazawiya, ʿArab el-Bašatwah, and ʿArab el-Buʿati, who were assembled in the Bēt She'an Valley, were connected to their main quarters in Transjordan.[41]

The government tightened control over the Bedouin tribes near the newly created political borders, for fear of smuggling, the spread of diseases, and border incidents. The established limitations had an effect on the traditional livelihood means of the tribes, but a new economic branch was opened: the tribes of ʿArab el-Hēb, ʿArab el-Ḥamām, and ʿArab el-ʿArāmša, which were located near the borders, made the smuggling industry a significant source of income.

In 1926, some arrangements were made between the British and the French that allowed some Bedouin tribes to cross the borders to find pasture and water. However, for this purpose, the Bedouins were forced, for the first time, to carry passports and mark their flocks.[42] The law required every tribe—whether nomadic or seminomadic—who wished to move to another territory to apply for a transit permit from the British district officer.

During the period of the Great Arab Revolt of 1936–39, cooperation between the Bedouin tribes in the Galilee and the Arab rural population increased in attacks on the British and Zionist establishment and infrastructure, under the common name of Palestinian Arab Nationalism. The cooperation accelerated the process of settlement of many Bedouins in the Arab villages.[43]

The British Mandate adopted a moderate policy toward the Bedouins until the early 1940s. The high commissioner felt committed to maintaining the law and refrained from intervening in the internal affairs of the Bedouins as long as the law was preserved. The Bedouins were not required to have work permits or licenses to carry weapons or to trade in animals. In drought years, the British authorities came to the aid of the Bedouins and saved their flocks by transferring them to the Bēt She'an Valley in 1928 and to the Carmel region in the drought of 1946. Simultaneously, the British prohibited the Bedouins from collecting sponsorship taxes from agricultural villages or weak tribes or conducting raids (ġazu) on agricultural villages. They introduced new regulations (Collective Punishments Ordinance, or CPO) that allowed for the collective punishment of the tribes and established the "indirect government" system, which placed the collective responsibility for tribal affairs on the head of the tribe.

In 1942, the British promulgated the Bedouin control regulations, the main purpose of which was to provide tools that would help the government control the tribes and convince them to move to a permanent settlement.[44] Along with the regional security increase, the Bedouin grazing areas decreased. Villagers began to cultivate lands where the Bedouin used to graze, far from the villages. Massive land purchases began by Jewish settlement bodies, municipal systems and industrial areas developed, and forests were planted. As a result, the Bedouin tribes' migratory areas diminished.[45]

The effect of the above developments on the lives of the Bedouins can be demonstrated in a 1946 letter to the Nazareth district commissioner: "You know very well that this is our only land left to our tribe for grazing, and if this land is taken by the afforestation department, we will not be left with any land to graze our flocks. . . .We will become prisoners in our homes and surrounded by barbed wire fences."[46]

As a result of increasing British control, we can see in the 1940s a clear trend among the Bedouins in the Galilee: purchasing land from anyone who agreed to sell. Since they did not have the capital to buy large plots of land, families bought small plots according to their ability and according to the village land offerings. They were sold marginal land, which was often very poor in quality, and cheap plots of land that were scattered.[47] However, these limited areas were sufficient to make the Bedouins feel that they had a home and an inheritance. As a result of this process, most of the major tribes, such as ʿArab el-Sawāʿed or ʿArab el-Neʿēm, were forced to disperse geographically, which led to their weakening.

According to the first population estimate conducted by the British authorities in 1922, the nomadic Bedouins in the Galilee numbered 17,000, while in the second population estimate in 1931, they numbered only 11,500. These numbers indicate an intensive settlement process both in independent Bedouin communities and in the Arab towns and villages in the Galilee. In the third population estimate conducted by the British authorities in 1946, the nomadic Bedouin in the Galilee numbered less than 10,000 residents. This indicates the continuation of the process of permanent settlement.[48]

The Bedouins, who were forced to reduce herds because of the reduction in migratory areas, had to find an alternative economic growth. One alternative created during the Mandate period was paid labor, mainly as unskilled workers in the construction, agriculture, and industrial sectors. The Bedouins quickly discovered that paid work was more economical than raising herds. There began a rapid transition to permanent housing, and the need for transportable tents decreased. The Bedouins began moving to settlements characterized by permanence, such as permanent tents, tin dwellings, shacks, and even stone houses.

The transition to permanent residence created a large number of permanent hamlets, usually in geographical locations where the tribe used to wander or, in some cases, on lands purchased by the tribe. In most cases the settlements, established without any planning or infrastructure, dispersed over very large areas.

Map 3, based on the map of Ashkenazi, with a few corrections, presents the spreading of the tribes at the end of the British Mandate period.

The Impact of the Early Jewish Settlement on the Bedouin Tribes in the Galilee

With the beginning of the Jewish settlement in the Galilee, the relationship between the Jewish settlers and the Bedouins began to crystallize. Most of the land purchases took place in the sparsely populated, uninhabited, and marshy areas where the land was cheap and available. These places were also favored by Bedouin tribes. Sawā'ed argues in his study that clashes between Bedouin and Jewish settlers did not usually deviate from the sphere of relations between neighbors.[49]

According to Falah, the purchase of land by the Jews in the Galilee in the 1920s and 1930s was mainly focused in areas with low agricultural populations, areas where Bedouin tribes' herds tended to graze: the Ḥula Valley, the Sea of Galilee area, the Bēt She'an Valley, the Jezreel Valley, and the coastal plain.[50] As a result, the first settlements in the Galilee were located mainly on lands that had previously served as grazing land for the Bedouins, and therefore the tribes' migratory space was restricted, limiting the tribal migration range. Thus, for example, the settlements of Yavne'el and Bēt Gan were established on land where the ʿArab el-Dalāiqa tribe lived. Mesḥa was established on lands where the ʿArab a-Ṣbēḥ tribe lived.[51] Rosh Pina, Yesod Ha-Maʿala, and Mishmar Ha-Yarden were established on lands where the ʿArab el-Sawāʿed tribe was located.[52] Kfar HaNasi was built on lands purchased from the ʿArab el-Hēb tribe.[53] Nahalal was established on the pasture of the Mazārīb tribe. The settlement of Yokne'am was established on lands purchased from the Kaʿabiyya tribe.[54]

The contacts between the populations were characterized by quarrels and provocations. The first settlers were foreign to the way of life that was common in Israel, and provocation erupted mainly as a result of mutual misunderstanding. The Bedouin tribes, which treated private property with contempt, ignored property rights over land and water sources. They used to go to the fields and use them as if they were their own. The small property found in the colonies, the flora and fauna, attracted their Bedouin neighbors who did not yet respect the property rights of others. They tried, both as a tribe and as individuals, to steal property from wherever they could. It was the Bedouin tradition that motivated them to robbery, a tradition that saw robbery as a legitimate source of income.[55]

In the Bedouin tradition, various laws relating to property on land, on crops, and on water were practiced according to the seasons of the year. As a result, disputes arose over the use of the settlement lands for grazing and for irrigation purposes.[56]

In the water sources, the Bedouin saw a gift of nature meant for all. When the Jewish settlers began to develop these water sources for irrigation purposes and expropriated them from general use, the Bedouins grew bitter and attacked the inhabitants of the *moshavot*. For example, Muhammad Sawā'ed reports on a quarrel that broke out in 1883 between the Arab tribe of Zanġariyya, which had migrated with their herds on the land east of Moshav Rosh Pina, and the settlement that had concentrated three springs into a channel for irrigating fields and a pond for watering the herds of the *moshava*.[57]

When the Jews appropriated the lands from their owners, they sought to exercise their rights: to settle and cultivate them. Acting in accordance with the principle that the owner of the land had the right to graze, they removed the shepherds by force. The water sources were also perceived as private property, and therefore they strongly opposed the Bedouins watering their flocks from the same sources of water. The Bedouins rebelled against the notion that it was not possible to graze on grass that was the gift from Allah, and was free to all, as it had been for generations. In many cases, tenant farmers lived on land purchased by the Jews; some were fellāḥīn, and some were Bedouins who refused to evacuate the land.[58] The Bedouins' difficulty in leaving the land given over to tenant farming was due, inter alia, to the fact that they did not have alternative places to move to.[59]

For example, in those days the Lower Galilee was a remote and forgotten area, a wild area that served as a convenient passage for the Bedouin tribes across the eastern Jordan to the Bēt She'an Valley for grazing and robbery. The purchase of the first lands in the Lower Galilee provoked unrest and resistance among the Bedouin tribes in the area.

The members of the ʿArab Dalāiqa tribe refused to leave the grazing lands in the area near the settlements of Yavne'el and Bēt Gan, which led to a bloody conflict with the settlements. The members of the tribe of ʿArab el-Ṣbēḥ refused to peacefully evacuate the lands of the settlement of Mesḥa, which were purchased by Yehoshua Hankin. On the other hand, there were tribes who preferred not to quarrel with the Jews and left the lands purchased for the establishment of the settlements. Thus behaved, for example, the tribe ʿArab el-Sawāʿed, which at the end of the nineteenth century had wandered into the region of Ḥula-Safed. Following the purchase of the land for the establishment of Rosh Pina, Yesod Hama'ala, and Mishmar Hayarden in 1882–84, the tribe left their grazing area and moved to Mount Kamon and the Zalmon Valley, which was lacking in population and good for grazing.

On the other side, the establishment of *moshavot* (settlements) in the Galilee also created wage-earning employment sources for the Bedouin, mainly in guard posts and as transporters of agricultural produce on camels. Thus, for example, the Rosh Pina settlement provided protection to Bedouins from the Zanġariyya tribe.[60] As a result, a relationship of interdependence ensued: the Bedouins who camped at the edge of the settlements with their flocks used to sabotage agricultural equipment and crops. The solution was to entrust the guard duty with them. At the same time, the settlers were completely dependent on the Bedouins for their agricultural produce and, therefore, tried very hard to cultivate a close and friendly relationship with them.[61]

The Jewish colonies refused to pay protection fees to the Bedouin tribes, and when they didn't, there was an increase in robbery and theft intended to force the settlers to pay. The thefts did not stop even when the *moshavim* surrendered and paid the guards for protection. Thus, the idea of the Hebrew watchmen developed. The foundation of the *Hashomer* (the Watchmen) organization (1920–90) pushed the Bedouins out of guard duty, and they remained disgruntled and resentful and felt free to harass the Jewish settlement.

The growth of the Jewish community in the Galilee coincided with the growth of the Arab national awakening. With the expansion of the areas of land purchased by the Zionist movement, the confrontation between Arabs and Jewish settlements increased. The Bedouins became embroiled in a growing political struggle between the Zionist movement and the Palestinian national movement.[62] The conflict sharpened relations between the Jewish community and Bedouin rivals or sympathizers. Some of the Bedouin tribes helped the Jewish community in its struggle against members of the Palestinian national movement because of personal connections created with Bedouin neighbors. For example, the Dayan family nurtured relations with the members of the ʿArab el-Mazārīb tribe. The citizens of Rosh Pina and the Alon family cultivated the members of the ʿArab el-Hēb tribe, and Giora Zaid nurtured a relationship with the members of the ʿArab el-Sawāʿed tribe. Moshe Dayan and Yigal Allon led their Bedouins with whom they had cultivated a relationship into the ranks of the Palmach ("strike force"), which was established in 1941, and into the Haganah's intelligence network, which was open to military service and fighting alongside the Jews during the War of Independence.[63] Some of the Bedouin tribes took part in the activities of the gangs and joined the Palestinian national camp. They were to pay a price during the War of Independence in 1948.

The Impact of the War of Independence on the Bedouin Tribes in the Galilee

The War of Independence was a fateful turning point for the Bedouin tribes. The immediate change was in the area of demographic and geographical expansion. In 1951, the Bedouins in the Galilee numbered less than 6,500 of the nearly 20,000 people listed in the British census in 1931.[64]

The war caused the flight of a significant portion of the Bedouin tribes in the Galilee to neighboring Arab countries. Many tribes that did not want to be controlled by the Jews or that believed the Jews would be defeated and they could return to their homes fled during the war to neighboring Arab countries: Lebanon, Syria, and Jordan. Bedouin tribes associated with the Arab gangs and the Arab Liberation Army fled for fear of Jewish revenge for their actions during the period of the state in the making. This is true of the Turkmens, ʿArab el-Dalāiqa, ʿArab el-Mawāsi, ʿArab el-Ṣaqr, ʿArab el-Qadriya, ʿArab el-Bawti, and others. There were also tribes such as the el-Rasatma branch from ʿArab el-Hēb, some of the Arabs of el-Samaniah, and some of the ʿArab el-Swēṭāt who fled from the Arab Liberation Army, which they feared because of their connections to Jewish settlements and especially because they feared they might be considered traitors because of the sale of land to Jews.[65]

There were tribes who left the country following the promises of Arab leaders that at the end of the fighting they would return to their homes. A number of tribes whose living areas were located on both sides of the international border preferred to move to a neighboring country. A clear example of this is the tribe of ʿArab el-Ṣaqr, whose living areas spread over both sides of the Jordan Valley. Other tribes, especially Bedouin tribes associated with the Arab gangs and the Arab Liberation Army, were expelled from Israel during the battles and in the early years of the state.[66]

Mazarib brings data about the impact of the war on Bedouin tribes in the Galilee. He claims that nearly 9,000 Bedouins moved to neighboring countries as a result of escape or deportation. The number of Bedouins who remained in the Galilee was estimated at 17,500 residents: about 13,000 in Arab towns and villages; 3,000 in Bedouin settlements; and about 1,500 nomadic Bedouins.[67]

Almost every tribe that migrated to a neighboring country left behind families or a fragment of a tribe who found refuge with Bedouin tribes that remained in the country or in Arab villages.[68] The Bedouin tribes that remained in the Galilee remained mostly in their prewar areas. Only tribes near the Syrian border were moved from there. The members of Krād el-Baqara and Krād el-Ġanameh, who lived in the demilitarized zone south of the Ḥula Lake, were transferred to Šaʿab and Šafarʿam. Some of them were even transferred to Syria in 1956. A group of residents of the ʿArab el-Ġawārna tribe, who lived in the Ḥula Valley, were transferred to Wādi Ḥamām at the foot of the Arbel.[69]

Bedouin tribes that stayed within the state area were mainly concentrated in five geographical areas:

1. Alonim-Shfarʿam Hills: The Bedouin tribes remained there mainly because of their economic and social relations with the Jewish settlements in the area. The relation of Nahalal people with the Mazārīb, el-Ġrifāt, el-Ğawamīs, and el-Ḥuğērāt tribes led these tribes to remain in Israel. The ʿArab el-Xawāled and el-ʿUmariyya tribes remained in the area as a result of their relations with Kibbutz Ramat Yohanan and Kfar HaMaccabi. The members of Zbēdāt were friends with Kibbutz Shaʿar Haʿamakim.

2. Bēt Netofa Valley: The Bedouin tribes of ʿArab el-Neğēdāt and ʿArab el-Hēb (the Falaḥāt branch) remained in Israel because of their connections with the Haganah.

3. The Zalmon bloc: The Bedouin tribes of ʿArab el-Sawāʿed, ʿArab el-Mresāt, ʿArab el-Ḥamdūn, and ʿArab el-Neʿēm remained in Israel because they were surrounded by the Israeli Defense Forces (IDF) during the occupation of the Galilee, and also because of their good relations with the Jews.

4. Mount Tabor area: Most of the ʿArab el-Ṣbēḥ tribe had joined the Arab Liberation Army in the region. Only the branch of Šibli remained in the area because of its relations with the Haganah. From the residents of the ʿArab el-Saʿāida tribe, only families who owned agricultural land remained in their place.

5. Ṭūba area: Here most of the residents of ʿArab el-Hēb and Zanġaria remained in their place because of their economic and security relations with the Jewish inhabitants of the *moshavot* (settlements) and kibbutzim in the area, as well as their military enlistment alongside the Jews in the war.

After the 1948 war, all the Bedouin tribes in the Galilee were under martial law (1948–66), which accelerated the process of transition to spontaneous settlement because of the limitations of work and movement that characterized the period.

The Great Tribes in the Galilee during the British Mandate Period

ʿArab el-Faḍel: They came from an ancient Bedouin tribe in Iraq that emigrated to the Golan in the fifteenth century. The tribe members attribute their origin to the family of the "sherifs," the family of the Prophet Muḥammad.[70] The tribe wandered in the area between the Bnot Yaakov Bridge in the south, Quneitra in the east, and Banias in the north. The tribe took control of most of the land in the Golan Heights, especially the fertile areas northwest of Quneitra. In the winter, they wandered to the area of Lake Ḥula and sometimes wandered to the Jezreel Valley. The head of the tribe also controlled the small tribes found in the Golan, which were mostly farmers.[71]

ʿArab el-Hēb: The tribe originated in Yemen and emigrated during the Islamic conquest of Iraq. The tribe entered the Land of Israel probably in the seventeenth century. During the Ottoman period, the tribe wandered in the Golan Heights and eventually settled in the Ḥula Valley in Ṭūba area. It was a strong tribe that imposed its authority over the villages and tribes of Safed and the Ḥula Valley. About one hundred years ago, the tribe was split by the Ottoman regime to weaken its great power, which was used to suppress the villages of fellāḥīn who lived in the Ḥula Valley. The tribe split into different tribes who lived in several geographical areas. ʿArab el-ʿAǧārma, which wandered in the Golan Heights; Attia, which was located in the area of Ṭūba, east of Rosh Pina, and which began building permanent dwellings in the 1940s; and the ʿArab el-Resatma clan, which dwelled in the area between Bar'am and Sasa northwest of Safed.[72] All the families fled to Lebanon in 1948. The Murdāt clan moved to the Dishon River area, and in 1948 most of the clan's residents fled to Lebanon. Nine families now live in the Jewish settlement Yaʿara. The Fuwwāz clan moved to the village of ʿĒlabūn. The clan of Fallāḥāt and the clan of Bešaira moved to the Bēt Netofa Valley area, on the northern slopes of

Mount Ṭur'an. Some of them bought land in the area of the village of 'Uzayer and some in Rūmat Hēb (Frush Rummāna). The Hēb Abu-Ṣiāḥ clan now has a neighborhood in Zarzīr, where they purchased land in 1943. They chose to move to the Alonim-Šfar'am hills because it was mostly a natural forest compared to the Bēt Netofa Valley, which was entirely cultivated by fellāḥīn from nearby villages.

'Arab el-Ḥuğērāt: Their origin is west of el-Liğah, in Syria, where single families joined a tribe that infiltrated the Land of Israel in the seventeenth century via northern Jordan and settled in several places in the Galilee. During the British Mandate, they found their livelihood in the Dahara area on Mount Atzmon. They mainly concentrated near Kafr Manda, Zippori, and Rommāna. Today most of them live in the village of Bīr-Maksūr, where they built their homes on privately owned land. Another part of the tribe settled in Dmēda, not far from Kafr Manda (the village got status of recognized settlement in 1995). Other parts settled near Acre and in the Bēt Netofa Valley.[73]

'Arab el-Ṣbēḥ: This tribe is considered one of the strongest in the Galilee. It originates from Ḥeğāz. Members of the tribe believe that they are descendants of Ṣabḥa—the daughter of the great Muslim commander Xālid Ibn el-Walīd. The tribe arrived to the Liğah area in the north of the Ḥauran, in southern Syria, and entered the Land of Israel through the Yarmuk Valley at the end of the seventeenth century. The tribe took control of much of the Lower Galilee, and its expansion spread over the Alonim-Šfar'am hills, Bēt Netofa, and around Mount Tabor.[74] Members of the tribe actively participated in the Arab revolt, primarily in the years 1936–39.[75] Most of the tribe fled to Jordan in 1948.[76] One clan, the Šibli clan, remained in Israel and lives in a recognized Bedouin village on the northern slope of Mount Tabor.

'Arab el-Rummāna-Ṣbēḥāt: A faction of the 'Arab-El-Ṣbēḥ tribe that moved to the village of Rummāna in the Bēt Netofa Valley in the late nineteenth century. Today most of them are located in the village of Zalafah and Salam by the 'Iron River, as well as in Basmat Ṭab'ūn.

'Arab el-Mawāsi: The tribe entered the Land of Israel in the nineteenth century, apparently from Egypt or Libya. During the British Mandate, it was considered the largest tribe in the Galilee. First, they settled in the Ḥula Valley and then wandered to other sites: near the village of Fasuta, northwest of Tiberias, and near Acre. Since many residents of the tribe participated in the Arab Revolt, they fled to southern Lebanon in 1948.[77]

'Arab el-Sawā'ed: One of the largest tribes in the Galilee, they settled in several places: near Acre, where they were known as 'Arab el-Ramel, and near Shfar'am, in a place called Ḥamīra. A third part wandered between Safed and Ḥula, and a fourth part in the Zalmon River area.[78] Today most of the tribe lives in the Bedouin settlements of Salāmeh and Kamāna in the area of the Zalmon River.

'Arab el-Turkmān: They settled in the southeastern part of the Jezreel Valley and in the sands between Caesarea and Binyamina. Another faction settled in the Golan Heights. The tribe belongs to the Turkish peoples. It originated in Anatolia. Their presence is known in the region from the Crusades' time. The penetration of the Turkmān tribes continued in the Mamluk period and after the Ottoman conquest.[79]

ʿArab el-Ṣaqr: They emigrated following the war with members of the Ṣaqr-Manǧad tribe. This tribe was considered the largest and most powerful in the Bēt She'an Valley. It originated in the Al-Sardiya tribe in Ḥeǧāz (Saudi Arabia) and wandered to the Ḥauran area.[80] In the seventeenth century, they entered the Land of Israel. The tribe's living area was part of the eastern side of the Jordan River and part of the southwestern section of the Bēt She'an Valley.[81]

ʿArab el-Bašātwa: Originating in Ḥeǧaz, they migrated to Iraq, then to Jordan, and from there they entered the Bēt She'an Valley. They settled east of the tribe of Bani Ṣaqr, between Gesher and Bēt She'an. Some claim that their Kurdish origin is similar to that of the Kurdish tribes in the Hula Valley.[82]

ʿArab el-Ġazwiyya: The tribe originated from the Gaza region, where it had migrated from Yemen before the Ottoman conquest of Yemen. During the period of Sultan Selim in the sixteenth century, they moved to Ḥauran. Eventually, they settled east and southeast of Bēt She'an, west of the Arab tribe of Bašatwa.[83]

ʿArab-Ṭabʿūn: This tribe includes two sociocultural groups: Kuskus and Ṭabʿūn. In the State of Israel, they received the united name Kuskus-Ṭabʿūn.[84]

ʿArab Zbēdāt: The origin of this tribe is the tribe of the el-Kaʿab in Ḥeǧāz. At the end of the nineteenth century, the tribe arrived there via Jordan and settled in the area of Sheikh Abrek and Ḥartiya (near Shaʿar Ha'amakim). Today most of them live in Basmat Ṭabʿūn.

ʿArab el-Ḥilf: This tribe was formed in the Galilee in the early 1920s as a result of the establishment of a protective alliance between families originating from different tribes. Today, they are two different tribes living in separate settlements two kilometers apart: Ḥilf Ṭabbāš, which belongs to the group of Kaʿabiyya, and Ḥilf Umm-Rashed, which joined the community in Basmat Ṭabʿūn. The origin of the members of ʿArab el-Ḥilf-Ṭabbāš is in the tribe of ʿArab el-Huzayel, a Negev tribe that lives north of Beersheba and that originated in the Sinai desert.

Krād el-Baqāra and Krād el-Ġanameh: The names of the tribes testify to their means of livelihood: sheep and cattle. Their origin is from Kurdistan. They probably came to the region in the twelfth century. The tribes were seminomadic, and they moved from Syria to the south of the Ḥula Valley. Over the years, many families of diverse origins, some of whom were slaves of African descent, have become clans. After the Independence War, their villages were found in the demilitarized zone between Israel and Syria. During the war, most of the residents fled to the Golan Heights (Syria). Some of the residents who remained in Israel were transferred to Shfarʿam in 1948, some to the village of Šaʿab, and some to Ṭūba Zanġaria. Some of the residents returned to their homes in the Ḥula Valley, and in 1956, the Israeli government decided to deport them to Syria, and their villages were destroyed.[85]

Zanġariyya: The tribe's origin is in Turkey. They apparently came from fellahin, and over the years, they lost their village characteristics and became semi-Bedouin. During the British Mandate period, the tribe lived in the Ḥula Valley. Today it is a branch of the village of Ṭūba-Zanġaria near Kibbutz Maḥanayim.[86]

ʿArab al-Dalāika: One of the largest Bedouin tribes that migrated south of the Sea of Galilee. Most of the tribe moved to a peasant lifestyle in the late nineteenth century. To supplement their income, they used to raid the Jewish colonies in the area. The settlements Kinneret, Degania, and Yavne'el were founded on the land sold in 1905 to the Jewish Colonization Association. The tribe was evacuated from the land only toward the end of the British Mandate period. Almost all of the tribe emigrated to Jordan in 1948.[87] Some families remained in Basmat Tav'un.

ʿArab-Ḥamdūn: During the British Mandate, the tribe lived in the Naftali Mountains around Nabi Yosha. Today, some of them are located near the settlement of Lotem and some in Yafiʿa near Nazareth.

ʿArab el-Neğēdāt: This tribe wandered in the 1940s into the Bēt Netofa Valley. Today they inhabit the village of Bʿēneh-Neğēdāt. The Neğēdāt are of Bedouin origin, and the people of Bʿēneh are villagers. According to the tribe tradition, they originate from Bedouin soldiers from Saudi Arabia, who fought in Ṣalāḥ al-Dīn's army, and the name of the tribe is derived from the name Nağed, an area in the middle of the Arabian Peninsula.

ʿArab el-Merisāt: The tribe emigrated from Syria in the middle of the eighteenth century. During the British Mandate period, they lived in the Shfarʿam region. Today, the tribe is scattered in several places: some of them live in Wādi Salāmeh, some in an unrecognized village near ʿAdi and Harduf, and others in ʿEilabun, Shfarʿam, Ṭamra, Yafiʿa, and Naḥef.

ʿArab el-ʿArāmšah: They still dwell today as they did during the Mandate period, on the border of the Lebanon, near Ḥanita. Part of the tribe moved to Lebanon in 1948.

ʿArab as-Saʿadiyya: This tribe is of Turkman origin, and they are also called Kaḥilāth. According to Yuval Arnon, the tribe came from Egypt and arrived at the area during the period of Muhammad Ali.[88] During the British Mandate, the tribe settled in the lands of Kira and Kammon in the Yokneʿam area. Following the purchase of the Kira and Kemon lands by the Jewish National Fund and Yehoshua Ḥankin in 1935, the tribe split into two groups. One group is now known as ʿArab el-Kaʿabiyyah and lives in the village of Kaʿabiyyah, a settlement established in 1941 with the help of compensation money the tribe received from Yehoshua Ḥankin. The second group settled in 1943 in Umm el-Ġanam. Another group lives in the village of Manšiyyat Zabda in the northern Jezreel Valley. Most of the tribe fled in 1948 to the Ğenin area.

ʿArab el-Ġrifāt: The origin of the tribe is the ʿArab el-Mawāli tribe, which is now in Syria and is probably descended from a Gypsy tribe from central Asia. In the middle of the eighteenth century, the tribe provided eighty guards to the son of Ḍaher al-ʿOmar of the Zaydān tribe, with whom they were in a defensive alliance. Over time, the number of people grew, and a new Bedouin tribe was created in the Galilee in the area of Shfarʿam. Over the years, the tribe wandered to the area of Kira (Yokneʿam), the tribe grew and became quite strong. In time, it split into several clans. The clan of Sirḥān migrated to the southern Carmel region of ʿEin Hod, the Šatweh clan migrated to the Bēt She'an Valley, the Tachmar clan migrated to the Tivʿon Forest area, the Nimrān clan migrated to the Alonim-Shfarʿam hills, and the Sahiyon clan moved to the Kurdani region of

Haifa Bay. At the end of the Ottoman period, the tribal *mukhtār* purchased lands from the Lebanese land dealer Sursuk in the hills of Alonim-Shfarʿam, and three of the five clans regrouped and today constitute the tribe of ʿArab el-Ġrifāt. Today the tribe is in a neighborhood in Bēt Zarzīr.

ʿArab el-Ġazālīn: The origin of the tribe is across the Jordan River. In the late Ottoman period, they wandered to the village of Iksāl in the Jezreel Valley. In the Alonim-Shfarʿam hills, the tribe had a number of *ʿizbāt* (seasonal tents). In 1948, many people of the tribe fled to Jordan. During the period of military rule, the remaining members of the tribe were transferred to the area of Bēt Zarzīr near the tribe of ʿArab el-Mazārīb. In the 1960s, some of them moved to Nazareth and Yafi'a, and some remained in a separate neighborhood in Bēt Zarzīr.

ʿArab el-Mazārīb: This tribe is not an organic Bedouin tribe but consists of individuals or individual families who have had to flee at various times from their mother tribes. They gathered together over time in the area of the Alonim-Shfarʿam hills. The Mazārīb is not a name based on a common ethnic origin but rather a geographical designation of their area of residence in the Alonim-Shfarʿam hills. This clan mainly includes members of four clans: Ḥanāḥna, ʿObeidāt, ʿAzav, and ʿAyadāt. The origin of each clan was different, and they were united at different times. The Ḥanāḥna clan originated in the ʿOqaba tribe from the Ṣalt area in northern Jordan. About three hundred years ago, a family from the tribe was forced to flee because of murder and fear of revenge. After many wanderings, they reached the area of the hills of Alonim-Shfarʿam. The ʿObēdāt clan originated in the Bedouin tribe of ʿArab el-Mrisāt. One member of the tribe was forced to flee because of blood revenge and was given shelter by the Ḥanāḥna clan and thus joined the Mazārīb tribe. Since he married a woman of African origin, their children were called *ʿobaid* (plural: ʿobēdāt, black slaves). The ʿAzav clan apparently originated in the Bedouin tribe in southwestern Iraq. In this case too, a member of the tribe was forced to flee because of murder and fear of revenge and was taken in by the Ḥanāḥna clan. The ʿIyadāt clan originated in the Bedouin tribe of ʿArab el-ʿArāmša, located in the northern Galilee on the Lebanese border. In this case too, a member of the tribe was forced to flee after a murder. In 1975 they were recognized by the Ministry of the Interior as an independent tribe in Bēt Zarzīr.

ʿArab el-Ḥağāğra: They originated in the tribe of Kaʿab in Ḥeğāz. The tribe came to Israel in the seventeenth century from a Bedouin group called Ḥağara in Syria. From Syria, the tribe passed through the Ḥauran and the Golan to the Galilee. Today they are a well-known community in the local council Kaʿabiyya-Ṭabbāš-Ḥağāğra.

ʿArab el-Ğawamīs: The tribe came from the Jammasīn tribe (they probably raised *ğamūs*, "buffalo"), which originated in the Golan Heights area around the city of Quneitra and the main area of Zarqa in northern Jordan. Two hundred years ago, the tribe migrated to the Mount Tabor area, where it remained for about fifty years. The tribe of Bēt Zarzīr arrived with families from the Bedouin tribe of ʿArab el-Ḥağāğra, with whom they had marriage relations and a common *muxtār*. The tribal grazing areas overlapped those of the Mazārīb and Ġrifāt tribes. During the British Mandate, the tribe was divided into two tribes. In time the original name of the tribe was changed from Ğammasīn to Ğawamīs. Today they constitute a neighborhood in Bēt Zarzīr.

ʿArab el-Neʿēm: Due to conflict, the tribe, which originated in Syria, migrated during the Ottoman period to the Kursi region by the Sea of Galilee. During the British mandate, the tribe lived in the vicinity of Givat Hamoreh (near Afula). Today the tribe is split and lives in several places. The largest faction is near the settlement of Ašḥar. Another concentration is found in Manšiyyat-ʿAla (Faḥūra) on the ʿAfula-Nazareth axis. Many families are living in Arab villages, mainly in Abu Snān, Taršīḥa, and Yafiʿa.[89]

ʿArab a-Saʿāideh: A peasant family from the village of Zipporia (Zippori). At the beginning of the twentieth century, the family left the village because of a dispute and moved to the oak forest near the Zbēdat tribe. The family adopted a Bedouin way of life, including marriage connections with ʿArab el-Ḥilf. Today they live in a neighborhood in north Basmat Ṭabʿūn near ʿArab el-Zbēdāt.

Notes

1. Ben David, *The Bedouins in Israel*, 36.
2. Ashkenazi, *The Bedouins in the Land of Israel*, 27–30.
3. Ben David, *The Bedouins in Israel*, 36.
4. Medzini, "Distribution of Bedouin Settlement in the Galilee," 13.
5. Kozali, *Israeli Institutional Policy towards the Bedouins*, 13.
6. Ashkenazi, *Tribus semi-nomades de la Palestine du nord*, 41.
7. Ben David, *The Bedouins in Israel*, 65.
8. Ben David, 65.
9. Golani, *On the Bedouins' Settlemental Development in Alonim-Shfar'am Hills*, 12.
10. Agmon, *Bedouin Tribes in the Hula Valley*, 96.
11. Kozali, *Israeli Institutional Policy towards the Bedouins*, 17n42.
12. Agmon, *Bedouin Tribes in the Hula Valley*, 97–96.
13. Arnon-Ohana, *A Saber from Within: The Internal Conflict in the Palestinian Movement 1929–1939*, 15.
14. Falah, *The Evolution of Semi-nomadism in Non-desert Environment*, 400.
15. Frantzman and Kark, *Bedouin Settlement in Late Ottoman and British Mandatory Palestine*.
16. Golani, *On the Bedouins' Settlement Development in Alonim-Shfar'am Hills*, 12.
17. Ben David, *The Bedouins in Israel*, 55.
18. Sawā'ed, *The Bedouins in the Land of Israel in the Years 1808–1904*.
19. Ashkenazi, *The Bedouins in the Land of Israel*, 51
20. Kozali, *Israeli Institutional Policy towards the Bedouins*, 13.
21. Ben-David, *The Bedouins in Israel*, 55.
22. Sawā'ed, *The Bedouins in the Land of Israel in the Years 1808–1904*, 17.
23. Dinur and Avigur, *Hagana History Book*, 60.
24. Sawā'ed, *The Bedouins in the Land of Israel in the Years 1808–1904*.
25. Kozali, *Israeli Institutional Policy towards the Bedouins*, 12.
26. Bitan-Buttenwieser 1969, 62.
27. Mazarib, *The Process of Bedouin Integration in the Arab Towns and Villages in the Galilee*, 54.

28. Sawā'ed, *The Bedouins in the Land of Israel in the Years 1808–1904*, 100.

29. Sawā'ed, *Bedouin-Jewish Relationship in the Land of Israel.*

30. Sawā'ed, *The Bedouins in the Land of Israel in the Years 1808–1904.*

31. Sawā'ed, *Bedouin-Jewish Relationship in the Land of Israel*, 32.

32. Ben-David and Barkai, *The Bedouins in the North of the Country in the Mirror of Changes*, 30; Ashkenazi, *The Bedouins in the Land of Israel*, 23.

33. Mazarib, *The Process of Bedouin Integration in the Arab Towns and Villages in the Galilee*, 68.

34. Ashkenazi, *The Bedouins in the Land of Israel*, 188.

35. Dinur and Avigur, *Hagana History Book*, 555.

36. *Haganah*, the Jewish defense
forces that would later become the Israeli army.

37. Dinur and Avigur, *Hagana History Book*, 593.

38. Dinur and Avigur..

39. Dinurand Avigur , 399.

40. Kozali, *Israeli Institutional Policy towards the Bedouins*, 15.

41. Falah, *The Development of the Planned Bedouin Settlement in Israel 1964–1982*, 7.

42. Falah, 9.

43. Mazarib, *The Process of Bedouin Integration in the Arab Towns and Villages in the Galilee*, 74.

44. Kozali, *Israeli Institutional Policy towards the Bedouins*, 18.

45. Falah, Pre-state Jewish Colonization in Northern Palestine, 293.

46. Sawā'ed, *Bedouin-Jewish Relationship in the Land of Israel*, 65.

47. Ben-David, *The Bedouins in Israel*, 66.

48. Mazarib, *The Process of Bedouin Integration in the Arab Towns and Villages in the Galilee*, 91.

49. Sawā'ed, *The Bedouins in the Land of Israel in the Years 1808–1904*, 124.

50. Falah, *Pre-state Jewish Colonization in Northern Palestine*, 303.

51. Yitshaki, *The Bedouin Tribes at the Foot of Mount Tabor*, 90.

52. Sawā'ed, *The Bedouins in the Land of Israel in the Years 1808–1904*, 129.

53. Dagan and Kozviner**,** *Pal-Heb: Bedouins in the Palmah during 1948*, 258.

54. Ben-David and Barkai, *The Bedouins in the North of the Country in the Mirror of Changes*, 81.

55. Sawā'ed, *The Bedouins in the Land of Israel in the Years 1808–1904*, 129.

56. Dinur and Shaul, *Hagana History Book*, 75.

57. Sawā'ed, *Bedouin-Jewish Relationship in the Land of Israel*, 44.

58. Sawā'ed, 64.

59. Ben David and Barkai, *The Bedouins in the North of the Country in the Mirror of Changes*, 84.

60. Sawā'ed, *The Bedouins in the Land of Israel in the Years 1808–1904*, 133.

61. Sawā'ed, *Bedouin-Jewish Relationship in the Land of Israel*, 32.

62. Sawā'ed, 53.

63. Sawā'ed.

64. Medzini, "Distribution of Bedouin Settlement in the Galilee," 38.

65. Ben-David and Barkai, *The Bedouins in the North of the Country in the Mirror of Changes*, 65.

66. Kozali, *Israeli Institutional Policy towards the Bedouins*, 42.

67. Mazarib, *The Process of Bedouin Integration in the Arab Towns and Villages in the Galilee*, 146.

68. Ben-David and Barkai, *The Bedouins in the North of the Country in the Mirror of Changes*, 27.

69. Kozali, *Israeli Institutional Policy towards the Bedouins*, 91.

70. Sawā'ed, *Bedouin-Jewish Relationship in the Land of Israel*, 14.

71. Ashkenazi, *The Bedouins in the Land of Israel*, 32.

72. Sawā'ed, *Bedouin-Jewish Relationship in the Land of Israel*, 14.

73. Sawā'ed, 14.

74. Yitshaki, *The Bedouin Tribes at the Foot of Mount Tabor*, 88.

75. Sawā'ed, *Bedouin-Jewish Relationship in the Land of Israel*, 213.

76. Shibli, *Bedouins in the Galilee*, 8.

77. Peled, *Noura's Dream: A Historical Portrait of a Bedouin Tribe*, 30–34, 117.

78. Sawā'ed, *Bedouin-Jewish Relationship in the Land of Israel*, 12.

79. Sawā'ed, 17.

80. Frantzman and Kark, *Bedouin Settlement in Late Ottoman and British Mandatory Palestine*, 4.

81. Sawā'ed, *Bedouin-Jewish Relationship in the Land of Israel*, 18.

82. Rabinowitz and Khawalde, *Demilitarized, Then Dispossessed: The Kirad Bedouins of the Hula Valley*, 518.

83. Sawā'ed, *Bedouin-Jewish Relationship in the Land of Israel*, 18.

84. Ben-David and Barkai, *The Bedouins in the North of the Country in the Mirror of Changes*, 31.

85. Ben-David and Barkay, *The Bedouins in the North of the Country in the Mirror of Changes*, 32; Rabinowitz and Khawalde, *Demilitarized, Then Dispossessed: The Kirad Bedouins of the Hula Valley*, 516–21.

86. Ben-David and Barkai, *The Bedouins in the North of the Country in the Mirror of Changes*, 32.

87. Falah, *Pre-state Jewish Colonization in Northern Palestine and Its Impact on Local Bedouin Sedentarization 1914–1948*, 303.

88. Arnon-Ohana, *A Saber from Within: The Internal Conflict in the Palestinian Movement 1929–1939*, 15.

89. Ben-David, *The Bedouins in Israel*, 67.

TABLE 1. Recognized Bedouin villages in the Galilee

Settlement name	Municipal status	Settlement makeup	Citizens' number (2014)
Ibṭin	Zevulun Regional Council (1963)	ʿAmariyya, ʿArab el-Xawāled, ʿArab el-Zbēdāt, ʿArab Ḥilf, ʿArab el-Turkman, some families from other tribes	2,670
Buʿeine Nuǧēdāt	Local council Bu'eine Nuǧēdat (1987)	Buʿēne—fallāḥīn, Nuǧēdat—ʿArab el-Nuǧēdāt	8,900
Bīr al-Maksūr	Local council Bīr al-Maksūr (1990)	ʿArab el-Ḥuǧerāt	8,500
Basmat Ṭab'ūn	Local council Basmat Tab'un (1972)	ʿArab el-Sʿadiyya, ʿArab el- Zbēdāt, ʿArab Ḥilf, ʿArab el-Xawāled	7,300
Dmēde	Misgav Regional Council (1995)	ʿArab el-Ḥuǧērāt	435
Wādi Ḥamām	al-Baṭūf Regional Council	ʿArab el-Ġawarna	1,370
Zarzīr	Local council Zarzīr (1996)	ʿArab el-Hēb (Abu-Ṣayāḥ), ʿArab el-Mazārīb, ʿArab el-Ġrifāt, ʿArab el-Ğawamīs, ʿIyadāt	7,200
Ḥusniyya	Misgav Regional Council (1996)	ʿArab el-Sawāʿed	620
Ṭūba-Zanġariyye	Local council Ṭūba-Zanġariyye (1988)	ʿArab el-Hēb, ʿArab el-Zanġariyye	6,100
Kammāneh	Misgav Regional Council (1995)	ʿArab el-Sawāʿed	1,390
Kaʿabiyya-Ṭabbāš-Ḥağāğra	Local council (1996)	ʿArab el-Kaʿabiyya, ʿArab Ḥilf (Ṭabbāš), ʿArab el-Ḥağāğra	4,800
Xawāled	Zevulun Regional Council (1993)	ʿArab el-Xawāled	420
Manšiyya Zabda	Jezreel Valley Regional Council (1979)	Fellaḥīn from ʿIlūt + Bedouins from the ʿArab el-Sʿadiyya	1,175
Sawā'ed Ḥamīra	Jezreel Valley Regional Council (1996)	ʿArab el-Sawāʿed	145
Sallāma	Misgav Regional Council (1986)	ʿArab el-Sawāʿed	3,000

TABLE 1. *(continued)*

Settlement name	Municipal status	Settlement makeup	Citizens' number (2014)
ʿArab el-ʿArāmšah	Mateh Asher Regional Council	ʿArab el-ʿArāmšah	1,565
Arab al-Neʿēm	Misgav Regional Council (1999)	Arab al-Neʿēm	725
Rās al-ʿĒn	Misgav Regional Council (1999)	ʿArab el-Sawāʿed + Christians of Nicola family	335
Rūmat al-Hēb	al-Baṭṭūf Regional Council (1969)	ʿArab el-Hēb	1,840
Šibli–Umm al-Ġanam	Local council Shibli (1984)	ʿArab el-Šibli (Ṣbēḥ), ʿArab el-Sʿadiyya	5,600
Total			**64,090**

TABLE 2. Bedouin citizens who live in Arab villages in the Galilee

Settlement name	Tribes in the settlement	Bedouin citizens estimation (2014)
Nazareth	ʿArab el-Naʿarāni, ʿArab el-Zayādne, ʿArab El-Rabīʿ, ʿArab el-Hēb	3,300
Sakhnin	ʿArab el-Zbēdāt, ʿArab el-Ṭarabiyya	4,950
Ṭámra	ʿArab el-Mrēsāt, el-Ḥabūzi, ʿArab el- Zayādne, ʿArab el-ʿabīd	2,160
Iʿbillin	ʿArab el-Mrisāt, ʿArab el-Sawā'ed, ʿArab el-Ḥuğerāt	1,240
Mġār	ʿArab el-Neʿēm, ʿArab el-Hēb, ʿArab el-Xeranba	1,430
Dēr Hanna	ʿArab al-Mawāsi, ʿArab el-Ḥamdūn, ʿArab el-Mrēsāt	410
Abu Snān	ʿArab el-Ne'ēm, ʿArab el-Sawāʿed, ʿArab el-Swēṭāt	2,440
Yāfa an-Naṣeriyye	ʿArab el-Ġazalīn, ʿArab el-Neʿēm, ʿArab el-Mazārīb	1,100
Tarshīha	ʿArab el-Neʿēm, ʿArab el-Swēṭāt, ʿArab el-Samniye	950
Šaʿab	Krād el-Bakāra, Krād el-Ġanāme	1,220
ʿEilabun	ʿArab al-Mawāsi, ʿArab el-Hēb	1,300
ʿIsfiya	Kaʿabiyya	950
Shfarʿam	ʿArab el-Sawāʿed, ʿArab el-Hanādi, ʿArab el-Zayādne, ʿArab el-Ḥuğerāt, ʿArab el-Samniyya, ʿArab el-zyūd, ʿArab el-Sawāʿed, Krād el-Ḥait	17,640
Yaʿara	ʿArab el-Hēb (Maradāt)	120
Total		**39,210**

TABLE 3. Bedouin diaspora settlements in the Galilee

Tribe	Size	Location
ʿArab el-Sawāʿed	12 families	About 1 km from Sawāʿed Ḥamīra
ʿArab el-Neʿēm	About 40 families	East to Karmiel
ʿArab el-Neʿēm	About 15 families	On Nazareth-ʿAfula road
ʿArab el-Hēb	About 5 families	In Bēt Netofa Valley
ʿArab el-Huğerāt	About 10 families	In Yodfat area
ʿArab el-Hēb (Batōf)	3 families	Rūmat al-Hēb (Xirbet Rūma)
ʿArab el-Ḥuğerāt	6 families	On Shfarʿam - Kiryat Ata axis
ʿArab el-Xawāled	8 families	Zippory River
ʿArab el-Ġrifāt	5 families	Al-ʿAkūb near Manshiyya Zabda
Total	**About 104 families**	

Source: Ben-David and Barkai 2012

Maps

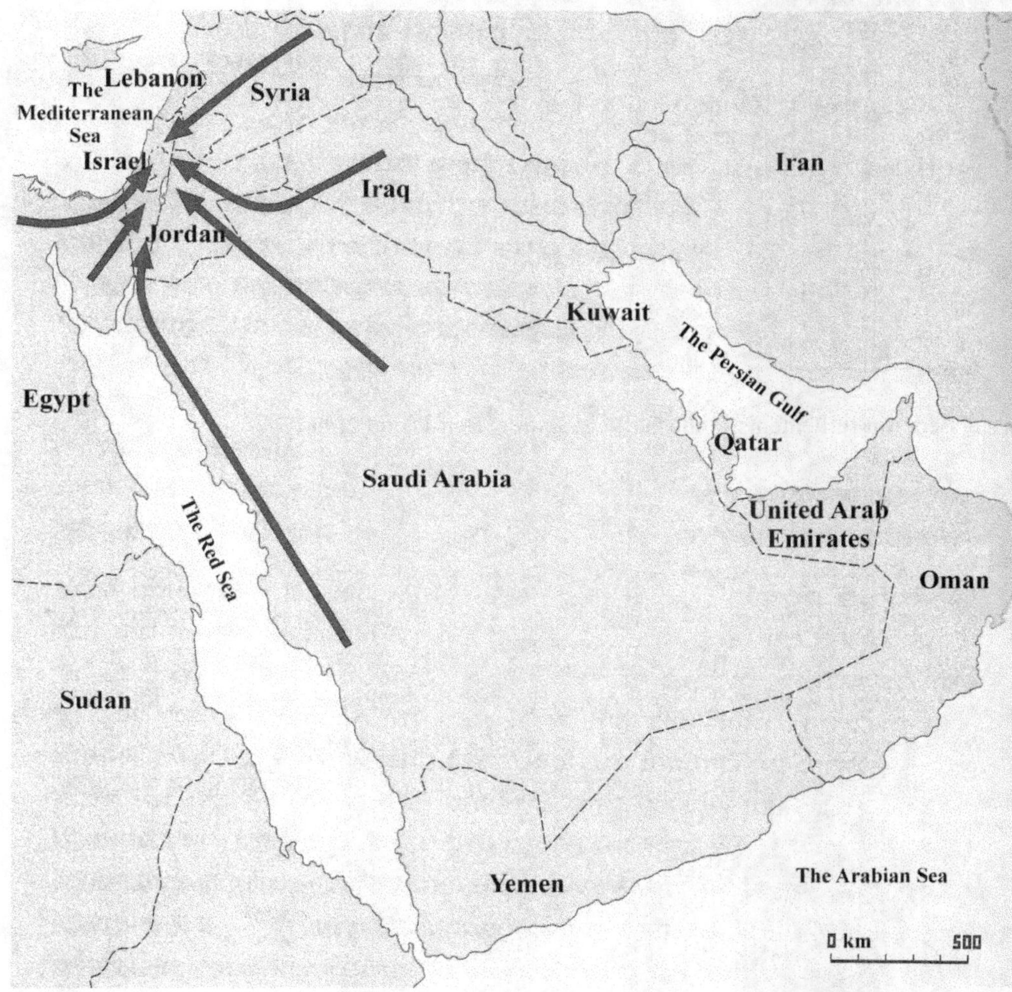

MAP 1. Directions of Bedouin tribes entering into Israel. Source: Ben-David 2014

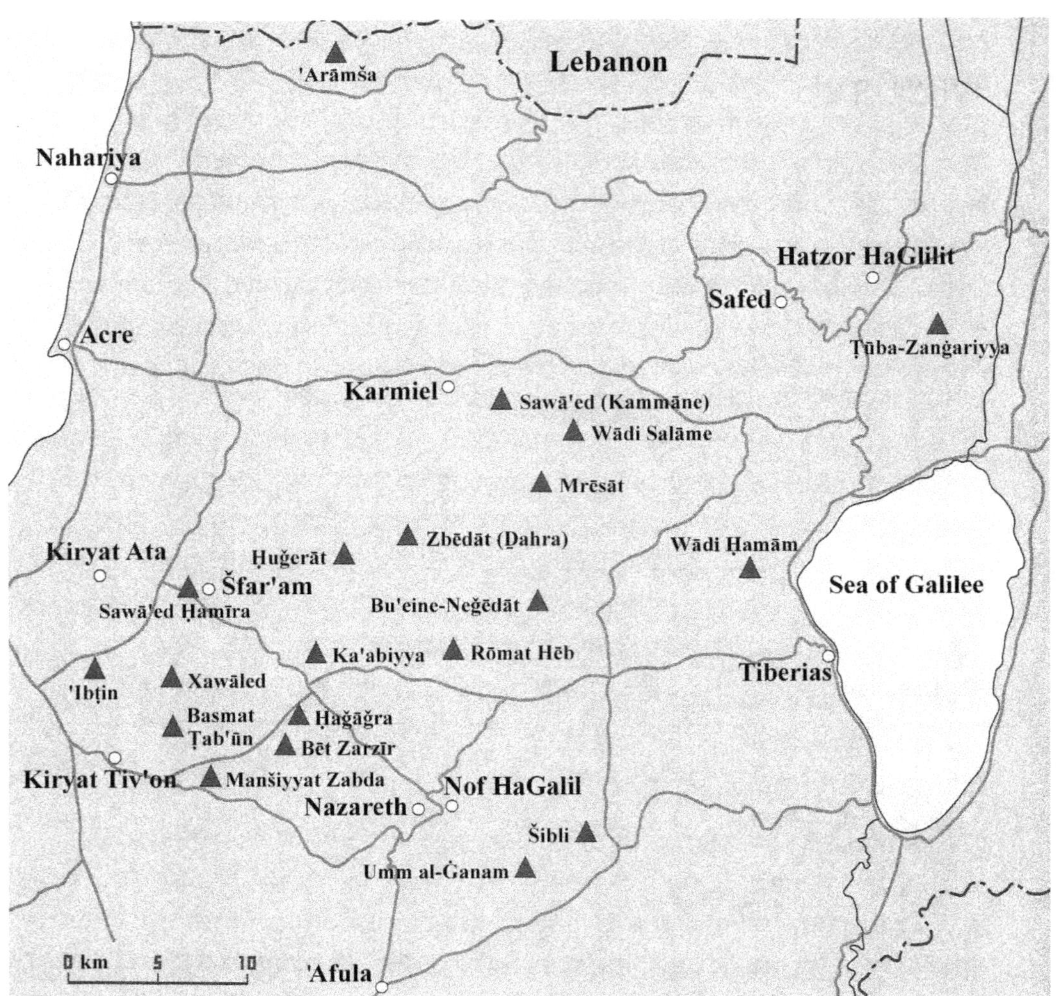

MAP 2. Bedouin settlements in the Galilee. Source: Ben-David 2014

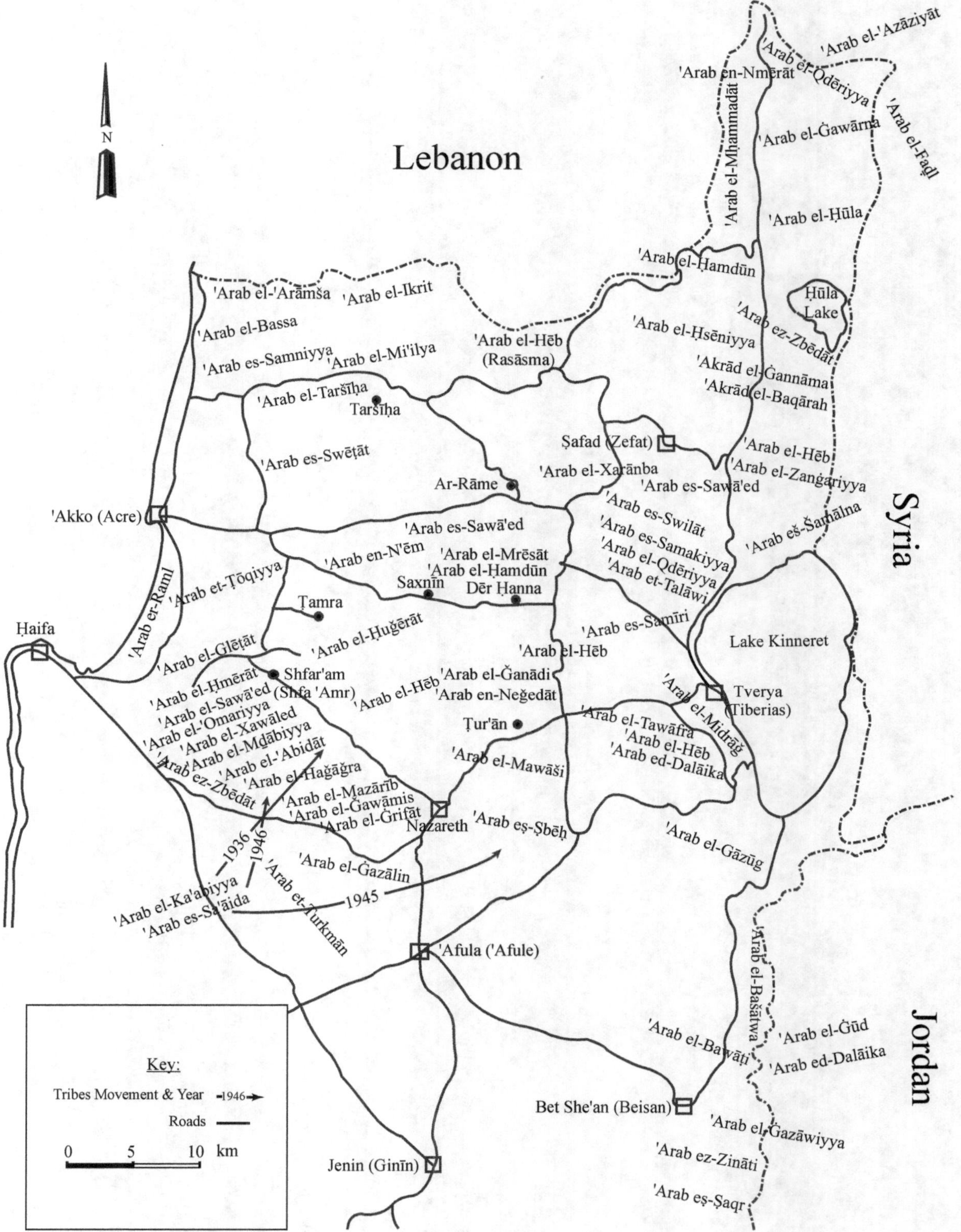

MAP 3. The Bedouin tribes in the Galilee according to Tovia Ashkenazi (1938). Sources: Ashkenazi (1938) and field survey (Medzini 1982)

Bibliography

Aarne, Antti. *The Types of the Folktale: A Classification and Bibliography.* Translated and edited by Stith Thompson. Helsinki: Finnish Academy of Science and Letters, 1961.

Aboab da Fonseca, *Menorat HaMa'or.* [In Hebrew.] Jerusalem, Mosad HaRav Kuk, 1961.

Abu Haidar, Farida. "Bedouinization." In *Encyclopedia of Arabic Language and Linguistics*, edited by Kees Versteegh, 1:269–74. Leiden: Brill, 2006.

Abu Rabi'a, Safa. *The Bedouin Woman: Changes and Transformations since the Establishment of the State up to the Present.* [In Hebrew.] 1996. http://beduin.snunit.org.il/doc/safa.htm.

Abu Risha, Zulaikha, ed. *Timeless Tales: Folktales Told by Syrian Refugees.* Translated by Serene Huleileh. Revised by Jack Lynch. N.p.: Hakawati Project Publications, 2016. http://chwb.org/wp-content/uploads/2015/02/CHwB_SyriskAntologi_eng_low.pdf.

Agmon, Iris. "Bedouin Tribes in the Hula Valley and Beth She'an Valley toward the End of the Ottoman Period." [In Hebrew.] *Kathedra*, 1987, 45:87–102. http://www.ybz.org.il/_Uploads/dbsAttachedFiles/Article_45.1.pdf.

Al-'Āref, 'Āref. *Bedouin Tribes in the Area of Be'er Sheva'.* [In Hebrew.] Translated by M. Kapeljuk. Tel-Aviv: Bustanay, 1938.

Al-Barghuthi, Abdullatif M. *Dictionary of Colloquial Palestinian Arabic Dialects.* [In Arabic.] Ramallah-Bireh: printed by the author, 2001.

Alexander, Tamar. "Haninat-Allah: The Yemenite Jewish Version of the Story of Cinderella and Its Parallels." [In Hebrew.] *Pe'amim* 53 (Autumn 1993): 124–48.

Alexander, Tamar, and Dov Noy. *The Treasure of Our Fathers: Judeo-Spanish Tales.* [In Hebrew.] Jerusalem: Misgav Yerushalayim, 1989.

Alexander-Frizer, Tamar. *The Story of a Beloved and a Half: The Folktale of Sephardi Jews.* [In Hebrew.] Jerusalem: Magnes; Beer-Sheba: Ben-Gurion University of the Negev Press, 2000.

Al-Rawi, Ahmed K. "The Arabic Ghoul and Its Western Transformation." *Folklore* 120 (December 2009): 291–306.

Arnon-Ohana, Yuval. *A Saber from Within: The Internal Conflict in the Palestinian Movement 1929–1939.* [In Hebrew.] Tel-Aviv: Yariv-Hadar, 1981.

Ashkenazi, Tovia. *The Bedouins in the Land of Israel.* [In Hebrew.] Jerusalem: Ariel, 2000.
———. *Tribus semi-nomades de la Palestine du nord.* Paris: Librairie Orientale Paul Geuthner, 1938.
Bailey, Clinton. *Bedouin Poetry from Sinai and the Negev.* Oxford: Clarendon, 1991.
Bar-Efrat, Shimon. *Narrative Art in the Bible.* [In Hebrew.] Tel-Aviv: Sifriat Poalim, 2004.
Barthélemy, Adrien. *Dictionnaire arabe-français: dialects de Syrie: Alep, Damas, Liban, Jérusalem.* Paris: Librairie Orientaliste Paul Geuthner, [1935–46, 1966?].
Bar-Zvi, Sasson. *Fable, Story and Legend in Arab Tents.* [In Hebrew.] Jerusalem: Ariel, 1998.
Bascom, William. *African Folktales.* Bloomington: Indiana University Press, 1992.
Basile, Giambattista. *Basile's "The Tale of Tales, or Entertainment for Little Ones."* Detroit: Wayne State University Press, 2007.
———. *Stories from the Pentamerone.* London: Macmillan, 1911.
Basset, René. "Salomon and the Griffin." In *Moorish Literature.* London: Colonial, 1901, 207. https://www.vonsteuben.org/ourpages/humanities/moorishlit.pdf.
Bauer, Leonhard. *Das palästinensische Arabisch. Die Dialekte des Städters und des Fellachen.* Leipzig: Hinrichs, 1910.
Behnsdtedt, Peter, and Aharon Geva-Kleinberger. *Dialects of Galilee (Israel) with Some Data for Adjacent Areas.* Leiden: Brill, 2019.
Behnstedt, Peter, and Manfred Woidich. *Arabische Dialektgeographie: Eine Einführung.* Leiden: Brill, 2005.
Ben-Amos, Dan. *Folktales of the Jews.* 3 vols. Philadelphia: Jewish Publication Society, 2006–11.
Ben-David, Yosef. *The Bedouins in Israel: Social and Soil Aspects.* [In Hebrew.] Jerusalem: Ben Shemesh Institute of the Study of Soil Policy and Soil Uses, 2004.
Ben-David, Yosef, and Amnon Barkai. *The Bedouins in the North of the Country in the Mirror of Changes.* [In Hebrew.] Jerusalem: Ariel, 2012.
Ben-Haim, Musa. *The Ox's Wisdom: Stories of the Arabic Life.* [In Hebrew.] Jerusalem: Akademon, 1966.
Ben-Shahar, Abraham. *From the Arabic Folklore: Stories and Fables, Legends and Proverbs from the Life of Our Arab Neighbors.* [In Hebrew.] Nazareth: Al-Nahda, 1976.
Berger, Yisrael. *Simchat Yisrael*, Pietrickov, Kleiman Press,1910.
Bergsträsser, Gotthelf. *Sprachatlas von Syrien und Palästina* [Speech atlas of Syria and Palestine]. Leipzig: J. C. Hinrichs, 1915.
Bettelheim, Bruno. *The Uses of Enchantment: The Meaning and Importance of Fairy Tales.* New York: Vintage Books, 1975.
Bettini, Lidia. *Contes Féminins de la Haute Jézireh Syrienne. Matériaux Ethno-Linguistiques d'un Parler Nomade Oriental.* Quaderni di Semitistica 26. Florence: University of Florence, Department of Linguistics, 2006.
Bin Gorion, Micha Joseph. *Mimekor Yisrael: Selected Classical Jewish Folktales.* Bloomington: Indiana University Press, 1990.
Bitan-Buttenwieser, Arieh. *Changes in the Settlement and Soil Use in the Eastern Lower Galilee since the Beginning of the 19th Century up to the Present.* [In Hebrew.] Jerusalem: Hebrew University of Jerusalem, 1969.
Blanc, Haim. "The Israeli Koiné as an Emergent National Standard." in:*Language Problems of Developing Nations*, edited by Joshua Fishman and Charles A. Ferguson, New York: John Wiley & Sons (1968): 237–251.
———. "The Arabic Dialects of the Negev Bedouins." *Proceedings of the Israel Academy of Sciences and Humanities* 4, no. 7 (1970): 112–50.
———. *Communal Dialects in Baghdad.* Boston: Harvard University Press, 1964.

———. "A Story of a Blue Wolf." In *Leshon Beney Adam* [Humans' language], collected by Moshe Singer, 112–15. Jerusalem: Bialik Institute, 1989.

———. *Studies in the North Palestinian Arabic: Linguistic Inquiries among the Druzes of Western Galilee and Mt. Carmel*. Jerusalem: Israel Oriental Society, 1953.

Borg, A. "Linguistic and Ethnographic Observations on the Color Categories of the Negev Bedouin." In *The Language of Color in the Mediterranean*, edited by Alexander Borg, 121–46. Stockholm: Almqvist and Wirkell International, 1999.

Bouhdiba, Abdelwahab. *Sexuality in Islam*. London: Routledge & Kegan Paul, 1985.

Brand, Sara. "Arabic-Hebrew Codeswitching among Arabic Speaking College Students: Structural, Sociopragmatic and Psycholinguistic Dimensions." [In Hebrew.] Unpublished PhD thesis, Bar-Ilan University, 2013.

Brinton, Laurel J. "Historical Discourse Analysis." In *Handbook of Discourse Analysis*, 2nd ed., edited by Deborah Tannen, Heidi E. Hamilton, and Deborah Schiffrin, 222–43. Chichester, UK: Wiley Blackwell, 2015.

Brosh, Na'ama. *Biblical Stories in Islamic Painting*. Jerusalem: Israel Museum, 1991.

Brunner-Traut, Emma. *Altägyptische Märchen: Mythen und andere volkstümliche Erzählungen*. Cologne: Diederichs Eugen, KG, 1963.

Buber, Shlomo, *Mavo Lemidrash Tanhuma (Introduction to Midrash Tanhuma)*. [In Hebrew.], Vilna (Vilnius) 1885, Jerusalem 1964. https://www.daat.ac.il/daat/vl/tanhumavo/tanhumavo07.pdf (p. 21).

Burton, Richard F. *Arabian Nights*. Oxford: Burton Club, 1885–88. http://www.burtoniana.org/books/1885-Arabian%20Nights/.

Bushnaq, Inea. *Arab Folktales*. New York: Pantheon Books, 1986.

Calame-Griaule, Geneviève. "Pour une étude ethnolinguistique litératures orales africaines." *Langages* 5, No. 18 (juin 1970), 22–47.

Calvino, Italo. *Italian Folktales*. Translated by George Martin. New York: Harcourt Brace Jovanovich, 1980.

Cantineau, Jean. "Études sur quelques parlers de nomades arabes d'Orient." *AIEO* 2 (1936): 1–119.

———. "Études sur quelques parlers de nomades arabes d'Orient." *AIEO* 3 (1937): 119–237.

Chang, Charles Bond. "First Language Phonetic Drift during Second Language Acquisition." PhD diss., University of California at Berkeley, 2010.

Crowfoot, Grace M., and Louise Baldensperger. *From Cedar to Hyssop: A Study in the Folklore of Plants in Palestine*. London: Sheldon, 1932.

Dagan, Shaul, and Kozviner Avner. *Pal-Heb: Bedouins in the Palmah during 1948*. [In Hebrew.] Ramat-Gan: Yisrael Galili Center for the History of the Hagana Defense Force and Touba Local Council, 1993.

Dakkur, Jihad Ahmad. *Galilee Stories*. [In Arabic.] Sur (Tyre), Lebanon: 2006.

Dinur, Ben-Zion, and Shaul Avigur, eds. *Hagana History Book*. [In Hebrew.] Tel-Aviv: Defense Ministry Publishing, 1954.

Dorson, Richard M. *Folktales Told around the World*. Chicago: University of Chicago Press, 1975.

Doughty, Charles. *Travels in Arabia Deserta*. New York: Liveright, 1955.

Elihay, Yohanan, *The Olive Tree Dictionary: A dictionary of Eastern Arabic Conversational Eastern Arabic (Palestinian)*. Jerusalem: Minerva Publishing House.

El-Shamy, Hasan. *Folktales of Egypt*. Chicago: University of Chicago Press, 1980.

———. *Tales Arab Women Tell, and the Behavioral Patterns They Portray*. Bloomington: Indiana University Press, 1999.

———. *Types of the Folktale in the Arab World*. Bloomington: Indiana University Press, 2004.

Elstein, Yoav. "The Theme 'The King's Daughter Locked-Up in a Tower': The Unfolding of the Versions from Midrash Tanhuma to Bialik's 'Legend of the Three and the Four.'" [In Hebrew.] In *Encyclopedia of the Jewish Story: Sippur Okev Sippur (A Story Follows a Story)*, 1:79–104, Ramat-Gan: Bar-Ilan University Press, 2005.

Epstein, Morris. *Tales of Sendebar*. Philadelphia: Jewish Publication Society of America, 1967.

Etkin, Tsevi. *On a Cup of Coffee: Arabic Legends and Folktales*. [Hebrew and Arabic transcription in Hebrew alphabet.] Jerusalem: Minerva, 2015.

Faitelovitz, Yaakov. *Stories of Beta Yisrael: Sixty Stories and a Story from Ethiopian Jews*. [In Hebrew.] Jerusalem: Haberman Institute for Literature Research, 1990.

Falah, Ghazi. "The Development of the Planned Bedouin Settlement in Israel 1964–1982: Evaluation and Characteristics." *Geoforum* 14 (1983): 311–23.

———. "The Evolution of Semi-nomadism in Non-desert Environment: The Case of Galilee in the 19th Century." *GeoJournal* 21, no. 4 (August 1990): 397–410.

———. "Pre-state Jewish Colonization in Northern Palestine and Its Impact on Local Bedouin Sedentarization 1914–1948." *Journal of Historical Geography* 17, no. 3 (1991): 289–309.

———. "The Role of the British Administration in the Sedentarization of the Bedouin Tribes in Northern Palestine 1918–1948." Working paper, University of Durham, Centre for Middle Eastern and Islamic Studies, 1983.

Ferguson, Charles Albert. "Diglossia." *Word* 15 (1959): 325–40. http://mapage.noos.fr/masdar/Ferguson-Diglossia.pdf.

Fischer, Wolfdietrich. *Die demonstrative Bildungen der neuarabischen Dialekte. Ein Beitrag zur historischen Grammatik des Arabischem*. The Hague: Mouton, 1959.

Fishbane, Michael. *Biblical Text and Texture: A Literary Reading of Selected Texts*. New York: Schocken Books, 1979.

Frantzman, Seth, and Ruth Kark. "Bedouin Settlement in Late Ottoman and British Mandatory Palestine: Influence on the Cultural and Environmental Landscape, 1870–1948." *New Middle Eastern Studies* 1 (2011): 1–24. http://geography.huji.ac.il/.upload/RuthPub/136.pdf.

Freud, Sigmund. *The Interpretation of Dreams*. Translated by A. A. Brill. London: Macmillan, 1913.

Freytagii, Georgii Wilhelmi. *Lexicon Arabico-Latinum*, Halis: Saxonum, 1830, 1833 (2 volumes).

Geva-Kleinberger, Aharon. *Die arabischen Stadtdialekte von Haifa in der ersten Hälfte des zwanzigsten Jahrhunderts*. Wiesbaden: Harrassowitz, 2004.

Goitein, Shelomo D. *Narrative Art in the Bible*. [In Hebrew.] Jerusalem: Jewish Agency of the Land of Israel, Department of Jews and Youth Immigration, 1956.

Golani, Gideon. "*Bedouins' Settlement in the Alonim-Shfar'am Hills Region*." [In Hebrew.] Jerusalem: Ministry of Interior, department of Minorities, and the Hebrew University of Jerusalem, Department of Geography, 1966.

Goldberg, Christine. "The Wolf and the Kids (ATU 123) in International Tradition." In *Erzählkultur, Beiträge zur kulturwissenschaftlichen Erzählforschung. Hans-Jörg Uther zum 65 Geburtstag*, edited by Rolf Wilhelm Brednich, 277–91. Berlin: Walter de Gruyter, 2009.

Green, André. *Le complexe de castration*. Que sais-je? Paris: Presses Universitaires de France, 2007.

Grimm, Jacob, and Wilhelm Grimm. *The Original Folk and Fairy Tales of the Brothers Grimm: The Complete First Edition*. Edited by Jack Zipes. Princeton, NJ: Princeton University Press, 2014.

Gruenwald, Max. *Tales, Songs & Folkways of Sephardic Jews*. [In Hebrew.] Edited by Dov Noy. Jerusalem: Magnes, 1982.

Habermann, A. M. "An Ancient Version of the Origin of 'The Legend of the Three and Four.'" [In Hebrew.] *Mo'znayim* 40, no. 2 (January 1975): 88–91.

Hanauer, James Edward. *Folk-lore of the Holy Land: Moslem, Christian and Jewish*. London: Duckworth, 1907. https://archive.org/details/cu31924029903816/page/n5.

Har-Shefi, Avisar. "The Rat and the Pit." [In Hebrew.] In *Encyclopedia of the Jewish Story: Sippur Okev Sippur (A Story Follows a Story)*, 3:181–210. Ramat-Gan: Bar-Ilan University.

Harrison, David K. *When Languages Die: The Extinction of the World's Languages and the Erosion of Human Knowledge*. Oxford: Oxford University Press, 2007.

Hasan-Rokem, Galit. *Web of Life: Folklore and Midrash in Rabbinic Literature*. Translated by Batya Stein. Stanford, CA: Stanford University Press, 2000.

Havelová, Andrea. "Arabic Dialects of Nazareth: A Dialectological and Sociolinguistic Description." PhD Thsis, University of Haifa, 2000.

Henkin, Roni. "Come, O Your Mother: Reverse Kinship Terms in the Negev Bedouin Dialects." [In Hebrew.] *Oryanut ve-Safa* [Literacy and language] 4, no. 201 (2012): 66–239.

———. "Diachronic and Synchronic Accommodation in Negev Arabic." In *Between the Atlantic and Indian Oceans: Studies on Contemporary Arabic Dialects; Proceedings of the 7th AIDA Conference, Held in Vienna from 5–9 September 2006*, edited by Stephan Prochazka and Veronika Ritt-Benmimoun, 237–50. Vienna: Neue Beihefte zur Wiener Zeitschrift für die Kunde des Morgenlandes, 2008.

———. "Hebrew and Arabic in Asymmetric Contact in Israel." *Lodz Papers in Pragmatics* 7, no. 1 (2011): 61–100.

———. "Narrative Styles of Negev Bedouin Men and Women." *Oriente Moderno* 80 (1) (2000): 59–81.

———. "Narrative Styles of Palestinian Bedouin Adults and Children." *Pragmatics* 8, no. 1 (1998): 47–78.

———. *Negev Arabic: Dialectal, Sociolinguistic, and Stylistic Variation*. Wiesbaden: Harrassowitz, 2010.

Hoberman, Robert D. "Pausal Forms." In *Encyclopedia of Arabic Language and Linguistics*, edited by K. Versteegh, 3:564–70. Leiden: Brill, 2009.

Homer. *The Essential Odyssey*, translated by Stanley Lombardo. Cambridge: Hackett Publishing, 2007.

Hone, William, *The Every-day Book, and Table Book*, 3 vols. 1, London, 1826.

Hujerat, Musa, *Widespread Customs in the Bedouin Society*. [In Hebrew.] *Masa*. March 13, 2006. http://folkmasa.org/asaf/bedouin_customs.htm.

Ibn Khaldun, 'Abd El-Rahman. *The Muqaddimah: Prolegomena to History*. Edited and abridged by N. J. Dawood. Translated by Franz Rosenthal. Princeton, NJ: Princeton University Press, 1966.

Jacobs, Joseph. *Celtic Fairy Tales*. New York: G. P. Putnam's Sons, 1892.

Jacobus de Voragine, *The Golden Legend: Readings on the Saints*, Princeton, NJ: Princeton University Press, 2012.

Jellinek, Aharon Ben Yitshaq Yehuda. *Bet Hamidrash* [House of study]. 6 vols. Vienna, 1857.

Kleinberg, Aviad. *Brother Ginepro's Pork Leg*. [In Hebrew.] Tel-Aviv: Zmora-Bitan, 2000.

Kozali, Sa'eed. *Israeli Institutional Policy towards the Bedouins*. [In Hebrew.] Master's thesis, University of Haifa, 2007.

Krumbacher, Karl. *Das Problem der Modern Griechishen Schriftsprache*. Munich, 1902.

Kúnos, Ignácz. *Forty Four Turkish Fairy Tales*. London: George G. Harrap, 1913.

Landau, Louis. "Contents and Forms in *Meam Loez* by Rabi Yaakov Khulî." [In Hebrew.] PhD thesis, Hebrew University of Jerusalem, 1980.

Lebling, Robert. *Legends of the Fire Spirits: Jinn and Genies from Arabia to Zanzibar.* London: I. B. Tauris, 2014.

Lerner, Amir. "Construction of 'The Banquet and the Beast's Tracks' Narrative: An Inquiry into Amalgamation of Plots in Medieval Jewish and Arabic Literature." [In Hebrew.] *Pe'amim* 132 (2012): 9–52.

Litani, Levana, and Yehuda Litani. *Irish Mythology.* [In Hebrew.] Tel-Aviv: Map—Mapping & Publishing, 2002.

Malka, Rafi. *The Animal Kingdom: Bedouin Legends and Folktales about Animals.* [In Hebrew.] Lahav: Joe Allon Center, Bedouin Culture Museum, 1996.

Ma'lūf, Lewis. *Al-Munjid fii al-Lugha wa-l-'Adab wa-l-'Uluum* [The supporter in the language, literature, and sciences]. 2 vols. Beirut: Al-Matba'a Al-Kathooliikiyya, 1960.

Mann, Thomas. *The Transposed Heads: A Legend of India.* Translated by H. T. Lowe-Porter. New York: Knopf, 1941.

Marçais, William. "La diglossie arabe." *L'Enseignement Publique* 97 (1930): 401–9.

Marom, Yafit. "The Bedouin Dialect of the Women of the Tarabīn Nuwēb'a Tribe: Sinai Peninsula, Egypt." [In Hebrew.] Unpublished PhD diss., Haifa University, 2012.

———. "The Fisherman and the Wishing Ring: A Text from the Tarabīn Nuwēb'a." *Jerusalem Studies in Arabic and Islam* 36 (2011): 177–204.

———. "Samḥa, the She-Camel: A Ghūl-Tale from Tarabīn Nuwēb'a." In *Proceedings of the 8th International Conference of AIDA—Colchester*, edited by Enam Al-Wer, Chryso Hadjidemetriou, Bruno Herin, and Uri Horesh, 95–101. Colchester, UK: University of Essex, 2015.

———. "The World of the Monsters: Fieldwork among the Women of the Tarabīn Nuwēb'a Tribe, Sinai Peninsula." In *Between the Atlantic and Indian Oceans: Studies on Contemporary Arabic Dialects; Proceedings of the 7th AIDA Conference, Held in Vienna from 5–9 September 2006*, edited by Stephan Procházka and Veronika Ritt-Benmimoun, 287–94. Münster-Wien: LIT, 2008.

Martin, Mary Lou, trans. *The Fables of Marie de France.* Birmingham, AL: Summa, 1984.

Maspero, Gaston. *Popular Stories of Ancient Egypt.* Translated by C. H. W. Johns. London: H. Grevel; New York: G. P. Putnam's Sons, 1915.

Mayno de' Mayneri, Pergaminus Nicolaus, and G. E Klemming. *Dialogus Creaturarum.* Stockholm: Johan Snell, 1483.

———. *Dialogus Creaturarum.* Translated by Pierre Ruelle. Brussels: Palais des Académies, 1985.

Mazārīb, Tomer. "The Process of Bedouin Integration in the Arab Towns and Villages in the Galilee: Historical, Social and Cultural Aspects (From the Beginning of the 18th Century to the End of the 20th Century)." [In Hebrew.] PhD thesis, University of Haifa, 2016.

Medzini, Arnon. "Distribution of Bedouin Settlement in the Galilee as a Product of Spontaneous Settlement and Intentional Governmental Policy." [In Hebrew.] *Monogeography* 1, Haifa: Haifa University, 1984.

Meron, Joram, and Riad Kabha. *Tales of the Wadi: Selected Folktales from Wadi Arah.* [In Hebrew and Arabic.] Givat Haviva: Institute for Arabic Studies, 1993.

Meron, Joram, Carmela Shehadi, and Nimer Ahmad Masarwi. *Seed of Pomegranate: The Woman in Arab Folktales* [In Hebrew and Arabic.] Givat Haviva: Jewish-Arab Center for Peace, 1997.

Meyuḥas, Yosef Baran. *Bible Tales in Arab Folk-lore.* Translated by Victor N. Levi. London: A. A. Knopf, 1928.

Muhawi, Ibrahim, and Sharif Kanaana. *Speak, Bird, Speak Again: Palestinian Arab Folktales*. Berkeley: University of California Press, 1989.

Nawi, Eliahu. *Arab Stories*. [In Hebrew.] Tel-Aviv: Ma'ariv Library, 1972.

Neishtadt, Mila. "The Lexical Component in the Aramaic Substrate of Palestinian Arabic." In *Semitic Languages in Contact*, edited by Aaron Michael Butts Leiden, 280–310. Boston: Brill, 2015.

Noy, Dov. "Family Conflict in Folktales of Jewish Communities." [In Hebrew.] In *Studies of the Center of Folklore Research*, 1:201–28. Jerusalem: Hebrew University of Jerusalem, 1970.

Oppenheimer, Max von. *Die Beduinen*. Vol. 2, *Palästina, Transjordanien, Sinai, Hedjaz*. Leipzig: Harrassowitz, 1943.

Owens, Jonathan. "The Historical Linguistics of the Intrusive *-n in Arabic and West Semitic." *Journal of the American Oriental Society* 133, no. 2 (2013): 217–47.

Palva, Heikki. "The Descriptive Imperative of Narrative Style in Spoken Arabic." *Folia Orientalia* 18 (1977): 5–26.

———. *Lower Galilean Arabic: An Analysis of its Anaptyctic and Prothetic Vowels with Sample Texts*. Studia Orientalia 32. Helsinki: Societas Orientalis Fennica, 1966.

Patai, Raphael. *Arab Folktales from Palestine and Israel*. Detroit: Wayne State University Press, 1998.

Patai, Rafael, and Yoseph Y. Rivlin, eds. *A Jerusalemite Story*. [In Hebrew.] Jerusalem: Institute for Folklore and Ethnology of the Land of Israel, 1947.

Peled, Kobi. *Noura's Dream: A Historical Portrait of a Bedouin Tribe*. [In Hebrew.] Haifa: University of Haifa; Tel-Aviv: Yedi'ot Ahronot, 2015.

Penard, A. P, and T. E. Penard. "Surinam Folk-Tales." *Journal of American Folklore* 30, no. 116 (April–June 1917): 239–50. http://folkmasa.org/yashpeh/mb_yashp.php?mishtane=3550].

Penzer, Norman Mosley. *The Ocean of Story*. London: Chas. J Sawyer, Grafton House, 1924.

Perez, Yoel Shalom. *Between the Sun and the Moon: Bedouin Folktales from the North of Israel*. [In Hebrew.] Jerusalem: Minerva, 2017.

———. "From the Source of Israel and Ishmael: Bedouin Parallels to Talmud and Midrash Stories." [In Hebrew.] *Mahut: Journal for Jewish Creation* 32 (Summer 2008): 9–32.

———. "Musical Instruments of the Bedouin Tribes in the North of Israel." [In Hebrew.] *Nature and Country* 22, no. 1 (November–December 1975): 9–11.

———. *The Prince of Aragon: A Collection of Sephardi Jews Tales*. [In Hebrew.] Hod-Hasharon: 'Agur, 1991.

Philippa, Kariem, Marlies Philippa, and Annelies Roeleveld. "Monophthongization of *ay/ai* and *aw/au*: A Comparison between Arabic and Germanic Dialects." *Amsterdamer Beiträge zur älteren Germanistik* 77, no. 3–4 (2017): 613–36.

Piamenta, Moshe. *Islam in Everyday Arabic Speech*. Leiden: E. J. Brill, 1979.

———. "A Linguistic System of Bedouin Manners in the Negev and Its Linguistic Description." [In Hebrew.] In *Oriental Studies in Memoriam D. H. Baneth*, 125–73. Jerusalem: Magnes, 1979.

———. *The Muslim Conception of God and Human Welfare as Reflected in Everyday Arabic Speech*. Leiden: E. J. Brill, 1983.

———. *The Use of Tenses, Aspects, and Moods in the Arabic Dialect of Jerusalem*. [In Hebrew.] Jerusalem: Prime Minister's Office, Bureau of the Adviser on Arab Affairs, 1964.

Plato. *The Dialogues of Plato* (Translator: B. Jowett), 5 vols. London: Oxford University Press, 1937. https://oll-resources.s3.us-east-2.amazonaws.com/oll3/store/titles/111/0131-01_Bk.pdf.

Pliny. *Natural History*, (Translators: H. Rackham, W.H.S. Jones & D.E. Eichholz), Cambridge, MA: Harvard University Press, 1949–54.
The Qur'ān. Translated by Alan Jones. Cambridge: Gibb Memorial Trust, 2007.
Rabinowitz, Dan, and Khawalde Sliman. "Demilitarized, Then Dispossessed: The Kirad Bedouins of the Hula Valley in the Context of Syrian-Israeli Relations." *International Journal of Middle East Studies* 32, no. 4 (2000): 511–30.
Radin, Paul. *The Trickster: A Study in American Indian Mythology*. New York: Schocken Books, 1972.
Ramanujan, A. K. *A Flowering Tree and Other Oral Tales from India*. Berkeley: University of California Press, 1997.
Raufman, Ravit. "Teaching Folklore in a Multi-culture Class: The Case of the Druze Versions of the Wolf and the Kids." [In Hebrew.] *Dameta Letamar (She Is Like a Palm)—Studies in Honor of Tamar Alexander, El Prezente, Studies of Sephardic Culture, 8–9 / Mikan (From Here)—Journal for Hebrew and Israeli Literature and Culture Studies* 2, no. 26 (2015): 607–25.
Rosén, Tova. *Hunting Gazelles: Reading Gender in Medieval Hebrew Literature*. [In Hebrew.] Tel-Aviv: Tel-Aviv University, 2006.
Rosenbaum, Gabriel Moshe. "Curses, Insults and Taboo Words in Egyptian Arabic: In Daily Speech and Written Literature." In *Romano-Arabica: Curses and Profanity in the Languages and Cultures of the Middle East and North Africa*, 19:153–88. Bucharest: University of Bucharest, 2019.
Rosenhouse, Judith. "An Arabic Story and Its Linguistic Analysis." *Zeitschrift für Arabische Linguistik* (ZAL) 30 (1995): 62–83.
———. *The Bedouin Arabic Dialects: General Problems and Close Analysis of North Israel Bedouin Dialect*. Wiesbaden: Harrassowitz, 1984.
———. "Colloquial Arabic and Hebrew Vowels in Bedouin and Druze Native Speakers' Spontaneous Speech (in Israel)." [In Hebrew.] In *Proceedings of the 31st–32nd Annual Meetings, No. XXXI*, edited by A. Amit and H. Bat-Zeev Shyldkrot, 102–21. Tel-Aviv: Haim B. Rosén Israeli Linguistic Society, Tel-Aviv University, 2017.
———. "A Comparative Analysis of Bedouin and Sedentary Men's and Women's Stories." In *Proceedings of the 3rd International Conference AIDA, Malta, 1998*, edited by M. Mifsud, 151–56. Valletta, Malta: AIDA, 2000.
———. "A Comparative Analysis of Stories Narrated by Bedouin and Sedentary Male and Female Speakers." *Zeitschrift für Arabische Linguistik* 39 (2001): 64–83.
———. "Features of Women's Speech in Arabic Dialects: An Interim Survey." In *Proceedings of the 2nd International Conference of AIDA, Cambridge, 1995*, edited by J. Cremona, C. Holes, and G. Khan, 207–16. Cambridge, 1995.
———. "Vocabulary Changes in an Eastern Arabic Region in the 20th Century." *Quaderni di Studi Arabic N.S. 9, The Language(s) of Arabic Literautre. Un Omaggio a Lidia Bettini* (2014): 99–114.
———. "Whose Child Is He? An Arabic Bedouin Story and an Analysis." *Fabula* 34, no. 1–2 (1993): 90–104.
Rosenhouse, Judith, and Yehuda Katz. *Texts in the Dialects of Bedouins in Israel*. [In Hebrew and phonetic transcription.] Occasional Papers on the Middle East (New Series) 3. Haifa: Jewish-Arab Center, Institute of Middle-East Studies, University of Haifa, 1980.
Runte, H. R., J. K. Wikeley, and A. J. Farrell, eds. *The Seven Sages of Rome and the Book of Sindbad: An Annotated Bibliography*. New York: Garland, 1984.
Ryder, Arthur W., trans. *The Panchatantra*. Chicago, University of Chicago Press, 1925.
Salamon, H. "Lame Bora: An Ethiopian Folktale." [In Hebrew.] In *Masoret Haya: 33 Essays in Folklore in Honor of Professor Haya Bar-Itzhak*, edited by Tsafi Sebba-Elron,

Haya Milo, and Idit Pintel-Ginsberg, 232–41. Haifa, Pardes Press and Haifa University Press, 2020.

Sawā'ed, Muḥammad. "Bedouin-Jewish Relationship in the Land of Israel in the Mandate Period, 1918–1948." [In Hebrew.] PhD thesis, Bar-Ilan University, 1998.

Sawā'ed, Muhammad Yusef. "The Bedouins in the Land of Israel in the Years 1808–1904." [In Hebrew.] Master's thesis, Bar-Ilan University, 1992.

Schmidt, Hans, and Paul Kahle. *Volkserzählungen aus Palästina*. 2 vols. Göttingen: Vandenhoeck & Ruprecht, 1918, 1930.

Schwarzbaum, Haim. *From the Source of Israel and Ishmael: The Folkloristic Aspects of Judaism and Islam*. [In Hebrew.] Tel-Aviv: Don, 1975.

Shabtai, Aharon. *Greek Mythology*. [In Hebrew.] Tel-Aviv: Map—Mapping & Publishing, 2000.

Shawarbah, Musa. *A Grammar of Negev Arabic: Comparative Studies, Texts and Glossary in the Bedouin Dialect of the 'Azāzmih Tribe*. Wiesbaden: Harrassowitz, 2012.

Shenhar, Aliza, "The Folkloristic Sources of Bialik's Agadat Shelosha ve-Arba'ah." [In Hebrew.] *Yeda-'Am*, 17, 28–32.

Shibli, Diab. A *Bedouin in the Galilee*. [In Hebrew.] Tel-Aviv: Tel-Aviv District Ministry of Education, 1992.

Shilo, Varda. *Lishana Deni (Our Language): A Collection of Legends and Folktales from the Tradition of Kurdistan Jews*. [In Hebrew and Zakho Aramaic., Jerusalem: Minerva, 2014.

Sowayan, Saad Abdulla. *The Arabian Oral Historical Narrative: An Ethnographic and Linguistic Analysis*. Wiesbaden: Otto Harrassowitz, 1992.

———. *Nabati Poetry: The Oral Poetry of Arabia*. Berkeley: University of California Press, 1985.

Spiegelberg, Wilhelm. *Der Ägyptische Mythus vom Sonnenauge (der Papyrus der Tierfabeln, Kufi). Nach dem Leidener demotischen Papyrus I 384*. Strasbourg: Strassburger Druckerei und Verlagsanstalt, 1917.

Stewart, Frank H. *Texts in Sinai Bedouin Law*. Part 1, *The Texts in English Translation*. With the assistance of H. Blanc and S. Hsen. Wiesbaden: Harrassowitz, 1988.

———. *Texts in Sinai Bedouin Law*. Part 2, *The Texts in Arabic, Glossary*. With the assistance of H. Blanc and S. Hsen. Wiesbaden: Harrassowitz, 1990.

Tatar, Maria. *The Annotated Brothers Grimm*. New York: W. W. Norton, 2004.

Teper, Yigal. "Game Boards in the Rock." [In Hebrew.] *Nature and Country* 20, no. 1 (November–December 1977): 21–23.

Thompson, Stith. *The Folktale*. Berkley: University of California Press, 1977. http://folkmasa.org/motiv/folktale.htm.

———. *Motif-Index of Folk Literature: A Classification of Narrative Elements in Folktales, Ballads, Myths, Fables, Mediaeval Romances, Exempla, Fabliaux, Jest-Books and Local Legends*. Rev. and enlarged ed. 6 vols. Bloomington: Indiana University Press, 1955–58.

Tolstoy, Leo. *Anna Karenina*, New Haven, CT: Yale University Press, 2014.

Uther, Hans-Jörg. *The Types of International Folktales: A Classification and a Bibliography, Based on the System of Antti Aarne and Stith Thompson*. Parts 1–3, FF Communications 284–86. Helsinki:, Academia Scientiarum Fennica, 2004.

Vicente, Angeles. "Demonstratives." In *Encyclopedia of Arabic Language and Linguistics*, edited by K. Versteegh, Leiden: Brill, 1:569–73. 2006.

Virgil. *Aeneid*. [In Hebrew.] Translated by Shelomo Dickman. Jerusalem: Bialik Institute, 1964.

Watson, Janet C. E., and Alex Bellem. "Glottalisation and Neutralization in Yemeni Arabic and Mehri: An Acoustic Study." In *Instrumental Studies in Arabic Phonetics*, edited by Z. M. Hassan and B. Hesselwood, 235–56. Amsterdam: John Benjamins, 2011.

Wehr, Hans. *A Dictionary of Modern Written Arabic*. Edited by J. Milton Cowan. Wiesbaden: Harrassowitz, 1971.

Wright, W. *A Grammar of the Arabic Language*. 2 vols. Cambridge: Cambridge University Press, 1962.

Yassif, Eli. *The Hebrew Collection of Tales in the Middle Ages*. [In Hebrew.] Tel-Aviv: Hakibbutz Hameuchad, 2004.

———. *The Hebrew Folktale: History, Genre, Meaning*. Translated by Jacqueline S. Teitelbaum. Bloomington: Indiana University Press, 1999.

Yitshaki, Arieh. "The Bedouin Tribes at the Foot of Mount Tabor." [In Hebrew.] *Qardom* 20 (1982): 88–92.

Yonai, Mordekhai. *Why Did the Earth Laugh? Bedouins Narrate*. [In Hebrew.] Tel-Aviv: Hakibbutz Hameuchad, 1994.

Yong, Rudolf Erik de. "The Bedouin Dialects of the Northern Dinai Littoral: Bridging the Linguistic Gap between the Eastern and Western Arab World." PhD thesis, University of Amsterdam, 1999.

Zubi, Amal. "Pausal Forms in the Arabic of Nazareth." *Mediterranean Language Review* 24 (2017): 159–74.

Index of Tale Types

Narrative Type	Narrative Type Name	Chapter Name
ATU 75	The Help of the Weak	43. The Lion Who Wanted to Know Man's Nature
ATU 123	The Wolf and the Kids	42. The Goat, the Kid, and the Ġūla
ATU 157A	The Lion Searches for Man	43. The Lion Who Wanted to Know Man's Nature
ATU 285A	The Man and the Wounded Snake	41. The Man and the Wounded Snake
ATU 300	The Dragon-Slayer	20. The Prince and His Two Wives; 23. The Dangerous Night-Watch; 31. The Sickle Hand
ATU 304	The Dangerous Night-Watch	23. The Dangerous Night-Watch
ATU 310	The Maiden in the Tower	32. Bells Sound
ATU 315A	The Cannibal Sister	24. My Mother Slew Me; My Father Ate Me; 30. The Girl and Her Seven Brothers; 31. The Sickle Hand
ATU 327A	Hansel and Gretel	34. The Children and the Ogre
ATU 327B	The Brothers and the Ogre	34. The Children and the Ogre
ATU 327C	The Devil (Witch) Carries the Hero Home in a Sack	34. The Children and the Ogre
ATU 327G	The Brothers at the Witch's House	38. The Two Brothers and the Ġūla
ATU 327H§	Foolish Husband Ignores His Wife's Advice and Leads Her and the Children to Ogress. He Is Devoured (El-Shamy)	37. The Ġūla, the Mallow Gatherer and His Daughter; 38. The Two Brothers and the Ġūla
ATU 328	The Boy Steals the Ogre's Treasure	34. The Children and the Ogre

Narrative Type	Narrative Type Name	Chapter Name
ATU 400	The Man on a Quest for His Lost Wife	8. The Doe
AT 401	The Princess Transformed into Deer	8. The Doe
ATU 425	The Search for the Lost Husband	33. The Golden Palm Tree
ATU 425B	Son of the Witch (AT 425B, The Disenchanted Husband: the Witch's Tasks)	33. The Golden Palm Tree
ATU 450	Little Brother and Little Sister	13. The Girl and Her Brother Who Became a Deer
ATU 451	The Maiden Who Seeks Her Brothers	31. The Sickle Hand
ATU 480D*	Tales of Kind and Unkind Girls	21. In the Family
ATU 510A	Cinderella	18. The Two Notes (Smart Ḥasan); 24. My Mother Slew Me; My Father Ate Me
ATU 516	Faithful John	19. The Kidnapped Bride
ATU 533	The Speaking Horsehead (The Geese Girl)	19. The Kidnapped Bride; 24. My Mother Slew Me; My Father Ate Me; 32. Bells Sound
ATU 533A§	Beautiful Maiden in Hideous Disguise. She Is Detected by the Prince (El-Shamy)	32. Bells Sound
ATU 551	Water of Life	20. The Prince and His Two Wives
ATU 572§	Bringing the Dumb Princess to Speak by Telling a Story That Ends with a Riddle (El-Shamy)	17. The Silent Princess and Smart Mḥammad
ATU 613	The Two Travelers	44. The Two Hunters
ATU 655	The Wise Brothers	26. The Inheritance Case
AT 655A	The Strayed Camel and the Clever Deductions	26. The Inheritance Case
ATU 705	Born from a Fish (Fruit)	28. Frēṭ Rummān (Snow White)
ATU 705A§	Born from Pregnant Man, Raised by Bird (Animal) (El-Shamy)	28. Frēṭ Rummān (Snow White)
ATU 707	The Three Golden Children	36. The Golden Children
ATU 709	Snow White	18. The Two Notes (Smart Ḥasan); 28. Frēṭ Rummān (Snow White)

Narrative Type	Narrative Type Name	Chapter Name
ATU 720	The Juniper Tree (AT 720, My Mother Slew Me; My Father Ate Me)	24. My Mother Slew Me; My Father Ate Me
ATU 725	A Dream about Future Greatness	1. Between the Sun and the Moon
ATU 736A	The Ring of Polycrates	14. Do Good and Throw It into the Sea
ATU 851	The Princess Who Cannot Solve the Riddle	16. The Son Who Obeyed His Mother; 17. The Silent Princess and Smart Mḥammad; 18. The Two Notes (Smart Ḥasan)
ATU 883A	The Innocent and Slandered Maiden	4. The Ḥağğ's Daughter and the Orator
ATU 884	The Forsaken Fiancée: Service as Menial	20. The Prince and His Two Wives
ATU 923B	The Princess Who Was Responsible for Her Own Fortune	6. The King's Wife and the Poor Man
ATU 930A f	The Weasel and the Pit	3. The Girl Who Fell into a Well
ATU 930A k	Solomon's Daughter in the Tower	2. The Princess on the Island
ATU 934 (AT 934B)	The Youth to Die on His Wedding Day	33. The Golden Palm Tree
ATU 945	Luck and Intelligence	17. The Silent Princess and Smart Mḥammad
ATU 960	The Sun Will Bring Everything to Light	10. The Raindrop Bubbles Will Testify
ATU 976	Which Was the Noblest Act?	26. The Inheritance Case
ATU 1137	The Blinded Ogre (Polyphemus, Tefegös)	27. The Giant
ATU 1350	The Soon-Consoled Widow	5. A Woman's Loyalty
ATU 1358C	Trickster Discovers Adultery: Food Goes to Husband Instead of Lover	25. The Boy, the Uncle, and the Lover
ATU 1510	The Matron of Ephesus	5. A Woman's Loyalty
ATU 1535	The Rich and the Poor Farmer	25. The Boy, the Uncle, and the Lover
ATU 1645	The Treasure at Home	10. The Raindrop Bubbles Will Testify
ATU 1645A	Dream of Treasure Bought	10. The Raindrop Bubbles Will Testify
ATU 1653	The Robbers under the Tree	38. The Two Brothers and the Ġūla

Index of Motifs

Motif No.	Description	Chapter No.
B. Animals		
B11.7.1	Dragon controls water-supply	31. The Sickle Hand
B11.10	Sacrifice of human being to dragon	20. The Prince and His Two Wives; 31. The Sickle Hand
B81	Mermaid. Woman with tail of fish (Sirens). Lives in sea.	9. The Woman from the Sea
B81.0.2	Woman from water world	9. The Woman from the Sea
B81.13.11	Woman from water world	9. The Woman from the Sea
B81.13.11.1	Mermaid caught by fishermen	9. The Woman from the Sea
B81.2	Mermaid marries man	9. The Woman from the Sea
B81.2.1	Mermaid has son by human father	9. The Woman from the Sea
B103.0.4.1	Grateful snake gives gold piece daily	41. The Man and the Wounded Snake
B517§	From random listening to the conversation of pigeons, it turns out that certain parts of their bodies are the only cure for the hero's healing	15. The Transposed Heads
B524.1.2	Dogs rescue fleeing master from tree refuge	31. The Sickle Hand
B765.6.1	Snake drinks milk	35. The Emīr's Daughter Who Flew to Switzerland; 41. The Shepherd and the Snake
‡B767.2	Snakes enjoy music	41. The Man and the Wounded Snake
C. Tabu		
C611	Forbidden chamber. Person allowed to enter all chambers of house except one	28. Frēṭ Rummān (Snow White)

Motif No.	Description	Chapter No.
C742	Tabu: striking monster twice. Though monster begs that hero strike him again, hero refuses. Monster would otherwise revive	23. The Dangerous Night-Watch 30. The Girl and Her Seven Brothers 35. The Emīr's Daughter Who Flew to Switzerland;
D. Magic		
D555.1	Transformation by drinking from animal's track	13. The Girl and Her Brother Who Became a Deer
D1311.6.1	Moon (stars) answers questions	28. Frēṭ Rummān (Snow White)
D1311.6.3	Sun answers questions	28. Frēṭ Rummān (Snow White)
D1451.2	Treasure falls from mouth	21. In the Family
D1505.1	Herbs restore sight	20. The Prince and His Two Wives
D1715	Magic power of dying man's words	10. The Rain Bubbles Will Testify
E. The Dead		
E11.1	Second blow resuscitates. First kills	23. The Dangerous Night-Watch 30. The Girl and Her Seven Brothers 35. The Emīr's Daughter Who Flew to Switzerland;
E34	Resuscitation with misplaced head. (Cf. M221.) In restoration of several persons simultaneously through reassembling of members, the heads are placed on the wrong bodies. Sometimes the damage is repaired, sometimes not	15. The Transposed Heads
E80	Water of Life. Resuscitation by water	33. The Golden Palm Tree
E710.1	Ferocious animal guardian of separable soul of ogress	23. The Dangerous Night-Watch
E711.1	Soul in egg	23. The Dangerous Night-Watch
E713	Soul hidden in a series of coverings. This motif is combined with several others. Usually the soul will be hidden in an egg, in a duck, in a well, in a church, or a similar series.	23. The Dangerous Night-Watch
E715.1	Separable soul in bird	23. The Dangerous Night-Watch
E721	Soul journeys from the body	10. The Rain Bubbles Will Testify
E730	Soul in animal form	10. The Rain Bubbles Will Testify
F. Marvels		
F647.1	Marvelous sensitiveness: meat (wine) tastes of corpse. Has been near grave	26. The Inheritance Case

Motif No.	Description	Chapter No.
F647.5.1	Marvelous sensitiveness: meat is dog's flesh. Animal has been suckled by a dog	26. The Inheritance Case
F661.1	Skillful marksman shoots meat from giant's hands	23. The Dangerous Night-Watch
F848.1	Girl's long hair as ladder into tower. Rapunzel	32. Bells Sound
F954	Dumb person brought to speak	16. The Son Who Obeyed His Mother
G. Ogres		
G30	Person becomes cannibal	31. The Sickle Hand
G33	Child born as cannibal	31. The Sickle Hand
G61	Relative's flesh eaten unwittingly	24. My Mother Slew Me; My Father Ate Me; 34. The Children and the Ogre
G82	Cannibal fattens victim	34. The Children and the Ogre
G249.1	Witches drive herds of deer	28. Frēṭ Rummān (Snow White)
G312.7	Ogress devours horses	31. The Sickle Hand
G441	Ogre carries victim in bag (basket)	34. The Children and the Ogre
G526	Ogre deceived by feigned ignorance of hero. Hero must be shown how to get into oven (or the like). Ogre shows him and permits himself to be burnt	34. The Children and the Ogre
G610.4§ (El-Shamy)	Stealing from ogre because of hunger (to avoid starvation)	38. The Two Brothers and the Ġūla
H. Tests		
H81.1	Hero lies by sleeping girl and leaves identification token with her	23. The Dangerous Night-Watch
H81.1.1	Hero takes token from sleeping princess	23. The Dangerous Night-Watch
H81.2	Clandestine visit of princess to hero betrayed by token	16. The Son Who Obeyed His Mother
H83	Rescue tokens. Proof that hero has succeeded in rescue	23. The Dangerous Night-Watch
H117	Identification by cut garment. Garment is cut and fragment taken as token	16. The Son Who Obeyed His Mother
H316	Suitor test: apple thrown indicates princess's choice. (Often golden apple)	23. The Dangerous Night-Watch
H343	Suitor test: bringing dumb princess to speak	17. The Silent Princess and Smart Mḥammad
H466	Feigned death to test wife's faithfulness	5. A Woman's Loyalty

Motif No.	Description	Chapter No.
H565	Riddle propounded from chance experience. On way to riddle trial youth sees things that give him a clue for his riddles	16. The Son Who Obeyed His Mother
H1023.2	Task: carrying water in a sieve	31. The Sickle Hand
H1324	Quest for marvelous remedy	20. The Prince and His Two Wives
J. The wise and the foolish		
J229.16.5.1§ (El-Shamy)	Captive man to ogress: who is captured by the monster turns to her and says, 'Devour me beginning with my little ears (beard) which did not heed my wife's fears (advice)	37. The Ġūla, the Mallow Gatherer, and His Daughter
J1661.1.1	Deduction: the one-eyed camel. A she-camel has passed, blind in one eye; on the one side she carries wine and on the other vinegar; two men lead her, one a heathen and the other a Jew. Solution: She is recognized as a she-camel by the footprints; she is blind because she feeds on only one side of the road; the wine dropping down has soaked into the earth; the vinegar makes bubbles; the heathen is not so careful in his manners as is the Jew	26. The Inheritance Case
K. Deceptions		
K521.1	Escape by dressing in animal (bird, human) skin	27. The Giant
K603	Escape under ram's belly. By hiding under the belly of a ram the hero escapes under the legs of the blind ogre	27. The Giant
K912	Robbers' (giants') heads cut off one by one as they enter house	23. The Dangerous Night-Watch
K1321.2	Man disguised as woman abducts princess	19. The Kidnapped Bride
K1344	Tunnel entrance to guarded maiden's chamber	19. The Kidnapped Bride
K1837	Disguise of woman in man's clothes	20. The Prince and His Two Wives
K1911.1.2	False bride takes true bride's place when child is born	13. The Girl and Her Brother Who Became a Deer
K2115	Animal-birth slander. A woman is accused of having given birth to animals. Her children are put out of the way and animals substituted	36. The Golden Children
K2284	Treacherous priest	4. The Ḥāğğ's Daughter and the Orator
M. Ordaining the future		
M341.1.1	Prophecy: death on wedding day	33. The Golden Palm Tree

Motif No.	Description	Chapter No.
N. Chance and fate		
N122.0.1	The choice of roads. At parting of three roads are equivocal inscriptions telling what will happen if each is chosen. Brothers each choose a different road.	23. The Dangerous Night-Watch
N211.1	Lost ring found in fish. (Polycrates)	14. Do Good and Throw It into the Sea
N271.1	The sun brings all to light. The murderer repeats as he sees the rays of the sun, the last words of the dying man, thus betraying the crime	10. The Raindrop Bubbles Will Testify
N271.2	Murder revealed by unusual names of boys. The dying man leaves message to name his sons "Oh Allah" and "Oh king" (or the like). This arouses the king's curiosity and brings the murder to light	10. The Raindrop Bubbles Will Testify
N531.3	Dream of treasure bought. Treasure has been seen by man's soul absent in sleep in form of a fly. The purchaser of the dream finds the treasure	10. The Raindrop Bubbles Will Testify
N571	Devil (Demon) as guardian of treasure	23. The Dangerous Night-Watch
N640	Accidental healing	7. Ǧuḥā and the Queen
N641.0.1§ (El-Shamy)	Patient laughs so hard at comic actions (scenes) about him, thus abscess breaks (object in throat dislodged) and he is healed.	7. Ǧuḥā and the Queen
N711	King (prince) accidentally finds maiden and marries her	28. Frēṭ Rummān (Snow White)
N711.2	Hero finds maiden in (magic) castle	23. The Dangerous Night-Watch
N773	Adventure from following animal to cave (lower world)	13. The Girl and Her Brother Who Became a Deer
P. Society		
P253.1	Brother about to drink blood of seemingly guilty sister	4. The Ḥāǧǧ's Daughter and the Orator
P253.2	Sister faithful to transformed brother	13. The Girl and Her Brother Who Became a Deer
R. Captive and fugitives		
R111.1.1	Rescue of princess from ogre	31. The Sickle Hand
R251	Flight on a tree, which ogre tries to cut down	31. The Sickle Hand
S. Unnatural cruelty		
S110.3	Princess builds tower of skulls of unsuccessful suitors	16. The Son Who Obeyed His Mother

Motif No.	Description	Chapter No.
T. Sex		
T231.3	Faithless widow ready to marry messenger who brings news of husband's death. The husband, however, has only feigned death to test her	5. A Woman's Loyalty
T475.2	Hero lies by princess in magic sleep and begets child	23. The Dangerous Night-Watch
T511.1.1	Conception from eating apple	29. The Man Who Delivered a Daughter; 34. The Children and the Ogre
T578	Pregnant man	29. The Man Who Delivered a Daughter
T581.12	Man gives birth to a daughter; woman gives birth to a son	28. Frēṭ Rummān (Snow White)
Z. Miscellaneous groups of motifs		
Z16	Tales ending with a question	16. The Son Who Obeyed His Mother

Narrators List

No.	Story No.	Story Name	Narrator	Tribe	IFA No.	Year	Comments
1	1	Between the Sun and the Moon	Ibrahim Qwēder Ṣbēḥāt	Rummāneh-Ṣbēḥāt	17414	1982	
2	2	The Princess on the Island	Ṯalǧe Mūsa	Ḥuǧērāt	17402	1982	
3	3	The Girl Who Fell into a Well	Nūra Ḥalīfa	ʿArāmša	14074		Recorder: Naomi Raies
4	4	The Ḥāǧǧ's Daughter and the Orator	Ṣabḥa ʿAbūd	Ḥuǧērāt	12718	1979	
5	5	A Woman's Loyalty	Ṣabḥa ʿAbūd	Ḥuǧērāt	12723	1979	
6	6	The King's Wife and the Poor Man	Zehiyya Ġrifāt	Ġrifāt	17411	1982	
7	7	Ǧuḥā and the Queen	Ṣabḥa ʿAbūd	Ḥuǧērāt	13259		
8	8	The Doe	Šḥāde Rxayyim	Saʿadiyya	17415	1982	
9	9	The Woman from the Sea	Unknown	ʿArāmša	17426		
10	10a	The Man and His Neighbor	Ṣabḥa ʿAbūd	Ḥuǧērāt	17406		
11	10b	Ḏāʿeq ʿAnṣāf (Tasting Justice)	Ibrahim ʿAli Ḥreb Ḥuǧērāt	Ḥuǧērāt	13247	1980	
12	11	The Coffee Server	Ṯalǧe Mūsa	Ḥuǧērāt		2015	

No.	Story No.	Story Name	Narrator	Tribe	IFA No.	Year	Comments
13	12	The Old Man and the Girl, the Old Woman and the Young Man	ʿĒide Xalīl Mrisāt	Mrēsāt	17417	1983	
14	13	The Girl and Her Brother Who Became a Deer	Ṭalǧe Mūsa	Ḥuǧērāt	15232	1982	
15	14	Do Good and Throw It into the Sea	Nūra Ḥalīfa	ʿArāmša	14075		
16	15	The Transposed Heads	Ṭarwa Yāsīn	Ḥaǧāǧra		1984	
17	16	The Son Who Obeyed His Mother	Zaid ʿAli Muḥammad Saʿadi	Saʿadiyya	13713	1981	
18	17	The Silent Princess and Smart Mḥammad	Ṭarwa Yāsīn	Ḥaǧāǧra	17393	1984	
19	18	The Two Notes (Smart Ḥasan)	Maḥmūd Muḥamad Mrisāt	Mrēsāt	17418	1982	
20	19	The Kidnapped Bride	Ṣabḥa ʿAbūd	Ḥuǧērāt	13260	1980	
21	20	The Prince and His Two Wives	Ṣabḥa ʿAbūd	Ḥuǧērāt	12721	1979	
22	21a	Between a Brother and His Sister	Ṭarwa Yāsīn	Ḥaǧāǧra	17397	1984	
23	21b	Between a Bride and Her Mother-in-Law	Maryam Šatwah	Ḥuǧērāt	18981	1982	
24	22	The Replaced Bride	Maryam Muṣṭafa Ṭabbāš	Ḥilf-Ṭabbāš	15229	1982	
25	23a	Šāṭer Ḥasan and His Nine Brothers	Unknown	Sawāʿed			
26	23b	Seven Brides for Seven Brothers	Ṣabḥa ʿAbūd	Ḥuǧērāt	17407	1980	
27	24a	The Green Bird	Ḥalīma Ḥasan Slimān	Zbēdāt	17429	1982	

No.	Story No.	Story Name	Narrator	Tribe	IFA No.	Year	Comments
28	24b	The Yellow Cow	Maryam Šatwah	Ḥuğērāt	17430	1982	
29	25	The Boy, the Uncle, and the Lover	Ṣabḥa ʿAbūd	Ḥuğērāt	18178		
30	26	The Inheritance Case	Ḥasan Maḥmūd Swēṭāt	Saʿadiyya	17423	1982	
31	27	The Giant	Warda Hawāš	Mazārīb	17420	1982	
32	28	Frēṭ Rummān (Snow White)	Zehiyya Ġrifāt	Ġrifāt	17413	1982	
33	29	The Man Who Delivered a Daughter	Ṭarwa Yāsīn	Ḥağāğra	18484	1984	
34	30	The Girl and Her Seven Brothers	Maryam Muṣṭafa Ṭabbāš	Ḥilf-Ṭabbāš	15230	1982	
35	31	The Sickle Hand	Ṭalğe Mūsa	Ḥuğērāt	15231	1985	
36	32a	Ǧbēna and the Jujube Tree	Zehiyya Ġrifāt	Ġrifāt	17412	1982	
37	32b	The Ǧinn and the Girl in Dog clothes	Ṣabḥa ʿAbūd	Ḥuğērāt	12720	1979	
38	33	The Golden Palm Tree	Unknown	Neʿēm			
39	34a	The Girls and the Ġūla	Warda Hawāš	Mazārīb	18171	1982	
40	34b	Grēʿa, Ḥmēda, and Ḥdaydūn	Maryam Muṣṭafa Ṭabbāš	Ḥilf-Ṭabbāš		1982	
41	34c	Nuṣṣ-ᵉNṣēṣ	Ṭalğe Mūsa	Ḥuğērāt	15231	1980	
42	35	The Emīr's Daughter Who Flew to Switzerland	Zehiyya Ġrifāt	Ġrifāt	17410	1982	
43	36a	The Three Siblings and the Talking Birds	Ḥalīma Ḥasan Slimān	Zbēdāt	17404	1982	
44	36b	The Wicked Old Woman	Warda Hawāš	Mazārīb		1982	

No.	Story No.	Story Name	Narrator	Tribe	IFA No.	Year	Comments
45	36c	The Emīr and the Slave	Unknown	Saʿadiyya	17421	1982	
46	37	The Ġūla, the Mallow Gatherer, and His Daughter	ʿĀlia Muḥammad Ḥrēb	Ḥuǧērāt	13252	1980	
47	38	The Two Brothers and the Ġūla	Ṯalǧe Mūsa	Ḥuǧērāt	17403	1982	
48	39a	The Young Man and the Ġūla	ʾUmm Mūsa Mizʿil	ʿArāmša			Recorder: Yehuda Katz
49	39b	The Ġūla Who Posed as a Tribe Member	Unknown	ʿArāmša	17427		
50	39c	The Groom and the Ġūla	Warda Hawāš	Mazārīb	18313	1982	
51	39d	The Ġūla in the Waterhole	Ibrāhīm ʿAli	Ḥuǧērāt	13248	1980	
52	39e	Abu Xiḏᵉr and the Ġūla	Nūra Ḥalīfa	ʿArāmša	17425		Recorder: Naomi Raies
53	40	The Old Woman and the Ḥūt	Ṯalǧe Mūsa	Ḥuǧērāt	17400	1982	
54	41a	The Snake Story	ʿAbdallah Asʿad Shibli	Šibli		1980	Recorder: Judith Rosen-house
55	41b	The Shepherd and the Snake	Nūra Ḥalīfa	ʿArāmša	14076	1981	Recorder: Naomi Raies
56	42	The Goat, the Kid, and the Ġūla	Maḥmūd Muḥammad Mrēsāt	Mrēsāt	17419	1982	
57	43	The Lion Who Wanted to Know Man's Nature	Zidān ʿAli Muṣṭafa	Sawāʿed	13258	1979	
58	44	The Two Hunters	Ḥasan Maḥmūd Swēṭāt	Saʿadiyya	17424	1982	

Subject and Name Index

Abu Haidar, Farida, 485
adultery, 54, 97, 224–225, 233–234, 529
Air Camel (huge mythical bird), 259–260, 263, 277, 279–280
Al-ʿĀref, ʿĀref. 467, 484
Al-Barghuthi, Abdullatif M., ix, 283, 359, 393
angel, 16, 24–25, 27, 78, 133, 133, 135, 171, 174, 338, 378
Aramaic, 359, 522
Ashkenazi, Tovia, 94, 100, 114, 118, 123–124, 156, 168, 484, 491, 497, 506–507, 515

Bailey, Clinton, 484n11
Barthélemy, Adrien, ix, 99n3, 99n7, 208n10, 210n21, 210n23, 254n3, 254nn6–7, 304n2, 358n4, 359n5, 402n3, 440n3, 461–462n4, 484n26
Bar-Zvi, Sasson, 96, 100, 438, 440, 484n12
Bascom, William, 293, 296
Basile, Giambattista, 113, 115, 157
Bauer, Leonhard, 466, 484n5
Behnsdtedt, Peter, and Aharon Geva-Kleinberger, 484n10
Ben-Amos, Dan, xi, 54, 66, 235, 270
Ben-David, Yosef, 488, 506n21, 507n47, 508n89, 518
Ben-David, Yosef, and Barkai, Amnon, 79n2, 484n3, 484n10, 507n32, 507n54, 507n65, 507n68, 508nn84–86, 511–512, 513–514
Berechiah Ben Natronai Ha-Nakdan Mishle Shualim (Fox Fables), 50
Bergsträsser, Gotthelf, 466, 484n4
Bettelheim, Bruno, 115, 263, 265, 317, 339–340, 444
Bettini, Lidia, 150n2
bird, 23–24, 27–28, 39–40, 51, 73, 77, 83, 93, 112, 129, 133–135, 139–143, 161–162, 168, 180–181, 193, 198–200, 203, 205–206, 210–216, 218, 220–221, 224, 229, 237–238, 250, 263, 270, 277, 279–280, 291, 298, 302, 316, 328, 338, 374–376, 378, 382, 386–388, 390–392, 406, 410–411, 459, 528, 532, 534
Blanc, Haim, 45, 144n4, 181n3, 218n3, 424n10, 467–468, 484n9, 484n14, 485n45, 518
blind, blindness, 8, 133, 136, 159, 161–162, 165–168, 174, 206, 228–229, 233, 236–237, 247–252, 298, 329, 369–370, 399, 459, 529, 534
Borg, A., 182n3
Burton, Richard, Arabian Nights, 64–66, 74, 78–79, 86, 163, 165, 205, 252, 256, 266, 299, 318, 359n18, 369–370, 391, 448, 450–451

Bushnaq, Inea, 11, 44, 180–181, 216, 391, 401, 444

cannibal(ism), 217, 250, 252, 293–298, 302–303, 340, 346, 349, 356, 401, 527, 533
Cantineau, Jean, 150n2, 444n1, 467, 484n7
code mixing, 117, 451, 461, 475
code switching, xiv, 480
colors, 6, 7, 62, 181, 182, 218, 297, 310. 311, 442, 479
cow, cow's dung, 171; demonic cow, 395, 400, 418, 446; eaten by a daemon, 262, 284–285, 294, 309; Ġūla maintains a herd of cows (or deer), 257, 265, 271, 403–405, 409–410, 428, 533; Ġūla turns herself into a cow, 401; provides food, 211, 213–217; speaking cow, 450, 539
Crowfoot, Grace M., and Baldensperger, Louise, 317, 398
Cyclops, 246, 249–251, 253, 428

demonstratives, 29, 75, 130, 175, 208, 209, 271, 358, 423, 440
dialects, Arabic: rural, 19, 62, 116, 123, 393, 412, 472–473. 483, 485; sedentary, viii–ix, 19, 45, 62, 75 87–88, 99, 105, 116–117, 123, 131, 150–151, 175, 182, 208–210, 218, 225, 241, 253–254, 282–283, 304, 320, 359, 371, 392–393, 402, 412, 423–424, 429, 443–444, 451, 461, 465–466, 468, 470–481, 483–485, 524; urban 19, 62, 116, 393, 424, 472, 483, 485
dialects in Arab countries: Arabian Peninsula, x, 104, 144, 465–466, 483, 504, 487; Bedouin, Galilee, ix, xi, 45, 62, 75, 87–88, 99, 104, 116–117, 130–131, 150–151, 208–210, 218, 241, 253, 266, 271, 282, 304, 321, 358–359, 393, 412, 423–424, 444, 461, 466–470, 472–483; Bedouin, lexical, ix– xi, 29, 88, 99, 181, 241, 254, 267, 283, 412, 461 467, 480–481, 483, 522; Bedouin, Negev, 75, 99, 104, 130, 144, 181–182, 208–210, 215, 218, 254, 271, 283, 321, 331, 423, 444, 461–462, 467–468, 472–473, 484; Egyptian, 62, 471, 524; Levant, ix, xi, 117, 254, 304, 359, 424, 461, 465; North African, 466, 483, 490
Diglossia, 484, 485, 520
diminutive, 99, 181, 331, 359, 393, 423, 473, 474

dog. A baby is replaced by a dog, 372–373, 376–377, 385–386, 392; barks as a sign of a man's death, 436, 438; carries a man in the sea, 22–23, 27; demon's dog, 290–291, 294, 312; as a derogatory nickname, 97, 457; dog meat, 230–231, 233–234, 236, 533; dragon behaves like a dog, 300; girl in dog clothes, 312–313, 315–316; guides children to the Ġūla, 348; Ġūla turns herself into a dog, 343–344, 401; hero asks dog a question, 142, 180; hero kills a watchdog, 203, 395, 400–401; hero's dog, 293–294, 296, 531; licks fawn face, 73; lamb grows on a dog's breasts, 237, 533; suckles a puppy, 237

El-Shamy, Hasan, xi, 72, 129, 134, 163, 142, 150, 216, 218, 270, 315, 332n7, 389–390, 398–399, 402, 444, 449, 527–528, 533–535
emphasis, 20, 36, 440, 468
emphatic(s), 266, 424, 468, 473
Etkin, Tsevi, 484n12
European, 62, 482

Falah, Ghazi, 490, 497, 520
Ferguson, Charles Albert, 484n2, 485n45, 518, 520
Fischer, Wolfdietrich, 75n3, 358n3
fox, 448–449, 453–455, 460, 462

Gaháwa, Gháwa syndrome, xiv, 41, 116, 189, 218, 282, 423, 458, 473, 476, 478
gender, 164, 168, 439, 443, 470–472, 476, 484
Genizah (Cairo Genizah), 24–25, 27, 234, 297
Geva-Kleinberger, Aharon, 480, 484n34
giant, 203, 205, 245, 247–253, 314, 318, 533–534
Ğinn (Jinn), 6, 70, 132–133, 166, 274, 278, 280, 309, 312, 314–315, 325–326, 352, 380, 421, 428
glottalization, 424
glottal stop, 62, 208, 209, 467, 472
goat. demonic goat, 91, 119–121, 132, 252–253, 261, 286–288, 403, 434–435; devoured by Ġūla, 294, 302; goat dung, 171; goat smell, 236; herded by Ġūla,

403–405, 409–410, 415; Jinn's goat, 187; mother goat, 317, 348, 441–444
goose, 51, 179–180, 221–222, 316–317
Grimm, Jacob, and Grimm, Wilhelm, 84, 113–114, 203, 224, 261, 264–265, 368, 410, 443, 448
Ġūl, Ġūla. adopts a girl (or a boy), 257, 265–266, 271, 281, 307, 309–311, 315, 317, 323, 329, 348, 357, 379, 388, 391; comes from the sea, 76; devours people, 44, 217–218, 251–252, 264–265, 276–277, 281, 297–298, 306, 317, 320, 334–342, 344–349, 352–353, 355–358, 375, 387, 396–403, 405, 407, 409–412, 415–417, 441–444; eats her own child, 281, 346; general description of Ġūl, 208–209, 321, 421–422, 428, 463; a girl turns to be a ġūla, 285, 295–298, 302; kidnaps a girl, 77, 251–252, 265, 307, 309, 314, 316–318, 325, 366, 374; poisons a girl (or people), 280–281, 364, 369–370; as robber, 203 turns a girl (or men) into a dove, 278, 302; in a well, 57, 61, 418

Ḥāmi (guarding ogre), 139, 142, 286
Hanauer, James Edward, 51, 297, 300, 315, 347, 359n16
Harrison, David K., 484n1
Havelová, Andrea, 480, 484n34, 521
Hebrew, viii, x, xi, xiv, 18, 87, 116, 117, 132, 154, 360, 368, 371, 382, 404, 409, 418, 426, 456, 458, 461, 464, 466, 467, 474, 481, 482, 483, 485, 499, 517–526
Henkin, Roni, x, 75, 99, 116n7, 130n1, 181n2, 208n8, 209, 215, 219n5, 254n7, 271n1, 282n2, 331n2, 393n12, 423n4, 444n1, 461n4, 462n4, 467, 484n9, 485n45, 521
Hesiod Theogony, 249
Hoberman, R. D., 424n10
Homer, *The Odyssey*, 78, 249–250
hūt: blocks water source, 139, 160–161, 167, 194–195, 286, 288–290, 292, 294–295, 298, 300–301; devours people, 251 general description of ḥūt, 206–207, 299; gives gifts to the hero, 139; helps the hero, 379–380, 388–389; hides someone's soul, 192, 199, 205–206; kidnaps a girl (or a woman), 192, 202–203, 205–206, 365–367, 425, 427–429; turns people to stone, 192, 199, 205; in a well, 57

Ibn Khaldun, 'Abd El-Rahman, 480, 482, 484n32, 485n44
'Imāla, 151, 181, 271, 360, 444, 473

Joseph, 12, 15–19, 43, 103, 303, 317, 355–356

Koineization, 483
Krumbacher, Karl, 484n2

LA (Literary Arabic), xiv, 87, 99, 104, 117, 144, 151, 208, 209, 225, 254, 267, 282, 283, 321, 331, 358–359, 392, 393, 412, 423, 424, 429, 444, 461, 466–482, 484
Lebling, Robert, xi n3, 209n11, 393n6, 521
Leveling, 62, 483
Lion: attacks the hero, 72, 460, 462; half-eagle and half-lion, 28; helps the hero, 73, 290–298; hero helps lioness to give birth, 287, 294–295; killed by Samson 135; learns man's character, 446–451, 527, 540; magic water turn a man to a lion, 379; prevents people from grazing, 285, 288

Māred (giant demon), 314, 318
Marom, Yafit, 209n11, 321n5, 393n6
Meron, Joram, and Kabha, Riad, 75n2, 84, 174, 264, 281, 298, 393n17, 401, 480, 484n34
Muhawi, Ibrahim, and Kanaana, Sharif, 216, 297, 299, 315–316, 332n7, 390–391, 401, 444
MSA (Modern Standard Arabic), xiv, 62, 87, 99, 104, 105, 117, 144, 151, 208, 209, 225, 226, 254, 267, 283, 321, 331, 358, 359, 392, 393, 412, 423, 424, 444, 461, 462, 466–479, 481, 482, 484
Musical Instruments. Meğna (coffee mortar), 320; Miğwez (a sort of clarinet), 318–320; Rabāba (a violin with one string), 93–95, 97–98, 162; Šubbābah (shepherd's flute), 439; Yarġūl (a sort of clarinet), 318–320

narrative imperative, 144, 175, 226, 424, 440, 523
negation, 99, 117, 393, 478, 479, 484
Nizami Seven Princesses, 235
nonpharyngeal, 117, 151
Number 469–471, 476, 477, 481, 490

Oppenheimer, Max von, 466, 484n6
Owens, Jonathan, 87n3, 131n2

Palva, Heikki, 144n4, 393n7, 440n5
Patai, Raphael, 368
Penzer, N. M., *Ocean of Stories*, 127–128, 205, 236
pharyngeal, xiv, 88, 117, 209, 467, 473, 478
pharyngealization, 468, 473
pharyngealized, xiv, 304, 473, 478, 483
phonetic, ix, xi, xiv, xv, 45, 87, 88, 116, 117, 158, 209, 241, 254, 304, 320, 412, 467, 472, 473, 475, 480, 483, 485
Piamenta, Moshe, xi n3, 62n5, 118n25, 207n1, 209nn15–16, 210n20, 267n4, 271n1, 271n3, 282n2, 423n8, 484n12
Pliny, *Natural History*, 437
pregnancy apples (pomegranates), 255, 262, 270, 315, 350, 354, 356–359, 536
pronouns: bound 45, 87, 131, 150, 209, 241, 331, 402, 412, 444, 477; free, 241, 271, 392, 476; suffixed, 45, 87, 131, 209, 283, 439, 440, 444, 473

Qur'ān, x, 12, 16, 43, 79, 94, 143, 237, 279, 317, 355; Koranic 241

Ram: buried instead of a man, 110; escaping under ram's belly, 248, 250–253, 534
Raṣād (a demon that guards properties and treasures), 61, 185, 189–190, 204, 208
riddle, 13–15, 17–18, 128, 130, 134–136, 142, 150, 164, 240, 381, 388, 528–529, 534
Rosenbaum, Gabriel Moshe, 62n5
Rosenhouse, Judith, ix, xi, 104, 105n5, 117n10, 239, 242n22, 254n7, 331n2, 424n10, 424n19, 433, 437, 440n13, 465, 480–482, 484n10, 484n12, 484nn17–18, 484n23, 484n25, 484n33, 485nn36–37, 485nn39–40, 524

Schmidt, Hans, and Kahle, Paul, 44, 46n10, 61, 62n10, 216–217, 219n7, 251, 391, 480, 484n34, 485n47, 524
Shawarbah, Musa, x, 99n10, 271n6, 321n5, 444n1, 467, 484n9, 525
Snake: drinks milk, 369, 531; gives gold, 333–336, 437–440, 531; jujube fruits replaced with snakes, 306; with magic scales 366; man-eater, 302–303, 369; poisons water, 364–366, 369–370; with seven heads 193, 205–206, 287–288, 292, 294; threatens a bride, 201, 207; tries to kill a princess, 207
Sowayan, Saad Abdulla, 75n2, 99n4
Stepmother, 112–113, 213–218, 261–262, 264, 338, 340–341, 356–357
Stewart, Frank H., 207n1, 484n11
Šūḥa (a giant bird) ,193, 198–200, 205–206, 210

thief, theives, 85, 104, 233, 235, 252–254

velar, 467, 468
velarization, 440, 468
velarized, xiv
verbs: conjugation(s), 225, 423, 469, 470, 474, 476, 477; measures 62, 87, 88, 151, 423, 424, 429, 440, 461, 469, 470, 473, 478
Virgil, Aeneas, 251
vocabulary, ix, x, 29, 99, 181, 254, 267, 461, 466, 479–482, 483, 484, 524

Watson, Janet C. E., and Bellem, Alex, 424n10
Wehr, Hans, ix, 99nn6–8, 105n4, 210n21, 254n3, 283n13, 393n13, 461n4, 525
wolf, 316, 347, 442–443, 445, 448–449, 453–455, 458–459, 460, 462
woman who dwells in the sea, 74, 76–79, 202, 204 374–387, 531
word stress, 116, 208, 475, 485
Wright, William, 282n2, 358n5
Wuhīf (a demon), 197, 198

Zubi, Amal, 424n10

Yoel Shalom Perez is Lecturer of Folklore at Ben-Gurion University of the Negev and Director of the Center of Folktales and Folklore. He is author of the preamble in *King Solomon and the Golden Fish: Tales from the Sephardic Tradition.*

Judith Rosenhouse is a retired faculty member and former Head of the Department of Humanities & Arts at Technion–Israel Institute of Technology. She is a linguist specializing in Arabic language, modern Hebrew, and Hungarian-Hebrew language contacts.

www.ingramcontent.com/pod-product-compliance
Lightning Source LLC
Chambersburg PA
CBHW081400090726
47908CB00012B/2744

* 9 7 8 0 2 5 3 0 6 3 8 3 0 *